Lecture Notes in Computer Science   3731

Commenced Publication in 1973
Founding and Former Series Editors:
Gerhard Goos, Juris Hartmanis, and Jan van Leeuwen

Editorial Board

David Hutchison
  Lancaster University, UK
Takeo Kanade
  Carnegie Mellon University, Pittsburgh, PA, USA
Josef Kittler
  University of Surrey, Guildford, UK
Jon M. Kleinberg
  Cornell University, Ithaca, NY, USA
Friedemann Mattern
  ETH Zurich, Switzerland
John C. Mitchell
  Stanford University, CA, USA
Moni Naor
  Weizmann Institute of Science, Rehovot, Israel
Oscar Nierstrasz
  University of Bern, Switzerland
C. Pandu Rangan
  Indian Institute of Technology, Madras, India
Bernhard Steffen
  University of Dortmund, Germany
Madhu Sudan
  Massachusetts Institute of Technology, MA, USA
Demetri Terzopoulos
  New York University, NY, USA
Doug Tygar
  University of California, Berkeley, CA, USA
Moshe Y. Vardi
  Rice University, Houston, TX, USA
Gerhard Weikum
  Max-Planck Institute of Computer Science, Saarbruecken, Germany

Farn Wang (Ed.)

Formal Techniques for Networked and Distributed Systems – FORTE 2005

25th IFIP WG 6.1 International Conference
Taipei, Taiwan, October 2-5, 2005
Proceedings

 Springer

Volume Editor

Farn Wang
National Taiwan University
Department of Electrical Engineering
1, Sec. 4, Roosevelt Rd., Taipei, Taiwan 106, ROC
E-mail: farn@cc.ee.ntu.edu.tw

Library of Congress Control Number: 2005932939

CR Subject Classification (1998): C.2.4, D.2.2, C.2, D.2.4-5, D.2, F.3, D.4

ISSN   0302-9743
ISBN-10   3-540-29189-X Springer Berlin Heidelberg New York
ISBN-13   978-3-540-29189-3 Springer Berlin Heidelberg New York

This work is subject to copyright. All rights are reserved, whether the whole or part of the material is concerned, specifically the rights of translation, reprinting, re-use of illustrations, recitation, broadcasting, reproduction on microfilms or in any other way, and storage in data banks. Duplication of this publication or parts thereof is permitted only under the provisions of the German Copyright Law of September 9, 1965, in its current version, and permission for use must always be obtained from Springer. Violations are liable to prosecution under the German Copyright Law.

Springer is a part of Springer Science+Business Media

springeronline.com

© 2005 IFIP International Federation for Information Processing, Hofstrasse 3, 2361 Laxenburg, Austria
Printed in Germany

Typesetting: Camera-ready by author, data conversion by Scientific Publishing Services, Chennai, India
Printed on acid-free paper   SPIN: 11562436   06/3142   5 4 3 2 1 0

Preface

FORTE (Formal Techniques for Networked and Distributed Systems) 2005 was sponsored by Working Group 6.1, Technical Committee 6 (TC6) of the International Federation for Information Processing (IFIP). The conference series started in 1981 under the name PSTV (Protocol Specification, Testing, and Verification). In 1988, a second series under the name FORTE was started. Both series merged to FORTE/PSTV in 1996. The conference name was changed to FORTE in 2001. During its 24-year history, many important contributions have been reported in the conference series. The last five meetings of FORTE were held in Pisa (Italy), Cheju Island (Korea), Houston (USA), Berlin (Germany), and Madrid (Spain).

The 25th FORTE was held from Sunday to Wednesday, October 2–5, 2005 on the beautiful campus of the National Taiwan University (NTU), Taipei, Taiwan, ROC. The scope covered formal description techniques (MSC, UML, Use cases, ...), semantic foundations, model-checking, SAT-based techniques, process algebrae, abstractions, protocol testing, protocol verification, network synthesis, security system analysis, network robustness, embedded systems, communication protocols, and several promising new techniques. In total, we received 88 submissions and accepted 33 regular papers and 6 short papers. All submissions received three reviews. The final program also included 3 keynote speeches, respectively by Prof. Amir Pnueli, Dr. Constance Heitmeyer, and Prof. Teruo Higashino, and 3 tutorials, respectively by Prof. Rance Cleaveland, Dr. Constance Heitmeyer, and Prof. Teruo Higashino. The proceedings also include the text of the keynote speeches. In addition, there were social events, including a reception, a banquet, and an excursion.

FORTE 2005 was co-located with ATVA (Automated Technology for Verification and Analysis) 2005 with a two-day overlap. Prof. Amir Pnueli was the joint keynote speaker. The participants of FORTE 2005 and ATVA 2005 also enjoyed a joint banquet/reception and a joint excursion.

FORTE 2005 was organized under the auspices of IFIP TC 6 by the Department of Electrical Engineering, NTU. It was generously supported by the National Science Council, Taiwan, ROC; the Ministry of Education, Taiwan, ROC; the Institute of Information Science, Academia Sinica, Taiwan, ROC; the Center for Information and Electronic Technologies, NTU; the Graduate Institute of Communication Engineering, NTU; and the Computer and Information Networking Center, NTU.

We would like to thank the Steering Committee members of FORTE for all their suggestions, guidance, and assistance. We also owe a lot to all the Program Committee members and reviewers for their effort in compiling rigorous reviews. Prof. Manuel Nunez deserves special thanks for unselfishly passing on his experience as organizer of FORTE 2004. We would also like to thank Prof. Jin-Fu Chang, Prof. Chuan Yi Tang, Prof. Wanjiun Liao, Prof. Sy-Yen Kuo, Prof. Ming-Syan Chen, Dr. Churn-Jung Liau, and Dr. Ching-Tarng Hsieh for their assistance. Finally special thanks go to Ms. Lih-Chung Lin, Ms. Tz-Hua Chen, Mr. Rong-Shiung Wu, and Mr. Zawa Chu for their energetic and careful planning in the local arrangements and webpage management.

October 2005   Farn Wang

Organization

Steering Committee

Gregor v. Bochmann (Canada) Tommaso Bolognesi (Italy)
John Derrick (UK) Guy Leduc (Belgium)
Ken Turner (UK)

General Chair

Jin-Fu Chang (Taiwan)

Program Chair

Farn Wang (Taiwan)

Program Committee

Gregor v. Bochmann (Canada) Tommaso Bolognesi (Italy)
Mario Bravetti (Italy) Ana Cavalli (France)
Jin Song Dong (Singapore) Khaled El-Fakih (UAE)
Colin Fidge (Australia) David de Frutos-Escrig (Spain)
Reinhard Gotzhein (Germany) Constance Heitmeyer (USA)
Holger Hermanns (Germany) Teruo Higashino (Japan)
Dieter Hogrefe (Germany) Gerald J. Holzmann (USA)
Ching-Tarng Hsieh (Taiwan) Claude Jard (France)
Myungchul Kim (Korea) Hartmut Koenig (Germany)
David Lee (USA) Chin-Laung Lei (Taiwan)
Wanjiun Liao (Taiwan) Churn-Jung Liau (Taiwan)
Huimin Lin (China) Nancy Lynch (USA)
Elie Najm (France) Manuel Nunez (Spain)
Kenji Suzuki (Japan) Alex Petrenko (Canada)
Ken Turner (UK) Chuan Yi Tang (Taiwan)
Farn Wang (Taiwan) Hasan Ural (Canada)
Tomohiro Yoneda (Japan) Hsu-Chun Yen (Taiwan)

Additional Reviewers

Akira Idoue   Alessandro Fantechi Alex Groce
Arnaud Dury Baptiste Alcalde   Bassel Daou and Daniel Amyot

Carlos Gregorio -Rodríguez Carron Shankland   Clara Segura
Claudio Guidi   Claudio Sacerdoti Coen   Constantin Werner
Dario VIEIRA   Dong Wang   Dongluo Chen
Elisangela Rodrigues-Vieira Fabio Martinelli   Fida Dankar
Guoqiang Shu   Hesham Hallal   Hidetoshi Yokota
Hong PAN   Ingmar Fliege   Ismael Rodriguez
Jalal Kawash   Jiale Huo   Jian Liu
Jinzhi Xia   Joachim Thees   Jun Lei
Jun Sun   Keqin Li   Li Jiao
Lijun Zhang   Luis Llana   Manuel Mazzara
Marco Zibull   Maurice ter Beek   Mercedes G. Merayo
Michael Ebner   Miguel Palomino   Natalia Lopez
Nicola Tonellotto   O. Marroquin-Alonso   Ping Hao
Rene Soltwisch   Robert Clark   Roberto Gorrieri
Roberto Lucchi   Rüdiger Grammes   Rui Xue
Salvatore Rinzivillo   Sam Owre   Savi Maharaj
Sebastian Schmerl   Serge Boroday   Soonuk Seol
Stefania Gnesi   Stephan Schröder   Stephane Maag
Sungwon Kang   Takashi Kitamura   Thomas Kuhn
Tomohiko Ogishi   Toru Hasegawa   Wenhui Zhang
Xinxin Liu   Yolanda Ortega-Mallén   Yuan Fang Li
Yutaka Miyake

Sponsoring Institutions

National Science Council, Taiwan, ROC
Ministry of Education, Taiwan, ROC
Institute of Information Science, Academia Sinica, Taiwan, ROC
Center for Information and Electronic Technologies, NTU
Graduate Institute of Communication Engineering, NTU
Computer and Information Networking Center, NTU

Table of Contents

KEYNOTE SPEECHES

Ranking Abstraction as Companion to Predicate Abstraction
  Ittai Balaban, Amir Pnueli, Lenore D. Zuck 1

Developing High Quality Software with Formal Methods:
What Else Is Needed?
  Constance Heitmeyer 13

A Testing Architecture for Designing High-Reliable MANET Protocols
  Teruo Higashino, Hirozumi Yamaguchi 20

REGULAR PAPERS

A Composition Operator for Systems with Active and Passive Actions
  Stefan Strubbe, Rom Langerak 24

A Formal Semantics of UML StateCharts by Means of Timed Petri Nets
  Youcef Hammal 38

A Hierarchy of Implementable MSC Languages
  Benedikt Bollig, Martin Leucker 53

Combining Static Analysis and Model Checking for Systems Employing
Commutative Functions
  A. Prasad Sistla, Min Zhou 68

Fast Generic Model-Checking for Data-Based Systems
  Dezhuang Zhang, Rance Cleaveland 83

Logic and Model Checking for Hidden Markov Models
  Lijun Zhang, Holger Hermanns, David N. Jansen 98

Proving $\forall \mu$-Calculus Properties with SAT-Based Model Checking
  Bow-Yaw Wang 113

Ad Hoc Routing Protocol Verification Through Broadcast Abstraction
  Oskar Wibling, Joachim Parrow, Arnold Pears 128

Discovering Chatter and Incompleteness in the Datagram Congestion Control Protocol
Somsak Vanit-Anunchai, Jonathan Billington, Tul Kongprakaiwoot 143

Thread Allocation Protocols for Distributed Real-Time and Embedded Systems
César Sánchez, Henny B. Sipma, Venkita Subramonian, Christopher Gill, Zohar Manna 159

A Petri Net View of Mobility
Charles A. Lakos 174

Modular Verification of Petri Nets Properties: A Structure-Based Approach
Kais Klai, Serge Haddad, Jean-Michel Ilié 189

An Improved Conformance Testing Method
Rita Dorofeeva, Khaled El-Fakih, Nina Yevtushenko 204

Resolving Observability Problems in Distributed Test Architectures
J. Chen, R.M. Hierons, H. Ural 219

Automatic Generation of Conflict-Free IPsec Policies
Chi-Lan Chang, Yun-Peng Chiu, Chin-Laung Lei 233

A Framework Based Approach for Formal Modeling and Analysis of Multi-level Attacks in Computer Networks
Gerrit Rothmaier, Heiko Krumm 247

Model Checking for Timed Statecharts
Junyan Qian, Baowen Xu 261

Abstraction-Guided Model Checking Using Symbolic IDA* And Heuristic Synthesis
Kairong Qian, Albert Nymeyer, Steven Susanto 275

Modeling and Verification of Safety-Critical Systems Using Safecharts
Pao-Ann Hsiung, Yen-Hung Lin 290

Structure Preserving Data Abstractions for Statecharts
Steffen Helke, Florian Kammüller 305

Amortised Bisimulations
Astrid Kiehn, S. Arun-Kumar 320

Proof Methodologies for Behavioural Equivalence in DPI
Alberto Ciaffaglione, Matthew Hennessy, Julian Rathke 335

Deriving Non-determinism from Conjunction and Disjunction
Naijun Zhan, Mila Majster-Cederbaum 351

Abstract Operational Semantics for Use Case Maps
Jameleddine Hassine, Juergen Rilling, Rachida Dssouli 366

ArchiTRIO: A UML-Compatible Language for Architectural Description and Its Formal Semantics
Matteo Pradella, Matteo Rossi, Dino Mandrioli 381

Submodule Construction for Extended State Machine Models
Bassel Daou, Gregor V. Bochmann 396

Towards Synchronizing Linear Collaborative Objects with Operational Transformation
Abdessamad Imine, Pascal Molli, Gérald Oster, Michaël Rusinowitch 411

Designing Efficient Fail-Safe Multitolerant Systems
Arshad Jhumka, Neeraj Suri 428

Hierarchical Decision Diagrams to Exploit Model Structure
Jean-Michel Couvreur, Yann Thierry-Mieg 443

Computing Subgraph Probability of Random Geometric Graphs: Quantitative Analyses of Wireless Ad Hoc Networks
Chang Wu Yu, Li-Hsing Yen 458

Formalising Web Services
Kenneth J. Turner 473

From Automata Networks to HMSCs: A Reverse Model Engineering Perspective
Thomas Chatain, Loïc Hélouët, Claude Jard 489

Properties as Processes: Their Specification and Verification
Joel Kelso, George Milne 503

SHORT PAPERS

Epoch Distance of the Random Waypoint Model in Mobile Ad Hoc Networks
Yueh-Ting Wu, Wanjiun Liao, Cheng-Lin Tsao 518

Automatic Partitioner for Behavior Level Distributed Logic Simulation
Kai-Hui Chang, Jeh-Yen Kang, Han-Wei Wang, Wei-Ting Tu, Yi-Jong Yeh, Sy-Yen Kuo 525

Expressive Completeness of an Event-Pattern Reactive Programming Language
  César Sánchez, Matteo Slanina, Henny B. Sipma, Zohar Manna 529

Formalizing Interoperability Testing: Quiescence Management and Test Generation
  Alexandra Desmoulin, César Viho 533

Formal Description of Mobile IPv6 Protocol
  Yujun Zhang, Zhongcheng Li 538

Incremental Modeling Under Large-Scale Distributed Interaction
  Horst F. Wedde, Arnim Wedig, Anca Lazarescu, Ralf Paaschen, Elisei Rotaru 542

The Inductive Approach to Strand Space
  Yongjian Li 547

Compositional Modelling and Verification of IPv6 Mobility
  Peng Wu, Dongmei Zhang 553

Author Index 557

Ranking Abstraction as Companion to Predicate Abstraction*

Ittai Balaban[1], Amir Pnueli[1,2], and Lenore D. Zuck[3]

[1] New York University, New York
{balaban, amir}@cs.nyu.edu
[2] Weizmann Institute of Science
[3] University of Illinois at Chicago
lenore@cs.uic.edu

Abstract. Predicate abstraction has become one of the most successful methodologies for proving safety properties of programs. Recently, several abstraction methodologies have been proposed for proving liveness properties. This paper studies "ranking abstraction" where a program is augmented by a non-constraining progress monitor, and further abstracted by predicate-abstraction, to allow for automatic verification of progress properties. Unlike most liveness methodologies, the augmentation does not require a complete ranking function that is expected to decrease with each step. Rather, the inputs are component rankings from which a complete ranking function may be formed.

The premise of the paper is an analogy between the methods of ranking abstraction and predicate abstraction, one ingredient of which is refinement: When predicate abstraction fails, one can refine it. When ranking abstraction fails, one must determine whether the predicate abstraction, or the ranking abstraction, need be refined. The paper presents strategies for determining which case is at hand.

The other part of the analogy is that of automatically deriving deductive proof constructs: Predicate abstraction is often used to derive program invariants for proving safety properties as a boolean combination of the given predicates. Deductive proof of progress properties requires well-founded ranking functions instead of invariants. We show how to obtain concrete global ranking functions from abstract programs.

We demonstrate the various methods on examples with nested loops, including a bubble sort algorithm on linked lists.

1 Introduction

Predicate abstraction has become one of the most successful methodologies for proving safety properties of programs. However, with no extension it cannot be used to verify general liveness properties. In this paper, we present a framework, based on predicate abstraction and *ranking abstraction*, for verification of both safety and progress properties. Ranking abstraction, introduced in [7], is based on an augmentation of the concrete program. The augmentation is parameterized by a set of well founded ranking

---

* This research was supported in part by NSF grant CCR-0205571, ONR grant N00014-99-1-0131, and Israel Science Foundation grant 106/02-1.

functions. Based on these, new *compassion* (strong fairness) requirements as well as transitions are generated, all of which are synchronously composed with the program in a non-constraining manner. Unlike most methodologies, the ranking functions are not expected to decrease with each transition of the program. Rather, a further step of state abstraction is performed such that, coupled with the new compassion, it serves to construct a complete ranking function.

The basic premise presented in this paper is that there is a duality between the activities that lead to verification of safety properties via predicate abstraction, and those that lead to verification of progress properties via ranking abstraction. This duality is expressed through the following components:

- *The initial abstraction.* Heuristics are applied to choose either an initial set of predicates, or a set of core well founded ranking functions.
- *Refinement.* A too-coarse initial abstraction leads to spurious abstract counterexamples. Depending on the character of the counterexample, either a predicate, or a ranking, refinement is performed.
- *Generation of deductive proof constructs.* Predicate abstraction is often used as an automatic method to generate an inductive invariant as a boolean combination of the given predicates. Dually, ranking abstraction can be used to generate a global concrete ranking function that decreases with every step of the program, as a lexicographical combination of the core ranking functions.

We demonstrate the use of ranking refinement in order to prove termination of a canonical program with nested loops and unbounded random assignments, as well as a bubble sort algorithm on unbounded linked lists. Both examples entail the use of additional heuristics in order to synthesize core ranking functions.

The framework, as well as all experiments, have been implemented using the TLV interactive model-checker [1]. The contribution of the paper is as follows: At the informal, philosophical level, it strives to convince the reader that the duality between invariance and progress, present in deductive frameworks, extends to how one approaches automatic verification of each kind of property. More concretely, it suggests a formal framework, based on two specific abstraction methods for proving both safety and progress properties. This includes heuristics for choosing separate refinement methodologies based on the form of counterexamples, and a method for automatically deriving a global well founded program ranking function.

The paper is organized as follows: Section 2 describes the computational model of *fair discrete systems* as well as predicate and ranking abstractions. Furthermore, it motivates the use of ranking abstraction by demonstrating its value, compared to a typical deductive method. Section 3 formalizes the different notions of abstraction refinement. Section 4 presents a method for extracting a global ranking function from an abstract program. Finally, Section 5 summarizes and concludes.

Related Work

Dams, Gerth, and Grumberg [6] point out the duality between verification of safety and progress of programs. Like us, they aim to lift this duality to provide tools for proving progress properties, whose functionality is analogous to similar tools used for safety. Specifically, they propose a heuristic for discovering ranking functions from a program's text. In contrast, we concentrate on an analogy with predicate abstraction, a particular method for safety. Our approach is broader, however, in that we suggest a general framework for safety and progress properties where each of the activities in a verification process has an instantiation with respect to each of the dualities.

In [10] Podelski and Rybalchenko present a method for synthesis of linear ranking functions. The method is complete for unnested loops, and is embedded successfully in a broader framework for proving liveness properties [9].

The topic of refinement of state abstraction, specifically predicate abstraction, has been widely studied. A number of existing works in this area are [5,3], and [4].

2 The Formal Framework

In this section we present our computational model, as well as the methods of predicate abstraction and ranking abstraction.

2.1 Fair Discrete Systems

As our computational model, we take a *fair discrete system* (FDS) $S = \langle V, \Theta, \rho, \mathcal{J}, \mathcal{C} \rangle$, where

- V — A set of *system variables*. A *state* of S provides a type-consistent interpretation of the variables V. For a state s and a system variable $v \in V$, we denote by $s[v]$ the value assigned to v by the state s. Let Σ denote the set of all states over V.
- Θ — The *initial condition*: An assertion (state formula) characterizing the initial states.
- $\rho(V, V')$ — The *transition relation*: An assertion, relating the values V of the variables in state $s \in \Sigma$ to the values V' in an S-successor state $s' \in \Sigma$.
- $\mathcal{J}$ — A set of *justice* (*weak fairness*) requirements (assertions); A computation must include infinitely many states satisfying each of the justice requirements.
- $\mathcal{C}$ — A set of *compassion (strong fairness)* requirements: Each compassion requirement is a pair $\langle p, q \rangle$ of state assertions; A computation should include either only finitely many p-states, or infinitely many q-states.

For an assertion ψ, we say that $s \in \Sigma$ is a ψ-state if $s \models \psi$.

A *computation* of an FDS S is an infinite sequence of states $\sigma : s_0, s_1, s_2, ...$, satisfying the requirements:

- *Initiality* — s_0 is initial, i.e., $s_0 \models \Theta$.
- *Consecution* — For each $\ell = 0, 1, ...$, the state $s_{\ell+1}$ is an S-successor of s_ℓ. That is, $\langle s_\ell, s_{\ell+1} \rangle \models \rho(V, V')$ where, for each $v \in V$, we interpret v as $s_\ell[v]$ and v' as $s_{\ell+1}[v]$.
- *Justice* — for every $J \in \mathcal{J}$, σ contains infinitely many occurrences of J-states.
- *Compassion* – for every $\langle p, q \rangle \in \mathcal{C}$, either σ contains only finitely many occurrences of p-states, or σ contains infinitely many occurrences of q-states.

2.2 Predicate Abstraction

The material here is a summary of [7] and [2]. We fix an FDS $S = \langle V, \Theta, \rho, \mathcal{J}, \mathcal{C} \rangle$ whose set of states is Σ. A *predicate abstraction* is a mapping $\alpha \colon \Sigma \to \{0,1\}^n$ for some positive n. The set of tuples $\{0,1\}^n$ is referred to as the set of *abstract states*. We focus on abstractions that can be represented by a set of equations of the form $\{u_i = P_i(V) \mid i = 1, \ldots, n\}$, where the P_i's are assertions over the concrete variables V, to which we refer as *predicates*, and $U = \{u_1, \ldots, u_n\}$ is the set of boolean *abstract variables*. The mapping α can also be expressed more succinctly by:

$$U = \mathcal{P}(V)$$

For an assertion $p(V)$, we define its abstraction by:

$$\alpha(p) \colon \exists V.(U = \mathcal{P}(V) \wedge p(V))$$

The semantics of $\alpha(p)$ is $\|\alpha(p)\| = \{\alpha(s) \mid s \in \|p\|\}$. Note that $\|\alpha(p)\|$ is, in general, an over-approximation – an abstract state is in $\|\alpha(p)\|$ iff *there exists* some concrete p-state that is abstracted into it. An assertion $p(V, V')$ over both primed and unprimed variables is abstracted by:

$$\alpha(p) \colon \exists V, V'.(U = \mathcal{P}(V) \wedge U' = \mathcal{P}(V') \wedge p(V, V'))$$

The assertion p is said to be *precise with respect to the abstraction* α if $\|p\| = \alpha^{-1}(\|\alpha(p)\|)$, i.e., if two concrete states are abstracted into the same abstract state, they are either both p-states, or they are both $\neg p$-states. For a temporal formula ψ in positive normal form (where negation is applied only to state assertions), ψ^α is the formula obtained by replacing every maximal state sub-formula p in ψ by $\alpha(p)$. The formula ψ is said to be *precise with respect to* α if each of its maximal state sub-formulas are precise with respect to α.

In all cases discussed in this paper, the formulae are precise with respect to the relevant abstractions. Hence, we can restrict to the over-approximation semantics.

The abstraction of S by α is the system

$$S^\alpha = \langle U, \alpha(\Theta), \alpha(\rho), \bigcup_{J \in \mathcal{J}} \alpha(J), \bigcup_{(p,q) \in \mathcal{C}} (\alpha(p), \alpha(q)) \rangle$$

The soundness of predicate abstraction is derived from [7]:

Theorem 1. *For a system S, abstraction α, and a positive normal form temporal formula ψ:*

$$S^\alpha \models \psi^\alpha \quad \Longrightarrow \quad S \models \psi$$

Thus, if an abstract system satisfies an abstract property, then the concrete system satisfies the concrete property.

2.3 Ranking Abstraction

State abstraction often does not suffice to verify progress properties. We consider *ranking abstraction*, a method of augmenting the concrete program in a non-constraining manner, in order to measure progress of program transitions, with respect to a ranking function. Once a program is augmented, a conventional state abstraction can be used to preserve this notion in the abstract system. This method was introduced in [7].

A ranking function is a function mapping program states to some domain $\mathcal{D}$. A ranking function is *well founded* if $\mathcal{D}$ is partially ordered by a relation $\succ$, which does not admit an infinitely descending chain of the form $a_0 \succ a_1 \succ a_2 \succ \cdots$. Throughout the rest of the paper we assume all ranking functions to be well founded. The augmentation of system S by a ranking function δ, written $S+\delta$, is the system

$$S+\delta: \langle V \cup \{dec\}, \Theta, \rho \wedge \rho_\delta, \mathcal{J}, \mathcal{C} \cup \{(dec > 0, dec < 0)\}\rangle$$

where dec is a fresh variable symbol, and the conjunct ρ_δ is defined as

$$\rho_\delta: dec' = \begin{cases} 1 & \delta \succ \delta' \\ 0 & \delta = \delta' \\ -1 & \text{otherwise} \end{cases}$$

The well foundedness of δ is abstracted by the augmentation into the compassion requirement $(dec > 0, dec < 0)$, stating that if dec is positive infinitely often in a computation, then it must also be negative infinitely often.

Since augmentation does not constrain the behavior of S, any property in terms of variables of S is valid over S iff it is valid over $S+\delta$. In order to verify a progress property ψ, an augmentation $S+\delta$ is abstracted using a standard state abstraction, as shown in Example 1.

$$\begin{array}{l} x, y : \textbf{natural init } x = 0, y = 0 \\ \left[\begin{array}{l} 0: x := ? \\ \textbf{while } x > 0 \textbf{ do} \\ \left[\begin{array}{l} 1: y := ? \\ \textbf{while } y > 0 \textbf{ do} \\ [\,2: y := y - 1\,] \\ 3: x := x - 1 \end{array}\right] \\ 4: \end{array}\right] \end{array}$$

Fig. 1. Program NESTED-LOOPS

Example 1 (Nested Loops). Consider the program NESTED-LOOPS in Fig. 1. In the program, the statements $x := ?, y := ?$ in lines 0 and 1 denote random assignments of arbitrary positive integers to variables x and y. An initial attempt to prove termination of this program is to define the ranking function $\delta_y = y$. The augmentation $S+\delta_y$ is shown in Fig. 2. Note that statements that in the original program assigned to y, are now replaced with a simultaneous assignment to both y and the augmentation variable dec_y.

While this augmentation is not sufficient to prove program termination, it can be used to show termination of the inner loop, expressed by

$$(\pi = 2) \Longrightarrow \Diamond(\pi = 3) \qquad (1)$$

where the variable π denotes the program counter. As a state abstraction we use

$$\alpha : (X = (x > 0)) \wedge (Y = (y > 0)) \wedge (Dec_y = dec_y)$$

$$
\begin{array}{|l|}
\hline
x, y \;:\; \text{natural} \quad \text{init } x = 0, y = 0 \\
dec_y \;:\; \{-1, 0, 1\} \\
\quad \text{compassion } (dec_y > 0, dec_y < 0) \\
\left[\begin{array}{l}
0: x := ? \\
\text{while } x > 0 \text{ do} \\
\quad \left[\begin{array}{l}
1: (y, dec_y) := (?, -1) \\
\text{while } y > 0 \text{ do} \\
\quad [\, 2: (y, dec_y) := (y-1, 1) \,] \\
3: x := x - 1
\end{array}\right] \\
4:
\end{array}\right] \\
\hline
\end{array}
$$

Fig. 2. Program AUGMENTED-NESTED-LOOPS

which results in the abstract program in Fig. 3. Notice that the abstraction has introduced nondeterministic assignments to both X and Y (lines 2 and 3). It is now possible to verify, e.g. by model-checking, the property (1) over the abstract program.

$$
\begin{array}{|l|}
\hline
X, Y \;:\; \{0, 1\} \quad \text{init } Y = 0, X = 0 \\
Dec_y \;:\; \{-1, 0, 1\} \\
\quad \text{compassion } (Dec_y > 0, Dec_y < 0) \\
\left[\begin{array}{l}
0: X := 1 \\
\text{while } X \text{ do} \\
\quad \left[\begin{array}{l}
1: (Y, Dec_y) := (1, -1) \\
\text{while } Y \text{ do} \\
\quad [\, 2: (Y, Dec_y) := (\{0, 1\}, 1) \,] \\
3: X := \{0, 1\}
\end{array}\right] \\
4:
\end{array}\right] \\
\hline
\end{array}
$$

Fig. 3. Program ABSTRACT-AUGMENTED-NESTED-LOOPS

In general, we consider simultaneous augmentation with sets of ranking functions. A *ranking* is a set of ranking functions. Let Δ be the ranking $\{\delta_1, \ldots, \delta_k\}$. Then the augmentation $S+\Delta$ is the system

$$S+\Delta : S+\delta_1 + \cdots + \delta_k$$

Just like the case of predicate abstraction, we lose nothing (except efficiency) by adding potentially redundant rankings. The main advantage here over direct use of ranking functions within deductive verification is that one may contribute as many elementary ranking functions as one wishes. It is then left to a model-checker to sort out their interaction and relevance. To illustrate this, consider a full termination proof of the program NESTED-LOOPS. Due to the unbounded non-determinism of the random assignments, a termination proof needs to use a ranking function ranging over lexicographic tuples, whose elementary ranking components are $\{\pi = 0, x, y\}$. With ranking abstraction, however, one need only provide the well founded ranking $\Delta = \{x, y\}$.

3 Abstraction Refinement

3.1 Preliminaries

In the following sections we refer to finite sequences of consecutive states, known as *traces*, as well as composite transition relations denoted by traces. Fix a trace

$\sigma : \sigma_1 \ldots \sigma_\ell$, where the σ_i are program states. An alternate representation of σ is as the sequence of transitions $\rho_1 \ldots \rho_{\ell-1}$, with ρ_i defined as $\sigma_i \wedge \sigma'_{i+1}$ for each $i < \ell$.

A composition of two transition relations ρ_1 and ρ_2, denoted by $\rho_1 \circ \rho_2$, is defined as $\exists V'. \rho_1(V, V') \wedge \rho_2(V', V'')$. The transition relation denoted by the trace σ, written ρ_σ, is the composition of its transition relations, given by $\rho_\sigma : \rho_1 \circ \ldots \circ \rho_{\ell-1}$.

A *cycle* is a trace of the form $\sigma_1 \ldots \sigma_\ell \sigma_1$. In the following sections we discuss both cycles and *control flow loops*, the difference being that while in a cycle the initial and last states are identical, a control flow loop is a trace where the initial and last states assign identical values to the program counter π, but not necessarily to other variables.

3.2 Refinement

The process of proving or refuting a progress property ψ over a program begins with a user-provided initial ranking Δ and an abstraction α. Following [11], the initial predicate abstraction is chosen as follows: Let $\mathcal{P}$ be the (finite) set of atomic state formulas occurring in ρ, Θ, $\mathcal{J}$, $\mathcal{C}$ and the concrete formula ψ that refer to non-control and non-primed variables. Then the abstraction α is the set of equations $\{B_p = p : p \in \mathcal{P}\}$.

The formula ψ^α is then model-checked over $(S+\Delta)^\alpha$. If ψ^α is valid then we can conclude that $S \models \psi$. Otherwise, a counterexample is found, in the form of a computation of S^α that does not satisfy ψ^α. If such a computation exists then a standard model checker will return a counter-example that is finitely represented as a "lasso" – a finite initial trace followed by a cycle. The following scenarios may give rise to a counterexample:

1. The property ψ is not valid: The concrete system indeed has a computation in which a cycle is repeated infinitely
2. The state abstraction is too coarse: The abstract system has a finite trace with no concrete counterpart
3. The concrete system has a finite acyclic trace that cannot be extended to an infinite computation, such that its abstraction contains a cycle.

In case 1, a valid counterexample to ψ has been found, and we conclude that ψ indeed is not valid over S. Cases 2 and 3 represent different forms of infeasibility of the counterexample, and are handled by different means of refinement.

Case 2 represents a typical scenario in state abstraction refinement, in the following way: Although the counterexample may be a lasso, say (σ_1, σ_2), we consider the finite trace $\sigma_1 \sigma_2$ and the fact that it is *spurious*, i.e., cannot be concretized. This case is therefore handled by refining the abstraction with a new predicate that eliminates the spurious trace. Any one of existing refinement methods may be applied (see, for example, [5,3,4]).

Case 3 implies the following situation: A cyclic trace is present in the abstract system, the concretization of which is a control-flow loop. Furthermore, the loop is *well-founded*, in that there exists no infinite sequence of iterations of the loop. To preserve this property in the abstract program, we search for a ranking function that proves the loop's well-foundedness. Formally, if ρ_σ is the loop transition relation, then our goal is to find a ranking function δ over a domain $(\mathcal{D}, \succ)$ such that $\rho_\sigma \to \delta \succ \delta'$. A number of methods have been proposed to synthesize such functions, among them in [10,6]. In

Subsection 3.3 we present an additional heuristic for the domain of unbounded linked lists.

Cases 2 and 3 both result in a refined abstraction and a refined ranking, respectively. Therefore, the verification process continues with a new iteration of augmentation and abstraction. The process repeats until success — ψ is proven to be valid or invalid — or the refinement reaches a fixpoint, in which case the process fails.

Example 2 (Termination of NESTED-LOOPS). Recall the program NESTED-LOOPS in Fig. 1, for which we wish to prove termination, expressed as $(\pi = 0) \implies \Diamond(\pi = 4)$. We begin with the initial abstraction and ranking used in Example 1:

$$\alpha : (X = (x > 0)) \land (Y = (y > 0)) \land (Dec_y = dec_y)$$
$$\Delta : \{\delta_1 = y\}$$

An initial iteration of abstraction and model-checking results in an abstract lasso counterexample consisting of the prefix

$$\langle \Pi = 0, X, \neg Y, Dec_y = 0 \rangle$$

and the cycle

$$\langle \Pi = 1, X, \neg Y, Dec_y = 0 \rangle$$
$$\langle \Pi = 2, X, Y, Dec_y = -1 \rangle$$
$$\langle \Pi = 3, X, \neg Y, Dec_y = 1 \rangle$$

with Π denoting the program counter in the abstract program. The lasso can be concretized, as shown by the concrete trace

$$s_1 : \langle \pi = 0, x = 0, y = 0, dec_y = 0 \rangle$$
$$s_2 : \langle \pi = 1, x = 4, y = 0, dec_y = 0 \rangle$$
$$s_3 : \langle \pi = 2, x = 4, y = 1, dec_y = -1 \rangle$$
$$s_4 : \langle \pi = 3, x = 4, y = 0, dec_y = 1 \rangle$$
$$s_5 : \langle \pi = 1, x = 3, y = 0, dec_y = 0 \rangle$$

Therefore the counterexample falls under Case 3 above, and we examine a concretization of the cyclic portion of the lasso, i.e., the subtrace $\sigma : s_2 \ldots s_5$. Forming its transition relation ρ_σ, we now examine its implication on transitions of the program variables, in the hope of proving well-foundedness. Specifically, we discover that the constraint $x > x'$ is implied by ρ_σ. This suggests refining Δ with the ranking function $\delta_2 = x$, to form $\Delta' : \{\delta_1 = y, \delta_2 = x\}$. At this point, the abstraction of $S+\Delta'$ by α is sufficient to verify the termination property.

3.3 Synthesizing Elementary Ranking Functions

A number of methods have been suggested for synthesis of ranking functions. In our examples we have used the general heuristic of searching for simple linear constraints implied by the transition relation of a control-flow loop ([10] provides a less naïve method for doing this. Indeed, their method is complete). For example, given a set of variables V and the transition relation ρ_σ of a loop, we check validity of implications such as $\rho_\sigma \to v > v'$, for each $v \in V$. As demonstrated, this has been sufficient in dealing with the NESTED-LOOPS program.

We have used a variant of this heuristic to deal with programs that manipulate unbounded pointer structures. One such program is BUBBLE SORT, shown in Fig. 4. This is a parametrized system with H denoting the maximal size of a singly-linked pointer structure (or *heap*). The heap itself is represented by the array Nxt. In addition there are a number of *pointer* variables, such as x and y, that are also parametrized by H.

$$
\begin{array}{l}
x, y, yn, prev, last : [0..H] \\
Nxt \qquad\qquad\qquad : \textbf{array } [0..H] \textbf{ of } [0..H] \text{ where } Nxt^*(x, nil) \\
D \qquad\qquad\qquad\quad : \textbf{array } [0..H] \textbf{ of bool} \\
\left[
\begin{array}{l}
0: \quad (prev, y, yn, last) := (nil, x, Nxt[x], nil); \\
1: \quad \textbf{while } last \neq Nxt[x] \textbf{ do} \\
\quad \left[
\begin{array}{l}
2: \textbf{while } yn \neq last \textbf{ do} \\
\quad \left[
\begin{array}{l}
3: \textbf{if } (D[y] > D[yn]) \textbf{ then} \\
\quad \left[
\begin{array}{l}
4: \ (Nxt[y], Nxt[yn]) := (Nxt[yn], y); \\
5: \textbf{if } (prev = nil) \textbf{ then} \\
\quad 6: \ x := yn \\
\quad \textbf{else} \\
\quad\quad 7: \ Nxt[prev] := yn; \\
8: \ (prev, yn) := (yn, Nxt[y])
\end{array}
\right] \\
\textbf{else} \\
\quad 9: \ (prev, y, yn) := (y, yn, Nxt[y])
\end{array}
\right] \\
\end{array}
\right] \\
10: \ (prev, y, yn, last) := (nil, x, Nxt[x], y); \\
11:
\end{array}
\right]
\end{array}
$$

Fig. 4. Program BUBBLE SORT

In order to synthesize a ranking function for BUBBLE SORT and similar programs, our strategy is to seek constraints on graph reachability. One such form of constraint is

$$\rho_\sigma \to (reach(v, v') \land v \neq v')$$

where ρ_σ is a loop transition relation and v is a pointer variable. Under the assumption that a singly-linked list emanating from v is acyclic, such a constraint suggests the ranking function $\{i \mid reach(v, i)\}$ over the domain $(2^\mathbb{N}, \supset)$. Indeed, while proving termination of BUBBLE SORT, one of the functions discovered automatically by refinement was $\{i \mid reach(yn, i)\}$, a function that serves to prove termination of the nested loop (lines $2 \ldots 9$).

4 Extracting Complete Ranking Functions

This section provides an overview of an algorithm that extracts a ranking function from a program constructed by a joint (ranking and predicate) abstraction. The algorithm manipulates a symbolic (BDD-based) representation of the system, and is an adaptation of the explicit state version in [8].

The algorithm EXTRACT-RANKING, shown in Fig. 5, is based on a partitioning of the control flow graph of an abstract program into strongly connected components. It distinguishes between components that are singletons with no edges, and components with

```
ranking                    : Σ → rankings
{(p₁,q₁),...,(pₙ,qₙ)}     : set of compassion requirements

EXTRACT-RANKING(S          : state assertion;
                ρ          : transition relation;
                ⟨r₁,...,rₖ⟩ : rₖ ∈ ℕ,
                             rⱼ ∈ ℕ or rⱼ = δᵢ, for some i ≤ n,
                             for all j < k) :
⎡ if S is satisfiable
⎢  ⎡ let s = S ∧ deadlock
⎢  ⎢ if s is satisfiable
⎢  ⎢   ⎡ ranking[α⁻¹(s)] := ⟨r₁,...,rₖ⟩
⎢  ⎢   ⎢ EXTRACT-RANKING(S ∧ ¬s;
⎢  ⎢   ⎢                 ρ ∧ ¬s';
⎢  ⎢   ⎣                 ⟨r₁,...,rₖ + 1⟩)
⎢  ⎢ else
⎢  ⎢   ⎡ let s = the set of pᵢ-states in S such that
⎢  ⎢   ⎢         s ∘ ρ* → ¬qᵢ ∧
⎢  ⎢   ⎢         s ∘ ρ* ↔ ρ* ∘ s,
⎢  ⎢   ⎢         for some 1 ≤ i ≤ n
⎢  ⎢   ⎢ let scc = S ∧ (s ∘ ρ*)
⎢  ⎢   ⎢ EXTRACT-RANKING(scc;
⎢  ⎢   ⎢                 ρ ∧ ¬s';
⎢  ⎢   ⎢                 ⟨rᵢ,...,rₖ,δᵢ,0⟩)
⎢  ⎢   ⎢ EXTRACT-RANKING(S ∧ ¬scc;
⎢  ⎢   ⎢                 ρ ∧ ¬scc ∧ ¬scc';
⎣  ⎣   ⎣                 ⟨r₁,...,rₖ⟩)
```

Fig. 5. Ranking Extraction Algorithm. The notations $s \circ \rho^*$ and $\rho^* \circ s$ denote, respectively, the sets of eventual successors and eventual predecessors of s.

at least one transition. The observation is that zero-edge singleton components represent program states that reside outside of any control-flow loop, while other components represent loops. A further observation is that if an always-decreasing ranking function indeed exists, any loop is necessarily *unfair*, i.e. there exists some fairness requirement that is not satisfied by a run that never escapes the loop. For clarity of presentation we assume that there are no justice requirements, only compassion. We also assume that all compassion requirements have been generated as a result of ranking abstraction, and hence each requirement (p_i, q_i) is associated with a component ranking function δ_i.

The algorithm iterates over the set of components, singleton or otherwise, while constructing a mapping between state sets and rankings. A ranking is a lexicographic tuple of the form $\langle r_1, \ldots, r_k \rangle$, where for all $j < k$, r_j is either a nonnegative integer, or the ranking function δ_i associated with the compassion (p_i, q_i). The element r_k is always a nonnegative integer.

Initially the algorithm is called with the set of reachable abstraction states, the abstract transition relation, and the tuple $\langle 0 \rangle$ as inputs. At every iteration, the algorithm first attempts to prune all deadlock states. It assigns the ranking $\langle r_1, \ldots, r_k + 1 \rangle$ to the concretization of every such state, where $\langle r_1, \ldots, r_k \rangle$ is the the ranking assigned

$$
\begin{array}{l}
X, Y \,:\, \{0,1\} \qquad \text{init } Y = 0, X = 0 \\
Dec_y \,:\, \{-1, 0, 1\} \\
Dec_x \,:\, \{-1, 0, 1\} \\
\text{compassion } \{(Dec_x > 0, Dec_x < 0), (Dec_y > 0, Dec_y < 0)\} \\
\left[\begin{array}{l}
0 : (X, Dec_x) := (1, -1) \\
\quad \textbf{while } X \textbf{ do} \\
\quad \left[\begin{array}{l}
1 : (Y, Dec_y) := (1, -1) \\
\quad \textbf{while } Y \textbf{ do} \\
\quad \left[\, 2 : (Y, Dec_y) := (\{0,1\}, 1) \,\right] \\
3 : (X, Dec_x) := (\{0,1\}, 1)
\end{array}\right] \\
4 :
\end{array}\right]
\end{array}
$$

Fig. 6. Abstraction of Program NESTED-LOOPS augmented with ranking functions $\delta_1 = y$ and $\delta_2 = x$.

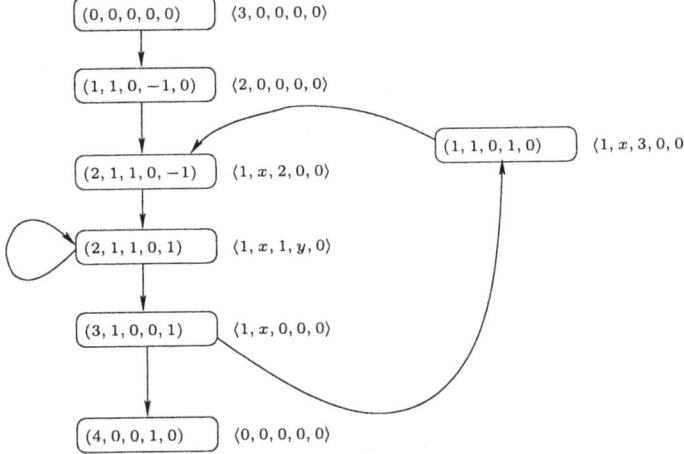

Fig. 7. Abstract Control Flow Graph and Ranking Function of NESTED-LOOPS. Each tuple (a, b, c, d, e) denotes the abstract program state ($\Pi = a, X = b, Y = c, Dec_x = d, Dec_y = e$).

in the previous iteration. If no deadlock exists, an arbitrary component is picked that has no outgoing edge and violates a compassion requirement (p_i, q_i), for some i. That is, the component contains one or more p_i-states, but no q_i-state. At this point the outgoing edges of the p_i-states are pruned from the graph. The algorithm is then applied recursively on what remains of the component, with the input ranking of $\langle r_1, \ldots, r_k + 1, \delta_i, 0 \rangle$, where $\langle r_1, \ldots, r_k \rangle$ is the ranking assigned in the previous iteration. This means that all rankings assigned by the recursive call will contain the prefix $\langle r_1, \ldots, r_k + 1, \delta_i \rangle$.

Example 3 (Extracting a Ranking Function of NESTED-LOOPS*).* We illustrate the algorithm by extracting a ranking function for NESTED-LOOPS, given the abstract program shown in Fig. 6. This is a version of the augmented abstract version from Fig. 3, after refinement with the ranking function $\delta_2 = x$.

Fig. 7 shows the control flow graph of the abstract program, with a ranking associated with each state. The interpretation of this diagram is a ranking function defined as follows: For any concrete state s that abstracts to a graph state $\alpha(s)$, the rank of s is the lexicographic tuple associated with $\alpha(s)$.

Space limitations prevent us from presenting a proof that the resulting ranking function is in fact always-decreasing.

5 Conclusion

The work in this paper is a direct continuation of [2], where a framework was presented for automatic computation of predicate and ranking abstractions, with a specific application to the domain of unbounded pointer structures (aka Shape Analysis). That framework requires all predicates and component ranking functions to be provided by the user. Here we have extended it with dual means of refinement for both types of abstraction.

We have shown two heuristics for synthesizing component ranking functions, one for a linear domain and another for a domain of unbounded pointer structures. These have been surprisingly effective in proving termination of a number of example programs. In the near future we plan to explore richer heuristics in the domain of shape analysis.

References

1. A. Pnueli and E. Shahar. A platform combining deductive with algorithmic verification. In Rajeev Alur and Thomas A. Henzinger, editors, *Proceedings of the Eighth International Conference on Computer Aided Verification CAV*, volume 1102, page 184, New Brunswick, NJ, USA, / 1996. Springer Verlag.
2. I. Balaban, A. Pnueli, and L. D. Zuck. Shape analysis by predicate abstraction. In *VMCAI'2005: Verification, Model Checking, and Abstraction Interpretation*, pages 164–180, 2005.
3. T. Ball, A. Podelski, and S. K. Rajamani. Relative completeness of abstraction refinement for software model checking. In *Tools and Algorithms for Construction and Analysis of Systems*, pages 158–172, 2002.
4. T. Ball and S. K. Rajamani. Automatically validating temporal safety properties of interfaces. *Lecture Notes in Computer Science*, 2057:103+, 2001.
5. E. M. Clarke, O. Grumberg, S. Jha, Y. Lu, and H. Veith. Counterexample-guided abstraction refinement. In *Computer Aided Verification*, pages 154–169, 2000.
6. D. Dams, R. Gerth, and O. Grumberg. A heuristic for the automatic generation of ranking functions. In G. Gopalakrishnan, editor, *Workshop on Advances in Verification*, pages 1–8, 2000.
7. Y. Kesten and A. Pnueli. Verification by augmented finitary abstraction. *Information and Computation*, 163(1):203–243, 2000.
8. O. Lichtenstein and A. Pnueli. Checking that finite-state concurrent programs satisfy their linear specification. In *Proc. 12th ACM Symp. Princ. of Prog. Lang.*, pages 97–107, 1985.
9. A. Podelski and A. Rybalchenko. Software model checking of liveness properties via transition invariants. Research Report MPI-I-2003-2-004, Max-Planck-Institut für Informatik, Stuhlsatzenhausweg 85, 66123 Saarbrücken, Germany, December 2003.
10. A. Podelski and A. Rybalchenko. A complete method for the synthesis of linear ranking functions. In *Verification, Model Checking, and Abstract Interpretation*, pages 239–251, 2004.
11. S. Graf and H. Saïdi. Construction of abstract state graphs with PVS. In O. Grumberg, editor, *Proc. 9th International Conference on Computer Aided Verification (CAV'97)*, volume 1254, pages 72–83. Springer Verlag, 1997.

Developing High Quality Software with Formal Methods: What Else Is Needed?

Constance Heitmeyer

Naval Research Laboratory, Washington, DC 20375
heitmeyer@itd.nrl.navy.mil

Abstract. In recent years, many formal methods have been proposed for improving software quality. These include new specification and modeling languages, whose purpose is to precisely describe the required software behavior at a high level of abstraction, and formal verification techniques, such as model checking and theorem proving, for mechanically proving or refuting critical properties of the software. Unfortunately, while promising, these methods are rarely used in software practice. This paper describes improvements in languages, specifications and models, code quality, and code verification techniques that could, along with existing formal methods, play a major role in improving software quality.

1 Introduction

During the past two decades, many specification and modeling languages have been introduced whose purpose is to precisely describe the required software behavior at a higher level of abstraction than the code. Examples of these languages include the synchronous languages, such as Lustre [Halbwachs1993]; the design language Statecharts [Harel1987]; requirements languages such as RSML [Heimdahl and Leveson1996], and SCR [Heitmeyer et al.2005]; and design languages offered by industry, such as UML and Stateflow [Mathworks1999], a version of Statecharts included in Matlab's Simulink graphical language.

Specifications and models expressed in these languages can have important advantages in software development. First, they provide a solid basis for both evaluating and improving the software code. Moreover, because they usually exclude design and implementation detail, these specifications and models are more concise than code. As a result, they can serve as an effective medium for customers and developers to communicate precisely about the required software behavior. In addition, they allow both manual and automated analysis of the required software behavior. Analyzing and correcting a software specification is usually cheaper than analyzing and correcting the code itself because the specification is most often smaller—thus finding and correcting bugs in a specification is easier than finding and correcting bugs in code.

Significant advances have also occurred in formal verification. These advances include automated analysis of software or a software artifact using an automated theorem prover such as PVS [Owre et al.1993] or a model checker, such as Spin

[Holzmann1997] or SMV [McMillan1993]. Such analysis is useful in analyzing a software specification, a model, or software code for critical properties, such as safety and security properties. Because the analysis is largely mechanical, these techniques can be a cost-effective means of either verifying or refuting that a software artifact or software code satisfies a specified property.

Unfortunately, while promising, formal specifications, models and verification techniques are rarely used by most software developers. After reviewing how formally-based tools can help developers improve the quality of both software and software artifacts, this paper describes four enhancements to the software development process which should not only improve software quality directly but should also encourage the use of existing formal methods.

2 On the Role of Tools

Many automated techniques and tools have been developed in recent years to improve the quality of software and to decrease the cost of producing quality software [Heitmeyer2003]. Such tools can play an important role in obtaining high confidence that a software system is correct, i.e., satisfies its requirements. Described below are five different roles that tools can play in improving the quality of both software and software artifacts. The first four help improve the quality of a specification or model. The fifth uses a high-quality specification to construct a set of tests for use in checking and debugging the software code.

2.1 Demonstrate Well-Formedness

A *well-formed* specification is syntactically and type correct, has no circular dependencies, and is *complete* (no required behavior is missing) and *consistent* (no behavior in the specification is ambiguous). Tools, such as NRL's consistency checker [Heitmeyer et al.1996], can automatically detect well-formedness errors.

2.2 Discover Property Violations

In analyzing software or a software artifact for a property, a tool, such as a model checker, can uncover a property violation. By analyzing the counterexample returned by the model checker, a developer may trace the problem to either a flaw in the specification or to one or more missing assumptions. Alternatively, the formulation of the property, rather than the specification, may be incorrect. Detecting and correcting such defects can lead to higher quality specifications and to higher quality code.

2.3 Verify Critical Properties

Either a theorem prover or a model checker may be used to verify that a software artifact, such as a requirements specification or a design specification, satisfies a critical property. Verifying that an artifact satisfies a set of properties can help practitioners develop high confidence that the artifact is correct.

2.4 Validate a Specification

A developer may use a tool, such as a simulator or animator, to check that a formal specification captures the intended software behavior. By running scenarios through a simulator (see, e.g., [Heitmeyer et al.2005]), the user can ensure that the system specification neither omits nor incorrectly specifies the software system requirements.

2.5 Automatically Construct a Suite of Test Cases

Specification-based testing can automatically derive a suite of test cases satisfying some coverage criterion, such as *branch coverage*, from a formal specification [Gargantini and Heitmeyer1999]. Automated test case generation can be enormously useful to software developers because 1) the cost and time needed to automatically construct tests is much lower than the cost and time needed in manually constructing tests, and 2) a suite of test cases mechanically generated from a specification usually checks a wider range of software behaviors than manually generated tests and hence may uncover more software defects.

3 What Else Is Needed?

For practitioners to apply existing formal methods more widely, a number of improvements in the software development process are needed. Described below are four areas where improvements are needed—in specification and modeling languages, in the quality of specifications and models, in the quality of manually generated code, and in improved techniques for software verification.

3.1 Improved Languages

One area that should be revisited is specification and modeling languages. In recent years, researchers have proposed many new languages for specifying and modeling software. Although these languages have been applied effectively in some specialized areas, for example, in control systems for nuclear power plants and in avionics systems, they are still not used widely by software practitioners. While languages introduced by industry, such as UML and Stateflow, are more widely used, they lack a formal semantics. Moreover, the specifications and models that practitioners produce using these languages usually include significant design and implement detail. Given the lack of formal semantics and the large specifications and models that result when design and implementation detail are included, the opportunity to analyze these specifications and models using formally-based tools is severely limited.

Hence, existing languages either need to be enhanced with features (such as fancy graphical interfaces) to encourage practitioners to use them, or new languages need to be invented. One promising approach is to design languages for specialized domains. For example, one or more languages could be designed to specify and model the required behavior of networks and distributed systems. Significantly different specification and modeling languages are likely to be needed to specify and model the required behavior of software used in automobiles or in avionics systems.

The benefits of using specification and modeling languages with an explicit formal semantics and which minimize implementation detail could be enormous. First, precise, unambiguous specifications can be analyzed automatically for well-formedness, such as syntax and type correctness, consistency (no unwanted non-determinism), and completeness (no missing cases), for critical application properties, such as security and safety properties, and for validity (a check that the specification captures the intended behavior). Specifications that are well-formed, correct with respect to critical application properties, and validated using simulation also provide a solid foundation both for automatic test generation and for generating efficient, provably correct source code.

3.2 Improved Specifications and Models

The specifications and models produced by practitioners (and some researchers) usually include significant design and implementation detail (i.e., are close to the code). Moreover, often they do not use abstraction effectively to remove redundancy and to enhance readabililty. The result is large, hard to understand specifications and models, filled with unnecessary detail and redundancy, which do not distinguish between the required software behavior and implementation detail. In part, this problem can be solved through education. The attributes of good specifications and models and how to construct them are topics that need to be taught and emphasized in software engineering curricula. The problem of poor quality specifications and models can also be ameliorated by improved specification and modeling languages. Such languages should reduce the opportunity for implementation bias and contain mechanisms which encourage the construction of precise, concise, and readable specifications and models. Well-thought out examples of high-quality specifications and models would also help practitioners produce better specifications and models.

3.3 Improved Methods for Building Code

However, improved specification and modeling languages and improved specifications and models are not enough. In the end, what is needed is correct, efficient code. As noted above, an important benefit of a formal specification is that it provides a solid basis for automatically generating provably correct, efficient code. While many techniques have been proposed for constructing source code from specifications, and many software developers use automatic code generators developed by industry, the code produced by these generators is often inefficient and wasteful of memory. Urgently needed are improved, more powerful methods for automatic generation of provably correct, efficient code from specifications.

Another promising approach to producing high quality code is to use "safe" languages, such as Cyclone [Trevor et al.2002]. Using a language such as Cyclone, which is designed to improve the quality of C programs, can reduce code vulnerabilities, such as uninitialized variables and potential sources of buffer overflows and arithmetic exceptions. A third promising approach to constructing high quality code is to encourage programmers to annotate their code with assertions that a compiler can check at run-time. Hardware designers routinely include such assertions in their designs. Moreover, some C, C++, and Java programmers routinely use assertions as an aid in both detecting and correcting software bugs. Increased use of both safe languages and the annotation of programs with assertions should help improve the quality of software code.

3.4 Improved Methods for Verifying Code

Although improved specifications and models and automatic code generation from high quality specifications can help improve the quality of software, it is highly likely that in the near future, most source code will be generated manually. Urgently needed therefore are improved methods for demonstrating that a manually generated program satisfies critical properties.

One promising approach is to encourage programmers to annotate their code with assertions and to then check those assertions automatically. While current compilers for C, C++, and Java, support and check assertions that annotate the code, the set of assertions that can be analyzed is very limited. Needed are compilers that can not only check simple Boolean inequalities, e.g., $x > 0$, but more complex assertions, e.g., $\text{priv}(P, x) = \text{R}$, which means that process P has read privileges for variable x. Such assertions can be translated into logic formulae, such as first-order logic formulae, and then a compiler should be able to use decision procedures to check that the code satisfies these logic assertions. In addition to helping practitioners document and detect bugs in their code, such assertions may also be used to prove that the code satisfies critical properties, such as security and safety properties.

Recently, we applied this approach to a software-based cryptographic system called CD (Cryptographic Device) II, the second member of a family of systems, each of which decrypts and encrypts data stored on two or more communication channels [Kirby et al.1999]. An essential property of this system is to enforce *data separation*, that is, to guarantee that data stored on one channel does not influence nor is influenced by data stored on a different channel. Satisfying this property is critical since data stored on one channel may be classified at a different level (e.g., Top Secret) than data stored on another channel (e.g., Unclassified).

A technique which could automatically check code annotated with assertions for a security property such as data separation would be extremely useful. However, rather than directly checking the code for conformance to the security property, an alternative is to construct a high-level formal specification of a system's required behavior, check the high-level specification for the property, and then check that the code is a refinement of the specification. The benefit of the high-level specification is that it describes precisely the set of services that the software is required to support. In checking CD II for data separation, we followed the latter approach: we constructed a high-level specification of the required behavior of CD II, used PVS to prove that the specification satisfied the data separation property, and then used inspection to show that the CD code, annotated with assertions, satisfied the high-level specification.

More automation of the process we used in verifying that the CD II code satisfies the data separation property would have been extremely useful. Not only would more automation dramatically reduce the human effort need to construct and check the code assertions against both the code and the formal specification, it would also significantly enhance our confidence that the code satisfied the assertions and therefore enforced data separation since manual construction and manual checking of assertions is somewhat error-prone. Two steps were especially labor-intensive: 1) annotating the code with assertions and 2) verifying that the code satisfied the assertions. Also expensive in terms of human effort was the process of demonstrating that the code assertions satisfied the high-level specification.

Adding some annotations to code is straightforward and, as mentioned above, automatic checking of simple code annotations is already supported by many source language compilers. However, generating more complex annotations from code (e.g., constructing inductive invariants from loops) is a problem that requires more research. Checking the conformance of the code with a set of assertions using decision procedures is a promising approach that should be explored by researchers and should help in automating the second step described above. Finally, checking the conformance of a set of validated assertions with a formal specification is also a problem that may require further research.

4 Summary

The improvements described above will require new research in specification and modeling languages, in checking and constructing more complex code assertions, in automatic code generation, and in code verification. They will also require the transfer of existing research, for example, the use of safe languages such as Cyclone, and of formal techniques, such as model checking, theorem proving, and decision procedures, into programming practice. In addition, better educated software developers are needed; such developers will know how to build high quality specifications and models and will routinely include assertions in their code. Finally, existing methods and tools must be better engineered. The result of improved and more automated methods, better educated practitioners, and better engineered tools should allow software practitioners to construct software in an environment in which tools do the tedious analysis and book-keeping and software developers are liberated to transform vague notions of the required software behavior into precise, readable specifications that minimize design and implementation detail and into code that is both provably correct and efficient.

Acknowledgments

Section 3.4, which proposes improved methods for verifying code, benefited from discussions with my NRL colleagues, Michael Colon, Beth Leonard, Myla Archer, and Ramesh Bharadwaj.

References

[Gargantini and Heitmeyer1999] Angelo Gargantini and Constance Heitmeyer. 1999. Using model checking to generate tests from requirements specifications. In *Proceedings, 7th European Software Engineering Conference and 7th ACM SIGSOFT Symposium on the Foundations of Software Engineering (ESEC/FSE-7)*, LNCS 1687, pages 146–162, Toulouse, FR, September. Springer-Verlag.

[Halbwachs1993] Nicolas Halbwachs. 1993. *Synchronous Programming of Reactive Systems*. Kluwer Academic Publishers, Boston, MA.

[Harel1987] David Harel. 1987. Statecharts: A visual formalism for complex systems. *Science of Computer Programming*, 8(3):231–274, June.

[Heimdahl and Leveson1996] Mats P. E. Heimdahl and Nancy Leveson. 1996. Completeness and consistency in hierarchical state-based requirements. *IEEE Transactions on Software Engineering*, 22(6):363–377, June.

[Heitmeyer et al.1996] C. L. Heitmeyer, R. D. Jeffords, and B. G. Labaw. 1996. Automated consistency checking of requirements specifications. *ACM Transactions on Software Engineering and Methodology*, 5(3):231–261.

[Heitmeyer et al.2005] C. Heitmeyer, M. Archer, R. Bharadwaj, and R. Jeffords. 2005. Tools for constructing requirements specifications: The SCR toolset at the age of ten. *Computer Systems Science and Engineering*, 20(1):19–35, January.

[Heitmeyer2003] Constance Heitmeyer. 2003. Developing high assurance systems: On the role of software tools. In *Proceedings, 22nd Internat. Conf. on Computer Safety, Reliability and Security (SAFECOMP 2003)*, Edinburgh, September. (invited).

[Holzmann1997] G. J. Holzmann. 1997. The model checker Spin. *IEEE Transactions on Software Engineering*, 23(5):279–295, May.

[Kirby et al.1999] J. Kirby, M. Archer, and C. Heitmeyer. 1999. SCR: A practical approach to building a high assurance COMSEC system. In *Proceedings, 15th Annual Computer Security Applications Conference (ACSAC '99)*, pages 109–118, Phoenix, AZ, December. IEEE Computer Society.

[Mathworks1999] The Mathworks Inc. 1999. Stateflow for use with Simulink, User's Guide, Version 2 (Release 11). Natick, MA.

[McMillan1993] K. L. McMillan. 1993. *Symbolic Model Checking*. Kluwer Academic Pub., Englewood Cliffs, NJ.

[Owre et al.1993] Sam Owre, Natarajan Shankar, and John Rushby. 1993. User guide for the PVS specification and verification system (Draft). Technical report, Computer Science Lab, SRI Int'l, Menlo Park, CA.

[Trevor et al.2002] Jim Trevor, Greg Morrisett, Dan Grossman, Michael Hicks, James Cheney, and Yanling Wang. 2002. Cyclone: A safe dialect of C. In *Proceedings, USENIX Annual Technical Conf.*, pages 275–288, Monterey, CA, June.

A Testing Architecture for Designing High-Reliable MANET Protocols

Teruo Higashino and Hirozumi Yamaguchi

Graduate School of Information Science and Technology,
Osaka University, Suita, Osaka 565-0871, Japan
{higashino, h-yamagu}@ist.osaka-u.ac.jp

Abstract. In future ubiquitous communication environments, broadband wireless communication will become popular. Also, wireless LAN devices such as IEEE802.11a/b/g and wireless PAN devices such as Bluetooth and ZigBee may be integrated into mobile terminals with reasonable cost and complementarily used with existing cellular networks. This means that mobile ad-hoc networks (MANETs), which are composed between these narrow range communication devices without fixed network infrastructures will be seamlessly connected to global networks (IP networks). For future deployment of MANET protocols, we discuss their testing issues with some experimental results.

1 Introduction

MANETs are getting recognized as one of key infrastructures to realize future ubiquitous communication environments. However, testing functional and performance validity of MANET applications and protocols is not an easy task. Even if given IUTs (Implementation Under Test) of mobile nodes have independently passed general conformance tests, they might not work correctly (or might not achieve reasonable performance) if they work together collaboratively to provide services and functionalities such as distributed content search and routing. Additionally, mobility of nodes makes the problem much more difficult. It is known that mobility models strongly make influence for their performance and correctness [1].

In this paper, we focus on functional and performance testing for MANET protocols. We discuss what properties should be validated in testing, and accordingly how we model the environments of target protocols. Then we propose a testing architecture for MANET protocols. The architecture is based on our network simulator MobiREAL [2,3]. We basically use passive testing methods where we observe sequences of data transmission between IUTs. Given IUTs to be tested and properties to be validated, the environments including mobility models and underlying wireless transmission layers can be virtually provided to IUTs as if they are executed on real mobile terminals. The architecture supports not only to provide environments but also to observe the results of passive testing visually. Some experimental results are also shown in this paper.

2 Passive Testing of MANET Protocols

When we consider passive testing in the higher layer (layer 4 and the above) of MANET protocols, we may simply abstract the communication channel between them as single unreliable channel. On the other hand, testing the network layer protocols of MANETs needs much consideration mainly because of (i) mobility modeling and (ii) upper/lower layer modeling.

Let us consider DSR (Dynamic Source Routing) [4] as an example. DSR finds multiple potential routes at the route request phase. Then one of them is selected and the others are kept in route cache of the nodes for some period. If the current route is broken, the route is re-established using the cache at the nodes. In this situation, if we would like to validate such property that the route can be re-established *in any situation of node mobility, topology and density*, we have to test given IUTs in many cases, giving many types of mobility models with different numbers of nodes. We may refer to Ref. [1] where several mobility models have been introduced. However, it is hard for designers to imagine mobility patterns of mobile nodes and choose ones that generate node mobility, topology and density that totally generates the desired situations. To cope with this problem, we may use several metrics to characterize the mobility [5–7].

The modeling of the upper/lower layers of the target layer might make some influence. In the lower layers, packet delay by collision avoidance and/or retransmission might make some influence to the performance of the network layer. The packet duplication by retransmission and packet regulation by rate control in the upper layers also might make some influence. Here, we assume that the implementation in the lower layers is correct. Also, we assume that we use general functions and applications in the upper layers (*e.g.* we assume that we use CBR (Constant Bit Rate)).

Under these assumptions, we assume that IUTs are provided as executable codes (thus they are black-boxes), and provide an architecture for passive testing. For given properties to be validated (*e.g.* communication between source and destination nodes can take place correctly in DSR), we observe communications between IUTs. We use a mobile ad-hoc network simulator called MobiREAL[2,3] which can control the mobility of each mobile node using a set of events with pre- and post-conditions. For macroscopic control of mobile nodes, mobility scenarios can be given. The simulator can provide implementation of the other layers such as CBR, TCP, IEEE802.11 MAC, and radio propagation. We are now planning to provide a virtual environment in the MobiREAL simulator where given IUTs can be executed as if they are executed on the real terminals. But actually these terminals are emulated using implementations of the other layer protocols of MobiREAL simulator.

3 Impact of Mobility – Experimental Results –

In this section, we present the experimental results of performance evaluation of DSR using MobiREAL. The results will show the difference of performance depending on mobility, and encourage us to provide our testing architecture.

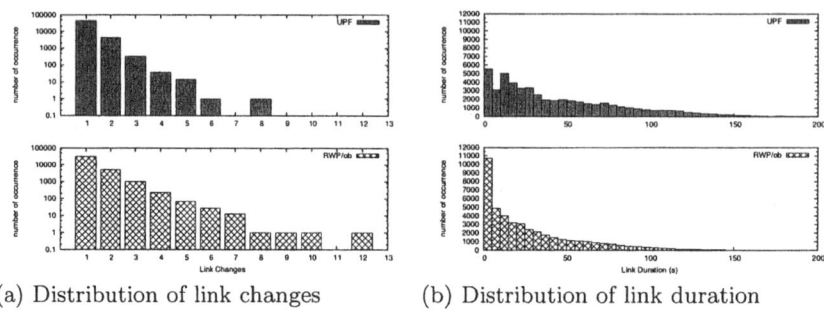

(a) Distribution of link changes   (b) Distribution of link duration

Fig. 1. Mobility Metrics

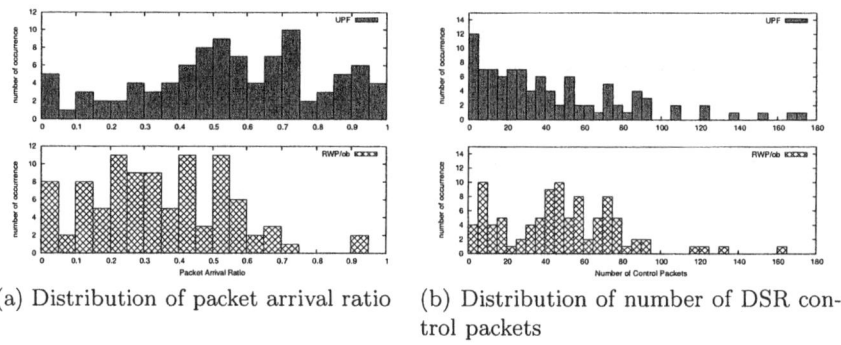

(a) Distribution of packet arrival ratio   (b) Distribution of number of DSR control packets

Fig. 2. DSR Performance

We have used different mobility models to see the impact of mobility models to MANET protocols. We have modeled a real 500m×500m region including buildings in downtown Osaka city. We have used two mobility models, (i) UPF (Urban Pedestrian Flow) mobility[8] which represents realistic movement of pedestrians in city sections, and (ii) a modified version of RWP (random way point) mobility denoted as RWP/ob ("ob." stands for obstacles). In RWP/ob, each node moves between intersections. At each intersection, the node randomly decides the next direction, avoiding to go backward. Then we have measured the metrics presented in Ref. [7] that characterize mobility. (i) link changes (*i.e.* the number of link creations between two nodes) and (ii) link duration (*i.e.* the longest time interval during which two nodes are in the transmission range of each other).

The distributions of these metrics are shown in Fig. 1. Clearly, RWP/ob model has several cases with larger link changes (*e.g.* 9 and the above) compared with UPF mobility. This is natural because in the UPF mobility, more neighboring nodes are going to the same destination than RWP mobility and thus link changes do not occur many times. This observation is endorsed by the link duration result, where UPF has longer durations clearly.

Then we have measured several metrics that show the performance of DSR. We have selected two application users in the same pedestrian flow but away from each other. The results are shown in Fig. 2.

In the UPF mobility, DSR route was established along the flow. Therefore, the route is stabler than RWP/ob. This observation is endorsed by Fig. 2(a) and Fig. 2(b). The packet arrival ratio becomes lower and the number of control packet is larger if the route is instable, since there are many disconnections of the route.

4 Conclusion

In this paper, we have discussed a passive testing architecture of MANET protocols, and have presented a future direction to design high-reliable MANET protocols. Our ongoing work is to design the presented architecture.

References

1. T. Camp, J. Boleng, and V. Davies. A survey of mobility models for ad hoc network research. *Wireless Communication & Mobile Computing (WCMC)*, pages 483–502, 2002.
2. K. Konishi, K. Maeda, K. Sato, A. Yamasaki, H. Yamaguchi, K. Yasumoto, and T. Higashino. MobiREAL simulator – evaluating MANET applications in real environments –. In *Proc. of the 13th IEEE Int. Symp. on Modeling, Analysis, and Simulation of Computer and Telecommunication Systems (MASCOTS 2005)*, 2005. (to appear).
3. MobiREAL web page. http://www.mobireal.net.
4. D. Johnson and D. Maltz. Dynamic source routing in ad hoc wireless networks. *Mobile Computing*, 1996.
5. P. Johansson, T. Larsson, N. Hedman, B. Mielczarek, and M. Degermark. Scenario-based performance analysis of routing protocols for mobile ad-hoc networks. In *Proc. of ACM/IEEE Mobicom*, pages 195–206, 1999.
6. X. Hong, T.J. Kwon, M. Gerla, D. L. Gu, and G. Pei. A mobility framework for ad hoc wireless networks. In *Proc. of the ACM 2nd Int. Conf. on Mobile Data Management (MDM2001) (LNCS Vol.1987)*, pages 185–196, 2001.
7. F. Bai, N. Sadagopan, and A. Helmy. The IMPORTANT framework for analyzing the impact of mobility on performance of routing for ad hoc networks. *AdHoc Networks Journal*, pages 383–403, November 2003.
8. K. Maeda, K. Sato, K. Konishi, A. Yamasaki, A. Uchiyama, H. Yamaguchi, K. Yasumoto, and T. Higashino. Getting urban pedestrian flow from simple observation : Realistic mobility generation in wireless network simulation. In *white paper (available on MobiREAL web page)*, 2005. (an extended version has been submitted to a conference).

A Composition Operator for Systems with Active and Passive Actions

Stefan Strubbe* and Rom Langerak

Twente University, PO BOX 217, 7500AE Enschede, The Netherlands
s.n.strubbe@math.utwente.nl, langerak@cs.utwente.nl

Abstract. We investigate requirements for a composition operator for complex control systems. The operator should be suitable for a context where we have both supervisory control and a system that consists of multiple (two or more) components. We conclude that using both passive (observing) and active (controlling) transitions is advantageous for the specification of supervisory control systems. We introduce a composition operator that meets the requirements. We give both operational and trace semantics for this operator and give necessary and sufficient conditions for commutativity and associativity.

Keywords: Compositional modelling, supervisory control.

1 Introduction

A complex system typically consists of multiple components which are running simultaneously and which are interacting with each other. Modelling these complex systems in a compositional way can be done by using a composition operator which combines the different components of the system. If we denote the composition operator by $||$, then $A||B$ is the system that is composed out of subsystems A and B. The interaction between the two subsystems is regulated by the composition rules of the operator $||$. Because the systems A and B run in parallel (or concurrently), we call $||$ the parallel composition operator.

The goal of this paper is to make clear that for the modelling of many types of systems, it is advantageous and natural to use two types of interaction: blocking-interaction and non-blocking-interaction. We show that this idea can be formalized by distinguishing active and passive actions. The operator we define via structured operational semantics ([1]) can be used with any transition-based model like automata or process algebra. The focus of this paper is to give a careful motivation for this operator.

In Section 2, which is the main part of the paper, we introduce the active/passive framework and we develop a composition operator that can establish several types of interaction between systems (that are built out of active and passive transitions). While we develop the operator step by step, we motivate each step by means of simple and clear examples. Some of these examples

---

* Supported by the EU-project HYBRIDGE (IST-2001-32460).

are about supervisory control systems because we think that supervisory control systems provide natural examples for our modelling framework. After the framework has been introduced (including a structural operational semantics for the composition operator), we give a more extensive example in Section 2.4 which shows all features of the framework and the composition operator. In Section 2.5 we take a closer look at supervisory control systems. We explain why we think that our framework has certain advantages over other frameworks in modelling supervisory control systems. Section 2 ends with a technical result on the operator.

In Section 3 we give a denotational semantics in terms of an extension of traces. We think that this semantics gives more insight in the composition operation and consequently more justification for the use of this specific operator.

In the last section we draw some conclusions and point out directions for future research.

2 The Active/Passive Framework

We can distinguish two types of interactions between processes. First, *blocking*-interaction: both partners (for example the controller and the process) need to be able to do the action, otherwise the action will not take place. This is the type of interaction that we see in many process algebra models (e.g. [2,3]). Secondly, *non-blocking*-interaction: one of the partners (the passive one) is not able to block the other (the active one). For example if a person (the passive partner) observes that a light (the active partner) is switched on. The person observes, but is not able to block the switching, i.e. the light could also be switched on without the person observing it.

Non-blocking-interaction can already be found in the literature, e.g. in broadcast systems ([4]) where several listening processes can receive (but not block) a signal, or in I/O automata ([5,6]), where processes should be input-enabled, i.e. ready to receive an input in any state of the process, such that an output will never be blocked.

We see that most formalisms support only blocking interaction and that some formalisms (broadcasting systems, I/O automata) support only non-blocking interaction. However, there exists no formalism that supports both blocking and non-blocking interaction. We will motivate that for our purposes, it is desirable to have a formalism that supports both types of interaction.

The context of processes that we want to specify is the following:

1. We want to specify *supervisory control systems*. We will see that we need both blocking and non-blocking interaction for this.
2. We are also interested in *modular supervisory control*, where a controller may consist of several modules. We will motivate that for this, in addition to blocking and non-blocking interaction, we need to control the scope of non-blocking interaction.
3. We want to specify *complex processes that consist of interacting subprocesses*. Here we will argue that we need the possibility to have multi-way synchronizations.

Now we will introduce our framework, which is based on active and passive actions and which supports both blocking and non-blocking interaction. We introduce the framework in three steps, corresponding to the three points in the above context. In each step we give motivating examples. In the first step we explain how active and passive actions can be used to establish blocking and non-blocking interaction. In the second step we explain how to deal with observations in systems that consist of more than two components. In the third step we treat the issue of multi-way synchronization (can one active action synchronize with multiple passive actions or only with one passive action?).

2.1 Step 1: Establishing Blocking and Non-blocking Interaction

We consider two types of actions: *active* actions (denoted as a, b etc.) and *passive* actions (which are observing actions and are denoted as $\bar{a}, \bar{b}$, etc.). Because we want to have both blocking and non-blocking interactions, we have to make clear which interactions are blocking and which are non-blocking. Therefore, we introduce the set A which contains all actions that are involved in blocking interaction. The composition operator will now be denoted by $|A|$. We still use $\|$ to denote the composition operator in cases where A is unspecified or irrelevant. Blocking-interaction is now expressed by the following operational rule ([1]):

$$r1. \frac{L_1 \xrightarrow{a} L_1', L_2 \xrightarrow{a} L_2'}{L_1|A|L_2 \xrightarrow{a} L_1'|A|L_2'} (a \in A),$$

which says that a blocking-synchronization (or active-active synchronization) on a from joint location $L_1|A|L_2$ to $L_1'|A|L_2'$, can only happen when both partners have the action a available from locations L_1 and L_2 to locations L_1' and L_2' respectively (In order to comply with the terminology used in timed and hybrid automata, we use the term *locations* to designate the *states* in an automaton). In Figure 1, where $a \in A$, we see that both the process P and the controller C have transitions labelled with a from their initial locations P_1 and C_1. This results in the (synchronized) a-transition in the composite system $P\|C$. In location P_3, P can do an a-action, but because $a \in A$ and C does not have an

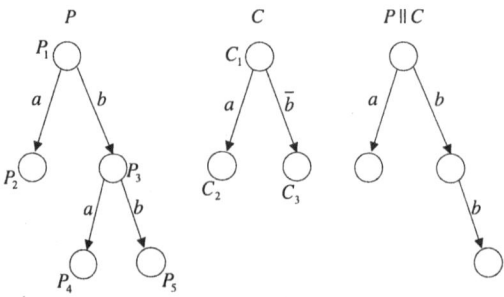

Fig. 1. Process P controlled by C

active a-transition in location C_3, this transition is blocked by C and therefore the transition is not present in $P||C$.

Blocking as expressed in rule r1 can be used in supervisory control where a controller C blocks certain actions of the process P. Another situation where active actions must synchronize (i.e. are in A) is where two partners cooperate on a certain task. If two persons are chatting with each other, then they are cooperating on the chat-task so to say. In other words, both are chatting or both are not chatting, one cannot chat without the other (this situation will be described in the example in Section 2.4). For a situation where two persons P_1 and P_2 can both do a specific action (like hanging up the phone as described in Section 2.4) independently of the other person, then the action can be independently performed (i.e. should not be in A).

For non-blocking-interaction, we need an active a with $a \notin A$ in one partner and a passive $\bar{a}$ in the other partner. Non-blocking interaction is now expressed by

$$r2. \frac{L_1 \xrightarrow{a} L_1', L_2 \xrightarrow{\bar{a}} L_2'}{L_1|A|L_2 \xrightarrow{a} L_1'|A|L_2'} (a \notin A),$$

which means that L_1 executes an a, which is observed by a $\bar{a}$-transition outgoing from L_2. In Figure 1 we see for example that the b-transition from location P_1 in P, is observed by the $\bar{b}$-transition in C. We also need rule r2', which is the mirror rule of r2 (i.e. $L_1 \xrightarrow{\bar{a}} L_1', L_2 \xrightarrow{a} L_2'$ instead of $L_1 \xrightarrow{a} L_1', L_2 \xrightarrow{\bar{a}} L_2'$ etc.).

If L_2 can not observe a-actions (i.e. there is no outgoing $\bar{a}$-transition), L_1 should still be able to execute a, since this execution does not depend on whether or not some other process is observing the action. This is expressed by

$$r3. \frac{L_1 \xrightarrow{a} L_1', L_2 \not\xrightarrow{\bar{a}}}{L_1|A|L_2 \xrightarrow{a} L_1'|A|L_2} (a \notin A)$$

and its mirror rule

$$r3'. \frac{L_1 \not\xrightarrow{\bar{a}}, L_2 \xrightarrow{a} L_2'}{L_1|A|L_2 \xrightarrow{a} L_1|A|L_2'} (a \notin A).$$

In Figure 1 we see for example that P has a b-transition from location P_3, which cannot be observed by C, but which is still present in $P||C$.

Note that because rules r2, r3 and r3' are the only rules from which active transitions can be derived, it follows that if L_2 *can* observe a, then it also *will* observe a, i.e. if L_2 has a $\bar{a}$-transition, then it can not choose not to observe an a executed by the other component. This makes sense in many situations, e.g. when some system broadcasts a radio signal a and a receiver is able to receive the signal (i.e. it has a passive $\bar{a}$-transition), then we should not allow the possibility that the signal is broadcast while the receiver does not receive (i.e. does not synchronize its passive $\bar{a}$-action with the active a-action).

Negative premises in rules (as in rule r3) may in general lead to complications (see [7]), however in our rules there are no problems, as can easily be seen from the fact that $\xrightarrow{\bar{a}}$ transitions never depend on $\xrightarrow{a}$ transitions, and therefore no circularities may arise.

In the supervisory control context, observing as active/passive-synchronization means that the controller observes actions of the process. Outside the supervisory control context, this mechanism can be used for other kinds of observation (e.g. a person that observes an alarm signal as described in Section 2.4).

2.2 Step 2: Controlling the Scope of the Observations

Passive transitions are intended to observe active transitions. This means that outside an open-systems context (i.e. when the system is closed and will not interact with other systems), passive transitions are supposed not to be present, since there is nothing to observe. Suppose we have a system that consists of a process P and a controller C, where the controller observes the actions of P. One could argue that $|A|$ should be defined such that after composition, there are no passive transitions anymore (which is the case if we only consider rules r1,r2 and r3). But that would not be suitable for a broader composition context like modular supervisory control: Suppose we have a system with one process P and two controllers C_1 and C_2, where both C_1 and C_2 are concurrently observing P. If we define $C := C_1 || C_2$ as the composed controller, then C should still observe P, with other words, C should still contain the passive transitions from C_1 and C_2 to observe P. This means that the 'real' observations happen when we compose C with P and not when we compose C_1 with C_2.

One solution one could think of is to indicate within the composition operator where the 'real' observations take place. We could use an observation set O and then $||_O$ (or together with A, $|_A^O|$) means that observations take place in this composition for the events in O. Then in the compound $(C_1||C_2)||_O P$ there are no passive transitions with labels from O anymore.

For the double-controller situation, $||_O$ seems to be a good solution. However, it seems that for modelling the following situation, we need a different solution: Suppose three persons P_1, P_2 and P_3 are working on a problem. All persons start working independently on this problem. Once one of the persons found the solution, all three persons stop with the problem. This can be modelled as in Figure 2, where the signal *ready* is 'broadcast' by one of the persons as soon as this person solved the problem, and is then received by the others. In this situation, every P_i should be able to hear every P_j ($i \neq j$). With $||_O$ we can not express this. (In $(P_1||P_2)||_O P_3$, P_1 does not observe P_2. In $(P_1||_O P_2)||P_3$, P_3 does not observe P_1 and P_2 etc.).

Instead of using $||_O$, we use the closing operator $[\cdot]_C$. $[X]_C$ discards all passive transitions in X with labels from C. With this closing operator, we can solve both the double-controller and the 'three persons' problem. The composition rules for this operator are

$$r7. \frac{L \xrightarrow{a} L'}{[L]_C \xrightarrow{a} [L']_C}$$

$$r8. \frac{L \xrightarrow{\bar{a}} L'}{[L]_C \xrightarrow{\bar{a}} [L']_C} (\bar{a} \notin C).$$

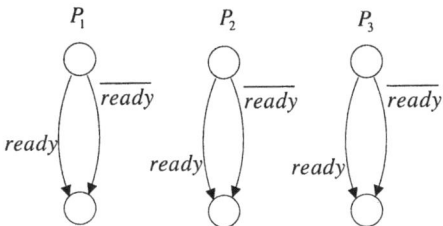

Fig. 2. Situation where all persons can observe all others

With $[\cdot]_C$ we can control the scope of the observations. Now, $\|$ should be defined such that in $X\|Y$, X can observe Y (and vice versa), but also $X\|Y$ can still observe Z in $(X\|Y)\|Z$. This is expressed by

$$r4. \frac{L_1 \xrightarrow{\bar{a}} L_1'}{L_1|A|L_2 \xrightarrow{\bar{a}} L_1'|A|L_2}$$

and its mirror r4' which say that after the composition, every passive transition 'remains', such that the component to which this transition belongs, is still able to observe a new component which might be added to the composite system in a new composition operation. If, for example, we know that X and Y only observe each other and will (or can) not observe Z or other components, then we could specify this as $[X\|Y]\|Z$. ($[\cdot]$ is shorthand for $[\cdot]_{\bar{\Sigma}}$ with $\bar{\Sigma}$ the set of all passive actions).

2.3 Step 3: Multi-way Synchronization

Consider the modular supervisory control situation again where we have two controllers C_1 and C_2 and a process C_3. Now suppose that C_3 has an action a which can be observed by both C_1 and C_2 (i.e. both controllers have $\bar{a}$-transitions). If we allow that both controllers can observe a concurrently (which is most natural), then we need to express the possibility of a multi-way synchronization (in this case: two passive actions and one active action). Another example (outside the supervisory control context) where we need a multi-way synchronization is the situation where an alarm signal in an office is heard (observed) by two different employees working in that office (this example is also described in Section 2.4).

The question now is whether there are situations we want to model that do not allow multi-way synchronizations. One such example (also considered in Section 2.4) is the telephone situation: a telephone in an office rings and only one of the employees may answer the call. Although both employees hear the telephone, only one may answer it (i.e. may synchronize its passive action with the active telephone signal).

We see that it is desirable to distinguish two types of passive actions: passive actions for which multi-way synchronization is allowed and passive actions for which this is not allowed. Therefore we introduce the set P, which contains all passive actions for which multi-way synchronization is allowed. The composition operator will now be denoted by $|_A^P|$. Multi-way synchronization is expressed by

$$r5. \frac{L_1 \xrightarrow{\bar{a}} L_1', L_2 \xrightarrow{\bar{a}} L_2'}{L_1|_A^P|L_2 \xrightarrow{\bar{a}} L_1'|_A^P|L_2'} (\bar{a} \in P),$$

which means that two passive $\bar{a}$-transitions, one in C_1 and one in C_2, synchronize, which results in a $\bar{a}$-transition for the composite system $C_1||C_2$. This synchronized passive transition can observe an a in C_3, which results in a new (multi-way) synchronized transition in $(C_1||C_2)||C_3$ which then expresses that C_1 and C_2 concurrently observe C_3.

If $a \in P$ and C_1 can observe a, but C_2 cannot observe a, then in $(C_1||C_2)||C_3$, C_1 should synchronize its passive $\bar{a}$ with the active a of C_3, while C_2 idles. This situation is expressed by

$$r6. \frac{L_1 \xrightarrow{\bar{a}} L_1', L_2 \not\xrightarrow{\bar{a}}}{L_1|_A^P|L_2 \xrightarrow{\bar{a}} L_1'|_A^P|L_2} (\bar{a} \in P)$$

and its mirror rule r6'. In the new situation (where we have introduced the set P), we can see that rule r4 (which expresses that passive transitions should interleave) only applies for passive actions not in P. Therefore r4 should be changed to

$$r4. \frac{L_1 \xrightarrow{\bar{a}} L_1'}{L_1|_A^P|L_2 \xrightarrow{\bar{a}} L_1'|_A^P|L_2} (\bar{a} \notin P).$$

With the set P as part of the operator, rules r1,r2 and r3 should be changed to

$$r1. \frac{L_1 \xrightarrow{a} L_1', L_2 \xrightarrow{a} L_2'}{L_1|_A^P|L_2 \xrightarrow{a} L_1'|_A^P|L_2'} (a \in A),$$

$$r2. \frac{L_1 \xrightarrow{a} L_1', L_2 \xrightarrow{\bar{a}} L_2'}{L_1|_A^P|L_2 \xrightarrow{a} L_1'|_A^P|L_2'} (a \notin A),$$

$$r3. \frac{L_1 \xrightarrow{a} L_1', L_2 \not\xrightarrow{\bar{a}}}{L_1|_A^P|L_2 \xrightarrow{a} L_1'|_A^P|L_2} (a \notin A).$$

Now rules r1 till r6 (and the mirror rules r2',r3',r4' and r6') form the structural operational semantics for $|_A^P|$ and rule r7 and r8 form the structural operational semantics for $[\cdot]_C$.

Note that the synchronization-mechanisms for active transitions and passive transitions are different. If an active action a is synchronizing (i.e. $a \in A$), then a component can execute the action only when the other component in the composition can also execute the action (and vice versa). If a passive action $\bar{a}$ is synchronizing (i.e. $\bar{a} \in P$), then if both components can execute the action, they have to synchronize. However, if only one component can execute the action, the action can still be executed without the other component synchronizing with it.

This is expressed in rule r6. For active-active synchronization we do not have an equivalent rule as r6. Because of this difference between the synchronization-mechanisms, we need to use different composition rules for both the active and the passive actions (i.e. we can not combine active and passive synchronization in the same rules).

2.4 Example

In Figure 3 we see an example where we find back all interaction structures we described before: non-synchronizing active transitions, synchronizing active transitions, non-synchronizing passive transitions, synchronizing passive transitions and active-passive synchronization.

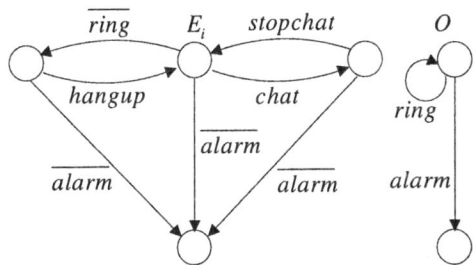

Fig. 3. Example with different kinds of interaction

The example of Figure 3 concerns an office O with two employees E_1 and E_2. In the office there are two sources which can produce a signal: A telephone and an alarm. The telephone rings when somebody calls the office, the alarm fires when there is danger, which means that the employees should leave the office when they hear the alarm. Both the telephone and the alarm execute their signals independently from the employees. Therefore they are modelled as active transitions labelled *ring* and *alarm* respectively (see Figure 3). If the telephone rings, O makes a self-loop which means that O stays in the same location. This location has the meaning of 'normal-working-conditions'. If the alarm goes, O jumps to a second location which has as meaning 'dangerous-working-conditions'.

E_1 and E_2 have the same automaton-structure. From E_1 (or E_2), the employee can exhibit three different actions: He can chat with his fellow employee, he can pick up the phone and he can leave the office. Leaving the office only happens when the alarm goes off. This action is modelled as a passive transition which synchronizes with the independent active alarm-transition in O. We see that from every location, the employee can react on the alarm. When the phone rings, the employee can pick up the phone by synchronizing its passive *ring* event with the active *ring* from O. The employee hangs up with an active *hangup* event. The employee can start a chat with his office-mate via the active *chat* event. This should synchronize with an active *chat* event of the office-mate (both should be willing or able to chat). The chat will be ended with an active-active synchronization of *stopchat*.

From the model we see that if the employees are chatting, they first have to end the chat before one of them can pick up the phone. This means that they will probably miss the first *ring* signal, but can maybe interact on the second *ring* signal (the phone might give multiple *ring* signals when somebody calls). Also, if one employee is phoning, he first has to hang up before a chat can be started.

Where do we see the different kinds of interaction? The passive *ring* transitions of E_1 and E_2 should be non-synchronizing since only one passive transition is allowed to synchronize with the active *ring* transition in O. The passive *alarm* transitions in E_1 and E_2 should synchronize because both employees react synchronously on the alarm. The active *hangup* transitions in E_1 and E_2 should be non-synchronizing (only one employee hangs up). The active *chat* and *stopchat* transitions in E_1 and E_2 should synchronize (both employees chat).

From the above follows that for the composition $E_1|_A^P|E_2$ we get $A = \{chat, stopchat\}$ and $P = \{\overline{alarm}\}$. For the composition $(E_1|_{chat,stopchat}^{\overline{alarm}}|E_2)|_A^P|O$ we get $A = \emptyset$ and $P = \bar{\Sigma}$. The total specification is then

$$(E_1|_{chat,stopchat}^{\overline{alarm}}|E_2)|_\emptyset^{\bar{\Sigma}}|O. \qquad (1)$$

If (1) is the system that we want to analyze, then we could close down all observation channels (i.e. the passive transitions) with the $[\cdot]$ operator. Now suppose that (1) is only one chamber of a bigger office consisting of multiple chambers. Then this chamber is only one unit and lets call it U_1. The other units then are $U_2 = (E_1'|_{chat,stopchat}^{\overline{alarm}}|E_2')|_\emptyset^{\bar{\Sigma}}|O'$, $U_3 = (E_1''|_{chat,stopchat}^{\overline{alarm}}|E_2'')|_\emptyset^{\bar{\Sigma}}|O''$ etc., where $E_i = E_i' = E_i''$, $O = O' = O''$ etc. The telephones in each office are local. With other words, if a telephone rings in one office, only the employees in that office hear the phone and can answer it. The alarm however is global. If there is danger in the building, the alarm goes synchronously in all offices. To specify that the phones are local, we use $[\cdot]$ and get $[U_i]_{ring}$. To specify that the alarm is global, we use *alarm* as a synchronization event in the composition of the units. The total composition of the whole building is then

$$U_1'|_{alarm}U_2'|_{alarm}U_3'|_{alarm}\cdots,$$

where $U_i' = [U_i]_{ring}$.

2.5 Supervisory Control with $|_A^P|$

In this section we want to take a closer look at supervisory control. We will shortly describe the main concepts of supervisory control and thereafter we compare how specification of control systems can be done in our active/passive framework to how it can be done in a framework where there is only blocking-interaction.

In the supervisory control paradigm ([8,9]), the actions of a process can be observable or unobservable and they can be controllable or uncontrollable. Observable actions can be observed by the controller (and unobservable actions can not). Controllable actions can be controlled by the controller (and uncontrollable actions can not). This means that the controller can block these actions, i.e. can prevent them from happening.

If we specify the control system within an automata framework, then the process and the controller are modelled as two separate automata which can interact. The plant executing an action is then modelled as a transition (labelled with this action) from one process-location to another process-location. The controller observing an action is then modelled as a transition in the controller that synchronizes with the to-be-observed transition in the process.

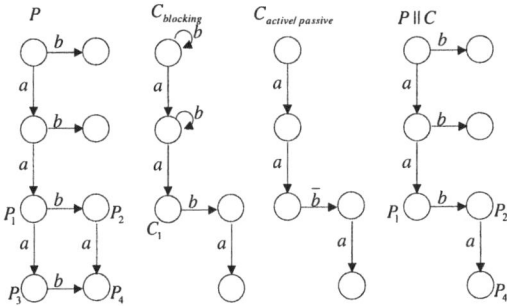

Fig. 4. Control in only-blocking framework and in active/passive framework

Consider the process P in Figure 4 with a controllable/observable and b uncontrollable/observable. We want to control this process such that the behavior of P is restricted to $P||C$ in Figure 4.

First lets see how this can be done in the only-blocking-interaction framework. Since a and b are both observable, we mark them as synchronization actions (i.e. in the composition operation these actions must synchronize while non-synchronization actions will be interleaved). The controller that does the job is $C_{blocking}$ in Figure 4. We see that we need two self-loops on action b, because otherwise the two upper b-transitions of P are blocked and that is not what we want according to $P||C$. We see that, according to the specification $P||C$, transition $P_1 \xrightarrow{a} P_3$ of P is blocked because of the absence of an a-transition in $C_{blocking}$ at location C_1.

For the active/passive framework, $C_{active/passive}$ from Figure 4 does the job. Because a is controllable (i.e. blockable), $a \in A$ and because b is not controllable, $b \notin A$. Blocking the a transition from P_1 to P_3 is done in the same way as in the only-blocking framework. The difference however is, that here we do not need the self-loops on b.

We could say that in the active/passive framework, the controller will observe only (by means of a passive transition) when it needs the information. In Figure 4, $C_{active/passive}$ observes $P_1 \xrightarrow{b} P_2$, but does not observe the upper b-transitions of P, because P may execute them without the controller 'knowing' it. In the only-blocking framework, the controller must also synchronize on the upper b-transitions, because otherwise they will be blocked. We think that this is an important advantage of using active/passive transitions: for uncontrollable/observable actions, transitions are only needed where observations are needed. If there is only blocking-interaction, transitions in the controller are needed everywhere the process executes an uncontrollable/observable action (otherwise they will be blocked and that is not allowed).

In fact we can say that in the supervisory control context, A (from $P|_A^P|C$) contains the controllable actions of the process P. Then, we resume: uncontrollable actions are observed by passive transitions and controllable actions are observed and controlled by active transitions. Note that an active transition of C labelled with a controllable event of P is both controlling (it allows P to execute the action) and observing (the controller synchronizes this transition with the one from P).

2.6 Commutativity and Associativity of $|_A^P|$

Theorem 1. $|_A^P|$ *is commutative for all A and P. $|_A^P|$ is associative if and only if for all events a we have: $a \notin A \Rightarrow \bar{a} \in P$.*

The proof of this theorem can be found on www.cs.utwente.nl/~strubbesn.

If, according to the above theorem, $|_{A_1}^P|$ and $|_{A_2}^P|$ are associative operators, we have $(X|_{A_i}^P|Y)|_{A_i}^P|Z = X|_{A_i}^P|(Y|_{A_i}^P|Z)$ for $i = 1, 2$, and therefore we could write $X|_{A_i}^P|Y|_{A_i}^P|Z$ instead. Note, however, that in general $(X|_{A_1}^P|Y)|_{A_2}^P|Z \neq X|_{A_1}^P|(Y|_{A_2}^P|Z)$ just as in general we do not have $(X|A_1|Y)|A_2|Z \neq X|A_1|(Y|A_2|Z)$ in for example CSP or LOTOS.

3 Trace Semantics

We want to give a trace semantics for the operator $|_A^P|$. This operator is used in a context where we have active actions (like a) and passive actions (like $\bar{a}$). A trace of an automaton could then be $ab\bar{a}$ for example. However, this notion of trace is not strong enough to give a trace semantics for composition (i.e. the sets of traces of the components are not enough to determine the set of traces of the composition).

See for example Figure 5. There the set of traces of X_1 and X_2 are both equals to $\{\epsilon, a, ab, aba, a\bar{c}\}$. The set of traces of Y equals $\{\epsilon, c\}$. If we could determine the trace set of a composite system from the trace sets of the components, then $X_1||Y$ and $X_2||Y$ should have the same trace set (because X_1 and X_2 have the same trace set). But this is not the case, since $acba$ is a trace of $X_1||Y$ while it is not a trace of $X_2||Y$. Therefore this notion of traces is not strong enough for a trace semantics of $|_A^P|$.

Another option for a trace semantics would be to look at traces of the form σP with $\sigma \in (\Sigma \cup \bar{\Sigma})^*$ and $P \subset \bar{\Sigma}$, where σP means that the process can execute the trace σ such that it ends up in a state where the set of passive events that are enabled equals P. This can be seen as an analogy of refusal traces in [10]. However, this notion of trace is also not strong enough because the processes

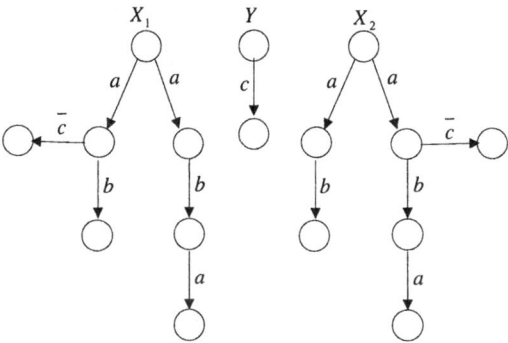

Fig. 5. Processes X_1, X_2 and Y

X_1 and X_2 in Figure 5 have the same traces of the form σP, while $X_1 \| Y$ and $X_2 \| Y$ have different traces.

We now introduce a trace concept called pie-traces (which stands for passive-information-extended-traces). We will see that this notion of trace is indeed strong enough to give a trace semantics for $|_A^P|$. A pie-trace in this semantics looks like

$$P_1 \alpha_1 P_2 \alpha_2 \cdots P_n \alpha_n,$$

where $\alpha_i \in \Sigma \cup \bar{\Sigma}$ and $P_i \subset \bar{\Sigma}$. We could say that part of the tree-structure (as far as it concerns the passive actions) is contained in these pie-traces. $P_1 \alpha_1 P_2 \alpha_2 \cdots P_n \alpha_n$ means that within the transition system, there exists an execution of trace $\alpha_1 \cdots \alpha_n$ such that at the state in the transition system where α_i is to be executed there are outgoing passive transitions for each $\bar{\alpha} \in P_i$ ($i = 1 \cdots n$) and there are no outgoing passive transitions for α if $\alpha \notin P_i$.

The processes in figure 5 have the following pie-traces: $Tr_{pie}(X_1) = \{a[\bar{c}]b, aba, ab, a\}$. Here $a[\bar{c}]b$ means $P_1 a P_2 b$ with $P_1 = \emptyset$, $P_2 = \{\bar{c}\}$ etc. $Tr_{pie}(X_2) = \{a[\bar{c}]ba, ab, a[\bar{c}]b, a\}$ and $Tr_{pie}(Y) = \{c\}$. With this notion of trace semantics, X_1 and X_2 have different semantics, thus they are not equivalent with respect to this notion of trace semantics. We now show that our notion of trace semantics is strong enough for a trace semantics of the composition operator $|_A^P|$:

Let σ_1 and σ_2 be pie-traces. Then we define $\sigma_1 |_A^P| \sigma_2$, which will turn out to be the set of interleavings of σ_1 and σ_2 with respect to $|_A^P|$, as follows:

- $\epsilon |_A^P| \epsilon := \{\epsilon\}$
- $(R_1 \alpha_1 \sigma_1') |_A^P| \epsilon := \{\epsilon\} \cup S_1$, where $S_1 := R_1 \alpha_1 (\sigma_1' |_A^P| \epsilon)$ if ($\alpha_1 \in \Sigma$ and $\alpha_1 \notin A$) or $\alpha_1 \in \bar{\Sigma}$ else $S_1 := \emptyset$.
- $\epsilon |_A^P| (R_2 \alpha_2 \sigma_2') := \{\epsilon\} \cup S_1$, where $S_1 := R_2 \alpha_2 (\epsilon |_A^P| \sigma_2')$ if ($\alpha_2 \in \Sigma$ and $\alpha_2 \notin A$) or $\alpha_2 \in \bar{\Sigma}$ else $S_1 := \emptyset$.
- $(R_1 \alpha_1 \sigma_1') |_A^P| (R_2 \alpha_2 \sigma_2') := \{\epsilon\} \cup S_1 \cup S_2 \cup S_3 \cup S_4$, where
  $S_1 := (R_1 \cup R_2) \alpha_1 (\sigma_1' |_A^P| \sigma_2)$ if one of the cases r3,r4 or r6 is true, else $S_1 := \emptyset$,
  $S_2 := (R_1 \cup R_2) \alpha_1 (\sigma_1' |_A^P| \sigma_2')$ if one of the cases r1,r2 or r5 is true, else $S_2 := \emptyset$,
  $S_3 := (R_1 \cup R_2) \alpha_2 (\sigma_1 |_A^P| \sigma_2')$ if one of the cases r3',r4' or r6' is true, else

$S_3 := \emptyset$,
$S_4 := (R_1 \cup R_2)\alpha_2(\sigma_1'|_A^P|\sigma_2')$ if case r2' is true, else $S_3 := \emptyset$.

Cases:
r1: $\alpha_1 = \alpha_2 \in \Sigma$ and $\alpha_1 \in A$
r2: $\alpha_1 \in \Sigma$ and $\alpha_2 = \bar{\alpha}_1$ and $\alpha_1 \notin A$
r3: $\alpha_1 \in \Sigma$ and $\bar{\alpha}_1 \notin R_2$ and $\alpha_1 \notin A$
r4: $\alpha_1 \in \bar{\Sigma}$ and $\alpha_1 \notin P$
r5: $\alpha_1 = \alpha_2 \in \bar{\Sigma}$ and $\alpha_1 \in P$
r6: $\alpha_1 \in \bar{\Sigma}$ and $\alpha_1 \notin R_2$ and $\alpha_1 \in P$
r2': $\alpha_2 \in \Sigma$ and $\alpha_1 = \bar{\alpha}_2$ and $\alpha_2 \notin A$
r3': $\alpha_2 \in \Sigma$ and $\bar{\alpha}_2 \notin R_1$ and $\alpha_2 \notin A$
r4': $\alpha_2 \in \bar{\Sigma}$ and $\alpha_2 \notin P$
r6': $\alpha_2 \in \bar{\Sigma}$ and $\alpha_2 \notin R_1$ and $\alpha_2 \in P$

Theorem 2. σ is a pie-trace of $X|_A^P|Y$ if and only if there exist pie-traces σ_x and σ_y of X and Y respectively such that $\sigma \in \sigma_x|_A^P|\sigma_y$.

Proof. It can be seen that the cases r1 till r6 and r2',r3',r4' and r6' correspond to the composition rules r1 till r6, r2',r3',r4' and r6'. This correspondence is such that when case r1 is true (from the initial states), then composition rule r1 can be applied in the composition and when case r2 is true then composition rule r2 can be applied, etc. Now it is easy to check that $\sigma_x|_A^P|\sigma_y$ is exactly the set of all interleavings (including synchronizations) of σ_x and σ_y that are accepted by the composition rules of $|_A^P|$, from which the result follows.

Similar to the definition of refusals in [10], we can now define pie-refusal traces of the form σX, where σ is a pie-trace and X a set of active actions that can be refused after σ. In this way a semantics is defined that reduces to the standard testing semantics in the absence of passive actions.

4 Conclusions and Outlook

In this paper we used active and passive transitions to model both blocking and non-blocking interaction between processes. We motivated that the use of active/passive transitions is particularly interesting for modelling supervisory control systems. Supervisory controllers have two distinct actions: observing and controlling, which can be modelled naturally with passive and active transitions respectively. With the use of active/passive transitions, we are able to avoid the problems that arise in the 'blocking' framework when it comes to modelling uncontrollable process actions.

We introduced the composition operator $|_A^P|$ for the active/passive framework by means of structural operational rules. By using *pie-traces*, we have also given a trace semantics for this operator.

With the active/passive framework and the operators $[\cdot]_C$ and $|_A^P|$, we have given two tools for the modular specification of control systems. First, with

$[\cdot]_C$ we can control the scope of the observations within the composite system. Secondly, with $|^P_A|$ we can establish synchronization of observations (which results in multi-may synchronizations) via the set P.

We think that many phenomena, in particular supervisory control systems, can be modelled naturally within the active/passive framework by making use of operators like $|^P_A|$ and $[\cdot]_C$. For future research, we want to explore the use of $|^P_A|$ in a hybrid (supervisory control) context. First steps in this direction can be found in [11]. Another interesting question is whether stochastic aspects can be incorporated in the $|^P_A|$-active/passive framework. In [12], we see the use of $|^{\bar{\Sigma}}_{\emptyset}|$ enhanced with stochastic aspects for the specification of Piecewise Deterministic Markov Processes.

References

1. Plotkin, G.D.: A structural approach to operational semantics. Technical Report DAIMI FN-19, Aarhus University, Comp. Sci. Dept. (1981)
2. Hoare, C.: Communicating Sequential Processes. Prentice-Hall (1985)
3. Bolognesi, T., Brinksma, E.: Introduction to the iso specification language lotos. Comp. Networks and ISDN Systems 14 (1987) 2559
4. Prasad, K.: A Calculus of Broadcasting Systems. In: Proc. 16th Colloquium on Trees in Algebra and Programming. Volume 493. (1991) 338358
5. Lynch, N.A., Segala, R., Vaandrager, F.W.: Hybrid I/O automata. Information and Computation 185(1) (2003) 105157
6. Lynch, N.A., Tuttle, M.R.: An introduction to input/output automata. CWI Quarterly 2 (1988) 219246
7. Groote, J.F.: Process Algebra and Structured Operational Semantics. PhD thesis, University of Amsterdam (1991)
8. Ramadge, P., Wonham, W.: The control of discrete event systems. Proceedings of the IEEE 77 (1989) 8198
9. Cassandras, C.G., Lafortune, S.: Introduction to discrete event systems. Kluwer Academic Publishers (1999)
10. Hennesy, M.: Algebraic Theory of Processes. MIT Press (1988)
11. Julius, A.A., Strubbe, S.N., van der Schaft, A.J.: Control of hybrid behavioral automata by interconnection. In: Preprints Conference on Analysis and Design of Hybrid Systems ADHS 03. (2003) 135140
12. Strubbe, S.N., Julius, A.A., van der Schaft, A.J.: Communicating piecewise deterministic markov processes. In: Preprints Conference on Analysis and Design of Hybrid Systems ADHS 03. (2003) 349354

A Formal Semantics of UML StateCharts by Means of Timed Petri Nets

Youcef Hammal

LSI, Département d'Informatique, Faculté d'Electronique & Informatique,
Université des Sciences et de la Technologie Houari Boumediene,
BP 32, El-Alia 16111, Bab-Ezzouar, Algiers, Algeria
yhammal@wissal.dz

Abstract. This paper deals with the formalization of Unified Modeling language (UML) by means of Petri Nets. In order to improve the semantics of UML dynamic diagrams, we define a new method of embedding UML StateCharts into Interval Timed Petri Nets (ITPN). This method considers all kinds of hierarchical states together with the most of pseudo-states like history ones. Besides consistencies analysis, time intervals of ITPN model well event generation and dispatching delays making it possible to achieve performance and time properties analysis of complex systems.

1 Introduction

Complex systems are typically large and reactive systems containing a great number of different kinds of hardware and software components that may operate concurrently by means of various synchronization and communication mechanisms. They are also characterized by very high-level interactions with their environment and reactions to external stimuli must be achieved within given time intervals. Otherwise, violation of those temporal constrains produces critical consequences. Therefore, modeling and analysis of functional requirements are not enough and other concepts like reliability and safety become as important as the previous ones.

Obviously a multi-paradigm modeling language is needed to design and analyze such critical systems. Hence the Unified Modeling language offers a collection of visual, friendly and flexible notations for expressing the artifacts representing various aspects of complex systems ranging from business applications to real time systems.

This OMG standard language [13] is based on object-orientation involving high-quality design concepts such as abstraction, encapsulation and decomposition of systems into objects. Besides, UML is also supported by wide-established tools and environments for specification, design and automatic code generation. Moreover its extensibility faculties make it easier to improve UML notations to address issues of critical systems with respect to the profile for schedulability, performance and time specification [14]. However in spite of the precise syntactic aspects of UML notations, their semantics remain too imprecise and lack verifiability capabilities [6][8]. So considering the semi-formal aspect of UML, it is imperative to define mapping methods of UML diagrams into other formal modeling languages to take advantage of their tools developed for analysis, simulation and verification of parts of produced models. Thus, the lack of formality can be overcome by providing a dynamic semantics to UML by means of various rigorous mathematical formalisms such as Petri Nets and Formal Specification Techniques (FST).

In this way our approach focuses on ascribing behavioral diagrams of UML (mainly StateCharts) with formal semantics in terms of temporal nets in order to allow both the verification of consistency of the different dynamic diagrams and the analysis of timeliness and performance of an UML model.

In this paper we deal with UML StateCharts that are state machines increasing the modeling power of classical state transition diagrams by introducing superstates and the hierarchical decomposition of superstates. On the other hand, the target formalism is a derived Petri net [1] enhanced with time intervals to represent timing information about event transmission delays. We proceed with our method by steps to overcome the arising difficulties relating to the boundary-crossing arcs that transgress the good compositional properties of StateCharts like those described in [16].

The paper is structured as follows: The next section presents the related work and the motivation of our work. Section 3 shows the basic features of UML StateCharts and in section 4 we present the interval timed Petri nets. Then in section 5, the patterns of our translation method are given for more comprehensibility and section 6 presents the main algorithms which map StateCharts into ITPN formalism. Finally a conclusion is given in section 7 where some remarks and future works are outlined.

2 Motivation and Related Work

The UML specification document [13] provides the description of any UML diagram in three parts: the abstract syntax, the well-formedness rules for the abstract syntax and then its semantics. The well-formedness rules are formulated in the Object Constraint Language OCL and the semantics is given in a natural language.

Thus the architects of UML use the meta-modeling level to describe UML using class diagrams and OCL to capture the static relationship between modeling concepts. However this approach is not adequate since class diagrams and OCL are too little precise to describe the language semantics [6]. Furthermore using natural language or OCL makes it hard to discover inconsistencies among various diagrams of an UML model. Moreover the lack of precise semantics of UML can lead to a number of problems relating to readability and interpretation, use of rigorous design process, rigorous semantic analysis and tool support limited only to syntactic concerns [6], [8].

Hence many proposals are issued giving formal meaning to UML Models in order to overcome the above problems and achieve their analysis by means of verification and validation tools. Among them we distinguish two families of approaches:

The first family includes approaches that improve the meta-model of UML to overcome the ambiguities of standard UML semantics. For instance the authors of [7] add Dynamic Meta Modeling rules for the specification of UML consistency constraints and provide concepts for an automated testing environment.

Another work [15] exploits the profile extension mechanism [14] to add definitions of some stereotypes and a set of UML diagrams that enable specification of real-time systems and their properties. To specify properties of such systems, specification-classes are defined having predefined constraints presented in an extended variant of Timed Computation Tree Logic (TCTL).

Likewise, [3] proposes a formalization of an extension of UML state diagrams for specification of real-time behavior. This enhancement is achieved by the timed statecharts formalism of Kesten and Pnueli. But the next translation step into timed automata is not defined to take advantage of their analysis tools like model-checkers.

The second family defines mappings from UML constructs into rigorous formalisms such as Petri nets and Formal Specification Techniques (FST) to accomplish consistency checking. This way, the approach of [8] exploits a formal notation like Z instead of OCL to formalize UML Components so that the usual facilities for Z become available for type checking and proving properties about components. But the main disadvantage of using Z is that faithfully mapping the UML semantics to Z can result in very verbose and cumbersome specifications.

In a similar work [17] the author proposes a mapping using the incremental two-way translation between UML and SDL concepts. The translation of a subset of UML state diagrams to the SDL ones proceeds by flattening a fragment of nested states. Nevertheless, several suitable concepts for reactive systems are abandoned like concurrent hierarchical states, history states and boundary-crossing transitions of which handling needs complex redefinitions of the translation.

In a same way, the approach of [5] defines a mapping from UML models consisting of use case, class and interaction diagrams to their equivalent in E-LOTOS to form a single formal model in E-LOTOS. However the synchronous communication mode of LOTOS compels adoption of the zero-time semantics and excludes many situations where asynchronous communication is necessary.

There are also works based on graphs as target models, like that of [9] transforming a subset of UML state diagrams into graphs via rewriting rules. Likewise the authors of [4][2][10][11] indicate too dynamic semantics of fragments of UML models based on enhanced Petri nets (respectively high-level Petri nets, object Petri Nets and Generalized Stochastic Petri Nets). Draft heuristics are given in both these papers to transform parts of the UML models into the target formalism.

Another alike paper [12] extends UML with performance annotations (paUML) to deal with the performance indices in mobile agent systems that are modeled in conjunction with design patterns. Then the paUML models are semi-automatically translated to generalized stochastic Petri nets (GSPN).

In a particular way, the author of [18] defines a toolkit of specification techniques for requirements and design engineering (TRADE) where some choices close to the Statemate semantics of StateCharts are adopted to define transition system semantics for UML specifications.

However, the works mentioned above (including GSPN-based ones) deal only with a subset of state diagrams close to particular application domains and the translation rules are not well formalized. Moreover discarded concepts such as concurrent composite states and history vertices are important for modeling reactive and concurrent systems. Also events queuing patterns do not fit for situations where one event may trigger many transitions at once in various orthogonal regions.

Accordingly we define in this paper a new translation method using timed Petri nets as target model. Instead of using time tag over transitions as done in [10], we prefer tag each event token with a time interval because this seems more faithful to model any dispatching delay. Our method allows also enabling many transitions with respect to the same trigger event. Furthermore, we deal with all kinds of hierarchical states and the most of pseudo-states like history ones. Obviously, introducing these concepts both with boundary-crossing arcs raises many problems we resolve by means of our enhanced model so that UML semantics [13] remain preserved.

Once the stateChart of an UML model is translated into a timed Petri net, we could achieve a consistency validation of the dynamic view with respect to sequence diagrams. The methodology may consist in checking whether event sequences are consistent with those of the reachability graph of the resulting net. Also it may find out whether and how temporal constraints of events paths could be fulfilled with respect to time intervals on the arcs of the reachability graph.

3 UML StateChart Features

The UML State Machines are an object-based variant of HAREL StateCharts that can model discrete behavior of objects through finite state-transition systems [13].

A StateChart (called also state diagram) shows the sequences of states that an object goes through during its lifetime in response to events, together with its response to those events. Note that an event can be a (asynchronous) signal, (synchronous) operation invocation, a time passing or a condition change.

A state is a condition or situation during the life of an object during which it satisfies some condition, performs some activity or waits for some event. Here an event is an occurrence of stimulus that can trigger a state transition. Note that a state may be either simple or composite. Any state enclosed within a composite state is called a substate of that composite state. It is called a direct substate when it is not contained by any other state; otherwise it is referred to as a transitively nested substate. When substates can execute concurrently, they are called orthogonal regions.

So a transition (arc) is a relationship between two states indicating that an object in the first (source) state will perform certain actions and enter the second (target) state when a specified event occurs and specified conditions are satisfied.

In general a state has several parts:

- *"Entry/exit"* actions are executed on entering and exiting the state, respectively.
- *"Do"* activity is executed while being in a state. It stops itself, or the state is exited, whichever comes first.
- *Substates* represent the nested structure of a state, involving sequentially or concurrently active substates connected via *internal* transitions.

When dealing with composite and concurrent states, the simple term "current state" can be quite confusing because more than one state can be active at once. If the control is in a simple state then all the composite states that either directly or transitively contain this simple state are also active.

Furthermore, since some of the composite states in this hierarchy may be concurrent, the current active state is actually represented by a tree of states starting with the single top state at the root down to the individual simple states at the leaves. We refer to such a state tree as a state configuration.

Also any transition originating from the boundary of composite state is called a high-level or group transition. If triggered, it results in exiting of all the substates of that composite state executing their exit actions starting with the innermost (deepest) states in the active state configuration.

3.1 Some Preliminary Expansion Rules

The pseudo-states are not states but only transient vertices used for more convenience when modeling the state machine graph. Thus, in order to simplify our translation method we remove all pseudo-states. But before erasing them, expansion rules below must be done with respect to the well-formedness rules defined in [13]:

- Any composite state containing a *shallow history* pseudo-state, should be labeled with the "history" tag.
- Any state containing a *deep history* pseudo-state, is labeled with the "history" tag and all its direct and transitively nested substates are also labeled with the "history" tag. This rule guarantees the handling of the history property in all transitively nested substates of any composite state owning a deep history pseudo-state.
- Any target state of a transition originating from an *initial* pseudo-state, is labeled with the "initial" tag.
- Target states of a transition originating from a *fork* pseudo-state are labeled with the "initial" tag. Obviously each initial state must belong to one orthogonal region of a concurrent composite state. The transition arc incoming to the fork vertex will be replaced by an incoming transition arc to the edge of the composite state
- All substates (in different orthogonal regions of a composite state) of which transitions merge into a join (terminator) pseudo-state, are labeled with the "final" tag. The transition arc outgoing from a join vertex to one target state, will be a triggerless outgoing arc from the edge of the composite state to the target state.

3.2 Mathematical Structure of a StateChart

Consequently to this previous operation and before defining the translation method of a state machine D into its equivalent Petri net, we use for more convenience the below mathematical structure to model the StateChart D.

A StateChart is a tuple: $D = <S, K, Tag, C, TA, S_0, L, E, G, A>$ where:

- S : set of states with the topmost state S_0.
- K : S→{Simple State, Sequential Composite State, Concurrent Composite State}.
- Tag : S→{Initial, Final, History}.
- C : S → 2^S is a mapping that gives to each composite state its nested states.

Note that $s \not\subset C^*(s)$ where $C^*(s) = \cup_i C^i(s)$ and $C^{i>0}(s) = \cup\{C^{i-1}(s_j)$ for $s_j \in C(s)\}$.
This mapping defines a partial order relation ($\subset$) among states we can depict as a tree.

- TA ⊆ SxS: Set of transition arcs.
- L is a labeling mapping: TA→ExGxA where E is the set of events, A is the set of actions and G is the set of guards.

4 Target Model of Translation

The target model of the translation is a kind of interval timed Petri net denoted by ITPN [1]. A marked ITPN is a tuple R = <P, T, Pre, Post, L_1, L_1, Prior, M_I > where:
- P is the places set and T is the transitions set.
- Pre: $T \rightarrow 2^P$ is a backward incidence function giving the inplaces (input places) of transitions and Post: $T \rightarrow 2^{P \times INT}$ is a forward incidence function giving the outplaces (output places) of transitions with the corresponding delay intervals.
- INT = { $[t_1,t_2] \in \Re^{\geq 0} \times \Re^{\geq 0}$ / $t_1 \leq t_2$ } the set of time intervals.
- L_1 and L_2 are labeling functions. L_1: P$\rightarrow$EVT (EVT is the set of events) and L_2: T$\rightarrow$ACT (ACT is the set of actions).
- Prior $\subseteq$ T x T is a priority relationship between transitions in conflict.
- M_I : P $\rightarrow$ $\aleph$ is the initial marking of the net at instant 0 from system starting.

A transition "t" is *enabled* within a marking M if the required tokens in inplaces are available: $\forall p \in$ Pre(t) : M(p)=1. Because the arcs are weighted with 1, when a transition "t" fires, a new marking M' is produced as follows: M' = M$\cup$Post(t)–Pre(t).

"t" consumes a token in each of its inplaces and generates one in each of its outplaces. However the timing policy of this ITPN requires any transition to be fired as soon as it is enabled. The produced tokens become available in outplaces only after freeze-up delays that are sampled respectively from the time intervals relating to the arcs joining the transition "t" to its outplaces. If there's no time interval on an arc, we consider the default interval [0,0].

The priorities between transitions aim at setting in order the simultaneous executions of several boundary-crossing arcs originating from transitively nested substates of a same superstate. According to [13] the priority level decreases from innermost substates down to the outermost ones such that when triggered at once, exit actions from the former substates execute before those of the former ones.

In the next sections we denote respectively by *entry* and *exit* places some initial and final places in a Petri net component. These particular places provide the links to connect together subnets relating to substates of any composite state.

In addition, each action will be mapped into an event raise, so that it makes it possible to join any net transition triggering one event to inplaces of another transition triggered by this specific event.

5 Transformation Patterns

Below we present the main patterns about different cases of translation where we use "transition arcs" to mean UML transitions in contrast with Petri net transitions.

5.1 Transition Arc Between Two Simple States

Given one transition arc between two simple states S_1 and S_2 belonging to the same containing state, we distinguish two cases requiring different treatments:
1. The trigger event may be a call event or signal event,
2. The trigger event may be a time event.

Case 1: The trigger event is a call event or signal event. The transition arc is mapped here into a net transition as follows (Fig.1):

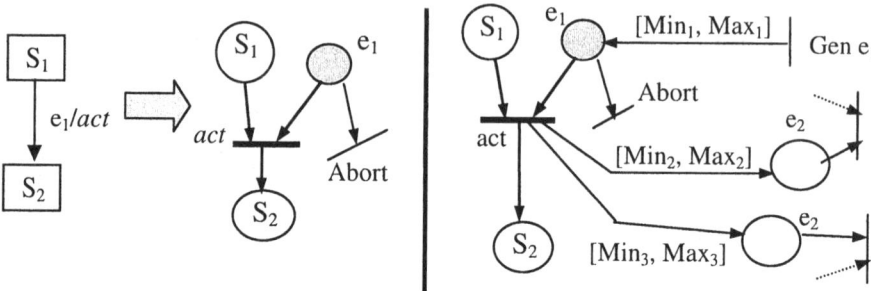

Fig. 1. Arc labeled by a call/signal event   **Fig. 2.** Connecting trigger event places

The source state S_1 is translated into an inplace of *act* depicting the incoming control flow and the target state S_2 is related to an outplace depicting the outgoing control flow. For the trigger event of the transition *act*, we generate another inplace called event place that depicts the event flow. This special place would be an outplace of any transition raising the relating event e_1.

In the same way, the action *act* labeling the net transition may consist in generating some event e_2 used by other transitions in the StateChart. Hence we should link later our net transition *act* to all (event) places labeled with the trigger event e_2.

Note that the abort transition models the possibility to discard the event e_1 if the state machine in not yet in S_1 with respect to UML semantics. Since any transition must fire whenever it becomes enabled, we must make the priority of the transition *act* superior than that of the abort transition (see Fig.2).

Furthermore, we can label with a time interval any outgoing arc from a net transition to a trigger event place. This interval models well the minimal and maximal time delays between the queuing and dispatching instants of the event. The variable transmission delays depend on the properties of the communication medium and other factors. For instance the possibility of event loss can be depicted by an interval $[x,\infty[$ where x denotes the minimal delay to deliver that event for processing. However, if we would model the synchronous communication we can do it by using the only interval [0,0] so that trigger events become available as soon as they are raised.

Case 2: The trigger event is a time event (when d). The translation of a time event arc into a net transition needs also an event inplace we should join as an outplace to the transition "T" which produces a token in the related place of S_1 (Fig.3).

However the net arc between "T" and the event place would be tagged with a time interval [d,d]. So if "T" fires, it produces a token in each of the two places relating respectively to the state S_1 and the event e. Here the place S_1 is marked immediately, whereas the place e receives its token after d time units. Once this token becomes available and if S_1 is still marked then the transition act is fired. Otherwise, the abort transition is performed consuming the time event token (Fig.3). Note that other transitions outgoing from S_1 may fire so that the transition *act* becomes disabled.

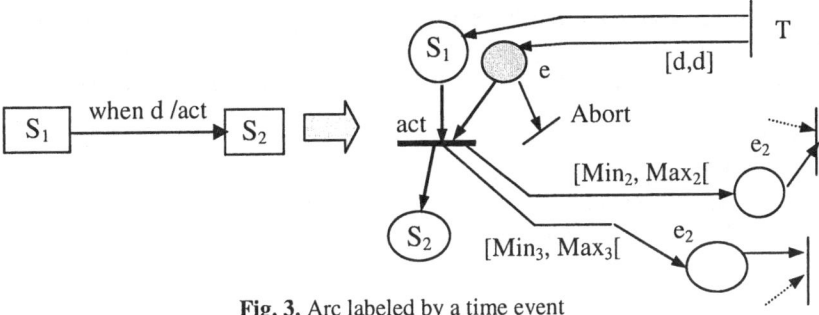

Fig. 3. Arc labeled by a time event

5.2 Transition Arc from a Simple State to a Composite State Without a History Tag

When the trigger event e_1 is dispatched, the system processes the transition action *act* immediately if the state machine is in the suitable state S_1 that has an outgoing arc triggered by e_1. Otherwise, this event e_1 is discarded.

As the arc tagged with e_1 goes to the edge of the composite state S_2, the outplace of the *act* transition is the initial place of the related net to S_2 if this one is sequential (Fig.4). But if S_2 is a concurrent state (Fig.5), all places relating to respectively initial states of concurrent regions of S_2 will be outplaces of the *act* transition. Hence when firing this transition, a token is produced in the initial place of each region of the state S_2, making it possible to activate both all those concurrent regions in the same time.

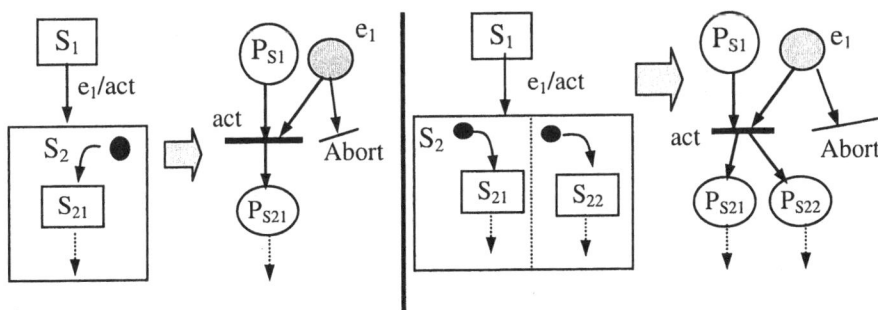

Fig. 4. Sequential composite state   **Fig. 5.** Concurrent composite state

5.3 Transition Arc from a Composite State Without History Tag

In Fig.6 there are three kinds of transition arcs exiting from the state X.

The simple one is a triggerless transition outgoing to the state G. In this case, we connect the subnet relating to the final substate D of X with the subnet relating to the target state G (the subnets of simple states are single places).

The second kind is a high-level transition outgoing from the edge of X to the state E. Here we have to connect each one of subnets relating to the direct substates of X with the place of G via a transition p triggered by the event e2. However instead of duplicating three times the transition p in X for each substate of which place becomes its inplace, it is more suitable to use (in Fig.6) all places related to X/B, X/C, X/D as optional inplaces for a single transition that is triggered by e_2. This feature is depicted by dashed lines joining the inplaces (B, C and D) to the transition p.

The third transition is an exit arc from only one direct substate C to the new target state F. So we have to connect only the subnet of C with the subnet relating to F.

Note that when exiting one region to somewhere outside its concurrent composite state, the other orthogonal regions of X should be also disabled [13].

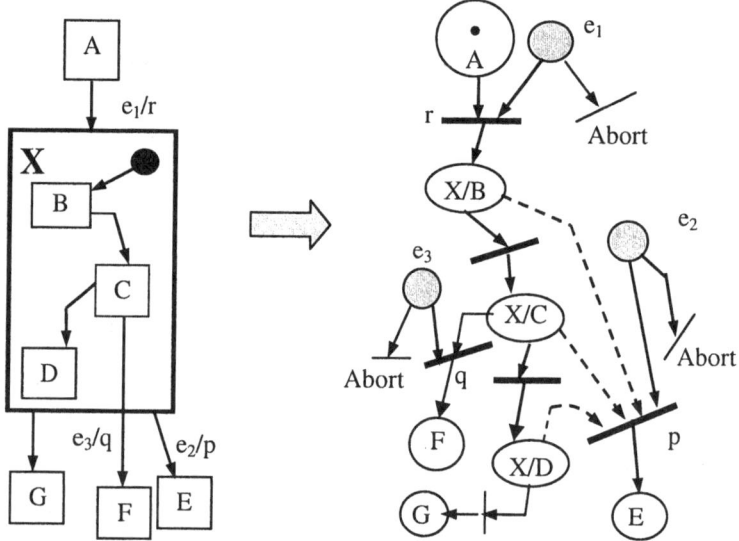

Fig. 6. Source state of an arc is a sequential composite state

5.4 Transition Arc from a Simple State to a Composite State with a History Tag

In Fig.7, the state S_2 is a sequential composite state with the history tag. So when this state is exited and then reentered again, the system should return to its most recent active configuration; that's the state configuration that was active when the composite state was last exited.

Therefore we use a *"thread"* place P_H as entry place to model control passing between substates of S_2.

Remind that an entry place is not marked at start but during net execution it may receive a token from a previous transition so that it activates S_2.

Moreover the place P_{S21} relating to the first substate S_{21} will be initially marked. When firing some internal transitions in S_2, the token of P_{S21} moves to the next places relating to substates of S_2 making it possible to determine every time the current marked place and consequently the related active substate.

Hence if the system leaves S_2 (removing P_H token) while a token is in an intermediate place and if it returns to S_2 (renewing a token in P_H), the recent active

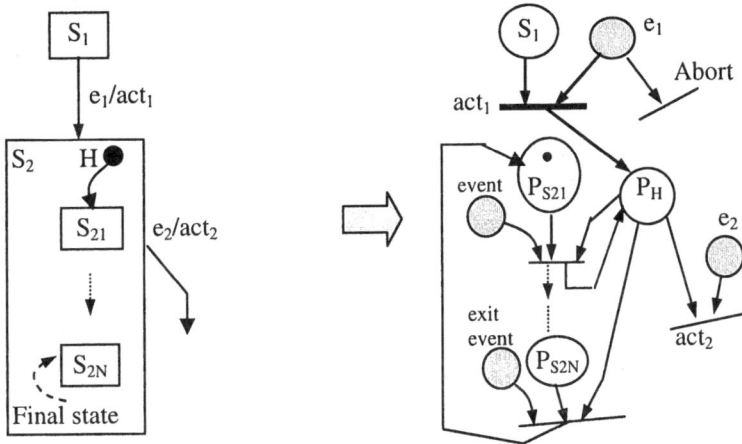

Fig. 7. Sequential composite state with history tag

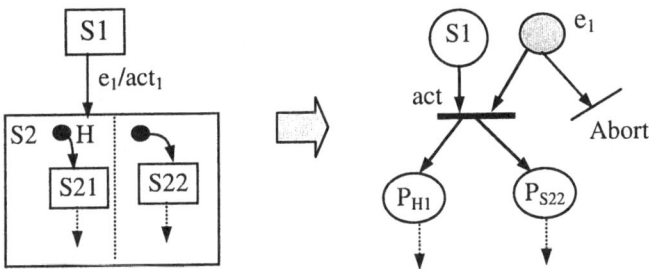

Fig. 8. Concurrent composite state with history tag

configuration is restored because the intermediate place remains marked until the control of S_2 is restored. However if a triggerless exit transition fires, the P_H token is finally consumed whereas a new token is produced in the initial place P_{S21}.

In Fig.8, S_2 is a concurrent composite state with two orthogonal regions of which one is labeled with the history tag. Here we apply to each region the suitable handling method among those we have presented above. It is obvious that the firing of act_1 transition produces a token in the appropriate entry place of each region. Whenever the region is tagged with "History", we consider its thread place P_H as an entry place. Otherwise, the place relating to the first substate of a region is taken as entry place.

5.5 Transition Arc from a Composite State with a History Tag to Other States

To simplify the resulting net in Fig.9, we do not add the transitions that represent event discarding. The dashed lines mean that the transitions p and q should have Y_1, Y_2 and Y_3 as optional inplaces. We recall that exit transitions of orthogonal regions must synchronize. So the exit arc, which is event triggerless, requires joining the final place of each region to that transition q. In addition we join X/P_H to the transition q which firing renews a token only in the initial place X_1 of the history tagged region.

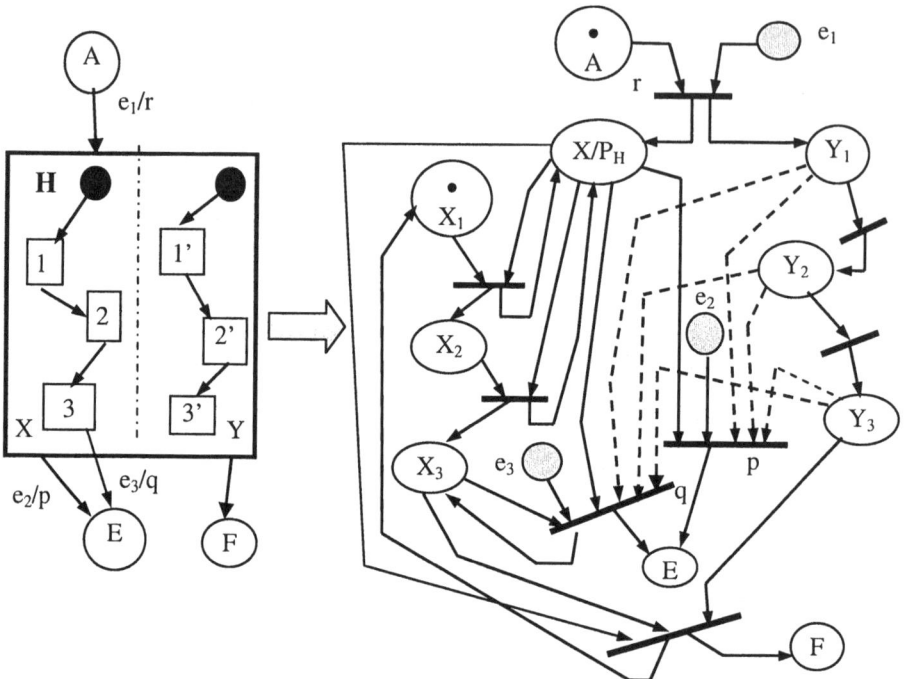

Fig. 9. Concurrent composite state with history tag

If the exit transition is a compound one (i.e. e_2/p) outgoing from the edge of a composite state, then we use as inplace the thread place of the history tagged region and as optional places all the places of the other orthogonal region without history tag.

6 Outlines of the Translation Algorithms

In the first step of the translation, we discard the boundary-crossing arcs that transgress the encapsulation concept of states [16]. Note that high-level transitions are also boundary-crossing transitions which are handled in the same manner.

As handling boundary-crossing arcs together with history vertices is too complex, we prefer go by steps and defer their treatment to the second step of the translation.

Once we obtain all related nets of a whole system, we combine them by means of the parallel operator. Every transition raising an event must have as outplace each one labeled with this event. Afterward, we could tag these added arcs with time intervals modeling dispatching delays of events or time constraints on StateCharts arcs.

6.1 First Step of Translation

Given some state machine D that consists of one topmost level state S_0. We discard all boundary-crossing arcs and then we construct the related net as follows:

Let $S_1,...,S_N$ be the direct substates of S_0 that may be connected together either sequentially or concurrently. First we construct the net $|[S_i]|$ relating to each substate S_i by applying recursively the same *algorithm1*. Then we use one of the two algorithms *Algo1-Seq* and *Algo1-Par* to combine together the resulting nets |[S$_i$]| by means of one of two connecting operators; the used operator may be either a parallel composition connector || (if S$_0$ is a concurrent state) or a sequential composition ⊗ (if S$_0$ is a sequential state).

If K(S$_0$) = Concurrent then |[S$_0$]| = |[S$_1$]| || ... || |[S$_N$]|.
If K(S$_0$) = Sequential then |[S$_0$]| = |[S$_1$]| ⊗ ... ⊗ |[S$_N$]|.

The same approach is then employed recurrently to each substate whenever this one is a composite state. The sketch of *algorithm1* is a follows:

```
Algorithm1 (S : IN UML State Machine) → |[S]| : ITPN
Begin
    if S is a simple state then  Algo1-Simple-State (S, N)
    else begin
            let Subnets-List := ∅;        // Subnets relating to
            for each substate SSi of S    // direct substates of S
              do begin   N_i := Algorithm1(SSi);
                         Add(Subnets-List, N_i);
                 end
            if K(S)=Sequential then Algo1-Seq(S, Subnets-List);
            if K(S)=Concurrent then Algo1-Par(S, Subnets-List);
         end
end Algorithm1.
```

Algo1-Simple-State handles only simple states by translating each one "S" of them into one place P$_S$. If S has not entry/exit actions, P$_S$ becomes both an entry and a final place of that related subnet |[S]|. Otherwise, the simple state with entry/exit actions is translated into three places, P$_{Entry}$, P$_S$ and P$_{Exit}$ that are linked by means of the entry/exit transitions as depicted in Fig.10.

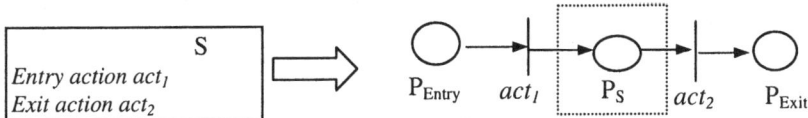

Fig. 10. Entry/exit actions handling in a simple state

The same approach is also applied to a composite state (both in *Algo1-Seq* and *Algo1-Par*) by substituting Ps with the subnet |[S]| related to this state S considered without its entry and exit actions. P$_{Entry}$ is linked by means of the *act$_1$* transition to the initial places of the subnet |[S]|, namely those which would receive the tokens to initiate the activity in that part of the system. Likewise, all final places of the subnet |[S]| have to be linked to P$_{Exit}$ by means of the transition *act2*.

Below we give the core of the subroutines Algo1-Seq and Algo1-Par:

```
Algo1-Seq (S: StateChart; Subnets-List: List of ITPN)→ ITPN
Begin
    for each arc Arc between SS_i and SS_j ∈ Substates(S)
      do if SS_i is a simple state or Arc is triggerless then
            begin   Add a transition T;
                    Join |[SS_i]| & |[SS_j]|∈ Subnets-List via T;
                    Label T with the action name of Arc;
                    Add an inplace of T that is labeled with
                         the trigger event name if it exits;
```

```
            end
        if S is history state   then   add a thread place P_H ;
        Link P_H at the same time as inplace and outplace of the
            each transition of all substates of S;
        Handle the entry and exit actions if they exist.
end Algo1-Seq.
```

Note that if the exit action exists in a history tagged state S then we should add in |[S]| an exit transition which is joined to P_H only as inplace such that when T_{exit} fires it consumes the P_H token. Thus any activity in |[S]| will be disabled. We should also reset the net by joining T_{exit} to the initially marked place of the first substate of S.

```
Algo1-Par (S: StateChart; Subnets-List: List of ITPN) → ITPN
Begin
    Juxtapose together all regions nets ∈ Subnets-List;
    Link each transition generating an event e to all event
        places labeled with e as outplaces;
    Add a fork place P_entry;
    Join P_entry to the entry places of subnets through an entry
        transition T_entry;
    Label T_entry with the entry action name if it exits;
    Add a join place P_exit;
    Join P_exit to the final places of subnets through an exit
        transition T_exit;
    Label T_exit with the exit action name if it exits;
end Algo1-Par.
```

6.2 Second Step of Translation

In this step we treat boundary-crossing arcs which triggering causes exiting also the concerned superstates starting from the innermost one in the active configuration.

We recall that high-level transitions belong also to this category of arcs. Indeed a high-level transition originates from the boundary of a composite state S and so it can occur wherever the substate the control is in. Therefore we expand any transition of this kind into a group of simple boundary-crossing arcs where each one of them originates from one simple substate of the composite state.

For each boundary-crossing arc *Arc*, *Algorithm2* generates a transition T with an inplace labeled with the triggering event of *Arc*. Then it simply joins T to the entry place of the subnet related to the target state of *Arc*.

However it is more difficult to cope with the source state (S) of *Arc*. Obviously we join its related place Ps to T as inplace to disable |[S]| when *Arc* occurs. Especially T will have a list of labels, which contains at least the exit action name of S and the name of the action on *Ac*.

The next subroutine of *Algorithm2* depends on whether the superstates of S have a history tag. When the state S is exited, the next procedure assures that any superstate of S of which the superstate is history tagged, should become active when their outermost state is reentered later. The main idea is to regenerate a token through *Arc* in the entry place of any superstate S' that is itself enclosed within a history tagged state. Obviously the entry place depends on whether S' is history tagged (Fig.11).

```
Handle-Boundary-Crossing-Arc (Arc: IN OUT StateChart Arc)
    Begin
        S':= Source state of Arc;    // S' is a simple state
```

```
    S":= SuperState(S');
while S" does not contain the target state of Arc
   do begin
         Add to Label(T) the exit action name of S";
         if S" has a history tag then
             if S' has not a history tag
                  then join T to the entry place of |[S']|
                  else join T to the thread place of |[S']|;
         S' := S";    S" := SuperState(S");
       end
end Handle-Boundary-Crossing-Arc.
```

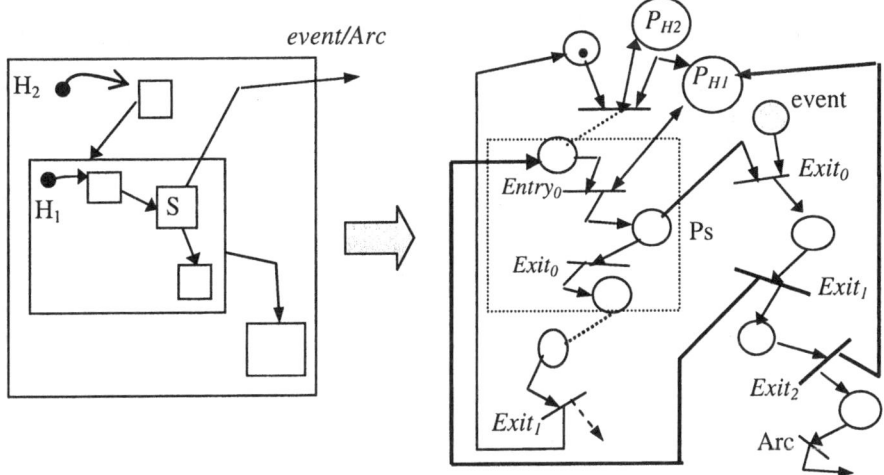

Fig. 11. Boundary-crossing arcs

Remark. Whenever one region of a concurrent state is exited by a boundary-crossing arc, all of orthogonal regions should also be exited. Therefore we add as *optional* inplaces some adequate places of the other orthogonal regions to the exit transition which becomes enabled only when its standard inplaces are marked. But when it fires, tokens in both usual and optional inplaces are consumed wherever the latter ones are available. Hence even if an optional inplace is not marked, the enabled transition fires. Here, thread places of the orthogonal regions are joined as optional inplaces to the exit transition which firing disables the subnets of the other regions.

7 Conclusion

This paper presents a new approach towards the formalization of UML by translating the StateCharts into a rigorous language, namely Interval Time Petri Nets (ITPN). We enhanced the previous formalism with some suitable concepts so that our method deals with both all kinds of composite states and pseudo-states and allows us to model the various dispatching delays of events and timing information on StateChart arcs.

Once an UML State diagram is converted into a Petri net, we can make use of existing tools for Petri net analysis [1] or check the semantically and temporal consistencies with reference to sequences diagram. In this setting, the intended methodology consists of generating the reachability graph from the related Petri net of any UML model and mapping the sequence diagram into a set of execution paths. Afterward, one can find out whether our graph embeds all these paths and whether timing constraints on events sequences are fulfilled considering the time intervals on graph transitions.

Similarly our approach can also be generalized to the activity diagrams since they are based on UML state machines. However some improvements would be performed to take into account some specific aspects of this kind of UML diagrams.

References

1. W.M.P. van der Aalst. Interval Timed Petri Nets and their analysis. Computing Science Notes 91/09, Eindhoven University of Technology, May 1991.
2. Luciano Baresi. Some Preliminary Hints on Formalizing UML with Object Petri Nets. Integrated Design and Process Technology IDPT-2002, June 2002.
3. Vieri Del Bianco, Luigi Lavazza, Marco Mauri. A Formalization of UML Statecharts for real-time software modeling. Integrated Design and Process Technology IDPT-2002.
4. Luciano Baresi, Mauro Pezzè. Improving UML with Petri Nets. Electronic Notes in Theoretical Computer Science 44 N° 4 (2001).
5. Robert G.Clark, Ana D. Moreira. Use of E-LOTOS in adding Formality to UML. Journal of Universal Computer Science 6(3) 1071-1087, 2000
6. A.Evans, J-M Bruel, R.France, K.Lano. Making UML Precise. In Proc. of the OOPSLA'98 Workshop on Formalizing UML, 1998.
7. Gregor Engels, Jan Hendrik Huasmann, Reiko Heckel, Stefan Sauer. Testing the Consistency of Dynamic UML Diagrams. Integrated Design and Process Technology IDPT-2002.
8. R.France, A.Evans, K.Lano, B.Rumpe. The UML as a formal Notation. UML'98 – Beyond Notation First International Workshop, Mulhouse, France, June 1998.
9. M. Gogolla, F.P. Presicce. State diagrams in UML: A formal semantics using graph transformations. In Proc. of PSMT'98 workshop precise semantics for modeling techniques.
10. G. Huszerl, I. Majzik, A. Pataricza, K. Kosmidis and M. Dal Cin. Quantitative Analysis of UML Statechart Models of Dependable Systems. The Computer Journal, Vol.45, N°3, 2002.
11. Peter King and Rob Pooley. Derivation of Petri Net Performance Models from UML specifications of Communications Software. B.R.Haverkort et al.(Eds.): TOOLS 2000, LNCS 1786, pp.262-276, 2000.
12. J. Merseguer, J. Campos, E. Mena. A pattern approach to model software performance using UML and Petri Nets: Application to Agent-based Systems. Workshop on software and performance, Ottawa, Sept.2000
13. Object Management Group, Inc. OMG Unified Modeling Language Specification. March 2003, Version 1.5, Formal/03-03-01.
14. Object Management Group, Inc. UML Profile for Schedulability, Performance, and Time Specification. September 2003, Version 1.0, Formal/03-09-01.
15. E.E.Roubtsova, J.van Katwijk, W.J.Toetenel, C.Ponk, R.C.M de Rooij. Specification of Real-Time Systems in UML. Electronic Notes in Theoretical Computer Science 39(3), 2000.
16. Anthony J.H. Simons. On the Compositional Properties of UML Statechart Diagrams. Rigorous Object-Oriented Methods, 2000.
17. K. Verschaeve, A.Ek. Three scenarios for combining UML and SDL'96. Eighth SDL Forum, Montréal, Canada, 1999.
18. Roel Wieringa. Formalizing the UML in a Systems Engineering Approach. In Proc. of second ECOOP workshop on precise behavioral semantics, 1998.

A Hierarchy of Implementable MSC Languages

Benedikt Bollig[1] and Martin Leucker[2]

[1] Lehrstuhl für Informatik II, RWTH Aachen, Germany
bollig@informatik.rwth-aachen.de
[2] Institut für Informatik, TU Munich, Germany
leucker@in.tum.de

Abstract. We develop a unifying theory of message-passing automata (MPAs) and MSC languages. We study several variants of *regular* as well as *product* MSC languages, their closure under finite union and their intersection. Furthermore, we analyse the expressive power of several variants of MPAs and characterize the language classes of interest by the corresponding classes of MPAs.

1 Introduction

A common design practice when developing communicating systems is to start with drawing scenarios showing the intended interaction of the system to be. The standardized notion of *message sequence charts* (MSCs, [ITU99]) is widely used in industry to formalize such typical behaviors.

A message sequence chart defines a set of processes and a set of communication actions between these processes. In the visual representation of an MSC, processes are drawn as vertical lines and interpreted as time axes. A labeled arrow from one line to a second corresponds to the communication event of sending a message from the first process to the second. Collections of MSCs are used to capture the scenarios that a designer might want the system to follow or to avoid. Figure 1 shows four simple MSCs.

The next step in the design process is to come up with a high-level model of the system to be. Such a model is usually formalized as a state machine or as an automaton. In the setting of MSCs, where the notion of distributed processes is central, one asks for distributed automata models. The components of such a distributed automaton should communicate by message passing to reflect the message flow indicated by MSCs. Thus, we are after message-passing automata (MPA) *realizing* or *implementing* the behavior given in form of scenarios.

In the setting of finite words, there has been an extensive study of several classes of languages and corresponding characterizations by means of automata. Algebraic and logical characterizations have been obtained as well.

In the setting of MSCs, however, a correspondence of languages and characterizing automata models or characterizing logical specifications is still at the beginning. In this paper, we provide a comprehensive study of MSC languages and message-passing automata. Our work can be summarized in two pictures, Figure 2 and Figure 3, which we explain in the rest of this introduction.

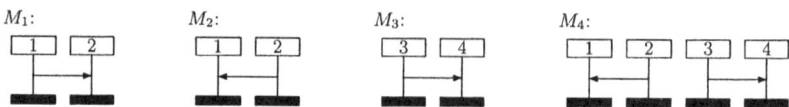

Fig. 1. The language of a finite MPA

When realizing communicating systems, two dimensions are important: *finiteness* and *independence*.

Finiteness. Most often, the intended system is required to have a finite set of (control) states. In the case of words, *regular* languages admit a characterization in terms of *finite* state machines. In general, the notion of *regularity* aims at *finite* representations. Thus, as in the word case, one is interested in *regular* MSC languages. While for the word case a consensus is reached for the notion of a regular language, this is not the case for MSC languages.

There have been several proposals for the *right* notion of regularity for MSC languages. Henriksen et al. started in [HMKT00], proposing that an MSC language is regular when its set of linearizations is regular. We denote this class of languages by $\mathcal{R}$ (see Figure 2).

One could likewise argue to call a set of MSCs regular, when it is definable by monadic second-order (MSO) logic (adjusted to MSCs), since this important property for verification holds for regular sets of words. This view was also pursued in [HMKT00] and it is shown that this class coincides with $\mathcal{R}$ when formulas are supposed to define *bounded* MSC languages. Intuitively, an MSC language is bounded iff its structure exhibits a bound on the number of send events that have not been received yet by the receiving process. For example, the MSC language $\{M_1\}^*$ (where M_1 is taken from Figure 1) is not bounded and hence not regular. It induces the set of MSCs that send arbitrarily many messages from process 1 to process 2. The set of all its linearizations gives rise to the set of all words that have the same number of send and receive events, where, for every prefix, the number of send events is larger or equal to the number of receive events. This language is not regular, since, intuitively, we would need an unbounded counter for the send events. In [GMK04], a more general notion of regularity was studied, which gives rise to *existentially* bounded MSC languages. Those languages require any MSC to exhibit at least one linearization that is compatible with a fixed channel capacity.

Independence. On the other hand, the systems exemplified by MSCs are distributed in nature and the notion of a *process* is central. It is therefore natural to consider every process to be represented as a single state machine or transition system. Furthermore, one defines a notion of communication, describing the way these parallel systems work together.

Languages defined by finite transition systems working in parallel are known as *product languages* and were initially studied in [Thi95] for Mazurkiewicz traces. That paper discusses finite-state systems. There is a common initial state and two different notions of acceptance condition. Either the acceptance condition is *local*, i.e. every process decides on its own when to stop, or it is *global*,

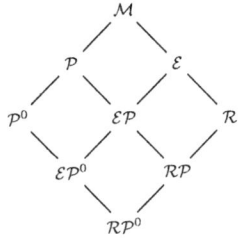

Fig. 2. The hierarchy of regular and product MSC languages

which allows to select certain combinations of local final states to be a valid point for termination. It is clear that (provided the system has a single initial state) the latter notion of acceptance is more expressive than local acceptance.

In the context of MSC languages, [AEY00] studied classes of MSCs taking up the idea of product behavior. Languages of MSCs are required to be closed under *inference*. The idea can be described looking at the setting in Figure 1. When realizing the behavior described by M_2 and by M_3, it is argued that the behavior of M_4 is also a possible one: Since processes 1 and 2 do not synchronize with processes 3 and 4, the four processes do not know whether the behavior of M_2 should be realized or that of M_3. We call the class of MSC languages that is closed under such inference *weak product MSC languages* and denote it by $\mathcal{P}^0$ (see Figure 2). Note that, in [AEY00], no finiteness condition was studied.

In simple words, *product languages* respect *independence*.

Extensions. Let us study extensions of the two existing approaches. When thinking about an automata model realizing MSC languages, the allowance of different initial states or global final states will give us classes of languages closed under finite union. For example, one could realize exactly the set consisting of M_2 and M_3 (without M_4). Thus, when considering finite unions of sets of $\mathcal{P}^0$ languages, one obtains the richer class of *product MSC languages*, denoted by $\mathcal{P}$. Combining the ideas of *independence* and *finiteness*, we get $\mathcal{RP}^0$ or $\mathcal{RP}$.

The drawback of the regularity notion used for $\mathcal{R}$ is that the simple language $\{M_1\}^*$ is not regular, as mentioned before. Let us once again turn to the logical point of view. Recall that MSO logic interpreted over bounded MSCs captures regular and, thus, bounded behavior. It was shown in [BL04] that MSO logic interpreted over the whole class of MSCs turns out to be too expressive to be compatible with certain finite message-passing automata as introduced beneath. These automata, though they employ finite state spaces for each process (but not globally), are capable of generating unbounded behavior using a priori unbounded channels. In [BL04], existential MSO, a fragment of MSO was shown to be expressively equivalent to finite message-passing automata. We therefore introduce the class of *EMSO-definable languages* ($\mathcal{E}$), which lifts the boundedness restriction without abandoning the existence of a finite automata-theoretic counterpart. Together with independence, we obtain the class $\mathcal{EP}$ or, when starting from $\mathcal{RP}^0$, the class, $\mathcal{EP}^0$.

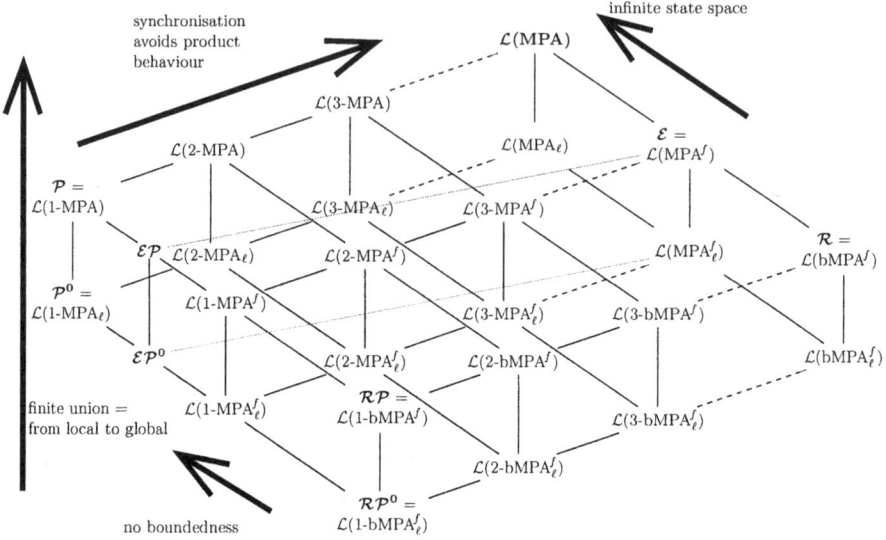

Fig. 3. A Hierarchy of MSC Languages

This completes the explanation of the languages shown in Figure 1, and, one main result of the paper is to show that languages actually form the hierarchy that is suggested in the figure.

Automata Models. So let us exhibit corresponding machine models and call our attention to Figure 3. We study several variants of message-passing automata (MPA), which consist of components that communicate through channels. All studied systems have a single initial state. We use (variations of) n-bMPA$_\ell^f$ to indicate several classes of MPAs. Dropping the requirement that the local state spaces are finite is indicated by the missing superscript f. When considering finite unions of languages, we have to move towards global acceptance conditions (rather than local), indicated by a missing ℓ.

When extending the expressiveness from regularity to EMSO-definable languages, we drop the boundedness condition of MSCs. This is represented in Figure 3 by a missing b. It can be shown that, when realizing regular languages, one needs so-called *synchronization messages* that are used to tell other components which transition was taken. They are used in [HMKT00] and [GMSZ02] to extend expressiveness. We show that the more of these messages are allowed, the more expressive power we have. The restriction to n synchronization messages is described by a preceding n- in Figure 3.

MPAs are subject to active research. However, there is no agreement which automata model is the right one to make an MSC language *implementable*: While, for example, [GMSZ02] is based on MPA$_\ell^f$, [AEY00, Mor02] focus on 1-MPA$_\ell$. In [HMKT00], though a priori unbounded channels are allowed, the bounded model bMPA$_\ell^f$ suffices to implement regular MSC languages. We provide a unifying framework and classify automata models according to their state-space, synchronization behavior, acceptance mode, and, on a rather semantical level, whether they generate bounded or unbounded behavior.

Our second main result is to show the correspondence indicated in Figure 3.

2 Preliminaries

Let us recall some basic definitions and let Σ be an alphabet. A finite Σ-*labeled partial order* is a triple $\mathcal{P} = (E, \leq, \ell)$ where E is a finite set, $\leq$ is a partial-order relation on E, i.e., it is reflexive, transitive, and antisymmetric, and $\ell : E \to \Sigma$ is a *labeling function*. For $e, e' \in E$, we write $e \lessdot e'$ if both $e < e'$ and, for any $e'' \in E$, $e < e'' \leq e'$ implies $e'' = e'$. A linearization of $\mathcal{P}$ is an extension $(E, \leq', \ell)$ of $\mathcal{P}$ such that $\leq' \supseteq \leq$ is a linear order. As we will identify isomorphic structures in the following, a linearization of $\mathcal{P}$ will be seen as a word over Σ. The set of linearizations of $\mathcal{P}$ is denoted by $Lin(\mathcal{P})$.

Let us fix a finite set *Proc* of at least two *processes*, which communicate with one another via message passing.[1] Communication proceeds through channels via executing communication actions. We denote by Ch the set $\{(p,q) \mid p, q \in \textit{Proc}, p \neq q\}$ of reliable FIFO *channels*. Given a process $p \in \textit{Proc}$, we furthermore set $\mathcal{C}_p$ to be $\{\texttt{send}(p,q) \mid (p,q) \in Ch\} \cup \{\texttt{rec}(p,q) \mid (p,q) \in Ch\}$, the set of *actions* of process p. The action $\texttt{send}(p,q)$ is to be read as "p sends a message to q", while $\texttt{rec}(q,p)$ is the complementary action of receiving a message sent from p to q. Accordingly, we set $Com := \{(\texttt{send}(p,q), \texttt{rec}(q,p)) \mid (p,q) \in Ch\}$. Moreover, let $\mathcal{C}$ stand for the union of the $\mathcal{C}_p$. Observe that an action $p\theta q$ ($\theta \in \{!,?\}$) is performed by process p, which is indicated by $P(p\theta q) = p$. A *message sequence chart* (MSC) (over *Proc*) is a tuple $(E, \{\leq_p\}_{p \in \textit{Proc}}, <_c, \ell)$ such that

- E is a finite set of *events*,
- ℓ is a mapping $E \to \mathcal{C}$,
- for any $p \in \textit{Proc}$, $\leq_p$ is a linear order on $E_p := \ell^{-1}(\mathcal{C}_p)$,
- $<_c \subseteq E \times E$ such that both, for any $e \in E$, there is $e' \in E$ satisfying $e <_c e'$ or $e' <_c e$ and, for any $(e_1, e'_1) \in <_c$, there are $p, q \in \textit{Proc}$ satisfying
  - $\ell(e_1) = \texttt{send}(p,q)$
  - $\ell(e'_1) = \texttt{rec}(q,p)$
  - for any $(e_2, e'_2) \in <_c$ with $\ell(e_1) = \ell(e_2)$, it holds $e_1 \leq_p e_2$ iff $e'_1 \leq_q e'_2$,
- $\leq := \left(<_c \cup \bigcup_{p \in \textit{Proc}} \leq_p\right)^*$ is a partial-order relation on E.

The set of MSCs is denoted by $\mathbb{MSC}$. (As *Proc* will be fixed in the following, a corresponding reference is omitted.) Let $M = (E, \{\leq_p\}_{p \in \textit{Proc}}, <_c, \ell) \in \mathbb{MSC}$. The behavior of M might be split into its components $M \upharpoonright p := (E_p, \leq_p, \ell_{|E_p})$, $p \in \textit{Proc}$, each of which represents the behavior of one single agent and can be seen as a word over $\mathcal{C}_p$. In turn, given a collection of words $w_p \in \mathcal{C}_p^*$, there is at most one MSC M such that, for any $p \in \textit{Proc}$, $w_p = M \upharpoonright p$. We will write $Lin(M)$ to denote $Lin((E, \leq, \ell))$, which extends to sets of MSCs as usual. Given

---

[1] In proofs, we sometimes silently assume the existence of more than two processes.

a set of words $L' \subseteq \mathcal{C}^*$, we say L' is an *MSC word language* if $L' = Lin(L)$ for some $L \subseteq \mathbb{MSC}$. In turn, a set $L \subseteq \mathbb{MSC}$ is uniquely determined by $Lin(L)$.

Let $B \geq 1$. We call a word $w \in \mathcal{C}^*$ *B-bounded* if, for any prefix v of w and any $(p,q) \in Ch$, $|v|_{\mathtt{send}(p,q)} - |v|_{\mathtt{rec}(q,p)} \leq B$ where $|v|_\sigma$ denotes the number of occurrences of σ in v. An MSC $M \in \mathbb{MSC}$ is called *B-bounded* if, for any $w \in Lin(M)$, w is B-bounded. The set of B-bounded MSCs is denoted by $\mathbb{MSC}_B$. An MSC language $L \subseteq \mathbb{MSC}$ is called B-bounded if $L \subseteq \mathbb{MSC}_B$. Moreover, we call L bounded if it is B-bounded for some B. In other words, boundedness is safe in the sense that any possible execution sequence does not claim more memory than some given upper bound (whereas existential boundedness, which, however, is not considered in this paper, allows an MSC to be executed even if this does not apply to each of its linear extensions [GMK04]).

3 Implementable MSC Languages

3.1 Regular MSC Languages

There have been several proposals for the *right* notion of regularity for MSC languages. In their seminal work [HMKT00, HMK+04], Henriksen et al. consider an MSC language to be regular if its set of linearizations forms a regular word language. For example, the MSC language $\{M_1\}^*$ (where M_1 is taken from Figure 1), which allows to concatenate M_1 arbitrarily often[2], is not bounded and hence cannot be regular. It induces the set of MSCs that send arbitrarily many messages from process 1 to process 2. The corresponding set of linearizations gives rise to a set of words that show the same number of send and receive events. This language is not recognizable in the free word monoid. In contrast, the language $\{M_1 \cdot M_2\}^*$ is regular, as its word language can be easily realized by a finite automaton. Thus, regularity aims at finiteness of the underlying *global* system, which incorporates the state of a communication channel.

Definition 1 ([HMKT00]). *A set $L \subseteq \mathbb{MSC}$ is called* regular *if $Lin(L)$ is a regular word language over $\mathcal{C}$.*

The class of regular MSC languages is denoted by $\mathcal{R}$.

Corollary 1 ([HMKT00]). *Any regular MSC language is bounded.*

As mentioned above, $\{M_1\}^*$ with M_1 again taken from Figure 1 is not regular. However, it is *existentially*-bounded [GMK04] and, as we will see in the next section, there is a simple finite message-passing automaton accepting $\{M_1\}^*$. Thus, we are looking for another, extended notion of *regularity*.

3.2 (E)MSO-Definable MSC Languages

Formulas from monadic second-order (MSO) logic (over *Proc*) involve first-order variables $x, y, \ldots$ for events and second-order variables $X, Y, \ldots$ for sets of events.

---
[2] Here, concatenation is meant to be asynchronous.

They are built up from the atomic formulas $\ell(x) = \sigma$ (for $\sigma \in \mathcal{C}$), $x \in X$, $x <_p y$ (for $p \in Proc$), $x <_c y$, and $x = y$ and furthermore allow the connectives $\neg$, $\vee$, $\wedge$, $\rightarrow$, $\leftrightarrow$ as well as the quantifiers $\exists$, $\forall$, which can be applied to either kind of variable. Formulas without free variables, which do not occur within the scope of a quantifier, are called sentences. Given an MSC $M = (E, \{\leq_p\}_{p \in Proc}, <_c, \ell)$ and an MSO sentence φ, the validity of the satisfaction relation $M \models \varphi$ is defined canonically with the understanding that first-order variables range over events from E and second-order variables over subsets of E. The *language* of φ, denoted by $L(\varphi)$, is the set of MSCs M with $M \models \varphi$. The class of subsets of $\mathbb{MSC}$ that can be defined by some MSO sentence φ is denoted by $\mathcal{MSO}$. An important fragment of MSO logic is captured by *existential* MSO (EMSO) formulas, which are of the form $\exists X_1 \ldots \exists X_n \varphi$ where φ does not contain any set quantifier. In many cases, the restriction to EMSO formulas suffices to characterize recognizability in terms of automata, e.g., in the domains of words, trees, and Mazurkiewicz traces. Sometimes, however, we even have to restrict to EMSO formulas not to exceed recognizability in terms of automata, because full MSO logic is too expressive in general. In fact, the latter applies to MSCs [BL04]. The class of EMSO-definable MSC languages will be denoted by $\mathcal{E}$.

3.3 Product MSC Languages

Languages defined by finite transition systems working in parallel are known as *product languages* and were initially studied by Thiagarajan in [Thi95] in the domain of Mazurkiewicz traces where distributed components communicate executing actions simultaneously rather than sending messages. Taking up the idea of product behavior, [AEY00] considers MSC languages that are closed under *inference*, which can be described by the setting depicted in Figure 1. Attempting to realize the MSC language $\{M_2, M_3\}$, one might argue that the behavior of M_4 is a feasible one, too. As processes 1 and 2 do not get in touch with processes 3 and 4, it is not clear to a single process whether to realize the behavior of M_2 or that of M_3 so that, finally, M_4 might be *inferred* from $\{M_2, M_3\}$. We call a set of MSCs that is closed under such an inference a *weak product MSC language*. Let us be more precise and, given $L \subseteq \mathbb{MSC}$ and $M \in \mathbb{MSC}$, write $L \vdash_{Proc} M$ if $\forall p \in Proc : \exists M' \in L : M' \upharpoonright p = M \upharpoonright p$.

Definition 2. *A set $L \subseteq \mathbb{MSC}$ is called a* weak product MSC language *if, for any $M \in \mathbb{MSC}$, $L \vdash_{Proc} M$ implies $M \in L$ [AEY00]. The finite union of weak product MSC languages is called a* product MSC language.

We let $\mathcal{P}^0$ and $\mathcal{P}$ denote the classes of weak product languages and, respectively, product languages.

In other words, an MSC language L is a weak product MSC language if every MSC that agrees on each process line with some MSC from L is contained in L, too. Getting back to Figure 1, M_4 agrees with M_2 on the first two process lines and with M_3 on the remaining two. Thus, M_4 belongs to any weak product language containing both M_2 and M_3. As global knowledge of an underlying system, one often allows several global initial or final states. This is the reason for

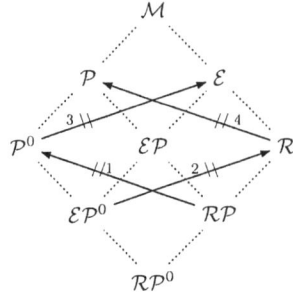

1	$\{M_2, M_3\}$
2	$\{M_2\}^*$
3	[BL04]
4	L_{N+1} with $N \geq 1$ (cf. Lemma 10)

Fig. 4. Strictness and incomparability in the hierarchy

considering finite unions of weak product languages. For example, $\{M_2, M_3\}$ is a product MSC language, while $\{M_4\}^*$ is not. Let us bring together the concepts of product behavior and regularity.

Definition 3. *We call* $\mathcal{R} \cap \mathcal{P}^0$ *the class of* weak regular product MSC languages *and denote it by* $\mathcal{RP}^0$. *Furthermore, an MSC language L is a* regular product MSC language, *denoted by $L \in \mathcal{RP}$, if it is the finite union of sets from $\mathcal{RP}^0$.*

Let us now extend our study towards product languages in combination with EMSO-definable languages. As the class of EMSO-definable languages turned out to capture exactly the class of languages implementable in terms of a finite message-passing automaton, we rather concentrate on EMSO-definable languages than on MSO-definable ones [BL04].

Definition 4. *We call* $\mathcal{E} \cap \mathcal{P}^0$ *the class of* weak EMSO-definable product MSC languages *and denote it by* $\mathcal{EP}^0$. *An MSC language L is an* EMSO-definable product MSC language *($L \in \mathcal{EP}$) if it is the finite union of sets from $\mathcal{EP}^0$.*

Theorem 1. *The classes of languages proposed so far draw the picture shown in Figure 2. The hierarchy is strict.*

Proof. $\mathcal{R} \subseteq \mathcal{E}$ has been shown, for example, in [BL04]. The other inclusions are straightforward. It remains to show strictness and incomparability. Consider the MSCs M_2 and M_3 from Figure 1. For a (crossed) arrow from a class of MSC languages $\mathfrak{C}_1$ to a class $\mathfrak{C}_2$ in Figure 4, the tabular aside specifies an MSC language L with $L \in \mathfrak{C}_1$ and $L \notin \mathfrak{C}_2$.

3.4 Product MSC Languages vs. Product Trace Languages

Product languages have been introduced first in the framework of (Mazurkiewicz) traces. So let us compare traces and MSCs in the scope of regular MSC languages and justify that, in this respect, we have chosen the same terminology for traces and MSCs. In particular, we raise the hope that results and logics regarding product trace languages are amenable to MSCs, such as the local temporal logic PTL, which is tailored to systems that support product behavior [Thi95].

Like MSCs, traces preserve some partial-order properties of a distributed system. Given a set $[K] := \{1, \ldots, K\}$ of *agents*, $K \geq 1$, they are based on a distributed alphabet $(\Sigma_1, \ldots, \Sigma_K)$, a tuple of (not necessarily disjoint) alphabets. Elements from Σ_i are understood to be actions that are performed by agent i. Let in the following $\tilde{\Sigma} = (\Sigma_1, \ldots, \Sigma_K)$ be a distributed alphabet, let Σ stand for the union of alphabets Σ_i, and let, for $a \in \Sigma$, $loc(a) := \{i \in [K] \mid a \in \Sigma_i\}$ denote the set of agents that are involved in the action a. A distributed alphabet $\tilde{\Sigma}$ determines a *dependence relation* $\mathcal{D}_{\tilde{\Sigma}} = (\Sigma, D)$ where $D = \{(a,b) \in \Sigma \times \Sigma \mid loc(a) \cap loc(b) \neq \emptyset\}$ is a reflexive and symmetric binary relation on Σ. Thus, actions a and b are understood to be *dependent* if they can both be performed by one and the same sequential agent.

A *(Mazurkiewicz) trace* over $\tilde{\Sigma}$ is a Σ-labeled partial order $(E, \leq, \ell)$ such that, for any $e, e' \in E$, $e \lessdot e'$ implies $(\ell(e), \ell(e')) \in D$ and $(\ell(e), \ell(e')) \in D$ implies $e \leq e'$ or $e' \leq e$. The set of traces over $\tilde{\Sigma}$ is denoted by $\mathbb{TR}(\tilde{\Sigma})$. As in the MSC case, the behavior of a trace $T \in \mathbb{TR}(\tilde{\Sigma})$ can be split into components $T \restriction i := (E_i, \leq \cap (E_i \times E_i), \ell_{|E_i})$ (where $E_i := \ell^{-1}(\Sigma_i)$), each of which can be seen as a word over Σ_i and represents the behavior of one single agent. Also, given a collection of words $w_i \in \Sigma_i^*$, there is at most one trace T such that, for any $i \in [K]$, $w_i = T \restriction i$. A set $L \subseteq \mathbb{TR}(\tilde{\Sigma})$ is called *regular* if $Lin(L)$ is a regular word language over Σ. The class of regular trace languages over $\tilde{\Sigma}$ is denoted by $\mathcal{R}_{\mathbb{TR}(\tilde{\Sigma})}$. Let $L \subseteq \mathbb{TR}(\tilde{\Sigma})$ and $T \in \mathbb{TR}(\tilde{\Sigma})$. Similarly to MSCs, we write $L \vdash_{\tilde{\Sigma}} T$ if, for any $i \in [K]$, there is $T' \in L$ such that $T' \restriction i = T \restriction i$. A set $L \subseteq \mathbb{TR}(\tilde{\Sigma})$ is called a *weak product trace language* (over $\tilde{\Sigma}$) ($L \in \mathcal{P}^0_{\mathbb{TR}(\tilde{\Sigma})}$) if, for any $T \in \mathbb{TR}(\tilde{\Sigma})$, $L \vdash_{\tilde{\Sigma}} T$ implies $T \in L$. A set $L \subseteq \mathbb{TR}(\tilde{\Sigma})$ is called a *product trace language* ($L \in \mathcal{P}_{\mathbb{TR}(\tilde{\Sigma})}$) if it is the finite union of weak product trace languages [Thi95]. The classes $\mathcal{RP}^0_{\mathbb{TR}(\tilde{\Sigma})}$ and $\mathcal{RP}_{\mathbb{TR}(\tilde{\Sigma})}$ are defined as expected.

We now recall in how far bounded MSC languages can be seen as trace languages over an appropriate alphabet [Kus03]. Let B be a positive natural. We define $\mathcal{D}_B$ to be the dependence alphabet $(\mathcal{C} \times \{1, \ldots, B\}, D_B)$ where $(\sigma_1, n_1) D_B (\sigma_2, n_2)$ if $P(\sigma_1) = P(\sigma_2)$ or $((\sigma_1, \sigma_2) \in Com \cup Com^{-1}$ and $n_1 = n_2)$. Setting Co to be $\{(\sigma, \tau, n) \mid (\sigma, \tau) \in Com, \ n \in \{1, \ldots, B\}\}$, let $\tilde{\Sigma}_B$ be the distributed alphabet $(\overline{\mathcal{C}}_\gamma)_{\gamma \in Proc \cup Co}$ where, for $p \in Proc$, $\overline{\mathcal{C}}_p := \mathcal{C}_p \times \{1, \ldots, B\}$ and, for $(\sigma, \tau, n) \in Co$, $\overline{\mathcal{C}}_{(\sigma,\tau,n)} := \{(\sigma, n), (\tau, n)\}$. Note that, given $B \geq 1$, $\mathcal{D}_{\tilde{\Sigma}_B} = \mathcal{D}_B$. To an MSC $M = (E, \{\leq_p\}_{p \in Proc}, <_c, \ell) \in \mathbb{MSC}_B$, we assign the Mazurkiewicz trace $Tr_B(M) := (E, \leq, \ell')$ where for each $e \in E$, we define $\ell'(e)$ to be the new labeling $(\ell(e), |\{e' \in E_{P(\ell(e))} \mid e' \leq e\}| \mod B)$. According to [Kus03], $Tr_B(M)$ is a trace over $\tilde{\Sigma}_B$ for any $M \in \mathbb{MSC}_B$. Note that the mapping $Tr_B : \mathbb{MSC}_B \to \mathbb{TR}(\tilde{\Sigma}_B)$ is injective. It is canonically extended towards MSC languages. Thus, involving some relabeling, an MSC language $L \subseteq \mathbb{MSC}_B$ can be converted into some trace language $Tr_B(L) \subseteq \mathbb{TR}(\tilde{\Sigma}_B)$.

To make clear in the following when we address a class of MSC languages rather than trace languages, we write, for example, $\mathcal{R}_{\mathrm{MSC}}$ instead of simply $\mathcal{R}$.

Lemma 1 ([Kus02]). *For any $B \geq 1$ and any $L \subseteq \text{MSC}_B$, $L \in \mathcal{R}_{\text{MSC}}$ iff $Tr_B(L) \in \mathcal{R}_{\mathbb{TR}(\tilde{\Sigma}_B)}$.*

We now show that the above correspondence carries over to product behavior.

Lemma 2. *For any $B \geq 1$ and $L \subseteq \text{MSC}_B$, $L \in \mathcal{RP}^0_{\text{MSC}}$ iff $Tr_B(L) \in \mathcal{RP}^0_{\mathbb{TR}(\tilde{\Sigma}_B)}$.*

Proof. According to Lemma 1, Tr_B and its inverse both preserve regularity.

"only if": Suppose $L \subseteq \text{MSC}_B$ to be a weak regular product MSC language. Recall that $Tr_B(L)$ is a regular trace language over $\tilde{\Sigma}_B = (\overline{C}_\gamma)_{\gamma \in Proc \cup Co}$. Moreover, let $T \in \mathbb{TR}(\tilde{\Sigma}_B)$ such that, for any $\gamma \in Proc \cup Co$, there is a trace $T_\gamma \in Tr_B(L)$ satisfying $T_\gamma \upharpoonright \gamma = T \upharpoonright \gamma$. Then, $T \in Tr_B(\text{MSC}_B)$ and, in particular, we have $T_p \upharpoonright p = T \upharpoonright p$ and, thus, $Tr_B^{-1}(T_p) \upharpoonright p = Tr_B^{-1}(T) \upharpoonright p$ for any $p \in Proc$, which implies $Tr_B^{-1}(T) \in L$ and $T \in Tr_B(L)$.

"if": Suppose $L \subseteq \text{MSC}_B$ to generate a weak regular trace language over $\tilde{\Sigma}_B$, i.e., $Tr_B(L) \in \mathcal{RP}^0(\tilde{\Sigma}_B)$, and let $M \in \text{MSC}_B$ such that, for any $p \in Proc$, there is $M_p \in L$ with $M_p \upharpoonright p = M \upharpoonright p$. Trivially, we have that, for any $p \in Proc$, $Tr_B(M_p) \upharpoonright p = Tr_B(M) \upharpoonright p$. Moreover, for any $\gamma = (\text{send}(p,q), \text{rec}(q,p), n) \in Co$, $Tr_B(M_p) \upharpoonright \gamma = Tr_B(M) \upharpoonright \gamma$ (note that also $Tr_B(M_q) \upharpoonright \gamma = Tr_B(M) \upharpoonright \gamma$). This is because, in the trace of a B-bounded MSC, the n-th receipt of a message through (p,q) is ordered before sending from p to q for the $(n+B)$-th time. Altogether, we have $Tr_B(M) \in Tr_B(L)$ and, consequently, $M \in L$. □

Corollary 2. *For any $B \geq 1$ and any $L \subseteq \text{MSC}_B$, $L \in \mathcal{RP}_{\text{MSC}}$ iff $Tr_B(L) \in \mathcal{RP}_{\mathbb{TR}(\tilde{\Sigma}_B)}$.*

4 Message-Passing Automata

We now introduce and study *message-passing automata* (MPAs), our model of computation, which is is close to a real-life implementation of a message-passing system. MPAs can be considered to be the most common computation model for MSCs. An MPA is a collection of state machines that share one global initial state and several global final states. The machines are connected pairwise with a priori unbounded reliable FIFO buffers. The transitions of each component are labeled with send or receive actions. Hereby, a send action $p!q$ puts a message at the end of the channel from p to q. A receive action can be taken provided the requested message is found in the channel. To extend the expressive power, MPAs can send certain *synchronization messages*. Let us be more precise:

Definition 5 (Message-Passing Automaton). *A* message-passing automaton *(MPA) is a structure $\mathcal{A} = ((\mathcal{A}_p)_{p \in Proc}, \mathcal{D}, \overline{s}^{in}, F)$ such that*

- $\mathcal{D}$ *is a nonempty finite set of synchronization messages,*
- *for each $p \in Proc$, $\mathcal{A}_p$ is a pair (S_p, Δ_p) where S_p is a nonempty set of (p-)local states and $\Delta_p \subseteq S_p \times \mathcal{C}_p \times \mathcal{D} \times S_p$ is the set of (p-)local transitions,*

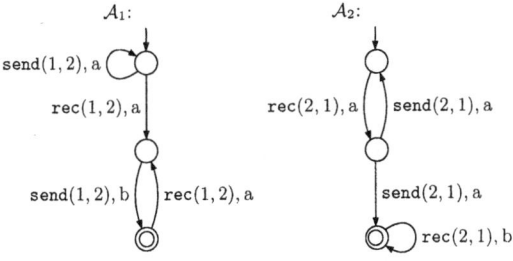

Fig. 5. A message-passing automaton

- $\overline{s}^{in} \in \prod_{p \in Proc} S_p$ is the global initial state, and
- $F \subseteq \prod_{p \in Proc} S_p$ is a finite set of global final states.

An MPA $\mathcal{A} = ((\mathcal{A}_p)_{p \in Proc}, \mathcal{D}, \overline{s}^{in}, F)$, $\mathcal{A}_p = (S_p, \Delta_p)$, is called

- an N-MPA, $N \geq 1$, if $|\mathcal{D}| = N$,
- *finite* if, for each $p \in Proc$, S_p is finite, and
- *locally-accepting* if there are sets $F_p \subseteq S_p$ such that $F = \prod_{p \in Proc} F_p$.

The class of MPAs is denoted by MPA, the class of finite MPAs by MPA^f. Furthermore, for a set $\mathfrak{C}$ of MPAs, we denote by N-$\mathfrak{C}$ the class of N-MPAs $\mathcal{A}$ and by $\mathfrak{C}_\ell$ the class of locally-accepting MPAs $\mathcal{A}$ with $\mathcal{A} \in \mathfrak{C}$, respectively. A locally-accepting finite 2-MPA with set of synchronization messages $\{a, b\}$ is illustrated in Figure 5.

In defining the behavior of an MPA, we adopt the view taken, for example, in [HMKT00, Mor02, GMSZ02], who suppose an MPA to run on linearizations of MSCs rather than on MSCs to reflect an operational behavior. Usually, such a view relies on the *global transition relation* of $\mathcal{A}$, which, in turn, defers to the notion of a *configuration*. Let us be more precise and consider an MPA $\mathcal{A} = ((\mathcal{A}_p)_{p \in Proc}, \mathcal{D}, \overline{s}^{in}, F)$, $\mathcal{A}_p = (S_p, \Delta_p)$. The set of *configurations* of $\mathcal{A}$, denoted by $Conf_\mathcal{A}$, is the cartesian product $S_\mathcal{A} \times \mathcal{C}_\mathcal{A}$ where $\mathcal{C}_\mathcal{A} := \{\chi \mid \chi : Ch \to \mathcal{D}^*\}$ is the set of possible *channel contents* of $\mathcal{A}$. Now, the *global transition relation* of $\mathcal{A}$, $\Longrightarrow_\mathcal{A} \subseteq Conf_\mathcal{A} \times C \times \mathcal{D} \times Conf_\mathcal{A}$, is defined as follows:

- $((\overline{s}, \chi), \mathtt{send}(p, q), m, (\overline{s}', \chi')) \in \Longrightarrow_\mathcal{A}$ if $(\overline{s}[p], \mathtt{send}(p, q), m, \overline{s}'[p]) \in \Delta_p$, $\chi' = \chi[(p, q)/m \cdot \chi((p, q))]$ (i.e., χ' maps (p, q) to $m \cdot \chi((p, q))$ and, otherwise, coincides with χ), and for all $r \in Proc \setminus \{p\}$, $\overline{s}[r] = \overline{s}'[r]$.
- $((\overline{s}, \chi), \mathtt{rec}(p, q), m, (\overline{s}', \chi')) \in \Longrightarrow_\mathcal{A}$ if there is a word $w \in \mathcal{D}^*$ such that $(\overline{s}[p], \mathtt{rec}(p, q), m, \overline{s}'[p]) \in \Delta_p$, $\chi((q, p)) = w \cdot m$, $\chi' = \chi[(q, p)/w]$, and for all $r \in Proc \setminus \{p\}$, $\overline{s}[r] = \overline{s}'[r]$.

Let $\chi_\varepsilon : Ch \to \mathcal{D}^*$ map each channel onto the empty word. When we set $(\overline{s}^{in}, \chi_\varepsilon)$ to be the *initial configuration* and $F \times \{\chi_\varepsilon\}$ to be the set of *final configurations*, $\mathcal{A}$ defines in the canonical way an MSC word language $L_w(\mathcal{A}) \subseteq \mathcal{C}^*$. The corresponding MSC language will be denoted by $L(\mathcal{A})$ and is called the *language* of $\mathcal{A}$. Given a class $\mathfrak{C}$ of MPAs, let furthermore $\mathcal{L}(\mathfrak{C}) := \{L \subseteq \mathbb{MSC} \mid \text{there is } \mathcal{A} \in \mathfrak{C} \text{ such that } L = L(\mathcal{A})\}$ denote the *class of languages* of $\mathfrak{C}$.

For configurations $(\bar{s}, \chi), (\bar{s}', \chi') \in \mathit{Conf}_\mathcal{A}$, we write $(\bar{s}, \chi) \Longrightarrow_\mathcal{A} (\bar{s}', \chi')$ if $((\bar{s}, \chi), \sigma, m, (\bar{s}', \chi')) \in \Longrightarrow_\mathcal{A}$ for some $\sigma \in \mathcal{C}$ and $m \in \mathcal{D}$. We call a configuration $(\bar{s}, \chi) \in \mathit{Conf}_\mathcal{A}$ *reachable* from another configuration $(\bar{s}', \chi') \in \mathit{Conf}_\mathcal{A}$ if $(\bar{s}', \chi') \Longrightarrow^*_\mathcal{A} (\bar{s}, \chi)$. Moreover, we say $(\bar{s}, \chi) \in \mathit{Conf}_\mathcal{A}$ is *productive* if there is a final configuration that is reachable from $(\bar{s}, \chi)$.

For $B \geq 1$, an MPA $\mathcal{A}$ is called *B-bounded* if, for any $(p, q) \in Ch$ and any configuration $(\bar{s}, \chi)$ that is productive and reachable from the initial configuration, it holds $|\chi((p,q))| \leq B$. According to [HMKT00], who use a slightly different notion of bounded MPAs, we call an MPA $\mathcal{A}$ *strongly-B-bounded* for some $B \geq 1$ if, for any $(p, q) \in Ch$ and any configuration $(\bar{s}, \chi)$ that is reachable from the initial configuration, $|\chi((p,q))| \leq B$. Furthermore, $\mathcal{A}$ is called *(strongly) bounded* if it is B-bounded (strongly-B-bounded, respectively) for some $B \geq 1$. Given a class $\mathfrak{C}$ of MPAs, let b$\mathfrak{C}$ (sb$\mathfrak{C}$) denote the set of (strongly, respectively) bounded MPAs $\mathcal{A}$ with $\mathcal{A} \in \mathfrak{C}$.

Sometimes, it is more convenient to consider MPAs with a set of global initial states instead of one global initial state. So let an *extended MPA* be an MPA $\mathcal{A} = ((\mathcal{A}_p)_{p \in \mathit{Proc}}, \mathcal{D}, S^{in}, F)$ where, though, $S^{in} \subseteq \prod_{p \in \mathit{Proc}} S_p$ is a finite *set of global initial states*. The language of $\mathcal{A}$ is defined analogously to the MPA case.

Lemma 3. *Let $N \geq 1$ and L be an MSC language. Then L is the language of a (bounded/finite/bounded and finite) N-MPA iff it is the language of an extended locally-accepting (bounded/finite/bounded and finite, respectively) N-MPA.*

Proof. "only if": Let $\mathcal{A} = ((\mathcal{A}_p)_{p \in \mathit{Proc}}, \mathcal{D}, \bar{s}^{in}, F)$, $\mathcal{A}_p = (S_p, \Delta_p)$, be an MPA. For each state $\bar{s} \in F$, introduce a global initial state running a distinct copy $\mathcal{A}(\bar{s})$ of $\mathcal{A}$ with local state spaces $S_p^{\bar{s}}$ (in the following, a copy of a local state $s \in S_p$ in $\mathcal{A}(\bar{s})$ is denoted by $s^{\bar{s}}$). The set of global final states is henceforth the cartesian product $\prod_{p \in \mathit{Proc}} \bigcup_{\bar{s} \in F} \{\bar{s}[p]^{\bar{s}}\}$. The resulting MPA is locally-accepting and, obviously, recognizes the same language as $\mathcal{A}$ without having affected the number of messages, boundedness, or finiteness properties.

"if": Let $\mathcal{A} = ((\mathcal{A}_p)_{p \in \mathit{Proc}}, \mathcal{D}, S^{in}, F)$, $\mathcal{A}_p = (S_p, \Delta_p)$, be an extended MPA where F is the product $\prod_{p \in \mathit{Proc}} F_p$ of sets $F_p \subseteq S_p$. The basic idea is to create a copy $S_p^{\bar{s}_0} = S_p \times \{\bar{s}_0\}$ of S_p for any global initial state $\bar{s}_0 \in S^{in}$. Starting in some new global initial state $\bar{s}^{in}$ and switching to some state $(s, \bar{s}_0)$ now settles for simulating a run of $\mathcal{A}$ from $\bar{s}_0$ by henceforth allowing to enter no other copy than $S_p^{\bar{s}_0}$. In a global final state, it is then checked whether the other processes agree in their choice of $\bar{s}_0$. More formally, we may have local transitions $((s, \bar{s}_0), \sigma, m, (s', \bar{s}_0))$ with $\bar{s}_0 \in S^{in}$ if (s, σ, m, s') is a local transition of $\mathcal{A}$. Moreover, we add kind of initial transitions $(\bar{s}^{in}[p], \sigma, m, (s, \bar{s}_0))$ if $(\bar{s}_0[p], \sigma, m, s)$ is some p-local transition of $\mathcal{A}$ with $\bar{s}_0 \in S^{in}$. It remains to reformulate the acceptance condition: $\bar{s}$ is a global final state if there is $\bar{s}_0 \in S^{in}$ such that, for any $p \in \mathit{Proc}$, either $\bar{s}[p] = \bar{s}^{in}[p]$ and $\bar{s}_0[p] \in F_p$ or $\bar{s}[p] \in F_p \times \{\bar{s}_0\}$. $\square$

Lemma 4 ([AEY00]). $\mathcal{P}^\diamond = \mathcal{L}(1\text{-MPA}_\ell)$

Corollary 3. $\mathcal{P} = \mathcal{L}(\text{1-MPA})$

Proof. "$\supseteq$": According to Lemma 3, a 1-MPA can be transformed into an equivalent extended locally-accepting 1-MPA $((\mathcal{A}_p)_{p \in Proc}, \mathcal{D}, S^{in}, F)$, which then recognizes $\bigcup_{\overline{s} \in S^{in}} L(((\mathcal{A}_p)_{p \in Proc}, \mathcal{D}, \overline{s}, F))$. The assertion follows from Lemma 4 and Definition 2.

"$\subseteq$": Similarly, any MSC language $L \in \mathcal{P}$ is the union of finitely many languages $L_1, \ldots, L_k \in \mathcal{P}^0$, which, according to Lemma 4 are recognized by locally-accepting 1-MPAs $\mathcal{A}^1, \ldots, \mathcal{A}^k$ (each employing, say, a as synchronization message) with global initial states $\overline{s}_1, \ldots, \overline{s}_k$ and sets of global final states $F^1, \ldots, F^k$, respectively, where, for each $i \in \{1, \ldots, k\}$, $F^i = \prod_{p \in Proc} F_p^i$ for some $F_p^i \subseteq S_p^i$ (let hereby S_p^i be the set of p-local states of $\mathcal{A}^i$). Without loss of generality, $\mathcal{A}^1, \ldots, \mathcal{A}^k$ have mutually distinct local state spaces. The extended locally-accepting 1-MPA recognizing L processwise merges the state spaces and transitions of $\mathcal{A}^1, \ldots, \mathcal{A}^k$, employs $\{\overline{s}_1, \ldots, \overline{s}_k\}$ being the set of global initial states, and, similarly to the proof of Lemma 3, sets the set of global final states to be $\prod_{p \in Proc} \bigcup_{i \in \{1, \ldots, k\}} F_p^i$. The assertion then follows from Lemma 3. $\square$

Lemma 5. $\mathcal{RP}^0 = \mathcal{L}(\text{1-bMPA}_\ell^f)$

Proof. "$\supseteq$": This direction directly follows from Lemma 4 and Lemma 7 below.
"$\subseteq$": Let $L \in \mathcal{RP}^0$ and, for $p \in Proc$, $\mathcal{A}_p = (S_p, \Delta_p, \overline{s}_p^{in}, F_p)$ be a finite automaton over $\mathcal{C}_p$ satisfying $L(\mathcal{A}_p) = L \upharpoonright p := \{M \upharpoonright p \mid M \in L\}$. Consider the MPA $\mathcal{A} = ((\mathcal{A}_p')_{p \in Proc}, \mathcal{D}, \overline{s}^{in}, F)$ with $\mathcal{D} = \{a\}$, $\overline{s}^{in} = (\overline{s}_p^{in})_{p \in Proc}$, $F = \prod_{p \in Proc} F_p$, and $\mathcal{A}_p' = (S_p, \Delta_p')$ where, for any $s, s' \in S_p$ and $\sigma \in \mathcal{C}_p$, $(s, \sigma, \text{a}, s') \in \Delta_p'$ if $(s, \sigma, s') \in \Delta_p$. We claim that both $\mathcal{A} \in$ 1-bMPA$_\ell^f$ and $L(\mathcal{A}) = L$. First, it is easy to see that $L \subseteq L(\mathcal{A})$. Now assume an MSC M to be contained in $L(\mathcal{A})$. For each $p \in Proc$, $M \upharpoonright p \in L(\mathcal{A}_p) = L \upharpoonright p$ so that there is an MSC $M' \in L$ with $M' \upharpoonright p = M \upharpoonright p$. From the definition of $\mathcal{P}^0$, it then immediately follows that M is contained in L, too. Clearly, $\mathcal{A}$ is finite, locally-accepting, and bounded. $\square$

Lemma 6. $\mathcal{RP}^0 \supsetneq \mathcal{L}(\text{1-sbMPA}_\ell^f)$

Proof. It remains to show strictness. Let $L = \{M_1\}^* \cup \{M_2\}^*$ with M_1 and M_2 given by Figure 6, and suppose there is an MPA $\mathcal{A} \in$ 1-MPA$_\ell^f$ with $L(\mathcal{A}) = L$. Then, for each natural $n \geq 1$, the word

$$\text{send}(1,2)^2 \left(\text{send}(3,1)\,\text{rec}(1,2)\,\text{send}(1,2)^2\,\text{rec}(2,1)\,\text{send}(2,3)\,\text{rec}(3,2)\right)^n$$

from $\mathcal{C}^*$ leads from the initial configuration of $\mathcal{A}$ via $\Longrightarrow_\mathcal{A}$ to some configuration (s, χ) with $\chi((1,2)) = n + 3$. Thus, $\mathcal{A}$ cannot be strongly-bounded. Nevertheless, L is contained in $\mathcal{RP}^0$ and 2-bounded. $\square$

Corollary 4. $\mathcal{RP} = \mathcal{L}(\text{1-bMPA}^f)$

Lemma 7 ([HMKT00]). $\mathcal{R} = \mathcal{L}(\text{bMPA}^f) = \mathcal{L}(\text{sbMPA}^f)$

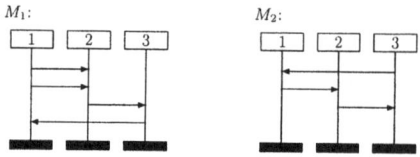

Fig. 6. Universal boundedness vs. strong boundedness

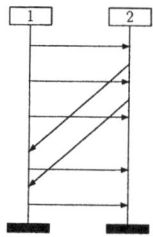

Fig. 7. $M(3,2)$

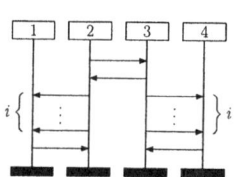

Fig. 8. MSC $M(i)$

In [BL04], it has been shown that any EMSO-definable MSC language is implementable as a finite MPA and vice versa.

Lemma 8 ([BL04]). $\mathcal{E} = \mathcal{L}(\text{MPA}^f)$

Lemma 9. *We have the following strict inclusion:*

(a) $\mathcal{L}(\text{1-MPA}^f_\ell) \subsetneq \mathcal{EP}^0$
(b) $\mathcal{L}(\text{1-MPA}^f) \subsetneq \mathcal{EP}$

Proof. Inclusion of (a) follows from Lemma 4 and Lemma 8. Inclusion of (b) then proceeds as the proof for Corollary 3. Let us turn towards strictness. For naturals $m, n \geq 1$, let the MSC $M(m,n)$ be given by its projections according to $M(m,n) \upharpoonright 1 = \text{send}(1,2)^m \, (\text{rec}(1,2) \, \text{send}(1,2))^n$ and $M(m,n) \upharpoonright 2 = (\text{rec}(2,1) \, \text{send}(2,1))^n \, \text{rec}(2,1)^m$. The MSC $M(3,2)$ is depicted in Figure 7. Now consider the EMSO-definable MSC language $L = \{M(n,n) \mid n \geq 1\}$, which is recognized by the finite locally-accepting 2-MPA from Figure 5. We easily verify that L is a weak product MSC language. However, L is not contained in $\mathcal{L}(\text{1-MPA}^f)$. Because suppose there is $\mathcal{A} = ((\mathcal{A}_p)_{p \in \{1,2\}}, \mathcal{D}, \bar{s}^{in}, F) \in \text{1-MPA}^f$ with $L(\mathcal{A}) = L$. As $\mathcal{A}$ is finite, there is $n \geq 1$ and an accepting run of $\mathcal{A}$ on $M(n,n)$ such that $\mathcal{A}_1$, when reading the first n letters $\text{send}(1,2)$ of $M(n,n) \upharpoonright 1$, goes through a cycle, say of length i (≥ 1), and $\mathcal{A}_2$, when reading the last n letters $\text{rec}(2,1)$ of $M(n,n) \upharpoonright 2$, goes through another cycle, say of length j (≥ 1). But then there is also an accepting run of $\mathcal{A}$ on $M(n+(i \cdot j), n) \notin L$. □

Lemma 10. *For each* $N \geq 1$, $\mathcal{L}((N+1)\text{-bMPA}^f_\ell) \setminus \mathcal{L}(N\text{-MPA}) \neq \emptyset$.

For $N \geq 1$, consider the MSC language $L_{N+1} = \{M(i) \mid i \in \{1,\ldots,N^2+1\}\}^*$ where $M(i)$ is depicted in Figure 8. Though L_{N+1} is realizable by means of $N+1$ synchronization messages, N messages turn out to be insufficient.

Lemma 11. $\mathcal{L}(1\text{-bMPA}^f) \setminus \mathcal{L}(\text{MPA}_\ell) \neq \emptyset$

Proof. Let L^f consist of the MSCs M_1 and M_2 given by Figure 1. Then L^f is contained in $\mathcal{L}(1\text{-bMPA}^f) \setminus \mathcal{L}(\text{MPA}_\ell)$. In contrast, a bounded finite 1-MPA recognizing L^f has some global knowledge employing global final states. □

Theorem 2. *The classes of MSC languages proposed in Sections 3 and 4 draw the picture given by Figure 3.*

We did not pay special attention to the relation between (weak) EMSO-definable product languages and the classes of languages defined by (locally-accepting) finite N-MPAs for $N \geq 2$, which is indicated by the light-gray line in Figure 3. We believe that it is possible to show incomparability respectively witnessed by a language depending on N and similar to the suggested one.

References

[AEY00] R. Alur, K. Etessami, and M. Yannakakis. Inference of Message Sequence Charts. In *Proceedings of the 22nd International Conference on Software Engineering*. ACM, 2000.

[BL04] B. Bollig and M. Leucker. Message-Passing Automata are expressively equivalent to EMSO Logic. In *Proceedings of CONCUR 2004*, volume 3170 of *LNCS*. Springer, 2004.

[GMK04] B. Genest, A. Muscholl, and D. Kuske. A Kleene theorem for a class of communicating automata with effective algorithms. In *Proceedings of DLT 2004*, volume 3340 of *LNCS*. Springer, 2004.

[GMSZ02] B. Genest, A. Muscholl, H. Seidl, and M. Zeitoun. Infinite-state high-level MSCs: Model-checking and realizability. In *Proceedings of ICALP 2002*, volume 2380 of *LNCS*. Springer, 2002.

[HMK+04] J. G. Henriksen, M. Mukund, K. Narayan Kumar, M. Sohoni, and P. S. Thiagarajan. A theory of regular MSC languages. *Information and Computation*, 2004. to appear.

[HMKT00] J. G. Henriksen, M. Mukund, K. Narayan Kumar, and P. S. Thiagarajan. Regular collections of message sequence charts. In *Proceedings of MFCS 2000*, volume 1893 of *LNCS*. Springer, 2000.

[ITU99] ITU-TS Recommendation Z.120: Message Sequence Chart 1999 (MSC99), 1999.

[Kus02] D. Kuske. A further step towards a theory of regular MSC languages. In *Proceedings of STACS 2002*, volume 2285 of *LNCS*. Springer, 2002.

[Kus03] D. Kuske. Regular Sets of Infinite Message Sequence Charts. *Information and Computation*, 187:80–109, 2003.

[Mor02] R. Morin. Recognizable sets of message sequence charts. In *Proceedings of STACS 2002*, volume 2285 of *LNCS*. Springer, 2002.

[Thi95] P. S. Thiagarajan. A trace consistent subset of PTL. In *Proceedings of CONCUR 1995*, volume 962 of *LNCS*. Springer, 1995.

Combining Static Analysis and Model Checking for Systems Employing Commutative Functions*

A. Prasad Sistla and Min Zhou

University of Illinois at Chicago
{sistla, mzhou}@cs.uic.edu

Abstract. The two main hindrances for a wider application of the model checking approach for verification of concurrent and distributed systems are the *state explosion* problem and its limitation in handling infinite state systems. We consider a class of infinite state systems given by certain types of Transition Diagrams (TDs), called *simple TD*s, that employ commutative functions for updating variables. For such systems, we presented model checking methods that combine bi-simulation reductions with static analysis. The new methods are extensions of earlier methods where static analysis was not employed. These methods can be applied to a wider class of systems.

1 Introduction

The two main hindrances for a wider application of the model checking approach for verification concurrent and distributed programs are the *state explosion* problem and its limitation in handling infinite state systems. In our earlier work [7], we considered a class of infinite state systems given by certain types of Transition Diagrams (TDs), called *simple TD*s, that employ commutative functions for updating variables. For these systems, we presented model checking methods that use reductions with respect to a class of bi-simulation relations which can be checked on-the-fly. Experimental results showing the effectiveness of these approaches were also given. In this paper, we further extend these methods by combining them with static analysis to define larger bi-simulation relations. We give some applications of these results.

We assume that the concurrent program is given by a Transition Diagram (TD) [4] which is an edge labeled directed graph. Each edge label consists of a condition, called guard, and an action which is a concurrent assignment of values to variables. A TD is called a simple TD if the expression that is assigned to a variable x is either a constant, or a variable, or of the form $f(x)$ where f is a unary function. Further more, we require that the functions, that are used, are mutually commutative, that is, for any two functions f, g, $fg = gf$. We consider only simple TDs. It should be noted that such TDs are as powerful as Turing machines.

---

* This work is supported in part by the NSF grants CCR-9988884 and CCR-0205365.

In [7], we defined an infinite sequence of non-decreasing bi-simulations, for simple TDs. These bi-simulations, denoted as $\sim_k$ for each $k \geq 0$, are defined over the *symbolic state* graph of the TD. Some of the techniques of [7] were implemented and applied to some practical protocols such as the sliding window protocol, producer-consumer protocols, etc.

In this paper, we extend the methods of [7] by combining them with simple techniques from static analysis. The combination of these techniques allows us to model check a wider class of programs, i.e., TDs. In the definition of $\sim_k$ introduced in [7], we defined two symbolic states s and t to be equivalent with respect to $\sim_k$ if the predicates obtained by instantiating certain *predicate templates* in these two states are equivalent; these templates are derived from the guards of the transitions of the TD and also from the temporal formula that one wants to check. The equivalence of the predicates assumes an implicit universal quantification over their free variables. We show that by analyzing the TD in advance, the domain over which the universal quantifiers range can be reduced. We actually give methods for obtaining constraints that restrict the domains of the quantifiers. This allows more states to be considered equivalent.

We give some applications of the above results. First, we consider simple TDs over integer domains where the functions updating the variables increment or decrement them by some constants. For such TDs, we show that we can define bi-simulations directly on their standard reachability graphs. For many integer TDs, we show that our method can be used to obtain finite quotient structures. We believe that our results can be applied to analyze real examples involving processes communicating through queues at certain level of abstraction.

Finally, we also show how the commutative requirement for simple TDs can be relaxed.

The paper is organized as follows. Section 2 briefly reviews the approach given in [7] and defines the notation. Section 2 also proves additional properties of the bi-simulations that were defined in [7]. Section 3 gives methods that combine static analysis and bi-simulations. Section 5 shows how the commutativity requirement can be relaxed. Section 6 disusses related work.

2 Background and Notation

2.1 Transition Diagram

A TD is a triple $G = (Q, X, E)$ such that Q denotes a set of nodes, X is a set of variables, and E is a set of transitions which are quadruples of the form $\langle q, C, \Lambda, q' \rangle$ where $q, q' \in Q$, C is a condition involving the variables in X and Λ is a set of assignments of the form $x := \rho$ where $x \in X$ and ρ is an expression involving the variables in X. For a transition $\langle q, C, \Lambda, q' \rangle$, we call C the condition part or *guard* of the transition and Λ the action part of the transition and we require that Λ contains at most one assignment for each variable.

For any node q of G, we let $guards(q)$ denote the set of guards of transitions from the node q. We also let $guards(G)$ denote the set of guards of all transitions of G.

The semantics of a TD is defined in the usual way. A state of a TD $G = (Q, X, E)$ is a pair (q, h) where $q \in Q$, called location, and h is an evaluation of X. A transition $e = (q_1, C, \Lambda, q_2)$ is enabled in the state (q, h) if $q = q_1$ and the condition C is satisfied by h. Let $s = (q, h)$ be a state and $e = (q_1, C, \Lambda, q_2)$ be a transition that is enabled in s. The transition e can be executed in the state s to obtain a successor state which is defined in the usual way.

A path in G from node q to node r is a sequence of transitions starting with a transition from q and ending with a transition leading to r such that each successive transition starts from the node where the preceding transition ends. The left part of figure 1 shows a TD with 3 nodes. Notice that the transitions t_1 and t_2 both have empty guards meaning that they are always enabled.

2.2 Kripke Structures, Bi-simulation, etc.

A labeled Kripke structure H over a set of atomic propositions AP and over a set of labels Σ is a triple (S, R, L) where S is a set of states, $R \subseteq S \times \Sigma \times S$ and $L : S \to 2^{AP}$ associates each state with a set of atomic propositions. The Kripke structure H is said to be deterministic if for every $s \in S$ and every $\alpha \in \Sigma$ there exists at most one $s' \in S$ such that $(s, \alpha, s') \in R$.

For the Kripke structure $H = (S, R, L)$, an execution/computation σ is an infinite sequence $s_0, e_0, s_1, e_1, ..., s_i, e_i, ...$ of alternating states and labels in Σ such that for each $i \geq 0$, $(s_i, e_i, s_{i+1}) \in R$. A finite execution/computation is a finite sequence of the above type ending in a label in a state. Corresponding to a finite execution $\sigma = s_0, e_0, s_1, ..., s_m$ let $trace(\sigma)$ denote the finite sequence $L(s_0), e_0, ..., L(s_i), e_i, ...L(s_m)$. The length of a finite trace is the number of transitions in it. For any integer $k > 0$, let $Finite\_Traces_k(H, s)$ denote the set of finite traces of length k from s.

Let $H = (S, R, L)$ and $H' = (S', R', L')$ be two structures over the same set of atomic propositions AP and the same set Σ of labels. A relation $B \subseteq S \times S'$ is a bi-simulation between H and H' iff for all $s \in S$ and $s' \in S'$, if $(s, s') \in B$, then $L(s) = L'(s')$ and the following conditions hold: (a) for every $(s, \alpha, s_1) \in R$, there exists a state $s_1' \in S'$ such that $(s', \alpha, s_1') \in R'$ and $(s_1, s_1') \in B$; (b) similarly, for every $(s', \alpha, s_1') \in R'$, there exists a state $s_1 \in S$ such that $(s, \alpha, s_1) \in R$ and $(s_1, s_1') \in B$. A *sub-bi-simulation* between H and H' is any subset of a bisimulation relation between H and H'.

Suppose $G = (Q, X, E)$ is a TD and u is a state. The semantics of G starting from the state u can be defined by a Kripke structure $Reach(G, u) = (S, R, L)$ over the set of atomic propositions AP and the set of labels E as follows: S is the set of reachable states obtained by executing the TD G from u; R is the set of triples (s, e, s') such that the transition $e \in E$ is enabled in state s and s' is obtained by executing e in state s; for any $s \in S$, $L(s)$ is the set of atomic propositions in AP that are satisfied in s. Computations of the TD G are computations of $Reach(G, u)$. Let $\pi = e_0, e_1, ..., e_{m-1}$ be a path in G from node q and let $s_0 = (q, h_0)$ be a state. We say that π is *feasible* from s_0 if there exists a finite computation of the form $s_0, e_0, s_1, ..., e_{m-1}$ in the $Reach(G, s_0)$. In this case, we say that s_m is the state obtained by executing the path π from

s_0. For the TD given in 1, it is easy to see that the reachability graph from the state $(0, h)$, where h assigns 0 to all the variables, is infinite since x, y can grow arbitrarily large.

Let B be any sub-bi-simulation relation from $Reach(G, u)$ to itself. Instead of constructing $Reach(G, u)$, we can construct a smaller structure using the relation B. We incrementally construct the structure by executing G starting from u. Whenever we get a state w by executing a transition from an already reached state v, we check if there exists an already reached state w' such that (w, w') or (w', w) is in B; if so, we simply add an edge to w' otherwise we include w into the set of reached states and add an edge to w. This procedure is carried until no more new nodes can be added to the set of reached states. We call the resulting structure the reduction of $Reach(G, u)$ with respect to B. This reduction has the property that no two states in it are related by B. The number of states in this reduction may not be unique and may depend on the order of execution of the enabled transitions. However, if B is an equivalence relation then the number of states in the reduction is unique and equals the number of equivalence classes of S with respect to B.

We use the temporal logic CTL* [1] to specify properties of $Reach(G, u)$. Each atomic proposition in the formulas is a predicate involving variables in X or the special variable lc which refers to the nodes of G. We let AP be the set of predicates that appear in the temporal formula that we want to check. The atomic propositions refering to lc are of the form $lc = q$ where q is a node of G. For any formula or predicate p, we let $var(p)$ denote the set of variables appearing in it.

If K is a reduction of $Reach(G, u)$ with respect to a sub-bisimulation relation then a state which is present in both $Reach(G, u)$ and K satisfies the same set of CTL* formulas in both structures. Also, any two states in $Reach(G, u)$, that are related by a sub-bi-simulation, satisfy the same set of CTL* formulas.

2.3 Symbolic Graph

For an expression Φ, we use $\Phi\{\beta/\alpha\}$ denote the expression obtained from Φ by substituting β for α.

Let $G = (Q, X, E)$ be a TD, $u = (q_0, h_0)$ be the initial state of G. $Sym\_Reach(G, u) = (S', R', L')$, called *symbolic graph*, is a Kripke structure obtained by the symbolic execution of G starting from u. Each state s in S', called a *symbolic state*, is a triple of the form $(s.lc, s.val, s.exp)$ where $s.lc \in Q$, $s.val$ is an evaluation of the variables in X and $s.exp$ is a function that assigns each variable x an expression which involves only the variable x itself. Intuitively, $s.lc$ denotes the node in Q where the control is, $s.val(x)$ denotes the latest constant assigned to x and $s.exp(x)$ denotes the composition of functions that were applied to x since then. It is easy to see that a symbolic state s corresponding to the actual state $(s.lc, h)$ where $h(x) = s.exp(x)\{s.val(x)/x\}$ for each $x \in X$. We let $act\_state(s)$ denote the actual state corresponding to the symbolic state s. Each member of R' is a triple of the form (s, e, s') where $s \in S$ and $e \in E$ that is enabled in s and $s' \in S$ is the successor of s after the execution of e. L' is a labeling function that associates with each symbolic state s, the set of predicates in $AP \cup guards(G)$ that are satisfied in the corresponding actual state. Note that the predicate $lc = q$ is satisfied in a symbolic state s, if $s.lc = q$. We say that a transition e is enabled in a symbolic state s if it is enabled in the corresponding actual state, i.e., in the state $act\_state(s)$.

The successor states of a symbolic state s are defined as follows. Assume that a transition $e = (q, C, \Lambda, q')$ is enabled in s. The new symbolic state s' obtained by executing e from s is defined as follows: $s'.lc = q'$ and for each variable x, if there is no assignment to x in Λ then $s'.val(x) = s.val(x)$ and $s'.exp(x) = s.exp(x)$. If there is an assignment of the form $x := c$ where c is a constant then $s'.val(x) = c$ and $s'.exp(x) = x$. If there is an assignment of the form $x := \psi(x)$ in Λ then $s'.val(x) = s.val(x)$ and $s'.exp(x) = \psi(s.exp(x))$; that is the value remains unchanged and the new expression is obtained by applying the function ψ to the old expression. If there is an assignment of the form $x := y$ in Λ then $s'.val(x) = s.val(y)$ and $s'.exp(x) = s.exp(y)\{x/y\}$; that is the value of $s.val(y)$ is copied and the expression of y in s is also copied after replacing every y by x in the expression. If s' is obtained by executing an enabled transition e from a state s in S', then s' is a state in S' and $(s, e, s') \in R'$.

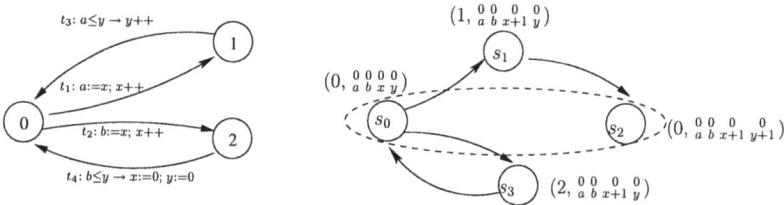

Fig. 1. Example of a TD and its reduced symbolic state graph with respect to $\sim_0$

For the TD given in the left part of figure 1 with initial value $a = b = x = y = 0$, the right part of figure 1 gives part of its symbolic state graph. The initial state s_0 is $(0, \begin{smallmatrix} 0 & 0 & 0 & 0 \\ a & b & x & y \end{smallmatrix})$, where the first 0 denotes the node, the vectors $(0, 0, 0, 0)$ and (a, b, x, y) represent the functions $s_0.val$ and $s_0.exp$ respectively.

It should be noted that an actual state may be represented by several symbolic states which are obtained by different execution paths in our symbolic state graph.

2.4 Predicate Templates and Definition of $\sim_0$

Let π be a path in G. Such path denotes a possible execution in G. For the path π, we define a function $depends_\pi$ from X to $X \cup \{*\}$ as follows. Intuitively, if $depends_\pi(x)$ is a variable, say y, this means the value of x after the execution of π depends on the value of y before the execution of π. We define $depends_\pi$ inductively on the length of π. If π is a single transition $\langle q, C, \Lambda, q' \rangle$ then $depends_\pi(x)$ is given as follows: if Λ has the assignment

$x := y$ then $depends_\pi(x) = y$; if Λ has no assignment to x or has an assignment of the form $x := \psi(x)$ then $depends_\pi(x) = x$; when x is assigned a constant, $depends_\pi(x) = *$. If π is the path consisting of π_1 followed by π_2 then $depends_\pi$ is defined as follows: for each $x \in X$, if $depends_{\pi_2}(x)$ is a variable then $depends_\pi(x) = depends_{\pi_1}(depends_{\pi_2}(x))$, otherwise $depends_\pi(x) = *$.

A predicate template is a pair (p, f) where p is a predicate and f is function from X to $X \cup \{*\}$. With each node q we associate a set $ptemplates(q)$ defined as follows: $ptemplates(q) = \{(p, depends_\pi) : \pi$ is a path from node q to some node r and $p \in guards(r) \cup AP\}$. An efficient method to compute $ptemplates(q)$ without examining all the paths from q is given in [7].

Now we define the instantiation of a predicate template in a symbolic state. Suppose s is a state of the symbolic state graph $Sym\_Reach(G, u)$, (p, f) is a predicate template and $x_1, x_2, \cdots, x_n$ are variables appearing in p. Let p' be the predicate obtained by replacing every occurrence of the variable x_i (for $1 \le i \le n$), for those x_i such that $f(x_i) \ne *$, by the expression $s.exp(y_i)\{x_i/y_i\}$ where y_i is the variable $f(x_i)$. Note that the variables x_i for which $f(x_i) = *$ are not replaced. We define $(p, f)[s]$ to be p' as given above.

Definition 1. *Define relation $\sim_0$ as follows: For any two states s and t, $s \sim_0 t$ iff $s.lc = t.lc$, $s.val = t.val$ and for each $(p, f) \in ptemplates(s.lc)$, $(p, f)[s] \equiv (p, f)[t]$ is a valid formula.*

The following theorem is proved in [7] and its proof crucially depends on the commutativity requirement.

Theorem 1. *$\sim_0$ is a bi-simulation on the symbolic state graph $Sym\_Reach(G, u)$.*

2.5 Extended Predicate Templates and $\sim_k$

In order for two symbolic states s and t to be related by $\sim_0$, we required that $s.lc = t.lc$ and for every guard p of a transition from a node r that is reachable from $s.lc$ in the TD and for every template $(p, f) \in ptemplates(s.lc)$, we required that the instantiations of (p, f) in s and t be equivalent. This requirement can be relaxed as follows. If none of the paths leading to r is feasible then, in the above requirement, we do not need to consider templates of the form (p, f) where p is a guard of some transition from r'. Now we define a bi-simulation relation $\sim_k$ in which we relax the equivalence condition. Roughly speaking, in the definition of $\sim_k$, we require s and t to be equivalent with respect to guards of node r only when there exists a path of length at least k leading to r which is feasible for both s and t.

Let π be a path in G, $|\pi|$ be the length of π and p be any predicate. Also, let $\pi' \circ \pi''$ denote the path π' followed by π''. Now we define the weakest precondition of p with respect to π, denoted by $WP(\pi, p)$ as follows.

$$WP(\pi, p) = \begin{cases} p & \text{if } |\pi| = 0 \\ p\{\rho_i/x_i\} & \text{if } |\pi| = 1 \wedge \text{ the assignments are } x_i := \rho_i \\ WP(\pi', WP(e, p)) & \text{if } \pi = \pi' \circ e \end{cases}$$

It has been shown [7] that if path π of G is feasible from state s, and s' is the state obtained by executing π from s, then s' satisfies p iff s satisfies $WP(\pi, p)$.

Suppose $\pi = e_0 \circ e_1 \circ ..., e_{k-1}$ be a path in G and for $0 \leq i < k$, C_i is the guard of the transition e_i. For each i, $0 < i \leq k$, let $\pi(i)$ denote the prefix of π consisting of the first i transitions, i.e., the path from e_0 to e_{i-1}. Define $Cond(\pi)$ to be the predicate $C_0 \wedge \bigwedge_{0<i<k} WP(\pi(i), C_i)$. It has be shown [7] that a path π of G is feasible from state s iff s satisfies the predicate $Cond(\pi)$.

The set $extended\_templates(q, k)$ is defined to be the set of triples which are of the form $(Cond(\pi''), WP(\pi'', p), depends_{\pi'})$ where π', π'' are paths such that $\pi'\pi''$ (i.e., π' followed by π'') is a path from q to some node r, the length of π'' is k and $p \in guards(r) \cup AP$. Similar to $ptemplates(q)$, we have an efficient method to compute $extended\_templates(q, k)$ without examining all the paths from q. Note that unlike $ptemplates(q)$, $extended\_templates(q, k)$ are triples.

Definition 2. *Define relation $\sim_k$ on the states of $Sym\_Reach(G, u)$ as follows. $\sim_k$ is the set of all pairs (s, t) where s, t are states of $Sym\_Reach(G, u)$ such that:*

1. *$s.lc = t.lc$ and $s.val = t.val$*
2. *$Finite\_Traces_k(s) = Finite\_Traces_k(t)$ and*
3. *for every $(p_1, p_2, f) \in extended\_templates(s.lc, k)$ the formula $((p_1, f)[s] \wedge (p_1, f)[t]) \supset ((p_2, f)[s] \equiv (p_2, f)[t])$ is a valid formula.*

Theorem 2, 3 and 4 are from [7].

Theorem 2. *For each $k > 0$, $\sim_k$ is a bi-simulation relation.*

Theorem 3. *For every $k \geq 0$, every TD G, and for every set AP of atomic predicates, $\sim_k \subseteq \sim_{k+1}$.*

Theorem 4. *For every $k \geq 0$, there exists a TD G and a set of atomic predicates AP for which the above containment is strict, i.e. $\sim_k \subset \sim_{k+1}$.*

2.6 Relationships Among the Bisimulation Relations

In this sub-section we state theorems strengthing previously stated results. We can strengthen theorem 4 as follows.

Theorem 5. *Given any integer $k \geq 0$, there exists a TD such that $\sim_{k+1}$ gives finite quotient structure while $\sim_k$ does not.*

Theorem 6. *There exists a TD for which $\forall k > 0$, $\sim_k \subset \sim_{k+1}$.*

3 Using Static Analysis to Constrain the Quantifiers' Range

Recall that in the definition of $\sim_0$, for $s \sim_0 t$, we require that for each template $(p, f) \in ptemplates(s.lc)$, $(p, f)[s] \equiv (p, f)[t]$. It should be noted that there is an implicit universal quantification on variables when we assert the validity of the

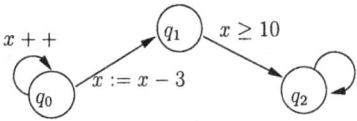

Fig. 2. Example of a TD which can get finite reduction by a simple static analysis

equivalence $(p, f)[s] \equiv (p, f)[t]$. This universal quantification can be restricted to range over a smaller set of values in some cases. By this change, we get another bi-simulation relation which is larger than $\sim_0$.

Example: Consider figure 2 which is a TD over a single integer variable x. The transition from q_1 to q_2 has null action and the guards of all other transitions are "true". The initial state is $u = (q_0, h)$ where $h(x) = 0$. For this TD, it can be shown that $\sim_0$ is the identity relation and hence the reduction of $Sym\_Reach(G_1, u)$ with respect to $\sim_0$ is infinite. By a simple static analysis, one can show that the value of x, when control is at node q_1, is greater than or equal to -3. We show below that, the quantifier over x correspoding to the predicate template for the predicate $x \geq 0$ can be restricted to the values of $x \geq -3$. Using this modification, we define another bi-simulation $\sim_0'$ which gives a finite reduction for $Sym\_Reach(G_1, u)$; the number of states in this reduction is 13.

Now consider simple TD G and any state s in $Sym\_Reach(G, u)$. Let (p, f) be any predicate template in $ptemplates(s.lc)$ such that $p \in guards(G) \cup AP$. Let $\{x_1, ..., x_n\}$ be all the variables in $var(p)$ and $Q_p \subseteq Q$ be as defined below: if $p \in AP$ then $Q_p = Q$, otherwise Q_p is the set of all nodes q in G such that $p \in guards(q)$.

Let G' be the TD obtained from G by replacing all guards in its transitions by the constant predicate $True$. Now let $T_{p,s}$ be the set $\{h : h$ is a valuation and for some $q \in Q_p$ the state (q, h) is reachable from the state $(s.lc, s.val)$ in $Reach(G', u)\}$. Essentially, $T_{p,s}$ is the set of valuations for the variables in X when the control is at some node in Q_p when the TD G' is executed starting from the state $(s.lc, s.val)$. Let $g_{p,s}$ be a formula, with free variables from X, that defines the set $T_{p,s}$, i.e., $T_{p,s}$ is exactly the set of valuations that satisfy the constraint given by $g_{p,s}$. (Note that we are assuming that the assertion logic is expressive enough to express this set). Essentially, $g_{p,s}$ defines a constraint on the values of the variables when the control is at some node in Q_p. Let $\sim_0'$ be the set of (s, t) such that s, t are symbolic states, $s.lc = t.lc$, $s.val = t.val$, and for all $(p, f) \in ptemplates(s.lc)$ the formula $g_{p,s} \supset ((p, f)[s] \equiv (p, f)[t])$ is valid. Thus we see that the quantifiers over the variables in X are restricted to the valuations that satisfy $g_{p,s}$, i.e., to the valuation in $T_{p,s}$. Observe that $T_{p,s} = T_{p,t}$; thus it does not matter whether we use s or t for obtaining these sets and the formulas $g_{p,s}$. Note that if we replace $g_{p,s}$ by $True$ then we get $\sim_0$. From this, it should be easy to see that $\sim_0' \supseteq \sim_0$.

Theorem 7. $\sim_0'$ *is a bi-simulation on symbolic state graph $Sym\_Reach(G, u)$.*

Proof: Assume that $s \sim_0' t$. Clearly, $s.lc = t.lc$ and $s.val = t.val$. Let $p \in (AP \cup guards(s.lc))$. From the definition of $ptemplates(s.lc)$, we see that $(p, f_{id}) \in$

$ptemplates(s.lc)$. By the definition of $\sim'_0$, $g_{p,s} \supset (p, f_{id})[s] \equiv (p, f_{id})[t]$ is valid. The tuple of values of variables defined by $s.val$ belongs to $T_{p,s}$ and hence it satisfies the formula $g_{p,s}$. As a consequence, the two predicates $(p, f_{id})[s]$ and $(p, f_{id})[t]$ evaluate to the same truth value, when the variables in them are substituted by the values given by $s.val(x)$. It is also not difficult to see that these truth values, respectively, are the truth value of the predicate p in the actual states $act\_state(s)$ and $act\_state(t)$. It is easy to see that the symbolic state s satisfies p iff t satisfies p. Since this property holds for every $p \in (AP \cup guards(s.lc))$, it is easily seen that $L'(s) = L'(t)$ and every transition e from node $s.lc$ is enabled in s iff it is enabled in t. Now assume $(s, e, s') \in R'$ which means there is an enabled transition e in s and s' is reached after the execution of e. From above analysis, we know that e is also enabled in t. Let t' be the symbolic state obtained by executing e from t. We show that $s' \sim'_0 t'$. Obviously, $s'.lc = t'.lc$ and $s'.val = t'.val$.

Now, we show that for all $(p, f') \in ptemplates(s'.lc)$, $g_{p,s'} \supset ((p, f')[s'] \equiv (p, f')[t'])$ is a valid formula. Consider a template $(p, f') \in ptemplates(s'.lc)$. From the definition of $ptemplates(s.lc)$, it is seen that there exists a $(p, f) \in ptemplates(s.lc)$ satisfying the following conditions for every x in $var(p)$. These conditions are divided into five cases. The first case is when $f'(x) = *$; in this case, $f(x) = *$ and the variable x in p remains unchanged when we obtain $(p, f)[s]$ and $(p, f')[s']$ from p. In the other cases $f'(x) \neq *$, i.e., $f'(x)$ is a variable. Let $f'(x)$ be the variable y. The remaining cases depend on whether there is an assignment to y in the action part of e and if so, what is assigned to it. The second case is when there is no assignment for the variable y. In this case, $f(x) = y$ and $s'.exp(y) = s.exp(y)$; hence the expressions substituted for x in p to obtain $(p, f)[s]$ and $(p, f')[s']$ are identical. The third case is when y is assigned a constant; in this case, $f(x) = *$ and from the construction of $Sym\_Reach(G, u)$, we see that $s'.exp(y) = y$ and hence the expressions substituted for x in p to obtain $(p, f)[s]$ and $(p, f')[s']$ are both x itself. The fourth case is when y is assigned a variable z; in this case, $f(x) = z$ and $s'.exp(y) = s.exp(z)\{y/z\}$; from this it should be easy to see that the expressions substituted for x in p to obtain $(p, f)[s]$ and $(p, f')[s']$ are identical.

In all above four cases, we see that the same expression is substituted for x in p to obtain both $(p, f)[s]$ and $(p, f')[s']$. The fifth and last case is when there is an assignment of the form $y := \psi(y)$ where ψ is a unary function; in this case, $f(x) = y$ and $s'.exp(y) = \psi(s.exp(y))$; since the function ψ is commutative with the functions appearing in $s.exp(y)$, it is easy to see that $s'.exp(y) = s.exp(y)\{\psi(y)/y\}$; it should be noted that the variable x in p is substituted by $s.exp(y)\{x/y\}$ and by $s'.exp(y)\{x/y\}$ respectively to obtain $(p, f)[s]$ and $(p, f')[s']$. From the above observations, we see that the expression substituted for x in p to obtain $(p, f')[s']$ is $s.exp(y)\{\psi(x)/y\}$. Let $x_1, ..., x_n$ be the variables in $var(p)$ to which this last case applies. For each $i = 1, ..., n$, let $f'(x_i) = y_i$ and $y_i := \psi_i(y_i)$ be the assignment to y_i in the action part of e.

From the above observations, we see that the expression substituted for x_i in p to obtain $(p, f)[s]$ is $s.exp(y_i)\{x_i/y_i\}$, while the expression substituted for x in

p to obtain $(p, f')[s']$ is $s.exp(y_i)\{\psi_i(x_i)/y_i\}$. Using this fact for each $i = 1, ..., n$ and the fact that in all the first four cases the same expressions are substituted for x in p to obtain both $(p, f)[s]$ and $(p, f')[s']$, it is not difficult to see that $(p, f')[s'] = (p, f)[s]\{\psi_1(x_1)/x_1, ..., \psi_n(x_n)/x_n\}$. By the same argument, we see that $(p, f')[t'] = (p, f)[t]\{\psi_1(x_1)/x_1, ..., \psi_n(x_n)/x_n\}$.

Now we relate the sets $T_{p,s}$, $T_{p,s'}$, and consequently, the formulas $g_{p,s}$, $g_{p,s'}$. Recall that $T_{p,s}$ denotes the set of valuations for variables in X when control is in some location in Q_p in a computation of the TD G' starting from the state $(s.lc, s.val)$. Using the same argument as given above, it is easy to see that for every $h' \in T_{p,s'}$ there exists a $h \in T_{p,s}$ satisfying the following condition: for $1 \leq i \leq n$, $h(x_i) = \psi_i(h(x_i))$; for every $z \in X - \{x_i : 1 \leq i \leq n\}$, $h(z) = h'(z)$. From this it follows that the formula $g_{p,s'} \supset g_{p,s}\{\psi_1(x_1)/x_1, ..., \psi_n(x_n)/x_n\}$ is a valid formula.

Since, $g_{p,s} \supset (p, f)[s] \equiv (p, f)[t]$ is valid, its validity holds even when we replace each x_i by $\psi(x_i)$ for $i = 1, ..., n$. When this replacement is done, we get that $g_{p,s}\{\psi_1(x_1)/x_1, ..., \psi_n(x_n)/x_n\} \supset ((p, f')[s'] \equiv (p, f')[t'])$ is valid. Since $g_{p,s'} \supset g_{p,s}\{\psi_1(x_1)/x_1, ..., \psi_n(x_n)/x_n\}$ is a valid formula, we see that $g_{p,s'} \supset ((p, f')[s'] \equiv (p, f')[t'])$ is a valid formula. □

Now consider the the example TD G_1 given by figure 2. Let $u = (q_0, h)$ where $h(x) = 0$. Let p be the guard $x \geq 10$ which is the guard of the transition from q_1 to q_2. Let s and t be two states in $Sym\_Reach(G_1, u)$ with $s.lc = q_0$, $t.lc = q_0$, $s.exp(x) = x + c$ and $t.exp(x) = x + d$. Observe that $c, d \geq 0$. It should be easy to see that $g_{p,s}$ is the constraint $x \geq -3$. The template $(x \geq 10, f_{id})$ is the only non-trivial predicate template in $ptemplates(q_0)$. From our definition of $\sim_0'$, it is easily seen that $s \sim_0' t$ iff the formula $x \geq -3 \supset (x + c \geq 10 \equiv x + d \geq 10)$ is a valid formula. This gives us 13 equivalence classes and hence the reduction of $Sym\_Reach(G, u)$ has 13 states. (Note that in the definition of $\sim_0$, the equivalence $(x + c \geq 10 \equiv x + d \geq 10)$ is required to hold for all values of x including all negative values; due to this reason, $\sim_0$ is an identity relation as pointed out at the beginning of the section).

The above defintion of $\sim_0'$ can be naturally extended to $\sim_i$ for every $i \geq 0$ giving us the relations $\sim_i'$.

In the above definitions, we see that the formula $g_{p,s}$ depends on p, $s.lc$ and $s.val$. Note that the set of possible values of $s.val$ can be determined from static analysis of G. Essentially, for any variable x, $s.val(x)$ is a constant that is assigned to x in the action part of some transition. Since we ignore all the guards when we compute $T_{p,s}$, it is not difficult to see that $T_{p,s}$ or $g_{p,s}$ can be computed by static analysis of G. The number of values of $s.val$ can be exponential. Many times we can get a constraining formula $g_{p,s}$ which is independent of $s.val$. For example, consider the example given in figure 3, a possible $g_{p,s}$ can be $(x_1 \geq 0 \land x_2 \geq 0)$ for every predicate p and state s since all the updating functions increment variables.

Now, we consider the TD G given in figure 3 with initial state (q_0, h) where $h(x_1) = h(x_2) = 0$. We show that $\sim_0 \subset \sim_0' \subset \sim_1'$ for this TD. First, it is easy to see that $ptemplates(q_0) = \{(x_1 = 0, f_{id}), (x_2 = 0, f_{id}), (x_1 \geq 20, f_{id}), (x_2 \geq$

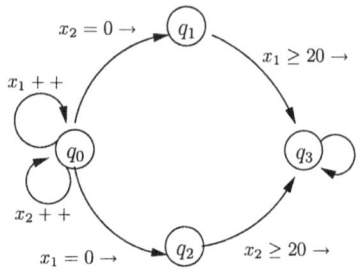

Fig. 3. Example of a TD for which $\sim_0 \subset \sim_0' \subset \sim_1'$

$20, f_{id})\}$. For every state s in $Sym\_Reach(G, u)$ and for every guard p, $g_{p,s}$ is the constraint $(x_1 \geq 0 \land x_2 \geq 0)$. Also, for any state s in $Sym\_Reach(G, u)$ such that $s.lc = q_0$ it is the case that $s.val(x_1) = s.val(x_2) = 0$. Let s, t be any two states such that $s.lc = t.lc = 0$. Let $s.exp(x_1) = x_1 + c_1$ and $s.exp(x_2) = x_2 + c_2$; similarly, let $t.exp(x_1) = x_1 + d_1$ and $s.exp(x_2) = x_2 + d_2$. Now, s and t are related by $\sim_0'$ if the values c_1, c_2, d_1, d_2 are all ≥ 20. (As in the previous example, the relation $\sim_0$ is simply the identity relation).

Now consider the relation $\sim_1'$. From the definitions, it can be seen that $extended\_templates(q_0, 1) = \{(x_2 = 0, x_1 \geq 20, f_{id}), (x_1 = 0, x_2 \geq 20, f_{id}), (true, x_1 = 0, f_{id}), (true, x_2 = 0, f_{id})\}$. By a detailed combinatorial analysis, it can be shown that the set of states in $Sym\_Reach(G, u)$ form into $21^2 - 21$ classes with respect to $\sim_0'$ and 42 classes with respect to the bi-simulation $\sim_1'$. In a more general case, if the constant in the transitions entering node q_3 is c then the set of states of the form (q_0, h) will be divided in to $(c+1)^2 - (c+1)$ and $2(c+1)$ classes with respect to the bi-simulations $\sim_0', \sim_1'$ respectively. Thus in the general case, the total number of states in the reductions with respect to $\sim_0', \sim_1'$ are given by $(c+1)^2 + 2(c+1)$ and $3(c+1) + 3$ respectively. Thus $\sim_1'$ gives more reduction. In general, we can generalize the example by introducing n arbitrary variables where $\sim_1'$ has much more reduction than $\sim_0'$.

The above analysis assumes that the set $T_{p,s}$ is definable by a formula $g_{p,s}$. This would require that the logic used for obtaining the formula is expressive enough. This may not always be the case. Even if the logic is expressive enough, computing a formula that exactly defines $T_{p,s}$ may be expensive. On the other hand, it may be easier to compute a formula that defines a super set of $T_{p,s}$. Let $f_{p,s}$ be a formula that defines any superset of $T_{p,s}$. Let $\sim_0''$ be the relation obtained by replacing the formula $g_{p,s}$ by the formula $f_{p,s}$ in the definition of $\sim_0'$. Since $g_{p,s} \supset f_{p,s}$ is a valid formula, it is easy to see that $\sim_0'' \subseteq \sim_0'$ and hence $\sim_0''$ is a sub-bi-simulation relation. As indicated in sub-section 2.2, we can use $\sim_0''$ to construct a reduction of $Sym\_Reach(G, u)$ and perform model checking on this reduction.

4 Transition Diagrams over Integer Domains

The use of symbolic graphs can be avoided for certain cases. Consider transition diagrams where the variables are integer variables and the functions updating them either increment or decrement them by some constants. Let $f_c(x)$ be the function $x + c$ where c is a constant. Obviously for any two constants c and d, the functions f_c and f_d are commutative.

Without constructing the symbolic state graph, we can directly define a bi-simulation on the standard reachability graph $Reach(G, u)$. Recall that each state of $Reach(G, u)$ is of the form (q, h) where $q \in Q$ and h assigns values to variables in X. Let $s = (q, h)$ be a state in $Reach(G, u)$. For a predicate template (p, f), define $(p, f)[s]$ to be the predicate obtained by replacing each occurrence of a variable x in p by $x + h(f(x))$ if $f(x)$ is a variable. We don't replace x if $f(x) = *$. Let $\approx_0$ be the set of pairs of states (s, t), where $s = (q, h)$ and $t = (q, h')$ for some $q \in Q$, such that for each $(p, f) \in ptemplates(q)$, $(p, f)[s] \equiv (p, f)[t]$ is valid. This construction can be employed for a general case where "+" is any commutative and associative binary operator over the domain of the variables.

Theorem 8. $\approx_0$ *is a bi-simulation on* $Reach(G, u)$. □

Now we show, how to efficiently check if $s \approx_0 t$ for a TD G where each predicate $p \in guards(G) \cup AP$ is linear, i.e. is of the form $\Sigma_{1 \leq i \leq n} a_i x_i > d'$ where $x_i \in X$ and $a_1, ..., a_n$ are integer constants. Let $s = (q, h)$ and $t = (q, h')$ be any two states. Let $I = \{i : 1 \leq i \leq n \text{ and } f(x_i) \neq *\}$. It is not difficult to see that $(p, f)[s] \equiv (p, f)[t]$ is valid if $\Sigma_{i \in I} a_i h(f(x_i)) = \Sigma_{i \in I} a_i h'(f(x_i))$. This condition can be checked efficiently. It is easy to see that checking equivalence can also be done efficiently when p is of the form $(\Sigma_{1 \leq i \leq n} a_i x_i) \bmod c = c'$ where c, c' are constants. Thus, if for every predicate p of the form $\Sigma_{1 \leq i \leq n} a_i x_i > d'$ in $guards(G) \cup AP$, the set $\{\Sigma_{i \in I} a_i h(f(x_i)) : s = (q, h) \text{ is a state in } Reach(G, u)$ and $(p, f) \in templates(q)$ and $I = \{i : f(i) \neq *\}\}$ is finite then $\approx_0$ has a finite quotient.

A subclass of integer domain TDs are those in which the variables range over natural numbers; this occurs if all the constants in the transitions are positive and the initial state u assigns only positive values to the variables. Furthermore, we require that each predicate p is a linear predicate and the coefficients of variables in the predicate are all positive. Let $s = (q, h)$ and $t = (q, h')$ be two states. Now consider any template (p, f) in $ptemplates(s.lc)$ where p is given by $\Sigma_{1 \leq i \leq n} a_i x_i > d'$. Let $I = \{i : f(x_i) \neq *\}$. It is not difficult to see that $(p, f)[s] \equiv (p, f)[t]$ is valid if either the two values $\Sigma_{i \in I} a_i h(f(x_i))$ and $\Sigma_{i \in I} a_i h'((f(x_i))$ are equal, or both of them are greater than d'.

4.1 Static Analysis for Integer TDs

Using Linear Equations for Static Analysis
For any state s, any $(p, depends_\pi) \in ptemplates(s.lc)$, we define $T_{p,s}$ to be the set of all h such that, for some $q \in Q_p$, the state (q, h) is reachable from the state $(s.lc, \mathbf{0})$ in the $Reach(G', u)$. Here Q_p is the set of nodes as given in the beginning of the previous section and $\mathbf{0}$ is the valuation that gives zero value to all the variables. Note that in the above definition we are considering execution from the state $(s.lc, \mathbf{0})$ not from the state $(s.lc, s.val)$ as in the previous section.

Therefore, $T_{p,s}$ does not depend on the values of the variables in s. This set only depends on p, i.e., Q_p and on $s.lc$. As given in the previous subsection, using formulas that define the sets of $T_{p,s}$, we can define a bi-simulation $\approx'_0$ that is bigger than $\approx_0$. Such formulas can be obtained by static analysis.

For each $i > 0$, we define the bi-simulations $\approx_i$ and $\approx'_i$ just like $\sim_i$ and $\sim'_i$ excepting that these are defined on the structure $Reach(G, u)$ (they are defined on the same lines as $\approx_0$ and $\approx'_0$).

Now we consider a subclass of integer domain TDs in which every assignment of a variable either increments or decrements it by a constant, i.e., a variable is not assigned another variable or a constant. We call such a TD as a *restricted* TD. Now we give a general procedure for obtaining formulas that define supersets of the sets $T_{p,s}$ as defined above. Observe that these formulas only depend on p and $s.lc$. Actually, for each $q \in Q$ and for each $r \in Q$, we give a formula $f_{q,r}$ that defines a superset of all valuations h such that the state (r, h) is reachable from $(q, \mathbf{0})$ in $Reach(G, u)$.

General Procedure for $f_{q,r}$: Now we give a general procedure to compute $f_{q,r}$ for a restricted TD G where q, r are nodes in G. let π be a path from q to r, for every transition e, let y_e to denote the number of times e is traversed in the path π. For every node u, let $d^+(u)$ denote the set of edges starting at u, $d^-(u)$ denote the set of edges ending in u. Then for every node $u \neq q, r$, we will have $\Sigma_{e \in d^+(u)} y_e = \Sigma_{e \in d^-(u)} y_e$. Also we will have $\Sigma_{e \in d^+(q)} y_e = \Sigma_{e \in d^-(q)} y_e + 1$ and $\Sigma_{e \in d^+(r)} y_e = \Sigma_{e \in d^-(r)} y_e - 1$. Note that above equations are satisfied by any path from q to r. Let $w(x_i, e)$ denote the value by which x_i is increased in the transition e. In the case x_i is not updated in e, let $w(x_i, e) = 0$. Now Let $x_i = \Sigma y_e w(x_i, e)$. Let $g_{q,r}$ be the conjunction of all above equations. For any $p \in (AP \cup guards(G))$ and state s, let $e_{p,s}$ be the disjunction of all $g_{p.lc,r}$ such that $r \in Q_p$. It should be easy to see that $e_{p,s}$ defines a superset of $T_{p,s}$. As in section 3, we can use the formulas $e_{p,s}$ to define a sub-bi-simulation relation $\approx''_0$ similar to $\sim''_0$, and use it to construct a reduction of $Reach(G, u)$.

The above procedure, given for restricted TDs, can be extended to any simple TD with minor modifications.

Using Shortest Path Algorithms

Now, we give a more efficient method for using static analysis in any restricted TD G in which every guard of a transition is a conjunction of conditions of the form $x \# c$ where $\#$ is a relation operator and c is a constant. A cycle in G is a simple path starting and ending in the same node. We say that a cycle is a positive cycle or a negative cycle for a variable x if the sum of all the changes of the value of x along this cycle is positive(> 0) or negative (< 0) respectively. For any path π in G and variable x, let $weight(\pi, x)$ denote the sum of the changes in value of x along π. For any pair of nodes q, r and variable x, let $low(q, r, x), high(q, r, x)$ be the minimum or maximum of $weight(\pi, x)$ of all paths π from q to r respectively. It is easy to see that if there is a path from q to r passing through a negative cycle for x, then $low(q, r, x)$ is $-\infty$; otherwise $low(q, r, x)$ is a finite number. Similar relation holds for $high(q, r, x)$ and positive cycles. Note that the value $low(q,r,x)$ or $high(q,r,x)$ can be computed in polynomial time using shortest path algorithm over graphs [2]. For nodes q,r, $f_{q,r} = \wedge_{x \in X} low(q,r,x) \leq x \leq high(q,r,x)$. As in the earlier paragraph, for any $p \in (AP \cup guards(G))$ and state s, let $e_{p,s}$ be the disjunction of all $f_{s.lc,r}$ such that $r \in Q_p$ and $\approx_0''$ be the corresponding sub-bi-simulation relation. It can be shown that if for every node q and for every variable x, all the paths from the initial node to q pass through only positive cycles for x or all such paths pass through only negative cycles, the reduction of $Reach(G,u)$ with respect to $\approx_0''$ is finite.

5   Relaxing the Commutativity Requirement

So far in this paper, we required that the set of all functions applied to variables of the same type are mutually commutative. This requirement can be relaxed as follows. Recall that for any path π in the G, $depends_\pi$ is a function that specifies dependencies of values of the variables at the end π to their values at the beginning of π. Now we introduce a binary relation $depends\_on$ on variable-node pairs, i.e., pairs of the form (x,r) where $x \in X$ and r is a node in G. The pair (y,r) $depends\_on$ the pair (x,q) if there exists a path π in G from node q to r such that $depends_\pi(y) = x$. It is easy to see that for the TD given in Figure 4, (x,q_2) $depends\_on$ (x,q_1) while (x,q_3) does not $depends\_on$ (x,q_2) because the only transition from q_2 to q_3 assigns a constant to x. On the other hand, if t_2 did not have this assignment for x then (x,q_3) $depends\_on$ (x,q_2), and in addition if we had $x := y$ as the assignment in t_1 then (x,q_3) $depends\_on$ (y,q_1).

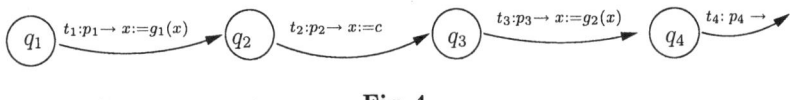

Fig. 4.

Using the relation $depends\_on$, we specify the less restrictive commutative requirement. Let Π be the set of all functions that are applied to variables in the transitions of G. Let $\{\Pi_1, ..., \Pi_m\}$ be the finest partition of Π which satisfies the following condition: two functions ψ_1 and ψ_2 are in the same set Π_i if there exist pairs (y,r) and (x,q) such that (y,r) $depends\_on$ (x,q) and there exist transitions $(q', C_1, \Lambda_1, q), (r, C_2, \Lambda_2, r')$ such that the assignment $x := \psi_1(x)$ is in Λ_1 and the assignment $y := \psi_2(y)$ is in Λ_2. It is easy to see that the partition can be computed efficiently from G using standard graph algorithms. Consider the example of Figure 4, the functions g_1, g_2 are in the different sets of the partition and hence they need not be commutative. On the other hand, if t_2 did not have any assignment for x then both g_1, g_2 would be in the same set of the partition and they would need to be commutative. Now, the commutativity requirement is relaxed by requiring that any two functions $f, g \in \Pi$ be commutativity only if they belong to the same set in the partition, i.e., if $f, g \in \Pi_i$ for some i, $1 \leq i \leq m$.

6 Discussion and Related Work

As indicated in the introduction, this work is an extension of our earlier work [7]. We have essentially extended that work by combining it with static analysis. The static analysis techniques employed here involve the variable value range analysis. Such techniques have been employed earlier in static analysis of programs [6]. Our innovative idea is to combine them with bi-simulation reductions and to employ them in model checking.

The paper [7] discusses the relationship of the original work presented there with the approach given in [5] and with other works based on bi-simulation reduction given in [3]. It is to be noted that none of these works employ static analysis.

References

1. E. M. Clarke, E. A. Emerson, and A. P. Sistla. Automatic verification of finite state concurrent system using temporal logic specifications: a practical approach. In *POPL '83: Proceedings of the 10th ACM SIGACT-SIGPLAN symposium on Principles of programming languages*, pages 117–126, New York, NY, USA, 1983. ACM Press.
2. T. H. Cormen, C. E. Leiserson, and R. L. Rivest. *Introduction to Algorithms*. MIT Press/McGraw-Hill, Cambridge, Massachusetts, 1990.
3. D. Lee and M. Yannakakis. Online minimization of transition systems (extended abstract). In *Proceedings of the twenty-fourth annual ACM symposium on Theory of computing*, pages 264–274. ACM Press, 1992.
4. Z. Manna and A. Pnueli. *The Temporal Logic of Reactive and Concurrent Systems: Specification*. Springer-Verlag, Berlin, Jan. 1992.
5. K. S. Namjoshi and R. P. Kurshan. Syntactic program transformations for automatic abstraction. In *CAV2000*, pages 435–449, 2000.
6. F. Nielson, H. R. Nielson, and C. L. Hankin. *Principles of Program Analysis*. Springer, 1999.
7. A. P. Sistla, M. Zhou, and X. Wang. Model checking of systems employing commutative functions. In R. Cousot, editor, *6th International Conference on Verification, Model Checking and Abstract Interpretation*, Lecture Notes in Computer Science. Springer, 2005.

Fast Generic Model-Checking for Data-Based Systems

Dezhuang Zhang and Rance Cleaveland

Department of Computer Science,
State University of New York at Stony Brook, NY 11794-4400, USA
{dezhuang, rance}@cs.sunysb.edu

Abstract. This paper shows how *predicate equation systems* (PESs) may be used to solve model-checking problems for systems, such as those involving real-time or value passing, that manipulate data. PESs are first defined and the encoding of model-checking problems described; then generic global and local approaches for solving PESs are given. Real-time model checking is then considered in detail, and a new, efficient on-the-fly technique for real-time model checking based on proof search in PESs is developed and experimentally shown to significantly outperform existing approaches when system specifications or formula specifications contain errors and to be competitive when both are correct.

1 Introduction

Temporal-logic model checkers [8, 9, 24] automatically establish whether or not a system satisfies a specification given as a formula in temporal logic. The model-checking problem has been studied most intensively in the area of finite-state systems but also for real-time systems and systems involving integer-valued variables. An interesting insight to emerge in the area of finite-state model checking is that model-checking questions can be reduced to solving systems of propositional equations [2, 11] called *boolean equation systems*. This observation leads to a uniform framework for understanding a number of different model-checking techniques, including so-called *symbolic* approaches [7]. It has also served as a basis for new algorithms, including efficient on-the-fly model-checkers for the mu-calculus [2] and symbolic algorithms based on Gaussian elimination [22].

The goal of this paper is to develop a similar framework for model checking of *data-based* systems that manipulate values and thus may not be finite-state. The proposed formalism, *predicate equation systems* (PESs), generalizes boolean equation systems to full first-order logic. We indicate how different model-checking techniques for systems that process data, including Presburger systems [6] and real-time model checking [18], may be cast in terms of PESs, and we also discuss how generic model-checking techniques may be derived based on PESs. We then use a proof system for PESs as a basis for deriving a new, very efficient on-the-fly technique for model-checking real-time systems. Experimental data is presented suggesting that our prototype implementation significantly outperforms existing real-time model checkers when system specifications or formulas contain errors (the most likely scenario) and is competitive with these checkers when specifications and formulas are correct. Thus, in addition to serving as a uniform framework for describing existing model-checking routines, PESs also open new avenues for model checking as well.

2 Defining Predicate Equation Systems

Predicate equation systems consist of systems of simultaneous equations whose right-hand sides are first-order formulas. This section defines PESs and other terminology and notation used in the rest of the paper.

If $\mathcal{Q}$ and $\mathcal{X}$ are sets, then the set $\mathcal{Q}^{\mathcal{X}}$ consists of all functions mapping $\mathcal{X}$ to $\mathcal{Q}$. We assume that if $f \in \mathcal{Q}^{\mathcal{X}}$ and $f \in \mathcal{Q}^{\mathcal{X}'}$ then $\mathcal{X} = \mathcal{X}'$, and we write $\mathrm{dom}(f) = \mathcal{X}$ for the *domain* of f. We sometimes write $\mathcal{Q}^{\mathcal{X}}$ as $\mathcal{X} \to \mathcal{Q}$. If $f \in \mathcal{Q}^{\mathcal{X}}$ and $f' \in \mathcal{Q}'^{\mathcal{X}'}$, then $f[f']$ represents the function in $(\mathcal{Q} \cup \mathcal{Q}')^{(\mathcal{X} \cup \mathcal{X}')}$ defined as follows.

$$(f[f'])(x) = \begin{cases} f'(x) & \text{if } x \in \mathcal{X}' \\ f(x) & \text{otherwise} \end{cases}$$

Also, if $f \in \mathcal{Q}^{\mathcal{X}}$ and $\mathcal{X}' \subseteq \mathcal{X}$, then $f \lceil \mathcal{X}'$ denotes the function in $\mathcal{Q}^{\mathcal{X}'}$ defined by $(f \lceil \mathcal{X}')(x) = f(x)$ if $x \in \mathcal{X}'$. Finally, if $\mathcal{X} = \{x_1, \ldots, x_n\}$ and $\{q_1, \ldots, q_n\} \subseteq \mathcal{Q}$ then $(x_1 := q_1, \ldots, x_n := q_n)$ represents the function that maps each x_i to q_i.

2.1 Basic Data Theories

The predicate calculus we consider is parameterized with respect to the *basic data theory* used to specialize the domain of discourse.

Definition 1. *Let $\mathcal{D}$ be a set of* data values *and $\mathcal{X}$ a set of* data variables. *A basic data theory over $\mathcal{X}$ and $\mathcal{D}$ is a tuple $\langle \mathcal{BExp}, \mathcal{DExp}, fv, \langle - \rangle, \models, |-| \rangle$, where:*

1. $\mathcal{BExp}$ *is a set of* data predicates;
2. $\mathcal{DExp}$ *is a set of* data expressions;
3. $fv : (\mathcal{BExp} \cup \mathcal{DExp}) \to 2^{\mathcal{X}}$ *is the* free-variable mapping;
4. $\langle - \rangle : (\mathcal{BExp} \cup \mathcal{DExp}) \times \mathcal{DExp}^{\mathcal{X}} \to (\mathcal{BExp} \cup \mathcal{DExp})$ *is the* substitution function *(notation: $b\langle f \rangle$ for $\langle - \rangle(b, f)$);*
5. $\models \subseteq \mathcal{D}^{\mathcal{X}} \times \mathcal{BExp}$ *is the* interpretation relation *(notation: $\rho \models b$ for $\models (\rho, b)$);*
6. $|-| : \mathcal{DExp} \times \mathcal{D}^{\mathcal{X}} \to \mathcal{D}$ *is the* evaluation function *(notation: $|b|_\rho$ for $|-|(b, \rho)$)*

and such that the following hold.

1. $(b\langle f \rangle)\langle g \rangle = b\langle f \triangleleft g \rangle$, *where* $(f \triangleleft g)(x) = \begin{cases} g(x) & \text{if } x \in \mathrm{dom}(g) - \mathrm{dom}(f) \\ f(x)\langle g \rangle & \text{otherwise} \end{cases}$
2. $|e\langle f \rangle|_\rho = |e|_{\rho[|f|_\rho]}$, *where $|f|_\rho$ is defined by: $(|f|_\rho)(x) = |f(x)|_\rho$.*

In $\langle \mathcal{BExp}, \mathcal{DExp}, fv, \langle - \rangle, \models, |-| \rangle$, $\mathcal{BExp}$ is a set of atomic predicates about data values; $\mathcal{DExp}$ is a set of data-valued expressions; $fv(b)$ the set of free data variables in b; and $b\langle f \rangle$ is the result applying substitution f to expression b. If $\rho \models b$ then ρ makes b true, while $|e|_\rho$ is the result of evaluating e in ρ. If $\mathcal{I} = \{x_1, \ldots, x_n\} \subseteq \mathcal{X}$ is a finite subset of $\mathcal{X}$ we use the term *assignment* for the function $(x_1 := e_1, \ldots x_n := e_n)$ in $\mathcal{DExp}^{\mathcal{I}}$. We often use $\bar{x} := \bar{e}$ to represent an assignment and call elements of $\mathcal{D}^{\mathcal{X}}$ data states.

2.2 The Predicate Calculus

The predicate calculus is used to define the right-hand sides of predicate equation systems. Our account of the predicate calculus is parameterized with respect to a set $\mathbb{X}$ of *predicate variables*, a set $\mathcal{D}$ of data values, a set $\mathcal{X}$ of data variables, and a basic data theory $B = \langle \mathcal{BExp}, \mathcal{DExp}, fv, \models, |-| \rangle$ over $\mathcal{X}$ and $\mathcal{D}$. The formulas are given as follows, where $b \in \mathcal{BExp}$, $X \in \mathbb{X}$, $x \in \mathcal{X}$, and A is an assignment.

$$\phi ::= b \mid \neg b \mid \phi_1 \vee \phi_2 \mid \phi_1 \wedge \phi_2 \mid X \mid \phi[A] \mid \exists x.\phi \mid \forall x.\phi \tag{1}$$

The operators are standard, except for X and $\phi[A]$. As formulats may contain predicate variables, substitution, $\phi[A]$, which is usually a meta-operation, must be included as an operator in the language (since, e.g., $X[\overline{x} := \overline{e}]$ cannot be rewritten). The definition $fdv(\phi)$ of free (data) variables in ϕ is given in the usual manner, based on the definition of fv given in the basic data theory; the definition $fpv(\phi)$ of free predicate variables is standard. We call a formula ϕ *predicate-closed* if $fpv(\phi) = \emptyset$ and *closed* if $fpv(\phi) = fdv(\phi) = \emptyset$. We often call formulas generated by the above grammar *predicates*.

Predicates are interpreted with respect to a data state ρ and a *predicate state* $\theta \in (2^{(\mathcal{D}^{\mathcal{X}})})^{\mathbb{X}}$ mapping predicate variables to sets of data states. We write $\rho \models_\theta \phi$ to denote that formula ϕ holds in data state ρ and predicate state θ. The definition is as follows.

$$\begin{aligned}
\rho \models_\theta b &\quad \text{iff } \rho \models b \text{ (i.e. wrt basic data theory)} \\
\rho \models_\theta \neg b &\quad \text{iff } \rho \not\models b \\
\rho \models_\theta \phi_1 \vee \phi_2 &\quad \text{iff } \rho \models_\theta \phi_1 \text{ or } \rho \models_\theta \phi_2 \\
\rho \models_\theta \phi_1 \wedge \phi_2 &\quad \text{iff } \rho \models_\theta \phi_1 \text{ and } \rho \models_\theta \phi_2 \\
\rho \models_\theta X &\quad \text{iff } \rho \in \theta(X) \\
\rho \models_\theta \phi[A] &\quad \text{iff } \rho[|A|_\rho] \models_\theta \phi \\
\rho \models_\theta \exists x.\phi &\quad \text{iff for some } d \in \mathcal{D}, \rho[x := d] \models_\theta \phi \\
\rho \models_\theta \forall x.\phi &\quad \text{iff for all } d \in \mathcal{D}, \rho[x := d] \models_\theta \phi
\end{aligned}$$

We use $[\![\phi]\!]_\theta$ to represent the set $\{\rho \mid \rho \models_\theta \phi\}$. If a formula ϕ is predicate-closed, then $[\![\phi]\!]_\theta = [\![\phi]\!]_{\theta'}$ for any θ and θ'; in this case we write $[\![\phi]\!]$ for this common value. Finally, while negation is restricted in the logic, every predicate-closed formula ϕ has a formula $\text{not}(\phi)$ that is semantically equivalent to ϕ's negation.

2.3 Predicate Equation Systems

Predicate Equation Systems (PESs) consist of blocks of equations of the form $X = \phi$, where X is a predicate variable and ϕ is a predicate. Such a system is intended to define a mutually recursive family of predicates, one for each equation. Since a given equation can have several solutions, blocks in PESs are equipped with an indication as to whether the "least" (most restrictive) "greatest" (most permissive) solution is intended.

Definition 2. *A predicate equation block has form $\langle p, \overline{E} \rangle$, where $p \in \{\mu, \nu\}$ is the parity indicator and $\overline{E} = \langle E_1, \ldots, E_n \rangle$ is a finite sequence of equations of form $X_i = \phi_i$, with the X_i distinct predicate variables and each ϕ a predicate.*

In predicate block $\langle p, \overline{E} \rangle$ p determines whether the "greatest" (ν) or "least" (μ) solution of the equations is intended. We write $\text{lhs}(B) = \{X_1, \ldots, X_n\}$ for the left-hand-side variables in block B and $\text{rhs}(B) = \{\phi_1, \ldots, \phi_n\}$ for the right-hand-side predicates.

Definition 3. *A predicate equation system (PES) is a finite sequence $\langle B_1, \ldots, B_n \rangle$ of predicate equation blocks with the property that if $i \neq j$, then $\text{lhs}(B_i) \cap \text{lhs}(B_j) = \emptyset$.*

The notions of lhs and rhs can be extended in the obvious manner to PESs. We call a PES P predicate-closed if $\bigcup_{\phi \in \text{rhs}(P)} fpv(\phi) \subseteq \text{lhs}(P)$.

PESs are interpreted using fixpoints of monotonic functions defined over the complete lattice given by $2^{(\mathcal{D}^{\mathcal{X}})}$ (i.e. the lattice of sets of data states, ordered by set inclusion). Given a predicate environment θ, a predicate ϕ containing free predicate variable X may be seen as a function f_θ over this lattice as follows: $f_\theta(S) = [\![\phi]\!]_{\theta[X:=S]}$. A complete account of fixpoint equation systems is given in [30], and the semantics of

PESs may be seen as an instance of this, where the lattice Q is taken to be $2^{(\mathcal{D}^{\mathcal{X}})}$. Given a "starting" environment θ, the semantics, $[\![P]\!]_\theta$, of PES P is an environment θ' that, for any equation $X = E$ of P, satisfies: $\theta'(X) = |E|_{\theta'[X:=\theta'(X)]}$. and is appropriately extremal. Note that if P is predicate-closed, then $[\![P]\!]_\theta(X) = [\![P]\!]_{\theta'}(X)$ for any $X \in \mathsf{lhs}(P)$ and θ, θ'. Based on this observation, it follows that if ϕ is a predicate, P is predicate-closed, and $\mathit{fpv}(\phi) \subseteq \mathsf{lhs}(P)$, then $[\![\phi]\!]_{[\![P]\!]_\theta} = [\![\phi]\!]_{[\![P]\!]_{\theta'}}$ for any θ, θ'. In this case we write $[\![\phi]\!]_P$ for this common value, and if $\sigma \in [\![\phi]\!]_P$ we represent this notationally as $\sigma \models_P \phi$.

3 Transition Systems and the Modal Mu-Calculus

A goal of this paper is to reduce model checking to computing solutions of PESs. The basic approach consists of showing how, given a symbolic system model and a formula in the first-order mu-calculus, a PES may be generated whose "solutions" are answers for the model-checking problem. This section lays the foundation for this approach by introducing our system model, *parameterized symbolic transition graphs with assignment* (PSTGAs), and our temporal logic, the first-order mu-calculus.

3.1 Concrete Transition Systems

Fix a set of data values $\mathcal{D}$, a set of data variables $\mathcal{X}$, and a set Λ of communication port names not containing a distinguished value τ. The set of *concrete actions* $\mathcal{A}ct_c$ is given as $\mathcal{A}ct_c = \{\lambda!d \mid \lambda \in \Lambda, d \in D\} \cup \{\lambda?d \mid \lambda \in \Lambda, d \in D\} \cup \{\tau\}$. Actions have the usual interpretation: $\lambda!d$ represents the emission of value d on port λ, and $\lambda?d$ the receipt of value d on λ. τ denotes the internal action.

Definition 4. *A concrete transition system (CTS) is a tuple $\langle \Sigma, V \to_c, \Sigma_I \rangle$, where Σ is the set of states, $V : \Sigma \to \mathcal{D}^{\mathcal{X}}$ the valuation function, $\to_c \subseteq \Sigma \times \mathcal{A}ct_c \times \Sigma$ the transition relation, and $\Sigma_I \subseteq \Sigma$ the set of start states.*

A CTS models the behavior of a system. We write $\sigma \xrightarrow{a}_c \sigma'$ for $\langle \sigma, a, \sigma' \rangle \in \to_c$.

3.2 The First-Order Modal Mu-Calculus

To specify system properties, we use first-order modal mu-calculus [29] and modal equation systems (MESs). The former enhances the predicate calculus with modal operators; MESs are like PESs whose right-hand sides of MESs are mu-calculus formulas. Fix basic data theory $\langle \mathcal{B}\mathrm{Exp}, \mathcal{D}\mathrm{Exp}, \mathit{fv}, \langle - \rangle, \models, |-| \rangle$ and set Λ of port names. Then first-order mu-calculus formulas have the following form, where $e \in \mathcal{D}\mathrm{Exp}$ and $\lambda \in \Lambda$.

$$\phi ::= \langle \text{operators from Equation 1} \rangle \mid \langle \tau \rangle \phi \mid [\tau]\phi \mid \langle \lambda!e \rangle \phi \mid [\lambda!e]\phi \mid \langle \lambda?e \rangle \phi \mid [\lambda?e]\phi$$

The notions *fpv* and *fdv* of free formula / data variables may be adapted in the obvious manner. We call a mu-calculus formula ϕ *formula-closed* if $\mathit{fpv}(\phi) = \emptyset$.

The semantics of modal mu-calculus formulas is given with respect to a CTS $C = \langle \Sigma, V, \to_c, \Sigma_I \rangle$, and takes the form of a relation $\langle \sigma, \rho \rangle \models_{C,\theta} \phi$, which, given an environment $\theta \in (2^{(\Sigma \times (\mathcal{D}^{\mathcal{X}}))})^{\mathcal{X}}$ mapping predicate variables to sets consisting of states paired with *alternative data assignments* (used to handle bound variables), determines whether or not CTS state σ paired with ρ satisfies ϕ. This relation is given as follows (obvious cases omitted).

$\langle \sigma, \rho \rangle \models_{C,\theta} X$ iff $\langle \sigma, \rho \rangle \in \theta(X)$
$\langle \sigma, \rho \rangle \models_{C,\theta} \exists x.\phi$ iff for some d, $\langle \sigma, \rho[x := d] \rangle \models_{C,\theta} \phi$
$\langle \sigma, \rho \rangle \models_{C,\theta} \langle \tau \rangle \phi$ iff there is σ' s.t. $\sigma \xrightarrow{\tau}_c \sigma'$ and $\langle \sigma', \rho \rangle \models_{C,\theta} \phi$
$\langle \sigma, \rho \rangle \models_{C,\theta} [\tau] \phi$ iff for all σ' s.t. $\sigma \xrightarrow{\tau}_c \sigma'$, $\langle \sigma', \rho \rangle \models_{C,\theta} \phi$
$\langle \sigma, \rho \rangle \models_{C,\theta} \langle \lambda!e \rangle \phi$ iff there is σ' s.t. $\sigma \xrightarrow{\lambda!d}_c \sigma'$, $|e|_{V(\sigma)[\rho]} = d$, and $\langle \sigma', \rho \rangle \models_{C,\theta} \phi$
$\langle \sigma, \rho \rangle \models_{C,\theta} \langle \lambda?e \rangle \phi$ iff there is σ' s.t. $\sigma \xrightarrow{\lambda?d}_c \sigma'$, $|e|_{V(\sigma)[\rho]} = d$, and $\langle \sigma', \rho \rangle \models_{C,\theta} \phi$

Note that the semantics of the modal operators are different from the ones given in [21, 26]. Here, in $\langle \lambda?x \rangle \phi$ the x in ϕ is not bound, while in the other work this is the case. Our logic only permits variables to be bound using $\forall$ and $\exists$.

We sometimes write $\sigma \models_{C,\theta} \phi$ if $\langle \sigma, \emptyset \rangle \models_{C,\theta} \phi$, where $\emptyset$ is the empty data assignment. We also define $[\![\phi]\!]_{C,\theta} = \{\langle \sigma, \rho \rangle \mid \langle \sigma, \rho \rangle \models_{C,\theta} \phi\}$. We may now apply the general fixpoint-equation system theory in [30] to define the semantics of mu-calculus equation systems (MESs). The lattice in question is $2^{(\Sigma \times \mathbb{A}(\mathcal{D},\mathcal{X}))}$ ordered by set inclusion, where $\mathbb{A}(\mathcal{D}, \mathcal{X}) = \bigcup_{\mathcal{I} \subseteq \mathcal{X}} \mathcal{D}^{\mathcal{I}}$ is the set of assignments; the semantics, $[\![M]\!]_{C,\theta}$, of mu-calculus equation system M is an environment mapping each $X \in \mathsf{lhs}(M)$ to a set of state / assignment pairs that is the appropriate solution for the equation defining X.

We also adapt the definitions of formula/predicate-closed-ness from PESs in the obvious manner. If MES M is formula-closed then $[\![M]\!]_{C,\theta}(X) = [\![M]\!]_{C,\theta'}(X)$ for any $X \in \mathsf{lhs}(M)$ and θ, θ', and we write $[\![M]\!]_C$ for this value. It also follows that if M is formula-closed and ϕ is such that $fpv(\phi) \subseteq \mathsf{lhs}(M)$, then $[\![\phi]\!]_{[\![M]\!]_{C,\theta}} = [\![\phi]\!]_{[\![M]\!]_{C,\theta'}}$ for any θ, θ'. When this holds we use $[\![\phi]\!]_{C,M}$ for this value, and we write $\langle \sigma, \rho \rangle \models_{C,M} \phi$ if $\langle \sigma, \rho \rangle \in [\![\phi]\!]_{C,M}$, and $\sigma \models_{C,M} \phi$ if $\langle \sigma, V(\sigma) \rangle \in [\![\phi]\!]_{C,M}$.

3.3 Parameterized Symbolic Transition Graphs with Assignment

Our symbolic system model, Parameterized Symbolic Transition Graphs with Assignment (PSTGAs), extends the STGA formalism of [21] with a facility for *parameterized transitions*. This enables them to encode a range of other symbolic system formats, including the value-passing CCS in [10], Linear Process Equations [16], the event-action language in [6], and timed automata [18].

Fix value set $\mathcal{D}$, variable set $\mathcal{X}$, and data theory $\langle \mathcal{BE}xp, \mathcal{DE}xp, fv, \langle - \rangle, \models, |-| \rangle$ over $\mathcal{D}$ and $\mathcal{X}$. Let Φ be the associated set of predicate-calculus formulas. Also fix a set Λ of communication port names not containing the distinguished name τ, and define the set of symbolic actions $\mathcal{A}ct_s = \{\lambda?x \mid c \in \Lambda, x \in \mathcal{X}\} \cup \{\lambda!e \mid c \in \Lambda, e \in \mathcal{DE}xp\} \cup \{\tau\}$.

Definition 5. *A PSTGA is a tuple* $G = \langle S, \mathcal{I}, R, S_I, \mathit{InitC} \rangle$, *where:*

1. *S is a finite set of control locations;*
2. *$\mathcal{I} \subseteq \mathcal{X}$ is a finite set of assignable data variables;*
3. *$R \subseteq S \times (\mathcal{X} - \mathcal{I}) \times \Phi \times \Phi \times \mathbb{A}(B, \mathcal{I}) \times \mathcal{A}ct_s \times S$ is a finite set of parameterized transitions satisfying: if $\langle s, k, \kappa, \beta, A, \lambda?x, s' \rangle \in R$ then $x \in \mathcal{I}$;*
4. *$S_I \subseteq S$ are the initial locations; and*
5. *$\mathit{InitC} \in \mathcal{BE}xp$ is the initial condition.*

In PSTGA $G = \langle S, \mathcal{I}, R, S_I, \mathit{InitC} \rangle$, S_I contains the possible starting locations and InitC the initial condition on data variables. Based on the current control location and data state, transitions may fire, with data variables and control locations being updated.

With this intuition in mind, let us more closely examine the structure of parameterized transitions in a PSTGA. Each transition is a tuple $\langle s, k, \kappa, \beta, A, \alpha, s'\rangle$, where s and s' are the source and target control location, respectively. The k and κ are used to parameterize, or "index", the transition. Roughly speaking, each value d, that, when substituted for k, makes κ "true", defines a transition, in the STGA sense, consisting of: a boolean guard $\beta\langle k := d\rangle$ determining when the transition can "fire"; an assignment $A_d^k = (A \lhd (k := d))\lceil \mathrm{dom}(A)$ to variables in $\mathcal{I}$; and a communication action $\alpha[k := d]$ (defined as the replacement of free occurrences of data variable k in the action expression by d). STGA transitions, in contrast, omit k and κ. The utility of our more complex model will become apparent when we consider timed automata.

Semantically, a PSTGA $G = \langle S, \mathcal{I}, R, S_I, \mathrm{Init}\mathcal{C}\rangle$ is interpreted as a CTS $C_G = \langle \Sigma, V, \to_c, \Sigma_I\rangle$ as follows.

1. $\Sigma \subseteq S \times \mathcal{D}^{\mathcal{X}}$. Note that in $\langle s, \rho\rangle$, ρ provides values to the data variables.
2. $V(\langle s, \rho\rangle) = \rho$.
3. $\langle s, \rho\rangle \xrightarrow{a}_c \langle s', \rho'\rangle$, iff there is $\langle s, k, \kappa, \beta, A, \alpha, s'\rangle \in R$, $d' \in D$, and ρ'' with:
   (a) $\rho \models \kappa[k := d']$, $\rho \models \beta[k := d']$, $\rho'' = \rho'[k := d'][\!| A_d^k|_\rho]$, and
   (b) either: (i) $a = \tau$ and $\rho' = \rho''$; or (ii) $a = \lambda!d$, $\alpha[k := d'] = \lambda!e$, $|e|_\rho = d$, and $\rho' = \rho''$; or $a = \lambda?d$, $\alpha[k := d'] = \lambda?x$, and $\rho' = \rho''[x := d]$.
4. $\sigma_I = \{\langle s_I, \rho\rangle \mid s_I \in S_I, \rho \models \mathrm{Init}\mathcal{C}\}$

PSTGAs and the Mu-Calculus. The definition of C_G implies an immediate interpretation of the mu-calculus with respect to PSTGA G. In addition to the other notations defined for the mu-calculus, we also introduce the following. Let ϕ be a mu-calculus formula, and s a control location in PSTGA G, and let θ be a mapping of mu-calculus formula variables to sets of states in C_G paired with assignments. Then $[\![\phi]\!]_\theta(s) = \{\rho \mid \langle\langle s, \rho\rangle, \rho\rangle \in [\![\phi]\!]_{C_G, \theta}\}$. That is, the "semantics" of a control location s vis à vis a formula is the set of data states that, when combined with s, make the formula "true". Similarly, if M is a formula-closed MES, and ϕ is a mu-calculus formula with $fpv(\phi) \subseteq \mathrm{lhs}(M)$, we write $[\![\phi]\!]_{G,M}(s)$ for $\{\rho \mid \langle\langle s, \rho\rangle, \rho\rangle \in [\![\phi]\!]_{C_G, M}\}$. In this case, we also say that a PSTGA G satisfies a mu-calculus formula ϕ with respect to equation system M (written $G \models_M \phi$) if for all $s_I \in S_I$, $\{\rho \mid \rho \models \mathrm{Init}\mathcal{C}\} \subseteq [\![\phi]\!]_{G,M}(s_I)$.

4 From Model Checking to Predicate Equation Systems

The model-checking problem for PSTGAs is: given PSTGA G, formula-closed MES M and $X \in \mathrm{lhs}(M)$, does $G \models_M X$? This section shows how to translate this question into an equivalent one involving PESs. The key problem to be addressed is the symbolic representation of the set $[\![X]\!]_{G,M}(s_I)$ for every $s_I \in S_I$. This is achieved by constructing a PES equation for each state in G and equation in M. Formally, we define a function F that, given a PSTGA G and formula-closed mu-calculus equation system M, yields a predicate-closed PES $F(G, M)$. F is applied on a block-by-block basis; that is, $F(G, \langle B_1, \ldots, B_n\rangle) = \langle F(G, B_1), \ldots, F(G, B_n)\rangle$. $F(G, B) = F(G, \langle p, \overline{E}\rangle)$ in turn yields a predicate equation block of form $\langle p, \overline{E'}\rangle$, where for each equation $X = \phi$ in $\overline{E}$ and control location s in G, there is an equation of form $Y_{s,X} = F(s, \phi)$ in $\overline{E'}$. $F(s, \phi)$ is defined in Figure 1.

Theorem 1. *Let $G = \langle S, \mathcal{I}, R, S_I, \mathrm{Init}\mathcal{C}\rangle$ be a PSTGA, and let M be a closed MES. Then for any $s \in S$ and any $X \in \mathrm{lhs}(M)$, $[\![X]\!]_{G,M}(s) = [\![Y_{s,X}]\!]_{F(G,M)}$.*

$$
\begin{aligned}
F(s,b) &= b & F(s,\neg b) &= \neg b \\
F(s,\phi_1 \vee \phi_2) &= F(s,\phi_1) \vee F(s,\phi_2) & F(s,\phi_1 \wedge \phi_2) &= F(s,\phi_1) \wedge F(s,\phi_2) \\
F(s,X) &= Y_{s,X} & F(s,\exists x.\phi) &= \exists x.F(s,\phi) \\
F(s,\forall x.\phi) &= \forall x.F(s,\phi) & F(s,\phi[x := e]) &= F(s,\phi)[x := e] \\
F(s,\langle\tau\rangle\phi) &= \bigvee\{\exists k.\kappa \wedge \beta \wedge F(s',\phi)[A] \mid \langle s,k,\kappa,\beta,A,\tau,s'\rangle \in R\} \\
F(s,[\tau]\phi) &= \bigwedge\{\forall k.(\kappa \wedge \beta) \to F(s',\phi)[A] \mid \langle s,k,\kappa,\beta,A,\tau,s'\rangle \in R\} \\
F(s,\langle c!e\rangle\phi) &= \bigvee\{\exists k.\kappa \wedge \beta \wedge F(s',\phi)[A] \mid \langle s,k,\kappa,\beta,A,\alpha,s'\rangle \in R \wedge (\alpha = c!e)\} \\
F(s,[c!e]\phi) &= \bigwedge\{\forall k.(\kappa \wedge \beta) \to F(s',\phi)[A] \mid \langle s,k,\kappa,\beta,A,\alpha,s'\rangle \in R \wedge (\alpha = c!e)\} \\
F(s,\langle c?e\rangle\phi) &= \bigvee\{\exists k.\kappa \wedge \beta \wedge F(s',\phi)[A][x := e] \mid \langle s,k,\kappa,\beta,A,\alpha,s'\rangle \in R \wedge \alpha = c?x\} \\
F(s,[c?e]\phi) &= \bigwedge\{\forall k.\kappa \wedge \beta \to F(s',\phi)[A][x := e] \mid \langle s,k,\kappa,\beta,A,\alpha,s'\rangle \in R \wedge \alpha = c?x\}
\end{aligned}
$$

Fig. 1. Translation Function for PESs

5 Encoding Real Time Model Checking Via PESs

Different model-checking problems may be uniformly captured in terms of PESs, from boolean equation systems (BESs) [2, 23] and Presburger systems [6] to real-time model checking [18]. To illustrate this we detail an encoding of real-time model checking.

The framework we consider is given in [18], which models real-time systems using so-called *guarded-command real-time programs* (which are expressively equivalent to the better-known timed-automaton formalism) and uses the timed modal mu-calculus to define properties. Let R^+ be the set of nonnegative real numbers, $C = \{x_1, \ldots, x_n\}$ be a finite set of clock variables, and $\mathcal{P}$ be a finite set of boolean variables. The set of state predicates is defined by the following grammar, where $p \in \mathcal{P}$, $x, y \in C$, and $c, d \in \mathbb{N}$ are nonnegative integer constants.

$$\phi := p \mid x \leq d \mid c \leq y \mid x + c \leq y + d \mid \neg\phi \mid \phi_1 \vee \phi_2$$

A (clock) state $\rho \in (R^+)^{(C \cup \mathcal{P})}$ satisfies: $\rho(p) \in \{0, 1\}$ if $p \in \mathcal{P}$ (here 0 is interpreted as "false", and 1 as "true"). If ρ is a state and $\delta \in R^+$ then $\rho + \delta$ is the new state $\rho[x_1 := \rho(x_1) + \delta, \ldots, x_n := \rho(x_n) + \delta]$. State predicates are interpreted with respect to states in the usual fashion; we write $\rho \models \phi$ when this is the case. Then a real-time program has form $R = \langle G, \phi \rangle$, where:

- G is a finite set of guarded commands of form $\psi \to A$, with ψ a state predicate and A an assignment of form $v_1 := e_1, \ldots, v_n := e_n$. If $v_i \in \mathcal{P}$, then e_i must either be 0 or 1; if $v_i \in C$, then e_i must either be 0 (reset) or v (no change).
- State predicate ϕ, the *invariant*, is past-closed: if $\rho + \delta \models \phi$ then $\rho \models \phi$.

In state ρ program R executes as follows. If a $\psi \to A$ is such that $\rho \models \psi$, then the assignment A is "executed" in the usual manner, updating ρ to ρ', provided that $\rho' \models \phi$ also. In addition, provided $\rho + \delta \models \phi$, R may "idle".

The syntax of the timed mu-calculus extends the state-predicate language.

$$\phi ::= \langle \text{state-predicate operators} \rangle \mid X \mid \phi_1 \triangleright \phi_2 \mid z.\phi \mid \mu X.\phi$$

The new operators include capabilities for recursive definition (X, $\mu X.\phi$), a modal operator ($\phi_1 \triangleright \phi_2$), and the *freeze quantifier* ($z.\phi$), which sets "specification clock" z to 0. The formula $\phi_1 \triangleright \phi_2$ has the following meaning: $\phi_1 \vee \phi_2$ holds as time elapses, until a guarded-command fires, at which point ϕ_2 holds.

Our translation of timed model-checking into PESs converts a real-time-program / timed-mu-calculus formula into a PSTGA (the formula is needed for the specification clocks). Then the timed mu-calculus formula is translated into a MES, and our generic generator applied. Let $R = \langle G, \phi \rangle$ be a real-time program and γ be a timed mu-calculus formula, with $\S(\gamma) = \{s_1, \ldots, s_m\}$ the names of the specification clocks used in γ. To define a PSTGA, we introduce the following basic data theory (take $\mathcal{D} = \mathbb{R}^+$).

- $\mathcal{X} = C \cup \S(\gamma) \cup \mathcal{P} \cup \{k\}$, where $k \notin C \cup \S(\phi) \cup \mathcal{P}$
- $\mathcal{B}\mathrm{Exp} = \{p = 1 \mid p \in \mathcal{P}\} \cup \{x + c \leq y + d \mid x, y \in C, c, d \in \mathbb{N}\}$
- $\mathcal{D}\mathrm{Exp} = \{0, 1\} \cup \{x + k \mid x \in C \cup \S(\gamma)\}$
- $fv, \langle - \rangle, \models, |-|$ defined in the usual manner

We now define the PSTGA $G_{R,\gamma} = \langle S, \mathcal{I}, R, S_I, \mathrm{Init}\mathcal{C}\rangle$ associated with R and ϕ as follows. We take $S = \{s\}$ (i.e. there is one control location) and $\mathcal{I} = C \cup \S(\gamma)$. For each $\psi \to A \in G$, R contains a transition $\langle s, k, k = 0, \psi, A, \tau, s \rangle$, a τ-labeled transition corresponding to each guarded command in R. Note that k cannot appear free in ψ or A. There is also a parameterized transition of form $\langle s, k, \phi[x_1 := x_1 + k, \ldots, x_n := x_n + k], tt, [\bar{x} := \bar{x} + k], t!k, s\rangle$. The notation $\bar{x} := \bar{x} + k$ is shorthand for $x_1 := x_1 + k, \ldots, x_n := x_n + k$, etc. This transition models the ability of time to advance, so long as the state invariant remains true. The action label $t!k$ uses a special port t on which the delay k is written. Finally, we set $S_I = \{s\}$ and $\mathrm{Init}\mathcal{C} = \phi \wedge \bigwedge_{x \in \mathcal{X}} x = 0$.

The translation of the timed mu-calculus formula γ is omitted; we only comment on $\phi_1 \triangleright \phi_2$ and $z.\phi$. The former is given as $\exists \delta. \langle t!\delta \rangle \langle \tau \rangle \phi_2 \wedge \forall \epsilon. \epsilon \leq \delta \to \langle t!\epsilon \rangle (\phi_1 \vee \phi_2)$. The latter is $\phi[z := 0]$. Once all instances of these operators have been eliminated, the resulting formula can be easily converted into an MES.

6 Generic Algorithmic Approaches

The previous section suggested how model-checking problems can be encoded as PESs. This section discusses algorithmic issues involved in computing solutions to PESs and their relation to the specific algorithms given by researchers studying the aforementioned problems.

Global Approaches. The paper [30] gives an iterative strategy for computing the solution to fixpoint equation systems that is based on the following technique for computing solutions to basic blocks.

1. Assign each lhs variable the correct extremal value ($\top$ for ν, $\bot$ for μ).
2. "Iterate" by evaluating the right-hand side of each equation using the current assignment to derive a new assignment. Terminate when there is no change.

For PESs, this strategy has an obvious symbolic implementation: for a ν-block, initialize each lhs predicate variable to tt, then iterate by replacing the lhs variables by their definitions in rhs predicates and checking if the old predicates imply the new ones; terminate if they do. Note that in general, this strategy might not terminate. First, the basic data theory may not decidable, so checking formula equivalence cannot be automated. Second, the number of iterations needed may not be finite. Traditional global finite-state model checkers use this strategy, as do both [6] and [18]. In [6], the authors note that, even though Presburger arithmetic is decidable, their procedure may not terminate. In contrast, the restrictions in state predicates in [18] do guarantee termination.

The paper [12] restricts the allowed form of predicates mentioned in [6] so that the only basic comparisons allowed mirror those of [18], albeit for integers rather than real numbers. In this case, the iterative fixpoint calculation is guaranteed to terminate. This fact, together with the PES formulation of real-time model-checking, therefore suggests a novel symbolic approach to discrete-time model checking. Rather than expand

$$
\vee_1 \frac{\Phi \vdash \psi_1 \vee \psi_2}{\Phi \vdash \psi_1} \quad \vee_2 \frac{\Phi \vdash \psi_1 \vee \psi_2}{\Phi \vdash \psi_2} \quad \vee_3 \frac{\Phi \vdash \phi \vee \psi}{\Phi, \mathsf{not}(\phi) \vdash \psi} \quad \vee_4 \frac{\Phi \vdash \psi \vee \phi}{\Phi, \mathsf{not}(\phi) \vdash \psi}
$$

$$
\exists \frac{\Phi \vdash \exists x.\psi}{\Phi \vdash \psi[x := t]} \ (t \in \mathcal{D}\mathsf{Exp}) \qquad \forall \frac{\Phi \vdash \forall x.\psi}{\Phi \vdash \psi[x := x']} \ (x' \text{ a fresh data variable})
$$

$$
\mathsf{Cut} \frac{\Phi \vdash \psi}{\Phi \vdash \psi \vee \phi \ ; \ \Phi, \phi \vdash \psi} \qquad S \frac{\Phi, \phi \vdash \psi}{\Phi \vdash \mathsf{not}(\phi) \vee \psi} \quad T \frac{\Phi, \phi \vdash \psi}{\Phi \vdash \psi}
$$

$$
\wedge \frac{\Phi \vdash \psi_1 \wedge \psi_2}{\Phi \vdash \psi_1 \ ; \ \Phi \vdash \psi_2} \quad \vee \frac{\Phi, \phi_1 \vee \phi_2 \vdash_P \psi}{\Phi, \phi_1 \vdash_P \psi \ ; \ \Phi, \phi_2 \vdash_P \psi} \quad [] \frac{\Phi \vdash \psi[A_1][A_2]}{\Phi \vdash \psi[A_1 \triangleleft A_2]]}
$$

$$
[b] \frac{\Phi \vdash b[A]}{\Phi \vdash b\langle A \rangle} \ (b \in \mathcal{B}\mathsf{Exp}) \qquad [\neg b] \frac{\Phi \vdash (\neg b)[A]}{\Phi \vdash \neg(b\langle A\rangle)} \ (b \in \mathcal{B}\mathsf{Exp})
$$

$$
[\vee] \frac{\Phi \vdash (\psi_1 \vee \psi_2)[A]}{\Phi \vdash \psi_1[A] \vee \psi_2[A]} \qquad [\wedge] \frac{\Phi \vdash (\psi_1 \wedge \psi_2)[A]}{\Phi \vdash \psi_1[A] \wedge \psi_2[A]}
$$

$$
[\exists] \frac{\Phi \vdash (\exists x.\psi)[A]}{\Phi \vdash \psi[x := t][A]} \ (t \in \mathcal{D}\mathsf{Exp}) \quad [\forall] \frac{\Phi \vdash (\forall x.\psi)[A]}{\Phi \vdash \psi[x := x'][A]} \ (x' \text{ a fresh data variable})
$$

$$
C \frac{\Phi \vdash X}{\Phi \vdash \psi} \ (X = \psi \text{ an equation}) \qquad [C] \frac{\Phi \vdash X[A]}{\Phi \vdash \psi[A]} \ (X = \psi \text{ an equation})
$$

Fig. 2. A Gentzen-like Proof System for PESs

a discrete-time model into a CTS by "exploding" delays into sequence of clock ticks, mirror the definitions of timed-automata / real-time programs, albeit in the setting of integers, then use the symbolic approach here combined with the observation of [12].

Local Approaches. Significant attention has been paid to local, or on-the-fly, approaches to finite-state model checking. In the setting of BESs, this amounts to computing the solution of a single (propositional) variable rather than the values of all variables. In the case of data-based model checking, on-the-fly techniques have received little attention, although in the case of real-time model checking the subject is discussed in [27]. In the remainder of this section, we present a local model-checking framework for PESs that is based on a Gentzen-style, goal-directed proof system related to ones given in [5, 19].

The proof rules operates on *sequents* of the form: $\Phi \vdash \psi$, where $\Phi = \{\phi_1, \ldots \phi_n\}$ is a set of predicate-closed formulas, and ψ is a predicate. We interpret $\Phi \vdash \psi$ as the formula $\bigwedge \Phi \to \psi$. The rules for the proof system are given in Figure 2 and follow the following syntactic conventions: ϕ, ϕ_i are predicate closed, while ψ, ψ_i need not be; Φ, ϕ is short-hand for $\Phi \cup \{\phi\}$. Conclusions are also written above subgoals, which are separated by a ";". Rules $\vee_1 - \wedge$ are familiar from the predicate calculus; note that instead of left- and right- rules for each construct as in [28], we rely on rule S combined with the fact that the not function "drives" negations inside. The remaining rules are for the substitution operator and predicate variables.

The rules also share an implicit side condition: they may only be applied to *non-leaf* sequents in a sequent. These are defined as follows.

Definition 6. *Let σ be a sequent of form $\Phi \vdash_P \psi$.*

1. *Let ϕ be a predicate-closed formula and $A \stackrel{\text{def}}{=} [\bar{x} := \bar{e}]$ an assignment. Then the strongest postcondition, $\mathsf{post}(\phi, A)$, of ϕ wrt A is defined as*

$$\mathsf{post}(\phi, \bar{x} := \bar{e}) \stackrel{\text{def}}{=} \exists \bar{v}.(\bar{x} = (\bar{e}[\bar{x} := \bar{v}]) \wedge \phi[\bar{x} := \bar{v}])$$

2. σ is a (successful) leaf *if one of the following conditions holds. (a).* $\psi \in \mathcal{BExp}$ *or* $\psi = \neg b$ *for some* $b \in \mathcal{BExp}$ *(successful if* $[\![\bigwedge \Phi \to \psi]\!] = \mathcal{D}^{\mathcal{X}}$). *(b).* $\psi \in \Phi$ *(always successful). (c).* $\psi = X[A]$ *(A may be empty) with parity p, and there is another sequent* σ' *of form* $\Phi' \vdash_P X[A']$ *on the path from the root node of the proof to* σ *with the property that no* $\sigma'' \vdash_P X''[A'']$ *such that* X'' *has parity different than p and* X'' *is defined in an earlier block in the PES than* X, *and* $\mathsf{post}(\Phi, A)$ *logically implies* $\mathsf{post}(\Phi', A')$. *Such a leaf is successful if the parity of* X *is* ν.

A proof built using these rules is *valid* if and only if it is finite, every path ends in a leaf, and every leaf is successful. The following is true.

Theorem 2. *The proof rules in Figure 2 are sound: if* $\Phi \vdash \psi$ *has a valid proof wrt PES* P *then* $[\![\Phi \to \psi]\!]_P = \mathcal{D}^{\mathcal{X}}$.

In general, the proof rules are not complete; proofs may require the Cut rule, and the data theory may not be expressive enough to define the necessary property. One must also be able to determine the validity of implications in the basic data theory. One may identify data theories for which completeness does hold. For example, we conjecture the following: If any predicate is semantically equivalent to a finite boolean combination of data predicates, the proof system for this data theory is complete.

7 On-the-Fly Real-Time Model Checking

This section shows how ideas from the previous section may be used to develop a novel efficient on-the-fly model-checking algorithm for real-time systems. The essential idea is to search for proofs of PESs using the proof rules given there.

Three key challenges exist for efficient proof search. The first involves computing implications in the basic data theory (here, the theory of clock constraints). For real-time model checking, efficient data structures for this problem have been proposed, including difference-bound matrices (DBMs) [14], constraint-decision diagrams (CDDs) [20] and clock restriction diagrams (CRDs) [31]. Because of ease of implementation, our prototype uses DBMs. The second challenge is to reuse sequents whose truth has been previously established, which we achieve by sequent caching. The third challenge is to devise derived proof rules from the generic ones to afford efficient proof generation. The generic rules are intended for arbitrary predicates; for specific applications, like real-time model checking, special forms of predicates predominate, and developing special-purpose proof rules can speed proof search significantly. In the case of real-time model checking, for example, quantifiers only appear in formulas of the form $\exists k.\phi[x_i := x_i + k]$ or $\forall k.\phi[x_i := x_i + k]$, where the x_i are clocks. Instead of using the generic rules for quantifiers, we use rules specialized for these formulas. Note that these rules are derived from the generic ones, and hence are guaranteed to be sound. This, plus an additional argument (omitted here) establishing the completeness of these derived rules for real-time, ensures the correctness of our algorithm.

A final observation is in order. A significant difficulty in automating proof search involves the Cut rule: automatically inferring the "cutting predicates" is non-obvious. In our approach, we defer the computation of these predicates by introducing placeholders for them and using a "backward" analysis of the proof tree to infer values for these placeholders. This strategy is inspired by the *splitting* technique used in [27].

We now give the derived rules used in our algorithm by first introducing two derived operators, where $\mathsf{pre}(\phi, A) \stackrel{\text{def}}{=} \phi[A]$ is the weakest precondition operator.

- $suc_t(\phi) \stackrel{\text{def}}{=} \exists k.\text{post}(\phi, \bar{x} := \bar{x} + k)$, time successor of ϕ.
- $pre_t(\phi) \stackrel{\text{def}}{=} \exists k.\text{pre}(\phi, \bar{x} := \bar{x} + k)$, time predecessor of ϕ.

In the rules that follow, s, s' are placeholders.

(1) $\dfrac{\Phi \vdash_P \forall k.\psi[\bar{x} := \bar{x} + k]}{suc_t(\Phi) \vdash_P \psi}$ (2) $\dfrac{\Phi, s \vdash_P \forall k.\psi[\bar{x} := \bar{x} + k]}{suc_t(\Phi), s' \vdash_P \psi \; ; \; suc_t(\Phi \wedge s) \vdash_P suc_t(\Phi) \wedge s'}$

(3) $\dfrac{\Phi \vdash_P pre_t(\psi)}{suc_t(\Phi), s \vdash_P \psi \; ; \; \Phi \vdash_P pre_t(s)}$ (4) $\dfrac{\Phi, s \vdash_P pre_t(\psi)}{suc_t(\Phi), s' \vdash_P \psi \; ; \; s \vdash_P pre_t(s')}$

(5) $\dfrac{\Phi \vdash_P \psi[A]}{\text{post}(\Phi, A) \vdash_P \psi}$ (6) $\dfrac{\Phi, s \vdash_P \psi[A]}{\text{post}(\Phi, A), s' \vdash_P \psi \; ; \; s \vdash_P \text{pre}(s', A)}$

(7) $\Phi, s \vdash_P \varphi$ $\begin{cases} \text{if } \Phi \to \varphi \text{ a tautology,} & s \stackrel{\text{def}}{=} \text{true} \\ \text{if } \Phi \to \varphi \text{ a contradiction,} & s \stackrel{\text{def}}{=} \text{false} \\ \text{otherwise} & s \stackrel{\text{def}}{=} \varphi \end{cases}$

Rules (1)–(4) are specialized for real-time from the general quantifier elimination rules. Rules (5) and (6) are used for the time reset operation. Rule (7) is used to determine the values of placeholders. Recall that Φ, ϕ, φ are predicate-closed, while ψ need not to be.

The algorithm uses a generic, depth-first search technique, with caching; the proof rules above are used to generate sequents needed to be proved next in order for the goal sequent to be true. When a sequent is generated, the cache is first checked to see if it is implied by something in the cache; then the leaf is examined to see if it is a leaf, and if not, rules are then recursively applied to it. The same basic algorithm can easily be adapted to other settings by changing the proof rules uses.

Experimental Evaluation. We have implemented a prototype, which we call CWB-RT, of the abovementioned algorithm. The effort took approximately one month, with a week devoted to DBM implementations and the rest to building the proof-search infrastructure. C++ was used as the implementation language. To assess the performance of CWB-RT, we ran it on several examples taken from the literature and compared the results with those from the most recent available versions of Kronos (2.5i.2), UPPAAL (3.4.7, with both breadth-first (-b) and depth-first (-d) search options) and RED (5.3, with both forward and backward analysis). The experimental platform used was an Intel Pentium IV 2.8GHz with 2GB memory running Linux. The systems are listed below, together with properties (a) that should hold of correct implementations and properties (b) containing a bug that should not hold of correct implementations. The "formula bugs" include both logical errors and errors that could result from typographical mistakes (i.e. typing "2" rather than "1" by accident).

1. *Fischer's timed Mutual Exclusion (MUX)* [1, 31]. We verify that (a). at any time, no more than one process is in its critical section. (b). at most four processes could be in their waiting states at the same time.
2. *FDDI token-ring mutual exclusion protocol* [13,31]. We want to verify that (a). at any moment, at most one station is holding the token. (b). station i is in its asynchronous mode at time $20 * i$ of the network clock.
3. *Scheduling problem of real-time operating system (PATHOS)* [3,31]. The property verified is that (a). no deadlines will be missed. (b). no new deadlines (2 units ahead of time) will be missed.

4. *Safeness of a leader-election algorithm (LEADER)* [31]. We check that (a).at any time there is at least one process who is a child to no other processes. (b).at any time there is at least three processes, each of which is a child to no other processes.
5. *Bounded liveness of a leader-election algorithm (LBOUND)* [31]. We verify that (a). after $2\lceil log_2 m \rceil$ time units, where m is the number of processes, the algorithm will terminate. (b). after 3 time units, the algorithm will terminate.
6. *CSMA/CD benchmark* [31, 32]. We check that (a). at any moment, at most one process is in the transmission mode for no less than 52 time units. (b). a third process could retry to send while two are already in the transmission status.

One of the motivations for on-the-fly model checking is that bugs can be caught much more quickly than with global approaches since computation can be short-circuited when errors are found. We tested this hypothesis in two ways. First, for each buggy formula (b) and correct system specification, we collected comparative performance data for the model checkers in question. These figures in Table 1 indicate that CWB-RT performs much better than the other tools in this case.

Table 1. Performance data when correct systems fail buggy (i.e. (b)) properties. The numbers in the names of the systems refer to the numbers of processes in the models. Times represent CPU time in seconds, "O/M" means "out-of-memory".

Example	CWB-RT	Kronos 2.5i.2	UPPAAL 3.4.7 (-b)	UPPAAL 3.4.7 (-d)	RED 5.3 (forward)	RED 5.3 (backward)
MUX-20-b	7.83s	O/M	O/M	24.55s	O/M	O/M
MUX-40-b	372.81s	O/M	O/M	1139.57s	O/M	O/M
MUX-50-b	2653.00s	O/M	O/M	O/M	O/M	O/M
FDDI-30-b	0.20s	O/M	O/M	O/M	22.85s	15.96s
FDDI-40-b	0.58s	O/M	O/M	O/M	92.92s	78.57s
FDDI-60-b	2.76s	O/M	O/M	O/M	1788.43s	1053.06s
PATHOS-7-b	10.58s	O/M	O/M	O/M	O/M	3582.55s
PATHOS-8-b	48.32s	O/M	O/M	O/M	O/M	O/M
PATHOS-9-b	212.66s	O/M	O/M	O/M	O/M	O/M
LEADER-10-b	0.00s	O/M	O/M	O/M	21.32s	264.46s
LEADER-20-b	0.03s	O/M	O/M	O/M	O/M	O/M
LEADER-120-b	26.50s	O/M	O/M	O/M	O/M	O/M
LBOUND-10-b	0.01s	O/M	O/M	O/M	O/M	O/M
LBOUND-40-b	1.92s	O/M	O/M	O/M	O/M	O/M
LBOUND-120-b	284.42s	O/M	O/M	O/M	O/M	O/M
CSMA/CD-20-b	0.02s	O/M	6.11s	0.12s	O/M	O/M
CSMA/CD-40-b	0.15s	O/M	O/M	2.41s	O/M	O/M
CSMA/CD-100-b	3.81s	O/M	O/M	232.32s	O/M	O/M

We then studied situations in which correct formulas were used but buggy system specifications given. The data we obtained is given in Table 2, where the error for MUX originates in a misassignment to the global lock with the difference between the number of processes and the process identifier; the destination of the transition from the asynchronous state is misset to itself for the first station in FDDI; the error in PATHOS involves an ommitted clock reset, which would be a typical programming error one might observe; and the error in CSMA/CD is caused by missing a collision signal, thus it leads to an incomplete system specification; the error in LBOUND is caused by setting the parent to NULL in the requester-responder pair, and to the identifier complemented by the number of processes in LEADER.

Table 2. Performance data for buggy system specifications and correct (i.e. (a)) properties

Example	CWB-RT	Kronos 2.5i.2	UPPAAL 3.4.7 (-b)	UPPAAL 3.4.7 (-d)	RED 5.3 (forward)	RED 5.3 (backward)
MUX-14-e	1.32s	O/M	O/M	O/M	O/M	O/M
MUX-16-e	13.00s	O/M	O/M	O/M	O/M	O/M
MUX-18-e	257.02s	O/M	O/M	O/M	O/M	O/M
FDDI-30-e	0.24s	O/M	1.81s	2.54s	67.09s	14.15s
FDDI-40-e	0.70s	O/M	6.09s	9.39s	351.09s	39.37s
FDDI-60-e	3.16s	O/M	44.43s	63.26s	7066.18s	308.60s
PATHOS-5-e	0.51s	O/M	1.02s	109.56s	215.04s	24.33s
PATHOS-6-e	19.71s	O/M	354.40s	O/M	O/M	250.64s
PATHOS-7-e	2283.13s	O/M	O/M	O/M	O/M	O/M
LEADER-60-e	0.02s	O/M	21.18s	21.04s	O/M	O/M
LEADER-70-e	0.03s	O/M	O/M	O/M	O/M	O/M
LEADER-150-e	0.26s	O/M	O/M	O/M	O/M	O/M
LBOUND-10-e	0.00s	O/M	O/M	62.33s	O/M	O/M
LBOUND-20-e	0.02s	O/M	O/M	O/M	O/M	O/M
LBOUND-120-e	1.16s	O/M	O/M	O/M	O/M	O/M
CSMA/CD-10-e	65.19s	O/M	O/M	O/M	2057.94s	2389.87s
CSMA/CD-11-e	200.50s	O/M	O/M	O/M	O/M	O/M
CSMA/CD-12-e	670.95s	O/M	O/M	O/M	O/M	O/M

Again, the figures show that CWB-RT significantly outperforms the other tools on these case studies. We conjecture that CWB-RT's superior performance in this and the preceding case is due to the combined forward / backward analysis of our algorithm. The logical infrastructure of our algorithm is useful to detect errors quickly while most of other tools are devoted to compute a fixpoint before it could find an error.

An often-mentioned criticism of on-the-fly model checking is that when system specifications and formulas are both correct, these algorithms perform very poorly. To test the validity of this statement, we ran CWB-RT on all (a) properties for correct versions of the case studies. The performance figures are given in Table 3 and tend to refute the assertion just given. Specifically, it can be seen that CWB-RT generally outperforms Kronos and is often better, though sometimes worse, than UPPAAL3.4.7. RED5.3 generally outperforms CWB-RT on these examples, although it should be noted that while Kronos [32] was implemented with DBMs, as CWB-RT is, UPPAAL [4] use CDDs and RED5.3 CRDs [31]. We conjecture that CWB-RT would see considerable performance improvement if we used CDDs / CRDs in place of DBMs. Also, CWB-RT's competitiveness does suggest that our proof-search strategy, which combines forward (proof search) and backward (sequent caching) analysis, offers peformance improvements over the "pure forward" or "pure backward" strategies favored by these tools.

8 Conclusions

In this paper we have presented predicate equation systems (PESs) as a generic model-checking framework for data-based systems. We illustrated the flexibility of PESs by showing model-checking problems for real time may be captured uniformly using them, and we developed generic global and local approaches to computing solutions of PESs. Finally, we developed a new model-checking algorithm for real-time based on proof search in the setting of PESs and gave experimental data showing that the algorithm is competitive with, and often superior to, existing approaches.

Table 3. Performance data for correct systems and properties (i.e. (a) properties)

Example	CWB-RT	Kronos 2.5i.2	UPPAAL 3.4.7 (-b)	UPPAAL 3.4.7 (-d)	RED 5.3 (forward)	RED 5.3 (backward)
MUX-5-a	0.23s	0.48s	0.77s	4.12s	4.67s	1.36s
MUX-6-a	4.03s	O/M	68.87s	927.79s	66.89s	3.92s
MUX-7-a	115.53s	O/M	O/M	O/M	778.48s	10.32s
FDDI-20-a	0.21s	O/M	O/M	O/M	2.02s	2.25s
FDDI-40-a	2.29s	O/M	O/M	O/M	16.91s	24.39s
FDDI-60-a	11.03s	O/M	O/M	O/M	60.07s	85.99s
PATHOS-4-a	4.19s	O/M	0.21s	0.14s	10.15s	6.07s
PATHOS-5-a	2824.96s	O/M	2.14s	55.27s	353.98s	360.06s
PATHOS-6-a	O/M	O/M	O/M	O/M	12053.26s	31190.21s
LEADER-6-a	0.24s	O/M	1.32s	1.53s	0.43s	1.28s
LEADER-7-a	12.74s	O/M	136.29s	142.02s	1.18s	3.73s
LEADER-8-a	1888.35s	O/M	O/M	O/M	2.97s	9.80s
LBOUND-6-a	0.35s	O/M	2.53s	1.64s	67.70s	33.17s
LBOUND-7-a	15.22s	O/M	145.86s	153.59s	453.58s	193.68s
LBOUND-8-a	2431.69s	O/M	O/M	O/M	2933.81s	892.97s
CSMA/CD-6-a	3.89s	0.32s	2.55s	5.15s	709.12s	0.52s
CSMA/CD-7-a	56.62s	O/M	218.81s	182.49s	12109.23s	1.26s
CSMA/CD-8-a	1584.76s	O/M	O/M	O/M	O/M	3.15s

Related Work. Both [23] and [25] propose model checkers for the value-passing mu-calculus, although these algorithms only work for finite systems. Groote et al. [16] define first-order boolean equation systems, which are very similar to our PESs. That work does not consider proof systems or on-the-fly algorithms, however, and it did not study the real-time model-checking problem. Tableau methods [26, 17] can be cast into a local algorithms for PESs in a way simliar to [22]. Finally, [27] also gives an on-the-fly algorithm for model-checking real-time systems and [15] proposes a computational framework based on logic programming for verifying real-time systems. Our method is different in being based on proof search; this basis permitted us to identify situations, specifically in the checking of invariance properties, in which we can avoid clock-zone-splitting operations that their algorithm requires. Consequently, we conjecture that our algorithm will significantly outperform that one for checking safety properties.

References

1. R. Alur, C. Courcoubetis, D. Dill, N. Halbwachs, and H. Wong-Toi. An implementation of three algorithms for timing verification based on automata emptiness. In *RTSS92*, 1992.
2. H. R. Andersen. Model checking and boolean graphs. *Theoretical Computer Science*, 126(1), 1994.
3. F. Balarin. Approximate reachability analysis of timed automata. In *IEEE RTSS96*, 1996.
4. G. Behrmann, J. Bengtsson, A. David, K. G. Larsen, P. Pettersson, and W. Yi. Uppaal implementation secrets. In *FTRTFT02*, 2002.
5. S. Berezin. *Model Checking and Theorem Proving: a Unified Framework*. PhD thesis, Carnegie Mellon University, 2002.
6. T. Bultan, R. Gerber, and W. Pugh. Symbolic model checking of infinite state systems using presburger arithmetic. In O. Grumberg, editor, *CAV97*, 1997, LNCS 1254, Springer-Verlag.

7. J. R. Burch, E. M. Clarke, K. L. McMillan, D. L. Dill, and L. J. Hwang. Symbolic model checking: 10^{20} states and beyond. In *Proceedings of the 5th IEEE Symposium on Logic in Computer Science*, pages 428–439, Philadelphia, PA, 1990.
8. E. M. Clarke and E. A. Emerson. Design and synthesis of synchronization skeletons using branching-time temporal logic. In D. Kozen, editor, *Proceedings of the Workshop on Logic of Programs,* Yorktown Heights, LNCS 131, pages 52–71, 1981.
9. E. M. Clarke, O. Grumberg, and D. Peled. *Model Checking.* MIT Press, 1999.
10. R. Cleaveland and J. Riely. Testing-based abstractions for concurrent systems. In *CONCUR94*, LNCS 836, pages 417–432, 1994
11. R. Cleaveland and B. Steffen. A linear-time model-checking algorithm for the alternation-free modal mu-calculus. In *CAV91*, LNCS 575, pages 48–58, 1991.
12. H. Comon and Y. Jurski. Multiple counters automata, safety analysis and presburger arithmetic. In *CAV98*, LNCS 1427, pages 268–279. Springer-Verlag, 1998.
13. C. Daws, A. Olivero, S. Tripakis, and S. Yovine. The tool kronos. In *DIMACS Workshop on Verification and Control of Hybrid Systems*, LNCS 1066. Springer-Verlag, 1995.
14. D. L. Dill. Timing assumptions and verification of finite-state concurrent systems. In *CAV89*. LNCS 407, 1989.
15. X. Du, C.R. Ramakrishnan, and S.A. Smolka. Tabled resolution + constraints: A recipe for model checking real-time systems. In *RTSS00*, 2000.
16. J.F. Groote and T.A.C. Willemse. A checker for modal formulas for processes with data. Technical report, Technische Universiteit Eindhoven, The Neitherlands, 2002.
17. M. Hennessy and X. Liu. A modal logic for message passing processes. *Acta Informatica*, 32(4):375–393, 1995.
18. T. A. Henzinger, X. Nicollin, J. Sifakis, and S. Yovine. Symbolic model checking for real-time systems. *Information and Computation*, 111(2), 1994.
19. J.Bradfield and C.Stirling. Local model checking for infinite state spaces. *Theoretical Computer Science*, 96:157–174, 1992.
20. K. G. Larsen, P. Pettersson, and W. Yi. UPPAAL in a nutshel. *Software Tools for Technology Transfer*, 1:134–152, 1997.
21. H. Lin. Symbolic graphs with assignment. In *CONCUR96*, LNCS 1119, pages 50–65, 1996.
22. A. Mader. *Verification of Modal Properties Using Boolean Equation Systems.* PhD thesis, Müchen, Techn-Univ., 1997.
23. R. Mateescu. Local model-checking of an alternation-free value-based modal mu-calculus. In *VMCAI98*, September 1998.
24. J. P. Queille and J. Sifakis. Specification and verification of concurrent systems in Cesar. In *Proceedings of the International Symposium in Programming*, LNCS 137, Springer-Verlag, 1982.
25. C.R. Ramakrishnan. A model checker for value-passing mu-calculus using logic programming. In *PADL01*, LNCS 1990, Las Vegas, Nevada, March 2001. Springer-Verlag.
26. J. Rathke and M. Hennessy. Local model checking for value-passing processes. In *Proceedings of the International Symposium on Theoretical Aspects of Computer Software (TACS '97)*, LNCS 1281, Springer-Verlag, 1997.
27. O. Sokolsky and S. Smolka. Local model checking for real-time systems. In P. Wolper, editor, *CAV 95*, LNCS 939, Liège, Belgium, July 1995.
28. A. Szalas. Logic for computer science. lecture notes. URL http://www.ida.liu.se/~andsz.
29. A. Szałas. On natural deduction in first-order fixpoint logics. *Fundamenta Informaticae*, 26:81–94, 1996.
30. L. Tan and R. Cleaveland. Evidence-based model checking. In *CAV*, LNCS 2404, 2002.
31. F. Wang. Efficient verification of timed automata with bdd-like data-structures. In *VMCAI 2003*, LNCS 2575, pages 189–205, 2003.
32. S. Yovine. Kronos: A verification tool for real-time systems. *Software Tools for Technology Transfer*, 1:123–133, 1997.

Logic and Model Checking for Hidden Markov Models*

Lijun Zhang[1], Holger Hermanns[1,2], and David N. Jansen[2]

[1] Department of Computer Science, Saarland University,
D-66123 Saarbrücken, Germany

[2] Department of Computer Science, University of Twente,
Enschede, The Netherlands

Abstract. The branching-time temporal logic PCTL* has been introduced to specify quantitative properties over probability systems, such as discrete-time Markov chains. Until now, however, no logics have been defined to specify properties over hidden Markov models (HMMs). In HMMs the states are hidden, and the hidden processes produce a sequence of observations. In this paper we extend the logic PCTL* to POCTL*. With our logic one can state properties such as "there is at least a 90 percent probability that the model produces a given sequence of observations" over HMMs. Subsequently, we give model checking algorithms for POCTL* over HMMs.

1 Introduction

Hidden Markov models (HMMs) [17] were developed in the late 1960's and have been proven to be very important for many applications, especially speech recognition [13], character recognition [22], biological sequence analysis [5], and protein classification problems [15]. Lately, HMMs receive increased attention in the context of communication channel modelling [20] and of QoS properties in wireless networks [9].

An HMM is a doubly embedded stochastic process with an underlying stochastic process over some state space, which is *hidden*. The occupied state can only be observed through another set of stochastic processes that produce a sequence of observations. Given the sequence of observations, we do not exactly know the occupied state, but we do know the probability distribution over the set of states. This information is captured by a so-called belief state.

For a given HMM, one is often interested in the properties of the underlying stochastic process. In addition, one is also interested to reason about properties over the other set of stochastic processes which produce the observations. In this

---

* Parts of this work was carried out while the third author was with the Max-Planck-Institut für Informatik, Saarbrücken. This work is partially supported by the NWO-DFG bilateral project VOSS, the NWO Vernieuwingsimpuls award 016.023.010, and by the DFG as part of the Transregional Collaborative Research Center SFB/TR 14 AVACS.

paper, we introduce a logic called POCTL*, which consists of state formulas, path formulas and belief state formulas. POCTL* allows us to specify properties of interests over HMMs. We consider the property:

There is at least a 90 percent probability that the model produces the sequence of observations $O = (o_0, o_1, \ldots, o_n)$.

This property can be expressed in POCTL* by $\mathcal{P}_{\geq 0.9}(\mathbf{X}_{o_0}\mathbf{X}_{o_1}\ldots\mathbf{X}_{o_n}tt)$. As indicated by Rabiner [17], this probability can be viewed as the score which specifies how well a given model matches the observations. In *Speech Recognition* [13], we want to find out the most likely sentence (with the highest score) given a language and some acoustic input (observations). Assuming that we know that the HMM for the word "Need" produces the acoustic observations O with probability at least 0.9, then we can almost conclude that this acoustic input represents the word "Need". In the protein classification problem, we want to classify the new protein to one known class. The idea is to construct an HMM for every known class, and calculate the score of the new protein under every class. The new protein belongs to the class which matches it (produces it with the highest probability).

On one hand, POCTL* is basically an extension of PCTL* where the next operator is equipped with an observation constraint. On the other hand, POCTL* can also be considered as a variant of the temporal logic ACTL*, presented by De Nicola *et al.* [14], in which the usual next operator is extended to constrain the action label of the transition.

The PCTL* model checking [2, 1, 11] problem can be reduced to the QLS (quantitative LTL specification) model checking problem. For QLS model checking, one constructs first a Büchi automaton for an LTL formula using well-known methods [23, 21, 10], and then builds the product of the system and the constructed Büchi automaton. Finally, the QLS model checking problem can be reduced to a probabilistic reachability analysis in the product system.

Following the same line, we shall present the POCTL* model checking algorithm as follows. First, it will be reduced to the QOS (quantitative OLTL specification, where OLTL abbreviates Observational LTL) model checking problem. The latter can be further reduced to a probabilistic reachability analysis in the product automaton. To that end, we construct a Büchi automaton for a given OLTL formula. The construction is an adaption of the one presented in [10].

2 Preliminaries

Rabin Automaton. A deterministic *Rabin automaton* [18, 2] is a tuple $\mathcal{R}_\phi = (\Sigma, Q, q_{in}, \delta, U)$ where Σ is a nonempty finite alphabet, Q is a finite set of states, $q_{in} \in Q$ is the initial state, $\delta : Q \times \Sigma \to Q$ is the transition function, and $U = \{(P_i, R_i) \mid i = 1, \ldots, r\}$ is the Rabin acceptance condition where $P_i, R_i \subseteq Q$.

We call an infinite sequence $w = w_1, w_2, \ldots$ over Σ a *word* over Σ. w induces an unique path $\pi = q_0, q_1, \ldots$ in $\mathcal{R}$ where $q_0 = q_{in}$, and $q_{i+1} = \delta(q_i, w_i)$ for $i = 0, 1, \ldots$ π is an *accepting* path if $\inf(\pi) \subseteq P_j$ and $\inf(\pi) \cap R_j \neq \emptyset$ for some $j \in \{1, \ldots, r\}$ where $\inf(\pi)$ denotes the set of states that occur infinitely often in π.

Discrete-time Markov Chains. A labeled discrete-time Markov chain (DTMC) is a tuple $\mathcal{D} = (S, \mathbf{P}, L)$ where S is a finite set of states, $\mathbf{P} : S \times S \to [0,1]$ is a probability matrix satisfying $\sum_{s' \in S} \mathbf{P}(s, s') \in \{0, 1\}$ for all $s \in S$, and $L : S \to 2^{AP}$ is a labeling function.

3 Hidden Markov Models

This section first recalls the concept of HMM, then defines belief states, paths over HMM, and probability spaces for a given HMM.

3.1 Labeled Discrete-Time HMMs

An HMM [17] is a doubly embedded stochastic process with an underlying stochastic process that is *hidden*, but can only be observed through another set of stochastic processes that produce a sequence of observations. We add a labeling function to the standard definition of HMMs, in other words, we consider an HMM as an extension of a labeled DTMC:

Definition 1. *A labeled discrete-time HMM $\mathcal{H}$ is a tuple $(S, \mathbf{P}, L, \Theta, \mu, \alpha)$ where $(S, \mathbf{P}, L)$ is a labeled DTMC, Θ is a finite set of observations, $\mu : S \times \Theta \longrightarrow [0,1]$ is an observation function satisfying $\sum_{o \in \Theta} \mu(s, o) = 1 \; \forall s \in S$, and α is an initial distribution on S such that $\sum_{s \in S} \alpha(s) = 1$.* □

The observation set Θ corresponds to the output of the model. By definition, $\mu(s, \cdot)$ is a distribution on Θ, and $\mu(s, o)$ indicates the probability that the state s produces the observation o. For the sake of brevity, we write $\mu_s(o)$ instead of $\mu(s, o)$. The probability that the model starts with state s is $\alpha(s)$. In what follows we use the term HMM to refer to a labeled discrete-time HMM. For technical reasons, we assume there is no absorbing state in an HMM throughout our discussion[1].

3.2 Belief State

The observation depends stochastically and exclusively on the current state. In general, the same observation could be emitted by several different states; therefore, we are uncertain about the current state, but, we can summarize the historical observations in a *belief state* (or *information state*) [12, 16] which is a distribution over S. A belief state is not really a state of the HMM. Rather, it is a way to describe what we know about the state, given the history of observations. The set of all possible belief states is called the *belief space*, and is denoted by $\mathcal{B}$. We use S^t with $S^t \in S$ to denote the state at time t, and $O^t \in \Theta$ to denote the observation at time t. We write b_t to denote the belief state at time t.

---

[1] As indicated by Baier [2] (for concurrent probabilistic systems), this is a harmless restriction since any system can be transformed into an "equivalent" system without absorbing states. For an HMM $\mathcal{H}$ with absorbing states, we insert just a special state † with a self-loop and transitions from any absorbing state in $\mathcal{H}$ to †.

Definition 2. Let $o_i \in \Theta$ where $i = 0, \ldots, t$. The belief state b_t at time t, is the distribution over S at time t given the observation history $o_0, \ldots, o_t$:

$$b_t(s) = P(S^t = s | O^0 = o_0, \ldots, O^t = o_t, \mathcal{H}) \ \forall s \in S \qquad \square$$

Now given the historical observations $o_0, \ldots, o_t$, the question is how to calculate the belief state b_n. The belief state at time 0 only depends on the initial distribution and the first observation. The belief state at time t captures all of our information about the past. As a result, we can inductively calculate the current belief state b_t based on the previous belief state b_{t-1} and the current observation o_t. This is illustrated in Figure 1.

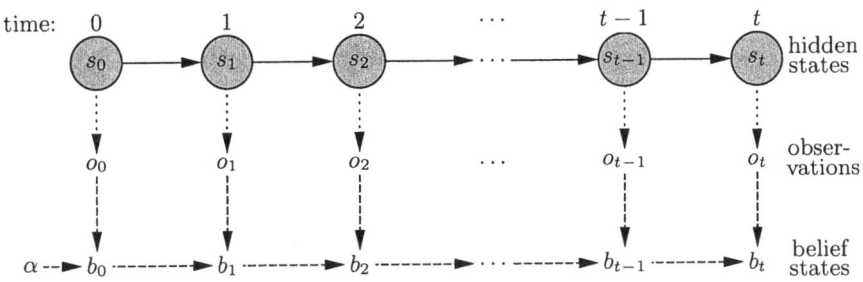

Fig. 1. Updating belief states

We depict the states in gray circles to indicate that they are hidden. The states together with the solid arrows between them represent the underlying state evolvement. The dotted arrows between states and observations mean that the observation o_t is produced from the state s_t according to the observation function μ. As a particular case, b_0 is a function of o_0 and the initial distribution α. Applying the Bayesian rule and the definition of b_0 we get: $b_0(s) = \frac{\alpha(s)\mu_s(o_0)}{K_0}$ where K_0 is a normalizing constant with value $\sum_{s \in S} \alpha(s)\mu_s(o_0)$.

The dashed arrows, between the current observation o_t, previous belief state b_{t-1} and the current belief state b_t, mean that b_t depends on o_t and b_{t-1} for all $t = 1, \ldots, n$. Again, applying the Bayesian rule and the definition of b_t we have: $b_{t+1}(s) = \frac{\sum_{s_t \in S} b_t(s_t)\mathbf{P}(s_t, s)\mu_s(o_{t+1})}{K_{t+1}}$ where K_{t+1} is a normalizing constant with value: $\sum_{s \in S} \left(\sum_{s_t \in S} b_t(s_t)\mathbf{P}(s_t, s)\mu_s(o_{t+1}) \right)$. Hence, given the historical observations, we are able to calculate the current belief state.

3.3 Paths in HMM and Probability Spaces over Paths

Given $\mathcal{H} = (S, \mathbf{P}, L, \Theta, \mu, \alpha)$, let $s_i \in S$ and $o_i \in \Theta$ for all $i \in \mathbb{N}$. A path σ of $\mathcal{H}$ is a sequence $(s_0, o_0), (s_1, o_1) \ldots \in (S \times \Theta)^\omega$ where $\mu_{s_i}(o_i) > 0, \mathbf{P}(s_i, s_{i+1}) > 0$ for all $i \in \mathbb{N}$ and $(S \times \Theta)^\omega$ denotes the set of infinite sequences of elements of $S \times \Theta$.

For a path σ and $i \in \mathbb{N}$, let $\sigma_s[i] = s_i$ denote the $(i+1)$st state of σ, and $\sigma_o[i] = o_i$ denote the $(i+1)$st observation of σ. Let $\sigma[i]$ denote the suffix path of σ starting with $\sigma_s[i]$, i.e., $(s_i, o_i), (s_{i+1}, o_{i+1}), \ldots$. Note that $\sigma[0] = \sigma$.

Let $Path^{\mathcal{H}}$ denote the set of all paths in $\mathcal{H}$, and $Path^{\mathcal{H}}(s)$ denote the set of paths in $\mathcal{H}$ that start in s. The superscript $\mathcal{H}$ is ommitted whenever convenient. We define a probability space on paths of $\mathcal{H}$ using the standard cylinder construction. For a path $(s_0, o_0), (s_1, o_1), \ldots$, we define the *basic cylinder set* induced by the prefix of this path as follows:

$$\mathcal{C}((s_0, o_0), (s_1, o_1), \ldots, (s_n, o_n)) := \{\sigma \in Path \mid \forall i \leq n . \sigma_s[i] = s_i \wedge \sigma_o[i] = o_i\}$$

If it is clear from the context, we use just $\mathcal{C}$ to denote this cylinder set. $\mathcal{C}$ consists of all paths σ starting with $(s_0, o_0), (s_1, o_1), \ldots (s_n, o_n)$. Let $\mathcal{C}yl$ contain all sets $\mathcal{C}((s_0, o_0), \ldots, (s_n, o_n))$ where $s_0, \ldots, s_n$ range over all state sequences and $o_0, \ldots, o_n$ range over all observation sequences. Let $\mathcal{F}$ be the σ-algebra on $Path$ generated by $\mathcal{C}yl$. Let $\mathbf{i}(s, s_0) = 1$ if $s = s_0$, and $\mathbf{i}(s, s_0) = 0$ if $s \neq s_0$. The probability measure[2] $\Pr_s$ on $\mathcal{F}$ is defined by induction on n by $\Pr_s(\mathcal{C}(s_0, o_0)) = \mathbf{i}(s, s_0) \mu_{s_0}(o_0)$ and, for $n > 0$:

$$\Pr_s(\mathcal{C}((s_0, o_0), \ldots, (s_n, o_n)))$$
$$= \Pr_s(\mathcal{C}((s_0, o_0), \ldots, (s_{n-1}, o_{n-1}))) \cdot \mathbf{P}(s_{n-1}, s_n) \mu_{s_n}(o_n)$$

By induction on n, we obtain:

$$\Pr_s(\mathcal{C}((s_0, o_0), \ldots, (s_n, o_n))) = \mathbf{i}(s, s_0) \mu_{s_0}(o_0) \prod_{i=1}^{n} \mathbf{P}(s_{i-1}, s_i) \mu_{s_i}(o_i) \quad (1)$$

Lemma 3. *Let $s \in S$. The triple $(Path, \mathcal{F}, \Pr_s)$ on domain $Path$ is a probability space, where $\mathcal{F}$ is the σ-algebra generated by the set of basic cylinder sets $\mathcal{C}yl$, and $\Pr_s$ is the probability measure which is described by Equation 1.* □

Let $b \in \mathcal{B}$ be a belief state, and $C \in \mathcal{C}yl$ be a basic cylinder set. We extend the probability measure with respect to a belief state b by: $\Pr_b(C) = \sum_{s \in S} b(s) \cdot \Pr_s(C)$. Similar to Lemma 3, the triple $(Path, \mathcal{F}, \Pr_b)$ on domain $Path$ is also a probability space.

4 The Logic POCTL*

This section presents the branching-time temporal logic Probabilistic Observation CTL* (POCTL*) which allows us to specify properties over HMMs. We have indicated in the introduction that for an HMM, one wants to specify properties over the underlying DTMC and in addition, one is also interested in reasoning

---

[2] We define here actually a probability function $\Pr_s$ on the set $\mathcal{C}yl$. For $\mathcal{F}$ is a σ-algebra generated by $\mathcal{C}yl$, this probability function can be extended to a unique probability measure on $\mathcal{F}$.

about properties over the other set of stochastic processes which produce observations. The logic PCTL* is interpreted over DTMCs to express quantitative stochastic properties [2, 7, 6]. We extend PCTL* to POCTL* such that the next operator is equipped with an observation constraint. In this way we can state properties over the observations, e.g., $X_o \phi$ means that the next observation is o and the subsequent path satisfies ϕ.

POCTL* can be also considered as a variant of the temporal logic ACTL* introduced by De Nicola et al. [14]. ACTL* is interpreted over Labeled Transition Systems (LTS) and has been proven to have the same power as CTL*. In ACTL* the usual next operator is extended to interpret the labeled action of the transition (e.g., $X_a \phi$ means the next transition is labeled with an action a and the subsequent path satisfies ϕ).

4.1 Syntax of POCTL*

Let $\mathcal{H} = (S, \mathbf{P}, L, \Theta, \mu, \alpha)$ be an HMM with $o \in \Theta$. The syntax of the logic POCTL* is defined as follows:

$$\Phi := a \mid \neg \Phi \mid \Phi \wedge \Phi \mid \epsilon$$
$$\phi := \Phi \mid \neg \phi \mid \phi \wedge \phi \mid \mathbf{X}_o \phi \mid \phi \mathcal{U}^{\leq n} \phi$$
$$\epsilon := \mathcal{P}_{\trianglelefteq p}(\phi) \mid \neg \epsilon \mid \epsilon \wedge \epsilon$$

where $n \in \mathbb{N}$ or $n = \infty$, $0 \leq p \leq 1$ and $\trianglelefteq \in \{\leq, <, \geq, >\}$. □

The syntax of POCTL* consists of state formula, path formula and belief state formula. As in CTL*, we use Φ, Ψ for state formula and ϕ, ψ for path formula. The formula ϵ is called belief state formula. In HMMs, we are uncertain about the current state, but we always know the current belief state. Therefore, we want to know if some (probabilistic) properties are valid in belief states. We consider the example in the introduction:

> There is at least a 90 percent probability that the model produces a sequence of observations $O = (o_0, o_1, \ldots, o_n)$.

This can be expressed by a belief state formula $\epsilon = \mathcal{P}_{\geq 0.9}(\mathbf{X}_{o_0} \mathbf{X}_{o_1} \ldots \mathbf{X}_{o_n} tt)$. Intuitively, a belief state b satisfies ϵ if the probability measure w.r.t. b, i.e., Pr_b, of the set of paths satisfying $\mathbf{X}_{o_0} \mathbf{X}_{o_1} \ldots \mathbf{X}_{o_n} tt$ meets the bound ≥ 0.9. In *Speech Recognition* [13], we want to find out the most likely sentence given a language and some acoustic input. For example, if we know that the HMM for the word "Need" produces the acoustic observations with probability at least 0.9, we can almost conclude that this acoustic input represents the word "Need". We indicate that this property cannot be expressed by any sublogics of POCTL* that we shall define later.

For the sake of simplicity, we do not consider the exist operator. The formula $\exists \phi$ is almost equivalent to the probability formula $\mathcal{P}_{>0} \phi$. The standard (i.e., unbounded) until formula is obtained by taking n equal to ∞, i.e., $\phi \mathcal{U} \psi = \phi \mathcal{U}^{\leq \infty} \psi$. We use the abbreviations $\wedge, \diamond, \square$ which are defined in the same way as for CTL*. The timed variants of the temporal operators can be derived, e.g., $\diamond^{\leq n} \phi = tt \mathcal{U}^{\leq n} \phi$, $\square^{\leq n} \phi = \neg \diamond^{\leq n} \neg \phi$.

4.2 Semantics of POCTL*

Let $\mathcal{H} = (S, \mathbf{P}, L, \Theta, \mu, \alpha)$ be an HMM with $s \in S$ and $\sigma \in Path$. The semantics of POCTL* is defined by a satisfaction relation (denoted by $\models$) either between a state s and a state formula Φ, or between a path σ and a path formula ϕ, or between a belief state b and a belief state formula ϵ. We write $\mathcal{H}, s \models \Phi$, $\mathcal{H}, \sigma \models \phi$ and $\mathcal{H}, b \models \epsilon$ if state s, path σ and belief state b satisfy state formula Φ, path formula ϕ and belief state formula ϵ, respectively. If the model $\mathcal{H}$ is clear from the context, we simply write $s \models \Phi$, $\sigma \models \phi$ and $b \models \epsilon$.

Let b_s be the belief state with $b_s(s) = 1$ and $b_s(s') = 0$ for $s' \neq s$. The satisfaction relation $\models$ is defined in Figure 2 where $\Pr_b\{\sigma \in Path \mid \sigma \models \phi\}$, or $\Pr_b(\phi)$ for short, denotes the probability measure of the set of all paths which satisfy ϕ and start states weighted by b.

$s \models a$	iff	$a \in L(s)$
$s \models \neg \Phi$	iff	$s \not\models \Phi$
$s \models \Phi \wedge \Psi$	iff	$s \models \Phi \wedge s \models \Psi$
$s \models \epsilon$	iff	$b_s \models \epsilon$
$\sigma \models \Phi$	iff	$\sigma_s[0] \models \Phi$
$\sigma \models \neg \phi$	iff	$\sigma \not\models \phi$
$\sigma \models \phi \wedge \psi$	iff	$\sigma \models \phi \wedge \sigma \models \psi$
$\sigma \models \mathbf{X}_o \phi$	iff	$\sigma_o[0] = o \wedge \sigma[1] \models \phi$
$\sigma \models \phi \mathcal{U}^{\leq n} \psi$	iff	$\exists 0 \leq j \leq n.(\sigma[j] \models \psi \wedge \forall i < j.\sigma[i] \models \phi)$
$b \models \mathcal{P}_{\trianglelefteq p}(\phi)$	iff	$\Pr_b\{\sigma \in Path \mid \sigma \models \phi\} \trianglelefteq p$
$b \models \neg \epsilon$	iff	$b \not\models \epsilon$
$b \models \epsilon \wedge \epsilon'$	iff	$b \models \epsilon \wedge b \models \epsilon'$

Fig. 2. Semantics of POCTL*

A path satisfies the new operator $\mathbf{X}_o \phi$ if it starts with the observation o and the suffix[3] $\sigma[1]$ satisfies ϕ. Let Ω be a set of observations, i.e., $\Omega \subseteq \Theta$. We use the abbreviation $\mathbf{X}_\Omega \phi$ for $\bigvee_{o \in \Omega} \mathbf{X}_o \phi$ to shorten our notations.

By the definition of $\mathbf{X}_\Omega \phi$, we obviously have $\sigma \models \mathbf{X}_\Omega \phi$ iff $\sigma_o[0] \in \Omega \wedge \sigma[1] \models \phi$. The usual next operator can be described as $\mathbf{X}\phi \equiv \mathbf{X}_\Theta \phi$. Thus, the logic PCTL* can be considered as a sublogic of POCTL*.

4.3 The Sublogics

An LTL formula together with a bound (QLS formula) can be interpreted over probabilistic models [2]. Recall that the logic PCTL* is a combination of PCTL

---

[3] This suffix $\sigma[1]$ is well-defined for we have previously assumed that the model does not contain any absorbing states.

and QLS. In PCTL, arbitrary combinations of state formulas are possible, but the path formulas consists of only the next and until operators. The logic LTL allows arbitrary combinations of path formulas but only propositional state formulas. This section introduces the sublogics POCTL, OLTL and QOS of POCTL*. They can also be considered as extensions of the logics PCTL, LTL and QLS where the next operator is equipped with an observation (or a set of observations) constraint.

POCTL. We define the logic POCTL as a sublogic of POCTL* by imposing the restriction on POCTL* formulas that every next and until operator ($\mathbf{X}, \mathcal{U}^{\leq n}$) should be immediately enclosed in the probabilistic operator $\mathcal{P}$. The syntax of state and belief state formulas is the same as POCTL*, and the path formulas are given by:

$$\phi := \mathbf{X}_\Omega \Phi \mid \Phi \mathcal{U}^{\leq n} \Phi$$

where $\Omega \subseteq \Theta$.

Since we have $\mathbf{X}\phi \equiv \mathbf{X}_\Theta \phi$, the logic PCTL is naturally a sublogic of POCTL. POCTL is a proper sublogic of POCTL*. For example, we let $a, a' \in AP$, then the formulas $\mathcal{P}_{<p}(\mathbf{XX}a)$ and $\mathcal{P}_{<p}(a\mathcal{U}(\mathbf{X}a'))$ are not valid POCTL formulas, but are valid POCTL* formulas.

OLTL. In OLTL, we allow arbitrary combinations of path formulas, but only propositional state formulas. Formally, OLTL formulas are the path formulas defined by:

$$\phi := a \mid \neg \phi \mid \phi \wedge \phi \mid \mathbf{X}_o \phi \mid \phi \mathcal{U}^{\leq n} \phi$$

QOS. Now we extend QLS to QOS (quantitative OLTL specification) which shall contribute to POCTL* model checking.

A QOS formula is a pair $(\phi, \trianglelefteq p)$ where ϕ is an OLTL formula, $\trianglelefteq \in \{\leq, <, \geq, >\}$ and $p \in [0,1]$. Let $\mathcal{H} = (S, \mathbf{P}, L, \Theta, \mu, \alpha)$ be an HMM with $s \in S$. The semantics of the QOS formula is given by:

$$\mathcal{H}, s \models (\phi, \trianglelefteq p) \iff \Pr_s(\phi) \trianglelefteq p$$

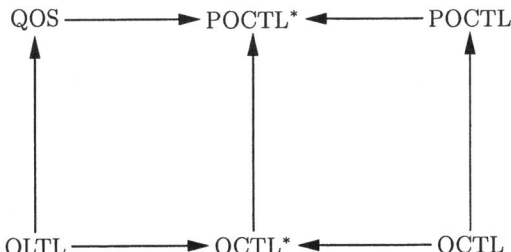

Fig. 3. Relationship of the logic POCTL* and its sublogics

The logics OCTL* and OCTL can be defined as extensions of CTL* and CTL, in which the next operator is equipped with an observation, and a set of observations respectively. The semantics of the sublogics are intuitively clear from the interpretation of POCTL*.

Relationship of POCTL and Its Sublogics.* Figure 3 shows an overview of the relationship of the logic POCTL* and its sublogics. There is an arrow from a logic A to another logic B if A is a proper sublogic of B. The logics in the upper part can be considered as the probabilistic counterpart of the corresponding one in the lower part.

4.4 Specifying Properties in POCTL*

First, we indicate that we cannot calculate an exact probability by a POCTL* formula, however, we can specify a bound on the probability measure instead. Actually, we do not need the exact values in most cases. To illustrate the expressiveness of POCTL*, we consider following properties:

- The probability that the next observation is *head* and then the model goes to state *fair* meets the bound < 0.2.

$$\mathcal{P}_{<0.2}(\mathbf{X}_{head} at_{fair})$$

This formula can be considered as a state formula or a belief state formula. A state (belief state) satisfies this formula if the probability calculated using the measure w. r. t. the state (belief state) meets the bound < 0.2.
- The probability is at most 0.05, that we eventually get an observation *head* and then move to state *fair*, whereas at any moment before we are either in state u_1 or state u_2.

$$\mathcal{P}_{\leq 0.05}((at_{u_1} \vee at_{u_2}) \,\mathcal{U}\, \mathbf{X}_{head} at_{fair})$$

- With probability at least 0.9, the model generates the observation sequence $(o_0, o_1, \ldots, o_n)$.

$$\mathcal{P}_{\geq 0.9}(\mathbf{X}_{o_0} \mathbf{X}_{o_1} \ldots \mathbf{X}_{o_n} tt)$$

- The probability that the state sequence $(s_0, s_1, \ldots, s_n)$ produces the observation sequence $(o_0, o_1, \ldots, o_n)$ is at most 0.1.

$$\mathcal{P}_{\leq 0.1}(s_0 \wedge \mathbf{X}_{o_0}(s_1 \wedge \mathbf{X}_{o_1}(\ldots (s_n \wedge \mathbf{X}_{o_n} tt)\ldots)))$$

where s denotes the atomic proposition that the system is now in state s.

5 Model Checking

In this section, we present model checking algorithms for the logics POCTL*, POCTL and QOS. The model checking algorithm for POCTL* follows the same lines as the one for PCTL* [2, 7, 6]. It will first be reduced to the QOS model checking problem. The latter can further be reduced to a probabilistic reachability analysis. To that end, we construct a Büchi automaton for a given OLTL formula. The POCTL model checking algorithm can be adapted from the one presented by Hansson & Jonsson [11].

5.1 POCTL* Formulas

Let $\mathcal{H} = (S, \mathbf{P}, L, \Theta, \mu, \alpha)$ be an HMM with $s \in S$, and Φ be a POCTL* formula. The POCTL* model checking problem is to check whether $\mathcal{H}, s \models \Phi$ (or $s \models \Phi$ for short). The model checking algorithm for POCTL* is an adaption of the one presented in [2] for PCTL*.

The algorithm is based on a recursive procedure that computes the sets $Sat(\Psi)$ for all state subformulas Ψ of Φ. The cases where Ψ is an atomic proposition or a negation or a conjunction is given by: $Sat(a) = \{s \in S \mid a \in L(s)\}$, $Sat(\neg\Psi_1) = S \backslash Sat(\Psi_1)$ and $Sat(\Psi_1 \wedge \Psi_2) = Sat(\Psi_1) \cap Sat(\Psi_2)$.

The case that Ψ is the probabilistic operator $\mathcal{P}_{\trianglelefteq p}(\phi)$ is more involved. By the semantics, it is equivalent to check whether $\mathrm{Pr}_{b_s}(\phi)$ meets the bound $\trianglelefteq p$, i.e., whether $\mathrm{Pr}_s(\phi) \trianglelefteq p$. Let $\Psi_1, \ldots, \Psi_k$ be the maximal state subformulas of ϕ. The sets $Sat(\Psi_i)$ can be calculated recursively. Then, we replace $\Psi_1, \ldots, \Psi_k$ by the new atomic propositions $n_1, \ldots, n_k$ and extend the label of state s by n_i if $n_i \in Sat(\Psi_i)$.

We replace the subformulas $\Psi_1, \ldots, \Psi_k$ by new atomic propositions $n_1, \ldots, n_k$. The so obtained path formula ϕ' is an OLTL formula, and obviously we have $\mathrm{Pr}_s(\phi) = \mathrm{Pr}_s(\phi')$. Now we apply the QOS model checking algorithm to calculate $\mathrm{Pr}_s(\phi')$, which will be discussed in Section 5.3. Hence, the complexity of the POCTL* model checking algorithm is dominated by the one for QOS.

Belief State. Now, we show how to check whether a belief state b satisfies a belief state formula ϵ, i.e., $b \models \epsilon$. The most interesting case is $\epsilon = \mathcal{P}_{\trianglelefteq p}(\phi)$ where ϕ is a POCTL* path formula. By definition,

$$b \models \mathcal{P}_{\trianglelefteq p}(\phi) \iff p_b(\phi) \trianglelefteq p \iff \sum_{s \in S} b(s) \mathrm{Pr}_s(\phi) \trianglelefteq p$$

therefore, it is sufficient to calculate $\mathrm{Pr}_s(\phi)$ for all $s \in S$.

5.2 POCTL Formulas

Let $\mathcal{H} = (S, \mathbf{P}, L, \Theta, \mu, \alpha)$ with $s \in S$, and Φ be a POCTL formula. The algorithm to check whether $s \models \Phi$ can be adapted from the one presented by Hansson & Jonsson [11]. In case Φ is of the form $a, \neg\Phi', \Phi_1 \wedge \Phi_2, \mathcal{P}(\Phi_1 \mathcal{U}^{\leq n} \Phi_2), \mathcal{P}(\Phi_1 \mathcal{U} \Phi_2)$, the set $Sat(\Phi)$ can be determined using the same strategy as for PCTL. Let $p \in [0, 1]$, $\Omega \subseteq \Theta$ and $\trianglelefteq \in \{\leq, <, \geq, >\}$. We only need to consider the case that $\phi = \mathcal{P}_{\trianglelefteq p}(\mathbf{X}_\Omega \Phi')$. We observe that

$$p_s(\mathbf{X}_\Omega \Phi') = \mu_s(\Omega) \cdot \sum_{s' \in Sat(\Phi')} \mathrm{P}(s, s')$$

where $\mu_s(\Omega) = \sum_{o \in \Omega} \mu_s(o)$ and the set $Sat(\Phi') = \{s \in S \mid s \models \Phi'\}$ can be recursively evaluated. Thus, $s \models \mathcal{P}_{\trianglelefteq p}(\mathbf{X}_\Omega \Phi')$ iff $p_s(\mathbf{X}_\Omega \Phi') \trianglelefteq p$.

5.3 QOS Formulas

This section presents the model checking algorithm for QOS formulas. We introduce two methods, an automaton based approach, which is based on the algorithm introduced by Baier et al [2, 4], and a direct method, where we reduce the problem to a PCTL* model checking problem over a DTMC, and apply the efficient algorithm presented by Courcoubetis et al [7].

An automaton based approach. The input is $\mathcal{H} = (S, \mathbf{P}, L, \Theta, \mu, \alpha)$ with $s \in S$ and a QOS formula $(\phi, \trianglelefteq p)$ where $p \in [0, 1]$. We shall check whether $\mathcal{H}, s \models (\phi, \trianglelefteq p)$. We first construct a Büchi automaton $\mathcal{A}_\phi$ for ϕ. This construction is an extension of the one presented by Gerth et al. [10] (for space reason, we present it in [24, Appendix A]). By the result of Safra [18, 19], the Büchi automaton can be translated to a deterministic Rabin automaton. Let $\mathcal{R}_\phi = (\Sigma, Q, q_{in}, \delta, U)$ denote the Rabin automaton for ϕ. (Note that $\Sigma = \mathcal{P}(AP) \times \Theta$.) Next, we build the product automaton $\mathcal{H} \times \mathcal{R}_\phi$. Finally, the problem to calculate the measure of paths in $Path^{\mathcal{H}}(s)$ satisfying ϕ is reduced to a probabilistic reachability analysis in the product automaton. The method we shall present is an adaption of the one introduced by Bianco & de Alfaro [4], where we follow the presentation in [2].

The product automaton $\mathcal{H} \times \mathcal{R}_\phi = (S', \mathbf{P}', L')$ is given by: $S' = S \times Q$, $\mathbf{P}'((s, q), (s', q')) = \mathbf{P}(s, s') \cdot \mu_{s'}(o)$ if $q' \in \delta(q, (L(s'), o))$ and 0 otherwise.

For $s \in S$ and $o \in \Theta$, we define $s_R = (s, \delta(q_{in}, (L(s), o)))$. Let σ denote the path $(s_0, o_0), (s_1, o_1) \ldots$ in $\mathcal{H}$. Since $\mathcal{R}_\phi$ is a deterministic automaton, we define the unique induced path $\sigma_R(s_0, q_0), (s_1, q_1), (s_2, q_2) \ldots$ in $\mathcal{H} \times \mathcal{R}_\phi$, where $q_0 = \delta(q_{in}, (L(s_0), o_0))$, $q_{i+1} = \delta(q_i, (L(s_{i+1}), o_{i+1}))$.

Theorem 4. *Let $P'_i = S \times P_i$ and $R'_i = S \times R_i$. We define $U' = \cup_{1 \leq j \leq r} U'_j$, where U'_j is the largest subset of P'_j such that, for all $u' \in U'_j$: $reach^{\mathcal{H} \times \mathcal{R}_\phi}(u') \subseteq U'_j$ and $reach^{\mathcal{H} \times \mathcal{R}_\phi}(u') \cap R'_j \neq \emptyset$. Then,*

$$\Pr_s^{\mathcal{H}}(\phi) = \sum_{o \in \Theta} \mu_s(o) \cdot \Pr_{s_R}^{\mathcal{H} \times \mathcal{R}_\phi}(reach(U'))$$

where $s_R = (s, \delta(q_{in}, (L(s), o)))$, and $\Pr_s^{\mathcal{H}}(\phi) = \Pr_s\{\sigma \in Path^{\mathcal{H}}(s) \mid \sigma \models \phi\}$ and $reach(U')$ denote the set of path which can reach U', i.e. $\{\sigma' \in Path^{\mathcal{H} \times \mathcal{R}_\phi}(s_R) \mid \exists i \text{ such that } \sigma'[i] \in U'\}$.

Proof. Let $\mathcal{C}((s, o_0), (s_1, o_1), \ldots, (s_n, o_n))$ be a basic cylinder set in $\mathcal{H}$ such that every path σ in $\mathcal{C}$ satisfies ϕ. The measure of $\mathcal{C}$ is $\mu_s(o_0) \prod_{i=1}^{n} \mathbf{P}(s_{i-1}, s_i) \mu_{s_i}(o_i)$. The induced unique cylinder set in $\mathcal{H} \times \mathcal{R}_\phi$ is $\mathcal{C}'((s, q_0), (s_1, q_1), \ldots, (s_n, q_n))$ where $q_0 = \delta(q_{in}, (L(s), o_0))$ and $q_{i+1} = \delta(q_i, (L(s_{i+1}), o_{i+1}))$ for $i = 1, \ldots, n$. Obviously, σ_R is in $\mathcal{C}'$. Since σ satisfies ϕ, the path $\pi = q_{in}, q_0, \ldots, q_n, \ldots$ must be an accepting path. Hence, there exists an i such that $\inf(\pi) \subseteq P_i$ and

$\inf(\pi) \cap R_i \neq \emptyset$. By the definition of U', σ_R must contain at least one state which belongs to U'.

By construction of $\mathcal{H} \times \mathcal{R}_\phi$, the measure of $\mathcal{C}'$ is simply $\prod_{i=1}^n \mathbf{P}(s_{i-1}, s_i) \mu_{s_i}(o_i)$. Since $\mathcal{C}$ is an arbitrary cylinder set of interest, the above result is true for all $o_0 \in \Theta$. Let C_1, C_2 be two different cylinder sets in $\mathcal{H}$. Obviously, either one cylinder set includes another, or they are disjoint. Hence, summing up over all possible observations, we are done. □

Complexity. In [24, Appendix A] we show that the Büchi automaton for the OLTL formula is exponential in the size of the formula. By the results of Safra [18, 19], the deterministic Rabin automaton for ϕ is double exponential in the size of the formula. So the overall complexity of the product automaton is linear in the size of the model, and double exponential in the size of the formula.

It thus remains to compute the reachability probability $\Pr_{s_R}^{\mathcal{H} \times R_\phi}(reach(U'))$ in the product automaton. To obtain this quantity, we can apply the method presented by de Alfaro [8, page 52]. The complexity is polynomial in the size of the product automaton.

A direct approach. The main idea of this approach is to construct a DTMC from the HMM, and transform the QOL formula ϕ to a QLS formula. Then, the original problem can be reduced to DTMC model checking problem.

We extend the set of atomic propositions by $AP' = AP \cup \{\Omega \mid \Omega \subseteq \Theta\}$. Given $\mathcal{H} = (S, \mathbf{P}, L, \Theta, \mu, \alpha)$ and a QOS formula $(\phi, \trianglelefteq p)$, we define the DTMC $\mathcal{D} = (S', \mathbf{P}', L')$ where $S' = S \times \Theta$, $\mathbf{P}'((s,o), (s',o')) = \mathbf{P}(s,s') \cdot \mu_{s'}(o')$ and $L'(s,o) = L(s) \cup \{\Omega \subseteq \Theta \mid o \in \Omega\}$. Furthermore, we define a QLS formula $(\phi', \trianglelefteq p)$ as follows: Let $\mathbf{X}_\Omega \psi$ be a subformula of ϕ, we replace it by $\Omega \wedge \mathbf{X}\psi$, where Ω is a new atomic proposition. We proceed this process repeatedly until there is no next formula indexed with observations.

Lemma 5. $p_s^{\mathcal{H}}(\phi) = \sum_{o \in \Theta} \mu_s(o) \cdot p_{(s,o)}^{\mathcal{D}}(\phi')$

Proof. Similar to Lemma 4. □

Complexity. The constructed DTMC can be, in the worst case, $\mathcal{O}(|S|^2 |\Theta|^2)$. We need still to calculate the probability measure of $\{\sigma \in Path^{\mathcal{D}} \mid \sigma \models \phi'\}$ in the DTMC. The optimal algorithm for that is given by Courcoubetis *et al* [7], and the complexity is polynomial in the size of the model, and exponential in the size of the formula.

In comparison to the other method, this method is single exponential in the size of the formula, but the DTMC suffers from the size $\mathcal{O}(|S|^2 |\Theta|^2)$.

5.4 Improving the Efficiency

In this section, we discuss some efficiency issues for some special POCTL* formulas. After that we give some further improvements.

The Formula $s_0 \wedge \mathbf{X}_{o_0}(s_1 \wedge \mathbf{X}_{o_1}(\ldots(s_n \wedge \mathbf{X}_{o_n} tt)\ldots))$. For state $s \in S$, we let s denote also the atomic propositions which asserts that the model resides in state s. Given a basic cylinder set $\mathcal{C}((s_0, o_0), \ldots, (s_n, o_n))$, we define a formula $\phi = s_0 \wedge \mathbf{X}_{o_0}(s_1 \wedge \mathbf{X}_{o_1}(\ldots(s_n \wedge \mathbf{X}_{o_n} tt)\ldots))$ which is called the characteristic formula of this basic cylinder set. Obviously, $\{\sigma \in Path \mid \sigma \models \phi\} = \mathcal{C}((s_0, o_0), \ldots, (s_n, o_n))$. Hence, to check whether $s \models \mathcal{P}_{\trianglelefteq p}(\phi)$ boils down to checking whether the probability measure of the basic cylinder set, i.e., $\mathrm{Pr}_s(\mathcal{C})$, meets the bound $\trianglelefteq p$.

The Formula $\mathbf{X}_{o_0}\mathbf{X}_{o_1}\ldots\mathbf{X}_{o_n} tt$. We define a path formula $\phi = \mathbf{X}_{o_0}\mathbf{X}_{o_1}\ldots\mathbf{X}_{o_n} tt$ given the cylinder set $\mathcal{C}(o_0, \ldots, o_n) = \{\sigma \in Path \mid \forall i \leq n.\sigma_o[i] = o_i\}$. Obviously, $\{\sigma \in Path \mid \sigma \models \phi\} = \mathcal{C}(o_0, \ldots, o_n)$, which implies that to check whether $\alpha \models \mathcal{P}_{\trianglelefteq p}(\phi)$ boils down to checking whether $\sum_{s \in S} \alpha(s) \mathrm{Pr}_s(\mathcal{C})$ meets the bound $\trianglelefteq p$. The value $\mathrm{Pr}_s(\mathcal{C})$ can be calculated using Forward-Backward method presented in [17], with complexity $\mathcal{O}(|S|^2 n)$.

Building the Automaton by Need. The set of states of the product automaton contains all pairs $(s, q) \in S \times Q$. In case Φ is a simple probabilistic operator, i.e., $\mathcal{P}_{\trianglelefteq p}(\phi)$ where there is no probabilistic operator in ϕ, we only need the states of the product automaton which are reachable from initial states s_R. So in this case we can construct the states of the product automaton as needed.

Reducing to POCTL Model Checking. Since the POCTL model checking algorithm is more efficient, we can use it to deal with QOS formulas of the form $(\phi \,\mathcal{U}\, \psi, \trianglelefteq p)$ (or $(\phi \,\mathcal{U}^{\leq n}\, \psi, \trianglelefteq p)$) where ϕ and ψ are POCTL* path formulas which can be verified recursively.

6 Conclusion and Future Work

6.1 Conclusion

In this paper, we have defined probability spaces (w.r.t. state and belief state) for a given HMM. We have presented the temporal logic POCTL* with which we can specify state-based, path-based and belief state-based properties over HMMs. With POCTL* one can specify properties not only over the underlying DTMC, but also over the set of processes producing observations. Finally, we have focused on the POCTL* model checking algorithm. The most interesting case is to deal with the probabilistic operator, and we have shown that this can be reduced to QOS model checking. Then, the QOS model checking problem is reduced to a probabilistic reachability analysis in the product automaton of the HMM and a deterministic Rabin automaton. The complexity of our model checking algorithm is polynomial in the size of the model and exponential in the length of the formula.

6.2 Future Work

In this section, we consider some interesting directions for future work.

HMDP. We plan to extend an HMM to a Hidden Markov decision process (HMDP) [4, 8] where probabilistic and nondeterministic choices coexist. In an HMM, a successor of a state s is selected probabilistically according to the transition matrix. On the contrary, in an HMDP, for a state s, one first selects a probabilistic distribution over actions nondeterministically. Then, a successor can be chosen probabilistically according to the selected distribution over actions.

The nondeterminism is resolved by *schedulers* [3] (called *strategy* in [4, 8], *adversary* in [2]). A scheduler η assigns a distribution over actions to a finite sequence of states (history). Given a scheduler η, one can select a successor of a state probabilistically, as in an HMM. Moreover, we can get a probability measure [4] $\Pr_s^\eta$ w.r.t. the scheduler η and a state s. Thus, the logic POCTL* can be extended to interpret properties over HMDPs in the following way:

$$s \models \mathcal{P}_{\trianglelefteq p}(\phi) \quad \text{iff} \quad \forall \eta. \Pr_s^\eta \{\sigma \in Path^\eta \mid \sigma \models \phi\} \trianglelefteq p$$

Since a belief state is a distribution over states, we can extend the probability measure w.r.t. s and η to the one w.r.t. a belief state and η. The semantics that a belief state satisfies a belief state formula can also be defined in a similar way. The model checking algorithm can be adapted from the one presented by de Alfaro for PCTL* formulas over MDPs.

HMDP with Fairness. Baier [2] extended the logic PCTL* to interpret properties over concurrent probabilistic systems (similar to MDPs) with fairness assumptions. She also presented a PCTL* model checking algorithm over concurrent probabilistic systems with fairness assumptions which is adapted from the one by de Alfaro. It could be extended to a POCTL* model checking algorithm over HMDPs with fairness assumptions.

Acknowledgements. The authors are grateful to Christel Baier (University of Bonn) and Frits Vaandrager (Radboud University Nijmegen) for helpful comments at an early state of the work presented in this paper.

References

1. Suzana Andova, Holger Hermanns, and Joost-Pieter Katoen. Discrete-time rewards model-checked. In *FORMATS, LNCS 2791:88-104*. Springer, 2003.
2. C. Baier. On Algorithmic Verification Methods for Probabilistic Systems, 1998. Habilitations- schrift zur Erlangung der venia legendi der Fakultät für Mathematik und Informatik, Universität Mannheim.
3. C. Baier, B.R. Haverkort, H. Hermanns, and J.-P. Katoen. Efficient computation of time-bounded reachability probabilities in uniformized continuous-time Markov decision processes. In *TACAS, LNCS 2988:61-76*. Springer, 2004.
4. A. Bianco and L. de Alfaro. Model Checking of Probabilistic and Nondeterministic Systems. In *FSTTCS, LNCS 1026:499-513*. Springer, 1995.
5. E. Birney. Hidden Markov models in biological sequence analysis. *IBM Journal of Research and Development*, 45(3):449-454, 2001.

6. C. Courcoubetis and M. Yannakakis. Verifying Temporal Properties of Finite-State Probabilistic Programs. In *FOCS:338-345*. IEEE Computer Society Press, October 1988.
7. C. Courcoubetis and M. Yannakakis. The Complexity of Probabilistic Verification. *Journal of the ACM*, 42(4):857–907, 1995.
8. L. de Alfaro. *Formal Verification of Probabilistic Systems*. PhD thesis, Stanford University, 1997. Technical report STAN-CS-TR-98-1601.
9. J.-M. François and G. Leduc. Mobility prediction's influence on QoS in wireless networks: A study on a call admission algorithm. In *3rd International Symposium on Modeling and Optimization in Mobile, Ad-Hoc and Wireless Networks*, pages 238–247. IEEE Computer Society, 2005.
10. R. Gerth, D. Peled, M.Y. Vardi, and P. Wolper. Simple On-the-fly Automatic Verification of Linear Temporal Logic. In *PSTV 38:3-18*. Chapman & Hall, 1995.
11. H. Hansson and B. Jonsson. A Logic for Reasoning about Time and Reliability. *Formal Aspects of Computing*, 6(5):512–535, 1994.
12. M. Hauskrecht. Value-Function Approximations for Partially Observable Markov Decision Processes. *Journal of Artificial Intelligence Research*, 13:33–94, 2000.
13. D. Jurafsky and J.H. Martin. *Speech and Language Processing: An Introduction to Natural Language Processing, Computational Linguistics, and Speech Recognition*. Prentice Hall, 2000.
14. R. D. Nicola and F. W. Vaandrager. Action versus state based logics for transition systems. In *Semantics of Systems of Concurrent Processes, LNCS 469:407-419*. Springer, 1990.
15. P.A. Pevzner. *Computational Molecular Biology: An Algorithmic Approach*. The MIT Press, 2000.
16. P. Poupart. Approximate Value-Directed Belief State Monitoring for Partially Observable Markov Decision Processes. Master's thesis, University of British Columbia, November 2000.
17. L.R. Rabiner. A Tutorial on Hidden Markov Models and Selected Applications in Speech Recognition. *Proceedings of the IEEE*, 77(2):257–286, February 1989.
18. S. Safra. On the complexity of ω-automata. In *FOCS*, pages 319–327, 1988.
19. S. Safra. Exponential determinization for ω-automata with strong-fairness acceptance condition. In *STOC*, pages 275–282, 1992.
20. K. Salamatian and S. Vaton. Hidden markov modeling for network communication channels. In *SIGMETRICS*, pages 92–101. ACM Press, 2001.
21. M. Y. Vardi and P. Wolper. An Automata-Theoretic Approach to Automatic Program Verification. In *LICS*, pages 332–345. IEEE Computer Society Press, June 1986.
22. J. A. Vlontzos and S. Y. Kung. Hidden Markov models for character recognition. *IEEE Transactions on Image Processing*, 1:539–543, October 1992.
23. P. Wolper, M. Y. Vardi, and A. P. Sistla. Reasoning about Infinite Computation Paths. In *FOCS '83*, pages 185–194. IEEE Computer Society Press, 1982.
24. L. Zhang, H. Hermanns, and D. N. Jansen. Logic and Model Checking for Hidden Markov Chais. AVACS Technical Report No. 6, SFB/TR 14 AVACS, May 2005. ISSN: 1860-9821, http://www.avacs.org.

Proving ∀μ-Calculus Properties with SAT-Based Model Checking*

Bow-Yaw Wang

Institute of Information Science, Academia Sinica,
Taipei, Taiwan

Abstract. In this paper, we present a complete bounded model checking algorithm for the universal fragment of μ-calculus. The new algorithm checks the completeness of bounded proof of each property on the fly and does not depend on prior knowledge of the completeness thresholds. The key is to combine both local and bounded model checking techniques and use SAT solvers to perform local model checking on finite Kripke structures. Our proof-theoretic approach works for any property in the specification logic and is more general than previous work on specific properties. We report experimental results to compare our algorithm with the conventional BDD-based algorithm.

1 Introduction

Due to the limitation of BDD-based model checking on large designs, SAT-based bounded model checking has become a supplementary verification technique in recent years [1, 2]. Different from model checking [3, 4], bounded model checking focuses on catching design flaws within a bounded number of steps, and therefore does not guarantee the design to be free from errors. Naturally, one wonders whether bounded model checking can be extended to be complete.

There is a bound (called *completeness threshold*) such that the absence of flaws within the completeness threshold implies the satisfiability of the property [1, 5]. One often uses over-approximations of the completeness threshold in practice since computing the exact value is hard. But redundant computation incurred by approximations may impede the performance. Promising alternatives are available for checking linear properties, where the completeness of bounded model checking can also be determined dynamically [6–9]. However, the dynamic completeness criteria for branching-time properties are still missing.

In this paper, we propose a new framework for proving temporal properties by bounded model checking. Similar to [6–9], our algorithm determines the completeness of bounded model checking on the fly to avoid redundant computation. We use the universal fragment of propositional μ-calculus as the formalism for property specification. With the standard embedding [10–12], linear- and fragments of branching-time temporal logics are subsumed by our framework. Our

---
* This work was supported in part by NSC grand NSC 93-2213-E-001-012-.

technique therefore opens up opportunities for developing new complete bounded model checking algorithms.

The key concept is to combine bounded and local model checking techniques. Local model checking (also known as tableau-based model checking) tries to find a proof for the property by exploring neighboring states [13–15]. The proof search in local model checking algorithms is not unlike those of bug hunting in bounded model checking: a flaw is nothing but a "local" proof of the negation of the given property. The completeness of the proof rules in local model checking ensures that a flaw can always be found in finite models, should one exist.

We therefore propose an algorithm that reduces the proof search in local model checking to Boolean satisfiability. Since the negation of any formula in the universal fragment of μ-calculus belongs to the existential fragment of μ-calculus, we look for design flaws by finding proofs for arbitrary formula in the fragment. For any formula in the fragment, we construct a Boolean formula for it. The satisfiability of the Boolean formula is shown to be equivalent to the existence of a bounded proof in local model checking. Additionally, we show that the unsatisfiability of a similar Boolean formula implies the absence of proofs. The latter formula allows our algorithm to check the completeness criterion dynamically. Since the criterion is proof-theoretic, it is valid for *all* properties in the specification logic. Our technique gives a proof-theoretic interpretation of the completeness criteria and is more general than those in [6, 7, 9].

A major advantage of our technique is to verify many more properties by the use of standard encodings. For instance, ∀CTL [10, 12] and the universal fragment of Fair CTL [16] can be verified by embedding them into the universal fragment of μ-calculus. Our framework gives a unified theory of completeness criteria, which cannot be found in previous works. Additionally, the verification of linear-time temporal logic can be reduced to checking fairness constraints by the automata-theoretic technique [11]. Our technique is also applicable for linear properties.

The remainder of this paper is organized as follows. After discussing related work in Section 1.1, preliminaries are given in Section 2. Section 3 recalls the local model checking proof rules. The main technical results are shown in Section 4. Experimental results are presented in Section 5. Finally, in Section 6, we present our conclusions and discuss the future work.

1.1 Related Work

The inductive method was originally proposed as a heuristic for proving properties in bounded model checking. Later, it was improved and made complete for safety [6, 7] and liveness [17] properties. In the complete inductive method, if the induction proves the property or the completeness criterion is met, the algorithm reports that the property is satisfied. Otherwise, it looks for design flaws within the current bound.

A more direct approach for LTL model checking is reported in [9]. The authors give characterizations for LTL formulae of the form $\neg Gp$, $\neg FG\neg p$, and $\neg Fp$. Using the automata-theoretic technique developed in [11], the LTL model checking problem is reduced to verifying $FG\neg p$ and solved in [9]. For special cases such as Gp and Fp, [9] shows how to verify these properties directly.

State traversal can be simulated by exploiting conflict analysis in SAT solvers as well [8]. Given two conflicting Boolean formulae A and B, an interpolant P of A and B is a formula that is implied by A but conflicts with B. If A represents the initial states and B represents the set of states that violate the property, their interpolants can be understood as under-approximations of "bad" states. The interpolation is then combined with bounded model checking to verify linear temporal properties in [8].

The reduction of proof search in local model checking to satisfiability can also be found in [18, 19], in which the authors reduce the local model checking problem to Presburger arithmetic for infinite-state systems. Due to the undecidability of the μ-calculus model checking problem on infinite-state systems, the completeness of the algorithms in [18, 19] is not the main concern of the authors. For the invariant and inevitable properties on finite-state systems, the present work extends and subsumes the complete algorithms in [20].

To the best of our knowledge, estimating the completeness threshold is still required in order to prove fragments of branching-time temporal logics in bounded model checking [1]. Ideally, one would like to apply the techniques in [6–9] to develop similar on-the-fly completeness criteria for branching-time temporal logics. However, the techniques used in [6–9] are based essentially on closely examining paths of interest. It is unclear whether the approach would work for branching-time temporal logics. Additionally, our proof-theoretic approach gives general completeness criteria for fragments of branching-time temporal logics, not only particular temporal properties.

2 Preliminaries

We use the universal fragment of μ-calculus as the specification logic for temporal properties [21]. A μ-calculus formula ψ is defined recursively as follows.

- Propositional variables (PV): $X, Y, Z, \ldots$;
- Atomic propositions (AP): $p, q, \ldots$;
- Boolean operators: $\neg \psi$, $\psi \wedge \psi'$;
- The modal existential next-state operator: $\Diamond \psi$;
- The least fixed-point operator: $\mu X.\psi$, where the bound propositional variable X occurs positively in ψ.

As usual, derived operators such as the disjunctive operator $\psi \vee \psi'$ ($\equiv \neg(\neg \psi \wedge \neg \psi')$), the modal universal next-state operator $\Box \psi$ ($\equiv \neg \Diamond \neg \psi$) and, the greatest fixed-point operator $\nu X.\psi$ ($\equiv \neg \mu X.\neg \psi[\neg X/X]$, where $\neg \psi[\neg X/X]$ is obtained by substituting $\neg X$ for X in $\neg \psi$) are used. A μ-calculus formula ψ is *normal* if all negations only apply to atomic propositions. The universal fragment of μ-calculus (denoted $\forall \mu$-calculus) formulae are those without modal existential next-state operators in their normal forms. Similarly, $\exists \mu$-calculus formulae are those without modal universal next-state operators. By α-conversion, it suffices to consider μ-calculus formula ψ whose nested bound propositional variables are distinct.

Let $\mathbb{B} = \{\text{false}, \text{true}\}$ be the Boolean domain and $\mathbb{N}$ the natural numbers (non-negative integers). A *state* (denoted by $\bar{r}, \bar{s}, \bar{t}, \ldots$) is a Boolean vector of size $n > 0$. Let V be a set of Boolean variables, and $\bar{u}, \bar{v}, \bar{w} \in V^n$ be vectors of Boolean variables of size n. Equivalently, we may think of a state as a *valuation* $[\![\bar{u}]\!]\rho$ for $\bar{u}$, where $\rho \in V \to \mathbb{B}$ is an assignment of Boolean variables. A *Kripke structure* is a tuple $K = (\mathbb{B}^n, I, \to, L)$, where $I \subseteq \mathbb{B}^n$ is the set of initial states, $\to \subseteq \mathbb{B}^n \times \mathbb{B}^n$ is the total transition relation, and $L : \mathbb{B}^n \to 2^{AP}$ is the labeling function that maps each state to the atomic propositions satisfied in that state. We write $\bar{s} \to \bar{t}$ for $(\bar{s}, \bar{t}) \in \to$.

Let $\epsilon \in PV \to 2^{\mathbb{B}^n}$ be an environment for propositional variables. Given a propositional variable X and a set of states R, the environment $\epsilon[X \mapsto R]$ assigns X to R, but keeps other propositional variables Y assigned to $\epsilon(Y)$. The semantic function $[\![\psi]\!]\epsilon \subseteq \mathbb{B}^n$ for the μ-calculus formula ψ and the environment ϵ is defined as follows.

$$[X]\epsilon = \epsilon(X)$$
$$[p]\epsilon = \{\bar{s} \in \mathbb{B}^n : p \in L(\bar{s})\}$$
$$[\neg\psi]\epsilon = \mathbb{B}^n \setminus [\psi]\epsilon$$
$$[\psi \wedge \psi']\epsilon = [\psi]\epsilon \cap [\psi']\epsilon$$
$$[\Diamond\psi]\epsilon = \{\bar{s} \in \mathbb{B}^n : \exists \bar{t} \in \mathbb{B}^n. \bar{s} \to \bar{t} \text{ and } \bar{t} \in [\psi]\epsilon\}$$
$$[\mu X.\psi]\epsilon = \bigcap \{R \subseteq \mathbb{B}^n : [\psi](\epsilon[X \mapsto R]) \subseteq R\}.$$

The characteristic functions of p, I, and $\to$ are denoted by χ_p, χ_I, and $\chi_\to$ respectively. Let $\bar{u}$ and $\bar{u}'$ be vectors of Boolean variables representing current and next states respectively. Then $\chi_p(\bar{u})$ is satisfied by ρ if and only if $[\![\bar{u}]\!]\rho$ is a state satisfying the atomic proposition p. Similarly, $\chi_I(\bar{u})$ is satisfied by an assignment ρ if and only if the state $[\![\bar{u}]\!]\rho$ is an initial state, and $\chi_\to(\bar{u}, \bar{u}')$ is satisfied by ρ if and only if the state $[\![\bar{u}]\!]\rho$ is followed by $[\![\bar{u}']\!]\rho$ in K.

Let ψ be a μ-calculus formula, $K = (\mathbb{B}^n, I, \to, L)$ a Kripke structure and $\bar{s}$ a state. We write $K, \bar{s} \models \psi$ if $\bar{s} \in [\psi]\emptyset$; if $K, \bar{s}_0 \models \psi$ for all initial states $\bar{s}_0 \in I$, we denote it by $K \models \psi$. The model checking problem is to determine whether $K \models \psi$.

In [13–15], several tableau-based μ-calculus model checking algorithms were developed. The proof rules in [13,14] were simplified in [22,15] by extending fixed point operators to:

$$\sigma X\{\bar{r}_0 \cdots \bar{r}_m\}\Phi,$$

where σ can be either of the fixed point operators and $\bar{r}_0, \ldots, \bar{r}_m$ are states. Intuitively, $\bar{r}_0, \ldots, \bar{r}_m$ record visited states in the fixed-point formulae. The semantics of the new operators are defined accordingly:

$$[\mu X\{\bar{r}_0 \cdots \bar{r}_m\}\psi]\epsilon = \bigcap \{R \subseteq \mathbb{B}^n : [\psi](\epsilon[X \mapsto R]) \setminus \{\bar{r}_0 \cdots \bar{r}_m\} \subseteq R\}$$
$$[\nu X\{\bar{r}_0 \cdots \bar{r}_m\}\psi]\epsilon = \bigcup \{R \subseteq \mathbb{B}^n : R \subseteq [\psi](\epsilon[X \mapsto R]) \cup \{\bar{r}_0 \cdots \bar{r}_m\}\}.$$

The *extended µ-calculus* uses extended fixed point operators instead. Note that $\sigma X\{\}\psi \equiv \sigma X.\psi$; hence, any µ-calculus formula can be transformed into an equivalent extended µ-calculus formula syntactically.

3 Proof Rules

Different from global model checking algorithms in [10, 12, 4], the algorithms developed in [13–15, 22] search for a proof for the given µ-calculus property at an initial state by exploring the Kripke structure locally. It is noted that the worst-case complexity of the tableau-based algorithms remains the same as the conventional algorithms [13]. However, the proof-theoretic algorithms would be more efficient if the property could be proved locally.

Figure 1 shows the proof rules for $\exists$µ-calculus model checking. Given a Kripke structure K, a state $\bar{s}$, and a µ-calculus formula ψ, a *judgment* is of the form $K, \bar{s} \vdash \psi$. Given a judgment, a *proof* is a tree constructed according to the proof rules in Figure 1. Note that the rules ($\neg\neg$), ($\vee$L), ($\vee$R), ($\neg\vee$), ($\wedge$), ($\neg\wedge$L), ($\neg\wedge$R), ($\Diamond$), ($\neg\Box$), (σ-Unroll), and ($\neg\sigma$-Unroll) reduce the current judgment to one or more judgments to be justified later. We therefore say a proof is *full* if all of its leaves are instances of the rules (AP), ($\neg$AP), (ν-Term), or ($\neg\mu$-Term).

Since we are interested in constructing Boolean formulae for $\exists$µ-calculus in this work, Figure 1 omits the corresponding rules for the universal modal operator, which are given in [13–15]. The full proof rules are sound and complete for finite Kripke structures:

Theorem 1. *([13–15]) Let $K = (\mathbb{B}^n, I, \rightarrow, L)$ be a Kripke structure, $\bar{s} \in \mathbb{B}^n$, and ψ a µ-calculus formula. Then*

$$K, \bar{s} \vdash \psi \text{ has a full proof if and only if } K, \bar{s} \models \psi.$$

4 Proof Search by SAT

To motivate our reduction of proof search to Boolean satisfiability, consider the safety property AGp. Suppose a flaw satisfying $EF\neg p (\equiv \neg AGp \equiv \mu X\{\}\neg p \vee \Diamond X)$ is found in one step. The corresponding Boolean formula generated by one of the complete inductive methods in [6] is

$$\chi_I(\bar{v}_0) \wedge \chi_\rightarrow(\bar{v}_0, \bar{v}_1) \wedge \neg\chi_p(\bar{v}_1) \wedge \bigwedge_{0 \leq i < j \leq 1} \bar{v}_i \neq \bar{v}_j. \tag{1}$$

Let the satisfying Boolean assignment be ρ. The following full proof for the judgment $K, [\![\bar{v}_0]\!]\rho \vdash \mu X\{\}\neg p \vee \Diamond X$ can be constructed by the proof rules in Figure 1,

$$\frac{p \in L(\bar{s})}{K, \bar{s} \vdash p} \text{ (AP)} \qquad \frac{p \notin L(\bar{s})}{K, \bar{s} \vdash \neg p} \text{ (}\neg\text{AP)}$$

$$\frac{K, \bar{s} \vdash \psi}{K, \bar{s} \vdash \neg\neg\psi} \text{ (}\neg\neg\text{)}$$

$$\frac{K, \bar{s} \vdash \psi}{K, \bar{s} \vdash \psi \vee \psi'} \text{ (}\vee\text{L)} \qquad \frac{K, \bar{s} \vdash \psi'}{K, \bar{s} \vdash \psi \vee \psi'} \text{ (}\vee\text{R)}$$

$$\frac{K, \bar{s} \vdash \neg\psi \quad K, \bar{s} \vdash \neg\psi'}{K, \bar{s} \vdash \neg(\psi \vee \psi')} \text{ (}\neg\vee\text{)}$$

$$\frac{K, \bar{s} \vdash \psi \quad K, \bar{s} \vdash \psi'}{K, \bar{s} \vdash \psi \wedge \psi'} \text{ (}\wedge\text{)}$$

$$\frac{K, \bar{s} \vdash \neg\psi}{K, \bar{s} \vdash \neg(\psi \wedge \psi')} \text{ (}\neg\wedge\text{L)} \qquad \frac{K, \bar{s} \vdash \neg\psi'}{K, \bar{s} \vdash \neg(\psi \wedge \psi')} \text{ (}\neg\wedge\text{R)}$$

$$\frac{K, \bar{t} \vdash \psi \quad \bar{s} \rightarrow \bar{t}}{K, \bar{s} \vdash \Diamond\psi} \text{ (}\Diamond\text{)} \qquad \frac{K, \bar{t} \vdash \neg\psi \quad \bar{s} \rightarrow \bar{t}}{K, \bar{s} \vdash \neg\Box\psi} \text{ (}\neg\Box\text{)}$$

$$\frac{\bar{s} \in \{\bar{r}_0 \cdots \bar{r}_m\}}{K, \bar{s} \vdash \nu X\{\bar{r}_0 \cdots \bar{r}_m\}\psi} \text{ (}\nu\text{-Term)}$$

$$\frac{K, \bar{s} \vdash \psi[\nu X\{\bar{r}_0 \cdots \bar{r}_m \bar{s}\}\psi/X] \quad \bar{s} \notin \{\bar{r}_0 \cdots \bar{r}_m\}}{K, \bar{s} \vdash \nu X\{\bar{r}_0 \cdots \bar{r}_m\}\psi} \text{ (}\nu\text{-Unroll)}$$

$$\frac{K, \bar{s} \vdash \neg\psi[\nu X\{\bar{r}_0 \cdots \bar{r}_m \bar{s}\}\psi/X] \quad \bar{s} \notin \{\bar{r}_0 \cdots \bar{r}_m\}}{K, \bar{s} \vdash \neg\nu X\{\bar{r}_0 \cdots \bar{r}_m\}\psi} \text{ (}\neg\nu\text{-Unroll)}$$

$$\frac{\bar{s} \in \{\bar{r}_0 \cdots \bar{r}_m\}}{K, \bar{s} \vdash \neg\mu X\{\bar{r}_0 \cdots \bar{r}_m\}\psi} \text{ (}\neg\mu\text{-Term)}$$

$$\frac{K, \bar{s} \vdash \neg\psi[\mu X\{\bar{r}_0 \cdots \bar{r}_m \bar{s}\}\psi/X] \quad \bar{s} \notin \{\bar{r}_0 \cdots \bar{r}_m\}}{K, \bar{s} \vdash \neg\mu X\{\bar{r}_0 \cdots \bar{r}_m\}\psi} \text{ (}\neg\mu\text{-Unroll)}$$

$$\frac{K, \bar{s} \vdash \psi[\mu X\{\bar{r}_0 \cdots \bar{r}_m \bar{s}\}\psi/X] \quad \bar{s} \notin \{\bar{r}_0 \cdots \bar{r}_m\}}{K, \bar{s} \vdash \mu X\{\bar{r}_0 \cdots \bar{r}_m\}\psi} \text{ (}\mu\text{-Unroll)}$$

Fig. 1. Proof Rules

where Γ and Δ stand for $[\![\bar{v}_1]\!]\rho \notin \{[\![\bar{v}_0]\!]\rho\}$ and $[\![\bar{v}_0]\!]\rho \rightarrow [\![\bar{v}_1]\!]\rho$ respectively:

$$\cfrac{\cfrac{\cfrac{\cfrac{p \notin L([\![\bar{v}_1]\!]\rho)}{K, [\![\bar{v}_1]\!]\rho \vdash \neg p} \text{ (}\neg\text{AP)}}{K, [\![\bar{v}_1]\!]\rho \vdash \neg p \vee \Diamond \mu X\{[\![\bar{v}_0]\!]\rho[\![\bar{v}_1]\!]\rho\}\neg p \vee \Diamond X} \text{ (}\vee\text{L)} \quad \Gamma}{\cfrac{K, [\![\bar{v}_1]\!]\rho \vdash \mu X\{[\![\bar{v}_0]\!]\rho\}\neg p \vee \Diamond X}{\cfrac{K, [\![\bar{v}_0]\!]\rho \vdash \Diamond \mu X\{[\![\bar{v}_0]\!]\rho\}\neg p \vee \Diamond X}{\cfrac{K, [\![\bar{v}_0]\!]\rho \vdash \neg p \vee \Diamond \mu X\{[\![\bar{v}_0]\!]\rho\}\neg p \vee \Diamond X}{K, [\![\bar{v}_0]\!]\rho \vdash \mu X\{\}\neg p \vee \Diamond X} \text{ (}\vee\text{R)}} \text{ (}\Diamond\text{)}} \text{ (}\mu\text{-Unroll)}} \text{ (}\mu\text{-Unroll)}} \Delta$$

It is easy to see that the Boolean formula $\chi_\to(\bar{v}_0, \bar{v}_1)$ in (1) corresponds to the second antecedent of the rule ($\Diamond$), and the formula $\bigwedge_{0 \leq i < j \leq 1} \bar{v}_i \neq \bar{v}_j$ to the second antecedent of the rule (μ-Unroll). Finally, the antecedent of rule ($\neg$AP) is discharged by the satisfiability of $\neg\chi_p(\bar{v}_1)$. Roughly, there is a Boolean subformula for each application of the proof rule ($\neg$AP), ($\Diamond$), and (μ-Unroll) respectively. We generalize the idea and construct a Boolean formula for each rule in Figure 1 so that the satisfiability of the Boolean formula is equivalent to the existence of subproofs.

A syntactic extension of μ-calculus formulae is needed in the following presentation. Consider the formula $\sigma X\{\bar{r}_0 \cdots \bar{r}_m\}\psi$, where $\bar{r}_0 \cdots \bar{r}_m$ are states. Since states $\bar{r}_i$'s are denoted by variable vectors $\bar{v}_i$'s to be determined by SAT solvers, we allow the syntactic extension $\sigma X\{\bar{v}_0 \cdots \bar{v}_m\}\psi$ in our construction. Formulae constructed by Boolean operators, modal operators, and the syntactic extension of fixed point operators are called *schematic μ-calculus* formulae. If ρ is an assignment to Boolean variables, define

$$[\![p]\!]\rho = p$$
$$[\![X]\!]\rho = X$$
$$[\![\neg\varphi]\!]\rho = \neg[\![\varphi]\!]\rho$$
$$[\![\varphi \vee \varphi']\!]\rho = [\![\varphi]\!]\rho \vee [\![\varphi']\!]\rho$$
$$[\![\varphi \wedge \varphi']\!]\rho = [\![\varphi]\!]\rho \wedge [\![\varphi']\!]\rho$$
$$[\![\Diamond\varphi]\!]\rho = \Diamond[\![\varphi]\!]\rho$$
$$[\![\Box\varphi]\!]\rho = \Box[\![\varphi]\!]\rho$$
$$[\![\sigma X\{\bar{v}_0 \cdots \bar{v}_m\}\varphi]\!]\rho = \sigma X\{[\![\bar{v}_0]\!]\rho \cdots [\![\bar{v}_m]\!]\rho\}[\![\varphi]\!]\rho.$$

The mapping $[\![\bullet]\!]\rho$ assigns states to variable vectors appearing in a schematic μ-calculus formula and thereby yielding an extended μ-calculus formula. We say an extended μ-calculus formula ψ is an *instance* of a schematic μ-calculus formula φ if there is an assignment ρ such that $[\![\varphi]\!]\rho = \psi$.

Let $K = (\mathbb{B}^n, I, \to, L)$ be a Kripke structure, $\bar{u} \in V^n$ and $d \in \mathbb{N}$. Figure 2 shows the translation rules to construct a Boolean formula $\Theta_K(\bar{u}, \varphi, d)$ for any schematic $\exists\mu$-calculus formula φ. Intuitively, the vector of Boolean variables $\bar{u}$ corresponds to the current state, φ the sub-property to be fulfilled at the current state, and d the bound of unrolling. The translation ensures that the satisfiability of the Boolean formula $\Theta_K(\bar{u}, \varphi, d)$ witnessed by the assignment ρ is equivalent to the existence of proof for $[\![\varphi]\!]\rho$ at state $[\![\bar{u}]\!]\rho$. For Boolean and next-state modal operators, consider the rule ($\neg\Box$) as an example. If there is a proof for $[\![\neg\Box\varphi]\!]\rho$ at state $[\![\bar{u}]\!]\rho$, then there is a proof for $[\![\neg\varphi]\!]\rho$ at state $[\![\bar{u}']\!]\rho$ for some $[\![\bar{u}']\!]\rho$ with $[\![\bar{u}]\!]\rho \to [\![\bar{u}']\!]\rho$. The corresponding Boolean formula is therefore $\chi_\to(\bar{u}, \bar{u}') \wedge \Theta_K(\bar{u}', \neg\varphi, d)$. Other rules can be derived similarly.

For proof of correctness, note that the unrolling of fixed-point subformulae increases the length of a formula. Induction on the lengths of formulae would not work. The following definition is needed in our doubly-inductive proof:

$\Theta_K(\bar{u}, \nu X\{\bar{v}_0 \ldots \bar{v}_m\}\varphi, d) =$
$$\begin{cases} (\bigwedge_{k=0}^{m} \bar{u} \neq \bar{v}_k) \Leftrightarrow c_i & \text{if } d = 0 \\ (\bigvee_{k=0}^{m} \bar{u} = \bar{v}_k) \vee \Theta_K(\bar{u}, \varphi[\nu X\{\bar{v}_0 \ldots \bar{v}_m \bar{u}\}\varphi/X], d-1) & \text{if } d \neq 0 \end{cases}$$
where $c_i \in V$ is a fresh Boolean variable

$\Theta_K(\bar{u}, \neg\nu X\{\bar{v}_0 \ldots \bar{v}_m\}\varphi, d) =$
$$\begin{cases} (\bigwedge_{k=0}^{m} \bar{u} \neq \bar{v}_k) \wedge c_i & \text{if } d = 0 \\ (\bigwedge_{k=0}^{m} \bar{u} \neq \bar{v}_k) \wedge \Theta_K(\bar{u}, \neg\varphi[\nu X\{\bar{v}_0 \ldots \bar{v}_m \bar{u}\}\varphi/X], d-1) & \text{if } d \neq 0 \end{cases}$$
where $c_i \in V$ is a fresh Boolean variable

$\Theta_K(\bar{u}, \mu X\{\bar{v}_0 \ldots \bar{v}_m\}\varphi, d) =$
$$\begin{cases} (\bigwedge_{k=0}^{m} \bar{u} \neq \bar{v}_k) \wedge c_i & \text{if } d = 0 \\ (\bigwedge_{k=0}^{m} \bar{u} \neq \bar{v}_k) \wedge \Theta_K(\bar{u}, \varphi[\mu X\{\bar{v}_0 \ldots \bar{v}_m \bar{u}\}\varphi/X], d-1) & \text{if } d \neq 0 \end{cases}$$
where $c_i \in V$ is a fresh Boolean variable

$\Theta_K(\bar{u}, \neg\mu X\{\bar{v}_0 \ldots \bar{v}_m\}\varphi, d) =$
$$\begin{cases} (\bigwedge_{k=0}^{m} \bar{u} \neq \bar{v}_k) \Leftrightarrow c_i & \text{if } d = 0 \\ (\bigvee_{k=0}^{m} \bar{u} = \bar{v}_k) \vee \Theta_K(\bar{u}, \neg\varphi[\mu X\{\bar{v}_0 \ldots \bar{v}_m \bar{u}\}\varphi/X], d-1) & \text{if } d \neq 0 \end{cases}$$
where $c_i \in V$ is a fresh Boolean variable

$\Theta_K(\bar{u}, p, d) = \chi_p(\bar{u})$

$\Theta_K(\bar{u}, \neg p, d) = \neg\chi_p(\bar{u})$

$\Theta_K(\bar{u}, \neg\neg\varphi, d) = \Theta_K(\bar{u}, \varphi, d)$

$\Theta_K(\bar{u}, \varphi \wedge \varphi', d) = \Theta_K(\bar{u}, \varphi, d) \wedge \Theta_K(\bar{u}, \varphi', d)$

$\Theta_K(\bar{u}, \neg(\varphi \wedge \varphi'), d) = \Theta_K(\bar{u}, \neg\varphi, d) \vee \Theta_K(\bar{u}, \neg\varphi', d)$

$\Theta_K(\bar{u}, \varphi \vee \varphi', d) = \Theta_K(\bar{u}, \varphi, d) \vee \Theta_K(\bar{u}, \varphi', d)$

$\Theta_K(\bar{u}, \neg(\varphi \vee \varphi'), d) = \Theta_K(\bar{u}, \neg\varphi, d) \wedge \Theta_K(\bar{u}, \neg\varphi', d)$

$\Theta_K(\bar{u}, \Diamond\varphi, d) = \chi_\rightarrow(\bar{u}, \bar{u}') \wedge \Theta_K(\bar{u}', \varphi, d)$
where $\bar{u}' \in V^n$ is a vector of fresh Boolean variables

$\Theta_K(\bar{u}, \neg\Box\varphi, d) = \chi_\rightarrow(\bar{u}, \bar{u}') \wedge \Theta_K(\bar{u}', \neg\varphi, d)$
where $\bar{u}' \in V^n$ is a vector of fresh Boolean variables

Fig. 2. Translation Rules

Definition 1. *Let Γ be a full proof. The* unrolling depth *of a leaf is the number of unrolling rules applied along the path from the root of Γ to the leaf. The unrolling depth of Γ is the maximum over the unrolling depths of all leaves.*

Since the proof of $\neg(\psi \vee \psi')$ is established by the proofs of $\neg\psi$ and $\neg\psi'$, naive structural induction is not applicable in the inner induction. Instead, the following ordering of extended μ-calculus formulae is used:

Definition 2. *Let ψ be an extended μ-calculus formula, then define*

$$\omega(p) = \omega(X) = \omega(\sigma X\{\bar{r}_0 \cdots \bar{r}_m\}\psi) = 0$$
$$\omega(\neg\psi) = \omega(\Diamond\psi) = \omega(\Box\psi) = \omega(\psi) + 1$$
$$\omega(\psi \vee \psi') = \omega(\psi \wedge \psi') = \max(\omega(\psi), \omega(\psi')) + 1$$

Since the function $\omega(\bullet)$ can be extended to schematic μ-calculus formulae straightforwardly, we abuse the notation and write $\omega(\varphi)$ when φ is a schematic μ-calculus formula as well.

Our results can be demonstrated in three steps. First, we consider proofs without unrolling fixed-point subformulae (Lemma 1 and 2). Using atomic propositions and fixed-point subformulae as the basis of inner induction, it can be shown that the existence of proofs is equivalent to the satisfiability of a Boolean formula ($\Omega_K(\bar{u}, \psi, d)$ in Theorem 2). Finally, the unsatisfiability of another Boolean formula ($\Lambda_K(\bar{u}, \psi, d)$ in Theorem 3) can be shown to imply the absence of proofs.[1]

Lemma 1. *Consider any schematic $\exists \mu$-calculus formula φ recursively constructed by $\neg\neg\varphi', \varphi' \wedge \varphi'', \neg(\varphi' \wedge \varphi''), \varphi' \vee \varphi'', \neg(\varphi' \vee \varphi''), \Diamond\varphi'$, or $\neg\Box\varphi'$. Let $\bar{u} \in V^n$ be a vector of Boolean variables and $d \in \mathbb{N}$. Suppose*

- *for all φ' with $\omega(\varphi') < \omega(\varphi)$, if $\Theta_K(\bar{u}, \varphi', d)$ is satisfied by some Boolean assignment ρ', then there is a full proof of unrolling depth d for $\psi' = [\![\varphi']\!]\rho'$ at $\bar{s}' = [\![\bar{u}]\!]\rho'$; and*
- *$\Theta_K(\bar{u}, \varphi, d)$ is satisfied by some Boolean assignment ρ.*

Then, there is a full proof of unrolling depth d for $\psi = [\![\varphi]\!]\rho$ at $\bar{s} = [\![\bar{u}]\!]\rho$.

Lemma 2. *Consider any extended $\exists \mu$-calculus formula ψ recursively constructed by $\neg\neg\psi', \psi' \wedge \psi'', \neg(\psi' \wedge \psi''), \psi' \vee \psi'', \neg(\psi' \vee \psi''), \Diamond\psi'$, or $\neg\Box\psi'$. Let φ be a schematic $\exists\mu$-calculus formula, $\bar{u} \in V^n$ a vector of Boolean variables, and $d \in \mathbb{N}$. Suppose*

- *ψ is an instance of φ;*
- *for all ψ' with $\omega(\psi') < \omega(\psi)$, if there is a full proof of unrolling depth d for ψ' at $\bar{s}'$ and ψ' is an instance of φ', then $\Theta_K(\bar{u}, \varphi', d)$ is satisfied by some Boolean assignment ρ' with $[\![\varphi']\!]\rho' = \psi'$ and $[\![\bar{u}]\!]\rho' = \bar{s}'$; and*
- *there is a full proof of unrolling depth d for ψ at $\bar{s}$.*

Then, $\Theta(\bar{u}, \varphi, d)$ is satisfied by some Boolean assignment ρ with $[\![\varphi]\!]\rho = \psi$ and $[\![\bar{u}]\!]\rho = \bar{s}$.

Lemmas 1 and 2 establish the correspondence between the satisfiability of Boolean formulae and proofs without further unrolling. The following lemma states that the required schematic μ-calculus formula φ in Lemma 2 does indeed exist.

Lemma 3. *Given a proof of an $\exists \mu$-calculus formula at state $\bar{s}_0$, if a judgment $K, \bar{s} \vdash \psi$ occurs in the proof, there is a schematic $\exists \mu$-calculus formula φ such that ψ is an instance of φ.*

For the translation of fixed-point formulae, consider $\nu X\{\bar{v}_0 \cdots \bar{v}_m\}\varphi$ as an example. If there is a proof of unrolling depth d for $[\![\nu X\{\bar{v}_0 \cdots \bar{v}_m\}\varphi]\!]\rho$ at $[\![\bar{u}]\!]\rho$,

---

[1] For the proofs of technical results, please see [23].

then either $[\![\bar{u}]\!]\rho = [\![\bar{v}_k]\!]\rho$ for some $0 \leq k \leq m$, or $[\![\bar{u}]\!]\rho \neq [\![\bar{v}_k]\!]\rho$ for all $0 \leq k \leq m$ and there is a proof of unrolling depth $d-1$ for $[\![\varphi[\nu X\{\bar{v}_0\cdots\bar{v}_m\bar{u}\}\varphi/X]]\!]\rho$ at $[\![\bar{u}]\!]\rho$. Thus, we have

$$\Theta_K(\bar{u},\nu X\{\bar{v}_0\cdots\bar{v}_m\}\varphi,d) = \bigvee_{k=0}^{m} \bar{u}=\bar{v}_k \vee \Theta_K(\bar{u},\varphi[\nu X\{\bar{v}_0\cdots\bar{v}_m\bar{u}\}\varphi/X],d-1).$$

Now suppose the number of unrolling has reached the limit ($d=0$). The proof of $[\![\nu X\{\bar{v}_0\cdots\bar{v}_m\}\varphi]\!]\rho$ may be full at $[\![\bar{u}]\!]\rho$, or need be justified by further unrolling. In the translation rule

$$\Theta_K(\bar{u},\nu X\{\bar{v}_0\cdots\bar{v}_m\}\varphi,0) = (\bigwedge_{k=0}^{m} \bar{u}\neq\bar{v}_k) \Leftrightarrow c_i,$$

the fresh variable c_i indicates which of the two cases occurs. If c_i is set to false, then $\bigvee_{k=0}^{m}\bar{u}=\bar{v}_k$ must be true and the proof would be full at $[\![\bar{u}]\!]\rho$. On the other hand, if c_i is true, it implies that $\bigwedge_{k=0}^{m}\bar{u}\neq\bar{v}_k$. The proof need be justified by further unrolling.

We call the fresh Boolean variable c_i used in the translation of $\sigma X\{\bar{v}_0\cdots\bar{v}_m\}\varphi$ (or $\neg\sigma X\{\bar{v}_0\cdots\bar{v}_m\}\varphi$) an *expansion variable*. The following theorem states that the existence of proofs and the satisfiability of certain Boolean formulae are equivalent.

Theorem 2. *Let $\bar{u}$ be a vector of Boolean variables, $d \in \mathbb{N}$, ψ an $\exists\mu$-calculus formula, and $c_0,\ldots,c_\ell$ the expansion variables in $\Theta_K(\bar{u},\psi,d)$. Define $\Omega_K(\bar{u},\psi,d)$ to be*

$$\Theta_K(\bar{u},\psi,d) \wedge \bigwedge_{i=0}^{\ell} \neg c_i.$$

- *If $\Omega_K(\bar{u},\psi,d)$ is satisfied by ρ, then there is a full proof of unrolling depth d for ψ at $\bar{s} = [\![\bar{u}]\!]\rho$.*
- *If there is a full proof of unrolling depth d for ψ at $\bar{s}$, then $\Omega_K(\bar{u},\psi,d)$ is satisfied by ρ with $[\![\bar{u}]\!]\rho = \bar{s}$.*

With a predetermined completeness threshold CT for the $\exists\mu$-calculus formula ψ and Kripke structure K, the satisfiability of $\Omega_K(\bar{u},\psi,CT)$ is equivalent to the existence of a full proof for ψ by Theorem 2. Hence, we have a complete algorithm for $\forall\mu$-calculus properties using completeness thresholds. Since $\forall\mu$-calculus is more expressive than $\forall$CTL, our construction subsumes those in [1].

Determining exact completeness thresholds, however, is hard. We prefer an algorithm that does not use completeness thresholds, but determines the completeness of proofs on the fly. Recall that the expansion variables c_i's are false in Theorem 2. This indicates that proofs do not need further unrolling. If we assume the subproofs of all unjustified fixed-point subformulae indeed exist by setting expansion variables to true, the unsatisfiability of the modified Boolean formula implies the absence of proof with additional unrolling. The following theorem gives us a completeness criterion in the flavor of [6,9]:

Theorem 3. *Let $\bar{u}$ be a vector of Boolean variables, $d \in \mathbb{N}$, ψ an $\exists\mu$-calculus formula, and $c_0, \ldots, c_\ell$ the expansion variables in $\Theta_K(\bar{u}, \psi, d)$. Define $\Lambda_K(\bar{u}, \psi, d)$ to be*

$$\Theta_K(\bar{u}, \psi, d) \wedge \bigwedge_{i=0}^{\ell} c_i.$$

If there is a full proof of unrolling depth greater than d for ψ at the state $\bar{s}$, then $\Lambda_K(\bar{u}, \psi, d)$ is satisfied by some Boolean assignment ρ with $[\![\bar{u}]\!]\rho = \bar{s}$

Theorems 2 and 3 are summarized by the algorithm in Figure 3. The algorithm searches proofs incrementally. In each iteration, it first checks whether there is a full proof. If so, it reports "$K, [\![\bar{u}]\!]\rho \vdash \neg\psi$" where ρ is a satisfying assignment. Otherwise, it checks whether full proofs may exist with more unrolling. If not, it reports "ψ is satisfied." Else, the loop is repeated by incrementing the number of unrolling. Observe that the expansion variable c_i forces the condition $\bigwedge_{k=0}^{m} \bar{u} \neq \bar{v}_k$ in $\Theta_K(\bar{u}, \psi, d)$ to be satisfied for each unrolling of fixed-point subformula. Since the number of states is finite, $\bigwedge_{k=0}^{m} \bar{u} \neq \bar{v}_k$ will be unsatisfiable after a finite number of unrolling. By Theorem 3, we conclude that there is no full proof.

Analysis. By generalizing the formula $\sigma X\{\}(\Diamond X \vee \sigma Y\{\}\Diamond(Y \vee X))$, it is easy to see that our construction requires $O(n2^d)$ Boolean variables in general. However,

>Let ψ be an $\forall\mu$-calculus formula
>$d \leftarrow 0$
>**loop**
>   **if** $I(\bar{u}) \wedge \Omega_K(\bar{u}, \neg\psi, d)$ is satisfied by ρ **then**
>   report "$K, [\![\bar{u}]\!]\rho \vdash \neg\psi$"
>   **if** $I(\bar{u}) \wedge \Lambda_K(\bar{u}, \neg\psi, d)$ is unsatisfiable **then**
>   reports "ψ is satisfied"
> $d \leftarrow d+1$
>**end**

Fig. 3. An Algorithm for Checking $\forall\mu$-Calculus Properties

if we consider $\forall$CTL properties, it can be shown that our algorithm requires $O(nd^\kappa)$ Boolean variables where κ is the maximal depth of nested temporal operators in the $\forall$CTL property.

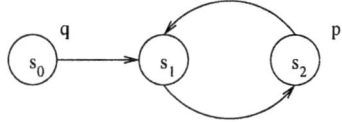

Fig. 4. A Simple Kripke Structure

As an example, consider the sample Kripke structure in Figure 4. The labels p and q denote $L(s_0) = \{q\}$, $L(s_2) = \{p\}$, but $L(s_1) = \emptyset$. Let Ψ stand for $\nu Y\{\}p \wedge \Box Y$. Suppose we wish to check whether $\neg q \vee (\mu X\{\}\Psi \vee \Box X)$ is satisfied by the Kripke structure. The corresponding Boolean formula for $\neg(\neg q \vee (\mu X\{\}\Psi \vee \Box X))$ is: (for detailed derivation, please see [23])

$$\Theta_K(\bar{u}, \neg(\neg q \vee (\mu X\{\}\Psi \vee \Box X)), 2))$$
$$= \chi_q(\bar{u}) \wedge (\neg\chi_p(\bar{u}) \vee (\chi_\rightarrow(\bar{u}, \bar{w}) \wedge (\bar{w} \neq \bar{u} \wedge c))) \wedge$$
$$(\chi_\rightarrow(\bar{u}, \bar{v}) \wedge (\bar{v} = \bar{u} \vee (c' \wedge (\chi_\rightarrow(\bar{v}, \bar{x}) \wedge ((\bar{x} \neq u \wedge \bar{x} \neq \bar{v}) \Leftrightarrow c'')))))$$

It is easy to see that there is no satisfying assignment for $\Omega_K(\bar{u}, \neg(\neg q \vee (\mu X\{\}\Psi \vee \Box X)), 2)$. By Theorem 2, there is no counterexample at unrolling depth 2. On the other hand, take the assignment ρ, where $[\![\bar{u}]\!]\rho = s_0$, $[\![\bar{v}]\!]\rho = s_1$, $[\![\bar{x}]\!]\rho = s_2$, and $[\![c]\!]\rho = [\![c']\!]\rho = [\![c'']\!]\rho =$ true. It is straightforward to verify that ρ is a satisfying assignment for $\Lambda_K(\bar{u}, \neg(\neg q \vee (\mu X\{\}\Psi \vee \Box X)), 2)$. Hence there may be a full proof of unrolling depth greater than 2 for $\neg(\neg q \vee (\mu X\{\}\Psi \vee \Box X))$ by Theorem 3.

5 Experimental Results

We are interested in the analysis of an n-process agreement protocol. Initially, process i has a random local bit v_i. All processes collect and distribute information with one another concurrently. At the end of the protocol, they will have the same value assigned to their local bits. In case of system failure, the faulty process stops updating its local bit nor exchanging information with others.

In addition to the local bit v_i, a program counter pc_i is used to indicate the current status (normal, failed, or decided) of process i. Firstly, we are interested in knowing whether all processes have agreed on their private bits when they all make their decisions. We therefore check that the following predicate is indeed invariant in the protocol:

$$good_n \triangleq (\bigwedge_{i=1}^{n} pc_i = decided) \Rightarrow ((\bigwedge_{i=1}^{n} v_i) \vee (\bigwedge_{i=1}^{n} \neg v_i))$$

Secondly, we verify the following CTL property in the protocol:

$$up_n \triangleq AG(v_1 \Rightarrow AF((\bigwedge_{i=1}^{n} pc_i = decided) \Rightarrow (\bigwedge_{i=1}^{n} v_i)))$$

The property up_n states that if the local bit of process 1 is true, then all computation paths will eventually make all local bits to be true when all processes decide. It is impossible to turn them back to be false in the protocol.

Thirdly, we verify that either all processes decide their local bits or some of them have failure almost surely along all computation. It can be specified by the following LTL formula:

$$ltl\_stable_n \stackrel{\triangle}{=} \Diamond(\Box((\bigwedge_{i=1}^{n} pc_i = decided) \vee (\bigvee_{i=1}^{n} pc_i = failed)))$$

In other words, no process can stay in a normal but undecided state forever. A weaker but similar property can be specified in Fair CTL. We now consider fair paths where no process is in the failed state infinitely often ($\Psi = \bigwedge_{i=1}^{n} F^{\infty}(pc_i \neq failed)$ in [10]). We would like to know whether all parties will decide their local bits eventually for all computation. In FCTL, we can specify the property as follows.

$$fctl\_stable_n \stackrel{\triangle}{=} A_\Psi F \bigwedge_{i=1}^{n} pc_i = decided$$

It is straightforward to rewrite the properties $good_n$, up_n, and $fctl\_stable_n$ in $\forall\mu$-calculus by standard encoding. For the LTL property ltl_stable_n, we apply the technique reported in [12, 24] and verify the existence of fair paths satisfying a $\forall\mu$-calculus formula. Observe that the completeness criteria for these properties are uniformly obtained by our framework. Once the property is rewritten as a $\forall\mu$-calculus formula, our proof-theoretic technique is able to verify it by any SAT solver.

Figure 5 compares the performance of our algorithm with the conventional BDD-based μ-calculus model checking algorithm. In our experiments, we use the CUDD package (release 2.4.0) with the sifting algorithm to implement the BDD-based algorithm. The zchaff SAT solver (release November 15th, 2004) is used as our SAT solver. All experiments were conducted on a Linux workstation (Pentium 4 2.8GHz with 2 GB memory).

Our experiments show that BDD-based algorithms perform consistently for different properties. If the BDD model representation can be built, these four properties can be verified with similar cost. On the other hand, the performance of SAT-based algorithm differs significantly in these properties. This is due to the fact that our algorithm requires different number of variables for these properties. It therefore does not perform so uniformly for various properties.

	$good_n$		up_n		ltl_stable_n		$fctl\_stable_n$	
n	BDD	SAT	BDD	SAT	BDD	SAT	BDD	SAT
3	0.13	0.77	0.19	0.99	0.2	2.33	0.11	7.36
4	1.2	1.44	1.06	4.09	2.80	10.76	1.36	31.00
5	11.91	3.86	10.55	9.45	17.21	29.12	12.95	112.82
6	17.44[2]	9.43	15.09[2]	34.94	15.19[2]	61.12	9.69[2]	232.63
7	timeout	18.23	timeout	75.86	timeout	157.21	timeout	553.02

(verification time in seconds)

Fig. 5. Experimental Results

---

[2] CUDD runs out of time with the sifting algorithm. The data is obtained without dynamic variable ordering.

For the invariant property $good_n$, our SAT-based algorithm is better than BDD-based algorithm for $n \geq 5$. For branching-time properties (up_n, ltl_stable_n, and $fctl\_stable_n$), the BDD-based algorithm cannot finish in 10 minutes for $n = 7$. With our algorithm, we are able to verify all these properties within 10 minutes. Surprisingly, our SAT-based algorithm performs better than BDD-based algorithm for some branching-time properties in this experiment.

6 Conclusion and Future Work

A complete SAT-based $\forall\mu$-calculus model checking algorithm is presented in the paper. Unlike previous works on proving branching-time temporal logics, our algorithm does not depend on completeness thresholds. Instead, it determines the completeness of proofs on the fly. The novelty of the new algorithm is that it combines both local and bounded model checking, and essentially reduces proof search in local model checking to Boolean satisfiability.

Our technique uses a proof-theoretic approach to develop completeness criteria. We feel our technique may give new insights into devising complete SAT-based model checking algorithms. Currently, it is unclear whether induction or interpolation can be applied in our framework. It would be interesting to have proof-theoretic interpretations of these heuristics as well.

Our experimental results suggest that our algorithm may perform better than a typical BDD-based model checker in some cases. In the future, we would like to conduct more experiments to support our preliminary findings.

Acknowledgments. The author would like to thank anonymous reviewers for their constructive comments and suggestions in improving the paper.

References

1. Biere, A., Cimatti, A., Clarke, E., Zhu, Y.: Symbolic model checking without BDDs. In Cleaveland, W.R., ed.: Tools and Algorithms for the Construction and Analysis of Systems. Volume 1579 of LNCS., Springer-Verlag (1999) 193–207
2. Biere, A., Cimatti, A., Clarke, E.M., Fujita, M., Zhu, Y.: Symbolic model checking using SAT procedures instead of BDDs. In: Proceedings of the 36th Design Automation Conference (DAC' 99), New York, ACM Press (1999) 317–320
3. Emerson, E., Clarke, E.: Using branching-time temporal logic to synthesize synchronization skeletons. Science of Computer Programming **2** (1982) 241–266
4. Clarke, E.M., Grumberg, O., Peled, D.A.: Model Checking. The MIT Press, Cambridge, Massachusetts (1999)
5. Clarke, E., Kroening, D., Ouaknine, J., Strichman, O.: Completeness and complexity of bounded model checking. In Steffen, B., Levi, G., eds.: Verification, Model Checking, and Abstract Interpretation. Volume 2937 of LNCS., Springer-Verlag (2004) 85–96
6. Sheeran, M., Singh, S., Stålmarck, G.: Checking safety properties using induction and a SAT-solver. In Jr., W.A.H., Johnson, S.D., eds.: Formal Methods in Computer-Aided Design. Volume 1954 of LNCS., Springer-Verlag (2000) 108–125

7. Leonardo de Moura, H.R., Sorea, M.: Bounded model checking and induction: From refutation to verification. In Jr., W.A.H., Somenzi, F., eds.: Computer Aided Verification. Volume 2725 of LNCS., Springer Verlag (2003) 14–26
8. McMillan, K.L.: Interpolation and sat-based model checking. In Jr., W.A.H., Somenzi, F., eds.: Computer-Aided Verification. Volume 2725 of LNCS., Springer Verlag (2003) 1–13
9. Awedh, M., Somenzi, F.: Proving more properties with bounded model checking. In Alur, R., Peled, D.A., eds.: Computer Aided Verification. Volume 3114 of LNCS., Springer Verlag (2004) 96–108
10. Emerson, E.A., Lei, C.L.: Efficient model-checking in fragments of the propositional mu-calculus. In: Proceedings First Annual IEEE Symposium on Logic in Computer Science, IEEE Computer Society Press (1986) 267–278
11. Vardi, M., Wolper, P.: An automata-theoretic approach to automatic program verification. In: Proceedings First Annual IEEE Symposium on Logic in Computer Science, IEEE Computer Society Press (1986) 332–344
12. Burch, J.R., Clarke, E.M., McMillan, K.L., Dill, D.L., Hwang, L.J.: Symbolic model checking: 10^{20} states and beyond. Information and Computation **98** (1992) 142–170
13. Cleaveland, R.: Tableau-based model checking in the propositional mu-calculus. Acta Informatica **27** (1989) 725–747
14. Stirling, C., Walker, D.: Local model checking in the modal mu-calculus. Theoretical Computer Science **89** (1991) 161–177
15. Andersen, H.R., Stirling, C., Winskel, G.: A compositional proof system for the modal μ-calculus. In: Proceedings, Ninth Annual IEEE Symposium on Logic in Computer Science, Paris, France, IEEE Computer Society Press (1994) 144–153
16. Emerson, E., Lei, C.: Modalities for model-checking: Branching time logic strikes back. In: Proceedings of the 12th ACM Symposium on Principles of Programming Languages, ACM Press (1985) 84–96
17. Schuppan, V., Biere, A.: Efficient reduction of finite state model checking to reachability analysis. Software Tools for Technology Transfer **5** (2004) 185–204
18. Schuele, T., Schneider, K.: Global vs. local model checking: A comparison of verification techniques for infinite state systems. In: International Conference on Software Engineering and Formal Methods (SEFM), Beijing, IEEE Computer Society Press (2004)
19. Schuele, T., Schneider, K.: Bounded local model checking. private communication (2005)
20. Wang, B.Y.: Unbounded model checking with sat - a local model checking approach. unpublished manuscript (2004)
21. Kozen, D.: Results on the propositional μ-calculus. Theoretical Computer Science **27** (1983) 333–354
22. Winskel, G.: A note on model checking the modal nu-calculus. Theoretical Computer Science **83** (1991) 157–167
23. Wang, B.Y.: Proving $\forall\mu$-calculus properties with sat-based model checking. Technical Report TR-IIS-05-003, Institute of Information Science, Academia Sinica (2005) http://www.iis.sinica.edu.tw/LIB/TechReport/tr2005/tr05003.pdf.
24. Clarke, E., Grumberg, O., Hamaguchi, K.: Another look at LTL model checking. In Dill, D.L., ed.: Computer Aided Verification. Volume 818 of LNCS., Springer-Verlag (1994) 415–428

Ad Hoc Routing Protocol Verification Through Broadcast Abstraction

Oskar Wibling, Joachim Parrow, and Arnold Pears

Department of Information Technology, Uppsala University,
Box 337, SE-751 05 Uppsala, Sweden
{oskarw, joachim, arnoldp}@it.uu.se

Abstract. We present an improved method for analyzing route establishment in ad hoc routing protocols. An efficient abstraction for Propagating Localized Broadcast with Dampening (PLBD) is developed. Applying this result we are able to verify networks and topology changes for ad hoc networks up to the limits currently envisaged for operational mobile ad hoc networks (MANETS). Results are reported for route discovery in the Lightweight Underlay Network Ad hoc Routing protocol (LUNAR) using UPPAAL and we provide an outline of how similar verifications can be conducted for DSR.

Keywords: Mobile ad hoc networks, routing protocols, formal verification, model checking, UPPAAL, LUNAR, DSR.

1 Introduction

Delivering data in an ad hoc network with mobile nodes requires new protocols. Traditional routing protocols are incapable of routing data packets efficiently in this type of situation, motivating emergence of new protocol proposals. Validation of these new protocols is principally through simulation. Simulation often fails to discover subtle design errors, and therefore formal verification is a promising approach.

In this work, we verify correct operation of the LUNAR [1] protocol route establishment in realistic general scenarios using a network diameter of up to eleven hops. We further describe how the route discovery phase in the DSR [2] protocol can be verified in a similar way. We have aimed for the modeling to be fairly straightforward and for the verification procedure to require a minimum amount of user interaction. The verification properties are formulated at a high and easily assimilated level, e.g. "route possible to set up".

The operation responsible for most of the complexity in the verification of a LUNAR network scenario is Propagating Localized Broadcast with Dampening (PLBD). PLBD is used in the route discovery phase where a node tries to find a path to another node in the network. Each PLBD phase that is initiated at a node contains a globally unique identifier in order for nodes to keep track of which PLBD:s they have seen. As the name implies, the broadcast propagates through the network, which causes many message exchanges between nodes.

This in turn yields many possible interleavings and leads to exponential growth in verification complexity with regard to increasing number of nodes as well as topological changes in the network.

We show that in any network topology where nodes are positioned so that at a certain time it is *possible* to transmit a message over a link chain between two nodes, the PLBD reaches the intended receiver. Furthermore, we show that if there is at least one such path available then there is always a fastest path. This means that a PLBD initiated by a sender will reach the receiver first along this path. Moreover, all the nodes along the path are the first to receive the PLBD. In LUNAR, network nodes only react to the first specific PLBD they receive; subsequent ones are dropped. Therefore, we model reactions on the first PLBD packet of each type and can safely ignore the rest.

Using this technique, we can model LUNAR with timed automata and perform verifications for realistic network sizes using the UPPAAL [3] tool. Variations on the PLBD operation are also used for route discovery in other ad hoc routing protocols; one example is the DSR protocol. The DSR variant of PLBD differs in that other nodes than the intended receiver can respond to a route discovery, if they happen to possess a cached route to the destination. Therefore, instead of studying just the fastest path, we need to study a number of disjoint paths. This increases the verification complexity, but the saving is still substantial in comparison to studying all possible packet interleavings.

The remainder of this paper is organized as follows. Section 2 covers preliminaries needed to assess the subsequent sections. Section 3 describes our new verification strategy in general and Section 4 provides more detail regarding the actual modeling of LUNAR. Verification results are presented in Section 5. Section 6 describes how the DSR protocol can be verified in a similar way, and Section 7 gives an overview of related efforts in verifying MANET protocols. Finally, Section 8 contains conclusions and describes opportunities for future work in the area.

2 Preliminaries

2.1 Previous Work

In previous work [4] our result was to formally verify important properties of ad hoc routing protocols acting in realistic network scenarios. The scenarios we used are repeated in Figure 1 for clarity. We studied the LUNAR protocol since it combines simplicity with the key properties of more complex ad hoc routing protocols. The protocol was modeled by seeing each node in the network as a separate entity. Each propagating broadcast then hugely increased the complexity because of the possible interleavings of messages. When using this approach we quickly ran out of memory due to verification state space explosion. We were unable to verify networks with more than six participating nodes and very simple topology changes. Here, we refine our method and extend it to verifying significantly larger networks.

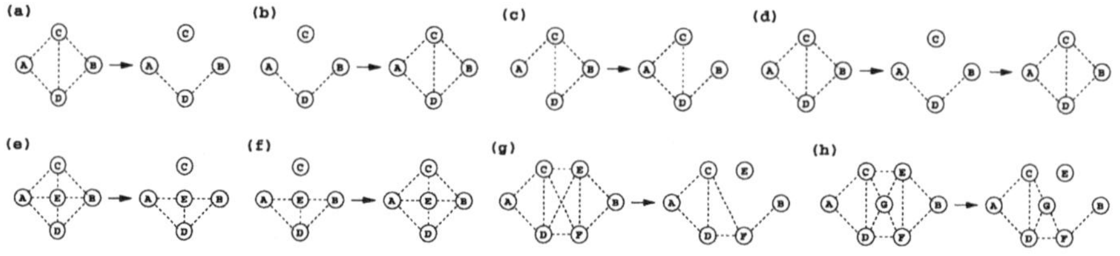

Fig. 1. Example classes of topology changes used in previous work

2.2 The Propagating Localized Broadcast with Dampening (PLBD) Operation

The reason for the state space explosion in the verification of LUNAR is the propagating localized broadcast operation (aka flooding) which works as follows:

- The broadcast is referred to as "localized" since each broadcast in a wireless network only reaches direct neighbors of the transmitting node and not nodes outside transmission range.
- Each node that initiates such a broadcast, tags the broadcast packet with a unique identifier (called the "series selector" in LUNAR).
- At each receiving node the broadcast identifier is compared with a local list to see if this particular packet has been seen before. If that is the case, the packet is just ignored. This mechanism prevents broadcast loops arising in the network.
- If the packet has not been seen before, and the receiving node is not the intended destination, the identifier is stored after which the packet is rebroadcast. Each neighbor, who has not seen the packet before will receive it together with neighbors that may already have seen the packet.
- The intended destination node also stores the identifier when and if it receives the packet, in order to be able to discard subsequent copies it might receive.

In our verification, we assume that this mechanism works, i.e. PLBD can be used as a primitive operation. In making this choice we run the risk of failing to detect subtle operational errors in the PLBD operation, potentially causing failure of the routing protocol. However, this risk is minimized by the analysis of the PLBD process needed to formulate the model.

When using PLBD, the only possible paths that packets can follow from a source to a destination are disjoint. That is, if the destination node receives a number of copies of the same PLBD, these must all have been transmitted through completely disjoint transmission chains. If two transmission chains should coincide at a node, then, since we assume that only one packet at a time can be delivered to each node, one of the packets would have been dropped and the other propagated. Different variants of PLBD have been proposed and used in other protocols [5]. The goal of these is to minimize the number of rebroadcasts needed to reach all connected nodes.

2.3 Brief Description of Ad Hoc Routing and LUNAR

A mobile ad hoc network (MANET) is a transient network that is set up to serve a temporary need, e.g. the exchange of files at a conference. It is assumed that nodes are mobile and that their location can change frequently. Therefore, node connectivity can also vary heavily. In the networks we study, multiple hops are possible between a source and a destination. This, in contrast to a fully connected network, means that nodes outside direct transmission range can be reached by traversing other intermediate nodes. In order to realize this, a routing protocol must be running on each node to forward packets from source to destination.

We study a basic version of the LUNAR protocol and use our earlier pseudo code description [6] to aid us in the modeling. The situation in which we wish to verify correct operation arises when one network node, S, has an IP packet to deliver to another node, D, but there is no route to that node available. In this situation the LUNAR route formation process is initiated at node S, which sends out a route request (RREQ) for the sought node using PLBD. On every retransmitting node, return information for the reply is temporarily stored. If the RREQ reaches D, that node will initiate a unicast route reply (RREP) destined for the node from which it received the RREQ. This node, as well as subsequent ones use the stored return information to re-address the unicast RREP for its next hop. On every step of the way back to node S, relays are also set up for label switching of wrapped IP packets later traveling along the found route. If node S does not receive a RREP within a certain time, it will issue a number of retries (using new PLBD identifiers). After that, the protocol will not take action until there is another IP packet that needs to be delivered.

2.4 General Assumptions

We use the following assumptions throughout this work.

- Unique id:s. It is possible for each network node to generate unique identifiers in isolation from the other nodes. In practice this can be implemented by appending the MAC address of a node to a monotonically increasing sequence number.
- Sequential delivery. Each node in the network can only receive and handle one message at a time. This means that we assume that relatively standard hardware is used in an actual implementation with no parallel processing of messages sent on different channels. Packets thus arrive at each network node in a strict time order.
- Bidirectional links. Only bidirectional links are possible in the network. Since 802.11 requires a bidirectional frame exchange as part of the protocol [2] this is not a significant limitation. It is, however, relevant since it affects the caching strategy of DSR.
- No persistent memory on nodes. If they go down, they lose their current route caches etc.

3 A Refined Modeling Strategy

3.1 Correct Operation of an Ad Hoc Routing Protocol

The definition of correct operation of an ad hoc routing protocol is taken from our previous work [4].

Definition 1. Correct operation of an ad hoc routing protocol
If there at one point in time exists a path between two nodes, then the protocol must be able to find some path between the nodes. When a path has been found, and for the time it stays valid, it shall be possible to send packets along the path from the source node to the destination node.

We said that "a path exists between two nodes", meaning that the path is valid for some time longer than what is required to complete the route formation process. A route formation process is the process at the end of which a particular routing protocol has managed to set up a route from a source node to a destination node, possibly traversing one or more intermediate nodes.

In the following, we will need a more detailed definition of path existence which pertains only to the unidirectional case. The reason is to be specific about what nodes are connected at different time periods for use in the proofs that follow.

Definition 2. Existence of a unidirectional path
Assume nodes $X_0 = S, X_1, \ldots, X_N = D$ (where $N \geq 1$). At time τ_0 a unidirectional path exists from network node S to D if, for all $n \in [0, N-1]$, between times τ_n and τ_{n+1} node X_n has connectivity and can transmit to node X_{n+1}. Furthermore, between these times, node X_n does not have connectivity to any of the nodes $X_m : m \in [n+2, N]$.

We require that $(\tau_{n+1} - \tau_n) = T_n : n \in [0, N-1]$ where T_n is the time required by node X_n to transmit a message to any (or all) of its neighboring nodes (i.e. over one hop), plus the time for the receiving node(s) to handle the packet and prepare for possible retransmission.

Note that we do not limit ourselves to unicast transmission. In the case of LUNAR, the first phase of the route formation process is to send a route discovery along a path from source to destination. We only require this path to be unidirectional. For LUNAR, our previous definition of path existence thus implies Definition 2. Therefore, if the preconditions of Definition 1 hold, then we know there is a unidirectional path at that point in time. In our verification, we will (as before) also make sure that these conditions hold.

3.2 Focusing on the Packet Transformation

We here describe a remedy for the state space explosion problem whilst still being able to model check scenarios of interesting proportion.

In LUNAR, two types of message transfer are used: unicast and PLBD. This is the case for other (reactive) ad hoc routing protocols as well, although some in addition use regular broadcast e.g. for neighbor sensing. Here, instead of being node centered, we focus on the packet. The idea is that every full (route setup - initial IP packet delivery) session begins with the source node, S, sending out a PLBD packet containing a RREQ for a particular destination, D. When this packet hits one or more other nodes, it can be viewed as being transformed into new packets. Once one of the rebroadcast packets reaches D (provided there is connectivity), this node will generate a RREP unicast packet destined for the node from which it received the RREQ. The RREP then traverses back through the network to S, all the time rewriting addresses. When the last RREP reaches S, it can send its initial IP packet along the found path.

The transformation is probably most easily seen in the case of the unicast chains: one packet comes into a node and another leaves. In the case of broadcast, we would like to be able to ignore all receiving nodes except one, which can then act as a message transformer.

3.3 Disregarding Unimportant Broadcast Receivers

To be able to motivate our claim that we can, at each step, disregard packets received by all broadcast receivers but one, whilst still being able to show important properties of the protocol we will need Theorem 2 below. First, however, we need a theorem that guarantees that we find a path if we use PLBD.

Theorem 1. Existence of a PLBD path
In a finite mobile network, if there at time τ_0 exists a possible unidirectional path between two nodes S and D, according to Definition 2, then a PLBD initiated from node S at this time will reach node D. The PLBD path is then the inverse of the following sequence of nodes: Node D, the node that broadcast the PLBD to D, and so on all the way back to node S.

Proof. See Figure 2 for an illustration. A PLBD with unique identifier β initiated by node S at time τ_0 will reach the direct neighbors of S. According to Definition 2 these direct neighbors either contain node D, or some intermediate node X_1. If node D was reached directly, it cannot have seen the PLBD with identifier β before and will receive the packet.

If node D was not in the direct neighbor set of S, then we know (according to our definition) that one of the other nodes in this set, say X_1, will receive the PLBD and, at time τ_1 be able to retransmit it to its neighbors. These neighbors

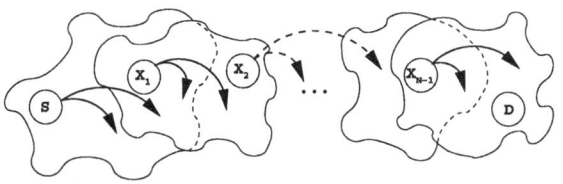

Fig. 2. Localized broadcast traversing network

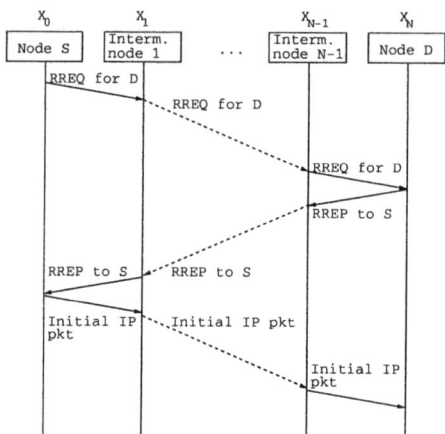

Fig. 3. LUNAR MSC with RREQ PLBD only along fastest path

may partially overlap the neighbor set of node S, but, according to Definition 2 the set will either contain node D or at least one other node, X_2, that has not previously seen this PLBD (with id β).

Continuing in this fashion, since the network is finite, we will eventually have transmitted to the final connected node(s) that had not yet heard the PLBD with identifier β. According to our definition, node D will then also be among the nodes that have received this PLBD.

Definition 3. Fastest path
A path ξ between two nodes S and D is faster than another path ρ at some point in time, if, at this time it is possible to deliver a packet from S to D faster along path ξ than along path ρ. A path χ is the fastest path between two nodes at some point in time, if, at this time it is faster than all other paths between the two nodes.

Theorem 2. Uniqueness of a PLBD path
If there at one point in time exists at least one PLBD path, from one network node to another one, then during the same time there must exist exactly one PLBD path.

Proof. Because the number of loop free paths in a finite graph is finite, the number of paths between two nodes, S and D, in a finite network is also finite. Then, if packets are sent from node S along all (disjoint) paths, one of them will be the first to reach node D, namely the one sent along the fastest path. The fastest path will also be the unique path, since node D will henceforth disregard all PLBD packets it receives containing that particular identifier.

Thus, to recapitulate, PLBD:s can effectively be studied as propagating unicasts. We illustrate this for LUNAR in Figure 3, describing the protocol with the help of a message sequence chart. We can see that, for the case of LUNAR, it is completely packet driven and in essence only reacts to incoming packets by updating internal tables and generating a new unicast or PLBD packet. If we always study the fastest path for every PLBD we cannot get any interference from other copies of the same broadcast packet since these will be dropped everywhere but along the fastest path according to our assumptions. Nodes that are not on the fastest path will therefore not be part of a chain forwarding the packet all the way to the intended destination node. Thus, we have fully motivated our packet transformation model and can go on to describing the model itself. What we essentially do is to reduce it from a parallel to a sequential one whereby complexity is significantly reduced.

4 Modeling Approach

4.1 The UPPAAL LUNAR Model and Verification Properties

UPPAAL [3] is a tool for simulation and verification of systems modeled as timed automata. Verification properties are passed to the system as Linear Temporal Logic (LTL) formulae. We have chosen to use UPPAAL in our work because of its powerful model checking capabilities and because we can use time in our models in a straightforward way. This further enables us to extract time bounds for route formation and initial IP packet delivery.

The LUNAR timed automata model includes a template (lunar_message) which models a packet in transit between two nodes. We use a system definition with three processes, representing the initial route discovery and two retries. Thus, a delay is passed as a parameter in order to model the timeout triggered resend. As in previous work we do not model any expanding ring search, but use a timeout value of 75 ms corresponding to three times the ring timeout in current LUNAR implementations and settle for two resends. Time only passes when messages are transmitted between network nodes, and we have used a range of [2,4] ms to model this delay. This represents four to eight times the theoretical delay lower limit (DLL) for the basic access mechanism of IEEE 802.11b [7]. Note that intermittent transmission failures on lower layers (e.g. due to packet collisions) are treated as link breakages in our model. In addition to the general assumptions in Section 2.4 we assume route caches to be initially empty.

Our model is to some extent less abstract than in previous work since we now model the selector tables explicitly. This is done through arrays (since there are no more complex data structures available), but it is still feasible since we gain state space usage from the PLBD abstraction. When a packet arrives at a node it needs to be switched so as to use new selectors. These are modeled using global arrays that for each node (MAC address) map selector value to a (MAC address, selector) pair.

Along the path of a PLBD, symbolic addresses of the intermediate nodes are generated as we go. These can be seen as pointers to the real addresses. Therefore, we select them from a limited range of numbers, e.g. [0,8] if we admit a maximum of 9 intermediate nodes along the fastest path. For each new route request the symbolic addresses are selected from different ranges, even though they may in reality point to the same node. Errors due to subtle faults in the algorithm that allocates selectors might elude our analysis as a result of this assumption.

We choose to verify deadlock freedom as well as route formation and initial IP packet delivery. These are verified by checking that we can eventually get to the snd_node_rec_lunar_rrep (sender node received LUNAR RREP) and message_del (IP packet delivered) states along all execution paths. To extract the time bounds, a global timeout is used and experimentally tuned for the upper range. For the lower range we instead use LTL formulae to check possibility for route formation and initial IP packet delivery along at least one execution path.

4.2 Correspondence Between Scenarios

Instead of specifying each individual scenario exactly, we are now able to parameterize on the following:

- Maximum network diameter (number of hops), d_{max}. The maximum number of possible intermediate nodes on the unique PLBD path between source and destination, plus one.
- Number of possible link failures, f, during playout of the scenario. Note that these represent critical link failures in the sense that we model them by dropping a packet nondeterministically along the fastest path.
- (Minimum network diameter, $d_{min} \leq d_{max}$; but this value should be set to 1 to allow for all possibilities of communicating nodes' positions. The only time we use a different value is when checking correspondence to previous scenarios where positions of source and destination nodes were specified.)

The scenarios we can study using the new model encompass all the ones in our previous work (shown in Figure 1). Our definition does not require the routing protocol to find a route (or send an initial IP packet along the route) if all paths are broken. We can include link breaks if we make sure that the protocol is given the chance to find a path along some other route, in accordance with the requirement of Definition 2. The inclusion of link breaks is important in order to verify that the protocol copes with those situations as well, in the case of LUNAR by initiating another route discovery after a timeout.

Scenario (g) in previous work corresponds to setting up our new model with minimum and maximum path lengths of three and with one possible link break. This is because in scenario (g) there is one link break that can occur at any time. The minimum and maximum path lengths are three, both before and after the link break. As an illustration see Figures 4 and 5 which show two possibilities for the packet traversal. Here, solid lines denote packets that are delivered, and dotted lines denote packets that are dropped because the receiver has already seen that particular PLBD identifier. Other traversals are possible and node E may go down at other times, but because of the dampening, it should be quite clear that the maximum path length will be three regardless of the order in which packets are delivered.

We validate that this is correct with our new model by extracting a bound on initial message delivery time, which is [18,111] just as in our previous work.

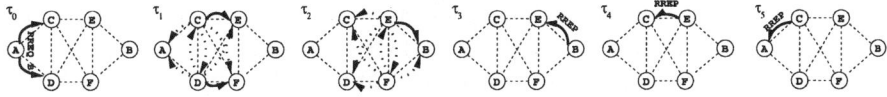

Fig. 4. Stepwise traversal of scenario (g) - Route setup initiated before link break

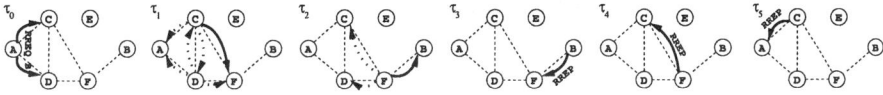

Fig. 5. Stepwise traversal of scenario (g) - Route setup initiated after link break

Using the same reasoning, we can easily translate all the previous scenarios to parameters in our new model.

5 Verification Results and Analysis

We have performed verification of LUNAR networks for the properties of interest (see Section 4.1). For general networks, i.e. where $d_{min} = 1$, we are able to verify route setup up to a diameter (d_{max}) of eleven hops, when using $f = 1$. For the same value of f we can verify initial IP packet delivery using $d_{max} = 8$ before running out of memory. This greatly surpasses the network size for which LUNAR is meant to operate (3 hops), this limit being due to the so called ad hoc network horizon [1]. Each verification takes less than a few minutes on a Macintosh PowerBook G4 laptop computer with a 1.33 GHz processor and 1.25 GB of memory. We also include some measurements from using the same processing power and verification software configuration as in our previous work. These data are presented in Table 1 together with our previous results to illustrate how substantial the performance increase is.

Due to space constraints, we are here only able to include one of our result plots. Figure 6 shows bounds on route formation and initial IP packet delivery times for the case when $d_{min} = d_{max}$ and $f = 1$. The same results as in corresponding scenarios of our previous work are obtained. As mentioned, we can also

Table 1. Comparison of UPPAAL verification results

	Explicit broadcast modeling			Using broadcast abstraction		
Scenario	States searched	Time used	Search completed	States searched	Time used	Search completed
(a)	15072	3.89 s	Yes	487	< 1 s	Yes
(e)	123196	57.91 s	Yes	487	< 1 s	Yes
(g)	2.01e+06	11:43 min:s	Yes	910	< 1 s	Yes
(h)	2.97e+07	1:59 h:min	No	910	< 1 s	Yes

verify the more general case where $d_{min} = 1$, and the difference in time bounds is that they then reach down to 4 ms for the route setup time and to 6 ms for the initial message delivery. The reason is that the most extreme case then is when source and destination are in direct contact, whereby the route setup can be completed in two transmissions. With this setting of d_{min} the verification also includes all intermediate situations, which increases the complexity.

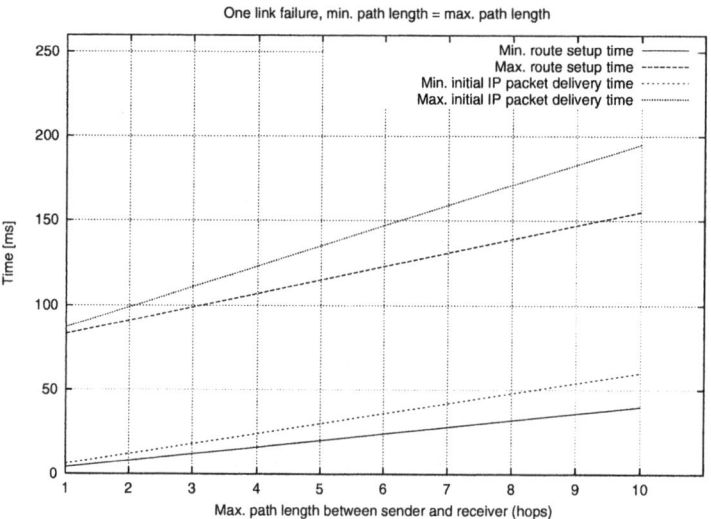

Fig. 6. Example plot showing time ranges extracted

Thus, since we are able to use a rather high number for the network diameter we are in fact able to study all networks of practical significance even though we have not produced a general proof. Our results are general in the sense that any mobility model can be accommodated. We only require that it, at some point, yields a network configuration with a unidirectional path between a given pair of nodes. Link breakages affect the initial state of route caches in the network. It is therefore important to study if different settings for f cause the protocol to behave differently. When increasing f from 1 to 2, and using $d_{min} = 1$, we can verify route setup up to $d_{max} = 8$ and initial IP packet delivery up to $d_{max} = 6$. Introducing more link breaks thus reduces the maximum network diameter that can be used. Due to the routing protocol structure of LUNAR its worst case behavior is captured by admitting the same number of link breaks as resends. The protocol cannot be expected to guarantee successful route discovery if more link breaks occur, since all retries may then be lost. Given that we only model two LUNAR resends (see Section 4.1) we therefore choose to set the limit at $f \leq 2$ in this study.

We can perform verification of all the scenarios studied in previous work, but considerably faster. Furthermore, we are able to study more general network configurations of much greater size. In a related project we are currently performing real world experimental evaluation of a number of ad hoc routing protocols. There, scenarios with a maximum of four nodes are used and even then, we note trouble in forming multi-hop paths which causes severe performance penalties for TCP [8].

6 Comparison of Route Discovery in DSR and LUNAR

DSR [2] and LUNAR can both be considered as on-demand protocols because neither of them relies on any kind of periodic packets to be exchanged between nodes. In the basic route discovery phase, the two protocols operate in a similar way. However, there are some important differences:

- DSR is a source route protocol which means that the RREQ packet includes addresses of all the nodes passed along the path from source to destination. This list is then returned to the source node and used as header for each IP packet that is subsequently to be routed. At each step, nodes use the next address in the header as new destination. In the case of LUNAR, label switching is instead used in nodes for the rewriting of addresses.
- LUNAR only stores the first response received from a route discovery. In DSR, on the other hand, a node may learn and cache multiple routes to any destination. This is also possible through overhearing routing information from packets sent by others as opposed to in LUNAR where nodes only use information they have themselves requested.
- In DSR, nodes which are not themselves the sought destination may answer with one of their routes. The answer will contain the list of addresses traversed thus far concatenated with the cached route. Loop segments are identified and removed, and a node cannot return a route in which it is not itself included.

In a DSR model we need to account for these differences properly. Instead of one destination for the PLBD, we need to study a set of answering nodes, $\mathcal{D}$. As an upper bound for this set we have the number of disjoint paths originating from network node S. We can, however, settle for all those that reach a neighbor of D, since the others will not be valid at the time of the RREQ. In the DSR draft it is said that the number of hops will often be small (e.g. perhaps 5 or 10 hops). It is also stated that the DSR protocol is designed mainly for mobile ad hoc networks of up to about 200 nodes. In a finite network, the set of answering nodes is also finite. The maximum value will be the total number of nodes in the network minus one (the sending node). This case appears if S and D are directly connected and all other nodes are also connected to both the source and destination. The implication for verification is, however, not as severe as it may first seem since no path can then be longer than two hops.

7 Related Work

Chiyangwa and Kwiatkowska [9] have studied timing properties of AODV [10] using UPPAAL. Their model uses a linear topology with specialized sender, receiver and intermediate nodes. The authors investigate how network diameter affects the protocol. They report that at 12 intermediate nodes, the recommended setting for route lifetime starts to prevent long routes from being discovered. They propose adaptive selection of this parameter to compensate for the behavior in large networks. This work is related to ours, but the linear scenario type contains a static number of nodes and its motivation is to discover a maximum diameter. Apart from providing a formal motivation to a single network path, our methodology encompasses a variety of topologies. Their method involves constructing a specialized model where we use the same protocol instance at each node which simplifies the modeling process.

Obradovic et al [11] have used the SPIN [12] model checker and the HOL [13] theorem prover to verify route validity and freedom from routing loops in AODV. They used conditions on next node pointers, sequence numbers and hop counters to form a path invariant on pairs of nodes (on the path from source to destination). Three lemmas were then verified using SPIN after which HOL was used to prove that the three lemmas imply the path invariant theorem (using standard deductive reasoning). The approach requires a significant amount of user interaction and is not directly applicable to other protocols.

Das and Dill [14] also prove absence of routing loops in a simplified version of AODV. The strategy is similar to that of Obradovic et al, but more automated. They use predicate abstraction and can discover most of the quantified predicates automatically by analyzing spurious abstract counter-example traces, albeit with some mechanical human involvement. The initial predicate set is formulated in a manual step where conditions on next node pointers, hop counters, and existence of routes are constructed. The method successfully discovers all required predicates for the version of AODV considered. Proficiency in formal verification is required in order to make general use of their method.

de Renesse and Aghvami [15] have used SPIN to model check the ad hoc routing protocol WARP. They use a general 5-node topology, and provide a nonexhaustive verification (using the approximating bitstate hashing mode [12]), covering 98% of the state space.

Xiong et al [16,17] have modeled AODV using Petri nets. A topology approximation mechanism describes dynamic topology changes. They report on a looping situation found during a state space search of a general ten node topology. Their broadcast model uses an average number of messages based on the average degree and the total number of nodes in the graph. The resulting PLBD implementation is less abstract than ours and models redundant packet transfers between nodes not on the fastest path between the sender and receiver. In contrast to our approach link failure effects are also not included in their model as they assume unicast transmissions to be globally receivable regardless of topology.

With our method we can use the same protocol instance for each symbolic node and easily verify high level properties of ad hoc routing protocols, such as "initial IP packet delivered". We do not put strict requirements on the topologies, but admit for general networks of a certain diameter and a given number of link breakages. The modeling and verification processes are thus quite simple and applicable to a range of different protocols.

8 Conclusions and Future Work

We have developed a new efficient method for modeling PLBD, one of the operations in ad hoc routing protocols most responsible for state space explosion in previous approaches. We applied the technique, verifying the operation of route establishment in the ad hoc protocol LUNAR, and derived upper and lower time bounds for both route establishment and first packet delivery over the resulting route. We verified route setup in networks of up to eleven hops in diameter, well over the envisioned upper limit for practical application of ad hoc routing in realistic scenarios.

For our future work we intend to perform the same verification for the DSR protocol, which we have only sketched here. We want to see if there are other protocols that utilize primitive operations, responsible for much of the complexity, which can be abstracted away from in order to enable for verification in realistic networks. These analyses can further be used to compare the quality of competing protocols.

References

1. Tschudin, C., Gold, R., Rensfelt, O., Wibling, O.: LUNAR: a lightweight underlay network ad-hoc routing protocol and implementation. In: Proc. Next Generation Teletraffic and Wired/Wireless Advanced Networking (NEW2AN). (2004)
2. Johnson, D.B., Maltz, D.A., Hu, Y.C.: Internet draft: The dynamic source routing protocol for mobile ad hoc networks (DSR). http://www.ietf.org/internet-drafts/draft-ietf-manet-dsr-10.txt (2004)
3. Larsen, K.G., Pettersson, P., Yi, W.: UPPAAL in a Nutshell. Int. Journal on Software Tools for Technology Transfer 1 (1997) 134–152
4. Wibling, O., Parrow, J., Pears, A.: Automated verification of ad hoc routing protocols. In: Proc. 24th IFIP WG 6.1 International Conference on Formal Techniques for Networked and Distributed Systems (FORTE). (2004)
5. Ni, S.Y., Tseng, Y.C., Chen, Y.S., Sheu, J.P.: The broadcast storm problem in a mobile ad hoc network. In: Proc. ACM MobiCom. (1999) 151–162
6. Wibling, O.: LUNAR pseudo code description. http://user.it.uu.se/~oskarw/lunar_pseudo_code/ (2005)
7. Xiao, Y., Rosdahl, J.: Throughput and delay limits of IEEE 802.11. IEEE Communications Letters 6 (2002) 355–357
8. Lundgren, H.: Implementation and Experimental Evaluation of Wireless Ad Hoc Routing Protocols. Phd thesis, Uppsala University (2005)
9. Chiyangwa, S., Kwiatkowska, M.: A timing analysis of AODV. In: Proc. Formal Methods for Open Object-Based Distributed Systems: 7th IFIP WG 6.1 International Conference (FMOODS). (2005)
10. Perkins, C.E., Royer, E.M.: Ad hoc on-demand distance vector routing. In: Proc. 2nd IEEE Workshop on Mobile Computing Systems and Applications. (1999) 90–100

11. Obradovic, D.: Formal Analysis of Routing Protocols. Phd thesis, University of Pennsylvania (2002)
12. Holzmann, G.: The Spin Model Checker, Primer and Reference Manual. Addison-Wesley, Reading, Massachusetts (2003)
13. University of Cambridge Computer Laboratory: Automated reasoning group HOL page. http://www.cl.cam.ac.uk/Research/HVG/HOL/ (2005)
14. Das, S., Dill, D.L.: Counter-example based predicate discovery in predicate abstraction. In: Formal Methods in Computer-Aided Design, Springer-Verlag (2002)
15. de Renesse, R., Aghvami, A.: Formal verification of ad-hoc routing protocols using SPIN model checker. In: 12th Mediterranean Electrotechnical Conference (IEEE MELECON). (2004)
16. Xiong, C., Murata, T., Tsai, J.: Modeling and simulation of routing protocol for mobile ad hoc networks using colored Petri nets. In: Proc. Workshop on Formal Methods Applied to Defence Systems in Formal Methods in Software Engineering and Defence Systems. (2002)
17. Xiong, C., Murata, T., Leigh, J.: An approach to verifying routing protocols in mobile ad hoc networks using Petri nets. In: Proc. IEEE 6th CAS Symposium on Emerging Technologies: Frontiers of Mobile and Wireless Communication. (2004)

Discovering Chatter and Incompleteness in the Datagram Congestion Control Protocol

Somsak Vanit-Anunchai[1], Jonathan Billington[1], and Tul Kongprakaiwoot[2]

[1] Computer Systems Engineering Centre, University of South Australia,
Mawson Lakes Campus, SA 5095, Australia
Somsak.Vanit-Anunchai@postgrads.unisa.edu.au
Jonathan.Billington@unisa.edu.au
[2] TextMe Co., Ltd., 20 North Sathorn Rd, Bangkok 10500, Thailand
tul@textme.co.th

Abstract. A new protocol designed for real-time applications, the Datagram Congestion Control Protocol (DCCP), is specified informally in a final Internet Draft that has been approved as an RFC (Request For Comment). This paper analyses DCCP's connection management procedures modelled using Coloured Petri Nets (CPNs). The protocol has been modelled at a sufficient level of detail to obtain interesting results including pinpointing areas where the specification is incomplete. Our analysis discovers scenarios where the client and server repeatedly and needlessly exchange packets. This creates a lot of unnecessary traffic, inducing more congestion in the Internet. We suggest a modification to the protocol that we believe solves this problem.

Keywords: DCCP, Internet Protocols, Coloured Petri Nets, State space methods.

1 Introduction

Streaming media applications and online games are becoming increasingly popular on the Internet. Because these applications are delay sensitive, they use the User Datagram Protocol (UDP) rather than the Transmission Control Protocol (TCP). The users then implement their own congestion control mechanisms on top of UDP or may not implement any control mechanism at all. The growth of these applications therefore poses a serious threat to the Internet. To tackle this problem, an Internet Engineering Task Force (IETF) working group is developing a new transport protocol, called the Datagram Congestion Control Protocol (DCCP) [5–8]. The purpose of DCCP is to support various congestion control mechanisms that suit different applications. It therefore could replace TCP/UDP for delay sensitive applications and become the dominant transport protocol in the Internet. Hence we consider that it is important to verify DCCP as soon as possible, to remove errors and ambiguities and ensure its specification is complete before implementation.

In this paper, Coloured Petri Nets (CPNs) [4] are used to model and analyse DCCP's connection management procedures. We chose CPNs because they are used widely to model and analyse concurrent and complex systems [1,4] including transport protocols like TCP [2,3]. We have previously applied our methodology [2] to earlier versions of DCCP. We demonstrated [11] that a deadlock occurs in DCCP version 5 [6] during DCCP connection setup. Further work [9] upgraded the model to version 6 [7] and also discovered undesired terminal states. These models [11,9] were incomplete, in that they did not include DCCP's synchronisation procedures, which are used in conjunction with connection management.

As far as we are aware, this paper describes the first formal specification of DCCP's connection establishment, close down and synchronisation procedures for version 11 [8] of the specification. Further, using a set of initial configurations, we incrementally analyse the connection management procedures including the synchronization mechanism. Although no deadlock or livelock is found, we discover some chatter in the protocol where both ends repeatedly exchange packets, creating a lot of unnecessary traffic. We canvass a possible solution to this problem. A further contribution of this paper is the identification of areas where the specification is incomplete.

This paper is organised as follows. To make the paper self-contained, section 2 summarises DCCP's connection management procedures. The CPN model of DCCP is illustrated in section 3, which starts with a statement of scope and modelling assumptions, and closes with a discussion of areas of incompleteness in the specification. Section 4 presents our analysis results and section 5 summarises our work.

2 Datagram Congestion Control Protocol

DCCP [8] is a connection oriented protocol designed to overcome the problem of uncontrolled UDP traffic. The connection management procedures have some similarities with TCP, with some states being given the same names. However, DCCP's procedures are substantially different from those of TCP. For example, connection establishment uses a 4-way handshake (rather than 3), there is no notion of simultaneously opening a connection, connection release is simpler, as it does not aim to guarantee delivery of data in the pipeline, and the use of sequence numbers is quite different. There is also a procedure which allows a server to request that the client closes the connection and waits for 2 Maximum packet lifetimes (MPL) to ensure all old packets are removed, before a new instance of the connection can be established, rather than the server having to wait for this period. Further, DCCP includes procedures for resynchronizing sequence numbers. This section summarises the key features of DCCP connection management that we wish to model and analyse.

2.1 DCCP Packet Format

Like TCP, DCCP packets comprise a sequence of 32 bit words as shown in Fig. 1. The DCCP header contains 16 bit source and destination port numbers, an 8 bit data offset, a 16 bit checksum and sequence and acknowledgement numbers in a very similar way to TCP. However, there are significant differences. DCCP

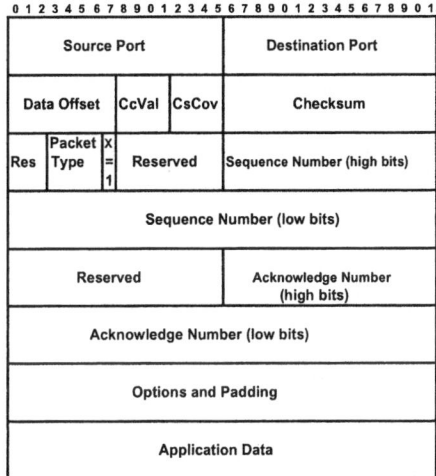

Fig. 1. DCCP Packet Format

defines 10 packets that are encoded using a 4 bit Packet Type field, rather than the control bits used in TCP (for SYN, FIN, RST, ACK). The packets are: Request, Response, Data, DataAck, Ack, CloseReq, Close, Reset, Sync and SyncAck. Sequence (and acknowledgement) numbers are 48 bits long (instead of 32 bits) and number packets rather than octets. The sequence number of a DCCP-Data, DCCP-Ack or DCCP-DataAck packet may be reduced to 24 bits by setting the X field to 0. CCVal, a 4 bit field, contains a value that is used by the chosen congestion control mechanism [8]. Checksum Coverage (CsCov), also a 4 bit field, specifies how much of the packet is protected by the 16 bit Checksum field. Finally, the Options field can contain information such as Cookies and time stamps but also allows DCCP applications to negotiate various features such as the Congestion Control Identifier (CCID) and the size (width) of the Sequence Number validity window [8].

2.2 Connection Management Procedures

The state diagram, shown in Fig. 2, illustrates the connection management procedures of DCCP. It comprises nine states rather than TCP's eleven states. The typical connection establishment and close down procedures are shown in Fig. 3. Like TCP, a connection is initiated by a client issuing an "active open" command. We assume that the application at the server has issued a "passive open" command. After receiving the "active open", the client sends a DCCP-Request packet to specify the client and server ports and to initialize sequence numbers. On receiving the DCCP-Request packet, the server replies with a DCCP-Response packet indicating that it is willing to communicate with the client. The response includes the server's initial sequence number and any features and options that the server agrees to. It also directly acknowledges re-

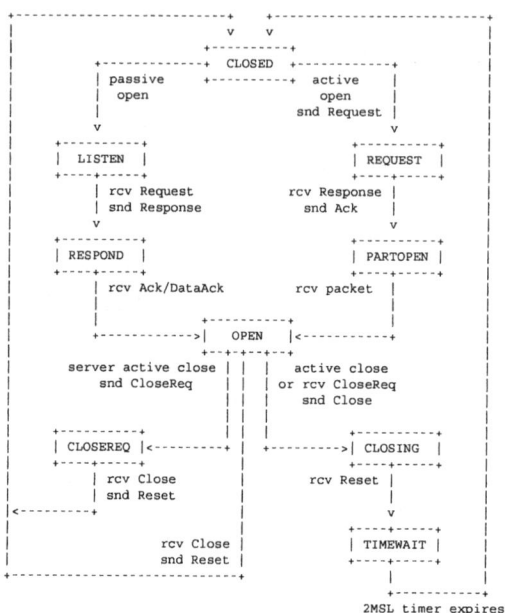

Fig. 2. DCCP State Diagram [8]

ceiving the DCCP-Request. Note that acknowledgements are not cumulative. The client sends an DCCP-Ack or DCCP-DataAck packet to acknowledge the DCCP-Response packet and enters PARTOPEN (this is a new state introduced in version 6 of the protocol). On receiving an acknowledgement from the client, the server enters the OPEN state and is ready for data transfer. At the client, after receiving one of a DCCP-Data, DCCP-DataAck, DCCP-Ack or DCCP-SyncAck packet, the client enters OPEN indicating that the connection is established. During data transfer, the server and client may exchange DCCP-Data, DCCP-Ack and DCCP-DataAck packets (for piggybacked acknowledgements).

Fig. 3 (b) shows the typical close down procedure. The application at the server issues a "server active close" command. The server sends a DCCP-CloseReq packet and enters the CLOSEREQ state. When the client receives a DCCP-CloseReq packet, it must generate a DCCP-Close packet in response. After the server receives a DCCP-Close packet, it must respond with a DCCP-Reset packet and enter the CLOSED state. When the client receives the DCCP-Reset packet, it holds the TIMEWAIT state for 2 MPL[1] before entering the CLOSED state.

Alternatively, either end will send a DCCP-Close packet to terminate the connection when receiving an "active close" command from the application. The end that sends the DCCP-Close packet will hold the TIMEWAIT state

---

[1] Maximum packet lifetime time (MPL) = Maximum Segment Lifetime (MSL) in TCP.

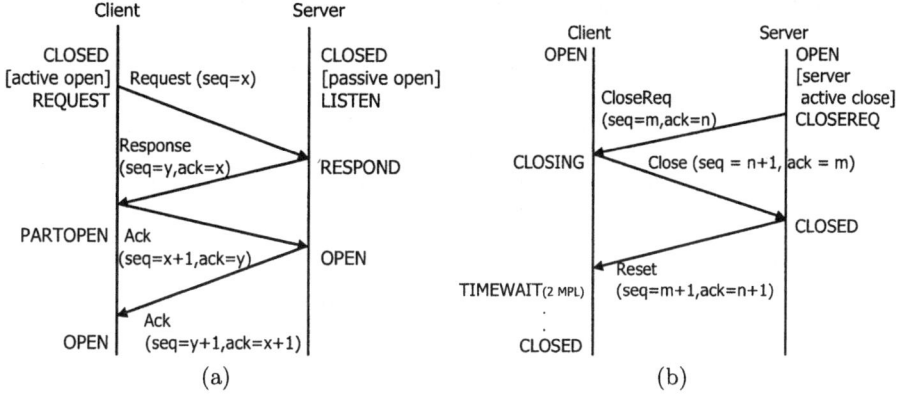

Fig. 3. Typical Connection Establishment and Release Scenarios

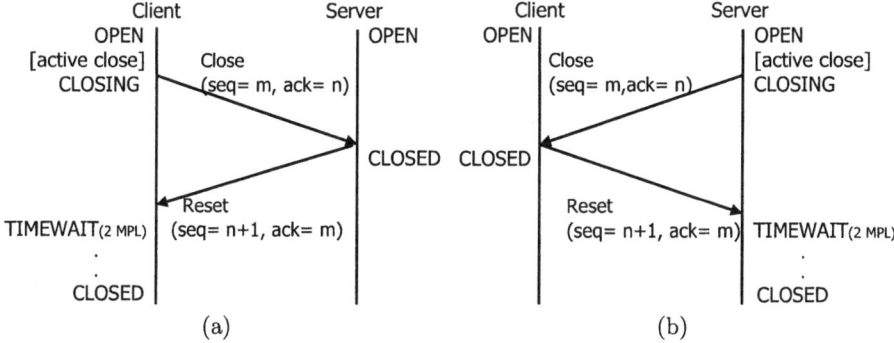

Fig. 4. Alternative Close Down Procedures

as shown in Fig. 4. Beside these three closing procedures, there are another 2 possible scenarios concerned with simultaneous closing. The first procedure is invoked when both users issue an "active close". The second occurs when the client user issues an "active close" and the application at the server issues the "server active close" command.

2.3 Retransmission and Back-Off Timers

Besides the timer (2MPL) in the TIMEWAIT state, DCCP defines two further timers: Retransmission and Back-off. When the sending client does not receive an answer, the timeout period that it waits before retransmitting a packet is determined by the Retransmission Timer (typically 2RTT[2]). After retransmitting for a period (typically 4MPL), it sends a DCCP-Reset and enters the CLOSED state. This timeout period is determined by the Back-off Timer. Generally, if the

---

[2] RTT = Round Trip Time.

Table 1. Validity Condition for Sequence and Acknowledgement Numbers

Packet Type	Sequence Number Check	Acknowledgement Number Check
Request	SWL $\leq$ seqno $\leq$ SWH	N/A
Response	SWL $\leq$ seqno $\leq$ SWH	AWL $\leq$ ackno $\leq$ AWH
Data	SWL $\leq$ seqno $\leq$ SWH	N/A
Ack	SWL $\leq$ seqno $\leq$ SWH	AWL $\leq$ ackno $\leq$ AWH
DataAck	SWL $\leq$ seqno $\leq$ SWH	AWL $\leq$ ackno $\leq$ AWH
CloseReq	GSR $<$ seqno $\leq$ SWH	GAR $\leq$ ackno $\leq$ AWH
Close	GSR $<$ seqno $\leq$ SWH	GAR $\leq$ ackno $\leq$ AWH
Reset	GSR $<$ seqno $\leq$ SWH	GAR $\leq$ ackno $\leq$ AWH
Sync	SWL $\leq$ seqno	AWL $\leq$ ackno $\leq$ AWH
SyncAck	SWL $\leq$ seqno	AWL $\leq$ ackno $\leq$ AWH

server does not receive a timely response (typically 4MPL), it sends a DCCP-Reset and enters CLOSED. This timeout period is also governed by the Back-off Timer. However when in CLOSEREQ if no response is received within 2 RTT, the server retransmits DCCP-CloseReq. Retransmissions typically occur for 4 MPL but if no response is received, a DCCP-Reset is sent and the server enters the CLOSED state. The sequence number of every retransmitted packet is always increased by one.

2.4 Variables and Sequence Validity

For each connection, DCCP entities maintain a set of state variables. Among those, the important variables are Greatest Sequence Number Sent (GSS), Greatest Sequence Number Received (GSR), Greatest Acknowledgement Number Received (GAR), Initial Sequence Number Sent and Received (ISS and ISR), Valid Sequence Number window width (W) and Acknowledgement Number validity window width (AW). Based on the state variables, the valid sequence and acknowledgement number intervals are defined by Sequence Number Window Low and High [SWL,SWH], and Acknowledgement Number Window Low and High [AWL,AWH] according to the equations of pages 40–41 of the DCCP Definition [8]. Additionally the SWL and AWL are initially not less than the initial sequence number received and sent respectively.

Generally, received DCCP packets that have sequence and acknowledgement numbers inside these windows are valid, called "sequence-valid". Table 1 shows the window ranges for each packet type. The DCCP-CloseReq, DCCP-Close and DCCP-Reset are valid only when seqno $>$ GSR and ackno $\geq$ GAR.

However, there are some exceptions to Table 1, depending on state. According to the pseudo code (see [8] pages 54–58), no sequence validity check is performed in the CLOSED, LISTEN and TIMEWAIT states. In the REQUEST state, only the acknowledgement numbers of the DCCP-Response and DCCP-Reset packets are validated. Other packet types received are responded to with a DCCP-Reset. The acknowledgement number of a DCCP-Reset received in the REQUEST state is validated using [AWL,AWH] instead of [GAR,AWH].

2.5 DCCP-Reset Packets

An entity in the CLOSED, LISTEN or TIMEWAIT state ignores a DCCP-Reset packet while replying to any other unexpected packet types with DCCP-Reset. In other states on receiving a sequence-valid DCCP-Reset packet, the entity goes to TIMEWAIT for 2MPL and then enters the CLOSED state. If the DCCP-Reset packet received is sequence-invalid, the entity responds with a DCCP-Sync. However a sequence-invalid DCCP-Response or DCCP-Reset received in the REQUEST state will be responded to with a DCCP-Reset instead of a DCCP-Sync. When the client is in the REQUEST state, it has not received an initial sequence number (no GSR). In this case the acknowledgement number of the DCCP-Reset is set to zero.

2.6 Resynchronizing Sequence Numbers

Malicious attack or a burst of noise may result in state variables and sequence and acknowledgement number windows being unsynchronized. The DCCP-Sync and DCCP-SyncAck packets are used to update GSR and to resynchronize both ends. When receiving a sequence-invalid packet, an end must reply with a DCCP-Sync packet. It does not update GSR because the sequence number received could be wrong. However the acknowledgement number in the DCCP-Sync packet is set equal to this invalid received sequence number. After receiving a sequence-valid DCCP-Sync, the end must update its GSR variable and reply with a DCCP-SyncAck. It does not update GAR. After receiving a sequence-valid DCCP-SyncAck, an end updates GSR and GAR. An end ignores sequence-invalid DCCP-Sync and DCCP-SyncAck packets, except in the CLOSED, TIMEWAIT, LISTEN and REQUEST states where a DCCP-Reset is sent in response.

3 Modelling DCCP's Connection Management Procedures

3.1 Modelling Scope and Assumptions

Our model comprises all the state transitions of Fig. 2, including the following details from the DCCP Definition [8]: the pseudo code of section 8.5 (pages 54–58); the narrative description of DCCP's event processing in section 8 (pages 48–54); and packet validation in section 7 (pages 38–44). We also make the following assumptions regarding DCCP connection management when creating our CPN model.

1. We only consider at single connection instance while ignoring the procedures for data transfer, congestion control and other feature options. A DCCP packet is modelled by its packet type, sequence number and acknowledgement number. Other fields in the DCCP header are omitted because they do not affect the operation of the connection management procedure.

2. Sequence numbers are assumed not to wrap.

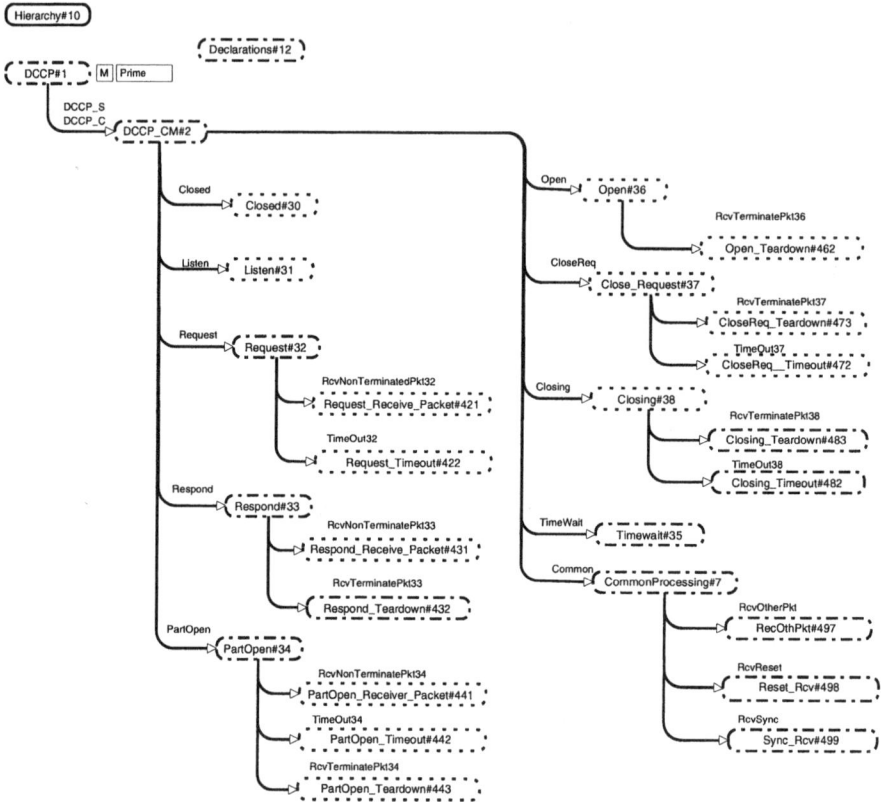

Fig. 5. Hierarchy Page

3. We do not consider misbehaviour or malicious attack.

4. Reordered or lossy channels may mask out possible deadlock, such as unspecified receptions. Thus we incrementally study [2] the CPN model with the following channel characteristics: FIFO without loss, reordered without loss, FIFO with loss, and reordered with loss. However due to space limitations, we only discuss the case when the communication channels can delay and reorder packets without loss.

5. We set the window size to 100 packets because it is specified as the initial default value in the specification (page 31 of DCCP [8]).

6. Without loss of generality, we only use DCCP-Ack and not DCCP-DataAck in order to reduce the size of the state space.

3.2 Structure

The structure of our DCCP CPN model has been influenced by our earlier work [3,11]. It is structured into four hierarchical levels shown in Fig. 5, and comprises 6 places, 27 substitution transitions, 63 executable transitions and 9 func-

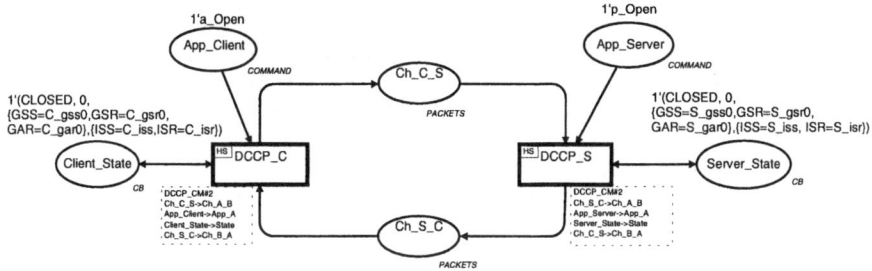

Fig. 6. The DCCP Overview Page

```
1 color PacketType1 = with Request | Data;
2 color PacketType2 = with Sync | SyncAck | Response | Ack | DataAck
                        | CloseReq | Close | Rst;
3 var p_type1:PacketType1;
4 var p_type2:PacketType2;
5 color SN = IntInf with ZERO..MaxSeqNo;              var sn:SN;
6 color SN_AN = record SEQ:SN*ACK:SN;                 var sn_an:SN_AN;
7 color PacketType1xSN = product PacketType1*SN;
8 color PacketType2xSN_AN = product PacketType2*SN_AN;
9 color PACKETS = union PKT1:PacketType1xSN+PKT2:PacketType2xSN_AN;
```

Fig. 7. Definition of DCCP PACKETS

tions. The first level is named DCCP. This level calls a page named DCCP_CM (DCCP connection management) twice (for the client and the server). This allows one DCCP entity to be defined and instantiated as either a client or server, greatly simplifying the specification and its maintenance. This has proven to be very beneficial due to there being 6 revisions since we first modelled DCCP [11]. The third level has ten pages, describing the procedures that are followed in each DCCP state. Processing common to several states is specified in the Common Processing page. For convenience of editing and maintaining the model, we group the transitions that have common functions into the fourth level pages. Significant effort has gone into validating this model against the DCCP definition [8] by using manual inspection and interactive simulation [2].

3.3 DCCP Overview

The top level, corresponding to DCCP#1 in the hierarchy page, is the DCCP Overview Page shown in Fig. 6. It is a CPN diagram comprising 6 *places* (represented by ellipses), two *substitution transitions* (represented by rectangles with an HS tag) and *arcs* which connect places to transitions and vice versa. The client is on the left and the server on the right and they communicate via two channels, shown in the middle of Fig. 6. We model unidirectional and re-ordering channels from the client to the server and vice versa by places named Ch_C_S

```
1 color STATE = with CLOSED | LISTEN | REQUEST | RESPOND |
          PARTOPEN | S_OPEN | C_OPEN | CLOSEREQ | CLOSING | TIMEWAIT;
2 color RCNT = int;    var rcnt:RCNT;  (*Retransmit Counter *)
3 color GS = record GSS:SN*GSR:SN*GAR:SN;       var g:GS;
4 color ISN = record ISS:SN*ISR:SN;             var isn:ISN;
5 color CB = product STATE*RCNT*GS*ISN;
6 color COMMAND = with p_Open | a_Open | server_a_Close | a_Close;
```

Fig. 8. DCCP's Control Block and User Commands

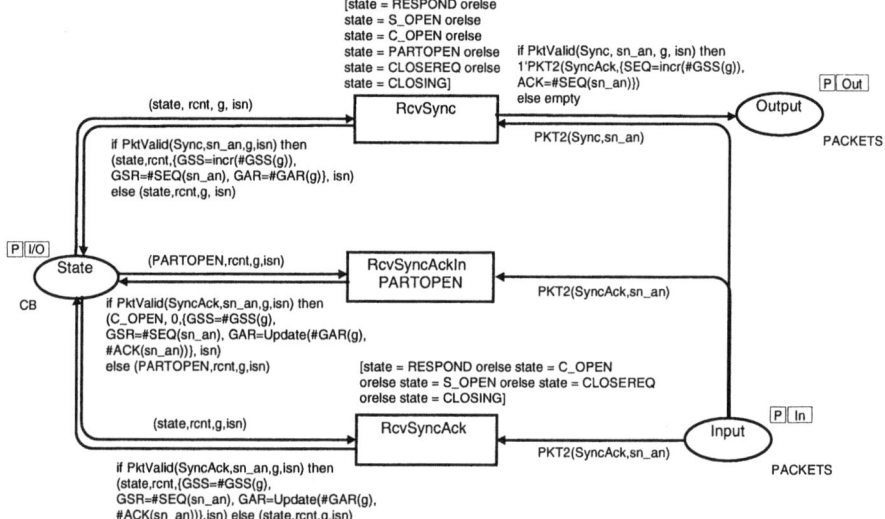

Fig. 9. The Sync_Rcv Page

and Ch_S_C which are typed by PACKETS. Fig. 7 declares PACKETS (line 9) as a union of packets with and without acknowledgements.

Places, Client_State and Server_State, typed by CB (Control Block), store DCCP state information. Fig. 8 defines CB (line 5) as a product comprising STATE, RCNT (Retransmit Counter), GS (Greatest Sequence Number) and ISN (Initial Sequence Number). Places named App_Client and App_Server, typed by COMMAND, model DCCP user commands. Fig. 8 also defines COMMAND (line 6). Tokens associated with these places shown on the top of ellipses, for example "a_Open", are called initial markings. They represent the initial state of the system.

3.4 Second, Third and Fourth Level Pages

The substitution transitions DCCP_C and DCCP_S in Fig. 6 are linked to the second level page named DCCP_CM (as shown in Fig. 5). DCCP_CM is organized into a further ten substitution transitions linked to the third level pages,

```
1  fun incr(sn:SN) = if (sn = MaxSeqNo) then ZERO else IntInf.+(sn, ONE);
2  fun Update(new:SN,old:SN) = if (IntInf.>(new,old)) then new else old;
3  val W  = IntInf.fromInt(100); val AW = IntInf.fromInt(100);
4  fun SeqValid(p_type2:PacketType2, s2:SN_AN, g:GS, isn:ISN) =
5   let                          (* Sequence Number Validity *)
6   val SWL=IntInf.max(IntInf.-(IntInf.+(#GSR(g),ONE),
7                      IntInf.div(W,IntInf.fromInt(4))),#ISR(isn));
8   val SWH=IntInf.+(IntInf.+(#GSR(g),ONE),
9                      RealToIntInf 4((IntInfToReal 4 W)*3.0/4.0+0.5));
10  in  case p_type2 of Response => IntInf.>=(#SEQ(s2),SWL)
11                                 andalso IntInf.<=(#SEQ(s2),SWH)
12   | Ack =>      IntInf.>=(#SEQ(s2),SWL) andalso IntInf.<=(#SEQ(s2),SWH)
13   | DataAck =>  IntInf.>=(#SEQ(s2),SWL) andalso IntInf.<=(#SEQ(s2),SWH)
14   | CloseReq => IntInf.>(#SEQ(s2),#GSR(g)) andalso IntInf.<=(#SEQ(s2),SWH)
15   | Close =>    IntInf.>(#SEQ(s2),#GSR(g)) andalso IntInf.<=(#SEQ(s2),SWH)
16   | Rst =>      IntInf.>(#SEQ(s2),#GSR(g)) andalso IntInf.<=(#SEQ(s2),SWH)
17   | Sync =>     IntInf.>=(#SEQ(s2),SWL)
18   | SyncAck =>  IntInf.>=(#SEQ(s2),SWL)
19   | _ => false
20  end;
21 fun AckValid(p_type2:PacketType2, s2:SN_AN, g:GS, isn:ISN) =
22  let                          (* Acknowledgement Number Validity*)
23   val AWL = IntInf.max(IntInf.-(IntInf.+(#GSS(g),ONE),AW),#ISS(isn));
24   val AWH = #GSS(g);
25  in case p_type2 of Response =>   IntInf.>=(#ACK(s2),AWL)
26                                 andalso IntInf.<=(#ACK(s2),AWH)
27   | Ack =>     IntInf.>=(#ACK(s2),AWL) andalso IntInf.<=(#ACK(s2),AWH)
28   | DataAck => IntInf.>=(#ACK(s2),AWL) andalso IntInf.<=(#ACK(s2),AWH)
29   | CloseReq =>IntInf.>=(#ACK(s2),#GAR(g)) andalso IntInf.<=(#ACK(s2),AWH)
30   | Close =>   IntInf.>=(#ACK(s2),#GAR(g)) andalso IntInf.<=(#ACK(s2),AWH)
31   | Rst =>     IntInf.>=(#ACK(s2),#GAR(g)) andalso IntInf.<=(#ACK(s2),AWH)
32   | Sync =>    IntInf.>=(#ACK(s2),AWL) andalso IntInf.<=(#ACK(s2),AWH)
33   | SyncAck => IntInf.>=(#ACK(s2),AWL) andalso IntInf.<=(#ACK(s2),AWH)
34   | _ => false
35  end;
36 fun PktValid(p_type2:PacketType2, s2:SN_AN, g:GS, isn:ISN) =
37   SeqValid(p_type2:PacketType2,s2:SN_AN,g:GS,isn:ISN)
38   andalso AckValid(p_type2:PacketType2,s2:SN_AN, g:GS, isn:ISN);
```

Fig. 10. Functions used in the Sync Rcv Page

representing the processing required in each DCCP state. We group the transitions that have common functions into the fourth level pages. In particular, we model the behaviour of DCCP in the RESPOND, PARTOPEN, OPEN, CLOSEREQ and CLOSING states when receiving DCCP-Reset and DCCP-Sync packets into pages named Reset_Rcv and Sync_Rcv pages under the Common Processing page in the third level. The RcvOthPkt page models DCCP's behaviour in the OPEN, CLOSEREQ and CLOSING states when receiving packets other than DCCP-CloseReq, DCCP-Closing, DCCP-Reset, DCCP-Sync and DCCP-SyncAck. Space limits prevent us from including all pages, but a representative example is given in Fig. 9. The figure shows the level of detail required to capture the procedures to be followed by both the client and the server when receiving the DCCP-Sync and DCCP SyncAck packets. Fig. 10 shows functions incr(), Update() and PktValid() used in the Sync_Rcv page.

3.5 Incompleteness in the Specification

User commands appear in the state diagram of Fig. 2 but the specification [8] does not provide any detail. As stated in version 5 [6], the application may try to close during connection establishment. Thus an "active close" command could occur in the REQUEST, RESPOND, PARTOPEN and OPEN states. Similarly, at the server, a "serve active close" command could also occur in the RESPOND and OPEN states. We assume this to be the case in our model, but do not analyse it in this paper.

When the server enters the RESPOND state, it has no information about GAR which is needed to validate the acknowledgement number of DCCP-CloseReq, DCCP-Close and DCCP-Reset. We believe that the specification does not currently cater for the situation when the server receives one of these packets in the RESPOND state. This may happen when the client's user issues an "active close" command while it is in the REQUEST state. The solution to this problem needs further investigation and we do not analyse these scenarios in this paper.

4 Analysis of DCCP CPN Model

4.1 Initial Configuration

Using an incremental approach [2] we analyse different connection management scenarios by choosing a number of different initial markings. This is to gain confidence in the model and to provide insight into DCCP's behaviour. In this paper we limit the maximum number of retransmissions to one to make the generation of the state space tractable. We analyse the DCCP model using Design/CPN 4.0.5 on a Pentium-IV 2 GHz computer with 1GB RAM. Initial markings of each scenario are shown in Table 2.

Case I is for connection establishment. The client and server are both CLOSED with ISS set to five. The client issues an "active Open" command while the server issues a "passive Open" command. There are five scenarios of connection termination when both ends are in the OPEN state. Cases II, III and IV model the case when only one end issues a close command. Cases V and VI represent the simultaneous close scenarios when both ends issue close commands at the same time. Each end has the initial values of GSS, GSR and GAR shown in Table 2, and the channels are empty.

Table 2. Initial Configurations

Case	App_Client	App_Server	Client_State	Server_State
I	1'a_Open	1'p_Open	CLOSED GSS=0,GSR=0,GAR=0 ISS=5,ISR=0	CLOSED GSS=0,GSR=0,GAR=0 ISS=5,ISR=0
II	1'a_Close		OPEN GSS=200,GSR=200,GAR=200	OPEN GSS=200,GSR=200,GAR=200
III		1'a_Close	OPEN GSS=200,GSR=200,GAR=200	OPEN GSS=200,GSR=200,GAR=200
IV		1'Server a_Close	OPEN GSS=200,GSR=200,GAR=200	SOPEN GSS=200,GSR=200,GAR=200
V	1'a_Close	1'a_Close	OPEN GSS=200,GSR=200,GAR=200	OPEN GSS=200,GSR=200,GAR=200
VI	1'a_Close	1'Server a_Close	OPEN GSS=200,GSR=200,GAR=200	OPEN GSS=200,GSR=200,GAR=200

4.2 State Space Results

Table 3 summarizes the state space statistics. The last column shows the number of terminal states which have the same pair of states but different value of GSS, GSR and GAR. In all cases nothing is left in the channels.

In case I, connection establishment, there are three different types of terminal states. The first type is desired when both ends are in OPEN. The second type is when both ends are CLOSED. This can occur when the request or response is sufficiently delayed so that the Back-off timer expires, closing the connection. The third type is when the client is CLOSED, but the server is in the LISTEN state. This situation can happen when the server is initially CLOSED and thus rejects the connection request. After that the server recovers and moves to the LISTEN state. Although we are unable to obtain the full state space for case VI because of state explosion, we can obtain partial state spaces. Case VI a) is when there is no retransmission. Case VI b) is when only one DCCP-Close is retransmitted. Case VI c) is when only one DCCP-CloseReq is retransmitted. Cases II, III, IV, V, VI a), VI b) and VI c) have only one type of terminal state when both ends are in CLOSED.

The Strongly Connected Component (SCC) graphs of all cases (except case VI) were generated. The size of each SCC graph is the same as the size of the state space. This indicates that there are no cycles and hence no livelocks in the state spaces.

4.3 DCCP Chatter During Connection Establishment

Further analysis of case I shows that the state space size grows almost linearly with ISS, as illustrated in Table 4. We have investigated how ISS affects the state space size and found an interesting result. Fig. 11 shows a trace illustrating chatter for the case when ISS=2. The values in brackets, for instance (7,2,3), are (GSS,GSR,GAR). The server, in the CLOSED state, repeatedly sends a

Table 3. State Space Results

Case	Nodes	Arcs	Time (sec)	Dead Markings		
				Client_State	Server_State	Number
I	171,040	457,535	1,067	OPEN	OPEN	67
				CLOSED	CLOSED	1,153
				CLOSED	LISTEN	4
II	73	119	0	CLOSED	CLOSED	8
III	73	119	0	CLOSED	CLOSED	8
IV	30,787	76,796	62	CLOSED	CLOSED	645
V	3,281	8,998	3	CLOSED	CLOSED	64
VI	>545,703	>1,475,936	>152,200	CLOSED	CLOSED	>702
VI a)	437	828	0	CLOSED	CLOSED	33
VI b)	3,324	8,381	3	CLOSED	CLOSED	89
VI c)	33,644	85,926	74	CLOSED	CLOSED	642

Table 4. Growth of the State Space as a Function of ISS

ISS	Nodes	Arcs	Time (sec)	Dead Markings		
				Client_State	Server_State	Number
1	86,058	225,485	325	OPEN	OPEN	67
				CLOSED	CLOSED	733
				CLOSED	LISTEN	4
2	104,464	275,540	457	OPEN	OPEN	67
				CLOSED	CLOSED	823
				CLOSED	LISTEN	4
3	124,763	330,900	596	OPEN	OPEN	67
				CLOSED	CLOSED	923
				CLOSED	LISTEN	4
4	146,955	391,565	785	OPEN	OPEN	67
				CLOSED	CLOSED	1,022
				CLOSED	LISTEN	4
5	171,040	457,535	1,067	OPEN	OPEN	67
				CLOSED	CLOSED	1,153
				CLOSED	LISTEN	4

sequence-invalid DCCP-Reset packet while the client in PARTOPEN repeatedly responds with DCCP-Sync. The sequence and acknowledgement numbers in both packets increase over time until the sequence number of the DCCP-Reset received is greater than the client's GSR and becomes sequence-valid according to Table 1. Fig.11 shows the sequence number of the DCCP-Reset generated increases from zero to three while the client's GSR is equal to two. When receiving the sequence-valid DCCP-Reset (with seq=3), the client enters the TIMEWAIT state and then CLOSED after 2 MPL. A similar situation happens when the server enters the LISTEN state after sending the DCCP-Reset with sequence number zero. This behaviour creates unnecessary traffic, adversely affecting congestion in the Internet. It will be particularly severe if the initial sequence number is even moderately large, which will often be the case.

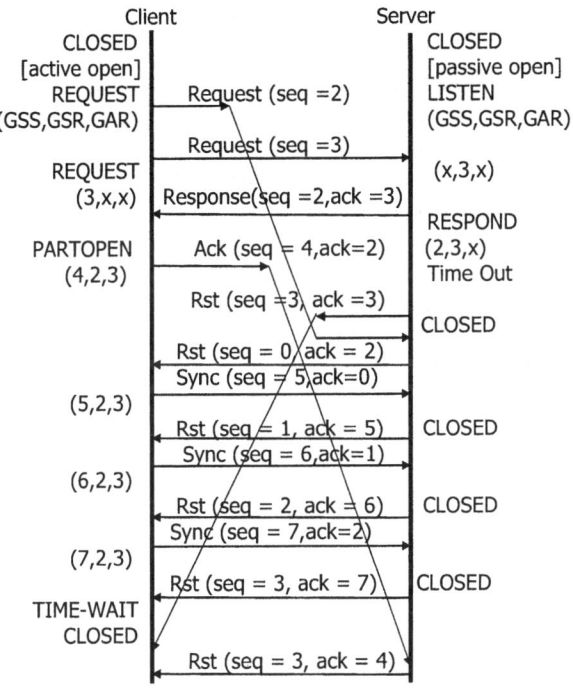

Fig. 11. Repeatedly Exchanged Messages for Case I with ISS=2

This problem is caused by the invalid DCCP-Reset packet having sequence number zero. Because there are no sequence number variables in the CLOSED or LISTEN state, according to the specification [8] section 8.3.1, the sequence number of the DCCP-Reset packet generated in the CLOSED and LISTEN states is the received acknowledgement number plus one. If there is no received acknowledgement number because the received packet type is DCCP-Request (or DCCP-Data), the sequence number of the DCCP-Reset packet is set to zero and the acknowledgement number is set to the received sequence number.

In versions 5 and 6 of the draft specification[6,7], the DCCP-Reset packet with sequence number zero is specified as a valid packet. However, our previous work [9,11] shows that this valid DCCP-Reset causes deadlocks where the server is in the CLOSED state and the client is in OPEN. Since draft specification version 7, a DCCP-Reset with sequence number zero is no longer considered a valid packet. A solution may be to ignore an incoming packet without an acknowledgement number when received in the CLOSED or LISTEN state. This is because every state (except CLOSED and LISTEN) has a Back-off timer, which will guarantee that the other end will eventually go to the CLOSED state.

5 Conclusion

This paper has illustrated a formal specification and has provided an initial but detailed analysis of DCCP's connection management procedures. Significant effort has been spent on ensuring that the CPN specification accurately captures the pseudo code and narrative description in the final Internet Draft version 11 [8]. This has revealed areas in the specification which we believe to be incomplete as discussed in section 3.5. Our analysis has discovered scenarios where the client keeps sending DCCP-Sync packets in response to the server sending sequence-invalid DCCP-Reset packets. This may have an adverse effect on congestion in the Internet, if the initial sequence number chosen is even moderately large. Future work will involve modifying the procedures to eliminate this problem and verifying that the revised model works correctly. We need to analyse our model when an application closes during connection establishment as was discussed in section 3.5. We would also like to extend our work to include Option/Feature negotiation.

References

1. Billington, J., Diaz, M. and Rozenberg, G., editors (1999), *Application of Petri Nets to Communication Networks*, Advances in Petri Nets, LNCS Vol 1605, Springer-Verlag.
2. Billington, J., Gallasch, G.,E. and Han, B. (2004), "A Coloured Petri Net Approach to Protocol Verification" in *Lectures on Concurrency and Petri Nets*, LNCS Vol 3098, pp. 210-290, Springer-Verlag.
3. Han, B. and Billington, J. (2002), "Validating TCP connection management" in *Workshop on Software Engineering and Formal Methods, Conferences in Research and Practice in Information Technology*, ACS, Vol. 12, pp. 47-55.
4. Jensen, K. (1997), *Coloured Petri Nets: Basic Concepts, Analysis Methods and Practical Use*. Volumes1-3, Monographs in Theoretical Computer Science, Springer-Verlag, Berlin.
5. Kohler, E. and Floyd, S. (2003), "Datagram Congestion Control Protocol (DCCP) overview", http://www.icir.org/kohler/dcp/summary.pdf.
6. Kohler, E. and Floyd, S. (2003), *Datagram Congestion Control Protocol, Internet-Draft version 5.* draft-ietf-dccp-spec-05.ps, October 2003, http://www.icir.org/kohler/dcp/.
7. Kohler, E. and Floyd, S. (2004), *Datagram Congestion Control Protocol, Internet-Draft version 6.* draft-ietf-dccp-spec-06.ps, February 2004, http://www.icir.org/kohler/dcp/.
8. Kohler, E. and Floyd, S. (2005), *Datagram Congestion Control Protocol, Internet-Draft version 11.* draft-ietf-dccp-spec-11.ps, March 2005, http://www.icir.org/kohler/dcp/.
9. Kongprakaiwoot, T. (2004), *Verification of the Datagram Congestion Control Protocol Using Coloured Petri Nets*. Master of Engineering Minor Thesis, Computer Systems Engineering Centre, University of South Australia.
10. University of Aarhus (2004), Design/CPN Online. http://www.daimi.au.dk/ designCPN/.
11. Vanit-Anunchai, S. and Billington, J. (2004), "Initial Result of a Formal Analysis of DCCP Connection Management", *Proc. Fourth International Network Conference*, Plymouth, UK, 6-9 July 2004, pp. 63–70.

Thread Allocation Protocols for Distributed Real-Time and Embedded Systems[*]

César Sánchez[1], Henny B. Sipma[1],
Venkita Subramonian[2], Christopher Gill[2], and Zohar Manna[1]

[1] Computer Science Department,
Stanford University, Stanford, CA 94305, USA
{cesar,sipma,manna}@CS.Stanford.EDU
[2] Department of Computer Science and Engineering,
Washington University, St. Louis, MO 63130, USA
{venkita, cdgill}@CSE.wustl.EDU

Abstract. We study the problem of thread allocation in asynchronous distributed real-time and embedded systems. Each distributed node handles a limited set of resources, in particular a limited thread pool. Different methods can be invoked concurrently in each node, either by external agents or as a remote call during the execution of a method. In this paper we study thread allocation under a *WaitOnConnection* strategy, in which each nested upcall made while a thread is waiting must be made in a different thread.

We study protocols that control the allocation of threads to guarantee the absence of deadlocks. First, we introduce a computational model in which we formally describe the different protocols and their desired properties. Then, we study two scenarios: a single agent performing sequential calls, and multiple agents with unrestricted concurrency. For each scenario we present (1) algorithms to compute the minimum amount of resources to avoid deadlocks, and (2) run-time protocols that control the allocation of these resources.

1 Introduction

In this paper we present a computational model for thread allocation in distributed real-time and embedded (DRE) systems. The model is targeted at component middleware architectures in which components make remote two-way method calls to other components. In particular, we consider the case where a remote method call f by component A to component B may result in one or more method calls from B (or other components) to A before f returns. These method calls are known as "nested upcalls".

Nested upcalls can occur in the context of a variety of middleware concurrency architectures, including the Leader/Followers [16] approach used in

---

[*] This research was supported in part by NSF grants CCR-01-21403, CCR-02-20134, CCR-02-09237, CNS-0411363, and CCF-0430102, by ARO grant DAAD19-01-1-0723, and by NAVY/ONR contract N00014-03-1-0939.

TAO [15, 10] and the Half-Sync/Half-Async [16] approach used in the variant of nORB [4] used to integrate actual and simulated system components [18]. These kinds of middleware have been used in turn to build a wide range of DRE systems for applications ranging from avionics mission computing information systems [6] to active damage detection using MEMS vibration sensor/actuators [20].

Ensuring the safety and liveness of concurrent nested upcalls in middleware for DRE systems is thus an important and compelling problem. In current practice, middleware concurrency architectures are realized in software frameworks designed according to documented best practices, but it is still possible for unforeseen factors introduced during the design to result in safety and liveness violations [17]. Hence, a more formal basis can have a significant impact on the correctness of these systems, which motivates the work presented here.

There are two main strategies to deal with nested upcalls. The first is known as *WaitOnConnection*, where component A holds on to the thread from which method call f was invoked. With this strategy any nested calls to A will have to acquire a new thread to run. The second approach relies on the use of a *reactor*, a well-known technique for multiplexing asynchronously arriving events onto one or more threads [16]. This approach is known as *WaitOnReactor*, in which component A releases the thread after the method call is made. To preserve the semantics of the two-way call, it maintains a stack to keep track of the order in which methods were invoked, such that they can be exited in reverse order. Both approaches have advantages and disadvantages. A disadvantage of the first approach is that threads cannot be reused while the reactor is waiting for the method to return, which can lead to deadlock. A disadvantage of the second approach is that the stack must be unwound in *last-in-first-out* order, resulting in blocking delays for the completion of methods initiated earlier, which can lead to deadline violations. This may be especially problematic in systems with multiple agents.

In other complementary research [19] we have examined safety and liveness for the *WaitOnReactor* approach. In this paper we only consider the *WaitOnConnection* approach, and focus on deadlock avoidance in that context. We assume we are given a set of reactors $\mathcal{R}$, hosting components of the system, and a set of call-graphs $\mathcal{G}$, representing the possible call sequences that components can invoke. We also assume that each call graph may be invoked multiple times concurrently. The goals are: (1) to determine what minimum number of threads is necessary in each reactor to avoid deadlock; and (2) to construct protocols that are deadlock free and make efficient use of the threads available (that is, they do not unnecessarily block invocations). We will consider two cases: (1) the number of concurrent processes is fixed in advance (which is common in DRE systems), and (2) the number of concurrent processes is not bounded (such as in network services).

Related Work. Deadlocks have been studied in many contexts. In computer science, one of the first protocols for deadlock avoidance was Dijkstra's Banker's algorithm [5], which initiated much follow-up research [7–9, 1], and which is still the basis for most current deadlock avoidance algorithms. In the control community, deadlock avoidance mechanisms have been studied in the context of Flexible Manufacturing Systems (FMSs) [14, 3, 21, 13]. In contrast with the Banker's algorithm, in which only the maximum amount of resources is taken into account, protocols for FMSs take into account more information about the processes to maximize concurrency without sacrificing deadlock freedom.

In the distributed systems community (see, for example, [11]), general solutions to distributed deadlock tend to be considered impractical. For example, global consistency and atomicity would be a prerequisite for a "distributed version" of the Banker's algorithm. Most approaches so far have focused on deadlock detection and roll-back (e.g. in distributed databases) and deadlock prevention by programming discipline (e.g. by observing a partial order on locks acquired).

The protocols presented in this paper can be viewed as a practical solution to the case where extra information is available in the form of call graphs, which is common in DRE systems. We show that the incorporation of this information enables efficient "local" protocols (that is, no communication between distributed nodes is required at runtime) that guarantee absence of deadlock.

2 Computational Model

We define a system $\mathcal{S}$ as a tuple $\langle \mathcal{R}, \mathcal{G} \rangle$ consisting of a set of reactors $\mathcal{R}$: $\{r_1, \ldots, r_k\}$ and a set of distinct call graphs $\mathcal{G} : \{G_1, \ldots, G_m\}$.

Definition 1 (Call-graph). *Given a set of method names N, a call-graph is a finite tree $\langle V = (N \times \mathcal{R}), E \rangle$ with nodes consisting of a method name and a reactor. A node (f, r) denotes that method f runs in reactor r. An edge from (f_1, r_1) to (f_2, r_2) denotes that method f_1, in the course of its execution may invoke method f_2 in reactor r_2.*

For ease of exposition we assume that methods of child nodes are hosted in a different reactor than their parent nodes. Local calls can always be run in the same thread, implemented as conventional method calls, and are not considered here. We use the notation $f{:}r$ to represent that method f runs in reactor r.

Example 1. Figure 1 shows an example of a call-graph. The methods f_i run in reactor r, the method g runs in reactor s, and the methods h_i run in reactor t. Method f_1 may invoke the remote methods g and h_1.

We assume that each reactor r has a fixed number of pre-allocated threads. Although in many modern operating systems threads can be spawned dynamically, many DRE systems pre-allocate fixed sets of threads to avoid the relatively large and variable cost of thread creation and initialization. We assume that each reactor r has a set of local variables V_r that includes the constant $T_r \geq 1$ denoting the number of threads present in r, and a variable t_r representing the number of available threads.

A *protocol* for controlling thread allocation is implemented by code executed in a reactor before and after each method is dispatched. This code can be dependent on the call graph node. The structure of a protocol is shown in Figure 2

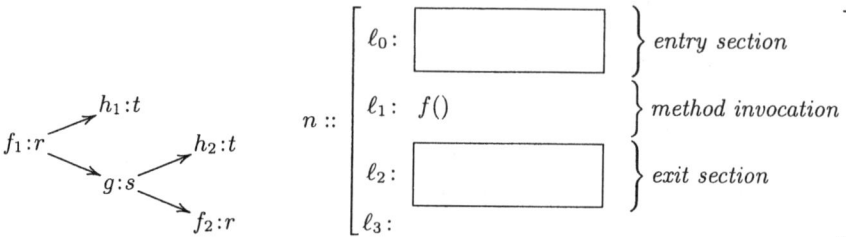

Fig. 1. A sample call graph G **Fig. 2.** Protocol schema

for a node $n = f{:}r$. The entry and exit sections implement the thread allocation policy. Upon invocation, the entry section typically checks thread availability by inspecting local variables V_r of reactor r and assigns a thread if one is available. The method invocation section executes the code of f; it terminates after all its descendants in the call graph have terminated and returned. The exit section releases the thread and may update some local variables in reactor r.

Multiple instances of these protocols may execute concurrently, one for each invocation. Each instance is called a *task*. Thus the local variables of the reactor are shared between tasks running in the same reactor, but are not visible to tasks that reside in other reactors.

The global behavior of a system S is represented by sequences of (global) states, where a state $\sigma : \langle \mathcal{P}, s_\mathcal{R} \rangle$ contains a set of tasks together with their local states, $\mathcal{P}$, and a valuation $s_\mathcal{R}$ of the local variables in all reactors. To describe a task state we use the notion of labeled call graph:

Definition 2 (Labeled Call Graph). *Let ℓ_0, ℓ_1, ℓ_2, and ℓ_3 be protocol location labels representing the progress of a task, as illustrated in Figure 2. A labeled call graph (G, γ) is an instance of a call graph $G \in \mathcal{G}$ and a labeling function $\gamma : N_G \mapsto \{\bot, \ell_0, \ell_1, \ell_2, \ell_3\}$ that maps each node in the call graph to a protocol location, or to $\bot$ for method calls that have not been performed yet.*

Then, formally, the state of a task is modeled as a labeled call graph. A subtree of a labeled call graph models the state of a *sub-task*. When the context of the subtree is not relevant, we will write task to refer to the corresponding sub-task. A task is *active* if its root is labeled ℓ_1 or ℓ_2, *waiting* if it is labeled ℓ_0, and *terminated* if it is labeled ℓ_3. We use upper-case letters $P, Q, P_1, \ldots$ to denote tasks and lower case letters $n, n_1, \ldots$ to denote call-graph nodes. To simplify the presentation, given a task $P = (G, \gamma)$ we use $\gamma(P)$ as an alias of $\gamma(\text{root}(P))$. We also say that task P is in location ℓ if $\gamma(P) = \ell$.

A *system* $S : \langle \mathcal{R}, \mathcal{G} \rangle$ gives rise to the *state transition system* (see [12]) $\Psi : \langle V, \Theta, \mathcal{T} \rangle$ consisting of the following components:

- $V : \{I\} \cup V_R$: a set of variables, containing the variable I denoting a set of labeled call graphs (tasks and their state), and the local variables $V_R = \bigcup_{r \in \mathcal{R}} V_r$ of each reactor.

- $\Theta : I = \emptyset \wedge \bigwedge_{r \in \mathcal{R}} \Theta_r$: the initial condition, specifying initial values for the local reactor variables and initializing the set of tasks to the empty set.
- $\mathcal{T}$: a set of state transitions consisting of the following global transitions:
  1. **Creation:** A new task P, with $\gamma(n) = \bot$ for all nodes n in its call graph, is added to I:

  $$\tau_1 : I' = I \cup \{P\} \wedge pres(V_R)$$

  where $pres(V_R)$ states that all variables in V_R are preserved.

  2. **Method invocation:** Let $P \in I$ and Q be a sub-task of P such that either (a) $Q = P$ or (b) $\gamma(Q) = \bot$ and its parent node is in ℓ_1. A function invocation changes the annotation of Q to ℓ_0:

  $$\tau_2 : \gamma(Q) = \bot \wedge \gamma'(Q) = \ell_0 \wedge pres(V_R)$$

  3. **Method entry:** Let Q be a waiting task whose enabling condition is satisfied. The method entry transition marks Q as ℓ_1 and updates the local variables in its reactor according to the protocol of the node $n = root(Q)$. Formally, let $En_n(V_r)$ be the enabling condition of the entry of the protocol of Q, and $Act_n(V_r, V_r')$ represent the change in variables of reactor r after the entry is executed; then:

  $$\tau_3 : \gamma(Q) = \ell_0 \wedge En_n(V_r) \wedge \gamma'(Q) = \ell_1 \wedge Act_n(V_r, V_r') \wedge pres(V_R - V_r)$$

  4. **Method execution:** Let Q be a task in ℓ_1 such that all its descendants are labeled $\bot$ or ℓ_3. This transition denotes the termination of Q. The status of Q is updated to ℓ_2:

  $$\tau_4 : \gamma(Q) = \ell_1 \wedge \bigwedge_{R \in descs(Q)} (\gamma(R) = \bot \vee \gamma(R) = \ell_3) \wedge \gamma'(Q) = \ell_2 \wedge pres(V_R)$$

  5. **Method exit:** Let Q be a task in ℓ_2; the method-exit transition moves Q to ℓ_3 and updates the variables in its reactor according to the exit of the protocol for $n = root(Q)$. Formally, let $Out_n(V_r, V_r')$ represent the transformation that the exit protocol for n performs on the variables of reactor r; then

  $$\tau_5 : \gamma(Q) = \ell_2 \wedge \gamma'(Q) = \ell_3 \wedge Out_n(V_r, V_r') \wedge pres(V_R - V_r)$$

  6. **Deletion:** A task P in ℓ_3 is removed from I:

  $$\tau_6 : \gamma(P) = \ell_3 \wedge I' = I - \{P\}$$

  7. **Silent:** All variables are preserved: $\quad \tau_7 : pres(V)$

All transitions except **Creation** and **Silent** are called *progressing* transitions, since they correspond to the progress of some existing task. The system as defined is a nondeterministic system. It assumes an external environment that determines creation of new tasks, and a scheduler that selects which task progresses. In particular, the scheduler decides which task in the entry transition proceeds to the method section. If any progressing transition *can* occur, then some progressing transition will be taken in preference to any non-progressing transition. Therefore, unless the system is deadlocked, an infinite sequence of silent transitions cannot occur because a progressing transition will occur eventually. If in state σ there are k active tasks corresponding to methods in reactor r, then we say that there are k threads allocated in r.

Definition 3 (Run). *A* run *of a system Ψ is a sequence of $\sigma_0, \sigma_1, \ldots$ of states such that σ_0 is an initial state, and for every i, there exists a transition $\tau \in \mathcal{T}$ such that σ_{i+1} results from taking τ from σ_i.*

3 Properties

In this section we formally define some properties to study the correctness of the protocols. Most properties will be presented as *invariants*. Figure 3(a) illustrates the simplest possible protocol, EMPTY-P, in which the entry and exit sections do nothing with the reactor variables.

Definition 4 (Invariant). *Given a system $\mathcal{S}$, an expression φ over the system variables of $\mathcal{S}$ is an* invariant *of $\mathcal{S}$ if it is true in every state of every run of $\mathcal{S}$.*

An expression can be proven invariant by showing that it is inductive or implied by an inductive expression. An expression φ is *inductive* for a transition system $\mathcal{S} : \langle V, \Theta, \mathcal{T} \rangle$ if it is implied by the initial condition, $\Theta \rightarrow \varphi$, and it is preserved by all its transitions, $\varphi \wedge \tau \rightarrow \varphi'$, for all $\tau \in \mathcal{T}$.

Definition 5 (Adequate). *A protocol is* adequate *if the number of threads allocated in every reactor r never exceeds the total number of threads in r, T_r.*

Adequacy is a fundamental property, required in every reasonable protocol, since no more resources than available can possibly be granted. ADEQUATE-P is a simple adequate protocol, shown in Figure 3(b), in which the entry section (ℓ_0) blocks further progress until the guard expression $1 \leq t_r$ evaluates to true. Its adequacy is a consequence of the following invariants:

$$\psi_1 : \forall r \in \mathcal{R} \,.\, t_r \geq 0$$
$$\psi_2 : \forall r \in \mathcal{R} \,.\, T_r = t_r + at\_\ell_{1,r} + at\_\ell_{2,r}$$

where, $at\_\ell_{1,r}$ and $at\_\ell_{2,r}$ denote the total number of active sub-tasks in reactor r. It is easy to show that ψ_1 and ψ_2 are inductive.

Definition 6 (Deadlock). *A state σ is a* deadlock *if some task is in ℓ_0, but only non-progressing transitions are enabled.*

If a deadlock is reached, the tasks involved cannot progress. Intuitively, each of the tasks has locked some resources—threads in our case—that are necessary for other tasks to complete, but none of them has enough resources to terminate. The following example shows that ADEQUATE-P does not guarantee absence of deadlock.

$$n :: \begin{bmatrix} \ell_0: & \text{skip} \\ \ell_1: & f() \\ \ell_2: & \text{skip} \\ \ell_3: & \end{bmatrix} \qquad n :: \begin{bmatrix} \ell_0: & \begin{bmatrix} \text{when } 1 \leq t_r \text{ do} \\ \quad t_r \text{--} \end{bmatrix} \\ \ell_1: & f() \\ \ell_2: & t_r \text{++} \\ \ell_3: & \end{bmatrix}$$

(a) The protocol EMPTY-P (b) The protocol ADEQUATE-P

Fig. 3. Protocols EMPTY-P and ADEQUATE-P for node $n = (f{:}r)$

Example 2. Consider the system $\mathcal{S} : \langle \{r, s\}, \{G_1, G_2\} \rangle$ with two reactors r and s, and two call graphs

$$G_1 : n_{11} : \langle f{:}r \rangle \longrightarrow n_{12} : \langle g_2{:}s \rangle \quad \text{and} \quad G_2 : n_{21} : \langle g{:}s \rangle \longrightarrow n_{22} : \langle f_2{:}r \rangle.$$

Both reactors have one thread ($T_r = T_s = 1$). Assume the protocol for all nodes is ADEQUATE-P. Let $\sigma : \langle \{P_1, P_2\}, t_r = 0, t_s = 0 \rangle$ be a state with two tasks: P_1 an instance of G_1 with $\gamma(n_{11}) = \ell_1$ and $\gamma(n_{12}) = \ell_0$, and P_2 an instance of G_2 with $\gamma(n_{21}) = \ell_1$ and $\gamma(n_{22}) = \ell_0$. It is easy to see that σ is a deadlock: no progressing transition is enabled. Furthermore, σ is reachable from an initial state and hence appears in some run.

In a deadlock state, independent of the protocol used, any task that is active must have a descendant task that is waiting for a thread, as expressed by the following lemma.

Lemma 1. *In a deadlock state, any active task has a waiting descendant.*

Proof. Let σ be a deadlock state and P an active task. Then $\gamma(P) = \ell_1$, since for $\gamma(P) = \ell_2$, transition τ_5 is enabled, contradicting deadlock. We prove that P has at least one waiting descendant by induction on the position of P in the call graph. For the base case, let P correspond to a leaf node. But then transition τ_4 is enabled, contradicting deadlock. Thus a leaf node cannot be active in a deadlock state. For the inductive case, let $Q_1, \ldots, Q_n$ be the descendants of P. If some Q_i is waiting we are done. If some Q_i is active, by the inductive hypothesis, it has a waiting descendant, and hence P has a waiting descendant. Otherwise for all Q_i, $\gamma(Q_i) = \bot$ or $\gamma(Q_i) = \ell_3$. But then τ_4 is enabled, contradicting deadlock. □

Another desirable property of thread allocation protocols is absence of starvation, that is, every task eventually progresses. A task P starves in a run of a system if, after some prefix run, the labeling of P never changes thereafter. A system prevents starvation if no task starves in any of its runs.

Deadlock implies starvation, but the converse does not hold. For example, if other tasks are scheduled in preference to it throughout the run, but the task could have made progress had it been scheduled, that constitutes starvation but not deadlock. This raises the question of schedulers to enforce particular (possibly application-specific [2]) policies for process scheduling, but a detailed consideration of that issue is outside the scope of this paper.

4 Deadlock-Avoidance Protocols

This section introduces several protocols and studies whether they prevent deadlocks in different scenarios. The protocols have the structure shown in Figure 2, where the entry and exit sections may be different for different nodes in the call graph. More precisely, the protocols are parameterized by an annotation of the call graphs, $\alpha : V \mapsto \mathbb{N}^+$, that maps nodes of all call graphs to the positive natural numbers. Intuitively, the annotation provides a measure of the resources—threads in our case—needed to complete the task corresponding to the node. We consider two annotations: *height* and *local height*. Height of a node in a call graph is the usual height of a node in a tree. Local height only takes into account nodes in the same reactor.

Definition 7 (Height). *Given a call graph G, the height of a node n in G, written $h(n)$, is*

$$h(n) = \begin{cases} 1 & \text{if } n \text{ is a leaf, and} \\ 1 + max\{h(m) \mid n \to m\} & \text{otherwise.} \end{cases}$$

where $n \to m$ denotes that m is a child node of n.

Definition 8 (Local Height). *Given a call graph G, the local height of a node $n = f{:}r$ in G, written $lh(f{:}r)$ is*

$$lh(f{:}r) = \begin{cases} 1 & \text{if } f{:}r \text{ is a leaf, and} \\ 1 + max\{lh(g{:}s) \mid f{:}r \to^+ g{:}s \text{ and } r = s\} & \text{otherwise.} \end{cases}$$

where $n \to^+ m$ denotes that m is a descendant of n.

Example 3. Figure 4 shows a call-graph (left) and its local height (center) and height (right) annotations. Here, $n = f_1 : r$ has local height 2, since f_1 may indirectly call f_2 in the same reactor through a nested call.

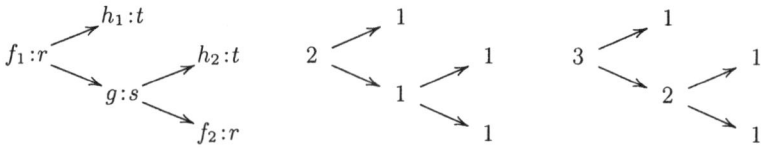

Fig. 4. Sample call graph (left) and its local-height (center) and height (right) annotations

4.1 Single Agent

We first consider the scenario of a single agent sequentially activating tasks, also studied in [17]. This scenario represents an environment that cannot make any

$$n :: \begin{bmatrix} \ell_0: & \begin{bmatrix} \textbf{when } \alpha(n) \leq t_r \textbf{ do} \\ \quad t_r\text{--} \end{bmatrix} \\ \ell_1: & f() \\ \ell_2: & t_r\text{++} \\ \ell_3: & \end{bmatrix}$$

Fig. 5. The protocol BASIC-P for call-graph node $n = (f:r)$

concurrent calls. In terms of our model, this corresponds to systems in which the number of tasks in any state is at most 1, that is, systems for which $|I| \leq 1$ is an invariant. In this scenario the following theorem establishes a necessary and sufficient condition to guarantee absence of deadlocks.

Theorem 1 (from [17]). *To perform a call with local-height n with absence of deadlock, at least n available threads in the local reactor are needed.*

Theorem 1 provides a simple, design-time method to compute the minimum number of threads, T_r, needed in each reactor r to guarantee absence of deadlock: T_r must be at least the maximum local height for any node in any call graph whose method call resides in r. The condition is necessary, because if it is violated a deadlock will occur, independent of the protocol used. The condition is sufficient, because if it is met, no deadlock will occur. Thus, in the single agent case the trivial protocol EMPTY-P, shown in Figure 3(a), will guarantee absence of deadlock, provided all reactors have the required number of threads.

4.2 Multiple Agents: Generic Protocols

In case of multiple agents performing multiple concurrent calls, the condition expressed in Theorem 1 is necessary but not sufficient to guarantee the absence of a deadlock (using EMPTY-P) as illustrated by the following example.

Example 4. Consider again the system of Example 2. This system satisfies the condition of Theorem 1: the local heights of the nodes are $lh(n_{11}) = lh(n_{12}) = lh(n_{21}) = lh(n_{22}) = 1$ and $T_r = T_s = 1$. A deadlock is produced however, if P_1, an instance of G_1, takes the thread in r and P_2, an instance of G_2, takes the thread in s.

Indeed, it can be shown that no number of pre-allocated threads in reactors r and s in the above example can prevent deadlock in the presence of an unbounded number of multiple concurrent calls. Thus more sophisticated protocols are needed to control access to the threads.

We propose two such protocols: BASIC-P and EFFICIENT-P, both parameterized by the annotation function $\alpha : V \mapsto \mathbb{N}^+$. In this section we present some properties for generic annotations α; in the next section we analyze deadlock avoidance and resource utilization for some specific height annotations.

The first protocol, BASIC-P, is shown in Figure 5. The reactor variable t_r is used to keep track of the threads currently available in the reactor. In the entry section access is granted only if the number of resources indicated by the annotation function at that node, $\alpha(n)$, is less than or equal to the number of threads available. When access is granted, t_r is decremented by one, reflecting that one thread has been allocated. Note that not all resources requested are reserved.

The second protocol, EFFICIENT-P, shown in Figure 6, exploits the observation that every task that needs just one resource can always, independently of other tasks, terminate once it gets the resource. The protocol has two reactor variables, t_r and p_r, where t_r, as in BASIC-P, keeps track of the number of threads currently available, and p_r tracks the threads that are potentially available. The difference with BASIC-P is that the number of *potentially* available threads is not reduced when a thread is granted to a task that needs only one thread. With EFFICIENT-P fewer tasks are blocked, thus increasing potential concurrency and improving resource utilization.

Example 5. Consider the system $\mathcal{S}: \langle \{r,s\}, \{G_1, G_2\}\rangle$ with $T_r = T_s = 2$ and

$$G_1 : n_{11} : \langle f_1{:}r\rangle \quad \text{and} \quad G_2 : n_{21} : \langle f_2{:}r\rangle \longrightarrow n_{22} : \langle g{:}s\rangle.$$

with annotations $\alpha(n_{11}) = \alpha(n_{22}) = 1$ and $\alpha(n_{21}) = 2$. Assume the following arrival of tasks: P_1: an instance of G_1 and P_2 an instance of G_2. With BASIC-P, P_2 is blocked until P_1 is finished and has released the thread, while with EFFICIENT-P, P_2 can run concurrently with P_1.

To study the properties of different annotations, we first establish some properties that hold for EFFICIENT-P [1] for any annotation α. We first introduce some notation and abbreviations. Let $at\_\ell_{i\_j,r}$ denote the number of tasks in a reactor r that are at location ℓ_{i_j}. Then the number of active tasks P with annotation $\alpha(P) = 1$ in r is equal to $act_{1,r} \stackrel{\text{def}}{=} at\_\ell_{1\_1,r} + at\_\ell_{2\_1,r}$, and the number of tasks in r with $\alpha(P) > 1$ is $act_{>1,r} \stackrel{\text{def}}{=} at\_\ell_{1\_2,r} + at\_\ell_{2\_2,r}$. Let $act_{>k,r}$ denote the number of tasks in r with annotation greater than k. With initial condition $\Theta_r : t_r = p_r \wedge T_r = t_r$, it is easy to verify that the following are inductive invariants for all reactors.

$$\varphi_1 : t_r \geq 0$$
$$\varphi_2 : p_r \geq 1$$
$$\varphi_3 : p_r = t_r + act_{1,r}$$
$$\varphi_4 : T_r = p_r + act_{>1,r}$$

The following lemmas apply to all reactors.

Lemma 2. *If $t_r = 0$ then there exists at least one active task with annotation 1 in r, that is, $\varphi_5 : t_r = 0 \rightarrow act_{1,r} \geq 1$ is an invariant.*

Proof. Follows directly from φ_2 and φ_3. □

---
[1] The same properties hold for BASIC-P, but we will not prove them here.

$$n :: \begin{bmatrix} \ell_{0\_1}: & \begin{bmatrix} \text{when } 1 \leq t_r \text{ do} \\ t_r\text{--} \end{bmatrix} \\ \ell_{1\_1}: & f() \\ \ell_{2\_1}: & t_r\text{++} \\ \ell_{3\_1}: & \end{bmatrix} \qquad n :: \begin{bmatrix} \ell_{0\_2}: & \begin{bmatrix} \text{when } \alpha(n) \leq p_r \wedge 1 \leq t_r \text{ do} \\ \langle p_r\text{--}, \ t_r\text{--} \rangle \end{bmatrix} \\ \ell_{1\_2}: & f() \\ \ell_{2\_2}: & \langle t_r\text{++}, \ p_r\text{++} \rangle \\ \ell_{3\_2}: & \end{bmatrix}$$

If $\alpha(n) = 1$ \qquad\qquad If $\alpha(n) > 1$

Fig. 6. The protocol EFFICIENT-P for node $n = (f\!:\!r)$

Lemma 3. *The number of active tasks P with annotation $\alpha(P) > k$, for $0 \leq k \leq T_r$, is less than or equal to $T_r - k$, that is, φ_6 : $\text{act}_{>k,r} \leq T_r - k$ is an invariant.*

Proof. To show that φ_6 is an invariant, it suffices to show that in a state where $\text{act}_{>k,r} = T_r - k$, a waiting task Q with $\alpha(Q) > k$ cannot proceed. For $k = 0$ we have $\text{act}_{>0,r} = T_r$. By φ_3 and φ_4, $T_r = t_r + \text{act}_{>1,r} + \text{act}_{1,r} = t_r + \text{act}_{>0,r}$, and thus $t_r = 0$. Consequently, the transitions for both ℓ_{0_1} and ℓ_{0_2} are disabled for Q. For $k > 0$, note that $\text{act}_{>k,r} \leq \text{act}_{>1,r}$, and thus in a state where $\text{act}_{>k,r} = T_r - k$, we have $T_r - k \leq \text{act}_{>1,r}$. By φ_4, $p_r = T_r - \text{act}_{>1,r}$, and thus $p_r \leq k$. Consequently, transition ℓ_{0_2} is disabled for k, as by assumption $\alpha(Q) > k$. □

Lemma 4. *If a task P is in location ℓ_{0_2} in r and the transition for ℓ_{0_2} is not enabled for P, then there is an active task Q in r with annotation $\alpha(Q) \leq \alpha(P)$.*

Proof. Note that $\alpha(P) > 1$. Transition ℓ_{0_2} is disabled for P if $t_r = 0$ or if $\alpha(P) > p_r$. If $t_r = 0$, then by Lemma 2 there exists an active task Q with annotation 1, and hence $\alpha(Q) < \alpha(P)$. If $\alpha(P) > p_r$ then by φ_4, $\text{act}_{>1,r} > T_r - \alpha(P)$. However, by Lemma 3, $\text{act}_{>\alpha(P),r} \leq T_r - \alpha(P)$. Thus there must at least be one active task Q in r such that $\alpha(Q) \leq \alpha(P)$. □

4.3 Protocols Based on Height and Local Height

In Section 4.2 we introduced the protocol EFFICIENT-P for a generic call graph annotation α that provides a measure of the number of resources required to complete the task. In this section we analyze two such measures: local height (Def. 8) and height (Def. 7). Local height requires the least resources. Unfortunately it does not guarantee freedom of deadlock. We prove that using height does guarantee absence of deadlock. However, for many designs it is too conservative in its requirements for resources. Therefore in Section 4.4 we propose a less conservative annotation, based on the combination of all graphs rather than on individual call graphs, that still guarantees deadlock freedom.

Local Height. Using local height, as defined in Def. 8 for α in the protocols BASIC-P and EFFICIENT-P does not guarantee absence of deadlock. A simple counterexample is provided by Example 4 for both protocols.

Height. We will now prove that using height, as defined in Def. 7 for α guarantees absence of deadlock. We assume that for every reactor the number of threads T_r is greater than or equal to the highest annotation of any node that runs in r in any call graph in the system. We first prove one more auxiliary lemma.

Lemma 5. *With the use of* EFFICIENT-P *with the height annotation, every task P with $h(P) = 1$ can complete.*

Proof. Note that P can always progress when it is active, since it is a leaf node. Thus it is sufficient to show that it can eventually progress when it is waiting at ℓ_{0_1}. If $t_r \geq 1$ it can obviously progress. If $t_r = 0$, then by Lemma 2, there exists an active task Q in r with $h(Q) = 1$. This task can terminate, thereby incrementing t_r, and thus unblocking P. □

Theorem 2. EFFICIENT-P *with height annotation guarantees absence of deadlock.*

Proof. By contradiction, suppose that σ is a reachable deadlock state. Let $P \in I$ be a task in σ such that $h(P)$ is minimal in I. Consider two cases: (1) $h(P) = 1$. By Lemma 5, P can eventually progress, contradicting deadlock. (2) $h(P) > 1$. If P is active, then by Lemma 1 it must have a waiting descendant, contradicting that P has minimal height. If P is waiting, then by Lemma 4 there exists an active task Q with $h(Q) \leq h(P)$. Again $h(Q) < h(P)$ contradicts the minimality of P. If $h(Q) = h(P)$, then Q, being active, must have a waiting descendant by Lemma 1, contradicting the minimality of P. □

Thus, if every call graph is annotated with height and every reactor r is provided with at least as many threads as the maximum height of a node that runs in r, then EFFICIENT-P guarantees deadlock-free operation. The disadvantage of using height as an annotation is that the number of threads to be provided to each reactor can be much larger than is strictly necessary. This not only wastes resources, it may also make some systems impractical, as illustrated by the following example.

Example 6. Consider a system $\mathcal{S} : \langle \mathcal{R}, \{G_1, \ldots, G_m\}\rangle$. A simple way to force invocations of $G_1, \ldots, G_m$ to be performed sequentially is to introduce a new reactor r— called the *serializer*—and to merge $G_1, \ldots, G_m$ into a single call graph by adding a root node n, and making $G_1, \ldots, G_m$ its subtrees. When using EFFICIENT-P with the height annotation, the new node node n is annotated with $h(n) = max(h(G_1), \ldots, h(G_m)) + 1$, which may be large. Now r needs to be provided with this many threads, while one would have sufficed.

Clearly, using height may be wasteful of resources. In the next section we propose a more efficient annotation that addresses this problem.

4.4 A More Efficient Annotation

Deadlock is caused by cyclic dependencies. Using EFFICIENT-P with an annotation without cyclic dependencies prevents deadlock. Example 4 showed that the

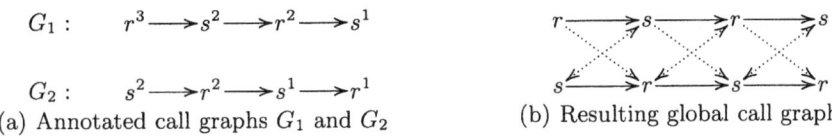

Fig. 7. Global call graph for two call graphs G_1 and G_2

deadlock produced with local height as annotation was caused by the interaction of multiple call graphs. Thus, a check for cyclic dependencies must consider the union of all call graphs.

Definition 9 (Global Call Graph). *Given a system* $S : \langle \mathcal{R}, \{G_1, \ldots, G_m\}\rangle$ *with* $G_i : \langle V_i, E_i\rangle$, *where* V_i, V_j *are assumed to be disjoint for* $i \neq j$, *and annotation function* $\alpha : \bigcup_i V_i \mapsto \mathbb{N}$, *the global call graph for* S *and* α, $G_{S,\alpha} : \langle V_S, E_D, E_A\rangle$ *consists of*

- V_S: $\bigcup_i V_i$;
- E_D: $\bigcup_i \to_i^+$, *the union of the descendant relations of all call graphs, where* $\to^+$ *is the transitive closure of* E_i;
- E_A: $\{(v_1 : \langle f : r\rangle, v_2 : \langle g : s\rangle) \mid \alpha(v_1) \geq \alpha(v_2) \text{ and } r = s\}$ *where* v_1 *and* v_2 *may belong to different call graphs* G_i.

Example 7. Figure 7(b) shows the global call graph for two annotated call graphs G_1 and G_2, where the solid lines indicate edges in E_D (no composed edges are shown) and the dotted lines indicate edges in E_A.

Definition 10 (Dependency Relation). *Given global call graph* $G_{S,\alpha} : \langle V_S, E_D, E_A\rangle$, $v_1 \in V_S$ *is dependent on* $v_2 \in V_S$, *written* $v_1 \succ v_2$, *if there exists a path from* v_1 *to* v_2 *consisting of edges in* $E_A \cup E_D$ *with at least one edge in* E_D.

A global call graph has a *cyclic dependency* if for some node v, $v \succ v$.

Theorem 3 (Annotation). *Given a system* S *and annotation* α, *if the global call graph* $G_{S,\alpha}$ *does not contain any cyclic dependencies, then* EFFICIENT-P *used with* α *guarantees absence of deadlock for* S.

Proof. We first observe that, in the absence of cyclic dependencies, the dependency relation $\succ$ is a partial order on the nodes in all call graphs, the proof closely follows that of Theorem 2.

By contradiction, suppose that σ is a reachable deadlock state. Let $P \in I$ be a task in the set of tasks in σ such that P resides in reactor r and is minimal with respect to $\succ$. Consider three cases: (1) P is active. Then, by Lemma 1, P must have a waiting descendant Q, but then $P \succ Q$, contradicting the minimality of P. (2) P is waiting and $\alpha(P) = 1$. Then $t_r = 0$ (otherwise P could proceed, contradicting deadlock), and by Lemma 2, there exists an active task Q in r with annotation 1, and thus there exists an edge in E_A from P to Q. But by Lemma 1, Q has a waiting descendant R, and thus $P \succ R$, contradicting minimality of P.

(3) P is waiting and $\alpha(P) > 1$. By Lemma 4, there exists an active task Q with $\alpha(Q) \le \alpha(P)$, and, as for case (2) there exists a task R such that $P \succ R$, contradicting minimality of P. □

It is easy to see that the conditions posed by Theorem 3 require the annotation to subsume local height. On the other hand, height clearly satisfies the conditions. For many systems, however, the annotation can be significantly lower than height. For example, in Example 6, the serializer node can safely be given annotation 1, instead of the maximum height of all call graphs.

5 Conclusions and Future work

We have formalized thread allocation in DRE systems and proposed several "local" protocols that guarantee absence of deadlock with respect to availability of threads. We have assumed static call graphs, which are the norm in many DRE systems.

These protocols are of practical as well as theoretical interest: they can be implemented (1) *transparently*, *e.g.*, by using the protocols to filter which enabled handles in a reactor's handle set will be dispatched in each iteration of a reactor's event loop [16]; (2) *efficiently*, *e.g.*, by storing pre-computed call graph annotation constants and references to protocol variables for each method in a hash map, to allow constant time lookup at run-time; and (3) *effectively*, *e.g.*, by checking for cyclic dependencies in annotations, as we have done previously for scheduling dependencies between avionics mission computing operations [6].

As future work we will examine optimizations where the protocol can reduce pessimism dynamically at run-time, *e.g.*, upon taking particular branches that require fewer threads than other alternatives. This will involve (1) maintaining a representation of the call graph and its annotations, as objects register and deregister with each reactor at run-time; (2) distributed consistent communication of relevant changes to the graph, annotations, and task progress variables; and (3) re-evaluation of safety and liveness properties at each relevant change.

References

1. Toshiro Araki, Yuji Sugiyama, and Tadao Kasami. Complexity of the deadlock avoidance problem. *2nd IBM Symposium on Mathematical Foundations of Computer Science*, pages 229–257, 1971.
2. Tejasvi Aswathanarayana, Venkita Subramanian, Douglas Niehaus, and Christopher Gill. Design and performance of configurable endsystem scheduling mechanisms. In *Proceedings of 11th IEEE Real-Time and Embedded Technology and Applications Symposium (RTAS)*, 2005.
3. Zbignew A. Banaszak and Bruce H. Krogh. Deadlock avoidance in flexible manufacturing systems with concurrently competing process flow. *IEEE Transactions on Robotics and Automation*, 6(6):724–734, December 1990.
4. Center for Distributed Object Computing. nORB—Special Purpose Middleware for Networked Embedded Systems. http://deuce.doc.wustl.edu/nORB/, Washington University.

5. Edsger W. Dijkstra. Cooperating sequential processes. Technical Report EWD-123, Technological University, Eindhoven, the Netherlands, 1965.
6. Christopher D. Gill, Jeanna M. Gossett, Joseph P. Loyall, Douglas C. Schmidt, David Corman, Richard E. Schantz, and Michael Atighetchi. Integrated Adaptive QoS Management in Middleware: An Empirical Case Study. *Journal of Real-time Systems*, 24, 2005.
7. Arie N. Habermann. Prevention of system deadlocks. *Communications of the ACM*, 12:373–377, 1969.
8. James W. Havender. Avoiding deadlock in multi-tasking systems. *IBM Systems Journal*, 2:74–84, 1968.
9. Richard C. Holt. Some deadlock properties of computer systems. *ACM Computing Surveys*, 4:179–196, 1972.
10. Institute for Software Integrated Systems. The ACE ORB (TAO). http://www.dre.vanderbilt.edu/TAO/, Vanderbilt University.
11. Nancy A. Lynch. *Distributed Algorithms*. Morgan Kaugmann, 1996.
12. Zohar Manna and Amir Pnueli. *Temporal Verification of Reactive Sytems: Safety*. Springer, 1995.
13. Philip M. Merlin and Paul J. Schweitzer. Deadlock avoidance in store-and-forward networks–I: Store-and-forward deadlock. *IEEE Transactions on Communications*, 28(3), March 1980.
14. Spiridon A. Reveliotis, Mark A. Lawley, and Placid M. Ferreira. Polynomial-complexity deadlock avoidance policies for sequential resource allocation systems. *IEEE Transactions on Automatic Control*, 42(10):1344–1357, October 1997.
15. Douglas C. Schmidt. Evaluating Architectures for Multi-threaded CORBA Object Request Brokers. *Communications of the ACM Special Issue on CORBA*, 41(10), October 1998.
16. Douglas C. Schmidt, Michael Stal, Hans Rohnert, and Frank Buschmann. *Pattern-Oriented Software Architecture: Patterns for Concurrent and Networked Objects, Volume 2*. Wiley & Sons, New York, 2000.
17. Venkita Subramonian and Christopher D. Gill. A generative programming framework for adaptive middleware. In *Proceedings of the 37th Hawaii International Conference on System Sciences (HICSS'04)*. IEEE, 2004.
18. Venkita Subramonian and Christopher D. Gill. Middleware Design and Implementation for Networked Embedded Systems. In Richard Zurawski, editor, *Embedded Systems Handbook*, chapter 30, pages 1–17. CRC Press, Boca Raton, FL, 2005.
19. Venkita Subramonian, Christopher D. Gill, César Sánchez, and Henny B. Sipma. Composable timed automata models for real-time embedded systems middleware. http://www.cse.seas.wustl.edu/techreportfiles/getreport.asp?440, Washington University CSE Department Technical Report 2005-29.
20. Venkita Subramonian, Guoliang Xing, Christopher D. Gill, Chenyang Lu, and Ron Cytron. Middleware specialization for memory-constrained networked embedded systems. In *Proceedings of 10th IEEE Real-Time and Embedded Technology and Applications Symposium (RTAS)*, 2004.
21. Ke-Yi Xing, Bao-Sheng Hu, and Hao-Xun Chen. Deadlock avoidance policy for petri-net modeling of flexible manufacturing systems with shared resources. *IEEE Transactions on Automatic Control*, 41(2):289–295, February 1996.

A Petri Net View of Mobility

Charles A. Lakos*

School of Computer Science, University of Adelaide,
Adelaide, SA 5005, Australia
Charles.Lakos@adelaide.edu.au

Abstract. Mobile systems explore the interplay between *locality* and *connectivity*. A subsystem may have a connection to a remote subsystem and use this for communication. Alternatively, it may be necessary or desirable to move the subsystem *close to* the other in order to communicate. This paper presents a Petri Net formalisation of mobile systems so as to harness the intuitive graphical representation of Petri Nets and the long history of associated analysis techniques.

The proposed formalism starts with modular Petri Nets, where a net is divided into modules which can interact via place and transition fusion. The first change is that the flat module structure is replaced by fully nested modules, called *locations*. The nesting of locations provides a notion of *locality* while their fusion context determines their *connectivity*. The transitions constituting a location are constrained so that we can determine when a location is occupied by a subsystem, and when the subsystem shifts from one location to another.

The colourless version of the formalism is conceptually simpler, while the coloured version caters for more dynamic configurations and helps identify isolated subsystems for which garbage collection may be appropriate.

1 Introduction

There has been considerable interest in mobility and mobile agent systems. Here, components or subsystems migrate from one location to another. When present at a location, the subsystem can interact more readily with co-located subsystems, and less readily (if at all) with remote subsystems. In formalising mobile systems, it is important to be able to evaluate their correctness, the security implications, and the efficiency gains of moving subsystems to avoid latency costs of complex communication protocols.

Mobile systems expose the interplay between locality and connectivity [17]. Connectivity allows one subsystem to interact with another by virtue of having a connection or reference. In a distributed environment, the access from one subsystem to another via a reference is constrained by locality or proximity. It is desirable to capture mobility in a Petri Net formalism, so as to build on the intuitive graphical representation of Petri Nets, the long history of associated analysis techniques [18,19], and to be able to reason about causality and concurrency [6]. However, a simple and general (even elegant) formulation has proved elusive. This paper is an attempt to address this deficiency.

In our presentation, we consider that an appropriate point of departure is that of *Modular Petri Nets* [3,4]. Here, a net is made up of a number of subnets, which interact

---

* Supported by an Australian Research Council (ARC) Discovery Grant DP0210524.

in the standard Petri Net way by place and transition fusion. (This makes it possible to model both asynchronous and synchronous interaction, respectively.) It is common to distinguish between nets and systems, where nets capture the structure, and where systems augment the net with the state or marking. We find it convenient to distinguish between subnets, locations and subsystems. A *subnet* is a Petri Net that captures the structure of a module. It can be considered as a type or class for a set of instances. A *location* is a subnet in a particular fusion environment. In other words, a location can be considered to be a type with a range of possible interaction capabilities. Finally, a *subsystem* is a location with a non-empty marking. In other words, it represents an instance of a subnet with a range of interaction capabilities.

Thus, we first extend modular nets with the notion of *locations*, which are subnets with a specific fusion environment. Locations are nested and thus capture the notion of locality or proximity. The fusion environment determines the connectivity or interaction possibilities for a subsystem. Secondly, modular nets are extended with the capability of *shifting locations*, which is represented by having transitions with arcs incident on locations. In other words, a subsystem resident in one location can be shifted to another location by firing such a transition. This implies that it is possible to manipulate the marking of a location as a unit.

By analogy with Petri Net theory, it is convenient to distinguish colourless and coloured varieties of mobile systems, which are respectively based on colourless and coloured versions of modular nets [3,4]. In the colourless version, each location may have at most one resident subsystem — the so-called *unfolded* representation. In the coloured version, multiple subsystems can be resident at a given location, but then the place markings will need to distinguish which tokens belong to which subsystem. This is a so-called *folded* representation — it requires that each token is associated with a subsystem by including a data value called an *identifier*.

The paper is organised as follows: Section 2 presents a motivating example of a simple mail agent system. Section 3 presents the formal definitions for a colourless version of mobile systems, while Section 4 presents a coloured version. Section 5 considers possible variations of the formalism and compares it with other approaches in the literature. Section 6 presents the conclusions and avenues for further work.

2 Example

We informally introduce the proposed concepts by considering a simple mail agent (shown in Fig. 1) and its associated system (shown in Fig. 2). A Petri Net (as in Fig. 1) consists of places, transitions and arcs, together with annotations of these. The *places* are depicted as ovals and can hold tokens, which then determine the state of the system. The *transitions* are depicted as rectangles, and determine the possible changes of state. The arcs indicate how the transitions affect the places. In a colourless net, each place holds a number of undifferentiated tokens, and the arcs indicate how many tokens are consumed or generated. So, if an arc from a place to a transition is annotated by the number 2, then that transition can occur only if two tokens in the place can be consumed.

In the example of Fig. 1, there are three places and six transitions. The initial marking shows that place *empty* is marked while the places *has1* and *has2* are not. In this

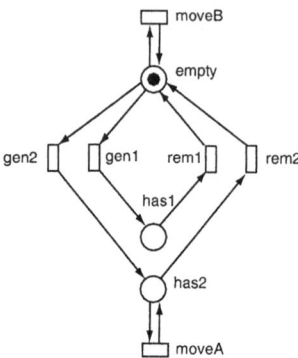

Fig. 1. Subnet for the Agent processes

state, either transition *gen1* or *gen2* can fire — so far, the choice is non-deterministic. This subnet is meant to represent a simple mail agent. With place *empty* marked, the agent has no mail to deliver, while if place *has1* or *has2* is marked, then the agent has mail to deliver to site 1 or site 2, respectively. The transitions *gen1* and *gen2* generate these mail messages, while transitions *rem1* and *rem2* consume (or deliver) them. Transitions *moveA* and *moveB* are used to constrain or allow movement of the agent.

The composite mail system is shown in Fig. 2. Each rounded rectangle is a *location*, which is a subnet together with a fusion environment. The main or root location is labelled *System*, and it contains three locations labelled *Site0*, *Site1* and *Site2*. Within each of these locations is a nested location for the mail agent, labelled *Loc0*, *Loc1* and *Loc2*, respectively. This example uses transition fusion but not place fusion, and this fusion is indicated in one of three ways — by name correspondence, by a double line, or by a line through the transition (which is used to indicate that it is blocked in this location, i.e. fused to a disabled transition in the environment, which is then not shown to avoid clutter).

At *Site0*, the agent resides in location *Loc0*. Its transitions *gen1* and *gen2* can occur, while the others are blocked. These are fused (as indicated by name correspondence) with transitions *gen1* and *gen2* of *Site0*. Thus, at *Site0* it is possible to generate a message destined for *Site1* or *Site2*, in which case the corresponding place *has1* or *has2* of the agent will become marked. Once this has occurred, transition *mov01* is enabled. As indicated by the double lines, this transition is fused with the transition *mov01* in the location *System*, which is also fused with the transition *mov01* in location *Site1*. The transition *mov01* in location *Site0* has a broad input arc incident on location *Loc0*, while transition *mov01* in location *Site1* has a broad output arc incident on location *Loc1*. This is shorthand for shifting the location of a subsystem — the broad input arc removes all the tokens from the source location, and the broad output arc deposits the tokens into the target location. We comment further on this below.

At *Site1*, the agent resides in location *Loc1*. Its transitions *rem1*, *moveA* and *moveB* can occur, while the others are blocked. Transition *rem1* in the agent is fused with the similarly-named transition in *Site1*. This transition allows *Site1* to accept a message destined for here. The transition *moveA/B* in *Site1* is fused with either transition *moveA*

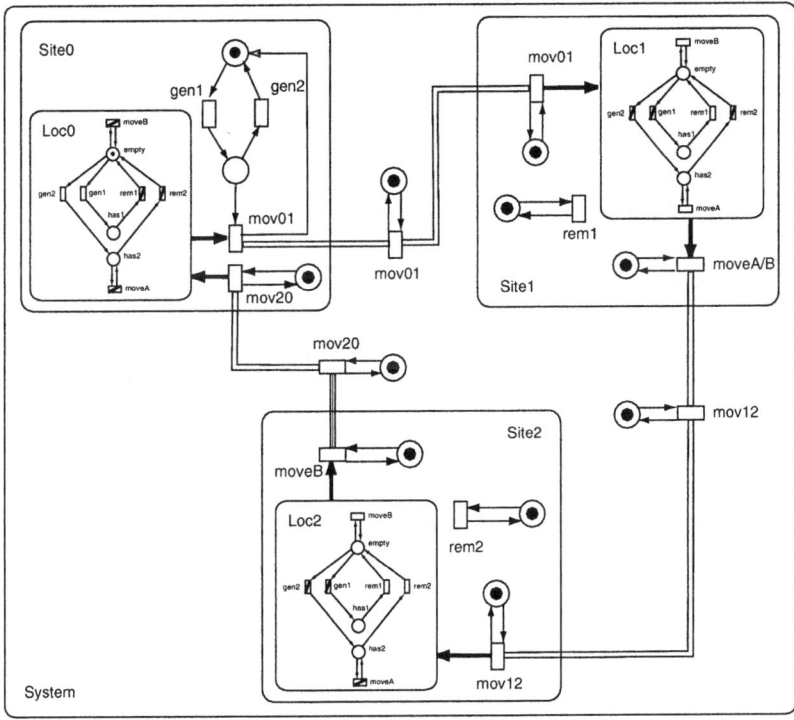

Fig. 2. Composite mail system

or *moveB* of the agent. This, in turn, is fused with the transition *mov12* of the root instance, and a similarly named transition at *Site2*. *Site2* has a similar structure, and transition *rem2* causes the message destined for this site to be removed.

A location is occupied if at least one of the local places is marked. Thus, in our example, the initial marking indicates that locations *System*, *Site0*, *Site1*, *Site2* and *Loc0* are occupied, while locations *Loc1* and *Loc2* are not. In order to ensure that transitions are only enabled for occupied locations, we insist that such transitions have at least one input and one output arc incident on a local (as opposed to a fused) place. Hence, all the side conditions shown in the figure — a side condition is a place with both an input and an output arc incident on an adjacent transition.

The transitions like *mov01* which shift the location of a subsystem (or more generally consume a subsystem at a location or generate a subsystem at a location) are shown with a broad arc. This is a shorthand notation for indicating that all the tokens in the local places are consumed. Where a consume is paired with a corresponding generate, it is assumed that the marking is shifted from one location to another. This description is informal, and the notation is syntactic sugar. It is made precise by identifying *vacate* and *occupy* transitions. Vacate transitions (if enabled) will have the effect of clearing the marking of its location, i.e. they have input arcs but no output arcs. Dually, occupy transitions (if enabled) will have the effect of setting the marking of its location, i.e. they have output arcs but no input arcs. It is expected that such vacate and occupy transitions will normally be fused with environment transitions, and that a vacate transition fused directly or indirectly with an occupy transition will have the effect of shifting the subsystem. The broad arcs incident on a location are thus syntactic sugar for a number of such vacate and occupy transitions — one for every possible marking of the location. This has theoretical implications which we consider in Section 3.

It is worth noting that for *Site0*, the shifting of the agent is determined solely by the site, whereas for *Site1* and *Site2* the agent collaborates with the shift transition.

3 Modular Petri Nets for Mobility

In this section we present a definition of mobile systems in terms of Modular Petri Nets. In Section 4 we present a definition in terms of Modular Coloured Petri Nets.

Definition 1 (Multiset). *A multiset over set S is a mapping $m : S \to \mathbb{N}$, where $m(s)$ gives the number of occurrences of s. The set of all multisets over set S is denoted $\mu(S)$.*

Definition 2 (Petri Net). *A Petri Net (PN) is a tuple $PN = (P, T, W)$ where:*

1. *P is a finite set of places.*
2. *T is a finite set of transitions with $P \cap T = \emptyset$.*
3. *$W : (P \times T) \cup (T \times P) \to \mathbb{N}$ is an arc weight function.*

The arc weight function W indicates the number of tokens consumed or generated by the firing of the transition. If an arc weight is zero, the arc is not drawn.

Definition 3 (PN Markings and Steps). *For a Petri Net PN, a marking is a mapping $M : P \to \mathbb{N}$, i.e. $M \in \mu(P)$, and a step is a mapping $Y : T \to \mathbb{N}$, i.e. $Y \in \mu(T)$. A Petri Net System is a Petri Net together with an initial marking.*

The example of Fig.1 is a Petri Net System where the arcs shown have a weight of *1* and the arcs which have not been drawn have a weight of *0*. Further, the initial marking of place *empty* is one token, while other places hold no tokens.

Definition 4 (PN Behaviour). *For a Petri Net PN, a step Y is enabled in marking M, denoted $M[Y\rangle$, if $\forall p \in P : \Sigma_{t \in Y} W(p,t) \leq M(p)$. If step Y is enabled in marking M, then it may occur, leading to marking M', denoted $M[Y\rangle M'$, where $\forall p \in P : M'(p) = M(p) - \Sigma_{t \in Y} W(p,t) + \Sigma_{t \in Y} W(t,p)$. We write $[M\rangle$ for the markings reachable from M by the occurrence of zero or more steps.*

The above definitions are quite conventional. They capture the requirement that a place must have sufficient tokens to satisfy all consume demands of the step, and that when the step occurs, a place receives tokens from all generate actions. We now depart from convention by defining *locations* and *mobile systems*. These have been motivated by *Modular Petri Nets* [4], but here we retain the nested structure of the modules, which we call *locations*, and thereby capture the notion of locality.

Definition 5 (PN Location). *A Petri Net Location is a tuple $L = (S_L, P_L, T_L, W_L)$ where:*

1. S_L is a finite set of locations. We define $loc(L) = \bigcup_{s \in S_L} loc(s) \cup \{L\}$. We require $\forall s \in S_L : loc(s) \cap \{L\} = \emptyset$.
2. (P_L, T_L, W_L) is a Petri Net. We define $plc(L) = \bigcup_{s \in S_L} plc(s) \cup \{P_L\}$ and $trn(L) = \bigcup_{s \in S_L} trn(s) \cup \{T_L\}$.

Thus, locations are properly nested nets. Locations are unique, as are places and transitions (which are differentiated by the location in which they reside). We can define markings, steps and behaviour for individual locations just as for Petri Nets, but we defer such definitions to mobile systems.

Definition 6 (Mobile System). *A Mobile System is a tuple* $MS = (L_0, PF, TF, M_0)$ *where:*

1. L_0 is a location, called the root location. We define $P = plc(L_0)$ and $T = trn(L_0)$.
2. PF is a set of place fusion sets where $\bigcup_{pf \in PF} pf = P$ and $\forall pf_1, pf_2 \in PF : pf_1 \cap pf_2 \neq \emptyset \Rightarrow pf_1 = pf_2$.
3. TF is a set of transition fusion sets where $\bigcup_{tf \in TF} tf = T$ and $\forall tf_1, tf_2 \in TF : tf_1 \cap tf_2 \neq \emptyset \Rightarrow |tf_1| = |tf_2|$.
4. M_0 is the initial marking of the location.

The set of place fusion sets covers all places and the fusion sets cannot partially overlap. This is in contrast to the definition of Modular Petri Nets [4], where the transitive closure of the fusion sets is used to determine the equivalence classes over places, which are then called place instance groups. Our approach means that each place fusion set corresponds to one place instance group. Similarly, the set of transition fusion sets is required to cover all transitions and if one transition occurs in more than one transition fusion set then these sets must have the same size. Again, this is more restricted than that of Modular Petri Nets, but it is not a theoretical restriction given that every transition can be duplicated so there is one duplicate per occurrence in a fusion set.

Definition 7 (MS Markings and Steps). *For mobile system MS, a marking is a mapping* $M : P \to \mathbb{N}$, *where* $\forall pf \in PF : \forall p_1, p_2 \in pf : M(p_1) = M(p_2) = M(pf)$, *and a step is a mapping* $Y : T \to \mathbb{N}$, *where* $\forall tf \in TF : \forall t_1, t_2 \in tf : Y(tf) = Y(t_1) = Y(t_2)$.

In a mobile system, as in modular nets, the markings of fused places are identical, and the multiplicity of fused transitions in a step are identical. This justifies defining the markings and steps of such a system in terms of place fusion sets and transition fusion sets. It is then appropriate to extend the definition of the arc weight function W to apply to place fusion sets and transition fusion sets, i.e.

$$\forall (f_1, f_2) \in (PF \times TF) \cup (TF \times PF) : W(f_1, f_2) = \Sigma_{x \in f_1, y \in f_2} W(x, y)$$

Definition 8 (MS Behaviour). *For a mobile system MS, a step* Y *is* enabled *in marking* M *if* $\forall pf \in PF : \Sigma_{tf \in Y} W(pf, tf) \leq M(pf)$. *If step* Y *is enabled in marking* M, *then it* may *occur, leading to marking* M' *where* $\forall pf \in PF : M'(pf) = M(pf) - \Sigma_{tf \in Y} W(pf, tf) + \Sigma_{tf \in Y} W(tf, pf)$.

Definition 9. *For a Mobile System MS we classify places and transitions as follows:*

1. $LP = \{p \in P \mid \exists pf \in PF : pf = \{p\}\}$ *is the set of* local places.
2. $EP = P - LP$ *is the set of* exported places.
3. $LT = \{t \in T \mid \exists tf \in TF : tf = \{t\}\}$ *is the set of* local transitions.
4. $ET = T - LT$ *is the set of* exported transitions.
5. $VT = \{t \in T \mid \exists p \in LP : W(p,t) > 0 \land \forall p \in P : W(t,p) = 0\}$ *is the set of* vacate transitions.
6. $OT = \{t \in T \mid \exists p \in LP : W(t,p) > 0 \land \forall p \in P : W(p,t) = 0\}$ *is the set of* occupy transitions.
7. $RT = \{t \in T \mid \exists p_1, p_2 \in LP : W(t,p_1) > 0 \land W(p_2,t) > 0\}$ *is the set of* regular transitions.

We distinguish local as opposed to exported places and transitions — exported entities are fused to at least one other. With the notion of mobility, we are interested in whether a transition interacts with local places, since this determines if the location is occupied. Accordingly, we classify transitions by their interaction with local places.

Definition 10 (Well-formed). *A Mobile System MS is* well-formed *if:*

1. All transitions are vacate, occupy or regular transitions, i.e. $T = VT \cup OT \cup RT$.
2. Vacate transitions empty a location for all reachable markings, i.e. $\forall L \in loc(L_0)$: $\forall t \in VT \cap T_L : \forall M \in [M_0\rangle : M[t\rangle M' \Rightarrow \forall p \in LP \cap plc(L) : M'(p) = \emptyset$.
3. Occupy transitions fill a location for all reachable markings, i.e. $\forall L \in loc(L_0)$: $\forall t \in OT \cap T_L : \forall M \in [M_0\rangle : M[t\rangle M' \Rightarrow \forall p \in LP \cap plc(L) : M(p) = \emptyset$.

The above definition of a *well-formed mobile system* is the key definition that supports mobility. We identify a location as being *occupied* if a local place is marked. A *vacate* transition has the effect of transforming an occupied location (and its nested locations) to unoccupied, while an *occupy* transition has the effect of transforming an unoccupied location (and its nested locations) to occupied. A *regular* transition has the effect of ensuring that an occupied location stays occupied.

The requirement that all transitions fall into one of these three categories ensures that occupy transitions are the only ones that can become enabled if the location to which they belong is unoccupied. The requirements that vacate transitions make a location unoccupied and that occupy transitions make a location occupied apply to all reachable markings. It is therefore debatable whether these should be classified as requirements for being *well-formed* or *well-behaved*. Our choice of terminology reflects our intention that these conditions should be determined from the structure of the net, without the need for reachability analysis. Essentially, the problem is one of incorporating *clear* and *set* arcs [12] — the nature of these arcs determines whether reachability and boundedness are decidable for this form of Petri Net [7]. If all places in all locations are bounded, then it will be possible to incorporate complementary places and there will be a finite number of possibilities for the clear and set arcs, and hence for clearing and setting the marking of the location. If there are unbounded places, then we will need the generalised form of clear and set arcs [12] which make reachability and boundedness undecidable [7].

We refer to a location together with a non-empty marking as a *subsystem*. By incorporating vacate and occupy transitions, the above formalism is sufficient for studying mobility — fusing a vacate transition in one location with an occupy transition in another corresponds to shifting the location of a subsystem. For notational convenience, we introduce the broad arcs incident on locations, as in Section 2. These are a shorthand for sets of vacate and/or occupy transitions — one for each possible reachable marking of the location. They summarise the possibility of shifting the location of a subsystem whatever its current state. Again, with bounded places, the possible alternatives can be enumerated. With unbounded places, the generalised clear and set arcs are required.

Definition 11 (Isolated subsystem). *Given a Mobile System MS in marking M, a transition sequence $t_1 t_2 ... t_n$ is a* causal sequence *if there are markings $M_1, M_2, ... M_n$ such that $M[t_1\rangle M_1[t_2\rangle M_2...[t_n\rangle M_n$ and $\forall k \in 1..(n-1) : \exists p \in P : W(t_k, p) > 0 \land W(p, t_{k+1}) > 0$. Given a Mobile System MS, a subsystem resident in location L is* isolated *in marking M if there is no causal sequence $t_1 t_2 ... t_n$ with $t_1 \in T_L$ and $t_n \in T_{L_0}$.*

The definition of a *causal sequence* is derived from *causal nets* [5]. It captures the notion of causal dependency between transitions t_1 and t_n, since the output of each transition is consumed by the subsequent transition. We then say that the subsystem in location L is *isolated* if there is no such causal sequence with t_1 in location L and t_n in the root location. In other words, the firing of transitions of the subsystem in location L cannot affect, directly or indirectly, the root location.

If we are only interested in studying the behaviour of the root location, we can reduce the size of the state space by eliminating isolated subsystems. For the moment, this observation seems somewhat pointless because we need the reachability graph to determine whether a location is isolated. We revisit this issue in the coloured version of mobile systems.

4 Modular Coloured Petri Nets for Mobility

We now extend the definition of mobile systems to incorporate colour, i.e. data values. One of the benefits of doing so — just as for coloured nets — is to have a more concise notation. It will now be possible to have multiple subsystems resident in the one location, provided that the elements of the subsystems are differentiated by the use of identifiers, a special kind of data value from a set *ID*. Local places will have tokens tagged by the subsystem identifier, and local transitions will have firing modes similarly tagged. Fused places will have tokens tagged by the identifiers of all subsystems with one of the fused places, and similarly, fused transitions will have firing modes tagged by identifiers of all participating subsystems. Thus, we dictate that tokens and transition firing modes have colour sets which are tuples, the first element of which is the multiset of identifiers which determine the subsystem(s) to which they belong. We use a projection function π_1 to select the first element of such tuples. The constraints on the consistent use of identifiers are found in Definition 20.

Definition 12 (Coloured Petri Net). *A Coloured Petri Net (CPN) is a tuple $CPN = (\Sigma, P, T, \theta, W)$ where:*

1. Σ is a set of colour sets (or types).
2. P is a finite set of places.
3. T is a finite set of transitions with $P \cap T = \emptyset$.
4. $\theta : P \cup T \to \Sigma$ is a colour function giving the colour set associated with each place and transition.
5. $W : (P \times T) \cup (T \times P) \to \Sigma \to \Sigma$ is an arc weight function where $W(p,t), W(t,p) \in \mu(\theta(t)) \to \mu(\theta(p))$.

The definition of CPNs is simplified to that of [3]. As in Definition 2, we combine the specification of arcs and their inscriptions into one entity, namely the arc weight function W. We use θ to specify the colour set associated with each place. Symmetrically, we also use θ to specify the colour set associated with each transition — the values of this colour set determine the allowable firing modes of the transition, thus making it superfluous to specify a transition guard.

Definition 13 (CPN Markings and Steps). *For a Coloured Petri Net a* marking *is a mapping* $M : P \to \Sigma$, *where* $M(p) \in \mu(\theta(p))$, *and a* step *is a mapping* $Y : T \to \Sigma$, *where* $Y(t) \in \mu(\theta(t))$. *A* Coloured Petri Net System *is a Coloured Petri Net together with an initial marking.*

Definition 14 (CPN Behaviour). *For a Coloured Petri Net CPN, a step Y is* enabled *in marking M if* $\forall p \in P : \Sigma_{(t,c) \in Y} W(p,t)(c) \leq M(p)$. *If step Y is enabled in marking M, then it may* occur, *leading to marking M' where* $\forall p \in P : M'(p) = M(p) - \Sigma_{(t,c) \in Y} W(p,t)(c) + \Sigma_{(t,c) \in Y} W(t,p)(c)$.

Given our use of transition firing modes, the elements of a step are transition-mode pairs, rather than transition-binding pairs, as in [3]. Otherwise, the above definitions are quite conventional.

Definition 15 (Coloured Location). *A Coloured Location is a tuple* $CL = (S_{CL}, \Sigma_{CL}, P_{CL}, T_{CL}, \theta_{CL}, W_{CL})$ *where:*

1. S_{CL} *is a finite set of locations. We define* $loc(CL) = \bigcup_{s \in S_{CL}} loc(s) \cup \{CL\}$.
2. $(\Sigma_{CL}, P_{CL}, T_{CL}, \theta_{CL}, W_{CL})$ *is a Coloured Petri Net. We define* $plc(CL) = \bigcup_{s \in S_{CL}} plc(s) \cup \{P_{CL}\}$ *and* $trn(CL) = \bigcup_{s \in S_{CL}} trn(s) \cup \{T_{CL}\}$.

Coloured locations, like colourless locations of Definition 5, are modules which retain the nesting structure. As before, we can define markings, steps and behaviour for individual coloured locations, but we defer such definitions to coloured mobile systems.

Definition 16 (Coloured Mobile System). *A Coloured Mobile System is a tuple* $CMS = (CL_0, PF, TF, M_0)$ *where:*

1. CL_0 *is a coloured location, called the* root *location. We define* $P = plc(CL_0)$ *and* $T = trn(CL_0)$.
2. PF *is a set of place fusion sets where* $\bigcup_{pf \in PF} pf = P$ *and* $\forall pf_1, pf_2 \in PF : pf_1 \cap pf_2 \neq \emptyset \Rightarrow pf_1 = pf_2$.
3. TF *is a set of transition fusion sets where* $\bigcup_{tf \in TF} tf = T$ *and* $\forall tf_1, tf_2 \in TF : tf_1 \cap tf_2 \neq \emptyset \Rightarrow |tf_1| = |tf_2|$.
4. M_0 *is the initial marking of the location.*

As in Definition 6, the set of place fusion sets covers all places and the fusion sets do not partially overlap. Thus, each place fusion set corresponds to a place instance group of [3]. Similarly, the set of transition fusion sets covers all transitions and if one transition occurs in more than one fusion set, then the sets must have the same size.

Definition 17 (CMS Markings and Steps). *For a Coloured Mobile System CMS, a marking is a mapping* $M : P \to \Sigma$, *where* $M(p) \in \mu(\theta(p))$ *and* $\forall pf \in PF : \forall p_1, p_2 \in pf : M(p_1) = M(p_2) = M(pf)$, *and a step is a mapping* $Y : T \to \Sigma$, *where* $Y(t) \in \mu(\theta(t))$ *and* $\forall tf \in TF : \forall t_1, t_2 \in tf : Y(tf) = Y(t_1) = Y(t_2)$.

In a coloured mobile system, as in coloured modular nets, the markings of fused places are identical, and the multiplicity of fused transitions in a step are identical. As for colourless mobile systems, this justifies defining the markings and steps of such a system in terms of place fusion sets and transition fusion sets. It is also appropriate to extend the definition of the arc weight function W to apply to place fusion sets and transition fusion sets in the same way as for colourless mobile systems.

Definition 18 (CMS Behaviour). *For a coloured mobile system CMS, a step* Y *is enabled in marking* M *if* $\forall pf \in PF : \Sigma_{(tf,c) \in Y} W(pf, tf)(c) \leq M(pf)$. *If step* Y *is enabled in marking* M, *then it may occur, leading to marking* M' *where* $\forall pf \in PF : M'(pf) = M(pf) - \Sigma_{(tf,c) \in Y} W(pf, tf)(c) + \Sigma_{(tf,c) \in Y} W(tf, pf)(c)$.

Definition 19. *For a Coloured Mobile System CMS we define:*

1. $LP = \{p \in P \mid \exists pf \in PF : pf = \{p\}\}$ *is the set of* local places.
2. $EP = P - LP$ *is the set of* exported places.
3. $LT = \{t \in T \mid \exists tf \in TF : tf = \{t\}\}$ *is the set of* local transitions.
4. $ET = T - LT$ *is the set of* exported transitions.
5. $VT = \{t \in T \mid \exists p \in LP : \forall c \in \theta(t) : W(p,t)(c) > \emptyset \land \forall p \in P : \forall c \in \theta(t) : W(t,p)(c) = \emptyset\}$ *is the set of* vacate transitions.
6. $OT = \{t \in T \mid \exists p \in LP : \forall c \in \theta(t) : W(p,t)(c) > \emptyset \land \forall p \in P : \forall c \in \theta(t) : W(p,t)(c) = \emptyset\}$ *is the set of* occupy transitions.
7. $RT = \{t \in T \mid \exists p_1, p_2 \in LP : \forall c \in \theta(t) : W(t,p_1)(c) > \emptyset \land W(p_2,t)(c) > \emptyset\}$ *is the set of* regular transitions.

As in Definition 9, we distinguish local versus exported places and transitions, and we classify transitions by their interaction with local places.

Definition 20 (Consistent). *A Coloured Mobile System CMS is consistent if:*

1. *The colour set for a place is given by a tuple with the first element being a multiset of identifiers, the size being determined by the size of the relevant fusion set, i.e.* $\forall pf \in PF : \forall p \in pf : \theta(p) = \mu(ID) \times ... \land |\pi_1(\theta(p))| = |pf|$.
2. *The colour set for a transition is given by a tuple with the first element being a multiset of identifiers, the size being determined by the size of the relevant fusion set, i.e.* $\forall tf \in TF : \forall t \in tf : \theta(t) = \mu(ID) \times ... \land |\pi_1(\theta(t))| = |tf|$.
3. *The firing mode of each transition shares an identifier with the consumed tokens, i.e.* $\forall p \in P : \forall t \in T : \forall c \in \theta(t) : \forall c' \in W(p,t)(c) : \pi_1(c) \cap \pi_1(c') \neq \emptyset$.

4. *The firing mode of each transition shares an identifier with the generated tokens, i.e.* $\forall p \in P : \forall t \in T : \forall c \in \theta(t) : \forall c' \in W(t,p)(c) : \pi_1(c) \cap \pi_1(c') \neq \emptyset$.
5. *Distinct subsystems have distinct identifiers, i.e.* $\forall M \in [M_0\rangle : \forall CL_1, CL_2 \in loc(CL_0) : \forall p_1 \in LP \cap CL_1 : \forall p_2 \in LP \cap CL_2 : \forall c_1 \in M(p_1) : \forall c_2 \in M(p_2) : CL_1 \neq CL_2 \Rightarrow \pi_1(c_1) \cap \pi_2(c_2) = \emptyset$.
6. *The consumed tokens provide all the identifiers found in the transition firing modes, i.e.* $\forall t \in T : \forall c_1, c_2 \in \theta(t) : (\forall p \in P : W(p,t)(c_1) = W(p,t)(c_2)) \Rightarrow c_1 = c_2$.

As discussed earlier, we use identifiers from the set $ID \in \Sigma$ to differentiate the multiple subsystems resident in the one location and we require that those identifiers be used consistently. Since tokens in a fused place belong to multiple subsystems, they are identified by all the associated subsystem identifiers. The same applies to fused transitions, and hence points *1* and *2* above. (We use multisets of identifiers so as to handle fusion of places and transitions from the same subsystem.) Furthermore, the firing of a transition should only remove or generate tokens for matching subsystems, and hence points *3* and *4*. Finally, we do not wish to allow transitions to *invent* identifiers, which may or may not be associated with existing subsystems. Therefore, we require that a transition's firing mode is solely determined by the consumed tokens, which is point *6* above. We now define well-formed nets by extending the constraints on vacate and occupy transitions to cater for coloured nets.

Definition 21 (Well-formed). *A Coloured Mobile System CMS is* well-formed *if:*

1. *All transitions are vacate, occupy or regular transitions, i.e.* $T = VT \cup OT \cup RT$.
2. *Vacate transitions empty a location of a subsystem for all reachable markings, i.e.* $\forall CL \in loc(CL_0) : \forall t \in VT \cap T_{CL} : \forall M \in [M_0\rangle : M[(t,c)\rangle M' \Rightarrow \forall p \in LP \cap plc(CL) : \forall c' \in M'(p) : \pi_1(c) \cap \pi_1(c') = \emptyset$.
3. *Occupy transitions fill an empty location with a subsystem for all reachable markings, i.e.* $\forall CL \in loc(CL_0) : \forall t \in OT \cap T_{CL} : \forall M \in [M_0\rangle : M[(t,c)\rangle M' \Rightarrow \forall p \in LP \cap plc(CL) : \forall c' \in M(p) : \pi_1(c) \cap \pi_1(c') = \emptyset$.

Definition 22 (Isolated subsystem). *Given a Coloured Mobile System CMS in marking M, a transition sequence* $(t_1, c_1)(t_2, c_2)...(t_n, c_n)$ *is a* causal sequence *if there are markings* $M_1, M_2, ...M_n$ *such that* $M[(t_1, c_1)\rangle M_1[(t_2, c_2)\rangle M_2...[(t_n, c_n)\rangle M_n$ *and* $\forall k \in 1..(n-1) : \exists p \in P : W(t_k, p)(c_k) \cap W(p, t_{k+1})(c_{k+1}) \neq \emptyset$. *Given a Coloured Mobile System CMS, a subsystem resident in location CL is* isolated *in marking M if there is no causal sequence* $(t_1, c_1)(t_2, c_2)...(t_n, c_n)$ *with* $t_1 \in T_{CL}$ *and* $t_n \in T_{CL_0}$.

The definition of an *isolated subsystem* is simply a coloured version of Definition 11. However, with the use of colours and the differentiation of subsystems by identifiers, it is possible to approximate the identification of isolated subsystems. Suppose that a subsystem with identifier *id* is resident in location *CL*. Suppose further that there is no place outside *CL* holding tokens which include the value *id*. Then the subsystem is isolated and can be eliminated provided we are only interested in the behaviour of the root location.

This follows from the fact that there can only be an appropriate causal sequence if location *CL* can fire a fused transition or can access tokens from a fused place. In the former case, the fusion partner will have to have a firing mode which includes *id*, which in turn will need to come from a consumed token (points *2*, *4*, *6* from Definition 20). In the case of fused places, the accessed token will need to have an identifier which includes *id* (point *1* of Definition 20). Both of these are excluded if there is no place outside of *CL* which holds tokens including the value *id*.

The above is essentially garbage collection for mobile systems. It provides a sufficient condition for a subsystem being isolated, but it is not a necessary condition.

5 Variations and Related Work

The above Petri Net formalisms for mobile systems can be varied in a number of ways. As is common with Petri Nets, this formulation appears to be rather static — the number of locations and the communication partners at each location are determined in advance. However, a more dynamic version can be achieved by suitable use of colours or types. Firstly, we could annotate transitions with expressions of the form $v = new$ $S(arguments)$ and $v.connect(arguments)$. These would, respectively, generate a new instance of subnet S and move the subsystem identified by v, with the arguments in both cases indicating the new fusion context. However, the possible fusion contexts can be enumerated in advance by analysing the syntax of those calls. Secondly, we could use synchronous channels [2] to determine communication partners dynamically — it has been shown that synchronous channels are semantically equivalent to the standard transition fusion that we adopted [2]. Thirdly, we could use colours not just to distinguish multiple subsystems resident in the one location but also to fold multiple locations (with similar fusion contexts) onto one, with colours identifying the different locations.

The formulation above can be interpreted as a variant of *Object-Based Petri Nets* (OBPNs) where the subnets correspond to classes and the subsystems correspond to instances. An earlier formulation of OBPNs [13], with a view to capturing inheritance, constrained classes to interact either by place fusion or transition fusion. The current proposal allows both. There, explicit destruction of objects was assumed — here we allow for garbage collection. There, catering for multi-level activity was rather complex — here we have a simpler formulation based on Modular Petri Net semantics. A simplifying factor is that shifting the location of a subsystem is not combined with other internal activity, since vacate and occupy transitions cannot, respectively, generate and consume tokens. However, such an extension could be incorporated.

The Nets-within-Nets paradigm proposed by Valk has been the focus of a significant effort in terms of object-oriented design and mobility [8,9,10,20]. The fundamental notion is that there are (at least) two levels of Petri Nets — the system net provides the most abstract view of the system. The tokens resident in the places of the system net may be black tokens (with no associated data) or representations of object nets. The two-level hierarchy can be generalised to an arbitrary number of levels, but that is not necessary for our purposes. Three different semantics have been proposed for the nets-within-nets paradigm — a reference semantics (where tokens in the system net are references to common object nets), a value semantics (where tokens in the system net are distinct object nets), and a history process semantics (where tokens in the system net are object net processes) [20]. The reference semantics (as supported by the Renew tool [11]) has been used to model mobile agent systems [8,9]. However, a reference semantics provides a global reference scope, so that connectivity is enhanced but locality becomes meaningless. These authors have acknowledged that a value semantics is really required for mobility [10]. Then, locality is meaningful but connectivity is more constrained — an object net residing in a system place can primarily synchronise with the system transitions adjacent to the place. In other words, the object net token has to be removed from the place in order to interact with it. The interaction between co-resident tokens has more recently been added using another form of synchronous channel. However, the notation in Renew suggests that the interaction is achieved by the two object nets being accessed as side conditions of a system net transition.

Our proposal has certain points of contact with the nets-within-nets paradigm. The notation of having arcs incident on locations is akin to system net places containing object nets which can be removed (or added) by adjacent system net transitions. However, our locations have a more general fusion context. We have also refined the results of [10] in noting that if locations have bounded places, then we obviate the need for generalised clear and set arcs for shifting subsystem locations, and hence reachability and boundedness can remain decidable.

There have been a number of calculi proposed for working with mobility. Mobility was one of the key motivations behind the π-calculus [16]. However, the π-calculus did not explore the interplay between connectivity and locality — it had a flexible method for exchanging names and thus modifying connectivity, but there was no sense in which the connectivity was limited by locality. (The scope rules simply limited the accessibility to names.)

The ambient calculus [1] identifies *ambients* as a sphere of computation. They are properly nested which then determines locality. Capabilities are provided for entering, leaving and dissolving ambients. Movement across ambient boundaries can be *subjective* — the process in the ambient decides to employ the capability — or *objective* — the process outside the ambient dictates the move. As in the π-calculus, connectivity is provided by the ability to communicate capabilities or names over channels.

The seal calculus [21] identifies *seals* as agents or mobile computations. Here, seal boundaries are the main protection mechanism and seal communication is restricted to a single level in the hierarchy. Mobility is not under the control of a seal but of its parent — thus subjective moves of the ambient calculus are not supported.

The capabilities of the above calculi can be broadly mapped into the formalisms of this paper which can make it possible to specify and reason about causality and concurrency, as in [6]. Ambients and seals can be mapped to locations. We can cater for synchronous and asynchronous communication. Moves are objective, and fusion can be constrained to the enclosing location as in the Seal calculus.

6 Conclusions

This paper has proposed a Petri Net formalism suitable for studying mobility, and specifically the interplay between locality and connectivity. It has extended Modular Petri Nets with the notion of nested modules called *locations*. The nesting of modules determines locality while the fusion context of each module determines connectivity.

Locations are constrained so that the firing of their transitions depends on the locations being occupied. Another key extension is the identification of *vacate* and *occupy* transitions, which change the occupied status of locations. For notational convenience, we add arcs incident on locations to represent multiple vacate and occupy transitions. We have also identified isolated subsystems which cannot affect, either directly or indirectly, the root location. The analysis of the system could be simplified by removing such isolated subsystems from further consideration. In the coloured version of mobile systems, the question of isolated subsystems can be resolved with techniques similar to garbage collection for object-oriented systems.

The proposed Petri Net formalism for mobility is quite simple and general even though the changes to Modular Petri Nets are not extensive. Consequently, it will be relatively simple to study mobile systems using currently available modular analysis tools such as Maria [15], which already has support for nested modules. With a bit more effort, it is also possible to map these mobile systems into Hierarchical Coloured Petri Nets and analyse them in the tool Design/CPN [14].

Future work will explore front ends to existing tools in order to facilitate the modelling of mobile systems, as well as their analysis. We are also interested in exploring the analysis possibilities for realistic case studies.

Acknowledgements

The author acknowledges early discussions with Thomas Mailund about state space exploration of Object-Based systems, and the helpful comments of Glenn Lewis.

References

1. L. Cardelli and A. Gordon. Mobile Ambients. In M. Nivat, editor, *Foundations of Software Science and Computational Structures*, volume 1998 of *Lecture Notes in Computer Science*, pages 140–155. Springer Verlag, 1998.
2. S. Christensen and N.D. Hansen. Coloured Petri Nets Extended with Channels for Synchronous Communication. In R. Valette, editor, *15th International Conference on the Application and Theory of Petri Nets*, volume 815 of *Lecture Notes in Computer Science*, pages 159–178, Zaragoza, 1994. Springer-Verlag.
3. S. Christensen and L. Petrucci. Modular State Space Analysis of Coloured Petri Nets. In G. De Michelis and M. Diaz, editors, *Application and Theory of Petri Nets*, volume 935 of *Lecture Notes in Computer Science*, pages 201–217. Springer-Verlag, Berlin, 1995.
4. S. Christensen and L. Petrucci. Modular analysis of Petri Nets. *The Computer Journal*, 43(3):224–242, 2000.
5. J. Desel and W. Reisig. Place/Transition Petri Nets. In W. Reisig and G. Rozenberg, editors, *Lectures on Petri Nets I: Basic Models*, volume 1491 of *Lecture Notes in Computer Science*, pages 122–173. Springer, Dagstuhl, 1998.
6. R. Devillers, H. Klaudel, and M. Koutny. Petri Net Semantics of the Finite π-Calculus. In D.de Frutos-Escrig and M. Nunez, editors, *Formal Techniques for Networked and Distributed Systems*, volume 3235 of *Lecture Notes in Computer Science*, pages 309–325, Madrid, 2004. Springer-Verlag.

7. C. Dufourd, A. Finkel, and Ph. Schnoebelen. Reset nets between decidability and undecidability. In K. Larsen, S. Skyum, and G.Winskel, editors, *25th International Colloquium on the Automata, Languages and Programming*, volume 1443 of *Lecture Notes in Computer Science*, pages 103–115, Aalborg, 1998. Springer-Verlag.
8. M. Köhler, D. Moldt, and H. Rölke. Modelling the Structure and Behaviour of Petri Net Agents. In J.-M. Colom and M. Koutny, editors, *International Conference on the Application and Theory of Petri Nets*, volume 2075 of *Lecture Notes in Computer Science*, pages 224–241, Newcastle, 2001. Springer-Verlag.
9. M. Köhler, D. Moldt, and H. Rölke. Modelling Mobility and Mobile Agents Using Nets within Nets. In W. van der Aalst and E. Best, editors, *International Conference on the Application and Theory of Petri Nets*, volume 2679 of *Lecture Notes in Computer Science*, pages 121–139, Eindhoven, 2003. Springer-Verlag.
10. M. Köhler and H. Rölke. Properties of Object Petri Nets. In J. Cortadella and W. Reisig, editors, *International Conference on the Application and Theory of Petri Nets*, volume 3099 of *Lecture Notes in Computer Science*, pages 278–297, Bologna, 2004. Springer-Verlag.
11. O. Kummer, F. Wienberg, M. Duvigneau, J. Schumacher, M. Köhler, D. Moldt, H. Rölke, and R. Valk. An extensible editor and simulation engine for Petri nets: Renew. In J. Cortadella and W. Reisig, editors, *25th International Conference on Application and Theory of Petri Nets (ICATPN 2004)*, volume 3099 of *Lecture Notes in Computer Science*, pages 484–493, Bologna, Italy, 2004. Springer.
12. C. Lakos and S. Christensen. A General Systematic Approach to Arc Extensions for Coloured Petri Nets. In R. Valette, editor, *15th International Conference on the Application and Theory of Petri Nets*, volume 815 of *Lecture Notes in Computer Science*, pages 338–357, Zaragoza, 1994. Springer-Verlag.
13. C.A. Lakos. From Coloured Petri Nets to Object Petri Nets. In G. De Michelis and M. Diaz, editors, *16th International Conference on the Application and Theory of Petri Nets*, volume 935 of *Lecture Notes in Computer Science*, pages 278–297, Torino, Italy, 1995. Springer.
14. C.A. Lakos. State Space Exploration of Object-Based Systems. Technical Report TR05-01, Department of Computer Science, University of Adelaide, April 2005.
15. M. Mäkelä. Maria: Modular Reachability Analyser for Algebraic System Nets. In J. Esparza and C. Lakos, editors, *23rd International Conference on the Application and Theory of Petri Nets*, volume 2360 of *Lecture Notes in Computer Science*, pages 434–444, Adelaide, Australia, 2002. Springer.
16. R. Milner. Elements of Interaction. *Communications of the ACM*, 36(1):78–89, 1993. ACM.
17. R. Milner. The Flux of Interaction. In J.-M. Colom and M. Koutny, editors, *International Conference on the Application and Theory of Petri Nets*, volume 2075 of *Lecture Notes in Computer Science*, pages 19–22, Newcastle, 2001. Springer-Verlag.
18. W. Reisig and G. Rozenberg, editors. *Lectures on Petri Nets I: Basic Models*, volume 1491 of *Lecture Notes in Computer Science*. Springer, Berlin, 1998.
19. W. Reisig and G. Rozenberg, editors. *Lectures on Petri Nets II: Applications*, volume 1492 of *Lecture Notes in Computer Science*. Springer, Berlin, 1998.
20. R. Valk. Object Petri Nets — Using the Nets-within-Nets Paradigm. In J. Desel, W. Reisig, and G. Rozenberg, editors, *Lectures on Concurrency and Petri Nets*, volume 3098 of *Lecture Notes in Computer Science*, pages 819–848. Springer-Verlag, 2004.
21. J. Vitek and G.Castagna. Towards a Calculus of Secure Mobile Computations. In *IEEE Workshop on Internet Programming Languages*, Chicago, 1998. IEEE.

Modular Verification of Petri Nets Properties: A Structure-Based Approach

Kais Klai[1], Serge Haddad[2], and Jean-Michel Ilié[3]

[1] LaBRI CNRS UMR 5800, Université de Bordeaux I, Talence, France
kais.klai@labri.fr
[2] LAMSADE CNRS UMR 7024, Université de Paris Dauphine, France
haddad@lamsade.dauphine.fr
[3] LIP6 CNRS UMR 7606, Université de Paris 6, France
Jean-Michel.ilie@lip6.fr

Abstract. In this paper, we address the modular verification problem for a Petri net obtained by composition of two subnets. At first, we show how to transform an asynchronous composition into a synchronous one where the new subnets are augmented from the original ones by means of linear invariants. Then we introduce a non-constraining relation between subnets based on their behaviour. Whenever this relation is satisfied, standard properties like the liveness and the boundedness and generic properties specified by a linear time logic may be checked by examination of the augmented subnets in isolation. Finally, we give a sufficient condition for this relation which can be detected modularly using an efficient algorithm.

Keywords: Abstraction, modular verification, (de)composition, Petri nets.

1 Introduction

The validation of complex distributed systems must come up to the well-known state explosion problem. Thus, numerous validation techniques have been proposed in order to reduce the number of states to be explored.

Among them, the modular verification approaches aim to take benefit from some knowledge about the components of the system and the way they communicate. The synchronous composition between components is very popular in system verification since, from properties of the components, one can deduce those of the system. For instance, the finiteness of the system is directly deduced from the fact that the composed modules are finite. Asynchronous composition usually better corresponds to systems where the modules are distributed and weakly coupled. In such a case, modules communicate asynchronously by message sending. Taking asynchronous communication into account during the validation process is generally a difficult task: for instance the system can be infinite even if the composed modules are finite.

In a verification process, the properties which are validated at first are the standard ones with respect to the model used. For instance, the boundedness or the liveness properties of a Petri net ensure a positive *a priori* on the correctness of the design. The finiteness of the system is directly deduced from the fact that it is bounded, while the liveness property indicates that all the pieces of codes within a system remain available whatever the evolution of the system. The validation of the specific properties of a system often requires specification languages like temporal logic, able to express the causality between the state changes. Our work deals with the linear time logic LTL. Such a logic views the system like a set of runs. LTL may be checked on the fly, which means that the state space of the system is constructed step by step as the need of the verification occurs. Moreover whenever the property to be checked is detected false, a run highlighting the problem is exhibited for free to the designer.

Without any restriction on the composition, the efficiency of the modular verification rather depends on the system to be analyzed. For instance in [2], it is possible to minimize the reachable states of each module by hiding the internal moves, before the synchronization of modules. Reachability analysis has been proved to be effective on the resulting structure in [6] and the method has been extended to operate the model checking of LTL-X formulae (LTL without the "next" operator). Anyway, experimental results show that this technique is efficient for some models, but for others the combinatorial explosion is not really attacked.

Other approaches have proposed to restrict the application domain by laying some construction rules down, either for the modules or their communication medium. The general idea consists in replacing the analysis of the global state space by the analysis of the state spaces of modules. Actually, the verification of system properties consists in checking separately some properties on each module then piecing the results together in order to conclude whether the system is correct. General properties are addressed as well as some sets of temporal properties. In general, the brute force approach which consists in partitioning the system in whatever subnets is bound to fail. Different approaches of composition have been proposed depending in particular, on the way each module can abstract its environment (see [10,9,1]). At first, some general properties of a Petri net were initially considered (boundedness, liveness); henceforth, the model checking problem of temporal formulae was investigated [5,8]. Anyway, rather restrictive conditions are forced, thus reducing drastically the application to concrete systems.

In this paper, we propose a new structure-based modular approach starting from a non-constraining relation between components. We start from a specification of the system in Petri nets without restriction and address the verification of both standard properties and linear time temporal logics (LTL-X). We then decompose the Petri net in two components such that their (common) interface only contains transitions. In order to abstract the environment of a component, we propose to take benefit from the existence of linear positive place-invariants. Such invariants which often exist in well-specified system, are used to enrich each subnet by some abstraction of the other subnet. However, to check the system properties in isolation on a component, one may need to check whether the other component does not constrain its behaviour. Thus we develop a modular test of this constraining relation by analyzing in isolation the behaviour of the component which must be non-constraining. The principal contribution of our modular approach w.r.t. the existent works is the combination of structural and behavioural aspects. From the structural point of view, we furnish a general composition model where the system invariants are originally exploited in order to abstract modules. While, from the behavioural point of view, and in opposition to some existent techniques (see [11,2,6]), the synchronized product between the system components is avoided.

The paper is organized as follows: in section 2, we introduce our decomposition scheme showing how to handle asynchronous communication and deducing some useful properties. In section 3, we define the non-constraining relation between components, we propose a sufficient condition, show how to check it efficiently and bring out our compositionality results. At last, concluding remarks and perspectives are given in section 4.

2 Decomposition Scheme

2.1 Preliminaries and Notations

In this section we recall the definition of a Petri net and some basic notions of Petri net theory. In order to decompose Petri nets, we also formalize the notion of subnets.

Vectors and matrices. Let v be a vector or a matrix, then v^T denotes its transpose. So if v, v' are two vectors then $v^T.v'$ corresponds to their scalar product. Let v be a vector of $\mathbb{N}^P$ then the support of v, denoted $||v||$, is defined by $||v|| = \{p \in P \mid v(p) > 0\}$.

Petri nets. Let P and T be disjoint finite sets of places and transitions respectively, the elements of $P \cup T$ are called nodes. A net is a tuple $N = \langle P, T, Pre, Post \rangle$ with the backward and forward incidence matrices Pre and $Post$ defined by Pre (resp. $Post$): $(P \times T) \longrightarrow \mathbb{N}$. We denote by $Pre(t)$ (resp. $Post(t)$) the column vector indexed by t of the matrix Pre (resp. $Post$). $W = Post - Pre$ is the incidence matrix of N. The preset of a place p (resp. a transition t) is defined as $^{\bullet}p = \{t \in T \mid Post(p,t) > 0\}$ (resp. $^{\bullet}t = \{p \in P \mid Pre(p,t) > 0\}$), and its postset as $p^{\bullet} = \{t \in T \mid Pre(p,t) > 0\}$ (resp. $t^{\bullet} = \{p \in P \mid Post(p,t) > 0\}$). The preset (resp. postset) of a set X of nodes is given by the union of the presets (resp. postsets) of all nodes in X. $^{\bullet}X^{\bullet}$ denotes the union of the preset and the postset of X.

In case of ambiguity the name of the corresponding net is specified: $^{\bullet}X(N)$, $X^{\bullet}(N)$ and $^{\bullet}X^{\bullet}(N)$.

A marking of a net is a mapping $P \longrightarrow \mathbb{N}$. We call $\Sigma = \langle N, m_0 \rangle$ a net system with initial marking m_0 of N. A marking m enables the transition t ($m \xrightarrow{t}$) if $m(p) \geq Pre(p,t)$ for each $p \in {}^{\bullet}t$. In this case the transition can occur, leading to the new marking m', given by: $m'(p) = m(p) + W(p,t)$ for every place $p \in P$. We denote this occurrence by $m \xrightarrow{t} m'$. If there exists a chain $(m_0 \xrightarrow{t_1} m_1 \xrightarrow{t_2} m_2 \longrightarrow \ldots \xrightarrow{t_n} m_n)$, denoted by $m_0 \xrightarrow{\sigma} m_n$, the sequence $\sigma = t_1 \ldots t_n$ is also called a computation. A computation of infinite length is called a run. We denote by T^* (resp. T^∞) the set of finite (resp. infinite) sequences of T. T^ω denotes the set of all sequences of T ($T^\omega = T^* \cup T^\infty$). The finite (resp. infinite) language of (N, m_0) is the set $L^*(\langle N, m_0 \rangle) = \{\sigma \in T^* \mid m_0 \xrightarrow{\sigma} \}$ (resp. $L^\infty(\langle N, m_0 \rangle) = \{\sigma \in T^\infty \mid m_0 \xrightarrow{\sigma} \}$), also $L^\omega(\langle N, m_0 \rangle) = L^*(\langle N, m_0 \rangle) \cup L^\infty(\langle N, m_0 \rangle)$. Moreover, $[N, m_0\rangle = \{m \text{ s.t. } \exists \sigma \in T^*, m_0 \xrightarrow{\sigma} m\}$ represents the set of reachable markings of $\langle N, m_0 \rangle$.

Subnets. Let $N = \langle P, T, Pre, Post \rangle$ be a Petri net. N' is a subnet of N induced by (P', T'), $P' \subseteq P$ and $T' \subseteq T$, if $N' = \langle P', T', Pre', Post' \rangle$ is a Petri net s.t. $\forall (p,t) \in P' \times T'$, $Pre'(p,t) = Pre(p,t)$ and $Post'(p,t) = Post(p,t)$. If m is a marking of N then we define its restriction to places of N' as follows: $\forall p \in P'$ $m'(p) = m(p)$. The restriction of m to P' is denoted by $m_{\lfloor P'}$.

Linear invariants. Let v be a vector of $\mathbb{N}^P$, v is a positive linear invariant iff $v.W = 0$. If v is a positive linear invariant and $m \xrightarrow{\sigma} m'$ is a firing sequence then $v^T.m' = v^T.m$.

Sequences. Let σ be a sequence of transitions ($\sigma \in T^\omega$). λ denotes the empty sequence. For a transition t in T, we define $|\sigma|_t$ by:
If t occurs infinitely often in σ then $|\sigma|_t = \infty$ else $|\sigma|_t = k$ where, k is the number of occurrences of t in σ. We extend this notation to subsets X of transitions: $|\sigma|_X = \sum_{t \in X} |\sigma|_t$. Moreover, $|\sigma|$ is the number of transitions in σ. By analogy to the notations introduced on sets of nodes, we define:
$^\bullet \sigma = \cup_{t,[|\sigma|_t > 0]} {}^\bullet t$, $\sigma^\bullet = \cup_{t,[|\sigma|_t > 0]} t^\bullet$ and $^\bullet \sigma^\bullet = {}^\bullet \sigma \cup \sigma^\bullet$.
The set of transitions which occur infinitely often in σ is denoted by $inf(\sigma)$.
The projection of a sequence σ on a set of transitions $X \subseteq T$ is the sequence obtained by removing from σ all transitions that do not belong to X. It is defined as follows: $\lfloor : T^\omega \times 2^T \longrightarrow T^\omega$ s.t.:

- $\lambda_{\lfloor X} = \lambda$,
- $\forall \sigma \in T^\omega$ and $t \in T$ if $t \in X$ then $(t.\sigma)_{\lfloor X} = t.\sigma_{\lfloor X}$ else $(t.\sigma)_{\lfloor X} = \sigma_{\lfloor X}$.

The projection function is extended to sets of sequences (i.e. languages) as follows: $\forall \Gamma \subseteq T^\omega$, $\Gamma_{\lfloor X} = \{\sigma_{\lfloor X} \mid \sigma \in \Gamma\}$.

2.2 Synchronous Decomposition

In this section, we define the decomposition of a Petri net N into two subnets N_1 and N_2 through a set of interface transitions T_I.

Definition 1 (Decomposable Petri net). *Let $N = \langle P, T, Pre, Post \rangle$ be a Petri net and T_I a non empty subset of T. N is said to be decomposable into $N_1 = \langle P_1, T_1 = T_{11} \cup T_I, Pre_1, Post_1 \rangle$ and $N_2 = \langle P_2, T_2 = T_{21} \cup T_I, Pre_2, Post_2 \rangle$ through the interface T_I if:*

- *$P = P_1 \cup P_2$ and $T = T_1 \cup T_2$,*
- *$P_1 \cap P_2 = \emptyset$, $T_{11} \cap T_{21} = \emptyset$,*

- $\forall i \in \{1,2\}$, $\forall (p,t) \in P_i \times T_i$, $Pre_i(p,t) = Pre(p,t)$ and $Post_i(p,t) = Post(p,t)$,
- $\forall i,j \in \{1,2\}$, $i \neq j$, $\forall (p,t) \in P_i \times (T_j \setminus T_I)$, $Pre(p,t) = Post(p,t) = 0$

Notation: From now on, tuple $N_d = \langle N_1, T_I, N_2 \rangle$ denotes the decomposition of the net N into N_1 and N_2 through T_I.

Note that the composition of subnets by fusion of transitions occurs in a large class of Petri net models. Even if this kind of interface is especially used to model synchronous composition, we will see that our modular technique allows one to handle asynchronous composition as well, thanks to the exploitation of the positive linear invariants of the system. Figure 1 illustrates an example of a decomposable Petri net model. It models a simplified *client-server* system. The server switches between states *Passive* and *Active* on reception of *On* and *Off* signals respectively. On the other side, the client is initially *Idle*. When it wants to send a message, it waits for the server to be *Active* (place *Wserv*). Then, it sends its message and waits for a positive or negative acknowledgement (place *Wack*). In the case of a positive acknowledgement, it becomes again *Idle*. Otherwise, it tries to retransmit the message (place *Fail*). On reception of a message, the server analyzes it and sends a positive or negative acknowledgement (place *Analyze*).

The considered set of transitions T_I is $\{Send, Cons, Ncons\}$ (the full transitions of Figure 1). Here the subnet of the server (generated by the bold places of Figure 1) is unbounded due to the place *Mess* and any other choice of interface between the client and the server will lead to similar problems. A correct modular approach should analyze a component of the system completed by an abstraction of its environment. In the next subsection, we show how to exploit system invariants in order to automatically construct such an abstraction.

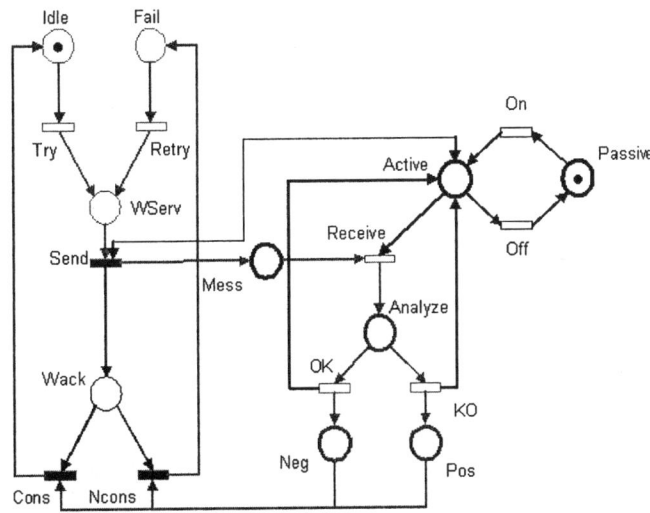

Fig. 1. A decomposable Petri net

2.3 Exploiting the Linear Invariants

A linear invariant of a Petri net corresponds to a safety property of the modelled system. Due to the equation defining such invariants, their computation is reduced to find a generative family of positive solutions of a linear equation system. Although the worst case time complexity of this computation is not polynomial, in practice the algorithm behaves efficiently and its usual time complexity is negligible w.r.t. the reachability graph construction. Thus, this approach is widely used for analysis of Petri nets and integrated in numerous softwares.

Here, we propose to use a linear invariant as a witness of the synchronization between two subnets. Consequently, we look for linear invariants whose support intersects the places of the two subnets. Let V_{dec} be the subset of positive place-invariants which fulfill the above condition, picked from a generative family of a decomposable Petri net N. With each item $v \in V_{dec}$, we associate two places $a_1^{(v)}, a_2^{(v)}$ where $a_i^{(v)}$ is added to the subnet N_j in such a way that its current marking summarizes the information given by the positive place-invariant v. The obtained net is called *component subnet* and denoted from now on by $\widehat{N_i}$. V_{dec} will be called the set of global invariants. Given a place p, the vector 1_p in the following definition denotes the vector of $\mathbb{N}^P$ where each element is zero except the one indexed by the place p.

Definition 2 (*Component subnet*). *Let $N_d = \langle N_1, T_I, N_2 \rangle$ be a decomposition of a Petri net N. The component subnet related to $N_i = \langle P_i, T_i, Pre_i, Post_i \rangle$ ($\{i, j\} = \{1, 2\}$) is a Petri net $\widehat{N_i} = \langle \widehat{P_i}, \widehat{T_i}, \widehat{Pre_i}, \widehat{Post_i} \rangle$ such that:*

- $\widehat{T_i} = T_i$,
- $\widehat{P_i} = P_i \cup A_j$, with $A_j = \{a_j^{(v)} | v \in V_{dec}\}$ *the set of abstraction places.*

Let Φ be a mapping from $P \cup A_1 \cup A_2$ to $\mathbb{N}^{P \cup A_1 \cup A_2}$ defined by:
$\forall p \in P, \Phi(p) = 1_p$ *and* $\forall a_i^{(v)} \in A_i, \Phi(a_i^{(v)}) = \Sigma_{p \in P_i} v(p).1_p$
- $\forall p \in \widehat{P_i}, \forall t \in \widehat{T_i}, \widehat{Pre_i}(p, t) = Pre(t)^T.\Phi(p)$ *and* $\widehat{Post_i}(p, t) = Post(t)^T.\Phi(p)$

We illustrate the concept of *component subnets* on the client-server model of Figure 1. This model has the following generative family of invariants:

1. $Idle + Fail + Wserv + Wack$
2. $Active + Passive + Analyze$
3. $Idle + Fail + Wserv + Mess + Analyze + Pos + Neg$

The first two invariants are local to one subnet. Thus, only the third one, which covers both subnets, is used for the *component subnets* construction, leading to the components described in Figure 2. These subnets have been enlarged with two abstraction places, called here Abs_1 and Abs_2. Let us explain for instance the underlying meaning of the abstraction place Abs_1. Since $\Phi(Abs_1) = 1_{Idle} + 1_{Fail} + 1_{Wserv} + 1_{Mess}$, this place contains the sum of tokens of the four previous places. As $Wserv$ is an input place of the transition $Send$ and the three others ones aren't, $Pre(Abs_1, Send) = 1$. The other arcs are similarly deduced.

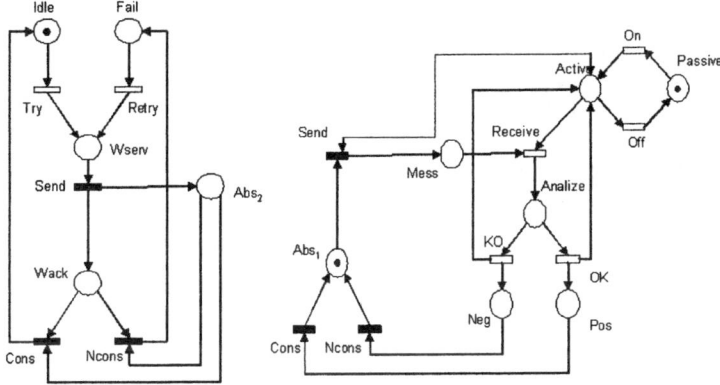

Fig. 2. The two component subnets

According to this interpretation, the following definition defines the mapping from a *global* marking (a marking of the original net) to markings of the component subnets.

Definition 3. *Let $N_d = \langle N_1, T_I, N_2 \rangle$ be the decomposition of a Petri net N and let $\widehat{N_i}$ ($i = 1, 2$) be the induced component subnets. For each marking m of N, Φ_i the projection mapping on $\widehat{N_i}$ is defined by: $\forall p \in P_i, \Phi_i(m)(p) = m^T.\Phi(p)$*

The following proposition and corollary summarize what can be directly deduced from this decomposition about the relative behaviours of the net and its component subnets.

Proposition 1. *Let $N_d = \langle N_1, T_I, N_2 \rangle$ be a decomposition of a marked Petri net $\langle N, m \rangle$ and let $\widehat{N_i}$ ($i = 1, 2$) be the induced component subnets. Then, the following assertion holds:*
$\forall \sigma \in T^*$, *if* $m \xrightarrow{\sigma} m'$ *then* $\Phi_i(m) \xrightarrow{\sigma \lfloor \widehat{T_i}} \Phi_i(m')$

Proof. We prove the proposition for $\sigma = t$ being a single transition. The proposition follows by a straightforward induction. We consider the following cases.

case 1: $t \in \widehat{T_i}$
$m \xrightarrow{\sigma} m' \Rightarrow m \geq Pre(t) \Rightarrow \forall p \in \widehat{P_i}, m^T.\Phi(p) \geq Pre(t)^T.\Phi(p)$ (by positivity of $\Phi(p)$) $\Leftrightarrow \forall p \in \widehat{P_i}, \Phi_i(m)(p) \geq \widehat{Pre_i}(p, t)$. Thus $\Phi_i(m) \xrightarrow{t}$.
$m' = m - Pre(t) + Post(t) \Rightarrow \forall p \in \widehat{P_i}, m'^T.\Phi(p) = m^T.\Phi(p) - Pre(t)^T.\Phi(p) + Post(t)^T.\Phi(p) \Leftrightarrow \forall p \in \widehat{P_i}, \Phi_i(m')(p) = \Phi_i(m)(p) - \widehat{Pre_i}(p, t) + \widehat{Post_i}(p, t)$.
Thus $\Phi_i(m) \xrightarrow{t} \Phi_i(m')$.

case 2: $t \notin \widehat{T_i}$
$\forall p \in P_i, p \notin {}^\bullet t^\bullet$. Thus $\Phi_i(m')(p) = m'(p) = m(p) = \Phi_i(m)(p)$
Let $v \in V_{dec}$, since v is a flow: $m'^T.(\Phi(a_i^{(v)}) + \Phi(a_j^{(v)})) = m^T.(\Phi(a_i^{(v)}) + \Phi(a_j^{(v)}))$

Thus, $\Phi_i(m')(a_j^{(v)}) - \Phi_i(m)(a_j^{(v)}) = m'^T.\Phi(a_j^{(v)}) - m^T.\Phi(a_j^{(v)})$
$= m'^T.\Phi(a_i^{(v)}) - m^T.\Phi(a_i^{(v)}) = \Sigma_{p \in P_i} v(p).(m'(p) - m(p)) = 0$
(since any such $p \notin {}^\bullet t^\bullet$)
Thus $\Phi_i(m') = \Phi_i(m)$.

The assertions given in the following corollary are immediate consequences of the above proposition.

Corollary 1. *Let $N_d = \langle N_1, T_I, N_2 \rangle$ be a decomposition of a marked Petri net $\langle N, m \rangle$ and let $\widehat{N_i}$ ($i = 1, 2$) be the induced component subnets. Then, the following assertions hold:*

- $L^\omega(N, m)_{\lfloor \widehat{T_i}} \subset L^\omega(\widehat{N_i}, \Phi_i(m))$
- $\{\sigma_{\lfloor \widehat{T_i}} \mid \sigma \in L^\infty(N, m) \text{ and } Inf(\sigma) \cap \widehat{T_i} \neq \emptyset\} \subset L^\infty(\widehat{N_i}, \Phi_i(m))$
- (N, m) *is unbounded* $\Rightarrow \exists i \, (\widehat{N_i}, \Phi_i(m))$ *is unbounded*

3 Preservation of Properties

3.1 The Non-constraining Relation

In this section, we define the *non-constraining relation*: an asymmetric property to be checked between two given marked *component subnets* obtained from a decomposition of a net: $(\widehat{N_2}, \widehat{m_2})$ does not constrain $(\widehat{N_1}, \widehat{m_1})$ if for any firing sequence enabled from $(\widehat{N_1}, \widehat{m_1})$, there exists a firing sequence enabled from $(\widehat{N_2}, \widehat{m_2})$, which both have the same projection on the interface transitions. Under such a relation, we prove that the firing sequences enabled in the non constrained component exactly represent the firing sequences of the global net, up to the projection on the transition interface.

Definition 4 (Non-constraining relation). *Let $\langle \widehat{N_1}, \widehat{m_1} \rangle$ and $\langle \widehat{N_2}, \widehat{m_2} \rangle$ be the two component subnets induced by a decomposition of a Petri net $\langle N, m \rangle$: $\langle \widehat{N_2}, \widehat{m_2} \rangle$ does not constrain $\langle \widehat{N_1}, \widehat{m_1} \rangle$ iff $L^\omega_{\lfloor T_I}(\langle \widehat{N_1}, \widehat{m_1} \rangle) \subseteq L^\omega_{\lfloor T_I}(\langle \widehat{N_2}, \widehat{m_2} \rangle)$.*

When each component doesn't constrain the other one we say that they are *mutually non-constraining*.

Proposition 2. *Let $\langle \widehat{N_1}, \widehat{m_1} \rangle$ and $\langle \widehat{N_2}, \widehat{m_2} \rangle$ be the two marked component subnets induced by a decomposition of a marked Petri net $\langle N, m \rangle$. If $\langle \widehat{N_2}, \widehat{m_2} \rangle$ does not constrain $\langle \widehat{N_1}, \widehat{m_1} \rangle$ then the following assertion holds:*
$\forall \sigma_1 \in \widehat{T_1}^*: \widehat{m_1} \xrightarrow{\sigma_1} \widehat{m_1'} \Rightarrow \exists \sigma \in T^*$ *and* $\exists m' \in \mathbb{N}^P$ *s.t.:*
$\sigma_{\lfloor T_1} = \sigma_1, m \xrightarrow{\sigma} m'$ *(and $\Phi_1(m') = \widehat{m_1'}$ by proposition 1).*

Proof. Let $\sigma_1 = \sigma_1^0.t^1. \cdots .t^k.\sigma_1^k$ with $\forall m, \sigma_1^m \in T_{11}$ and $t^m \in T_I$.
By hypothesis, there exists a firing sequence σ_2 in $(\widehat{N_2}, \widehat{m_2})$:
$\sigma_2 = \sigma_2^0.t^1. \cdots .t^k.\sigma_2^k$ with $\forall m, \sigma_2^m \in T_{21}$.
We claim that $\sigma = \sigma_1^0.\sigma_2^0.t^1. \cdots .t^k.\sigma_1^k.\sigma_2^k$ is the required sequence. We prove it by induction on the prefixes of σ.

Let $\sigma'.t$ be a prefix of σ such that σ' is a firing sequence, i.e. $m\xrightarrow{\sigma'}m''$.
By proposition 1, $\forall i \in \{1,2\}, \widehat{m_i} = \Phi_i(m)\xrightarrow{\sigma'_{\lfloor \widehat{T_i}}}\Phi_i(m'')$
By construction $\forall i \in \{1,2\}, (\sigma'.t)_{\lfloor \widehat{T_i}}$ is a prefix of σ_i. Thus $\Phi_i(m'')\xrightarrow{t_{\lfloor \widehat{T_i}}}$

Case 1: $t \in T_I$
Let $p \in {}^\bullet t$, $p \in P_i$ for some $i \in \{1,2\}$,
since $\Phi_i(m'')\xrightarrow{t}$, $m''(p) = \Phi_i(m'')(p) \geq Pre(p,t)$, we conclude that $m''\xrightarrow{t}$.

Case 2: $t \in T_{i1}$ for some $i \in \{1,2\}$
Let $p \in {}^\bullet t$ since $t \in T_{i1}$ then $p \in P_i$,
since $\Phi_i(m'')\xrightarrow{t}$, $m''(p) = \Phi_i(m'')(p) \geq Pre(p,t)$, we conclude that $m''\xrightarrow{t}$.

The non-constraining relation can be regarded as an inclusion relation between the languages of the components subnets, once projected on the shared transition interface. Checking such a property represents the main difficulty of our approach. A naive test of this relation would result in building the synchronized product of the components subnets reachability graphs, which could drastically limit the interests of our methods.

Here, we propose a new approach based on an abstraction of the system, namely, the *interface component subnet*, which allows one to represent the language of the global net compactly, up to a projection on the transition interface. It is obtained by connecting the interface transitions to the abstraction places of both components subnets. Figure 3 represents the interface component subnet of the net depicted in Figure 1.

Definition 5 (*Interface component subnet*). Let $N_d = \langle N_1, T_I, N_2 \rangle$ be the decomposition of a Petri net N and let $\widehat{N_i}$ ($i = 1,2$) be the induced component subnets. The interface component subnet related to N_d is a Petri net $\widehat{N_{int}} = \langle \widehat{P_{int}}, \widehat{T_{int}}, \widehat{Pre_{int}}, \widehat{Post_{int}} \rangle$ such that, for $i,j \in \{1,2\}$ and $i \neq j$:
- $\widehat{T_{int}} = T_I$,
- $\widehat{P_{int}} = A_1 \cup A_2$, with $A_i = \{a_i^{(v)} | v \in V_{dec}\}$ the set of abstraction places of $\widehat{N_i}$,
- $\forall a \in A_i, \forall t \in \widehat{T_{int}}, \widehat{Pre_{int}}(a,t) = \widehat{Pre_j}(a,t)$ and $\widehat{Post_{int}}(a,t) = \widehat{Post_j}(a,t)$.

Using Proposition 1, one can immediately state the following: $\forall i \in \{1,2\}$, $L^\omega_{\lfloor T_I}(\widehat{N_i},\widehat{m_i}) \subseteq L^\omega(\widehat{N_{int}},\widehat{m_{int}})$.

Proposition 3. Let $N_d = \langle N_1, T_I, N_2 \rangle$ be a decomposition of a marked Petri net $\langle N, m \rangle$ and let $\widehat{N_i}$ ($i = 1,2$) and $\widehat{N_{int}}$ be the induced component subnets.

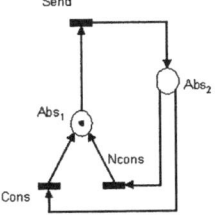

Fig. 3. The Client-Server interface component subnet

Then, the following assertion holds:
$\langle \widehat{N_i}, \widehat{m_i} \rangle$ *is non-constraining for* $\langle \widehat{N_{int}}, \widehat{m_{int}} \rangle \Rightarrow \langle \widehat{N_i}, \widehat{m_i} \rangle$ *is non-constraining for* $\langle \widehat{N_j}, \widehat{m_j} \rangle$ *(*$j \in \{1,2\}$ *and* $j \neq i$*)*

The proof is obvious since from proposition 1, one can immediately state that $L^\omega_{\lceil T_I}(\widehat{N_i}, \widehat{m_i}) \subseteq L^\omega(\widehat{N_{int}}, \widehat{m_{int}})$ (for $i \in \{1,2\}$). This proposition will be exploited in the next subsection, in order to restrain the test of the non-constraining relation between two component subnets, to a lighter relation between a component subnet and the interface component subnet. The non-constraining relation can thus be checked modularly, since one component subnet is considered at a time. It is worth noting that the component subnet is computed only once even if a mutual non-constraining relation is checked.

3.2 The Non-constraining Test Algorithm

Now we explain how to check whether a given somponent subnet $\langle \widehat{N_i}, \widehat{m_i} \rangle$ is non-constraining for $\langle \widehat{N_{int}}, \widehat{m_{int}} \rangle$. The proposed algorithm 3.2 works on the fly and focusses on the behaviour of the $\langle \widehat{N_i}, \widehat{m_i} \rangle$ around the interface. Its local moves induced by the local transitions are hence abstracted (unobserved) since they are not directly involved in the inclusion test. This allows us to reuse the concept of observation graph proposed in [4] to represent a reachability graph compactly. Here, the observed transitions are those of the interface transitions. The observation graph of $(\widehat{N_i}, \widehat{m_i})$ is a graph where each node is a set of markings linked by local (unobserved) transitions and each arc is labelled with an interface transition. Nodes of the observation graph are called meta-states and may be represented and managed efficiently by using *decision diagram techniques* (BDD for instance). In practice, the efficiency of this approach is obtained whenever the number of observed transitions is small with respect to the total number of transitions ([4], [7]). In order to check the non-constraining relation, the observation graph of $(\widehat{N_i}, \widehat{m_i})$ is synchronized against the reachability graph of the interface component subnet $\langle \widehat{N_{int}}, \widehat{m_{int}} \rangle$. However, the required synchronized product is widely reduced comparing to the general one. In fact, each reachable meta-state of $\langle \widehat{N_i}, \widehat{m_i} \rangle$ leads, by construction, to a unique reachable state of $\langle \widehat{N_{int}}, \widehat{m_{int}} \rangle$. In other words, a meta-state is never synchronized with two different states of the interface component subnet. Obviously, the reciprocal doesn't hold: a state of $\langle \widehat{N_{int}}, \widehat{m_{int}} \rangle$ could be synchronized with many meta-states of $\langle \widehat{N_i}, \widehat{m_i} \rangle$. Thus, in the worst case, the complexity of the non-constraining test is given by the number of reachable meta-states of $\langle \widehat{N_i}, \widehat{m_i} \rangle$ instead of (classically) the size of the synchronized product. The data structures used by Algorithm 3.2 are the following ones:

- a set H_{int} represents a heap to store the states of $\langle \widehat{N_{int}}, \widehat{m_{int}} \rangle$ that are visited,
- a table $Synch$ is used to associate a subset of meta-states (set of states) with each state of H_{int}. For any state s in H_{int}, we ensure that the meta-states of $Synch[s]$ are incomparable.

- a stack st, the items of which are tuples $\langle S, s, f \rangle$ composed of a meta-state of $\langle \widehat{N_i}, \widehat{m_i} \rangle$, a state of $\langle \widehat{N_{int}}, \widehat{m_{int}} \rangle$ and a set of interface transitions enabled from both nodes.

Algorithm 3.1 Non-constraining of $(\langle \widehat{N_i}, \widehat{m_i} \rangle$ w.r.t. $\langle \widehat{N_{int}}, \widehat{m_{int}} \rangle)$

```
 1: state s_int = m̂_int, s'_int;
 2: Events f^i, f^int, Obs = T_I, Unobs = T̂_i \ Obs;
 3: Set S_i, S'_i, H_int; Set of Set Synch;
 4: stack st(⟨Set, state, Events⟩);
 5: S_i = Saturate({m̂_i}, Unobs);
 6: f^int = firable({s_int}, Obs); f^i = firable(S_i, Obs);
 7: if (¬(f^i ⊇ f^int)) then
 8:     return false
 9: end if
10: H_int = {s_int}; Synch[s_int] = {S};
11: st.Push(⟨S_i, s_int, f^int⟩);
12: repeat
13:     st.Pop(⟨S_i, s_int, f^int⟩);
14:     for t ∈ f^int do
15:         S'_i = Img(S_i, t); S'_i = Saturate(S'_i, Unobs);
16:         s'_int = Img({s_int}, t);
17:         if s'_int ∉ H_int then
18:             H_int = H_int ∪ {s'_int}; Synch[s'_int] = ∅
19:         end if
20:         if ∄ S ∈ Sync[s'_int] s.t. S ⊆ S'_i then
21:             for each S ∈ Synch[s'_int] s.t. S'_i ⊆ S do
22:                 Sync[s'_int] = Sync[s'_int] \ {S};
23:             end for
24:             Sync[s'_int] = Sync[s'_int] ∪ {S'_i};
25:             f^i = firable(S'_i, Obs)); f^int = firable(s'_int, Obs)
26:             if (¬(f^i ⊇ f^int)) then
27:                 return false
28:             end if
29:             st.Push(⟨S'_i, s'_int, f^int⟩);
30:         end if
31:     end for
32: until st == ∅;
33: return true
```

Three builder functions are used (all can be implemented symbolically using BDD notations) : $img(S, t)$ returns the immediate successors of the set of states S, through the firings of the transition t. $firable(S, o)$ is defined from a set of states S and a set of transitions o. It returns the subset of transitions in o that are enabled from a state of S (not necessarily the same). $saturate(S, u)$ returns a meta-state from a subset of states S and a set of (unobserved) transitions u.

Starting from each state of S, it infers all possible firings of the u transitions until a fix point is reached. The resulting meta-state consists of the states of S and all the reached states w.r.t. u.

The first stage of Algorithm 3.2 allows one to compute the first elements of the data structures, in particular the first items of the H_{int}, $Synch$ and st. For that, the initial meta-state S_i of $\langle \widehat{N_i}, \widehat{m_i} \rangle$ is computed. The transitions f^{int} enabled from the initial state s_{int} of $\langle \widehat{N_{int}}, \widehat{m_{int}} \rangle$ are evaluated. If the enabled set of observable transitions from S_i doesn't contain the enabled set f^{int} the non-constraining test is stopped with a negative answer. Otherwise, the tuple $\langle S_i, s_{int}, f^{int} \rangle$ is pushed on the stack. Then, the algorithm iterates to synchronize successors items from an element of the stack, e.g. $\langle S_i, s_{int}, f^{int} \rangle$. According to each transition t in f^{int}, it computes and processes the successor s'_{int} from s_{int} in $\langle \widehat{N_{int}}, \widehat{m_{int}} \rangle$ and the successor S'_i from S_i in $\langle \widehat{N_i}, \widehat{m_i} \rangle$.

In order to be efficient, we propose to decrease the number of (successors) tuples to be pushed on the stack. This is why we maintain the set $Sync[s'_{int}]$ of meta-states of $\langle \widehat{N_i}, \widehat{m_i} \rangle$ for each visited state s'_{int} of $\langle \widehat{N_{int}}, \widehat{m_{int}} \rangle$. Actually, a newly computed meta-state S'_i synchronized with s'_{int} can be discarded if a larger meta-state already exists in $Sync[s'_{int}]$. Otherwise, the meta-states in $Sync[s'_{int}]$, the set of states of which properly contains S'_i, are removed.

The algorithm will return false as soon as the sets of enabled interface transitions from both sides don't match with each other, meaning that the component subnet is constraining for the interface component subnet. Conversely, the algorithm will return true at the end of the synchronization product (the stack is empty), meaning that the component subnet does not constrain the interface component subnet.

3.3 Compositionality Results

With respect to the decomposition, we study two kinds of systems properties: generic properties like liveness and boundedness, and specific properties expressed by action-based temporal logics (logics using actions as atomic propositions) based on infinite observed sequences (sequences where some observed transitions occur infinitely often).

Preservation of generic properties. In this part, we prove that given a decomposable Petri net N, and under a mutual non-constraining condition between the corresponding *component subnets* $\widehat{N}_1$ and $\widehat{N}_2$, liveness (resp. boundedness) of N is completely characterized by the liveness (resp. boundedness) of $\widehat{N}_1$ and $\widehat{N}_2$.

Proposition 4. *If $\langle \widehat{N}_1, \widehat{m}_1 \rangle$ and $\langle \widehat{N}_2, \widehat{m}_2 \rangle$ are mutually non-constraining, then the following assertion holds:*
$\langle N, m \rangle$ *is live* $\Leftrightarrow \langle \widehat{N}_1, \widehat{m}_1 \rangle$ *and* $\langle \widehat{N}_2, \widehat{m}_2 \rangle$ *are live.*

Proof. ($\Rightarrow$) Assume that $\langle N, m \rangle$ is live. Let $\widehat{m}_1'$ be a reachable marking in $\langle \widehat{N}_1, \widehat{m}_1 \rangle$ and t a transition of $\widehat{T}_1$. Let us prove that there exists a sequence ending by t which is enabled by the marking $\widehat{m_1}'$. Since $\langle \widehat{N_2}, \widehat{m_2} \rangle$ is non-constraining for $\langle \widehat{N_1}, \widehat{m_1} \rangle$ and according to the proposition 2, there exists a sequence σ and a marking m' such that $m \xrightarrow{\sigma} m'$ and $\Phi_1(m') = \widehat{m_1}'$. On the other hand, since the marked net $\langle N, m \rangle$ is live, there exists a sequence σ' having t as the last transition and which is enabled by the marking m'. Let m'' be the marking reached by this sequence.

Let us now consider the sequence $\sigma\sigma'$, enabled by $\langle N, m \rangle$, according to the proposition 1, the projected sequence $\sigma\sigma'_{\lfloor \widehat{T_1}}$ is enabled by $\langle \widehat{N_1}, \widehat{m_1} \rangle$ and the marking reached is equal to $\Phi_1(m'')$. We conclude that $\sigma'_{\lfloor \widehat{T_1}}$ (having t as a last transition) is enabled by $\widehat{m_1}'$.

By symmetry, we prove that $\langle \widehat{N_2}, \widehat{m_2} \rangle$ is live.

($\Leftarrow$) Assume that que $\langle \widehat{N_1}, \widehat{m_1} \rangle$ and $\langle \widehat{N_2}, \widehat{m_2} \rangle$ are mutually non-constraining and live. Let m' be a reachable marking in $\langle N, m \rangle$ and t a transition of T, let us prove that there exists a sequence, having t as the last transition, which is enabled by marking m'.

Due to the symmetry of the problem, we assume that the transition t belongs to $\widehat{T_1}$. According to proposition 1, there exists a sequence σ_1 which is enabled by $\langle \widehat{N_1}, \widehat{m_1} \rangle$ and leading to the marking $\widehat{m_1'} = m'_{\lfloor \widehat{T_1}}$. On the other hand, there exists a sequence σ'_1 having t as the last transition and which is enabled by $\widehat{m_1'}$ (because $\langle \widehat{N_1}, \widehat{m_1} \rangle$ is live). Moreover, since $\langle \widehat{N_2}, \widehat{m_2} \rangle$ is non-constraining for $\langle \widehat{N_1}, \widehat{m_1} \rangle$, we deduce the existence of a sequence σ', which is enabled by $\langle N, m' \rangle$, such that $\sigma'_{\lfloor \widehat{T_1}} = \sigma'_1$. The sequence satisfying the former condition has t as the last transition. Thus, we deduce that $\langle N, m \rangle$ is live.

Proposition 5. *Let $\langle N, m \rangle$ be a Petri net and let $N_d = \langle N_1, T_I, N_2 \rangle$ be a decomposition of N leading to the component subnets $\langle \widehat{N_1}, \widehat{m_1} \rangle$ and $\langle \widehat{N_2}, \widehat{m_2} \rangle$. If $\langle \widehat{N_1}, \widehat{m_1} \rangle$ and $\langle \widehat{N_2}, \widehat{m_2} \rangle$ are mutually non-constraining, then:*
$\langle N, m \rangle$ is bounded $\Leftrightarrow \langle \widehat{N_1}, \widehat{m_1} \rangle$ and $\langle \widehat{N_2}, \widehat{m_2} \rangle$ are bounded.

Proof. $\Leftarrow$ (Corollary 1)
$\Rightarrow$ Assume that $\langle N, m \rangle$ is bounded. We suppose that $\langle \widehat{N_i}, \widehat{m_i} \rangle$ is unbounded, for $i \in \{1, 2\}$. This means that there exists a run (an infinite computation) $\xi_i = \widehat{m_i}^0 \xrightarrow{t_1^i} \widehat{m_i}^1 \xrightarrow{t_2^i} \ldots$ and a place $p \in \widehat{P_i}$ such that $\forall \widehat{m_i}^k \in \xi_i, \exists \widehat{m_i}^l \in \xi_i$ with $l > k$ s.t. $\widehat{m_i}^k(p) < \widehat{m_i}^l(p)$. Since $\langle \widehat{N_j}, \widehat{m_j} \rangle$ ($j \in \{1, 2\}$, $j \neq i$) doesn't constrain $\langle \widehat{N_i}, \widehat{m_i} \rangle$, there exists a run $\xi = m_0 \xrightarrow{\sigma_1} m_1 \xrightarrow{\sigma_2} \ldots$ in $\langle N, m \rangle$ s.t. $\xi_{\lfloor \widehat{T_i}} = \xi_i$ and $\forall k = 1, 2, \ldots \widehat{m_i}^k = \Phi_i(m_k)$.

Case 1: $p \notin A_j$
In this case, $p \in P$ and $\forall m_k \in \xi, \exists m_l \in \xi$ with $l > k$ s.t. $m_k(p) < m_l(p)$ which means that $\langle N, m \rangle$ is unbounded and then contradicts the hypothesis.

Case 2: $p \in A_j$, let v be the corresponding positive invariant.
In this case, $\forall m_k \in \xi, \exists m_l \in \xi$ with $l > k$ s.t. $v^T.m_k < v^T.m_l$. This means that there exists, at least, one place in $\|v\|$ for which the marking can be infinitely

increased through ξ (v is a positive invariant). This contradicts the hypothesis that $\langle N, m \rangle$ is bounded.

Preservation of action-based temporal properties. Let us consider a Petri net N and an action-based temporal logic formula f relative to the infinite observed sequences of N. Assuming that the transitions occurring in f belong to one component subnet, we show how to exploit our approach in order to modularly check f. First, the following proposition states that, checking if a particular transition $t \in \widehat{T_1}$ (for instance) appears infinitely often in a firing sequence of a decomposable Petri net $\langle N, m \rangle$ is reduced to the analysis of firing sequences of $(\widehat{N_1}, \widehat{m_1})$ if it is not constrained by $(\widehat{N_2}, \widehat{m_2})$.

Proposition 6. *Let $N_d = \langle N_1, T_I, N_2 \rangle$ be a decomposition of a Petri net $\langle N, m \rangle$ leading to the component subnets $(\widehat{N_1}, \widehat{m_1})$ and $(\widehat{N_2}, \widehat{m_2})$. Let t be a transition in $\widehat{T_1}$. If $(\widehat{N_2}, \widehat{m_2})$ is non-constraining for $(\widehat{N_1}, \widehat{m_1})$, then:*
$$\exists \sigma \in L^\omega(N, m) \text{ s.t. } t \in inf(\sigma) \iff \exists \sigma_1 \in L^\omega(\widehat{N_1}, \widehat{m_1}) \text{ s.t. } t \in inf(\sigma_1)$$

Proof. ($\Longrightarrow$) Let $\sigma \in L^\omega(N, m)$ a firing sequence in $\langle N, m \rangle$ such that $t \in inf(\sigma)$ and $\sigma_1 = \sigma_{\lfloor \widehat{T_1}}$. Following the proposition 1, we deduce that $\widehat{m_1} \xrightarrow{\sigma_1}$. Because $t \in \widehat{T_1}$, one concludes that $t \in inf(\sigma_1)$.
($\Longleftarrow$) Let $\sigma_1 \in L^\omega(\widehat{N_1}, \widehat{m_1})$ such that $\widehat{m_1} \xrightarrow{\sigma_1} \widehat{m_1}'$ and $t \in inf(\sigma_1)$. According to proposition 2, there exists a firing sequence $\sigma \in L^\omega(N, m)$ such that $\sigma_1 = \sigma_{\lfloor \widehat{T_1}}$. Since $t \in inf(\sigma_1)$, one deduces that $t \in inf(\sigma)$.

Proposition 6 leads to a modular model checking approach dealing with infinite observed sequences. Given a decomposable Petri net N and a formula f such that the set $Occ(f)$ (set of transitions occurring in f) is a subset of $\widehat{T_i}$ ($i \in \{1, 2\}$), checking f on N can be reduced to check f on $\widehat{N_i}$ in the two following cases:

- f holds on $\widehat{N_i}$,
- f doesn't hold on $\widehat{N_i}$ and $\widehat{N_i}$ is non constrained by $\widehat{N_j}$.

4 Conclusion

In this paper, we have presented a decomposition approach which allows the modular verification of Petri nets properties. The liveness and boundedness of the system components can be used to check these properties for the system. This is also the case for any linear time property whenever its checking relates to the infinite observed executions of some component of the system. In contrast to previous techniques, we do not force any specific (restrictive) structure at the interface of the modules, but we exploit the linear invariants (that are usually common in well-specified system models) of the system. Our main contribution is the definition of a sufficient condition to test the non-constraining relation w.r.t. a component subnet. In order to be general, it is tested behaviourally but modularly with respect to a component subnet.

The limit of the presented work occurs when the non-constraining relation is required for a component subnet but does not hold. Concerning LTL properties, our first solution is an iterative technique presented in [3]. Starting from the smallest component subnet to check the satisfaction of an LTL property, it automatically enlarges the component subnet whenever the property is detected false and the environment is constraining.

From a practical point of view, we have shown how the observation-based approach presented in [4] can be adapted to reduce the representation of the reachability graph of a component subnet (using symbolic decision diagram techniques) leading to an efficient modular test of the non-constraining relation. We are currently developping a tool in order to test our method on real case studies.

References

1. Mohamed-Lyes Benalycherif and Claude Girault. Behavioural and structural composition rules preserving liveness by synchronisation for colored FIFO nets. In *Lecture Notes in Computer Science; Proc. 17th International Conference in Application and Theory of Petri Nets (ICATPN'96), Osaka, Japan*, volume 1091, pages 73–92. Springer-Verlag, June 1996.
2. S. Christensen and L. Petrucci. Modular analysis of petri nets. *Computer Journal*, 43(3):224–242, 2000.
3. S. Haddad, J.-M. Ilié, and K. Klai. An incremental verification technique using decomposition of petri net. In *proc. of the IEEE SMC'02 - Systems, Man and Cybernetics, Hammamet, Tunisia*, 2002.
4. S. Haddad, J.-M. Ilié, and K. Klai. Design and evaluation of a symbolic and abstraction-based model checker. In *Proc. of Automated Technology for Verification and Analysis: Second International Conference, ATVA 2004, Taipei, Taiwan, ROC, October 31-November 3*, 2004.
5. J.-M. Ilié, K. Klai, and B. Zouari. A modular verification methodology for d-nri petri nets. In *in proc. of the International Conference ACS/IEEE 2003 on Computer Systems and Applications (AICCSA-03), Tunis, Tunisia*, pages 14–18, 2003.
6. T. Latvala and M. Makela. Ltl model checking for modular Petri nets. In *in proc. of ICATPN'04*, pages 298–311, 2004.
7. V. Noord. Treatment of epsilon moves in subset construction. In *Computational Linguistics, MIT Press for the Association for Computational Linguistics*, volume 26. 2000.
8. A. Santone. Compositionality for Improving Model Checking. In *In proc. of FORTE'00*, in proc. of Formal Methods for Distributed System Development, October 2000.
9. C. Sibertin-Blanc. A client-server protocol for composition of Petri nets. In *in proc. of ICATPN'93*, LNCS, June 1993.
10. Y. Souissi and G. Memmi. Compositions of nets via a communication medium. *LNCS*, 483:457–470, 1991.
11. A. Valmari. Compositional state space generation. In *in proc. of ICATPN'90*, LNCS, May 1990.

An Improved Conformance Testing Method

Rita Dorofeeva[1], Khaled El-Fakih[2], and Nina Yevtushenko[1]

[1] Tomsk State University, Russia
[2] American University of Sharja, UAE
drf@kitidis.tsu.ru, kelfakih@aus.ac.ae,
yevtushenko@elefot.tsu.ru

Abstract. In this paper, we present a novel conformance test suite derivation method. Similar to the HIS method, our method uses harmonized state identifiers for state identification and transition checking and can be applied to any reduced possibly partial deterministic or nondeterministic specification FSM. However, in contrast with the HIS method, in the proposed method appropriate state identifiers are selected on-the-fly (for transition checking) in order to shorten the length of the obtained test suite. Application examples and experimental results are provided. These results show that the proposed method generates shorter test suites than the HIS method. Particularly, on average, the ratio of the length of the test suites derived using the proposed method over the length of corresponding suites derived using the HIS method is 0.66 (0.55) when the number of states of an implementation equals to (is greater than) the number of states of the specification. These ratios are almost independent of the size of specifications.

1 Introduction

Many FSM-based test derivation methods have been developed for conformance testing of communication protocols and other reactive systems [2,3,10,12,14,15,17]. Well-known methods are called the W [2, 14], partial W (Wp) [3], HIS [10,17], and generalized Wp (GWp) [7, 8] test derivation methods. For related surveys the reader may refer to [1,6,13,16]. In [2,3,10,14,15,17] testing methods, one usually assumes that not only the specification, but also the implementation can be modeled as a deterministic FSM, while in [7,8] the specification and the implementation are modeled as non-deterministic FSMs (NFSMs). If the behavior of a (deterministic/non-deterministic) implementation FSM is different than the specified behavior, the implementation contains a fault.

The above methods, each provides the following fault coverage guarantee: If the specification can be modeled by a (reduced) FSM with n states and if a corresponding implementation can be modeled by an FSM with at most m states, where m is larger or equal to n, then a test suite can be derived by the method (for this given m) and the implementation passes this test suite if and only if it conforms (i.e. is equivalent) to the specification. A test suite is called *m-complete* [11] if it detects any nonconforming implementation with at most m states. Guessing the bound of m is an intuitive process based on the knowledge of a specification, the class of implementations which have to be tested for conformance and their interior structure [1]. All of the above methods assume that a reliable reset is available for each implementation under test (written as 'r'). This implies that a test suite can be composed of several individual test cases, each starting with the reset operation.

The HIS, Wp, and UIOv methods are modifications of the so-called W method. All these methods have two phases. Tests derived for the first phase check that each state presented in the specification also exists in the implementation, while tests derived for the second phase check all (remaining) transitions of the implementation for correct output and ending state as defined by the specification. For identifying the state during the first phase and for checking the ending states of the transitions in the second phase, certain state distinguishing input sequences are used. The only difference between the above methods is how such distinguishing sequences are selected. In the original W method, a so-called characterization set W is used to distinguish the different states of the specification. The Wp method uses the W set during the state identification phase (the first phase) while only an appropriate subset, namely a corresponding state identifier, is used when checking the ending state of a transition. In the UIOv method, which is a proper sub-case of the Wp method, the ending state of a transition is identified by the output obtained in response to a single input sequence. Such a Unique Input/Output sequence, called *UIO*, allows distinguishing the expected ending state from all other states of the specification. However, a *UIO* sequence may not exist for some states of a given specification FSM. Moreover, a W set also may not exist for a partially specified specification [16,17]. In this case, only the HIS method can be used where a family of state identifiers [9,10,16] is used for state identification as well as for transition checking.

The GWp method is a generalization of the Wp method to the case when the system specification and implementation are modeled as non-deterministic FSMs. For nondeterministic FSM implementations, in order to guarantee a full-fault detection power, the GWp method assumes that all possible observations of the non-deterministic implementation to a given test can be obtained by repeatedly executing this test. This assumption is called the *complete testing assumption* [7,8]. The GWp method uses a characterization set W to distinguish the different states of the specification. However, a W set may not exist for partially specified NFSMs. In this case, only the generalized HIS method [8] can be used where a family of harmonized state identifiers is used instead of a characterization set for state identification and transition checking.

The length of a derived test suite essentially depends on how a family of state identifiers is selected. In the above methods, for every state of the specification FSM, only one state identifier is selected (in advance) for testing all the incoming transitions of the state. In this paper, we propose an improved method that for every incoming transition of a state selects (on-the-fly) an appropriate state identifier that shortens the length of the resulting test suite. Our method generalizes the method (called H method) originally proposed for complete deterministic FSMs [5]. First we extend the H method for partial deterministic machines and we present more detailed sufficient conditions for having a complete test suite when the system specification and implementation have equal number of states. Then, we experiment with the extended H (hereafter also called as H method) method in order to compare the length of its test suites with test suites derived using the HIS method. The experiments are conducted for the case when $m = n$ and for the case when $m > n$. Experiments with the case when $m = n$ show that on average, the ratio of the length of H over the length of the HIS test suites is 0.66 and experiments with the case when $m = n + 1$ and $m = n + 2$ show that on average this ratio is 0.55. Moreover, the experiments show that these ratios are almost independent of the size of the specification machines. Finally, we extend the H test derivation method for partial nondeterministic machines. We note that the H method, as the HIS, generates complete test suites and is applicable to any complete or partial reduced specification machine.

This paper is organized as follows. Section 2 defines notations for describing finite state machines. Section 3 includes the H method for deterministic partial FSMs and Section 4 includes related experimental results. Section 5 includes the generalization of the H method for non-deterministic partial machines and Section 6 concludes the paper.

2 Finite State Machines

A non-deterministic finite state machine (NFSM) is an initialized non-deterministic Mealy machine that can be formally defined as follows. A *non-deterministic finite state machine* M is a 6-tuple $\langle S, X, Y, h, D_M, s_0 \rangle$, where S is a finite nonempty set of states with s_0 as the initial state; X and Y are input and output alphabets; D_M is the specification domain that is a subset of $S \times X$; and $h: D_M \to 2^{S \times Y} \setminus \emptyset$ is a behavior function where $2^{S \times Y}$ is the set of all subsets of the set $S \times Y$. The behavior function defines the possible transitions of the machine. Given a present state s_i and an input symbol x, each pair $(s_j, y) \in h(s_i, x)$ represents a possible transition to the next state s_j with the output y.

An NFSM M is *observable* if for each pair $(s, x) \in D_M$ and each output y there is at most one state $s' \in S$ such that $(s', y) \in h(s, x)$. In this paper, we consider only observable NFSMs. Each NFSM is known to have an observable FSM with the same behavior [7, 8]. If $D_M = S \times X$ then M is said to be a *complete* FSM; otherwise, it is called a *partial* FSM. In the complete FSM we omit the specification domain D_M, i.e. complete FSM is 5-tuple $M = \langle S, X, Y, h, s_0 \rangle$. If for each pair $(s, x) \in D_M$ it holds that $|h(s, x)| = 1$ then FSM M is said to be *deterministic*. In the deterministic FSM (DFSM) M instead of behavior function h we use two functions, transition function $\delta_M: D_M \to S$ and output function $\lambda_M: D_M \to Y$.

We use the notation "$(s_i\text{-}x/y\text{->}s_j)$" to indicate that the FSM M at state s_i responds with an output y and makes the transition to the state s_j when the input x is applied. State s_i is said to be the *starting* state of the transition, while s_j is said to be the *ending* state of the transition. If we are not interested in the output we write "$s_i\text{-}x\text{->}s_j$" when an input x is applied at state s_i.

The concatenation of sequences v_1 and v_2 is the sequence $v_1.v_2$. For a given alphabet Z, Z^* is used to denote the set of all finite words over Z including the empty word ε while Z^m denotes the set of all the words of length m. Let V be a set of words over alphabet Z. The prefix closure of V, written $\mathit{Pref}(V)$, consists of all the prefixes of all words in V, i.e. $\mathit{Pref}(V) = \{\alpha \mid \exists \gamma \, (\alpha.\gamma \in V)\}$. The set V is *prefix-closed* if $\mathit{Pref}(V) = V$.

As usual, the behavior function h of a FSM M can be extended to the set X^* of finite input sequences. Given state s and input sequence $x_1...x_k$, the pair $(s', y_1...y_k) \in$

$h(s, x_1...x_k)$ if and only if there exists states $s_1',..., s_{k+1}'$ such that $s_1' = s$ and $(s_{j+1}', y_j) \in h(s_j', x_j)$ for each $j = 1, ..., k$. In this case, the sequence $x_1 ... x_k$ is called a *defined input sequence* at state s. The set of all defined input sequences at state s of M is denoted **DIS**$_M(s)$; while the set of defined input sequences at the initial state is denoted **DIS**$_M$, for short.

Given an input sequence $\alpha = x_1 ... x_k$ and an FSM M, we let the set $out_M(s, \alpha)$ denote the set of output projections (i.e. responses) of M to the input α. Formally, $out_M(s, \alpha) = \{\gamma | \exists s' \in S\ [(s', \gamma) \in h(s, \alpha)]\}$. If M is deterministic then $|out_M(s, \alpha)| \leq 1$. The FSM is called *connected* if for each state $s \in S$ there exists an input sequence α_s that takes the FSM from the initial state to state s. The sequence α_s is called a *transfer sequence* for the state s. We further consider only connected FSMs. A set Q of input sequences is called a *state cover set* of FSM M if for each state s_j of S, there is an input sequence $\alpha_j \in Q$ such that $s_1 \text{-} \alpha_j \text{->} s_j$. A state cover set exists for every connected FSM. We further consider prefix-closed state cover sets, i.e., we include the empty sequence ε in Q.

Let $M = (S, X, Y, h_M, D_M, s_1)$ and $I = (T, X, Y, h_I, D_I, t_1)$ be two FSMs. In the following sections M usually represents a specification while I denotes an implementation. We say that state t of I is *quasi-equivalent* to state s of M [4, 10, 8], written $t \sqsupseteq s$, if **DIS**$_M(s) \subseteq$ **DIS**$_I(t)$, and for each input sequence $\alpha \in$ **DIS**$_M(s)$ it holds that $out_M(s, \alpha) = out_I(t, \alpha)$. In other words, FSM I at state t can have "more defined" behavior than FSM M at state s. However, for each defined input sequence at state s, the output responses of FSMs M and I coincide. FSM I is *quasi-equivalent* to M if $t_1 \sqsupseteq s_1$. We also say that states s and t are *distinguishable*, written $s \not\cong t$, if there exists an input sequence $\alpha \in$ **DIS**$_M(s) \cap$ **DIS**$_I(t)$ such that $out_M(s, \alpha) \neq out_I(t, \alpha)$; the sequence α is said to *distinguish* the states s_j and t_j. Two FSMs M and I are said to be *distinguishable* if their initial states are distinguishable. An FSM is said to be *reduced* if its states are pair-wise distinguishable.

When testing NFSMs, the specification M of the given system is assumed to be a partial/complete non-deterministic finite state machine while an implementation I of M is assumed to be a complete and non-deterministic. However, it is assumed that the specification M has so-called *harmonized traces* [10] such that for each input sequence $\alpha = x_1...x_k$ defined at the initial state and each two pairs $(s', y_1...y_k)$, $(s'', y_1...y_k) \in h_M(s_1, x_1...x_k)$ the sets of defined input sequences at states s' and s'' coincide. The reason is a test suite is derived in advance and each input sequence is applied independently of the output response of an implementation at hand. When testing DFSMs, the specification M of the given system is assumed to be a deterministic partial/complete finite state machine while an implementation I of M is assumed to be complete and deterministic.

We say that implementation I *conforms to* the specification M if and only if FSM I is quasi-equivalent to M. In other words, for each input sequence that is defined in the specification the output responses of M and I coincide [4,16,8]. Otherwise, I is called a *nonconforming* (or *faulty*) implementation of M. In this case, an input sequence α that distinguishes initial states of FSMs I and M is said to *distinguish* the implementation I from the specification M or α is said to *detect* the faulty implementation I.

Given the input alphabet X, we denote $J_m(X)$ the set of all complete deterministic machines over the input alphabet X with up to m states. Given a deterministic specification FSM M, a *test suite TS* is a finite set of finite input sequences of the FSM M. A test suite *TS* is *m-complete* for the specification FSM M if for each implementation $I \in J_m(X)$ that is distinguishable from M, there exists a sequence in *TS* that distinguishes M and I.

3 An Improved Test Generation Method

Given a deterministic reduced possibly partial specification FSM M with n states, in this section, we first establish sufficient conditions for having an m-complete test suite. This is done for the cases when $m > n$ and when $m = n$. Based on these conditions, in the following two subsections we present a novel test derivation method with related experimental results. In Section 5, we generalize the method for the case when the specification and implementation machines are non-deterministic.

3.1 Sufficient Conditions for an M-Complete Test Suite

Given a reduced deterministic specification machine M with n states, the following theorem establishes sufficient conditions for a given test suite to be m-complete assuming that $m \geq n$. The theorem extends a related theorem given in [5] for partial deterministic specification machines.

Theorem 1. Given a reduced deterministic specification M with n states and a state cover set Q of M, let *TS* be a finite set of defined finite input sequences of M that contains the set of sequences $Q.X^{m-n+1} \cap \mathbf{DIS}_M$. The test suite *TS* is m-complete if the following conditions hold:

1. For each two (different) states of M reachable through sequences α and β in Q, *TS* has sequences $\alpha.\gamma$ and $\beta.\gamma$ where γ is a distinguishing sequence of the states $\delta_M(s_1, \alpha)$ and $\delta_M(s_1, \beta)$ reachable by the sequences α and β, respectively.
2. For each sequence $\alpha.\beta$, $\alpha \in Q$, $|\beta| = m - n + 1$, and each non-empty prefix β_1 of β that takes the specification FSM M to state s from state $\delta_M(s_1, \alpha)$, *TS* has the sequences $\alpha.\beta_1.\gamma$ and $\omega.\gamma$, where $\omega \in Q$ and $\delta_M(s_1, \omega) \neq s$, and γ is a distinguishing sequence of states $\delta_M(s_1, \alpha\beta_1)$ and $\delta_M(s_1, \omega)$.
3. For each sequence $\alpha.\beta$, $\alpha \in Q$, $|\beta| = m - n + 1$, and each two non-empty prefixes β_1 and β_2 of β that take the specification FSM M from state $\delta_M(s_1, \alpha)$ to two different states, *TS* has sequences $\alpha.\beta_1.\gamma$ and $\alpha.\beta_2.\gamma$, where γ is a distinguishing sequence of states $\delta_M(s_1, \alpha\beta_1)$ and $\delta_M(s_1, \alpha\beta_2)$.

Proof. Consider a test suite *TS* that satisfies the conditions of the theorem and assume that there exists a complete FSM $I = \langle T, X, Y, \delta_I, \lambda_I, t_1 \rangle$ with m states that is distinguishable from the specification FSM $M = \langle S, X, Y, \delta_M, \lambda_M, D_M, s_1 \rangle$ but for each input sequence of the set *TS*, the output responses of M and I to the input sequence coincide. Let P be the set of states that are reachable in I via sequences of the state cover set Q, and v be a shortest input sequence from some state $\delta_I(t_1, \alpha_j)$ of the set P that distinguishes states $\delta_M(s_1, \alpha_j)$ and $\delta_I(t_1, \alpha_j)$. By definition, TS has a sequence $\alpha_j\beta$, where β has length $m - n + 1$ and β is a prefix of v.

Consider the set R of sequences that is the union of sequences in the state cover set and the set of sequences $\alpha_j\beta'$ over all non-empty prefixes β' of β. The number of such sequences equals to $n + (m - n + 1) = m + 1$ and since I has at most m states there are two sequences in the set that take FSM I from the initial state to the same state. Let $R = \{\alpha_1, ..., \alpha_n, ..., \alpha_{m+1}\}$ where $\alpha_i = \alpha_j\beta_i$ for $i = n + 1, ..., m + 1$, and $\delta_I(t_1, \alpha_i) = \delta_I(t_1, \alpha_r)$.

Considering i and r, there are three possible cases: $i, r \leq n$; $i \leq n < r$; or $i, r > n$.

1) $i, r \leq n$. In this case, $\alpha_i, \alpha_r \in Q$ and the set TS has sequences $\alpha_i \gamma$ and $\alpha_r \gamma$ where γ distinguishes states $\delta_M(s_1, \alpha_i)$ and $\delta_M(s_1, \alpha_r)$. Thus, this case is not possible for FSM I that passes the test TS.

2) $i \leq n < r$. In this case, $\alpha_i \in Q$ and the trace v', where v' is obtained from v by deleting the prefix β_r, distinguishes states $\delta_M(s_1, \alpha_i)$ and $\delta_I(t_1, \alpha_r)$. The latter contradicts the fact that the trace v that contains β as a prefix is a shortest trace with such feature.

3) $i, r > n$. In this case, the trace v could be shortened by deleting the part between two states $\delta_M(s_1, \alpha_i)$ and $\delta_M(s_1, \alpha_r)$.

Thus, given an FSM I with at most m states that is not quasi-equivalent to M, there exists an input sequence of the test TS such that output response of I to the sequence is different from that of the specification FSM M, i.e., TS is m-complete. □

According to Theorem 1, given a state s of M, different state identification sequences can be used when checking different incoming transitions of state s. When $m = n$, Theorem 1 can be refined and the following theorem establishes sufficient conditions for a given test suite to be n-complete.

Theorem 2. Given a reduced deterministic specification M with n states and state cover set Q of M, let TS be a finite set of defined finite input sequences of M that contains the set $Q.X \cap \mathbf{DIS}_M$. The set TS is n-complete if the following conditions hold:

1. For each two different states of M reachable through sequences α and β in Q, TS has the sequences $\alpha.\gamma$ and $\beta.\gamma$ where γ is a distinguishing sequence of the states $\delta_M(s_1, \alpha)$ and $\delta_M(s_1, \beta)$.
2. For each defined transition (s, x) of the specification M, TS has a sequence $\alpha.x$ with the following properties:
    a) $\delta_M(s_1, \alpha) = s$.
    b) For each state reachable through a sequence $\beta \in Q$ such that state $\delta_M(s_1, \beta) \neq s$, TS has sequences $\alpha.\gamma$ and $\beta.\gamma$ where γ is a distinguishing sequence of states s and $\delta_M(s_1, \beta)$.
    c) For each state reachable through sequence $\beta \in Q$ such that state $\delta_M(s_1, \beta) \neq \delta_M(s, x)$, TS has sequences $\alpha.x.\gamma$ and $\beta.\gamma$, where γ is a distinguishing sequence of states $\delta_M(s, x)$ and $\delta_M(s_1, \beta)$.

In the following section, we consider a simple application example that shows how test suites derived by other methods can be shortened by use of Theorems 1 and 2. We also illustrate by an example that the conditions stated in Theorems 1 and 2 are not necessary conditions.

3.2 Application Example

Consider the specification FSM shown in Fig. 1. We derive a 4-complete test suite based on the HIS method [10, 17] using $Q = \{\varepsilon, a, b, c\}$ as a state cover set and $F = \{H_1, H_2, H_3, H_4\}$ with $H_1 = \{a, bb\}$, $H_2 = \{a, b\}$, $H_3 = \{a\}$, $H_4 = \{a, bb\}$, as a separating family of state identifiers. For state identification, we use the sequences: $r.\varepsilon.H_1 + r.a.H_3 + r.b.H_4 + r.c.H_2$. For testing transitions we use the sequences: $r.a.H_3 + r.b.H_4 + r.c.H_2 + r.a.a.H_2 + r.a.b.H_1 + r.b.a.H_3 + r.b.b.H_2 + r.b.c.H_3 + r.c.a.H_4 + r.c.b.H_3$. We replace the H's in the above sequences by their corresponding values and then remove from the obtained set those sequences that are proper prefixes of other sequences. The obtained 4-complete test suite TS_{HIS} = {raaa, raab, raba, rabbb, rbaa, rbba, rbbb, rbca, rcaa, rcabb, rcba} with total length 46. However, due to Theorem 1, we do not need to append sequence $r.aa$ with a, as b already distinguishes state $2 = \delta_M(1, aa)$ from any other state reachable through the sequences of the state cover set. For the same reason, without loss of the completeness of the test suite the following sequences can be deleted from TS_{HIS}: rbba and rcaa. Moreover, transition $4-b\to 2$ can be checked by the sequences rcabb, while transition $2 - b \to 3$ can be checked by the sequence raaba; thus, the sequence rcba and rbbb can be deleted from the test suite. As a result, we obtain a 4-complete test suite {raaba, raba, rabbb, rbaa, rbca, rcabb} with total length 27.

We further show that the conditions of Theorems 1 and 2 are not necessary conditions. The reason is that two states can be implicitly distinguished if their successor states under some input are different. Consider the FSM B shown in Fig. 2.

	1	2	3	4
a	3/1	4/1	2/0	3/1
b	4/0	3/1	1/0	2/0
c	2/1	-	-	3/1

Fig. 1. Specification FSM M

	1	2	3
a	2/0	1/1	2/1
b	3/0	1/1	3/1

Fig. 2. Specification FSM B

The FSM B has the set $Q = \{\varepsilon, a, b\}$ as a state cover. We consider the test suite TS_1 of all prefixes of the set $\{raaa, rabb, rbaba, rbbab\}$; the set TS_1 contains all the sequences of the set $r.Q.\{a, b\}$. We first observe that states 2 and 3 that are reachable through sequences a and b in Q are not distinguished with suffixes aa, bb and aba, bab applied after ra and rb in the test suite. Nevertheless, if an implementation at hand passes the test suite TS_1 then the states reachable after the sequences ra and rb are different. Otherwise, the states reachable after the sequence raa (rab) and after the sequence rba (rbb) coincide and thus we have four different output responses to the sequences $r.a$ and $r.b$:

	a	b
t_1	0	0
$\delta_B(t_1, a) = \delta_B(t_1, b)$	1	1
$\delta_B(t_1, a.a) = \delta_B(t_1, b.a)$	0	1
$\delta_B(t_1, a.b) = \delta_B(t_1, b.b)$	1	0

If an implementation I has at most three states and passes TS_1, we can draw the following conclusions:

a) States $t_2 = \delta_I(t_1, a)$ and $t_3 = \delta_I(t_1, b)$ of I are two different states;
b) Input a distinguishes the initial state of I from the other states of I;
c) $\delta_I(t_2, a) = \delta_I(t_2, b) = t_1$.

Thus, $\delta_I(t_3, a) = t_2$ since $\lambda_I(t_3, ba) = 11$, and $\delta_I(t_3, b) = t_3$ since $\lambda_I(t_2, ab) = 10$ and $\delta_I(t_2, a) = t_1$. Therefore, any implementation that passes TS_1 is equivalent to the given specification FSM B, i.e., TS_1 is a 3-complete test suite.

As demonstrated by the above example, the possibility to distinguish two states based on their successor states depends on the number of states of an implementation at hand. Based on this, more rigorous analysis is needed to determine related conditions that can be used for shortening the length of a test suite.

3.3 Test Derivation Method

Let A be a specification FSM, $A = (S,X,Y,\delta,\lambda,s_0)$, where $|S|=n$. Below we present a test generation method that derives an *m-complete* test suite for A, where $m \geq n$.

Algorithm 1. Test Generation Method
Input : A reduced deterministic specification FSM $M = (S,X,Y,\delta,\lambda,D_M,s_0)$ with n states, a prefix-closed state cover set Q of M, and an upper bound m on the number of states of an implementation FSM of M, where $m \geq n$.
Output : An *m*-complete test suite TS
Step 1. Derive the set of sequences $TS = QPref(X^{m-n+1}) \cap \mathbf{DIS}_M$
Step 2. For each two sequences α_i and α_j of the state cover set Q check if the set TS has sequences $\alpha_i.\omega$ and $\alpha_j.\omega$ such that ω distinguishes states $\delta(s_0, \alpha_i)$ and $\delta(s_0, \alpha_j)$ in the specification FSM. If there are no such sequences select a

sequence ω that distinguishes states $\delta(s_0, \alpha_i)$ and $\delta(s_0, \alpha_j)$ and add to TS sequences $\alpha_i.\omega$ and $\alpha_j.\omega$.

Step 3. For each sequence $\alpha_i.\beta \in QPref(X^{\leq m-n+1}) \cap \mathbf{DIS}_M$, $\alpha_i \in Q$, let s_i be the state reachable from the initial state of M by the sequence α_i. Check if the set TS has sequences $\alpha_i.\beta.\omega$ and $\alpha_j.\omega$, $\alpha_j \in Q$, $\delta(s_0, \alpha_j) \neq s$, such that ω distinguishes states $\delta(s_0, \alpha_i.\beta)$ and $\delta(s_0, \alpha_j)$ in the specification FSM. If there are no such sequences select sequence ω that distinguishes states $\delta(s_0, \alpha_i.\beta)$ and $\delta(s_0, \alpha_j)$ and add to TS sequences $\alpha_i.\beta.\omega$ and $\alpha_j.\omega$.

Step 4. For each sequence $\alpha_i.\beta \in QPref(X^{\leq m-n+1}) \cap \mathbf{DIS}_M$, $\alpha_i \in Q$, and each two non-empty prefixes β_1 and β_2 of the sequence β, check if the set TS has sequences $\alpha_i.\beta_1.\omega$ and $\alpha_i.\beta_2.\omega$ such that ω distinguishes states $\delta(s_0, \alpha_i.\beta_1)$ and $\delta(s_0, \alpha_i.\beta_2)$ in the specification FSM. If there are no such sequences select sequence ω that distinguishes states $\delta(s_0, \alpha_i.\beta_1)$ and $\delta(s_0, \alpha_i.\beta_2)$ and add to TS sequences $\alpha_i.\beta_1.\omega$ and $\alpha_i.\beta_2.\omega$.

Due to Theorem 2, the following statement holds.

Theorem 3. The set of input sequences TS obtained with Algorithm 1 is an m-complete test suite for the given specification FSM M.

Intuitively, the above method uses an appropriate sequence for testing each transition of the implementation. The prefix of the sequence takes the implementation to the starting state of the tested transition and its suffix distinguishes the expected final state of the tested transition from all other states of the specification using an appropriate state identification sequence. Unlike the HIS method, the identification sequence of the starting state of the tested transition has to be harmonized only with other state identification sequences of the states of the state cover set Q and of the states reachable from the initial state by the prefix of the sequence. Moreover, for the same state of the specification, we can use different state identification sequences when testing different transitions.

To illustrate the method we derive a 5-complete test suite for the specification FSM in Figure 1. We first use the HIS method to obtain an 5-complete test suite and obtain the set {*raaaa, raaabb, raaba, rabaa, rabba, rabbbb, rabca, rabcb, rbaaa, rbaab, rbaba, rbabbb, rbbaa, rbbabb, rbbba, rbcaa, rbcab, rbcba, rbcbbb, rcaaa, rcaba, rcabb, rcaca, rcbaa, rcbab, rcbba, rcbbbb*} with total length 141. We use state identifiers {*a*} and {*b*} to check states 3 and 2, as both of them are applied after sequences of the state cover set Q, state identifier *bb* to check state 4, state identifiers {*a, bb*} to check state 1, and obtain the test suite {*raaabb, raaba, rabaa, rabbbb, rabcb, rbaab, rbaba, rbabbb, rbbabb, rbbba, rbcab, rbcba, rbcbbb, rcaaa, rcabb, rcaca, rcbab, rcbba, rcbbbb*} that is 5-complete and has total length 101.

4 Experimental Results

In this section we experiment with the HIS and H methods in order to compare the length of their test suites. Table 1 provides a comparison between the length of the test suites obtained by these methods for the case when the number of states of an implementation of a given system equals to the number of states of the given specification (i.e. $m = n$) and Table 2 provides a comparison for the case when $m > n$. The comparison in Tables 1 and 2 is based on randomly generated completely specified reduced deterministic specifications with a varying number of states (n).

Each row of Tables 1 (2) corresponds to a group of 50 randomly generated completely specified reduced specifications. For each of these specifications we use the HIS and H methods to derive corresponding test suites. Then, we calculate the average length of the test suites generated for each group using each of these methods as shown in Columns IV and V (V and VI), respectively.

Table 1. A summary of experiments for the case when number of inputs/outputs equals to 10 and $m=n$

I- Groups of 50 Experiments	II- Number of States	III- Number of Transitions	IV- Average Length HIS Test Suites	V- Average Length H Test Suites
1	30	300	2243	1568
2	50	500	4375	2852
3	60	600	5490	3656
4	70	700	6694	4344
5	80	800	7892	5216
6	90	900	9194	6078
7	100	1,000	10503	6880

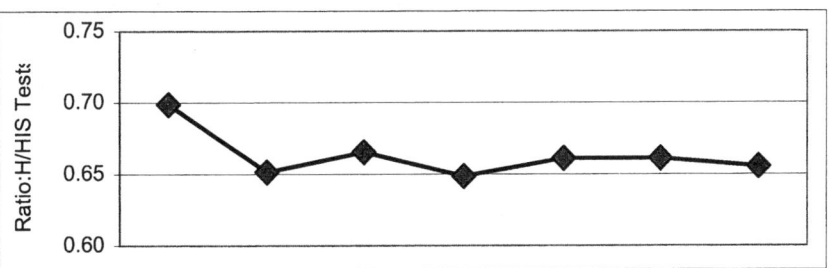

Fig. 3. Rations of average length H/HIS Test Suites when $m = n$ for the experiments in Table 1

Figure 3 depicts the ratios of length of the test suites of the H method over the length of the HIS based test suites for the experiments shown in Table 1. On average, the H test suites are 0.66 percent of the HIS test suites. Moreover, according to the experiments this ratio is almost independent of the size of the specification.

Table 2. A summary of experiments for the case when number of inputs/outputs equals 4 and $m=n+1$ and $m=n+2$

I- Groups of 50 Experiments	II- Number of States of the specification	III- Number of States of an implementation	IV- Number of Transitions	V- Average Length HIS Test Suites	VI- Average Length H Test Suites
1	10	11	44	1399	883
2	20	21	84	3773	2212
3	30	31	124	6432	3560
4	40	41	164	9272	5188
5	50	51	204	12494	6837
6	10	12	48	6790	4181
7	20	22	88	17238	9565
8	30	32	128	29860	15115
9	40	42	168	44137	21919
10	50	52	208	58949	28813

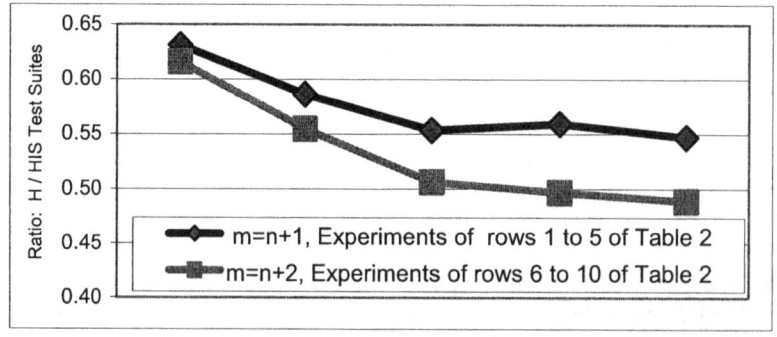

Fig. 4. Ratios of average length H/HIS Test Suites when $m=n+1$ and $m=n+2$

Figure 4 depicts the ratios of length of the test suites of the H method over the length of the HIS based test suites for the experiments depicted in rows 1 to 5 and rows 6 to 10 of Table 2. On average, the H test suites are 0.55 percent of the HIS test suites. Moreover, according to the experiments this ratio slightly decreases as the size of the specification increases.

5 Generalizing the H Method for Nondeterministic Machines

When the specification FSM M is reduced, possibly partial, nondeterministic with harmonized traces, the fault domain $R_m(X)$ contains all complete observable NFSM implementations of M, defined over the input alphabet X of M, with at most m states. A test suite TS is m-complete for M if for each implementation $I \in R_m(X)$ that is distinguishable from M, there exists a sequence in TS that distinguishes M and I.

Due to the complete testing assumption [7, 8], the procedure used for deriving an m-complete test suite for deterministic machines can be adapted for deriving an m-complete test suite for nondeterministic machines. First, we derive a state cover set of the NFSM specification $M = (S, X, Y, h_M, D_M, s_1)$ [7, 8]. However, in this case, differently from deterministic FSMs, the number of sequences in a state cover set can be less than the number of states n of the specification machine. This is due to the fact that the specification machine in response to a single defined input sequence, repeatedly applied at the initial state, can reach several states and produce in response different output sequences.

For each state $s_i \in S$, we consider the sequences $\alpha_i.X^{m-n+1} \cap \mathbf{DIS}_M(s_i)$, where $\alpha_i \in Q$ is the sequence of Q that takes the NFSM specification to state s_i from the initial state and $\mathbf{DIS}_M(s_i)$ is the set of all defined input sequences at state s_i. We let $Q.X^{m-n+1} \cap \mathbf{DIS}_M$ denote the set of all obtained sequences. Since the specification FSM has harmonized traces, the sets of defined input sequences of the states reachable by any initially defined input sequence coincide. For every sequence $\alpha_i \in Q$, we denote $S_i \in S$ the subset of states for which we use $\alpha_i \in Q$. The subsets S_i form a partition of the set S.

As an application example of the HIS method [8], consider the NFSM M shown in Fig. 5. M admits the set $\{\varepsilon, a, b\}$ as a state cover set. The NFSM M is reduced; state 3 can be distinguished from all other states by the input sequence a, state 2 can be distinguished from all other states by the input sequence aa, and states 1 and 4 can be distinguished by the input sequence b. Moreover, M has harmonized traces since it has the same set of defined inputs at states 2 and 3. Let $m = 4$. Then the set $Q.X^{m-n+1} \cap \mathbf{DIS}_M = \{a, b, c, aa, ac, ba, bb, bc\}$.

The FSM M has the following sets of harmonized state identifiers, $H_1 = \{aa, b\}$, $H_2 = \{aa\}$, $H_3 = \{a\}$ and $H_4 = \{aa, b\}$. For each sequence in the set $Q.X^{m-n+1} \cap \mathbf{DIS}_M$, we determine the states reached by this sequence and append the sequence with corresponding sets of harmonized state identifiers. The union of all obtained test sequences is the 4-complete test suite $TS_{HIS} = \{raaaa, racaa, racb, rbaaa, rbbaa, rbbb, rbcaa, rcaa, rcb\}$ which is of length 40. Here we note that state 1 has also the sequence cc as a state identifier which is shorter than the sequences of H_1, but cc is not used since it is not harmonized with the identifiers of all other states. We note that the GWp [7] method can not be applied to this example since M does not have a characterization set. States 1 and 4 of M can be distinguished only by an input sequence b or by an input sequence with the head symbol c. However, by direct inspection, one can observe that states 2 and 3 can not be distinguished with these sequences.

	1	2	3	4
a	3/1; 2/0	2/1; 3/0	2/0	3/1; 2/0
b	4/0,1	-	-	1/1
c	1/1	1/0	1/0	2/1

Fig. 5. Partial NFSM specification M

Similar to Theorem 1, the following theorem allows us to use non-harmonized state identifiers when deriving an m-complete test suite.

Theorem 4. Given a set TS of defined input sequences of the specification NFSM M, let TS contain the set $Q.X^{m-n+1} \cap \mathbf{DIS}_M$. The set TS is m-complete if

- For each two sequences α_i and $\alpha_j \in Q$, for each two states $s_i \in S_i$ and $s_j \in S_i$, the set TS has sequences $\alpha_i \sigma$ and $\alpha_j \sigma$ where σ distinguishes states s_i and s_j;
- For each sequence $\alpha_i.v \in Q.(X^{\leq m-n+1}) \cap \mathbf{DIS}_M$, $\alpha_i \in Q$, each state $s_i \in S_i$, and each state s reachable from state s_i via the sequence v and each state $s_j \in S_j$, $s_j \neq s$ and $\alpha_j \in Q$ the set TS has sequences $\alpha_i.v\sigma$ and $\alpha_j.\sigma$, where σ distinguishes state s from state s_j.
- For each sequence $\alpha_i.\beta$, $\alpha_i \in Q$, $|\beta| = m - n + 1$, each state $s_i \in S_i$ and each two non-empty prefixes β_1 and β_2 of β that take the specification FSM M from state s_i to the subsets of states P_1 and P_2, for each two states $s_1 \in P_1$ and $s_2 \in P_2$, TS has sequences $\alpha.\beta_1.\gamma$ and $\alpha.\beta_2.\gamma$, where γ is a distinguishing sequence of states s_1 and s_2.

In other words, similar to the case of deterministic FSMs, we do not need to derive in advance state distinguishing sequences for the specification FSM. These sequences can be derived on-the-fly starting with the set $Q.X^{m-n+1} \cap \mathbf{DIS}_M$. Moreover, different state identifiers can be used for checking incoming transitions of states. These identifiers do not have to be harmonized with the identifiers of all other states. In our working example, we observe that the state identifier $\{cc\}$ can be used for identifying state 1 despite of the fact that this identifier is not harmonized with the identifiers of all other states. Due to the above theorem, the test suite $TS_2 = \{raaaa, raccc, rbaaa, rbbcc, rbcaa, rbcc, rccc\}$ of length 33 is also 4-complete.

Algorithm 2. Test Generation Method
Input : The reduced nondeterministic specification FSM $M = (S,X,Y,\delta,\lambda,D_M,s_0)$ with n states and harmonized traces, a prefix-closed state cover set Q of M, and an upper bound m on the number of states of an implementation FSM, where $m \geq n$.

Output : An m-complete test suite TS

Step 1. Derive the set of sequences $TS = QPref(X^{m-n+1}) \cap \mathbf{DIS}_M$ and fix for each $\alpha_i \in Q$ the subset S_i of states for which we use the sequence α_i.

Step 2. For each two sequences α_i and α_j of the state cover set Q and each two states $s_i \in S_i$ and $s_j \in S_j$, check if the set TS has sequences $\alpha_i.\omega$ and $\alpha_j.\omega$ such that ω distinguishes states s_i and s_j in the specification FSM. If there are no such sequences select a sequence ω that distinguishes states s_i and s_j and add into TS sequences $\alpha_i.\omega$ and $\alpha_j.\omega$.

Step 3. For each sequence $\alpha_i.\beta \in QPref(X^{\leq m-n+1}) \cap \mathbf{DIS}_M$, $\alpha_i \in Q$, each state $s_i \in S_i$, each state s reachable from s_i via sequence β and each state $s_j \in S_j$, $\alpha_j \in Q$, check if the set TS has sequences $\alpha_i.\beta.\omega$ and $\alpha_j.\omega$, $s_j \neq s$, such that ω distinguishes states s_j and s in the specification FSM. If there are no such sequences select sequence ω that distinguishes states s_j and s and add to TS sequences $\alpha_i.\beta.\omega$ and $\alpha_j.\omega$.

Step 4. For each sequence $\alpha_i.\beta \in QPref(X^{\leq m-n+1}) \cap \mathbf{DIS}_M$, $\alpha_i \in Q$, each state $s_i \in S_i$, and each two non-empty prefixes β_1 and β_2 of the sequence β, let P_1 and P_2 be the sets of states reachable from state s_i via sequences β_1 and β_2. For each two states $s_1 \in P_1$ and $s_2 \in P_2$, check if the set TS has sequences $\alpha_i.\beta_1.\omega$ and $\alpha_i.\beta_2.\omega$ such that ω distinguishes states s_1 and s_2 in the specification FSM. If there are no such sequences select sequence ω that distinguishes states s_1 and s_2 and add to TS sequences $\alpha_i.\beta_1.\omega$ and $\alpha_i.\beta_2.\omega$.

Due to Theorem 4, the following statement holds.

Theorem 5. The set of input sequences TS obtained using Algorithm 2 is an m-complete test suite for the given specification FSM M.

6 Conclusion

An improved HIS based test derivation method has been presented in this paper. The method can be applied for any reduced possibly partial and nondeterministic specification machine. In comparison with the HIS method, in the proposed method state identifiers are derived on-the-fly and different state identifiers can be used when checking different incoming transitions of a state. Experimental results show that the proposed method returns shorter test suites than the HIS method. In particular, on average, the length of a test suite derived using the H method is 0.66% (0.55%) of the length of a test suite derived using the HIS method when the number of states of an implementation equals to (is greater than) the number of states of the specification. The length of a test suite returned by the proposed method essentially depends on the order in which transitions are checked. Accordingly, currently, we are incorporating into our method an optimization procedure that determines an order that provides a shortest length test suite.

References

1. G. v. Bochmann, A. Petrenko, "Protocol testing: review of methods and relevance for software testing," *Proc. International Symposium on Software Testing and Analysis*, Seattle, 1994, pp. 109-123.
2. T. S. Chow, "Test design modeled by finite-state machines," *IEEE Trans. SE*, vol. 4, no.3, 1978, pp. 178-187.
3. S. Fujiwara, G. v. Bochmann, F. Khendek, M. Amalou, and A. Ghedamsi, "Test selection based on finite state models," *IEEE Trans. SE*, vol. 17, no. 6, 1991, pp. 591-603.
4. AGill, *Introduction to the Theory of Finite-State Machines*, McGraw-Hill, 1962.
5. I. Koufareva, M. Dorofeeva. *A novel modification of W-method*. Joint Bulletin of the Novosibirsk computing center and A.P. Ershov institute of informatics systems. Series: Computing science, issue: 18, 2002, NCC Publisher, Novosibirsk. - PP. 69-81.
6. D. Lee and M. Yannakakis, "Principles and methods of testing finite state machines-a survey", *Proceedings of the IEEE*, vol. 84, no. 8, 1996, pp. 1090-1123.
7. G. L. Luo, G. v. Bochmann, and A. Petrenko, "Test Selection Based on Communicating Nondeterministic Finite-State Machines Using a Generalized Wp-method", *IEEE Transactions on Software Engineering*, 20(2):149–161, 1994.
8. G. Luo, A. Petrenko, G. v. Bochmann, "Selecting Test Sequences for Partially Specified Nondeterministic Finite State Machines", *Proc. 7th IWPTS*, Japan, 1994.
9. A. Petrenko, "Checking experiments with protocol machines," *Proc. 4th Int. Workshop on Protocol Test Systems*, 1991, pp. 83-94.
10. A. Petrenko, N. Yevtushenko, A. Lebedev, and A. Das, "Nondeterministic state machines in protocol conformance testing," *Proc. of the IFIP 6th IWPTS*, France, 1993, pp. 363-378.
11. A. Petrenko and N. Yevtushenko, "On Test Derivation from Partial Specifications", Proc. of the IFIP Joint International Conference, FORTE/PSTV'2000, Italy, 2000, pp. 85-102.
12. K. Sabnani and A. Dahbura, "A protocol test generation procedure," Computer Networks and ISDN Systems, vol. 15, no. 4, 1988, pp. 285-297.
13. D. P. Sidhu, and T. K. Leung, "Formal methods for protocol testing: a detailed study," *IEEE Trans. SE*, vol. 15, no. 4, 1989, pp. 413-426.
14. M. P. Vasilevskii, "Failure diagnosis of automata," translated from Kibernetika, No.4, 1973, pp. 98-108.
15. S. T. Vuong, W.W.L. Chan, and M.R. Ito, "The UIOv-method for protocol test sequence generation," *Proc. of the IFIP TC6 2nd IWPTS*, North-Holland, 1989, pp. 161-175.
16. M. Yannakakis and D. Lee, "Testing finite state machines: fault detection", *Journal of Computer and System Sciences*, 50, 1995, pp. 209-227.
17. N. Yevtushenko and A. Petrenko, *Test derivation method for an arbitrary deterministic automaton*, Automatic Control and Computer Sciences, Allerton Press Inc., USA, #5, 1990.

Resolving Observability Problems in Distributed Test Architectures

J. Chen[1], R.M. Hierons[2], and H. Ural[3]

[1] School of Computer Science, University of Windsor,
Windsor, Ontario, Canada N9B 3P4
xjchen@uwindsor.ca
[2] Department of Information Systems and Computing, Brunel University,
Uxbridge, Middlesex, UB8 3PH United Kingdom
rob.hierons@brunel.ac.uk
[3] School of Information Technology and Engineering, University of Ottawa,
Ottawa, Ontario, Canada K1N 6N5
ural@site.ottawa.ca

Abstract. The introduction of multiple remote testers to apply a test or checking sequence in a test architecture brings out the possibility of controllability and observability problems. These problems often require the use of external coordination message exchanges among testers. In this paper, we consider constructing a test or checking sequence from the specification of the system under test such that it will be free from these problems and will not require the use of external coordination messages. We give an algorithm that can check whether it is possible to construct subsequences from a given specification that eliminate the need for using external coordination message exchanges, and when it is possible actually produces such subsequences.

Keywords: Finite state machine, testing, test architecture, observability, controllability.

1 Introduction

In a distributed test architecture, a tester is placed at each port of the system under test (SUT) N to apply an input sequence constructed from the specification M of N. When N is a state based system whose externally observable behaviour is specified as a finite state machine (FSM) M, the input sequence applied to N is called a test sequence [13,14] or a checking sequence [6,8,10]. The application of a test/checking sequence in the distributed test architecture introduces the possibility of controllability and observability problems. These problems occur if a tester cannot determine either when to apply a particular input to N, or whether a particular output from N has been generated in response to a specific input, respectively [12].

It is nessesary to construct a test or checking sequence that causes no controllability or observability problems during its application in a distributed test architecture (see, for example, [1,5,7,9,11,15–17]). For some specifications, there exists such an input sequence in which the coordination among testers is achieved indirectly via their interactions with N [14,12]. However, for some other specifications, there may not exist an input sequence in which the testers can coordinate solely via their interactions with N [1,15]. In this case it is necessary for testers to communicate directly by exchanging external coordination messages among themselves over a dedicated channel during the application of the input sequence [2].

It is argued that both controllability and observability problems may be overcome through the use of external coordination messages among remote testers [2]. However, there is often a cost associated with the use of such messages which is composed of the cost of setting up the infrastructure required to allow the exchange of such messages and the cost of delays introduced by exchanging these messages. It is thus desirable to construct a test or checking sequence from the specification of the system under test such that it will not cause controllability and observability problems and will not require the use of external coordination message exchanges.

In [4] we have given a necessary and sufficient condition so that each transition *involved in a potentially undetectable output shift fault* can be *independently verified at port p*. By *verified at port p*, we mean we are able to conclude that the output of this transition at port p is correct according to the correct output sequence of a certain transition path. By *indepedently*, we mean that the above conclusion on the output at port p of each transition does not rely on the correctness of any other transitions. Independence here can be helpful for fault diagnoses: in the case that the system under test contains only undetectable output shift faults, we will be able to identify them. In [3] we have given a necessary and sufficient condition so that each transition involved in a potentially undetectable output shift fault *and has a non-empty output at port p* can be *independently verified at port p*. Based on this we can conclude that each transition involved in a potentially undetectable output shift fault can be *verified at port p*. In this way, we have a weaker condition than that of [4] but we will no more be able to diagnose the undetectable output shift faults: in the case that the system under test contains only undetectable output shift faults, we can only identify those incorrect *non-empty outputs* at port p. In this paper, we do not consider the fault diagnosis problem and we show that in this context, we can have more specifications than those satisfying the conditions in [4] or [3] with which we can construct a subsequence for each transition involved in a potentially undetectable output shift fault so that we can conclude that the outputs at port p of these transitions are correct according to the correct output sequences of the constructed subsequences. We present an algorithm that identifies whether a given specification falls in this category and when it does so constructs the subsequences.

The rest of the paper is organized as follows. Section 2 introduces the preliminary terminology. Section 3 gives a formal definition of the problem and identifies the condition that the specification of the system under test is checked against. Section 4 presents an algorithm for constructing subsequences that eliminate the need for using external coordination messages, proves the correctness of the algorithm, and gives its computational complexity. Section 5 discusses the related work. Section 6 gives the concluding remarks.

2 Preliminaries

An n-port *Finite State Machine* M (simply called an FSM M) is defined as $M = (S, I, O, \delta, \lambda, s_0)$ where S is a finite set of states of M; $s_0 \in S$ is the initial state of M; $I = \bigcup_{i=1}^{n} I_i$, where I_i is the input alphabet of port i, and $I_i \cap I_j = \emptyset$ for $i, j \in [1, n]$, $i \neq j$; $O = \prod_{i=1}^{n}(O_i \cup \{-\})$, where O_i is the output alphabet of port i, and $-$ means null output; δ is the transition function that maps $S \times I$ to S; and λ is the output function that maps $S \times I$ to O. Each $y \in O$ is a *vector of outputs*, i.e., $y = <o_1, o_2, ..., o_n>$ where $o_i \in O_i \cup \{-\}$ for $i \in [1, n]$. We use $*$ to denote any possible output, including $-$, at a port and $+$ to denote non-empty output. We also use $*$ to denote any possible input or any possible vector of outputs. In the following, $p \in [1, n]$ is a port. A *transition* of an FSM M is a triple $t = (s_1, s_2; x/y)$, where $s_1, s_2 \in S$, $x \in I$, and $y \in O$ such that $\delta(s_1, x) = s_2$, $\lambda(s_1, x) = y$. s_1 and s_2 are called the *starting state* and the *ending state* of t respectively. The *input/output pair* x/y is called the *label* of t and t will also be denoted as $s_1 \xrightarrow{x/y} s_2$. p will denote a port and we use $y\mid_p$ or $t\mid_p$ to denote the output at p in output vector y or in transition t respectively. We use T to denote the set of all transitions in M.

A *path* $\rho = t_1\, t_2\, \ldots\, t_k$ ($k \geq 0$) is a finite sequence of transitions such that for $k \geq 2$, the ending state of t_i is the starting state of t_{i+1} for all $i \in [1, k-1]$. When the ending state of the last transition of path ρ_1 is the starting state of the first transition of path ρ_2, we use $\rho_1@\rho_2$ to denote the *concatenation* of ρ_1 and ρ_2. The *label* of a path $(s_1, s_2, x_1/y_1)\, (s_2, s_3, x_2/y_2) \ldots (s_k, s_{k+1}, x_k/y_k)$ ($k \geq 1$) is the sequence of input/output pairs $x_1/y_1\, x_2/y_2\, \ldots\, x_k/y_k$ which is an *input/output sequence*. The *input portion* of a path $(s_1, s_2, x_1/y_1)\, (s_2, s_3, x_2/y_2)$ $\ldots (s_k, s_{k+1}, x_k/y_k)$ ($k \geq 1$) is the input sequence $x_1 x_2 \ldots x_k$. We say t is *contained in* ρ if t is a transition along path ρ.

When ρ is non-empty, we use *first*(ρ) and *last*(ρ) to denote the first and last transitions of path ρ respectively and *pre*(ρ) to denote the path obtained from ρ by removing its last transition.

We will use 2-port FSMs to show some examples. In a 2-port FSM, ports U and L stand for the upper interface and the lower interface of the FSM. An output vector $y = \langle o_1, o_2 \rangle$ on the label of a transition of the 2-port FSM is a pair of outputs with $o_1 \in O_1$ at U and $o_2 \in O_2$ at L.

Given an FSM M and an input/output sequence $x_1/y_1\, x_2/y_2\, \ldots\, x_k/y_k$ of M a *controllability* (also called *synchronization*) *problem* occurs when, in the labels x_i/y_i and x_{i+1}/y_{i+1} of two consecutive transitions, there exists $p \in [1, n]$ such that $x_{i+1} \in I_p$, $x_i \notin I_p$, $y_i\mid_p = -$ ($i \in [1, k-1]$). If this controllability problem occurs then the tester at p does not know when to send x_{i+1} and the test/checking sequence cannot be applied. Consecutive transitions t_i and t_{i+1} form a *synchro-*

nizable pair of transitions if t_{i+1} can follow t_i without causing a synchronization problem. Any path in which every pair of transitions is synchronizable is called a *synchronizable path*. An input/output sequence is *synchronizable* if it is the label of a synchronizable path.

We assume that for every pair of transitions (t, t') there is a synchronizable path that starts with t and ends with t'. If this condition does not hold, then the FSM is called *intrinsically non-synchronizable* [1].

A *same-port-output-cycle* in an FSM is a path $(s_1, s_2, x_1/y_1)$ $(s_2, s_3, x_2/y_2)$ ... $(s_k, s_{k+1}, x_k/y_k)$ $(k \geq 2)$ such that $s_1 = s_{k+1}$, $s_i \neq s_{i+1}$ for $i \in [1, k]$, and there exists a port p with $y_i \mid_p \neq -$ and $x_i \notin I_p$ for all $i \in [1, k]$. An *isolated-port-cycle* in an FSM is a path $(s_1, s_2, x_1/y_1)$ $(s_2, s_3, x_2/y_2)$ ... $(s_k, s_{k+1}, x_k/y_k)$ $(k \geq 2)$ such that $s_1 = s_{k+1}$, $s_i \neq s_{i+1}$ for $i \in [1, k]$, and there exists a port p with $y_i \mid_p = -$ and $x_i \notin I_p$ for all $i \in [1, k]$.

A transition t is involved in a potentially undetectable output shift fault at p if and only if there exists a transition t' and a transition path ρ such that at least one of the following holds.

1. $t\rho t'$ is a synchronizable path, no transition in $\rho t'$ contains input at p, the ouputs at p in all transitions contained in ρ are empty, and $t \mid_p = - \Leftrightarrow t' \mid_p \neq -$. In this case an undetectable output shift fault can occur between t and t' in $t\rho t'$. If $t \mid_p = -$ we call it a *backward* output shift fault and if $t \mid_p \neq -$ we call it a *forward* output shift fault.

2. $t'\rho t$ is a synchronizable path, no transition in ρt contains input at p, the ouputs at p in all transitions contained in ρ are empty, and $t \mid_p = - \Leftrightarrow t' \mid_p \neq -$. In this case an undetectable output shift fault can occur between t and t' in $t'\rho t$. If $t \mid_p = -$ we call it a *forward* output shift fault and if $t \mid_p \neq -$ we call it a *backward* output shift fault.

When ρ is empty, we also say that t is involved in a potentially undetectable *1-shift* output fault.

The observability problem occurs when we have potentially undetectable output shift faults in the specification of the FSM.

We will use T_p to denote the set of transitions that are involved in potentially undetectable output shift faults at p. Let $T'_p = T_p \cap \{t \mid t\mid_p \neq -\}$. T'_p denotes the set of transitions that are involved in potentially undetectable output shift fault at p and whose output at p are non-empty.

A relation R between elements of a set A and elements of a set B is a subset of $A \times B$. If (a, b) is an element of relation R then a is related to b under R and we also write aRb. The set of elements related to $a \in A$ under R is denoted $R(a)$ and thus $R(a) = \{b \in B | (a, b) \in R\}$.

Given a set A, a relation R between A and A is a *partial order* if it satisfies the following conditions.

1. For all $a \in A$, aRa.
2. If aRa' and $a'Ra$ then $a = a'$.
3. If $a_1 R a_2$ and $a_2 R a_3$ then $a_1 R a_3$.

3 Verifiability of Outputs

To verify the output of transition t at port p, we search for a path ρ containing t such that

- ρ is synchronizable;
- we are able to determine the output sequence of ρ at p from applying the input portion of ρ from the starting state of ρ;
- from the correct output sequence of ρ at p we can determine that the output of t at p is correct.

We require that $first(\rho)$ and $last(\rho)$ have input at p in order to identify a certain output sequence: no matter how ρ is concatenated with other subsequences, we can always determine the output sequence produced at p in response to the first $|pre(\rho)|$ inputs of ρ since this output sequence is immediately preceded and followed by input at p.

To determine the correct output of (t, p) from the correct output sequence of ρ at p, we require that

- If the output of (t, p) is nonempty, then all the outputs at p in $pre(\rho)$ are either also nonempty or already known to be correct.
- If the output of (t, p) is empty, then all the outputs at p in $pre(\rho)$ are either also empty or already known to be correct.

Example 1. In the given specification in Figure 1, there is an undetectable output shift fault in $t_1 t_3$ at port U, because the input of t_3 is not at U while there is a potential output shift of o from t_3 to t_1. We are interested in constructing a path to verify that the output of transition t_1 and that of t_3 at this port are correct.

$\rho_1 = t_1 t_2$ is such a synchronizable path for t_1: it has input at U in t_1 ($first(\rho)$) and input at U in t_2 ($last(\rho)$), and according to the output at U between these two inputs when ρ_1 is applied as a subsequence, we are able to verify that the output of t_1 at U is correct.

If we know that the output of t_1 at U is correct, then $\rho_2 = t_1 t_3 t_1$ is also a desirable synchronizable path for t_2: it has input at U in t_1 (for both $first(\rho)$ and $last(\rho)$), and according to the output at U between these two inputs when ρ_2 is applied as a subsequence, we are able to verify that the output of t_2 at U is correct since we already know that the output of t_1 at U is correct.

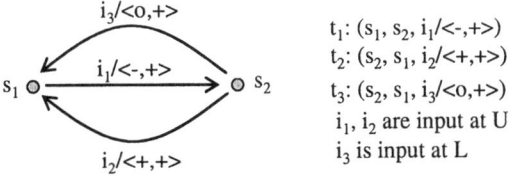

Fig. 1. An example where $\mathcal{T}_p$ is verifiable at U

Formally, we introduce the following concept.

Definition 1. *Let t be a transition, and v a set of transitions in M. ρ is an absolute verifying path upon v for (t, p) if*

- *ρ is a synchronizable path;*
- *t is contained in pre(ρ);*
- *first(ρ) and last(ρ) and only these two transitions in ρ have input at p;*
- *$t \notin v$ and for all t' contained in pre(ρ), either $t' \in v$ or $t'\,|_p = -\,\Leftrightarrow\, t\,|_p = -$.*

Note that given t and ρ we will typically consider a minimal set v that satisfies the above conditions: if $t'\,|_p = -\,\Leftrightarrow\, t\,|_p = -$ then $t' \notin v$.

Example 2. In Example 1,

- $t_1 t_2$ is an absolute verifying path upon $\emptyset$ for (t_1, U).
- $t_1 t_3 t_1$ is an absolute verifying path upon $\{t_1\}$ for (t_3, U).

Directly from this definition, we have:

Proposition 1. *If ρ is an absolute verifying path upon v for (t, p) and v is a minimal such set, then ρ is an absolute verifying path upon v for (t', p) for any t' contained in pre(ρ) such that $t'\,|_p = -\,\Leftrightarrow\, t\,|_p = -$.*

Proposition 2. *Let v be a set of transitions in M, ρ an absolute verifying path upon v for (t, p). If for every transition t' in v, the output at p of t' in the SUT is correct, then the correct output sequence at p in response to the first $|\text{pre}(\rho)|$ inputs of ρ implies the correct output of (t,p).*

Proof. Suppose $t\,|_p \neq -$ (The proof for the case when $t\,|_p = -$ is analogous).

Suppose that m inputs from pre(ρ) lead to non-empty output at p in M. Thus, if we observe the correct output sequence in response to the first $|\text{pre}(\rho)|$ inputs of ρ then we must observe m outputs at p in response to these inputs.

Since $t\,|_p \neq -$, and ρ is an absolute verifying path upon v for (t, p), we know by definition that for all t' in ρ' such that $t'\,|_p = -$, the output of t' at p is correct (and so is $-$) in the SUT. So, we know that the corresponding $|\text{pre}(\rho)| - m$ inputs in pre(ρ) lead to empty output at p. Thus we can map the observed outputs at p, in response to the input portion of pre(ρ), to the inputs that caused them and so if the correct output sequence is observed then the output of p at t must be correct.

To verify the output of (t, p), we try to find a path ρ that is an absolute verifying path upon v for (t, p) for some set v such that the output at p for every transition in v is verified. So in general, we search for an acyclic digraph of transitions such that each transition in this digraph has an absolute verifying path upon a set of transitions that appear as its successors in the digraph. Such an acyclic graph can be represented as a partial order in the following way.

Definition 2. *Suppose that $\mathcal{U}$ is a set of transitions of M, $\mathcal{R}$ is a relation from $\mathcal{U}$ to $\mathcal{U}$, and $\mathcal{P}$ is a function from $\mathcal{U}$ to synchronizable paths of M. Let p be any port in M. The set $\mathcal{U}$ of transitions is verifiable at p under $\mathcal{R}$ and $\mathcal{P}$ if the following hold.*

(a) For all $t \in \mathcal{U}$, $\mathcal{P}(t)$ is an absolute verifying path upon $\mathcal{R}(t)$ for (t,p);
(b) $\mathcal{R} \cup \{(t,t)|t \in \mathcal{U}\}$ is a partial order.

Where such $\mathcal{R}$ and $\mathcal{P}$ exist we also say that $\mathcal{U}$ is verifiable at p.

Suppose that $\mathcal{U}$ is verifiable at p under $\mathcal{R}$ and $\mathcal{P}$ and we observe correct output sequence corresponding to the first $|pre(\mathcal{P}(t))|$ output of $\mathcal{P}(t)$ for each $t \in \mathcal{U}$. Then according to Proposition 2, we know that the output of t at p is correct for each $t \in \mathcal{U}$. So our goal is to find a set $\mathcal{U}$ that is verifiable at p such that $\mathcal{T}_p \subseteq \mathcal{U}$.

Example 3. In Example 1, for port U, we have $\mathcal{T}_U = \{t_1, t_3\}$. $\mathcal{T}_U$ is verifiable at U because

- $t_1 t_2$ is an absolute verifying path upon $\emptyset$ for (t_1, U).
- $t_1 t_3 t_1$ is an absolute verifying path upon $\{t_1\}$ for (t_3, U).

So let $\mathcal{P}(t_1) = t_1 t_2$, $\mathcal{P}(t_3) = t_1 t_3 t_1$, $\mathcal{R}(t_1) = \emptyset$, $\mathcal{R}(t_3) = \{t_1\}$ (i.e. $\mathcal{R} = \{(t_3, t_1)\}$), then $\mathcal{T}_p = \{t_1, t_3\}$ is verifiable at U under $\mathcal{P}$ and $\mathcal{R}$.

Proposition 3. *If ρ is an absolute verifying path upon v for (t,p) and v is a minimal such set then $v \subseteq \mathcal{T}_p$.*

Proof. Let $\rho = t_1 \ldots t_k$ (for $k \geq 2$) where $t = t_i$ for some $i \in [1, k-1]$. Suppose $t_i |_p \neq -$ (the case for $t_i |_p = -$ is analogous). Consider an arbitrary transition $t' \in v$: it is sufficient to prove that $t' \in \mathcal{T}_p$.

By the minimality of v we have t' is contained in $pre(\rho)$ and so $t' = t_j$ for some $j \in [1, k-1]$. Since ρ is an absolute verifying path upon v for (t_i, p), $t_i \notin v$ and so $j \neq i$. Suppose $i < j$ (the case for $i > j$ is analogous).

Since $t_j \in v$, by the minimality of v we have that $t_j |_p = -$. Now as $i < j$, $t_i |_p \neq -$, $t_j |_p = -$, there exists some maximal l with $i \leq l < j$ such that $t_l |_p \neq -$. Let $\rho' = t_l \ldots t_j$. By Definition 1, no transition in ρ' has input at p. By considering ρ' we see that $t_j \in \mathcal{T}_p$.

This result allows us to consider only transitions in $\mathcal{T}_p$ for $\mathcal{U}$.

Proposition 4. *Suppose M is an FSM that is not intrinsically non-synchronizable, p is a port of M and $\mathcal{U}$ is a set of transitions verifiable at port p. If $\mathcal{T}'_p \subseteq \mathcal{U}$ or $\mathcal{T}_p - \mathcal{T}'_p \subseteq \mathcal{U}$, then $\mathcal{T}_p$ is verifiable at p.*

Proof. Suppose $\mathcal{U}$ is verifiable under $\mathcal{R}$ and $\mathcal{P}$ and that $\mathcal{R}$ is a minimal such relation (i.e. $\mathcal{U}$ is not verifiable using a relation that contains fewer pairs).

First, consider the case that $\mathcal{T}'_p \subseteq \mathcal{U}$. According to Theorem 2 in [3], there exists an absolute verifying path upon $\mathcal{T}'_p$ for (t,p) for every $t \notin \mathcal{T}'_p$. Since $\mathcal{T}'_p \subseteq \mathcal{U}$, there exists $\rho'_{p,t}$, the absolute verifying path upon $\mathcal{T}'_p$ for (t,p), for $t \in \mathcal{T}_p - \mathcal{U}$. Now define relation $\mathcal{R}'$ and function $\mathcal{P}'$ in the following way.

1. $\mathcal{R}' = \mathcal{R} \cup \{(t,t')|t \in \mathcal{T}_p - \mathcal{U} \wedge t' \in \mathcal{T}_p'\}$
2. $\mathcal{P}' = \mathcal{P} \cup \{(t, \rho'_{p,t})|t \in \mathcal{T}_p - \mathcal{U}\}$

It is easy to check that $\mathcal{T}_p$ is verifiable at p under $\mathcal{R}'$ and $\mathcal{P}'$ as required.

Now consider the case that $\mathcal{T} - \mathcal{T}_p' \subseteq \mathcal{U}$. Similar to Theorem 2 in [3], we can prove that there exists an absolute verifying path upon $\mathcal{T}_p - \mathcal{T}_p'$ for (t, p) for every $t \notin \mathcal{T} - \mathcal{T}_p'$. The proof is then similar to that for the case where $\mathcal{T}_p' \subseteq \mathcal{U}$.

4 Algorithm

To calculate $\mathcal{T}_p'$ and $\mathcal{T}_p - \mathcal{T}_p'$, we can first determine all transitions involved in potentially undetectable *1-shift* output fault. This can be done by comparing every two transitions $s_1 \xrightarrow{x_1/y_1} s_2$ and $s_2 \xrightarrow{x_2/y_2} s_3$ where x_2 is not at p. If y_1 has nonempty output at p while y_2 does not, or vice versa, then t_1 and t_2 are involved in potentially undetectable 1-shift output fault and we can put them into $\mathcal{T}_p'$ and $\mathcal{T}_p - \mathcal{T}_p'$ respectively. In particular, for the purpose of the next step of the calculation, we can mark those transitions put into $\mathcal{T}_p - \mathcal{T}_p'$ as *backward* or *forward* to indicate whether it is involved in a potentially undetectable backward or forward output shift. This step takes $\mathcal{O}(v^2)$ time where v is the number of transitions in the given specification. At the end of this step, the set $\mathcal{T}_p'$ calculated is what we want. Then we can calculate all of the other transitions in $\mathcal{T}_p - \mathcal{T}_p'$ that have empty output at p and are involved in potentially undetectable output fault. We can keep adding transitions $s_1 \xrightarrow{x_1/y_1} s_2$ into $\mathcal{T}_p - \mathcal{T}_p'$ if the output of y_1 at p is empty and one of the following holds:

- There exists $s_2 \xrightarrow{x_2/y_2} s_3$ in $\mathcal{T}_p - \mathcal{T}_p'$ marked as *backward* and x_2 is not at p. In this case, the added transition is also marked as *backward*.
- There exists $s_3 \xrightarrow{x_2/y_2} s_1$ in $\mathcal{T}_p - \mathcal{T}_p'$ marked as *forward* and x_1 is not at p. In this case, the added transition is also marked as *forward*.

This step also takes $\mathcal{O}(v^2)$ time.

Next, we consider an algorithm:

- to check if $\mathcal{T}_p$ is verifiable at p. According to Proposition 4, this amounts to check if there exists $\mathcal{U}$ such that $\mathcal{U}$ is verifiable at p and $\mathcal{T}_p' \subseteq \mathcal{U}$ or $\mathcal{T}_p - \mathcal{T}_p' \subseteq \mathcal{U}$;
- when $\mathcal{T}_p$ is verifiable at p, construct absolute verifying paths for each transition in $\mathcal{T}_p$.

Figure 2 gives such an algorithm. Here, $\mathcal{U}$ is a set of transitions that is verifiable at p. It is initially set to empty. We search for transitions to be added into $\mathcal{U}$ and try to make $\mathcal{U} \supseteq \mathcal{T}_p$. According to Proposition 3, we only need to consider transitions in $\mathcal{T}_p$ to be added into $\mathcal{U}$, so in fact, we seek a set $\mathcal{U}$ such that $\mathcal{U} = \mathcal{T}_p$.

If we succeed, we have an absolute verifying path $\rho_{p,t}$ kept in $\mathcal{P}(t)$ for each $t \in \mathcal{U}$. Of course, if we do not need the absolute verifying paths but just want to

```
1:  input: M and a port p of M
2:  output: answer if $T_p$ is verifiable at p, and if so, provide $\rho_{p,t}$ for each transition t
    in $T_p$
3:  $\mathcal{U} := \emptyset$
4:  for all $t \in T_p$ do
5:      $\mathcal{P}(t) := null$
6:  end for
7:  if $T_p = \emptyset$ then
8:      success := true
9:      goto line 27
10: end if
11: success := false
12: checkset := $T_p$
13: checkset' := $\emptyset$
14: while checkset $\neq \emptyset \land$ checkset' $\neq$ checkset do
15:     checkset' := checkset
16:     if we can find an absolute verifying path $\rho_{p,t}$ upon $\mathcal{U}$ for $(t,p)$ for some $t \in$
        checkset then
17:         for $t'$ contained in $pre(\rho_{p,t})$ such that $(t' \notin \mathcal{U})$ and $(t'|_p = - \Leftrightarrow t|_p = -)$ do
18:             add $t'$ to $\mathcal{U}$
19:             $\mathcal{P}(t') := \rho_{p,t}$
20:         end for
21:         checkset := $T_p - \mathcal{U}$
22:         if checkset := $\emptyset$ then
23:             success := true
24:         end if
25:     end if
26: end while
27: if success then
28:     output("success", $\mathcal{P}$)
29: else
30:     output("no such set of sequences exists.")
31: end if
```

Fig. 2. Algorithm 1: generating a set of paths

check whether T_p is verifiable at p, the algorithm can be easily modified so that it stops whenever $T_p \subseteq \mathcal{U}$ or $T_p' \subseteq \mathcal{U}$ (Proposition 4).

If T_p is empty, then we do not need to do anything (lines 7-10). If $T_p \neq \emptyset$, then we start to check if there exists a transition $t \in T_p$ that has an absolute verifying path (upon $\emptyset$) for (t,p). We use checkset to denote the current set of transitions that we need to search for absolute verifying paths and initially checkset = T_p. Thus if checkset becomes $\emptyset$ then we terminate the loop and the algorithm has found a sufficient set of paths. At the end of an iteration the set checkset' denotes the value of checkset before the iteration of the while loop and thus if there is no progress (checkset' = checkset at this point) the algorithm terminates with failure.

Whenever we find an absolute verifying path $\rho_{p,t}$ upon $\mathcal{U}$, we can add t' to $\mathcal{U}$ for all t' contained in $pre(\rho)$ and $t'|_p = - \Leftrightarrow t|_p = -$. This is based on Proposition 1. At the same time, we update checkset.

To find an absolute verifying path ρ upon $\mathcal{U}$ for (t,p), we can construct $G[t,\mathcal{U}]$ which is obtained from G by removing all edges except those corresponding to a transition t' in one of the following cases:

- t' has input at p;
- $t'\mid_p = -$ iff $t\mid_p = -$;
- $t' \in \mathcal{U}$.

We then search for a synchronizable path in $G[t,\mathcal{U}]$ that contains t, starts with input at p, and ends with input at p. We can search for such a path similar to standard algorithms (e.g. find all vertices reachable from all ending vertex of edges representing t and all vertices that get us to the starting vertex of edges representing t). Note that we do not need to consider cycles in $G[t,\mathcal{U}]$: if there exists an absolute verifying path with a cycle then there is such a path that has no cycles.

The following two results show that Algorithm 1 is correct.

Theorem 1. *Suppose that Algorithm 1 outputs "success" and $\mathcal{P}$. Then there exists a relation $\mathcal{R}$ such that $\mathcal{T}_p$ is verifiable at p under $\mathcal{R}$ and $\mathcal{P}$.*

Proof. Define a relation $\mathcal{R}$ in the following way. Given a transition $t \in \mathcal{T}_p$ consider the iteration in which t is added to $\mathcal{U}$ and let $\mathcal{U}_t$ denote the value of $\mathcal{U}$ at the beginning of this iteration. Then, since we could add t to $\mathcal{U}$ on this iteration, there is an absolute verifying path upon $\mathcal{U}_t$ for (t,p). Thus, we let $\mathcal{R}$ be the relation such that for all $t \in \mathcal{T}_p$, $\mathcal{R}(t) = \mathcal{U}_t$. Clearly $\mathcal{T}_p$ is verifiable at p under $\mathcal{R}$ and $\mathcal{P}$ as required.

Theorem 2. *Suppose that Algorithm 1 does not output "success". Then $\mathcal{T}_p$ is not verifiable at p.*

Proof. Proof by contradiction: suppose that there exists $\mathcal{R}$ and $\mathcal{P}$ such that $\mathcal{T}_p$ is verifiable at p under $\mathcal{R}$ and $\mathcal{P}$ and that Algorithm 1 terminates with a set $\mathcal{U}$ such that $\mathcal{T}_p \not\subseteq \mathcal{U}$.

Define a function *depth* from $\mathcal{T}_p$ to the integers in the following way. The base case is $depth(t) = 1$ if $\mathcal{R}(t) = \{t\}$. The recursive case is if $\mathcal{R}(t) \neq \{t\}$ then $depth(t) = 1 + max_{t' \in \mathcal{R}(t) \setminus \{t\}} depth(t')$. Let t denote an element of $\mathcal{T}_p \setminus \mathcal{U}$ that minimises $depth(t)$. But, every element of $\mathcal{R}(t)$ is in $\mathcal{U}$ and thus there exists an absolute verifying path upon $\mathcal{R}(t)$ for (p,t). This contradicts the algorithm terminating with set $\mathcal{U}$ such that $\mathcal{T}_p \not\subseteq \mathcal{U}$ as required.

Now we turn to the complexity of the algorithm.

Let $m = |\mathcal{T}_p|$ be the number of transitions involved in output shift faults at p. For each while-loop (line 14-26), we construct an absolute verifying path upon $\mathcal{U}$ for one of the transitions in *checkset*, and we can remove at least one transition from *checkset*. As initially $|checkset| = m$, the while-loop will be executed at most m times.

Within each while-loop in lines 14-26, we need to check if we can find an absolute verifying path $\rho_{p,t}$ upon $\mathcal{U}$ for (t,p) for some $t \in checkset$. This can be realized by trying to construct $\rho_{p,t}$ for each $t \in checkset$ until such a $\rho_{p,t}$ is found. This takes at most $|checkset|$ times of effort for each attempt.

For each attempt to construct an absolute verifying path upon $\mathcal{U}$ for a given transition t, it takes $\mathcal{O}(wv)$ times to construct a path where w is the number of the states in M and v is the number of transitions in M.

For the for-loop in lines 17-20, we can keep a set α of all transitions t' contained in $pre(\rho_{p,t})$ such that $t' \notin \mathcal{U}$ and $t'|_p = - \Leftrightarrow t|_p = -$ during the construction of $\rho_{p,t}$. This does not affect our estimated time $\mathcal{O}(wv)$. After we have found such an $\rho_{p,t}$ successfully, we can move all transitions in α from $checkset$ to $\mathcal{U}$. For each such move, there will be one less while-loop executed, and thus the time for the operation of the for-loop in lines 17-20 can be ignored.

In summary, the time complexity of Algorithm 1 is $\mathcal{O}(m^2wv)$.

5 Relationship with Previous Work

To make sure that each transition involved in a potentially undetectable output shift fault can be *independently* verified at port p, we need to have $\rho_1@t@\rho_2$ as an absolute verifying path upon $\emptyset$ for (t,p) for all transition t involved in a potentially undetectable output shift fault. If $\rho_1@t@\rho_2$ is an absolute verifying path upon $\emptyset$ for (t,p), then $\rho_1@t$ and $t@\rho_2$ correspond to the absolute leading path and absolute trailing path respectively defined in [4], where we have presented a necessary and sufficient condition to guarantee the existence of absolute leading path and absolute trailing path for (t,p) for each t involved in a potentially undetectable output shift fault:

Given an FSM with no same-port-output-cycles or isolated-port-cycles, for any transition t involved in a potentially undetectable 1-shift output faults, there is an absolute leading path and an absolute trailing path for (t,p) if and only if for any pair of transitions $s_1 \xrightarrow{*/*} s$ and $s \xrightarrow{*/*} t_1$ in the FSM,

a *if there exists a potential undetectable forward shift of an output at port p, then there exists at least one transition to s with a null output at port p, and at least one transition from s with either an input or a non-empty output at port p.*

b *if there exists a potential undetectable backward shift of an output at port p, then there exists at least one transition to s with a non-empty output at port p, and at least one transition from s with either an input or a null output at port p.*

This result is presented in terms of 1-shift output faults while it holds also for general output shift faults.

Apparently, when the above condition holds, there exists an absolute verifying path upon $\emptyset$ for (t,p) for every $t \in \mathcal{T}_p$, and thus $\mathcal{T}_p$ is verifiable. In other words, we presented in [4] a condition to guarantee that for each $t \in \mathcal{T}_p$, there exists an absolute verifying path upon $\emptyset$ for (t,p), and this condition is sufficient for $\mathcal{T}_p$ to be verifiable.

In [3], we have given a weaker condition than the one in [4]:

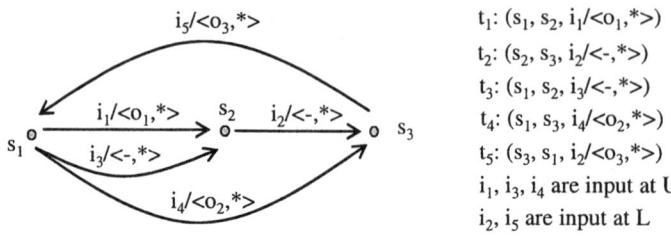

Fig. 3. Example to show the relationship with previous work

Theorem 3. *Let M be a given FSM which is not intrinsically non-synchronizable and has no same-port-output-cycles. Let p be any port of M.*

(i) (t_0, p) has an absolute leading path for every $t_0 \in \mathcal{T}'_p$, if and only if

$\forall t = s_1 \xrightarrow{x/y} s_2 \in \mathcal{T}'_p$, $x \notin I_p$ *implies* $\exists s_3 \xrightarrow{x'/y'} s_1 \in T$ *synchronizable with t such that $y'|_p \neq -$;*

(ii) (t_0, p) has an absolute trailing path for every $t_0 \in \mathcal{T}'_p$, if and only if

$\forall t = s_1 \xrightarrow{x/y} s_2 \in \mathcal{T}'_p$, $\exists s_2 \xrightarrow{x'/y'} s_4 \in T$ *synchronizable with t such that $x' \in I_p \lor y'|_p \neq -$.*

The above theorem gives a condition and declares that under this condition, it is guaranteed the existence of absolute leading path and absolute trailing path for (t, p) only for all those transitions involved in potentially undetectable output shift *and have non-empty output at p*. So it guarantees that for each transition t of this category, (t, p) has an absolute verifying path upon $\emptyset$.

Then it is proved there that for other transitions t' involved in potentially undetectable output shift but with empty output at p, there is an absolute verifying path upon $\mathcal{T}'_p$ for (t', p):

Theorem 4. *Given any FSM M that is not intrinsically non-synchronizable and port p, every $t \notin \mathcal{T}'_p$ has an absolute verifying path upon $\mathcal{T}'_p$.*

According to these two theorems, the condition in Theorem 3 is sufficient for $\mathcal{T}_p$ to be verifiable.

On the other hand, the conditions in [4,3] are not necessary for $\mathcal{T}_p$ to be verifiable.

Example 4. In Example 1 we have shown that $\mathcal{T}_p$ is verifiable at U. However, the conditions in [4,3] do not hold. This is because for (t_3, U), t_3 does not have input at U and there is no transition ending at s_2 with non-empty output at U.

The following shows another example where $\mathcal{T}_p$ is verifiable at U while the conditions in [4,3] do not hold.

Example 5. In Figure 3, there are undetectable output shift faults at port U in $t_1 t_2$ and in $t_2 t_5$. $\mathcal{T}_U = \{t_1, t_2, t_5\}$. $\mathcal{T}'_U = \{t_1, t_5\}$.

The conditions in [4,3] do not hold because for (t_1, U), there is no transition starting from s_2 that has either input at U or non-empty output at U.

However, $\mathcal{T}_U$ is verifiable at U:

- $t_4 t_5 t_1$ is an absolute verifying path upon $\emptyset$ for (t_5, U).
- $t_3 t_2 t_5 t_1$ is an absolute verifying path upon $\{t_5\}$ for (t_2, U).
- $t_1 t_2 t_5 t_1$ is an absolute verifying path upon $\{t_2, t_5\}$ for (t_1, U).

6 Conclusion

This paper has presented a sound procedure to check for the possibility of constructing a test/checking sequence that will not cause controllability and observability problems and will not require external coordination message exchanges among remote testers during its application in a distributed test architecture. This is realized by constructing a path that can help checking the output of a transition t at a certain port p, for each transition t involved in a potentially undetectable output shift fault. The effectiveness of this path on checking the output of transition t at port p must not be affected by controllability and observability problems. The correct output of transition t at port p is actually derived from the correct output sequence when applying the input portion of this path during the test. It remains as an interesting problem to produce an *efficient* test or checking sequence from an FSM, that is guaranteed to determine the correctness of the SUT for the considered fault model.

Acknowledgements

This work was supported in part by Natural Sciences and Engineering Research Council (NSERC) of Canada under grant RGPIN 976 and 209774, Leverhulme Trust grant number F/00275/D, Testing State Based Systems, and Engineering and Physical Sciences Research Council grant number GR/ , Formal Methods and Testing (FORTEST).

References

1. S. Boyd and H. Ural. The synchronization problem in distributed testing. complexity. Information Processing Letters, 40:1?
2. L. Cacciari and O. Rafiq. Controllability and observability problems in distributed testing. Information and Software Technology, 41:76?
3. J. Chen, R. M. Hierons, and H. Ural. On resolving observability problems in distributed test architectures. Submitted to al Conference on Formal Techniques for Networked and Distributed Systems (FORTE 2004), volume 3235 of LNCS, pages 229–242. Springer.
4. J. Chen, R. M. Hierons, and H. Ural. Resolving observability problems in distributed testing. In 24rd ? sequences based on multiple UIO sequences. IEEE/ACM T? king, 3:152–157, 1995.
5. W. Chen and H. Ural. Sync?

6. A. Gill. Introduction to the Theory of Finite-State Machines. New York: McGraw-Hill, 1962.
7. S. Guyot and H. Ural. Synchronizable checking sequences based on UIO sequences. In Proc. of IFIP IWPTS95, pages 395407, Evry, France, September 1995.
8. F.C. Hennie. Fault detecting experiments for sequential circuits. In Proc. of Fifth Ann. Symp. Switching Circuit Theory and Logical Design, pages 95110, Princeton, N.J., 1964.
9. R. M. Hierons. Testing a distributed system: generating minimal synchronised test sequences that detect output-shifting faults. Information and Software Technology, 43(9):551560, 2001.
10. D. Lee and M. Yannakakis. Principles and methods of testing finitestate machines a survey. Proceedings of the IEEE, 84(8):10891123, 1996.
11. G. Luo, R. Dssouli, and G. v. Bochmann. Generating synchronizable test sequences based on finite state machine with distributed ports. In The 6th IFIP Workshop on Protocol Test Systems, pages 139153. Elsevier (North-Holland), 1993.
12. G. Luo, R. Dssouli, G. v. Bochmann, P. Venkataram, and A. Ghedamsi. Test generation with respect to distributed interfaces. Computer Standards and Interfaces, 16:119132, 1994.
13. K.K. Sabnani and A.T. Dahbura. A protocol test generation procedure. Computer Networks, 15:285297, 1988.
14. B. Sarikaya and G. v. Bochmann. Synchronization and specification issues in protocol testing. IEEE Transactions on Communications, 32:389395, April 1984.
15. K.C. Tai and Y.C. Young. Synchronizable test sequences of finite state machines. Computer Networks, 13:11111134, 1998.
16. H. Ural and Z. Wang. Synchronizable test sequence generation using UIO sequences. Computer Communications, 16:653661, 1993.
17. Y.C. Young and K.C. Tai. Observation inaccuracy in conformance testing with multiple testers. In Proc. of IEEE WASET, pages 8085, 1998.

Automatic Generation of Conflict-Free IPsec Policies*

Chi-Lan Chang, Yun-Peng Chiu, and Chin-Laung Lei

Department of Electrical Engineering, National Taiwan University,
No.1, Sec. 4, Roosevelt Road, Taipei, Taiwan 106
{qlchang, frank}@fractal.ee.ntu.edu.tw, lei@cc.ee.ntu.edu.tw

Abstract. IPsec (IP security) will function correctly only if its security policies satisfy all the requirements. If the security policies cannot meet a set of consistent requirements, we said there are policy conflicts. In this paper, we analyze all situations which could possibly lead to a policy conflict and try to resolve all of them. We induce only two situations which could cause conflicts and also propose an algorithm to automatically generate conflict-free policies which satisfy all requirements. We also implement our algorithm and compare the results of simulation with the other approaches and show that it outperforms existing approaches in the literature.

1 Introduction

IPsec (IP security) provides authentication and confidentiality and is widely used in building a VPN (Virtual Private Network) of an organization or a business. Because that IPsec implements security services at IP layer and directly protects all the packets to achieve its security goal, the applications at upper layer do not need to make any change. According to the security requirements of an organization, security policies are configured on every security gateway or router in the VPN to enforce the required protections. Security requirements are goals we want to reach, and security policies which are configured in all involved computers are the detailed methods to reach those requirements.

({10.1.2.1},{10.2.2.1},any,any,any) → enforce (encryption, strong, 10.1.2.*, 10.2.2.*)

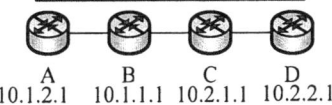

A   B   C   D
10.1.2.1   10.1.1.1   10.2.1.1   10.2.2.1

Fig. 1. An encryption requirement example

Basically, security policies are generated according to the security requirements. Correctly producing security policies from requirements is an important issue, because if there is an error setting on one of these gateways or routers, packets will be

---

* This work was supported in part by Taiwan Information Security Center (TWISC), National Science Council under the grants No. NSC 94-3114-P-001-001Y

dropped and the whole network will be blockaded, or the security will be breached. For example, in **Fig. 1**, we have a simple network topology of four nodes, A, B, C, and D, and we also have one encryption requirement which is to protect the traffic from node A to node D, including the network links A to B, B to C, and C to D. Node A is the gateway of domain 10.1.2.1/24, node B is the gateway of domain 10.1.1.1/16, node C is the gateway of domain 10.2.1.1/16, and node D is the gateway of domain 10.2.2.1/24. The form of requirement we used in this paper is defined in [1]. For more explanations, the readers can refer to Section 3.

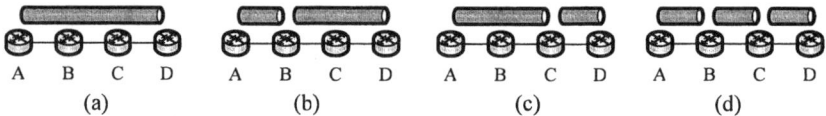

Fig. 2. Four different configurations of security policies that satisfy our requirement

There are many possible ways to generate security policies to satisfy our requirements. For example, in **Fig. 2**, we show four different configurations of security policies to satisfy the requirement of **Fig. 1**. Security policies decide how the IPsec tunnels will be build. In (a) of **Fig. 2**, the policy builds an encryption tunnel directly from node A to node D. Therefore, all the packets which are subject to our requirement will be protected from this tunnel, and we can say this policy **satisfies** our requirement. In (b) of **Fig. 2**, two security policies were generated. One is to protect the traffic from node A to node B, and the other is to protect the traffic from node B to node D. Obviously, the packets subject to our requirement will go through the first tunnel from A to B, and then go through the second tunnel from B to D. Assume the node B is trusted and data decryption is permitted on this node, we can see these two security policies satisfy our requirement. In (c) and (d) of **Fig. 2**, the security policies also satisfy our requirement.

However, there may be some conflicts between policies, and not every possible configuration of security policies will satisfy the requirements. This issue was first addressed in [1]. Therefore, we bring up a policy-generation algorithm to produce security policies to satisfy all the requirements, and try to minimize not only the number of total tunnels but also the number of tunnels passed by all possible traffic. The reason to minimize the number of total tunnels is that if there are more tunnels, the network topology will be more complicated, and the network management and analysis will be more difficult, too. On the other hand, if there are fewer tunnels which are passed by all possible traffic, we can save more computational power and improve the efficiency of the entire network. In this paper, we present our algorithm for automatic generation of conflict free policies, and compare the results with other three algorithms which are proposed by the predecessors.

The rest of the paper is organized as follows. The policy conflict problem is described in Section 2. Related works are addressed in Section 3. In Section 4, we present the proposed algorithm for generating conflict-free IPsec policies. Some simulation results are given in Section 5, and finally we make a conclusion of this paper in Section 6.

2 Policy Conflict Problem

The cause of a policy conflict is more than one policies have certain kind of intersection. More precisely, a conflict happens when the packets in one tunnel pass through a network node (a security gateway, a router, or any IPsec-enabled machine), but the packets are pulled down into another tunnel by the policy of that network node. Only in such situation, the policy conflict might have a chance to happen. Although not every intersection of tunnels will lead to a policy conflict, we can simplify the problem to consider only two tunnels and all kinds of intersection relationships between them. Since a policy conflict might happen only when packets in the first tunnel are pulled down into the second tunnel, we only need to consider the linear network area between the starting node and the end node of the second tunnel, and all the nodes of the first tunnel in this linear network area. Therefore, we only need to consider one-dimensional relationships between two tunnels. Here we refer to a tunnel as "first" or "second" depends on the order the packets encounter them. If two tunnels have no one dimensional intersection relationship, they will not conflict with each other.

For example, in **Fig. 3**, although the two tunnels are in two-dimensional, we could consider their one dimensional intersection part, which is the three points 2, 4, and 3. The point 2 and point 3 are the starting point and the end point of the second tunnel, so both of them are always on the same line. As for the point 4, it is the last node of the first tunnel in the line segment between point 2 and point 3.

Fig. 4 lists all intersection relationships between two tunnels in one-dimension, and we will analyze these relationships to find in what situations there will be policy conflicts. We omit other situations in which two tunnels do not intersect with each other. In the case (A) of **Fig. 4**, the upper tunnel and the lower tunnel have the same starting point and the same end point, and there will be no policy conflicts. In the case (B), the upper tunnel is the first tunnel and it starts at the same point where the second (lower) tunnel starts, and the traffic will be encapsulated twice at this starting point and decapsulated at the end point of the second tunnel. When the traffic is decapsulated at the end point of the second tunnel, it will be sent back to the end point of the first tunnel, and there might be a policy conflict because of the sending-back phenomenon.

In the case (C), the traffic is encapsulated at the starting point of the first (lower) tunnel. When the traffic travel the network to the starting point of the second (upper) tunnel, the traffic will be encapsulated again and sent to the end point of the second tunnel, which is also the end point of the first tunnel. So, the traffic will be decapsulated twice at the most right node, which is the end point of both of tunnels, and there will be no policy conflicts here. In the case (D), the traffic is encapsulated twice at the most left node, which is the starting point of both of tunnels, and then the traffic will be decapsulated and leave the second (lower) tunnel at the middle node, which is the end point of the second tunnel. Finally, the traffic is sent to the end point of the first (upper) tunnel and decapsulated there. In this case, there will be no policy conflicts, either. In the case (E), the traffic is encapsulated in the starting point of the first (upper) tunnel. At the middle node, which is the starting point of the second (lower) tunnel, the traffic will be encapsulated again at this middle node. Then, the traffic will be directly sent to the most right node, which is the end point of the second tunnel, and the traffic will be decapsulated and sent back to the end point of the first tunnel. After arriving at the end point of the first tunnel, the traffic will leave the first tunnel and be sent to the most right node. Therefore, in the case (E), the policy conflict might happen. In the case (F), at first, the traffic is encapsulated by the longer (upper) tunnel, and then the traffic will encounter the shorter (lower) tunnel. The traffic will leave the shorter tunnel first and then leave the longer tunnel in the end. The length of a tunnel is defined as the hop count it passed. We make a summary of all the cases in which the policy conflict might happen in **Fig. 5**. There are only two situations which might cause the policy conflicts. The situation (1) has not been addressed yet in other papers before. The proposed algorithm could handle these two situations and generate conflict-free policies to meet the security requirements.

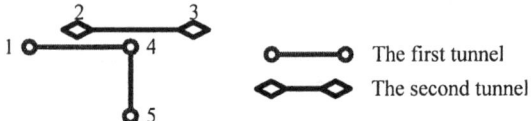

Fig. 3. An example: the intersection of two tunnels

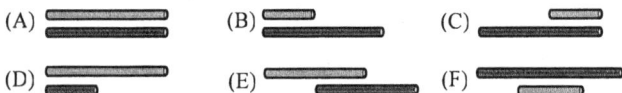

Fig. 4. All intersection relationships between two tunnels

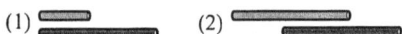

Fig. 5. Two situations which cause the policy conflicts

3 Related Works

In this section, we describe the definitions and syntax for security requirements and security policies we used in this paper. Security requirements are high-level goals we want to achieve, and security policies are actually configured at all related machines in a virtual private network. We also describe three existing algorithms which automatically generate security policies for the requirements. These algorithms were described in [2] and [3].

3.1 Security Requirements

In [1], the authors clearly defined two levels of security policies, which are the requirement level and the implementation level. A security policy set is **correct** if and only if it satisfies all the requirements. A requirement R is a rule of the following form: If condition C then action A:

$$R = C \rightarrow A$$

There are four kinds of requirements in [1]:

- Access Control Requirement (ACR):

    flow id → *deny | allow*

- Security Coverage Requirement (SCR):

    flow id → *enforce (sec-function, strength, from, to, [trusted-nodes])*

- Content Access Requirement (CAR):

    flow id, [sec-function, access-nodes] → *deny | allow*

- Security Association Requirement (SAR):

    flow id, [SA-peer1, SA-peer2] → *deny | allow*

flow id is used to identify a traffic flow, and is composed of 5 to 6 sub-selectors including *src-addr, dst-addr, src-port, dst-port, protocol,* and optional *user-id*. A requirement is **satisfied** if and only if all packets selected by the condition part execute the action part of the requirement.

3.2 Security Policies

For different implementations of IPsec, there are different ways to specify these policies. For convenience, we choose the syntax specified in **setkey** of the IPsec-Tools project [5] to describe a security policy in this paper. The IPsec-Tools project is a port of KAME's IPsec utilities to Linux-2.6 IPsec implementation. It supports NetBSD and FreeBSD as well. The **setkey** is a tool of the IPsec-Tools project to manipulate IPsec policies. According to the manual of **setkey**, the syntax to describe a security policy is as the following:

  src_range dst_range upperspec policy;

src_range and *dst_range* are selections of the secure communication specified as IPv4/v6 address or address range, and it may accompany TCP/UDP port specification. *upperspec* is the upper-layer protocol to be used, such as TCP, UDP, or ICMP, and it can be specified as **any** for "any protocol." *policy* uses the format:

  -P direction [priority specification] ***discard/none/ipsec*** *protocol/mode/src-dst/level [...]*

For instance, the configuration (a) of **Fig. 2**, which builds a tunnel from node 10.1.2.1 to node 10.2.2.1, has the policies as follows.
At node 10.1.2.1 (the gateway of domain 10.1.2.1/24):
  *10.1.2.1/24 10.2.2.1/24 any -P **out** ipsec esp/tunnel/10.1.2.1-10.2.2.1/require;*
At node 10.2.2.1 (the gateway of domain 10.2.2.1/24):
  *10.1.2.1/24 10.2.2.1/24 any -P **in** ipsec esp/tunnel/10.1.2.1-10.2.2.1/require;*

3.3 The Bundle Approach

The bundle approach is the first algorithm for solving the IPsec policy-conflict problem, and it was proposed in [2]. The bundle approach has two phases. First, it

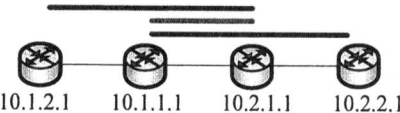

Fig. 6. The three requirements example

Table 1. The three requirements of **Fig. 6**

R_1	$(\{10.1.*.*\}, \{10.2.*.*\}) \to$ (encryption, weak, 10.1.*.*, 10.2.*.*)
R_2	$(\{10.1.2.*\}, \{10.2.*.*\}) \to$ (authentication, strong, 10.1.2.*, 10.2.*.*)
R_3	$(\{10.1.*.*\}, \{10.2.2.*\}) \to$ (encryption, strong, 10.1.*.*, 10.2.2.*)

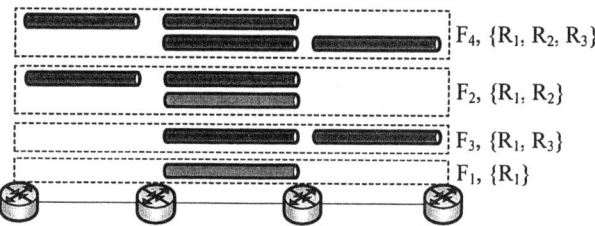

Fig. 7. The solution of bundle approach for the three requirements example

separates the entire traffic into several disjoint traffic flow sets, called bundles, each of which is subject to a unique set of security requirements. Second, given a set of requirement actions for each bundle, the bundle approach generates corresponding security policies.

For example, in **Fig. 6**, we use a simple network for explanation. The node 10.1.2.1 is the gateway of domain 10.1.2.1/24, the node 10.1.1.1 is the gateway of domain 10.1.1.1/16, the node 10.2.1.1 is the gateway of domain 10.2.1.1/16, and the node 10.2.2.1 is the gateway of domain 10.2.2.1/24. The specifications of the three requirements are listed in **Table 1**. In the first phase, the bundle approach separates the entire traffic into four traffic filters: $F_1 = (\{10.1.*.*\}, \{10.2.*.*\})$, $F_2 = (\{10.1.2.*\}, \{10.2.*.*\})$, $F_3 = (\{10.1.*.*\}, \{10.2.2.*\})$, $F_4 = (\{10.1.2.*\}, \{10.2.2.*\})$. Then, the approach generates a set of policies for each filter and the solution is shown in **Fig. 7**.

3.4 The Direct Approach

The direct approach [2] builds tunnels directly and makes sure new tunnels do not overlap with any existing old tunnels. If a new tunnel overlaps with an existing tunnel, the approach builds two new connecting tunnels that do not overlap with others instead. Although the direct approach builds fewer tunnels than the bundle approach and has better efficiency, the paper [2] told us that there would be no solution using the direct approach if it could not find non-overlapped solution for one requirement. However there might be solution using bundle approach. Therefore, the paper suggested a combined approach which uses the direct approach first and if it cannot find the solution, uses the bundle approach instead. The solution for the three requirements example is shown in **Fig. 8**.

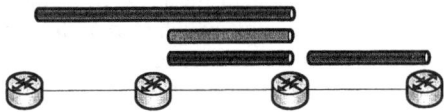

Fig. 8. The solution of direct approach for the three requirements example

3.5 The Ordered-Split Algorithm

The ordered-split algorithm was proposed in [3]. It handles the requirements of authentication and the requirements of encryption separately. It first converts original requirements into tie-free requirement sets and then generates minimal size canonical solutions for the new requirements. A canonical solution is defined as a solution with no two tunnels start at the same place or end at the same place. A Tie-free requirement set is defined as a requirement set with no two requirements share the same *from* values and the same *to* values. The *from* and *to* values of one requirement determine the network area which needs to be proteced. According to the simulation and analysis of [3], this algorithm generates fewer tunnels than the bundle/direct approach and the enhanced bundle/direct approach. The solution for the three requirements example is shown in **Fig. 9**. There are three tunnels in this solution, and the middle tunnel will provide both the encryption and authentication.

These algorithms are used to find correct security policy sets and minimize the total number of tunnels. As we said before, if the total number of tunnels is small, the network topology will be simpler and the policy management will be much easier. Generally speaking, if there are fewer tunnels, there would be fewer tunnels packets are needed to pass. The total computational cost will decrease, and all the security requirements are still satisfied. However, a question is, if two security policy sets have the same number of total tunnels, which policy set is a better solution? The answer is the policy set which has longer average tunnel length will be a better choice. It is because that we will need the tunnel length to be as long as possible in order to avoid traffic being encapsulated and decapsulated many times. In this paper, we present a policy-generation algorithm achieve these goals: (1) generates correct security policies, (2) minimizes total number of tunnels, and (3) makes every tunnel as long as possible.

Fig. 9. The solution of the ordered-split algorithm for the three requirements example

4 Policy-Generation Algorithm

Our algorithm will handle the two situations which cause policy conflicts, and will generate the correct security policies according to the security requirements. In **Fig. 5**, the situation (1) is a kind of nested tunnels and can be avoided if we always set the priority of the longer tunnel higher than the priority of the shorter tunnel. In other words, if there are more than two tunnels which start at the same point, we will set the policies at the starting point so that a longer tunnel will always be processed earlier than a shorter one. In most implementations of IPsec, the priorities of security policies at a network node are decided by the order with which we specify. If we always process a longer tunnel first, we will never encounter the situation (1) in **Fig. 5**. This is the reason for our algorithm to keep the policies in the descending order regarding the lengths.

Table 2 lists our algorithm. First, the algorithm takes the **Network**, and **Reqs** as its arguments. The **network** is a general graph structure and represents the entire network. We need to know the entire network topology to build each tunnel. And **Reqs** represents the list of security requirements. At first, according to the network range given by the requirements, we directly build a tunnel (policy) for each

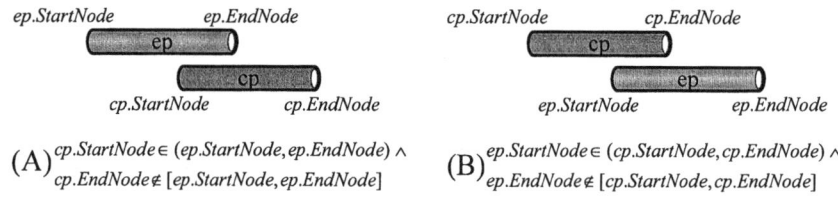

Fig. 10. Two possibilities of situation (2) in **Fig. 5**

Table 2. The policy generation algorithm

```
1  PolicyList
2  Policy_Gen_Algorithm(Graph Network, ReqList Reqs) {
3     PolicyList    policies;
4     policies = Directly_Build_A_Tunnel_For_Each_Requirement(Network, Reqs);
5     Sort_By_Length_Descending(policies);
6     Resolve_If_Tunnel_Overlapped(policies);
7     Delete_Redundant_ Tunnels(policies);
8     return policies;
9  }
```

requirement. And then, all tunnels are sorted in the descending order with respect to their lengths.. The reason for doing this is to avoid the situation (1) in **Fig. 5**, which may incur a policy conflict. Then, we check if there are overlapped tunnels and resolve them. In **Fig. 10**, **cp** means the current policy we want to check and **ep** means the existing policy which is build. The resolving process is simple, because now we only need to worry about the situation (2) in **Fig. 5**. There are two possibilities: one is

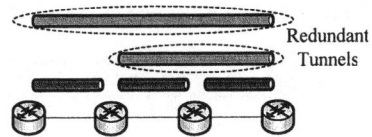

Fig. 11. An example of redundant tunnels

ep is "first" tunnel and **cp** is the "second", and the other is **cp** is the "first" tunnel and **ep** is the "second" tunnel. A tunnel is "first" or "second" depends on the order with which the packets encounter. The expressions (A) and (B) in the bottom of **Fig. 10** represent the logical relationships between **cp** and **ep**. If a policy conflict happens, we will cut the overlapped tunnel into two pieces. We cut **cp** because the length of cp is always less than or equal to the length of each existing policy **ep**. We want to keep all tunnels as long as possible, so we cut a short tunnel. In practice, we can check the *trusted_nodes* attribute of the requirements to see if the cutting node is trusted. In the final phase of our algorithm, we delete all the redundant long tunnels. A tunnel is redundant if there exist another tunnels with the same beginning point and the end point. **Fig. 11** shows an example of redundant tunnels.

We take the example in **Fig. 6** and **Table 1** to illustrate our algorithm and compare it with other three algorithms. At first, we directly build three tunnels for the three requirements individually, and sort them regarding their length. The result is shown in **Fig. 12**. In the second phase, we check if there are any overlapped tunnels like the situation (2) of **Fig. 5** and resolve these tunnels. The result of this checking process is shown in **Fig. 13**. Finally, we delete all redundant tunnels and get the final solution shown in **Fig. 14**.

We compare the four solutions for the three requirements example in the **Table 4**. The "tunnels passed" is the accumulated number of tunnels which are passed by the six possibilities of the traffic with the same direction (from left to right) listed in **Table 3**.

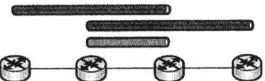

Fig. 12. Directly build a tunnel for each requirement

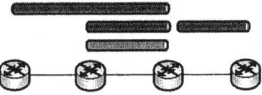

Fig. 13. Check the overlapped tunnels and resolve them

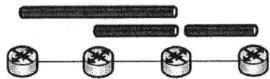

Fig. 14. The final solution for the three requirements example by our algorithm

Table 3. The six possibilities of the traffic

From	To
10.1.2.1/24	10.1.1.1/16 - 10.1.2.1/24[1]
10.1.1.1/16	10.2.1.1/16
10.2.1.1/16 - 10.2.2.1/24	10.2.2.1/24
10.1.2.1/24	10.2.1.1/16
10.1.1.1/16	10.2.2.1/24
10.1.2.1/24	10.2.2.1/24

Table 4. Comparison of four solutions

	Number of Tunnels	Tunnels Passed
Bundle	10	36
Direct	4	13
Ordered-Split	3	10
Ours	3	9

Table 5. An example of four requirements

Req1	(3, 7) → (E, 3, 7)
Req2	(1, 4) → (E, 1, 4)
Req3	(2, 7) → (A, 2, 7)
Req4	(2, 5) → (E, 2, 5)

We give the other example in **Table 5** and **Fig. 15**. There are four security requirements in this example. We use a concise form to describe a requirement. We use the node identifier number to replace the IP address, and we use the notations E and A to represent the encryption and authentication. Our solution is shown in **Fig. 16**. **Fig. 17** is the solution by using the direct approach. There is one problem may occur in this solution. At node 4, there are three tunnels and the processing order of these three tunnels is undefined in the direct approach. So it is possible to cause a policy conflict if the situation (1) in **Fig. 5** happened. In fact, [2] and [3] did not consider this kind of the policy conflict. When we compare our algorithm with the algorithms in [2] and [3], we assume the situation (1) in **Fig. 5** will not cause a conflict. In the end, **Fig. 18** shows the solution by using the ordered-split algorithm, and we eliminate the tunnel which is an authentication tunnel from node 2 to node 7, because the other short tunnels T2, T3, T4, and T5 already provide both the encryption and authentication.

Table 6 shows the results of these algorithms. By using the direct approach, if we send traffic from node 3 to node 7, the traffic will pass through the tunnels T6, T3,

---

[1] The minus operator means that the network domain 10.1.2.1/24 is excluded.

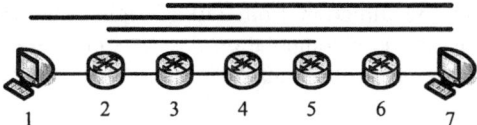

Fig. 15. An example of four requirements

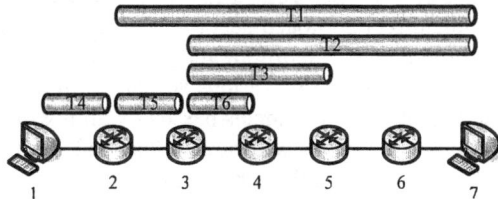

Fig. 16. The solution for the example of **Fig. 15** by using our algorithm

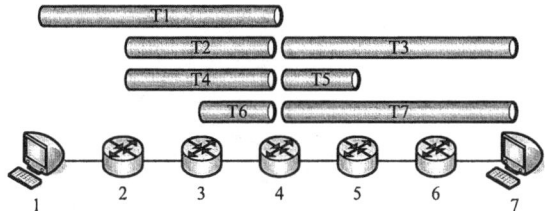

Fig. 17. The solution for **Fig. 15** by using the direct approach

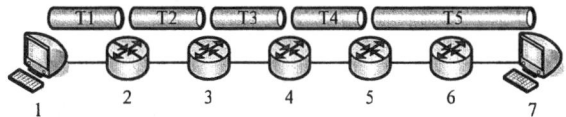

Fig. 18. The solution for **Fig. 15** by using the ordered-split algorithm

Table 6. The compare of three algorithms

	Total Number of Tunnels	Accumulated Number of Tunnels Passed
Direct	7	52
Ordered-Split	5	45
Ours	5	40

T5, and T7 in **Fig. 17**. By using the ordered-split algorithm, the same traffic will pass through the tunnels T3, T4, and T5 in **Fig. 18**. And by using our algorithm, the same traffic will pass through the tunnels T2, T3, and T6 in **Fig. 16**. The rest may be deduced by analogy. We calculate the accumulated number of tunnels passed by all possible traffic with the direction from left to right. The fewer the accumulated number of tunnels is, the less computation power is consumed. As we can see, our algorithm has fewer accumulated number of tunnels.

5 Simulation

From the previous section, we observed that our algorithm has fewer tunnels and less waste of computational power when comparing to the ordered-split algorithm, which is better than the bundle/direct approach according to the analysis of [3]. Therefore, we implemented the ordered-split algorithm and our algorithm in C++, and compare the results of these two algorithms for various scenarios. We will focus on the total number of tunnels and the number of tunnels passed by all possible traffic. If there are fewer tunnels, the network topology will be simpler, and the network management and analysis will be easier, too. On the other hand, if there are fewer tunnels passed by all possible traffic, we can avoid unnecessary encryptions/decryptions. Therefore our algorithm consumes less computation power and improves the efficiency of the entire network.

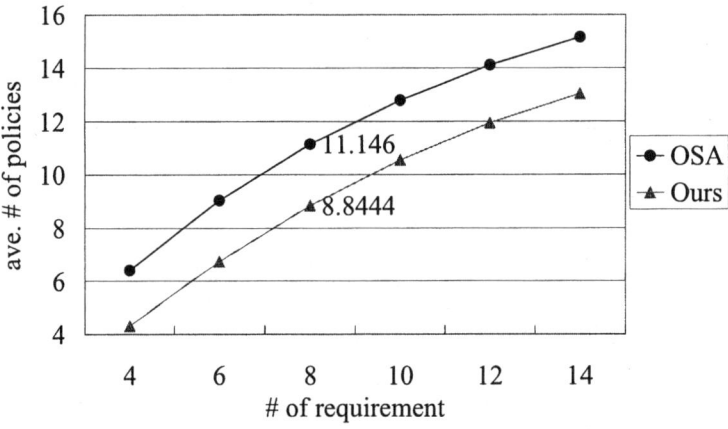

Fig. 19. The average numbers of policies in the network of 20 routers

Fig. 19 compares the result of our algorithm and order-split algorithm (shown as OSA in the graph) in the network of 20 routers. The X-axis is the average number of policies, and the Y-axis is the number of requirements. Our simulation program randomly generates 10,000 cases and calculates the average values produced by both algorithms. We can see our algorithm generates fewer tunnels than the ordered-split algorithm. **Fig. 20** shows the average number of tunnels passed by all possible traffic in the network of 20 routers. The X-axis of **Fig. 20** is the number of requirements, and the Y-axis is the average number of tunnels passed by traffic. **Fig. 21** and **Fig. 22** show the comparison in the network 50 routers. In practice, a VPN of a business or an organization seldom has more than 50 routers. By observing every simulated case, we can see that our algorithm generates fewer tunnels and requires fewer computational costs than the ordered-split algorithm.

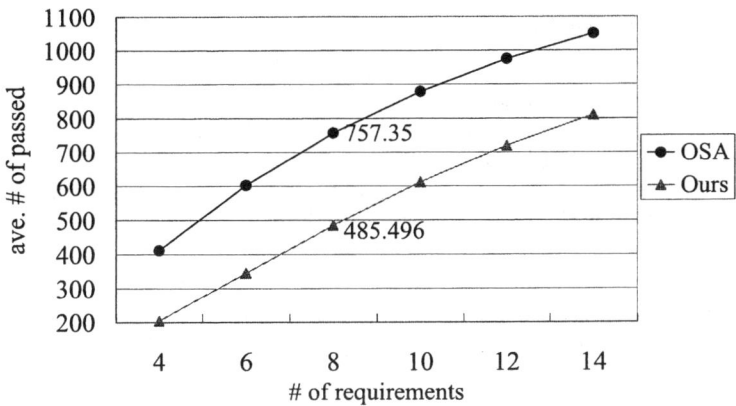

Fig. 20. The average number of tunnels passed by traffic in the network of 20 routers

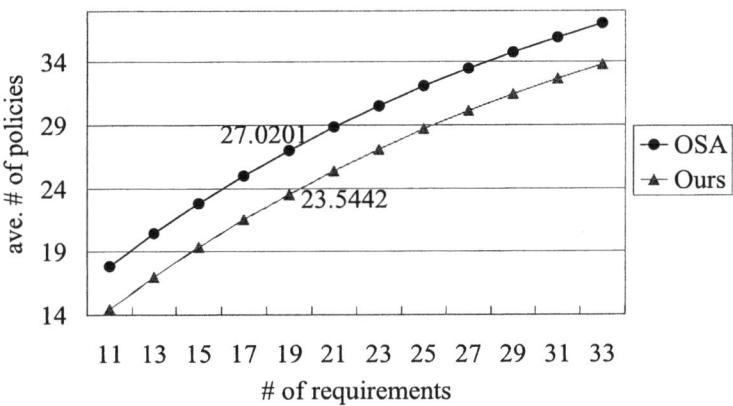

Fig. 21. The average numbers of policies in the network of 50 routers

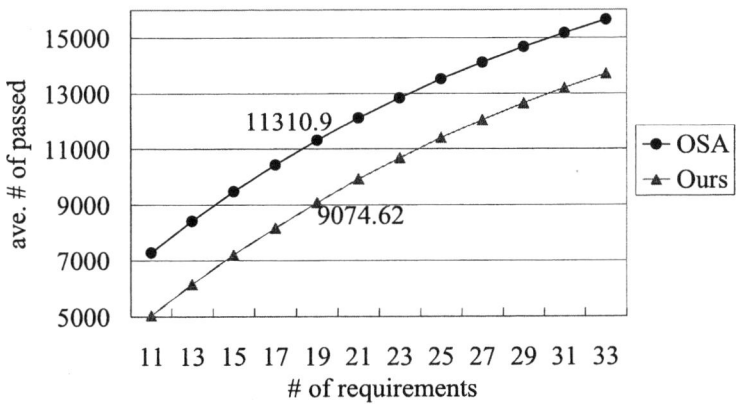

Fig. 22. The average number of tunnels passed by traffic in the network of 50 routers

6 Conclusions and Future Work

In this paper, we analyzed what situations would cause the policy conflicts. And we induced only two situations would cause conflicts. Then, we proposed an algorithm to automatically generate conflict-free policies and satisfy all the security requirements. Our algorithm generates fewer tunnels and save more computational power than other existing approaches in the literature. Our algorithm is "off-line," and there might be more improvement to speed up this algorithm. In the future, we can try to find a solution to resolve the policy conflict problem online. Besides, the delivery of policies is still a problem. If we have generated correct and efficient policies, how do we deliver them to each network node and configure them? Every security gateway, router, or network device may have different implementation of IPsec, and we need different ways to configure them. Therefore, it is our future work to develop a uniform interface of delivering and configuring policies.

References

1. Z. Fu, S. F. Wu, H. Huang, K. Loh, F. Gong, I. Baldine, and C. Xu, "IPsec/VPN Security Policy: Correctness, Conflict Detection, and Resolution," IEEE Policy 2001 Workshop, 2001.
2. Z. Fu and S. F. Wu, "Automatic Generation of IPsec/VPN Security Policies in an Intra-Domain Environment," 12th International Workshop on Distributed Systems: Operations & Management (DSOM 2001), 2001.
3. Y. Yang, C. U. Martel, and S. F. Wu, "On Building the Minimal Number of Tunnels - An Ordered-Split approach to manage IPsec/VPN policies," 9th IEEE/IFIP Network Operations and Management Symposium (NOMS 2004), April 2004.
4. W. Stallings, "Cryptography and Network Security: Principles and Practices," 3/e, Prentice Hall, 2002.
5. The IPsec-Tools Project, http://ipsec-tools.sourceforge.net/
6. S. Kent and R. Atkinson, "Security Architecture for the Internet Protocol," RFC 2401, Internet Society, Network Working Group, November 1998.
7. S. Kent and R. Atkinson, "IP Authentication Header," RFC 2402, Internet Society, Network Working Group, November 1998.
8. S. Kent and R. Atkinson, "IP Encapsulating Security Payload (ESP)," RFC 2406, Internet Society, Network Working Group, November. 1998.
9. D. Maughan, M. Schertler, M. Schneider, and J. Turner, "Internet Security Association and Key Management Protocol (ISAKMP)," RFC 2408, Internet Society, Network Working Group, November 1998.
10. J. Jason, L. Rafalow, E. Vyncke, "IPsec Configuration Policy Information Model," RFC 3585, Internet Society, Network Working Group, August 2003.
11. J. D. Moffett, "Requirements and Policies," Position paper for Policy Workshop 1999, November 1999.

A Framework Based Approach for Formal Modeling and Analysis of Multi-level Attacks in Computer Networks

Gerrit Rothmaier[1] and Heiko Krumm[2]

[1] Materna GmbH, Dortmund, Germany
gerrit.rothmaier@materna.de
[2] Universität Dortmund, Dortmund, Germany
krumm@cs.uni-dortmund.de

Abstract. Attacks on computer networks are moving away from simple vulnerability exploits. More sophisticated attack types combine and depend on aspects on multiple levels (e.g. protocol and network level). Furthermore attacker actions, regular protocol execution steps, and administrator actions may be interleaved. Analysis based on human reasoning and simulation only has a slim chance to reveal attack possibilities. Formal methods are in principle well-suited in this situation. Since complex scenarios have to be considered, however, high efforts are needed for modeling. Furthermore, automated analysis tools usually fail due to state space explosion. We propose a novel approach for modeling and analyzing such scenarios. It combines the high-level specification language cTLA with a computer network framework, optimization strategies, a translation tool, and the SPIN model checker. As a proof of feasibility we apply our approach to a multi-LAN scenario.

1 Introduction

Current trends [Ver04] show an increasing number of attacks. Especially attacks that are more sophisticated than just simple vulnerability exploitations are on the rise. Frequently, commonly deployed protocols and services are misused. This is facilitated by the fact that many basic protocols and services have long known security problems (cf. [Bel89]).

In the analysis of such attacks, multiple levels have to be considered simultaneously. For example, an attack on a routing protocol in a multi-LAN scenario may be feasible only with a specific update packet propagation. Propagation in turn depends on low level aspects like network topology and connectivity besides the protocol level flooding algorithm used. Furthermore, attacker position and administrator actions may matter as well. *Multi-level attacks* are attacks which combine and depend on aspects on multiple levels. Because of the complexity involved with simultaneously regarding multiple levels, manual analysis of such attack types is very difficult. Simulation techniques tend to provide good coverage only for very small systems. Thus the likelihood of finding potential attack sequences by means of simulation in a more extensive system is very low.

In this context we recognize the need for a suitable approach to formal modeling and automated analysis of complex attack types, especially multi-level attacks, in computer networks. We aim to learn about attack processes, their impacts on the network components and their inferences with network administration processes. This shall help to predict relevant attack scenarios and provide means for the clear description of attacks, advice and countermeasures.

For our network modeling and attack analysis we resort to formal techniques. We combine the flexible and modular specification technique *cTLA* [HK00] with the model checker *SPIN* [Hol03], which is currently one of the most powerful and elaborated automated process system verification tools. *cTLA* supports the efficient and structured description of broad models. Using *cTLA2PC*, our translation tool, the *cTLA* specifications are transformed to the more low level process system description language *Promela*, which is input to the automated model checker *SPIN*.

We successfully applied a preliminary version of our approach to the analysis of low-level *ARP* attacks and administrator actions in a single LAN scenario [RPK04]. When starting with larger and more complex examples we, however, experienced high model development efforts. Initial analysis runs showed serious state explosion effects exceeding given memory limits. Therefore we developed further enhancements of our approach with respect to two aspects: First, we developed a *cTLA*-based modeling framework. It defines suitable network model architecture principles and supplies corresponding re-usable model elements thus supporting the efficient development of models. Second, we investigated *SPIN*'s automated model evaluation procedure in order to develop model optimizations. *SPIN* performs model evaluation by means of the computation of the set of reachable system states. This corresponds to the execution of all possible system behavior steps. Thus *SPIN* executes the model, and suitable model optimization conceptions can be adopted from the field of efficient protocol implementation (cf. [Svo89]). In particular, activity thread approaches – coarsening the execution step granularity – and buffer management approaches – reducing the size of interface parameters – were applied. Furthermore, *cTLA2PC* has been optimized to produce *Promela* code with less possible execution traces and to save state components. After these refinements, the modeling and automated analysis of the example scenario described in this paper became possible.

This paper reports on our refined formal modeling and analysis approach. Its main focus is the presentation of the modeling framework and the model optimizations. Section 2 deals with related work. The modeling framework is described in section 3. Section 4 outlines the *cTLA* modeling language. Subsequently, as a proof of feasibility, a medium size example scenario is considered in section 5. Section 6 gives an overview of optimizations on different levels and describes the results of the automated scenario analysis with *SPIN*. Concluding remarks are given in section 7.

2 Related Work

Approaches for the formal analysis and verification of security properties can generally be structured in program and protocol verification. Program verification shall enhance the trustworthiness of software systems (e.g. [BR00]). Protocol verification shall detect vulnerabilities of cryptographic protocols (e.g. [Mea95]). In both fields, a variety of basic methods are applied including classic logic and algebraic calculi (e.g. [KK03]), special calculi (e.g. [BAN89]), and process system modeling techniques (e.g. [LBL99]). Moreover the approaches differ with respect to tool support. Many tools take advantage of existant more general analysis tools like *Prolog*, expert system shells, theorem provers, algebraic term rewriting systems, and reachability analysis based model checkers like *SPIN* (e.g. [RRC03]). Some powerful tools combine several analysis techniques [Mea96].

Formal modeling and analysis of network attack sequences combining aspects on different levels – e.g. protocol and network level – is a relatively new field. Ramakrishnan and Sekar [RS02] report on the analysis of vulnerabilities resulting from the combined behavior of system components. They consider a single host only, however. A process model is used which is specified in a *Prolog* variant. In the focus are simple security properties, expressed by labeling states safe and unsafe. A custom model checker built on top of a *Prolog* programming environment searches execution sequences which lead to unsafe states and correspond to vulnerability exploitations. Noel et al [NBR02] report on *topological vulnerability analysis*, i.e. checking networks of hosts for vulnerability combinations. A network is statically modeled by a set of tables representing hosts, predefined vulnerabilities, attacker access levels per host, and a connectivity matrix. The analysis investigates the possible combinations of the given vulnerabilities and their stepwise propagation in the network using *SMV* [Ber01]. Protocol level aspects, however, can only be modeled in a very limited way using symbolic constants in the connectivity matrix.

With respect to the simplification of models, our work is on the one hand related to techniques for efficient protocol implementation which were developed about 20 years ago in the course of the upcoming high-speed communication. In particular we learned from the activity thread implementation model which schedules activities of different protocol layers in common sequential control threads [Svo89], and from integrated layer processing which combines operations of different layers [AP93]. On the other hand, approaches for direct *SPIN* model reductions have to be mentioned. Particularly, Ruys [Ruy01] introduces low-level *SPIN*-specific optimizations. Partial order reductions, proposed by Alur et al. [ABH97], have a strong relationship to the activity thread implementation model providing the basis for the elimination of non-deterministic execution sequences.

3 Framework

Designing computer network specifications suitable for automated analysis is difficult. Particularly, the right abstraction level must be chosen. On the one hand, relevant details of a given scenario have to be captured. On the other hand, detailed models naturally have a very large state vector. Furthermore, the number of potential states grows exponentially with the state-vector size. Thus even a small addition to the model can lead to a prohibitive increase in the number of states. This effect is known as *state space explosion*. Automated analysis is rendered impossible because given time and memory constraints are quickly exceeded.

We aim to support the design process for computer network specifications in a way which fosters reuse of tried and tested abstractions and simplifies key design decisions. In the world of object-oriented programming patterns and frameworks are used for this task (cf. Gamma's definition in [GHJ95, pp. 26-27]). Thus we decided to carry over the framework concept to computer network specifications. While designing computer network specifications for different scenarios, we identified common architectural elements. These elements form the basis of the *cTLA* computer network modeling framework. It defines both basic structure, i.e. typical elements like nodes, interfaces and media with their coupling, and basic behavior, i.e. sending and receiving actions, of computer networks. A specific model has to add its own elements (e.g. *RIP* capable nodes), but the overall architecture is given by the framework.

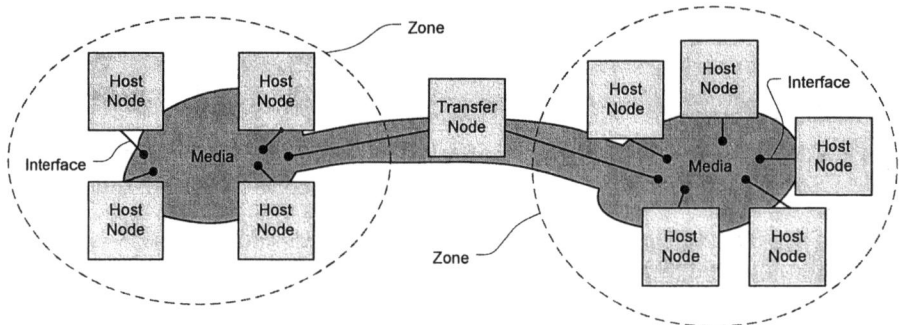

Fig. 1. Framework's large scale network view

3.1 Fundamentals

Our framework is based on the large scale view of computer networks exemplified by **Figure 1**. It shows two zones, each containing several nodes. The nodes inside a zone can directly communicate with any other node in the same zone. Zones can also be interpreted as network broadcast segments or subnets. All active network elements are modeled by *nodes*. Nodes communicate using *interfaces*. A node is said to belong to a zone if it has an interface in the zone. Interfaces transmit *packets* over *media*. Media is partitioned according to the zones. The two zones are connected by a *transfer node*. A *transfer node* is a special node with at least two interfaces in two different zones. It enables inter-zone communication. A node with just one interface is a *host node*.

On a small scale or node-oriented view packets are processed, sent and received through actions. Inside a node, the packet processing is structured into layers. A valid packet that is received from media by an interface is stored in the interface's receive buffer and then processed through the layers (action rpcs). A packet which shall be sent is processed (action spcs) the other way around, down the layers until it has reached the interface level. A node's snd and media's in actions respectively node's rcv and media's out actions are coupled. If media does not already contain a packet from the zone it can be sent (i.e. moved from the node's to media's packet buffer). The exact layer and address types used in a node vary depending on the specific node and scenario.

Most of today's computer networks employ the internet standard protocols. Thus our framework particularly supports *TCP/IP* based node types.

3.2 Architecture

An overview of the framework as a *UML* class diagram is depicted in **Figure 2**. The most current version of the framework's elements can be retrieved via our web site [Rot04].

According to the syntactical level of the elements, the framework is structured into the packages *Enumerations & Functions* (1), *Data Types* (2), and *Process Types* (3). The package *Enumerations & Functions* is used to define the network topology, initial address assignment and protocols desired for a model. For example, the enumeration ZoneIdT contains the model's zones, the function fSrcToIa assigns the initial addresses and the enumeration ProtocolT lists the required protocols.

The package *Data Types* contains common date types for interfaces, packets and buffers used throughout the framework. For instance, the type InterfaceT combines attributes of an interface, PacketT is used to represent a packet and PacketBufT defines a buffer for packets.

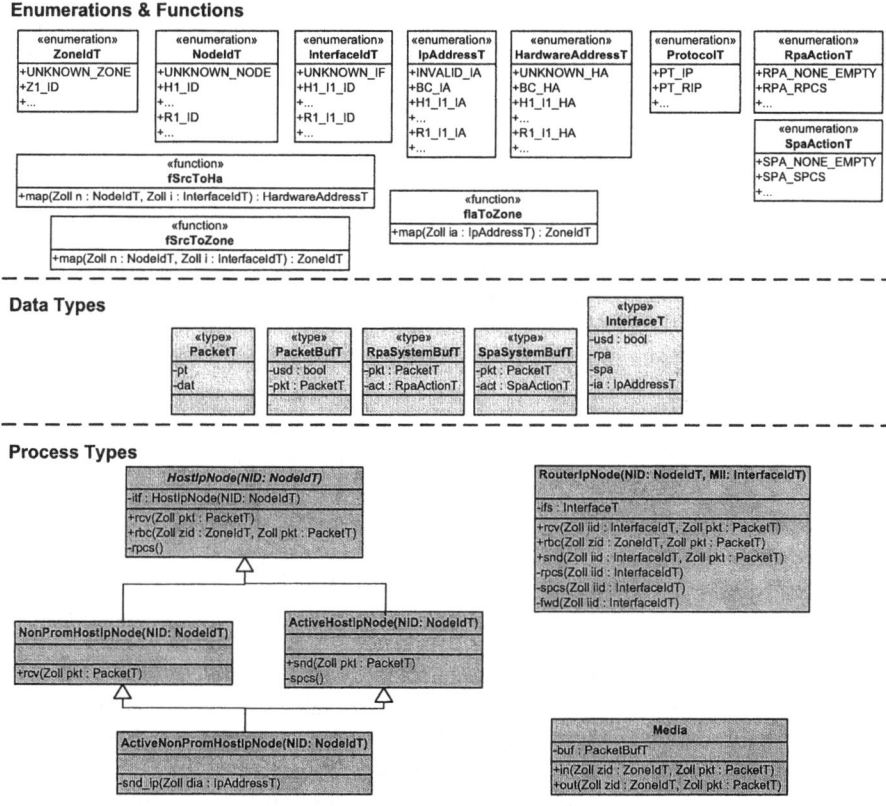

Fig. 2. Framework structure

Finally, the package *Process Types* provides process types media and nodes. For example process type RouterIpNode contains the behavior of a *IP* transfer node and

`HostIpNode` represents a *IP* host node. Through inheritance behavior is specialized. For example, `ActiveHostIpNode` adds behavior for the processing and sending of packets.

From a functional viewpoint framework elements of several packages usually collaborate to model a conception. For example, a scenario's network topology is modeled by several functions (e.g. `fSrcToZone`) and enumerations (e.g. `ZoneIdT`), together with appropriate handling by processes (e.g. `Media`, `HostIpNode`, `RouterIpNode`) and their actions (e.g. `out`, `rcv`).

Another example is packets and their processing. Packets are sent to and received from `Media` by nodes using interfaces. Interfaces are represented through the `InterfaceIdT` data type, their send and receive buffer's with the `PacketBufT` data type. Packets themselves are mapped to the `PacketT` data type. A packet's interpretation depends on its protocol type (`PacketT.pt`, `ProtocolT` enumeration). Packets currently in processing at a node are stored between layers using the `SystemBufT` data type. The processing actions are defined via the `ActionT` enumeration, usually depending on the protocol type. Similarly addressing depends on intertwined framework elements as well: functions (e.g. `fSrcToIa`), enumerations (e.g. `IpAddressT`), data types (e.g. `PacketT`) and node process types.

4 cTLA

Compositional TLA (cTLA) is based on Lamport's *temporal logic of actions (TLA)* [Lam94]. Explicit notions of modules, process types and composition of process types [HK00] are added, however. The following section gives a short overview of the *cTLA 2003* process types, a more detailed description is contained in [RK03].

The *simple process type* defines a state transition system directly. The state space is spanned by the local variables of the process type. For example, in `HostIpNode` the variable `itf` is a user defined record type containing the network interface's attributes. The set of initial states is defined by the *Init*-predicate (*cTLA* keyword `INIT`). The *actions*, keyword `ACTIONS`, directly constitute the *next-state relation*. Syntactically, actions are predicates over state variables (referring to the current state, e.g. v), so-called primed state variables (referring to the successor state, e.g. v'), and action parameters. Parameters support the communication between processes.

An internal action defines a set of state transitions in exactly the same way as a normal action. Internal actions, however, cannot be coupled with actions of other processes. Thus in the composed system each internal action is accompanied by stuttering steps of all other system components.

A *process extension type* (keyword `EXTENDS`) specializes or augments other process types. This resembles inheritance in object-oriented programming. For example, the `ActiveHostIpNode` process type uses this mechanism to add the action `snd` to `HostIpNode`. The state space is spanned by the vector of all state variables of the extended processes plus extra state variables defined by the extending process. *Init*-predicates and actions are merged through logical conjunction.

The *process composition type* describes systems which are composed from subsystems (keyword `CONTAINS`). These subsystems may in turn be further subsystems or sets of process instances. For example, the system process IpMultiLevelExample of the example scenario is defined using process composition. Its actions are conjunctions of contained processes' actions which have to be performed jointly in order to realize an action of the system. Each process can contribute to a system action by at most one process action. If a process does not contribute to a system action, it performs a *stuttering step*. In *cTLA 2003* [RK03] process stuttering steps do not have to be explicitly listed on the right hand side of system actions.

The state transition system which models an instance of a process composition type is defined indirectly. The state space of the composed process is spanned by the vector of all state variables of the contained processes. Its *Init*-predicate is the conjunction of the *Init*-predicates of the contained processes. The *next-state relation* is the disjunction of the system actions defined in the composing process itself.

The *TLA* formula describing a *cTLA* process system is equivalent to a conjunction of the process formulas and consequently a system implies its constituents.

5 Example Scenario

To demonstrate the feasibility of our approach, we describe the formal modeling and analysis of an example scenario. It consists of multiple hosts in different LANs which are interconnected by routers as depicted in **Figure 3**. In particular, the routers R1, R2, R3 are connected in a triangle fashion forming an internal backbone. We aim to model and analyze this scenario for attack sequences along the lines of the routing and tunneling protocol attack ideas described at the Blackhat Europe Conference [BHE01]. All hosts are *TCP/IP* nodes. The routers additionally run *RIP*, which is still one of the most widely used *interior gateway* routing protocols.

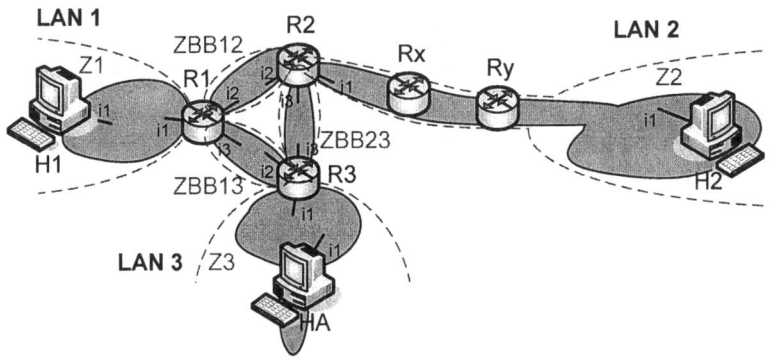

Fig. 3. Example scenario

5.1 Protocol Modeling

The *TCP/IP* modeling is inherited from the framework's HostIpNode and RouterIpNode process types. So it suffices to implement *RIP* handling with a new process type. RipRouterIpNode extends process type RouterIpNode – which can only statically route – with actions for handling *RIP* updates and updating the routing table dynamically.

We only give a short overview of *RIP* here, a more detailed description is given by Perlman [Per00]. Each router uses a *routing information base (RIB)* to store entries of the form (dst, nho, itf, met). The field dst contains the final destination and nho the *IP* address of the *next-hop*, i.e. the next router on the way to the destination. If the current router is directly connected to the final destination's network, this field contains a special value (NHO_DIRECT in our modeling). The itf field contains the interface connected to the next-hop or the final destination's network. The met field is used for storing a *cost metric*, usually the number of *hops*, from the current router to the final destination. A metric of 1 denotes that the current router is directly connected to the final destination's network. On the other hand, a metric of 16 := MET_INF means infinite cost.

RIP works with two stages, *input processing* and *output processing*. Input processing handles received *RIP* update packets. The critical element of a *RIP update packet* is the pair (dst', met'). A *RIP* update packet may contain several such pairs. For our modeling, however, without loss of generality, we assume that all update packets contain only one pair. The fields describe the best route (in terms of metric) to the destination as known by the router from which the packet originated. If the update packet passes basic sanity checks the packet is considered for updating the router's *RIB*. Usually the *RIB* will only be updated if the update packet's metric is better than the existing metric. A packet from the *next-hop* of an already existing route, however, is allowed to update the *RIB* even if the new metric is worse.

If a *RIB* entry has been changed (no matter which case applied), its *route change flag* is set. *Output processing* will then send a *triggered update*. We only model triggered updates, because regular updates are mainly useful for debugging purposes.

All updates are sent observing the *split horizon* principle. That means the updates are sent to all neighboring routers with the exception of the router from which this route was received (i.e. the *next-hop* nho).

5.2 Network and System Modeling

We compose our system model using the framework's basic process types (e.g. Media) and the specific process types required for the example scenario (e.g. RipRouterIpNode). To simplify our modeling, the "straight through" routers Rx and Ry are not represented by RipRouterIpNode instances. We just represent them in the metric of the others routers. Furthermore, we select fixed host roles. HA models the attacker host, H1 is the victim and H2 its intended communication partner. The attacker HA is modeled by type RipAttackerHostIpNode which extends ActiveHostIpNode with the ability to create and send fake *RIP* update packets. ActiveHostIpNode is a basic *TCP/IP* processing node from the framework based on HostIpNode. The victim (H1) is represented by type ActiveNonPromHostIpNode and H2 by NonPromHostIpNode type, both directly from the framework.

For each analysis run, we pick fixed locations for HA, H1, and H2. For example, the attacker, HA, is located in LAN 3, the victim, H1, is placed in LAN1 and H1's communication partner, host H2, is a member of LAN 2 (cf. **Figure 3**).

We label each node's interfaces (e.g. i1, i2, i3) and define the assigned *IP* addresses. For each router, the initial routing tables have to be defined. For example, R1 is directly connected (i.e. metric 1) to zones ZBB12 and ZBB13 over interfaces 2 respectively 3. The route to Z2 is given indirectly via next-hop R2 (interface 2) with metric 4 (i.e. R1, R2, Rx, Ry). We start with fully initialized routing tables. Finally, the *cTLA* modeling is completed with the definition of the system process type `Ip-MultiLevelExample`.

We still have to define the security property to be analyzed. *Promela* includes `assert` statements for the *SPIN* model checker. For simplicity, we check the following confidentiality property: `assert( (ha_itf.rpa.pkt.dat_ida == HA_I1_IA) );`

It expresses that host HA only receives packets which are destined for it. After translation of the scenario model to *Promela* with *cTLA2PC*, this assertion has to be inserted into the *Promela* representation of the `rcv_ha` action (i.e. host HA's non broadcast packet receive action). Broadcast packets can not trigger the assertion, because they are received by the `rbc` action instead of `rcv_ha`.

6 Optimizations and Analysis Results

After translation to Promela the example system had an initial state vector size of about 630 bytes. That was still too large for successful analysis. In *SPIN*'s full state-space search verification modes memory limits were exceeded quickly. Approximative verification modes did not produce any result in reasonable time. Thus we developed further optimization strategies.

6.1 Optimizations

Optimizations are generally feasible on several levels: Scenario level (1), *cTLA* level (2), *Promela* level (3), and on the verifier level through special *SPIN* verification options (4).

At the scenario level, abstractions are often most helpful. As described in section 5, fixed roles and attacker positions may suffice for each analysis run. Furthermore it may be possible to simplify the modeled protocols (e.g. by allowing only one update pair in each update packet). Such high-level optimizations often yield state space savings even before the specification design is started.

Regarding the second point, the modeling may be optimized at the *cTLA* level. For example, we are able to represent the nodes using fewer buffers and actions per layer with a smarter approach. Our framework's node modeling follows the *activity thread* approach known from efficient protocol implementation [Svo89]. Actions and working buffers of different layers which process the same packet can be combined. This approach requires less state space than a naive layer-by-layer modeling. Because of the framework, this *cTLA* level optimization is inherited by our modeling as well. At this stage, the example scenario modeling has the afore-mentioned state vector of about 630 bytes. This is our starting point for further optimizations.

Action parameters can be optimized on the *cTLA* level, too. First, an equivalent flat system, which contains only a system process and system actions has to be generated. This expansion can be done with the *cTLA2PC* tool. Generally, *cTLA* action parameters correspond to existentially quantified variables. But in the flat system, for most action parameters value determining equalities exist. This is due to the fact that all system actions are coupled process actions. Input parameters of one underlying action are output parameters of another. Therefore, it is possible to replace these input parameters with the corresponding symbolic output value. This *"paramodulated"* *cTLA* version usually leads to a noticeable smaller state vector. For example, the example scenario after this step has a state-vector of about 580 bytes.

To enable model checking with *SPIN*, we translate the *cTLA* specification to *Promela* using the *cTLA2PC* tool. Thus we can optimize our scenario modeling at the *Promela* level as well. A comprehensive summary of low-level *Promela/SPIN* optimizations is described by Ruys [Ruy01]. For instance, *SPIN's* built-in bit-arrays should be avoided. Mapping bit-arrays into bytes using macros decreases the required state space for such variables up to a factor of eight. *cTLA2PC* supports several such optimizations through specific switches during the translation process. With these optimizations the state-vector for our scenario decreases to about 320 bytes.

Furthermore, we acquire extra information from the *cTLA* origin of the *Promela* model. Thus more advanced optimizations are possible. From the *cTLA* specification we have a structuring of the model into parametrized system actions. The execution of these actions can be arbitrarily interleaved, but each action is atomic. So a single *Promela* process embedding all actions in a non-deterministic do-loop suffices. Because *cTLA* actions are deterministic, each action is embraced by the *Promela* d_step keyword. This optimization does not improve the state-vector, but reduces the required search depth for a specific sequence.

For the action parameters, we at first used *input generator processes*. For each parameter type input generator processes according to the maximum multiplicity of the parameter are needed. Each input generator sets a matching global variable to a random value. Because a model checker has to take each potential execution path into account, all possible parameter values are covered. The input generator approach works fine, but so far automated analysis efforts of the scenario described in this paper failed. We estimated that an attack sequence for the scenario would require about 32 steps, including about 10 *input generator steps* (i.e. value settings). But test runs of our model showed that *SPIN* exceeded 3 GB of memory (i.e. the practical x86 per process memory limit) after reaching search depth 23.

Thus we invented a totally different approach to handle parametrized actions. No input generators and no parameter variables are used. Instead, all parametrized actions are completely "unrolled". This means that each parametrized action is replaced by copies with fixed parameters for all possible parameter values. Because all variable types in *cTLA* (and in finite-state specification languages) are finite, this is accomplishable.

Of course, the *unroll approach* leads to a lengthy *Promela* level specification, but *SPIN* copes much better with such a specification than with a specification using the input generator approach. The size of the state-vector is not reduced very much, but the number of processes, actual transitions and the search depth required for a specific sequence are distinctly smaller, because no input generator steps exist.

Finally, *SPIN* supports different options during verification. For example, different *verification modes* (i.e. full state space search, approximative bit-state hashing) and state-vector representation schemes (i.e. compression, graph encoding) are available.

In our experience, these options offer only modest improvements relative to the default settings and each other. Thus most of the time the feasibility of automated analysis does not depend on the right choice of *SPIN* options, but much more on careful optimizations of the modeling.

6.2 Results

Following the optimizations described above we were able to reduce the state-vector for the example scenario to about 50% of its initial size (316 vs 630 bytes). Because input generator steps are no longer needed (unroll optimization), the depth required for a specific sequence is reduced as well.

Automated analysis of a scenario with *SPIN* requires that properties which shall not be violated (i.e. invariants) are included in the *Promela* specification. Then, *SPIN* can check if a sequence leading to a violation of such a property exists. The violation is saved to a trail file. Using *SPIN*'s guided simulation feature this trail file can be expanded to the sequence of executed *Promela* statements. A special feature of *cTLA2PC* (option --trace-points) helps to map the *Promela* statements back to actions in the original model.

```
pan: assertion violated (ha_itf.rpa.pkt.dat_ida==11) (at depth
  21)
pan: wrote ip-multilevel-example-veri-flat-para.promela.trail
(SPIN Version 4.2.0 -- 27 June 2004)
[...]
State-vector 316 byte, depth reached 21, errors: 1
5.5768e+06 states, stored
5.5768e+06 nominal states (stored-atomic)
4.28228e+08 states, matched
4.33804e+08 transitions (= stored+matched)
[...]
```

Listing 1. SPIN verifier output (assertion violated!)

We analyzed the described modeling for assertion violations using *SPIN* on a standard PC system. After about 40min and requiring slightly under 1 GB of RAM *SPIN* found an attack sequence of depth 21 (cf. **Listing 1**) violating the specified confidentiality property.

Using *SPIN*'s guided simulation feature and mapping of the results back to *cTLA* actions identified the attack sequence depicted in **Figure 4** (slightly simplified for clarity). The discovered attack sequence corresponds nicely with the routing and tunneling protocol attack ideas from the Blackhat Europe Conference [BHE01]. In a nutshell, after system initialization the host H1 submits a packet destined for host H2 to its router R1. Then, the attacker HA broadcasts a *RIP* update packet advertising a new route to zone Z2 with metric 1 from HA. This packet is then accepted and processed by router R3, which updates its routing table (new route to Z2 via HA has metric 2 = HA's metric + 1, existing route via R2 has metric 4) and prepares triggered *RIP* updates to the other zones (without the originating zone because of the *split horizon* principle). R3 then broadcasts the triggered update packet to zone ZBB13. R1 receives and processes the packet and updates its routing table (the new route to Z2 with metric 3 via R3 is better than the existing route with metric 3 via R2). Then R1 forwards the packet from H1 according to the changed table (next-hop R3) and sends it. R3 receives the packet and forwards it to its next-hop, the attacker, HA. Thus HA receives a packet from H1 to H2, violating the assertion.

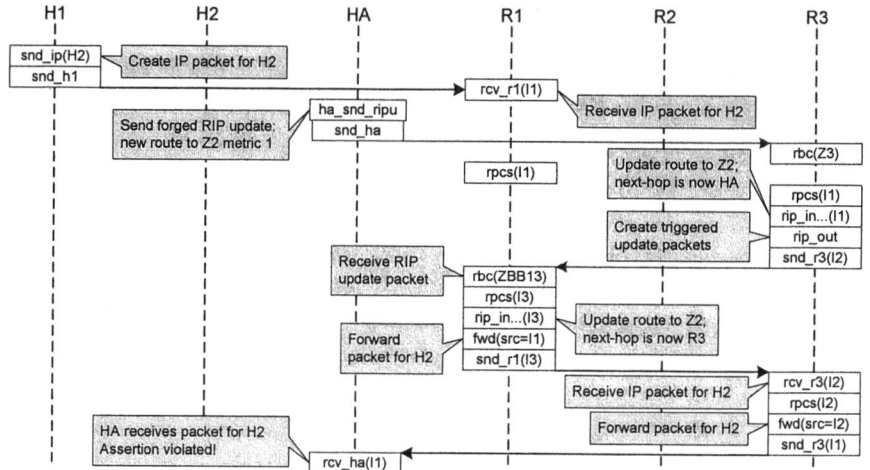

Fig. 4. Attack sequence found by SPIN

Attack sequences depend on the attacker position, update propagation, and initial routing tables which in turn depend on low-level network topology aspects. For example, an attack sequence like the one shown in **Figure 4** is not possible if H2 is connected directly to R2. First, the initial routing tables have other metrics. Second, the metric of the forged *RIP* update packet from HA is increased by each router on its way to R3. Thus the new route would not be better than the existing route, and R3's routing table would not be updated.

Because of the breadth first search the described sequence is minimal. Thus only necessary steps are included. Further variants are possible. For example, R3 will usually broadcast the triggered update packet to R2 as well. Because this step is not required for the violation of the stated confidentiality property, it is not included in the 21 step sequence.

Practical tools to facilitate attacks on routing protocols are widely available, e.g. [FX01]. More secure protocols (e.g. *S-RIP* [WKO04]) have been suggested but are rarely deployed. Widespread deployment is hindered by the usually required computationally expensive cryptographic operations. Furthermore, interoperability is a key requirement in heterogeneous networks but standardization of new protocols is a lengthy process.

7 Concluding Remarks

Attack types combining and depending on aspects on multiple levels, especially protocol and network levels, form an interesting class of advanced network attack types.

They can be modeled and analyzed by means of formal process systems. The presented approach combines the high level specification language *cTLA* with a modeling framework, a translator tool *(cTLA2PC)*, model optimization strategies, and the well-known model checker *SPIN*. Our results show that the analysis of practically relevant attack types in medium size scenarios is feasible.

Current work aims to a further enhancement of our approach which shall eventually enable the automated prediction of new network attack strategies. For that purpose framework extensions and additional model optimization strategies are under development. Moreover, model development and analysis experimentation will be supported by a workbench assembling the tool set. Another interesting aspect to be studied further is the integration of logical deduction-based analysis procedures which can exploit *TLA*'s symbolic logic proof techniques.

References

[AP93] M. Abbott, L. Peterson: *Increasing network throughput by integrating protocol layers*. IEEE/ACM Transactions on Networking, 1 (1993) 600–610.

[ABH97] R. Alur, R.K. Brayton, T.A. Henzinger, S. Qadeer, S.K. Rajamani: *Partial order reduction in symbolic state space exploration*. In Proc. of CAV 97: Computer-Aided Verification, LNCS 1254, pp. 340-351. Springer-Verlag, 1997.

[BR00] M. Balser, W. Reif et al.: *Formal System Development with KIV*. In: T. Maibaum (ed.), Fundamental Approaches to Software Engineering. Springer LNCS 1783, 2000.

[Bel89] S. M. Bellovin: *Security Problems in the TCP/IP Protocol Suite*. Computer Communication Review, Vol. 19, No. 2, pp. 32-48, 1989.

[Ber01] S. Berezin: *The SMV web site*. URL: http://www.cs.cmu.edu/~modelcheck/smv.html/, 1999.

[BHE01] Blackhat Europe Conference: *Routing and Tunneling Protocol Attacks*, URL: http://www.blackhat.com/html/bh-europe-01/bh-europe-01-speakers.html#FX, 2001.

[BAN89] M. Burrows, M. Abadi, R. Needham: *A Logic of Authentication*. In: Proceedings of the Royal Society, Volume 426, Number 1871, 1989, and in: William Stallings, Practical Cryptography for Data Internetworks, IEEE Computer Society Press, 1996.

[CM88] K.M. Chandy, J.Misra: *Parallel Program Design* - A Foundation, Addison-Wesley, Reading, 1988.

[FX01] FX of Phenoelit: *Internet Routing Protocol Attack Suite*, URL: http://www.phenoelit.de/irpas, 2001.

[GHJ95] E. Gamma, R. Helms, R. Johnson et al: *Design Patterns: Elements of Reusable Object-Oriented Software*. Addison-Wesley, 1995.

[HK00] P. Herrmann, H. Krumm: *A framework for modeling transfer protocols*. Computer Networks, 34(2000)317-337.

[Hol03] G. J. Holzmann: *The SPIN model checker*. Addison Wesley, 2003.

[KK03] K. Kawauchi, S. Kitazawa et al.: *A Vulnerability Assessment Tool Using First-Order Predicate Logic*. IPSJ SIGNotes Computer SECurity No.019 (2003)

[Lam94] L. Lamport: *The temporal logic of actions*, ACM Trans. Prog. Lang. and Sys. 16 (1994) 872-923.

[LBL99] G. Leduc, O. Bonaventure, L. Leonard et al: *Model-based verification of a security protocol for conditional access to services*. Formal Methods in System Design, Kluwer Academic Publishers, vol.14, no.2, March 1999 p.171-91.

[Mea95] C. Meadows: *Formal Verification of Cryptographic Protocols: A Survey*. In: Proc. Asiacrypt, Int. Conf. on Theory and Application of Cryptology, LNCS, Springer-Verlag, 1995.

[Mea96] C. Meadows: *The NRL Protocol Analyzer: An Overview*. Journal of Logic Programming, 26, 2 (1996) pp. 113-131.

[NB02] S. Noel, B. O' Berry, R. Ritchey: *Representing TCP/IP connectivity for topological analysis of network security*. Computer Society, IEEE (ed.), Proc. of the 18th Annual Computer Security Applications Conference, Dec. 2002, p. 25-31.

[Per00] R. Perlman: *Interconnections*. 2nd Edition, Addison-Wesley, 2000.

[RRC03] P. Romano, M. Romero, B. Ciciani, F. Quaglia: Validation *of the Sessionless Mode of the HTTPR Protocol*. Proc. of IFIP 23rd International Conference on Formal Techniques for Networked and Distributed Systems (FORTE'03), LNCS 2767, Springer-Verlag 2003.

[RS02] C. Ramakrishnan, R. Sekar: *Model-Based Analysis of Configuration Vulnerabilities*. Journal of Computer Security, Vol. 10, Nr. 1, Jan. 2002, p. 189-209.

[RK03] G. Rothmaier, H. Krumm: *cTLA 2003 Description*. Internal Technical Report, URL: http://ls4-www.cs.uni-dortmund.de/RVS/MA/hk/cTLA2003description.pdf, 2003.

[RPK04] G. Rothmaier, A. Pohl, H. Krumm: *Analyzing Network Management Effects with SPIN and cTLA*. Proc. of IFIP 18th World Computer Congress, TC11 19th International Information Security Conference, pp. 65-81, 2004.

[Rot04] G. Rothmaier: *cTLA Computer Network Specification Framework*. Internal Report. URL: http://www4.cs.uni-dortmund.de/RVS/MA/hk/framework.html

[Ruy01] T. C. Ruys: *Towards Effective Model Checking*. PhD Thesis, Univ. Twente, 2001.

[Svo89] L. Svobodova: *Implementing OSI Systems*. IEEE Journal on Selected Areas in Communications 7 (1989), pp.1115–1130, 1989.

[Ver04] Verisign: *Internet Security Intelligence Briefing / November 2004 / Vol. 2 / Issue II*. URL: http://www.verisign.com/ Resources/Intelligence_and_Control_Services_White_Papers/internet-security-briefing.html

[WKO04] T. Wan, E. Kranakis, P.C. van Oorschot: *S-RIP: A Secure Distance Vector Routing Protocol*. In Proc. of Applied Cryptography and Network Security (ACNS'04), Yellow Mountain, China, 2004.

Model Checking for Timed Statecharts

Junyan Qian[1,2] and Baowen Xu[1]

[1] Department of Computer Science and Engineering,
Southeast University, Nanjing 210096, China
http://cse.seu.edu.cn/people/bwxu/
[2] Department of Computer Science and Technology,
Guilin University of Electronic Technology, Guilin 541004, China
qjy@gliet.edu.cn, bwxu@seu.edu.cn

Abstract. Timed Statecharts, which can efficiently specify explicit dense time, is an extension to the visual specification language Statecharts with real-time constructs. We give a definition of timed Statecharts that specifies explicit temporal behavior as timed automata does. It is very difficult to verify directly whether timed Statecharts satisfies the required properties. However, by compiling it into timed automata, timed Statecharts may be checked using UPPAAL tool. In the paper, the state of timed Statecharts is represented by inductive term, and a step semantics of timed Statecharts is briefly described. The translation rules are shown by a compositional approach for formalizing the timed Statecharts semantics directly on sequences of micro steps. Timed automata corresponding to timed Statecharts was also discussed.

1 Introduction

Statecharts [1] is a visual language for specifying the behavior of complex reactive system. The formalism extends traditional finite state machines with notions of hierarchy, concurrency, and priority. In short, one can say: Statecharts = state-diagrams + depth + orthogonality + broadcast-communication. Now there also exists many related specification formalisms such as Modecharts [2] and RSML [3]. Statecharts is the most important UML component specifying complex reactive system such as communication protocol and digital control unit.

Statecharts, a synchronous visual modeling language, adopts *fictitious clock model* that only requires the sequence of integer times to be non-decreasing. All components are driven by common global clocks, called *tick* clock. However, it is not sufficient to specify time-critical systems with fictitious clock. Statecharts has to face the problems that it can't specify the required temporal behavior as timed automata does. In order to efficiently specify explicit dense time, Statecharts is extended with real-time constructs, including clocks, timed guards and invariants. The advantages of modeling complex reactive behavior with Statecharts are combined with the advantages of specifying temporal behavior with timed automata, resulting in the real-time extension of Statecharts; we call it *timed Statecharts*.

Model checking [4] is an automatic technique for verifying finite state reactive systems. In order to verify whether a timed Statecharts model satisfies the required properties, we present a model checking algorithm for timed Statecharts. Just as verifying

Statecharts, we first flat timed Statecharts and then apply a model checking tool to verify the resulting model. The translation rules that compile timed Statecharts into an equivalence timed automata are discussed by a compositional approach which formalizes the timed Statecharts semantics directly on sequences of micro steps and describes parallel behavior by process algebra.

Relate work. In the past two decades, model checking, which was first introduced for ordinary finite-state machines in Clarke and Emerson [5], has emerged as a promising and powerful approach to fully automatic verification of systems. Given a state transition system and a property, model checking algorithms exhaustively explore the state space to determine whether the system satisfies the property. The result is either a claim that the property is true or else a counterexample failing to the property.

It was very successful for the Statecharts language to specify reactive systems by its intuitive syntax and semantics. Since the original formalism of Harel, the theory of Statecharts has been under an extensive research and many different semantic approaches evolved from the academic world [6][7][8][9][10][11]. But for timed Statecharts, only hierarchical timed automata with an operational semantic to analyze timed Statecharts was discussed in [18][19].

Extended Hierarchical Automata, as the structural basis of Statecharts semantics, were introduced in [12] for Statemate and in [13] for UML. It translates Statecharts into PROMELA that is the input language of the SPIN model checker to perform the verification. Gnesi [14] uses a formal operational semantics for building a labeled transition system which is then used as a model to be checked against correctness requirements expressed in the action based temporal logics ACTL. In their reference verification environment JACK, automata are represented in a standard format, which facilitates the use of different tools for automatic verification. Pap [15] describes methods and tools for automated safety analysis of UML Statecharts specifications. Chan [16] and Schmidt [17] also contribute to mode checking for Statecharts. David [18] gives a formal verification of UML Statecharts with real-time extensions using hierarchical timed automata, while our method is to translate directly timed Statecharts to flat timed automata that can be used in UPPAAL.

The remainder of this paper is organized as follows. The next section introduces timed automata and its operational semantics, and section 3 defines timed Statecharts and its terms. Section 4 formulates a step semantics. Section 5 formalizes our compositional semantics and gives our translation rules from timed Statecharts to timed automata. Finally, section 6 provides our conclusions.

2 Timed Automata

Timed automaton [20] is an extended automaton to model the behavior of real time system over time. We consider a variant of timed automata without accepting states. The next subsection gives the operational semantics of the automata.

DEFINITION 1. (Clock) A clock is a variable ranging over R^+, the set of non-negative real numbers.

Let C be a finite set of variables called clocks. A clock valuation is a function that assigns a non-negative real-value to every clock. The set of valuations of C, denoted

V_C, is the set $[C \rightarrow R^+]$ of total mappings from C to R^+. Let $v \in V_C$ and $t \in R^+$, the clock valuation $v+t$ denotes that every clock is increased by t with respect to valuation v. It is defined by $(v+t)x=v(x)+t$ for every clock $x \in C$.

DEFINITION 2. (Clock constraints) For set C of clocks with $x, y \in C$, the set Ψ_C of clock constraints over C is defined by

$$\delta ::= x \prec c \mid x - y \prec c \mid \neg \delta \mid (\delta \wedge \delta)$$

where $c \in R^+$ and $\prec \in \{<, \leq\}$

Clock constraints are evaluated over clock valuations. For $x, y \in C$, $v \in V_C$ and let $\alpha, \beta \in \Psi_C$ we have

- $v \models x \prec c$ iff $v(x) \prec c$
- $v \models x - y \prec c$ iff $v(x) - v(y) \prec c$
- $v \models \neg \alpha$ iff $v \not\models \alpha$
- $v \models \alpha \wedge \beta$ iff $v \models \alpha$ and $v \models \beta$

DEFINITION 3. (Timed automaton) A timed automaton is a tuple TA = $(S, C, s_0, L, Inv, \rightarrow)$ where: S is a finite set of states, C a finite set of time clocks, $s_0 \in S$ an initial state, L a set of labels, $Inv: S \rightarrow \Psi_C$ a function that associates a timing constraint to each state, called state invariant, $\rightarrow \in S \times (L \times \Psi_C \times 2^C \times \{\text{true, false}\}) \times S$ a set of transitions, where a transition $t=(s, e, g, r, u, s')$ connects a source state s and a target state s' with label e, timing constraint guard g, clock resets r and urgency flag u.

The function Inv associates a time constraint to each state $s \in S$, i.e., the automaton can stay in the state only while the current time clock valuation satisfies $Inv(s)$. The state invariant forces the automaton to translate before it becomes **false**, so that it avoids the automaton to get stuck at the state s. when the time constraint g associated to the edge is satisfied by current values of time clocks, the automaton may perform a translation.

The transition system underlying timed automaton TA, denoted $\mathcal{M}(TA)$, be defined as $(Q, q_0, \rightarrow)$ where:

- $Q = \{(s, v) \in S \times V_C \mid v \models Inv(s)\}$;
- $q_0 = (s_0, v_0)$ where $v_0(x)=0$ for $x \in C$;
- The transition relation of timed automaton $t \in Q \times (L \times \Psi_C \times 2^C \times \{\text{true, false}\}) \times Q$, which describes how to evolve from one state to another, is defined by the following rules:

  - $(s_i, v) \xrightarrow{*} (s_j, \text{reset } R \text{ in } v)$ if the following conditions hold:
    i. $t = \langle s_i, E, A, G, R, u, j \rangle$;
    ii. E are satisfied;
    iii. $v \models G$;
    iv. $(\text{reset } R \text{ in } v) \models Inv(s_j)$;

  - $(s_i, v) \xrightarrow{d} (s_i, v+d)$, for positive real d, if the following condition holds:
    i. $\forall d' \leq d, v+d' \models Inv(s_i)$;
    ii. $\neg \textbf{urgent}(t)$, the urgency flag of transition $\hat{t}$ is **false**.

where clock valuation **reset R in** v, valuation v with clock x reset, is define by:

$$(\textbf{reset } x \textbf{ in } v)(y) = \begin{cases} v(y) & \text{if } x \neq y \\ 0 & \text{if } x = 0 \end{cases}$$

3 Timed Statecharts

In this section we firstly define the formal syntax of timed Statecharts and give a simple example of a timed Statecharts, and then represent timed Statecharts state not visually but by terms. A timed Statecharts is in fact a Statecharts equipped with a set of real-valued clocks. Clocks are used to precisely measure the elapse of time between events.

3.1 Timed Statecharts Definition

DEFINITION 4. (Time Statecharts) A timed Statecharts is an eight tuple TS=($\mathcal{N}$, $\mathcal{N}_0$, σ, type, C, I, $\mathcal{L}$, T), where:

1. a finite set $\mathcal{N}$ of states.
2. a subset $\mathcal{N}_0 \subseteq \mathcal{N}$ of initial states.
3. $\sigma: \mathcal{N} \rightarrow 2^{\mathcal{N}}$, $\sigma(n)$ gives the sub-states of n which are called sons of n, σ defines a tree structure.
4. type: $\mathcal{N} \rightarrow \{\text{AND, OR, BASIC}\}$ is the type function.
5. a finite set C of clocks.
6. $Inv: \mathcal{N} \rightarrow \Psi_C$, a function that assigns to each state an invariant.
7. A set of transition labels $\mathcal{L}$, partitioned into two disjoint sets $\mathcal{L} = L_T \cup L_E$, where $L_T \subseteq \Psi_C \times 2^C \times \mathcal{U}$ represents a set of clock constraints label, where $\mathcal{U} = \{\textbf{true}, \textbf{false}\}$ is a set of urgency flag; and $L_E \subseteq Event \times Cond \times Action$ a set of unclock constraints label, where $Event$ is a set of event, $Cond$ a set of condition, $Action$ a set of action..
8. $T \subseteq \mathcal{N} \times \mathcal{L} \times \mathcal{N}$ is a set of transition relation, where a transition $t=(n, e, c, a, g, r, u, n')$ connects two states n and n', and have a source state n, a target state n', a event e, a condition c, a action a, a guard g, an clock resets r and an urgency flag u.
   Properties of σ which assure the well-formed tree structure are:
   - disjoint super-states: if $n \neq n'$ then $\sigma(n) \cap \sigma(n') = \emptyset$;
   - no recursion: if $n' \in \sigma^*(n)$ then $n \notin \sigma(n')$;
   - $root$ has no ancestor: $\forall n \in \mathcal{N}, root \notin \sigma(n)$;
   - basic nodes are empty: type(n)=BASIC $\Leftrightarrow \sigma(n) = \emptyset$;
   - sub-states of AND are not BASIC: type(n)=AND $\wedge$ $n_1 \in \sigma(n) \Rightarrow \sigma(n_1) \neq \emptyset$;
   - if type(n)=AND then there is no $n_1 \rightarrow n_2$ for all $n_1, n_2 \in \sigma(n)$;

A traditional Statecharts models the system as being in a number of states that describe its operations. A state can be considered a point in the computation. States are denoted by rectangles with rounded corners and transitions as arrows. A state can be BASIC, AND or OR. If a state is BASIC, it has no sub-states, called BASIC-state. An OR-state has sub-states and exactly one of them is active at a certain point of time.

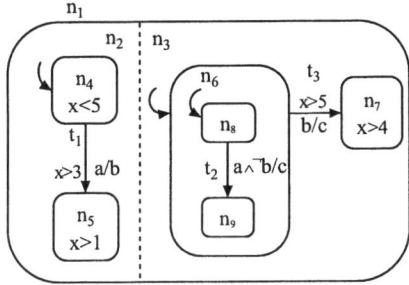 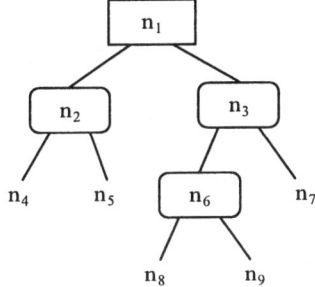

Fig. 1. A simple example of a timed Statecharts   **Fig. 2.** A state hierarchical structure

An AND-state has OR sub-states, and all of them are active if the parent state is active.

Figure 1 shows a simple example of a timed Statecharts. The state labeled n_1 is split into two concurrent sub-states n_2 and n_3 by the dashed line through its middle. n_1 is called an AND-state because it has these orthogonal components. n_2 is decomposed into sub-states labeled n_4 and n_5 to indicate that the model can be in only one of those states at any time, so n_2 is an OR-state. When a state is not decomposed into AND or OR-states, it is called a BASIC state. The State n_4 has the time invariant $x<5$, invariant of the n_5 is $x>1$ (x denotes clocks), and the two States are connected by transition t_1. In the simple case transitions are connected directly with a source and a target state. The transition t_1 is triggered by event a and timed constraint $x>3$.

If a state is entered, one direct sub-state is entered in the OR case and all direct sub-states are entered in the AND case. Exiting a state is analogous. AND, OR and BASIC states form a tree structure and this hierarchy allows for stepwise refinement of the behavior of complex systems. All states in the largest rounded corners rectangle come into being a hierarchical structure as a tree that is shown Fig. 2. State n_1 is an ancestor of State n_2 and n_3, while State n_2 and n_3 is an offspring of State n_1.

3.2 Statecharts Terms

For description convenience we assume that state and transition name of timed Statecharts are unique, clock invariants of OR-state and AND-state are always true, and also ignores interlevel transitions, i.e. transitions crossing borderlines of states. Timed Statecharts is represent by terms, as done in [6]. Formally, suppose $\mathcal{N}$ be a set of names for timed Statecharts states, $\mathcal{T}$ a set of names for timed Statecharts transitions, Π a countable set of timed Statecharts events, $\mathcal{G}$ a set of clocks constraints, $\mathcal{R}$ a set of clocks resets, an $\mathcal{U}=\{\textbf{true}, \textbf{false}\}$ represent a set of urgent flag. Inv is a set of invariant over timed Statecharts states. With every event $e \in \Pi$, we associate a negated counterpart $\bar{e}$ and $\bar{e}=_{def} e$ as well as $\bar{E}=_{def}\{\bar{e}\,|e \in E\}$ for $E \subseteq \Pi \cup \{\bar{e}\,|e \in \Pi\}$. The set SC of timed Statecharts terms is then defined by the following inductive rules.

BASIC-state: If $n \in \mathcal{N}$, $\xi \in Inv$, then $s=[n,\xi]$ is a timed Statecharts term.

OR-state: Suppose $n \in \mathcal{N}$, and that $s_1,...,s_k$ are timed Statecharts terms for k>0, with $\vec{s} =_{\text{def}} (s_1,...,s_k)$. Also let $\rho =_{\text{def}} \{1,...,k\}$ and $l \in \rho$, with $T \subseteq \mathcal{T} \times \rho \times 2^{\Pi \cup \neg \Pi} \times 2^{\Pi} \times \mathcal{G} \times \mathcal{R} \times \mathcal{U} \times \rho$. Then $s = [n: \vec{s} \ ;l;T]$ is a timed Statecharts term. Here $s_1,...,s_k$ are the sub-states of s, set T contains the transitions connecting these states, s_1 is the default state of s, and s_l is the currently active sub-state of s.

AND-state: If $n \in \mathcal{N}$, if $s_1,...,s_k$ are timed Statecharts terms for k > 0, and $\vec{s} =_{\text{def}} (s_1,...,s_k)$, then $s = [n: \vec{s} \ ]$ is a timed Statecharts term, where $s_1,...,s_k$ are the parallel sub-states of s.

$s_1 = [n_1: (s_1, s_2)]$
$s_2 = [n_2: (s_4, s_5); 1; \{t_1, 1, \{a\}, \{b\}, 2\}]$
$s_3 = [n_3: (s_6, s_7); 1; \{t_3, 1, \{b\}, \{c\}, 2\}]$
$s_6 = [n_6: (s_8, s_9); 1; \{t_2, 1, \{a \wedge \bar{b}\}, \{c\}, 2\}]$
$s_4 = [n_4, x<5] \ s_5 = [n_5, x>1] \ s_7 = [n_7, x>4]$
$s_8 = [n_8] \ s_9 = [n_9]$

Fig. 3. Statecharts terms

Transitions of OR-states $[n: \vec{s} \ ;l;T]$ are those of the form $\hat{t} = <t, i, E, A, G, R, u, j>$, where (i) t is the name of $\hat{t}$, **name**$(\hat{t}) =_{\text{def}} t$, (ii) **source**$(\hat{t}) =_{\text{def}} s_i$ is the source state of $\hat{t}$, (iii) **ev**$(\hat{t}) =_{\text{def}} E$ is the trigger of $\hat{t}$, (iv) **act**$(\hat{t}) =_{\text{def}} A$ is the action of $\hat{t}$, (v) **guard**$(\hat{t}) =_{\text{def}} G$ is the clock constraints of $\hat{t}$, (vi) **reset**$(\hat{t}) =_{\text{def}} R$ is the clock resets of $\hat{t}$, (vii) **urgent**$(\hat{t}) =_{\text{def}} u$ is the urgency flag of $\hat{t}$, and (viii) **target**$(\hat{t}) =_{\text{def}} s_j$ is the target state of $\hat{t}$. The timed Statecharts term corresponding to the time Statecharts depicted in Fig. 1 is term s_1, which is defined in Fig. 3.

4 A Step Semantics of Timed Statecharts

The transition relation of timed Statecharts $\hat{t} \in \mathcal{T} \times \rho \times 2^{\Pi \cup \neg \Pi} \times 2^{\Pi} \times \mathcal{G} \times \mathcal{R} \times \mathcal{U} \times \rho$, which describes how to evolve from one state to another, is defined by the following rules.

- $(s_i, v) \xrightarrow{*} (s_j, \text{reset reset}(\hat{t}) \text{ in } v)$ if the following conditions hold:
  i. $\hat{t} = <t, i, E, A, G, R, u, j>$;
  ii. **ev**$(\hat{t})$ are satisfied;
  iii. **guard**$(\hat{t}) \models G$;
  iv. (**reset reset**$(\hat{t})$ **in** v) $\models Inv(s_j)$;
  v. **act**$(\hat{t})$ are generated.

- $(s_i, v) \xrightarrow{d} (s_i, v+d)$, for positive real d, if the following condition holds:
  i. $\forall d' \leq d, v+d' \models Inv(s_i)$;
  ii. $\neg$**urgent**$(\hat{t})$, the urgency flag of transition $\hat{t}$ is **false**.

For BASIC-states of timed Statecharts, the transition relation is similar to the transition relation of timed automaton. However, in practice, we have to consider other property for timed Statecharts, such as hierarchy, concurrency and priority. Before defining translation rules for timed Statecharts based on its operational semantics, we discuss classical Statecharts semantics as proposed by Pnueli and Shalev [7].

We sketch the semantics of timed Statecharts terms adopted in [8], which is a slight variant of the classical Statecharts operation semantics. A timed Statecharts s reacts to the arrival of some external events by triggering and clock constraints enabled micro steps in a chain-reaction manner. When this chain reaction comes to a halt, a complete macro step has been performed. More precisely, a macro step comprises a maximal set of micro steps, or transitions, that (i) are *relevant*, (ii) are mutually *consistent*, (iii) are triggered by events $E \subseteq \Pi$ offered by the environment or generated by other micro steps, (iv) satisfy clock constraints $G \subseteq \mathcal{G}$, (v) satisfy invariant of target state, (vi) are mutually *compatible*, and (vii) obey the principle of *causality*. Finally, we say that transition t is enabled in $s \rightarrow s'$ with respect to event set E, clock constraints G and transition set T, if $t \in \mathbf{En}(s, E, G, T, s')$, $s' \in \mathbf{target}(T)$, which is defined as follows.

$\mathbf{En}(s, E, G, T) =_{\text{def}} \mathbf{relevant}(s) \cap \mathbf{consistent}(s, T) \cap (\mathbf{invariant}(s) \vee (\mathbf{invariant}(s)$
$\wedge \mathbf{urgent}(T))) \cap \mathbf{invariant}(s') \cap \mathbf{triggered}(s, (E \cup \bigcup_{t \in T} \mathbf{act}(t)) \cap G)$

where:

- **relevant**(s) is the set of transitions whose source is in the set s;
- **consistent**(s, T) is the set of transitions that do not conflict with anything in T;
- **invariant**(s) represents that state s satisfy invariant;
- **urgent**(T) represents that the urgency flag of transition T is **true**;
- **triggered**(s,($E \cap G$) is the set of transitions whose triggers are satisfied by the event set E and clock constraint G. This is where global in consistency is eliminated;
- **act**(t) is the set of events generated by transition t.

Given a time Statecharts term s, a set E of events, and a set G of clock constraints, the non-deterministic *step-construction* function presented in Fig. 4 computes a set T^* of transitions. By executing the transitions in T^*, timed Statecharts term s may evolve in the single macro step $s \xrightarrow[A,R]{E,G} s'$ to timed Statecharts term s', producing the events $A = \bigcup_{t \in T} \mathbf{act}(t)$ and clock reset $R = \bigcup_{t \in T} \mathbf{reset}(t)$. term s' can be derived from s by updating the index l in every OR-state $[n: \bar{s}\ ;l;T]$ of s satisfying $t \in T^*$ for some $t \in T$.

```
function step_construction(s, E);
var T:=∅;
begin
  while T⊂En(s,E,G,T) do
      choose  t∈En(s,E,G,T)\T;
      T := T∪{t};
  od;
  return T
end
```

Fig. 4. A step-construction function

5 Model Checking for Timed Statecharts

A macro step of Timed Statecharts comprises a maximal set of micro steps. We directly define the semantics on sequences of micro steps, and use timed automaton as the semantics domain. Given a timed Statecharts TS, we translate TS to timed automata TA by a mapping Δ: TS→TA, where TA-states model timed Statecharts terms, TA-labels describe unclock constraints labels L_E(i.e. event/action) of timed Statecharts, TA-clocks denote timed Statecharts clocks, TA-clock constraints express timed Statecharts clock constraints, TA-state invariants model timed Statecharts invariants, and TA-transitions is sequences of timed Statecharts micro steps.

5.1 Translation Rules for Time Statecharts Based on Operational Semantics

For convenience, we define $\vec{s}_{l\to s'} =_{def} (s_1,...,s_{l-1},s',s_{l+1},..., s_k)$ for all $1 \leq l \leq k$ and $s' \in SC$. Furthermore, we need function **default**: SC→SC which sets the default state for given a Statecharts term s. **default**$([n,\xi])=_{def}[n,\xi]$, **default**$([n:\vec{s};l;T])=_{def}$ **default**(s_1), **default**$([n:\vec{s}])=_{def}\bigcup_{1\leq i\leq k}$ **default**(s_i). Defining for function η: SC→$\mathcal{N}$, γ: SC→Inv, which sets the state and the invariant for given a Statecharts terms s. (i) $\eta([n,\xi])=\{\{n\}\}$, $\gamma([n,\xi])=\{\{\xi\}\}$; (ii) $\eta([n:\vec{s};l;T])= \bigcup_{1\leq i\leq k} \{\{n\}\cup q_i \mid q_i\in \eta(s_i)\}$, $\gamma([n:\vec{s};l;T])= \bigcup_{1\leq i\leq k} \{r_i \mid r_i\in\gamma(s_i)\}$; (iii) $\eta([n:\vec{s}])=\{\{n\}\cup \bigcup_{1\leq i\leq k} q_i \mid q_i\in \eta(s_i)\}$, $\gamma([n:\vec{s}])=\{\bigcap_{1\leq i\leq k} r_i \mid r_i\in\gamma(s_i)\}$.

However, it is practical and important to consider history states in OR-states. For recording a history state, we additionally define a flag of history state $\tau \in \{none, deep, shallow\}$. *None* means that history states are not considered. *Deep* means that the old active state of the or-state and the old active states of all its sub-states are restored. *Shallow* means that only the active state of the or-state is restored and that its sub-states are reinitialized as usual. The modification of function **default** that just has to replace function **default**(s) by function **default**(τ, s) is done by integrated a history mechanism. The terms **default**(*none*, s) and **default**(*deep*, s) are simply defined by **default**(s) and s, respectively. The definition of **default**(*shallow*, s) can be done along the structure of timed Statecharts terms as follows.

default(*shallow*, $[n,\xi]) =_{def} [n,\xi]$

default(*shallow*, $[n:\vec{s};l;T]) =_{def} [n:\vec{s}_{[l\to default(s_l)]};l;T]$

default(*shallow*, $[n:\vec{s}]) =_{def}$ **default**(*shallow*, $\vec{s}$)

Transition relation → is defined by using SOS rules by Plotkin [21] as follows.

$$name \frac{premise}{conclusion} \text{ (side condition)} \quad \text{as well as} \quad name \frac{premise}{conclusion} \text{(side condition)}$$

In this subsection, operational semantics of timed Statecharts transition in BASIC-states, AND-states and OR-states was defined. There are three rules about BASIC-states: **BAS-1** rule describes the execution from one BASIC-state to another, where **source**$(t)=[n,\xi]$, **target**$(t)=[n',\xi']$, if the event **ev**(t), the clock constraints **guard**(t) of

$t \in T$ and the invariants of the target state are satisfied, the transition be enabled, and the actions **act**(t) and the clock reset **reset**(t) are done.

$$\text{BAS-1} \frac{\text{En}([n,\xi], E, G, T, [n', \xi'])}{[n,\xi] \xrightarrow[\text{act}(t),\text{reset}(t)]{\text{ev}(t),\text{guard}(t)}_{\text{name}(t)} [n', \xi']}$$

$$\begin{pmatrix} t \in T, \text{source}(t) = [n,\xi], \\ \text{target}(t) = [n', \xi'], \\ (\textbf{reset } \text{reset}(t) \textbf{ in } v) \models \xi' \end{pmatrix}$$

BAS-2 rule describes the execution from one BASIC-state to one AND-state which is its brother. As noted above, for all super states (i.e. OR-state and AND-state), their state invariants are always true, but when an OR-state is entered, one direct sub-state is entered, and until a BASIC-state. So we need to consider state invariant which can get from function γ. **BAS-2** rule defines as follows.

$$\text{BAS-2} \frac{\text{En}([n,\xi], E, G, T, [n' : \vec{s}; l; T])}{[n,\xi] \xrightarrow[\text{act}(t),\text{reset}(t)]{\text{ev}(t),\text{guard}(t)}_{\text{name}(t)} [n : \vec{s}_{[l \to \text{default}(\tau, s_l)]}; l; T]}$$

$$\begin{pmatrix} t \in T, \text{source}(t) = [n,\xi], \\ \text{target}(t) = [n' : \vec{s}; l; T], \\ (\textbf{reset } \text{reset}(t) \textbf{ in } v) \models \gamma([n' : \vec{s}; l; T]) \end{pmatrix}$$

BAS-3 rule demonstrate the delay of BASIC-states, where $v+d$ stands for the current clock assignment plus the delay for all the clocks, we have

$$\text{BAS-3} \frac{(v+d) \models \text{Inv}([n,\xi]) \wedge \neg \text{urgent}(t)}{([n,\xi], v) \xrightarrow{d} ([n,\xi], v+d)}$$

$$(\forall d' \leq d, v+d' \models \text{Inv}([n,\xi]))$$

There are also three rules about OR-states: one rules describes the execution of a timed Statecharts transition $t \in T$ of an OR-state $[n: \vec{s}; i; T]$. It defines that the OR-state with currently active sub-state s_i may change to OR-state $[n: \vec{s}_{[l \to \text{default}(\tau, s_l)]}; l; T]$ with currently active sub-state s_l as rule **OR-1**.

$$\text{OR-1} \frac{\text{En}([n : \vec{s}; i; T], E, G, T, [n : \vec{s}; l; T])}{[n : \vec{s}; i; T] \xrightarrow[\text{act}(t),\text{reset}(t)]{\text{ev}(t),\text{guard}(t)}_{\text{name}(t)} [n : \vec{s}_{[l \to \text{default}(\tau, s_l)]}; l; T]}$$

$$\begin{pmatrix} t \in T, \text{source}(t) = [n : \vec{s}; i; T], \\ \text{target}(t) = [n' : \vec{s}; l; T], \\ (\textbf{reset } \text{reset}(t) \textbf{ in } v) \models \gamma([n' : \vec{s}; l; T]) \end{pmatrix}$$

Other rule that describes from the OR-state $[n: \vec{s}; l; T]$ to BASIC-state, is not discussed particularly due to similar to **BAS-1** rule. Another rule describes that the OR-state $[n: \vec{s}; l; T]$ with currently active sub-state s_l may change with same label to the OR-state $[n: \vec{s}_{[l \to s'_l]}; l; T]$ with currently active sub-state s'_l as rule **OR-2**.

$$\text{OR-2} \frac{s_l \xrightarrow[A,R]{E,G} s'_l}{[n:\vec{s};l;T] \xrightarrow[A,R]{E,G}_L [n:\vec{s}_{[l\to s'_l]};l;T]}$$

It is indispensable for transition rule of Statecharts AND-states to consider many enabled transitions to execute in parallel as rule **AND**. For AND-state's parallel description, we firstly introduce process algebra. Process algebra [22] is a powerful formal method for depicting algebra structure and analyzing parallel system. Basic process algebra (BPA) is a core in all process algebra theory. Basic process terms are built from atomic actions, alternative composition and sequential composition.

- An atomic action represents indivisible behavior, including event and action.
- The symbol · denotes sequential composition. The process term $p \cdot q$ executes p, and upon successful termination proceeds to execute q;
- The symbol + denotes alternative composition. The process term $p+q$ executes behavior of either p or q.

By appending merge $\|$, left merge $\lfloor$ and communication merge $|$, BPA is extended to express process communication in parallel system. The merge $\|$ executes the two process terms in its arguments in parallel, the left merge $\lfloor$ executes an initial transition of its first argument, and the communication merge $|$ executes a communication between initial transitions of its arguments. The process term $p\|q$ executes p and q in parallel; analogously, $p\lfloor q$ executes restrictedly p in an initial transition; $p|q$ executes a communication p and q.

AND-state of Statecharts specifies the parallel behavior of reactive system. In Fig. 1, the AND-state n_1 comprises two concurrent sub-states n_2 and n_3. Suppose the state configuration is currently in n_4 and n_8, if the event a and b occurs, the transition t_1 and t_3 is enabled. Because transitions can be taken in the sub-states of an AND-state simultaneously, the transition t_1 and t_3 is executed in parallel, as written $t_1\|t_3$. Based on parallel axiom of process algebra, merge $t_1 \| t_3 = (t_1\lfloor t_3 + t_3\lfloor t_1) + t_1 | t_3$.

$$\text{AND} \frac{\begin{array}{c}(\forall m \in M : s_m \xrightarrow[A_m,R_m]{E_m,G_m}_{L_m} s'_m) \\ \wedge (\forall i,j \in M : (\neg ev(t_i)) \cap act(t_j) = \varnothing)\end{array}}{[n:\vec{s}] \xrightarrow[\bigcup_{m\in M} A_m \cup \bigcup_{m\in M} R_m]{(\bigcup_{l\in H}(E_l \setminus \bigcup_{j=1}^{l-1} act(t_j))) \wedge \bigcup_{l\in H} G_l}_{\bigcup_{m\in M} L_m} [n:\vec{s}'_1]\|...\|[n:\vec{s}'_{|M|}]}$$

$$\begin{pmatrix} M \subseteq K = \{1,...,k\}, H = \{1,...,|M|\}, \\ \text{source}(L_m) = s_m, \text{target}(L_m) = s'_m \end{pmatrix}$$

When AND-state includes k OR sub-states, an execution of k transitions in parallel need be considered. As above-mentioned, we can define **AND** rule, which an execution of $|M|$ transitions in parallel in all sub-states s_m of AND-state $[n:\vec{s}\,]$ may be specified to $[n:\vec{s}'_1]\|...\|[n:\vec{s}'_{|M|}]$ by merge of process algebra.

5.2 Macro Step

The above rules realize a compositional semantics of timed Statecharts on sequences of the micro steps. However, we consider even more the classical macro-step semantics of timed Statecharts. Let s, $s' \in SC$, E, $A \subseteq \Pi$, $G \subseteq \mathcal{G}$ and $R \subseteq \mathcal{R}$, we write $s \Rightarrow s'$ and say s may perform a macro step with input E, output A, clock constraints G and clock reset R to s', if $\exists s_1, \ldots, s_m \in SC$, $\exists E_1, \ldots, E_m \subseteq \Pi \cup \Pi$, $\exists A_1, \ldots, A_m \subseteq \Pi$, $\exists G_1, \ldots, G_m \subseteq \mathcal{G}$, $\exists R_1, \ldots, R_m \subseteq \mathcal{R}$, such that (i) $s \xrightarrow[A_1, R_1]{E_1, G_1} s_1 \xrightarrow[A_2, R_2]{E_2, G_2} \ldots \xrightarrow[A_m, R_m]{E_m, G_m} s_m \rightarrow s'$, (ii) $\bigcup_{i=1}^{m} E_i \subseteq E$ and $\bigcup_{i=1}^{m} A_i \cap E = \emptyset$, (iii) $A = \mathbf{act}(s_m) \cap \Pi$, (iv) $\bigcup_{i=1}^{m} G_i \subseteq G$, (v) (**reset** R_i **in** v) $\models \xi_i$, $0 < i \leq m$, (vi) $\not\exists$ s_{m+1}, E_{m+1}, A_{m+1}, G_{m+1}, R_{m+1}, $s_m \xrightarrow[A_{m+1}, R_{m+1}]{E_{m+1}, G_{m+1}} s_{m+1}$, where $E_{m+1} \subseteq E$ and $A_{m+1} \cap E = \emptyset$. If timed Statecharts term s satisfies event E, clock constraints G, We may say, s may evolve in the single macro step $s \xrightarrow[A, R]{E, G} s'$ to timed Statecharts term s', generate action A and reset clock R.

5.3 Translate Time Statecharts into Timed Automata

Given timed Statecharts, it can be translated into timed automata by a mapping Δ: TS→TA. To define the mapping function Δ, we firstly suppose a timed Statecharts p by terms,, and define the entities $S(p)$, $C(p)$, $L(p)$, $\rightarrow_p$ and $Inv(p)$, which mean respectively the states set, the clock set, the label set, the set of transition relation and the state invariant function of TA $\Delta(p)$, where:

- $S(p)$ is a set of state configurations of Statecharts term p. The definition of $S(p)$ can be done as follows.
  i. $S([n,\xi]) = \{\{\eta([n,\xi])\}\} = \{\{n\}\}$
  ii. $S([n: \vec{s} ;l;T]) = \bigcup_{1 \leq i \leq k} \{\{\eta([n: \vec{s} ;l;T])\} \cup q_i \mid q_i \in S(s_i)\}$
  iii. $S([n: \vec{s}]) = \{\{\eta([n: \vec{s}])\} \cup \bigcup_{1 \leq i \leq k} q_i \mid q_i \in S(s_i)\}$
- $C(p) = C$ a set of the timed Statecharts clocks;
- $L(p) = 2^{\Pi_p \cup \neg \Pi_p} \times 2^{\Pi_p}$ represents the set of timed Statecharts event and action, written event/action;
- $\rightarrow_p \subseteq S(p) \times L(p) \times \mathcal{G} \times \mathcal{R} \times S(p)$ that operation rules have already been discussed in the above, represent the sequence macro step of Statecharts. Assume a translation $e = (s, L, G, R, s')$ connects two states s and s', describes $s \xrightarrow[A_1, R_1]{E_1, G_1} s_1 \xrightarrow[A_2, R_2]{E_2, G_2} \ldots \xrightarrow[A_m, R_m]{E_m, G_m} s_m \rightarrow s'$, where $L = E_1 \wedge E_2 \wedge \ldots \wedge E_m / A_1 \vee A_2 \vee \ldots \vee A_m$, $G = G_1 \wedge G_2 \wedge \ldots \wedge G_m$, $R = R_1 \vee R_2 \vee \ldots \vee R_m$;
- $Inv(p)$: $S(p) \rightarrow \Psi_C$, a function that assigns to each state an invariant, where $Inv([n,\xi]) = \chi([n,\xi])$, $Inv([n: \vec{s} ;i;T]) = \chi([n: \vec{s} ;l;T])$, $Inv([n: \vec{s}]) = \chi([n: \vec{s}])$
- $\varsigma(p)$ expresses the initial term set of timed Statecharts. We may define $\varsigma([n,\xi]) = \{n\}$, $\varsigma([n: \vec{s} ;i;T]) = \{n\} \cup s_1$, $\varsigma([n: \vec{s}]) = \{n\} \cup \bigcup_{1 \leq i \leq k} s_i$.

Considering our example of timed Statecharts of Fig. 1, its translation TA of timed Statecharts is depicted in Figure 5.

Without loss of generality, we wish to consider interlevel transitions and clock invariants of OR-state and AND-state for timed Statecharts. Harel considers interlevel transitions as important concept of the language [1]: "...as our methods does not necessarily advocate layer-by-layer development; it is more flexible and encourages interlevel connections too, whenever appropriate." Hence we can not rule them out. This intricacy is mainly caused by interlevel transitions, but we wish to describe interlevel transitions but have simple operational semantics. It is feasible and practical to change from interlevel transitions to non-interlevel transitions. Our approach that is similar to [12] is lift interlevel transitions to the uppermost states that are exited and entered when transitions is taken. Let $sr(t)$ (called *source restriction*) is a set of states which were the original states of the transition t, and $td(t)$ (called *target determinator*) is a set of states that were entered originally.

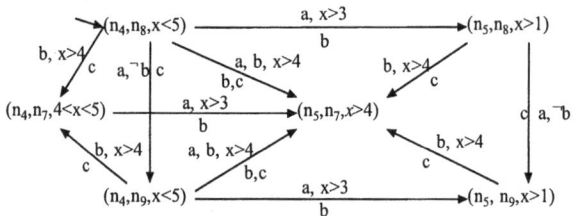

Fig. 5. Translation Timed Automata for timed Statecharts in Fig. 1

By transition label extensions added $sr(t)$ and $td(t)$, interlevel transitions can be compiled into non-interlevel transitions.

In the following, we will describe how to eliminate clock invariants for super state of timed Statecharts. Assume that two state of timed Statecharts $n_1, n_2 \in N$, n_1 be a super state, i.e. type(n_1)=AND or type(n_1)=OR, and n_2 may be a arbitrary type, including AND, OR and BASIC, and let $n_2 \in \sigma(n_1)$. According to the priority of transitions for timed Statecharts, we define the priority of state invariant that if sub-state n_2 invariant is satisfied but father-state n_1 invariant is not, then the current state configuration can not be in n_2, i.e. clock invariant of state n_1 is prior to clock invariant of sub-state n_2. In order to let that clock invariants of OR-state and AND-state always are true, only clock invariant of sub-states n_2 need be updated such as $Inv(n_2)=Inv(n_2) \wedge Inv(n_1)$. More precisely, we define formally as follows.
- $\forall n \in N$, and type(n)=AND or type(n)=OR, $Inv(n)$=true;
- $\forall n \in N$, $n \in \sigma^k(root)$, type(n)=BASIC, $Inv(n)=Inv(n) \wedge \bigcup_{1 \leq i \leq k} \sigma^{-i}(n)$.

where *root* is a unique root state and has no ancestor. $\sigma^k(root)=\sigma(\sigma^{k-1}(root))$, σ^{-1} that gives the father-state is a inverse of σ, and $\sigma^{-k}(n) = \sigma^{-1}(\sigma^{-(k-1)}(n))$.

5.4 Model Checking Timed Statecharts

Given a timed Statecharts TS, and TCTL formulae ϕ, the model checking timed Statecharts problem that we are interested in is to check whether TS satisfies ϕ, abbreviated TS $\models \phi$. According to the last translation rules, the equivalence model TA that results from timed Statecharts TS is called its timed automata. Thus, roughly speaking, model checking timed Statecharts against a TCTL-formula amounts to model checking its timed automata against a TCTL-formula. Formally, for any timed Statecharts TS, we have:

$$TS \models \phi \text{ if and only if } TA \models \phi$$

In summary we obtain the scheme for model checking the TCTL-formula ϕ over the timed Statecharts TS:

1. Construct the flat timed automata model TA $=(S, C, s_0, L, Inv, \rightarrow)$;
2. The model checking problem for TCTL, deciding whether TA, $s_0 \models \phi$, can be solved by constructing the region automaton $\mathcal{R}(TA)$ under the time equivalence classes under $\approx$;
3. Apply the CTL model checking procedure on $\mathcal{R}(TA)$.

Actually, the problem for model checking timed Statecharts can be converted to the classical problem for model checking timed automata [23][24].

6 Conclusion

Timed Statecharts is an extension of the visual specification language Statecharts with real-time constructs, and can efficiently specify explicit dense time. The timed Statecharts serves better the modeling of complex reactive real-time systems. The paper presented a new approach for formalizing timed Statecharts semantics, which is centered on the compositional principle. Based on timed Statecharts term syntax and formal operational semantics, and description of parallel behavior by process algebra, each timed Statecharts is mapped to a timed automaton. This makes it possible to translate our hierarchical structure to a flat one and thus provide a framework for formal verification of a real-time extension of Statecharts.

References

1. D. Harel. Statecharts: a Visual Formalism for Complex Systems. Science of Computing, 8(1987) 231-274
2. F. Jahanian and A.K. Mok. A Graph-theoretic Approach for Timing Analysis and its Imple-mentation. IEEE Transactions on Computers, C-36(1987) 961~975
3. Leveson NG, Heimdahl M, Hildreth H, Reese JD. Requirements Specification for Process-Control Systems. IEEE Transactions on Software Engineering, 20(1994) 684~707
4. E.M. Clarke, O. Grumberg, D.A. Peled. Model Checking. The MIT Press (2000)
5. E. M. Clarke, E. A. Emerson. Synthesis of synchronization skeletons for branching time temporal logic. In Logic of Programs: Workshop, Yorktown Heights. NY, LNCS 131, Springer-Verlag, (1981) 52-71
6. D. Harel, A. Pnueli, J.P. Schmidt, and R. Sherman. On the Formal Semantics of Statecharts. In Proceedings of the 2nd IEEE symposium on Logic in Computer science, Ithaca, New York, (1987) 54-64

7. G. Lüttgen, M. von der Beeck, and R. Cleaveland. Statecharts via Process Algebra. In 10th International Conference on Concurrency Theory(CONCUR '99), J. Baeten and S. Mauw, eds., Vol. 1664 of Lecture Notes in Computer Science, Eindhoven, The Netherlands, Springer-Verlag (1999) 399-414
8. A. Maggiolo-Schettini, A. Peron, and S. Tini. Equivalences of Statecharts. In 7th International Conference on Concurrency Theory (CONCUR '96), U. Montanari and V. Sassone, eds., Vol. 1119 of Lecture Notes in Computer Science, Pisa, Italy, Springer-Verlag (1996) 687-702
9. R. Heckel, J. Kuster, and G. Taentaer. Towards Automatic Translation of UML Models into Semantic Domains. In Proc. AGT 2002: Workshop on Applied Graph Transformation, Grenoble, France, (2002) 11-21
10. G. Lüttgen, M. von der Beeck, and R. Cleaveland. A Compositional Approach to Statecharts Semantics. NASA/CR-2000-2100086, ICASE Report No. 2000-12 (2000)
11. A. Pnueli and M. Shalev. What is in a Step: on the Semantics of Statecharts. In Theoretical Aspects of Computer Software (TACS '91), T. Ito and A. Meyer, eds., Vol. 526 of Lecture Notes in Computer Science, Sendai, Japan, Springer-Verlag (1991) 244-264
12. E. Mikk, Y. Lakhnech, and M. Siegel et al. Implementing Statecharts in PROMELA/SPIN. In: Proc of Workshop on Industrial-Strength Formal Specification Techniques(WIFT'98). BocaRaton, Florida: IEEE Computer Society (1998)
13. D. Latella, I. Majzik, and M. Massink. Automatic Verification of UML Statechat Diagrams Using the SPIN Model-checker. Formal Aspects of Computing, 11(1999): 637-664.
14. S. Gnesi, and D. Latella. Model Checking UML Statechart Diagrams Using JACK. In Proceedings of the 4th IEEE international Symposium on High-Assurance Systems Engineering (1999) 46-55
15. Z. Pap, I. Majzik, and A. Pataricza. Checking General Safety Criteria on UML Statecharts. In U. Voges, editor, SAFECOMP 2001, LNCS 2187, Springer-Verlag, (2001) 46-55
16. W. Chan, R. Anderson, P. Beame, and S. Burns et al. Model Checking Large Software Specifications. IEEE Transactions on Software Engineering, 24(1998) 498-520
17. A. Schmidt and D. Varro. CheckVML: A Tool for Model Checking Visual Modeling Languages. In the 6th International Conference on the Unified Modeling Language, LNCS 2863, Springer-Verlag, (2003) 92-95.
18. A. David, M. Oliver Möller, and Wang Yi. Formal Verification of UML Statecharts with Real-Time Extensions. In Proceedings of the 5th International Conference on Fundamental Approaches to Software Engineering, Vol. 2306 of Lecture Notes in Computer Science, Springer-Verlag, (2002) 218-232
19. H. Giese and S. Burmester. Real-Time Statechart Semantics. Technical Report tr-ri-03-239, Computer Science Department, University of Paderborn, (2003)
20. R. Alur and D. Dill. A Theory of Timed Automata. Theoretical Computer Science, 126(1994) 183-235.
21. G. D. Plotkin. A Structural Approach to Operational Semantics. Technical Report DAIMI FN-19, Computer Science Department, Aarhus University, (1981)
22. W. Fokkink. Introduction to Process Algebra. Springer, (2000)
23. R. Alur, C. Courcoubetis and D. Dill. Model Checking in Dense Real-time. Information and Computation, 104(1993) 2-34
24. S. Yovine. Model Checking Timed Automata. In Embedded Systems, LNCS, 1494, (1998)

Abstraction-Guided Model Checking Using Symbolic IDA* and Heuristic Synthesis

Kairong Qian, Albert Nymeyer, and Steven Susanto

School of Computer Science & Engineering,
The University of New South Wales, Sydney Australia
{kairongq, anymeyer, ssus290}@cse.unsw.edu.au

Abstract. A heuristic-based symbolic model checking algorithm, BDD-IDA* that efficiently falsifies invariant properties of a system is presented. As in bounded model checking, the algorithm uses an iterative deepening search strategy. However, in our case, the search strategy is guided by a heuristic that is computed from an abstract model, which is derived from the concrete model by a synthesis technique. Synthesis involves eliminating so-called weak variables from the concrete specification, where the weak variables are identified by a data-dependency analysis. Unique to this work is the use of the depth-first IDA* search algorithm in a BDD setting, and the automatic synthesis of the heuristic. The performance of the approach on a large number of small examples is compared with standard BDD-based approaches. Experiments on a variety of real-world models from different domains are also conducted. The approach reveals a consistent improvement on all models, and in some cases a speed-up of 2 orders of magnitude is obtained.

Keywords: Formal verification, symbolic model checking, heuristic search, data abstractions, model approximations.

1 Introduction

Model checking [7] is often used in preference to theorem proving for the verification of properties in finite-state systems because of its high level of automation as well as its ability to produce counter-examples when a given property is found not to hold. The safety properties of a system can often be captured by one or more system invariants that characterise the set of states within which the system must reside. This process of checking invariants is also called a reachability analysis. The aim of a reachability analysis is to detect error states, where the paths leading to these states determine counter-examples to the invariant. Counter-examples provide valuable information to system developers about potential design errors in a system. In this work we are more focussed on falsification of invariants than verification.

This work is based on the symbolic model checking approach [15] in which symbolic data structures called binary decision diagrams (BDDs) [2] are used to represent a finite-state space. Invariant checking in symbolic model checking is usually done by either BDD-based or SAT-based algorithms. The BDD-based algorithm, BDD-BFS, conducts a breadth-first search on the system state space and records all reachable states. The goal for the search algorithm usually captures those states in which the invariants are violated. Being 'blind', BDD-BFS is an inefficient way to find error states as typically many regions of the state space will needlessly be searched. A BFS strategy is more suited to correct models and is wasteful of space as generally all reachable states need to be stored. As well, for large systems, the sizes of BDDs in BDD-BFS can grow exponentially, making state space exploration almost impossible in realistic cases.

An alternative symbolic model checking approach is called bounded model checking[1]. Bounded model checking translates the bounded semantics of the invariant into Boolean expressions and uses SAT procedures to determine their satisfiability. By incrementally increasing the bound, the algorithm iteratively deepens the state space exploration. If an error state is encountered at some level, the algorithm will terminate and report a counter-example. In general, SAT-based algorithms tend to detect counter-examples quicker than BDD-BFS due to the inherent DFS search strategy that SAT solvers use [5] if the counter-examples are short. SAT-based approaches, however, can be handicapped by a huge number of clauses that need to be input to the SAT solver. In our work, we combine aspects of both techniques by using BDDs to represent the state space and a heuristic DFS strategy to locate error states.

Because a BDD-based, depth-first search (BDD-DFS) strategy is not naturally layered like BFS, it requires a special mechanism to partition each BDD frontier during the search. The integration of BDD-DFS with heuristic search provides this mechanism: the heuristic values of states are not only used to estimate the distances to the goal, they are also used to partition the frontier into sub-frontiers. Each sub-frontier, represented by a single BDD, is treated by BDD-DFS as a single node in the search graph.

Our integration of heuristics and symbolic data is yet another development in the growing field of guided model checking [10,17,19,20] whose aim is to apply 'smart' technology to model verification. In previous work [17], we integrated the A* search algorithm into a symbolic model checker. In this paper, we instead use a 'more efficient' version of A* called IDA* (iterative deepening A*), designed to minimise memory usage. A* is in essence a mixture of BFS and DFS. If the heuristic is informative, the search is more like DFS, otherwise, with poor direction, the search works on a broad front. The tendency to mimic BFS when poorly informed means that A* can have exponential memory requirements. In 1985, Korf [13] devised IDA* that is basically DFS, but has some BFS characteristics. He found this algorithm was often better than A* in solving hard AI problems [14].

The new, integrated algorithm we develop is called BDD-IDA*. The advantages of using BDD-IDA* are:

1. The iterative and bounded DFS strategy in IDA* detects so-called shallow and corner bugs that are difficult to detect by unbounded DFS.

2. In BFS, the frontier is layered. In A*, the frontier is typically 'onion shaped' because of the action of the heuristic (biasing the search towards a particular path that leads to a goal state). Pruning of the search space in fact occurs before the bound is reached, so the frontier is more pointed to the goal for each iteration.
3. IDA* has the same linear (in the search depth) space complexity as DFS. (But note, as we use BDDs to represent sets of states, the actual space requirement can be exponential in the number of states.)

A second important feature of our work is that we have extended the idea presented in earlier work [17] of using an abstract version of the concrete model as a heuristic (the so-called pattern database). In that work we did not address the problem of how to obtain the abstract model. In this work, we address this issue and present an automatic method to generate abstract models that is based on a data-dependency analysis of the concrete model specification. In this analysis, we determine the *strength* of each variable. This information is used by the heuristic generator to eliminate those variables that are considered less relevant (or weak), and thereby reduce the size of the model. We refer to this technique as *heuristic synthesis*. Being able to automatically determine a heuristic frees the system designer/verifier from this task, and makes the guided model checker fully automatic.

In summary, a number of model-checking and artificial intelligence approaches have been combined to produce an integrated, fully automatic framework that allows more efficient property falsification than alternative approaches. The rest of paper is organised as follows. Section 2 reviews the guided model checking framework we use and presents the BDD-based IDA* algorithm. In Section 3 the three-phase heuristic synthesis procedure based on abstractions is illustrated. We describe the tool that we have developed and the experiments in Section 4. Section 5 discusses related work from the literature and Section 6 concludes this work.

2   Guided Model Checking and Symbolic IDA*

The general framework for our abstraction-guided approach is based on work presented in [17]. We depict our approach in Figure 1. The process starts with the concrete model. In the first step we generate, automatically, a data abstraction of the concrete model using a data dependency analysis. The abstract model is taken as input by a standard model checker that uses a BFS search algorithm. If the model checker verifies the abstract model successfully, we terminate. If the abstract model fails the verification, we construct a heuristic using the abstract model. The guided model checking algorithm is then invoked to check the concrete system using the heuristic as guide. The outcome of the guided model checker is either that the concrete model is verified, or that a counter-example (*CX* in the figure) is produced. The approach in this paper differs from [17] in two aspects. 1) We use an automatic heuristic synthesis procedure, and 2) as our primary focus is on falsification and not verification, we use a DFS-based heuristic search algorithm, IDA*, and modify it to use BDDs.

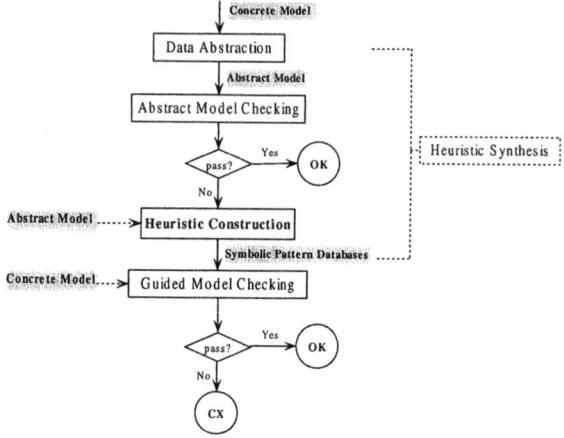

Fig. 1. The abstraction-guided model checking framework

The algorithm, called BDD-IDA*, is based on the explicit IDA* algorithm. The algorithm takes four inputs. The inputs S_0 and $\mathcal{G}$ of the algorithm are BDDs representing the initial set of states and the goal, i.e. set of "bad" states. The input BDD $\mathcal{R}$ is the transition relation. Note that we denote the calculation of the image of a given set of states S by $\mathcal{R}(S)$. The input σ is a heuristic that will be illustrated in next section. Finally, the input $Bound$ determines the search depth. We use an explicit stack where each element in the stack is of the form (g, h, S). The integer g indicates the actual number of transitions from S_0 to S and h the heuristic estimation of number of transitions from S to $\mathcal{G}$. In line 10, the algorithm calls the procedure **SplitAndPush**. This procedure uses the heuristic σ to partition a set of states S (that constitute the frontier of the IDA* search) into subsets, and together with their associated costs g and h, pushes each subset onto the stack. We show this procedure in the next session.

Procedure BDD-IDA* $(S_0, \mathcal{R}, \mathcal{G}, \sigma, Bound)$
1   $stack.push() \leftarrow (0, 0, S_0)$
2   $counter \leftarrow 1$
3   **while** $(counter \leq Bound)$ **do**
4   **while** $(stack \neq \phi)$ **do**
5         $(g, h, S) \leftarrow stack.pop()$
6   **if** $(S \wedge \mathcal{G} \neq \phi)$
7   **return** $Bound$
8   **if** $(h + g < counter)$
9            $S \leftarrow \mathcal{R}(S)$
10   **SplitAndPush**(g, S, σ)
11     $counter \leftarrow counter + 1$
12     $stack.push() \leftarrow (0, 0, S_0)$
13 **return** $NoErrorInBound$

Note that we do not memorise the set of reachable states in the algorithm as we are only interested in the falsification of invariant properties.

3 Heuristic Synthesis

In this section we will outline how the heuristic σ is synthesised. It is a three-phase process. (1) Abstraction: a data dependency analysis is used to automatically define an abstraction function for the concrete model. (2) Approximation: an approximation of the abstract model is then computed in order to avoid the computational penalty for exact abstraction. (3) Heuristic Construction: a standard BDD-BFS algorithm is used to compute all reachable frontiers in the approximate model. The result of this synthesis is a set of BDDs $\sigma = \{B_1, B_2, \ldots, B_n\}$ where each B_i represents a set of states in the abstract model with the same heuristic value.

Phase 1: Abstraction

Let $M = (S, R, S_0)$ denote a concrete model where S is a set of states, $S_0 \subseteq S$ is a set of initial states and R is the transition relation. Let $H : S \to \hat{S}$ be a surjection that maps the concrete state space onto an abstract space $\hat{S}$ with $|\hat{S}| \leq |S|$. H therefore induces an abstract model that is defined as follows.

Definition 1 (Abstraction). *The abstraction of M w.r.t. H is denoted by $\hat{M} = (\hat{S}, \hat{R}, \hat{S}_0)$, where*

- $\hat{S} = \{\hat{s} | s \in S \land \hat{s} = H(s)\}$
- $\hat{S}_0 = \{\hat{s} | \hat{s} \in \hat{S} \land \hat{s} = H(s) \land s \in S_0\}$
- $\hat{R} \subseteq \hat{S} \times \hat{S}$ *is a transition relation, where* $(\hat{s}_1, \hat{s}_2) \in \hat{R}$ *iff* $\hat{s}_1 = H(s_1) \land \hat{s}_2 = H(s_2) \land \exists s_1 \exists s_2 (s_1, s_2) \in R$

In symbolic model checking, S_0 and R of M are usually represented by two first-order formulas, $\mathcal{F}_0(x_1, x_2, \ldots, x_n)$ and $\mathcal{F}_R(x_1, x_2, \ldots, x_n, x'_1, x'_2, \ldots, x'_n)$, where $\{x_1, x_2, \ldots, x_n\}$ and $\{x'_1, x'_2, \ldots, x'_n\}$ are variables that represent the current state and next state of the model. Without loss of generality we assume all variables range over same domain D, hence the state set of M is $S = D \times D \times \ldots \times D$. Let $\{\hat{x}_1, \hat{x}_2, \ldots, \hat{x}_n\}$ and $\{\hat{x}'_1, \hat{x}'_2, \ldots, \hat{x}'_n\}$ be variables that represent the current state and next state of $\hat{M}$. We denote $H(x_i) = \hat{x}_i$ iff H maps every value of x_i to an abstract value of $\hat{x}_i$. Let $\hat{\mathcal{F}}_0$ and $\hat{\mathcal{F}}_R$ denote the formulas that represent $\hat{S}_0$ and $\hat{R}$ respectively. Using the quantification on $\mathcal{F}_0$ and $\mathcal{F}_R$, we construct $\hat{S}_0$ and $\hat{R}$ by evaluating the following formulas.

1. $\hat{\mathcal{F}}_0 = \exists x_1 \ldots \exists x_n (H(x_1) = \hat{x}_1 \land \ldots \land H(x_n) = \hat{x}_n \land \mathcal{S}_0(x_1, \ldots, x_n))$
2. $\hat{\mathcal{F}}_R = \exists x_1 \ldots \exists x_n \exists x'_1 \ldots \exists x'_n (H(x_1) = \hat{x}_1 \land \ldots \land H(x_n) = \hat{x}_n \land H(x'_1) = \hat{x}'_1 \land \ldots \land H(x'_n) = \hat{x}'_n \land \mathcal{R}(x_1, \ldots, x_n, x'_1, \ldots, x'_n))$

To build the abstraction from a concrete model, we first need to define H. In BDD-based symbolic model checking, every variable of the concrete model is encoded using a set of Boolean variables. Let V be a set of Boolean variables that encode all the variables in M. Following [5,17], we define H by restricting a subset $V_{inv} \subset V$ to a single-element domain, i.e. $H(\mathcal{F}) = \exists v_0...\exists v_m \mathcal{F}$ for all $v_i \in V_{inv}$, where $\mathcal{F}$ is formula representing a set of concrete states. This abstraction essentially makes the variables in V_{inv} invisible. Note that in our earlier work [17], the user had to provide V_{inv} to build the abstract model; possibly a difficult task. In this paper we describe an automated method to generate V_{inv} that is based on a data dependency analysis.

Data Dependency Analysis. The aim of this analysis is to estimate the strength of each variable v_i in V, and remove weak variables to form an abstract model. The analysis is based on the cone of influence (COI) abstraction techniques [7]. Let $V_p \subseteq V$ be a set of variables that appears in the specification φ. The COI of V_p, denoted by C, is the minimal set of variables such that:
- $V_p \subseteq C$
- if for some $v_i \in C$ its $next(v_i)$ depends on v_j, then $v_j \in C$

If $|C| < |V|$, then we construct a reduced model M' that only contains variables in C. It is proved in [7] that the reduced and original models form a bi-simulation relation w.r.t. all CTL specifications that only have variables from V_p, i.e. $M' \models \varphi \leftrightarrow M \models \varphi$. As a result, model checking can be performed on the reduced model. Of course, every variable in C must be included, otherwise the reduced model is not bi-similar.

We use abstraction only to synthesise the heuristics that guide the model checker of the concrete model, so we do not need to restrict ourself to removing only the variables outside of C (unlike [7]). Although all variables in C can influence the variables in φ, the degree of influence will not normally be the same. Some variables in V_p are more strongly influenced by variables in $C - V_p$ than others. To determine the subset of variables of V on which the truth of φ is heavily reliant, we build a dependency tree. Let $D(v)$ be the positive integer denoting the distance from v to the root of the dependency tree. The smaller $D(v)$ is, the stronger the influence of v on φ. The following algorithm computes $D(v)$ for all $v \in C$.

> initialise $i := 0$, $C := V_p$ and $V_t := V_p$;
> **while** C changes **do**
> $i := i + 1$;
>   **for** each $v_i \in V_t$, compute all its dependable variables;
>   put those who are not in C into V_{tt};
>   assign $D(v) := i$ for all $v \in V_{tt}$;
>   assign $C := C \cup V_{tt}$ and $V_t := V_{tt}$;

To determine V_{inv} we need to set the threshold d for $D(v)$, and compute $V_{inv} := (V - C) \bigcup \{v | v \in C \wedge D(v) \geq d\}$, where $(V - C)$ are all variables that are outside of the COI. (In our tool the value of d is a run-time option.)

Phase 2: Approximation

Having defined H, we need to evaluate $\hat{\mathcal{F}}_0$ and $\hat{\mathcal{F}}_R$ in order to compute $\hat{S}_0$ and $\hat{R}$ for $\hat{M}$. We could evaluate them directly, i.e. quantifier elimination. For asynchronous systems, $\hat{\mathcal{F}}_R$ is usually made up of a disjunction of transition blocks and existential quantification can distribute over them. Synchronous models however consist of conjunctions of small transition blocks and existential quantifiers do not distribute over them. This means that we need to build a monolithic BDD for the formulae $\mathcal{F}_0$ and $\mathcal{F}_R$ and then perform quantifier elimination on them. This is computationally very expensive, especially in the case of $\hat{\mathcal{F}}_R$.

This problem can be avoided if we allow the existential quantifiers to distribute over the conjunctions. In other words, we want to push the quantification to the small transition blocks. This computation can be relatively easy because the blocks are often small. But of course the resulting model is not $\hat{M}$ anymore, but an *approximation* of it, which we denote $\hat{M}_{app}$. It is proved in [6] that this approximation does not cause the loss of any initial states and transitions, i.e. $\hat{M}_{app}$ simulates $\hat{M}$ (see [6] or [16] for the definition of a simulation relation for Kripke structures). By transitivity of the simulation relation, $\hat{M}_{app}$ simulates M because $\hat{M}_{app}$ simulates $\hat{M}$ and $\hat{M}$ simulates M [16]. In order to show the correctness of the mechanism, we need to show that $\hat{M}_{app}$ contains the information that we can use to estimate the length of counter-examples of M. This we do in the following lemma.

Lemma 1. *If a state $s \in S$ is reachable in M from any state in S_0, then its abstract counterpart $\hat{s}$ is also reachable in $\hat{M}_{app}$ from any state in $\hat{S}_0$.*

The proof of this lemma is omitted. In essence, this lemma implies that if a counter-example is present in the original model, it must be manifest in the abstract model $\hat{M}$ as well as in the approximation $\hat{M}_{app}$. Note that both the abstraction and approximation do not 'lose' any transitions of the original system, although internal transitions with one abstract state are not visible in $\hat{M}$. Thus, the admissibility of the approach will therefore not be affected (see [17]). This guarantees the resulting counter-example will be the shortest.

Phase 3: Constructing a Heuristic

The purpose of a heuristic is to estimate the number of transitions from each concrete state to a goal state (or error state). The heuristic value for each state $s \in S$ in M is simply the number of transitions from $\hat{s} = H(s)$ to the abstract goal state in $\hat{M}_{app}$. This type of heuristic is usually referred to as a *pattern database* [8,11,17], where *pattern* is another term for abstraction. The term *database* means the heuristic is a memory-based heuristic that can be handled by a hash table, where the indices represent abstract states and the entries are heuristic values. As in our earlier work [17], we use a set of BDDs to store the heuristic, called symbolic pattern databases (SPDB) and denoted by $\sigma = \{B_1, B_2, ..., B_n\}$. Note that the set of states represented by these BDDs are disjoint, i.e. $B_1 \wedge B_2 \wedge ... \wedge B_n = \phi$. Each B_i represents a set of abstract states that have the same heuristic value, and hence have the same number of transitions to the abstract goal state. A SPDB can be constructed using both backward and forward blind BFS search in $\hat{M}_{app}$:

Backward Construction. Use a BDD-based BFS strategy to explore $\hat{M}_{app}$, and start at the abstract goal. Put each frontier-BDD into the heuristic hash table with the number of iterations as the entry in SPDB. Terminate if an abstract initial state is encountered.

Forward Construction. Instead, start at an abstract initial state, and store each frontier temporarily. If the search detects the abstract goal, then extract the path backward from the goal to the initial state. The set of BDDs that comprises the path is a forward SPDB. This process is the same as the counter-example extraction in standard invariant checking. The paths generated here are a subset of the paths extracted by backward SPDB.

It is of course possible that the heuristic synthesis procedure cannot find a trace in the approximation $\hat{M}_{app}$. In that case the original model M does not have a counter-example (by Lemma 1).

Splitting the BDD. Let $\sigma = \{B_1, B_2, \ldots, B_n\}$ be the heuristic (SPDB) that is synthesised by the the 3-phase process described above. The following algorithm splits a BDD into several BDDs that are the disjoint subsets of the original set of states. In order to contain the BDD size after splitting, we use the *restrict* operator on BDDs, denoted by $\downarrow$. Note the subscript i of each B_i indicates the number of transitions B_i to the error state in the abstract model. The heuristic of a concrete state is simply the value of i of its corresponding abstract state and is used by BDD-IDA* to prioritise the state space search and hence for efficient error detection.

Procedure SplitAndPush $(Cost, \mathcal{S}, \sigma)$
    for each $B_i \in \sigma$ do
        $I \leftarrow \mathcal{S} \downarrow B_i$
        if $(I \neq \phi)$
            $stack.push() \leftarrow (Cost + 1, i, I)$
        $\mathcal{S} \leftarrow \mathcal{S} \wedge \overline{I}$
    if $(\mathcal{S} \neq \phi)$
        $stack.push() \leftarrow (Cost + 1, \infty, \mathcal{S})$

4 The GOLFER Tool and Experiments

The algorithms described above have been implemented in an model checker called GOLFER. The tool GOLFER incorporates the heuristic search algorithms A*, IDA* and weighted A*, and will construct a SPDB as part of heuristic synthesis using the abstraction/approximation techniques described above.

GOLFER is built on top of the open-source model checker NuSMV [4], and offers almost all the BDD-based verification facilities included in the system. It allows, for example, the user to choose an input ordering and transition-partition heuristics. Additionally, we have implemented a frontier-partition heuristic that is important in the guided model checking algorithm. As well as the automatic abstraction construction that uses the data dependency analysis, GOLFER allows the user to input the abstraction H as a file of variable strength values.

The work is of course on-going and the current version of GOLFER consists of about 3200 lines of C code (not including the NuSMV code).

To evaluate the ideas presented in this paper we have experimentally compared the performance of BDD-IDA* in GOLFER and the standard algorithms in NuSMV (namely BDD-BFS and a SAT-based bounded model checking algorithm). Note that in our experiment both BDD-IDA* and BDD-BFS use the same transition partition method of NuSMV for each model. We compare the run-time and memory usage for these methods. These approaches all operate in a fully automated manner, without any user interference except that we need to set up a bound for our algorithm and the SAT-based algorithm. In the experiment we set the bound to 50 and use the zChaff solver for the SAT algorithm. We first compare the performance of GOLFER and NuSMV on a simple game. We then follow with more realistic models. In the experiment we used known good BDD variable orderings for both BDD-IDA* and BDD-BFS when they were available. We also tried random orderings and found both algorithm has similar sensitivity to the same ordering. All experiments were carried out using shell scripts. The timeout operation (set to 2 hours) was implemented by a perl script. All experiments were conducted in a shared Intel X86 machine (CPU P4 933MHz) running Linux with 6G RAM.

The Sliding-Tile Puzzle. consists of a board of $n \times n$ squares occupied by $n^2 - 1$ tiles. Each tile exactly fits on one square and is labelled by a number ranging from 1 to $n^2 - 1$. Starting in some given initial configuration of the tiles on the board, the aim of the game is to move the tiles one at a time by utilising the empty square until some given goal configuration is reached. Each state of the puzzle has between 2 and 4 successors, hence the branching factor for the search graph is small. In the experiment, we use a 3×3 board and 8 tiles. We encode the puzzle in the SMV input language and randomly generate 500 solvable initial configurations. We show the results for our algorithm BDD-IDA* and the standard BDD-BFS approach in NuSMV in Figure 2. (The SAT-based approach is not included at this stage as it is not competitive on small models.)

In Figure 2 we group, average and order the data for the runs that result in the same solution depth. Generally, but not always, the shorter the solution

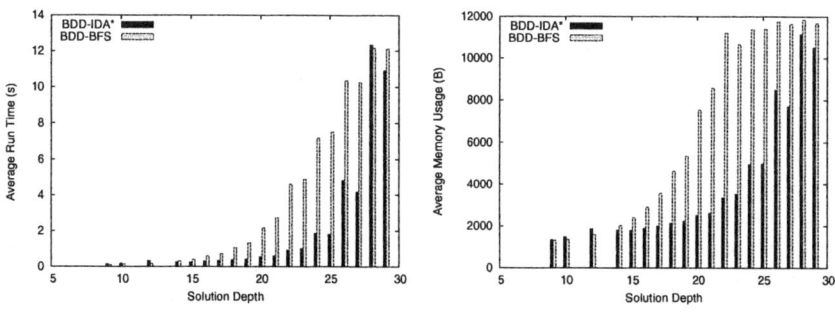

Fig. 2. Run-time and memory usage for IDA* and BFS for the sliding-tile puzzle

depth, the faster the model checker finds the solution. Most solutions for the 500 starting configurations were in the range 17 to 27. Within this solution range BDD-IDA* outperforms BDD-BFS in both time and memory. For configurations with shorter solutions, BDD-BFS is generally faster than BDD-IDA* because of the overhead of the abstraction process in BDD-IDA*, which dominates when the goal configuration is just a few transitions away. For configurations with the longest solutions, BDD-IDA* and BDD-BFS perform similarly. It is not clear why this is the case. It is true that there are few long solutions, so the sparseness of data may be contributing to this behaviour. However, we have observed the heuristic is quite poor for these configurations. If we manually generate a better heuristic for these configurations, we found that BDD-IDA* performed much better than BDD-BFS. We therefore feel that the data dependency analysis may be responsible, and conjecture that abstracting the system by eliminating supposedly weak variables loses validity in the longest runs. This may be an artifact of the particular data-dependency analysis that we have used.

While this data provides an interesting comparison between the 2 methods, one needs to remember that these methods are certainly not the best way to solve this kind of puzzle. An explicit-state model checker for example could be made to solve these puzzles faster than any of the above methods.

Real-World Examples. We applied the BDD-IDA* and BDD-BFS to the 8 models listed in Table 1. In this table, we show the type of model and the size of the SMV specification in each case. Some of the models can be found from

Table 1. Model used in the experimentation

Name	Description	Type	Lines SMV code
dme	distributed mutual exclusive ring	circuit	102
leader	concurrent leader election	protocol	129
mutex	mutual exclusion	protocol	116
ns	Needham-Schroeder public key protocol	protocol	319
peter	Peterson's mutual exclusion algorithm	protocol	126
sr	sender receiver protocol	protocol	106
tarb	tree arbiter	circuit	142
tcas	traffic collision avoiding system	controller	3269

Bwolen Yang's collection of SMV models. If a model is parameterised, the value of the parameter is indicated by a numerical suffix in the name of the model. We sometimes also used the same model with different invariants. These models contain a parenthesised 'p' suffix in the model name.

The experimental results for comparing BDD-IDA* and BDD-BFS are shown in Table 2. For each model, we show the number of Boolean variables (#Vars) that are used to encode the model, the length of the counter-examples (CX), and the run-time and the number of BDD nodes for each of the methods (when possible). The table shows that BDD-IDA* consistently outperforms BDD-BFS in all but one case, *peter-3*. Note that the run-times for BDD-IDA* include the time for heuristic synthesis. We believe that the poor performance in the case

Table 2. Experimental results for BDD-IDA*, BDD-BFS

			Run-time		# BDD Nodes	
Model	# Vars	CX	BDD-IDA*	BDD-BFS	BDD-IDA*	BDD-BFS
dme6	240	28	78.46	–	655163	–
dme8	320	30	7033.99	–	4499580	–
leader-3	85	16	1.01	1.65	305231	535585
leader-4	128	18	11.07	40.33	228193	223136
leader-5	168	20	111.62	502.18	981095	2335851
leader-6	200	22	1123.79	5486.61	3945215	4988551
mutex-16	141	10	0.66	11.13	208967	439208
mutex-20	175	10	1.01	36.13	320392	598775
mutex-24	207	10	1.56	87.59	461404	2486530
mutex-28	239	10	2.30	208.93	158186	4898940
ns (p1)	87	14	0.90	13.14	183538	117207
ns (p2)	133	14	7.43	341.80	103938	1267943
peter-3	72	26	0.59	0.42	151819	144783
peter-4	103	42	10.06	54.87	278411	542995
sr-11	273	14	0.44	67.14	177872	237768
sr-12	297	14	0.70	95.83	211911	262272
tarb-15	244	24	15.29	431.64	258489	6743882
tarb-17	276	24	32.11	712.31	464059	12649365
tarb-19	308	24	28.46	561.77	626627	11079508
tcas (p1)	292	12	4.44	25.07	190876	617102
tcas (p2)	292	16	3.43	92.11	536990	2918189
tcas (p3)	292	24	9.45	2364.88	328944	17165753
tcas (p4)	292	18	116.37	250.39	1745925	10673258
tcast (p1)	292	12	5.34	27.94	230336	623381
tcast (p2)	292	18	38.05	275.91	623307	6224724
tcast (p3)	292	16	4.37	107.33	562949	1625174
tcast (p4)	292	16	4.97	93.85	552857	1620110

Table 3. Experimental results for BDD-IDA*, BDD-BFS and SAT

	Run-time		
Model	BDD-IDA*	BDD-BFS	SAT
dme6	78.46	–	176.37
dme8	7033.99	–	521.77
ns (p2)	7.43	341.80	192.80
tarb-15	15.29	431.64	121.61
tarb-17	32.11	712.31	156.45
tarb-19	28.46	561.77	195.11

of *peter-3* is an artifact of its smallness: the run-time is short and the automatic heuristic synthesis is an overhead that BDD-BFS does not have. In the cases *mutex* and *tcas*, BDD-IDA* can be up to 2 orders of magnitude faster. In most cases, less BDD nodes are used, sometimes an order of magnitude less. In the few cases where more BDD nodes were used, it was the same order of magnitude.

We cannot see from this data how much of the improved run-times comes from the 'falsification superiority' of DFS over BFS (note the very different BDD-partitioning schemes used in both strategies clouds this issue somewhat as well), and how much is a result of the guided search. We have used the same run-time options in all cases. In a few cases, we did notice that by changing certain run-time options such as the threshold of partition size or partition heuristics, we could improve the performance for BDD-BFS. However, we could never make it perform better than BDD-IDA*. We have not tried to fine-tune the partitioning scheme used in BDD-IDA*. Placing this work in context we should note that all the models contain at most a few invariant properties, and we know these properties are false. The experimental context is hence somewhat artificial and

BDD-IDA*may not produce such performance improvements when used to verify models containing many properties. Furthermore, BDD-IDA* detects counter-examples. If the algorithm does not return before the timeout then we cannot say whether a counter-example exists or not.

We also compared the run-time of BDD-IDA*, BDD-BFS and SAT methods and the results are shown in Table 3. Note that we only do so if the SAT has better performance than BDD-BFS. Of 6 models we have experimented, BDD-IDA*detects error faster than SAT in 5 models. For model "dme8", our BDD-IDA* runs much slower than SAT for some unknown reason.

Optimality. The performance of BDD-IDA* is dependent on the quality of the heuristic. Suppose the heuristic cost for a BDD is h^* and the exact cost h, then the quality is determined by the smallness of $\mid h^* - h \mid$. We in fact don't care whether h^* over- or under-estimates the real cost, but if it does over-estimate the cost, then we cannot guarantee that the algorithm will find the shortest counter-example. In model checking this is not normally an issue, but in general, and in particular in artificial intelligence, it can be a very serious issue. In fact, the heuristic synthesis procedure used in this work always results in a heuristic that under-estimates the cost because it is based on homomorphic abstractions [17]. To improve the effectiveness of the heuristic, we could instead use the heuristic cost $a \times h^*$ instead of h^*, where $a > 1$ is a constant factor that can be tuned for specific applications. We could go a step further and use the total cost formula $f^* = b \times g + a \times h^*$ where a, b are constant values and g is the exact cost from the initial BDD (or state) to the current BDD (state). This may speed up the search dramatically, but optimality can no longer be guaranteed.

5 Related Work

The main work in BDD-based guided model checking uses prioritised traversal techniques. In [3] Cabodi et. al. proposed a mixed forward-backward prioritised traversal algorithm that checks invariant properties. This work is closely related to our approach as both share the idea of using prioritised traversal as well as abstractions and approximations. However, Cabodi et. al. differ in the way they combine these aspects:

- They construct an approximation of the concrete model and use it to approximate the forward reachable state set, which is then used to prioritise the backward traversal of the state space. They use a best-first search algorithm. We use approximation for the computationally-intensive abstraction process. The heuristic synthesis in our approach is goal-oriented and BDD-IDA* also takes the real cost into account. As well, the state space search of our approach is iterative deepening which characterises the SAT-based search strategy.
- They study only forward-backward traversal orders, which are more suited to circuits than communication protocols (for example) because traversals in both directions may not be possible even in the abstract model due to high branching factors. In our work we do not restrict ourselves in this way.

During the approximation phase, we do not have to traverse from the target to the initial states. Because our approximation is target-oriented, partial approximation traversal also serves as a heuristic for estimating the length of partial counter-examples.

In [18,12] prioritised traversal algorithms are proposed based on BDD partitioning (or subsetting). A so-called "high-density" reachability analysis is used as a BDD optimisation technique to traverse the state space of the system, and the density of a BDD is defined to be the ratio of states the BDD can represent over its size. The BDD with higher density will gain higher priority in the state space traversal. This technique only aims at optimising the size of BDDs and offers no guidance to the model checking algorithm in the search for error states. In our work, heuristics are synthesised from the abstract model, and provide direct information about potential error states in the model. The above approaches use the VIS language and we use SMV. It would be possible combine our work with the above approaches, but there would be difficulties.

Most work in guided model checking is based on the explicit-state representation [9,20,21]. The first work on guided model checking in [22] applies prioritised state space exploration to model checking and proposes practical heuristics to guide the search. Heuristic search algorithms such as A* and IDA* have also been used in explicit-state model checking in HFS-SPIN [9], recently Hopper (implemented on top of Murφ) [20] and FLAVERS [21]. All this work shows that the heuristic search algorithm can enhance the model checker's ability to detect counter-examples. The role of BDDs, particularly in combination with IDA*, is an important aspect of our work of course, as is the use of heuristic synthesis, which none of these authors above have addressed.

6 Conclusion and Future Work

In this work we have presented a fully automatic, symbolic, abstraction-guided model checker that builds its own abstract model, and uses this model as heuristic to guide the model checker. The main contribution of this work is its integration of:

- a data dependency analysis that is used to build an abstract model
- IDA* with heuristic synthesised from the abstract model, and
- a BDD partitioning algorithm in BDD-IDA* based on the heuristic.

The heuristic, which plays a vital role in guided search, is 'double-dipped' in this research: it not only guides the IDA* search strategy, it also provides a mechanism to partition the search space (i.e. BDDs). While it is true that the internal BDD operations are more complex than standard BDD-BFS, this is hidden from the user.

The 'bug-hunting' ability of DFS has long been recognised, as is attested by the huge popularity of SPIN. But SPIN is not symbolic of course, and is not guided, and being conventional DFS, is not always able to find the nearest bugs, which BFS does so well. The GOLFER tool adds a functionality to NuSMV that is all of the above, without the expense of BFS.

There is of course much work to be done. Foremost will be gaining a better understanding of the best type of data analysis to use to build the abstract model. It is not clear whether other notions of weak and strong may be more appropriate in determining whether a variable is important or not in guiding the search algorithm. For example, the current notion of eliminating weak variables does not work when all variables are equally related to the property variables. One direction for future research in this area is machine learning. Extending the framework to search for counter-examples for liveness properties is also an useful step to take.

Finally, in the abstraction-refinement framework Clarke et al. [5] uses abstraction in a very different way to us (we use it only to compute a heuristic). Nevertheless, the efficient way we detect counter-examples, which play an important role in refinement, could be usefully employed in that framework.

Acknowledgement. We would like to thank all anonymous referees for their corrections and suggestions.

References

1. A. Biere, A. Cimatti, E. M. Clarke, and Y. Zhu. Symbolic model checking without BDDs. In *TACAS '99: Proceedings of the 5th International Conference on Tools and Algorithms for Construction and Analysis of Systems*, pages 193–207. Springer-Verlag, 1999.
2. R. E. Bryant. Graph-based algorithms for Boolean function manipulation. *IEEE Transaction*, C-35(8):677–691, Aug 1986.
3. G. Cabodi, S. Nocco, and S. Quer. Mixing forward and backward traversals in guided-prioritized bdd-based verification. In *Proceedings of the 14th International Conference Computer Aided Verification, Copenhagen, Denmark, July 27-31*, volume 2404 of *LNCS*, pages 471–484. Springer, 2002.
4. A. Cimatti, E. M. Clarke, F. Giunchiglia, and M. Roveri. NuSMV: A new symbolic model verifier. In *Proceedings of the 11th International Conference on Computer Aided Verification, Trento, Italy, July 6-10*, volume 1633 of *LNCS*, pages 495–499. Springer, 1999.
5. E. Clarke, A. Gupta, J. Kukula, and O. Strichman. SAT based abstraction-refinement using ILP and machine learning techniques. In *Proceedings of the 14th International Conference on Computer Aided Verification, Copenhagen, Denmark, July 27-31*, volume 2404 of *LNCS*, pages 265–279. Springer, 2002.
6. E. M. Clarke, O. Grumberg, and D. E. Long. Model checking and abstraction. *ACM Transactions on Programming Languages and Systems*, 16(5):1512–1542, September 1994.
7. E. M. Clarke, O. Grumberg, and D. Peled. *Model Checking*. MIT Press, 1999.
8. J. C. Culberson and J. Schaeffer. Searching with pattern databases. In *Proceedings of the 11th Biennial Conference of the Canadian Society for Computational Studies of Intelligence, Toronto, Ontario, Canada, May 21-24*, volume 1081 of *LNCS*, pages 402–416. Springer, 1996.
9. S. Edelkamp, A. L. Lafuente, and S. Leue. Directed explicit model checking with HSF–SPIN. In *Model Checking Software, 8th International SPIN Workshop, Toronto, Canada, May 19-20, Proceedings*, volume 2057 of *LNCS*, pages 57–79. Springer, 2001.

10. S. Edelkamp, S. Leue, and A. Lluch-Lafuente. Directed explicit-state model checking in the validation of communication protocols. Technical report, Albert-Ludwigs-Universitt Freiburg, 2001.
11. S. Edelkamp and A. Lluch-Lafuente. Abstraction databases in theory and model checking practice. In *Proceedings of Workshop on Connecting Planning Theory with Practice, International Conference on Automated Planning and Scheduling (ICAPS), Whistler, Canada*, 2004.
12. R. Fraer, G. Kamhi, B. Ziv, M. Y. Vardi, and L. Fix. Prioritized traversal: Efficient reachability analysis for verification and falsification. In *Proceedings of 12th International Conference on Computer Aided Verification*, volume 1855 of *LNCS*, pages 389–402. Springer, 2000.
13. R. Korf. Iterative-deepening A*: An optimal admissible tree search. In *Ninth International Joint Conference on Artificial Intelligence(IJCAI-85)*, pages 1034–1036, LA,California,USA, 1985. Morgan Kaufmann.
14. R. Korf. Linear-space best-first search. *Artificial Intelligence*, 62(1):41–78, July 1993.
15. K. McMillan. *Symbolic model checking*. Kluwer Academic Publishers, Boston, MA, 1993.
16. K. Qian and A. Nymeyer. Abstraction-based model checking using heuristical refinement. In *Proceedings of the 2nd Internation Symposium on Automated Technology for Verification and Analysis (ATVA'04), to appear*, LNCS. Springer, 2004.
17. K. Qian and A. Nymeyer. Guided invariant model checking based on abstraction and symbolic pattern databases. In *Proceedings of the 10th Internation Conference on Tools and Algorithms for the Construction and Analysis of Systems, Barcelona, Spain,*, volume 2988 of *LNCS*, pages 497–511. Springer, 2004.
18. K. Ravi and F. Somenzi. High-density reachability analysis. In *ICCAD '95: Proceedings of the 1995 IEEE/ACM International Conference on Computer-Aided Design*, pages 154–158. IEEE Computer Society, 1995.
19. A. Santone. Heuristic search + local model checking in selective mu-calculus. *IEEE Transactions on Software Engineering*, 29(6):510–523, 2003.
20. K. Seppi, M. Jones, and P. Lamborn. Guided model checking with a bayesian meta-heuristic. In *Proceedings of the Fourth International Conference on Application of Concurrency to System Design (ACSD'04)*, pages 217–226. IEEE, 2004.
21. J. Tan, G. S. Avrunin, L. A. Clarke, S. Zilberstein, and S. Leue. Heuristic-guided counterexample search in flavers. In *SIGSOFT '04/FSE-12: Proceedings of the 12th ACM SIGSOFT Twelfth International Symposium on Foundations of Software Engineering*, pages 201–210. ACM Press, 2004.
22. C. H. Yang and D. L. Dill. Validation with guided search of the state space. In *Proceedings of the 35th Conference on Design Automation, Moscone Center, San Francico, California, USA, June 15-19*, pages 599–604. ACM Press, 1998.

Modeling and Verification of Safety-Critical Systems Using Safecharts

Pao-Ann Hsiung and Yen-Hung Lin

Department of Computer Science and Information Engineering,
National Chung Cheng University, Chiayi, Taiwan−621, ROC
hpa@computer.org

Abstract. With rapid development in science and technology, we now see the ubiquitous use of different types of *safety-critical systems* in our daily lives such as in avionics, consumer electronics, and medical systems. In such systems, unintentional design faults might result in injury or even death to human beings. To make sure that safety-critical systems are really safe, there is need to verify them formally. However, the verification of such systems is getting more and more difficult, because the designs are becoming very complex. To cope with high design complexity, currently model-driven architecture design is becoming a well-accepted trend. However, conventional methods of code testing and standards conformance do not fit very well with such model-based approaches. To bridge this gap, we propose a model-based formal verification technique for safety-critical systems. In this work, the *model checking paradigm* is applied to the *Safecharts model* which was used for modeling, but not yet used for verification. Our contributions are five folds. Firstly, the safety constraints in Safecharts are mapped to semantic equivalents in timed automata for verification. Secondly, the theory for safety constraint verification is proved and implemented in a compositional model checker (SGM). Thirdly, prioritized transitions are implemented in SGM to model the risk semantics in Safecharts. Fourthly, it is shown how the original Safecharts lacked synchronization semantics which could lead to safety hazards. A solution to this issue is also proposed. Finally, it is shown that priority-based approach to mutual exclusion of resource usage in the original Safecharts is unsafe and corresponding solutions are proposed here. Application examples show the feasibility and benefits of the proposed model-driven verification of safety-critical systems.

1 Introduction

Safety-critical systems are systems whose failure most probably results in the tragic loss of human life or damage to human property. There are numerous examples of these mishaps. The accident at the Three Mile Island nuclear power plant in Pennsylvania on 28th March, 1979 is just one unfortunate example. Moreover, as time goes on, there are more and more cars, airplanes, rapid transit systems, medical facilities, and consumer electronics, which are all safety-critical systems appearing in our daily lives. When some of them malfunction or fault, a tragedy is inevitable. The natural question that comes to mind is that can we use these systems without 100% warranty? Obviously, the answer is negative. That's why we need some methodology to exhaustively verify safety-critical systems.

Traditional verification methods such as simulation and testing can only prove the presence of faults and not their absence. Simulation and testing [11] both involve making experiments before deploying the system in the field. While simulation is performed on an abstract model of a system, testing is performed on the actual product. In the case of hardware circuits, simulation is performed on the design of the circuit, whereas testing is performed on the fabricated circuit itself. In both cases, these methods typically inject signals at certain points in the system and observe the resulting signals at other points. For software, simulation and testing usually involve providing certain inputs and observing the corresponding outputs. These methods can be a cost-efficient way to find many errors. However, checking all of the possible interactions and potential pitfalls using simulation and testing techniques is rarely possible. Conventionally, safety-critical systems are validated through standards conformance and code testing. Using such verification methods for safety-critical systems cannot provide the desired 100% confidence on system correctness.

In contrast to the traditional verification methods, formal verification is exhaustive and provides 100% guarantee. Further, unlike simulation, formal verification does not require any testbenches or stimuli for triggering a system. More precisely, formal verification is a mathematical way of proving a system satisfies a set of properties. *Formal verification* methods such model checking [4] are being taken seriously in the recent few years by several large hardware and software design companies such as Intel, IBM, Motorola, and Microsoft, which goes to show the importance and practicality of such methods for real-time embedded systems and SoC designs. For the above reasons, we will thus employ a widely popular formal verification method called *model checking* for the verification of safety-critical systems that are formally modeled.

In the course of developing a model-based verification method for safety-critical systems, several issues are encountered as detailed in the following. First and foremost, we need to decide how to model safety-critical systems. Our decision is to adopt Safecharts [4] as our models. Safecharts are a variant of Statecharts, especially for use in the specification and the design of safety-critical systems. The objective of the model is to provide a sharper focus on safety issues and a systematic approach to deal with them. This is achieved in Safecharts by making a clear separation between functional and safety requirements. Other issues encountered in designing the formal verification methodology for model-based safety-critical systems are as follows:

1. How to transform Safecharts into a semantically equivalent *Extended Timed Automata* (ETA) model that can be accepted by traditional model checkers? How can the transformation preserve the safety semantics in Safecharts?
2. What are the properties that must be specified for model checking Safecharts?
3. Basic states in Safecharts have a risk relation with each other specifying the comparative risk/safety levels. How do we represent such information in ETA for model checking?
4. Safecharts have safety loopholes due to the lack of synchronization mechanisms. A motivational example will be given in Section 4.4.

5. The current semantics of Safecharts states that mutual exclusion of resource usages can be achieved through priority. This is clearly insufficient as priorities cannot ensure mutual exclusion.

The remaining portion is organized as follows. Section 2 describes the background form our model including a comparison between conventional validation, such as simulation and testing, and formal verification. Basic definitions used in our work are given in Section 3. Section 4 will formulate each of our solutions to solving the above described problems in formally verifying safety-critical systems modelled by Safecharts. The article is concluded and future research directions are given in Section 6.

2 Related Work

A commonly-used method to demonstrate the safety of a system is *proof by contradiction* [13]. In this method, we assume that the unsafe states, identified by hazard analysis, can be reached by executing the program. We then systematically analyze the code and show that the pre-conditions for a hazardous state are contradicted by the post-conditions of all program paths leading to that state. If this is the case, the initial assumption of an unsafe state is incorrect. If this is repeated for all identified hazards, then the system is safe. However, to find and list all possible hazards of safety-critical systems is difficult. For example, a system may fail due to an unpredicted hazard that may lead to a serious tragedy. This is not allowed, and that's why we propose a more formal method to verify safety-critical systems that are modeled by Safecharts and verified by model checking as introduced in the rest of this Section.

Safecharts [4] is a variant of Statecharts intended exclusively for safety-critical systems design. With two separate representations for functional and safety requirements, Safecharts brings the distinctions and dependencies between them into sharper focus, helping both designers and auditors alike in modeling and reviewing safety features. Safecharts incorporates ways to represent equipment failures and failure handling mechanisms and uses a safety-oriented classification of transitions and a safety-oriented scheme for resolving any unpredictable nondeterministic pattern of behavior. It achieves these through an explicit representation of risks posed by hazardous states by means of an ordering of states and a concept called *risk band*. Recognizing the possibility of gaps and inaccuracies in safety analysis, Safecharts do not permit transitions between states with unknown relative risk levels. However, in order to limit the number of transitions excluded in this manner, Safecharts provides a default interpretation for relative risk levels between states not covered by the risk ordering relation, requiring the designer to clarify the risk levels in the event of a disagreement and thus improving the risk assessment process.

Timed Computation Tree Logic (TCTL) is a *timed* extension of the well-known temporal logic called *Computation Tree Logic* (CTL) which was proposed by Clarke and Emerson in 1981. We will use TCTL to specify system properties that are required to be satisfied.

Model checking [2,3,12] is a technique for verifying finite state concurrent systems. One benefit of this restriction is that verification can be performed automatically. The procedure normally uses an exhaustive search of the state space of a system to determine if some specification is true or not. Given sufficient resources, the procedure will always terminate with a *yes/no* answer. Moreover, it can be implemented by algorithms with reasonable efficiency, which can be run on moderate-sized machines. The process of model checking includes three parts: modeling, specification, and verification. *Modeling* is to convert a design into a formalism accepted by a model checking tool. Before verification, *specification*, which is usually given in some logical formalism, is necessary to state the properties that the design must satisfy. The *verification* is completely automated. However, in practice it often involves human assistance. One such manual activity is the analysis of the verification results. In case of a negative result, the user is often provided with an error trace. This can be used as a counterexample for the checked property and can help the designer in tracking down where the error occurred. In this case, analyzing the error trace may require a modification to the system and a reapplication of the model checking algorithm.

Our safety-critical system model and its model checking procedures are implemented in the *State-Graph Manipulators* (SGM) model checker [14], which is a high-level model checker for both real-time systems as well as systems-on-chip modeled by a set of timed automata.

3 System Model, Specification, and Model Checking

Before going into the details of how Safecharts are used to model and verify safety-critical systems, some basic definitions and formalizations are required as given in this Section. Both Safecharts and their translated ETA models will be defined. TCTL and model checking will also be formally described.

Definition 1. Statechart
Statecharts are a tuple $\mathcal{F} = (\mathcal{S}, \mathcal{T}, \mathcal{E}, \Theta, \mathcal{V}, \Phi)$, where $\mathcal{S}$ is a set of all states, $\mathcal{T}$ is a set of all possible transitions, $\mathcal{E}$ is a set of all events, Θ is the set of possible types of states in Statecharts, that is, $\Theta = \{AND, OR, BASIC\}$, $\mathcal{V}$ is a set of integer variables, and $\Phi ::= v \sim c \mid \Phi_1 \wedge \Phi_2 \mid \neg \Phi_1$, in which $v \in \mathcal{V}$, $\sim \in \{<, \leq, =, \geq, >\}$, c is an integer, and Φ_1 and Φ_2 are predicates. Let $\mathcal{F}_i$ be an arbitrary state in $\mathcal{S}$. It has the general form:

$$\mathcal{F}_i = (\theta_i, C_i, d_i, T_i, E_i, l_i)$$

where:

- θ_i : the type of the state $\mathcal{F}_i$; $\theta_i \in \Theta$.
- C_i : a finite set of direct substates of $\mathcal{F}_i$, referred to as *child states* of $\mathcal{F}_i$, $C_i \subseteq \mathcal{S}$.
- $d_i : d_i \in C_i$ and is referred to as the *default state* of $\mathcal{F}_i$. It applies only to OR states.
- T_i : a finite subset of $\mathcal{T}$, referred to as explicitly *specified transitions* in $\mathcal{F}_i$.
- E_i : the finite set of events relevant to the specified transitions in T_i; $E_i \subseteq \mathcal{E}$.
- l_i : a function $T_i \to \mathcal{E} \times \Phi \times 2^{E_i}$, labelling each and every specified transition in T_i with a triple, 2^{E_i} denoting the set of all finite subsets of E_i. □

Given a transition $t \in \mathcal{T}$, its label is denoted by $l(t) = (e, fcond, a)$, written conventionally as $e[fcond]/a$. e, $fcond$ and a in the latter, denoted also as $trg(t) =$

$e, con(t) = fcond$, and $gen(t) = a$, represent respectively the triggering event, the guarding condition and the set of generated actions.

Definition 2. Safechart
Safecharts $\mathcal{Z}$ extend Statecharts by adding a safety-layer. States are extended with a risk ordering relation and transitions are extended with safety conditions. Given two comparable states s_1 and s_2, a risk ordering relation $\sqsubseteq$ specifies their relative risk levels, that is $s_1 \sqsubseteq s_2$ specifies s_1 is safer then s_2. Transition labels in Safecharts have an extended form:

$$e[fcond]/a[l,u]\Psi[G]$$

where $e, fcond$, and a are the same as in Statecharts. The time interval $[l, u)$ is a real-time constraint on a transition t and imposes the condition that t does not execute until at least l time units have elapsed since it most recently became enabled and must execute strictly within u time units. The expression $\Psi[G]$ is a safety enforcement on the transition execution and is determined by the safety clause G. The safety clause G is a predicate, which specifies the conditions under which a given transition t must, or must not, execute. Ψ is a binary valued constant, signifying one of the following enforcement values:

- *Prohibition* enforcement value, denoted by ⇂. Given a transition label of the form ⇂ $[G]$, it signifies that the transition is forbidden to execute as long as G holds.
- *Mandatory* enforcement value, denoted by ↾. Given a transition label of the form $[l, u)$ ↾ $[G]$, it indicates that whenever G holds the transition is forced to execute within the time interval $[l, u)$, even in the absence of a triggering event. □

The Safecharts model is used for modeling safety-critical systems, however the model checker SGM can understand only a flattened model called *Extended Timed Automata* [6] as defined in the following.

Definition 3. Mode Predicate
Given a set C of clock variables and a set D of discrete variables, the syntax of a *mode predicate* η over C and D is defined as: $\eta := \mathit{false} \mid x \sim c \mid x - y \sim c \mid d \sim c \mid \eta_1 \wedge \eta_2 \mid \neg\eta_1$, where $x, y \in C$, $\sim \in \{\leq, <, =, \geq, >\}$, $c \in \mathcal{N}$, $d \in D$, and η_1, η_2 are mode predicates. □

Let $B(C, D)$ be the set of all mode predicates over C and D.

Definition 4. Extended Timed Automaton
An *Extended Timed Automaton* (ETA) is a tuple $\mathcal{A}_i = (M_i, m_i^0, C_i, D_i, L_i, \chi_i, T_i, \psi_i, \tau_i, \rho_i)$ such that: M_i is a finite set of modes, $m_i^0 \in M_i$ is the initial mode, C_i is a set of clock variables, D_i is a set of discrete variables, L_i is a set of synchronization labels, and $\epsilon \in L_i$ is a special label that represents asynchronous behavior (i.e. no need of synchronization), $\chi_i : M_i \mapsto B(C_i, D_i)$ is an *invariance* function that labels each mode with a condition true in that mode, $T_i \subseteq M_i \times M_i$ is a set of transitions, $\lambda_i : T_i \mapsto L_i$ associates a synchronization label with a transition, $\tau_i : T_i \mapsto B(C_i, D_i)$ defines the transition triggering conditions, and $\rho_i : T_i \mapsto 2^{C_i \cup (D_i \times \mathcal{N})}$ is an *assignment* function that maps each transition to a set of assignments such as resetting some clock variables and setting some discrete variables to specific integer values. □

A system state space is represented by a *system state graph* as defined in Definition 5.

Definition 5. System State Graph
Given a system $\mathcal{S}$ with n components modelled by $\mathcal{A}_i = (M_i, m_i^0, C_i, D_i, L_i, \chi_i, T_i, \psi_i, \tau_i, \rho_i)$, $1 \leq i \leq n$, the system model is defined as a state graph represented by $\mathcal{A}_1 \times \ldots \times \mathcal{A}_n = \mathcal{A}_\mathcal{S} = (M, m^0, C, D, L, \chi, T, \psi, \tau, \rho)$, where:

- $M = M_1 \times M_2 \times \ldots \times M_n$ is a finite set of system modes, $m = m_1.m_2.\ldots.m_n \in M$,
- $m^0 = m_1^0.m_2^0.\ldots.m_n^0 \in M$ is the initial system mode,
- $C = \bigcup_i C_i$ is the union of all sets of clock variables in the system,
- $D = \bigcup_i D_i$ is the union of all sets of discrete variables in the system,
- $L = \bigcup_i L_i$ is the union of all sets of synchronization labels in the system,
- $\chi : M \mapsto B(\bigcup_i C_i, \bigcup_i D_i)$, $\chi(m) = \wedge_i \chi_i(m_i)$, where $m = m_1.m_2.\ldots.m_n \in M$.
- $T \subseteq M \times M$ is a set of system transitions which consists of two types of transitions:
  - *Asynchronous transitions*: for each $e \in T$, $\exists i, 1 \leq i \leq n, e_i \in T_i$ such that $e_i = e$
  - *Synchronized transitions*: $\exists i, j, 1 \leq i \neq j \leq n, e_i \in T_i, e_j \in T_j$ such that $\psi_i(e_i) = (l, in), \psi_j(e_j) = (l, out), l \in L_i \cap L_j \neq \emptyset$, $e \in T$ is synchronization of e_i and e_j with conjuncted triggering conditions and union of all transitions assignments (defined later in this definition)
- $\psi : T \mapsto L \times \{in, out\}$ associates a synchronization label and a direction of communication with a transition, which represents a blocking signal that was synchronized, except for $\epsilon \in L$, ϵ is a special label that represents asynchronous behavior (i.e. no need of synchronization),
- $\tau : T \mapsto B(\bigcup_i C_i, \bigcup_i D_i)$, $\tau(e) = \tau_i(e_i)$ for an asynchronous transition and $\tau(e) = \tau_i(e_i) \wedge \tau_j(e_j)$ for a synchronous transition, and
- $\rho : T \mapsto 2^{\bigcup_i C_i \cup (\bigcup_i D_i \times \mathcal{N})}$, $\rho(e) = \rho_i(e_i)$ for an asynchronous transition and $\rho(e) = \rho_i(e_i) \cup \rho_j(e_j)$ for a synchronous transition. □

Definition 6. Safety-Critical System
A *safety-critical system* is defined as a set of *resource* components and *consumer* components. Each component is modeled by one or more Safecharts. If a safety-critical system $\mathcal{H}$ has a set of resource components $\{R_1, R_2, \ldots, R_m\}$ and a set of consumer components $\{C_1, C_2, \ldots, C_n\}$, $\mathcal{H}$ is modeled by $\{\mathcal{Z}_{R_1}, \mathcal{Z}_{R_2}, \ldots, \mathcal{Z}_{R_m}, \mathcal{Z}_{C_1}, \mathcal{Z}_{C_2}, \ldots, \mathcal{Z}_{C_n}\}$, where $\mathcal{Z}_X$ is a Safechart model for component X. Safecharts $\mathcal{Z}_{R_i}$ and $\mathcal{Z}_{C_j}$ are transformed into corresponding ETA $\mathcal{A}_{R_i}$ and $\mathcal{A}_{C_j}$, respectively. Therefore, $\mathcal{H}$ is semantically modeled by the state graph $A_{R_1} \times \ldots \times A_{R_m} \times A_{C_1} \times \ldots \times A_{C_n}$ as defined in Definition 5. □

For both hardware and software systems, a property or requirement can be specified in some *temporal logic*. The SGM model checker chooses TCTL as its logical formalism, as defined below.

Definition 7. Timed Computation Tree Logic (TCTL)
A *timed computation tree logic* formula has the following syntax:

$$\phi ::= \eta \mid EG\phi' \mid E\phi' U_{\sim c}\phi'' \mid \neg\phi' \mid \phi' \vee \phi'',$$

where η is a mode predicate, ϕ' and ϕ'' are TCTL formulae, $\sim \in \{<, \leq, =, \geq, >\}$, and $c \in \mathcal{N}$. $EG\phi'$ means there is a computation from the current state, along which ϕ' is always true. $E\phi' U_{\sim c}\phi''$ means there exists a computation from the current state, along which ϕ' is true until ϕ'' becomes true, within the time constraint of $\sim c$. Shorthands like EF, AF, AG, AU, $\wedge$, and $\rightarrow$ can all be defined [5]. □

Definition 8. Model Checking
Given a Safechart $\mathcal{Z}$ that represents a safety-critical system and a TCTL formula, ϕ, expressing some desired specification, model checking [2,3,12] verifies if $\mathcal{Z}$ satisfies ϕ, denoted by $\mathcal{Z} \models \phi$.

Model checking can be either explicit using a labeling algorithm or symbolic using a fixpoint algorithm. *Binary Decision Diagram* (BDD) and *Difference Bound Matrices* (DBM) are data structures used for Boolean formulas and clock zones [3], respectively. □

4 Model Checking Safecharts

Safecharts have been used to model safety-critical systems, but the models have never been verified. In this work, we propose a method to verify safety-critical systems modelled by Safecharts. Our target model checker is *State Graph Manipulators* (SGM) [14,6], which is a high-level model checker for both real-time systems, as well as, Systems-on-Chip modelled by a set of extended timed automata. As mentioned in Section 1, there are several issues to be resolved in model checking Safecharts.

Basically, a system designer models a safety-critical system using a set of Safecharts. After accepting the Safecharts, we transform them into ETA, while taking care of the safety characterizations in Safecharts, and then automatically generate properties corresponding to the safety constraints. The SGM model checker is enhanced with transition priority, synchronization, and urgency. Resource access mechanisms in Safecharts are also checked for satisfaction of modeling restrictions that prevent violation of mutual exclusion. Finally, we input the translated ETA to SGM to verify the safety-critical system satisfies functional and safety properties. Each of the issues encountered during implementation and the corresponding solutions are detailed in the rest of this section.

4.1 Flattening Safecharts and Safety Semantics

Our primary goal is to model check Safecharts, a variant of Statecharts. However, Safecharts cannot be accepted as system model input by most model checkers, which can accept only flat automata models such as the extended timed automata (ETA) accepted by SGM. As a result, the state hierarchy and concurrency in Safecharts must be transformed into semantically equivalent constructs in ETA. Further, besides the functional layer, Safecharts have an extra safety layer, which must be transformed into equivalent modeling constructs in ETA and specified as properties for verification.

There are three categories of states in Safechart: OR, AND, and $BASIC$. An OR-state, or an AND-state, consists generally of two or more substates. Being in an AND-state means being in all of its substates simultaneously, while being in an OR-state means being in exactly one of its substates. A $BASIC$-state is translated into an ETA *mode*. The translations for OR-states and AND-states are performed as described in [8].

Safety Semantics. The syntax for the triggering condition and action of a transition in Safecharts is:

$$e[fcond]/a[l,u)\Psi[G],$$

where e is the set of triggering events, $fcond$ is the set of guard conditions, a is the set of broadcast events, $[l,u)$ is the time interval specifying the time constraint, Ψ means the execution conditions for safety constraints, and G is the set of safety-layer's guards. In Safecharts, $e[fcond]/a$ appears in the *functional* layer, while $[l,u)\Psi[G]$ may appear in the *safety* layer. The two layers of Safecharts can be integrated into one in ETA as described in the following. However, we need to design three different types of transitions [1]:

- *Eager Evaluation* (ϵ) : Execute the action as soon as possible, i.e. as soon as a guard is enabled. Time cannot progress when a guard is enabled.
- *Delayable Evaluation* (δ) : Can put off execution until the last moment the guard is true. So time cannot progress beyond a *falling edge* of guard.
- *Lazy Evaluation* (λ) : You may or may not perform the action.

The transition condition and assignment $e[fcond]/a[l,u)\Psi[G]$ can be classified into three types as follows:

1. $e[fcond]/a$

    There is no safety clause on a transition in Safechart, thus we can simply transform it to the one in ETA. We give the translated transition a *lazy* evaluation (λ).

2. $e[fcond]/a \uparrow [G]$

    There is *prohibition* enforcement value on a transition t. It signifies that the transition t is forbidden to execute as long as G holds. During translation, we combine them as $e[fcond \wedge \neg G]/a$. We give the translated transition a *lazy* evaluation (λ). The transformation is shown in Fig. 1.

3. $e[fcond]/a[l,u) \uparrow [G]$

    There is *mandatory* enforcement value on a transition t. Given a transition label of the form $e[fcond]/a[l,u) \uparrow [G]$, it signifies that the transition is forced to execute within $[l,u)$ whenever G holds. We translate functional and safety layers into a transition t_1 and a path t_2, respectively. t_1 represents $e[fcond]/a$, which means t_1 is enabled if the triggering event e occurs and its functional conditional $fcond$ is true. We give t_1 a *lazy* evaluation (λ). Path t_2 is combined by two transitions, t_ϵ and t_δ. Transition t_ϵ is labeled $[G]/timer := 0$, where *timer* is a clock variable used for the time constraint, and we give t_ϵ an *eager* evaluation (ϵ). When G holds, t_ϵ executes as soon as possible, and t_ϵ's destination is a newly added mode, named *translator(t)*. t_δ's source is *translator(t)*, and its destination is t's destination. t_δ's guard is $[timer \geq l \wedge timer < u]$. However, we give t_δ a *delayable* evaluation (δ), which means it can put off execution until the last moment the guard is true. The procedure of translation is shown in Fig. 2.

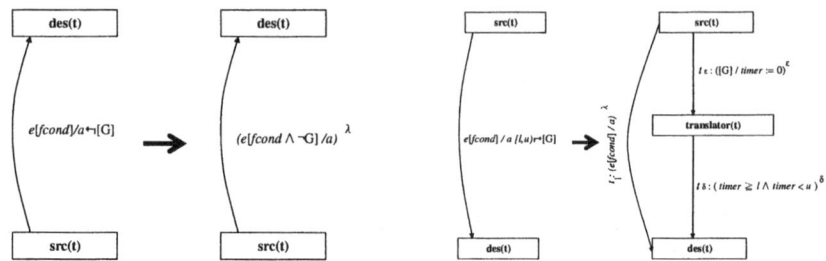

Fig. 1. Transformation of prohibition evaluation **Fig. 2.** Transformation of mandatory evaluation

4.2 Property Specification for Safecharts

In the safety-layer of Safecharts, there are two types of safety conditions on a transition, one is *prohibition* and the other is *mandatory*. After parsing the Safechart models of a safety-critical system, corresponding properties are automatically generated without requiring the user to specify again. Such properties are used to verify if the safety-layers work or not. As described in the following, to ensure that the safety constraints are working, two categories of properties are generated automatically for model checking.

1. $AG((src(t) \wedge G) \rightarrow \neg EX(des(t)))$
   If a transition t in Safechart has prohibition condition ⇃ $[G]$ in its safety-layer, it means that such transition is forbidden to execute as long as G holds. As shown in Fig. 1, t's source is *src(t)*, and its destination is *des(t)*. Due to ⇃ $[G]$, *src(t)* is not allowed to translate to *des(t)* as long as G holds. If such property is tenable in our system state graph, which means that there is no transition from *src(t)* to *des(t)* executing whenever G holds, then we can know that the safety-critical system won't become dangerous while G holds.

2. $AG((src(t) \wedge G \rightarrow \neg EX(\neg translator(t)))$ and $AG(translator(t) \wedge timer < u)$
   If a transition t in Safechart has $[l, u)$ ↾ $[G]$ in its safety-layer, it means that such transition is enabled and forced to execute within $[l, u)$ whenever G holds. As mentioned in former sections, we add two transitions for the safety-layer's behavior, namely t_ϵ and t_δ, and a mode, *translator(t)* between them.
   From Fig. 2, when G holds, t_ϵ must be executed as soon as possible due to its eager evaluation and the next active mode must be $translator(t)$. Moreover, we know that if the mode $translator(t)$ is active, then the next active state must be $des(t)$ within the time limit $timer \geq l \wedge timer < u$. If this constraint is violated, then the safety condition will not be satisfied.

4.3 Transition Priority

When modeling safety-critical systems, it is important to eliminate any non-deterministic behavior patterns of the system. Non-determinism arises if the triggering expressions of two transitions starting from a common state are simultaneously fulfilled. Because of its concern with safety-critical systems, Safecharts remove non-determinism in all cases except when there is no safety implication. In a Safechart model, a list of *risk*

Risk Band

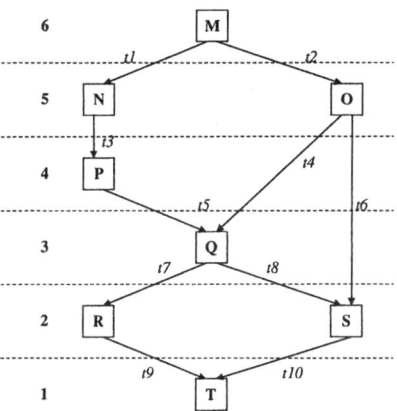

Fig. 3. Risk graph with risk band

relation tuples is used to represent a *risk graph* [10]. Non-comparable conditions may still exist in a risk graph. An example [9] is given in Fig. 3, where, relative to other states, the state O may have received less attention in the risk assessment, resulting in it becoming non-comparable with other states in the graph, namely, the states N and P. Consequently, Safecharts do not allow any transition between them, for instance, a transition such as $O \rightsquigarrow P$.

As a solution to the above problem, the authors of Safecharts proposed *risk band* [9], which can be used to enumerate all states in a risk graph to make precise their relative risk relations that were not explicitly described. To adopt this method, we implemented transition priorities based on the risk bands of a transition's source and destination modes. According to a list of risk relations, we can give modes different risk bands, as depicted in Fig. 3, where the maximum risk band, max_{rb}, is 6. We assign each transition a priority as follows:

$$pri(t) = max_{rb} - (rb_{src(t)} - rb_{des(t)}),$$

where $pri(t)$ is the priority assigned to transition t, $rb_{src(t)}$ is the risk band of transition t's source mode, and $rb_{des(t)}$ is the risk band of transition t's destination mode. Moreover, the smaller the value of $pri(t)$ is, the higher is the priority of transition t. In Fig. 3, $pri(t4)$ is 4, and $pri(t6)$ is 3. Obviously, when $t4$ and $t6$ are both enabled, $t6$ will be executed in preference to $t4$. With risk bands, we can give a transition leading to a lower risk band state a higher priority.

For implementing transition priorities into the SGM model checker, the triggering guards of a transition are modified as follows [1].

$$\tau'(t_i) = \tau(t_i) \wedge \bigwedge_{j \geq i} \neg \tau(t_j),$$

where $\tau(t_i)$ and $\tau(t_j)$ are the guard conditions of transitions t_i and t_j, $j \geq i$ means that t_j's priority is higher than or equal to t_i's, and $\tau'(t_i)$ is the modified guard condition of

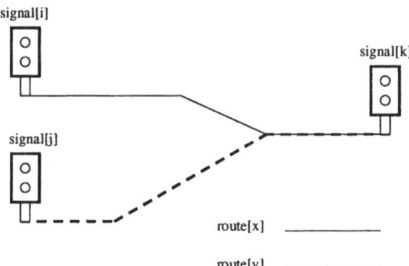

Fig. 4. Routes and signals

t_i. This application results in allowing t_i executed only if there is no enabled transition t_j which has priority over t_i.

4.4 Transition Urgency and Synchronization

Safecharts have a safety/security loophole due to the lack of synchronization mechanisms. A motivation example is the railway signal system illustrated in Fig. 4, where a route can be requested, evaluated, and set when the required signals on a route are operating without faults and are in the free state. The Safecharts for route[x] and signal[i] are given in Fig. 5 and Fig. 6, respectively. A signal breaks down when either its lamp or its sensor fails. The signal mode is changed from OPR to FAULTY upon receiving either ε_l (lamp fail event) or ε_s (sensor fail event). However, this mode change is not synchronized with ε_l or with ε_s, thus in-between these two actions, a route could have been evaluated and set, although the signal is faulty which is not detected because the signal's mode has not been changed as yet. Due to this lack of synchronization, safety loopholes exists in Safecharts. The route once set could allow a train to pass through a faulty signal endangering human lives as well as damaging properties. Safety-based resolution of non-determinism as proposed in [9,10,11] also does not solve this synchronization issue because non-determinism is resolved only among transition of the same Safechart and not among different Safecharts.

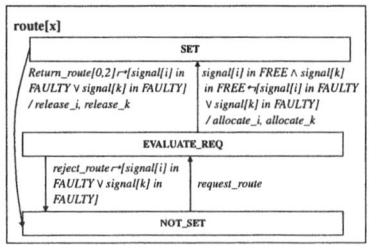

Fig. 5. Safechart for route[x]

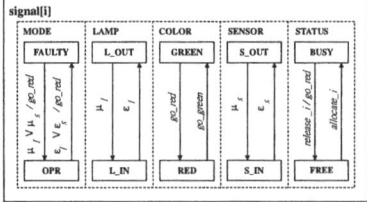

Fig. 6. Safechart for signal[i]

To solve the above problem, we propose the use of *transition urgency* as detailed in the following.

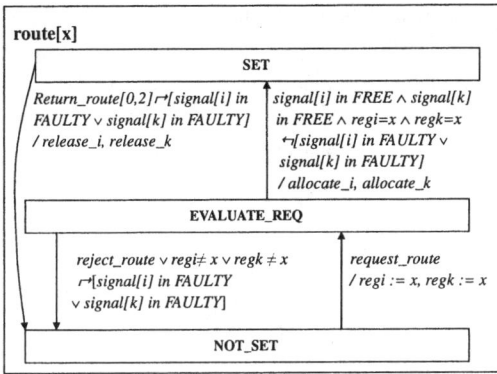

Fig. 7. Safechart for route[x] with mutual exclusion

Transition Urgency. As mentioned in Section 4.1, there are three types of transitions: *eager evaluation* (ϵ), *delayable evaluation* (δ), and *lazy evaluation* (λ). Transitions concerned with safety are given eager evaluation (ϵ) to ensure that when some malfunction or repair events happen, they can be executed first to reflect the correct status of a real-time system. In the railway signalling example, the model designer must give the transition with malfunctioning event ε an eager evaluation ϵ. As soon as the event ε occurs, the *signal*'s MODE is immediately changed to FAULTY. Thus *route* will not acquire the usage of *signal*, due to the safety-layer prohibiting guard condition $signal[i]$ in FAULTY $\vee$ $signal[k]$ in FAULTY.

To eliminate the safety-loopholes in Safecharts and avoid errors due to the loopholes, the above method must be used to extend Safecharts. We have implemented the proposed method in our Safecharts verification framework based on SGM.

4.5 Resource Access Mechanisms

Safecharts model both consumers and resources. However, when resources must be used in a mutually exclusive manner, a model designer may easily violate the mutual exclusion restriction by simultaneous checking and discovery of free resources, followed by their concurrent usages. A motivation example can be observed in the railway signalling system as illustrated in Fig. 4, Fig. 5, and Fig. 6, where signal[k] must be shared in a mutually exclusive way between route[x] and route[y]. However, each route checks if signal[k] is free and finds it free, then both route will be SET, assuming all signals are fault-free. This is clearly a modeling trap that violates mutually exclusive usages of resources. A serious tragedy could happen in this application example as two intersecting routes are set resulting in perhaps a future train collision.

From above we know that when consumers try to acquire resources that cannot be used concurrently, it is not safe to check only the status of resources. We need some kind of model-based mutual exclusion mechanism. A very simple policy would be like Fischer's mutual exclusion protocol [7]. For each mutually exclusive resource, a variable is used to record the id of the consumer currently using the resource. Before the consumer uses the resource, it has to check if the variable is set to its id. Fig. 7 is a corrected variant of the route Safechart from Fig. 5. When *route[id]* transits into EVALUATE_REQ, it sets variable *reg* to its id. When *route[x]* tries to transit into the SET mode to acquire the usage of *resource*, it needs to check if *reg* is still its id. If *reg* is still *x*, then *route[x]* acquires the usage of the resource. Other mechanisms such as atomic test-and-set performed on a single asynchronous transition can also achieve mutual exclusion.

5 Application Examples

The proposed model-based verification methodology for safety-critical systems was applied to several variants of the basic railway signaling system, which was illustrated in Fig. 4. The basic system was used to check the feasibility of the proposed methodology. The variants were used to check the scalability and efficiency of the methodology.

The basic system consists of two routes: route[x] and route[y], where route[x] requires signal[i] and signal[k], and route[y] requires signal[j] and signal[k]. The numbers and sizes of the Safecharts and the generated ETA are given in Table 1. As illustrated in Figs. 8 and 9, for each route Safechart, one ETA is obtained and for each signal Safechart, five ETA are generated. Thus, in the full system consisting of 5 Safecharts, 17 ETA are generated. It can be observed that the number of ETA modes, 40, is lesser than the number of Safecharts states, 56. The reason for this reduction is that hierarchical states do not exist in ETA. The synchronization and the mutual exclusion issues were both solved for this railway system as described in Sections 4.4 and 4.5, respectively.

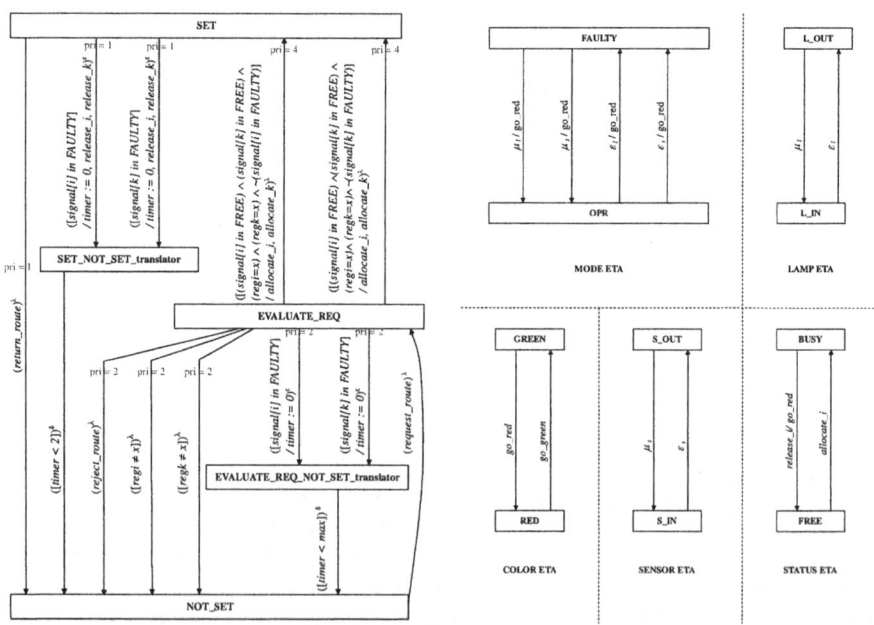

Fig. 8. ETA for route[x] **Fig. 9.** ETA for signal[i]

Table 1. Results of the Railway Signaling System

Component Name	Safecharts				ETA		
	#	#	$|S|$	$|T|$	#	$|M|$	$|T|$
route	2	1	4	4	1	5	13
signal	3	1	16	10	5	10	12
full system	5	5	56	38	17	40	62

Table 2. Results of Application Examples

	System		Safecharts			ETA			$|\phi|$	Issues Solved		Time	Mem
	$|R|$	$|S|$	#	$|S|$	$|T|$	#	$|M|$	$|T|$		Sync	ME	(μs)	(MB)
A	2	3(1)	5	56	38	17	40	62	16	3	1	230	0.12
B	2	4(1)	6	72	48	22	50	78	19	4	1	292	0.12
C	2	4(2)	6	72	48	22	50	82	22	4	2	337	0.13
D	3	4(1)	7	76	52	23	55	87	24	4	1	326	0.14
E	3	5(2)	8	92	62	28	65	111	33	5	2	515	0.14
F	4	5(1)	9	96	66	29	70	112	32	5	1	634	0.14

$|R|$: total num of routes, $|S|$: total num of signals (num of shared signals), $|\phi|$: num of properties generated. Sync: Num of synchronization issues solved, ME: Num of mutual exclusion issues solved

A number of variants of the basic railway signaling system were used for validating the proposed method's scalability and efficiency. Varying the number of routes and the number of signals in each route increases the complexity and the concurrency of the system. However, we can observe from the verification results in Table 2 that the amount of time and memory expended for verification do not increase exponentially and are very well acceptable. The number of properties to be verified also increase and thus their automatic generation is also a crucial step for successful and easily accessible verification of safety critical systems. The number of issues solved imply how the proposed solutions in this work are significant for the successful verification of complex systems modeled by Safecharts.

6 Conclusions

Nowadays, safety-critical systems are becoming more and more pervasive in our daily lives. To reduce the probability of tragedy, we must have a formal and accurate methodology to verify if a safety-critical system is safe or not. We have proposed a formal method to verify safety-critical systems. Our methodology can be applied widely to safety-critical systems with a model-driven architecture. We hope our methodology can have some real contribution such as making the world a safer place along with the development of science and technology.

References

1. K. Altisen, G. Gössler, and J. Sifakis. Scheduler modeling based on the controller synthesis paradigm. *Real-Time Systems*, 23:55–84, 2002.
2. E.M. Clarke and E.A. Emerson. Design and sythesis of synchronization skeletons using branching time temporal logic. In *Proceedings of the Logics of Programs Workshop*, volume 131 of *LNCS*, pages 52–71. Springer Verlag, 1981.
3. E.M. Clarke, O. Grumberg, and D.A. Peled. *Model Checking*. MIT Press, 1999.
4. H. Dammag and N. Nissanke. Safecharts for specifying and designing safety critical systems. In *Proceedings of the 18th IEEE Symposium on Reliable Distributed Systems*, pages 78–87, October 1999.
5. T.A. Henzinger, X. Nicollin, J. Sifakis, and S. Yovine. Symbolic model checking for reattime systems. In *Proceedings of the IEEE International Conference on Logics in Computer Science (LICS)*, pages 394–406, June 1992.
6. P.-A. Hsiung and F. Wang. A state-graph manipulator tool for real-time system specification and verification. In *Proceedings of the 5th International Conference on Real-Time Computing Systems and Applications (RTCSA)*, October 1998.
7. K.G. Larsen, B. Steffen, and C. Weise. Fischer's protocol revisited: A simple proof using model constraints. In *Hybrid System III*, volume 1066 of *LNCS*, pages 604–615, 1996.
8. L. Lavazza, editor. *A methodology for formalising concepts underlying the DESS notation*. ITEA, December 2001.
9. N. Nissanke and H. Dammag. Risk bands - a novel feature of Safecharts. In *Proceedings of the 11th International Symposium on Software Reliability Engineering (ISSRE)*, pages 293–301, October 2000.
10. N. Nissanke and H. Dammag. Risk ordering of states in Safecharts. In *Proceedings of the 19th International Conference on Computer Safety, Reliability, and Security*, volume 1943 of *LNCS*, pages 395–405. Springer Verlag, October 2000.
11. N. Nissanke and H. Dammag. Design for safety in safecharts with risk ordering of states. *Safety Science*, 40(9):753–763, December 2002.
12. J.-P. Queille and J. Sifakis. Specification and verification of concurrent systems in CESAR. In *Proceedings of the International Symposium on Programming*, volume 137 of *LNCS*, pages 337–351. Springer Verlag, 1982.
13. I. Sommerville. *Software Engineering*. Addison Wesley, 6th edition, 2001.
14. F. Wang and P.-A. Hsiung. Efficient and user-friendly verification. *IEEE Transactions on Computers*, 51(1):61–83, January 2002.

Structure Preserving Data Abstractions for Statecharts

Steffen Helke and Florian Kammüller

Technische Universität Berlin,
Institut für Softwaretechnik und Theoretische Informatik

Abstract. Hierarchical automata (HAs) represent a structured model of statecharts previously formalized in Isabelle/HOL. The present work extends this framework by an abstraction technique for HAs defined on infinite data spaces. This structure preserving abstraction enables the connection of the framework to the model checker SMV. This paper reports on the following results (a) We discuss abstractions of sequential automata, from which HAs are composed. Here we focus on the special problems of synchronous models and examine the feasibility of constructions for over- and underapproximations in order to preserve CTL properties. (b) Based on this results we describe a compositional abstraction technique, which can be applied to HAs. (c) We extend the formalization of HAs in Isabelle/HOL by suitable operators to construct abstractions inside the logic. (d) We present an efficient implementation of the abstraction process outside of the logic, which is integrated in the formalization by the oracle interface of Isabelle.

1 Introduction

In earlier work we already proposed a formalization of Hierarchical Automata (HAs) [KH00,HK01] in Isabelle/HOL [Pau94]. The motivation for this project has been, and still is, to provide a mechanized support for statecharts [HN96]. As Mikk [Mikk00] has already correctly observed, a formal treatment of statecharts needs an ameliorated calculus with an improved hierarchical structure that facilitates the analysis of (a) the typical hierarchical states of statecharts and (b) the consequently intricate structure of inter-level transitions. In the formalism of HAs these obvious problems can nicely be resolved. Therefore, we have adopted the HAs as well as a basis for the formalization in Isabelle/HOL.

The second major goal of the formalization of statecharts is to provide mechanized support for statecharts containing data. Therefore, in addition to the original formalization [KH00,HK01] we have furthermore suggested an extension in which finite HAs, i.e. HAs containing only finite data can already be verified by a connected model checker SMV efficiently [HK03]. However, the crux with data contained in a state transition model like statecharts or HAs, respectively, is that the state space can become infinite. Hence, the ultimate goal of the formalization of statecharts in Isabelle/HOL that has now been achieved has been to integrate the formalization with the well-known technique of abstract interpretation [CC77] in order to make any data containing statecharts amenable to automatic verification with the support of a connected model checker. To enable reasoning in the formalization at the concrete and abstract level and to improve readability we devise an abstraction in which the result of the abstraction is again a hierarchical automaton.

The basic idea of the integration of Isabelle/HOL with the SMV model checker (and in principle any model checker that is suitably adjusted to check finite HAs) is to host the HAs in an Isabelle/HOL embedding and control the abstraction process there. The connection to the model checker is realized via Isabelle's oracle interface. Although in principle feasible – as shown in this paper – to express a general abstraction operator based on Galois connections inside the Isabelle/HOL model, we provide in addition for practical purposes an ML implementation for the construction of the HA abstraction.

The most advanced result presented in this paper is the construction of an abstraction process for infinite HAs. The techniques used in the abstraction are based on earlier work [SS99,Dam96], but we go further than that as we do not consider just simple flat transition systems but realistic hierarchical state transition models as they are used in software engineering. For example, UML integrates state-machines that are basically the same as statecharts. Moreover in contrast to [SS99] the abstraction in the formalization inside Isabelle is not restricted to just boolean abstractions. Finally, this formalization is complemented with an implementation following the outline of [SS99] but lifted to hierarchical automata. The resulting integrated framework including model checking is better suited for handling case studies.

2 Abstraction of Sequential Automata

In [HK01,Mikk00] Sequential Automata (SAs) are the basic building block of HAs. They are similar to simple transition systems. The syntactic structure of an HA is described as a tree-like structure containing the SAs. This syntactic representation of HAs is complemented by a semantical model in our framework. Each level of hierarchy of an HA is represented by one SA.

In this section we propose a property preserving abstraction technique for SA, that are defined on infinite data spaces. The result of the abstraction is again an SA. In the next section we reuse this basic theory to explain the compositional abstraction for HAs.

2.1 Property Preservation and Galois Connections

The framework of [HK01] includes a formalization of CTL [CE81], which is interpreted on HAs and on SAs respectively. In the present work, we investigate property preserving abstraction for SAs in order to preserve CTL formulas. In the literature we can find basically two approaches: over- and underapproximation.

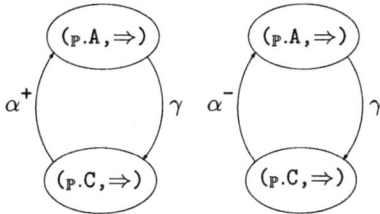

Fig. 1. Galois Connections for Over- and Underapproximation of Predicates

In an overapproximation the abstract model can contain new behaviour, but old behaviour cannot be lost. That is, properties of the universal fragment of CTL (∀CTL), that are valid on all paths of the overapproximated abstract model, must hold on the paths of the concrete model. In contrast, in an underapproximation new behaviour cannot be added, but old behaviour can be lost. Accordingly properties of the existential fragment of CTL (∃CTL) are preserved by underapproximated abstract models. In the work of Dams [Dam96] two automata representing these different kinds of abstractions are generated. Depending on the property that has to be verified the appropriate model has to be chosen.

In recent work [HJS01] the information for over- and underapproximation is represented in one so called modal transition system by *may* and *must* transitions. For verifying these transition systems special model checkers are proposed. Compared to a traditional symbolic model checker like SMV [McM93] such tools are inefficient. Moreover in our framework we like to generate SAs as abstractions, whose semantics is defined on traditional transition systems. Consequently, we chose to base our framework on the work of Dams and adapt his abstraction process to SAs. We must restrict the process to overapproximations, because SAs will not allow a reduction by underapproximation. Details are explained in the following subsection.

The theoretical basis for over- and underapproximations are galois connections [MSS86]. For complete lattices, C and A, a pair of monotone maps, $\alpha \colon \mathtt{C} \to \mathtt{A}$ and $\gamma \colon \mathtt{A} \to \mathtt{C}$ define a galois connection, written $\mathtt{gc}\,(\mathtt{A},\mathtt{C},\alpha,\gamma)$, iff $\alpha \circ \gamma \leq \mathtt{id}_\mathtt{A}$ and $\mathtt{id}_\mathtt{C} \leq \gamma \circ \alpha$. Furthermore the maps in a galois connection satisfy the following adjunction theorems, which allows to define α by γ and vice versa using the generalized meet and join $(\bigvee,\bigwedge)$ that exist in complete lattices.

$$\alpha.\mathtt{c} = \bigwedge \{\mathtt{a}\colon \mathtt{A} \mid \mathtt{c} \leq \gamma.\mathtt{a}\}$$
$$\gamma.\mathtt{a} = \bigvee \{\mathtt{c}\colon \mathtt{C} \mid \alpha.\mathtt{c} \leq \mathtt{a}\}$$

Figure 1 represents two instantiated galois connections relating spaces of abstract and concrete predicates. Accordingly the elements are ordered by $\Rightarrow$. On the left hand side of the figure we define a galois connection $\mathtt{gc}\,(\mathtt{P.A},\mathtt{P.C},\alpha^+,\gamma)$ for overapproximation to weaken concrete predicates by the abstraction α^+, which is reflected in the following galois property.

$$\mathtt{p}_c \Rightarrow \gamma.\alpha^+.\mathtt{p}_c$$

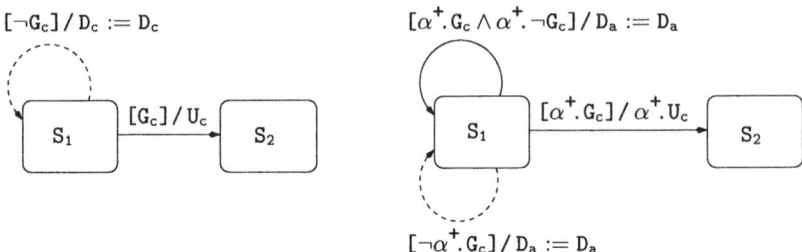

Fig. 2. Implicit Behaviour and Overapproximation of an SA

Correspondingly on the right hand side, a galois connection gc ($\mathbb{P}.C, \mathbb{P}.A, \gamma, \alpha^-$) for underapproximation is given, in order to strengthen concrete predicates by the abstraction α^-, which is reflected in the following galois property.

$$\gamma.\alpha^-.p_c \Rightarrow p_c$$

A special effect is, that overapproximations can be expressed by underapproximations.

$$\alpha^+.\neg p_c \Leftrightarrow \neg\alpha^-.p_c$$

We use this property for the definition of the construction operators and also to reduce the complexity in the ML implementation of an abstraction algorithm. Furthermore, we are going to use the fact that the strongest postcondition SP and the weakest precondition WP form a galois connection gc ($\mathbb{P}.A, \mathbb{P}.C, SP, WP$) to define the construction operators in Section 4.

The ML implementation of our abstraction technique is a predicate abstraction similar to the work of [SS99]. Usually the abstraction function α is defined for predicate abstractions by γ using the adjunction theorems (see above). We need this property in Section 5.

2.2 Generating Overapproximations for SAs

This paper is based on a formalization of statecharts as HAs [HK01,HK03]. It includes a formalization of SAs. The semantics of SAs is there a special case of the semantics of HAs, because SAs can be viewed as HAs without hierarchy. Based on this formalization we introduce an abstraction technique for overapproximation of SAs. Statecharts and consequently HAs – as the communication principles stay the same – belong to the family of synchronous languages. So the used formalization as HAs and SAs reflects the properties of synchronous languages and has to be respected in the abstraction process. One special property of synchronous languages is, that in each semantical status – synchronized by a global clock – the system performs a defined calculating step. Semantical statuses of SAs where no transitions fire, perform a trivial calculating step, in which the data variables are assigned to the previous value. This effect can be interpreted as complementation by implicit transitions.

On the left hand side in Figure 2 this is depicted by a dashed self-transition, where the guard $\neg G_c$ is constructed as the negated guard of the exiting transition. In general, this guard must be constructed as the conjunction of negated guards of all exiting transitions. Overapproximating an SA we construct an identical structured SA. We adopt the control states and abstract the transitions. Abstracting transitions we abstract guards and updates separately.

In general it is impossible to construct a guard in the abstraction by the given predicates exactly. Firstly, we propose to weaken a guard G_c by α^+ using overapproximation. Building such weaker guard adds new behaviour to the model, however it deletes some implicit behaviour simultaneously caused by the special semantics of synchronous languages. The reason is, that the guard of the implicit transition $\neg \alpha^+. G_c$ will be automatically stronger. Therefore, secondly we must add a suitable self transition, to adjust this unwanted effect. The guard of this self transition must be constructed by a conjunction of the overapproximated guard of G_c and the negated underapproximated guards of all exiting transitions. On the right hand side of Figure 2 this procedure is illustrated.

Abstracting the example only one exiting transition has to be considered. Firstly, we abstract the guard G_c by α^+ and introduce a self-transition. The guard of this self-transition is constructed by a conjunction of the overapproximated guard of the exiting transition $\alpha^+. G_c$ and the negation of the underapproximated guard of the exiting transition $\neg \alpha^-. G_c$. The latter can be expressed by α^+ using the theorem of subsection 2.1, so that finally we obtain the following guard for the self-transition.

$$[\alpha^+. G_c \wedge \alpha^+. \neg G_c]$$

Building traditional overapproximation of updates [SS99] is compatible with SAs, because a weaker update adds new behaviour to the system, but old behaviour cannot be lost. Accordingly on the right hand side of Figure 2 the update is overapproximated by α^+. However, in general, abstracting updates results in non-constructive predicates, so that the action language of SAs is violated. More precisely for each U_c we obtain in general more than one abstract update by α^+.

We must restrict to overapproximation, because SAs will not allow a reduction by underapproximation. This is caused by the special semantics of synchronous languages, which can be interpreted as a complementation by implicit transitions. This complementation restricts the possibility for reduction of the behaviour fundamentally. Consider the example in Figure 2 on the left hand side. If we propose to build a stronger guard of G_c by α^-, we obtain a weaker guard for the implicit transition consequently. That is, we add new behaviour to the abstract model, which is unsound for underapproximation. Hence, for the example on the left hand side of Figure 2 we cannot build an underapproxmiation, where the abstract model is again an SA. The only way out is to reduce nondeterministic branches to deterministic ones, however this is not sufficient as a general procedure. Consequently the result of an underapproximation cannot usually be expressed by an SA.

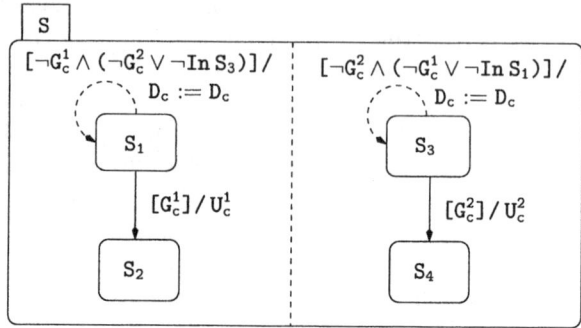

Fig. 3. Implicit Concrete Behaviour of HAs

3 Abstraction of Hierarchical Automata

In this section we introduce the lifting of the abstraction process to the level of HA. A HA is constructed from a finite set of SAs and a composition function CF that describes the hierarchical relation between those SAs. The first subsection 3.1 gives a brief introduction to semantical characteristics of HAs. In the following subsection we describe how we can handle global information of update-function locally by a generic parameter. The last subsection presents a structure preserving overapproximation for HAs.

3.1 Semantical Characteristics of HAs

The literature contains several accounts addressing the rather complex semantics of statecharts [HN96,Mikk00]. For a better understanding of the abstraction theory the interpretation of implicit behaviour as well as the partitioning of the data space are introduced in some detail as they play a central role for abstraction.

Implicit Concrete Behaviour: Implicit behaviour occurs in synchronous modelling languages whenever a transition cannot fire at the beginning of a clock cycle. In this situation the statechart executes a trivial calculation step that restores the data state. In Section 2 the implicit behaviour has been represented in the model by a dashed arrow (cf. Figure 2). This special transition only fires if no other transition of the model is enabled. As is shown in Figure 3 we can model the implicit behaviour of a HA explicitly in a similar fashion. Note, however, that with respect to compositional abstraction, the guard of the self-transition depends on context information that lies outside the SA in which the self-loop is defined. Considering the SA on the left hand side of the Figure, we observe that the guard of the implicit self-transition of the control state S_1 holds, if and only if the guard G_c^1 of the transition exiting S_1 does not hold. In addition a predicate of the parallelly composed SA must hold. Either the control state S_3 is not active or the guard of the transition exiting S_3 is not valid. More generally, in all parallelly composed SAs there must not be any transition that is enabled.

The modelling of implicit behaviour of HAs shown in Figure 3 may become complicated, because usually we have more than one local state in an SA. The concept of generic update functions – presented in the next subsection – can avoid this effect, because they abstract from the dependencies between parallelly composed SAs (cf. Figure 4). Additionally generic update functions can model partial updates, which is not supported by the modelling of Figure 3.

Partitions on Data Spaces and Partial Update-Functions: In general, the data space of an HA consists of a finite number of disjoint partitions. Update-functions can be defined in such a way that they do not write on all partitions. The semantics of HAs determines the values of partitions after transition execution also in cases in which a transition does not write on the partition.

That is, the update-functions are partial. More precisely, in one step of calculation of HA transitions of several SAs that are composed in parallel can be executed synchronously. If a transition does not write on a partition, it is first examined whether there is another synchronously executed transition writing on this partition. If this is the case, the value of the synchronously executed transition is selected. In case of a concurring write of several transitions on one partition (so-called racing) the resulting conflict is resolved by introducing a non-determinism (interleaving semantics). In contrast, if there is no transition writing on a partition, the semantics assigns to this partition the value prior to execution of the transition.

Note, that there already exists a complete formal semantics of HAs including data spaces in Isabelle/HOL [HK03]. Furthermore there the idea of generic update-functions is presented, which we will introduce in the next subsection.

3.2 Generic Update-Functions in an HA-Context

When considering SAs as constituents of an HA the individual data spaces of the SA have to be embedded into the global data space of the HA. There are two entities of an SA and its abstraction that are influenced by this embedding: the update-functions given in the action parts of the transitions of an SA and the self-loops that are added to the states of the SA during the abstraction. The embedding of an SA is simply given by adding an additional context parameter to the update-functions of the SA representing the remainder of the global data space. The effect of the update-functions is extended in the embedding by explicitly assigning those context parameter to their pre-state. We call these update-function generic as they abstract over context information and can thus be used for arbitrary contexts.

In Figure 4 we see the left SA of Figure 3. Differing from Figure 3 we used a generic update-function here. In this example we assume that the data space is

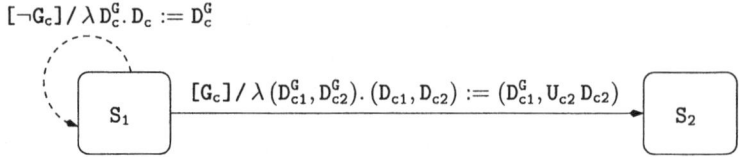

Fig. 4. Implicit Behaviour of SAs Including a Generic Update-Function

divided into two partitions represented by the Cartesian product[1]. We further assume that the update-function writes just on the second partition D_{c2} using the update-function U_{c2}. The update-function U_{c2} works on partitions and is derived from an update-function U_c that operates on the entire data space. The generic update-function abstracts over a context parameter (D^G_{c1}, D^G_{c2}) that has a partitioning identical to the data space. The generic parameter D^G_{c1} is passed on to the first partition of the data space. Here, the well-formedness of the update-function requires that D^G_{c1} must not be modified as this would lead to a kind of micro-step semantics that we do not intend.

Generic update-functions may be employed similarly for the description of implicit behaviour. In Figure 4 we use in contrast to Figure 3 a modified label to annotate the dashed self-transition. Using a generic update-function the guard can be weakened and may now be defined only using the information $\neg G_c$ locally available in the SA. The self-transition cannot describe more implicit behaviour, because the reachable data states in the post state coincide with data states of possibly synchronously firing transitions due to the generic parameter of the update-function.

When introducing the overapproximations for SAs in the Section 2 we assumed that update-functions always write on all partitions of the data space. The aim of the next subsection 3.3 is to adapt the given abstraction concept to generic update-functions that do not write on the entire data space, but only some of its partitions.

3.3 Overapproximations for HAs

The idea for the abstraction of the HA is to divide the HA into its defining SAs, define the abstraction functions for each of the SAs and compose the set of individual abstractions to an abstraction function for the HA.

The resulting abstraction method for HA preserves properties of the concrete HA in the constructed abstract HA because it respects the structure of the HA and the constituting SAs are adjusted prior to composition in such a way that they are properly embedded into the data space of the HA.

The latter step – realized by an extension of each update-function of an SA by a context parameter as explained in the last subsection – allows to abstract

---

[1] In our Isabelle theory of abstraction partitions are realized as a list of sum types (cf. Section 4).

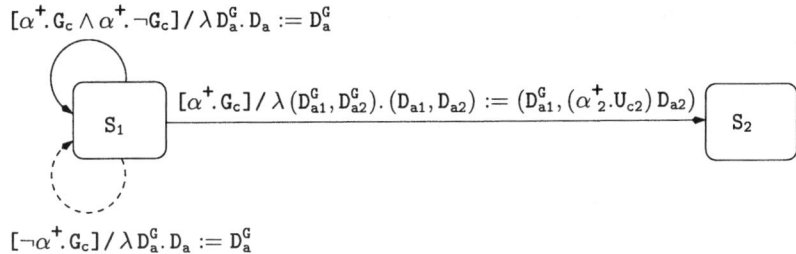

Fig. 5. Abstraction of SAs Including a Generic Update-Function

SAs separately. However we need a technique for dealing with the generic context parameters.

We suggest two possibilities for the abstraction of generic update-functions.

In the first naïve approach the generic context parameter of the update-function is not preserved during abstraction. This abstraction is rather rough. It assumes that in partitions, on which locally no write occurs, to which the context parameter has been passed on, arbitrary behaviour may occur. In Section 4 we define an operator that constructs such an abstraction.

The elaborated approach to the abstraction of generic update-functions is to preserve the generic parameter during abstraction. This is only possible if the given abstraction-function preserves the structure of the data space and each data partition of the concrete system is mapped independently of other partitions onto exactly one partition of the abstract data space. Figure 5 shows such an abstraction for the example introduced in Figure 4. In this example the concrete generic parameters (D_{c1}^G, D_{c2}^G) are replaced by corresponding abstract representations (D_{a1}^G, D_{a2}^G). The update-function U_{c2} can be overapproximated by α_2^+. Note, however, that α_2^+ can only be calculated precisely if the abstraction function respects, as described above, the structure of the data space. Otherwise the elaborated approach is not applicable and we have to use again the naïve alternative. Furthermore, α_2^+ calculates in general more than one abstract update-function.

4 Calculating Abstractions in Isabelle

The concepts presented in the previous section have been transformed into a theory of abstraction for the theorem prover Isabelle. This new theory extends the existing theory of HAs by calculating operators that enable the construction of an abstract HA from a concrete HA and an abstraction function.

4.1 Calculating Overapproximated SAs

In order to construct the abstraction of an SA inside the logic, we define in Isabelle/HOL (suitable) calculating operators that – given a concrete SA SA_c and an abstraction function R — construct an abstract SA using overapproximation. The construction operator $\text{AbsBy}^+_{\text{SA}}$ is defined in Isabelle as follows.

$$\text{SA}_c \text{ AbsBy}^+_{\text{SA}} \text{ R} \equiv_{df} \text{let } (s_c, i_c, ts_c) = \text{SA}_{\text{Rep}} \text{ SA}_c;$$
$$s_a = s_c;$$
$$i_a = i_c;$$
$$ts_a = ts_c \text{ AbsBy}^+_{\text{Ts}} \text{ R}$$
$$\text{in } \text{SA}_{\text{Cons}}(s_a, i_a, ts_a)$$

First the concrete SA SA_c is transformed into its representation. Thereby its concrete components, like the set of control states s_c, the initial set of control states i_c and the transition relation ts_c become accessible. Since we want to construct a structure preserving abstraction for the SA, we adopt the structural information from s_c and i_c as they are.

Abstracting the transition relation by the construction operator $\text{AbsBy}^+_{\text{Ts}}$ each transition of ts_c is abstracted separately. According to the presented procedure in Figure 2 we abstract a transition t_c in two steps. Firstly, we build an abstract transition replacing guard and update-function of t_c by corresponding overapproximated counterparts. Secondly, we generate a self transition on the source state of t_c, which is labeled by the negation of the underapproximated guard of t_c and an update-function, that assigns the previous value to the data variables. Note, that the construction of the self transition could be more precise, because we ignore the guards of other exiting transitions in the source state of t_c. The core of the construction lies on one side in the abstraction of the guard with the operator $\text{AbsBy}^+_{\text{G}}$ and on the other side in the abstraction of the update-function with the operator $\text{AbsBy}^+_{\text{U}}$. The following constant definition introduces the construction operator for the abstraction of a guard.

$$\text{G}_c \text{ AbsBy}^+_{\text{G}} \text{ R} \equiv_{df} \lambda d_a. \exists d_c. (\text{G}_c\, d_c) \wedge (\text{R}\, d_c) = d_a$$

The definition corresponds to a *strongest postcondition* and weakens the property G_c. The weakening can be proved as the following theorem. The proof is by stepwise simplification.

$$(\text{G}_c\, d_c) \Rightarrow (\text{G}_c \text{ AbsBy}^+_{\text{G}} \text{ R})(\text{R}\, d_c)$$
$$\Leftrightarrow (\text{G}_c\, d_c) \Rightarrow \exists d. (\text{G}_c\, d) \wedge (\text{R}\, d) = (\text{R}\, d_c)$$
$$\Leftrightarrow (\text{G}_c\, d_c) \Rightarrow (\text{G}_c\, d_c) \wedge (\text{R}\, d_c) = (\text{R}\, d_c)$$

In addition to the overapproximation of a guard we need to calculate the overapproximation of an update-function. First we consider the formal description of an operator that defines such an abstraction.

$$\text{U}_c \text{ AbsBy}^+_{\text{U}} \text{ R} \equiv_{df} \{\text{U}_a. \forall d_a. \exists d_c. d_a = (\text{R}\, d_c) \wedge \text{R}(\text{U}_c\, d_c) = \text{U}_a(\text{R}\, d_c)\}$$

The result of this overapproximation of a concrete update-function U_c is a finite set of abstract update-functions containing at least one element. The definition given above simulates the behaviour of an abstract update-function by the behaviour of a concrete update-function. Figure 6 illustrates graphically the encoded simulation property. Similar to the overapproximation of guards, the abstraction of an update-function may as well be described using the *strongest*

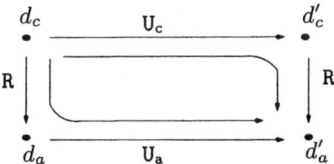

Fig. 6. Simulation Property for Abstraction of Update-Functions

postcondition. To this end, update-functions are interpreted as binary predicates defined over the pre-states and post-states of the data. Such a predicate may be derived directly from an update-function U using the operator UP.

$$\text{UP U} \equiv_{df} \lambda d\, d'.\ d' = (\text{U}\, d)$$

The operator $\text{AbsBy}^+_{\text{UP}}$ defines how the abstraction of a concrete update-function U_c can be expressed as an abstract binary predicate

$$U_c\ \text{AbsBy}^+_{\text{UP}}\ R \equiv_{df} \lambda d_a\, d'_a.\ \exists d_c\, d'_c.\ (U_c\, d_c) = d'_c \wedge (R\, d_c) = d_a \wedge (R\, d'_c) = d'_a$$

The fact that the operators $\text{AbsBy}^+_{\text{U}}$ and $\text{AbsBy}^+_{\text{UP}}$ describe equivalent abstract behaviour is proved in Isabelle by the following theorem.

$$\text{Surj R} \Rightarrow (U_c\ \text{AbsBy}^+_{\text{UP}}\ R = \bigvee \text{UP}\, `\, (U_c\ \text{AbsBy}^+_{\text{U}}\ R))$$

This equivalence holds under the assumption that the abstraction function R is surjective. To be able to compare the operators with each other we first transform the set of abstract update-functions in a set of abstract binary predicates using the operator UP. Finally, the disjunction of all those predicates is equivalent to the predicate constructed using the operator $\text{AbsBy}^+_{\text{UP}}$.

4.2 Calculating Overapproximated HAs

In order to provide a construction for HAs as well, we reuse the operator $\text{AbsBy}^+_{\text{SA}}$ introduced in the previous section and extended corresponding to Figure 5. The operator $\text{AbsBy}^+_{\text{HA}}$ implements this idea as follows.

$$\begin{aligned}
\text{HA}_c\ \text{AbsBy}^+_{\text{HA}}\ R \equiv_{df}\ &\text{let}\ (d_c, sas_c, es_c, cf_c) = \text{HA}_{\text{Rep}}\ \text{HA}_c\,; \\
&d_a &&= R\, d_c\,; \\
&sas_a &&= (\lambda sa_c.\, sa_c\ \text{AbsBy}^+_{\text{SA}}\ R)\, `\, \text{SA}_c\,; \\
&es_a &&= es_c\,; \\
&cf_a &&= cf_c \\
&\text{in}\ \text{HA}_{\text{Cons}}\,(d_a, sas_a, es_a, cf_a)
\end{aligned}$$

First we transform the concrete HA HA_c into its representation to gain access to the concrete components, like the initial data state d_c, the finite set of SAs sas_c, the set of events es_c, and the composition function cf_c. Since we want to construct a structure preserving abstraction for the HA, we adopt the structural information of es_c and cf_c as they are. In contrast, the two other components that involve data, have to be abstracted in a suitable fashion. To this end we abstract the initial data state of the HA using the abstraction-function R. To abstract the SAs the operator $\text{AbsBy}^*_{\text{SA}}$ is applied to each element of the set sas_c. Note, however, that the operator $\text{AbsBy}^*_{\text{SA}}$ has been adapted accordingly to enable in addition the abstraction of partial update-functions. The abstraction of partial update-functions is now discussed in more detail.

An update-function is a function that calculates a new data value from the data value prior to execution of a transition. This leads to the following polymorphic type definition in the Isabelle/HOL formalization.

$$\delta \, \text{update} \equiv_{df} \delta \to \delta$$

As described in Section 3 the polymorphic type δ^2 may consist of finitely many disjoint partitions. Furthermore, update-functions can only write on specific partitions of the global data space. In Isabelle/HOL all functions are total. Therefore, we had to develop an appropriate model of updates on partitions on which no write is performed that respects the statecharts semantics. To this end we extend the type of the update-function by an additional data parameter. That is, we define a kind of generic update-function as follows.

$$\delta \, \text{update} \equiv_{df} [\delta, \delta] \to \delta$$

Wellformedness of the update-function requires that the values of a partition contained in a generic parameter may only be passed on but must not be altered. In the semantics of HAs this parameter may be instantiated and evaluated by the context information that is then available. In this step it is checked whether synchronously firing transitions write on the partition. If there is no write, the old value that has been valid prior to the transition's execution is assigned. In addition we define an resolution for write conflicts (racing) using non-determinism in the semantics. A precise semantical foundation for update-functions is provided by earlier work [HK03].

The problem with compositional abstraction is that, in general, only local information is available, and therefore a technique is needed to abstract a generic update-function. For the abstraction of generic update-functions it is important to define a solution in which the abstract update-function is also well-formed. We suggest two solutions.

The first naïve solution does not permit generic parameters in an abstract update-function. When calculating abstract updates the post-state of any data partition may only depend on locally determined data values. Information passed by the generic data parameter may not be used for the calculation of the post-state. This may, in certain cases, lead to a rather rough approximation. More precisely, if we ignore the generic parameter for the abstraction, we get in a first step a set of concrete non-generic update-functions describing the possible effects.

$$\text{Updates UG}_c \equiv_{df} \{ \, \text{U}_c \, . \, \exists d^g_c \, . \, \text{U}_c = (\lambda \, d^p_c \, . \, \text{UG}_c \, d^g_c \, d^p_c) \, \}$$

---

[2] Defined using Isabelle/HOL's datatype package.

The following constant definition $\text{AbsBy}^+_{\text{UG}}$ constructs from this set of update-functions a set of non-generic abstract update-functions.

$$\text{UG}_c \text{ AbsBy}^+_{\text{UG}} \text{ R} \equiv_{df} \bigcup ((\lambda\, u_c.\, u_c \text{ AbsBy}^+_{U} \text{R}) \text{ ' (Updates UG}_c))$$

The naïve approach is feasible in cases where all concrete update functions write on the entire data space, because in this case the operator Updates yields just one function. However, in cases where generic update-functions write only on parts of the data space, the naïve approach leads to approximations that lack precision.

The presentation of the formalization of the elaborated solution is omitted here, but we give an outline. This approach requires that the abstraction function R is constructed such that for each partition there is a suitable abstraction that maps this partition independent of other partitions onto an abstract data partition. On one side, this procedure preserves the structure of the data space. On the other side, it enables the simulation of the behaviour of concrete generic update-functions by the behaviour of abstract generic update-functions. To this end, the previous polymorphic type δ is refined into a list of sum-types where each element of the list describes a partition of the data space. Based on this structured data-type, we can formalize the requirement on the abstraction function stated above and define a corresponding operator for the construction of generic update-functions.

5 Implementation of the Abstraction Process

Besides the Isabelle definitions of operators for the construction of overapproximated HAs from a given HA and an abstraction function, we have in addition implemented an abstraction algorithm that is connected via the so-called oracle-interface of Isabelle to our Isabelle theory. This algorithm has been developed as a diploma thesis. It adapts the algorithm for predicate abstraction of transition systems suggested by Shankar and Saïdi [SS99] to HAs. In this kind of abstraction data variables of a transition system, that are declared on infinite data domains, are interpreted abstractly by a finite number of characteristic predicates. Adapting this algorithm to HAs for each partition of the data space predicates will be defined independently. These predicates must be defined by an expert and will be given as an input to the abstraction process. In the construction of the abstract data space, concrete data variables on infinite domains are replaced by a finite number of boolean variables. Each boolean variable encodes whether a corresponding characteristic predicate is satisfied or not. Accordingly the concretization function γ of the galois connections for predicate abstraction is given by a substitution, that replaces in an abstract formula the boolean variables by the corresponding predicates. Usually the abstraction function α is defined by γ using the adjunction theorems (cf. Section 2). So we obtain for over- and underapproximation the following abstraction functions.

$$\alpha^+.p_c = \bigwedge \{p_a : \mathbb{P}.A \mid p_c \Rightarrow \gamma.p_a\}$$
$$\alpha^-.p_c = \bigvee \{p_a : \mathbb{P}.A \mid \gamma.p_a \Rightarrow p_c\}$$

In practice it is not feasible to calculate all formulas of p.A. So we must restrict ourselves to representative formulas. [SS99] proves that it is sufficient for calculating an overapproximation, to show $p_c \Rightarrow \gamma . p_a$ for all disjunctions, that can build on the introduced boolean variables. So the complexity can be reduced to at most $3^k - 1$ proof obligations, where k represents the number of boolean variables used to represent the predicates.

As a result of the implementation we found that already for small examples the number of abstract update functions calculated for one concrete update-function is rather high. This problem can be controlled if the predicates used for the abstract interpretation of a partition are chosen such that they are mutually exclusive and do not overlap.

6 Conclusions

In this paper we have presented a concept for the abstraction of statecharts containing data. The concept is based on a formalization in the generic interactive theorem prover Isabelle/HOL. Following the approach of [Mikk00], we use a representation of statecharts as hierarchical automata. The methodology of building the abstraction is similar to earlier work on abstract interpretation of transition systems by Cousot and Dams. However, the novelty here is that the existing concepts are transferred to the formalism of statecharts that (a) enable to structure the state space and (b) contain data. While there is some work on mechanical analysis of transition systems containing data using abstraction techniques [MN95] and some mechanizations of statecharts, e.g. [BW98], we are not aware of any work dedicated to the statecharts formalism combining theorem proving and model checking.

The embedding in the theorem prover represents a semantical foundation for data enriched statecharts enables the calculation of overapproximations, and serves well as a logical framework for mechanically proved abstractions. We have developed a structure preserving abstraction technique for HAs that can be applied in a compositional manner. To this end we extended the abstraction theory for transition systems to SAs. To keep our method compositional we use a novel technique that respects context informations. For the analysis of case studies we integrated an implementation of an algorithm for the abstraction process outside Isabelle.

In contrast to other approaches of abstraction theories for model checking we do not yet consider a complementary refinement process that is used to refine too rough abstractions in order to regain better approximations. Currently we plan to adapt our approach for detecting spurious counterexamples [CGJ+00] to refine the abstraction in a suitable way.

Acknowledgment. We would like to thank Dr. J.Sanders from PRG Oxford for his support and comments. This work has been partly supported by the DFG/BC ARC project.

References

[BW98] U. Brockmeyer and G. Wittich. Tamagotchis need not die – verification of statemate design. In B. Steffen, editors, *Tools and Algorithms for the Construction and Analysis of Systems, TACAS'98, Springer LNCS*, **1384**, 1998.

[CC77] P. Cousot and R. Cousot. Abstract Interpretation: A Unified Lattice Model for Static Analysis of Programs by Construction of Approximation of Fixed Points. In *Proceedings of the 4th ACM Symposium on Principles of Programming Languages, ACM*, New York, 1977.

[CE81] E. M. Clarke and E.A. Emerson. Synthesis of synchronization skeletons for branching time temporal logic. In D. Kozens, editor, *Logic of Programs: Workshop, Springer LNCS*, **131**, 1981.

[CGJ+00] E. Clarke, O. Grumberg, S. Jha, Y. Lu and H. Veit. Counterexample-guided Abstraction Refinement. In A.P. Sistla, E.A. Emerson, editors, *Computer Aided Verification, CAV00, Springer LNCS*, **1855**, 2000.

[Day93] N. Day. A model checker for statecharts. Technical Report TR-93-35, Department of Computer Science, University of British Columbia, October 1993.

[Dam96] D. Dams. Abstract Interpretation and Partition Refinement for Model Checking. PhD thesis, Eindhoven University of Technology, Netherlands, July 1996.

[HN96] D. Harel and D. Naamad. A STATEMATE semantics for statecharts. *ACM Transactions on Software Engineering and Methodology*, 5(4):293-333, Oct 1996.

[KH00] F. Kammüller and S. Helke. Mechanical Analysis of UML State Machines and Class Diagrams. In *Defining Precise Semantics for UML*, Sophia Antipolis, France, June 2000. Satellite Workshop, ECOOP 2000.

[HK03] S. Helke and F. Kammüller, Verification of Statecharts Including Data Spaces. In D. Basin, B. Wolff, editors, TPHOLs 2003: Emerging Trends Proceedings, *Technical Report Albert-Ludwigs-Universitat Freiburg* **189**, 2003.

[HK01] S Helke and F. Kammüller. Representing Hierarchical Automata in Interactive Theorem Provers. In R. J. Boulton, P. B. Jackson, editors, *Theorem Proving in Higher Order Logics, TPHOLs 2001, Springer LNCS*, **2152**, 2001.

[HJS01] M. Huth, R. Jagadeesan and D. Schmidt. Modal transition systems: a foundation for three-valued program analysis. , editors, *European Symposium on Programming, ESOP 2001, Springer LNCS*, **2028**, 2001.

[McM93] K. McMillan. Symbolic Model Checking: An Approach to the State Explosion Problem. Kluwer Academic Publishers, 1993.

[Mikk00] E. Mikk. Semantics and Verification of Statecharts. *PhD thesis, Christian Albrechts Universität Kiel*, 2000.

[MN95] O. Müller and T. Nipkow. Combining Model Checking and Deduction for I/O Automata. *In TACAS95, 1st International Workshop on Tools and Algorithms for the Construction and Analysis of Systems, Springer LNCS*, **1019**:116, 1995.

[MSS86] A. Melton, D.A. Schmidt and G. . Strecker. Galois connections and Computer Science applications,*Springer LNCS*, **240**:299-312, 1986.

[Pau94] L. C. Paulson. Isabelle: *A Generic Theorem Prover, Springer LNCS*, **828**, 1994.

[SS99] H. Saïdi and N. Shankar. Abstract and Model Check While You Prove. In N. Halbwachs and D. Peled, editors, *11th Interantional Conference on Computer Aided Verification, CAV99, Springer LNCS*, **1633**, 1999.

Amortised Bisimulations

Astrid Kiehn and S. Arun-Kumar

Department of Computer Science and Engineering,
Indian Institute of Technology Delhi, New Delhi 110016, India
{astrid, sak}@cse.iitd.ernet.in

Abstract. We introduce a quantitative concept for bisimulations by integrating the notion of amortisation (cf. [3]). This allows us to make behavioural comparisons between nondeterministic systems that are inherently non-terminating and to analyse the relative long-term costs of deploying them. To this end, we conservatively extend CCS to include a new set of cost-based actions and define a cost-based quantitative relation called amortised bisimulation. We demonstrate the applicability of our approach by two case studies. In both cases the cost of additional administration is shown to amortise. We furthermore show that the amortised preorder for speed introduced in [6] is naturally expressible in our setting.

1 Introduction

Bisimulation equivalence [7,8,11] has been developed as a notion of behavioural equivalence for nondeterministic, conceptually nonterminating systems. Loosely speaking, two systems are bisimilar (bisimulation equivalent) if each can simulate the other where the roles of who is simulating whom can interchange at any point of time. Bisimulation equivalence is a mathematically elegant, tractable concept and several tools mechanising or assisting the decision process have been developed (e.g. [2,5]).

However, bisimulation equivalence does not allow one to make any assessment about the relative expenses of the two systems being compared. For example, one would like to know whether one system (or a system's component) is more cost efficient than the other and to what extent. To make such assertions possible, we suggest the notion of amortised bisimulations.

The main idea is to consider actions together with their costs and to modify bisimulation equivalence in such a way that actions are matched with "functionally equivalent" actions. The difference in their costs adds to the credit which is accumulated during the mutual simulation. This accumulated credit is used as a parameter in the definition of amortised bisimilarity. For a system p to be considered less expensive than another system q, the amortised bisimulation containing (p, q) should have nonnegative credit everywhere.

In more detail, we conservatively extend CCS to include a new set of cost-based actions which cannot be hidden. We then define the cost-based quantitative relation called amortised bisimulation. CCS along with its classical equivalence relations of strong bisimilarity and observational equivalence on CCS processes may be recovered by simply discarding the new actions from the action set. We demonstrate the usefulness of amortised bisimulations by presenting two case studies. In both cases we show that the cost of additional administration gets amortised.

The first study (based on [9]) compares a model of communication called shared messaging communication (SMC) with the conventional message-passing (MP) model. The authors of the model show experimentally that when large data items are to be transferred as part of inter-task communication, the SMC model is more efficient than MP in terms of the communication costs involved. In fact, the truth of the authors' claims is intuitively quite straightforward. But those results cannot generally be proven without integrating costs into the operational model of the respective systems. We substantiate their claim by defining suitable amortised bisimulations.

The second case study considers a proxy server and is somewhat different in nature. Again, we use costs to describe the expense for long- and short-distance communication. Whether a proxy system is more efficient than a system without a proxy, however, depends on the frequency with which a page is updated relative to that of the accesses to it. The expense involved in a proxy server pays off, only if pages are more frequently accessed than updated. We therefore cannot establish any efficiency result without modelling this frequency in some way. We present a simplified model of the entire system comprising a client, a proxy server and a web server and show that under these assumptions the proxy server can reduce the communication costs involved in transferring a page. On the other hand, when pages are more frequently updated than accessed, the proxy server becomes a bottleneck and then it is more efficient to do without it.

While our notion of costs is fairly general, it applies when the cost is measured in terms of time. We pick the amortised faster-than preorder described in [6] and show that it may be captured in our framework.

2 Amortised Bisimulations

A *labelled transition system (LTS)* $\mathcal{L}$ is a 3-tuple $\langle \mathbf{P}, \mathcal{A}, \longrightarrow \rangle$, where $\mathbf{P}$ is a set of *process states* or *processes*, $\mathcal{A}$ is a (possibly countable) set of actions and $\longrightarrow \subseteq \mathbf{P} \times \mathcal{A} \times \mathbf{P}$ is the *transition relation*.

Our LTSs are generated by an extension of Milner's CCS – see [8] for an introduction –, where in addition to the normal set of actions $Act_\tau = Act \cup \{\tau\}$ there is a set of priced actions $CAct$ which have a cost assigned to them by a function $C : CAct \to I\!N$. Thus, the set of all actions is $\mathcal{A} = Act_\tau \cup CAct$, where Act, $\{\tau\}$ and $CAct$ are assumed to be pairwise disjoint. Priced actions differ from actions in Act – apart from carrying costs – in that they do not have complements. We assume the usual CCS operators with their usual interleaving operational semantics [8]. Specifically, we have action prefixing over $\mathcal{A}$, (binary) choice, (parallel) composition, restriction, relabelling (which is bijective by definition, cf. [7]) and process names (for recursion). With regard to $CAct$, a priced action cannot synchronize with any other action, it cannot be restricted away and it cannot be renamed ($\forall a \in CAct : f(a) = a$ and $f|_{Act} : Act \to Act$). Priced actions therefore are always visible. We use $\sim$ to denote strong bisimilarity and $\approx$ for observational equivalence (which treat priced and non-priced actions alike).

To capture the idea of "functional equivalence" formally, we introduce the relation ρ over priced actions. For example, consider the task of getting books from a library where costs are measured in terms of time. There are costs for getting to (and back from) the library (action get_to_lib) and costs for accessing the book of interest ($access\_book$). The walk to the local library might be short but as its stock of books is not well sorted accessing them is more time consuming than in the more distant, central library. Moreover, the book might not be in the stock at all and can only be reserved ($reserve\_book$) as it has to be ordered by an inter-library loan. Formulated in CCS, we obtain the two processes:

$Central\_Lib \stackrel{df}{=} get\_to\_lib_{cen}.access\_book_{cen}.Central\_Lib$
$Local\_Lib \stackrel{df}{=} get\_to\_lib_{loc}.(access\_book_{loc}.Local\_Lib + reserve\_book.Local\_Lib)$

where the costs of actions are $C(get\_to\_lib_{cen}) = 2$, $C(access\_book_{cen}) = 1$ and $C(get\_to\_lib_{loc}) = 1$, $C(access\_book_{loc}) = 2$ and $C(reserve\_book) = 4$. Clearly, $get\_to\_lib_{loc}$ and $get\_to\_lib_{cen}$ are functionally equivalent and so are $access\_book_{loc}$ and $access\_book_{cen}$. We also assume functional equivalence of $reserve\_book$ and $access\_book_{cen}$. Thus, all these pairs are in ρ. If we match actions according to ρ then $Central\_Lib$ and $Local\_Lib$ describe functionally equivalent processes. Moreover, given an initial credit of 1, $Central\_Lib$ is more cost efficient than $Local\_Lib$. The credit 1 is required to cover the expenses for the longer walk to the central library and it amortises with the cheap access of the book. So, in the setting of amortised bisimulations we can prove $Central\_Lib \prec_1^\rho Local\_Lib$.

Formally, $\rho \subseteq CAct_\tau \times CAct_\tau$ and to allow a uniform treatment of actions, we extend ρ and C to be defined over $\mathcal{A}$ with the following restrictions:

1. ρ restricted to Act_τ is the identity relation.
2. $C(a) = 0$ for all $a \in Act_\tau$.

We call ρ a $CAct$-association and abbreviate $C(a)$ to c_a for all $a \in \mathcal{A}$. In the examples, we define ρ by stating its definition over $CAct_\tau$, only.

Definition 1. *Let $\langle \mathbf{P}, \mathcal{A}, \longrightarrow \rangle$ be a labelled transition system over $\mathcal{A} = Act_\tau \cup CAct$ and let ρ be a $CAct_\tau$-association. A family $(R_i)_{i \in \mathbb{N}}$ of binary relations over $\mathbf{P}$ is a strong amortised ρ-bisimulation, if for all $i \in \mathbb{N}$, $(p, q) \in R_i$:*

1. $p \stackrel{a}{\longrightarrow} p'$ *implies* $\exists q', b$ *[$a \rho b$ and $q \stackrel{b}{\longrightarrow} q'$ and $(p', q') \in R_{i+c_b-c_a}$]*,
2. $q \stackrel{b}{\longrightarrow} q'$ *implies* $\exists p', a$ *[$a \rho b$ and $p \stackrel{a}{\longrightarrow} p'$ and $(p', q') \in R_{i+c_b-c_a}$]*,

where $a, b \in \mathcal{A}$. Each relation R_i is called an i-slice of the amortised ρ-bisimulation. We say p is amortised cheaper (more cost efficient) than q up to credit i, in notation, $p \prec_i^\rho q$, if $(p, q) \in R_i$ for some amortised strong ρ-bisimulation $(R_i)_{i \in \mathbb{N}}$.

In case that $i = 0$ we simply write $p \prec^\rho q$. The i-index gives the maximal credit which p requires to bisimulate q. The credit cannot be higher than i as we do not consider slices with a negative index.

To give a few simple examples, let $a, b, d, e \in CAct$, $c_a = c_d = 1$, $c_b = 2$ and $c_e = 3$. Then $a.b.0 \prec^\rho e.d.0$, $a.b.0 \prec^\rho b.a.0$, $a.b.0 \not\prec^\rho a.b.0$ and $b.a.0 \prec_1^\rho a.b.0$ where $\rho = \{(a,b), (b,a), (a,e), (b,d)\}$. The underlying amortised ρ-bisimulations are easily exhibited by the reader. To ease terminology, if ρ is understood from the context we simly omit mentioning it. Some facts on amortised bisimulations are given next.

Proposition 2. *Let $(R_i)_{i \in \mathbb{N}}$ be a family of relations satisfying the conditions of Definition 1.*

1. *If $CAct = \emptyset$ then each i-slice R_i is a strong bisimulation.*
2. $\bigcup_{i \in \mathbb{N}} R_i$ *is a strong bisimulation.*
3. $(S_j)_{j \in \mathbb{N}}$, *where for some constant $l \in \mathbb{N}$, $S_{i+l} = R_i$ and $S_j = \emptyset$ for all $j < l$, is a strong amortised ρ-bisimulation.*
4. $(T_j)_{j \in \mathbb{N}}$, *where $T_j = \bigcup_{i \leq j} R_i$, for all $j \in \mathbb{N}$, is a strong amortised ρ-bisimulation.*

In general, we could have relaxed the restriction to $\mathbb{N}$ in Definition 1 by allowing the family to be indexed over all the integers, provided a lower bound l exists such that for all $i < l$, $R_i = \emptyset$ and $p \prec^\rho q$ if $(p, q) \in R_l$. In fact, for convenience we will use negative indices in one example later and this is justified in view of part 3 of the proposition above.

A few basic properties of $\prec_i^\rho$ are given in the next proposition.

Proposition 3. *Let $i, j \in \mathbb{N}$.*

1. $(\prec_i^\rho)_{i \in \mathbb{N}}$ *is the component-wise largest strong amortised ρ-bisimulation.*
2. $\prec_i^\rho \subseteq \prec_{i+1}^\rho$.
3. $\sim \circ \prec_i^\rho = \prec_i^\rho = \prec_i^\rho \circ \sim$, *where $\circ$ denotes relational composition.*
4. *If ρ is reflexive then $\prec_i^\rho$ is reflexive and $\sim \subseteq \prec_i^\rho$.*
5. *If ρ is transitive then $\prec_i^\rho \circ \prec_j^\rho \subseteq \prec_{i+j}^\rho$.*
   In particular, $\prec^\rho$ is transitive if ρ is transitive.

To see that symmetry of ρ does not carry over to $\prec_i^\rho$ consider $p = a.0$, $q = b.0$, $c_a = 1$, $c_b = 2$ and $\rho = \{(a,b), (b,a)\}$. We next list the congruence properties of $\prec_i^\rho$ with respect to CCS-operators.

Proposition 4. *Let $p \prec_i^\rho q$ and $r \prec_j^\rho s$ where $i, j \in \mathbb{N}$.*

1. $a.p \prec_k^\rho b.q$ *whenever $a\rho b$ and $k \geq i + c_a - c_b \geq 0$ where $a, b \in A$.*
2. $p + r \prec_k^\rho q + s$ *for $k \geq \max\{i, j\}$.*
3. $p \mid r \prec_k^\rho q \mid s$ *for $k \geq i + j$.*
4. $p[f] \prec_k^\rho q[f]$ *for $k \geq i$*
5. $p \setminus a \prec_k^\rho q \setminus a$ *for any $a \in Act$.*

Note, that the congruence result for parallel composition only holds due to the fact that priced actions cannot communicate. As a corollary of this proposition we obtain the congruence results for $\prec^\rho$ where i and j are chosen as 0.

We now consider the generalization of amortised bisimilarity to its weak counterpart. A weak transition is defined as usual, just as $\hat{a} = a$ if $a \neq \tau$ and $\hat{\tau} = \varepsilon$. However, via ρ we can map priced actions to τ and the weak matching has to take these "visible τ-actions" into account. To formulate this, let $\varepsilon \rho u$ ($u \rho \varepsilon$, respectively) denote that $\tau \rho u_i$ for all i where $u = u_1 \cdots u_n$, $u_i \in CAct$. The cost function C is extended to words by $c_u = c_{u_1} + \cdots + c_{u_n}$.

Definition 5. *Let the preconditions be as in Definition 1. A family $(R_i)_{i \in \mathbb{N}}$ of binary relations over $\mathbf{P}$ is a weak amortised ρ-bisimulation, if for all $i \in \mathbb{N}$, $(p, q) \in R_i$:*

1. $p \xrightarrow{a} p'$ *implies* $\exists q', b, u, v \ [a \rho b, \ \varepsilon \rho uv, \ q \xRightarrow{u \hat{b} v} q'$ *and* $(p', q') \in R_{i + c_{u \hat{b} v} - c_a}]$,
2. $q \xrightarrow{b} q'$ *implies* $\exists p', a, u, v \ [a \rho b, \ uv \rho \varepsilon, \ p \xRightarrow{u \hat{a} v} p'$ *and* $(p', q') \in R_{i + c_b - c_{u \hat{a} v}}]$,

where $a, b \in \mathcal{A}$ and $u, v \in CAct^*$. Process p is (weakly) amortised cheaper (more cost efficient) than q up to credit i, $p \prec_i^\rho q$, if $(p, q) \in R_i$ for some weak amortised ρ-bisimulation $(R_i)_{i \in \mathbb{N}}$. We write $p \prec_i^\rho q$ if $(p, q) \in R_i$ for some i-slice R_i.

The assertions of Proposition 3 remain valid for the weak case. Additionally, we may replace $\sim$ by $\approx$ in clause 3 and clause 4. Finally, the congruence results stated in Proposition 4 carry over apart from closure under $+$ which is lost for standard reasons.

3 The Amortised Faster-Than Preorder

In [6], Lüttgen and Vogler consider a timed version of CCS incorporating urgent actions and a clock pulse action σ. They then define a preorder called the *amortised faster-than* preorder as the largest relation with index 0 in a family of bisimulation relations indexed by the natural numbers. In their treatment, every action is visible (this includes σ as well as τ). Hence they work within a strong bisimilarity setting. However, the conditions governing these bisimulation relations is reminiscent of the treatment of sequences of internal actions in the definition of weak bisimilarity. The number of clock actions executed up to a given state thus gives the time of the next visible action.

Definition 6. [the amortised faster-than preorder] *A family $(R_i)_{i \in \mathbb{N}}$ of relations over $\mathbf{P}$ is a family of amortised faster-than relations if, for all $i \in \mathbb{N}$, $(p, q) \in R_i$ and $a \in \mathcal{A}$:*

1. $p \xrightarrow{a} p'$ *implies* $\exists q', k, l \ [q \xrightarrow{\sigma}{}^k \xrightarrow{a} \xrightarrow{\sigma}{}^l q'$ *and* $(p', q') \in R_{i+k+l}]$.
2. $q \xrightarrow{a} q'$ *implies* $\exists p', k, l \ [k + l \leq i$ *and* $p \xrightarrow{\sigma}{}^k \xrightarrow{a} \xrightarrow{\sigma}{}^l p'$ *and* $(p', q') \in R_{i-k-l}]$.

3. $p \xrightarrow{\sigma} p'$ implies $\exists q', k$ $[k \geq 1 - i$ and $q \xrightarrow{\sigma}^k q'$ and $(p', q') \in R_{i-1+k}]$.
4. $q \xrightarrow{\sigma} q'$ implies $\exists p', k$ $[k \leq i + 1$ and $p \xrightarrow{\sigma}^k p'$ and $(p', q') \in R_{i+1-k}]$.

Process p is amortised faster than q if there is a family $(R_i)_{i \in \mathbb{N}}$ of amortised faster-than relations such that $(p, q) \in R_0$.

We give two embeddings of the faster-than preorder in our setting. As mentioned before, Definition 6 has similarities with both weak and strong bisimulation. Accordingly, we give two embeddings, one which characterizes the amortised faster-than preorder as a weak amortised bisimulation while the second identifies it with a strong amortised bisimulation.

In our first (straight forward) embedding we relate a clock pulse σ via ρ to τ and vice versa. We further assume that this internal transition is different from [6]'s τ as τ's are considered as visible there. Under these assumptions a transition sequence $p \xrightarrow{\sigma}^k \xrightarrow{a} \xrightarrow{\sigma}^l p'$ coincides with $p \overset{\sigma^k a \sigma^l}{\Longrightarrow} p'$ in our setting where $\varepsilon \rho \sigma^{k+l} \rho \varepsilon$. Thus, the faster-than preorder reduces to an instance of an amortised weak bisimilarity.

Proposition 7. *The amortised faster-than preorder is a weak amortised ρ-bisimulation ($\preceq^\rho$) where $CAct = \{\sigma\}$, $c_\sigma = 1$ and $\rho = \{(\tau, \sigma), (\sigma, \tau), (\sigma, \sigma)\}$.*

Note, that this amortised weak bisimulation also characterizes the weak amortised faster-than preorder which, however, has not been defined in [6].

For the second embedding, we reformulate the faster-than preorder such that the transition to be matched is a weak one in the sense that it may be preceded and followed by a sequence of clock transitions.

Lemma 8. Characterization *The faster-than preorder may be equivalently defined by varying conditions (1) to (4) as follows.*

1. $p \xrightarrow{\sigma}^k \xrightarrow{a} \xrightarrow{\sigma}^l p'$ implies $\exists q', m, n$ $[k - m \leq i$ and $q \xrightarrow{\sigma}^m \xrightarrow{a} \xrightarrow{\sigma}^n q'$ and $(p', q') \in R_{i-(k+l)+(m+n)}]$.
2. $q \xrightarrow{\sigma}^m \xrightarrow{a} \xrightarrow{\sigma}^n q'$ implies $\exists p', k, l$ $[k - m \leq i$ and $p \xrightarrow{\sigma}^k \xrightarrow{a} \xrightarrow{\sigma}^l p'$ and $(p', q') \in R_{i-(k+l)+(m+n)}]$.
3. $p \xrightarrow{\sigma}^k p'$ implies $\exists q', m$ $[k - m \leq i$ and $q \xrightarrow{\sigma}^m q'$ and $(p', q') \in R_{i-k+m}]$.
4. $q \xrightarrow{\sigma}^m q'$ implies $\exists p', k$ $[k - m \leq i$ and $p \xrightarrow{\sigma}^k p'$ and $(p', q') \in R_{i-k+m}]$.

For the embedding we need a refinement of the original definition of amortised ρ-bisimulation such that the matching of actions can be cost dependent. By itself, this seems to be a reasonable assumption as, for example, if one has accumulated in the simulation a huge credit one can be more generous in choosing matching actions which are expensive. To cover this aspect, we define ρ as a family $\rho = (\rho_i)_{i \in \mathbb{N}}$.

Definition 9. *Let $\rho = (\rho_i)_{i \in \mathbb{N}}$ and be a family of binary relations on $CAct_\tau$. A family of binary relations over $\mathbf{P}$, indexed by $\mathbb{N}$, is a cost dependent amortised ρ-bisimulation, if for all $i \in \mathbb{N}$, $(p, q) \in R_i$ and $a \in Act$:*

1. $p \xrightarrow{a} p'$ implies $\exists q', b \ [\ a\rho_i b$ and $q \xrightarrow{b} q'$ and $(p', q') \in R_{i+c_b-c_a}]$.
2. $q \xrightarrow{b} q'$ implies $\exists p', a \ [\ a\rho_i b$ and $p \xrightarrow{a} p'$ and $(p', q') \in R_{i+c_b-c_a}]$.

Let $p \sqsubseteq_i^\rho q$ denote the largest such relations.

The amortised faster-than preorder of [LV05] is a special case of the cost dependent set up.

Proposition 10. *The faster-than preorder is an instance of a cost dependent strong amortised ρ-bisimulation.*

Proof. We define $CAct = (I\!N \times Act \times I\!N) \cup I\!N$ and based on that cost function C and cost dependent relations ρ_i:

$$C(\alpha) = \begin{cases} k+l & \text{if } \alpha = (k, a, l) \\ k & \text{if } \alpha = k \end{cases}$$

For each $i \in I\!N$, $\rho_i \subseteq (I\!N \times Act \times I\!N)^2 \cup I\!N^2$. In its definition we distinguish between two cases. If $\alpha = (k, a, l)$ and $\beta = (m, b, n)$ then $\alpha \rho_i \beta$ if and only if $a = b$, $k - m \leq i$ and $(k+l) - (m+n) \leq i$. If, otherwise, $\alpha = k$ and $\beta = m$ then $\alpha \rho_i \beta$ if and only if $k - m \leq i$.

In the transition system we consider, $p \xrightarrow{(k,a,l)} p'$ if and only if $p \xrightarrow{\sigma}^k \xrightarrow{a} \xrightarrow{\sigma}^l p'$ and $p \xrightarrow{k} p'$ if and only if $p \xrightarrow{\sigma}^k p'$. It is now easily verified, that with Definition 8 and the instantiations given, amortised faster-than preorder is equal to the induced cost dependent amortised ρ-bisimulation.

In comparison, the weak amortised bisimulation certainly gives a more natural characterization of the faster-than preorder. In addition, the characterization as a strong amortised bisimulation has the following two drawbacks. First, its generalization to a weak faster-than preorder is not straight forward. Second, as priced actions cannot communicate, the parallel composition of transition systems in our and in the setting of [6] would yield different composed systems.

4 Shared Messaging Communication vs. Message Passing

In [9] the authors suggest and investigate a model called shared messaging communication (SMC) in which the advantages of message-passing (MP) and shared memory are combined. This is to reduce the communication costs (both in terms of communication latency and memory usage) of sending large payloads by allowing tasks to communicate data through special shared memory regions. The communication primitives are used only to send references (called *tokens*) to the shared memory region.

The following is a brief description of the system.

1. Each task operates on its private address space as well as on special memory regions which are used for inter-task communication.

2. Tasks communicate data in blocks of predefined size through *tokens*, which they are not allowed to copy or modify.
3. The system provides interfacial primitives for obtaining memory, composing a token and sending it. Correspondingly it also provides primitives for receiving a token, consuming it and releasing memory.

The authors consider an asynchronous communication model with a buffer for tokens. However, the basic principles and the motivation for the SMC model also hold in the synchronous communication setting.

The experimental results provided by the authors suggest that message-passing channels outperform shared messaging communication (due to the extra overhead involved in obtaining and releasing memory) when the payloads in communication are of small size. At higher sized payloads the SMC outperforms pure message-passing, since in SMC only a token is sent, as opposed to the message passing model where the entire contents of the message are sent.

We confirm these observations by proving (for our abstract processes) that up to a given credit, SMC is indeed amortised cheaper than MP. The credit given reflects the overheads of obtaining and releasing memory.

The following actions are necessary to control the access to the shared address space.

gum give unused memory (to be bound to a token t)
$\overline{uo}$ usage over (of the memory given by the token t)
$\overline{st}$ send token
rt receive token
$\overline{cps}$ compose token: write the data to the shared memory specified by the token
csm consume token: read the contents of the memory specified by the token.

The communicational behaviour of a *SMC* process is described by *SMC_Process*:

$$\begin{aligned}
SMC\_Process &\stackrel{df}{=} \tau.Request\_Token + \tau.Receive\_Token \\
Request\_Token &\stackrel{df}{=} gum.Compose\_Token \\
Compose\_Token &\stackrel{df}{=} \sum_{k \in \mathbb{N}-\{0\}} (\overline{cps}.)^k Send\_Token \\
Send\_Token &\stackrel{df}{=} \overline{st}.SMC\_Process \\
Receive\_Token &\stackrel{df}{=} rt.Consume\_Token \\
Consume\_Token &\stackrel{df}{=} \sum_{k \in \mathbb{N}-\{0\}} (csm.)^k Usage\_Over \\
Usage\_Over &\stackrel{df}{=} \overline{uo}.SMC\_Process
\end{aligned}$$

The definition of *Compose_Token* reflects the fact that depending on the size of the data to be transferred, it needs to be split into packets – the number of packets is given by the index k – which then are sent one by one. Similar arguments apply for receiving the data.

We may model the behaviour of a *MP* process as follows.

$$\begin{aligned}
MP\_Process &\stackrel{df}{=} \tau.Send\_Message + \tau.Receive\_Message \\
Send\_Message &\stackrel{df}{=} \sum_{k \in \mathbb{N}-\{0\}} (\overline{sm}.)^k MP\_Process \\
Receive\_Message &\stackrel{df}{=} \sum_{k \in \mathbb{N}-\{0\}} (rm.)^k MP\_Process
\end{aligned}$$

Comparing *SMC_Process* with *MP_Process*, it is clear, that *cps* should be matched with *sm* and *csm* with *rm*. The handling of tokens can be viewed as administrative overheads which may be matched with an idle action on the message passing side. For the sending of data, we therefore have the correspondence

$$SMC\_Process \xrightarrow{\tau} \xrightarrow{gum} \xrightarrow{cps} \cdots \xrightarrow{cps} \xrightarrow{st} SMC\_Process$$
$$MP\_Process \xrightarrow{\tau} \xrightarrow{\varepsilon} \underbrace{\xrightarrow{sm} \cdots \xrightarrow{sm}}_{k \text{ times}} \xrightarrow{\varepsilon} MP\_Process$$

and for receiving we have a respective matching. Clearly, sending or receiving a token should involve lower costs than sending/receiving data packets. Thus we associate with the former cost 1 and with the latter cost 2 (which could have been any $l > 1$, allowing for a similar analysis). This yields the following *CAct*-association ρ:

cost	SMC	MP	cost
1	gum	τ	0
1	$\overline{uo}$	τ	0
1	$\overline{st}$	τ	0
1	rt	τ	0
0	$\overline{cps}$	$\overline{sm}$	2
0	csm	rm	2

Proposition 11. *Let ρ and C as in the above table. Then SMC_Process is amortised cheaper than MP_Process up to credit 1: $SMC\_Process \preccurlyeq_1^\rho MP\_Process$.*

Proof. As it seems natural to start a simulation with credit 0, let us also consider bisimulation slices with index -1. So we have $(SMC\_Process, MP\_Process) \in R_0$ where $(R_i)_{i \in \mathbb{N} \cup \{-1\}}$ is the weak amortised ρ-bisimulation given by

	SMC_Process	MP_Process	condition on i	
1.	$SMC\_Process$	$MP\_Process$	$i = 2j,$	$j \geq 0$
2.	$Request\_Token$	$Send\_Message$	$i = 2j,$	$j \geq 0$
3.	$Receive\_Token$	$Receive\_Message$	$i = 2j,$	$j \geq 0$
4.	$Compose\_Token$	$Send\_Message$	$i = 2j - 1,$	$j \geq 0$
5.	$(\overline{cps}.)^k Send\_Token$	$(\overline{sm}.)^k MP\_Process$	$i = 2j - 1,$	$j \geq 1$
6.	$Consume\_Token$	$Receive\_Message$	$i = 2j - 1,$	$j \geq 0$
7.	$(csm.)^k Usage\_Over$	$(rm.)^k MP\_Process$	$i = 2j - 1,$	$j \geq 1$
8.	$Send\_Token$	$MP\_Process$	$i = 2j - 1,$	$j \geq 1$
9.	$Usage\_Over$	$MP\_Process$	$i = 2j - 1,$	$j \geq 1$

where a pair of processes of a line is contained in R_i if i satisfies the condition of the last column.

By the monotonicity property, $(SMC\_Process, MP\_Process) \in R'_1$ for the amortised ρ-bisimulation $(R'_i)_{i \in \mathbb{N}}$ where $R'_i = R_{i-1}$ for all $i \in \mathbb{N}$. This establishes $SMC\_Process \preccurlyeq_1^\rho MP\_Process$, i.e. $SMC\_Process$ is more cost efficient than $MP\_Process$ up to credit 1.

5 Web Access with and Without a Proxy Server

In most computing environments, it is fairly common to find a caching proxy server in operation. Caching proxy servers improve the performance of web-access within the network by caching most frequently accessed pages of a web server with predominantly static content and serving them to the clients in the network. The main communication overhead is restricted to receiving header information from the web-site. This information is used to determine whether the cached copy in the proxy is the latest or needs to be updated. Caching proxies also improve the performance of the web server by reducing the number of direct accesses to the web-site from distant clients for its content.

We model greatly simplified versions of the clients and the proxy server. We show that the use of the proxy server reduces the volume of traffic between the network and the web server, while still serving up-to-date information to each client.

Let $d\_request\_header$, d_serve_header $d\_request\_page$ and d_serve_page be all the visible actions. The prefix 'd' indicates direct access to the web server rather than via a proxy. In the absence of a proxy server, a typical client D_Client has the following definition.

$$D\_Client \stackrel{df}{=} \overline{d\_request\_page}.D\_Client'$$
$$D\_Client' \stackrel{df}{=} d\_serve\_page.D\_Client$$

With the introduction of a proxy, the clients communicate only with the proxy and are indeed set up to do just that. The actions involving communications of the clients with the proxy server are $p\_request\_page$ and p_serve_page which stand respectively, for requesting a page from the proxy and serving a page from the proxy.

$$P\_Client \stackrel{df}{=} \overline{p\_request\_page}.P\_Client'$$
$$P\_Client' \stackrel{df}{=} p\_serve\_page.P\_Client$$

The proxy server requests the web server for the page and caches it when it arrives (this initial request is done by $i\_request\_page$). For future requests, it merely asks for the header and compares it with its cached version. It requests the full page only if the header information is different. Again we simplify the design by assuming it serves only one request at a time.

$$
\begin{aligned}
Proxy_{start} &\stackrel{df}{=} p\_request\_page.First\_Copy \\
First\_Copy &\stackrel{df}{=} \overline{i\_request\_page}.Request\_Sent \\
\\
Proxy &\stackrel{df}{=} p\_request\_page.Client\_Wait \\
Client\_Wait &\stackrel{df}{=} \overline{d\_request\_header}.Check\_Update \\
Check\_Update &\stackrel{df}{=} d\_serve\_header.Decide \\
DECIDE &\stackrel{df}{=} \tau.No\_Update + \tau.Update \\
Update &\stackrel{df}{=} \overline{d\_request\_page}.Request\_Sent \\
No\_Update &\stackrel{df}{=} \overline{p\_serve\_page}.Proxy \\
Request\_Sent &\stackrel{df}{=} d\_serve\_page.Cached \\
Cached &\stackrel{df}{=} \overline{p\_serve\_page}.Proxy
\end{aligned}
$$

For the complete system, we consider just one client as this suffices to demonstrate the benefits of a proxy.[1] The entire system with the proxy server is

$$P\_System_{init} \stackrel{df}{=} (P\_Client \mid Proxy_{start}) \setminus \underbrace{\{p\_request\_page, p\_serve\_page\}}_{=:ProxyInt}$$

of which the main behaviour is given by

$$P\_System \stackrel{df}{=} (P\_Client \mid Proxy) \setminus ProxyInt.$$

It is clear that the two systems P_System and D_System, where

$$D\_System \stackrel{df}{=} D\_Client,$$

are not observationally equivalent since P_System may perform actions which are not in the sort of D_System. However they are both functionally equivalent from the point of view of the client. To set up ρ, we inspect how the actions of P_System and D_System correspond during one round of communication. In case that no updating is required the correspondence is

$$P\_System \xrightarrow{\tau} \xrightarrow{drh} \xrightarrow{dsh} \xrightarrow{\tau} P\_System$$
$$D\_System \xrightarrow{\varepsilon} \xrightarrow{drp} \xrightarrow{dsp} \xrightarrow{\varepsilon} D\_System$$

while in case of an updating we have:

$$P\_System \xrightarrow{\tau} \xrightarrow{drh} \xrightarrow{dsh} \xrightarrow{\tau} \xrightarrow{drp} \xrightarrow{dsp} \xrightarrow{\tau} P\_System$$
$$D\_System \xrightarrow{\varepsilon} \xrightarrow{drp} \xrightarrow{dsp} \xrightarrow{\varepsilon} \xrightarrow{\varepsilon} \xrightarrow{\varepsilon} D\_System$$

Note, that D_System is actually not capable of performing any τ-transition, so it can match $d\_request\_page$ and d_serve_page only by staying idle. Thus, we define ρ as given via the following table.

cost	P_System	abbr.	D_System	cost
w_1	$i\_request\_page$	irp	$d\_request\_page$	w_1
w_2	d_serve_page	dsp	d_serve_page	w_2
w_1	$d\_request\_page$	drp	τ	0
w_2	d_serve_page	dsp	τ	0
u_1	$d\_request\_header$	drh	$d\_request\_page$	w_1
u_2	d_serve_header	dsh	d_serve_page	w_2

We set $v_i := w_i - u_i$ for $i = 1, 2$, $u := u_1 + u_2$, $v := v_1 + v_2$ and $w := w_1 + w_2$. Thus, u gives the cost of a complete update round while v is the credit obtained from one round without update. As the cost of getting a page is much higher than that of getting a header, we have $v > u$ (as we may assume $w > u$). Furthermore, we require $u \neq 0$.

---

[1] Imagine a German living in India accessing the news *Tagesschau* every few minutes.

As discussed in the introduction, it is necessary to model the relative frequencies of update rounds against rounds without an update, in order to establish any efficiency result. We proceed by introducing a *decision maker DM*. Whenever the header of the page is provided by the web server, it has to be decided whether the copy in the cache has to be updated or not. This decision is taken by *DM*. Essentially, *DM*'s decision is nondeterministic, but we assume that the number of update-decisions ($\bar{b}$-actions) is never higher than n times the number of no-update decisions ($\bar{a}$-actions), for some fixed n. We then show for which n, depending on the costs for long distance communications, the proxy system is actually more efficient.

The decision maker is given by

$$DM \stackrel{df}{=} \bar{a}.(DM \mid \underbrace{\bar{b}.\cdots.\bar{b}}_{n \text{ times}}.0)$$

and to enable it to interact with *Proxy* we replace *DECIDE* by

$$Decide \stackrel{df}{=} a.No\_Update + b.Update.$$

The complete proxy-system now is

$$P\_System \stackrel{df}{=} (P\_Client \mid Proxy \mid DM) \backslash \underbrace{ProxyInt \cup \{a, b\}}_{=:H}$$

where we do not introduce fresh names for the modified systems.

Proposition 12. *Let u be the extra cost of one update of a page and v be the cost saved if an update is not necessary. Assume that at any state of a computation, the number of updates is never higher than n times the number of no-updates. Then whenever $n \leq \frac{v}{u}$, P_System is more cost efficient than D_System, that is*

$$P\_System_{init} \preccurlyeq^\rho D\_System$$

where ρ and C are given in the table on page 330.

Proof. For a derivative p of DM let $\Delta(p) := \max\{n \mid \exists p' : p \xrightarrow{b^n} p'\}$. It is easily verified that

$$p \sim q \text{ if and only if } \Delta(p) = \Delta(q).$$

Thus $\Delta(m) := \{p \mid \Delta(p) = m\}$ is an equivalence class of bisimilar processes and by the congruence properties for $\preccurlyeq^\rho$ we do not have to distinguish between different representatives in the semantic analysis. This reduces the cases to inspect in the proof considerably.

We define the weak amortised ρ-bisimulation $(R_i)_{i \in \mathbb{N}}$ as the smallest relation satisfying the conditions described by the following table[2].

---

[2] For the sake of readability, we omit the restriction set H in the proxy system.

	P_System$_{init}$			D_System	condition on i
1.	P_Client |	Proxy$_{start}$	| $\Delta(0)$	D_Client	$i = 0$
2.	P_Client' |	First_Copy	| $\Delta(0)$	D_Client	$i = 0$
3.	P_Client' |	Request_Sent	| $\Delta(0)$	D_Client'	$i = 0$

	P_System			D_System	
4.	P_Client |	Proxy	| $\Delta(m)$	D_Client	$i \geq m \cdot u$
5.	P_Client' |	Client_Wait	| $\Delta(m)$	D_Client	$i \geq m \cdot u$
6.	P_Client' |	Check_Update	| $\Delta(m)$	D_Client'	$i \geq m \cdot u + v_1$
7.	P_Client' |	Decide	| $\Delta(m)$	D_Client	$i \geq m \cdot u + v$
8.	P_Client' |	No_Update	| $\Delta(m)$	D_Client	$i \geq m \cdot u$
9.	P_Client' |	Update	| $\Delta(m)$	D_Client	$i \geq m \cdot u + w$
10.	P_Client' |	Request_Sent	| $\Delta(m)$	D_Client	$i \geq m \cdot u + w_2$
11.	P_Client' |	Cached	| $\Delta(m)$	D_Client	$i \geq m \cdot u$

As an example, we verify the properties of a weak amortised ρ-bisimulation (Definition 5) for case 7. All other cases are similar.

So assume $((P\_Client' \mid Decide \mid \Delta(m))\backslash H, D\_Client) \in R_i$ for some $i \geq m \cdot u + v$.

There are two transition possible for P_System's state.

One transition is

$$(P\_Client' \mid Decide \mid \Delta(m))\backslash H \xrightarrow{\tau} (P\_Client' \mid No\_Update \mid \Delta(m+n))\backslash H$$

where the τ-action is due to DM's decision that no update is required. This decision will release n more $\bar{b}$'s in DM and therefore the new state of the decision maker is $\Delta(m+n)$. D_System can match the τ-move only by staying idle. Hence, we have to show:

$$(*) \qquad ((P\_Client' \mid No\_Update \mid \Delta(m+n))\backslash H, D\_Client) \in R_i$$

However as $n \leq \frac{v}{u}$, we have $v \geq n \cdot u$. Thus,

$$i \geq m \cdot u + v \geq (m+n) \cdot u$$

and, thus, condition 8 is verified for $(*)$.

The other transition initially possible is – provided $m > 0$ –

$$(P\_Client' \mid Decide \mid \Delta(m))\backslash H \xrightarrow{\tau} (P\_Client' \mid Update \mid \Delta(m-1))\backslash H$$

where this τ-action is due to DM's decision to update. Again, D_System stays idle and it is easily verified that

$$((P\_Client' \mid Update \mid \Delta(m-1))\backslash H, D\_System) \in R_i$$

by case 9.

Now, assume D_System performs the first move which can only be

$$D\_Client \xrightarrow{\overline{d\_request\_page}} D\_Client'.$$

P_System can always match this (going via state No_Update) by

$$(P\_Client' \mid Decide \mid \Delta(m))\backslash H \xRightarrow{\overline{d\_request\_header}}$$

$$(P\_Client' \mid Check\_Update \mid \Delta(m+n))\backslash H$$

with cost u_1. We have to show that

$$((P\_Client' \mid Check\_Update \mid \Delta(m+n))\backslash H, D\_Client') \in R_{i+v_1}$$

which follows from case 6 if $i + v_1 \geq (m+n) \cdot u + v_1$. However, $(m+n) \cdot u \leq m \cdot u + v \leq i$ by the preconditions.

6 Conclusions

In this paper we have proposed amortised ρ-bisimulation as a behavioural relation which admits quantitative assertions on the cost relationship of the processes under comparison. To this end, we have enriched CCS by priced actions and studied basic properties of the resulting calculus. Depending on the relation ρ, which determines which actions can match which in the bisimulation game, amortised ρ-bisimulations can coincide with bisimilarity or just give a relation without preferred properties like reflexivity or transitivity. Though the latter can be considered as undesirable, we have pursued the policy of developing a calculus which would satisfy certain needs highlighted by the case studies. For example, the proof that in the presence of a proxy server, in general, a system is more cost efficient, would have been much less clear if ρ was deemed to be reflexive. But even in that case study, we were able to use the proof techniques of standard CCS. We therefore believe that the proposed theory may be useful for similar verifications, though, of course, more case studies are required to test its applicability. Another indicator, which makes us believe that our definitions are "right" or "natural" is the fact that only after we had fixed our notion of amortised bisimulations, we came across Lüttgen & Vogler's work on amortised faster-than preorders, which turned out just to be an instance of our more general set-up.[3] Aiming at expressing amortisation within bisimilarity it seems natural to consider bisimulations with an extra cost component.

There are various questions regarding the algebraic properties of the comparison relations that this work raises. For instance the properties of the ρ-relation between actions (or action sequences) largely influences the corresponding nature of the bisimilarity relation. The tradeoff between nice properties and wide applicability needs to be further studied. Another question we have not addressed

---

[3] We acknowledge that our notation is highly influenced by [6].

(and this is relevant in the context of CCS), is whether priced actions should be allowed to communicate and synchronize, and if so what would be the costs of such a communication and whether compatibility with parallel composition could be achieved.

Behavioural equivalences and preorders have largely dominated the analysis of the semantics of programs and systems. The literature does contain several works ([1,6,10,4]) in which authors have compared the relative efficiencies of systems by using time as a quantity to be captured behaviourally. The notion of time is implicit also in the notion of computation and may be viewed as a cost that may be captured behaviourally. However, the notion of cost in this paper goes further. Costs are explicitly assigned to actions and cannot necessarily be inferred from behaviour. The result is that the same behaviours under different cost functions could yield radically different decisions as to the relative costs of running competing systems. The analysis of long-term costs is important in nondeterministic systems which theoretically may run forever. We hope to have made a small step towards such an analysis.

References

1. S. Arun-Kumar and M. Hennessy. An efficiency preorder for processes. *Acta Informatica*, 1(29):737–760, 1992.
2. R. Cleaveland, J. Parrow, and B. Steffen. A semantics based verification tool for finite state systems. In *Proceedings of the 9th International Symposium on Protocol Specification, Testing and Verification*, North Holland, 1989.
3. T. Cormen, C. Leiserson, R. Rivest, and C. Stein. *Introduction to Algorithms.* Prentice-Hall India, 2004. (second edition).
4. M. Hennessy and T. Regan. A process algebra for timed systems. *Information and Computation*, 117(2):221–239, 1995.
5. H. Lin. A process algebra manipulator. *Formal Methods in Systems Design*, 7:243–259, 1995.
6. G. Lüttgen and W. Vogler. Bisimulation on speed: a unified approach. In *Proceedings of FOSSACS 2005*, number 3441 in Lecture Notes in Computer Science, pages 79–94. Springer–Verlag, 2005.
7. R. Milner. *A Calculus of Communicating Systems*, volume 92. Lecture Notes in Computer Science, 1980.
8. R. Milner. *Communication and Concurrency.* Prentice-Hall, 1989.
9. Satya Kiran M.N.V., Jayram M.N., Pradeep Rao, and S.K. Nandy. A complexity effective communication model for behavioral modeling of signal processing applications. In *Proceedings of DAC 2003*, 2003.
10. F. Moller and C. Tofts. Relating processes with respect to speed. In *Proceedings of CONCUR 91*, number 527 in Lecture Notes in Computer Science, pages 424–438. Springer–Verlag, 1991.
11. D. Park. Concurrency and automata on infinite sequences. In P. Deussen, editor, *Proceedings of ICALP 81*, number 104 in Lecture Notes in Computer Science. Springer–Verlag, 1981.

Proof Methodologies for Behavioural Equivalence in DPI

Alberto Ciaffaglione[1,2], Matthew Hennessy[2], and Julian Rathke[2]

[1] Dipartimento di Matematica e Informatica, Università di Udine, Italia
ciaffagl@dimi.uniud.it
[2] Department of Informatics, University of Sussex, United Kingdom
{A.Ciaffaglione, M.Hennessy, J.Rathke}@sussex.ac.uk

Abstract. We focus on techniques for proving behavioural equivalence between systems in DPI, a distributed version of the PICALCULUS in which processes may migrate between dynamically created locations, and where resource access policies are implemented by means of capability types.

We devise a tractable collection of auxiliary proof methods, relying mainly on the use of *bisimulations up-to β-reductions*, which considerably relieve the burden of exhibiting witness bisimulations. Using such methods we model simple distributed protocols, such as crossing a firewall, a server and its clients, metaservers installing memory services, and address their correctness in a relatively simple manner.

1 Introduction

Bisimulations [Mil89], and the related bisimulation equivalence, have been proved to be of central importance in the elaboration of semantic theories of processes, and in developing verification techniques for them. The purpose of this work is to demonstrate that they may be also employed for the verification of distributed systems, even when the correctness depends on access control policies.

We focus on an abstract system description language called DPI [HR02b], an extension of the well-known PICALCULUS [MPW92,SW01]. In this language a system consists of a collection of *processes*, or *agents*, distributed among different *sites*, where they can use *local resources*; these resources are modelled using *local* versions of PICALCULUS *communication channels*. Agents may migrate from site to site, generate new local resources, or indeed new sites.

Following ideas originally formulated in [PS00], DPI can be endowed with a system of *capability types*, with which access policies to both resources and sites can be expressed. Since the behaviour of systems is dependent on the access policy in force, a new theory of semantic equivalence is required to take this dependency into account. This was developed in [HR02a,HMR04], where the equivalence is expressed in the form of triples

$$\mathcal{I} \models M \approx_{bis} N$$

Intuitively this means that the systems M and N exhibit the same behaviour, from the point of view of a user constrained by the access policy $\mathcal{I}$; formally, $\mathcal{I}$ is simply a type environment, giving, for each resource and location, the capabilities which may be exercised by the user.

In this paper we show that this relativised notion of system behaviour can be effectively employed to demonstrate the correctness of access protocols for distributed

			$R, U ::=$	*Processes, or Agents*
			$u!\langle V\rangle R$	Output
$M, N ::=$		*Systems*	$u?(X) R$	Input
$l[\![P]\!]$		Located agents	goto $v.R$	Migration
$M \mid N$		Composition	(newc c : C) R	Local channel creation
(new e : E) M		Name Scoping	(newloc k : K) R	Location creation
$\mathbf{0}$		Termination	if $v_1 = v_2$ then R else U	Matching
			$R \mid U$	Parallelism
			$*R$	Iteration
			stop	Termination

Fig. 1. Syntax for D<small>PI</small>

systems. All the examples considered are simple; nevertheless, we feel that they at least demonstrate the feasibility of this approach to system verification.

In the next section we review the language D<small>PI</small>, its type system, and the relativised notion of bisimulation equivalence. This is followed by an exposition of some useful proof techniques, relying mainly on the use of bisimulations up-to in the spirit of [SM92], which alleviate the burden of exhibiting witness bisimulations. This is then followed by three sections, each considering a particular verification example. The final section is about related and future work.

2 D<small>PI</small>: A Synopsis

In this section we recall the essential features of the language D<small>PI</small>; readers are referred to [HMR04,HR02b,CHR05] for a more detailed description.

Syntax. The syntax of the language is given in Figure 1, and presupposes a set of *identifiers*; there are two syntactic categories, for systems, and agents.

A typical system takes the form (new e : E)($l[\![P]\!] \mid k[\![Q]\!]$) $\mid l[\![R]\!]$. This represents a system with two sites, l and k, with the agents P and R running at the former and Q at the latter; moreover P and Q, although executing at different sites, share some private information, e, of type E. The syntax for agents is an extension of that of the picalculus [SW01]. There is input and output on local channels, parallelism, matching of values, iteration, and a migration construct. For example, in the system $l[\![P \mid \text{goto } k.Q]\!] \mid k[\![R]\!]$, the process Q can migrate from l to k, leading to the resulting system $l[\![P]\!] \mid k[\![Q \mid R]\!]$. Finally, processes have the ability to create new instances of names (channels, newc, and sites, newloc); their declaration types dictate the use to which these will be put.

The values V communicated along channels consist of tuples of *simple values*, v. These, in turn, may be *identifiers*, u, or structured values, of the form $u_1 @ u_2$; the latter are used to represent channels which are not local to the site at which the communication takes place. In turn, the input construct $u?(X) R$ uses patterns, X, to deconstruct incoming values; these may be taken to be values constructed from variables, in which each variable has at most one occurrence.

Typing. D<small>PI</small> is a capability based language, in the sense that the behaviour of processes depends on the capabilities the various entities have received in their environment. Formally, these capabilities are represented as types, and the various categories of types we

Base Types: $\textbf{base} ::= \textbf{int} \mid \textbf{bool} \mid \textbf{unit} \mid \top \mid \ldots$
Value Types: $A ::= \textbf{base} \mid C \mid C@\textsf{loc} \mid K$

Local Channel types: $C ::= r\langle T \rangle \mid w\langle T \rangle \mid rw\langle T \rangle$
Location Types: $K ::= \textsf{loc}[c_1 : C_1, \ldots, c_n : C_n], n \geq 0$ (provided $c_i = c_j$ implies $i = j$)

Transmission Types: $T ::= (A_1, \ldots, A_n), n \geq 0$

Fig. 2. Types for DPI - informal

use are given in Figure 2. Apart from the standard base types, and the special *top* type $\top$, the main ones are

local channel types: these are ranged over by C and can take the form $rw\langle T \rangle$, giving the ability to both read and write values of type T, or the restricted supertypes $r\langle T \rangle$ and $w\langle T \rangle$;
non-local channel types: these take the form $C@\textsf{loc}$, and a value of this type is a structured value, $c@l$;
location types: these take the form $\textsf{loc}[c_1 : C_1, \ldots, c_n : C_n]$; receiving a value l of this type gives access to the channels, or resources, c_i at type C_i, for $1 \leq i \leq n$.

The types come equipped with a *subtyping* relation, which is defined inductively, from the standard requirements on channel types, and *record subtyping* on location types $\textsf{loc}[c_1{:}C_1, \ldots c_n{:}C_n] <: \textsf{loc}[c_1{:}C_1, \ldots c_k{:}C_k]$, whenever $k \leq n$. Viewing types (intuitively) as sets of capabilities, $T_1 <: T_2$ means that the capabilities of T_2 are a subset of those of T_1.

The static typing of a system, $\Gamma \vdash M$, indicates that M uses all its identifiers in accordance with the types designated in the *type environment* Γ, which gives the type of all the free names in M. Formally, a type environment Γ is a consistent list of entries, which must take one of the following forms

- $u : \textsf{loc}$, indicating u is to be used as a location;
- $u@w : C$, indicating that w is already known to Γ as a location, and u is a local channel at w with type C.

The typing of systems requires an auxiliary typing judgment for agents, $\Gamma \vdash_k P$, which needs to be parameterised relative to the current location k, because resources are located: they may be available at one site and not another.

Behaviour. The behaviour of a system, that is the ability of its agents to interact with other agents, depends on the knowledge these agents have of each other capabilities.

Definition 1 (Configurations). *A configuration consists of a pair $\mathcal{I} \triangleright M$, where*

- *$\mathcal{I}$ is a type environment which associates some type to every free name in M*
- *there is a type environment Γ such that $\Gamma \vdash M$ and $\Gamma <: \mathcal{I}$*

This latter requirement means that if $\mathcal{I}$ can assign a type $T_{\mathcal{I}}$ to a name n, then Γ can assign a type T_{Γ} such that $T_{\Gamma} <: T_{\mathcal{I}}$. Again, viewing types as sets of capabilities, this means that $T_{\mathcal{I}}$, representing the knowledge of the external user, is a subset of T_{Γ}, the actual set of capabilities used to type the system M. □

$$\frac{\text{(M-IN)}}{I \triangleright k[\![a?(X)R]\!] \xrightarrow{k.a?V} I \triangleright k[\![R\{V/x\}]\!]}$$

$$\frac{\text{(M-OUT)}}{I \triangleright k[\![a!\langle V\rangle P]\!] \xrightarrow{k.a!V} I, \langle V : I^r(k,a)\rangle @k \triangleright k[\![P]\!]}$$

$$\frac{\text{(M-WEAK)}}{I \triangleright M \xrightarrow{(\tilde{e}:\tilde{E})k.a?V} M} \frac{I,\langle e:\mathsf{E}\rangle \triangleright M \xrightarrow{(\tilde{d}:\tilde{D})k.a?V} I' \triangleright M'}{I \triangleright M \xrightarrow{(e:\mathsf{E};\tilde{d}:\tilde{D})k.a?V} I' \triangleright M'} \; \mathsf{bn}(e) \notin I$$

$$\frac{\text{(M-OPEN)}}{I, \langle e : \mathsf{T}\rangle \triangleright M \xrightarrow{(\tilde{d}:\tilde{D})k.a!V} I' \triangleright M'}{I \triangleright (\mathsf{new}\, e : \mathsf{E}) M \xrightarrow{(e:\mathsf{E};\tilde{d}:\tilde{D})k.a!V} I' \triangleright M'}$$

$$\text{(M-CTXT)} \quad \frac{I \triangleright M \xrightarrow{\mu} I' \triangleright M'}{I \triangleright M \mid N \xrightarrow{\mu} I' \triangleright M' \mid N} \; \mathsf{bn}(\mu) \notin \mathsf{fn}(N)$$
$$I \triangleright N \mid M \xrightarrow{\mu} I' \triangleright N \mid M'$$

$$\text{(M-NEW)} \quad \frac{I, \langle e : \mathsf{T}\rangle \triangleright M \xrightarrow{\mu} I', \langle e : \mathsf{T}\rangle \triangleright M'}{I \triangleright (\mathsf{new}\, e : \mathsf{E}) M \xrightarrow{\mu} I' \triangleright (\mathsf{new}\, e : \mathsf{E}) M'} \; \mathsf{bn}(e) \notin \mu$$

Fig. 3. External actions-in-context for DPI

$$\text{(M-COMM)} \quad \frac{I_1 \triangleright M \xrightarrow{(\tilde{e}:\tilde{E})k.a?V} I_1' \triangleright M'}{I_2 \triangleright N \xrightarrow{(\tilde{e}:\tilde{E})k.a!V} I_2' \triangleright N'}$$
$$I \triangleright M \mid N \xrightarrow{\tau} I \triangleright (\mathsf{new}\, \tilde{e} : \tilde{\mathsf{E}})(M' \mid N')$$

$$\text{(M-COMM)} \quad \frac{I_1 \triangleright M \xrightarrow{(\tilde{e}:\tilde{E})k.a!V} I_1' \triangleright M'}{I_2 \triangleright N \xrightarrow{(\tilde{e}:\tilde{E})k.a?V} I_2' \triangleright N'}$$
$$I \triangleright M \mid N \xrightarrow{\tau} I \triangleright (\mathsf{new}\, \tilde{e} : \tilde{\mathsf{E}})(M' \mid N')$$

(M-MOVE)
$$I \triangleright k[\![\mathsf{goto}\, l.P]\!] \xrightarrow{\tau}_\beta I \triangleright l[\![P]\!]$$

(M-EQ/NEQ)
$$I \triangleright k[\![\mathsf{if}\, v_1 = v_2 \,\mathsf{then}\, P \,\mathsf{else}\, Q]\!] \xrightarrow{\tau}_\beta I \triangleright k[\![P]\!] \quad (v_1 = v_2)$$
$$I \triangleright k[\![\mathsf{if}\, v_1 = v_2 \,\mathsf{then}\, P \,\mathsf{else}\, Q]\!] \xrightarrow{\tau}_\beta I \triangleright k[\![Q]\!] \quad (v_1 \neq v_2)$$

(M-SPLIT)
$$I \triangleright k[\![P \mid Q]\!] \xrightarrow{\tau}_\beta I \triangleright k[\![P]\!] \mid k[\![Q]\!]$$

(M-L.CREATE)
$$I \triangleright k[\![(\mathsf{newloc}\, l : \mathsf{L})\, P]\!] \xrightarrow{\tau}_\beta I \triangleright (\mathsf{new}\, l : \mathsf{L})\, k[\![P]\!]$$

(M-UNWIND)
$$I \triangleright k[\![*P]\!] \xrightarrow{\tau}_\beta I \triangleright k[\![*P \mid P]\!]$$

(M-C.CREATE)
$$I \triangleright k[\![(\mathsf{newc}\, c : \mathsf{C})\, P]\!] \xrightarrow{\tau}_\beta I \triangleright (\mathsf{new}\, c@k : \mathsf{C})\, k[\![P]\!]$$

Fig. 4. Internal actions-in-context for DPI

So we define the behaviour in terms of actions over configurations, that is

$$I \triangleright M \xrightarrow{\mu} I' \triangleright M' \tag{1}$$

where the label μ can take any of the following forms

- τ: an internal action, requiring no participation by the user;
- $(\tilde{e} : \tilde{\mathsf{E}})k.a?V$: the input of value V along the channel a, located at the site k. The bound names in $(\tilde{e})$ are freshly generated by the user;
- $(\tilde{e} : \tilde{\mathsf{E}})k.a!V$: the output of value V along the channel a, located at the site k. The bound names in $(\tilde{e})$ are freshly generated by the environment.

The rules for defining these actions are given in Figure 3 and Figure 4, a slightly different but equivalent formulation to that given in [HMR04]. The guiding principle for (1) to happen, is that M must be able to perform the action μ, and the user must have, in I, the capability to participate in the action. The rules use some new notation for looking up the types associated with channels in environments: the partial functions $I^r(k, a)$ and $I^w(k, a)$ return the read, respectively write, type associated with the channel a at the location k in I (of course these may not exist, and $I^w(k, a) \downarrow$, for example, indicates that the write type is indeed defined). We extract names from entries in environments with the function $\mathsf{bn}(-)$, defined by $\mathsf{bn}(u) = u$ and $\mathsf{bn}(u \bullet w) = u$; this is extended to actions μ in the obvious manner. Notice also that we use the notation $\mathsf{fn}(-)$ for free variables. Finally, we have labelled some internal actions in Figure 4 as β-actions, which will be useful in the next section; but for the moment these labels can be ignored.

We now have a labelled transition system in which the states are configurations, and we can apply the standard definition of (weak) bisimulation.

(S-EXTR) $(\text{new } e{:}E)(M \mid N) \equiv M \mid (\text{new } e{:}E) N$, if $\text{bn}(e) \notin \text{fn}(M)$
(S-COM) $M \mid N \equiv N \mid M$
(S-ASSOC) $(M \mid N) \mid O \equiv M \mid (N \mid O)$
(S-ZERO) $M \mid \mathbf{0} \equiv M$
            $k[\![\text{stop}]\!] \equiv \mathbf{0}$
(S-FLIP) $(\text{new } e{:}E)(\text{new } e'{:}E') M \equiv (\text{new } e'{:}E')(\text{new } e{:}E) M$, if $\text{bn}(e) \notin (e'{:}E')$, $\text{bn}(e') \notin (e{:}E)$

Fig. 5. Structural equivalence for DPI

Definition 2 (Bisimulations). *We say a binary relation over configurations is a bisimulation if both it, and its inverse, satisfy the following transfer property*

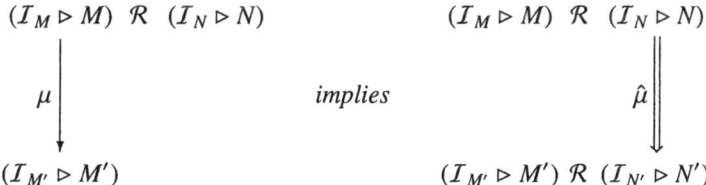

Here we use standard notation, see [MPW92], with $\stackrel{\mu}{\Longrightarrow}$ representing $\stackrel{\tau}{\longrightarrow}{}^* \circ \stackrel{\mu}{\longrightarrow} \circ \stackrel{\tau}{\longrightarrow}{}^*$, and $\stackrel{\hat{\mu}}{\Longrightarrow}$ meaning $\stackrel{\tau}{\longrightarrow}{}^*$, if μ is τ, and $\stackrel{\mu}{\Longrightarrow}$ otherwise. This allows a single internal move to be matched by zero or more internal moves.

We let $\approx_{bis}$ denote the largest bisimulation between configurations. □

Rather than writing $(\mathcal{I} \triangleright M) \approx_{bis} (\mathcal{I} \triangleright N)$, we use the more suggestive notation $\mathcal{I} \models M \approx_{bis} N$. This can be viewed as a relation between systems, parameterised over type environments which represent user's knowledge of system's capabilities.

It is this bisimilarity $\approx_{bis}$ which is the object of our study: we aim to show that, despite the complexity of its definition, tractable proof techniques can be developed for it. Finally, we should remark this is not an arbitrarily chosen version of bisimulation equivalence; in [HMR04] its definition is justified in detail: it is shown to be, in some sense, the largest reasonable typed equivalence between DPI systems.

3 Proof Techniques

The basic method for showing that two systems M and N are equivalent, relative to an environment $\mathcal{I}$, is to exhibit a parameterised relation $\mathcal{R}$ such that $\mathcal{I} \models M \mathcal{R} N$, and demonstrate that it satisfies the requirements of being a bisimulation. In this section we give a number of auxiliary methods, which can considerably relieve the burden of exhibiting such relations. The following Theorem is proved in [HMR04], and justifies a form of contextual reasoning.

Theorem 1 (Contextuality).

- $\mathcal{I} \models M \approx_{bis} N$ and $\mathcal{I} \vdash O$ imply $\mathcal{I} \models M \mid O \approx_{bis} N \mid O$
- $\mathcal{I}, \langle e : \mathsf{E} \rangle \models M \approx_{bis} N$ implies $\mathcal{I} \models (\text{new } e : \mathsf{E}) M \approx_{bis} (\text{new } e : \mathsf{E}) N$ □

We can also manipulate system descriptions. Let $\equiv$ be the least equivalence relation which satisfies the rules in Figure 5, and is preserved by the constructs $- \mid -$ and $(\text{new } e : \mathsf{E})(-)$; this is referred to as *structural equivalence*.

Proposition 1. $M \equiv N$ implies $M \approx_{bis} N$. □

This means that we can employ the axioms in Figure 5 as equations for manipulations of systems preserving the semantics. For example, we can omit the termination process stop, because $k[\![\text{stop}]\!] \equiv \mathbf{0}$ and $M \mid \mathbf{0} \equiv M$.

Further equations can be obtained by considering the internal actions in Figure 4. First observe that these actions do not change the environment of a configuration, and therefore, for convenience, let us abbreviate $\mathcal{I} \triangleright M \xrightarrow{\tau} \mathcal{I} \triangleright M'$ to the simpler $\mathcal{I} \triangleright M \xrightarrow{\tau} M'$.

Proposition 2. $\mathcal{I} \triangleright M \xrightarrow{\tau}_\beta^* N$ implies $\mathcal{I} \models M \approx_{bis} N$. □

This Proposition gives more valid equations for reasoning about systems. Typical examples, obtained just by examining those axioms in Figure 4 which describe β-actions, include $k[\![P \mid Q]\!] \approx_{bis} k[\![P]\!] \mid k[\![Q]\!]$ and $k[\![\text{goto } l.P]\!] \approx_{bis} l[\![P]\!]$ and $k[\![(\text{newc } c : C)\ P]\!] \approx_{bis} (\text{new } c@k : C)\, k[\![P]\!]$.

But these β-labelled internal actions also provide us with a very powerful method for approximating bisimulations.

Definition 3 (Bisimulations up-to-β). *A binary relation between configurations is said to be a bisimulation up-to-β if it, and its inverse, satisfy the following transfer property*

$$
\begin{array}{ccc}
(\mathcal{I}_M \triangleright M)\ \mathcal{R}\ (\mathcal{I}_N \triangleright N) & \qquad (\mathcal{I}_M \triangleright M) \quad \mathcal{R} \quad (\mathcal{I}_N \triangleright N) \\
\mu \downarrow \qquad\qquad\qquad & \text{implies} \qquad\qquad\qquad \hat{\mu} \Downarrow \\
(\mathcal{I}_{M'} \triangleright M') & \qquad (\mathcal{I}_{M'} \triangleright M')\ \mathcal{A}_l \circ \mathcal{R} \circ \mathcal{A}_r\ (\mathcal{I}_{N'} \triangleright N')
\end{array}
$$

where $\mathcal{A}_l$ is the relation $(\xrightarrow{\tau}_\beta^* \circ \equiv)$, and $\mathcal{A}_r$ is $\approx_{bis}$; strictly speaking, these relations are over systems, but they are lifted in the obvious manner to configurations. □

The idea of these approximate bisimulations is that to match an action $(\mathcal{I}_M \triangleright M) \xrightarrow{\mu} (\mathcal{I}_{M'} \triangleright M')$ it is sufficient to find a β-derivative of the residual $(\mathcal{I}_{M'} \triangleright M') \xrightarrow{\tau}_\beta^* (M'')$ and a matching action $(\mathcal{I}_N \triangleright N) \xRightarrow{\hat{\mu}} (\mathcal{I}_{N'} \triangleright N')$ such that, up-to structural equivalence and bisimilarity, respectively, the pairs $(\mathcal{I}_{M'} \triangleright M'')$ and $(\mathcal{I}_{N'} \triangleright N')$ are once more related. Intuitively, a configuration can represent all the configurations to which it can evolve using β-moves.

Proposition 3. *If $(\mathcal{I} \triangleright M)\mathcal{R}(\mathcal{I} \triangleright N)$, $\mathcal{R}$ a bisimulation up-to-β, then $\mathcal{I} \models M \approx_{bis} N$.* □

4 Crossing a Firewall

Let us consider the *firewall* example, first proposed in [CG98] and studied at length in [GC99,LS00,MN03] within versions of Mobile Ambients. Intuitively, a firewall is a domain to which access is restricted: only agents which are permitted, in some sense, by the firewall, are allowed in. A simple example takes the form

$$F \Leftarrow (\text{new } f : \mathsf{F})\, f[\![P \mid *\text{goto } a.\text{tell}!\langle f \rangle]\!]$$

Here f is the name of the firewall, which is created with the capabilities described in the location type F, and P is some code which maintains the internal business of the firewall. A typical example of the capabilities could be given by F = loc[info : rw⟨I⟩, req : rw⟨R⟩], which allow reading to and writing from two resources info and req in f. Then P could, for example, maintain appropriate services at the resources; of course, it would also be able to use non-local resources it knows about in its current environment.

The existence of the firewall is made known only to another domain, a, via the information channel tell located there. An example is the following

$$A \Leftarrow a[\![R \mid \text{tell}?(x) \text{ goto } x.Q]\!]$$

where a is informed of f by inputing on the local channel tell. If we consider an arbitrary type environment Γ, we have the execution

$$\Gamma \triangleright F \mid A \xrightarrow{\tau}{}^* (\text{new } f : \text{F})(f[\![P \mid {*}\text{goto } a.\text{tell}!\langle f \rangle \mid Q]\!]) \mid a[\![R]\!] \quad (2)$$

so the code Q is allowed to execute locally within the firewall.

Notice that the resources to which Q has access within the firewall are controlled by the capability type associated with the information channel tell. For example, suppose in Γ the type associated with this channel is rw⟨F_r⟩, where F_r = loc[info : w⟨I⟩, req : r⟨R⟩]. Then F_r is a supertype of the declaration type F: hence in (2), Q, having gained entry into the firewall, can only write to resource info and read from req.

Let us now consider the correctness of this simple protocol, which allows access of one agent, Q, to the firewall. Let Γ be any type environment such that

$$\Gamma \vdash F \mid A \quad (3)$$

Then one might expect to be able to derive

$$\Gamma \models F \mid A \approx_{bis} (\text{new } f : \text{F})(f[\![P \mid {*}\text{goto } a.\text{tell}!\langle f \rangle \mid Q]\!]) \mid a[\![R]\!] \quad (4)$$

But this happens not to be true, because of the implicit assumption that the information channel tell in a can only be accessed by partners in the entry protocol, f and a. But, in order for (3) to be true, we must have $\Gamma \vdash_a$ tell : rw⟨F_r⟩, and this allows other agents in the environment access to tell. For example, consider

$$\text{Rogue} \Leftarrow b[\![\text{goto } a.\text{tell}!\langle b \rangle]\!]$$

and suppose that the only type inference from Γ involving b is $\Gamma \vdash b$: loc; so Γ is not aware of any resources at b. Nevertheless $\Gamma \vdash$ Rogue, and therefore *Contextuality* (Theorem 1) applied to (4) would give

$$\Gamma \models F \mid A \mid \text{Rogue} \approx_{bis} (\text{new } f : \text{F})(f[\![P \mid {*}\text{goto } a.\text{tell}!\langle f \rangle \mid Q]\!]) \mid a[\![R]\!] \mid \text{Rogue}$$

But this is obviously not the case, as the left-hand system can reduce via a series of τ-steps (representing the interaction between A and Rogue) to the state

$$\Gamma \triangleright F \mid a[\![R]\!] \mid b[\![Q]\!]$$

Under reasonable assumptions about the code Q, the right-hand system has no corresponding reduction to a similar state. On the left-hand side the code Q, now located at b, can not run, while on the right-hand side, no matter what τ-steps are made, Q will be able to execute at f. Thus (4) can not be true.

However, our framework allows us to amend the correctness statement (4) above, taking into account the implicit assumption about the information channel tell. The essential point is that the protocol works provided that *only the firewall can write on* tell. This can be formalised by proving the equivalence between the two systems relative to a restricted environment, one which does not allow write access to tell.

First some notation. Let us write $\Gamma \vdash_k^{max} V : \mathsf{T}$ to mean

- $\Gamma \vdash_k V : \mathsf{T}$
- $\Gamma \vdash_k V : \mathsf{T}'$ implies $\mathsf{T} <: \mathsf{T}'$

In other words, T is the *largest* type which can be assigned to V. Now suppose $\mathcal{I}$ is a type environment which satisfies

(i) $\mathcal{I} \vdash_a^{max} \mathsf{tell} : \mathsf{r}\langle \mathsf{F} \rangle$
(ii) $\mathcal{I} \vdash a[\![R]\!]$
(iii) $\mathcal{I} \vdash (\mathsf{new}\, f : \mathsf{F})\, f[\![P]\!]$

The import of the first requirement, which is the most important, is that systems in the computational context can not write on tell. The other requirements, which are mainly for convenience, ensure that the residual behaviour at a and f is well-behaved, although a side-effect is that they also can not write on tell. Under these assumptions, we prove

$$\mathcal{I} \models F \mid A \approx_{bis} (\mathsf{new}\, f : \mathsf{F})(f[\![P \mid *\mathsf{goto}\, a.\mathsf{tell}!\langle f \rangle \mid Q]\!]) \mid a[\![R]\!] \qquad (5)$$

First note that (up-to structural equivalence)

$$\mathcal{I} \triangleright F \mid A \xrightarrow{\tau}_\beta F \mid A_t \mid a[\![R]\!]$$

via (M-SPLIT) and (M-CTXT), where we use A_t as a shorthand for $a[\![\mathsf{tell}?(x)\, \mathsf{goto}\, x.Q]\!]$. So, by Propositions 1 and 2, it is sufficient to prove

$$\mathcal{I} \models F \mid A_t \mid a[\![R]\!] \approx_{bis} (\mathsf{new}\, f : \mathsf{F})(f[\![P \mid *\mathsf{goto}\, a.\mathsf{tell}!\langle f \rangle \mid Q]\!]) \mid a[\![R]\!]$$

Here assumption (ii) comes in useful, as by *Contextuality* it is now sufficient to prove

$$\mathcal{I} \models F \mid A_t \approx_{bis} (\mathsf{new}\, f : \mathsf{F})(f[\![P \mid *\mathsf{goto}\, a.\mathsf{tell}!\langle f \rangle \mid Q]\!])$$

Then the left-hand side can be manipulated via the structural equivalence rule (S-EXTR), thereby reducing the proof burden to

$$\mathcal{I} \models (\mathsf{new}\, f : \mathsf{F})(f[\![P \mid *\mathsf{goto}\, a.\mathsf{tell}!\langle f \rangle]\!] \mid A_t) \approx_{bis} (\mathsf{new}\, f : \mathsf{F})(f[\![P \mid *\mathsf{goto}\, a.\mathsf{tell}!\langle f \rangle \mid Q]\!])$$

and another application of *Contextuality* reduces this further to

$$\mathcal{I}_f \models f[\![P \mid *\mathsf{goto}\, a.\mathsf{tell}!\langle f \rangle]\!] \mid A_t \approx_{bis} f[\![P \mid *\mathsf{goto}\, a.\mathsf{tell}!\langle f \rangle \mid Q]\!]$$

where $\mathcal{I}_f$ is a shorthand for $\mathcal{I}, \langle f : \mathsf{F} \rangle$. Now let F_g represent $f[\![*\mathsf{goto}\, a.\mathsf{tell}!\langle f \rangle]\!]$. Then we have

- $I_f \triangleright f[\![P \mid *\text{goto } a.\text{tell}!\langle f \rangle]\!] \mid A_t \xrightarrow{\tau}_\beta f[\![P]\!] \mid F_g \mid A_t$
- $I_f \triangleright f[\![P \mid *\text{goto } a.\text{tell}!\langle f \rangle \mid Q]\!] \xrightarrow{\tau}^*_\beta f[\![P]\!] \mid F_g \mid f[\![Q]\!]$

So, further applications of Proposition 2, *Contextuality* and assumption (iii), give the requirement

$$I_f \models F_g \mid A_t \approx_{bis} F_g \mid f[\![Q]\!] \tag{6}$$

This we establish directly by exhibiting a particular bisimulation.

We define the parameterised relation $\mathcal{R}$ by letting $\mathcal{J} \models M \mathcal{R} N$ whenever

(a) $\mathcal{J} \triangleright M$ is a configuration and N is the same as M
(b) or $\mathcal{J}$ is I_f and

- M has the form $F_g \mid A_t \mid \Pi_n (a[\![\text{tell}!\langle f \rangle]\!])^n$
- N has the form $F_g \mid f[\![Q]\!] \mid \Pi_n (a[\![\text{tell}!\langle f \rangle]\!])^n$

where $\Pi_n (a[\![\text{tell}!\langle f \rangle]\!])^n$, for some $n \geq 0$, means n copies of $a[\![\text{tell}!\langle f \rangle]\!]$ running in parallel.

Proposition 4. *The relation $\mathcal{R}$ defined above is a bisimulation up-to-β.*

Proof. Suppose $\mathcal{J} \models M \mathcal{R} N$. Let us consider all possible actions from $\mathcal{J} \triangleright M$. In fact, it is sufficient to consider the case (b) above, when $\mathcal{J}$ and M and N are of the prescribed form. The actions fall into one of three categories (for convenience we shorten $\Pi_n (a[\![\text{tell}!\langle f \rangle]\!])^n$ with Π_n).

- Here F_g is responsible, so the action takes the form $I_f \triangleright M \xrightarrow{\tau}_\beta f[\![*\text{goto } a.\text{tell}!\langle f \rangle \mid \text{goto } a.\text{tell}!\langle f \rangle]\!] \mid A_t \mid \Pi_n$. But $I_f \triangleright f[\![*\text{goto } a.\text{tell}!\langle f \rangle \mid \text{goto } a.\text{tell}!\langle f \rangle]\!] \mid A_t \mid \Pi_n \xrightarrow{\tau}_\beta F_g \mid a[\![\text{tell}!\langle f \rangle]\!] \mid A_t \mid \Pi_n$, and this can be matched, via clause (b), by $I_f \triangleright N \xrightarrow{\tau}^*_\beta F_g \mid a[\![\text{tell}!\langle f \rangle]\!] \mid f[\![Q]\!] \mid \Pi_n$, because $F_g \mid a[\![\text{tell}!\langle f \rangle]\!] \mid A_t \mid \Pi_n \equiv F_g \mid A_t \mid \Pi_{n+1}$ and $F_g \mid a[\![\text{tell}!\langle f \rangle]\!] \mid f[\![Q]\!] \mid \Pi_n \equiv F_g \mid f[\![Q]\!] \mid \Pi_{n+1}$ and $\equiv \subseteq \approx_{bis}$ (Proposition 1).
- The second possibility is that the third component, $\Pi_n (a[\![\text{tell}!\langle f \rangle]\!])^n$, is responsible for the action, which must be $a.\text{tell}!f$. It is easy to see that $I_f \triangleright N$ can perform exactly the same action, to a related configuration in clause (b).
- Finally, the middle component, A_t, might be involved in the action. Note that the action can not be external, as the action $a.\text{tell}?V$ (for some value V) is not allowed by the environment. So it must be a communication, of the form $I_f \triangleright M \xrightarrow{\tau} F_g \mid a[\![\text{goto } f.Q]\!] \mid \Pi_{n-1}$. But the following β-steps can be carried out starting from this configuration: $I_f \triangleright F_g \mid a[\![\text{goto } f.Q]\!] \mid \Pi_{n-1} \xrightarrow{\tau}^*_\beta F_g \mid a[\![\text{tell}!\langle f \rangle]\!] \mid f[\![Q]\!] \mid \Pi_{n-1} \equiv F_g \mid f[\![Q]\!] \mid \Pi_n$, and this can be matched in clause (a) by the empty sequence of internal actions from $I_f \triangleright N$.

Symmetrically, it is easy to see that every action from $\mathcal{J} \triangleright N$ can be matched by one from $\mathcal{J} \triangleright M$, possibly preceded by a number of τ-actions: these latter are required when $f[\![Q]\!]$ is responsible for the action to be matched. □

This, by using Proposition 3, completes our proof of (5) above.

Note that the firewall F allows, in principle, multiple entries of agents from a. So, for example, if R, in (5), had the form $R'\,|\,\mathsf{tell?}(x)\,\mathsf{goto}\,x.Q'$, then the reasoning we have just completed could be repeated, to prove

$$\mathcal{I} \models F\,|\,a[\![R]\!] \approx_{bis} (\mathsf{new}\,f:\mathsf{F})(f[\![P\,|\,*\mathsf{goto}\,a.\mathsf{tell!}\langle f\rangle\,|\,Q']\!])\,|\,a[\![R']\!] \qquad (7)$$

Moreover, we know f can not appear in Q; therefore, (S-EXTR) from Figure 5 together with (7) can be combined with (5), to prove

$$\mathcal{I} \models F\,|\,A \approx_{bis} (\mathsf{new}\,f:\mathsf{F})(f[\![P\,|\,*\mathsf{goto}\,a.\mathsf{tell!}\langle f\rangle\,|\,Q\,|\,Q']\!])\,|\,a[\![R']\!]$$

where the domain a has managed to send two separate agents into the firewall.

5 A Server and Its Clients

We consider in this section the canonical example of a *server* and its *clients*. A server is a domain providing services to potentially arbitrary clients, as e.g. the following

$$S \Leftarrow s[\![*\mathsf{req?}(x, y_\circledcirc z)\mathsf{goto}\,z.y!\langle \mathit{isprime}(x)\rangle\,|\,S']\!]$$

which provides an iterated service at resource req, and internal code, S', to setup and administrate the site. The channel req expects to receive a structured value of the form $(i, c_\circledcirc l)$. This is a pair, consisting of an integer i, and a return address $c_\circledcirc l$, that is the name of a reply channel, c, together with the location of that channel, l. The server then executes the procedure $\mathit{isprime}(-)$ on the incoming value, i, sends a process to the return site, and delivers the result on the return channel there. The procedure $\mathit{isprime}$ is not directly part of the language, but one can easily imagine an extension supporting let expressions, in which case the body of the server would be better represented as $*\mathsf{req?}(x, y_\circledcirc z)\mathsf{let}\,b = \mathit{isprime}(x)\,\mathsf{in}\,\mathsf{goto}\,z.y!\langle b\rangle$, thereby emphasising that the procedure is executed at the server's site.

Typical clients of the server are domains taking the form

$$C_i \Leftarrow c_i[\![(\mathsf{new}\mathsf{c}\,r:\mathsf{R})\;\mathsf{goto}\,s.\mathsf{req!}\langle v_i, r_\circledcirc c_i\rangle\,|\,C'_i]\!]$$

These generate a private reply channel r at the declaration type $\mathsf{R} = \mathsf{rw}\langle\mathbf{bool}\rangle$, and send a process to the server (whose address they need to know) asking for the primality of an integer; concurrently, the agent C'_i executes at the site.

As in the case of the firewall, the correctness of the protocol between the server S and its clients C_i depends on the proper management of the access to the request channel req: clients should only have write access, while the server only needs read access. So the correctness of the protocol can be expressed as an equivalence between two systems, relative to a restricted environment. Let $\mathcal{I}$ be a type environment satisfying

(i) $\mathcal{I} \vdash^{max}_s \mathsf{req}:\mathsf{w}\langle\,\mathbf{int},\mathsf{w}\langle\mathbf{bool}\rangle_\circledcirc\mathsf{loc}\,\rangle$
(ii) $\mathcal{I} \vdash s[\![S']\!]$
(iii) $\mathcal{I} \vdash C_i$

The first requirement establishes *the computational context can not read on* req, while the following points ensure that the residual behaviour at the server and the clients is well-behaved, with the side-effect that neither S' nor C'_i can read on req.

First, let us show that one client interacts correctly with the server

$$\mathcal{I} \models S \mid C_1 \approx_{bis} S \mid c_1[\![(\text{newc } r : \text{R}) \ r!\langle \textit{isprime}(v_1)\rangle \mid C'_1]\!] \tag{8}$$

Note that (up-to-structural equivalence)

$$\mathcal{I} \triangleright S \mid C_1 \xrightarrow{\tau}^*_\beta (\text{new } r@c_1 : \text{R}) \, S_r \mid s[\![S']\!] \mid s[\![\text{req}!\langle v_1, r@c_1\rangle]\!] \mid c_1[\![C'_1]\!]$$

where we use S_r as a shorthand for $s[\![*\text{req}?(x, y@z)\text{goto } z.y!\langle \textit{isprime}(x)\rangle]\!]$, and

$$\mathcal{I} \triangleright S \mid c_1[\![(\text{newc } r : \text{R}) \ r!\langle \textit{isprime}(v_1)\rangle \mid C'_1]\!] \xrightarrow{\tau}^*_\beta$$
$$(\text{new } r@c_1 : \text{R}) \, S_r \mid s[\![S']\!] \mid c_1[\![r!\langle \textit{isprime}(v_1)\rangle]\!] \mid c_1[\![C'_1]\!]$$

By Propositions 1, 2, *Contextuality*, and assumptions (ii), (iii), it is therefore sufficient to prove

$$\mathcal{I}_r \models S_r \mid s[\![\text{req}!\langle v_1, r@c_1\rangle]\!] \approx_{bis} S_r \mid c_1[\![r!\langle \textit{isprime}(v_1)\rangle]\!]$$

where $\mathcal{I}_r$ is a shorthand for $\mathcal{I}, \langle r@c_1 : \text{R}\rangle$. We establish this equivalence by exhibiting a particular bisimulation. Let $\mathcal{R}$ be the parameterised relation defined by letting $\mathcal{J} \models M \mathcal{R} N$ whenever

(a) $\mathcal{J} \triangleright M$ is a configuration and N is the same as M
(b) or $\mathcal{J}$ is $\mathcal{I}_r$ and
  - M has the form $S_r \mid s[\![\text{req}!\langle v_1, r@c_1\rangle]\!] \mid \Pi_n$
  - N has the form $S_r \mid c_1[\![r!\langle \textit{isprime}(v_1)\rangle]\!] \mid \Pi_n$
  where Π_n is a shorthand for $\Pi_n \, (s[\![\text{req}?(x, y@z)\text{goto } z.y!\langle \textit{isprime}(x)\rangle]\!])^n$
(c) or $\mathcal{J}$ is $\mathcal{I}'_r$, where the domain of $\mathcal{I}'_r$ is a superset of that of $\mathcal{I}_r$, and
  - M has the form $S_r \mid s[\![\text{req}!\langle v_1, r@c_1\rangle]\!] \mid \Pi_n \mid \Pi_{j\in J} \, (k_j[\![d_j!\langle \textit{isprime}(i_j)\rangle]\!])$
  - N has the form $S_r \mid c_1[\![r!\langle \textit{isprime}(v_1)\rangle]\!] \mid \Pi_n \mid \Pi_{j\in J} \, (k_j[\![d_j!\langle \textit{isprime}(i_j)\rangle]\!])$
  such that $\mathcal{I}'_r \vdash^{max}_s \text{req:w}\langle \text{int}, \text{w}\langle \textbf{bool}\rangle@\text{loc} \, \rangle$, and, for every $j \in J$: $\mathcal{I}'_r \vdash_{k_j} d_j:\text{w}\langle \textbf{bool}\rangle$.
  The notation $\Pi_{j\in J} \, (k_j[\![d_j!\langle \textit{isprime}(i_j)\rangle]\!])$ means (different) instances of systems running in parallel.

Proposition 5. *The relation $\mathcal{R}$ defined above is a bisimulation up-to-β.*

Proof. Suppose $\mathcal{J} \models M \mathcal{R} N$. The actions from $\mathcal{J} \triangleright M$ in the case (b) above fall into one of three categories.

- First S_r is responsible: $\mathcal{I}_r \triangleright M \xrightarrow{\tau}^*_\beta S_r \mid \Pi_1 \mid s[\![\text{req}!\langle v_1, r@c_1\rangle]\!] \mid \Pi_n$, and this can be matched by $\mathcal{I}_r \triangleright N \xrightarrow{\tau}^*_\beta S_r \mid \Pi_1 \mid c_1[\![r!\langle \textit{isprime}(v_1)\rangle]\!] \mid \Pi_n$, because both configurations belong to $\mathcal{R}$, clause (b), up-to structural equivalence.

- The third component, Π_n ($s[\![\mathsf{req}?(x, y@z)\mathsf{goto}\ z.y!\langle isprime(x)\rangle]\!])^n$, is responsible for the action, which is either $s.\mathsf{req}?\langle i_j, d_j@k_j\rangle$ or $(e{:}E)s.\mathsf{req}?\langle i_j, d_j@k_j\rangle$. These actions correspond to the delivery of (new) data by the environment (from which the system is allowed to learn infinitely new names), and are followed by the action (M-MOVE). However, it is easy to see that $\mathcal{I}_r \triangleright N$ can perform exactly the same actions, to a related configuration in clause (c).
- Finally, the middle component, $s[\![\mathsf{req}!\langle v_1, r@c_1\rangle]\!]$, may be involved in the action, which must be a communication: $\mathcal{I}_r \triangleright M \xrightarrow{\tau} S_r \mid s[\![\mathsf{goto}\ c_1.r!\langle isprime(v_1)\rangle]\!] \mid \Pi_{n-1}$. Then the following β-steps can be carried out: $\mathcal{I}_r \triangleright S_r \mid s[\![\mathsf{goto}\ c_1.r!\langle isprime(v_1)\rangle]\!] \mid \Pi_{n-1} \xrightarrow{\tau}^*_\beta S_r \mid \Pi_1 \mid c_1[\![r!\langle isprime(v_1)\rangle]\!] \mid \Pi_{n-1}$, and this configuration can be matched, in clause (a), by the empty sequence of actions from $\mathcal{I}_r \triangleright N$.

Symmetrically, every action performed by $\mathcal{I}_r \triangleright N$ can be matched by $\mathcal{I}_r \triangleright M$; for example, consider the output action by the 2nd component of N: $\mathcal{I}_r \triangleright S_r \mid c_1[\![r!\langle isprime(v_1)\rangle]\!] \mid \Pi_n \xrightarrow{c_1.r!\langle isprime(v_1)\rangle} \mathcal{I}_r \triangleright S_r \mid \Pi_n$. This can be easily matched by $\mathcal{I}_r \triangleright M$, via clause (a), using τ-steps followed by the same action.

Finally, it is not problematic to check that all configurations in $\mathcal{R}$ by virtue of clause (c) can have their respective actions properly matched. □

This completes our proof of (8), that one client can interact correctly with the server. Contextual reasoning can now be employed to generalise this result to an arbitrary number of clients. For example, let us show

$$\mathcal{I} \models S \mid C_1 \mid C_2 \approx_{bis} S \mid \Pi_{i \in \{1,2\}}\ c_i[\![(\mathsf{newc}\ r : \mathsf{R})\ r!\langle isprime(v_i)\rangle \mid C'_i]\!] \qquad (9)$$

Because of $\mathcal{I} \vdash C_2$ (requirement (iii) above), *Contextuality* applied to (8) gives

$$\mathcal{I} \models S \mid C_1 \mid C_2 \approx_{bis} S \mid c_1[\![(\mathsf{newc}\ r : \mathsf{R})\ r!\langle isprime(v_1)\rangle \mid C'_1]\!] \mid C_2 \qquad (10)$$

Repeating the analysis of C_1 on C_2, we obtain

$$\mathcal{I} \models S \mid C_2 \approx_{bis} S \mid c_2[\![(\mathsf{newc}\ r : \mathsf{R})\ r!\langle isprime(v_2)\rangle \mid C'_2]\!]$$

But $\mathcal{I} \vdash C_1$ (same requirement (iii)) also implies $\mathcal{I} \vdash c_1[\![(\mathsf{newc}\ r : \mathsf{R})\ r!\langle isprime(v_1)\rangle \mid C'_1]\!]$, and therefore by *Contextuality* we obtain

$$\mathcal{I} \models S \mid C_2 \mid c_1[\![(\mathsf{newc}\ r : \mathsf{R})\ r!\langle isprime(v_1)\rangle \mid C'_1]\!] \approx_{bis}$$
$$S \mid c_2[\![(\mathsf{newc}\ r : \mathsf{R})\ r!\langle isprime(v_2)\rangle \mid C'_2]\!] \mid c_1[\![(\mathsf{newc}\ r : \mathsf{R})\ r!\langle isprime(v_1)\rangle \mid C'_1]\!]$$

So we conclude (9) from (10), Proposition 1, and transitivity of $\approx_{bis}$.

It is then a simple matter to extend this reasoning, using induction, to show that an arbitrary number of clients can be handled

$$\mathcal{I} \models S \mid \Pi_{i \in \{1,\ldots,n\}}\ C_i \approx_{bis} S \mid \Pi_{i \in \{1,\ldots,n\}}\ c_i[\![(\mathsf{newc}\ r : \mathsf{R})\ r!\langle isprime(v_i)\rangle \mid C'_i]\!]$$

6 Metaservers

In this section we describe a *memory service* by involving the newloc operator of DPI, which allows the creation of new instances of sites. A (meta)server contains a resource setup, where requests are received, and installs the service at a new site, thus providing personalised treatment to its clients.

A first version of the server receives a return address, generates a new located memory cell, and installs some code there, meanwhile delivering the new location name at the reply address

$$S \Leftarrow s[\![*\mathsf{setup}?(y{\circledast}z)\,(\mathsf{newloc}\,m:\mathsf{M})\ \mathsf{goto}\,m.\mathsf{Mem}\mid \mathsf{goto}\,z.y!\langle m\rangle]\!]$$

where Mem is the code running at the location m, and for instance can take the form

$$\mathsf{Mem} \Leftarrow (\mathsf{newc}\,v:\mathsf{V})\ v!\langle 0\rangle \mid *\mathsf{get}?(y{\circledast}z)\,v?(w)\,(\mathsf{goto}\,z.y!\langle w\rangle \mid v!\langle w\rangle)$$
$$\mid *\mathsf{put}?(x, y{\circledast}z)\,v?(w)\,(\mathsf{goto}\,z.y!\mid v!\langle x\rangle)$$

Here we are using the channel v as a restricted form of memory cell: the value it contains (whose initial value is set to 0) disappears once it is read, therefore it has to be reinstated. The two methods get and put can be seen as the canonical ways to access the cell, therefore the declaration type of the new site can be set to $\mathsf{M} = \mathsf{loc}[\mathsf{get}:\mathsf{T}_g, \mathsf{put}:\mathsf{T}_p]$. Notice that we have chosen this particular instantiation for the running code Mem just for reasons of simplicity, as the proofs we are going to develop are, in principle, independent of it.

Clients of the memory service generate a new reply channel, send a request to the server, and wait for the server to deliver the new memory cell

$$C_i \Leftarrow c_i[\![(\mathsf{newc}\,r:\mathsf{R})\ \mathsf{goto}\,s.\mathsf{setup}!\langle r{\circledast}c_i\rangle \mid r?(x)\,P_i(x)]\!]$$

where $P_i(x)$ is parametric code which depends on (the name of) the new site, x, and $\mathsf{R} = \mathsf{rw}\langle \mathsf{M}\rangle$.

An alternative, slightly different version of the server leaves to the clients the responsibility to create the memory cells, just installing the servicing code at the proffered site

$$S' \Leftarrow s'[\![*\mathsf{setup}'?(x, y{\circledast}z)\ \mathsf{goto}\,x.\mathsf{Mem}\mid \mathsf{goto}\,z.y!]\!]$$

Correspondingly, clients generate an acknowledgement channel and a new location, send a request to the server, and await the server to acknowledge the service has been installed

$$C'_i \Leftarrow c_i[\![(\mathsf{newc}\,t:\mathsf{T})\,(\mathsf{newloc}\,m_i:\mathsf{M})\ \mathsf{goto}\,s'.\mathsf{setup}'!\langle m_i, t{\circledast}c_i\rangle \mid t?P_i(m_i)]\!]$$

where $\mathsf{T} = \mathsf{rw}\langle \mathsf{unit}\rangle$.

We want now to relate the two different approaches, therefore connecting the behaviour of the two following systems, relative to a typing environment $\mathcal{I}$

$$\mathcal{I} \models S \mid C_1 \mid C_2 \tag{11}$$
$$\mathcal{I} \models S' \mid C'_1 \mid C'_2 \tag{12}$$

Our goal is to establish that, from the point of view of the clients, under certain hypotheses the two kinds of servers S and S' lead to equivalent behaviour. This means finding a suitable type environment $\mathcal{I}$ such that

$$\mathcal{I} \models S \mid C_1 \mid C_2 \approx_{bis} S' \mid C'_1 \mid C'_2 \tag{13}$$

It is immediate to notice that the correctness of this protocol requires that *the computational context should have neither write nor read access to the* setup *and* setup' *channels*. Thus, the equivalence can be proved relative to a restricted environment $\mathcal{I}$, satisfying

$$\mathcal{I} \vdash_s^{max} \text{setup} : \mathsf{T} \qquad\qquad \mathcal{I} \vdash_s^{max} \text{setup}' : \mathsf{T}$$

Now, the internal actions allow to deduce a derivation from (11) and (12) to the systems

$$\mathcal{I} \models S \mid \Pi_{i \in \{1,2\}} (\text{new } m_i:\mathsf{M})(m_i[\![\text{Mem}]\!] \mid c_i[\![P_i(m_i)]\!]) \tag{14}$$

$$\mathcal{I} \models S' \mid \Pi_{i \in \{1,2\}} (\text{new } m_i:\mathsf{M})(m_i[\![\text{Mem}]\!] \mid c_i[\![P_i(m_i)]\!]) \tag{15}$$

Therefore we address (13) in three steps: first we prove that the two pairs of systems (11),(14) and (12),(15) are equivalent, then we connect the systems (14) and (15) by a technical lemma. That is

(i) $\mathcal{I} \models S \mid \Pi_{i \in \{1,2\}} C_i \approx_{bis} S \mid \Pi_{i \in \{1,2\}} (\text{new } m_i : \mathsf{M})(m_i[\![\text{Mem}]\!] \mid c_i[\![P_i(m_i)]\!])$
(ii) $\mathcal{I} \models S' \mid \Pi_{i \in \{1,2\}} C'_i \approx_{bis} S' \mid \Pi_{i \in \{1,2\}} (\text{new } m_i : \mathsf{M})(m_i[\![\text{Mem}]\!] \mid c_i[\![P_i(m_i)]\!])$
(iii) $\mathcal{I} \models l[\![*a?(x)P(x)]\!] \mid Q \approx_{bis} Q$ for every $\mathcal{I}, Q, l, a, P$ s. t. $\mathcal{I} \vdash_l^{max} a:\mathsf{T}$ and $a \notin \text{fn}(Q)$

The proof of the point (iii) is straightforward, as a witness bisimulation $\mathcal{R}$ can be promptly defined by letting $\mathcal{J} \models M \mathcal{R} N$ whenever

(a) $\mathcal{J} \triangleright M$ and $\mathcal{J} \triangleright N$ are configurations
(b) $\mathcal{J}$ is $\mathcal{I}$ and M has the form $l[\![*a?(x)P(x)]\!] \mid \Pi_n (l[\![a?(x)P(x)]\!])^n \mid N$

which can be easily proved to be a bisimulation up-to-β.

We argue below both the proof of (i) (the one of (ii) is completely similar) and how to get the proof of (13) from those of (i), (ii), (iii). Let us start from the latter.

Using the equations (i) and (ii), the equivalence (13) can be reduced to

$$\mathcal{I} \models S \mid \Pi_{i \in \{1,2\}} Q_i \approx_{bis} S' \mid \Pi_{i \in \{1,2\}} Q_i \tag{16}$$

where Q_i denotes $(\text{new } m_i : \mathsf{M})(m_i[\![\text{Mem}]\!] \mid c_i[\![P_i(m_i)]\!])$. It is natural now to assume that the conditions required by the lemma (iii) are satisfied by the code Q_i (setup, setup' $\notin$ fn(Q_i), in the case). Hence, it is possible to apply that lemma to both the sides of the equation (16), thus obtaining an identity.

Finally, we address the point (i). First notice that (up-to structural equivalence)

$$\mathcal{I} \triangleright S \mid \Pi_{i \in \{1,2\}} C_i \xrightarrow{\tau}_\beta^*$$
$(\text{new } r_1 \text{\textcircled{\tiny{o}}} c_1 : \mathsf{R}, r_2 \text{\textcircled{\tiny{o}}} c_2 : \mathsf{R}) \; S \mid \Pi_{i \in \{1,2\}} (s[\![\text{setup}!\langle r_i \text{\textcircled{\tiny{o}}} c_i \rangle]\!] \mid c_i[\![r_i?(x) \, P_i(x)]\!])$

and $S \mid \Pi_{i \in \{1,2\}} Q_i \equiv (\text{new } m_1 : \mathsf{M}, m_2 : \mathsf{M}) \; S \mid \Pi_{i \in \{1,2\}} (m_i[\![\text{Mem}]\!] \mid c_i[\![P_i(m_i)]\!])$. Therefore, by Propositions 1, 2, we reduce (i) to the following

$\mathcal{I} \models (\text{new } r_1 \text{\textcircled{\tiny{o}}} c_1 : \mathsf{R}, r_2 \text{\textcircled{\tiny{o}}} c_2 : \mathsf{R}) \; S \mid \Pi_{i \in \{1,2\}} (s[\![\text{setup}!\langle r_i \text{\textcircled{\tiny{o}}} c_i \rangle]\!] \mid c_i[\![r_i?(x) \, P_i(x)]\!]) \approx_{bis}$
$(\text{new } m_1 : \mathsf{M}, m_2 : \mathsf{M}) \; S \mid \Pi_{i \in \{1,2\}} (m_i[\![\text{Mem}]\!] \mid c_i[\![P_i(m_i)]\!])$

which we prove by exhibiting a particular bisimulation. Let us fix before some shorthand notation

$C_{1i} \triangleq c_i[\![r_i!\langle m_i \rangle]\!]$ $\qquad C_{?i} \triangleq c_i[\![r_i?(x) \, P_i(x)]\!]$
$M_i \triangleq m_i[\![\text{Mem}]\!]$ $\qquad S_{1i} \triangleq s[\![\text{setup}!\langle r_i \text{\textcircled{\tiny{o}}} c_i \rangle]\!]$
$C_{P_i} \triangleq c_i[\![P_i(m_i)]\!]$ $\qquad B \triangleq (\text{new } m_1, m_2 : \mathsf{M}) \; S \mid \Pi_n \mid M_1 \mid C_{P_1} \mid M_2 \mid C_{P_2}$

and $\Pi_n \triangleq \Pi_n$ (s[[setup?$(y@z)$ (newloc m : M) goto m.Mem | goto $z.y!\langle m \rangle$]])^n. We define the relation $\mathcal{R}$ by letting $\mathcal{J} \models P \mathcal{R} Q$ whenever $\mathcal{J} \triangleright P$ is a configuration and Q is the same as P, or $\mathcal{J}$ is $\mathcal{I}$ and Q has the form B and P has the form

(a) (new $r_1@c_1$: R, $r_2@c_2$: R) $S \mid \Pi_n \mid S_{!1} \mid S_{!2} \mid C_{?1} \mid C_{?2}$
(b) or (new $r_1@c_1$: R, $r_2@c_2$: R, m_1 : M) $S \mid \Pi_n \mid S_{!2} \mid C_{?2} \mid M_1 \mid C_{!1} \mid C_{?1}$
(c) or (new $r_1@c_1$: R, $r_2@c_2$: R, m_2 : M) $S \mid \Pi_n \mid S_{!1} \mid C_{?1} \mid M_2 \mid C_{!2} \mid C_{?2}$
(d) or (new $r_2@c_2$: R, m_1 : M) $S \mid \Pi_n \mid S_{!2} \mid C_{?2} \mid M_1 \mid C_{P_1}$
(e) or (new $r_1@c_1$: R, m_2 : M) $S \mid \Pi_n \mid S_{!1} \mid C_{?1} \mid M_2 \mid C_{P_2}$
(f) or (new $r_1@c_1$: R, $r_2@c_2$: R, m_1 : M, m_2 : M) $S \mid \Pi_n \mid M_1 \mid C_{!1} \mid C_{?1} \mid M_2 \mid C_{!2} \mid C_{?2}$
(g) or (new $r_2@c_2$: R, m_1 : M, m_2 : M) $S \mid \Pi_n \mid M_1 \mid C_{P_1} \mid M_2 \mid C_{!2} \mid C_{?2}$
(h) or (new $r_1@c_1$: R, m_1 : M, m_2 : M) $S \mid \Pi_n \mid M_1 \mid C_{!1} \mid C_{?1} \mid M_2 \mid C_{P_2}$

Proposition 6. *The relation $\mathcal{R}$ defined above is a bisimulation up-to-β.* □

We omit the proof of this Proposition, as no extra critical aspects arise with respect to the proofs detailed in the previous two sections. Summing up, we have shown (13) under the following assumptions

- $\mathcal{I} \vdash^{max}_s$ setup : T and $\mathcal{I} \vdash^{max}_{s'}$ setup' : T
- setup $\notin$ fn(Mem) and setup' $\notin$ fn(Mem)
- setup $\notin$ fn(P_i) and setup' $\notin$ fn(P_i)

It is then possible to consider an arbitrary number of clients. The correctness of these can once more be addressed using the techniques, such as *Contextuality*, discussed in the previous sections.

7 Related and Future Work

Proofs of correctness of protocols or language translations are often carried out with respect to *contextual* equivalences [GC99,LS00]. Nevertheless, the use of bisimulation-based notions of equivalences enables such proofs to be considerably simplified. For instance, in [MN03], two up-to proof techniques (up-to expansion and up-to context) are borrowed from the PICALCULUS and adapted to develop an algebraic theory and prove the correctness of the perfect firewall protocol [CG98]. Our paper tries to contribute to this second approach, using bisimulations, extending their application to situations in which the environment plays a significant role in system behaviour.

In this document, we have defined and illustrated a collection of methods for proving bisimulation equivalences for distributed, mobile systems, modelled with the DPI calculus [HR02b]. In order to cope with bisimulation equivalence in DPI [HMR04], it is natural to look for bisimulations up-to in the spirit of [SM92]. More precisely, we have introduced in our work *bisimulations up-to β-reductions*, which have been inspired by a similar approach to concurrent ML [JR04]. This technique relieves the burden of exhibiting witness bisimulations, and its feasibility has been proved to be successful, combined with *Contextuality*, for addressing the verification of sample access protocols, such as crossing a firewall, the interaction between a server and its clients, and metaservers providing memory services.

In the future, we plan to test further with the up-to β-reduction technique we have devised, by dealing with more involved protocols, possibly in the spirit of [US01]. That work uses a novel notion of coupled simulation that, despite not coinciding with any contextual equivalence, allows the proof of correctness of a simple central-forwarding-server algorithm.

We would like also to extend the results and techniques stated for DPI to the more involved SAFEDPI [HRY04], which takes into account extra safety aspects of distributed systems.

Acknowledgements. The authors would like to acknowledge the financial support of the two EU Global Computing projects, *Mikado* and *Myths*.

References

[CG98] Luca Cardelli and Andrew D. Gordon. Mobile ambients. In Proc. of *FoSSaCS*, *Lecture Notes in Computer Science* 1378, Springer, 1998.

[CHR05] Alberto Ciaffaglione, Matthew Hennessy, and Julian Rathke. Proof methodologies for behavioural equivalence in DPI. *Technical Report 03:2005, Department of Informatics, University of Sussex*, http://www.dimi.uniud.it/ ciaffagl, 2005.

[GC99] Andrew D. Gordon and Luca Cardelli. Equational properties of mobile ambients. In Proc. of *FoSSaCS*, *Lecture Notes in Computer Science* 1578, Springer, 1999.

[HMR04] Matthew Hennessy, Massimo Merro, and Julian Rathke. Towards a behavioural theory of access and mobility control in distributed systems. *Th. Comp. Science* 322(3), 2004.

[HR02a] Matthew Hennessy and Julian Rathke. Typed behavioural equivalences for processes in the presence of subtyping. *Electronic Notes in Th. Comp. Science* 61, 2002.

[HR02b] Matthew Hennessy and James Riely. Resource access control in systems of mobile agents. *Information and Computation* 173(1), 2002.

[HRY04] Matthew Hennessy, Julian Rathke, and Nobuko Yoshida. SAFEDPI: a language for controlling mobile code. In Proc. of *FoSSaCS*, *LNCS* 2987, Springer, 2004.

[JR04] Alan Jeffrey and Julian Rathke. A theory of bisimulation for a fragment of concurrent ML with local names. *Theoretical Computer Science* 323(1-3), 2004.

[LS00] Francesca Levi and Davide Sangiorgi. Controlling interference in ambients. In Proc. of *POPL*, 2000.

[Mil89] Robin Milner. *Communication and Concurrency*. Prentice Hall, 1989.

[MN03] Massimo Merro and Francesco Zappa Nardelli. Bisimulation proof methods for mobile ambients. In Proc. of *ICALP*, *Lecture Notes in Computer Science* 2719, Springer, 2003.

[MPW92] Robin Milner, Joachim Parrow, and David Walker. A calculus of mobile processes (I and II). *Information and Computation*, 100(1,2), 1992.

[PS00] Benjamin C. Pierce and Davide Sangiorgi. Behavioral equivalence in the polymorphic PICALCULUS. *Journal of ACM* 47(3), 2000.

[SM92] Davide Sangiorgi and Robin Milner. The problem of "weak bisimulation up to". In Proc. of *CONCUR*, *Lecture Notes in Computer Science* 630, Springer, 1992.

[SW01] Davide Sangiorgi and David Walker. *The PICALCULUS: a Theory of Mobile Processes*. Cambridge University Press, 2001.

[US01] Asis Unyapoth and Peter Sewell. Nomadic pict: correct communication infrastructure for mobile computation. In Proc. of *POPL*, 2001.

Deriving Non-determinism from Conjunction and Disjunction

Naijun Zhan[1,*] and Mila Majster-Cederbaum[2]

[1] Lab. of Computer Science, Institute of Software, Chinese Academy of Sciences, South Fourth Street No.4, Zhong Guan Cun, 100080, Beijing, P.R. China
[2] Lehrstuhl für Praktische Informatik II, Fakultät für Mathematik und Informatik, Mannheim Universität, D7,27, 68163, Mannheim, Deutschland

Abstract. In this paper, we show that the non-deterministic choice "+", which was proposed as a primitive operator in *Synchronization Tree Logic* (STL for short) can be defined essentially by conjunction and disjunction in the μ-calculus (μM for short). This is obtained by extending the μ-calculus with the non-deterministic choice "+" (denoted by μM^+) and then showing that μM^+ can be translated into μM. Furthermore, we also prove that STL can be encoded into μM^+ and therefore into μM.

Keywords: Non-determinism, Synchronization Tree Logic, μ-calculus, process algebra.

1 Introduction

Compositional methods allow one to build up a large system by composing existing systems with the defined constructors and reduce the problem of correctness for a complex system to similar and simpler correctness problems for the subsystems. Because the complexity of large systems is normally untractable, it is necessary that a method for developing these systems is compositional (vertically or horizontally) in order to avoid combinatorial explosion in specifying and verifying these systems.

It is widely agreed that modal and temporal logics such as the μ-calculus [5] and Hennessy-Milner Logic (HML for short) [4], are an appropriate tool for the specification and proof of reactive systems. In many cases, these systems can be modelled by the term language $\mathcal{T}[\{\epsilon\}, \{+\}, Act, \mathcal{X}]$ of an algebra with a congruence relation $\sim$, where $\mathcal{T}[\{\epsilon\}, \{+\}, Act, \mathcal{X}]$ is constructed from a constant ϵ by using a set Act of unary operators, a binary operator $+$ and *recursion*. $\mathcal{T}[\{\epsilon\}, \{+\}, Act, \mathcal{X}]$ is at the base of many process algebras, where Act represents a set of *action names*, $+$ the *non-deterministic choice* and ϵ the system performing no actions. The terms can be interpreted over trees labeled over Act - *synchronization trees* - following the terminology of [8]. It is required that modal logics $\mathcal{L}$ meet the condition of adequacy, namely,

$$\forall t_1, t_2 \in \mathcal{T}[\{\epsilon\}, \{+\}, Act, \mathcal{X}] \, (t_1 \sim t_2 \text{ iff } \forall \phi \in \mathcal{L}(t_1 \models \phi \text{ iff } t_2 \models \phi)).$$

---
* This work is supported in part by CNSF-60493200 and CNSF-60421001.

I.e, the congruence $\sim$ and the equivalence relation induced by the logic agree. For example, HML has the property, i.e., two CCS terms are equal up to strong bisimulation if and only if they satisfy the same HML properties, see [4].

On the other hand, it is desirable that the logics have compositionality, i.e. there exists a connection between the connectives of these logics and the constructors of programs so that one can reduce the problem of correctness for a complex system to similar and simpler correctness problems for the subsystems. It seems that many classic modal logics like the μ-calculus and HML do not have such a property.

Motivated by the above two requirements, Graf and Sifakis proposed a modal logic, called *Synchronization Tree Logic* (STL) [2]. The language of formulae of STL is generated from the constants $\epsilon, \top$ by using the *boolean connectives*, the set 2^{Act} of unary operators where Act is a set of actions, the binary operator $+$ and *fixpoint operators*. The operator $+$ of the logic is an extension of the one $+$ of programs. $P \models \phi_1 + \phi_2$ means that there exist P_1 and P_2 such that $P \sim P_1 + P_2$, $P_1 \models \phi_1$ and $P_2 \models \phi_2$. Therefore, $\mathcal{T}[\{\epsilon\}, \{+\}, Act, \mathcal{X}]$ is contained in STL, i.e., programs are formulae of the logic. In order to avoid confusions, we will use ϕ_P to denote the formula corresponding to the program P. So, the verification of an assertion $P \models \phi$ can be reduced to the syntax-directed proof of the validity of the formula $\phi_P \Rightarrow \phi$.

It is clear that STL is more expressive than μM since it is not hard to encode μM into STL, for example, $[A]\phi$ can be defined as $\neg(A \neg \phi_{STL} + \top)$ and $\langle A \rangle \phi$ as $A\phi_{STL} + \top$, where $A \subseteq Act$ and ϕ_{STL} stands for the counterpart of ϕ in STL. But for the converse direction, by our knowledge, it seems that until up to now it is still open.

In this paper, we will study the issue of the definability of $+$ in μM and give an affirmative answer. We show that the choice $+$ can be defined essentially by conjunction and disjunction in μM. This is captured by extending μM with the choice $+$ to μM^+ and then encoding μM^+ into μM. Furthermore, we show that STL can be translated into μM^+, and we can thus claim that μM is as expressive as STL.

The rest of this paper is organized as follows: Some basic notions are defined in Section 2. Section 3 briefly reviews μM firstly, then extends it with the nondeterministic choice $+$ to μM^+. Section 4 is devoted to encoding μM^+ into μM. STL and some related results are provided in Section 5. Section 6 is devoted to translating STL into μM^+. A short conclusion is given in Section 7.

2 Preliminaries

Consider a term language $\mathcal{T}$ built from the constants ϵ, τ, and a set $\mathcal{X}$ of process variables by using a set Act of unary operators, a binary operator $+$, and recursion.

Formally, $\mathcal{T}$ is formed according to the following rules:

- $\epsilon, \tau \in \mathcal{T}, \mathcal{X} \subseteq \mathcal{T}$,
- $aP, P_1 + P_2, rec\, x.P \in \mathcal{T}$ if $a \in Act, x \in \mathcal{X}, P, P_1, P_2 \in \mathcal{T}$.

We denote by $T[\{\epsilon\}, \{+\}, Act, \mathcal{X}]$ the sub-language which consists of all the well-guarded and closed terms in T, where $rec\ x.P$ is well-guarded means that any occurrence of the variable x in P is within the scope of an operator of Act.

For a given $P \in T$, the set of actions that occur in P is called its *sort*, denoted $S(P)$, inductively defined by $S(\epsilon) \stackrel{\frown}{=} \emptyset$, $S(\tau) \stackrel{\frown}{=} Act$, $S(x) \stackrel{\frown}{=} \emptyset$, $S(a\,P) \stackrel{\frown}{=} \{a\} \cup S(P)$, $S(P_1 + P_2) \stackrel{\frown}{=} S(P_1) \cup S(P_2)$, $S(rec\,x.P) \stackrel{\frown}{=} S(P)$.

Intuitively, we consider that elements of $T[\{\epsilon\}, \{+\}, Act, \mathcal{X}]$ represent programs: Act is a set of atomic actions; $+$ stands for *non-deterministic choice*; and ϵ for the program performing no actions; τ can be conceived as a program that behaves like **chaos** in CSP [3] which can do anything.

A structured operational semantics of T in Plotkin's Style is defined as follows:

Act $\dfrac{}{aP \stackrel{a}{\to} P}$ Nd $\dfrac{P_1 \stackrel{a}{\to} P_1'}{P_1 + P_2 \stackrel{a}{\to} P_1',\ P_2 + P_1 \stackrel{a}{\to} P_1'}$

Rec $\dfrac{P_1[rec\,x.P_1/x] \stackrel{a}{\to} P_1'}{rec\,x.P_1 \stackrel{a}{\to} P_1'}$ Chaos $\dfrac{}{\tau \stackrel{a}{\to} Q}$ for any $a \in Act$ and $Q \in T$.

A process term $P \in T$ determines a labelled *transition system*, i.e., a tuple $T(P) = (\Sigma, S(P), \to, P)$, where Σ is the set of states which is reachable from P, and $P \in \Sigma$ is the initial state, $\to \subseteq \Sigma \times S(P) \times \Sigma$ is the set of transitions, derived from the above operational semantics.

Remark 1. 1. Any transition system representing a term of $T[\{\epsilon\}, \{+\}, Act, \mathcal{X}]$ is always finitely branching as only well-guarded terms are admitted;
2. The sort of each term of $T[\{\epsilon\}, \{+\}, Act, \mathcal{X}]$ is finite as so is its syntax.

Definition 1. *A binary relation S over $T[\{\epsilon\}, \{+\}, Act, \mathcal{X}]$ is called a strong bisimulation if $(P, Q) \in S$ implies*

- *whenever $P \stackrel{a}{\to} P'$ then, for some $Q', Q \stackrel{a}{\to} Q'$ and $(P', Q') \in S$, for any $a \in Act$; and*
- *whenever $Q \stackrel{a}{\to} Q'$ then, for some $P', P \stackrel{a}{\to} P'$ and $(P', Q') \in S$ for any $a \in Act$.*

Given two processes $P, Q \in T[\{\epsilon\}, \{+\}, Act, \mathcal{X}]$, P and Q are strongly bisimilar, written $P \sim Q$, if $(P, Q) \in S$ for some strong bisimulation S.

It is shown in [7] that $\sim$ is a congruence on $T[\{\epsilon\}, \{+\}, Act, \mathcal{X}]$. [1] proved the following result, namely,

Lemma 1. *For each $P \in T[\{\epsilon\}, \{+\}, Act, \mathcal{X}]$, there exists a process of the form $\Sigma_{i=1}^{m} \Sigma_{j=1}^{i_{a_i}} a_i P_{i,j}$ such that $P \sim \Sigma_{i=1}^{m} \Sigma_{j=1}^{i_{a_i}} a_i P_{i,j}$, where $a_i \neq a_j$ if $i \neq j$.*

Note that an empty sum is abbreviated as ϵ.

3 The μ-Calculus and Its Extension with "+"

In this section, we first briefly review the μ-calculus; then extend the logic with the non-deterministic operator "+". We denote by μM^+ the extension.

For easing to encode STL into μM, we use the slightly generalized version of the μ-calculus (see [9]) in the sense that modalities on sets of actions are adopted rather than modalities on a single action, although the two formalisms are equivalent if the set of actions is assumed to be finite.

3.1 μM

Let Act be a set of atomic actions, ranged over by $a, b, c, \ldots$. $A, B, \ldots$ stand for the subsets of Act. Let tt be propositional constant as usual, and $\mathcal{X}$ be a set of variables, ranged over by $x, y, z, \ldots$.

Formulae of μM are generated by:

$$\phi ::= tt \mid x \mid \neg \phi \mid \phi \vee \phi \mid \langle A \rangle \phi \mid [A]\phi \mid \mu x.\phi,$$

where $A \subseteq Act$ and $x \in \mathcal{X}$.

The notions of *scope*, *bound* and *free occurrences* of variables, *closed* and *open formulae*, etc. are the same as in first-order predicate logic, where μx is treated as *quantifier*. We will use $fn(\phi)$ to stand for the variables that have some free occurrence in ϕ, and $bn(\phi)$ for the variables that have some bound occurrence in ϕ. We say that ϕ is *positive (negative) in the variable* x if every free occurrence of x in ϕ occurs within the scope of an even (odd) number of negations $\neg$. A formula ϕ is said *positive (negative)* if for every $x \in bn(\phi)$, its scope in ϕ is positive (negative) in x. A formula ϕ is called *strongly positive* if it is positive and each occurrence of x is within the scope of an even number of negations $\neg$ for any $x \in fn(\phi)$. For example, let $\phi_1 \hat{=} x \vee \mu x. \neg\neg x$, $\phi_2 \hat{=} \neg y \vee \mu x. \neg\neg x$. It is clear that ϕ_1 and ϕ_2 both are positive; however, ϕ_1 is strongly positive as well, but ϕ_2 is not. We say that x is *guarded* in ϕ if every occurrence of x in ϕ is within the scope of $\langle A \rangle$ or $[A]$ for some $A \subseteq Act$. A formula ϕ is called *guarded* if each variable in $bn(\phi)$ is guarded.

If $A = \{a\}$, we directly write $\langle a \rangle \phi$ and $[a]\phi$ instead of $\langle \{a\} \rangle \phi$ and $[\{a\}]\phi$ respectively.

We denote by $\mathcal{L}_\mu(Act)$ the language of formulae of μM that are positive and guarded, by $c\mathcal{L}_\mu(Act)$ the set of all closed formulae in $\mathcal{L}_\mu(Act)$. As [11] showed that any formula $\phi \in \mu$M is equivalent to a positive guarded formula ϕ', we theorefore only focus on $\mathcal{L}_\mu(Act)$ and $c\mathcal{L}_\mu(Act)$ in what follows.

A valuation ρ is a mapping with the type $\rho : \mathcal{X} \to 2^{\mathcal{T}[\{\epsilon\},\{+\},Act,\mathcal{X}]}$, which associates a set of processes with each propositional variable. $\rho[x \leadsto \mathcal{A}]$ agrees with ρ except for assigning $\mathcal{A}$ to x.

Definition 2. *The semantics of $\mathcal{L}_\mu(Act)$ under a valuation ρ is given by a satisfaction relation between $\mathcal{T}[\{\epsilon\},\{+\},Act,\mathcal{X}]$ and $\mathcal{L}_\mu(Act)$ relative to ρ, denoted by $\models^\rho_{\mu M}$, inductively defined as follows:*

$P \models^\rho_{\mu M} tt$,

$P \models^\rho_{\mu M} x$, iff $P \in \rho(x)$,

$P \models^\rho_{\mu M} \neg\phi$ iff $P \not\models^\rho_{\mu M} \phi$,

$P \models^\rho_{\mu M} \phi_1 \vee \phi_2$ iff $P \models^\rho_{\mu M} \phi_1$ or $P \models^\rho_{\mu M} \phi_2$,

$P \models^\rho_{\mu M} \langle A \rangle \phi$ iff $\exists a \in A, \exists P'. P \xrightarrow{a} P'$ and $P' \models^\rho_{\mu M} \phi$,

$P \models^\rho_{\mu M} [A]\phi$ iff $\forall a \in A, \forall P'. P \xrightarrow{a} P'$ implies $P' \models^\rho_{\mu M} \phi$,

$P \models^\rho_{\mu M} \mu x.\phi$ iff $P \in \bigcap \{\mathcal{A} \mid \{Q \mid Q \models^{\rho[x \leadsto \mathcal{A}]}_{\mu M} \phi\} \subseteq \mathcal{A}\}$,

where $P, P' \in \mathcal{T}[\{\epsilon\}, \{+\}, Act, \mathcal{X}]$ and $\mathcal{A} \subseteq \mathcal{T}[\{\epsilon\}, \{+\}, Act, \mathcal{X}]$.

Note that the restriction that all formulae of $\mathcal{L}_\mu(Act)$ are positive guarantees that the interpretation of a formula of the form $\mu x.\phi$ is well defined by the Tarski-Knaster Theorem [10].

Since the meaning of a closed formula ϕ is independent of valuations, we will abbreviate $P \models^\rho_{\mu M} \phi$ as $P \models_{\mu M} \phi$ for any valuation ρ.

The following derived operators are useful:

$$ff \triangleq \neg tt,$$
$$\phi_1 \wedge \phi_2 \triangleq \neg((\neg\phi_1) \vee (\neg\phi_2)),$$
$$\phi_1 \Rightarrow \phi_2 \triangleq (\neg\phi_1) \vee \phi_2,$$
$$\phi_1 \Leftrightarrow \phi_2 \triangleq (\phi_1 \Rightarrow \phi_2) \wedge (\phi_2 \Rightarrow \phi_1),$$
$$\nu x.\phi \triangleq \neg(\mu x.\neg\phi\{\neg x/x\}).$$

Convention: In order to improve the readability, in the later, we assume the binding precedence among the operators as "$\neg$" > "$\vee$" = "$\wedge$" > "μx" = "νx" > "$\Rightarrow$" = "$\Leftrightarrow$".

3.2 μM^+

μM^+ is an extension of μM with the non-deterministic choice "+". Informally, $\phi + \psi$ holds in a process P means that there exist P_1 and P_2 such that $P \sim P_1 + P_2$, P_1 satisfies ϕ and P_2 meets ψ.

Given a set Act of atomic actions and a set $\mathcal{X}$ of variables, formulae of μM^+ are generated as follows:

$$\phi ::= tt \mid x \mid \neg \phi \mid \phi \vee \phi \mid \langle A \rangle \phi \mid [A]\phi \mid \phi + \phi \mid \mu x.\phi,$$

where $x \in \mathcal{X}$ and $A \subseteq Act$.

Some notions for μM^+ can be defined same as in μM. We will use $\mathcal{L}^+_\mu(Act)$ to denote the language of formulae of μM^+ that are guarded and positive and $c\mathcal{L}^+_\mu(Act)$ to stand for the set of closed formulae in $\mathcal{L}^+_\mu(Act)$.

Definition 3. *A formula* $\phi \in \mathcal{L}_\mu^+(Act)$ *is called* strictly guarded, *if each variable* $x \in fn(\phi) \cup bn(\phi)$ *is guarded and does not occur in any sub-formula of the forms* $x + \psi$ *or* $\neg x + \psi$.

Note that strictly guarded is stronger than guarded, for instance, $\langle A \rangle(x + y)$ is guarded, but not strictly guarded.

Definition 4. *The semantics of* $\mathcal{L}_\mu^+(Act)$ *under a given valuation ρ is given by a satisfaction relation between* $\mathcal{T}[\{\epsilon\}, \{+\}, Act, \mathcal{X}]$ *and* $\mathcal{L}_\mu^+(Act)$ *relative to ρ, denoted by* $\models_{\mu M+}^\rho$. *The definition of* $\models_{\mu M+}^\rho$ *contains all clauses listed in Definition 2, in addition to including the following clause for interpreting "+":*

$$P \models_{\mu M+}^\rho \phi_1 + \phi_2 \text{ iff } \exists P_1 \exists P_2.P \sim P_1 + P_2, P_1 \models_{\mu M+}^\rho \phi_1 \text{ and } P_2 \models_{\mu M+}^\rho \phi_2,$$

where $P, P_1, P_2 \in \mathcal{T}[\{\epsilon\}, \{+\}, Act, \mathcal{X}]$.

Since the meaning of a closed formula ϕ is independent of valuations, we will abbreviate $P \models_{\mu M+}^\rho \phi$ as $P \models_{\mu M+} \phi$ for any valuation ρ. A formula ϕ is valid, written $\models_{\mu M+} \phi$, if $P \models_{\mu M+}^\rho \phi$ for any $P \in \mathcal{T}[\{\epsilon\}, \{+\}, Act, \mathcal{X}]$ and any valuation ρ. Sometimes, we write ϕ directly instead of $\models_{\mu M+} \phi$ for simplicity.

It is clear that $\mathcal{L}_\mu(Act) \subseteq \mathcal{L}_\mu^+(Act)$ and $c\mathcal{L}_\mu(Act) \subseteq c\mathcal{L}_\mu^+(Act)$.
Convention We will assume that "+" has a priority over all other binary operators, but "$\neg$" has a higher priority to it. Given a set $A \subset B$, we will use $\bar{A}$ to stand for the complement $B - A$.

3.3 Some Results on μM and μM^+

From Definition 4, it is easy to see that "+" is monotonic. That is,

Proposition 1. *If* $\phi_1 \Rightarrow \phi_2$ *and* $\psi_1 \Rightarrow \psi_2$ *then* $\phi_1 + \psi_1 \Rightarrow \phi_2 + \psi_2$.

Definition 5. *Given a set of process* $\mathcal{A} \subseteq \mathcal{T}[\{\epsilon\}, \{+\}, Act, \mathcal{X}]$, $\mathcal{A}$ *is bisimulation closed if* $\forall P \in \mathcal{A}$ *and* $\forall Q \in \mathcal{T}[\{\epsilon\}, \{+\}, Act, \mathcal{X}]$, $P \sim Q$ *implies that* $Q \in \mathcal{A}$. *For convenience, from now on, we will abbreviate* bisimulation closed *as* B.C.. *A valuation ρ is* B.C. *if for all* $x \in \mathcal{X}$ $\rho(x)$ *is* B.C..

Regarding the above definition, we have the following results:

Lemma 2. *If* $\mathcal{A}_1, \mathcal{A}_2 \subseteq \mathcal{T}[\{\epsilon\}, \{+\}, Act, \mathcal{X}]$ *are* B.C., *then*

1. $\bar{\mathcal{A}}_1, \mathcal{A}_1 \cap \mathcal{A}_2$ *and* $\mathcal{A}_1 \cup \mathcal{A}_2$ *are* B.C.,
2. $\{P \in \mathcal{T}[\{\epsilon\}, \{+\}, Act, \mathcal{X}] \mid \text{if } P \xrightarrow{a} P' \text{ and } a \in A \text{ then } P' \in \mathcal{A}_1\}$ *is* B.C.,
3. $\{P \in \mathcal{T}[\{\epsilon\}, \{+\}, Act, \mathcal{X}] \mid \exists P' \in \mathcal{A}_1.\exists a \in A.P \xrightarrow{a} P'\}$ *is* B.C.,
4. $\mathcal{A}_1 + \mathcal{A}_2$ *is* B.C., *where* $\mathcal{A}_1 + \mathcal{A}_2$ *denotes the set* $\{P \mid \exists P_1 \in \mathcal{A}_1.\exists P_2 \in \mathcal{A}_2.P \sim P_1 + P_2\}$.

For any set of processes $\mathcal{A} \subseteq \mathcal{T}[\{\epsilon\}, \{+\}, Act, \mathcal{X}]$, we can associate with it the following subset:

$$\mathcal{A}^d \triangleq \{P \in \mathcal{A} \mid \text{ if } P \sim Q \text{ and } Q \in \mathcal{T}[\{\epsilon\}, \{+\}, Act, \mathcal{X}] \text{ then } Q \in \mathcal{A}\}.$$

The set $\mathcal{A}^d$ is the largest bisimulation closed set contained in $\mathcal{A}$.

Lemma 3. *For any set $\mathcal{A}, \mathcal{A}_i \subseteq \mathcal{T}[\{\epsilon\}, \{+\}, Act, \mathcal{X}]$ for $i = 1, 2$,*
1. *$\mathcal{A}^d$ is B.C.,*
2. *$\mathcal{A}^d \subseteq \mathcal{A}$,*
3. *$\mathcal{A}^d = \mathcal{A}$ if $\mathcal{A}$ is B.C.,*
4. *$\mathcal{A}_1^d \subseteq \mathcal{A}_2^d$ if $\mathcal{A}_1 \subseteq \mathcal{A}_2$,*
5. *$\mathcal{A}_1^d + \mathcal{A}_2^d \subseteq \mathcal{A}^d$ if $\mathcal{A}_1 + \mathcal{A}_2 \subseteq \mathcal{A}$.*

We use ρ^d to stand for the valuation defined by $\rho^d(x) = \rho(x)^d$. By Lemma 3, it is clear that ρ^d is B.C. for any valuation ρ. From now on, we will use BCV to stand for the set of bisimulation closed valuations.

In the following, we will use $[\![\phi]\!]_\rho$ to denote the set of processes that meet ϕ under the valuation ρ, i.e., $[\![\phi]\!]_\rho \triangleq \{P \in \mathcal{T}[\{\epsilon\}, \{+\}, Act, \mathcal{X}] \mid P \models^\rho_{\mu M+} \phi\}$. We will write $\rho \subseteq \rho'$ if $\rho(x) \subseteq \rho'(x)$ for any $x \in \mathcal{X}$.

Proposition 2. *For any $\phi \in \mathcal{L}^+_\mu(Act)$, if ϕ is strongly positive and $\rho \subseteq \rho'$, then $[\![\phi]\!]_\rho \subseteq [\![\phi]\!]_{\rho'}$.*

Lemma 4. *For any $\phi \in \mathcal{L}^+_\mu(Act)$ which is strongly positive, any valuation ρ, and $\mathcal{A} \in \mathcal{T}[\{\epsilon\}, \{+\}, Act, \mathcal{X}]$, then*

1. *If ρ is B.C., then $[\![\phi]\!]_\rho$ is B.C. as well;*
2. *$[\![\phi]\!]_{\rho^d} \subseteq \mathcal{A}^d$ if $[\![\phi]\!]_\rho \subseteq \mathcal{A}$.*

Proof. Similar to the proof for Proposition 3 in Section 5.4 in [9], simultaneously proving these two statements by induction on ϕ, the proof is done. ⊣

As [9] pointed out that each formula of $c\mathcal{L}_\mu(Act)$ defines a bisimulation invariant property, the following theorem indicates that every formula in $c\mathcal{L}^+_\mu(Act)$ is bisimulation invariant as well. The forward direction of the theorem follows immediately from the above lemma; the converse direction comes from the fact $c\mathcal{L}_\mu(Act) \subseteq c\mathcal{L}^+_\mu(Act)$.

Theorem 1. *For any $P, Q \in \mathcal{T}[\{\epsilon\}, \{+\}, Act, \mathcal{X}]$, $P \sim Q$ iff for each $\phi \in c\mathcal{L}^+_\mu(Act)$, $P \models_{\mu M+} \phi$ iff $Q \models_{\mu M+} \phi$.*

The following lemmas can be proved by Definition 4.

Lemma 5.

(1) $\phi + f\!f \Leftrightarrow f\!f$
(2) $tt + tt \Leftrightarrow tt$
(3) $[A]tt \Leftrightarrow tt$
(4) $\langle A \rangle f\!f \Leftrightarrow f\!f$
(5) $\phi + \psi \Leftrightarrow \psi + \phi$
(6) $(\phi + \psi) + \varphi \Leftrightarrow \phi + (\psi + \varphi)$
(7) $\langle A \rangle \phi_1 \wedge [A \cup B]\phi_2 \Rightarrow \langle A \rangle (\phi_1 \wedge \phi_2)$
(8) $\phi + (\varphi \vee \psi) \Leftrightarrow (\phi + \varphi) \vee (\phi + \psi)$
(9) $\langle A \rangle \phi_1 \vee \langle A \rangle \phi_2 \Leftrightarrow \langle A \rangle (\phi_1 \vee \phi_2)$
(10) $[A]\phi_1 \wedge [A]\phi_2 \Leftrightarrow [A](\phi_1 \wedge \phi_2)$
(11) $\langle A_1 \cup A_2 \rangle \phi \Leftrightarrow \langle A_1 \rangle \phi \vee \langle A_2 \rangle \phi$
(12) $[A_1 \cup A_2]\phi \Leftrightarrow [A_1]\phi \wedge [A_2]\phi$

Lemma 6.

(1) $\neg[A]\phi \Leftrightarrow \langle A \rangle \neg \phi$
(2) $\neg \langle A \rangle \phi \Leftrightarrow [A]\neg \phi$
(3) $[A_1]\phi_1 \wedge [A_2]\phi_2 \Leftrightarrow [A_1 - (A_1 \cap A_2)]\phi_1 \wedge [A_1 \cap A_2](\phi_1 \wedge \phi_2) \wedge [A_2 - (A_1 \cap A_2)]\phi_2$

4 Reducing $c\mathcal{L}_\mu^+(Act)$ to $c\mathcal{L}_\mu(Act)$

In this section, we show that "+" is definable in μM by reducing $c\mathcal{L}_\mu^+(Act)$ into $c\mathcal{L}_\mu(Act)$. The encoding is completed via the following three steps: firstly, we prove that in some special cases, "+" can be defined by conjunction and disjunction; then we show that the problem of eliminating "+" in a strongly positive and strictly guarded formula ϕ can be reduced to one of the above special cases; and finally we complete the encoding by proving that for any $\phi \in c\mathcal{L}_\mu^+(Act)$, there is a formula $\phi' \in c\mathcal{L}_\mu^+(Act)$ which is strictly guarded such that $\phi \Leftrightarrow \phi'$.

We say that ϕ implies ψ w.r.t. bisimulation closed valuations, denoted by $\phi \overset{bc}{\Rightarrow} \psi$, if $[\![\phi]\!]_\rho \subseteq [\![\psi]\!]_\rho$ for any $\rho \in BCV$. $\phi \overset{bc}{\Leftrightarrow} \psi$ means $\phi \overset{bc}{\Rightarrow} \psi$ and $\psi \overset{bc}{\Rightarrow} \phi$. It is clear that $\phi \Rightarrow \psi$ implies $\phi \overset{bc}{\Rightarrow} \psi$, and $\phi \overset{bc}{\Rightarrow} \psi$ iff $\phi \Rightarrow \psi$ if $\phi, \psi \in c\mathcal{L}_\mu^+(Act)$.

In order to attain the first step, we need the following proposition:

Proposition 3. **1.** *For any* $P, Q \in \mathcal{T}[\{\epsilon\}, \{+\}, Act, \mathcal{X}]$, *if* $P \models_{\mu M+}^\rho \langle A \rangle \phi$ *then* $P + Q \models_{\mu M+}^\rho \langle A \rangle \phi$; *and*
2. *If* $P \models_{\mu M+}^\rho [A]\phi_1$ *and* $Q \models_{\mu M+}^\rho [A]\phi_2$ *then* $P + Q \models_{\mu M+}^\rho [A](\phi_1 \vee \phi_2)$.

The following lemma claims that in some special cases, "+" can be defined essentially by conjunction and disjunction.

Lemma 7.

$$(\bigwedge_{i=1}^n \bigwedge_{j=1}^{n_i} \langle A_i \rangle \phi_{i,j} \wedge \bigwedge_{i=1}^m [B_i]\psi_i) + (\bigwedge_{i=1}^k \bigwedge_{j=1}^{k_i} \langle C_i \rangle \varphi_{i,j} \wedge \bigwedge_{i=1}^m [B_i]\chi_i)$$

$$\overset{bc}{\Leftrightarrow} \bigwedge_{i=1}^n \bigwedge_{j=1}^{n_i} \langle A_i \rangle (\phi_{i,j} \wedge \psi_i) \wedge \bigwedge_{i=1}^k \bigwedge_{j=1}^{k_i} \langle C_i \rangle (\varphi_{i,j} \wedge \chi_i) \wedge \bigwedge_{i=1}^m [B_i](\psi_i \vee \chi_i)$$

where all conjuncts in the formula of the left side of $\overset{bc}{\Leftrightarrow}$ are strongly positive, $n, k \leq m$, $\forall 1 \leq i \leq n. A_i \subseteq B_i$, $\forall 1 \leq i \leq k. C_i \subseteq B_i$, and for any $1 \leq i, j \leq m$, if $i \neq j$ then $B_i \cap B_j = \emptyset$.

Proof. "$\overset{bc}{\Rightarrow}$" can be easily proved by Proposition 3 and Lemma 4. So, we only give a sketch for the proof of the converse direction. Assume

$$P \models_{\mu M+}^\rho \bigwedge_{i=1}^n \bigwedge_{j=1}^{n_i} \langle A_i \rangle (\phi_{i,j} \wedge \psi_i) \wedge \bigwedge_{i=1}^k \bigwedge_{j=1}^{k_i} \langle C_i \rangle (\varphi_{i,j} \wedge \chi_i) \wedge \bigwedge_{i=1}^m [B_i](\psi_i \vee \chi_i), \quad (1)$$

where ρ is B.C.. By Lemma 1, $P \sim \Sigma_{i=1}^l \Sigma_{j=1}^{ia_i} a_i P_{i,j}$, where $l \geq m$ and for any $1 \leq i, j \leq l$, if $i \neq j$ then $a_i \neq a_j$. So, we have $\Sigma_{i=1}^l \Sigma_{j=1}^{ia_i} a_i P_{i,j} \models_{\mu M+}^\rho \bigwedge_{i=1}^n \bigwedge_{j=1}^{n_i} \langle A_i \rangle (\phi_{i,j} \wedge \psi_i)$ by Lemma 4. This implies that for each $1 \leq i \leq n$ and

$1 \leq j \leq n_i$, there exist $1 \leq r_i \leq l$ and $1 \leq h_j \leq i_{a_{r_i}}$ such that $a_{r_i} \in A_i$ and $P_{r_i,h_j} \models^\rho_{\mu M+} \phi_{i,j} \wedge \psi_i$. Let $P' \hat{=} \Sigma_{i=1}^n \Sigma_{j=1}^{n_i} a_{r_i} P_{r_i,h_j}$. It is obvious that

$$P' \models^\rho_{\mu M+} \bigwedge_{i=1}^n \bigwedge_{j=1}^{n_i} \langle A_i \rangle \phi_{i,j} \wedge \bigwedge_{i=1}^m [B_i] \psi_i. \qquad (2)$$

Similarly, we get that for each $1 \leq i \leq k$ and $1 \leq j \leq k_i$, there exist $1 \leq r_i \leq l$ and $1 \leq h_j \leq i_{a_{r_i}}$ such that $a_{r_i} \in C_i$ and $P_{r_i,h_j} \models^\rho_{\mu M+} \varphi_{i,j} \wedge \chi_i$. Let $P'' \hat{=} \Sigma_{i=1}^k \Sigma_{j=1}^{n_i} a_{r_i} P_{r_i,h_j}$. It is easy to show that

$$P'' \models^\rho_{\mu M+} \bigwedge_{i=1}^k \bigwedge_{j=1}^{k_i} \langle C_i \rangle \varphi_{i,j} \wedge \bigwedge_{i=1}^m [B_i] \chi_i. \qquad (3)$$

Then, we add each summand of $\Sigma_{i=1}^l \Sigma_{j=1}^{i_{a_i}} a_i P_{i,j}$ to P' or P'' according to the following algorithm: For each $1 \leq i \leq l$, if $a_i \in B_j$ for some $j \in \{1, \ldots, m\}$ then let $I_1 \hat{=} \{h \mid P_{i,h} \models \psi_j\}$ and $I_2 \hat{=} \{h \mid P_{i,h} \models \chi_j\}$; otherwise, $I_1 \hat{=} \{1, \ldots, i_{a_i}\}$ and $I_2 = \emptyset$. Since $P \models^\rho_{\mu M+} [B_j](\psi_j \vee \chi_j)$, it is clear that $I_1 \cup I_2 = \{1, \ldots, i_{a_i}\}$. Then, let $P' := P' + \sum_{h \in I_1} a_i P_{i,h}$ and $P'' := P'' + \sum_{h \in I_2} a_i P_{i,h}$. Because $B_i \cap B_j = \emptyset$ if $i \neq j$, it is easy to show that (2) and (3) keep invariant for each cojoining. Additionally, it is easy to see that $P' + P'' \sim P$. Hence, from Lemma 4,

$$P \models^\rho_{\mu M+} (\bigwedge_{i=1}^n \bigwedge_{j=1}^{n_i} \langle A_i \rangle \phi_{i,j} \wedge \bigwedge_{i=1}^m [B_i] \psi_i) + (\bigwedge_{i=1}^k \bigwedge_{j=1}^{k_i} \langle C_i \rangle \varphi_{i,j} \wedge \bigwedge_{i=1}^m [B_i] \chi_i). \qquad \dashv$$

Furthermore, applying the above lemma, we can complete the second step by proving the following results:

Lemma 8. *For any $\phi \in \mathcal{L}^+_\mu(Act)$, if ϕ is strictly guarded and strongly positive, then there exists ϕ' in which no $+$ occurs such that $\phi' \stackrel{bc}{\Leftrightarrow} \phi$ and ϕ' is strictly guarded and strongly positive.*

Proof. By induction on the structure of ϕ. Here, we only list the proofs for some interesting cases.

- $\phi = \neg \psi$

    Suppose $\rho \in BCV$ and $fn(\phi) \subseteq \{x_1, \ldots, x_n\}$. Let $\neg \rho$ be defined by $\neg \rho(x) = \mathcal{T}[\{\epsilon\}, \{+\}, Act, \mathcal{X}] - \rho(x)$ for any $x \in \mathcal{X}$. By Lemma 2.1., $\neg \rho$ is B.C.. It is easy to see that $[\![\varphi]\!]_\rho = [\![\varphi\{\neg x_1/x_1, \ldots, \neg x_n/x_n\}]\!]_{\neg \rho}$ for any $\varphi \in \mathcal{L}^+_\mu(Act)$ whose free variables are in $\{x_1, \ldots, x_n\}$.

    Since ϕ is strictly guarded and strongly positive, so is $\psi\{\neg x_1/x_1, \ldots, \neg x_n/x_n\}$. By the induction hypothesis, there is ψ' in which no $+$ occurs such that $\psi\{\neg x_1/x_1, \ldots, \neg x_n/x_n\} \stackrel{bc}{\Leftrightarrow} \psi'$ and ψ' is strictly guarded and strongly positive. Besides,

$$\begin{aligned}
[\![\phi]\!]_\rho &= \mathcal{T}[\{\epsilon\}, \{+\}, Act, \mathcal{X}] - [\![\psi]\!]_\rho \\
&= \mathcal{T}[\{\epsilon\}, \{+\}, Act, \mathcal{X}] - [\![\psi\{\neg x_1/x_1, \ldots, \neg x_n/x_n\}]\!]_{\neg\rho} \\
&= \mathcal{T}[\{\epsilon\}, \{+\}, Act, \mathcal{X}] - [\![\psi'\{\neg x_1/x_1, \ldots, \neg x_n/x_n\}]\!]_\rho \\
&= [\![\neg\psi'\{\neg x_1/x_1, \ldots, \neg x_n/x_n\}]\!]_\rho
\end{aligned}$$

Hence, let $\phi' \widehat{=} \neg\psi'\{\neg x_1/x_1, \ldots, \neg x_n/x_n\}$. It is obvious that no + occurs in ϕ', ϕ' is strictly guarded and strongly positive and $\phi \overset{bc}{\Leftrightarrow} \phi'$.

- $\phi = \langle A \rangle \phi_1$

  As ϕ is strictly guarded and strongly positive, this implies the following two cases:
  1. ϕ_1 is equivalent to a disjunction of some formulae of the form $x_1 \wedge \cdots x_n \wedge \chi_1 \wedge \cdots \wedge \chi_\ell$, where $n, \ell \geq 0$, $x_1, \cdots, x_n \in Var$, and for each $1 \leq i \leq \ell$, $\chi_i \in \mathcal{L}_\mu(Act)$ which is strictly guarded and strongly positive;
  2. ϕ_1 is strictly guarded and strongly positive.

  In either of the two cases, by the induction hypothesis, it is easy to construct a formula ϕ' in which no + occurs such that ϕ' is strictly guarded and $\phi' \overset{bc}{\Leftrightarrow} \phi$.

- $\phi = \phi_1 + \phi_2$

  Since ϕ is strictly guarded and strongly positive, so are ϕ_1 and ϕ_2. By the induction hypothesis, there exist ϕ'_i such that ϕ'_i is strongly positive and strictly guarded, $\phi'_i \overset{bc}{\Leftrightarrow} \phi_i$ and no + occurs in ϕ'_i for $i = 1, 2$.
  We consider the following two cases:
  1. $\phi'_1 \overset{bc}{\Leftrightarrow} ff$ or $\phi'_2 \overset{bc}{\Leftrightarrow} ff$. If so, let $\phi' \widehat{=} ff$. By Lemma 5.(1), we have that $\phi'_1 + \phi'_2 \overset{bc}{\Leftrightarrow} ff$. On the other hand, by Proposition 1, it follows that $\phi \overset{bc}{\Leftrightarrow} ff$. Hence, ϕ' is what we want.
  2. $\phi'_1 \overset{bc}{\not\Leftrightarrow} ff$ and $\phi'_2 \overset{bc}{\not\Leftrightarrow} ff$. Using the laws of Boolean Algebra, Lemma 5.9–12 and Lemma 6, we can transform ϕ'_1 and ϕ'_2 equivalently as follows:

$$\phi'_1 \Leftrightarrow \bigvee_{i=1}^{m_1} (\bigwedge_{j=1}^{m_{1,i}} \bigwedge_{h=1}^{m_{1,i,j}} \langle A_{1,i,j} \rangle \phi_{1,i,j,h} \wedge \bigwedge_{j=1}^{m'_{1,i}} [B_{1,i,j}]\psi_{1,i,j}), \quad (4)$$

$$\phi'_2 \Leftrightarrow \bigvee_{i=1}^{m_2} (\bigwedge_{j=1}^{m_{2,i}} \bigwedge_{h=1}^{m_{2,i,j}} \langle A_{2,i,j} \rangle \phi_{2,i,j,h} \wedge \bigwedge_{j=1}^{m'_{2,i}} [B_{2,i,j}]\psi_{2,i,j}), \quad (5)$$

where
- $\forall 1 \leq i \leq 2, \forall 1 \leq j \leq m_i.(\forall 1 \leq k_1, k_2 \leq m_{i,j}.k_1 \neq k_2 \Rightarrow A_{i,j,k_1} \cap A_{i,j,k_2} = \emptyset) \wedge (\forall 1 \leq k_1, k_2 \leq m'_{i,j}.k_1 \neq k_2 \Rightarrow B_{i,j,k_1} \cap B_{i,j,k_2} = \emptyset) \wedge (\forall 1 \leq k_1 \leq m_{i,j}, \forall 1 \leq k_2 \leq m'_{i,j}.A_{i,j,k_1} \subseteq B_{i,j,k_2} \vee A_{i,j,k_1} \cap B_{i,j,k_2} = \emptyset))$;
- $B_{1,i_1,j_1} = B_{2,i_2,j_2}$ or $B_{1,i_1,j_1} \cap B_{2,i_2,j_2} = \emptyset$ for all $1 \leq i_1 \leq m_1$, $1 \leq j_1 \leq m'_{1,i_1}$, $1 \leq i_2 \leq m_2$, $1 \leq j_2 \leq m'_{1,i_2}$;

- for all $i = 1, 2$, $1 \leq j_1 \leq m_i$, $1 \leq k_1 \leq m_{i,j_1}$ $1 \leq j_2 \leq m_{3-i}$, $1 \leq k_2 \leq m'_{3-i,j_2}$, $A_{i,j_1,j_2} \subseteq B_{3-i,j_2,k_2}$ or $A_{i,j_1,j_2} \cap B_{3-i,j_2,k_2} = \emptyset$.

  By Lemma 5.5–8, we have

  $$\phi'_1 + \phi'_2 \overset{bc}{\Leftrightarrow} \bigvee_{i_1=1}^{m_1} \bigvee_{i_2=1}^{m_2} (\bigwedge_{j=1}^{m_{1,i_1}} \bigwedge_{h=1}^{m_{1,i_1,j}} \langle A_{1,i_1,j} \rangle \phi_{1,i_1,j,h} \wedge \bigwedge_{j=1}^{m'_{1,i_1}} [B_{1,i_1,j}]\psi_{1,i_1,j}) +$$

  $$(\bigwedge_{j=1}^{m_{2,i_2}} \bigwedge_{h=1}^{m_{2,i_2,j}} \langle A_{2,i_2,j} \rangle \phi_{2,i_2,j,h} \wedge \bigwedge_{j=1}^{m'_{2,i_2}} [B_{2,i_2,j}]\psi_{2,i_2,j}) \quad (6)$$

  Thus, according to Lemma 5 and Lemma 7, for each disjunct of the right hand of (6), there is a formula $\varphi_{i,j}$ that is equivalent to the disjunct w.r.t. BCV, strictly guarded, strongly positive and no $+$ occurs in it, where $1 \leq i \leq m_1$ and $1 \leq j \leq m_2$. So, let $\phi' \hat{=} \bigvee_{i=1}^{m_1} \bigvee_{j=1}^{m_2} \varphi_{i,j}$. It is easy to see that ϕ' meets the requirement.

- $\phi = \mu x.\phi_1$

  Since ϕ is strictly guarded and strongly positive, so is ϕ_1. Therefore, by the induction hypothesis, there exists ϕ'_1 in which no $+$ occurs such that ϕ'_1 is strictly guarded and strongly positive and $\phi'_1 \overset{bc}{\Leftrightarrow} \phi_1$. By Lemma 4, it is easy to see that $\mu x.\phi_1 \overset{bc}{\Leftrightarrow} \mu x.\phi'_1$. Thus, let $\phi' \hat{=} \mu x.\phi'_1$. ⊣

Finally, in order to encode $c\mathcal{L}^+_\mu(Act)$ into $c\mathcal{L}_\mu(Act)$, we need to show the following lemma:

Lemma 9. *For any $\phi \in c\mathcal{L}^+_\mu(Act)$, there exists $\phi' \in c\mathcal{L}^+_\mu(Act)$ such that ϕ' is strictly guarded and $\phi \Leftrightarrow \phi'$.*

Proof. In order to prove the lemma, we need to show the following equations:

$$\mu x.\phi_1[\langle A \rangle \phi_2[(x \odot \phi_3) + \phi_4]] \Leftrightarrow \mu x.\phi_1[\langle A \rangle \phi_2[\mu y.(\phi_1[\langle A \rangle \phi_2[y]] \odot \phi_3) + \phi_4]] \quad (7)$$
$$\nu x.\phi_1[\langle A \rangle \phi_2[(x \odot \phi_3) + \phi_4]] \Leftrightarrow \nu x.\phi_1[\langle A \rangle \phi_2[\nu y.(\phi_1[\langle A \rangle \phi_2[y]] \odot \phi_3) + \phi_4]] \quad (8)$$
$$\mu x.\phi_1[[A]\phi_2[(x \odot \phi_3) + \phi_4]] \Leftrightarrow \mu x.\phi_1[[A]\phi_2[\mu y.(\phi_1[[A]\phi_2[y]] \odot \phi_3) + \phi_4]] \quad (9)$$
$$\nu x.\phi_1[[A]\phi_2[(x \odot \phi_3) + \phi_4]] \Leftrightarrow \nu x.\phi_1[[A]\phi_2[\nu y.(\phi_1[[A]\phi_2[y]] \odot \phi_3) + \phi_4]] \quad (10)$$
$$\mu x.\phi_1[\langle A \rangle \phi_2[(\neg x \odot \phi_3) + \phi_4]] \Leftrightarrow \mu x.\phi_1[\langle A \rangle \phi_2[\nu y.(\neg \phi_1[\langle A \rangle \phi_2[y]] \odot \phi_3) + \phi_4]] \quad (11)$$
$$\nu x.\phi_1[\langle A \rangle \phi_2[(\neg x \odot \phi_3) + \phi_4]] \Leftrightarrow \nu x.\phi_1[\langle A \rangle \phi_2[\mu y.(\neg \phi_1[\langle A \rangle \phi_2[y]] \odot \phi_3) + \phi_4]] \quad (12)$$
$$\mu x.\phi_1[[A]\phi_2[(\neg x \odot \phi_3) + \phi_4]] \Leftrightarrow \mu x.\phi_1[[A]\phi_2[\nu y.(\neg \phi_1[[A]\phi_2[y]] \odot \phi_3) + \phi_4]] \quad (13)$$
$$\nu x.\phi_1[[A]\phi_2[(\neg x \odot \phi_3) + \phi_4]] \Leftrightarrow \nu x.\phi_1[[A]\phi_2[\mu y.(\neg \phi_1[[A]\phi_2[y]] \odot \phi_3) + \phi_4]] \quad (14)$$

where $\odot \in \{\wedge, \vee\}$, $\phi_i[\ ]$ stands for a formula with the hole $[\ ]$, the formula at the left side of each equation is guarded.

We only prove (9) as an example, the others can be proved similarly.[1]

Since $\phi_1[[A]\phi_2[(x \odot \phi_3) + \phi_4]]$ is guarded, by Knaster-Tarski Theorem, it is clear that $\mu x.\phi_1[[A]\phi_2[(x \odot \phi_3) + \phi_4]]$ is the unique least solution of the equation

$$x = \phi_1[[A]\phi_2[(x \odot \phi_3) + \phi_4]] \quad (15)$$

---

[1] Note that in the proofs for (15)–(14), we need to let $\neg y = (\neg x \odot \phi_3) + \phi_4$ in order to guarantee the resulted formulae are still positive.

Let y be a fresh variable and $y = (x \odot \phi_3) + \phi_4$. It is easy to see the least solution of (15) is equivalent to the x-component of the least solution of the following equation system:

$$x = \phi_1[[A]\phi_2[(x \odot \phi_3) + \phi_4]]$$
$$y = (x \odot \phi_3) + \phi_4$$

Meanwhile, it is easy to rewrite the above equation system to the following one

$$x = \phi_1[[A]\phi_2[y]]$$
$$y = (\phi_1[[A]\phi_2[y]] \odot \phi_3) + \phi_4$$

It is not hard to derive the least solution of the above equation system as

$$(\mu x.\phi_1[[A]\phi_2[\mu y.(\phi_1[[A]\phi_2[y]] \odot \phi_3) + \phi_4]], \mu y.(\phi_1[[A]\phi_2[y]] \odot \phi_3) + \phi_4.$$

Therefore, (9) follows.

Repeatedly applying (7)–(14), for any given formula $\phi \in c\mathcal{L}_\mu^+(Act)$, we can rewrite it to ϕ' which is strictly guarded such that $\phi \Leftrightarrow \phi'$. ⊣

Example 1. Let $\phi = \mu x.\langle A \rangle x + \mu y.[C]\neg(\langle B \rangle \neg y + \neg x) \vee \langle C \rangle tt$, where $A \cap B = B \cap C = A \cap C = \emptyset$. Applying the rewriting rule (13), it results that

$\phi \Leftrightarrow \mu x.\langle A \rangle x +$
$\quad \mu y.([C]\neg(\nu z.\neg(\langle A \rangle x + \mu y'.([C]\neg z \vee \langle C \rangle tt)) + \langle B \rangle \neg y) \vee \langle C \rangle tt$
$\Leftrightarrow \mu x.\langle A \rangle x + \mu y.([C]\neg(\nu z.\neg(\langle A \rangle x + ([C]\neg z \vee \langle C \rangle tt)) + \langle B \rangle \neg y) \vee \langle C \rangle tt$
$\Leftrightarrow \mu x.\langle A \rangle x + \mu y.([C]\neg(\nu z.\neg\langle A \rangle x + \langle B \rangle \neg y) \vee \langle C \rangle tt$
$\Leftrightarrow \mu x.\langle A \rangle x + \mu y.([C]\neg(\neg\langle A \rangle x + \langle B \rangle \neg y) \vee \langle C \rangle tt$
$\Leftrightarrow \mu x.\langle A \rangle x + \mu y.([C][B]y \vee \langle C \rangle tt)$
$\Leftrightarrow \mu x.\langle A \rangle x \vee (\langle A \rangle x \wedge \langle C \rangle tt)$
$\Leftrightarrow \mu x.\langle A \rangle x,$

where $\phi_1 = \langle A \rangle x + \mu y.([\ ] \vee \langle C \rangle tt), \phi_2 = \neg([\ ]), \phi_3 = tt, \phi_4 = \langle B \rangle \neg y$. ⊣

Note that in the above example, we can also unfold $\mu y.[C]\neg(\langle B \rangle \neg y + \neg x) \vee \langle C \rangle tt$ first, then apply Lemma 7 and obtain the same result.

Directly from Lemma 9 and Lemma 8, we can conclude:

Theorem 2. $\forall \phi \in c\mathcal{L}_\mu^+(Act), \exists \phi' \in c\mathcal{L}_\mu(Act).\phi \Leftrightarrow \phi'$.

In the later, we will use En to denote the above implicit translating function from $c\mathcal{L}_\mu^+(Act)$ to $c\mathcal{L}_\mu(Act)$.

5 Synchronization Tree Logic

[2] proposed a logic, called *Synchronization Tree Logic* (STL) for the specification and proof of programs, described by $T[\{\epsilon\}, \{+\}, Act, \mathcal{X}]$. Formulae of STL can

be obtained from the constants ϵ, $\top$ by using *logical connectives*, consistent extensions of the operators $a \in Act$, $+$ and *fixpoint operators*. Therefore, STL contains $T[\{\epsilon\}, \{+\}, Act, \mathcal{X}]$, i.e., terms of $T[\{\epsilon\}, \{+\}, Act, \mathcal{X}]$ are formulae of STL if we look recursive operators of $T[\{\epsilon\}, \{+\}, Act, \mathcal{X}]$ as greatest fixpoint operators. Its semantics is defined by associating with a formula a set of terms (synchronization trees) representing unions of congruence classes of the strong congruence relation.

Given a set Act of atomic actions and a set $\mathcal{X}$ of variables, formulae of STL are constructed by the rule:

$$\phi ::= \epsilon \mid \top \mid x \mid \neg \phi \mid B\phi \mid \phi + \phi' \mid \phi \vee \phi' \mid \mu x.\phi,$$

where $x \in \mathcal{X}$ and $B \subseteq Act$.

In what follows, we will use $\mathcal{L}_{\mathrm{STL}}(Act)$ to stand for the set of formulae of STL that are guarded and positive and $c\mathcal{L}_{\mathrm{STL}}(Act)$ for the subset of $\mathcal{L}_{\mathrm{STL}}(Act)$ in which all formulae are closed.

Definition 6. *Given a valuation $\rho \in BCV$, the semantics of $\mathcal{L}_{\mathrm{STL}}(Act)$ is given by a satisfaction relation between $T[\{\epsilon\}, \{+\}, Act, \mathcal{X}]$ and $\mathcal{L}_{\mathrm{STL}}(Act)$ relative to ρ, denoted by $\models^\rho_{\mathrm{STL}}$, inductively defined as follows:*

$$P \models^\rho_{\mathrm{STL}} \top,$$
$$P \models^\rho_{\mathrm{STL}} \epsilon \text{ iff } P \sim \epsilon,$$
$$P \models^\rho_{\mathrm{STL}} \neg \phi \text{ iff } P \not\models^\rho_{\mathrm{STL}} \phi,$$
$$P \models^\rho_{\mathrm{STL}} B\phi \text{ iff } \exists I \subseteq \mathrm{N}. I \neq \emptyset, I \text{ is finite},$$
$$\forall i \in I (\exists a_i \in B \text{ and } \exists P_i. P_i \models^\rho_{\mathrm{STL}} \phi), P \sim \Sigma_{i \in I} a_i P_i,$$
$$P \models^\rho_{\mathrm{STL}} \phi_1 \vee \phi_2 \text{ iff } P \models^\rho_{\mathrm{STL}} \phi_1 \text{ or } P \models^\rho_{\mathrm{STL}} \phi_2,$$
$$P \models^\rho_{\mathrm{STL}} \phi_1 + \phi_2 \text{ iff } \exists P_1, P_2. P_1 \models^\rho_{\mathrm{STL}} \phi_1, P_2 \models^\rho_{\mathrm{STL}} \phi_2 \text{ and } P \sim P_1 + P_2,$$
$$P \models^\rho_{\mathrm{STL}} \mu x.\phi \text{ iff } P \in \bigcap \{\mathcal{A} \mid \mathcal{A} \text{ is B.C. and } [\![\phi]\!]_{\rho[x \leadsto \mathcal{A}]} \subseteq \mathcal{A}\},$$

where $\mathcal{A} \subseteq T[\{\epsilon\}, \{+\}, Act, \mathcal{X}], B \subseteq Act$.

Some notions and derived operators can be defined similarly as in μM and μM$^+$. In what follows we will use $\bot$ to denote $\neg \top$. Note that in STL all valuations are restricted to be in BCV.

[2] proved the following results:

Proposition 4. $[\![\phi]\!]_\rho$ *is B.C., for any $\rho \in BCV$ and $\phi \in \mathcal{L}_{\mathrm{STL}}(Act)$.*

Proposition 5. *For each $P \in T[\{\epsilon\}, \{+\}, Act, \mathcal{X}]$,*

$$[\![\phi_P]\!] = \{P' \in T[\{\epsilon\}, \{+\}, Act, \mathcal{X}] \mid P \sim P'\}.$$

More results on STL can be found in [2].

6 Reducing $c\mathcal{L}_{\text{STL}}(Act)$ to $c\mathcal{L}_\mu(Act)$

In this section, we define a function $Tr : \mathcal{L}_{\text{STL}}(Act) \to \mathcal{L}_\mu^+(Act)$ such that for any $\phi \in \mathcal{L}_{\text{STL}}(Act)$, $P \in \mathcal{T}[\{\epsilon\}, \{+\}, Act, \mathcal{X}]$ and $\rho \in BCV$, $P \models_{\text{STL}}^\rho \phi$ iff $P \models_{\mu M+}^\rho Tr(\phi)$. Moreover, according to Theorem 2, for each $\phi \in c\mathcal{L}_{\text{STL}}(Act)$ and $P \in \mathcal{T}[\{\epsilon\}, \{+\}, Act, \mathcal{X}]$, $P \models_{\mu M+} Tr(\phi)$ iff $P \models_{\mu M} En(Tr(\phi))$. Thus, this completes the reduction from $c\mathcal{L}_{\text{STL}}(Act)$ to $c\mathcal{L}_\mu(Act)$.

Definition 7. *The function Tr is inductively defined as follows:* $Tr(\bot) \hat{=} ff$, $Tr(\top) \hat{=} tt$, $Tr(x) \hat{=} x$, $Tr(\epsilon) \hat{=} [Act]ff$, $Tr(\neg \phi) \hat{=} \neg Tr(\phi)$, $Tr(B\phi) \hat{=} [B]Tr(\phi) \wedge [\bar{B}]ff \wedge \langle B \rangle Tr(\phi)$, $Tr(\phi_1 \vee \phi_2) \hat{=} Tr(\phi_1) \vee Tr(\phi_2)$, $Tr(\phi_1 + \phi_2) \hat{=} Tr(\phi_1) + Tr(\phi_2)$, $Tr(\mu x.\phi) \hat{=} \mu x.Tr(\phi)$.

Theorem 3. *For any $P \in \mathcal{T}[\{\epsilon\}, \{+\}, Act, \mathcal{X}]$ and $\phi \in \mathcal{L}_{\text{STL}}(Act)$, $Tr(\phi) \in \mathcal{L}_\mu^+(Act)$ and $P \models_{\text{STL}}^\rho \phi$ iff $P \models_{\mu M+}^\rho Tr(\phi)$. Where $\rho \in BCV$.*

Proof. $Tr(\phi) \in \mathcal{L}_\mu^+(Act)$ is obvious by Definition 7, the proof for the second part can proceed by induction on the structure of ϕ. ⊣

The following theorem that follows directly from Theorem 3 and Theorem 2 indicates that applying Tr and En, STL can be translated into μM.

Theorem 4. *For all $P \in \mathcal{T}[\{\epsilon\}, \{+\}, Act, \mathcal{X}]$, $\phi \in c\mathcal{L}_{\text{STL}}(Act)$, $En(Tr(\phi)) \in c\mathcal{L}_\mu(Act)$ and $P \models_{\text{STL}} \phi$ iff $P \models_{\mu M} En(Tr(\phi))$.*

Corollary 1. *For any $P, Q \in \mathcal{T}[\{\epsilon\}, \{+\}, Act, \mathcal{X}]$, $Q \models_{\mu M} En(Tr(\phi_P))$ iff $P \sim Q$.*

Below we present an example to show how to translate a formula $\phi \in c\mathcal{L}_{\text{STL}}(Act)$ into $c\mathcal{L}_\mu(Act)$, and indicate that for any $P \in \mathcal{T}[\{\epsilon\}, \{+\}, Act, \mathcal{X}]$, $En(Tr(\phi_P))$ is exactly the characteristic formula of P up to $\sim$. Given an equivalence or preorder $\preceq$ over processes, the characteristic formula for a process P up to it is a formula ϕ_P such that given a process Q, $Q \models \phi_P$ if and only if $Q \preceq P$.

Example 2. Suppose $Act = \{a, b, c\}$, $P \hat{=} rec\, x.(a\, b\, x + a\, c\, \epsilon)$ and $Q \hat{=} rec\, x.[a\, (b\, x + c\, \epsilon)]$. Thus, by Definition 7,

$$Tr(\phi_P) \Leftrightarrow \nu x.[\langle a \rangle (\langle b \rangle x \wedge [\{\bar{b}\}]ff \wedge [b]x) \wedge [\{\bar{a}\}]ff \wedge [a](\langle b \rangle x \wedge [\{\bar{b}\}]ff \wedge [b]x)]$$
$$+ [\langle a \rangle (\langle c \rangle [Act]ff \wedge [\{\bar{c}\}]ff \wedge [c][Act]ff) \wedge [\{\bar{a}\}]ff \wedge [a](\langle c \rangle [Act]ff$$
$$\wedge [\{\bar{c}\}]ff \wedge [c][Act]ff)]$$

Moreover, we can get

$$En(Tr(\phi_P)) \Leftrightarrow \nu x.\langle a \rangle (\langle b \rangle x \wedge [\{\bar{b}\}]ff \wedge [b]x) \wedge \langle a \rangle (\langle c \rangle [Act]ff \wedge [\{\bar{c}\}]ff$$
$$\wedge [c][Act]ff) \wedge [\{\bar{a}\}]ff \wedge [a]((\langle b \rangle x \wedge [\{\bar{b}\}]ff \wedge [b]x)$$
$$\vee (\langle c \rangle [Act]ff \wedge [\{\bar{c}\}]ff \wedge [c][Act]ff))$$

It is easy to see that $En(Tr(\phi_P))$ is exactly the characteristic formula of P and $Q \not\models_{\mu M} En(Tr(\phi_P))$ since $P \not\sim Q$. ⊣

7 Concluding Remarks

In this paper, we investigated the definability of the non-deterministic operator $+$ introduced in STL as a primitive in the μ-calculus. This was captured via extending the μ-calculus with the non-deterministic operator $+$ to μM^+ first and then showing that μM^+ can be encoded into the modal μ-calculus.

Furthermore, we proved that STL can be translated into the modal μ-calculus by encoding it into μM^+. Thus, if Act is finite, we can get the decidability of STL by the decidability of the μ-calculus [5]. In fact, we could translate other STL-like modal logics into the μ-calculus, for example, it is easy to encode the modal process logic presented in [6] into the μ-calculus according to the results shown in this paper.

The converse procedure to translate $\mathcal{L}_\mu(Act)$ into $\mathcal{L}_{\text{STL}}(Act)$ can be obtained easily. Thus, we see that the μ-calculus is as expressive as STL.

In summary, the significance of this work lies in:

- We proved that the non-deterministic choice $+$ is definable in the μ-calculus, so that we can compare the expressiveness between the μ-calculus with process algebra-like modal logics such as STL, for example, it was shown in this paper that the μ-calculus is as expressive as STL.
- A connection between the connectives of the μ-calculus and the operators of $\mathcal{T}[\{\epsilon\}, \{+\}, Act, \mathcal{X}]$ has been established in this paper. This thus makes it possible that syntax-directed proofs for programs defined in terms of $\mathcal{T}[\{\epsilon\}, \{+\}, Act, \mathcal{X}]$ can be done in the μ-calculus;
- We indirectly presented an algorithm to construct the characteristic formula up to $\sim$ for a given finite-state process specified by $\mathcal{T}[\{\epsilon\}, \{+\}, Act, \mathcal{X}]$ syntactically and compositionally.

References

1. L. Aceto and M. Hennessy. Termination, deadlock, and divergence. *Journal of ACM, Vol. 39, No.1:147-187*. January, 1992.
2. S. Graf and J. Sifakis. A logic for the description of non-deterministic programs and their properties. *Information and Control*, 68:254-270. 1986.
3. C.A.R. Hoare. *Communicating Sequential Processes*. Prentice-Hall, 1985.
4. M. Hennessy and R. Milner. Algebraic laws for nondeterminism and concurrency. *Journal of ACM*, 32:137-161. Jan., 1985.
5. D. Kozen. Results on the propositional mu-calculus. *Theoretical Computer Science*, 27:333-354. 1983.
6. K.G. Larsen and B. Thomsen. A modal process logic. In the proc. of LICS'88, pp.203-210. IEEE Computer Science Society, 1988.
7. R. Milner. A complete inference system for a class of regular behaviours. *Journal of Computer and System Sciences*, 28:439-466. 1984.
8. R. Milner. *Communication and Concurrency*. Prentice Hall, 1989.
9. C. Stirling. *Modal and Temporal Properties of Processes*. Springer-Verlag, 2001.
10. A. Tarski. A lattice-theoretical fixpoint theorem and its application. *Pacific J. Math.*, 5:285-309. 1955.
11. I. Walukiewicz. Completeness of Kozen's axiomatisation of the propositional Mu-calculus. *Information and Computation*, 157:142–182. 2000.

Abstract Operational Semantics for Use Case Maps

Jameleddine Hassine[1], Juergen Rilling[1], and Rachida Dssouli[2]

[1] Department of Computer Science, Concordia University, Montreal, Canada
{j_hassin, rilling}@cs.concordia.ca
[2] Concordia Institute for Information Systems Engineering, Montreal, Canada
dssouli@ciise.concordia.ca

Abstract. Scenario-driven requirement specifications are widely used to capture and represent functional requirements. Use Case Maps (UCM) is being standardized as part of the User Requirements Notation (URN), the most recent addition to ITU−T's family of languages. UCM models allow the description of functional requirements and high-level designs at early stages of the development process. Recognizing the importance of having a well defined semantic, we propose, in this paper, a concise and rigorous formal semantics for Use Case Maps (UCM). The proposed formal semantics addresses UCM's operational semantics and covers the key language functional constructs. These semantics are defined in terms of Multi-Agent Abstract State Machines that describes how UCM specifications are executed and eliminates ambiguities hidden in the informal language definition. The resulting operational semantics are embedded in an ASM-UCM simulation engine and are expressed in AsmL, an advanced ASM-based executable specification language. The proposed ASM-UCM engine provides an environment for executing and simulating UCM specifications. We illustrate our approach using an example of a simplified call connection.

Keywords: Use Case Maps, user requirements notation, abstract state machines, formal semantics, simulation, AsmL.

1 Introduction

In the early stages of common development processes, system functionalities are defined in terms of informal requirements and visual descriptions. Scenario-driven approaches, although often semiformal, are widely accepted because of their intuitive syntax and semantics.(Amyot and Eberlein [4] provide an extensive survey of fifteen scenario notations)

Use Case Maps [12] is one of these scenario based languages that has gained momentum in recent years within the software requirements and specification community. Use Case Maps (UCMs) can be applied to capture and integrate functional requirements in terms of causal scenarios representing behavioral aspects at a higher level of abstraction, and to provide the stakeholders with guidance and reasoning about the system-wide functionalities and behavior. Use Case Maps [19] are part of a new proposal to ITU−T for a User Requirements Notation (URN) [18]. UCM notation has been baptized URN−FR, while another and complementary component for non-functional requirements is called URN−NFR. UCMs have been useful in a number of areas: Design and validation of telecommunication and distributed systems [2,3], detection and avoidance of undesirable feature interactions [13,21], evaluation of architectural alternatives [20], and performance evaluation [22].

However, the general lack of formalism and accuracy in requirement languages can cause ambiguities and misinterpretations of the specifications expressed by these languages and limit their use. This ambiguity can be removed by adding formal semantics to requirement specification languages. Moreover, this added formalism allows for a verification of specifications and their properties.

Currently, the UCM abstract syntax and static semantics are informally defined in an XML Document Type Definition [5]. However, to date the precise meaning of its execution semantics has not been captured.

In this paper, we present a formal operational semantics of UCM language in terms of *Abstract State Machines*(ASM) [16]. ASMs have been used to specify a wide variety of programming languages in particular C++ [24] and Java [10], logic programming languages such as Prolog [9] and its variants, and hardware languages such as VHDL [8]. ASMs have been also used to define the operational semantics of UML activity diagrams [7] and the formal definition of ITU−T standard SDL 2000 [15].

We tried to make this paper self-contained. In the next section, we provide an overview of the Use Case Maps notation. In section 3, we briefly introduce the basic concepts and notions of Abstract State Machines used in this paper. Section 4 gives the ASM models for Use Case Maps. In section 5, we provide an ASM-UCM engine, written in AsmL language [6], for simulating and executing UCM specifications. In section 6, we describe one possible scenario execution of the ASM model for the simplified call connection introduced in section 2.3. Finally, section 7 contains a brief discussion and a conclusion.

2 Use Case Maps Notation

2.1 Introduction

The Use Case Maps notation is a high level scenario based modeling technique used to specify functional requirements and high-level designs for various reactive and distributed systems. UCMs expressed by a simple visual notation allows for an abstract description of scenarios in terms of causal relationships between responsibilities (e.g. operation, action, task, function, etc.) along paths allocated to a set of components. These relationships are said to be causal because they involve concurrency, partial ordering of activities, and they link causes (e.g., preconditions and triggering events) to effects (e.g. postconditions and resulting events). With the UCM notation, scenarios are expressed above the level of messages exchanged between components, hence, they are not necessarily bound to a specific underlying structure (such UCMs are called *Unbound* UCMs). One of the strengths of UCMs is their ability to integrate a number of scenarios together (in a map-like diagram), and to reason about the architecture and its behavior over a set of scenarios. UCM specifications may be refined into more detailed models such as MSCs [20]. These detailed models may be transformed then into concrete implementations (possibly through automated code generation).

In the following section, we describe and illustrate the UCM core path notation. For a detailed description of the language, the reader is invited to consult [12] and [23].

2.2 UCM Functional Notation

A basic UCM path contains at least the following constructs: start points, responsibilities and end points. **Start points.** The execution of a scenario path begins at a start point. A start point is represented as a filled circle representing preconditions and/or triggering events. **Responsibilities.** Responsibilities are abstract activities that can be refined in terms of functions, tasks, procedures, events. Responsibilities are represented as crosses. **End points.** The execution of a path terminates at an end point. End points are represented as bars indicating post conditions and/or resulting effects.

UCMs help in structuring and integrating scenarios in various ways— sequentially, as alternatives (with OR-forks/joins as illustrated in Figure 1(a)) or concurrently (with AND-forks/joins as illustrated in Figure 1(b)). **OR-Forks.** represent a path where scenarios split as two or more alternative paths. An OR-Fork has one incoming hyperedge and two or more outgoing ones. Conditions (Boolean expression called guard) can be attached to alternative paths. **OR-Joins.** capture the merging of two or more independent scenario paths. **AND-Forks.** split a single control into two or more concurrent control. **AND-Joins.** capture the synchronization of two or more concurrent scenario paths.

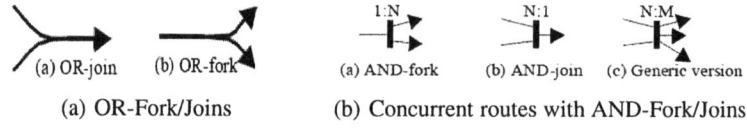

(a) OR-Fork/Joins (b) Concurrent routes with AND-Fork/Joins

Fig. 1. Structuring Scenarios

When maps become too complex to be represented as one single UCM, a mechanism for defining and structuring sub-maps becomes necessary. Path details can be hidden in sub-diagrams called plug-ins, contained in stubs (diamonds) on a path.

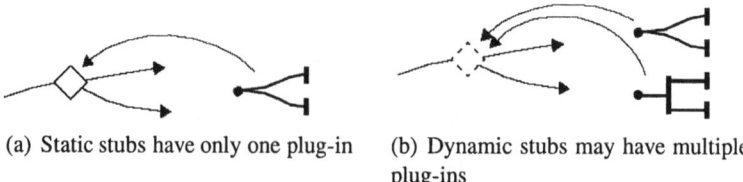

(a) Static stubs have only one plug-in (b) Dynamic stubs may have multiple plug-ins

Fig. 2. Stubs and plug-ins

2.3 Use Case Maps Example

Figure 3(a) shows a simplified call connection phase of a telephony system with one user-subscribed feature, *TeenLine* feature. This UCM is a modified version of the model originally introduced in [19]. The originating user can subscribe to the TeenLine feature which restricts outgoing calls based on the time of day (i.e., hours when homework should be the primary activity). This can be overridden on a per-call basis by anyone with the proper personal identification number. The causal path is initiated through the start point *req*. The dynamic stub *Originating* has two plug-ins:

- Default plug-in that represents how the basic call reacts in the absence of TeenLine feature (Figure 3(c)).
- TeenLine plug-in (Figure 3(b)) checks the current time (chkTime) and, if in the predefined range, requires a valid personal identification number (PIN) to be provided in a timely fashion for the call initiation to continue. If an invalid PIN is provided, or if a time-out occurs, then a denied reply is prepared (pd).

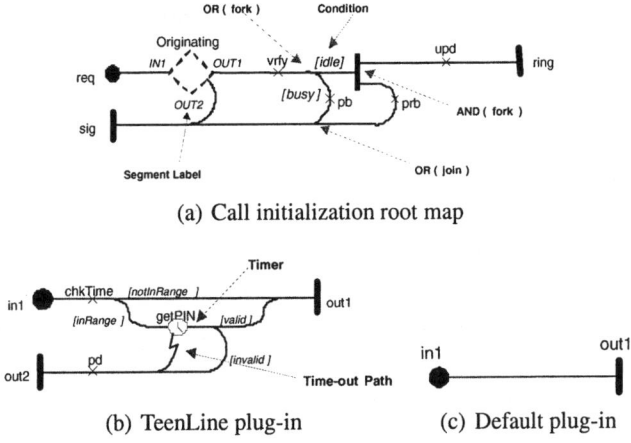

(a) Call initialization root map

(b) TeenLine plug-in   (c) Default plug-in

Fig. 3. UCM example

The stub selection policy is based on the global variable *SubTL* which determines whether the originating user has subscribed to TeenLine feature:

- *SubTL=true* → TeenLine plug-in.
- *SubTL=false* → Default plug-in.

Other global variables of the specification include also *getPIN* and *valid*. The binding relationship connects the stub path segments of the parent map to the start/end points of the plug-in. In our example, the binding relationship for the TeenLine plug-in is : {<TeenLine, IN1, in1>, <TeenLine ,OUT1, out1>,<TeenLine, OUT2, out2>} connects the stub path segments of the parent map to the start/end points of the plug-in. If the call is allowed, the system then verifies whether the called party is busy or idle (vrfy). The idle path splits the control into two concurrent paths: Ringing (ring) and signaling (sig) the occurrence of a prepared ringback reply (prb). In the case that the busy path is selected, it will result in the signaling of a prepared busy reply (pb).

3 Abstract State Machines

This section introduces some basic notions of ASM [16], that will be employed for the construction of our UCM model. For a rigorous mathematical definition of the semantic foundations of ASMs, we however refer to [11,16].

Abstract State Machines define a state-based computational model, where computations (runs) are finite or infinite sequences of states $\{S_i\}$ obtained from a given initial state S_0 by repeatedly executing transitions δ_i.

$$S_0 \xrightarrow{\delta_1} S_1 \xrightarrow{\delta_2} S_2 \quad \cdots \quad \xrightarrow{\delta_n} S_n$$

An ASM A is defined over a fixed vocabulary V, a finite collection of function names and relation names. Each function symbol has a fixed arity n and type $T_1,\ldots,T_n \to T$ where T_i and T are basic types. Names in V may be **(1) Static:** having the same (fixed) interpretation in each computation state of A **(2) Dynamic:** where function names can be altered by transitions fired in a computation step or, **(3) External:** its interpretation is determined by the environment (thus, not controlled by the system).

Given a vocabulary, A is defined by its program P and a set of distinguished initial states S_0. The program P consists of transition rules and specifies possible state transitions of A in terms of finite sets of local function *updates* on a given global state. Such transitions are atomic actions. A transition rule that describes the modification of the functions from one state to the next has the following form:
if Condition then <Updates> else <Updates> endif, where *Updates* is a set of function updates $f(t_1,t_2,\ldots,t_n) := t$ which are simultaneously executed when Condition is true. A state transition is performed by firing a set of rules in one step. Each function update changes a value at a specific location given by the left-hand-side of the update.

ASMs are multi-sorted based on the notion of universes. We presume the standard mathematic universes of Booleans, integers, lists, etc. as well as the standard operations on them such as the usual Boolean operations ($\land$, $\lor$ .etc.). A universe can be dynamically extended with individual objects by:
extend Universe with v <Rule> end extend, where v is a variable which is bound by the extend constructor.

The choose constructor defines an arbitrary selection of one element in a universe:
choose v in Universe <Rule> end choose, where v is non-deterministically selected from the given universe. The choose constructor can be qualified by a condition.

A distributed ASM (called also *Multi-Agent ASM*) involves a collection of agents that perform their computation concurrently. The agents are elements of a dynamic universe AGENT that may grow and shrink over a run. Each agent $a \in$ AGENT is viewed as an object of class AGENT and can identify itself by means of a special nullary function *me*:AGENT. The program of an agent a is a method of the class AGENT. The state of a (given by all fields of a) evolves in sequential steps with each invocation of its program. We assume that there is one program, prog, shared by all agents.

4 ASM Models for Use Case Maps

The definition of the ASM formal semantics of UCM consists of associating each UCM construct with an ASM which models its behavior. In this section, we associate an ASM signature to each UCM construct then we assign execution rules to them.

4.1 Signature of UCM Constructs

The UCM maps are modeled using the abstract sets: *StartPoint, EndPoint, Responsibility, AND-Fork, AND-Join, OR-Fork, OR-Join, Stub* and *Timer*. We define also the abstract set *HyperEdge* that represents the set of hyperedges connecting UCM constructs.

Start Points are of the form *StartPoint(PreCondition-set, TriggerringEvent-set, StartLabel, in, out)* where the parameter *PreConditions-set* is a list of conditions that must be satisfied in order for the scenario to be enabled (if no precondition is specified, then by default it is set to true). The parameter *TriggeringEvents-set* is a list that gives the set of events that can initiate the scenario along a path. One event is sufficient for triggering the scenario. The parameter *StartLabel* denotes the label of the start point. A start point should not have an incoming edge except when connected to an end point (called a waiting place). In such situation, we use the parameter *in* $\in$ *HyperEdge* to represent the connection with an end point. The parameter *out* $\in$ *HyperEdge* is the (unique) outgoing hyperedge.

End Points are of the form *EndPoint(PostCondition-set, ResultingEvent-set, EndLabel, in, out)* where the parameter *PostConditions-set* is a list of conditions that must be satisfied once the scenario is completed. The parameter *ResultingEvent-set* is a list that gives the set of events that result from the completion of the scenario path. The parameter *EndLabel* denotes the label of the end point; the parameter *in* $\in$ *HyperEdge* is the (unique) incoming hyperedge. End points have no target hyperedge except when connected to a start point (i.e. a waiting place). In such a case, *out* $\in$ *HyperEdge* represents such connection.

Responsibilities are of the form *Responsibility(in, Resp, out)* where *in* $\in$ *HyperEdge* is the incoming hyperedge, *Resp* is the responsibility to be executed (to be defined by a set of simultaneous ASM function updates), and *out* $\in$ *HyperEdge* is the outgoing hyperedge. A responsibility is connected to only one source hyperedge and to one target hyperedge.

OR-Forks are of the form *OR-Fork(in, $[Cond_i]_{i \leq n}$, $[out_i]_{i \leq n}$)* where *in* denotes the incoming hyperedge, $[Cond_i]_{i \leq n}$ is a finite sequence of Boolean expressions, and $[out_i]_{i \leq n}$ is a sequence of outgoing hyperedges.

OR-Joins are of the form *OR-Join($\{in_i\}_{i \leq n}$, out)* where $\{in_i\}_{i \leq n}$ denotes the incoming hyperedges and, *out* is the outgoing hyperedge.

AND-Forks are of the form *AND-Fork(in, $\{out_i\}_{i \leq n}$)* where *in* denotes the incoming hyperedge, and $\{out_i\}_{i \leq n}$ is a sequence of outgoing hyperedges.

AND-Joins are of the form *AND-Join($\{in_i\}_{i \leq n}$, out)* where $\{in_i\}_{i \leq n}$ denotes the incoming hyperedges, and *out* is the outgoing hyperedge.

Timers are of the form *Timer(in, TriggerringEvent-set, out, out_timeout)* where *in* denotes the incoming hyperedge. The parameter *TriggeringEvents-set* is the list that gives the set of events that can trigger the continuation path (i.e. represented by *out*) and the parameter *out_timeout* ∈ *HyperEdge* denotes the timeout path.

Stubs have the form $Stub(\{entry_i\}_{i \leq n}, \{exit_j\}_{j \leq m}, isDynamic, [Cond_k]_{k \leq l}, [plugin_k]_{k \leq l})$ where $\{entry_i\}_{i \leq n}$ and $\{exit_j\}_{j \leq m}$ denote respectively the set of the stub entry and exit points. *isDynamic* indicates whether the stub is dynamic or static. Dynamic stubs may contain multiple plug-ins, $[plugin_k]_{k \leq l}$ whose selection can be determined at run-time according to a selection-policy specified by the sequence of Boolean expressions $[Cond_k]_{k \leq l}$. The sequence Cond is empty for static stubs (i.e. *isDynamic=false*).

For each UCM construct we use a (static) function Param which, when applied to constructs yields the parameter. For example *in(StartPoint)* yields the incoming hyperedge of the construct StartPoint. We often suppress parameters notationally.

We formalize UCM maps by an abstract set MAPS. It contains the root map (i.e. the main UCM map) and all its submaps (i.e. plug-ins).

The nesting structure of a UCM specification is encoded in the following functions:

- UpMap: MAPS → MAPS ∪ $\{undef\}$, assigns to a plug-in its immediately enclosing map, if any. We assume that this function yields *undef* for the root map which is not enclosed in any map. Thus, *UpMap(rootMap)=undef*.
- StubBinding:$\{\{entry_i\} \cup \{EndPoints\}\} \times$ MAPS $\rightarrow \{\{StartPoints\} \cup \{exit_j\}\}$ specifies how a plug-in ∈MAPS is bound to a stub. The path segments that are connected to the stub need to be bound to the paths of the plug-ins in order to express continuity. This is done through explicit binding. An entry hyperedge joins a stub entry with a start point from the plug-in. An exit hyperedge joins a stub exit with an end point from the same plug-in.

In the following section, we define the ASM rules that define the operational semantics used to express the UCM control constructs.

4.2 ASM Rules of UCM Constructs

Let AGENT be the abstract set of agents *a* which move through their associated UCM map, by executing the UCM construct at the current active hyperedge, i.e. the hyperedge where the agent's control lies.

Every agent can mainly be characterized by three dynamic functions:

- active: AGENT→HyperEdge represents the identifier of the active hyperedge leading to the next UCM construct to be executed.
- mode: AGENT→ $\{running, inactive\}$. An agent may be running in normal mode or inactive once the agent has finished its computation.
- level: AGENT→MAPS gives the submap that the agent is currently traversing.

For the root map, it is required that there is an agent for each starting point, in running mode with active hyperedges positioned on the corresponding start points of the root map (i.e. active=in(StartPoint)). The creation of the initial ASM agents, their initialization and the initialization of the global variables used in the scenario definitions represent the initialization phase.

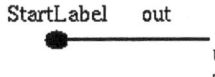

if CurrConstruct is StartPoint(PreCondition-set, TriggerringEvent-set, StartLabel, in, out) then
  if (EvaluatePreConditions & EvaluateTrigger) then me.active:= out
  where:
  - EvaluateTrigger: TriggerringEvent-set × {events} → Boolean; evaluates whether the set of events occurring at StartPoint are included in the TriggeringEvent-set.
  - EvaluatePreConditions: PreCondition-set → Boolean evaluates whether all preconditions are satisfied.

Fig. 4. Rule Start Point

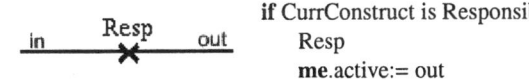

if CurrConstruct is Responsibility (in,Resp,out) then
  Resp
  me.active:= out

Fig. 5. Rule Responsibility

Typically, a running agent has to look at the target of its currently active hyperedge to determine the next action. CurrConstruct denotes the current UCM construct to be executed, i.e. the UCM construct where **me**.active=in(construct)∧**me**.mode=running.

In the following, we assign ASM execution rules to UCM constructs.

Start Points. If the control is on the hyperedge *in(StartPoint)*, the *PreCondition-set* is satisfied and there occurs at least one event from the *triggeringEvent-set*, then the start point is triggered and the control passes to the outgoing hyperedge of the StartPoint (Otherwise nothing happens and the control stays at the StartPoint). Figure 4 describes the start point rule.

Responsibilities. Responsibilites represent atomic actions, not to be decomposable, and their execution is not interruptible. If the control is on the hyperedge *in(Responsibility)* then *Resp* is performed and the control passes to the outgoing hyperedge.

If the control is on the incoming hyperedge of an OR-Fork, the conditions are evaluated and the control passes to the hyperedge associated to the true condition. If more than one condition evaluates to true (i.e. nondeterministic choice), the control passes randomly to one of the outgoing hyperedges associated to the true conditions. Figure 6 illustrates the OR-Fork rule.

When one or many flows reach an OR-Join, the control passes to the outgoing hyperedge. Figure 7 illustrates the OR-Join rule.

Note:An UCM loop can be modeled as an OR-Fork followed by an OR-Join. Their respective rules should be executed once encountered.

When the control is on an hyperedge entering an AND-Fork synchronization bar, then the flow is split into two or more flows of control. The currently running agent creates the necessary new subagents and sets their mode to running, then sets its mode to inactive. Each new ASM subagent inherits the program for executing UCMs, and its control is started on the associated outgoing hyperedge of the AND-Fork.

When many subagents running in parallel reach an AND-Join, their parallel flow must be joined. When all incoming hyperedges become active, a new agent is created

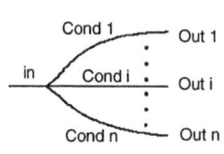

if CurrConstruct is OR-Fork(in, $[Cond_i]_{i \leq n}, [out_i]_{i \leq n}$)
then if NonDeterministicChoice($[Cond_i]_{i \leq n}$) **then**
  me.active:= (**choose** out_i **in** $[out_k]_{k \leq l}$)
 else if $Cond_1$ **then me**.active:=out_1
  ...
 if $Cond_n$ **then me**.active:= out_n
where NonDeterministicChoice:{Cond}→Boolean is a dynamic function that checks whether more than one condition evaluates to true and $[out_k]_{k \leq l}$ is the sequence of hyperedges associated to satisfied conditions.

Fig. 6. Rule OR-Fork

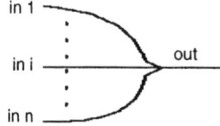

if CurrConstruct is OR-Join($\{in_i\}_{i \leq n}$, out) **then**
 me.active:= out

Fig. 7. Rule OR-Join

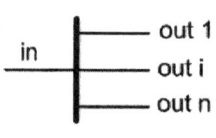

if CurrConstruct is AND-Fork(in, $\{out_i\}_{i \leq n}$) **then**
 me.mode:=inactive
 extend AGENT **with** $a_1, \ldots, a_n$
 do for all a_i, $1 \leq i \leq n$
  a_i.mode := running
  a_i.active := out_i

Fig. 8. Rule AND-Fork

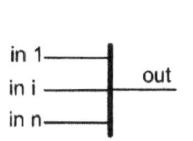

if CurrConstruct is AND-Join($\{in_i\}_{i \leq n}$, out)
then if not ($\forall a_1, \ldots, a_n \; in_i = active(a_i)$) **then**
  me.mode:= inactive
 else me.mode:= inactive
  extend AGENT **with** a_{n+1}
  a_{n+1}.active:= out
  a_{n+1}.mode:= running

Fig. 9. Rule AND-Join

and the control passes to the outgoing hyperedge. The last agent arriving to the AND-Join will fire the rule. Inactive agents are deleted after each rule's execution. For the clarity's sake, we have omitted the *Garbage Collection* from all our ASM rules.

Once the control reaches a stub, the control passes to the selected plug-in and the execution continues following the UCM semantics. No extra agents are needed to execute a *Stub* unless the selected plug-in contains a concurrent flow.

When the control reaches an end point, two cases should be considered, depending on whether the end point is inside a plug-in or part of the root map:

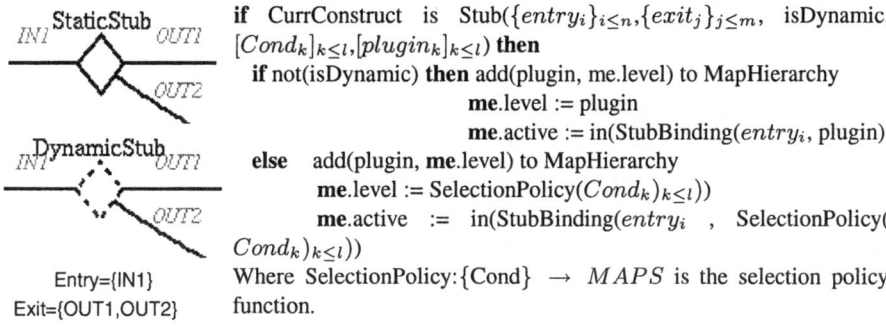

if CurrConstruct is Stub($\{entry_i\}_{i\leq n}, \{exit_j\}_{j\leq m}$, isDynamic, $[Cond_k]_{k\leq l}, [plugin_k]_{k\leq l}$) then
    if not(isDynamic) then add(plugin, me.level) to MapHierarchy
        me.level := plugin
        me.active := in(StubBinding($entry_i$, plugin)
    else add(plugin, me.level) to MapHierarchy
        me.level := SelectionPolicy($(Cond_k)_{k\leq l}$))
        me.active := in(StubBinding($entry_i$, SelectionPolicy($(Cond_k)_{k\leq l}$))
Where SelectionPolicy:{Cond} $\rightarrow$ $MAPS$ is the selection policy function.

Entry={IN1}
Exit={OUT1,OUT2}

Fig. 10. Rule Stub

if CurrConstruct is EndPoint(PostCondition-set,ResultingEvent-set, EndLabel, in, out)then if UpMap(me.level)$\neq$undef) then
        me.active:= out(StubBinding(EndPoint, me.level))
    elseif out$\neq$undef then me.active := out
    else me.mode:= inactive

Fig. 11. Rule End Point

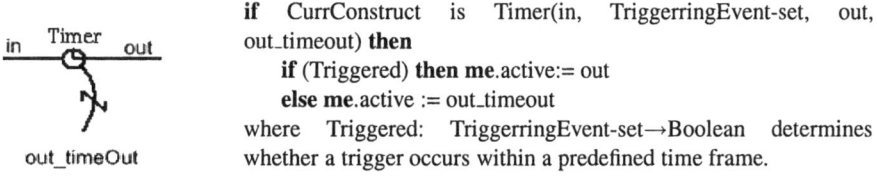

if CurrConstruct is Timer(in, TriggerringEvent-set, out, out_timeout) then
    if (Triggered) then me.active:= out
    else me.active := out_timeout
where Triggered: TriggerringEvent-set$\rightarrow$Boolean determines whether a trigger occurs within a predefined time frame.

Fig. 12. Rule Timer

1. End point is inside a plug-in: the control passes to the stub's exit point bound to the plug-in end point.
2. End point is part of the root map: the control passes to the out hyperedge if any (e.g. a waiting place) otherwise the running agent is stopped.

The exit from nested maps should be performed in the correct order of the stub structure. However, one control may exit the stub while another one is still inside the stub.

The timer rule is very similar to a basic OR-Fork rule with only two disjoint branches (out and out_timeOut).

5 ASM-UCM Simulation Engine

The ASM-UCM simulation engine is designed for simulating and executing UCM specifications. It is written in AsmL [6], a high level executable specification language developed by the Foundations of Software Engineering (FSE) group at Microsoft Research. AsmL is integrated with Microsoft's software development, documentation and runtime

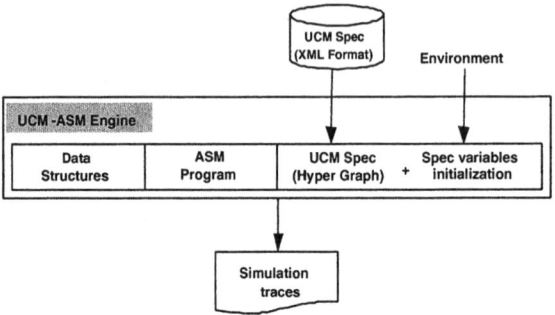

Fig. 13. ASM-UCM Simulation Engine Architecture

Enum Mode	**case** R_Construct
running	in_hy as HyperEdge
inactive	out_hy as HyperEdge
structure UCMElement	label as String
source as UCMConstruct	**case** OF_Construct
hyper as HyperEdge	in_hy as HyperEdge
target as UCMConstruct	Selec as Set of OR_Selection
type Maps = Set of UCMElement	**case** Stub_Construct
structure UCMConstruc	entry_hy as Set of HyperEdge
case SP_Construct	exit_hy as Set of HyperEdge
in_hy as HyperEdge	Selec_plugin as Set of Stub_Selection
out_hy as HyperEdge	Binding_Relation as Set of Stub_Binding
label as String	label as String
preCondition as Boolean	**case** ...

Fig. 14. Data Structures

environments including Visual Studio, Word and Component Object Model (COM). It has full .NET interoperability. Figure 13 shows the structure of the ASM-UCM simulation engine, which is composed of the following three components:

5.1 UCM Specification

In order to apply ASM rules defined in section 4, the UCM specification (originally described in XML format) should be translated into a hyper graph format where constructs are connected using hyperedges. For this purpose, we define a UCM specification as a hyper graph: SPEC = (C, H, λ) where:

- C is the set of UCM constructs composed of sets of typed constructs.
- H is the set of hyperedges
- λ is a transition relation (path connection) defined as: $\lambda = C \times H \times C$

Note: The translation from the XML format to hyper-graph format is done manually. Before a simulation can be run, the specification's global variables are initialized.

class Agent
    const id as String
    var active as HyperEdge
    var mode as Mode
    var level as Maps
Program()
step
    until me.mode = inactive **do**
        choose h **in** level **where** HyperExists(active, GetInHyperEdge(h.source))
        match (h.source)
    // Rule of Start Point
        SP_Construct (a,b,c,d): **me**.active := b
    // Rule of Responsibility
        R_Construct (a,b,c): Execute(h.source)
                             me.active := b
    // Rule of OR-Fork ...
	main()
	step
	    forall s in StartPoints
	        let ag=new Agent(label(s), in(s),
	running, RootMap, init_stub)
	            ag.Program()

Fig. 15. ASM-UCM program

5.2 Data Structures

The data structures maintained by the ASM-UCM engine are AsmL structures and dynamic sets. They encode the attribute information of UCM constructs and the structures that handle the dynamic flow of execution. The listing below shows part of the AsmL data structures used in ASM-UCM simulation engine. For instance, *Mode* is a static universe where each element is a static nullary function, *UCMElement* represents the structure of the transition relation λ, and *UCMConstruct* structure incorporates many case statements as a way of organizing different variant of UCM constructs.

5.3 ASM Program

The listing below illustrates the class *Agent* and the main program of the ASM-UCM simulation engine.

6 ASM Execution of the Simplified Call Connection

In this section, we will describe one possible scenario execution of the ASM model for the simplified call connection introduced in section 2.3.

During the initialization phase the main agent *Root* is created and the global variables are initialized (i.e.,SubTL=true;InRange=true;getPIN=true;valid=true). The start point *req* rule is executed, and the control goes to the hyperedge *IN1*. The Stub rule is then executed. The function *SelectionPolicy* selects the plug-in *TeenLine* and the control passes to *in(StubBinding(IN1, SelectionPolicy(SubTL)))* which is the incoming hyperedge of the startpoint in_1. Responsibility *ChkTime* is observed, control passes to hyperedge *e12*, then the timer is triggered and, a valid PIN is entered. When the control

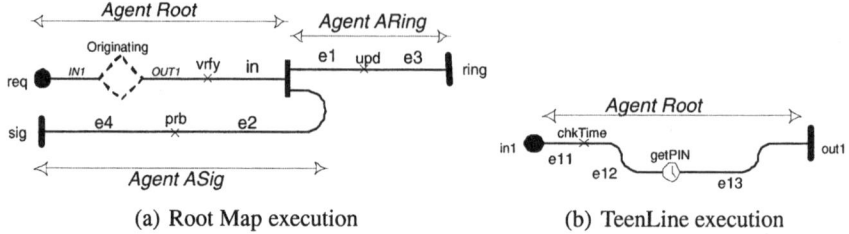

(a) Root Map execution (b) TeenLine execution

Fig. 16. Execution Trace

reaches the end point out_1, the EndPoint rule is executed, and the control passes to *out(StubBinding(EndPoint,level))* which is the hyperedge *OUT1*. Then the responsibility *vrf* is observed, and the control passes to the incoming hyperedge of the AND-Fork (i.e. hyperedge *in*). When the main agent *Root* reaches the AND-Fork, it creates two new agents *ARing* and *ASig* and changes it mode to *inactive*. These two agents start their execution respectively at the AND-Fork's upper and lower outgoing hyperedges (i.e. respectively hyperedges *e1* and *e2*). In our implementation, agents *ARing* and *ASign* evolve in an interleaving mode. Agent *ARing* executes responsibility *upd* and terminates while agent *ASig* executes *prb* then terminates. An ASM scheduler may be designed to have concurrent agents behave in true concurrency mode. Choosing the suitable concurrent execution semantics depends on the application domain and the design choices.

7 Discussion and Conclusion

In this paper, we have presented a formal operational semantics for Use Case Maps language based on Multi-Agent Abstract State Machines. Our ASM model provides a concise semantics of UCM functional constructs and describes precisely the control semantics.

Our approach based on ASM is more abstract and more flexible than the one given in [1] in terms of LOTOS [17]. Indeed, our ASM rules can be easily modified to accommodate language evolution. Considering new semantics for a UCM construct, result in changing the corresponding ASM rule without modifying the original specification. While in [1], one needs to redesign the mapping between UCM to LOTOS and to re-generate the LOTOS specification. Moreover, our ASM-UCM simulation engine may support different concurrency semantics at minimal cost. Agents may behave either in interleaving semantics with atomic actions (i.e. comparable to LOTOS processes) or in true concurrency mode. The choice of the suitable alternative depends on the application domain and the ASM program (i.e., ASM Scheduler) is designed accordingly.

We showed that ASMs are, in general, suitable to provide a formal representation of Use Case Maps constructs. The proposed semantics can be seen as a complementary, unambiguous documentation approach that provides additional insights of the UCM language and its notation, as well as a basis for future formal verification of UCM. As part of our future work, we will investigate the use of ASM model checking technique [14] to verify UCM specifications.

References

1. Amyot D., Formalization of Timethreads Using LOTOS. Master Thesis, Department of Computer Science, University of Ottawa, Canada, 1994.
2. Amyot D. and Andrade R., Description of wireless intelligent network services with Use Case Maps, SBRC'99, 17th Simpósio Brasileiro de Redes de Computadores, Salvador, Brazil, May 1999, pp. 418-433.
3. Amyot D., Buhr R.J.A., Gray T. and Logrippo L., Use Case Maps for the Capture and Validation of Distributed Systems Requirements. RE'99, Fourth IEEE International Symposium on Requirements Engineering, Limerick, Ireland, June 1999,44-53. http://www.UseCaseMaps.org/pub/re99.pdf
4. Amyot D. and Eberlein A., An Evaluation of Scenario Notations and Construction Approaches for Telecommunication Systems Development. In: Telecommunications Systems Journal, 24:1, 61-94, September 2003.
5. Amyot D. and Miga, A., Use Case Maps Document Type Definition 0.19. Working document, June 2000. http://www.UseCaseMaps.org/xml/
6. AsmL for Microsoft.Net, http://www.research.microsoft.com/foundations/asml, 2003
7. Börger E., Cavarra A. and Riccobene E., An ASM Semantics for UML Activity Diagrams. In T. Rus, editor, Proc. Algebraic Methodology and Software Technology, 8th International Conference, AMAST 2000, LNCS 1826. Springer, 2000.
8. Börger E., Glässer U. and Muller W., Formal Definition of an Abstract VHDL'93 Simulator By EA-Machines. In C. Delgado Kloos and P. T. Breuer, eds., Formal Semantics for VHDL, 107-139. Kluwer Academic Publishers, 1995.
9. Börger E. and Rosenzweig D., A mathematical definition of full Prolog. In Science of Computer Programming, vol. 24, 249-286. North-Holland, 1994.
10. Börger E. and Schulte W., Defining the Java Virtual Machine as Platform for Provably Correct Java Compilation. In L. Brim, J. Gruska, and J. Zlatuska, editors, Mathematical Foundations of Computer Science, MFCS 98, Lecture Notes in Computer Science. Springer, 1998.
11. Börger E. and Stärk R., Abstract State Machines: A Method for High-Level System Design and Analysis. Springer-Verlag, 2003.
12. Buhr, R. J. A., Use Case Maps as Architectural Entities for Complex Systems. In: IEEE Transactions on Software Engineering, 24(12) (Dec. 1998) 1131-1155.
13. Buhr R. J. A., Elammari M., Gray T. and Mankovski S., Applying Use Case Maps to multi-agent systems: A feature interaction example. In 31st Annual Hawaii International Conference on System Sciences, 1998.
14. Del Castillo G. and Winter K., Model checking support for the ASM high-level language. In S. Graf and M. Schwartzbach, editors, 6th International Conference for Tools and Algorithms for the Construction and Analysis of Systems (TACAS 2000), volume 1785 of LNCS, pp 331-346. Springer-Verlag, 2000.
15. Eschbach R., Glässer U., Gotzhein R., von Löwis M. and Prinz A., Formal Definition of SDL−2000 - Compiling and Running SDL Specifications as ASM Models. In Journal of Universal Computer Science, 7 (11): 1025-1050, Springer Pub. Co., Nov. 2001.
16. Gurevich Y., Evolving algebra 1993: Lipari guide. In E. Börger, editor, Specification and Validation Methods. Oxford University Press, Oxford, 1995.
17. ISO, Information Processing Systems, OSI: LOTOS - A Formal Description Technique Based on the Temporal Ordering of Observational Behaviour. IS 8807, Geneva, 1989.
18. ITU-T, Recommendation Z.150, User Requirements Notation (URN)- Language Requirements and Framework, Geneva, Switzerland. http://www.UseCaseMaps.org/urn/
19. ITU-T, URN Focus Group (2002), Draft Rec. Z.152 - UCM: Use Case Map Notation (UCM). Geneva.

20. Miga A., Amyot D., Bordeleau F., Cameron C. and Woodside M., Deriving Message Sequence Charts from Use Case Maps Scenario Specifications. Tenth SDL Forum (SDL'01), Copenhagen, 2001. LNCS 2078, 268-287.
21. Nakamura N., Kikuno T., Hassine J., and Logrippo L., Feature Interaction Filtering with Use Case Maps at Requirements Stage. In: Sixth International Workshop on Feature Interactions in Telecommunications and Software Systems (FIW'00), Glasgow, Scotland, UK, May 2000.
22. Petriu. D. C. and Woodside M., Software Performance Models from System Scenarios in Use Case Maps, Proceedings of the 12th International Conference on Computer Performance Evaluation, Modelling Techniques and Tools, p.141-158, April 14-17, 2002.
23. Use Case Maps Web Page and UCM Users Group, 1999. http://www.UseCaseMaps.org
24. Wallace C., The Semantics of the C++ Programming Language. In E. Börger, editor, Specification and Validation Methods. Oxford University Press, 1995.

ArchiTRIO: A UML-Compatible Language for Architectural Description and Its Formal Semantics

Matteo Pradella[2], Matteo Rossi[1], and Dino Mandrioli[1,2]

[1] Dipartimento di Elettronica e Informazione, Politecnico di Milano
[2] CNR IEIIT-MI, Piazza Leonardo da Vinci 32, 20133 Milano, Italy
{pradella, rossi, mandrioli}@elet.polimi.it

Abstract. ArchiTRIO [14] is a formal language, which complements UML 2.0 concepts with a formal, logic-based notation that allows users to state system-wide properties, both static and dynamic, including real-time constraints. In this paper we present the semantics of the core concepts of the ArchiTRIO language. As the core elements of ArchiTRIO coincide with those of UML 2.0 (operation, interface, port, class), the semantics of ArchiTRIO provides also a formal definition for the basic concepts on which UML 2.0 is built.

Keywords: UML, software architecture, formal methods, real-time.

1 Introduction

In the last few years, UML [8] has risen to the status of *de facto* standard for system modeling in industrial practice. Its appeal originates from a number of factors such as ease of use and a certain degree of intuitiveness and flexibility in the notation (probably rooted in the borrowing form previous, well-established notations), which reduce the effort needed to be able to write UML models to a minimum. In its 2.0 incarnation, UML includes constructs (e.g., component, connector, port) that were previously missing, which are necessary for describing system architectures. Alas, as with the previous versions, UML lack of formality hampers its applicability to critical systems, where precise and rigorous designs are of the utmost importance for the correct development of the application.

In [14] we sketched a novel approach to providing UML with the degree of formality that is necessary for rigorous modeling and verification, one that hinges on the idea of *complementing* the UML notation of class and composite structure diagrams [8] with a temporal logic-based notation. This combination of UML and logic-based notation results in a formal language, called ArchiTRIO. [14] presents the ArchiTRIO approach to system modeling, which falls essentially in the category of lightweight methods [16]; more precisely, ArchiTRIO allows developers to use standard UML 2.0 notation to describe non-critical aspects of systems, but it also offers a complementary formal notation, fully integrated with the UML one, to represent those system aspects that require precise modeling.

ArchiTRIO, then, adds expressive power to UML diagrams, rather than replacing or modifying any of them: a user who at first does not need full-blown ArchiTRIO can start by drawing bare UML class diagrams, and only later, when the need arises for clarity and precision (especially for temporal constraints), introduce ArchiTRIO-specific notation.

ArchiTRIO is based upon few selected UML 2.0 constructs especially suited for describing architectures, it gives them a formal meaning, and precisely defines their composition. [14] mainly focuses on the principles behind ArchiTRIO and suggests guidelines for its application. This paper presents in some detail the semantics of the language. The semantics of ArchiTRIO is given in terms of HOT (Higher-Order TRIO), which is a higher-order extension of our previous first-order temporal logic TRIO [4]. We chose to found ArchiTRIO on a higher-order logic to allow for the concise representation of mechanisms such as the passing of parameters that have an ArchiTRIO/UML class for a type.

In our opinion, the distinguishing feature of HOT is its simplicity, rooted in the rigorous application of the principle of identifying the concepts of class and of abstract data type (see, e.g. [1]), which is seldom completely pursued in traditional object-oriented languages. Since ArchiTRIO has many concepts in common with UML (class, port, etc.), providing a semantics for the former amounts also to giving a formal definition for a number of UML elements.

This paper is structured as follows: Section 2 briefly summarizes the features of ArchiTRIO presented in [14]; Section 3 provides an overview of HOT and of its set-theoretic semantics; Section 4 builds upon it to define the semantics of ArchiTRIO; Section 5 compares the present work with some relevant literature, and especially with the OCL [7]; finally, Section 6 draws some conclusions and hints at future works in this area of research.

2 A Brief Overview of ArchiTRIO

In this section, we briefly summarize the ArchiTRIO approach originally presented in [14], and introduce a simple running example, an access control system for a building divided into areas having different security levels, which we will use throughout this article to illustrate the features of ArchiTRIO.

Consider an Access Control System used in one or more corporate buildings having three different security levels: *low, medium,* and *high*. The building may contain zero or more areas of a given security level. The access control is enforced essentially through two kinds of entities: a local mechanism based on the concept of *security gate*, and a *central control* connected to a user database.

Figure 1 shows the UML class diagram describing the situation above. It depicts a `CentralControl` class, the main entity which enforces the prescribed security policy for user access; a `UserDB`, that is a database containing users' sensible data and their actual security clearance; and three kinds of `Gate` classes: `SimpleGate`, `MediumSecurityGate`, and `HighSecurityGate`, in charge of managing the local access to areas with low, medium, and high security level, respectively. Every gate has a *port* of type `GatePort`, while `CentralControl` has

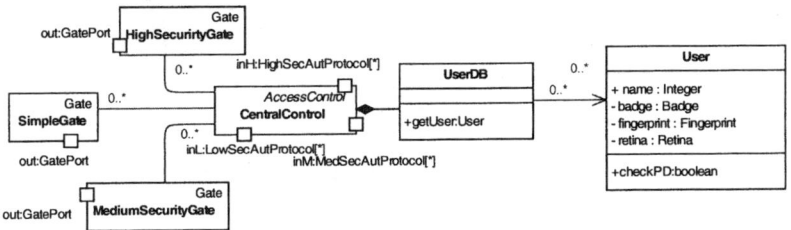

Fig. 1. Access Control System: the high-level class diagram

three different ports, LowSecAutProtocol, MedSecAutProtocol, and HighSec
AutProtocol that are used to communicate with SimpleGates, Medium
SecurityGates, and HighSecurityGates, respectively.

Moving in a top-down fashion, we now define the internal class structure
of the gates (for space reasons, we omit the corresponding diagram; the interested reader can refer to [14]). A SimpleGate is an entity having one or
more BadgeReaders (a subclass of IdRecognizer), managed by a local controller
LC_SimpleGate. Communication between BadgeReader and LC_SimpleGate is
based on the interface LocalControl, implemented by the latter.

A MediumSecurityGate is based on a more sophisticated IdRecognizer, i.e. a
FingerprintsReader, and has an EntrySensor. Analogously to the simple gate,
a medium security gate is supervised by a local controller, LC_MedSecGate, and
communication between the local controller and the sensors is based on the interface LocalControl. The most complex type of gate is the HighSecurityGate:
it consists of two kinds of IdRecognizers, a FingerprintsReader and a
RetinaScanner; an EntrySensor; and a local controller LC_HighSecGate. A high
security gate is opened only after both the user's fingerprints and retina are successfully checked.

Consider now for instance the structure of a high security gate (Figure 2). It
consists of a retina scanner (RS), a fingerprints reader (FR), an entry sensor (ES),
and a local control (LC). Every component is an instance of the corresponding class; LC exchanges data with the sensors by implementing the interface
LocalControl, while communication with the remote central control happens
through a replicated port of type GatePort.

Finally, consider the system high-level architecture (Figure 3). It consists of:
a central control (CC); two low security gates (Entrance and BackDoor); two

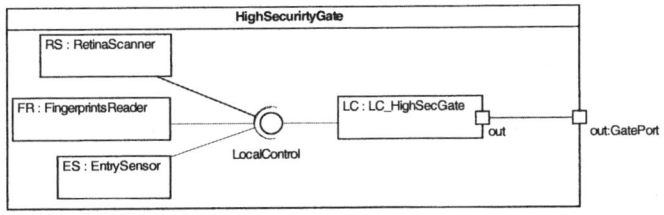

Fig. 2. Composite structure diagram of a high security gate

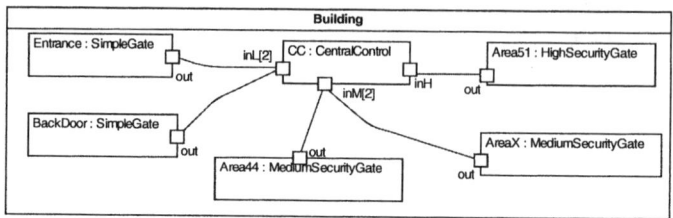

Fig. 3. The building structure: the high-level system architecture

medium security areas and their corresponding gates (`AreaX` and `Area44`); and one high security area reachable through a high security gate (`Area51`).

This concludes a first simple architectural description of the system, based exclusively on UML constructs. As we said in the introduction, UML *per se* does not precisely define many of the constructs we used for describing our system here. For instance, it lacks a precise definition of timeouts management and local control behavior. More generally, we would like to be able to precisely express a critical property and possibly to verify it. At this point the designer, e.g. of a critical system, could need something more than plain UML, to add desired properties and system requirements into its architecture. So ArchiTRIO appears in the picture: the designer needs a solid formal description of the used concepts (e.g. class, instance, interface, port, operation, connection, and so on), to state something more and more precisely of the system, well before implementing it.

The basic ArchiTRIO concepts mirror a subset of the elements one can find in UML 2.0. The core of the language is the *class*. A class defines *operations* and *attributes*, and can provide and require *interfaces*; *ports* are groups of required/provided interfaces, and can be used to define protocols. Classes can have *composite structures*, whose parts are connected by *connectors*. The graphical representation of those concepts that are common to both ArchiTRIO and UML is the same as in UML. Besides these UML elements, however, ArchiTRIO includes also concepts derived from temporal logic, which allow users to precisely define the behavior of a system modeled with ArchiTRIO.

For example, class `LC_HighSecGate` provides interface `LocalControl` and has a port of type `GatePort`; interface `LocalControl` defines two operations, `incomingData` and `personEntered`. In addition to the aforementioned UML port and interface, class `LC_HighSecGate` includes three logic items, `inGate`, `lastUser` and `gate_open`. Item `inGate` is time-independent (TI, meaning that its value is constant over time), and represents the identifier of the `Gate` to which the controller belongs; item `lastUser` is time-dependent (TD, that is its value depends on the time instant in which the item is evaluated) and models the data corresponding to the user who had either his/her fingerprints or his/her retina scanned; item `gate_open`, instead, is a state (which means that it is true/false in intervals of non-null duration), and models the intervals in which the gate is open.

In addition to the logic items explicitly declared in the class signature, an ArchiTRIO class includes a number of built-in items, which model the most significant features of the UML elements of the class (for example the parameters of an operation, an operation invocation, etc.). Then, the axioms of class LC_HighSecGate predicate over the logic items (explicitly declared or built-in) of the class to define its precise behavior. Axiom dataRelay shown below, for example, states that when an invocation of operation incomingData (exported through interface LocalControl) is received by the controller and the value of the rawData parameter is pd, within T time units in the future the controller will invoke (an instance of) operation sendPersData on port out, passing pd and the value corresponding to item inGate as parameters.

```
dataRelay:
    iD.inv_rec(pd) -> ex out.sPD(WithinF(out.sPD.invoke(pd, inGate), T));
```

In axiom dataRelay, iD and sPD are variables ranging over all possible *invocations* of operations incomingData and sendPersData, respectively. Then, ex out.sPD means that "there exists an invocation of operation sendPersData (within the scope of port out) such that...". inv_rec and invoke are built-in logic items (more precisely *events*, i.e. predicates that are true only in isolated time instants) modeling significant events of an operation invocation; in particular, event iD.inv_rec is true when invocation iD of operation incomingData is received by the local controller; similarly, event out.sPD.invoke is true when the controller issues invocation sPD on port out. WithinF is a temporal operator taken from the TRIO formal language (see [2] for its definition). pd is a variable of type PersonalData, where PersonalData is an ArchiTRIO class, not shown here for the sake of brevity, modeling either the badge, or the fingerprints, or the retina of a user.

Finally, a *port* is a collection of provided and required interfaces. It can be used to define a *protocol*, intended as a combination of invocations of operations that can be received (from a provided interface) or issued (to a required interface). Thus, an ArchiTRIO port can contain axioms defining the corresponding protocol in terms of the involved operation invocations. Consider, for example, port HighSecAutProtocol of Figure 1. It provides interface AccessControl, and requires one instance of interface FromAccessControl. The port defines the authentication protocol for gates that require that a user authenticates him/herself through both a fingerprint and a retina scan. More precisely, the two scans can occur in any order, but always within a maximum delay one from the other for the authentication to be successful (i.e. for the controller to allow the user to enter by opening the gate through an openGate command). Further details can be found in [14].

This concludes our simple and informal overview of ArchiTRIO. The next sections will cover these concepts more formally.

3   Higher-Order TRIO

Items are the founding elements of the HOT logic. HOT *items* correspond, in usual logic lore, to *constants*, *functions* or *predicates*. Items can have arguments (and return values), which are *typed* elements. The arguments (and returned values) of HOT items can be of any HOT type (see below). For example, we might define a HOT item it to be a time-dependent (TD) predicate with two arguments of type T1 and T2:

```
items:   TD it(T1, T2) : boolean;
```

Items are the building blocks for HOT *formulas*. HOT formulas are, as usual, a combination of functions, predicates (that is, items), logical connectors (&, |, ->, <->, not), temporal operators (Dist, Futr, Past, etc.) and quantifiers (all, ex). For example:

```
p1(f1, f2(c1)) -> Futr(all x(p2(x)), t);
```

Notice that every HOT variable (for example c1, x and t in the formula above) ranges over the values of some *type* (or *domain*), which is defined through a HOT *class*. A HOT class definition is essentially divided in two parts: the first part contains the local items; the second part contains the *axioms*. Axioms are formulas which model the behavior of the class; that is, they constrain its items. Given a HOT class, an element of the domain is called an *object*. The term object is synonym for *instance* (of a class) and *value* (of a type). A HOT object corresponds also to a *model* for the corresponding class (or, in TRIO terms, to a *history*); essentially, being HOT a temporal logic, an object is a function of time. As a consequence there is no notion of object creation and destruction as in operational languages. This approach differs from the usual related literature, but basically follows and extends the traditional TRIO class-oriented approach (see [2] for more details).

Modules. TRIO has a primitive notion of *module* that sharply distinguishes it from the notion of item: a module is an instance of a class contained in an instance of another class. HOT instead, thanks to being higher order does not need such a separation. Rather, it has linguistic constructs that allow one to obtain the same semantics as TRIO modules in HOT from basic HOT concepts. Thus, HOT offers the keyword module as a shorthand notation to automatically introduce the axioms and definitions corresponding to the semantics of TRIO modules, where essentially a module is represented through a HOT item. As a brief example, consider a class C containing an array m of n modules of class M:

```
modules: m[1..n] : M;
```

This array corresponds in HOT to the following time-independent item:

```
items: TI m(1..n) : M;
```

Inheritance. We distinguish two kinds of inheritance: *monotonic inheritance*, and *free, purely syntactic, inheritance*. Monotonic inheritance perfectly matches the notion of subtyping (in fact it is written C' subtype of C, or $C' \preceq C$):

1. every item and axiom defined in C is in C';
2. C' may add new items;
3. C' may add new axioms, thus more constraints w.r.t. C.

The subsection about semantics below shows how this simple notion of inheritance produces pure subtyping, as, e.g., in [1].

Instead, purely syntactic inheritance (written C' *redefines* C) is a free-form of inheritance: C' may modify, add, and delete any items and axioms of C.

We introduce both types of inheritance to make HOT a very free kind of logic language. Nonetheless, in our opinion the correct interpretation of inheritance is essentially subtyping. Although in this paper we do not deal with methodological aspects, we envisage a methodology where the specifier/designer could start with a class hierarchy in which both kinds of inheritance are used, being sometimes easier to work with a free form of inheritance, to later obtain, through some revision steps, a true tree in which only subtyping is used. For instance, consider the system presented in Section 2. The designer at first writes class SimpleGate, because it is the simplest kind of gate. Then, she decides to add another, more complex kind of gate: the MediumSecurityGate. She creates class MediumSecurityGate using syntactic inheritance from SimpleGate, replacing the BadgeReader component with one of type FingerprintsReader, then adding a new component of type EntrySensor. Later, rethinking about the relation between these two classes, she decides to collect all the concepts common in gates in a new class Gate, of which both SimpleGate and MediumSecurityGate become subtypes.

Genericity. HOT classes can be parametric with respect to values of classes and with respect to classes. The header of a generic HOT class has the syntax class <class_name> (<par_decls>) where parameters may be a type name or a value of a certain type.

Hints of HOT's Set-Theoretic Semantics. Given an item i of class C, let us call $sig(i)$ its signature[1]. Moreover, let us call $items(C)$ the set of items locally defined in C (e.g., if $items(C) = i_1, i_2$, and C' is a subtype of C that adds a single new item i_3 to C, then $items(C') = i_3$). Quite naturally, items are interpreted as (time dependent or independent) constants, functions or predicates, depending on their signature. Axioms are essentially constraints on the items. Classes are types, therefore are interpreted as sets of objects. An object x of class C is, in general, a function of time (τ):

$$x : \tau \to \underset{i \in I}{\times} sig(i), \text{ where } I = \bigcup_{C' \preceq C} items(C').$$

Therefore $x.i$ is interpreted as a projection of the range of x on the component $sig(i)$. For example, let C be a class with items n of type natural, and s of type string, with axioms stating that always $n = length(s)$. Let C' be a subtype of

---
[1] For simplicity, in the following we do not consider homonyms and name clashes.

C, containing a new item c of type char, and a new axiom which states that $c = s[0]$. Then, every object in C or C' can be interpreted as a function with signature: $\tau \to$ natural $\times$ string $\times$ char. The main difference is that C does not constrain in any way item c, therefore $C' \subseteq C$.

4 The Semantics of ArchiTRIO

We now define the semantics of the core elements of ArchiTRIO on the stage of HOT: classes (possibly composite), operations, interfaces/ports. For reasons of brevity, we do not present the full semantics of ArchiTRIO, but only a significant subset thereof; the elements presented here, however, should provide a meaningful enough picture.

4.1 ArchiTRIO Classes

An ArchiTRIO class is a HOT class, and defines a type; then, as in HOT, an ArchiTRIO object of type AT is an instance (i.e. a value) of class AT.

All ArchiTRIO classes are subtypes (in terms of HOT) of a HOT class ArchiRootClass; that is, all ArchiTRIO classes *implicitly* share a common root class, which thus defines a type that is common to all ArchiTRIO objects. A class can include *operations* and *attributes*. An attribute is, quite naturally, represented through an item modeling its value, and operations to get/set it. Then, its semantics does not raise specific issues besides those associated with the notion of operation.

4.2 Operations

The concept of ArchiTRIO (and, thus, UML) operation is defined through a HOT class Operation, which captures the core features shared by all operations. These features can be summed up as: 1) a set of items modeling the key aspects of an operation invocation (when the client object issues the invocation, when the server receives it, the parameters associated with the invocation, etc.), and 2) a set of axioms defining the constraints — time-related or not — over the aforementioned items (for example, the fact that a return must be preceded by the server object actually receiving the invocation, etc.). HOT class Operation defining the semantics common to all operations is sketched below.

```
class Operation
items:
  event invoke, inv_rec, reply; ...
axioms:
  Response_NC: reply -> SomP(inv_rec);
  ...
end
```

Class Operation introduces the logic items modeling the relevant features of an operation invocation (e.g. the invoke, inv_rec and reply events first introduced in Section 2), and the axioms defining the behavior that is common to all invocations. For example, axiom `Response_NC` defines a necessary condition for the reply event to occur: an operation invocation can return (occurrence of the reply event) only if the invocation was previously received by the called object (event `inv_rec`; see [2] for the definition of temporal operator SomP). Every instance o of class `Operation` corresponds to a *single* invocation of an operation. Then, for any instance o, the corresponding events `invoke`, `reply`, etc. are *unique*; that is, they can happen only *once* over the temporal domain. This property is defined by suitable axioms in HOT class `Operation`; for instance, formula `invoke_unique` states in an obvious way that, if event invoke occurs now, it cannot occur in any other instant of the temporal domain.

Every invocation is also characterized by a pair of objects: one that issues the invocation, and one that receives it. This is represented in the HOT semantics through a pair of items, `src` and `tgt`, both constants of type `ArchiRootClass`, modeling, respectively, the source of the invocation and its target.

A specific operation (e.g. sendPersData of interface `AccessControl`) is defined as a subtype of HOT class `Operation`. For example, class sendPersData below defines the semantics for the corresponding operation (see [14] for the complete declaration of the operation). Every instance spd of class sendPersData (i.e. every value of type sendPersData) is an invocation of the corresponding operation.

```
class AccessControl.sendPersData
subtype of: Operation;
items:
  TI rawData : PersonalData;
  TI gate : GateId;
  TI partial returned : User;
  TI partial raised : UserNonExistentException; ...
axioms: ...
end
```

The parameters of an operation are represented through constants having the same type of the parameter. For example parameter rawData of operation sendPersData corresponds to a constant with the same name in the HOT class sendPersData; then, given an instance sPD of class sendPersData, sPD.rawData is the value of parameter rawData for that invocation. Similarly, if an operation returns a value (resp. raises an exception), this is represented through a constant returned (resp. raised) of the same type as the returned value (resp. raised exception). Constant item returned is declared as partial, meaning that its value can be undefined, for example if the invocation ends with an exception (similarly, item raised is partial since its value is undefined if the invocation ends correctly). When the instance of an operation appears in a formula, the server object which it refers to is included, as a prefix, in the term identifying the instance (if the server object is not included, it defaults to this, i.e., the current object in which the formula is defined). For example, if sPD is a variable of type sendPersData and ac is a term corresponding to an instance of a class providing interface AccessControl (that is, operation sendPersData), to refer to an invocation of operation `sendPersData` on object `ac` we have to write `ac.sPD` (see for example formula `dataRelay` of class `LC_HighSecGate`). This corresponds to stating that the target object of invocation `sPD` is `ac` or, using the HOT semantics, that `sPD.tgt = ac`.

4.3 Interfaces and Ports

¿From a semantic point of view, an ArchiTRIO interface is a class that exports operations (and attributes), but cannot include other logic items (such as, for example, state `gate_open` of class `LC_HighSecGate`), nor can be decomposed into parts (i.e. it cannot be composite, but merely simple). The only possible associations that an interface can have are a generalization relationship with other interfaces, and a "provided by" relationship with an ArchiTRIO class; it cannot, for example, require an interface.

A class providing an interface I is a subtype of HOT class I. ArchiTRIO allows a class (resp. interface) to provide (resp. specialize) more than one interface. Then, the corresponding HOT class is a subtype of every and each one of the provided (resp. specialized) interfaces. An ArchiTRIO class requiring an interface I is a HOT generic (i.e. parametric) class with respect to a parameter of type I. For example, class `RetinaScanner` provides interface `IdRecognizer` and requires an interface `LocalControl`. The corresponding HOT class is shown below.

```
class RetinaScanner (lc : LocalControl)
subtype of: IdRecognizer; ...
end
```

As detailed above, HOT class `RetinaScanner` has one parameter, `lc`, of type `LocalControl`; that is, every object `rs` of class `RetinaScanner` must be instantiated with an object providing interface `LocalControl`. One way to provide an instance `c` of a class `C` requiring an interface `I` with the necessary instances of `I` is by *connecting* `c` with an object providing `I` in a Composite Structure Diagram, as explained in Section 4.4. A port in ArchiTRIO is a class that provides a (possibly empty) set of interfaces `PI`, and requires a (possibly empty) set of interfaces `RI`. In addition, an ArchiTRIO port can include a set of axioms, which define a protocol associated with the port. A port, like an interface, cannot include logic items, nor be decomposed further into parts; it may specialize another port, but not other kinds of classifiers (classes and interfaces). Only ArchiTRIO classes (neither interfaces, nor other ports) may offer a port.

Being an ArchiTRIO class, a port is defined as a HOT class that requires and provides the corresponding interfaces. For example, the HOT semantics of port `HighSecAutProtocol` shown in Figure 1 is the following:

```
class HighSecAutProtocol (fac : FromAccessControl)
subtype of: AccessControl; ...
end
```

The HOT semantics of an ArchiTRIO class C that offers a port p of type P is that of a class having a module p of type P. The multiplicity of every port component (i.e. how many instances of a port P an instance of C actually offers) is a parameter of the class offering it, if it is left open in the class definition (e.g., when defined as [1..*]). For example, class CentralControl of Figure 1 has three ports: inH of type HighSecAutProtocol, inM of type MedSecAutProtocol and inL of type LowSecAutProtocol. The actual multiplicity of these ports is decided when class CentralControl is instantiated (for example in the example of building of Figure 3, instance CC has two instances each of ports MedSecAutProtocol and LowSecAutProtocol, and one instance of port HighSecAutProtocol). Then, the HOT semantics of class CentralControl is the following[2]:

```
class CentralControl (N_inH : Natural, N_inM : Natural, N_inL : Natural,
                     inH_fac : FromAccessControl[1..N_inH], ...)
modules:
  inH[1..N_inH]: HighSecAutProtocol(inH_fac);
  inM[1..N_inM]: MedSecAutProtocol(...);
  inL[1..N_inL]: LowSecAutProtocol(...); ...
end
```

Note that the number of ports N_inH, N_inM and N_inL are parameters of class CentralControl, and are set when the class is instantiated.

4.4 Composite Classes

The parts of an ArchiTRIO composite class are defined, in a natural manner, through HOT modules. For example, the semantics of class HighSecurityGate of Figure 2 is the following (note the definition of port out as a module of the class, in accordance to the discussion of Section 4.3):

```
class HighSecurityGate (out_ac: AccessControl)
modules:
  out: GatePort(out_ac);
  LC: LC_HighSecGate;
  RS: RetinaScanner(LC);
  FR: FingerprintsReader(LC);
  ES: EntrySensor(LC); ...
end
```

As shown above, the HOT semantics of a connection between a provided and a required interface (such as the one between components LC and RS in Figure 2) is that of parameter instantiation. Then, for example, in object RC of class RetinaScanner (which requires an interface of type LocalControl) parameter lc is instantiated with object LC, which is precisely of type LocalControl (similarly for object FR and ES). There are two kinds of connectors between ports. The first one corresponds to the situation in which two ports of the same kind, one belonging to a composite class, and one belonging to one of its components, are connected with each other (this is, for example, the case of ports out of class HighSecurityGate and of its part LC). The second one,

---

[2] Parameter inH_fac is a sequence of N_inH objects of type FromAccessControl.

instead, corresponds to the configuration in which a port P providing interfaces PI1, ..., PIn and requiring interfaces RI1, ..., RIm is connected to a complementary port Pc *requiring* interfaces PI1, ..., PIn and *providing* interfaces RI1, ..., RIm. This second case occurs, for example, in class Building of Figure 3, where port inH of component CC, which has type HighSecAutProtocol, is connected to port out of Area51, which has type GatePort; in fact, port HighSecAutProtocol provides interface AccessControl and requires interface FromAccessControl, while port GatePort requires interface AccessControl and provides interface FromAccessControl, and is thus complementary to the former. Informally, in the first kind of connection between ports (the one exemplified by class HighSecurityGate and its part LC) the composite class relays *instantly* all signals arriving at the outermost port p_out to the innermost one p_in (and vice-versa). Then, all traces of port p_out are also traces for p_in. This corresponds to p_out and p_in actually being the *same* object. In the case of class HighSecurityGate, for example, this corresponds to stating that out = LC.out. The second kind of connection is instead an extended version of the connection between provided and required interfaces described above. Then, the connection between components CC and Area51 in class Building has the following semantics:

```
class Building ...
modules:
  CC: CentralControl(1, 2, 2, [Area51],...);
  Area51: HighSecurityGate(CC.inH); ...
end
```

where [Area51] is a sequence of exactly one object, Area51 (which has type FromAccessControl, as required by the definition of parameter inH_fac of class CentralControl above).

5 Related Works

ArchiTRIO is a formal language that includes a number of concepts from UML 2.0, and assigns them a precise semantics. As a consequence, it is related to a number of works that have appeared in the literature in recent years. In this section, we take into account some of the aforementioned works, and briefly analyze how our approach differs from previous ones.

ArchiTRIO is a logic-based language, and indeed the UML notation already includes a logic language, the Object Constraint Language (OCL) [7]. With respect to OCL, however, ArchiTRIO has larger scope and greater expressiveness. In fact, OCL is a language for specifying "[...] invariants on classes and types in the class model [...] pre- and post conditions on Operations and Methods [...] constraints on operations [...]" [7]. With ArchiTRIO one can express all of these properties and some more; for example, axiom dataRelay shown in Section 2, which defines neither a class invariant, nor a pre/post condition (nor a constraint) on an operation, but, rather, a dynamic relationship between two different operations, cannot be expressed as an OCL constraint[3]. In addition, OCL expressions are forbidden to "alter the state of the corresponding executing system" (i.e. they are *side-effect-free*), and they can describe the computation of an operation only if this is side-effect-free (in UML terms, only if it has an *isQuery* tag). ArchiTRIO formulas, on the other hand, do not have any of these restrictions, and can easily formalize properties such as "as a result of an invocation of operation Op, the value of attribute A becomes X".

Also, it is well-known that OCL cannot express real-time constraints. A real-time extension to OCL has been proposed in [15] to express real-time constraints on Statecharts. In the approach of [15], real-time OCL formulas can state that, for example, "if the class is in state X, then on all execution traces of the underlying Statechart state Y must follow after no less than T1 and no more that T2 time units" (where T1 and T2 must be either integer constants or the keyword inf); that is, RT-OCL formulas make sense only when interpreted with respect to the Statechart associated with the class. ArchiTRIO formulas, instead, are more expressive as far as temporal constraints are concerned (they allow quantifications over temporal variables, which can range not only over discrete, but also over continuous temporal domains), and have a higher level of abstraction. In fact, while RT-OCL formulas refer to a specific computational environment (i.e. the one given by the Statechart of the enclosing class), ArchiTRIO ones assume very little (for example that a reply must be preceded by an invoke), and they themselves define the possible computations of the class they refer to.

[9] presents a formal semantics for object systems with particular emphasis on how objects react to the stimuli (called *requests*) coming from other objects. In addition, it introduces a notion of *substitutability* between objects based on behavioral conformity. The present work exhibits some similarities with [9], in that we also provide a formal semantics for systems composed of communicating objects, and introduce a notion of *subtyping* that hinges on the principle that a subtype can be used wherever a parent type appears (in HOT/ArchiTRIO terms, it guarantees that the axiom formulas of the parent still hold). Notice, however, that while [9] refers to state-based specifications (for example ones given through Statecharts), ArchiTRIO belongs to the category of axiom systems, hence the two notions of substitutability and subtyping are inherently different, even if related (the former is based on the concept of trace containement/simulation, while the latter on the concept of subset/logical implication). In addition, while [9] basically offers a semantics of Statecharts describing communicating objects, ArchiTRIO has a wider reach, as it encompasses the definition of the whole system, in both its structural and dynamic features.

---

[3] One could argue that such a property (minus the real-time constraint) could be expressed in UML by means of a Statechart or an Activity Diagram. However, this only highlights the fact that while in ArchiTRIO there is a unique formalism for all aspects of the model (static and dynamic), basic UML relies on a number of overlapping views, which often express similar properties and can be difficult to reconcile with one another.

How to add formality to existing UML is a widely acknowledged problem. In this regard, a number of works in the literature have proposed an approach based on *translating* UML behavioral diagrams (especially Statecharts and sequence diagrams) into an existing formalism (be it π-Calculus [10], TRIO [11], Promela [13], and many others not listed here for the sake of brevity), or, alternatively, into an ad-hoc model [12]. The ArchiTRIO approach is different in that we do not translate any UML dynamic diagram into an existing formalism; on the contrary, we developed a formal language that is *integrated* into the UML 2.0 notation, which allows one to precisely describe both the structure and the dynamics of a system, of its components and their interactions, with particular attention to their temporal constraints.

Finally, [6] presents an approach to the analysis of system architectures based on a subset of UML 2.0 concepts and a formal semantics for time-annotated Statecharts. Again, with respect to this work, the scope of ArchiTRIO is wider, as it is intended for use in the whole system design phase, from modeling to verification. In fact, one could see the techniques presented in [6], and associated notations, as a target model, to be obtained through a suitable method from an ArchiTRIO design to perform subsequent verification.

6 Conclusions

We presented the semantics of the ArchiTRIO language [14]. Since ArchiTRIO shares many concepts with UML, its semantics effectively corresponds to a formal definition of a number of important UML concepts. The semantics of ArchiTRIO is given in terms of a higher-order temporal logic, HOT, which is endowed with a notion of subtyping built upon the simple and intuitive concept of subset.

Our further work on the ArchiTRIO language will follow a number of directions. First and foremost, we are currently developing an integrated tool-set, called TRIDENT, which is based on the Eclipse [3] platform, to support writing ArchiTRIO models. This tool, of which an early prototype exists, will be able to import UML diagrams from external tools, both commercial and non-commercial, and will allow users to add ArchiTRIO-specific details to those parts of the model that require a greater level of rigor and precision. Secondly, we will investigate verification techniques (to be supported by TRIDENT) to complement the modeling features presented in this paper. In this regard, the semantics of ArchiTRIO in terms of HOT suggests an encoding of ArchiTRIO classes into the higher-order logic of a theorem prover such as PVS, along the lines already followed for the TRIO language [5].

The ultimate goal of our research is the development of a complete "UML-compliant and compatible", fully tool supported methodology that allows one to move smoothly from a purely logic high-level specification to architectural design to implementation through a sequence of refinement steps, the correctness of each one being rigorously verified by exploiting several complementary methods.

Acknowledgements

The authors would like to thank the anonymous reviewers for their useful comments and suggestions.

References

1. H. Balsters and M. M. Fokkinga. Subtyping can have a simple semantics. *Theoretical Computer Science*, 87(1):81–96, 1991.
2. E. Ciapessoni, A. Coen-Porisini, E. Crivelli, D. Mandrioli, P. Mirandola, and A. Morzenti. From formal models to formally-based methods: an industrial experience. *ACM TOSEM*, 8(1):79–113, 1999.
3. Eclipse Foundation. http://www.eclipse.org.
4. C. A. Furia, D. Mandrioli, A. Morzenti, M. Pradella, M. Rossi, and P. San Pietro. Higher-order TRIO. Technical report, DEI, Politecnico di Milano, 2004.
5. A. Gargantini and A. Morzenti. Automated deductive requirements analysis of critical systems. *ACM TOSEM*, 3(3):225–307, 2001.
6. H. Giese, M. Tichy, S. Burmester, and S. Flake. Towards the compositional verification of real-time uml designs. In *Proc. of ESEC/FSE 2003*, pages 38–47, 2003.
7. Object Management Group. UML 2.0 OCL specification,. Technical report, OMG, 2003. ptc/03-10-14.
8. Object Management Group. UML 2.0 superstructure specification,. Technical report, OMG, 2003. ptc/03-08-02.
9. D. Harel and O. Kupferman. On object systems and behavioral inheritance. *IEEE Transactions on Software Engineering*, 28(9):889–903, 2002.
10. V. S. W. Lam and J. Padget. Formalization of uml statechart diagrams in the π-calculus. In *Proc. of the 2001 Australian Soft. Eng. Conf.*, pages 213–223, 2001.
11. L. Lavazza, G. Quaroni, and M. Venturelli. UML and formal notations for modelling real-time systems. In *Proc. of ESEC/FSE 2001*, pages 196–206, 2001.
12. X. Li, Z. Liu, and H. Jifeng. A formal semantics of UML sequence diagram. In *Proc. of the 2004 Australian Soft. Eng. Conf.*, pages 168–177, 2004.
13. W. E. McUmber and B. H. C. Cheng. A general framework for formalizing UML with formal languages. In *Proceedings of the 23rd ICSE*, pages 433–442, 2001.
14. M. Pradella, M. Rossi, and D. Mandrioli. A UML-compatible formal language for system architecture description. In *SDL 2005: Proc. of 12th SDL Forum*, volume 3530 of *Lecture Notes in Computer Science*, pages 234–246. Springer-Verlag, 2005.
15. S. Flake S. and W. Mueller. Formal semantics of static and temporal state-oriented OCL constraints. *Software and Systems Modeling*, 2(3):164–186, 2003.
16. H. Saiedian, J. P. Bowen, R. W. Butler, D. L. Dill, R. L. Glass, D. Gries, A. Hall, M. G. Hinchey, C. M. Holloway, D. Jackson, C. B. Jones, M. J. Luts, D. L. Parnas, J. Rushby, J. Wing, and P. Zave. An invitation to formal methods. *IEEE Computer*, 29(4):16–30, 1996.

Submodule Construction for Extended State Machine Models

Bassel Daou and Gregor V. Bochmann

School of Information Technology and Engineering (SITE),
University of Ottawa, Canada
{bdaou, bochmann}@site.uottawa.ca

Abstract. In this paper, we consider the problem of extending existing submodule construction techniques that have been developed for finite state models into more expressive and compact behavioral models that handle data through parameterized interactions, state variables and simple guards. We provide a behavioral model based on extended Input-Output Automata and describe an algorithm that provides the solution to the submodule construction problem in the context of this extended behavioral model. This algorithm is based on abstracting variable configurations using the concept of variable partitions, and splitting of states obtained from the finite state machine model in order to satisfy the constraints imposed by the values of exchanged interaction parameters.

1 Introduction

Submodule construction, also called equation solving or factorization, considers the following situation: An overall system is to be constructed which consists of several components. It is assumed that the specification S of the desired behavior of the system is given, as well as a specification of the behavior of all the components, except one. The process of submodule construction has the objective of finding a specification for the latter component such that all components together provide a behavior consistent with the behavior specification S. If the modeling paradigm for the behavior specifications is sufficiently limited, e.g. finite state models, an algorithm for submodule construction can be defined [MeBo83, Parr89, Shie89, LeQi90, DrBo99]. Submodule construction finds application in the synthesis of controllers for discrete event systems [BrWo94], communication gateway design and protocol conversion [KeHa93, KNM97, TBD97].

In this paper we consider submodule construction techniques for state transition models extended with state variables, interaction parameters and simple guards for transitions. We use a specification paradigm which is an extension of partially specified Input/Output Automata as discussed in [Boch02]. The main difficulties encountered when solving the submodule construction for such extended specification models are the following:

a. One has to keep track of the relationship between the variables of the new module X, the variables of the system specification and the variables of the existing component C.

b. For each of the input or output transitions of the new component X, one has to decide which local variables should be used to store parameter values received by an input, or which local variable should be used to define the value of an output parameter.

c. There may be many different global system states that may be reached depending on the choices that are taken under point (b) above. We want to find the most general specification for the component X such that without introducing not allowed output to the environment of the system nor unexpected input (for the existing component C) from the component X or from the environment.

Our approach for solving this problem without simply enumerating all possible choices for the new component X is based on the following two ideas:

1. In order to model the equivalence between different variables in a given state, we consider partitions over the set of all variables. A partition defines a set of non-overlapping subsets of variables, and our partitions have the property that all variables that belong to a given subset of the partition are equivalent, that is, known to have the same value.
2. After applying submodule construction for the IOA model (following known methods [QiLe91, BrWo94, KNM97, DriBo99]) we analyze the resulting state machine for X in order to determine which partitions may apply for each of its states. Since for a given state, some partitions may lead to invalid behavior, we introduce a transformation step in which the states of the component X are split according to the possible partitions that can be reached. The purpose of this splitting is to preserve the acceptable behavior (related to a particular partition) and eliminate invalid behaviors (related to other partitions). The splitting of one state often leads to the need for splitting other states from which the former can be reached. We therefore come up with a recursive splitting algorithm which allows us to eliminate all invalid behavior and keep all acceptable behavior, that is, we obtain the most general solution.

To simplify the problem we only deal with safety properties postponing issues related to liveness like blocking and progressiveness that has been solved for finite models [KNM97, DriBo99, BEYB03]. We note, however, that blocking will be partially solved in our context since we assume that the system component can not block any input from its environment.

The paper is structured as follows. In Section 2 we give the definition of our extended IOA specification formalism. Section 3 describes our submodule construction algorithm for extended IOA and gives some examples. Given the limited space in this paper, we concentrate on the definition of variable partitions and the state splitting algorithm.

2 Behavioral Model

We start by adopting a behavioral model that manipulates data and compactly represents large or infinite state systems. The model we suggest is an extension to the IO automata model [LyTu89].

2.1 Behavioral Model Properties

We stress mainly two aspects of the model: data manipulation and value passing, and differentiation between input and output in an assumption guarantee model.

2.1.1 Data Manipulation and Value Passing

The usage of dataflow information in models allows more compact and expressive representation of systems. Data manipulation and value passing can be achieved through extending finite automata models with parameterized interactions, local variables, simple transition guards and variable assignments. Parameterized interactions are used to represent the exchange of data between components and between components and the environment. Processing of data is done through saving values of input parameters in local variables, and using these values later to define the values of output parameters. Our model does not apply any operation on received data, and guards over data are simple equality checks used to represent the assignment of values to parameters, or in other words a restriction to the values that can be assigned to the parameters. Though the formal model that we present later allows for restrictions on input values, we assume that the behavior specification of C and S do not use this feature, since we are only using the guards to represent variable assignment to parameters.

2.1.2 Differentiation Between Input and Output in an Assumption Guarantee Model

As in the IOA model, a system has no control over its input interactions; however, it can assume that certain inputs are not possible. Similarly, a system might be required to give guarantees that it does not send certain interactions at certain states. This concept is generalized in our model to cover parameters sent and received alongside an interaction. So a machine can have assumptions that only specific values can be received using the transition guards and guarantees that it sends only specific values as parameters of output interactions it initiates. We use partial specification to indicate input assumptions and output guarantees, that is, if at a given state there was no transition labeled with a given interaction, then this indicates that the machine assumes that its environment will not generate that interaction at that state. Same applies to the case of output guarantees, where if an output interaction and a given output valuation of the interaction parameters was not specified, then that interaction and parameter valuation is guaranteed not to be generated by the machine.

2.2 Extended Input Output Transition Systems

In the following we present a formal definition of what we call Extended Input-Output Transition System (EIOTS), inspired from the Input Output symbolic Transition System IOSTS in [RBJ00], I/O Automata [LyTu89], and CSP [Hoar85]. An EIOTS is tuple $< S, V, s0, Se, \sum, T>$ where

- S is a nonempty finite set of states.
- V is a finite set of variables.
- $s0 \in S$ represents the initial state.

- Se ⊂ S represents the set of error states resulting from either a not allowed output or an unexpected input. All transitions starting at an error state should lead to an error state.
- Σ is a nonempty, finite alphabet, which is the disjoint union of a set Σ_{in} of input interactions, a set Σ_{out} of output interactions, and a set $\{i\}$ which has the special internal interaction i. For each interaction $\alpha \in \Sigma_{in} \cup \Sigma_{out}$, there is a (possibly empty) ordered set of interaction parameters Pm_α = <pm_1,..., pm_k>,
- $T \subseteq S \times 2^{Pm \times V} \times \Sigma \times 2^{V \times Pm} \times S$. Each tuple (s, γ, α, θ, s') ∈ T represents a transition where:
  - s ∈ S is the starting state of the transition.
  - $\gamma \subseteq Pm_\alpha \times V$. A couple (p,v) ∈ γ represents an equality condition of the form (p=v). If α is an input interaction then γ is interpreted as a transition guard formed by the conjunction of all constituting parameter conditions. If α is an output interaction then parameter conditions are interpreted as assignments of variables to parameters or in other words a restriction of the possible values that a parameter can take.
  - α ∈ Σ is the transition's interaction.
  - $\theta \subseteq V \times Pm_\alpha$. Each couple (v, p) ∈ θ represents an assignment of parameter p to variable v. The assignments in θ are executed during the transition after the assignments in γ; they assign new values to some of the variables in V. A variable is allowed to be assigned only once, this makes θ belong to the set of partial mapping relations in $V \times Pm_\alpha$
  - s' ∈ S is the end state of the transition.

The EIOTS shown in Figure 1 is taken as an example throughout this paper. It represents a desired system behavior S. In our notation, a question mark next to the interaction label represents an input, and an exclamation mark represents an output. Circles represent states and arrows represent transitions.

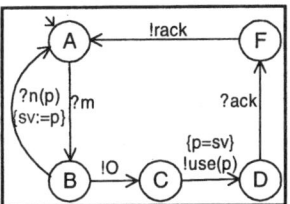

Fig. 1. EIOTS S

3 Submodule Construction Algorithm

The algorithm follows the general steps of submodule construction algorithm for finite state machines namely composition, hiding, determinization and bad or uncontrollable state removal. However, these steps have to be adapted for the new specification paradigm. To allow for determinization to take place we need to remove the effect of hidden guards and hidden variables. This is done through state splitting transformation.

In algorithm 1 we list the general steps of the submodule construction algorithm which basically include computing the unrestricted general behavior formed from the composition of the Chaos machine of X with the specification and the context. The chaos machine represents the most general behavior of X and uses as many variables as there are in S and C combined. To enable the composition between S and C we need to apply the duality operator to C which gives a machine that has the same structure as C with the exception of interchanging input and output interactions $\sum_{out}$ and $\sum_{in}$. The duality operator is applied as well to the composition so that we can compose it with the Chaos machine. Then, the resulting EIOTS is transformed using state splitting. After splitting we hide all interactions that are not visible to X and all variables coming from S and C. Finally, we handle the nondeterminism introduced by hiding, and we remove all uncontrollable behavior, that is, we mark all states that uncontrollably reach an error state as "bad", and add them to the set of error states.

Algorithm 1. Submodule Construction Algorithm:
Given C, S: EIOTS, $\sum_X$ Interaction Alphabet return EIOTS
- G1 := Chaos($\sum_X$, |S.V| +|C.V|) xDual(SxDual(C))
- G2 := Split(G1,$\sum_X$)
- G3 := Hide(G2, ($\sum_C$ U $\sum_S$) - $\sum_X$, S.V U C.V)
- G4 := Determinize(G3)
- G5 := RemoveUncontrollableBehavior(G4)
- Return EIOTS G5

To illustrate the algorithmic steps we use a submodule construction example. The general system specification S is given in Figure 1. Figure 2a below shows the behavior of the context and Figure 2b describes the general problem architecture. To distinguish variables of various machines, we use the name of the machine as a prefix when naming variables.

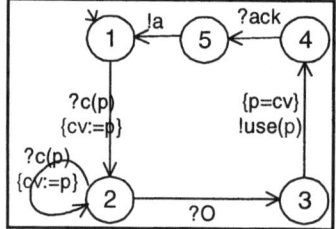
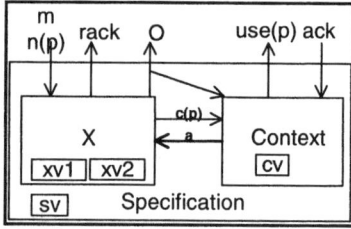

Fig. 2. (a) Context Behavior. (b) Example Architecture.

In the following sub sections we go through the operations on EIOTSs needed for the submodule construction algorithm stressing on composition, and state splitting operations.

3.1 Composition

The composition of EIOTS follows the composition of partially specified IO Automata [KeHa93]. That is, transitions with common interactions are executed synchronously and transition with interactions particular to each machine are executed independently, assuming that for each interaction there is only one initiator, which is one of the two composed machines or the environment.

Concerning the extended elements of the EIOTS model, the resulting composed machine will have a set of variables which is the disjoint union of the variables of the component machines, assuming that the machines have distinct variable names. When composing two input transitions, the resulting transition will be an input transition. Meanwhile, when composing an input transition with an output transition, the resulting transition will be an output transition. In both cases, the parameter conditions of the resulting transition will be the conjunction of the parameter conditions of the constituting transitions. Similarly, the variable assignments of the resulting transition will be the union of the variable assignments of the constituting transitions.

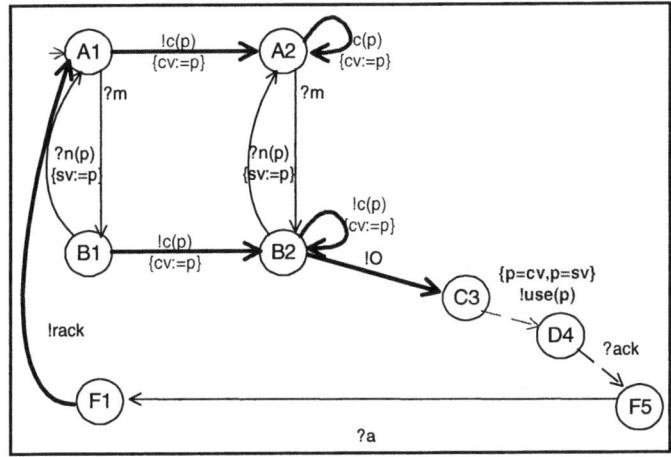

Fig. 3. Composition example. SxDual(C).

The composition of two EIOTSes E1 < S1, V1, s01, Se1, $\sum 1$, T1> and E2 < S2, V2, s02, Se2, $\sum 2$, T2> is an EIOTS E < S, V, s0, Se, $\sum$, T> that is formally defined as follows:
- S = {(s1,s2)| s1 ∈ S1 and s2 ∈ S2}
- V = V1UV2, the union of variables in E1 and E2.
- s0 = (s01, s02)
- Se = {(s1,s2) | s1∈ Se1 or s2 ∈ Se2}
- $\sum_{in.}$ = ($\sum 1_{in}$ - $\sum 2_{out}$) U ($\sum 2_{in}$ - $\sum 1_{out}$) *Note: Input interactions that are neither initiated by E1 nor by E2.*
- $\sum_{out.}$ = ($\sum 1_{out}$ U $\sum 2_{out}$). It is assumed that ($\sum 1_{out}$ ∩ $\sum 2_{out}$ = {})
- T = union of
  - {((s1,s2), γ1, α, θ1, (s1',s2)) | (s1, γ1, α, θ1, s1') ∈ T1, s2 ∈ S2, α ∈ $\sum 1$ - $\sum 2$} *Note: for transition with interactions in $\sum 1$ only.*
  - {((s1,s2), γ2, α, θ2, (s1,s2')) | (s2, γ2, α, θ2, s2') ∈ T2, s1 ∈ S1, α ∈ ($\sum 2$ - $\sum 1$)} *Note: for transition with interactions in $\sum 2$ only.*

○ {((s1,s2), γ1 U γ2, α, θ1U θ2, (s1',s2')) | (s1, γ1, α, θ1, s1') ∈ T1 and (s2, γ2, α2, θ2, s2') ∈ T2 and α ∈ ∑1 ∩ ∑2} *Note: for transitions with common interactions.*

Figure 3 shows the resulting machine of the composition operation of S and Dual(C) of our example. Notice in particular the output transition (C3, {p=cv; p=sv}, !use(p), {}, D4) which is the result of composing S's output transition (C, {p=sv}, !use(p), {}, D) and Dual(C)'s input transition (1, {p=cv},?use(p), {}, 4). An implicit condition that variables cv and sv should be equivalent to avoid an unspecified reception is created.

3.2 Chaos Machine

The notion of chaos was introduced by Hoare [Hoare85] to denote the most general behavior of a module. It was also used in several papers on submodule construction [PeYe98, DrBo99, Boch02]. For the case of submodule construction we can add variables as much as we want, since we have the full control over the new machine. However, to simulate S and C we only need as many variables as S and C combined.

For our EOITS model the chaos machine has one state which has a looping transition for each input interaction and each combination of assignments of interaction parameters to local variables. Similarly, it has an output transition for each output interaction and each combination of variable assignments to parameters. In Figure 4 we give the Chaos machine for the submodule construction example using two variables which correspond to the two variables of C and S; for the interaction ?n(p), for instance, this machine contains 4 transitions with different variable assignments.

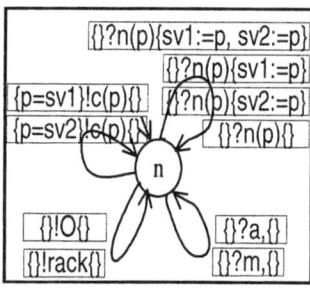

Fig. 4. Example Chaos machine: Chaos($\sum_x$, 2)

3.3 State Splitting

State splitting is done to separate variable configurations that cause guard failure into separate state splits. As outlined in the following algorithm, it is done in three steps, first a variable configuration information collection step in the form of variable partitions followed by two consecutive steps for state splitting.

Algorithm 2. State Splitting Algorithm:
Given G : EIOTS, $\sum_x$ Interaction Alphabet; return an EIOTS
- R := ComputePartitions(G)
- SplitPhaseOne(G, $\sum_x$, R, StateGroups)
- SplitPhaseTwo(G, $\sum_x$, R, StateGroups)
Return EIOTS G

3.3.1 Variable Partition Computation

The concept of variable partition is introduced for the purpose of statically analyzing an EIOTS machine. It mainly helps in providing an abstract representation of all variable configurations that are possible at each state of the machine. We are particularly interested in characterizing variable configurations that cause transition guards to fail.

After the execution of a given transition, some variables will be known to have same values (like those assigned the same input parameter). We say that such variables match, and we are interested in finding all variable matching relations at each and every state of the EIOTS. A variable matching relation is an equivalence relation, since it is reflexive, symmetric and transitive. Therefore, it can be represented by a partition over the set of variables since every equivalence relation over a set defines a unique partition of the elements in that set and vice versa. At any given state, more than one variable configuration or equivalence relation may exist since a state may be reached through different paths, and each execution path can create possibly a new variable configuration. However, since the number of variables is finite, there will be a finite number of possible variable relations and variable partitions at each state. Typically the initial configuration is represented with a single relation where no variable is known to be matching any other variable than itself. So, the initial partition is made of classes that have one variable each.

For a given variable configuration we can tell whether it conforms to a transition guard by checking whether its corresponding variable partition conforms to the guard. In the following we define the conformance predicate.

Definition 1: Partition Conformance Predicate. The predicate Conform is a mapping, $P \times 2^{PmxV} \rightarrow \{True, False\}$ where P is the set of all partitions of V (the set of all variables), and 2^{PmxV} represents the set of all possible transition guards, such that Conforms$(\pi, \gamma)=$
$\forall p \in Pm, \forall cl \in \pi, for\ E = \{v \in V \mid (p,v) \in \gamma\}\ (E \cap cl \neq \{\} \Rightarrow E \cap cl = E)$

Basically it says, if a parameter is restricted the value of several variables then these variables should be equivalent.

When a transition is executed it updates variables thus changing the variable configuration of the machine. In the following we define a transformation function that defines the partition representing the new variable configuration given the partition representing the old configuration and the executed transition.

Definition 2: Partition Transformation function. Each transition in the EIOTS defines a transformation function **Transform**: $P \times 2^{PmxV} \times 2^{VxPm} \rightarrow P\ \cup \{\}$, where Transform$(\pi, \gamma, \theta)$ is defined as follows: Let r be the relation in V×V corresponding to partition π. If Conforms (π, γ) then Transform$(\pi, \gamma, \theta) = \pi'$ where π' is the partition corresponding to relation r' in V×V such that for variables v1, v2 $\in$ V, (v1,v2) $\in$ r' if
 a) (v1,v2) $\in$ r and not $\exists$ (v1,p1) or (v2, p2) $\in$ θ, or
 b) $\exists$ p$\in$ Pm such that (v1,p) and (v2,p)$\in$ θ, or
 c) $\exists$ p$\in$ Pm, v3$\in$ V such that (v1,p)$\in$ θ, (p,v3)$\in$ γ, (v3,v2)$\in$ r, and not $\exists$ p' such that (v2,p') $\in$ θ

So there will be a resulting partition if the original partition conforms to the transition guard. And in the resulting partition two variables will be related or in other words, will be in the same class, if (a) they were in the same class of the original partition and neither is assigned by the transition, or (b) they are assigned the same parameter, or (c) one of them is assigned a parameter that is restricted to the value of a variable that was in the class of the second, while the second is not assigned a new value.

Using the partition transformation function we can define the concept of reachable partitions to a state as follows.

Definition 3: Reachable Partition to a State. We say that a partition π is reachable to a state s if and only if there exists a path from $s0$ to s such that a partition $\pi 0=\{\{v\} | v \in V\}$ will be transformed to π after successively applying on $\pi 0$ all the transformations defined by the transitions in the order defined by the path leading to s.

We can compute the set of reachable partitions for each state in an EIOTS machine by a recursive procedure described in the following.

Algorithm 3. Reachable Partitions Computation Algorithm:
Given E<S, V, s0, Se, $\sum$, T> returns R //$R=\{(s,\pi)\in S\times P | \pi$ is reachable to state $s\}$.
- $R := \{\}$
- $\pi 0 := \{\{v\} | v \in V\}$
- *newPartitions* = $\{(s0, \pi 0)\}$
- Loop while *newPartitions* $\neq \{\}$
  o Remove a couple $(s1, \pi)$ from *newPartitions*
  o $R = R \cup \{(s1, \pi)\}$
  o For each transition $(s, \gamma, a, \theta, s')$ in $\{(s, \gamma, a, \theta, s') \in T | s = s1\}$
    - if conforms(π, γ)
      o $\pi' = $ Transform(π, γ, θ)
      o If $(s', \pi') \notin R$
        - *newPartitions* = *newPartitions* $\cup \{(s', \pi')\}$

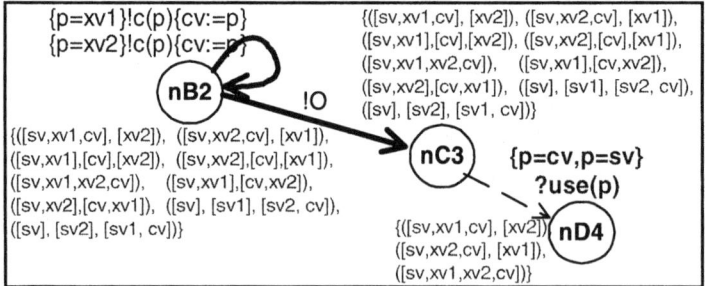

Fig. 5. Variable Partition Computation: part of Chaos(X.$\sum$, 2)xDual(SxDual(C))

The partition computation algorithm is a fixed point algorithm that loops until reaching a point where no progress can be made. Progress is evaluated in terms of finding new partitions possible in some state of the EIOTS. Since this algorithm only adds partitions and since the maximum number of partitions that can be introduced is bounded by the finite set of variable partitions, this algorithm is guaranteed to terminate.

In figure 5 we give part of the results of applying the partition computation algorithm to the composed behavior of X. Note how reachable partitions to state nD4 are only those variable partitions conforming to the guard {p=sv, p=cv} of the incoming transition.

3.3.2 Phase One

Once all variable partitions reachable at the states of the combined behavior are computed, we will be able to proceed with state splitting. In this phase of the algorithm we split into two each state that has an outgoing transition with a guard that fails for certain reachable variable partitions and succeeds for others. One state split will hold the failing partitions and the other will hold the succeeding ones.

Since each original state might have more than one outgoing transition, a state might be split into many state splits according to the different combinations of transition guards' successes and failures, and according to the availability of reachable partitions that satisfy each combination. Each group of states resulting from the splitting of one original state is saved together to be handled collectively in phase two. One element of each group is marked as the first state of the group to which all incoming transitions to the original state are still attached. These incoming transitions are to be handled in the second phase by either redirection or duplication and subsequent recursive state splitting.

Since we know that all uncontrollable behavior leading to an unsafe behavior will be eventually blocked, we treat this behavior collectively by using one state split to represent all partitions causing unsafe behaviors. Therefore, a one element of each state split group is marked as the uncontrollable split state and is used to hold all partitions that cause at least one guarded uncontrollable transition of the original state to fail. Uncontrollability in submodule construction is determined by the ability of the new module to control the execution of a given transition; therefore, we need to provide the algorithm with the set of interactions of the new module. A transition is controllable if (a)its interaction is initiated by the new module, or (b) if the interaction is an input to the new module and it is not the last transition from the same state with the same interaction that is not going to the error state. The second controllability condition is used to represent the ability of the new module to select a particular assignment of parameters to its local variables.

Next we give the algorithm for phase one. We use the function *copyState* as a shorthand for creating a new state as a copy of an existing state without copying incoming or outgoing transitions. We use as well the procedure *ReplaceState(old, s, G)* to replace state *old* by state *s* in *G* through diverting all incoming transition of state *old* to state *s*. Function *newErrorState* creates a new error state and returns it.

In Figure 6 we show the result of applying phase one of the splitting algorithm to the example used in Figure 5. In particular notice splitting state nC3 to two states nC3.1 and nC3.sE, where nC3.1 holds all partitions that conform to the guarded transition (nC3, {p=sv, p=cv}, ?use(p), {}, D4), and nC3.sE holds all partitions that do not conform, and since the mentioned transition is not controllable, nC3.sE is labeled as the error state of the state split group.

Algorithm 4. SplitPhaseOne Algorithm:
Given G < S, V, s0, Se, $\sum$, T>, $\sum$X Interaction Alphabet, R Set
// Note: $R = \{(s, \pi) \in SxP | \pi$ is reachable to state $s\}$.
- StateGroups:= { } // *this variable will hold tuples of the form (sSet: Set of States, f: State, sError: state) to store split state groups that will be later treated in Phase 2. f holds all incoming transitions to the group, and sError is the state with all partitions causing unsafe and uncontrollable behavior*
- For each state curS in G.S
  o sError := CopyState(G, curS)
  o first := curS
  o sSet:={curS} //*will hold states resulting from the splitting of one original state*
  o Tout := { (s, γ, a, θ, s') $\in$ T | s= curS }
  o Loop while Tout ≠ { }
    ▪ Remove any element (s1, γ1, a1, θ1, s1') from Tout
    ▪ BadPartitions = { π $\in$ P | $\exists$(s,π) $\in$ R where s1 = s and (not conforms(π, γ1) or s'$\in$ G.Se)}
    ▪ If BadPartitions ≠ { }
      • R = R − {(s, π) $\in$ SxP | s = s1 and π $\in$ BadPartitions}
      • If a1 $\in$ $\sum X_{out}$ or (a1 $\in$ $\sum X_{in}$ and cardinality({ (s, γ, a, θ, s',) $\in$ T | s = s1, a = a1 and s' $\notin$ G.Se}) > 1) // *transition is controllable*
      • //*Split the state, duplicate outgoing trans, disable nonconforming trans*
        o η := CopyState(G, s1)
        o sSet := sSet U {η}
        o T:=TU{(η, γ2, a2, θ2,s2') | $\exists$ (s2, γ2, a2, θ2, s'2) $\in$ T where s2 = s1}
        o Tout:=ToutU{(η,γ2,a2,θ2,s2')| $\exists$ (s2,γ2,a2,θ2,s'2)$\in$ Tout where s2=s1}
        o T = (T − {(η, γ1, a1, θ1, s1')}) U {(η, γ2, a1, θ2, newErrorState(G))}
      • else // *Transition is uncontrollable*
        o η := sError
      • R = R U {(s,π) $\in$ SxP | s = η and π $\in$ BadPartitions}
      • If {(s, π)$\in$ R| s=s1}={ }// *Delete state from group if it has no π's left*
        o sSet = sSet − {s1}
        o If s1 = first
          ▪ ReplaceState(first, η, G) // *redirects all incoming trans of first to η*
          ▪ first := η
  o If {(s,p) $\in$ R | s = sError} ≠ { }
    ▪ sSet := sSet U {sError}
    ▪ StateGroups:= StateGroups U {(sSet, first, sError)}
  o Else
    ▪ If |sSet| > 1
      o StateGroups:= StateGroups U {(sSet, first, null)}

3.3.3 Phase Two

In this phase of the algorithm each group of split states resulting from phase one is handled separately. The state designated first of its group has all incoming transitions of the original state. Each incoming transition to the group may lead to a recursive creation of a new state split group of the transition origin. For example transition (nB2, {}, !O, {}, nC3) in figure 6 will lead to the splitting of state nB2. At first nB2 is split into two states since nC3 group has only two states. However, due to incoming transitions to these states, the two nB2 states will be recursively split into states nB2.1, nB2.2, nB2.3, and nB2.4 as shown in figure 7.

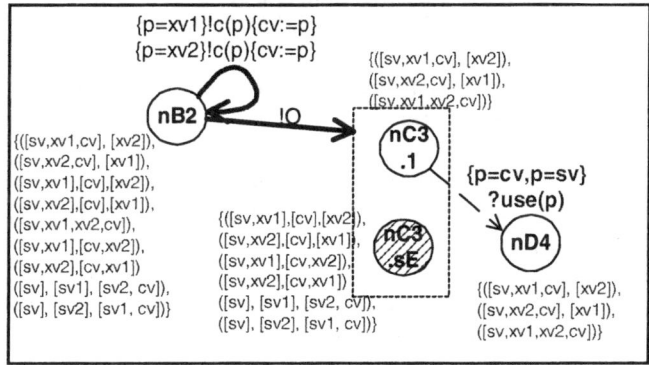

Fig. 6. Phase one of state splitting: part of Chaos(X.Σ, 2)xDual(SxDual(C))

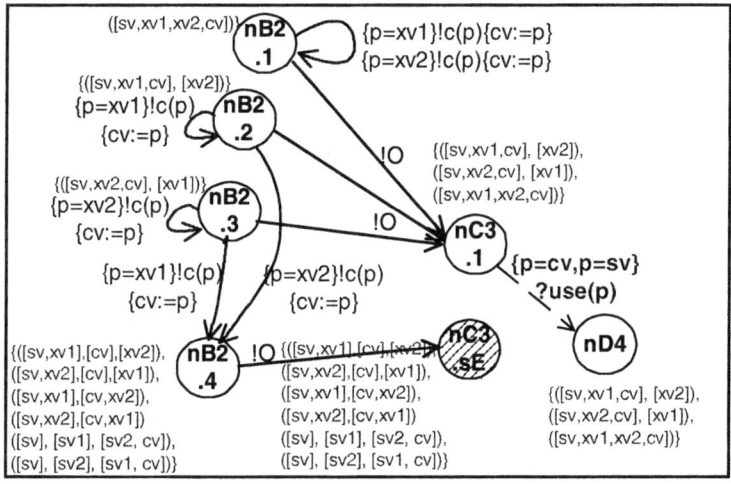

Fig. 7. Phase two of state splitting: part of Chaos(X.Σ, 2) x Dual(SxDual(C))

This algorithm is guaranteed to stop since it splits a state only if there are reachable partitions to be split. And it only adds partitions to state split that is designated an error state, but such a state split is not split any further. The maximum number of states that could result from splitting would be |R| where R is the state partition reachability relation. In the extreme, this is the case where each state is split into as many state splits as there are reachable partitions, that is, each split state will be holding a single partition.

Algorithm 5. SplitPhaseTwo Algorithm
Given G < S, V, s0, Se, $\sum$, T>, $\sum_X$ Interaction Alphabet , StateGroups, R Set // R
={(s, π)$\in$ SxP| π is reachable to state s}.
- Loop Until StateGroups= { }
  o Remove some element (StateSet, first, sError) from StateGroups
  o Tin := {(s, γ, a, θ, s')$\in$ T | s'= first}// all incoming transition to the current group
  o Loop Until Tin = { } //Handle each incoming transition separately
    ▪ Remove some element (s1, γ1, a1, θ1, s1') from Tin
    ▪ For each state curS in StateSet
      - // the inverse of Transform function for the partitions of the current state
      - PartitionSet := { π $\in$ P| (s1, π) $\in$ R and (curS, Transform(γ1,θ1, π)) $\in$ R}
      - If PartitionSet $\neq$ { }.
        o s1Group = {(sSet,e,f) $\in$ StateGroups| s1 $\in$ sSet}
        o If s1Group $\neq$ { }// s1 the starting state of the current transition belongs to a state group that is waiting to be handled
          ▪ Remove some (sSet, e, f) from s1Group
          ▪ StateGroups = StateGroups - s1Group
        o Else // Create new group
          ▪ sSet := {s1}
          ▪ f := s1
          ▪ e := null
        o If curS = sError and (a1 $\notin$ $\sum_{out}$ and (a1 $\notin$ $\sum_{in}$ or cardinality({ (s, γ,a, θ, s') $\in$ T| s = s1, a = a1 and s' $\notin$ G.Se }) = 1)// uncontrollable transition
          ▪ if e = null
            - e := copyState(G, s1)
          ▪ η:= e
        o Else
          ▪ η:= CopyState(G, s1)
          ▪ T:= TU{(η, γ2, a2, θ2, s'2)| $\exists$ (s2,γ2, a2,θ2, s'2)$\in$ T where s2 = s1}
          ▪ Tin:=TinU{(η,γ2,a2,θ2,s'2)|$\exists$ (s2,γ2,a2,θ2, s'2)$\in$ Tin where s2=s1}
          ▪ // Redirect η's transition that is the duplicate of the current transition to the current state.
          ▪ T:= (T – {(η, γ1, a1, θ1, s1')}) U {(η, γ2, a1, θ2, curS)}
        o sSet := sSet U {η}
        o R:= R U {(η, π) | π $\in$ PartitionSet}
        o R:= R - {(s, π) $\in$ R | s = s1 and π $\in$ PartitionSet}
        o If {(s, π) $\in$ R | s = s1} = { } //Delete state if it has no partitions left
          ▪ sSet:= sSet – {s1}
          ▪ If s1 = f
            - ReplaceState(f, η, G) // redirect all incoming transitions of f to η
            - f := η
        o If |sSet| > 1 or e $\neq$ null
          ▪ StateGroups:= StateGroupsU {(sSet, f,e)
  o G.Se = G.Se U {sError}

The state labeled as the error state of the currently handled group (such as state nC3.sE in Figure 8) receives special treatment. When handling an incoming transition to the error state of a group, the new state split of the transition's origin state corresponding to the error state is labeled itself as the error state of its group only if the transition is uncontrollable. In our example, new state split nB2.4 is not marked as the error state of its group since transition (nB2.4, { }, !O, { }, nC3.sE) is controllable.

3.4 Determinization and the Removal of Uncontrollable Behavior

Determinization or internal transition removal uses the usual subset construction algorithm for determinizing finite automata. As mentioned before, this is possible since the splitting algorithm removes the ambiguity created by transition guards.

The determinization results in new unsafe states due to unobservability. These states are removed together with all states from which the unsafe states can be reached through uncontrollable transitions. The same controllability criterion is used as in the case of splitting. This is similar to the case of submodule construction for simple finite state machine models.

4 Conclusion and Future Work

This paper addresses the problem of extending submodule construction techniques for finite state machine models to more expressive behavioral models that use variables, simple guards for transitions and exchange data with the environment through interaction parameters. We have defined a behavioral model with features based on an extended model of Input-Output Automata. The main contribution of this paper is the introduction of dataflow issues to submodule construction problem which has been limited in the past to control flow. However, we have only dealt with the simple usage of data, mainly saving and retransmission. We seek in the future to handle the control flow usage of data through building up on the current approach. We need to ease restrictions on guards such as allowing conjunction, disjunction, explicit negation and state variable equality predicates. This work will be as well the basis for further work on providing more efficient versions of the proposed algorithm through exploring the use of higher abstractions for representing variable partitions and taking into consideration undefined and dead variables.

References

[BEYB03] S. Buffalov, K. El-Fakih, N. Yevtushenko, G. V. Bochmann: Progressive Solutions to a Parallel Automata Equation. FORTE 03, pp. 367-382, 2003.
[Boch02] G. V. Bochmann. Submodule Construction for Specifications with Input Assumptions and Output Guarantees. FORTE 02, pp.17-33, 2002.
[BrWo94] B. A. Brandin, and W.M. Wonham. Supervisory Control of Timed Discrete Event Systems. IEEE Transactions on Automatic Control, Vol. 39, No. 2, pp. 329-342, 1994.
[DrBo99] J. Drissi, and G.V. Bochmann. Submodule Construction for Systems of I/O Automata. Tech. Rep. no. 1133, DIRO, University of Montreal, 1999.
[Hoar85] C. A. R. Hoare. Communicating Sequential Processes, Prentice Hall, Inc., 1985.

[KeHa93]   S.G. Kelekar, G. W. Hart. Synthesis of Protocols and Protocol Converters Using the Submodule Construction Approach. PSTV93, pp. 307-322, 1993.
[KNM97]   R. Kumar, S. Nelvagal, and S. I. Marcus. A Discrete Event Systems Approach for Protocol Conversion. Discrete Event Dynamical Systems: Theory and Applications, Vol. 7, No. 3, pp. 295-315, 1997.
[LeQi90]   P. Lewis and H. Qin. Factorization of finite state machines under observational equivalence. LNCS 458, Springer, 1990.
[LyTu89]   N. Lynch and M. Tuttle. An introduction to input/output automata, CWI Quarterly, Vol. 3, No. 2, pp. 219-246, 1989.
[MeBo83]   P. Merlin, and G. v. Bochmann. On The Construction of Submodule Specifications and Communication Protocols, ACM Trans. On Programming Languages and Systems. Vol. 5, No. 1, pp. 1-25, 1983
[NeBr95]   R. Negulescu, J. A. Brzozowski. Relative liveness: from intuition to automated verification. ASYNC 95, 108-117, 1995.
[Parr89]   J. Parrow. Submodule Construction as Equation Solving in CCS. Theoretical Computer Science, Vol. 68, 1989.
[PeYe98]   A. Petrenko and N. Yevtushenko. Solving Asynchronous Equations. In Proc. of IFIP FORTE/PSTV'98 Conf., Paris, Chapman-Hall, 1998.
[QiLe91]   H. Qin and P. Lewis. Factorisation Of Finite State Machines Under Strong and Observational Equivalences. Journal of Formal Aspects of Computing, Vol. 3, pp. 284- 307, 1991.
[RBJ00]   V. Rusu, L. du Bousquet, T. Jéron. An Approach to Symbolic Test Generation. IFM 2000: 338-357, 2000.
[Shie89]   M. W. Shields. Implicit system specification and the interface equation. The Computer Journal, Vol. 32, No. 5, pp. 399-412, 1989.
[TBD97]   Z. Tao, G. v. Bochmann and R. Dssouli. A Formal Method For Synthesizing Optimized Protocol Converters And Its Application To Mobile Data Networks. Mobile Networks & Applications, Vol.2, No. 3, pp. 259-69, 1997.

Towards Synchronizing Linear Collaborative Objects with Operational Transformation

Abdessamad Imine, Pascal Molli, Gérald Oster, and Michaël Rusinowitch

LORIA-INRIA Lorraine, France
{imine, molli, oster, rusi}@loria.fr

Abstract. A collaborative object represents a data type (such as a text document or a filesystem) designed to be shared by multiple geographically separated users. Data replication is a technology to improve performance and availability of data in distributed systems. Indeed, each user has a local copy of the shared objects, upon which he may perform updates. Locally executed updates are then transmitted to the other users. This replication potentially leads, however, to divergent (*i.e.* different) copies. In this respect, Operational Transformation (OT) algorithms are applied for achieving convergence of all copies, *i.e.* all users view the same objects. Using these algorithms users can apply the same set of updates but possibly in *different orders* since the convergence should be ensured in all cases. However, achieving convergence with the OT approach is still a critical and challenging issue. In this paper, we address an open convergence problem when the shared data has a linear structure such as list, text, ordered XML tree, etc. We analyze the source of this problem and we propose a generic solution with its formal correctness.

1 Introduction

Generally users involved in collaborative and mobile environments work on replicas of shared data. During disconnection periods, they can concurrently execute updates on replicas. This potentially leads to divergent replicas (*i.e.* different states). One of the main issues in such environments is how to maintain *consistency* (or convergence) among replicas after reconnection. Originating from real-time groupware research [2], the *Operational Transformation* (OT) approach provides an interesting solution [3,10]. Using this approach, after reconnection, a user A might get an operation op previously executed during disconnection by some other user B on replica of the shared data. User A does not necessarily integrate op by executing it as is on a replica. Instead, it might execute a variant of op, op' – called a *transformation* of op – that intuitively intends to achieve the same effect as op. When the transformed operations are executed, they create the illusion that all operations were executed in the intended execution context and in the intended order. Compared to other replication systems [12], the advantages of this approach are: (i) *it enables an unconstrained concurrency*, *i.e.* it requires no global order on concurrent operations unlike traditional consistency criteria such as linearizability [4]; (ii) *it transforms operations to run in any order even when they do not naturally commute*; (iii) *it produces a convergence state that precisely preserves the intentions of all the operations executed during disconnection periods.* Many collaborative applications are based on OT approach such as CoWord [18] (a collaborative word processor) and CoPowerPoint [15] (a real-time collaborative multimedia slides creation and presentation system).

The OT approach consists of application-dependent transformation algorithm. Thus, for every possible pair of concurrent operations, the application programmer has to define in advance how to merge these operations regardless of reception order. According to Ressel et al. [11], the OT algorithm needs to fulfill two conditions (which will be detailed in Section 2) in order to ensure convergence. Finding such an OT algorithm and proving that it satisfies the convergence conditions was always considered as a very hard task, because this proof is often difficult – even impossible – to produce by hand and unmanageably complicated [16]. To overcome this problem, we have proposed a formal framework to assist the development of correct OT algorithms by using a theorem prover [6,7].

However, although in theory [11], OT approach is able to achieve convergence in the presence of *arbitrary transformation orders*, some types of collaborative object still represent a serious handicap as for the application of the OT approach. Indeed, the convergence property has never been achieved when the collaborative object has a *linear structure* (such as list, text or ordered XML tree) and all proposed OT algorithms [2,11,17,14,5,8] fail to meet this property. In this paper, we analyse thoroughly the source of these failures and we propose an OT algorithm that ensures the convergence. Unlike previous works we have been able to completely give formal proof of its correctness by using a theorem prover. Furthermore, our OT algorithm is generic because it can be applied to any linear structure-based data.

The remainder of this paper is organized as follows. We present the operational transformation model in Section 2. Section 3 analyzes convergence problems that still remain and sketches an abstract solution. Section 4 presents the ingredients of our solution giving examples and proofs of correctness. The ingredients of our formalization for the linear collaborative object into a theorem prover language are given in Section 5. Section 6 discusses related work, and section 7 summarizes conclusions.

2 Operational Transformation Approach

2.1 The Model

OT considers n sites, where each site has a copy of the collaborative object. The collaborative object model we take is a *text object* modeled by a sequence of characters, where the position of its first character is zero. It is assumed that the text state can only be modified by executing the following two primitive editing operations: (i) $Ins(p, c)$ which inserts the character c at position p; (ii) $Del(p)$ which deletes the character at position p. It should be pointed out that the above text model is only an abstract view of many collaborative object models based on a linear structure. For instance the character parameter may be regarded as a string of characters, a line, a block of lines, an ordered XML node, etc.

We denote $st \odot op = st'$ when an editing operation op is executed on the text state st and produces text state st'. We say that op is *generated* on state st. Notation $[op_1; op_2; \ldots; op_n]$ represents an operation sequence. Applying an operation sequence to a text state st is recursively defined as follows: (i) $st \odot [\,] = st$, where $[\,]$ is the empty sequence and; (ii) $st \odot [op_1; op_2; \ldots; op_n] = (((st \odot op_1) \odot op_2) \ldots) \odot op_n$. Two operation sequences seq_1 and seq_2 are *equivalent*, denoted $seq_1 \equiv seq_2$, if $st \odot seq_1 = st \odot seq_2$ for all text states st.

To detect concurrency, we assume that there exists a Lamport's "happens before" partial ordering between the operations [12]. How this ordering relation is expressed is beyond the scope of this paper.

OT is an optimistic replication which lets many users concurrently update the shared data and next it synchronizes their divergent replicas in order to obtain the same data. The operations of each site are executed on the local replica immediately without being blocked or delayed, and then are propagated to other sites to be executed again. Accordingly, every operation is processed in four steps: (i) *generation* on one site; (ii) *broadcast* to other sites; (iii) *reception* on other sites; (iv) *execution* on other sites.

In the following, we give the conflict relation between two insert operations:

Definition 1. *(Conflict Relation) Two insert operations $op_1 = Ins(p_1, c_1)$ and $op_2 = Ins(p_2, c_2)$, generated on different sites, conflict with each other iff: (i) op_1 and op_2 are generated on the same text state; and, (ii) $p_1 = p_2$, i.e. they have the same insertion position.*

2.2 Transformation Principle

One of the significant issues when designing collaborative objects with a replicated architecture and an arbitrary communication of messages between sites is the *consistency maintenance* (or *convergence*) of all replicas. To illustrate this problem, consider the following example:

Example 1. Consider the following group text editor scenario (see Figure 1): there are two users (sites) working on a shared document represented by a sequence of characters. These characters are addressed from 0 to the end of the document. Initially, both copies hold the string "efecte". User 1 executes operation $op_1 = Ins(1, \text{"f"})$ to insert the character "f" at position 1. Concurrently, user 2 performs $op_2 = Del(5)$ to delete the character "e" at position 5. When op_1 is received and executed on site 2, it produces the expected string "effect". But, when op_2 is received on site 1, it does not take into account that op_1 has been executed before it and it produces the string "effece". The result at site 1 is different from the result of site 2 and it apparently violates the intention of op_2 since the last character "e", which was intended to be deleted, is still present in the final string. Consequently, we obtain a *divergence* between sites 1 and 2. It should be pointed out that even if a serialization protocol [2] was used to require that all sites execute op_1 and op_2 in the same order (*i.e.* a global order

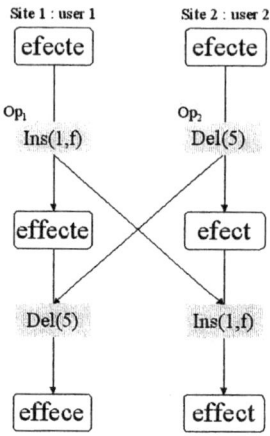
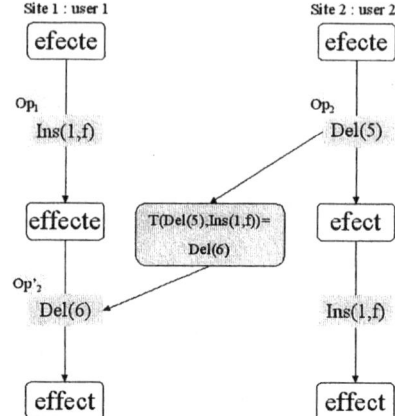

Fig. 1. Incorrect integration   **Fig. 2.** Integration with transformation

on concurrent operations) to obtain an identical result "effece", this identical result is still inconsistent with the original intention of op_2.

To maintain convergence, an OT approach has been proposed by Ellis and Gibbs [2] where a user X might get an operation op that was previously executed by some other user Y on the replica of the shared object. User X does not necessarily integrate op by executing it as it is on its replica. Instead, he might execute a variant of op, denoted by op' (called a *transformation* of op) that *intuitively intends to achieve the same effect as op*. This approach is based on an algorithm which takes two concurrent operations that are defined on the same object state. We denote this algorithm by a function T.

Example 2. In Figure 2, we illustrate the effect of T on the previous example. When op_2 is received on site 1, op_2 needs to be transformed according to op_1 as follows: $T((Del(5), Ins(1, \text{"f"}))) = Del(6)$. The deletion position of op_2 is incremented because op_1 has inserted a character at position 1, which is before the character deleted by op_2. Next, op'_2 is executed on site 1. In the same way, when op_1 is received on site 2, it is transformed as follows: $T(Ins(1, \text{"f"}), Del(5)) = Ins(1, \text{"f"})$; op_1 remains the same because "f" is inserted before the deletion position of op_2.

In the OT approach, every site is equipped by two main components [2,11]: the *integration component* and the *transformation component*. The integration component is an algorithm which is responsible for receiving, broadcasting and executing operations. It is *independent* of the semantics of the collaborative objects. Several integration algorithms have been proposed in the groupware area, such as dOPT [2], adOPTed [11], SOCT2,4 [14,19] and GOTO [16]. The transformation component is a set of OT algorithms which is responsible for merging two concurrent operations defined on the same state. Every OT algorithm is *specific* to the semantics of a collaborative object (text in our example). Every site generates operations sequentially and stores these operations in a data structure called *history*. When a site receives a remote operation *op*, the integration component executes the following steps:

1. from the local history it determines the sequence *seq* of operations that are concurrent to *op*;
2. it calls the transformation component in order to get operation *op'* that is the transformation of *op* according to *seq*;
3. it executes *op'* on the current state;
4. it adds *op'* to local history.

In this paper, we only deal with the design of OT algorithm for collaborative objects which have linear structure (such as list, text or ordered XML tree).

2.3 Convergence Conditions

Let *seq* be a sequence of operations. Transforming any editing operation *op* according to *seq*, denoted by $T^*(op, seq)$ is recursively defined as follows:

$$T^*(op, []) = op \text{ where } [] \text{ is the empty sequence;}$$
$$T^*(op, [op_1; op_2; \ldots; op_n]) = T^*(T(op, op_1), [op_2; \ldots; op_n])$$

Using an OT algorithm requires us to satisfy two conditions [11]. Given two operations op_1 and op_2, let $op'_2 = T(op_2, op_1)$ and $op'_1 = T(op_1, op_2)$, the conditions are as follows:

- **Condition** C_1: $st \odot [op_1; op'_2] = st \odot [op_2; op'_1]$, for every object state st.
- **Condition** C_2: if $[op_1; op'_2] \equiv [op_2; op'_1]$ then $T^*(op, [op_1; op'_2]) = T^*(op, [op_2; op'_1])$.

C_1 defines a *state identity* and ensures that if op_1 and op_2 are concurrent, the effect of executing op_1 before op_2 is the same as executing op_2 before op_1. This condition is necessary but not sufficient when the number of concurrent operations is greater than two. As for C_2, it ensures that transforming *op* along equivalent and different operation sequences will give the same operation. In previous work [11,9], the authors have proved that conditions C_1 and C_2 are sufficient to ensure the convergence property for *any number* of concurrent operations which can be executed in *arbitrary order*.

It should be pointed out that verifying that a given OT algorithm verifies C_1 and C_2 is a computationally expensive problem even for a simple document text. Using a theorem prover to automate the verification process is needed and would be a crucial step for building correct collaborative objects based on OT approach [5–7].

3 Convergence Problems

In order to illustrate the convergence problems encountered in building OT algorithm for linear collaborative objects, we present a well known transformation algorithm designed by Ellis and Gibbs [2] who are the pioneers of the OT approach. This algorithm is used to synchronize a collaborative text object, shared by two or more users. There are two editing operations: $Ins(p, c, pr)$ to insert a character c at position p and $Del(p, pr)$ to delete a character at position p. Operations Ins and Del are extended with another parameter pr[1]. This one represents a priority scheme that is used to solve a conflict occurring when two concurrent insert operations were originally intended to insert different characters at the same position. In Figure 3, we give the four transformation cases for Ins and Del proposed by Ellis and Gibbs. There are two interesting situations in the first case. The first situation is when the arguments of the two insert operations are equal (i.e. $p_1 = p_2$ and $c_1 = c_2$). In this case the function T returns the idle operation Nop that has a null effect on text state [2]. The second interesting situation is when only the insertion positions are equal (i.e. $p_1 = p_2$). Such conflicts are resolved by using the priority order associated with each insert operation. The insertion position will be shifted to the right ($p_1 + 1$) when Ins has a higher priority. The remaining cases of T are quite simple.

Using our theorem-proving approach [5,6], we have detected that the function T of Figure 3 contains some not obvious bugs that lead to divergence situations. These situations are detailed in the following.

3.1 Violation of C_1

The scenario violating C_1 is depicted in Figure 4 (for clarity we have omitted the priority parameter). There are two users: (i) $user_1$ inserts x in position 1 (op_1) while $user_2$ concurrently deletes the character at the same position (op_2). (ii) When op_2 is received by site 1, op_2 must be transformed according to op_1. So $T(Del(1), Ins(1, x))$ is called and $Del(2)$ is returned. (iii) In the same way, op_1 is received on site 2 and must be transformed according to op_2. $T(Ins(1, x), Del(1))$ is called and returns $Ins(0, x)$. Condition C_1 is violated. Accordingly, the final results on both sites are different.

The error comes from the definition of $T(Ins(p_1, c_1, pr_1), Del(p_2, pr_2))$. The condition $p_1 < p_2$ should be rewritten $p_1 \leq p_2$. This modification is sufficient to satisfy the condition C_1.

3.2 Violation of C_2

Even having corrected the previous error, we have detected that condition C_2 is not satisfied. Figure 5 presents a scenario for C_2 violation. In this scenario $seq = [op_2; op_3']$ and $seq' = [op_3; op_2']$ are two equivalent sequences. Using the function T of Figure 3 we must have $T(op_1, seq) = T(op_1, seq')$:

$$T^*(op_1, seq) = op_1' = T(T(op_1, op_2), op_3') = Ins(2, x)$$
$$T^*(op_1, seq') = op_1'' = T(T(op_1, op_3), op_2') = Ins(3, x)$$

---
[1] This priority is the site identifier where operations have been generated. Two operations generated from different sites have always different priorities.
[2] The definition of T is completed by: $T(Nop, op) = Nop$ and $T(op, Nop) = op$ for every operation op.

```
T(Ins(p_1,c_1,pr_1), Ins(p_2,c_2,pr_2)) =
if p_1 < p_2 then return Ins(p_1,c_1,pr_1)
elseif p_1 > p_2 then return Ins(p_1 + 1,c_1,pr_1)
    elseif c_1 == c_2 then return Nop()
        elseif pr_1 > pr_2 then return Ins(p_1 + 1,c_1,pr_1)
            else return Ins(p_1,c_1,pr_1)
endif;

T(Ins(p_1,c_1,pr_1), Del(p_2,pr_2)) =
if p1 < p2 then return Ins(p_1,c_1,pr_1)
else return Ins(p_1 − 1,c_1,pr_1)
endif;

T(Del(p_1,pr_1),Ins(p_2,c_2,pr_2)) =
if p_1 < p_2 then return Del(p_1,pr_1)
else return Del(p_1 + 1,pr_1)
endif;

T(Del(p_1,pr_1),Del(p_2,pr_2)) =
if p_1 < p_2 then return Del(p_1,pr_1)
elseif p_1 > p_2 then return Del(p_1 − 1,pr_1)
    else return Nop()
endif;
```

Fig. 3. Transformation function defined by Ellis and Gibbs [2]

As we can see, $op'_1 \neq op''_1$, C_2 is violated; and therefore the convergence is not achieved. The scenario illustrated in Figure 5 is called C_2 *puzzle*.

3.3 Analyzing the Problem

C_2 is considered as particularly difficult to satisfy. To better understand the source of this problem, we consider the previous scenario violating C_2 (see Figure 5). There are three concurrent operations $op_1 = Ins(3,x)$, $op_2 = Del(2)$ and $op_3 = Ins(2,y)$ where the insertion positions (*i.e.* $Pos(Ins(p,c,pr)) = p$) initially have the following relation: $Pos(op_1) > Pos(op_3)$.

According to Definition 1, op_1 and op_3 are not in conflict. In this scenario we have two equivalent operation sequences $S_1 = [op_2; op'_3]$ and $S_2 = [op_3; op'_2]$ where $op'_3 = T(op_3, op_2)$ and $op'_2 = T(op_2, op_3)$. The above relation between op_1 and op_3 is not preserved when transforming op_1 along sequence S_1 since $Pos(T(op_1, op_2)) = Pos(op'_3)$.

The transformation process may lead to two concurrent insert operations (with different original insertion positions) to get into a *false conflict situation* (to have the same insertion position). Unfortunately, the original relation between the positions of these operations is lost because of their transformations with other operations. Therefore, we need to know how the insert operations were generated in order to avoid divergence problems.

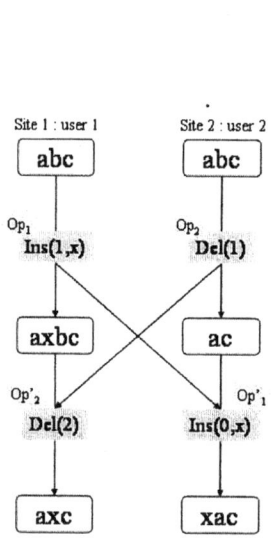

Fig. 4. Scenario violating C_1

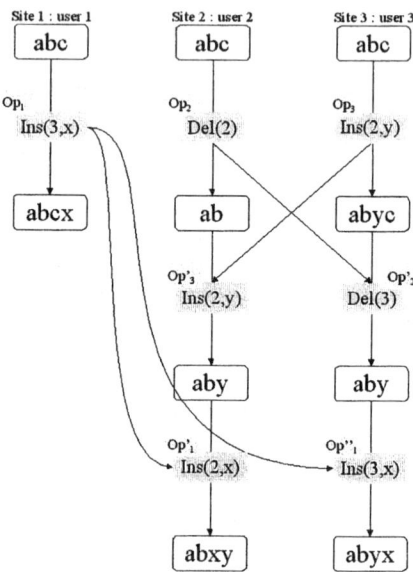

Fig. 5. Scenario violating C_2

In this paper, we propose a new approach to solve the divergence problem. Intuitively, we notice that storing previous insertion positions for every transformation step is sufficient to recover the original position relation between two insert operations.

4 Our Solution

In this section, we present our approach to achieving convergence. Firstly, we will introduce the key concept of position word for keeping track of insertion positions. Next, we will give our new OT function and how this function resolves the divergence problem. Finally, we will show the correctness of our approach.

4.1 Position Words

For any set of symbols Σ called an *alphabet*, Σ^* denotes the set of *words* over Σ. The empty word is denoted by ϵ. For $\omega \in \Sigma^*$, then $|\omega|$ denotes the *length* of ω. If $\omega = uv$, for some $u, v \in \Sigma^*$, then u is a *prefix* of ω and v is a *suffix* of ω. For every $\omega \in \Sigma^*$, such that $|\omega| > 0$, we denote $Base(\omega)$ (resp. $Top(\omega)$) the *last* (resp. *first*) symbol of ω. Thus, $Top(abcde) = a$ and $Base(abcde) = e$. We assume that Σ is totally ordered and denote the strict part of this order by $>$. If $\omega_1, \omega_2 \in \Sigma^*$, then $\omega_1 \preceq \omega_2$ is the *lexicographic ordering* of Σ^* if: (i) ω_1 is a prefix of ω_2, or (ii) $\omega_1 = \rho u$ and $\omega_2 = \rho v$, where $\rho \in \Sigma^*$ is the longest prefix common to ω_1 and ω_2, and $Top(u)$ precedes $Top(v)$ in the alphabetic order.

Definition 2. *(p-word)* We consider the natural numbers $\mathbb{N}$ as an alphabet. We define the set of p-words $\mathcal{P} \subset \mathbb{N}^*$ as follows: (i) $\epsilon \in \mathcal{P}$; (ii) if $n \in \mathbb{N}$ then $n \in \mathcal{P}$; (iii) if ω is a nonempty p-word and $n \in \mathbb{N}$ then $n\omega \in \mathcal{P}$ iff $n - Top(\omega) \in \{0, 1, -1\}$.

We observe immediately that we can concatenate two p-words to get another one if the origin of the first differs of at most 1 from the first letter of the second one:

Theorem 1. *Let ω_1 and ω_2 be two nonempty p-words. The concatenation of ω_1 and ω_2, written $\omega_1 \cdot \omega_2$ or simply $\omega_1 \omega_2$, is a p-word iff either $Base(\omega_1) = Top(\omega_2)$ or $Base(\omega_1) = Top(\omega_2) \pm 1$.*

For example, $\omega_1 = 00$, $\omega_2 = 1232$ and $\omega_1\omega_2 = 001232$ are p-words but $\omega_3 = 3476$ is not.

Definition 3. *(Equivalence of p-words)* The equivalence relation on the set of p-words $\mathcal{P}$ is defined by: $\omega_1 \equiv_\mathcal{P} \omega_2$ iff $Top(\omega_1) = Top(\omega_2)$ and $Base(\omega_1) = Base(\omega_2)$, where $\omega_1, \omega_2 \in \mathcal{P}$.

We can also show that this relation is a congruence using Definitions 2 and 3:

Proposition 1. *(Right congruence)* The equivalence relation $\equiv_\mathcal{P}$ is a right congruence, that is, for all $\rho \in \mathcal{P}$: $\omega_1 \equiv_\mathcal{P} \omega_2$ iff $\omega_1\rho \equiv_\mathcal{P} \omega_2\rho$.

4.2 OT Algorithm

In order to preserve the order relation between two insert operations, we propose to keep all different positions occupied by a character during the transformation process. It means that instead of the single position we maintain a stack of positions called a *p-word*. Each time an operation is transformed we push the last position before transformation in the *p*-word. The size of the stack is proportional to the number of concurrent operations. In Figure 6 we give the details of our new OT function. When two insertion operations insert two different characters at the same position (they are in conflict), a choice has to be made: which character must be inserted before the other? The solution that is generally adopted consists of associating a priority to each character (*i.e.*, the character's code or the site identifier). In our OT function, when a conflict occurs, the character whose code $Code(c)$ is the highest is inserted before the other.

If two *p*-words are identical it means that the two associated insert operations are equal. Otherwise the *p*-word allows to track the order relation between the two operations. We shall therefore redefine the insert operation as $Ins(p, c, w)$ where p is the insertion position, c the character to be added and w a *p*-word. When an operation is generated, the *p*-word is empty, *i.e.* $Ins(3, x, \epsilon)$. When an operation is transformed and the insertion position is changed, the original position is pushed to the *p*-word. For example, $T(Ins(3, x, \epsilon), Del(1)) = Ins(2, x, [3])$ and $T(Ins(2, x, [3]), Ins(1, x, \epsilon)) = Ins(3, x, [2 \cdot 3])$.

```
T(Ins(p₁,c₁,w₁),Ins(p₂,c₂,w₂)) =
let α₁=PW(Ins(p₁,c₁,w₁)) and α₂=PW(Ins(p₂,c₂,w₂))
if (α₁ ≺ α₂ or (α₁ = α₂ and Code(c₁) < Code(c₂)))
then return Ins(p₁,c₁,w₁)
elseif (α₁ ≻ α₂ or (α₁ = α₂ and Code(c₁) > Code(c₂)))
    then return Ins(p₁ + 1,c₁,p₁w₁)
    else return Nop
endif;

T(Ins(p₁,c₁,w₁),Del(p₂)) =
if p₁ > p₂ then return Ins(p₁ − 1,c₁,p₁w₁)
elseif p₁ < p₂ then return Ins(p₁,c₁,w₁)
    else return Ins(p₁,c₁,p₁w₁)
endif;

T(Del(p₁),Del(p₂)) =
if p₁ < p₂ then return Del(p₁)
elseif p₁ > p₂ then return Del(p₁ − 1)
    else return Nop
endif;

T(Del(p₁),Ins(p₂,c₂,w₂)) =
if p₁ < p₂ then return Del(p₁)
else return Del(p₁ + 1)
endif;
```

Fig. 6. New OT function

We define a function PW which enables to construct p-words from editing operations. It takes an operation as parameter and returns its p-word:

$$PW(Ins(p,c,w)) = \begin{cases} p & \text{if } w = \epsilon \\ pw & \text{if } w \neq \epsilon \text{ and} \\ & (p = Top(w) \\ & \text{or } p = Top(w) \pm 1) \\ \epsilon & \text{otherwise} \end{cases}$$

$$PW(Del(p)) = p$$

Figure 7 shows how the p-words solve the C_2 puzzle depicted in Figure 5. When op_1 is transformed according to op_3, $3 > 2$, so op_1 is inserted after op_3. This order relation must be preserved when $op'_1 = T(Ins(3,x,\epsilon), Del(2)) = Ins(2,x,[3])$ will be transformed according to op'_3. To preserve the relation detected between op_1 and op_3, we must observe $PW(op'_1) \succ PW(op'_3)$. As $[2;3] \succ [2;2]$ is true, the order relation is preserved.

There is still a problem. This solution leads to the convergence (*i.e.* the same states), but C_2 is not respected. Indeed, we can verify in Figure 7 that:

$$T^*(op_1, [op_2; op'_3]) \neq T^*(op_1, [op_3; op'_2])$$

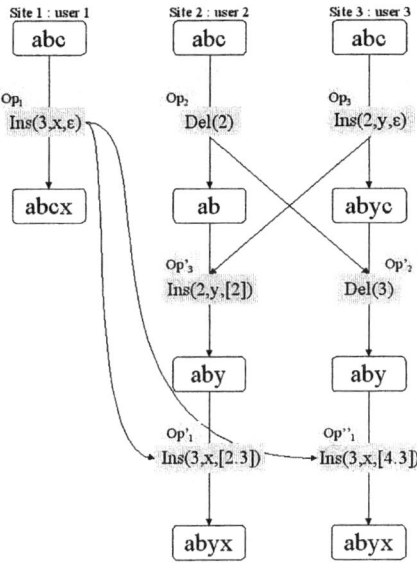

Fig. 7. Correct execution of C_2 puzzle

When two identical insertions operations are transformed according to two equivalent operation sequences, their p-words may get different. If they are different, they can be considered as equivalent if the top and the base of their p-words are equal. With the equivalence of p-words, we give the equivalence of two editing operations.

Definition 4. *(Operation equivalence)* Given two editing operations op_1 and op_2, we say that op_1 and op_2 are equivalent and we denote it also by $op_1 \equiv_\mathcal{P} op_2$ iff one of the following conditions holds: (i) $op_1 = Ins(p_1, c_1, w_1)$, $op_2 = Ins(p_2, c_2, w_2)$, $c_1 = c_2$ and $PW(op_1) \equiv_\mathcal{P} PW(op_2)$; (ii) $op_1 = Del(p_1)$, $op_2 = Del(p_2)$ and $p_1 = p_2$.

With the above operation equivalence we propose a weak form of the condition C_2 that still ensures the state convergence. This condition is called C'_2.

Definition 5. *(Condition C'_2)* For every editing operations op, op_1 and op_2, if the function T satisfies C_1 then:

$$T^*(op, [op_1\,;\,T(op_2, op_1)]) \equiv_\mathcal{P} T^*(op, [op_2\,;\,T(op_1, op_2)])$$

4.3 Correctness

In the following, we give the correctness of our approach by proving that:

1. our OT function does not lose track of insertion positions;
2. the original relation between two insert operations is preserved by transformation;
3. the conditions C_1 and C'_2 are satisfied.

Most of the proofs have been automatically checked by the theorem prover SPIKE [1].

Let $Char$ be the set of characters. We define the set of editing operations as follows: $\mathcal{O} = \{Ins(p, c, w) \mid p \in \mathbb{N}$ and $c \in Char$ and $w \in \mathcal{P}\} \cup \{Del(p) \mid p \in \mathbb{N}\}$.

Conservation of p-Words. In the following, we show that our OT function does not lose any information about position words.

Lemma 1. *Given an insert operation $op_1 = Ins(p_1, c_1, w_1)$. For every editing operation $op \in \mathcal{O}$ such that $op \neq op_1$, $PW(op_1)$ is a suffix of $PW(T(op_1, op))$.*

Proof. Let $op_1' = T(op_1, op)$ and $PW(op_1) = p_1 w_1$. Then, we consider two cases:

1. $op = Ins(p, c, w)$: Let $\alpha_1 = PW(op_1)$ and $\alpha_2 = PW(op)$.
   - if $\alpha_1 \prec \alpha_2$ or ($\alpha_1 = \alpha_2$ and $Code(c_1) < Code(c)$) then $op_1' = op_1$;
   - if $\alpha_1 \succ \alpha_2$ or ($\alpha_1 = \alpha_2$ and $Code(c_1) > Code(c)$) then $op_1' = Ins(p_1 + 1, c_1, p_1 w_1)$ and $p_1 w_1$ is a suffix of $PW(op_1')$;
2. $op = Del(p)$
   - if $p_1 > p$ then $op_1' = Ins(p_1 - 1, c_1, p_1 w_1)$ then $p_1 w_1$ is a suffix of $PW(op_1')$;
   - if $p_1 < p$ then $op_1' = op_1$;
   - if $p_1 = p$ then $op_1' = Ins(p_1, c_1, p_1 w_1)$ and $p_1 w_1$ is a suffix of op_1'. □

The following theorem states that the extension of our OT function to sequences, *i.e.* T^*, does not lose any information about position words.

Theorem 2. *Given an insert operation $op_1 = Ins(p_1, c_1, w_1)$. For every operation sequence seq, $PW(op_1)$ is a suffix of $PW(T^*(op_1, seq))$.*

Proof. By induction on n, the length of seq.

- *Basis step:* $n = 0$. Then seq is empty and we have $T^*(op_1, []) = op_1$.
- *Induction hypothesis:* for $n \geq 0$, $PW(op_1)$ is a suffix of $PW(T^*(op_1, seq))$.
- *Induction step:* Let $seq = [seq'; op]$ where seq' is a sequence of length n and $op \in \mathcal{O}$. We have $T^*(op_1, [seq'; op]) = T(T^*(op_1, seq'), op)$. By Lemma 1, $PW(T^*(op_1, seq'))$ is a suffix of $PW(T(op_1, [seq'; op])) = PW(T(T^*(op_1, seq'), op))$. By induction hypothesis and the transitivity of the suffix relation, we conclude that $PW(op_1)$ is a suffix of $PW(T^*(op_1, seq))$ for every sequence of operations seq. □

Position Relations. We can use the position relations between insert operations as an *invariant* which must be preserved when these operations are transformed and executed in all remote sites.

Lemma 2. *Given two concurrent insert operations op_1 and op_2. For every editing operation $op \in \mathcal{O}$ such that $op \neq op_1$ and $op \neq op_2$: $PW(op_1) \prec PW(op_2)$ implies $PW(T(op_1, op)) \prec PW(T(op_2, op))$*

Proof. We have to consider two cases: $op = Ins(p, c, w)$ and $op = Del(p)$.

The following theorem shows that the extension of our OT function to sequence, i.e. T^*, preserves also the invariance property.

Theorem 3. *Given two concurrent insert operations op_1 and op_2. For every sequence of operations seq: $PW(op_1) \prec PW(op_2)$ implies $PW(T^*(op_1, seq)) \prec PW(T^*(op_2, seq))$.*

Proof. By induction on the length of *seq*. □

Convergence Properties. Recall that the condition C_2' is a relaxed form of C_2. Indeed C_2' means that transforming an operation along two equivalent operation sequences will not give the same result but two equivalent operations. In the following, we sketch the proof that C_1 and C_2' are verified by our transformations and we can therefore conclude that it achieves convergence. The complete proofs of Theorems 4 and 5 below have been automatically checked by the theorem prover SPIKE. Due to lack of space we only give some representatives cases of the proofs.

The following theorem shows that our OT function satisfies C_1.

Theorem 4. *(Condition C_1). Given any editing operations $op_1, op_2 \in \mathcal{O}$ and for every object state st we have: $st \odot [op_1; T(op_2, op_1)] = st \odot [op_2; T(op_1, op_2)]$.*

Proof. Consider the following case: $op_1 = Ins(p_1, c_1, w_1)$, $op_2 = Ins(p_2, c_2, w_2)$ and $PW(op_1) \prec PW(op_2)$. According to this order, c_1 is inserted before c_2. If op_1 has been executed then when op_2 arrives it is shifted ($op_2' = T(op_2, op_1) = Ins(p_2 + 1, c_1, p_2 w_2)$) and op_2' inserts c_2 to the right of c_1. Now, if op_1 arrives after the execution of op_2, then op_1 is not shifted, i.e. $op_1' = T(op_1, op_2) = op_1$. The character c_1 is inserted as it is to the left of c_2. Thus executing $[op_1, op_2']$ and $[op_2, op_1']$ on the same object state gives also the same object state. □

Theorem 5 shows that our OT function also satisfies C_2'. This theorem means that if T satisfies condition C_1 then when transforming op_1 against two equivalent sequences $[op_2; T(op_3, op_2)]$ and $[op_3; T(op_2, op_3)]$ we will obtain two equivalent operations according to Definition 4.

Theorem 5. *(Condition C_2'). If the OT function T satisfies C_1 then for all op_1, op_2, $op_3 \in \mathcal{O}$ we have: $T^*(op_1, [op_2; T(op_3, op_2)]) \equiv_\mathcal{P} T^*(op_1, [op_3; T(op_2, op_3)])$.*

Proof. Consider the case of $op_1 = Ins(p_1, c_1, w_1)$, $op_2 = Del(p_2)$, $p_1 = p_2$ and $p > p_2 + 1$. Using our OT function (see Figure 6), we have $op_1' = T(op_1, op_2) = Ins(p_1, c_1, p_1 w_1)$ and $op_2' = T(op_2, op_1) = Del(p_2 + 1)$. When transforming op against $[Ins(p_1, c_1, w_2); Del(p_2 + 1)]$ we get $op' = Ins(p, c, (p + 1)pw)$ and when transforming op against $[Del(p_2); Ins(p_1, c_1, p_1 w_1)]$ we obtain $op'' = Ins(p, c, (p - 1)pw)$. Operations op' and op'' have the same insertion position and the same character. It remains to show that $PW(op') \equiv_\mathcal{P} PW(op'')$. As $p(p-1)p \equiv_\mathcal{P} p(p+1)p$ and the equivalence relation $\equiv_\mathcal{P}$ is a right congruence by Proposition 1 then op' and op'' are equivalent. □

5 Formal Specification

For modelling the structure and the manipulation of data in programs, *abstract data types* (ADTs) are frequently used [20]. Indeed, the *structure* of data is reflected by so called *constructors* (*e.g.*, 0 and successor $s(x)$, meaning $x+1$, may construct the ADT *nat* of natural numbers). Moreover, all (potential) data are covered by the set of *constructors terms*, exclusively built by constructors. An ADT may have different *sorts*, each characterized by a separate set of constructors. Furthermore, the *manipulation* of data is reflected by *function symbols* (*e.g.*, *plus* and *minus* on *nat*). The value computed by such functions are specified by *axioms*, usually written in equational logic. An *algebraic specification* is a description of one or more such abstract data types [20].

5.1 Collaborative Object Specification

More formally a collaborative object can be considered as a structure of the form $G = (O, T)$ where O is the set of operations applied to the object and T is the transformation function. In our approach, we construct an algebraic specification from a collaborative object. We define a sort *Opn* for the operation set O, where each operation serves as a constructor of this sort. These constructors are as follows: (i) $Ins(p, c, \omega)$ inserts element c at position p, (ii) $Del(p)$ deletes the element at position p.

We use the *List* ADT for specifying a linear collaborative object. The *List* ADT has two constructors: (i) $\langle \rangle$ (*i.e.*, an empty list); (ii) $l \circ x$ (*i.e.*, a list composed by an element x added to the end of the list l). The data type of *List*'s elements is only a template and can be replaced by each type needed. For instance, an element may be regarded as a character, a paragraph, a page, an XML node, etc. Because all operations are applied to the object structure in order to modify it, we give the following function: $\odot : List \times Opn \rightarrow List$. All appropriate axioms of the function $\odot$ describe the transition between the object states when applying an operation. For example, the operation $Del(p)$ changes *List* as follows:

$$l \odot Del(p) = \begin{cases} \langle \rangle & \text{if } l = \langle \rangle \\ l & \text{if } l = l' \circ c \text{ and } p \geq |l| \\ l' & \text{if } l = l' \circ c \text{ and } p = |l| - 1 \\ (l' \odot Del(p)) \circ c & \text{if } l = l' \circ c \text{ and } p < |l| - 1 \end{cases}$$

where $|l|$ returns the length of the list l.

In the same way, we define $Ins(p, c)$ modifications below:

$$l \odot Ins(p, c, \omega) = \begin{cases} \langle \rangle & \text{if } l = \langle \rangle \text{ and } p \neq 0 \\ l \circ c & \text{if } l = \langle \rangle \text{ and } p = 0 \\ (l' \odot Ins(p, c, \omega)) \circ d & \text{if } l = l' \circ d \text{ and } p < |l| \\ (l' \circ d) \circ c & \text{if } l = l' \circ d \text{ and } p = |l| \\ l & \text{if } l = l' \circ d \text{ and } p > |l| \end{cases}$$

An OT algorithm is defined by the following function: $T : Opn \times Opn \rightarrow Opn$. It takes two operation arguments. For example, the following transformation:

$T(Del(p_1), Ins(p_2, c_2, \omega_2)) =$ **if** $p_1 \geq p_2$ **then return** $Del(p_1 + 1)$ **else return** $Del(p_1)$

is defined by two conditional equations:

$$p_1 \geq p_2 \Longrightarrow T(Del(p_1), Ins(p_2, c_2, \omega_2)) = Del(p_1 + 1)$$
$$p_1 \not\geq p_2 \Longrightarrow T(Del(p_1), Ins(p_2, c_2, \omega_2)) = Del(p_1)$$

This example illustrates how it is easy to translate a transformation function into conditional equations. This task is straightforward and can be done mechanically.

We now express the convergence conditions as theorems to be proved in our algebraic setting. Both convergence conditions C_1 and C_2 are formulated as follows:

Theorem 6. (**Condition** C_1) $\forall op_1, op_2 \in Opn$ and $\forall st \in List$:

$$(st \odot op_1) \odot T(op_2, op_1) = (st \odot op_2) \odot T(op_1, op_2).$$

Theorem 7. (**Condition** C_2) $\forall op_1, op_2, op \in Opn$:

$$T(T(op, op_1), T(op_2, op_1)) = T(T(op, op_2), T(op_1, op_2)).$$

5.2 The Theorem Prover: SPIKE

To automatically check the convergence conditions C_1 and C_2 we have used SPIKE [1], an automated induction-based theorem prover. SPIKE was employed for the following reasons: (i) its high automation degree; (ii) its ability to perform case analysis (to deal with multiple methods and many transformation cases); (iii) its ability to find counter-examples; (iv) its incorporation of *decision procedures* (to automatically eliminate arithmetic tautologies produced during the proof attempt) [13].

6 Related Work

Several techniques have been proposed to address C_2. These may be categorized as follows.

The first approach tries to avoid the C_2 puzzle scenario. This is achieved by constraining the communication among replicas in order to restrict the space of possible execution order. For example, the SOCT4 algorithm [19] uses a sequencer, associated with a deferred broadcast and a sequential reception, to enforce a continuous global order on updates. This global order can also be obtained by using an undo/do/redo scheme like in GOTO [16].

The second approach deals with resolution of the C_2 puzzle. In this case, concurrent operations can be executed in any order, but transformation functions require to satisfy the C_2 condition. This approach has been developed in adOPTed [11], SOCT2 [14], and GOT [17]. Unfortunately, we have proved elsewhere [5] that all previously proposed transformation functions fail to satisfy this condition.

Recently, Li et al. [8] have tried to analyze the root of the problem behind C_2 puzzle. We have found that there is still a flaw in their solution. Let $op_1 =$

$Ins(p+1,x)$, $op_2 = Ins(p,z)$ and $op_3 = Del(p)$ be three concurrent operations generated on sites 1, 2 and 3 respectively. They use a function β that computes for every editing operation the original position according to the initial object state. For this case, it is possible to get: $\beta(op_1) = \beta(op_2) = \beta(op_3)$ whereas $Pos(op_1) > Pos(op_2)$. When a conflict occurs Li et al. use the site identifier to reorder the character to be inserted (see our OT function in Figure 6). Consider the following sequences:

$$S1 = [op_1; T(op_3, op_1)] = [Ins(p+1, z); Del(p)]$$
$$S2 = [op_3; T(op_1, op_3)] = [Del(p); Ins(p, z)]$$

Transforming op_2 against $S1$ does not give the same operation that transforming op_2 against $S2$. This case leads to divergence problem. Note that $Pos(T(op_2, op_3)) = Pos(T(op_1, op_3))$. Thus op_1 and op_2 lose their original relation after transformation according to op_3. The mistake is due to the definition of their β function. Indeed, their definition relies on the exclusion transformation function ET, which is the reversed function of T. For instance, if $T(op_1, op_2) = op'_1$ then $ET(op'_1, op_2) = op_1$. Due to the non-inversibility of T, ET is not always defined [16]. Consequently, the convergence property cannot be achieved in all cases.

7 Conclusion

OT has a great potential for generating non-trivial states of convergence. However, without a correct set of transformation functions, OT is useless. In this paper we have pointed out correctness problems of the existing OT algorithms used to synchronize linear collaborative objects (such as document text or XML trees) and we have proposed a solution based on a weak form of the condition C_2. Using our theorem-proving approach [5,6] we have provided a complete proof for our OT algorithm. Furthermore, our solution is generic because it can be applied to any linear structure-based data.

Although this weak form still ensures the convergence state, we cannot plug our OT algorithm in all integration algorithms based on the condition C_2, such as adOPTed [11] and SOCT2 [14]. So, we consider our work as a first step towards to build a generic integration algorithm based only on conditions C_1 and C'_2. Moreover, we plan to optimize our OT algorithm because the size of p-words increase according to the number of transformation steps.

References

1. A. Bouhoula, E. Kounalis, and M. Rusinowitch. Automated Mathematical Induction. *Journal of Logic and Computation*, 5(5):631–668, 1995.
2. C. A. Ellis and S. J. Gibbs. Concurrency Control in Groupware Systems. In *SIGMOD Conference*, volume 18, pages 399–407, 1989.
3. R. Guerraoui and C. Hari. On the consistency problem in mobile distributed computing. In *Proceedings of the second ACM international workshop on Principles of mobile computing*, pages 51–57. ACM Press, 2002.
4. M. P. Herlihy and J. M. Wing. Linearizability: a correctness condition for concurrent objects. *ACM Trans. Program. Lang. Syst.*, 12(3):463–492, 1990.

5. A. Imine, P. Molli, G. Oster, and M. Rusinowitch. Proving Correctness of Transformation Functions in Real-Time Groupware. In *8th European Conference of Computer-supported Cooperative Work*, Helsinki, Finland, 14.-18. September 2003.
6. A. Imine, P. Molli, G. Oster, and M. Rusinowitch. Deductive verification of distributed groupware systems. In *Algebraic Methodology and Software Technology, 10th International Conference, AMAST 2004*, volume 3116 of *Lecture Notes in Computer Science*, pages 226–240. Springer, 2004.
7. A. Imine, M. Rusinowitch, G. Oster, and P. Molli. Formal design and verification of operational transformation algorithms for copies convergence. *Theoretical Computer Science*, to appear (2005).
8. D. Li and R. Li. Ensuring Content Intention Consistency in Real-Time Group Editors. In *the 24th International Conference on Distributed Computing Systems (ICDCS 2004)*, Tokyo, Japan, March 2004. IEEE Computer Society.
9. B. Lushman and G. V. Cormack. Proof of correctness of ressel's adopted algorithm. *Information Processing Letters*, 86(3):303–310, 2003.
10. P. Molli, G. Oster, H. Skaf-Molli, and A. Imine. Using the transformational approach to build a safe and generic data synchronizer. In *Proceedings of the 2003 international ACM SIGGROUP conference on Supporting group work*, pages 212–220. ACM Press, 2003.
11. M. Ressel, D. Nitsche-Ruhland, and R. Gunzenhauser. An Integrating, Transformation-Oriented Approach to Concurrency Control and Undo in Group Editors. In *Proceedings of the ACM Conference on Computer Supported Cooperative Work (CSCW'96)*, pages 288–297, Boston, Massachusetts, USA, November 1996.
12. Y. Saito and M. Shapiro. Optimistic replication. *ACM Comput. Surv.*, 37(1):42–81, 2005.
13. S. Stratulat. A general framework to build contextual cover set induction provers. *Journal of Symbolic Computation*, 32(4):403–445, 2001.
14. M. Suleiman, M. Cart, and J. Ferrié. Concurrent Operations in a Distributed and Mobile Collaborative Environment. In *Proceedings of the Fourteenth International Conference on Data Engineering, February 23-27, 1998, Orlando, Florida, USA*, pages 36–45. IEEE Computer Society, 1998.
15. C. Sun. The copowerpoint project. http://reduce.qpsf.edu.au/copowerpoint/, 2004.
16. C. Sun and C. Ellis. Operational transformation in real-time group editors: issues, algorithms, and achievements. In *Proceedings of the 1998 ACM conference on Computer supported cooperative work*, pages 59–68. ACM Press, 1998.
17. C. Sun, X. Jia, Y. Zhang, Y. Yang, and D. Chen. Achieving convergence, causality-preservation and intention-preservation in real-time cooperative editing systems. *ACM Transactions on Computer-Human Interaction (TOCHI)*, 5(1):63–108, March 1998.
18. D. Sun, S. Xia, C. Sun, and D. Chen. Operational transformation for collaborative word processing. In *CSCW '04: Proceedings of the 2004 ACM conference on Computer supported cooperative work*, pages 437–446, New York, NY, USA, 2004. ACM Press.
19. N. Vidot, M. Cart, J. Ferrié, and M. Suleiman. Copies convergence in a distributed real-time collaborative environment. In *Proceedings of the ACM Conference on Computer Supported Cooperative Work (CSCW'00)*, Philadelphia, Pennsylvania, USA, December 2000.
20. M. Wirsing. Algebraic Specification. *Handbook of theoretical computer science (vol. B): formal models and semantics*, pages 675–788, 1990.

Designing Efficient Fail-Safe Multitolerant Systems

Arshad Jhumka[1] and Neeraj Suri[2]

[1] Department of Computer Science University of Warwick,
Coventry CV4 7AL, UK
arshad@dcs.warwick.ac.uk
[2] Department of Computer Science, TU - Darmstadt, Darmstadt, Germany

Abstract. In this paper, we propose a method for designing efficient fail-safe multitolerant systems. A multitolerant system is one that is able to tolerate multiple types of faults, and a fail-safe multitolerant system handles the various fault types in a fail-safe manner. Efficiency issues of interest are fault tolerance-related, and they are: (i) completeness, and (ii) accuracy. Based on earlier work, this paper makes the following contributions: (i) We develop a theory for design of efficient fail-safe multitolerance, (ii) based on the theory, we present a sound and complete algorithm that automates the addition of efficient fail-safe multitolerance, and (iii) we develop the example of an efficient fail-safe multitolerant token ring to show the viability of our approach. Our approach works for finite state systems.

Keywords: Detectors, fail-safe, multitolerance, program transformation, safety specification, automation, program synthesis.

1 Introduction

Fault tolerance is the ability of a program or system to satisfy its specification, even in the presence of external perturbations. Perturbations, or *faults*, are varied in nature, for example, computer intrusions, message losses, variable corruptions etc. Thus, a program intended to be deployed in such a faulty environment needs to be able to withstand the effect of these faults, i.e., we require the program to be tolerant to the faults. In other words, such a program needs to be *multitolerant*.

Alpern and Schneider showed that, in general, a specification [1] can be considered as the intersection of a *safety* specification, and a *liveness* specification. In the presence of faults, the need to satisfy both specifications is not mandatory, giving rise to different levels of fault tolerance. The more prominent of them being (i) fail-safe, (ii) non-masking and (iii) masking fault tolerance. In this paper, we focus on *fail-safe fault tolerance*. Fail-safe fault tolerance, informally, is the ability of a system to always satisfy its safety specification in the presence of faults, i.e., if the system is about to violate safety, then the system is halted. This type of fault tolerance is often used in safety critical systems, such as nuclear power plants, train control systems, where safety is more important than continuous provision of service. In practice, a backup system may be used after the original system is halted. Though a fail-safe fault-tolerant program does not have to guarantee liveness in presence of faults, some form of "controlled" liveness can be obtained [4].

Arora and Kulkarni [3] showed that there exists a class of program components, called *detectors* that is both necessary and sufficient to ensure fail-safe fault tolerance. A detector is a program component that asserts the validity of a given predicate in a given state of the program. Examples are run-time checks [9], executable assertions [5], error detection codes, comparators etc. Our focus on fail-safe fault tolerance design thus translates into focusing on the design of detectors.

Designing effective detectors is known to be a non-trivial task [9]. Composing[1] ineffective detectors with a given program will have some adverse effects, such as failures to detect erroneous states of the system, or the trigger of false alarms. To address these problems, Jhumka *et.al* [7,6] developed a theory of detectors that identified the properties that underpin the operational effectiveness of detectors. These properties are (i) *completeness*, and (ii) *accuracy*. The completeness property of a detector is linked with a detector's ability to detect erroneous states, while the accuracy property is linked with a detector's ability to avoid mistakes (false alarms). A complete and accurate detector is termed *perfect*. The completeness and accuracy properties represent the fault tolerance *efficiency* issues on which we focus in this paper.

Our approach to the design of multitolerance is based on the well-known software engineering principle of decomposition. Instead of trying to design detectors that are to efficiently tolerate a complex fault class F, we first decompose the complex fault class F into a sequence of basic fault classes $f_1 \ldots f_n$. We then design effective detectors that handle the first basic fault class f_1. Once done, we consider the next basic fault class f_2, and design effective detectors that not only handle f_2, but also do not interfere with the effectiveness of detectors that handle f_1. The idea is to incrementally design a multitolerant program such that, in any one step, effective tolerance to a new basic fault class is added, while all previous tolerances and effectivenesses are preserved.

1.1 Related Work

The first work on multitolerance design was proposed by Arora and Kulkarni in [2]. However, our work differs from that of Arora and Kulkarni [2] in the following ways: (i) fault tolerance efficiency issues are at the heart of the approach proposed in this paper, unlike in [2], (ii) we present a sound and complete algorithm for automating addition of multitolerance, unlike in [2]. Later, Kulkarni and Ebnenasir [8] proposed an automated approach, as in this paper, for the addition of multitolerance. Their approach differs from that proposed in this paper in two ways: (i) they tackle the problem in a different system model (where read/write restrictions are imposed), and (ii) they do not tackle efficiency properties, as in this paper.

Building on previous work [7,6], our contributions in this paper are: (i) We present a theory for efficient fail-safe multitolerance design, (ii) We provide a sound, and complete algorithm that automates the addition of efficient fail-safe

---

[1] We will formally define this term in the next section.

multitolerance, and (iii) we present a case study of the design of a fail-safe multitolerant token ring to show the applicability of our approach.

The paper is structured as follows: Sec. 2 introduces the assumed models and terminologies. Sec. 3 defines the problem of perfect fail-safe fault tolerance. In Sec. 4 addresses the problem of adding perfect fail-safe multitolerance to programs. An example of a fully distributed, fail-safe multitolerant program for a token ring is presented in Sec. 5.

2 Preliminaries

In this section, we recall the standard formal definitions of programs, faults, fault tolerance (in particular, fail-safe fault-tolerance), and of specifications [3].

2.1 Concurrent Systems

The work assumes an *interleaved* execution semantics together with the *shared variable* communication paradigm.

2.2 Programs

A *program* P consists of a set of processes $\{p_1 \ldots p_n\}$. Each process p_i contains a finite set of actions, and a finite set of variables. Each variable stores a value of a predefined nonempty finite domain and is associated with a predefined set of initial values. In this paper, we will use two representations of a program: (i) guarded command notation, and (ii) state transition system. While formal definitions/results will be based on the transition model, the guarded command notation provides a more "visual" basis.

In the guarded command notation, an action has the form

$$\langle \text{guard} \rangle \rightarrow \langle \text{statement} \rangle$$

where the guard is a predicate over the program variables, and the statement is either the empty statement or an instantaneous value assignment to one or more variables.

The *state space* S_P *of a program* P is the set of all possible value assignments to variables. A *state predicate of* P is a boolean expression over the state space of P. The *set of initial states* I_P is defined by the set of all possible assignments of initial values to variables of P.

An *action* ac *of* P *is enabled in a state* s if the guard of ac evaluates to "true" in s. An action ac can be represented by a set of state pairs. Note that programs are permitted to be non-deterministic as multiple actions can be enabled in the same state.

A *computation of* p is a weakly fair (finite or infinite) sequence of states $s_0, s_1, \ldots$ such that $s_0 \in I_p$ and for each $j \geq 0$, s_{j+1} results from s_j by executing the assignment of a single action which is enabled in s_j. *Weak fairness* implies that if a program action ac is continuously enabled, ac is eventually chosen to be executed. Weak fairness implies that a computation is *maximal* with respect to program actions, i.e., if the computation is finite then no program action is enabled in the final state.

A *state* s *occurs in a computation* $s_0, s_1, \ldots$ iff there exists an i such that $s = s_i$. Similarly, a *transition* (s, s') *occurs in a computation* $s_0, s_1, \ldots$ iff there exists an i such that $s = s_i$ and $s' = s_{i+1}$.

In the context of this paper, programs are equivalently represented as state machines, i.e., a program is a tuple $P = (S_P, I_P, \delta_P)$, where S_P is the state space and $I_P \subseteq S_P$ is the set of initial states. Transition $(s, s') \in \delta_P$ iff ac of P is enabled in state s and execution of ac in state s results in state s'. We say that ac *induces* these transitions. State s is called the *start state* and s' the *end state* of the transition.

2.3 Specifications

A *specification* for a program P is a set of computations which is *fusion-closed*. A *specification S is fusion-closed*[2] iff the following holds for finite computations α, β, and a state s: If $\alpha = \gamma \cdot s \cdot \rho$ and $\beta = \epsilon \cdot s \cdot \sigma$ are in S, then so are computations $\gamma \cdot s \cdot \sigma$ and $\epsilon \cdot s \cdot \rho$. A *computation c of P satisfies a specification S* iff $c \in S$. A *program P satisfies a specification S* iff all possible computation of P satisfies S.

Definition 1 (Maintains). *Let P be a program, S be a specification and α be a finite computation of P. We say that α maintains S iff there exists a sequence of states β of P such that $\alpha \cdot \beta \in S$.*

Definition 2 (Safety specification). *A specification S of a program P is a safety specification iff the following condition holds: $\forall$ computation σ that violates S, $\exists$ a prefix α of σ s.t $\forall$ state sequences β, $\alpha \cdot \beta$ violates S.*

Informally, the safety specification of a program states that "something bad never happens". More formally, it defines a set of "bad" finite computation prefixes that should not be found in any computation. Thus, satisfaction of a safety specification implies that the program should not display any violating (bad) computation prefix.

2.4 Fault Models and Fault Tolerance

All standard fault models from practice which endanger a safety specification (transient or permanent faults) can be modeled as a set of added transitions. We focus on the subset of these fault models which can potentially be tolerated: We disallow faults to violate the safety specification directly. For example, in the token ring protocol, at most one process can hold the token. We allow a fault to duplicate the token, however we rule out faults that "force" a second process to hold a duplicated token, as this kind of faults cannot be tolerated. Rather, faults can change the program state (e.g., duplication of token) such that subsequent program actions execution (holding of duplicate token) violate the safety specification. This can be potentially tolerated by asking any process to check if some other process is already holding a token, before accepting one.

We defer for future work investigation of fault tolerance under the fault model where safety is directly violated.

---

[2] Intuitively, fusion closure guarantees that history is available in each computation state.

Definition 3 (Fault model). *A fault model F for program P and safety specification SS is a set of transitions over the variables of P that do not violate SS, i.e., if transition (s_j, s_{j+1}) is in F and $s_0, s_1, \ldots, s_j$ is in SS, then $s_0, s_1, \ldots, s_j, s_{j+1}$ is in SS.*

We call members of F the *faults* affecting P. We say that a *fault occurs* if a fault transition is executed.

Definition 4 (Computation in the presence of faults). *A computation of P in the presence of faults F is a weakly P-fair sequence of states $s_0, s_1, \ldots$ such that s_0 is an initial state of P and for each $j \geq 0$, s_{j+1} results from s_j by executing a program action from P or a fault action from F.*

Weakly P-fair means that only the actions of P are treated weakly fair (fault actions must not eventually occur if they are continuously enabled). In the transition system view, a fault model F adds a set of (fault) transitions to δ_P. We denote the modified transition relation by δ_P^F. We call δ_P^F the program P in presence of F. Since fault actions are not treated fairly, their occurrence is not mandatory. Note that we do not rule out faults that occur infinitely often (as long as they do not directly violate the safety property).

Earlier, we discussed that a safety specification entails keeping track of bad prefixes that should not appear in any computation. The requirement of a safety specification being fusion-closed allows us to keep track of bad *transitions*, rather than of prefixes.

Definition 5 (bad transition). *Give a program P, fault model F, and fusion-closed safety specification $SSPEC$. A transition $t \in \delta_p^F$ is bad with respect to a safety specification SSPEC if for all computations σ of p holds: If t occurs in σ then $\sigma \notin SSPEC$.*

This is possible as fusion-closure implies availability of history in every computation state, and the history (prefix) can be encoded into that state. Note that, under our fault model assumption, a fault transition cannot be a bad transition.

Definition 6 (Fail-safe fault-tolerance). *Given a program P with safety specification SS, and a fault model F. The program P is said to be* fail-safe F-tolerant *for specification S iff all computations of P in the presence of faults F satisfy SS.*

If F is a fault model and SS is a safety specification, we say that a *program P is F-intolerant for SS* iff P satisfies SS in the absence of F but violates SS in the presence of F. For brevity, we will write *fault-intolerant* instead of *F-intolerant for SS* if F and SS are clear from the context.

Definition 7 (Reachable transition). *A transition (s,t) of P is reachable iff there exists a computation α of P such that (s,t) occurs in α.*

Definition 8 (Reachable transition in the presence of faults). *We say that a transition (s,t) is reachable by p in the presence of faults iff there exists a computation α of P in presence of faults such that (s,t) occurs in α.*

3 Addition of Fail-Safe Fault Tolerance

In this section, we explain the addition of fail-safe fault tolerance to a fault-intolerant program. We first briefly review the role of detectors in ensuring fail-safe fault tolerance.

3.1 Role of Detectors in Fail-Safe Fault Tolerance

Informally, a detector[3] is a program component that detects whether a given predicate is true in a given state. Arora and Kulkarni showed in [3] that, for every action ac of a program P with safety specification SS, there exists a predicate such that execution of ac in a state where this predicate is true satisfies SS. In other words, the action ac is transformed as follows: $(g \rightarrow st) \rightarrow (d \wedge g \rightarrow st)$, where d is the detector implementing the predicate. In this case, we say that action ac is composed with detector d (we sometimes say that detector d is monitoring ac). We say that a program P is composed with detector d if there is an action ac of P such that ac is composed with d. We also say that a program P is composed with a set of detectors D if $\forall d \in D \exists\ ac$ of P such that ac is composed with d. If a transition (s, s') induced by ac violates SS, then such a transition is a bad transition. Thus, any computation that violates SS contains a bad transition.

Given a program P with safety specification SS expressed as a temporal logic formula, the set of bad transitions (due to fusion closure) can be computed in polynomial time by considering all transitions (s, s') where $s, s' \in S_p$. For simplicity, we assume that the safety specification is concisely expressed as a set of bad transitions. The authors of [3] also show that fail-safe fault-tolerant programs contain detectors. However, [3] did not show how to design the required detectors. To address this problem, Jhumka et.al [6,7] developed a theory that underpins the design of effective (complete and accurate) detectors. We will develop the theory of multitolerance based on the theory of [6,7], which we will briefly introduce for sake of completeness.

3.2 Transformation Problem for Addition of Fail-Safe Fault Tolerance

The problem of adding fail-safe fault tolerance is formalized as follows:

Definition 9 (Fail-safe fault tolerance addition). *Let SS be a safety specification, F a fault model, and P an F-intolerant program for SS. The fail-safe transformation problem is defined as follows: Identify a program P' such that:*

1. *P' satisfies SS in the presence of F.*
2. *In the absence of F, every computation of P' is a computation of P.*
3. *In the absence of F, every computation of P is a computation of P'.*

A program p' that satisfies the above conditions is said to solve the fail-safe transformation problem for p. The second and third conditions imply that the detectors need to be transparent in the absence of faults, and should not add other ways of satisfying SS.

In the next section, we present a theory of detectors, based upon which, we provide an algorithm that synthesizes a program p' from a fault-intolerant program p, such that p' solves the fail-safe transformation problem.

---

[3] For a more formal introduction, we refer the reader to [3].

3.3 A Theory of Detectors

The detector theory of [6,7] is based on the concept of SS-inconsistency, where SS is the safety specification of a program P. The intuition behind the inconsistency is that if a given computation of P in the presence of faults violates the safety specification SS, then some "erroneous" transition has occurred in the computation, i.e., inconsistent with SS.

Definition 10 (SS-inconsistent transitions). *Given a fault-intolerant program P with safety specification SS, fault model F, and a computation α of P in the presence of F. A transition (s, s') is SS-inconsistent for P w.r.t. α iff*

- *there exists a prefix α' of α such that α' violates SS,*
- *(s, s') occurs in α', i.e., $\alpha' = \sigma \cdot s \cdot s' \cdot \beta$,*
- *all transitions in $s \cdot s' \cdot \beta$ are in δ_p, and*
- *$\sigma \cdot s$ maintains SS.*

Fig. 1 illustrates Definition 10. It shows the state transition relation of a program in the presence of faults (the transition (s_3, s_4) is introduced by F). The safety specification SS identifies a bad transition (s_6, s_7) which should be avoided. In the presence of faults, this transition becomes reachable and hence the program if F-intolerant since it exhibits a computation α_1 violating SS. In this computation, the three transitions following the fault transition match Definition 10 and hence are SS-inconsistent w.r.t. α_1 in the presence of F. Note that an SS-inconsistent transition is only reachable in the presence of faults.

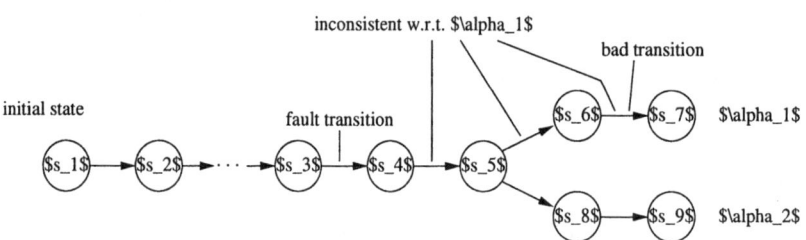

Fig. 1. Graphical explanation of SS-consistency

Intuitively, an SS-inconsistent transition for a given program computation is a program transition where the subsequent execution of a sequence of program transitions causes the computation to violate the safety specification. In a sense, SS-inconsistent transitions lead the program computation on the "wrong path".

Now we define SS-inconsistency independent of a particular computation.

Definition 11 (SS-inconsistent transition for P). *Given a program P, safety specification SS, fault model F. A transition (s, s') is SS-inconsistent for P iff there exists a computation α of P in the presence of F such that (s, s') is SS-inconsistent for p w.r.t. α.*

In general, due to non-determinism in program execution, a transition can be SS-inconsistent w.r.t. a computation α_1, and not be SS-inconsistent w.r.t. α_2.

If we cannot find a computation in the presence of faults for which a particular transition is SS-inconsistent then we say that this transition is SS-consistent.

The notion of SS-inconsistency is a characteristic for a computation which violates SS [6].

In the next section, we introduce the notion of perfect detectors using the terminology of SS-consistency.

3.4 Perfect Detectors

From Sec. 3.3, we observed that SS-inconsistent transitions are those transitions that can lead a program to violate its safety specification in the presence of faults if no precautions are taken. Perfect detectors are a means to implement these precautions. The definition of perfect detectors follows two guidelines: A detector d monitoring a given action ac of program P needs to (1) "reject" the starting states of all transitions induced by ac that are SS-inconsistent for P, and (2) "keep" the starting states of all induced transitions that are SS-consistent for P. These two properties are captured in the definition of *completeness* and *accuracy* of detectors.

Definition 12 (Detector accuracy). *Given a program P, safety specification SS, fault model F, and a program action ac of P. A detector d monitoring ac is SS-accurate for ac in P in presence of F iff for all transitions (s, s') induced by ac holds: if (s, s') is SS-consistent for P, then $s \in d$.*

Definition 13 (Detector completeness). *Given a program P with safety specification SS, fault class F, and a program action ac of P. A detector d monitoring action ac is SS-complete for ac in P in presence of F iff for all transitions (s, s') induced by ac holds: if (s, s') is SS-inconsistent for P, then $s \notin d$.*

Definition 14 (Perfect detector). *Given a program P, safety specification SS, fault class F, and a program action ac of P. A detector d monitoring ac is SS-perfect for ac in P in presence of F iff d is both SS-complete and SS-accurate for ac in P.*

Where the specification is clear from the context we will write *accuracy* instead of *SS-accuracy* (the same holds for completeness and perfection).

Intuitively, the completeness property of a detector is related to the safety property of the program p in the sense that the detector should filter out all SS-inconsistent transitions for p, whereas the accuracy property relates to the liveness specification of p in the sense that the detector should not rule out SS-consistent transitions. This intuition is captured by the following lemmas (for proof, refer to [6,7]).

Lemma 1 (Fault-free behavior).

Given a fault-intolerant program P and a set D of perfect detectors. Consider program P' resulting from the composition of P and D. Then the following statements hold:

1. In the absence of faults, every computation of P' is a computation of P.
2. In the absence of faults, every computation of P is a computation of P'.

```
add-perfect-fail-safe(δ_P, δ_F, ss: set of bad transitions):
{ ss_r := get-ssr(δ_P, δ_F, ss)
  return (P' = δ_P \ ss_r)}

get-ssr(δ_P, δ_F, ss: set of transitions):
{ ss_r := {(s,t)|(s,t) ∈ ss is reachable by P in presence of F}
  return (ss_r)}
```

Fig. 2. Algorithm that solves the fail-safe fault tolerance addition problem

Before we characterize the role of perfect detectors in presence of faults, we formally define critical actions of a program.

Definition 15 (Critical and non-critical actions). *Given a program P with safety specification SS, and fault class F. An action ac of P is said to be critical for P w.r.t SS in presence of F iff there exists a transition (s, s') induced by ac such that (s, s') is a bad transition that is reachable by P in presence of faults F (Definition 7). An action is non-critical for P w.r.t SS in presence of F iff it is not critical for P w.r.t SS in presence of F.*

Lemma 2 (Behavior in the presence of faults). *Given a fault-intolerant program P with safety specification SS, and fault class F. Given also a program P' by composing each critical action ac of P w.r.t SS in presence of F with a perfect detector for ac in presence of F. Then, P' satisfies SS in presence of faults F.*

Proofs of lemmas 1 and 2 can be found in [7]. From lemmas 1 and 2, we observe that a program P' obtained by composing each critical action ac of a fault-intolerant program P with a perfect detector for ac in P in presence of faults F (which can be shown to exist [6]) solves the fail-safe fault tolerance addition problem. When a fail-safe fault-tolerant program P' satisfies the three conditions for fail-safe fault tolerance addition problem, we say that P' is *perfectly fail-safe F-tolerant w.r.t SS* and that P' has *efficient fail-safe F-tolerance* (since P' is a *maximal* program that satisfies SS in presence of F).

3.5 Algorithm for Adding Perfect Fail-Safe Fault Tolerance

Having established the role of perfect detectors in fail-safe fault tolerance, in Fig. 2, we provide an algorithm that solves the fail-safe transformation problem, using perfect detectors. It takes as arguments the program P, the fault class F, and the set ss of bad program transitions encoding the safety specification (it can be shown that these are induced by critical actions of P in presence of F).

The theory (and algorithm) presented adds fail-safe fault tolerance to a single fault class. We now extend the results to handle multiple fault classes.

4 Addition of Perfect Fail-Safe Multitolerance

In this section, we consider the addition of perfect fail-safe fault tolerance for multiple fault classes. Specifically, the main question is whether perfect detectors are composable, i.e., whether the addition of two perfect detectors for two different fault classes in a program preserve each other efficiency properties (accuracy and completeness)?

4.1 A Stepwise Addition Approach

The approach adopted is stepwise, as also suggested by Arora and Kulkarni in [2]. One of the problems during the design of multitolerance is that a tolerance mechanism (detector in this case) for one fault class can interfere with the tolerance mechanism for another fault class. Thus, any synthesis method or automated procedure should ensure, by construction, that no interference exists between the tolerance mechanisms for different fault classes.

First, we define a fail-safe multitolerant program.

Definition 16 (Fail-Safe Multitolerant Program). *Given a program P with safety specification SS, and n fault classes $F_1 \ldots F_n$. A program P is said to be fail-safe multitolerant to $F_1 \ldots F_n$ for SS iff P is fail-safe F_i-tolerant for SS for each $1 \leq i \leq n$. A program P is said to be* perfectly *fail-safe multitolerant to $F_1 \ldots F_n$ for SS iff P is perfectly fail-safe F_i-tolerant to SS for each $1 \leq i \leq n$.*

The stepwise approach considers one fault class at a time, in some fixed order $F_1 \ldots F_n$. The fault-intolerant program P is transformed into a perfectly fail-safe multitolerant program to fault classes $F_1 \ldots F_n$. In the first step, P is augmented with detectors that will make the resulting program P_1 perfectly fail-safe fault-tolerant to F_1. Then, in the second step, P_1 is augmented with detectors that will make the resulting program P_2 perfectly fail-safe fault-tolerant to F_2, while preserving its perfect fail-safe fault tolerance to F_1. The same is repeated until all fault classes are tolerated. In other words, we want to know if perfect detectors for the various fault classes compose. This represents the main contribution (synthesis of perfect fail-safe multitolerance) of the paper. In contrast, [2,8] focused only only on fail-safe multitolerance (which can be trivially satisfied by using the empty program), whereas this paper focuses on the non-trivial provision of *perfect* fail-safe multitolerance. We provide below the non-interference conditions that need to be satisfied by a synthesis method:

Step 1 of Non-interference Conditions: Specifically, in the first step, when the fault-intolerant program P is augmented with detectors to obtain a program P_1, the following non-interference conditions need to be verified:

1. In the absence of F_1, the detector components added to P do not interfere with P, i.e., each computation of P is in the problem specification even if it executes concurrently with the new detector components.
2. In the presence of faults F_1, each computation of the detector components is in the components' specification even if they execute concurrently with P.
3. In the presence of faults F_1, the resulting program is perfectly fail-safe F_1-tolerant.

Step 2 of Non-interference Conditions: In the second step, when the fail-safe F_1-tolerant program p_1 is augmented with detectors that will make it fail-safe F_2-tolerant program, while preserving its fail-safe F_1 tolerance, the following non-interference conditions need to be satisfied:

1. In the absence of F_1 and F_2, the new detectors for fail-safe fault tolerance to F_2 do not interfere with p_1, i.e., each computation of p_1 satisfies the problem specification even if p_1 executes concurrently with the new detectors.
2. In the presence of F_1, the new detectors for fail-safe fault tolerance to F_2 do not interfere with the fail-safe fault tolerance to F_1 of p_1, i.e., every computation of p_1 is in the fail-safe fault-tolerance specification to F_1 even if p_1 executes concurrently with the new components.
3. In the presence of F_1, the new detectors for fail-safe fault tolerance to F_2 do not interfere with the perfect detection to F_1 of p_1.
4. In the presence of F_2, p_1 does not interfere with the new detectors that provide fail-safe fault-tolerance to F_2, i.e., every computation of the new component is in the new components specification.
5. In the presence of F_2, p_1 does not interfere with the perfect detection to F_2 provided by the new detector components.

These steps can be easily generalized to n steps. Observe that these sets of conditions specify the transformation problem for addition of perfect fail-safe multitolerance to an initially fault-intolerant program. Our next goal is to derive a sound, and complete algorithm that satisfies the various non-interference conditions during the addition of fail-safe multitolerance.

Before detailing our automated approach for addition of fail-safe multitolerance, we present a key result behind our approach.

Lemma 3 (Perfect detectors and multitolerance). *Given a fault-intolerant program P with safety specification SS, and fault classes $F_1 \ldots F_n$. Given a program P_{i-1} which is perfectly fail-safe multitolerant for SS with perfect detection to fault classes $F_1 \ldots F_{i-1}$. Given also a program P_i obtained from P_{i-1} s.t P_i is perfectly fail-safe fault-tolerant to F_i. Then, P_i is also perfectly fail-safe multitolerant to fault classes $F_1 \ldots F_{i-1}$.*

Proof Sketch: We can prove this by induction over the fault sequence. The base case is trivial, while for the inductive step, since all detectors added for F_i are perfect, they reject only SS-inconsistent transitions, i.e., they do not add any transition. Hence, the new set of perfect detectors added cannot interfere with the previous detectors. Thus, perfect detection for all previous fault classes is preserved.

P_i can be obtained from P_{i-1} by composing actions that are critical in the presence of F_i with the relevant perfect detectors (Lemma 2). Lemma 3 then shows that composition with perfect detectors preserves the perfect fail-safe fault tolerance to other classes. The lemma underpins the synthesis algorithm for perfect fail-safe multitolerance. The algorithm is sound (The returned program is indeed perfectly fail-safe multitolerant to all fault classes considered) and complete (if such a perfectly fail-safe multitolerant to all fault classes considered exists, then the algorithm will find it).

4.2 An Algorithm for Adding Efficient Fail-Safe Multitolerance

The algorithm for automatic synthesis of fail-safe multitolerant programs with perfect detection to all fault classes is shown in Fig. 3. The resulting program is fail-safe multitolerant to n fault classes by design (soundness).

Theorem 1. *Algorithm* add-perfect-fail-safe-multitolerance *is sound and complete.*

Proof. The algorithm is sound by construction, based on Lemma 3. Completeness of the algorithm is due to our assumption of finite state (bounded) programs and by construction.

---

add-perfect-fail-safe-multitolerance($P, [F_1 \ldots F_n]$, ss: set of transitions):

$\{i := 1; P_0 := P$
while $(i \leq n)$ do $\{$
$\quad P_i := $ add-perfect-fail-safe(P_{i-1}, F_i, ss);
$\quad i := i + 1;\}$ od
return$(P_n)\}$

Fig. 3. The algorithm adds fail-safe fault tolerance to n fault classes, with perfect detection to every fault class

It can also be shown that algorithm *add-perfect-fail-safe-multitolerance2* (see Fig. 4) is equivalent to algorithm *add-perfect-fail-safe-multitolerance*.

---

add-perfect-fail-safe-multitolerance2($P, [F_1 \ldots F_n]$, ss: set of transitions):

$P_n := $ add-perfect-fail-safe$(P, \bigcup_{i=1}^{n} F_i, ss)$;
return$(P_n)\}$

Fig. 4. The algorithm adds fail-safe fault tolerance to n fault classes, with perfect detection to every fault class

In the next section, we present a case study of the design of a perfect fail-safe multitolerant token ring.

5 Example of a Fail-Safe Multitolerant Token Ring

Processes $0 \ldots N$ are arranged in a ring. Process $k, 0 \leq k < N$ passes the token to process $k+1$, whereas process N passes the token to process 0. Each process k has a binary variable, $t.k$, and a process $k, k \neq N$ holds the token iff $t.k \neq t.(k+1)$, and process N holds the token iff $t.N = t.0$.

The fault-intolerant program for the token ring is as follows ($+_2$ is modulo-2 addition) :

ITR1 :: $k \neq 0 \land t.k \neq t.(k-1) \rightarrow t.k := t.(k-1)$

ITR2 :: $k = 0 \land t.k \neq t.N +_2 1 \rightarrow t.k := t.N +_2 1$

In the presence of faults, we do not want certain processes to take some steps. In particular, if the state of process k is corrupted, then process $k+1$ should not make any transition. The faults we consider here are general faults, such as timing, message loss or duplication, but such faults are detected by the process before any action inadvertently accesses that state. When a fault is detected by process k, the value of $t.k$ is set to $\bot$.

Fault Action: The first fault class F_1 that we consider is one that corrupts the state of a *single* process k, which can be any process.

$$F_1 :: t.k \neq \bot \wedge |\{k|t.k = \bot\}| = 0 \rightarrow t.k := \bot$$

Fail-Safe Fault Tolerance to Fault Class F_1: Running algorithm *add-perfect-fail-safe-multitolerance* will result in the following program after the first iteration.

1-FSTR1::$|\{k : t.k = \bot\}| \leq 1 \wedge t.(k-1) \neq \bot \wedge k \neq 0 \wedge t.k \neq t.(k-1) \rightarrow t.k := t.(k-1)$

1-FSTR2 :: $|\{k : t.k = \bot\}| \leq 1 \wedge t.N \neq \bot \wedge k = 0 \wedge t.k \neq t.N +_2 1 \rightarrow t.k := t.N +_2 1$

Theorem 2 (Fail-safe TR). *Program 1-FSTR is perfectly fail-safe fault-tolerant to F_1.*

Perfect Fail-Safe Fault Tolerance to Fault Classes F_1 and F_2: Second, we consider a fault class where the state of two processes k and l can be corrupted.

Fault Action: The fault action that we consider is

$$F_2 :: t.k \neq \bot \wedge |\{k|t.k = \bot\}| = 1 \rightarrow t.k := \bot$$

The second iteration of algorithm *add-perfect-fail-safe-multitolerance* on program 1-FSTR will result in the following program:

2-FSTR1 :: $|\{k : t.k = \bot\}| \leq 2 \wedge t.(k-1) \neq \bot \wedge k \neq 0 \wedge t.k \neq t.(k-1) \rightarrow t.k := t.(k-1)$

2-FSTR2 :: $|\{k : t.k = \bot\}| \leq 2 \wedge t.N \neq \bot \wedge k = 0 \wedge t.k \neq t.N +_2 1 \rightarrow t.k := t.N +_2 1$

Theorem 3 (Fail-safe TR). *Program 2-FSTR is perfectly fail-safe fault-tolerant to F_1 and F_2.*

Fail-Safe Fault Tolerance to Fault Class $F_1 \ldots F_{N+1}$: We then consider a fault class that can corrupt the state of i ($1 \leq i \leq (N+1)$) processes.

Fault Action: The fault action that we consider is

$$F_i :: t.k \neq \bot \wedge |\{k|t.k = \bot\}| = i - 1 \rightarrow t.k := \bot$$

The ith iteration of algorithm *add-perfect-fail-safe-multitolerance* on program (i-1)-FSTR will result in the following program:

i-FSTR1 :: $|\{k|t.k =\perp\}| \leq i \wedge t.(k-1) \neq \perp \wedge k \neq 0 \wedge t.k \neq t.(k-1) \rightarrow t.k := t.(k-1)$

i-FSTR2 :: $|\{k|t.k =\perp\}| \leq i \wedge t.N \neq \perp \wedge k = 0 \wedge t.k \neq t.N +_2 1 \rightarrow t.k := t.N +_2 1$

Theorem 4 (Fail-safe TR). *Program i-FSTR is perfectly fail-safe fault-tolerant to F_1 to F_i for $1 \leq i \leq (N+1)$.*

From program i-FSTR, it can be easily deduced that, when $i = N + 1$, $|\{k|t.k =\perp\}| \leq N + 1$ is always "True" (cannot corrupt more processes than there exist), so program $N+1$-FSTR (or MFSTR - Multitolerant Fail-Safe Token Ring) simplifies to:

MFSTR1 :: $t.(k-1) \neq \perp \wedge k \neq 0 \wedge t.k \neq t.(k-1) \rightarrow t.k := t.(k-1)$

MFSTR2 :: $t.N \neq \perp \wedge k = 0 \wedge t.k \neq t.N +_2 1 \rightarrow t.k := t.N +_2 1$

Program MFSTR is perfectly fail-safe fault tolerant to fault classes that can corrupt the state of any number of processes (up to every process), and is identical to the fail-safe fault-tolerant token ring program presented by Arora and Kulkarni in [2]. However, our approach (and results) differs from that of [2] in two important ways. First, our approach is automated, hence proofs of correctness are obviated. Second, our intermediate programs are different, i.e., the programs tolerating less than (N+1) faults are different. In effect, all the intermediate programs in [2] are exactly the same. This is because *bad* transitions, even those that are unreachable in the presence of certain faults were removed. As a matter of contrast, for every fault class, we remove only those bad transitions that are reachable. Thus, though the overall multitolerant program is correct, the approach is not efficient as they remove more transitions than is strictly necessary. Another important consequence of our theory is that for multitolerance, a system designer knows what are sufficient conditions to achieve this. As can be observed, when a fault occurs, the system may deadlock. However, Arora and Kulkarni argued in [2] that, towards adding masking fault tolerance (both safety and liveness preserved), a stepwise approach can be adopted where first fail-safe fault tolerance is added followed by liveness properties. Hence, as future work, we are looking to automate the addition of components that add liveness to fail-safe fault-tolerant programs.

6 Summary

In this paper, we have made the following contributions: Based on previous work, (i) we have developed a theory for perfect fail-safe multitolerance, (ii) We have provided a sound, and complete algorithm that automates addition of perfect fail-safe multitolerance, while guaranteeing the non-interference conditions, and

(iii) We have presented a case study of the design of a perfectly fail-safe multitolerant token ring that explains the working of our algorithm. The ability to automatically add fail-safe multitolerance to an initially fault-intolerant program is an important step in the design of fault-tolerant systems, the more so that the program is fail-safe multitolerant by design.

Acknowledgements. We wish to thank Felix Freiling for helpful discussions.

References

1. B. Alpern and F. B. Schneider. Defining liveness. Information Processing Letters, 21:181185, 1985.
2. A. Arora and S. S. Kulkarni. Component based design of multitolerant systems. IEEE Transactions on Software Engineering, 24(1):6378, Jan. 1998.
3. A. Arora and S. S. Kulkarni. Detectors and correctors: A theory of fault-tolerance components. In Proceedings of the 18th IEEE International Conference on Distributed Computing Systems (ICDCS98), May 1998.
4. C. Fetzer and F. Cristian. Fail-awareness: An approach to construct fail-safe applications. In Proceedings of The Twenty-Seventh Annual International Symposium on Fault-Tolerant Computing (FTCS97), pages 282291. IEEE, June 1997.
5. M. Hiller. Executable assertions for detecting data errors in embedded control systems. In Proceedings of the International Conference on Dependable Systems and Network (DSN 2000), pages 2433, 2000.
6. A. Jhumka, F. Freiling, C. Fetzer, and N. Suri. Automated synthesis of fail-safe fault-tolerance using perfect detectors. Technical report, University of Warwick, 2005.
7. A. Jhumka, M. Hiller, and N. Suri. An approach for designing and assessing detectors for dependable component-based systems. In HASE, pages 6978, 2004.
8. S. Kulkarni and A. Ebnenasir. Automated synthesis of multitolerance. In DSN, 2004.
9. N. G. Leveson, S. S. Cha, J. C. Knight, and T. J. Shimeall. The use of self checks and voting in software error detection: An empirical study. IEEE Transactions on Software Engineering, 16(4):432443, 1990.

Hierarchical Decision Diagrams to Exploit Model Structure

Jean-Michel Couvreur[1] and Yann Thierry-Mieg[2]

[1] Laboratoire Bordelais de Recherche en Informatique, France
`Couvreur@labri.u-bordeaux.fr`
[2] Laboratoire d'Informatique de Paris 6, France
`Yann.Thierry-Mieg@lip6.fr`

Abstract. Symbolic model-checking using binary decision diagrams (BDD) can allow to represent very large state spaces. BDD give good results for synchronous systems, particularly for circuits that are well adapted to a binary encoding of a state. However both the operation definition mechanism (using more BDD) and the state representation (purely linear traversal from root to leaves) show their limits when trying to tackle globally asynchronous and typed specifications. Data Decision Diagrams (DDD) [7] are a directed acyclic graph structure that manipulates(*a priori* unbounded) integer domain variables, and which offers a flexible and compositional definition of operations through inductive homomorphisms.

We first introduce a new transitive closure unary operator for homomorphisms, that heavily reduces the intermediate peak size effect common to symbolic approaches. We then extend the DDD definition to introduce hierarchy in the data structure. We define Set Decision Diagrams, in which a variable's domain is a *set of values*. Concretely, it means the arcs of an SDD may be labeled with an SDD (or a DDD), introducing the possibility of arbitrary depth nesting in the data structure. We show how this data structure and operation framework is particularly adapted to the computation and representation of structured state-spaces, and thus shows good potential for symbolic model-checking of software systems, a problem that is difficult for plain BDD representations.

1 Introduction

Model checking of concurrent systems is a difficult problem that faces the well known state-space explosion problem. Efficient techniques to tolerate extremely large state spaces have been developed however, using a compact representation based on decision diagrams [1,2]. However, these symbolic techniques suffer from the intermediate peak size effect : the size of intermediate results is sometimes out of proportion with the size of the result. This is particularly true of globally asynchronous systems [9]. To fight this effect, and its dual on the size of the BDD representing the transition relation, the works of [11,13,9] for example have shown how to exploit modularity to decompose a transition relation in various ways. This allows large gains with respect to a purely linear encoding in traditional BDD approaches. More recently Ciardo in [4] showed in the context of modular verification how a fixpoint evaluation that is guided by the variable ordering can dramatically reduce the peak size effect. This is due to a saturation algorithm that works from the leaves up, thus a large proportion of the nodes created at each iteration are retained in the result.

The structure of a model is essential from the architectural point of view, but is usually not well captured by symbolic representations. Indeed, in a BDD encoding, a system state is seen as a linear path that traverses all the (binary) variables that represent the system. This is a handicap for symbolic techniques when trying to tackle complex specifications, as structure information is lost in this state encoding. Gupta proposed in [10] an encoding of inductive Boolean functions using hierarchical BDD, in the context of parametric circuits. The complexity of the transition model used in that work has however prevented a more widespread use of this concept.

We define here a new hierarchical data decision structure, SDD, that allows to generalize some of these patterns of good decision diagram usage, in an open and flexible framework, inductive homomorphisms. SDD are naturally adapted to the representation of state spaces composed in parallel behavior, with event based synchronizations. The structure of a model is reflected in the hierarchy of the decision diagram encoding, allowing sharing of both operations and state representation. SDD allow to flexibly compute local fixpoints, and thus our model-checker though still very young offers performance an order above NuSMV [6] and comparable to SMaRT [4]. The DDD/SDD library is available under LGPL from ddd.lip6.fr.

The paper is structured as follows : we first present data decision diagrams (2.1) and labeled Petri nets (2.2) as the context in which we work. Section 3 shows how we integrated local saturation in our DDD operation framework. Section 4 introduces our new Set Decision Diagram hierarchical structure and operations. Section 5 explains how they can be used in the context of modular and hierarchical symbolic model checking for labeled transition systems, and in particular our chosen P/T nets. We give performances of our prototype in sections 3 and 5.

2 Context

2.1 Data Decision Diagram Definition

Data Decision Diagrams (DDD) [7] are a data structure for representing finite sets of assignments sequences of the form $(e_1 := x_1) \cdot (e_2 := x_2) \cdots (e_n := x_n)$ where e_i are variables and x_i are the assigned integer values. When an ordering on the variables is fixed and the values are booleans, DDD coincides with the well-known Binary Decision Diagram. When the ordering on the variables is the only assumption, DDD correspond to the specialized version of the Multi-valued Decision Diagrams representing characteristic function of sets [3]. However DDD assume no variable ordering and, even more, the same variable may occur many times in a same assignment sequence. Moreover, variables are not assumed to be part of all paths. Therefore, the maximal length of a sequence is not fixed, and sequences of different lengths can coexist in a DDD. This feature is very useful when dealing with dynamic structures like queues.

DDD have two terminals : as usual for decision diagram, 1-leaves stand for accepting terminators and 0-leaves for non-accepting ones. Since there is no assumption on the variable domains, the non-accepted sequences are suppressed from the structure. 0 is considered as the default value and is only used to denote the empty set of sequence.

This characteristic of DDD is important as it allows the use of variables of finite domain with *a priori* unknown bounds. In the following, E denotes a set of variables, and for any e in E, $Dom(e) \subseteq \mathbb{N}$ represents the domain of e.

Definition 1 (Data Decision Diagram). *The set $\mathbb{D}$ of DDD is defined by $d \in \mathbb{D}$ if:*

- $d \in \{0, 1\}$ or
- $d = \langle e, \alpha \rangle$ with:
  - $e \in E$
  - $\alpha : Dom(e) \to \mathbb{D}$, such that $\{x \in Dom(e) | \alpha(x) \neq 0\}$ is finite.

We denote $e \xrightarrow{x} d$, the DDD (e, α) with $\alpha(x) = d$ and for all $y \neq x$, $\alpha(y) = 0$. We call DDD sequence a DDD of the form $e_1 \xrightarrow{x_1} e_2 \xrightarrow{x_2} \ldots 1$.

Although no ordering constraints are given, DDD represent sets of *compatible DDD sequences*. Note that the DDD 0 represents the empty set and is therefore compatible with any DDD sequence. The symmetric compatibility property is defined inductively for two DDD sequences:

Definition 2 (Compatible DDD sequences).

- *Any DDD sequence is compatible with itself.*
- *Sequences 1 and $e \xrightarrow{x} d$ are incompatible*
- *Sequences $e \xrightarrow{x} d$ and $e' \xrightarrow{x'} d'$ are compatible iff. $e = e' \wedge (x = x' \Rightarrow d$ and d' are compatible)*

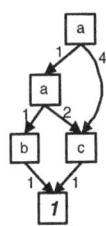

Fig. 1.
$a \xrightarrow{1} a \xrightarrow{1} b \xrightarrow{1} 1$
$+ a \xrightarrow{4} c \xrightarrow{1} 1$
$+ a \xrightarrow{1} a \xrightarrow{2} c \xrightarrow{1} 1$

As usual, DDD are encoded as (shared) decision trees (see Fig. 1 for an example DDD). Hence, a DDD of the form $\langle e, \alpha \rangle$ is encoded by a node labeled e and for each $x \in Dom(e)$ such that $\alpha(x) \neq 0$, there is an arc from this node to the root of $\alpha(x)$. By the definition 1, from a node $\langle e, \alpha \rangle$ there can be at most one arc labeled by $x \in Dom(e)$ and leading to $\alpha(x)$. This may cause conflicts when computing the union of two DDD, if the sequences they contain are incompatible, so care must be taken on the operations performed.

DDD are equipped with the classical set-theoretic operations. They also offer a concatenation operation $d_1 \cdot d_2$ which replaces 1 terminals of d_1 by d_2. Applied to well-defined DDD, it corresponds to a cartesian product. In addition, homomorphisms are defined to allow flexibility in the definition of application specific operations.

A basic homomorphism is a mapping Φ from $\mathbb{D}$ to $\mathbb{D}$ such that $\Phi(0) = 0$ and $\Phi(d + d') = \Phi(d) + \Phi(d'), \forall d, d' \in \mathbb{D}$. The sum and the composition of two homomorphisms are homomorphisms. Some basic homomorphisms are hard-coded. For instance, the homomorphism $d * Id$ where $d \in \mathbb{D}$, $*$ stands for the intersection and Id for the identity, allows to select the sequences belonging to d : it is a homomorphism that can be applied to any d' yielding $d * Id(d') = d * d'$. The homomorphisms $d \cdot Id$ and $Id \cdot d$ permit to left or right concatenate sequences. We widely use the left concatenation that adds a single assignment $(e := x)$, noted $e \xrightarrow{x} Id$.

Furthermore, application-specific mappings can be defined by *inductive* homomorphisms. An inductive homomorphism Φ is defined by its evaluation on the 1 terminal $\Phi(1) \in$, and its evaluation $\Phi' = \Phi(e \xrightarrow{x})$ for any $e \xrightarrow{x}$. Φ' is itself a (possibly inductive) homomorphism, that will be applied on the successor node d. The result of $\Phi(\langle e, \alpha \rangle)$ is then defined as $\sum_{x \in Dom(e)} \Phi(e \xrightarrow{x} \alpha(x))$. We give examples of homomorphisms in the next subsection which introduces a simple labeled P/T net formalism.

2.2 Labeled P/T Nets Definition

In this section, we introduce a class of modular Petri nets. We chose P/T nets for their simple semantics, but most of what is presented here is valid for other LTS.

A *Labeled P/T-Net* is a tuple $\langle P, T, Pre, Post, L, label \rangle$ where

- P is a finite set of places,
- T is a finite set of transitions (with $P \cap T = \emptyset$),
- *Pre* and *Post* : $P \times T \to \mathbb{N}$ are the pre and post functions labelling the arcs.
- L is a set of labels
- $label : L \times T \to \{True, False\}$ is a function labeling the transitions.

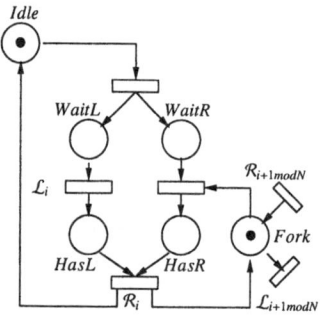

Fig. 2. Labeled PT net model of the philosophers

A marking m is an element of $\mathbb{N}^P$. A transition t is enabled in a marking m if for each place p, the condition $Pre(p,t)(m) \leq m(p)$ holds. The firing of a transition t from a marking m leads to a new marking m' defined by $\forall p \in P, m'(p) = m(p) - Pre(p,t) + Post(p,t)$.

Two labeled P/T nets may be composed by synchronization on the transitions that bear the same label. This is a parallel composition noted $/\!/$, with event-based synchronizations that yields a new labeled P/T net. This is a general compositional framework, adapted to the composition of arbitrary labeled transition systems (LTS).

This paper focuses on the representation of a state-space defined by composition of LTS, more than on a given formalism. We thus limit our discussion to ordinary nets, with only constant arc functions, and only pre and post arcs. However our implementations actually encompass a wider class of nets (with FIFO, queues...) described fully in [7]. Let us consider an encoding of a state space of a P/T net in which we use one variable for each place of the system. The domain of place variables is the set of natural numbers. The initial marking for a single place is encoded by: $d_p = p \xrightarrow{m_0(p)} 1$. For a given total order on the places of the net, the DDD encoding the initial marking is the concatenation of DDD $d_{p_1} \cdots d_{p_n}$. For instance, the initial state of a philosopher can be represented by : $Idle \xrightarrow{1} WaitL \xrightarrow{0} WaitR \xrightarrow{0} HasL \xrightarrow{0} HasR \xrightarrow{0} Fork \xrightarrow{1} 1$.

The symbolic transition relation is defined arc by arc in a modular way well-adapted to the further combination of arcs of different net sub-classes. The two following homomorphisms are defined to deal respectively with the pre (h^-) and post (h^+) conditions.

Both are parameterized by the connected place (p) as well as the valuation (v) labelling the arc entering or outing p.

$$h^-(p,v)(e,x) = \begin{cases} e \xrightarrow{x-v} Id & \text{if } e = p \wedge x \geq v \\ 0 & \text{if } e = p \wedge x < v \\ e \xrightarrow{x} h^-(p,v) & \text{otherwise} \end{cases}$$
$$h^-(p,v)(1) = \top$$

$$h^+(p,v)(e,x) = \begin{cases} e \xrightarrow{x+v} Id & \text{if } e = p \\ e \xrightarrow{x} h^+(p,v) & \text{otherwise} \end{cases}$$
$$h^+(p,v)(1) = \top$$

These basic homomorphisms are composed to form a transition relation. For a transition t, $^\bullet t$ (resp. $t^\bullet$) denotes the set of places $\{p \in P \mid Pre(p,t) \neq 0\}$ (resp. $\{p \in P \mid Post(p,t) \neq 0\}$). The full homomorphism h_{Trans} for a given transition t is obtained by :
$h_{Trans}(t) = \bigcirc_{p \in t^\bullet} h^+(p, Post(p,t)) \circ \bigcirc_{p \in {}^\bullet t} h^-(p, Pre(p,t))$

For instance the top-most transition in the model of Fig. 2 would have as homomorphism : $h_{Trans}(t) = h^+(WaitL, 1) \circ h^+(WaitR, 1) \circ h^-(Idle, 1)$.

When on a path a precondition is unsatisfied, the h^- homomorphism will return 0, pruning the path from the structure. Thus the h^+ are only applied on the paths such that all preconditions are satisfied.

3 Introducing Saturation

A first extension to the DDD homomorphism model was made to introduce the concept of local saturation. The idea, inspired by [4], is to compute fixpoint computations starting from internal nodes of the decision diagram structure, instead of having all fixpoint computations performed at the highest level. This is shown experimentally to considerably reduce the intermediate peak size effect that is one of the critical problems related to symbolic approaches (see [9] for a good overview of other intermediate size reduction techniques). In effect, by computing local fixpoints starting from the leaves of the structure and going up, and re-saturating lower nodes each time a variable is modified favors creation of "low" nodes that will indeed appear in the final result. The canonization process of decision diagrams is inductively based on the unicity of the terminal node(s), thus creating more saturated low nodes reduces the number of intermediate nodes at all levels in the structure.

To this end we introduce a new **transitive closure** * unary operator that allows to perform local fixpoint computations. For any homomorphism h, $h^*(d), d \in$ is evaluated by repeating $d \leftarrow h(d)$ until a fixpoint is reached. While this computation may not terminate, if it does its evaluation can be described as a finite composition using $\circ$ of h, thus is itself an inductive homomorphism. This operator is usually applied to $Id + h$ instead of h, allowing to cumulate newly reached paths in the result.

To use this operator efficiently, we need to set a starting level for each transition of the system. We define a transition t's top level, noted $top(t)$, as the variable of highest index (the last variable encountered in the DDD bears index 0) that is affected by a firing of t. We then define a table $TopTrans$ of size the number of variables of the system. This table contains in $TopTrans[i]$ a homomorphism that is a sum of the homomorphisms (constructed using the usual equation presented in section 2.2) of all transitions t such that $top(t) = i$, and of Id.

$$\mathcal{L}(e,x) = \begin{cases} e \xrightarrow{x} (TopTrans[e-1] \circ \mathcal{L}^*)^* & \text{if } e > 0 \\ e \xrightarrow{x} Id & \text{otherwise} \end{cases}$$
$$\mathcal{L}(1) = 1$$

We then define this new transition homomorphism $\mathcal{L}$ that exploits these aspects. $TopTrans$ is never modified, and is thus simply referenced in $\mathcal{L}$. The main application case consists in applying over the successor node of index $e-1$ a fixpoint of $\mathcal{L}$ (thus saturating all lower nodes of indexes strictly smaller than $e-1$) followed by all the transitions that start from node $e-1$ (plus Id) in a fixpoint. The last place in the structure is indexed by 0, and we stop the operation when we reach this level. For a system composed of N places, we compute the full state space by applying $(TopTrans[N-1] \circ \mathcal{L}^*)^*$ to the DDD representing the initial state.

Table 1 measures the impact of the use of fixpoint operators on state space construction. We use a benchmark of four models taken from [13]. Performance measures were run on a P4/2.4GHz/2GbRAM. The table shows the huge gain in complexity offered by local saturation. The number of nodes explored is however sometimes higher in the saturation approach; this effect is explained by the fact that every step of the fixpoint computations are cached, thus some transitions may be fired more times in the version with saturation. Ciardo et al. suggest in [4] that only the result of the full fixpoint

Table 1. Comparing our tool PNDDD with saturation activated or not. Benchmark models taken from [13]. We give for each model the final number of nodes and the total number of nodes explored (i.e. constructed at some point). Garbage collecting was deactivated to allow to measure this value; this is the default behavior anyway, we lazily collect garbage only once at the end of the construction.

Model	N	Nb. States	final nodes	PNDDD no sat total nodes	PNDDD no sat time (s)	PNDDD sat total nodes	PNDDD sat time (s)
Dining Philosophers	50	2.23e+31	1387	13123	11.6	10739	0.09
	100	4.97e+62	2787	26823	54.19	21689	0.18
	200	2.47e+125	5587	54223	234	43589	0.39
	1000	9.18e+626	27987	-	-	218789	2.1
Slotted Ring Protocol	10	8.29e+09	1281	35898	83.07	45970	0.8
	15	1.46e+15	2780	118054	595	132126	2.26
	50	1.72e+52	29401	-	-	3.58e+06	61.58
Flexible Manufacturing System	10	2.50+09	580	8604	2.06	11202	0.17
	25	8.54e+13	2545	50489	28.75	85962	1.58
	50	4.24e+17	8820	231464	240.4	490062	9.78
	80	1.58e+20	21300	-	-	1.72e+06	37.06
Kanban	10	1.01e+09	257	26862	20.47	5837	0.06
	50	1.04e+16	3217	-	-	209117	3.96
	100	1.73e+19	11417	-	-	1.32e+06	28.09
	200	3.17e+22	42817	-	-	9.23e+06	238.95

evaluation be cached, not its steps ; however we did not implement this tuning of our caching policy, which might reduce the *measure* (if we only count nodes actually created), but not truly the time/space complexity (as the extra nodes that we do count could be garbage colected at any time). Note that our fixpoint operator allows any library user to profit from leaves to root saturation instead of the traditional external fixpoint, thus generalizing the concept introduced in [4] to other applications.

The time complexity explosion in the version without local fixpoint is due to the cost of traversals of the structure and to the number of iterations required in this breadth-first evaluation scheme. The saturation process naturally applies transitions from their starting level as it is reached, whereas in a fixpoint "from outside", the transitions that target the bottom of the structure need to traverse a very large number of nodes.

4 Set Decision Diagrams

4.1 SDD Definition

DDD are a flexible data structure, and inductive homomorphisms give the user unprecedented freedom to define new symbolic operations. Since the work in [7], DDD have been used for instance to implement model checkers for a subset of VHDL in a project for the "Direction Générale des Armées" (DGA) called Clovis (the reports are however not public), for formal verification of LfP in MORSE, an RNTL project [12], and to construct a quotient state-space by exploiting the symmetries of a colored Well-Formed net model [15]. However, as we manipulated more and more complex data structures, such as the dynamically dimensioned tensors of [15], we encountered problems linked to the lack of structure of DDD. We therefore decided to extend the DDD definition to allow hierarchical nesting of DDD. This new data structure is called Set Decision Diagrams, as an arc of the structure is labeled by a *set* of values, instead of a single valuation. The set is itself represented by an SDD or DDD, thus in effect we label the arcs of our structure with references to SDD or DDD, introducing hierarchy in the data structure.

Set Decision Diagrams (SDD) are data structures for representing sequences of assignments of the form $e_1 \in a_1; e_2 \in a_2; \cdots e_n \in a_n$ where e_i are variables and a_i are sets of values. SDD can therefore simply be seen as a different encoding for set of assignment sequences of the same form as those of DDD, obtained by flattening the structure, i.e. as a DDD defined as $\bigcup_{x_1 \in a_1} \bigcup_{x_2 \in a_2} \cdots \bigcup_{x_n \in a_n} e_1 \xrightarrow{x_1} e_2 \xrightarrow{x_2} \cdots e_n \xrightarrow{x_n} 1$.

In this section we base our reasoning on the actual data structure that is used to store them, and as *sets* will label the arcs of our data structure, we use the $e_1 \in a_1 \cdots$ presentation. However the basic linearity operation properties over the sequences of the equivalent DDD must be ensured to allow correct computations. We assume no variable ordering, and the same variable can occur several times in an assignment sequence. We also make no assumptions on the domain of the variables. We encode SDD as shared decision trees. We define the usual terminals 0 and 1 to represent non-accepting and accepting sequences respectively. In the following, E denotes a set of variables, and for any e in E, $\text{Dom}(e)$ represents the domain of e,

Definition 3 (Set Decision Diagram). *The set of SDD is defined by $d \in $ if:*

- $d \in \{0,1\}$ *or*
- $d = (e, \alpha)$ *with:*
  - $e \in E$
  - α: *is a finite set of pairs (a_i, d_i) where $a_i \subseteq \text{Dom}(e)$ and $d_i \in $ *

We denote $e \xrightarrow{a_i} d_i$, the SDD (e,α) with $\alpha(a_i) = d$ and for all $a_j \neq a_i$, $\alpha(a_j) = 0$. We call SDD sequence an SDD of the form $e_1 \xrightarrow{a_1} e_2 \xrightarrow{a_2} \ldots 1$ where $\forall i, |a_i| = 1$.

We further introduce a canonical representation for SDD, essential to allow use of a unicity table and cache. The SDD we manipulate are canonized by construction, through the union operation given in proposition 1 below.

Definition 4 (Canonical Set Decision Diagram). *An SDD d is said to be canonical if and only if:*

- $d = 0$ *or* $d = 1$
- $d = (e, \alpha)$ *and* $\forall (a_i, d_i), (a_j, d_j) \in \alpha, i \neq j,$ $\begin{cases} 1.\ a_i \cap a_j = \emptyset \\ 2.\ d_i \neq d_j \\ 3.\ a_i \neq \emptyset \text{ and } d_i \neq 0 \end{cases}$

Intuitively this definition sets the constraints that:

1. The number of sets of values that are mapped to a non-zero SDD be finite. This is required so that the number of arcs leading from a node be finite, since *only the arcs labeled with sets that map to a non-zero SDD are stored in the data structure*;
2. For a value x of $\text{Dom}(e)$, at most one non zero SDD is associated. In other words the sets referenced on the arcs outgoing from a node are disjoint. This is required to allow existence of a unique canonical representation of sets, hence unicity and comparison of SDD nodes.
3. No two arcs from a node may lead to the same SDD. This is the crucial point, any time we are about to construct $e \xrightarrow{a} d + e \xrightarrow{a'} d$, we will construct $e \xrightarrow{a \cup a'} d$ instead. This corresponds to fusing arcs that would have led to the same node.
4. By definition, the empty set maps to 0 and is not represented.

Some immediate effects of this definition should be highlighted :

- This definition assumes that sets of values can be (efficiently) represented, as an arc of the shared decision tree representing the SDD is labeled with a set of values. As an SDD itself represents a set, we can use variables of domain itself, introducing hierarchy in the data structure.
- In practice, the requirements on the data sets that label the arcs of an SDD are that they offer the usual set theoretic operations (union, intersection and set difference) and the ability to compute a hash key for the set stored. These requirements are captured by an abstract interface class, thus labeling an SDD with any type of decision diagram (i.e. from existing libraries) should be very easy if it is written in C or C++.

- Another effect is that we no longer have the constraint of DDD that the number of values taken by a variable x be finite. This constraint expressed in DDD that the number of outgoing arcs from a node be finite, but is reduced for SDD to the constraint that the number of sets of values that lead to different nodes be finite. This subtle difference means that we could represent infinite sets provided an efficient set representation is used (intervals in $\mathbb{R}$ for instance). This possibility has not yet been fully explored, and stresses the limits of our definition however, as we can no longer consider our model equivalent to a linear DDD like finite representation.

To handle paths of variable lengths, SDD are required to represent a set of compatible assignment sequences. An operation over SDD is said partially defined if it may produce incompatible sequences in the result.

Definition 5 (Compatible SDD sequences).

- *Any SDD sequence is compatible with itself.*
- *1 and $e \xrightarrow{a} d$ are incompatible*
- *$e \xrightarrow{a} d$ and $e' \xrightarrow{a'} d'$ are compatible if* $\begin{cases} e = e' \\ \wedge a \text{ and } a' \text{ are compatible} \\ \wedge (a = a' \Rightarrow d \text{ and } d' \text{ are compatible}) \end{cases}$

The compatibility of a and a' is defined as SDD compatibility if $a, a' \in$ or DDD compatibility if $a, a' \in$. DDD and SDD are incompatible. Other possible referenced types should define their own notion of compatibility.

4.2 Operations on SDD

Set Theoretic Operations. First, we generalize the usual set-theoretic operations – sum (union), product (intersection) and difference – to sets of set assignment sequences expressed in terms of SDD.

Definition 6 (Finite Mapping and Union). *A mapping $\alpha : 2^{\text{Dom}(e)} \to$ is said to be finite if it respects the property that $\{a \subseteq \text{Dom}(e) | \alpha(a) \neq 0\}$ is finite. Such a mapping has a finite number k of sets $a_i \subseteq \text{Dom}(e)$ such that $\alpha(a_i) \neq 0$, and can be explicitly represented by the enumeration of the non-zero mappings it defines : $\alpha = \bigcup_{i=1}^{k} \{a_i \to d_i\}$ where $\forall i, a_i \subseteq \text{Dom}(e), d_i \in$. Let $\alpha = \bigcup_{i=1}^{k} \{a_i \to d_i\}$ and $\alpha' = \bigcup_{i=1}^{k'} \{a'_i \to d'_i\}$ be two finite mappings.*

We define the square union $\sqcup$ as :
$$\alpha \sqcup \alpha' = \bigcup_{i=1}^{k} \{a_i \to d_i\} \sqcup \bigcup_{i=1}^{k'} \{a'_i \to d'_i\}$$
$$= \bigcup_{i=1}^{k} \bigcup_{j=1}^{k'} \{a_i \cup a'_j \to d_i \text{ if } d_i = d'_j\}$$
$$\cup \bigcup_{i=1}^{k} \{a_i \to d_i \text{ if } \forall j \in [1 \cdots k'], d_i \neq d'_j\}$$
$$\cup \bigcup_{i=1}^{k'} \{a'_i \to d'_i \text{ if } \forall j \in [1 \cdots k], d'_i \neq d_j\}$$

Intuitively this operation performs part of the son-based canonization scheme necessary for SDD : it ensures that no two arcs from an SDD node lead to the same SDD (requirement 3 of SDD definition 3). It is easily implemented by a hash map of keys d_is and values a_is. However it should be noted that this operation does not preserve requirement 2 of definition 3, as nothing ensures that the sets mentionned on the arcs are disjoint. Indeed, a given value x in $\text{Dom}(e)$ may be included in more than one a_i set of the result. But this $\sqcup$ operation over mappings will serve as a basis to define the sum $+$, the difference $\setminus$, and the product $*$ of two SDD Mappings.

Definition 7 (Compatible SDD set theoretic operations). *By definition, set theoretic operations are only offered over compatible SDD.*

- $0 + d = d + 0 = d, 0 * d = d * 0 = 0, 0 \setminus d = 0$ and $d \setminus 0 = d, \forall d \in$;
- $1 + 1 = 1 * 1 = 1, 1 \setminus 1 = 0$
- $\langle e, \alpha \rangle \diamond \langle e, \alpha' \rangle = \langle e, \alpha \diamond \alpha' \rangle, \forall \diamond \in \{+, *, \setminus\}$

Proposition 1 (Mapping operations). *The sum $+$ (respectively product $*$ and difference $\setminus$) of two SDD mappings $\alpha = \bigcup_{i=1}^{k} \{a_i \to d_i\}$ and $\alpha' = \bigcup_{i=1}^{k'} \{a'_i \to d'_i\}$ can be defined inductively by :*

$$\alpha + \alpha' = \bigsqcup_{i=1}^{k} \{(a_i \setminus \bigcup_{j=1}^{k'}(a'_j)) \to d_i\}$$
$$\sqcup \bigsqcup_{i=1}^{k'} \{(a'_i \setminus \bigcup_{j=1}^{k}(a_j)) \to d'_i\}$$
$$\sqcup \bigsqcup_{i=1}^{k} \bigsqcup_{j=1}^{k'} \{a_i \cap a'_j \to d_i + d'_j\}$$

$$\alpha * \alpha' = \bigsqcup_{i=1}^{k} \bigsqcup_{j=1}^{k'} \{(a_i \cap a'_j) \to d_i * d'_j\}$$

$$\alpha \setminus \alpha' = \bigsqcup_{i=1}^{k} \{(a_i \setminus \bigcup_{j=1}^{k'}(a'_j)) \to d_i\}$$
$$\sqcup \bigsqcup_{i=1}^{k} \bigsqcup_{j=1}^{k'} \{a_i \cap a'_j \to d_i \setminus d'_j\}$$

Proof. We need to show the equivalence of the above propositions with a straight definition reasoning on the actual individual assignments in a sequence. The proof is relatively straightforward and is based on considering the different intersection possibilities between the operands' α mappings. It is omitted here due to lack of space as it requires introduction of additional definitions and notations for reasoning with the sequences of the equivalent DDD.

It should be noted that using $\sqcup$ to compose the terms constituting the result may produce some simplifications, as sets that map to the same value will be unioned, and the $d_i \diamond d'_j$ terms may produce already existing SDD. Furthermore, by definition the empty set $\emptyset$ maps to 0, this produces further simplification as both the $(a_i \setminus \bigcup_{j=1}^{k'}(a'_j))$ and the $a_i \cap a'_j$ terms are liable to be empty sets. We should remind here that the union $+$ operation defined above is the core of the canonisation procedure, as it is in charge of ensuring the canonicity of SDD by construction.

SDD Homomorphisms. By analogy with DDD, SDD allow the definition of user defined operations through a recursive and compositional definition : inductive homomorphisms. The essential constraint over homomorphisms is linearity over the set of sequences contained in an SDD. Homomorphisms can then be combined by sum and composition.

Definition 8 (Homomorphism). *A mapping Φ on SDD is a fully defined homomorphism if $\Phi(0) = 0$ and $\forall d_1, d_2 \in \ : \Phi(d_1) + \Phi(d_2) = \Phi(d_1 + d_2)$*

Proposition 2 (Sum and composition). *Let Φ_1, Φ_2 be two homomorphisms. Then $\Phi_1 + \Phi_2$, $\Phi_1 \circ \Phi_2$ are homomorphisms.*

The **transitive closure** * is also introduced, and allows to perform a local fixpoint computation. It follows the same definition as for DDD transitive closure : for a homomorphism h, $h^*(d)$ is computed by repeating $d \leftarrow h(d)$ until a fixpoint is reached. Again we usually use $(h + Id)^*$ in our fixpoint computations. From here we can allow the definition of user-defined inductive homomorphisms:

Proposition 3 (Inductive homomorphism). *The following recursive definition of mappings $(\Phi_k)_k$ defines a family of homomorphisms called inductive homomorphisms.:*

$$\forall d \in \ , \Phi_k(d) = \begin{cases} 0 & \text{if } d = 0 \\ d' \in & \text{if } d = 1 \\ \alpha' = \sum_{i=1}^{k} \Phi_k(e, a_i)(d_i) & \text{if } d = (e, \alpha = \bigcup_{i=1}^{k} \{a_i \rightarrow d_i\}) \end{cases}$$

$\Phi_k(e, a)$ is inductively defined as a sum $\Phi_k(e, a) = \sum_l \pi_l(e, a) \circ \Phi_l + \pi_0(e, a)$ where all $\pi_l(e, a)$ are SDD homomorphisms, linear over the elements of a ($\forall a, a' \subseteq \text{Dom}(e)$: $\pi_l(e, a \cup a') = \pi_l(e, a) + \pi_l(e, a')$).

To define a family of inductive homomorphisms Φ, one has just to set the homomorphisms for the symbolic expression $\Phi(e, a_i)$ for any variable e and set a_i and the SDD $\Phi(1)$. It should be noted that this definition differs from the DDD inductive homomorphism in that $\Phi(e, a_i)$ is defined over the *sets* ($a_i \subseteq \text{Dom}(e)$) of values of the variable e's domain $\text{Dom}(e)$. This is a fundamental difference as it requires Φ to be defined in an ensemblist way: we cannot by this definition define the evaluation of Φ over a single value of e. However Φ must be defined for the *set* containing any single value.

In addition we must respect the linearity constraint over the sequences of the equivalent DDD. Thus $\pi(e, a)$ must be an SDD homomorphism linear over the element of a.

We use most commonly homomorphisms of the form $e \xrightarrow{\phi(a)} Id$ which allows a linear operation on the values labeling the arc, and by composition with another inductive homomorphism, to realize an operation on the rest of the paths of the SDD.

As in [13], we require that the partition of the system into modules be *consistent*. This constraint allows the definition of a transition relation $\mathcal{N}$ in a partitioned disjunctive or conjunctive (i.e. $\mathcal{N} = \bigwedge_i \mathcal{N}_i$) form [11]. This allows one not to explicitly construct the full BDD (or Kronecker representation [13,5]) that corresponds to $\mathcal{N}$, allowing to tackle larger systems. In effect, consistency means each term composing $\mathcal{N}$ can be evaluated independently and in any order, and $\mathcal{N}(S) = \bigcap_i \mathcal{N}_i(S)$. For our ordinary Petri net model, this is not a problem as any partition is consistent [13], however more complex operations require some care in the definition of modules.

5 SDD and Modular Petri Nets

In this section we present how the SDD hierarchy can be exploited to efficiently generate and store the state-space of a labeled Petri net, itself a composition of labeled Petri nets.

In previous works, we had shown how to use DDD for non-modular Petri nets [7]. The key idea is to use a variable to represent the state of a *set* of places, instead of having one variable per place of the net. In Miner and Ciardo's work on Smart [13], a variable represented a set of places or module, but the states of the module were represented in an explicit fashion using splay trees. Here we propose a purely symbolic approach as we use an SDD variable to represent the state of a module entering the composition of the full model, the value domain of which is a DDD with one variable per place of the module.

Definition 9 (Structured state representation). *Let M be a labeled P/T net, we inductively define its representation $r(M)$ by :*

- *If M is a unitary net, we use the encoding of section 2.2 $r(M) = d_{p_1} \cdot d_{p_2} \cdots d_{p_n}$, with $d_p = p \xrightarrow{m_0(p)} 1$.*
- *If $M = M_1 \parallel M_2$, $r(M) = m_{M_1} \xrightarrow{r(M_1)} m_{M_2} \xrightarrow{r(M_2)} 1$. Thus the parallel composition of two subnets will give rise to the concatenation of their representations.*
- *If $M = (M_1)$, $r(M) = m_{(M_1)} \xrightarrow{r(M_1)} 1$. Thus parenthesizing an expression gives rise to a new level of hierarchy in the representation.*

A state is thus encoded hierarchically in accordance with the module definitions. We define a total order over the N subnets or modules composing a model, used to index these submodels. Indeed the parallel composition operation is commutative and symmetric, therefore a net can always be seen as a "flat" parallel composition of its subnets. Such a composition which does not use any parenthesizing, would produce a DDD representation. However, using different parenthesizing(s) yields a more hierarchical vision (nested submodules), that can be accurately represented and exploited in our framework.

Thus for a parenthesizing of the composition in the manner $M_0 \parallel (M_1 \parallel (M_2 \cdots \parallel (M_{n-1} \parallel (M_n) \cdots))$ we have n levels of depth in the SDD, with at each level k two variables : a variable m_k with the states of a unitary module of the form M_k, and a variable $m_{(M_k^+)}$ that in effect represents the states of all the modules of index greater than k.

We partition the transitions of the system into *local* and *synchronization* transitions. A transition t is local to unitary module M_n iff $\forall p \in {}^\bullet t \cup t^\bullet, p \in M_n$. For each unitary module of index n, we construct a DDD homomorphism $\mathcal{L}_n$ built using DDD saturation as presented in section 3.

For synchronization transitions that are not local to a single module, we define the projection of a transition on a module of index n as:

$$\Pi_n(t) = \bigcirc_{p \in t^\bullet \wedge p \in M_n} h^+(p, Post(p,t)) \circ \bigcirc_{p \in {}^\bullet t \wedge p \in M_n} h^-(p, Pre(p,t))$$

We further define for a synchronization transition t, $Top(t)$ as the most internal parenthesised group (M_k) such that M_k wholly contains t. So in effect t is local to this group, and this is the most internal level we can apply t from. When nesting occurs at more than one level of depth t has a top and bottom at each level of depth in the structure. $Bot(t)$ is defined as the lowest variable index that is used by t. Our full transition relation is then inductively defined by:

Let $\tau_k = \bigcup_{\{t|Top(t)=(M_k)\}} \tau(t)$ represent the transitions local to a parenthesized group (M_k); we define $\tau_{-1} = Id$.

$$\tau(t)(e,x) = \begin{cases} e \xrightarrow{\mathcal{L}_k^* \circ \Pi_k(t) \circ \mathcal{L}_k^*(x)} \tau_{e-1}^* & \text{if } e = m_{M_k} \wedge bot(t) \geq e \\ e \xrightarrow{\mathcal{L}_k^* \circ \Pi_k(t) \circ \mathcal{L}_k^*(x)} \tau_{e-1}^* \circ \tau(t) & \text{if } e = m_{M_k} \wedge bot(t) < e \\ e \xrightarrow{\tau_k^* \circ \tau(t) \circ \tau_k^*(x)} \tau_{e-1}^* \circ \tau(t) & \text{if } e = m_{(M_k)} \end{cases}$$
$$\tau(t)(1) = 1$$

This algorithm thus performs *local saturation* of nested subnets. Like the algorithms of [4], it performs local saturation on the lower nodes as soon synchronization transitions are fired. This avoids the creation of intermediate nodes which will not appear in the

Table 2. Performances of our prototype over some bench models. We compare our tool's run time with the run times of Smart. Indicatively we also give the runtimes of NuSMV [6], the emblematic tool for symbolic representations (these values were not measured by us, but are directly taken from [5]). Some are missing as indicated by ?. The Lotos model is obtained from a true industrial case-study. It was generated automatically from a LOTOS specification (8,500 lines of LOTOS code + 3,000 lines of C code) by Hubert Garavel from INRIA. AGV (automated guided vehicle) is a flexible manufacturing problem, with synthesis of controllers in mind : we give the statistics with and without the controller enabled. Example witness trace construction is possible, yielding the shortest path to (un)desirable states. Run time is 1h20 for finding a *shortest* witness trace enabling each of the 776 transitions of the Lotos model, the longest is 28 transitions in length.

Model	N (#)	States (#)	final SDD (#)	final DDD (#)	total SDD (#)	total DDD (#)	PNDDD SDD time (sec)	NuSMV time (sec)	SMaRT time (sec)
Philosophers	100	4.97+62	398	21	2185	70	0.21	990.8	0.43
	200	2.47+125	798	21	4385	70	0.43	18129	0.7
	1000	9.18e+626	3998	21	21985	70	2.28	-	5.9
	5000	6.52+3134	19998	21	109985	70	11.7	-	83.7
Ring	10	8.29e+09	61	44	2640	150	0.4	6.1	0.11
	15	1.65e+16	288	44	8011	150	1.21	2853	0.29
	50	1.72e+52	2600	44	238400	150	34.01	-	5.6
FMS	25	8.54e+13	55	412	346	11550	0.26	41.6	0.36
	50	4.24e+17	105	812	671	38100	1.02	17321	1.33
	80	1.58e+20	165	1292	1064	89760	2.59	-	4
	150	4.8e+23	305	2412	1971	294300	10.52	-	20.7
Kanban	10	1.01e+09	15	46	129	592	0.02	?	0.48
	50	1.04+16	55	206	1589	9972	1.08	?	43
	100	1.73e+19	105	406	5664	37447	8.79	?	474
	200	3.17e+22	205	806	21314	144897	93.63	?	13920
Lotos [8]	N/A	9.79474e+21	326	759	125773	34298	265.28	?	?
AGV [14]	N/A	3.09658e+07	12	34	135	234	0.01	?	?
AGV Controlled	N/A	1.66011e+07	95	124	2678	349	0.38	?	?

final state-space representation, hence it limits the peak number of nodes that needs to be stored.

The following table shows the performance of our prototype tool over models taken from [13]. We use here a simple $(M_1) /\!/ (M_2) /\!/ \cdots /\!/ (M_n)$ parenthesizing scheme in these performance runs, thus only one level of depth is used in the data structure. This is a parenthesizing scheme that most closely relates to the experiments of [4]; indeed the number of SDD nodes is identical to the number of MDD nodes reported by Smart.

We can observe that the encoding is much more compact than with plain DDD, and the run times are a factor below those obtained with the flat DDD representation. The exception is the philosophers model, which actually gives better run times in the flat DDD representation (though at a cost in terms of representation size). The slotted ring example shows the superiority of the MDD access procedure, which allows direct access to all the nodes of any level k. Thus MDD saturation more efficiently fights the intermediate size problem than our own transitive closure operator. We believe this might be improved by tuning the caching policy, but this remains to be proved.

The Kanban model shows the advantage of SDD over MDD when the number of states per submodel grows : in this model each submodule has a number of states factorial with respect to N, while the number of modules stays constant. Smart's MDD representation represents one arc for each state value of a submodule, as an arc bearing the index of the state in a splay tree explicit (but quite compact) representation. Thus although we may have the same number of nodes, the number of arcs in the MDD representation explodes exponentially with N, while our referenced DDD scheme allows to factorize all the arcs that lead from a node d_1 to a node d_2 in the referenced DDD. This is an important point as larger software examples present modules with a sometimes very large reachability set.

6 Conclusion

We have presented Set Decision Diagrams, a hierarchical directed acyclic graph structure, with a canonical representation that allows use of a BDD-like cache and unicity table. SDD operations are defined through a general and flexible model, inductive homomorphisms, that give exceptional freedom to the user. This structure is particularly well adapted to the construction and storage of the state space of hierarchical and modular models. Thanks to local fixpoint computations and improved sharing in the representation with respect to the purely linear encoding of usual decision diagram libraries, exceptional performances can be attained.

The principles of our parenthesized parallel composition can be generalized to a wide range of models that can be seen as LTS. The choice of a correct parenthesizing is an open problem : the separation into parts should highlight parts that are similar at least structurally. One easy choice for typed specifications is to assign an encoding to each type (record, vectors, lists, basic types...). This will increase representation sharing. Our library, available under LGPL from ddd.lip6.fr, can be extended through inheritance to use other decision diagram packages than DDD to represent the states of a module.

We are currently working at extending [15] to exploit symmetries in a hierarchical SDD representation, as coloration can be seen as an important structural information, that can guide the process of choosing an appropriate parenthesizing. We are also using the SDD in a project to model-check Promela specifications. Finally we aim at defining a framework for operations that do not respect the module consistency constraint, as our current solutions lacks generality in this respect.

References

1. R. Bryant. Graph-based algorithms for boolean function manipulation. *IEEE Transactions on Computers*, 35(8):677–691, August 1986.
2. J.R. Burch, E.M. Clarke, and K.L. McMillan. Symbolic model checking: 10^{20} states and beyond. *Information and Computation (Special issue for best papers from LICS90)*, 98(2):153–181, 1992.
3. G. Ciardo, G. Lüttgen, and R. Siminiceanu. Efficient symbolic state-space construction for asynchronous systems. In *Proc. of ICATPN'2000*, volume 1825 of *Lecture Notes in Computer Science*, pages 103–122. Springer Verlag, June 2000.
4. G. Ciardo, R. Marmorstein, and R. Siminiceanu. Saturation unbound. In H. Garavel and J. Hatcliff, editors, *Proc. Tools and Algorithms for the Construction and Analysis of Systems (TACAS'03)*, pages 379–393, Warsaw, Poland, April 2003. Springer-Verlag LNCS 2619.
5. Gianfranco Ciardo. Reachability set generation for petri nets: Can brute force be smart. In J. Cortadella and W. Reisig, editors, *Application and Theory of Petri Nets 2004. 25th International Conference, ICATPN 2004.*, volume 3099 of *LNCS*, pages 17–34, 2004.
6. A. Cimatti, E. Clarke, E. Giunchiglia, F. Giunchiglia, M. Pistore, M. Roveri, R. Sebastiani, and A. Tacchella. NuSMV Version 2: An OpenSource Tool for Symbolic Model Checking. In *Proc. International Conference on Computer-Aided Verification (CAV 2002)*, volume 2404 of *LNCS*, Copenhagen, Denmark, July 2002. Springer.
7. J.-M. Couvreur, E. Encrenaz, E. Paviot-Adet, D. Poitrenaud, and P.-A. Wacrenier. Data decision diagrams for Petri net analysis. In *Proc. of ICATPN'2002*, volume 2360 of *Lecture Notes in Computer Science*, pages 101–120. Springer Verlag, June 2002.
8. H. Garavel. A net generated from lotos by cadp (http://www.inrialpes.fr/vasy/cadp). In PetriNets@daimi.au.dk *mailing list.*, Posted 28/07/03 and follow-up with performance of 4 tools on 26/09/03.
9. J. Geldenhuys and A. Valmari. Techniques for smaller intermediary bdds. In *CONCUR 2001 - Concurrency Theory, 12th International Conference, Aalborg, Denmark, 2001*, volume 2154 of *Lecture Notes in Computer Science*, pages 233–247, 2001.
10. A. Gupta and A. L. Fisher. Representation and symbolic manipulation of linearly inductive boolean functions. In *ICCAD'93*, pages 111–116, 1993.
11. J.R. Burch, E.M. Clarke, and D.E. Long. Symbolic model checking with partitioned transition relations. In A. Halaas and P.B. Denyer, editors, *International Conference on Very Large Scale Integration*, pages 49–58, Edinburgh, Scotland, 1991. North-Holland.
12. F. Kordon and M. Lemoine, editors. *Formal Methods for Embedded Distributed Systems How to master the complexity*. Kluwer Academic, 2004.
13. A.S. Miner and G. Ciardo. Efficient reachability set generation and storage using decision diagrams. In *Proc. of ICATPN'99*, volume 1639 of *Lecture Notes in Computer Science*, pages 6–25. Springer Verlag, 1999.
14. L. Petrucci. Design and validation of a controller. In *Proceedings of the 4th World Multiconference on Systemics, Cybernetics and Informatics (SCI 2000)*, pages 684–688, Orlando, Florida, USA, July 2000.
15. Y. Thierry-Mieg, J-M. Ilie, and D. Poitrenaud. A symbolic symbolic state space. In *Proc. of the 24th IFIP WG 6.1 Int. Conf. on Formal Techniques for Networked and Distributed Systems (FORTE'04)*, volume 3235 of *LNCS*, pages 276–291, Madrid, Spain, September 2004. Springer.

Computing Subgraph Probability of Random Geometric Graphs: Quantitative Analyses of Wireless Ad Hoc Networks

Chang Wu Yu and Li-Hsing Yen

Department of Computer Science and Information Engineering,
Chung Hua University, Taiwan, R. O. C
{cwyu, lhyen}@chu.edu.tw

Abstract. This paper undergoes quantitative analyses on fundamental properties of ad hoc networks including estimating the number of hidden-terminal pairs and the number of exposed-terminal sets. To obtain these results, we propose a paradigm to systematically derive exact formulas for a great deal of subgraph probabilities of random geometric graphs. In contrast to previous work, which established asymptotic bounds or approximation, we obtain closed-form formulas that are fairly accurate and of practical value.

Keywords: Ad hoc networks, sensor networks, analytical method, random geometric graphs, performance evaluation, hidden terminal, exposed terminal, quantitative analysis.

1 Introduction

Ad hoc networks (MANETs), which are wireless networks with no fixed infrastructure, have received extensive attentions [1, 5, 8, 12, 38-41, 46, 49-52]. Each mobile node in the network functions as a router that discovers and maintains routes for other nodes. These nodes may move arbitrarily, and therefore network topology changes frequently and unpredictably. Other limitations of ad hoc networks include high power consumption, scare bandwidth, and high error rates. Applications of ad hoc networks are emergency search-and-rescue operations, meetings or conventions in which persons wish to quickly share information, data acquisition operations in inhospitable terrain, and automated battlefield [38]. Bluetooth networks [53] and sensor networks [35, 42] are commercial products of ad hoc networks.

A *geometric graph* $G=(V, r)$ consists of nodes placed in 2-dimension space R^2 and edge set $E=\{(i,j) \mid d(i,j) \leq r\}$, where $i, j \in V$ and $d(i,j)$ denotes the Euclidian distance between node i and node j. Let $X_n = \{x_1, x_2, \ldots, x_n\}$ be a set of independently and uniformly distributed random points. We use $\Psi(X_n, r, A)$ to denote the *random geometric graph* (RGG) [29] of n nodes on X_n with radius r and placed in an area A. RGGs consider geometric graphs on random point configurations. Applications of RGGs include communications networks, classification, spatial statistics, epidemiology, astrophysics, and neural networks [29].

A RGG $\Psi(X_n, r, A)$ is suitable to model an ad hoc network $N=(n, r, A)$ consisting of n mobile devices with transmission radius r unit length that are independently and uniformly distributed at random in an area A. When each vertex in $\Psi(X_n, r, A)$ represents a mobile device, each edge connecting two vertices represents a possible communication link as they are within the transmission range of each other. A random geometric graph and its representing network are shown in Figure 1. In the example, area A is a rectangle that is used to model the deployed area such as a meeting room. Area A, however, can be a circle, or any other shape, and even infinite space.

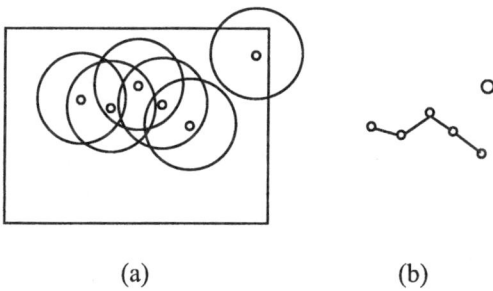

(a) (b)

Fig. 1. (a) An ad hoc network $N=(6, r, A)$, where A is a rectangle. (b) Its associated random geometric graph $\Psi(X_6, r, A)$.

RGGs are different from well-known *random graphs* [3, 13, 28]. One kind of random graph can be characterized by two parameters n and p, where n represents the number of nodes and p represents the probability of the existence of each possible edge. Edge occurrences in the random graph are independent to each other, which is not the case in MANETs. Therefore the fruitful results of random graphs cannot be directly applied to MANETs. Other graph models proposed for MANETs are interval graphs [16], unit disk graph [7, 17], proximity graphs [29], and indifference graphs [37].

Many fundamental properties of ad hoc networks are related to subgraphs in RGGs. For example, the IEEE 802.11 CSMA/CA protocol suffers from the hidden and the exposed terminal problem [41, 45]. The hidden terminal problem is caused by concurrent transmissions of two nodes that cannot sense each other but transmit to the same destination. We call such two terminals a *hidden-terminal pair*. The existence of hidden-terminal pairs in an environment seriously results in garbled messages and increases communication delay, thus degrading system performance [24, 25, 45].

A hidden-terminal pair can be represented by a pair of edges (x, y) and (x, z) of $G=(V, E)$ such that $(x, y) \in E$ and $(x, z) \in E$, but $(y, z) \notin E$. In graph terms, such a pair of edges is an induced subgraph p_2 that is a path of length two (See Figure 2). Counting the occurrences of p_2 in a given RGG helps counting the number of hidden-terminal pairs in the network.

The exposed terminal problem is due to prohibiting concurrent transmissions of two nodes that sense each other but can transmit to different receivers without conflicts [41]. The problem results in unnecessary reduction in channel utilization and throughput. We name these nodes an *exposed-terminal set*. Similarly, the problem can be modeled as a subgraph H of $G=(V, E)$ with four vertices $\{x, y, z, w\} \subseteq V$ such that $\{(x, y), (y, z), (z, w)\} \subseteq E$, but $(x, z) \notin E$ and $(y, w) \notin E$ (See Figure 2).

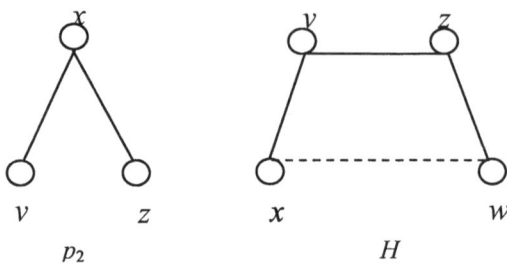

Fig. 2. The subgraphs of hidden-terminal pair p_2 and exposed-terminal set H

Quantitative analyses on specific subgraphs of a given RGG are of importance for understanding and evaluating the fundamental properties of MANETs. There is extensive literature on the subgraph probability of RGGs [29]. Penrose had shown that, for arbitrary feasible connected subgraph Γ with k vertices, the number of induced subgraphs isomorphic to Γ satisfies a Poisson limit theorem and a normal limit theorem [29]. To the best of our knowledge, previous related results are all asymptotic or approximate.

In the paper, we make the first attempt to propose a paradigm to systematically derive the exact formulas for a great deal of subgraph probabilities in RGGs. In contrast to previous asymptotic bounds or approximation, the closed-form formulas we derived are fairly accurate and of practical value. With the paradigm, we undergoes quantitative analyses on fundamental properties of ad hoc networks including the number of hidden-terminal pairs and the number of exposed-terminal sets.

Computing the probability of occurrence of RGG subgraphs is complicated by the assumption of finite plane. For example, one device in Figure 1 is deployed nearby the boundary of rectangle A so its radio coverage region (often modeled by a circle) is not properly contained in A. This is due to *border effects*, which complicate the derivation of closed formulas. Previous discussions usually circumvent the border effects by using *torus convection* [1, 20]. Torus convention models the network topology in a way that nodes nearby the border are considered as being close to nodes at the opposite border and they are allowed to establish links. Most of the time, we adopt *torus convention* to deal with border effects in the paper. However, we also obtain an exact formula for the single edge probability of RGGs when confronting the border effects.

Our definition of random geometric graphs $\Psi(X_n, r, A)$ is different from those of Poisson point process [1, 12], which assume that the distribution of n points (vertices) on a possibly infinite plane follows a Poisson distribution with parameter λ (the given density). In Poisson point process, the number of vertices can only be a random number rather than a tunable parameter. In practice, however, some MANET modeling requires a fixed input n or a finite deployed area.

The rest of the paper is organized as follows. In Section 2, some definitions and notations are introduced. In Section 3, we briefly survey related results on RGGs. A paradigm for computing the subgraph probability of RGGs with torus convention is presented in Section 4. Section 5 presents those derivations when confronting border effects. In Section 6, quantitative analyses on ad hoc networks are discussed. Finally, Section 7 concludes the paper.

2 Definitions and Notations

A *graph* $G=(V, E)$ consists of a finite nonempty vertex set V and edge set E of unordered pairs of distinct vertices of V. A graph $G=(V, E)$ is labeled when the $|V|$ vertices are distinguished from one another by names such as $v_1, v_2, \ldots, v_{|V|}$. Two labeled graphs $G=(V_G, E_G)$ and $H=(V_H, E_H)$ are identical, denoted by $G=H$ if $V_G=V_H$ and $E_G=E_H$. A graph $H=(V_H, E_H)$ is a *subgraph* of $G=(V_G, E_G)$ if $V_H \subseteq V_G$ and $E_H \subseteq E_G$. Suppose that V' is a nonempty subset of V. The subgraph of $G=(V, E)$ whose vertex set is V' and whose edge set is the set of those edges of G that have both ends in V' is called the subgraph of G *induced* by V', denoted by $G_{V'}$. The *size* of any set S is denoted by $|S|$. The *degree* of a vertex v in graph G is the number of edge incident with v. The notation $\binom{n}{m}$ denotes the number of ways to select m from n distinct objects.

The *subgraph probability* of RGGs is defined as follows. Let $\Omega=\{G_1, G_2, \ldots, G_k\}$ represent every possible labeled graphs of $\Psi(X_n, r, A)$, where $k=2^{\binom{n}{2}}$. When G_x is a labeled subgraph in Ω, we use $\Pr(G_x)$ to denote the probability of the occurrence of G_x. Suppose $S \subseteq V$ and $T \subseteq V$, we define $\Pr(G_s) = \sum_{\forall G_w \in \Omega \text{ and } G_s \subseteq G_w} \Pr(G_w)$, when $1 \leq w \leq k$.

A *walk* in $G=(V, E)$ is a finite non-null sequence $W=v_0e_1v_1e_2\ldots e_kv_k$, where $v_i \in V$ and $e_j \in E$ for $0 \leq i \leq k$ and $1 \leq j \leq k$. The integer k is the *length* of the walk. When $v_0, v_1, \ldots, v_k$ are distinct, W is called a *path*. A path is *a cycle* if its origin and terminus are the same. An induced subgraph that is a path of length i is denoted by p_i. Similarly, an induced subgraph that is a cycle of length i is denoted by c_i; c_3 is often called a *triangle*. A set of vertices is *independent* if no two of them are adjacent. An induced subgraph which is an independent set of size i is denoted by I_i. The notational conventions used in the paper can be found in [4].

3 Related Work in RGG

A book written by Penrose [29] provides and explains the theory of random geometric graphs. Graph problems considered in the book include subgraph and component counts, vertex degrees, cliques and colorings, minimum degree, the largest component, partitioning problems, and connectivity and the number of components.

For n points uniformly randomly distributed on a unit cube in $d \geq 2$ dimensions, Penrose [32] showed that the resulting geometric random graph G is k-connected and G has minimum degree k at the same time when $n \to \infty$. In [9, 10], Díaz et al. discussed many layout problems including minimum linear arrangement, cutwidth, sum cut, vertex separation, edge bisection, and vertex bisection in random geometric graphs. In [11], Díaz et al. considered the clique or chromatic number of random geometric graphs and their connectivity.

Some results of RGGs can be applied to the connectivity problem of ad hoc networks. In [39], Santi and Blough discussed the connectivity problem of random geometric graphs $\Psi(X_n, r, A)$, where A is a d-dimensional region with the same length size. In [1], Bettstetter investigated two fundamental characteristics of wireless networks: its minimum node degree and its k-connectivity. In [12], Dousse et al. obtained analytical expressions of the probability of connectivity in the one dimension case. In [18], Gupta and Kumar have shown that if $r = \sqrt{\frac{\log n + c(n)}{\pi n}}$, then the resulting network is connected with high probability if and only if $c(n) \to \infty$. In [47], Xue and Kumar have shown that each node should be connected to $\Theta(\log n)$ nearest neighbors in order that the overall network is connected.

Recently, Yen and Yu have analyzed link probability, expected node degree, and expected coverage of MANETs [49]. In [48], Yang has obtained the limits of the number of subgraphs of a specified type which appear in a random graph.

4 A Paradigm for Computing Subgraph Probability

In the section, we develop a paradigm for computing subgraph probability of RGGS. First of all, we are to prove that the occurrences of arbitrary two distinct edges in RGGs are independent in the next subsection. The property of edge independence greatly simplifies our further calculations. For simplicity, we always assume that A is sufficiently large to properly contain a circle with radius r in a $\mathcal{Y}(X_n, r, A)$ throughout the paper; that implies $\pi r^2 \leq |A|$. In the paper, notation $E_i(E_i')$ denotes the event of the occurrence (absence) of edge e_i.

Since we adopt torus convention to avoid border effects in the section, single-edge probability in RGG is obtained trivially and listed below.

Theorem 1: We have $\Pr(E_j) = \pi r^2 / |A|$, for an arbitrary edge $e_j = (u, v)$ and $u \neq v$, in a $\mathcal{Y}(X_n, r, A)$.

4.1 Edge Independence in RGGs

The next theorem will indicate that the occurrences of arbitrary two distinct edges in RGGs are independent. The result is somewhat difficult to be accepted as facts at first glance for some scholars. The following theorem shows that the occurrences of arbitrary two distinct edges in RGGs are independent even if they share one end vertex.

Theorem 2 [49]: For arbitrary two distinct edges $e_i = (u, v)$ and $e_j = (w, x)$ in a $\mathcal{Y}(X_n, r, A)$, we have $\Pr(E_i E_j) = \Pr(E_i) \Pr(E_j)$.

Note that Theorem 2 does not imply that the occurrences of more than two edges in RGGs are also independent. In fact, we will show their dependence later.

By Theorem 1 and 2, we obtain the probability of two-edge subgraphs immediately.

Corollary 3: For arbitrary two distinct edges $e_i = (u, v)$ and $e_j = (w, x)$ in a $\mathcal{Y}(X_n, r, A)$, we have $\Pr(E_i E_j) = (\pi r^2 / |A|)^2$.

4.2 Base Subgraphs

In this subsection, we consider eight labeled subgraphs with three vertices as *base subgraphs*, the probabilities of which will be used to compute the probability of larger subgraphs later. Based on the number of edges included, subgraphs of three vertices can be classified into four groups: a triangle (c_3), an induced path of length two (p_2), an edge with an isolated vertex ($p_1 + I_1$), and three isolated vertices (I_3) (See Figure 3).

To compute the probability of c_3, we need the following lemma. Two equal-sized circles are *properly intersecting* if one circle contains the center of the other. Due to page limit, we omit the proofs of Lemma 4-5 and Theorem 6-9 intentionally.

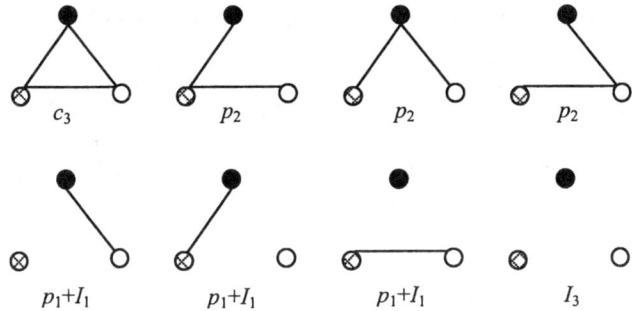

Fig. 3. Eight base subgraphs

Lemma 4: The expected overlapped area of two properly intersecting circles with the same radius r is $\left(\pi - \frac{3\sqrt{3}}{4}\right)r^2$ in a $\mathcal{Y}(X_n, r, A)$.

The following conditional probability is a consequence of Lemma 4.

Lemma 5: For three distinct edges $e_i=(u, v)$, $e_j=(u, w)$, and $e_k=(v, w)$ in a $\mathcal{Y}(X_n, r, A)$, we have $\Pr(E_iE_j | E_k) = \left(\pi - \frac{3\sqrt{3}}{4}\right)r^2/|A|$, where $u \neq v \neq w$.

The probability of the first base subgraph c_3 (triangle) can then be obtained.

Theorem 6: For three distinct edges $e_i=(u, v)$, $e_j=(u, w)$, and $e_k=(v, w)$ in a $\mathcal{Y}(X_n, r, A)$, we have $\Pr(E_iE_jE_k) = \left(\pi - \frac{3\sqrt{3}}{4}\right)\pi r^4/|A|^2$, where $u \neq v \neq w$.

Next, we consider the subgraph of an edge with an isolated vertex (p_1+I_1).

Theorem 7: For three distinct edges $e_i=(u, v)$, $e_j=(u, w)$, and $e_k=(v, w)$ in a $\mathcal{Y}(X_n, r, A)$, we have $P(E_iE_j'E_k') = \frac{\pi r^2}{|A|}\left(1 - \frac{\pi r^2}{|A|} - \frac{3\sqrt{3}}{4|A|}r^2\right)$, where $u \neq v \neq w$.

We have shown that the occurrences of two distinct edges in a $\mathcal{Y}(X_n, r, A)$ are independent (Theorem 2). The next theorem, however, shows that edge independence does not exist for subgraphs with three or more edges.

Theorem 8: The occurrences of arbitrary three distinct edges in a $\mathcal{Y}(X_n, r, A)$ are dependent.

The next base subgraph we considered is an induced path p_2, which will be used to model a hidden-terminal pair.

Theorem 9: For arbitrary three distinct edges $e_i=(u, v)$, $e_j=(u, w)$, and $e_k=(v, w)$ in a $\mathcal{Y}(X_n, r, A)$, we have $\Pr(E_iE_jE_k') = \left(\frac{3\sqrt{3}}{4}\right)\pi r^4/|A|^2$, where $u \neq v \neq w$.

The last base subgraph we considered is I_3.

Theorem 10: For arbitrary three distinct edges $e_i=(u, v)$, $e_j=(u, w)$, and $e_k=(v, w)$ in a $\mathcal{Y}(X_n, r, A)$, we have $\Pr(E_i'E_j'E_k') = 1 - \frac{\pi r^4}{|A|} - \frac{\frac{3\sqrt{3}}{4}}{|A|^2}\pi r^4$, where $u \neq v \neq w$.

Proof: (Omitted.) ∎

4.3 A Paradigm for Computing Subgraph Probability of RGGs

To simplify calculation, we adopt the following graph drawings. A solid line denotes an edge of G; a broken line denotes a possible edge between them; two vertices without a line denote a non-edge of G. Note that such graph drawing represent a class of graphs $G=(V, E_S, E_B)$, where $E_S(E_B)$ denotes solid-line edge (broken-line edge) set. For example, the following graph denotes eight base graphs depicted in Figure 3.

We list some subgraphs discussed in Section 4.1 or 4.2 with their notations, drawings, and probabilities in Table 1.

Table 1. Probabilities of subgraphs with three vertices or less in a RGG

Notation	p_1	E^2	c_3	p_2	E^1+I_1	I_3
G	(edge)	(triangle with broken base)	(triangle)	(path)	(edge + isolated)	(three isolated)
$\Pr(G)$	$\pi r^2/\|A\|$	$(\pi r^2/\|A\|)^2$	$\left(\pi - \dfrac{3\sqrt{3}}{4}\right)r^4/\|A\|^2$	$\left(\dfrac{3\sqrt{3}}{4}\right)r^4/\|A\|^2$	$\dfrac{\pi r^2}{\|A\|}(1-\dfrac{\pi r^2}{\|A\|}-\dfrac{\frac{3\sqrt{3}}{4}}{\|A\|}r^2)$	$1-\dfrac{\pi r^4}{\|A\|}-\dfrac{\frac{3\sqrt{3}}{4}}{\|A\|^2}\pi r^4$

Note that we have $\Pr(E^2)=\Pr(c_3)+\Pr(p_2)$ in Table 1. This equation can be derived by the following two types of derivation rules.

Type I   Type II

In fact, type I (type II) graph derivation rule can be applied on any broken-line edge (non-edge) of any graph. That is, for any $e \in E_B$, we have $G(V, E_S, E_B)=G_1(V, E_S \cup \{e\}, E_B-\{e\})+G_2(V, E_S, E_B-\{e\})$. Similarly, for any $e \notin E_S \cup E_B$, we have $G(V, E_S, E_B)=G_1(V, E_S, E_B \cup \{e\})-G_2(V, E_S \cup \{e\}, E_B)$ equivalently. We will show how these derivation rules can be used to systematically compute subgraph probability of RGGs.

Given a subgraph of a RGG, we try to obtain its probability by following three basic steps in the paradigm:

(1) Decompose the graph into a linear combination of base graphs by recursively applying the derivation rules.
(2) Compute the probabilities of base graphs.

(3) Compute the probability of the graph by manipulating the probabilities of base graphs.

We have established probability formulas for essential components (*i.e.* base graphs) in Section 4.2. The following example demonstrates the great convenience of this paradigm. A graph H (representing the exposed-terminal set) is decomposed into a set of subgraphs according to the derivation rules.

Graph H turns out to be a linear combination of three graphs. Although these subgraphs are not base graphs, we can obtain their probabilities with the help of base graphs. The first graph (denoted by E^3) consists of three solid edges (which form a path of length three) and three other broken edges; therefore we can obtain its probability by applying Theorem 1 three times; that is, we have $\Pr(E^3)=(\pi r^2/|A|)^3$. The second graph (denoted by E^1+c_3) consists of a triangle and a solid edge; then its probability can be obtained by applying Theorem 6 and Theorem 1 once; that is, we have $\Pr(E^1+c_3)=\left(\pi-\frac{3\sqrt{3}}{4}\right)\frac{\pi r^4}{|A|^2}\times\frac{\pi r^2}{|A|}$. The last graph (denoted by c_3^2) consists of two triangles with a common edge; we can also obtain its probability by applying Theorem 1 once and Lemma 5 twice; that is, we have $\Pr(c_3^2)=\left(\left(\pi-\frac{3\sqrt{3}}{4}\right)\frac{r^2}{|A|}\right)^2\times\frac{\pi r^2}{|A|}$. According to above discussion, we have

$\Pr(H)=\Pr(E^3)-2\times\Pr(E^1+c_3)+\Pr(c_3^2)=(\pi r^2/|A|)^3-2\times\left(\pi-\frac{3\sqrt{3}}{4}\right)\frac{\pi^2 r^6}{|A|^3}+\left(\pi-\frac{3\sqrt{3}}{4}\right)^2\frac{\pi r^6}{|A|^3}=\frac{27}{16}\frac{\pi r^6}{|A|^3}$.

In summary, we have the following theorem.

Theorem 11: For arbitrary four distinct nodes x, y, z, and w in a $\Psi(X_n, r, A)$, we have $\Pr(G_S=H)=\frac{27}{16}\frac{\pi r^6}{|A|^3}$, where $S=\{x, y, z, w\}$ and $H=(V_H, E_H)$ with $V_H=S$ and $\{(x, y), (y, z), (z, w)\}\subseteq E_H$, but $(x, z)\notin E_H$ and $(y, w)\notin E_H$.

Table 2 lists subgraphs and associated probabilities mentioned above.

Table 2. Probabilities of some subgraphs with four vertices in a RGG

Notation	E^3	E^1+c_3	c_3^2	H
G				
$\Pr(G)$	$(\pi r^2/|A|)^3$	$\left(\pi - \dfrac{3\sqrt{3}}{4}\right)\dfrac{\pi^2 r^6}{|A|^3}$	$\left(\pi - \dfrac{3\sqrt{3}}{4}\right)^2 \dfrac{\pi r^6}{|A|^3}$	$\dfrac{27}{16}\dfrac{\pi r^6}{|A|^3}$

Following our paradigm, the probability formulas of a great deal of subgraphs (in RGGs) can be obtained systematically. In Section 6, we will demonstrate that such specific subgraphs with their properties have considerable merit in quantitative analyses of wireless ad hoc networks.

5 Computing Subgraph Probability in the Face of Border Effects

In the section, we restrict the deployed area A to an $l \times m$ rectangle. We make an attempt to face border effects and obtain a closed-form formula of computing the single edge probability of RGGs. The results derived in the section can be used to measure the extent of coverage and connectivity of ad hoc networks [23].

Due to page limit, the main result and its corollaries are listed only.

Theorem 12 [49]: Given a $\Psi(X_n, r, A)$ and an $l \times m$ rectangle A, the single edge probability considering border effects is $\dfrac{\frac{1}{2}r^4 - \frac{4}{3}lr^3 - \frac{4}{3}mr^3 + \pi r^2 ml}{m^2 l^2}$.

Corollary 13: The average (expected) degree of a vertex in a $\Psi(X_n, r, A)$ considering border effects is $(n-1) \times (\dfrac{\frac{1}{2}r^4 - \frac{4}{3}lr^3 - \frac{4}{3}mr^3 + \pi r^2 ml}{m^2 l^2})$, where A is an $l \times m$ rectangle.

Corollary 14: The expected edge number of a $\Psi(X_n, r, A)$ considering border effects is $(\dfrac{n(n-1)}{2}) \times (\dfrac{\frac{1}{2}r^4 - \frac{4}{3}lr^3 - \frac{4}{3}mr^3 + \pi r^2 ml}{m^2 l^2})$, where A is an $l \times m$ rectangle.

To obtain these results, we first derive some necessary lemmas. Let $X_n=\{x_1, x_2, \ldots, x_n\}$ be a set of independently and uniformly distributed random points in a given $\Psi(X_n, r, A)$, where $x_i=(X_i, Y_i)$ and $0 \leq X_i \leq l$ and $0 \leq Y_i \leq m$, for $1 \leq i \leq n$. Clearly, X_i's (and Y_i's) are independent, identically distributed random variables with probability density function (p.d.f.) $f(x)=1/l$ ($g(y)=1/m$) over the range $[0, l]$ ($[0, m]$).

Lemma 15 [49]: Given a $\Psi(X_n, r, A)$ and any two distinct nodes $x_i=(X_i, Y_i)$ and $x_j=(X_j, Y_j)$, we have $\Pr[|X_i-X_j| \leq z] = \dfrac{-z^2 + 2lz}{l^2}$ and $\Pr[|Y_i-Y_j| \leq w] = \dfrac{-w^2 + 2mw}{m^2}$ where $0 \leq z \leq l$ and $0 \leq w \leq m$.

Lemma 16 [49]: Given a $\Psi(X_n, r, A)$ and any two distinct nodes $x_i=(X_i, Y_i)$ and $x_j=(X_j, Y_j)$, we have that: (1) the p.d.f. of $(X_i-X_j)^2$ is $f(u)=\dfrac{lu^{-\frac{1}{2}}-1}{l^2}$ where $0\leq u\leq l^2$, and (2) the p.d.f. of $(Y_i-Y_j)^2$ is $g(v)=\dfrac{mv^{-\frac{1}{2}}-1}{m^2}$, where $0\leq v\leq m^2$.

Lemma 17 [43]: $\int u^{-\frac{1}{2}}\sqrt{a^2-u}\,du = u^{\frac{1}{2}}\sqrt{a^2-u}+a^2\sin^{-1}\dfrac{\sqrt{u}}{a}+c$, where c is a constant.

We conclude that border effect does affect the value of the single edge probability of $\Psi(X_n, r, A)$. If A is an $l\times m$ rectangle, the difference between the single edge probabilities with and without avoiding border effects (by adopting torus convention) is $\dfrac{\frac{4}{3}mr^3+\frac{4}{3}lr^3-\frac{1}{2}r^4}{m^2l^2}$.

6 Quantitative Analyses of Wireless ad Hoc Networks

In the section, we make use of the derived results to develop quantitative analyses of ad hoc (sensor) networks including the number of hidden-terminal pairs and the number of exposed-terminal sets.

6.1 The Number of Hidden-Terminal Pairs

First, we compute the expected number of hidden-terminal pairs in any RGG. The performance of media access control (MAC) scheme is in close relation to the number of hidden-terminal pair of a given wireless network [24, 25, 45]. In literature, a hidden-terminal pair can be modeled by Hearing graph [45]; RTS/CTS mechanism and other methods have been designed for alleviate the hidden terminal problems [2, 14].

Since each hidden-terminal pair consists of three distinct labeled vertices, we set S to be the selected three-vertex set. There are $\binom{n}{3}$ different combinations for selecting three from n vertices, and three different settings for labeling one from three as the center of the hidden-terminal pair (*i.e.* the internal node of the induced path with length 2). Therefore, we have the number of hidden-terminal pairs $\binom{n}{3}\times 3\times \Pr(G_S=p_2)=3\binom{n}{3}\left(\dfrac{3\sqrt{3}}{4}\right)\pi r^4/|A|^2$ by Theorem 9.

Theorem 18: The expected number of hidden-terminal pairs in a $\Psi(X_n, r, A)$ is $3\binom{n}{3}\left(\dfrac{3\sqrt{3}}{4}\right)\pi r^4/|A|^2$.

Since $3\binom{n}{3}\left(\dfrac{3\sqrt{3}}{4}\right)\pi r^4/|A|^2 = 3\times\left(\dfrac{n\times(n-1)\times(n-2)}{1\times 2\times 3}\right)\times\left(\dfrac{3\sqrt{3}}{4}\right)\pi r^4/|A|^2 = (n^3-3n^2+2n)\left(\dfrac{3\sqrt{3}}{8}\right)\pi r^4/|A|^2$, we conclude that the hidden terminal pairs grow as like $O(n^3r^4)$, where n is the number of mobile nodes and r is the range of power.

In [24], Khurana et al. have shown that if the number of hidden terminal pairs is small and when collisions are unlikely, the RTS/CTS exchange is a waste of bandwidth. On the other hand, if the number of hidden terminal pairs is large, RTS/CTS mechanism helps avoid collision. Moreover, the optimal value for the RTS_Threshold in IEEE 802.11 [24] depends on the number of hidden terminals.

In [25], Khurana et al. have shown that hidden terminals can have a detrimental effect on the performance (including throughput, packet delay, and blocking probability) of the IEEE 802.11 MAC protocol. Specifically, they have showed that throughput is acceptable when the number of hidden-terminal pairs is less than 10%, beyond which throughput can fall sharply [25]. When determining a network-level simulation of a mobile ad hoc network or designing a wireless network, we can (with Theorem 18) precisely control the quantity of hidden terminal pairs by adjusting the number of mobile nodes or the power range.

6.2 The Number of Exposed Terminal Sets

To derive a tight bound of the number of exposed-terminal sets in a given RGG, we need to compute first the subgraph probability of c_4 (a cycle of length four). The paradigm proposed in Section 5 can be applied to tackle a great deal of subgraphs, but not some types of subgraphs such as cycles. We try to obtain tight bounds for $\Pr(c_4)$ in a different way.

Theorem 19: For arbitrary four distinct nodes u, v, w, and x in a $\mathcal{Y}(X_n, r, A)$, we have $\Pr(G_S=c_4) \leq \left(\dfrac{3\sqrt{3}}{4}\right)\dfrac{\pi r^6}{|A|^3}$, where $S=\{u, v, w, x\}$.

Proof: Consider the geometric graph c_4 and its circle model (See Figure 4(a) and Figure 4(b)). These four nodes need to be placed properly near to each other in order to form the cycle of length four. Since the longest distance between every two neighboring centers is r, the four centers in the circle model must be placed in a convex quadrilateral with the same size length r (See Figure 4(c)).

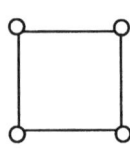 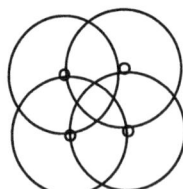 

Fig. 4. (a) A cycle of length four. (b) Its circle model. (c) The convex quadrilateral in the circle model.

Since the subgraph c_4 consists of a induced path p_2 and another nearby vertex, we have $\Pr(G_S=c_4)\leq\Pr(G_S=p_2)\times\Pr(\text{the remaining vertex is near } p_2 \text{ properly})$. Because $\Pr(\text{the remain vertex is near } p_2 \text{ properly})$ is the probability of putting the center of the remaining node in the convex quadrilateral, we have $\Pr(\text{the remaining vertex is near } p_2 \text{ properly})\leq(r^2/|A|)$. In a sequel, we have $\Pr(G_S=c_4) \leq \dfrac{r^2}{|A|} \times \left(\dfrac{3\sqrt{3}}{4}\right)\dfrac{\pi r^4}{|A|^2} = \left(\dfrac{3\sqrt{3}}{4}\right)\dfrac{\pi r^6}{|A|^3}$ by Theorem 9. ∎

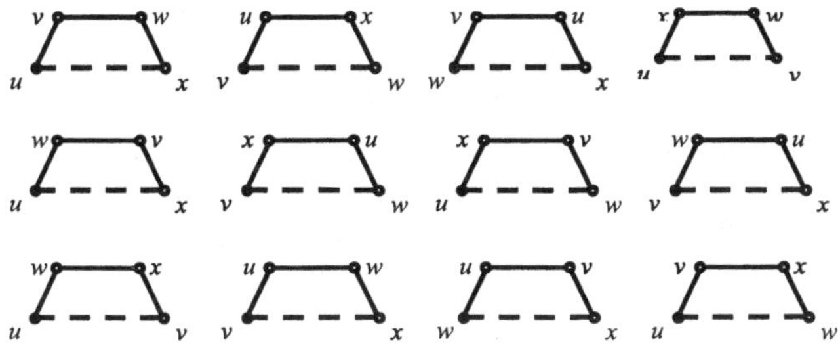

Fig. 5. Twelve different ways of labeling H graph

Counting the number of exposed-terminal sets is equivalent to counting the number of labeled subgraph H (See Table 2). There are $\binom{n}{4}$ ways to select four from n elements. Each has $\binom{4}{2} \times 2 = 12$ ways in forming the subgraph H (Figure 5).

Note that every graph in the same row contains the same subgraph (cycle of length four). Therefore the number of exposed-terminal sets is equal to the number of labeled H graphs minus the number of the duplicated cycles (=3(duplicated counting)×3(rows)):

$$\binom{4}{2} \times 2 \times \binom{n}{4} \times \Pr(G_S=H) - 3 \times 3 \times \binom{n}{4} \times \Pr(G_S=C_4)$$

$$= \frac{3^4}{4} \binom{n}{4} \frac{\pi r^6}{|A|^3} - 9 \times \binom{n}{4} \times \Pr(G_S=C_4) \qquad \text{(by Theorem 11)}$$

$$\geq \frac{3^4}{4} \binom{n}{4} \frac{\pi r^6}{|A|^3} - 9 \times \binom{n}{4} \times \left(\frac{3\sqrt{3}}{4}\right) \frac{\pi r^6}{|A|^3} \qquad \text{(by Theorem 19)}$$

$$\geq \left(\frac{3^4 - 27\sqrt{3}}{4}\right) \binom{n}{4} \frac{\pi r^6}{|A|^3}.$$

Theorem 20: The expected number of exposed-terminal sets in a $\mathcal{H}(X_n, r, A)$ is no less than $\left(\frac{3^4 - 27\sqrt{3}}{4}\right) \binom{n}{4} \frac{\pi r^6}{|A|^3}$.

Similarly, we conclude that the exposed-terminal sets grow as like $O(n^4 r^6)$, where n is the number of mobile nodes and r is the range of power. In [41], Shukla *et al.* have mitigated the exposed terminal problem by identifying exposed terminal sets and scheduling concurrent transmissions whenever possible. Combing with Theorem 20, we can estimate the extent of performance degradation due to the exposed-terminal problem, and adopt similar techniques used in [41] to improve system performance.

7 Conclusions

We have proposed a paradigm for computing the subgraph probabilities of RGGs, and have shown its applications in finding fundamental properties of wireless networks. We are surprised at finding some interesting properties:

1. The occurrences of two distinct edges in RGG are independent.
2. The occurrences of three or more distinct edges in RGG are dependent.
3. Probabilities of some specific subgraphs in RGG can be estimated accurately.

Many interesting subgraph probabilities and their applications in MANETs are still uncovered. For example, we are now interested in accurately estimating the diameter of RGGs. We also believe that the techniques developed in the paper can be exploited to conduct quantitative analysis on other fundamental properties of wireless ad hoc networks.

Acknowledgements

We would like to thank Dr. Jau-Ling Shih for her invaluable help.

References

1. Christian Bettstetter, "On the minimum node degree and connectivity of a wireless multi-hop network," *MobiHoc*, 2002, pp. 80-91.
2. V. Bharghavan, A. Demers, S. Shenker, and L. Zhang, "MACAW: a media access protocol for wireless LANs," *ACM SIGCOMM*, 1994, pp. 212-215.
3. B. Bollobas, *Random Graphs*, London: Academic Press, 1985.
4. J. A. Bondy and U. S. R. Murty, *Graph Theory with Applications*, Macmillan Press, 1976.
5. Josh Broth, David A. Maltz, David B. Johnson, Yih-Chun Hu, and Jorjeta Jetcheva, "A performance comparison of multi-hop wireless ad hoc network routing protocols," *Mobicom*, 1998, pp. 85-97.
6. C.-L. Chang and R. C. T. Lee, *Symbolic Logic and Mechanical Theorem Proving*, Academic Press, New York, 1973.
7. B. N. Clark, C. J. Colbourn, and D. S. Johnson, "Unit disk graphs," *Discrete Mathematics*, vol. 86, pp. 165-177, 1990.
8. Bevan Das and Vaduvur Bharghavan, "Routing in ad-hoc networks using minimum connected dominating sets," *IEEE International Conference on Communications*, 1997, pp. 376-380.
9. J. Díaz, M. D. Penrose, J. Petit, and M. Serna, "Convergence theorems for some layout measures on random lattice and random geometric graphs," *Combinatorics, Probability, and Computing*, No. 6, pp. 489-511, 2000.
10. J. Díaz, M. D. Penrose, J. Petit, and M. Serna, "Approximating layout problems on random geometric graphs," *Journal of Algorithms*, vol. 39, pp. 78-116, 2001.
11. J. Díaz, J. Petit, and M. Serna, "Random geometric problems on [0, 1]2, "*Lecture Notes in Computer Science*, vol. 1518, Springer-Verlag, New York/ Berlin, 1998.
12. O. Dousse, P. Thiran, and M. Hasler, "Connectivity in ad-hoc and hybrid networks," *Infocom*, 2002.
13. P. Erdös and A. Rénye, "On Random Graphs I," *Publ. Math. Debrecen*, vol. 6, pp. 290-297, 1959.
14. C. Fullmer and J. Garcia-Luna-Aceves, "Solutions to hidden terminal problems in wireless networks," *ACM SIGCOMM*, 1997, pp. 39-49.
15. E.N. Gilbert, "Random Graphs," *Ann. Math. Stat.*, vol. 30, pp. 1141-1144, 1959.
16. M. C. Golumbic, *Algorithmic Graph Theory and Perfect Graphs*, Academic Press, New York, 1980.
17. A. Gräf, M. Stumpt, and G. Wei β enfels, "On coloring unit disk graphs," *Algorithmica*, vol. 20, pp. 277-293, 1998.

18. P. Gupta and P. R. Kumar, "Critical power for asymptotic connectivity in wireless networks," *Stochastic Analysis, Control, Optimization and Applications*, pp. 547-566, 1998.
19. P. Gupta and P. R. Kumar, "The capacity of wireless networks," *IEEE Transactions on Information Theory*, vol. 46, no. 2, pp. 388-404, 2000.
20. Peter Hall, *Introduction to the Theory of Coverage Process*, John Wiley and Sons, New York, 1988.
21. Paul G. Hoel, Sidney C. Port, and Charles J. Stone, *Introduction to Probability Theory*, Houghton Mifflin Company, Boston, Mass., 1971.
22. T. Hou and V. Li, "Transmission range control in multihop packet radio networks, "*IEEE Transaction on Communications*, vol. 34, pp. 38-44, 1986.
23. C.-F. Hsin and M. Liu, "Network coverage using low duty-cycled sensors: Random and coordinated sleep algorithm," *International Symposium on Information Processing in Sensor Networks*, 2004.
24. S. Khurana, A. Kahol, S. K. S. Gupta, and P. K. Srimani, "Performance evaluation of distributed co-ordination function for IEEE 802.11 wireless LAN protocol in presence of mobile and hidden terminals," *International Symposium on Modeling, Analysis and Simulation of Computer and Telecommunication Systems*, 1999, pp. 40-47.
25. S. Khurana, A. Kahol, and A. Jayasumana, "Effect of hidden terminals on the performance of the IEEE 802.11 MAC protocol," Proceedings of Local Computer Networks Conference, 1998.
26. L. Kleinrock and J. Silvester, "Optimum transmission radii for packet radio networks or why six is a magic number," *Proc. IEEE National Telecom. Conf.*, 1978, pp. 4.3.1-4.3.5.
27. S.-J. Lee and M. Gerla, "AODV-BR: Backup routing in Ad hoc Networks," *IEEE Wireless Communications and Networking Conference*, 2000, vol. 3, pp. 1311-1316.
28. Edgar M. Palmer, *Graphical Evolution: An Introduction to the Theory of Random Graphs*, New York: John Wiley and Sons, 1985.
29. Mathew D. Penrose, *Random Geometric Graphs*, Oxford University Press, 2003.
30. M. D. Penrose, "A strong low for the longest edge of the minimal spanning tree," *The Annals of Probability*, vol. 27, no. 1, pp. 246-260, 1999.
31. M. D. Penrose, "The longest edge of the random minimal spanning tree," *The Annals of Applied Probability*, vol. 7, no. 2, pp. 340-361, 1997.
32. M. D. Penrose, "On k-connectivity for a geometric random graph," *Random structures and Algorithms*, vol. 15, no. 2, pp. 145-164, 1999.
33. T. K. Philips, S. S. Panwar, and A. N. Tantawi, "Connectivity properties of a packet radio network model," *IEEE Transactions on Information Theory*, pp. 1044-1047, 1989.
34. P. Piret, "On the connectivity of radio networks," *IEEE Transactions on Information Theory*, pp. 1490-1492, 1991.
35. G. J. Pottie and W. J. Kaiser, "Wireless integrated network sensors," *Commun. ACM*, vol. 43, no. 5, pp. 51–58, May 2000.
36. V. Ravelomanana, "Extremal Properties of three-dimensional sensor networks with applications," *IEEE Transactions on Mobile Computing*, vol. 3, no. 3, pp. 246-257, 2004.
37. F. S. Roberts, "Indifference graphs," in *Proof Techniques in Graph Theory*, F. Harary (editor), Academic Press, New York, pp. 139-146, 1969.
38. E.M. Royer and C-K Toh, "A Review of Current Routing Protocols for Ad Hoc Mobile Wireless Networks," *IEEE Personal Communication*, pp. 46-55, 1999.
39. Paolo Santi and Douglas M. Blough, "The critical transmitting range for connectivity in sparse wireless ad hoc networks," *IEEE Transactions on Mobile Computing*, vol. 2, no. 1, pp. 25-39, 2003.
40. Paolo Santi and Doulas M. Blough,"A probabilistic analysis for the radio range assignment problem in ad hoc networks," *MobiHoc*, 2001, pp. 212-220.

41. D. Shukla, L. Chandran-Wadia, and S. Iyer, "Mitigating the exposed node problem in IEEE 802.11 ad hoc networks," *International Conference on Computer Communications and Networks*, 2003, pp. 157-162.
42. K. Sohrabi, J. Gao, V. Ailawadhi, and G. J. Pottie, "Protocols for self-organization of a wireless sensor network, " *IEEE Personal Commun.*, vol. 7, no. 5, pp. 16–27, Oct. 2000.
43. J. Stewart, *Calculus*, 4th ed., Gary W. Ostedt, 1999.
44. H. Takagi and L. Kleinrock, "Optimal transmission ranges for randomly distributed packet radio terminals," *IEEE Transaction on Communications*, vol. 32, pp. 246-257, 1984.
45. F. Tobagi and L. Kleinrock, "Packet switching in radio channels, Part II-The hidden terminal problem in carrier sense multiple access and the busy tone solution," *IEEE Trans. Commun.*, vol. COM-23, no. 12, pp. 1417-1433, 1975.
46. J. Wu and H. Li, "Domination and its application in ad hoc wireless networks with unidirectional links," *International Conference on Parallel Processing*, 2000, pp. 189 – 197.
47. F. Xue and P. R. Kumar, "The number of neighbors needed for connectivity of wireless networks," *Wireless Networks*, vol. 10, pp. 169-181, 2004.
48. K. J. Yang, *On the Number of Subgraphs of a Random Graph in [0, 1]d*, Unpublished D.Phil. thesis, Department of Statistics and Actuarial Science, University of Iowa, 1995.
49. L.-H. Yen and C. W. Yu, "Link probability, network coverage, and related properties of wireless ad hoc networks," *The 1st IEEE International Conference on Mobile Ad-hoc and Sensor Systems*, 2004, pp. 525-527.
50. C. W. Yu, L.-H. Yen, and Yang-Min Cheng, "Computing subgraph probability of random geometric graphs with applications in wireless ad hoc networks," Tech. Rep., CHU-CSIE-TR-2004-005, Chung Hua University, R.O.C.
51. Chang Wu Yu, Li-Hsing Yen, Kun-Ming Yu, and Zhi Pin Lee, "An Ad Hoc Routing Protocol Providing Short Backup Routes," *Eighth IEEE Internation Conference on Communication Systems*, 2002, Singapore, pp.1052-1056.
52. Kun-Ming V. Yu, Shi-Feng Yand, and Chang Wu Yu, "An Ad Hoc Routing Protocol with Multiple Backup Routes," *Proceedings of the IASTED International Conference Networks, Parallel and Distributed Processing, and Applications*, 2002, pp. 75-80.
53. The Bluetooth Interest group," http://www.bluetooth.com."

Formalising Web Services

Kenneth J. Turner

Computing Science and Mathematics, University of Stirling, Scotland FK9 4LA
kjt@cs.stir.ac.uk

Abstract. Despite the popularity of web services, creating them manually is an intricate task. Composite web services are defined using the evolving standard for BPEL (Business Process Execution Logic). It is explained how CRESS (Chisel Representation Employing Systematic Specification) has been extended to meet the challenge of graphically and formally describing web services. Sample CRESS descriptions are presented of web services. These are automatically translated into LOTOS, permitting rigorous analysis and automated validation.

1 Introduction

1.1 Background

Web services have become a popular way of providing access to distributed applications. These may be legacy applications given a web service wrapping, or purpose-designed applications. This paper describes an unusual application of formal methods (LOTOS) to modern developments in communications systems (web services).

The interface to a web service is defined in WSDL (Web Services Description Language). However this is purely syntactic and does not define the semantics of a web service. Although WSDL can be manually created and edited, this is an intricate and error-prone task. For this reason, most commercial solutions aim to create WSDL automatically from the code of an application.

WSDL describes an *isolated* web service. The current thrust in web service research is on composing them into what are called *business process*. (Other terms used include business flow and web service choreography.) Assume that the following web services exist: airlines take flight bookings, hotels reserve rooms, car hire firms book vehicles, and banks accept electronic payments. A travel agency can then build a business process that arranges all these aspects of a trip through a single web service.

Unfortunately, many competing standards emerged for composing web services. Harmonisation was achieved with the multi-company specification for BPEL4WS (Business Process Execution Language for Web Services [1]). This is being standardised as WS-BPEL (Web Services Business Process Execution Language [2]). BPEL4WS is stable, and has been used for most of the work reported here. However it has shortcomings, so WS-BPEL has also been used for reference. For brevity, this paper refers to BPEL and web services with all the interpretations discussed above.

BPEL is a recent and evolving language, so tool support is still developing. It can be very difficult to understand a complex flow from the XML in BPEL. A graphical view of composed web services is thus very desirable. BPMN (Business Process Modeling Notation [3]) has been developed to give a high-level graphical view of such services.

This paper emphasises the *composition* of web services, not the description of *isolated* web services. This is partly because web service creation is now well automated, and partly because many web services already exist. Composing web services, i.e. defining web-based business processes, has attracted considerable industrial interest.

The author has previously developed CRESS (Chisel Representation Employing Structured Specification) as a general-purpose graphical notation for services. CRESS has been used to specify and analyse voice services from the IN (Intelligent Network) [6], Internet Telephony [7], and IVR (Interactive Voice Response) [8]. Service descriptions in CRESS are graphical and accessible to non-specialists. A major advantage of CRESS descriptions is that they are automatically translated into formal languages for analysis, as well as into implementation languages for deployment. CRESS offers benefits of comprehensibility, portability, rigorous analysis and automated implementation.

Essentially, CRESS describes the flow of actions in a service. It was therefore natural to investigate whether CRESS might be used for describing web service flows. This has proven to be an appropriate application of CRESS. CRESS is designed to be extensible, with plug-in modules for each application domain and each target language. Substantial work has been required because web services are quite distinctive. However, adding web services as a new CRESS domain has benefited from much of the existing CRESS framework. For example, CRESS has explicit support for features that allow a base service to be extended in a modular manner. The existing CRESS lexical analyser, parser and code generators have also been reused for web services.

The work described in this paper discusses how composed web services are represented using CRESS and translated into LOTOS. This automatically creates formal models of web services, and allows them to be rigorously analysed. Since web developers are unlikely to be familiar with formal methods, the use of LOTOS is hidden as much as possible in the approach. CRESS descriptions can be formally validated without seeing or understanding the underlying LOTOS. In additional work not reported here, the *same* CRESS descriptions of web services are automatically translated into BPEL and WSDL for implementation and deployment of web services.

1.2 Relationship to Other Work

Web services are well established and are widely supported by commercial tools; it would not be sensible to try competing with these. However the focus of this paper is on web service composition. Due to the relative newness of BPEL, support is only now maturing. Major products include IBM's WebSphere, Microsoft's BizTalk Server, Active EndPoint's ActiveBPEL, and Oracle's BPEL Process Manager. None of these provides a formal basis or rigorous analysis.

BPMN can be viewed as a competitor notation to CRESS for describing web services. However, BPMN is a very large notation (the standard runs to almost 300 pages). It also has a single purpose: describing business processes. BPMN is only a front-end for creating web services; tool support for creating (say) BPEL is only now emerging. In contrast, CRESS is a compact and general-purpose notation that has now been proven on services from four different domains. CRESS offers automated translation to formal languages (e.g. LOTOS, SDL) as well as to implementations (e.g. BPEL, VoiceXML). CRESS also introduces a feature concept that is lacking in other web service approaches.

There has been only limited research on formalising web services. [4] is closest to the present paper. This work supports automated conversion between BPEL and LOTOS. CRESS differs in using a more abstract, graphical description that is translated into BPEL and LOTOS; there is no interconversion among these representations.

LTSA-WS (Labelled Transition System Analyzer for Web Services [5]) is also close in aim to CRESS. LTSA-WS allows composed web services to be described in a BPEL-like manner. Service compositions and workflow descriptions are automatically translated into FSP (Finite State Processes) to check safety and liveness properties. CRESS differs in being a multi-purpose approach that works with many different kinds of services and with many different target languages. CRESS may be used with any analytic technique using on the formal languages it supports, although it offers its own approach based on scenario validation.

The CRESS notation is described and illustrated elsewhere (e.g. [6,7,8]). Only a brief overview is therefore given here; the notation is explained through examples. Section 2 illustrates how CRESS is used to describe business processes. Section 3 outlines the translation of CRESS service descriptions into LOTOS. Section 4 shows how the resulting specifications can be formally analysed in a variety of useful ways.

2 CRESS Description of Business Processes

A brief introduction is given to the concepts of business processes. The CRESS representation of these is then explained, mainly with reference to some realistic examples.

2.1 CRESS for Business Processes

A composite web service is termed a *business process*. It exchanges messages with *partner* web services, considered as service providers. A web service may be invoked *synchronously* (a request and immediate response) or *asynchronously* (a request followed by a later response). A business process is itself a web service with respect to its users. Web services have communication *ports* where *operations* are invoked. An unsuccessful operation gives rise to a *fault*. *Compensation* applies where work has to be undone due to a fault (e.g. a partial travel booking has to be cancelled). *Correlation* is used to link asynchronous messages to the correct business process instance.

A CRESS diagram is a directed graph that shows the flow of activities. In BPEL terms, a CRESS diagram defines an executable business process. Numbered nodes in a CRESS diagram correspond to BPEL activities. These are inputs and outputs (communications with other web services) or actions (internal to the web service). A BPEL activity is considered to terminate successfully or to fail (due to a fault).

In a CRESS diagram, arcs (BPEL links) join the nodes. CRESS nodes and arcs may have assignments in the form / *variable* <— *expression*. Arcs may be labelled by expression guards or event guards. Expression guards control alternative choices (switches in BPEL). Event guards introduce behaviour that is conditional on some event occurring (handlers in BPEL). The CRESS concept of event encompasses BPEL events, faults, requests for compensation and correlation requests.

For business processes, CRESS is required to offer sophisticated flow of control. Branches in a CRESS diagram normally reflect alternatives. However business processes need fine-grained control over parallelism. Although BPEL has separate constructs for sequence, iteration and graph-like flows, CRESS models them all in a uniform way.

2.2 CRESS for Business Activities

CRESS names are given in simple or hierarchic form. Operation names have the format *partner.port.operation*. Fault names have the format *fault.variable*, the fault variable being optional. Simple variables have the types defined by XSD (XML Schema Definition, e.g. **Float** f, **Natural** n, **String** s). CRESS can also define structured types, e.g. the following that defines two *offer* variables:

{**Natural** reference **String** dealer **Float** price **Natural** delivery} offer, offer2

Such a structured type is named implicitly after the first variable: *Offer*. Structured variables accesses have the form *offer.price*.

The subset of CRESS activities appearing in this paper is explained below; CRESS supports more than is described here. As usual, '?' means optional, '*' means zero or more times, and '|' denotes choice.

Invoke *operation output* (*input faults**)? An asynchronous (one-way) invocation sends only an output. A synchronous (two-way) invocation exchanges an output and an input with a partner web service. CRESS requires potential faults to be declared statically, though their occurrence is dynamic. The faults that may arise in a business process are implied by **Invoke**, **Reply** and **Throw**.

Receive *operation input* Typically this is used at the start of a business process to receive a request for service. An initial **Receive** creates a new instance of the process; a correlation handler is used to match incoming messages to the correct instance. Each such **Receive** is matched by a **Reply** for the same operation. **Receive** also accepts an asynchronous response to an earlier one-way **Invoke**.

Reply *operation output | fault* Typically this is used at the end of a business process to provide a response. Alternatively, a fault may be signalled.

Fork *strictness*.? This is used to introduce parallel paths; further forks may be nested to any depth. Normally, failure to complete parallel paths as expected leads to a fault. This is strict parallelism, and may be indicated explicitly as **strict** (the default). If this is too stringent, **loose** may be used instead.

Join *condition*.? Each **Fork** is matched by **Join**. By default, only one of the parallel paths leading to **Join** must terminate successfully. However, an explicit join condition may be defined over the termination status of parallel activities. In CRESS, the expression uses the node numbers of immediately prior activities. For example, 1 && (2 || 3) means that activity 1 and either activity 2 or 3 must terminate successfully. In turn, this means that activities prior to 1, 2 and 3 must also succeed.

Throw *fault*. This reports a fault as an event to be caught elsewhere by a fault handler.

Compensate *scope*? This is called after a fault to undo previous work. An explicit scope (CRESS node number) indicates which compensation to perform. In the absence of this, compensation handlers are called in reverse order of completion.

The **Throw** and **Compensate.** actions cause a CRESS event handler to be invoked. In BPEL these may be defined inside any scope of a process. In CRESS, scopes are implicit. As a consequence, event handlers may only be global or associated with an **Invoke**. (This is a small restriction that accords with common BPEL practice anyway.) The handlers appearing in this paper are as follows:

Catch *fault*. This defines how to handle the specified fault. If a fault has just a name and no value, it is handled by a **Catch** with a matching fault name only. A fault with name and value is handled by a **Catch** with matching fault name and variable type, otherwise by a **Catch** without a fault name but a matching type of fault value. (Although not illustrated in this paper, **CatchAll** handles any fault.) A fault handler applies where it is defined, and to subsidiary activities. If a fault occurs, it is considered by the current scope; if unmatched, it is considered by higher-level scopes until a matching handler is found. No match for a fault terminates the application.

Compensation. This defines how to undo work due to a fault. A compensation handler applies only where it is defined, and is enabled only once the corresponding activity completes successfully. If a compensation handler is executed, it expects to see the process state at the time it was enabled. It also cannot alter the current process state. In effect, the process must maintain a stack of compensation states.

2.3 A Lender Web Service

A loan service is a frequent example for business processes; the one here is based on that in the BPEL standard. LoanStar is a *lender* that offers a loan to an online customer, who submits a *proposal* containing name, address and loan amount. If the amount is 10000 or more, LoanStar asks its business partner FirstRate to perform a full assessment. FirstRate is an *approver* that thoroughly evaluates a loan proposal. The loan rate it determines is returned by LoanStar to its customer. FirstRate may cause a *refusal* fault (e.g. error message 'unacceptable') because a loan cannot be offered.

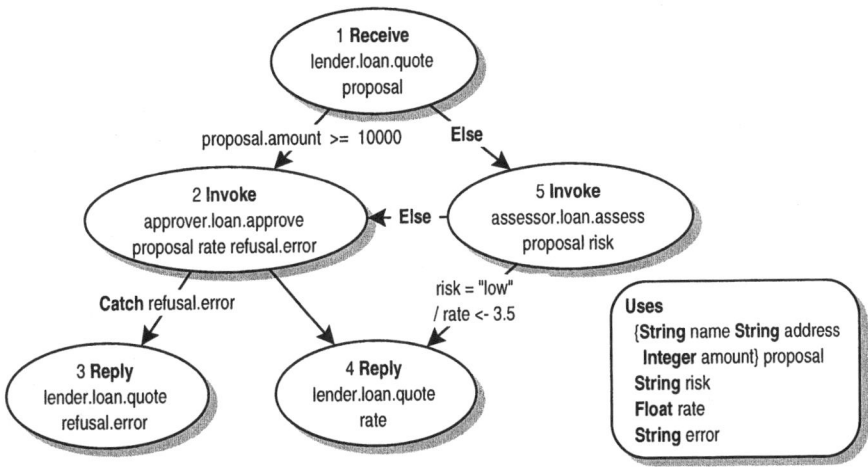

Fig. 1. Lender Business Process

A full assessment is costly, so a loan for less than 10000 is evaluated more simply. LoanStar asks its business partner RiskTaker to make a simple assessment. RiskTaker is an *assessor* that evaluates the risk of a loan. If the risk is low, LoanStar offers to lend at a basic rate of 3.5%. If the risk is not low, LoanStar asks FirstRate for a full assessment.

This example involves multiple web services: two partner web services (*assessor*, *approver*), and the business process itself (*lender*). The loan customer acts like a web service, and may be one. The CRESS description of the business process is in figure 1. The concepts needed to understand this have been explained earlier. Nodes (inputs, outputs, actions) in ellipses are linked by arcs (plain or guarded). If the *approver* invocation causes a *refusal* fault (node 2), this is caught by the associated handler (node 3).

The rounded rectangle at the bottom right of figure 1 is a CRESS rule box. **Uses** declares diagram variables, here *proposal*, *risk*, *rate* and *error*. Rule boxes have other purposes such as defining macros, event-triggered assignments and subsidiary diagrams.

An input or output names the partner, port and operation (e.g. *lender.loan.quote*). In this example, all the web services happen to communicate via port *loan*, but the port names could vary among services. The lender operation is *quote*, the approver operation is *approve*, and the assessor operation is *assess*.

2.4 A Car Supplier Web Service

As a further example, DoubleQuote is a *supplier* that offers online customers a good deal on car orders. A customer provides a *need* containing name, address and car model. The request for a quotation is passed to two dealers, each of which responds with an *offer* giving the dealer reference, name, price and delivery period.

DoubleQuote works with two business partners: BigDeal (acting as *dealer1*) and WheelerDealer (acting as *dealer2*). A dealer indicates that it cannot supply the model by replying with infinite price. (It would alternatively be possible to signal this by a fault.) The better offer is selected: the lower price, or the earlier delivery date if equal. This offer is sent to the appropriate dealer as a definite order. If necessary, the customer may later cancel the order corresponding to the selected offer.

Again, there are multiple web services: the dealers (*dealer1*, *dealer2*), the business process itself (*supplier*), and possibly the customer. The CRESS description of *supplier* is in figure 2. All partners happen to have the same port name *car*. The supplier operations are *order* and *cancel*, while the dealer operations are *quote*, *order* and *cancel*.

In figure 2, the supplier obtains dealer quotations in parallel (nodes 2 to 5) in order to save time. Both quotes must be obtained (3 && 4 in node 5) for the quotation process to terminate successfully. Whichever dealer offer is selected leads to a reply (node 7 or 9). Since a definite order is placed, it may be necessary to undo this if the DoubleQuote buyer renegues (or the calling web service faults). DoubleQuote therefore allows a previous order to be cancelled by the relevant dealer (nodes 10 to 12).

2.5 A Car Broker Web Service

As a final example, CarMen is a *broker* that provides an online service to negotiate car purchases and loans for these. A customer provides a *need* with name, address and car model. CarMen first uses its business partner DoubleQuote (section 2.4) to order the car on the best terms. If the car is unavailable (the price is infinite), CarMen informs its customer of refusal by causing a fault with error message 'car unavailable'. Otherwise, CarMen asks its business partner LoanStar (section 2.3) to arrange a loan for the car price. If a loan can be provided, the customer receives a *schedule* containing the dealer reference, name, price, delivery period and loan rate. If a loan is refused (e.g. because the customer financial record is bad), a loan refusal fault will occur. Since the car has already been ordered, compensation requires the order to be cancelled. The refusal is then returned to the customer.

The CRESS description of this business process is in figure 3. This time, the **Uses** clause also references the subsidiary services *lender* and *supplier*. If the *lender* invocation in node 3 causes a *refusal* fault, it is intercepted by the global fault handler (nodes 7, 8). This calls the compensation handler in node 6 and returns the fault to the customer.

The situation with web services is now very complex. The *broker* (figure 3) invokes the *supplier* to order the car (figure 2) and the *lender* to arrange a loan (figure 1). In turn, each of these invokes two further web services. A total of seven web services is therefore involved. The beauty of web services is that this is all invisible to CarMen's customer, who sees a single web service for ordering and financing the purchase of a car. In fact, the internal details of a business process are intentionally hidden since this is confidential. This also allows businesses to change their internal procedures, e.g. the supplier may change dealers or may use more than two dealers.

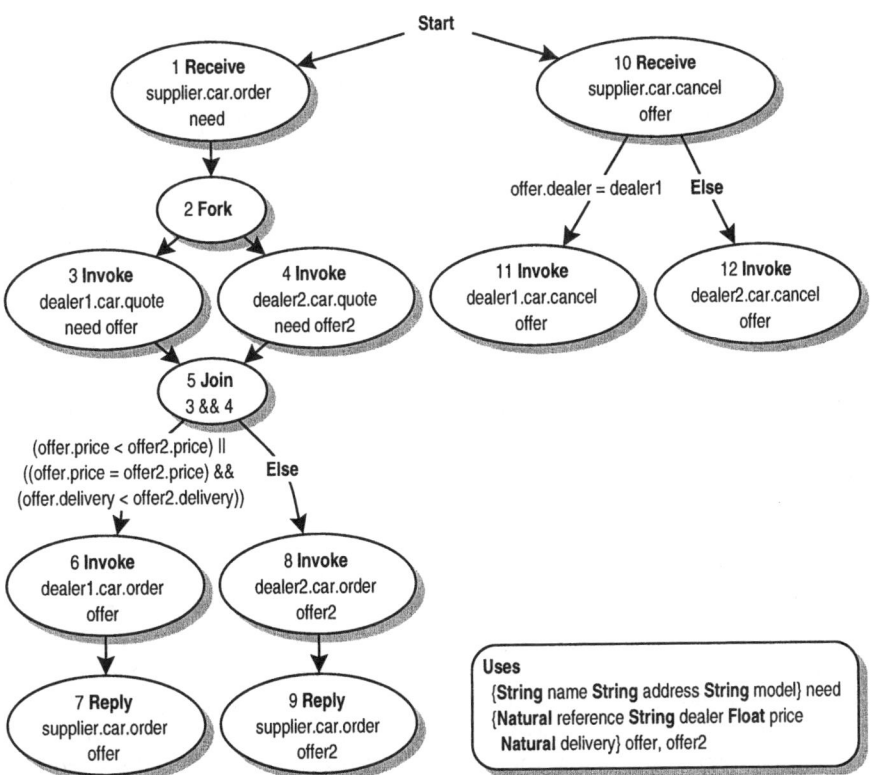

Fig. 2. Car Supplier Business Process

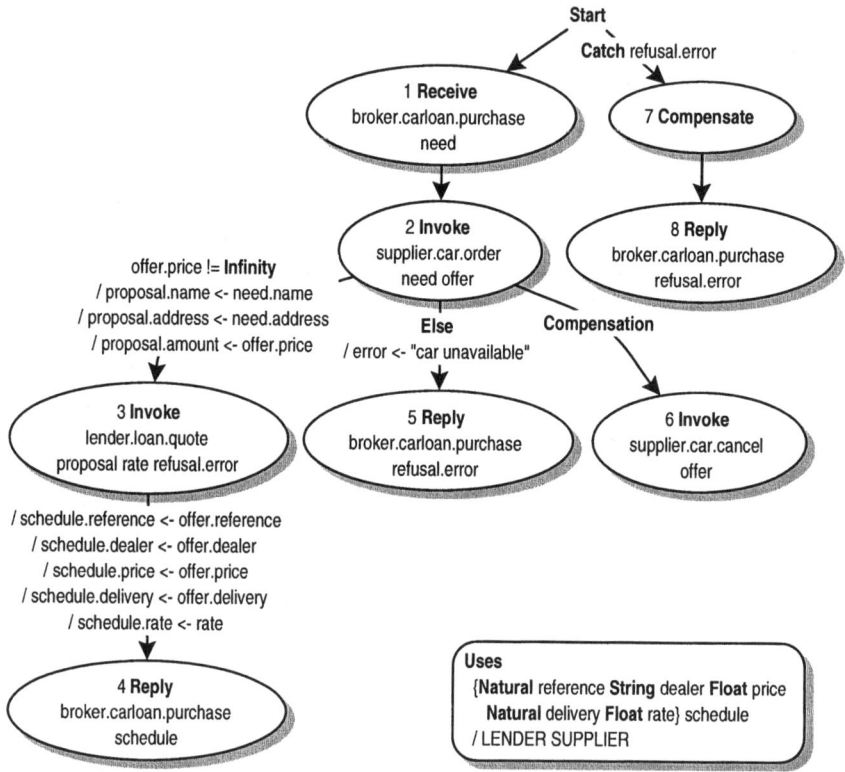

Fig. 3. Car Broker Business Process

3 Translating Web Services to LOTOS

The general principles of translating CRESS diagrams into LOTOS are explained in [6,8]. The generated code is neatly laid out and well commented. The CRESS framework is largely reusable for web services. However, web services have distinct characteristics that require extension to this approach. The translation strategy is illustrated in this section with extracts from the LOTOS generated by the examples in figures 1, 2 and 3.

3.1 Data Handling

BPEL simple types are translated into a limited range of LOTOS types. BPEL *boolean* corresponds to LOTOS *Bool*, BPEL *natural* to LOTOS *Nat*, and variations on BPEL *string* to LOTOS *Text*. Other numeric types in BPEL are mapped to LOTOS type *Number*. Numbers are problematic to handle in LOTOS since floating point numbers are required. BPEL 1.1 allows floating point variables, but fortunately requires only simple integer arithmetic. Text strings are also awkward in LOTOS since there is no character type. LOTOS has no lexical shorthands for numbers or strings, so an ugly syntax is required; their conventional form is shown in the code extracts that follow.

Expressions are translated into their obvious LOTOS equivalents. BPEL uses XPATH as its expression language, and so has access to a wide range of functions. The LOTOS framework has support for those required by BPEL 1.1, i.e. a subset of the arithmetic, logical and string functions in XPATH 1.0. Expression guards become LOTOS guarded choices. Assignments are turned into LOTOS **Let** statements.

BPEL requires use of structured variables. Each structured type is automatically translated into a LOTOS type with fields as operations. For example, *proposal* in figure 1 generates the type *Proposal*, with field operations such as *getName* and *setName*.

3.2 Basic Behaviour

Outputs (**Reply**, **Invoke**) and inputs (**Receive**, **Invoke**) correspond to LOTOS events. An activity sequence in a CRESS diagram becomes a sequence in LOTOS. However, parts of a CRESS diagram often have to be translated as separate LOTOS processes. This happens, for example, when part of a diagram is reached by different paths or is invoked as an event handler. A BPEL activity results in successful termination or failure. LOTOS behaviours therefore exit with state *True* or *False*. For simple behaviours, this is the *States* result of a process. It will be seen later that states are generalised when dealing with compensation handling or with concurrency.

All the aspects considered so far are illustrated in the following code for nodes 1, 2 and 5 in figure 1:

```
Process LENDER_1 [lender,approver,assessor]                    (* LENDER from 1 *)
  (error:Text,proposal:Proposal,rate:Number,risk:Text) : Exit(States) :=
  lender !loan !quote ?proposal:Proposal;                      (* LENDER receive 1 *)
  (
    [getAmount(proposal) Ge 10000] ->                          (* check proposal.amount >= 10000 *)
        LENDER_2 [lender,approver,assessor]                    (* LENDER invoke 2 (again) *)
           (error,proposal,rate,risk)
  []
    [Not(getAmount(proposal) Ge 10000)] ->                     (* Else after proposal.amount >= 10000 *)
        assessor !loan !assess !proposal;                      (* LENDER invoke 5 request *)
        assessor !loan !assess ?risk:Text;                     (* LENDER invoke 5 response *)
        (
          [risk Eq "low"] ->                                   (* check risk = "low" *)
            (
              Let rate:Number = 3.5 In                         (* update local *)
                LENDER_4 [lender,approver,assessor]            (* LENDER reply 4 (again) *)
                  (error,proposal,rate,risk)
            )
        []
          [Not(risk Eq "low")] ->                              (* Else after risk = "low" *)
              LENDER_2 [lender,approver,assessor]              (* LENDER output 2 (again) *)
                (error,proposal,rate,risk)
        )
  )
EndProc                                                        (* end LENDER_1 *)
```

3.3 Event Handling

For each web service, the CRESS translator statically discovers where event handlers are defined and the scopes where these apply (global, or associated with an **Invoke**). An event dispatcher process is then generated with reference to these handlers according to their scopes. If a fault handler does not exist for the current scope, the global handler (if any) is tried. Faults have to be matched against handlers in a particular order: **Catch** with a matching fault name, **Catch** with a matching fault name and type, **Catch** with a matching fault type, **CatchAll**. A fault means unsuccessful termination, so event handlers always exit with a *False* status.

A **Compensate** action, a **Throw** action or a fault invokes the event dispatcher with information about the scope, fault name and fault value type. The fault handling rules of BPEL require fault values to be coerced into a single LOTOS type *Value*. This is needed so that the kind of value can be matched against **Catch**. For example, a fault handler expecting a string must check if the value is indeed a string; another handler for the same fault name might deal with floating point fault values.

As an example, **Invoke** in node 2 of figure 1 may generate a *refusal* fault. This calls the *LENDER_EVENT* dispatcher for scope 0 associated with node 2; there is just one event scope in this example. The *Match* operation compares the given fault name and value type with those in the event (*refusal* and *Text* in this case). When node 3 is called, the fault value (*error*) is set to a string by operation *Text*.

```
Process LENDER_2 [lender,approver,assessor]                    (* LENDER from 2 *)
  (error:Text,proposal:Proposal,rate:Number,risk:Text) : Exit(States) :=
    approver !loan !approve !proposal;                         (* LENDER invoke 2 request *)
    (
      approver !loan !approve !refusal ?error:Text;            (* LENDER invoke 2 fault *)
      LENDER_EVENT [lender,approver,assessor]                  (* call event dispatcher *)
        (error,proposal,rate,risk,0 Of Nat,refusal,Value(error))
    []
      approver !loan !approve ?rate:Number;                    (* LENDER invoke 2 response *)
      LENDER_4 [lender,approver,assessor]                      (* LENDER reply 4 (again) *)
        (error,proposal,rate,risk)
    )
EndProc                                                        (* end LENDER_2 *)
Process LENDER_EVENT [lender,approver,assessor]                (* event dispatcher *)
  (error:Text,proposal:Proposal,rate:Number,risk:Text, scope:Nat,event:Event,value:Value) :
    Exit(States) :=
    [scope Eq 0] ->                                            (* scope 0 ? *)
    (
      [Match(event,kind,refusal,TextKind)] ->                  (* match for 'refusal.error'? *)
        LENDER_3 [lender,approver,assessor]                    (* call event handler *)
          (Text(value),proposal,rate,risk)
    )
EndProc                                                        (* end LENDER_EVENT *)
```

Compensation handling is much more complex to translate than fault handling. A compensation handler becomes available only when its associated scope has terminated successfully. The state of the process must also be stored for use by the compensation handler in case it is called later. When compensation is in use, LOTOS processes must therefore carry a *states* parameter as the history of compensation states.

As each activity with compensation completes, it prefixes the current state (i.e. the process parameters) to the previous state list. In this way, a stack of compensation states is maintained. The following extract is from nodes 1 and 2 of figure 3. The first parameter of operation *State* is a *True* status (all that is used in simple processes), while the second parameter is the compensation scope (1 in this case, 0 being the global scope).

```
Process BROKER_1 [broker,supplier,lender]                    (* BROKER from start *)
   (error:Text,need:Need,offer:Offer,proposal:Proposal,rate:Number,
    schedule:Schedule,states:States) : Exit(States) :=
      broker !carloan !purchase ?need:Need;                  (* BROKER receive 1 *)
      supplier !car !order !need;                            (* BROKER invoke 2 request *)
      supplier !car !order ?offer:Offer;                     (* BROKER invoke 2 response *)
      (
        Let states:States =                                  (* store state *)
          State(True,1,error,need,offer,proposal,rate,schedule) + states In ...
      )
EndProc                                                      (* end BROKER_1 *)
```

A **Compensate** action for a given scope invokes the event dispatcher. This searches the stored states for a matching compensation state. If found, the handler for this state is called. If not found (or no scope was specified by **Compensate**), the default action is to call all compensation handlers in reverse order of activity completion. The net effect is that compensation undoes previous work. In figure 3, for example, failure to obtain a loan causes the car order to be cancelled.

3.4 Concurrency

Parallel execution in BPEL (**Fork, Join**) is very tricky to render in LOTOS, despite the fact that LOTOS can readily specify concurrency. This is largely because BPEL has global variables that are shared among parallel execution paths, whereas LOTOS has only local state. It is also necessary to deal with the effects of event handlers during parallel execution, e.g. a fault may prematurely terminate one path and trigger compensation. By default, BPEL allows execution to continue if only one of the preceding parallel paths terminates successfully. However, an arbitrary combination of path termination statuses may be used to determine this.

The CRESS translation to LOTOS handles concurrency by collecting an exit state from each path. The status of each is then evaluated. If the **Join** condition is satisfied, execution can continue. If the condition is not satisfied, a *JoinFailure* fault is caused. However if the **Fork** specifies *loose* concurrency, the activity following **Join** is simply considered to have failed. This may allow other parts of the web service to continue.

Concurrency is a second reason for processes to carry their state as a parameter. Each parallel path exits with the current process state. The states from each path are reconciled, and the current process parameters are computed. In fact, BPEL acknowledges but does not solve the problem that the same variables may be altered in parallel path. The CRESS toolset performs a data flow analysis of diagrams as they are translated. This is essential anyway, for example to decide whether variables should be read

('?') or written ('!') in LOTOS events. The same data flow analysis detects variables that are altered on parallel paths, causing a warning to be issued during translation.

The following shows the translation of node 5 in figure 2 where the parallel paths from nodes 3 and 4 converge. As will be seen, the translation has to be very complex.

```
(
  (
    SUPPLIER_3 [supplier,dealer1,dealer2]              (* SUPPLIER output 3 *)
      (need,offer,offer2,states)
    >> Accept states:States In                          (* accept fork states *)
      Exit(states,Any States)                                    (* fork exit *)
  )
|||
  (
    SUPPLIER_4 [supplier,dealer1,dealer2]              (* SUPPLIER output 4 *)
      (need,offer,offer2,states)
    >> Accept states:States In                          (* accept fork states *)
      Exit(Any States,states)                                    (* fork exit *)
  )
)
>> Accept states0,states1:States In                     (* accept join states *)
(
  Let state:State = State(AnyBool,need,offer,offer2) In    (* get state updates *)
  Let state0:State = Head(states0) In                  (* get SUPPLIER 3 state *)
  Let state1:State = Head(states1) In                  (* get SUPPLIER 4 state *)
  Let status0:Bool = getStatus(state0) In             (* get SUPPLIER 3 status *)
  Let status1:Bool = getStatus(state1) In             (* get SUPPLIER 4 status *)
  Let state:State = getState(state,state0,state1) In       (* reconcile states *)
  Let need:Need = getNeed(state) In            (* set need from combined state *)
  Let offer:Offer = getOffer(state) In        (* set offer from combined state *)
  Let offer2:Offer = getOffer2(state) In     (* set offer2 from combined state *)
  Let states:States = getStates(Tail(states0),Tail(states1)) In  (* combine states *)
    [Not(status0 And status1)] ->                              (* join failed? *)
      SUPPLIER_EVENT [supplier,dealer1,dealer2]        (* call event dispatcher *)
        (need,offer,offer2,states,AnyNat,JoinFailure,AnyValue)
  []
    [status0 And status1] ->                            (* check join condition *)
      SUPPLIER_5 [supplier,dealer1,dealer2]            (* SUPPLIER from join 5 *)
        (need,offer,offer2,states)
)
```

3.5 Partner Processes

Partner web services are translated as separate LOTOS processes, synchronised in parallel with the main LOTOS process. If the partner is an external web service (e.g. *approver* or *assessor* in figure 1), a skeleton specification is generated to match its port/operation signature. For example, the default specification of *approver* is:

```
Process APPROVER [approver] : Exit(States) :=              (* APPROVER partner *)
  approver !loan !approve ?proposal:Proposal;        (* APPROVER 'approve' input *)
```

```
(
    approver !loan !approve !AnyNumber;        (* APPROVER 'approve' output *)
    APPROVER [approver]                         (* repeat APPROVER *)
[]
    approver !loan !approve !refusal !AnyText;  (* APPROVER 'refusal' fault *)
    APPROVER [approver]                         (* repeat APPROVER *)
)
EndProc                                         (* end APPROVER *)
```

This is sufficient for basic validation of the *lender* web service, but does not permit useful analysis. It is therefore possible to give a more realistic specification of external partners. If the CRESS translator finds the file *<partner>.lot*, it uses this specification of the partner instead of the default one. In fact these specifications can be arbitrarily complex. The four external partners in figures 1 and 2 were given realistic specifications. For example, the *dealer* partners maintain 'databases' (lists) of car information, customer quotations and customer orders.

3.6 Overall Specification Structure

When the broker service in figure 3 is translated, the services in figures 1 and 2 are also incorporated. The result is 330 lines of automatically generated LOTOS data types and 310 lines defining LOTOS processes. To this must be added the 400 lines of manually specified partner processes. The generated code is embedded in a specification framework that provides generic support for any web service. This consists of 590 lines of LOTOS (mostly complex data types). In total, this amounts to just over 1600 lines of LOTOS – a manageable specification.

The translation of exactly the same services to BPEL makes an interesting comparison. For this, CRESS generates 60 source files and 3300 lines of code (mostly BPEL, WSDL and Java). So whether the translation to LOTOS or BPEL is considered, it is evident that the CRESS notation is very compact.

4 Rigorous Analysis of Web Services

4.1 The Value of Formalising Web Services

Developing a formal interpretation of BPEL has been valuable in its own right. For example, a number of errors, omissions and ambiguities have been found in the standard (mainly in complex areas such as event handling and data handling). A number of these errors in BPEL4WS have already been corrected in WS-BPEL. The formalisation of BPEL also provides a precise interpretation of the standard.

More importantly, the formalisation supports a wide variety of analyses. Some of the investigations have used the TOPO (and LOLA) tools for LOTOS, while others have used CADP. Both offer distinct capabilities. LOLA has the advantage of using LOTOS data types as specified; this is beneficial since web services are supported by some rather complex types. LOLA is particularly useful for performing formally-based validation. CADP complements this through capabilities such as state space minimisation, equivalence checking and model checking. The penalty in using CADP is that it places certain requirements on the LOTOS, mainly on the data types. Some of these issues are addressed by annotations, but actualised data types have to be expanded manually, and some data types need manual realisations.

Rigorous analysis aims to find problems with a web service viewed as a black box. Formal verification indicates where the LOTOS is incorrect; the automatically generated comments show where the CRESS description needs to be improved. Formal validation, however, is performed at a higher level, so the CRESS changes are more obvious.

4.2 Formal Checking

When web services are composed, there is a danger that they do not synchronise properly due to a misunderstanding over the interface. In LOTOS terms, this manifests itself as a deadlock. (A LOTOS web service either performs **Exit** or recurses.) This is easily checked by LOLA using its expansion capabilities. When using BPEL (or more exactly WSDL), it is difficult to manually check services for compatibility since WSDL interface descriptions can be written in different ways and yet be consistent.

The internal design of a web service is proprietary. The owner may, however, wish to publish an abstraction for public use. There is then a question of whether the private and public specifications are consistent with each other. Essentially the public specification must be equivalent (e.g. observationally) to the private specification. Web services also evolve, e.g. the external partners used by a business process may change. Again, there is an issue of whether an updated web service is equivalent to the former one. CADP supports these kind of analyses with the specifications generated from web services.

CADP also allows model checking of web service properties. Safety and liveness properties can be formulated in ACTL (Action-based Computational Temporal Logic). For example, the *lender* service must not fault (safety), and every invocation of the *broker* service must eventually receive a response (liveness).

4.3 Rigorous Validation

In practice, web services have to be manually debugged like any other program, though tools like ActiveBPEL provide visual simulation. The LOTOS generated for web services can, of course, be manually simulated – but again this is just debugging.

The author has developed MUSTARD (Multiple-Use Scenario Test and Refusal Description [10]) as a language-independent and tool-independent approach for expressing use case scenarios. These are translated into the chosen language (LOTOS here) and automatically validated against the specification (using LOLA). This is useful for initial validation of a specification, and also for later 'regression testing' following a change in the service description.

There is insufficient space here to explain the MUSTARD notation, so reference to [10] and to the following example must suffice. Briefly, MUSTARD allows scenarios with sequences, alternatives, non-determinism and concurrency. The following MUSTARD scenario checks simultaneous requests to the *supplier* process. The first sequence requests an Audi A5, and expects to receive a schedule with dealer reference 8, name WheelerDealer, price 33000, delivery 30 days, loan rate 3.5%. The second requests a Ford Mondeo, and allows a specified schedule or an unavailable message in return.

```
test(Simultaneous_Purchases,                    % simultaneous purchases scenario
  succeeds(                                     % behaviour must succeed
    interleaves(                                % behaviours are interleaved
      sequences(                                % need request, schedule response
        send(broker.carloan.purchase,Need('Ken Turner,'Stirling Scotland,'Audi A5)),
        read(broker.carloan.purchase,Schedule(8,'WheelerDealer,33000,30,3.5))),
      sequences(                                % need request, choice response
        send(broker.carloan.purchase,Need('Kurt Jenner,'London England,'Ford Mondeo)),
        offers(                                 % choice of schedule or fault
          read(broker.carloan.purchase,Schedule(6,'BigDeal,20000,10,4.1)),
          read(broker.carloan.purchase,refusal,'car unavailable))))))
```

Of course, there is then the issue of where such scenarios come from. The author has separately developed PCL (Parameter Constraint Language [9]) for this kind of purpose. Trying to generate useful tests from a complex specification is generally infeasible. PCL is therefore used to annotate a specification with constraints on interesting input values and on useful orderings over inputs. This makes test generation practicable for specifications with complex data types, infinite data sorts or concurrency – all characteristic of web service specifications.

4.4 Interaction Among Services

Scenario-based validation is also a useful way of checking for interference among supposedly independent services. In telecommunications, this is called the feature interaction problem. Interactions may arise for technical reasons (e.g. conflicting services are activated by the same trigger) or for resource reasons (e.g. the services have a shared resource or external partner). One way of interpreting service interaction is that a service behaves differently in the presence of some other service.

Web services are formally validated by a range of MUSTARD scenarios that address all the critical characteristics of their behaviour. It then becomes possible to check services in isolation as well as in combination. This can effectively and efficiently detect interactions among services, though failure to detect interactions is not a guarantee that the services are interaction-free.

Web services are usually viewed as atomic and therefore do not incorporate add-on features (unlike telecommunications services). However it is useful to have a feature concept for web services. CRESS readily supports this in the same way as features can be added to voice services. A range of generic features has therefore been defined for web services; space does not allow them to be presented in detail here.

Consider the sample web services discussed earlier. They all make use of a customer name and address. The services could also perform other operations such as setting up an account or checking the status of a request. In all cases, it would be useful to validate the name and address provided. In fact this is a fraught problem, as all maintainers of mailing lists are aware.

A *name* feature has therefore been defined for normalising names. This is automatically invoked when a web service receives a given request with a name. It sets the name into a normal form (e.g. 'KJ Turner'). A *contact* feature has also been defined for checking whether a name and address are known to be associated. This is automatically invoked when a given request with name and address is received by a web service.

When services are validated with MUSTARD using *contact* alone or with *name* as well, it is found that they behave differently (i.e. feature interaction occurs). The problem is obvious: if the *name* feature normalises a name, this may be inconsistent with the name recorded for an address. Of course, most feature interactions are obvious with hindsight. The value of automated analysis is that such problems are detected without detailed manual investigation when a new feature is added.

5 Conclusions

Business processes can benefit from formal models of their behaviour. A graphical description is much more understandable than the raw BPEL and WSDL. A high degree of automation is strongly desirable in the creation of web-based business processes. CRESS meets all of these requirements. Compared to commercial tools, CRESS does not support the entirety of web services. It handles nearly everything used in practice, a lack of timers being the main omission. However CRESS confers distinctive benefits: applicability to many domains, human-readable code for translated services, features as service add-ons, and translation to formal languages for rigorous analysis.

CRESS has now shown its worth in four rather different application domains: IN, Internet Telephony, IVR and web services. The toolset is portable, having been used on four different platforms. CRESS accepts diagrams drawn with three existing graphical editors, and generates code in five different languages. It is therefore an approach of wide practical and theoretical benefit.

References

1. T. Andrews *et al.*, editors. *Business Process Execution Language for Web Services*. Version 1.1. BEA, IBM, Microsoft, SAP, Siebel, May 2003.
2. A. Arkin *et al.*, editors. *Web Services Business Process Execution Language*. Version 2.0. OASIS, Billerica, Massachusetts, Feb. 2005.
3. BPMI. *Business Process Modeling Notation*. Version 1.0. Business Process Management Initiative, May 2004.
4. A. Ferrara. Web services: A process algebra approach. In *Proc. 2nd. Intl. Conf. on Service-Oriented Computing*, 242–251. ACM Press, New York, Nov. 2004.
5. H. Foster, S. Uchitel, J. Kramer, and J. Magee. Compatibility verification for web service choreography. In *2nd. Intl. Conf. on Web Services*, San Diego, California, July 2004.
6. K. J. Turner. Formalising the CHISEL feature notation. In M. H. Calder and E. H. Magill, editors, *Proc. 6th. Feature Interactions*, 241–256. IOS Press, Amsterdam, May 2000.
7. K. J. Turner. Modelling SIP services using CRESS. In D. A. Peled and M. Y. Vardi, editors, *Proc. FORTE XV*, LNCS 2529, 162–177. Springer, Berlin, Nov. 2002.
8. K. J. Turner. Analysing interactive voice services. *Computer Networks*, 45(5):665–685, Aug. 2004.
9. K. J. Turner. Test generation for radiotherapy accelerators. *Software Tools for Technology Transfer*, Oct. 2004, in press.
10. K. J. Turner. Validating feature-based specifications. *Software Practice and Experience*, May 2005, in press.

From Automata Networks to HMSCs:
A Reverse Model Engineering Perspective

Thomas Chatain[1], Loïc Hélouët[2], and Claude Jard[3]

[1] IRISA/ENS Cachan-Bretagne, Campus de Beaulieu,
F-35042 Rennes cedex, France
Thomas.Chatain@irisa.fr
[2] IRISA/INRIA, Campus de Beaulieu,
F-35042 Rennes cedex, France
Loic.Helouet@irisa.fr
[3] IRISA/ENS Cachan-Bretagne, Campus de Ker-Lann,
F-35170 Bruz cedex, France
Claude.Jard@bretagne.ens-cachan.fr

Abstract. This paper considers the problem of automatic abstraction, from a low-level model given in term of network of interacting automata to a high-level message sequence chart. This allows the designer to play in a coherent way with the local and global views of a system, and opens new perspectives in reverse model engineering. Our technique is based on a partial order semantics of synchronous parallel automata and the construction of a finite complete prefix of an event-structure coding all the behaviors. We present the models and algorithms. The examples presented in the paper have been processed by a small software prototype we have implemented.

1 Introduction

Designing a distributed application is a complex task. At the final stage of the modeling, once the different architectural decisions have been made, designers usually obtain a set of communicating sequential components. During earlier stages of software development, designers use more abstract and visual representations such as scenarios. For instance, Message Sequence Charts (MSCs) [9] are an appealing visual formalism to capture system requirements. They are particularly suited for describing scenarios of distributed telecommunication software [7]. Several variants of MSCs appear in the literature (sequence diagrams, message flow diagrams, object interaction diagrams, Live Sequence Charts) and are used in a number of software engineering methodologies including UML [8]. They provide the designer with a global view of the dynamic behavior of the system, given in a declarative manner.

However, there is often a gap between the local view defined as sequential components and the more global view described by scenarios. Some scenarios cannot be implemented by sequential machines, and some compositions of sequential machines do not have finite representation in terms of MSCs. This is why a lot of recent works have been developed to automatically generate communicating automata (at least a skeleton) from MSCs [1,5] in the context of a top-down design methodology. Obviously, building a bridge in the opposite direction is also an interesting problem, as it would allow designers to play freely with any style of specification (global declarative or distributed imperative) while preserving the coherence of both views. A solution to this problem could also be the basis of another important challenge called "aspect modeling", in which a new feature described as a set of scenarios can be added safely to an already existing model of communicating machines. This will imply sophisticated formal techniques, since the required transformations modify dramatically the structure of the automata.

This context motivates our work on some "reverse distributed model engineering". We begin with simple models, which are networks of synchronous parallel finite state automata for the imperative aspect, and MSCs for the declarative aspect. The problem is thus to automatically obtain a MSC from an automata network, which codes all the runs of the system, runs being defined as partial orders of transition occurrences. The finiteness of the automata and the synchronous communication ensure that such a transformation is possible. This question has already been addressed from the theoretical point of view in term of formal languages in [3]. They show that any single Büchi automaton with a structural property, called diamond, and with all its states accepting, is able to generate the language of a bounded MSC. However, this problem is undecidable for asynchronous communicating finite state machines. This justifies our choice to consider synchronous networks and to propose an original algorithm to produce a concrete MSC, as readable as possible. Figure 1 shows an example of such network, which consists of two automata A_0 and A_1, synchronized on their common event x. Figure 1 gives the corresponding MSC we would like to compute. Notice that the MSC graph is complex due to the fact that this example was designed to show all the tricky aspects of the transformation. A more realistic example is treated in Section 4.

We will use the notion of unfolding, and the fact it can be finitely generated by a finite complete prefix. This is based on the unfolding theory, as presented in [4,2]. In the paper, we adopt nevertheless a direct approach, without using Petri nets as usual, in order to avoid to introduce a new intermediary formal model. The question of using the finite prefix as a generator of the unfolding is also new up to our knowledge.

The rest of the paper is organized as follows. Section 2 defines formally automata networks, MSCs and the notion of runs. The next section 3 is devoted to the generation of possible runs by the construction of a finite complete prefix of the unfolding. Section 4 presents how the MSC automaton and the referenced basic MSCs are extracted from the prefix. We conclude by a discussion summarizing the approach and proposing a few perspectives. All the proofs of the propositions and theorems are available in the research report [10].

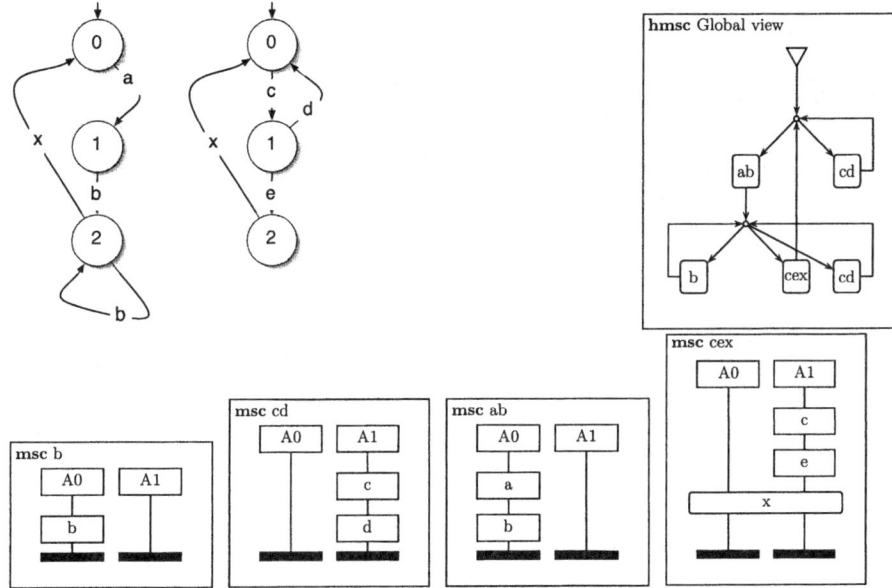

Fig. 1. A network of two synchronized automata and its scenario view

2 Definition of Automata Networks and MSCs

2.1 Networks

An *initialized labelled automaton* is a tuple $A = \langle S, \Sigma, \rightarrow, s^0 \rangle$ where S is a finite set of *states*, Σ is a set of labels, $\rightarrow \, \subseteq S \times \Sigma \times S$ is a set of *labelled transitions*, and $s^0 \in S$ is the initial state. For a transition $t = (s, a, s') \in \, \rightarrow$, we denote $\alpha(t) \stackrel{def}{=} s$ its *source*, $\beta(t) \stackrel{def}{=} s'$ its *target*, and $\lambda(t) \stackrel{def}{=} a$ its *label*.

$I \stackrel{def}{=} \{1, \ldots, n\}$ denotes a finite set of indices. We consider the *synchronous parallel composition of the initialized labelled automata* $A_i = \langle S_i, \Sigma_i, \rightarrow_i, s_i^0 \rangle_{i \in I}$

The network of Figure 1 is formally defined by:

$$S_0 = \{0, 1, 2\} \qquad S_1 = \{0, 1, 2\}$$
$$\Sigma_0 = \{a, b, x\} \qquad \Sigma_1 = \{c, d, e, x\}$$
$$s_0^0 = 0 \qquad s_1^0 = 0$$
$$\rightarrow_0 = \{(0, a, 1), (1, b, 2), (2, x, 0), (2, b, 2)\}$$
$$\rightarrow_1 = \{(0, c, 1), (1, e, 2), (2, x, 0), (1, d, 0)\}$$

In an interleaving semantics, the network behavior is defined as the (global) initialized labelled automaton $A = \langle S, \Sigma, \rightarrow, s^0 \rangle$ where:

- $S \stackrel{\text{def}}{=} S_1 \times \cdots \times S_n$
- $\Sigma \stackrel{\text{def}}{=} \bigcup_{i \in I} \Sigma_i$
- $((s_i)_{i \in I}, a, (s'_i)_{i \in I}) \in \rightarrow$ iff $\begin{cases} \forall i \in \{1, \ldots, n\} \\ \wedge \exists i \in \{1, \ldots, n\} \end{cases} \begin{cases} (s_i, a, s'_i) \in \rightarrow_i \\ \vee (s_i = s'_i \wedge a \notin \Sigma_i) \\ (s_i, a, s'_i) \in \rightarrow_i \end{cases}$
- $s^0 \stackrel{\text{def}}{=} (s_1^0, \ldots, s_n^0)$

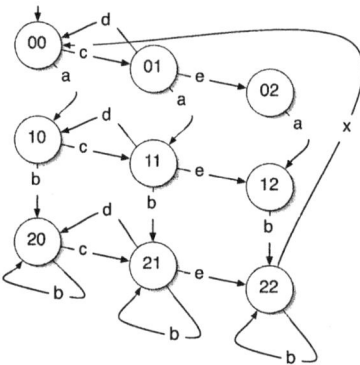

Fig. 2. The synchronized product

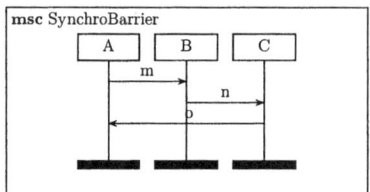

Fig. 3. bMSC representation of rendez-vous

Intuitively, we force the automata to evolve synchronously when they execute a transition labelled by the same name. In the other case, they evolve independently. Figure 2 shows the product automaton of our example. Sequential runs are the different paths in the graph of the product automaton. Unfortunately, this notion of run does not enlight the causal relations between the different occurrences of transitions (seen as atomic events), as done in MSCs. In our context, the right notion of run is the partial ordering of events that have occurred. Hence, runs of a system will be defined as basic MSCs.

2.2 Message Sequence Charts

MSCs are composed of basic scenarios (or bMSCs), that depict interactions among several objects. These interactions are then composed hierarchically by means of operators (loop, choice, sequence, ...). For the sake of simplicity, we will only consider a single hierarchical level. Interactions in the automata networks we consider are synchronous (i.e. Rendez-vous communication): they are blocking, and involve several participants. For this reason, communications in bMSCs will be represented by references to other bMSCs describing how a communication mechanism is implemented. Such Rendez-vous can be implemented using a synchronization barrier, as depicted in Figure 3. In MSCs, referencing inside a diagram is allowed by inline expressions. Here, we will only consider references to simple bMSCs depicting communications among a given set of components. We do not allow reference nesting, and will not use inline expressions with opt, alt or loop.

In our framework, a bMSC is defined as a finite set of events. Each event is represented as the vector of its predecessors on each instance. The absence of predecessor on an instance is denoted by the null event •. We associate a label to each event, which will serve to note the corresponding transition of the automata. For example, considering a system with three instances, the event e_3 denoted by $((e_1, (1, a, 2)), •, (e_2, (3, a, 4)))$ is a synchronization event between the first and the third instance, and having the events e_1 and e_2 as immediate predecessors on these instances. There is no immediate predecessor on the second instance since it does not participate in the synchronization. The labels are $(1, a, 2)$ and $(3, a, 4)$, denoting for instance the transitions to synchronize in an automata network. Formally, a $bMSC$ over a set of instances I is a tuple $B = (E, \Sigma, A, \Theta)$, where $E = \{(e_i, \sigma)_{i \in I}, \sigma \in \Sigma\}$ is a set of events such that each $e_i \in \{•\} \cup E \times \Sigma$. E contains *local events* (events such that $|\{e_i \neq •\}| = 1$) and *interactions* (events such that $|\{e_i \neq •\}| > 1$). Σ is a local alphabet, A is an alphabet of local actions and interaction names, and $\Theta : \Sigma \longrightarrow A$ assigns a global name to events.

When $f_i = (e, \sigma)$, we denote $\pi_i(f) = e$. We will say that e is a predecessor of f, and write $e \rightarrow f$ when $\exists i \in I$ such that $\pi_i(f) = e$. E also contains a specific event $\bot = (•, \ldots, •)_{i \in I}$ called the *initial event* that has no predecessor. We will say that an event is *minimal* in a bMSC iff $\bot$ is the unique predecessor of all its components. A bMSC must also satisfy the following properties :

i) the reflexive and transitive closure $\rightarrow^*$ of $\rightarrow$ is a partial order.
ii) (synchronization) $\forall e = (e_i)_{i \in I} \in E$, we require that $\exists ! a, \forall i \in I, e_i \neq • \implies \Theta(\sigma_i) = a$. This property means that all components participating to an event must synchronize.
iii) (local sequencing) $\forall i \in I, \forall e \in E, e_i \neq • \implies \pi_i(e) = \bot$ or $(\pi_i(e))_i \neq •$
iv) (no choice) $\forall (e, e') \in E^2, \forall i \in I, e \neq e' \implies \pi_i(e) \neq \pi_i(e')$. This property forbids the introduction of choices in a bMSC.

bMSCS are good candidates to model causal relations in runs of a distributed system. *Causality* between events is defined by $\rightarrow^*$. When neither $e \rightarrow^* e'$, nor $e' \rightarrow^* e$, we will say that e and e' are independent (or *concurrent*). The set of minimal events in B w.r.t $\rightarrow^*$ is denoted by $min(E)$. We will say that an event is minimal for an instance $i \in I$ if the predecessor event on component i is $\bot$. It is maximal for this instance if it is not a predecessor event for an event on this instance. The minimal (resp. maximal) event on instance i (when it is defined) will be denoted by $min_i(E)$(resp. $max_i(E)$). A bMSC $B1$ is a prefix of a bMSC $B2$ if and only if $E_1 \subseteq E_2$ and $\forall e \in E_1, \Theta_1(e) = \Theta_2(e)$. The empty bMSC is the tuple $B_\emptyset = (\{\bot\}, \emptyset, \emptyset, \emptyset)$. Figure 4 is an example of bMSC. This bMSC defines the behavior of 2 instances $A0$ and $A1$. Events a, b, c, e are local actions, and reference x represents a synchronous interaction between $A0$ and $A1$.

The *sequential composition* of two bMSCs $B1 = (E_1, \Sigma_1, A_1, \Theta_1)$, $B2 = (E_2, \Sigma_2, A_2, \Theta_2)$ is the bMSC $B = (E, \Sigma_1 \cup \Sigma_2, A_1 \cup A_2, \Theta)$, where :

$$E = \begin{aligned} &E_1 \cup \left(E_2 \setminus (\{\bot\} \cup \{min_i(E_2) | i \in I\}) \right) \\ &\cup \left\{ (e'_1, \ldots e'_n) | \exists i \in I, \exists (e_1, \ldots, e_n) \in min_i(E_2) \atop \wedge \forall j \in I, e'_j = \left\{ {(max_j(E_1), \sigma) \text{ if } e_j = (\bot, \sigma) \atop e_j \text{ otherwise}} \right. \right\} \end{aligned}$$

$\Theta(\sigma) = \Theta_1(\sigma)$ if $\sigma \in \Sigma_1$, $\Theta_2(\sigma)$ otherwise

More intuitively, sequential composition merges two bMSCs along their common instances axes by addition of an ordering between the last event on each instance of B_1 and the first event on the same instance in B_2.

A *High-level Message Sequence Chart* (HMSC) is a tuple $H = (N, \rightarrow, \mathcal{M}, n_0, F)$, where N is a set of nodes, $\rightarrow \subseteq N \times \mathcal{M} \times N$ is a transition relation, $\mathcal{M}$ is a set of bMSCs, n_0 is the initial node, and F is a set of accepting nodes. HMSCs can be considered as finite state automata labelled by bMSCs. A HMSC H defines a set of paths $\mathcal{P}_H$. For a given path $p = n_0 \xrightarrow{M_1} n_1 \xrightarrow{M_2} n_2 \ldots \xrightarrow{M_k} n_k \in \mathcal{P}_H$ we can associate a bMSC $B_p = M_1 \circ M_2 \circ \cdots \circ M_k$. The runs of a HMSC H are the prefixes of all bMSCs generated by paths of H. The run associated to the empty path is $B_\emptyset$.

2.3 Runs as Partial Orders

A *run* of an automata network $A_i = \langle S_i, \Sigma_i, \rightarrow_i, s_i^0 \rangle_{i \in I}$ is defined as a bMSC $M = (E, \Sigma, A, \Theta)$, with the following properties:

i) $\Sigma = \bigcup_{i \in I} \rightarrow_i$. Hence, for an event $e = (e_i)_{i \in I}$, each e_i is of the form $e_i = (e', t)$, and we will denote $\tau_i(e) \stackrel{def}{=} t$, $\alpha_i(e) \stackrel{def}{=} \alpha(t)$ and $\beta_i(e) \stackrel{def}{=} \beta(t)$. We define $\beta_i(\bot) \stackrel{def}{=} s_i^0$.

ii) $A = \bigcup_{i \in I} \Sigma_i$.

iii) $\Theta(t) = \lambda(t)$

iv) (local sequencing) $\forall i \in I \quad e_i \neq \bullet \implies \alpha_i(e) = \beta_i(\pi_i(e))$

As Σ, A, Θ are implicit for a given set of events E, we will often denote a bMSC $B = (E, \Sigma, A, \Theta)$ by its set of events E. Intuitively, an event $e \neq \bot$ represents the synchronization of actions of the automaton A_i such that $e_i \neq \bullet$; and $e_i = (e', t)$ means that the local action on automaton A_i is t, and the

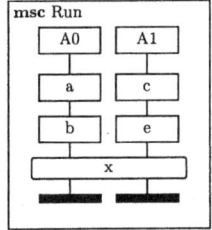

Fig. 4. A run as defined as a bMSC with inline references

previous action that concerned the automaton A_i was e'. Note that property
iii) implies that for a given component $i \in I$ and for any chain $\bot \longrightarrow e^1 = (\bot, t_1) \longrightarrow e^2 = (e^1, t_2) \ldots \longrightarrow e^k = (e^{k-1}, t_k)$ such that $\forall j \in 1..k, e^j{}_i \neq \bullet$, the sequence $t_1.t_2 \ldots t_k$ is a path of automaton A_i.

This run corresponds to the concatenation of the bMSCs AB and CEX of Figure 1. Its events are:

$$
\begin{aligned}
&0 = \bot, & &3 = ((1,(1,b,2)),\bullet), \\
&1 = ((0,(0,a,1)),\bullet), & &4 = (\bullet,(2,(1,e,2))), \\
&2 = (\bullet,(0,(0,c,1))), & &5 = ((3,(2,x,0)),(4,(2,x,0)))
\end{aligned}
$$

The question now is to represent all the possible runs. This is the role of the *unfolding*, which superimposes all the runs, shares the common prefixes and distinguishes the different histories using the notion of *conflict*.

3 Generation of Runs

3.1 Unfolding

We consider the union of all possible runs, forming a new event set E. The absence of choices is no more guaranteed. This is why we define the conflict relation $\#$ on the events as follows:

$$
e \# e' \quad \text{iff} \quad \exists f, f' \in E \begin{cases} f \neq f' \\ f \to^* e \\ f' \to^* e' \\ \exists i \in I \quad \pi_i(f) = \pi_i(f') \end{cases}
$$

Informally, two events are in conflict if they have a common ancestor event that branches on a **same** instance.

The *unfolding* of the synchronous parallel composition of the initialized labelled automata $A_i = \langle S_i, \Sigma_i, \to_i, s_i^0 \rangle_{i \in I}$ is the set U of all events that are not in self-conflict: $U \stackrel{\text{def}}{=} \{e \in E \mid \neg(e \# e)\}$. Graphically, we draw a circle for each event, and an arc from e' to e, labelled by i each time $e_i = (e', t)$. Figure 5 shows the shape of the unfolding of the network of Figure 1.

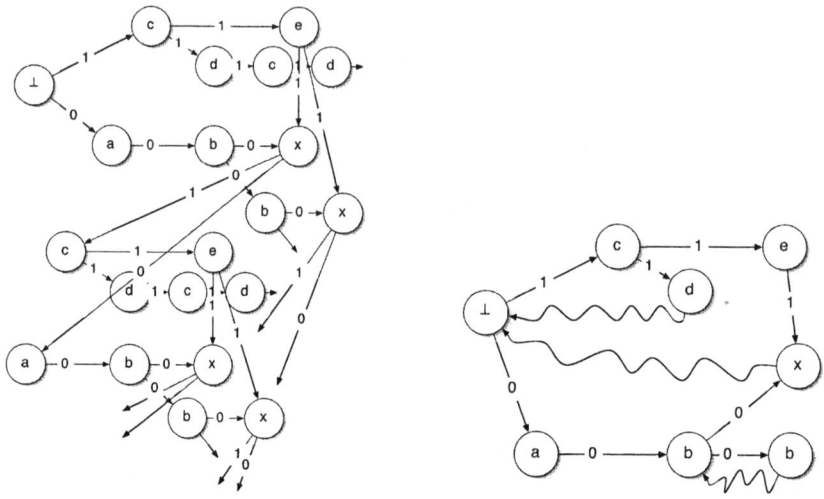

Fig. 5. The unfolding of the network of Figure 1 and its finite complete prefix

A (finite) run (also called a *configuration*) of the unfolding is a bMSC $B = (F, \Sigma, A, \Theta)$ where Σ, A, Θ are defined as usual, and F is a finite subset of E which is conflict-free and causally closed, i.e:$\begin{cases} \forall e, f \in F \quad \neg(e \# f) \\ \forall f \in F \quad \forall e \in E \quad e \to^* f \implies e \in F \end{cases}$

Proposition 1. *The unfolding contains all the possible runs.*

3.2 A Trivial Solution for MSC Extraction

As explained previously, our goal is to compute a global declarative view defined as a MSC from a distributed imperative view of a distributed system given by a network of automata. The existence of a trivial solution to this problem is guaranteed by the following proposition.

Proposition 2. *Let $A = (S, \Sigma, \longrightarrow, s^0)$ be the global initialized labelled automaton obtained by synchronous product of automata $(A_i)_{i \in I}$. Let $H = (S, b(\Sigma), \longrightarrow', s^0, S)$ be the HMSC where $b(\sigma)$ is the bMSC containing a single local action performed by an automaton or a single interaction performed by all automata involved in a synchronous communication, and $\longrightarrow' = \{(n, b(\sigma), n') | (n, \sigma, n') \in \longrightarrow)\}$. Then, the set of runs of H and the set of runs of $(A_i)_{i \in I}$ are equivalent.*

We can imagine the resulting HMSC by having a look on Figure 2. Clearly, it does not fulfill our goal of reverse model engineering. We must try to fill as much as possible the bMSCs.

3.3 Finite Complete Prefix

The unfolding U of an automata network is an infinite structure. However, it is possible to work on a finite representation of U called a *finite complete prefix*.

For a configuration $c \subseteq U$ and for an automaton $i \in I$, we define the *last event* $\uparrow_i c$ that concerned i in c as the event $f \in c$ such that:

$$(f_i \neq \bullet \ \lor \ f = \bot) \ \land \ \nexists f' \in c \quad \pi_i(f') = f$$

Proposition 3. *For a configuration $c \subseteq U$ and for an automaton $i \in I$, $\uparrow_i c$ is unique.*

We denote $\uparrow c$, the vector $(\uparrow_i c)_{i \in I}$ of last events. The *global state* vector associated with a configuration c is also defined as the states of each automaton after having performed the event $\uparrow_i c$, i.e.

$$GState(c) \stackrel{\text{def}}{=} (\beta_i(\uparrow_i c))_{i \in I}$$

For all $e \in U$, $\lceil e \rceil \stackrel{\text{def}}{=} \{f \in E \mid f \to^* e\}$ is a configuration, called the *local configuration of e*. We define the set C of *cut-off events* of an unfolding as:

$$e \in C \quad \text{iff} \quad \exists f \in \lceil e \rceil \setminus \{e\} \quad GState(\lceil f \rceil) = GState(\lceil e \rceil)$$

Actually the event f for a cut-off event e is generally not unique. We define the *regeneration configuration*, denoted ∂e of a cut-off event $e \in C$ as the intersection of the local configurations $\lceil f \rceil$ of the events $f \in \lceil e \rceil \setminus \{e\}$ such that $GState(\lceil f \rceil) = GState(\lceil e \rceil)$:

$$\partial e \stackrel{\text{def}}{=} \bigcap_{\substack{f \in \lceil e \rceil \setminus \{e\} \\ GState(\lceil f \rceil) = GState(\lceil e \rceil)}} \lceil f \rceil.$$

Proposition 4. *For all $e \in C$, $GState(\partial e) = GState(\lceil e \rceil)$.*

The set $\{e \in U \mid \nexists f \in C \quad f \to^+ e\}$ is a *finite complete prefix* of the unfolding U.

Theorem 1. *The finite complete prefix is a finite generator of the unfolding.*

Figure 5 (right) shows the prefix obtained from our example. Let us consider the event e, labelled by x. It is a cut-off event. Its regeneration configuration ∂e is $\{\bot\}$. This is graphically represented by an oscillating arrow pointed to $\bot$, knowing that $\partial e = \lceil \bot \rceil$.

The following algorithm computes the finite complete prefix U.

Initialization

1. create the initial event: $U = \bot = (\bullet)_{i \in I}$, with $GState(\{\bot\}) = (s_i^0)_{i \in I}$;
2. $C \leftarrow \emptyset$;

Repeat until deadlock

1. select a tuple $(x_i)_{i \in I}$ where $x_i \in \{\bullet\} \cup \rightarrow_i$, such that:
   - $\exists a \in \Sigma \quad \forall i \in I \quad \begin{cases} x_i = \bullet \implies a \notin \Sigma_i \\ x_i \neq \bullet \implies \lambda_i(x_i) = a \end{cases}$
   - $\forall i \in I \quad x_i \neq \bullet \implies \exists e_i' \in U \setminus C, \quad \beta_i(e_i') = \alpha_i(x_i)$
2. build the event $e = (e_i)_{i \in I}$, where $\begin{cases} e_i = (e_i', x_i) & \text{if } x_i \neq \bullet \\ e_i = \bullet & \text{otherwise} \end{cases}$
3. if $e \notin U \wedge \neg(e \# e)$ in $U \cup \{e\}$
   - $U \leftarrow U \cup \{e\}$;
   - if $\exists e' \in \lceil e \rceil$ with $GState(\lceil e' \rceil) = GState(\lceil e \rceil)$:
     then $C \leftarrow C \cup \{e\}$;
   $$\partial e \leftarrow \bigcap_{\substack{f \in \lceil e \rceil \setminus \{e\} \\ GState(\lceil f \rceil) = GState(\lceil e \rceil)}} \lceil f \rceil$$

---

4 MSC Extraction

MSC extraction starts with the abstraction of the prefix. Intuitively, for a given finite complete prefix, we define X as a subset of configurations that contains the local configuration of the cut-off events, their regeneration configuration, the local configuration of the terminal events, and that is closed under intersection. X can be projected on each instance in order to obtain a network of "abstract automata". The product forms the HMSC automaton. Basic MSCs are obtained by considering all the events occuring in an interval between two configurations of X, and transitions are deduced from configurations inclusion.

We denote by P the finite complete prefix of the unfolding U of an automata network. An event e is *terminal* if there exists no $f \in U$ such that $e \rightarrow f$. Let X be the set of configurations inductively defined as:

- $\{\bot\} \in X$
- for all e cut-off event, $\lceil e \rceil \in X \wedge \partial e \in X$;
- for all terminal event e, $\lceil e \rceil \in X$;
- for all $x, x' \in X$, $x \cup x'$ is a configuration $\implies x \cap x' \in X$.

We denote by $Y \stackrel{\text{def}}{=} \{\lceil e \rceil \mid e \in C\}$ the local configurations of cut-off events.
For all $x \in X$, let us define $E_x \stackrel{\text{def}}{=} x \setminus \bigcup_{\substack{x' \in X \\ x' \subsetneq x}} x'$. The sets E_x are subsets of elements that are not contained in any smaller configuration of X. They define the bMSCs that will be extracted from the prefix.

For all $x \in X$, the sets $E_{x'}$ with $x' \in X$, $x' \subseteq x$ are a partition of x. For all event $e \in x$ we denote $E^{-1}(e, x)$ the unique configuration $x' \in X$ such that $x' \subseteq x$ and $e \in E_{x'}$. Let us define an abstraction of the prefix P, where the elements of X play the role of "macro-events". For all $i \in I$ we define the set X_i of macro-events that concern i as:

$$X_i \stackrel{\text{def}}{=} \{x \in X \mid \exists e \in E_x, e_i \neq \bullet \vee e = \bot\}$$

For the example of Figure 5, we have:

- $X = \{\bot, \bot cd, \bot ab, \bot abcex, \bot abb\}$
- $E_\bot = \bot$, $E_{\bot cd} = cd$, $E_{\bot ab} = ab$, $E_{\bot abcex} = cex$, $E_{\bot abb} = b$
- $X_0 = \{\bot, \bot ab, \bot abcex, \bot abb\}$, $X_1 = \{\bot, \bot cd, \bot abcex\}$
- $Y = \{\bot cd, \bot abcex, \bot abb\}$

For all $i \in I$ and for all $x \in X_i \setminus \{\{\bot\}\}$, the last event that concerned i in $x \setminus E_x$ is $\uparrow_i (x \setminus E_x)$. We define the macro-event that immediately precedes x on i as $\pi_i(x) \stackrel{\text{def}}{=} E^{-1}(\uparrow_i (x \setminus E_x), x)$.

Using this definition, for each $i \in I$ we can now define the initialized labelled macro-automaton

$$\mathcal{A}_i \stackrel{\text{def}}{=} \langle X_i \setminus Y, \{E_x \mid x \in X_i\}, \rightarrow_i, \{\bot\}\rangle$$

where

$$\rightarrow_i = \begin{array}{l}\{(\pi_i(x), E_x, x) \mid x \in X_i \setminus \{\{\bot\}\} \wedge x \notin Y\} \\ \cup \{(\pi_i(x), E_x, E^{-1}(\uparrow_i \partial e, \partial e)) \mid x \in X_i \wedge x = \lceil e \rceil \text{ with } e \text{ cut-off event}\}\end{array}$$

Figure 6 shows the network of macro-automata obtained from our example. Let $\mathcal{A} = \langle S, \Sigma, \longrightarrow, s^0\rangle$ be the synchronous product $\mathcal{A}_1 \times \mathcal{A}_2 \times \cdots \times \mathcal{A}_n$. The HMSC extracted from a finite complete prefix P is defined as $H_P = (S, \longrightarrow', b(\Sigma), s^0, S)$, where $\forall \sigma \in \Sigma, b(\sigma)$ is the bMSC obtained by adding $\bot$ as predecessor of all minimal events to σ, and $\longrightarrow' = \{(s, b(\sigma), s') \mid \exists s, \sigma, s') \in \longrightarrow\}$. For our example, the HMSC computed from the synchronous product in Figure 6 is the resulting HMSC of Figure 1 announced in the beginning.

Theorem 2. *Let P be a finite complete prefix of an automata network unfolding, and let $(A_i)_{i \in I}$ be the set of "macro-automata" obtained from P. Let H be the HMSC obtained from the synchronous product $(A_i)_{i \in I}$. The runs of $(A_i)_{i \in I}$ and the runs of H are equivalent.*

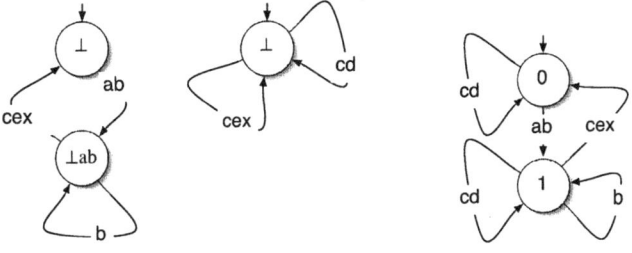

Fig. 6. The network of macro-automata and its product

Let us consider the more realistic example shown in Figure 7 (left). It is a simple connection and release protocol between two peers. The two peers (sender and receiver) are presented on top of the figure. They are connected through channels of size one. The automata of channels are given at the bottom of the figure. In this protocol, the sender can initiate a connection by sending the $Creq$ message ("!" and "?" characters denote the send and receive actions respectively). After that, it can decide locally to close the connection by sending the message $Dreq$, or receives the message $Ddreq$ indicating that a distant disconnection has been made by the receiver. In case of collision (reception of $Ddreq$ in state 2), the connection is also closed. On the receiver side, after having received the $Creq$, the received may decide to close the connection by sending the distant disconnection message $Ddreq$. If not, the $Dreq$ message is received in state 1. In that case, it is required that the receiver alerts the sender by the $Dconf$ message to allow it to close locally the connection. Note that in case of collision, it is possible to receive a message $Dreq$ in state 0, which must be skipped.

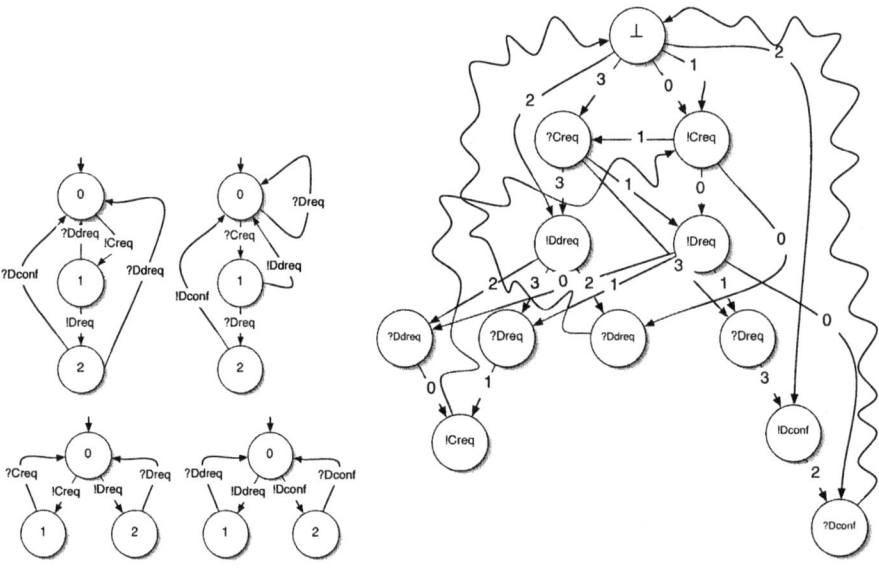

Fig. 7. The Connect-Disconnect protocol with channels of size one and its prefix

Figure 7 (right) shows the prefix of the unfolding of this example. We show three cut-off events, corresponding to the three basic patterns of the protocol, which are local disconnection, distant disconnection and collision. The MSC view produced by our method is shown in Figure 8.

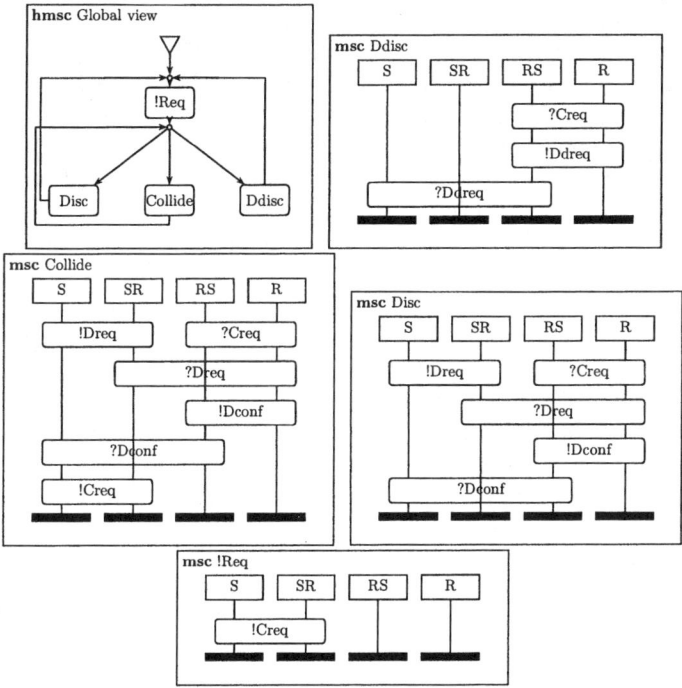

Fig. 8. MSC extracted from Automata of Figure 7

5 Discussion

We have addressed the problem of reverse model engineering, and more precisely the automatic translation of synchronous networks of finite automata into message sequence charts. A trivial solution is to build the product automaton and to interpret transition labels as basic MSCs. Unfortunately, this degenerated MSC does not fulfill the requirements of reverse engineering, which are to present the concurrent histories of the system using as much as possible a partial order view.

This work introduces new techniques that permit to recover a global partial-order based view of a system described by composition of sequential components, and hence seems relevant for reverse model engineering. The main algorithm is the unfolding of the network of automata. It computes the set of all partial order runs. Thanks to the finiteness of the system, this set is finitely generated by a prefix. From this prefix, we showed a way to extract basic partial order patterns (bMSCs). The removal of these patterns in the prefix, followed by a local projection lead to an abstract network of "macro-automata". A HMSC with the same behavior as the initial automata network can then be produced by computing the product of macro automata. An alternative could be to consider a parallel construct in the HMSC, as proposed for instance in netcharts [6].

The algorithms have been implemented in a software prototype (a few thousand of lines of C-code). The next step will be to be able to deal with more complex systems. First, we have to relax the synchronous assumption to take benefit of the asynchronous communication in MSCs. We think it is possible to find a class of systems in which synchronous communication can be safely replaced by an asynchronous one without changing the set of partial runs. Let us recall nevertheless that asynchronous communicating automata and MSC define uncomparable languages. This means that a translation of automata into MSC may not exists. Furthermore, deciding whether a network of asynchronous automata defines a MSC language is an undecidable problem. Hence, to be effective in an asynchronous framework, our approach will necessarily apply to a restricted class of automata. Secondly, the MSCs we obtain are dependent of two things: the definition of cut-off events and the definition of configurations that are extracted from the finite complete prefix. So far, an event is a cut off event if its configuration has already been seen in its causal past. This leads to some duplications of events in the finite complete prefix. The definition of cut-off events can be refined using the adequate orders proposed by J. Esparza in [2]. This enhancement will reduce the duplication of events. Concerning the definition of configurations to extract (the X set), we can decide to share more or less common prefixes in the bMSCs, and find a tradeoff between the number of duplications and the size of the considered bMSCs. This could be parameterized.

References

1. L. Hélouët and C. Jard. Conditions for Synthesis of Communicating Automata from HMSCs, 5th International Workshop on Formal Methods for Industrial Critical Systems (FMICS), ARE. Stefania-Gnesi, I. Schieferdecker (ed), GMD FOKUS, Apr. 2000.
2. J. Esparza and S. Römer. An Unfolding Algorithm for Synchronous Products of Transition Systems, Proc. of Concur 1999, Lecture Notes in Computer Science 1664, pp. 2-20, 1999.
3. A. Muscholl and D. Peled. From Finite State Communication Protocols to High-Level Message Sequence Charts, Proc. of ICALP'01, Lecture Notes in Computer Science 2076, pp. 720-731, 2001.
4. K. Mac Millan. A Technique of State Space Search Based on Unfolding, Journal of Formal Methods and System Design, 9, 1-22 (1992), Kluwer.
5. M. Abdallah, F. Khendec, and G. Butler. New Results on Deriving SDL Specifications from MSCs, Proc. of 9th SDL Forum, pp. 51-66, Montreal.
6. M. Mukund, K.N. Kumar, and P.S. Thiagarajan. Netcharts: Bridging the Gap between HMSCs and Executable Specifications, Proc. of Concur 2003, Lecture Notes in Computer Science 2761, pp. 296-310, 2003.
7. E. Rudolph, O. Graubmann and J. Grabowski. Tutorial on Message Sequence Charts, Computer Networks and ISDN Systems - SDL and MSC, Vol. 28, 1996.
8. G. Booch, I. Jacobson and J. Rumbaugh. Unified Modeling Language User Guide, Addison-Wesley, 1997.
9. ITU, Message Sequence Charts, standard Z.120, 2000.
10. C. Jard, L. Hélouët and T. Chatain. From Automata Networks to HMSCs: a Reverse Model Engineering Perspective, INRIA/IRISA Research Report, Aug. 2005, 22 pages.

Properties as Processes: Their Specification and Verification

Joel Kelso and George Milne

School of Computer Science and Software Engineering,
University of Western Australia
{joel, george}@csse.uwa.edu.au

Abstract. This paper presents a novel application of an untimed process algebra formalism to a class of timing-critical verification problems usually modelled with either timed automata or timed process algebra. We show that a formalism based on interacting automata can model system components, behavioural constraints and properties requiring proof without elaborating the underlying process-algebraic formalism to include explicit timing constructs; and that properties can be verified without introducing temporal logic, model-checking, or refinement relation checking. We demonstrate this technique in detail by application to the Fischer mutual-exclusion protocol, an archetypal example of a system that depends of timing constraints to operate correctly.

1 Introduction

Many complex systems are most naturally modelled as collections of components that operate and interact concurrently. Such modelling allows a problem to be decomposed into parts having behaviour that is, in isolation, readily described. To operate correctly, some complex systems rely on timing relationships between certain critical actions shared by two or more components. In order to verify the correctness of such systems, the tools and methodologies used must be capable of expressing timing constraints and temporal properties in a manner clearly comprehensible to the user.

The contribution of this paper is twofold. Firstly, it demonstrates an intuitive way of describing relative orderings among timing intervals as processes (i.e., as state machines), which can be naturally composed with system model processes to supply the timing-critical aspects of the model's behaviour. This separation of timed and untimed behaviour helps specification, as it allows greater freedom in partitioning the work of constructing complex models.

Secondly, this paper describes how formal protocol verification may be achieved by use of a process algebraic equivalence checker coupled with the *concurrent composition* of (1) a system description, as a process, and (2) a process which describes the property requiring proof, which is also presented as a state / action / new-state type process. When both types of object are modelled as processes, there is no need for design engineers to learn a separate property description language or model checking tool in addition to a language with which to express system behaviour.

We believe that this simplification, and the ability to express properties requiring verification in a state machine type manner, is of real value in encouraging engineers to adopt formal description and verification methods.

This paper uses the well-known Fischer protocol to illustrate both this treatment of timing representation, and the composition-based property verification technique.

A key feature of the methodology described in this paper is the central role of the concurrent composition operator. Concurrent composition is the fundamental mechanism for constructing system models in the process algebra paradigm; its use for this purpose warrants no additional comment. In our methodology, concurrent composition plays two further significant roles, namely to *enforce* timing constraints, and as the core of the *composition-based verification* technique.

1.1 Timing Constraints as Processes

Rather than encoding timing constraints as an integral part of a system model (which is the usual case with timed automata [2] and timed process algebra [20] modelling), timing constraints are encoded as separate processes that express relationships between time intervals.

This is accomplished by first determining which actions in the system model signify the boundaries of time critical time intervals, and then defining *timing constraint processes* which express the allowable sequences of occurrences of these events. When these processes are *composed* with the system model, they enforce the timing relationships that they encode.

In this way the modelling of system behaviour can be decoupled from the timing constraints. This simplifies model development and experimentation, since timed aspects of a model can be altered without modification of the time-insensitive aspects.

1.2 Properties as Processes

The idea of expressing properties requiring proof as processes is a well-known process algebraic technique, described for example in [6, 18, 22]. In the case where a correctness specification is a complete description of a system, verification proceeds by checking that the system implementation process is *equivalent* to the specification process according to some semantic equivalence relation.

Frequently, however, total behavioural equivalence between two processes is not the goal of the proof process. For certain systems, verifying correctness consists of determining that certain properties do in fact hold for an implemented system. Such properties do not constitute a complete specification but are rather a particular relationship between a number of distinct actions. Verification of such properties then requires the demonstration that the occurrence of the property actions in the constructed system model process have the same sequence of occurrence designated by the property process.

One technique for accomplishing this is to *abstract* all non-property actions from the model process, and then check that the model *refines* the property process according to a semantic ordering relation (see [22] chapter 14 for example).

In this paper we describe an alternative proof mechanism that avoids the introduction of the concept of process refinement orderings, and in which concurrent composition plays a crucial role.

A similar approach to using a single language to specify system behaviour, constraints and properties is explored for the Temporal Logic of Actions ([16]) in [1], where a close relationship between logical conjunction of formulæ and concurrent composition of processes is shown.

In section 2 we present the mechanism which underlies our property verification technique. In section 3 we demonstrate the technique by application to the Fischer protocol, showing in detail how timing constraints *and* correctness properties are formulated as processes. In section 4 we discuss the significance of this work and contrast it with related work.

2 Checking Properties via Composition

We show how the verification of a class of properties, safety properties, can be performed in an process algebra (or *interacting automata*) based framework by making use of the concurrent composition of processes and process equivalence testing – provided that the process composition operation has certain features.

Our description of this technique is framed in terms of the Structural Operational Semantics approach to formalising process behaviour [21]. Under this approach, processes are identified with *labelled transition systems* (LTS). A LTS is a rooted directed graph where each edge is labelled with an *action*. Each vertex of the graph is a distinct *state* of the process, and each edge represents a *transition* between states, with transition labels determining the interaction between the process and its environment (or with other processes).

Labelled transition systems admit a variety of different equivalence relations and orderings, such as *trace equivalence*, *testing equivalence* and *bisimulation*. The technique we present here can be used with any of these process equivalence relations, yielding criteria for the fulfillment of safety properties which vary in sensitivity to internal (unobserved) process nondeterminism. Trace equivalence is assumed here, since it is both simple and sufficiently discriminating for the examples in this paper.

2.1 Safety Properties and Concurrent Composition

A *safety property* of a system is a property which states that "nothing bad" will ever happen. When expressed as a process, a *safety property process* exhibits only allowable behaviours – the set of behaviours that a system must not overstep if it is to fulfill that property.

The concurrent composition of processes is used to verify that a system correctly satisfies a particular safety property using the following procedure:

1. The system model process is composed with the property process so that *they synchronise only for the events in the property process.*
2. This composite process is compared to the system model process: if the two are equivalent, then the system fulfills the safety property.

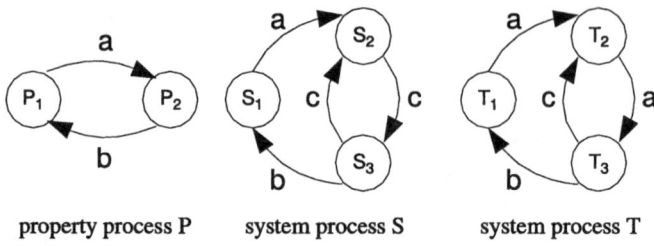

Fig. 1. Example property and system processes

This procedure is summarised by an equation that must hold in order for system S to fulfill property P:

$$S * P \cong S \quad (1)$$

where $S * P$ denotes the concurrent composition of S and P.

To see how the *concurrent composition* of processes can be used to perform a safety property check, consider an example property process P and two different system component processes S and T, pictured in Figure 1. Process P represents the property that all occurrences of actions a and b must begin with a and then strictly alternate.

By having P operate in parallel with S and synchronising on actions a and b, P can be considered to be "supervising" S, watching for occurrences of actions a and b. Let us follow the possible activity of the combined process $S * P$.

Both processes begin in state 1. In state S_1, S can perform action a and transition to state S_2. Since P and S synchronise on action a, P participates in this action and also transitions from state P_1 to state P_2.

In state S_2, S can perform action c and transition to state S_3. Since P is uninterested in action c, S is free to perform this action without any change in P. In state S_3, S may again perform c and return to state S_2. S may thus perform any number of c actions while P remains in state P_2.

In state S_3, S may also perform a b action. In this case, P must be in state P_2, and is also ready to perform action b, returning both processes to state 1.

In this example, process S is never prevented from performing an action by P. The behaviour of the composite process $S * P$ is thus equivalent to S, so S satisfies property P.

Process T provides a contrasting example of a process that fails to satisfy property P. By again following the concurrent behaviour of T and P we can see how this is detected.

The initial behaviour of T and P is the same as S and P – both participate in action a and transition to state 2. In state T_2, T can only perform action a. Since T and P synchronise on action a, P must also perform a. But in state P_2, P is only ready to perform action b. Neither process allows the other to continue, and so the composite behaviour of T and P ends at this point. This behaviour (a single occurrence of a) is clearly not equivalent to the behaviour of T, so T does not satisfy property P.

These examples are extremely simple, but the technique operates correctly for arbitrarily complex processes, including those where both system and property are nondeterministic. The soundness of this property checking technique is proven in [10].

In order for this proof technique to work, the concurrent composition operation must have two important characteristics. Firstly, the operator must be able to enforce synchronisation for actions in the property process, while allowing free asynchronous activity for other actions. Secondly, the operator must allow *multi-way synchronisation*. It must allow two *or more* processes to participate in an interaction, so that property processes can synchronise on the *same actions* present in the system processes. This enables a property process to monitor system processes and restrict their behaviour to activity that correctly satisfies the property. If the system processes *do* contravene the specified property, then the equivalence check will detect the fact that the composite system's activity has been curtailed, signifying that the safety property is not satisfied.

The concurrent composition operator of the CIRCAL formalism [17], used in this paper, has these characteristics. The CCS [19] parallel composition operator cannot be used in this manner since CCS synchronisation operates with complementary pairs of events, which are eliminated in the resulting composite process. The CSP [9] *generalised parallel* operator is suitable since the set of synchronisation events is an explicit parameter to the operator, and the operator allows multi-way composition.

2.2 Modelling With CIRCAL

In this paper we adopt the CIRCAL process algebra [17, 18] for our definition of model components, constraints and properties. Several different notations and toolsets have been developed for defining complex systems as CIRCAL processes. XCircal [18], used in this paper, is a C-like language in which the CIRCAL process algebra operators have been embedded, while [6] defines an intuitive and precise diagrammatic notation for CIRCAL processes. Also under development is a library of functional language combinators (in Haskell) for defining and manipulating CIRCAL processes [11], and a visual programming interface for building processes in diagrammatic form.

These representations build upon the same underlying CIRCAL process formalism, and enable modellers to exploit the formalism's important features. Three of the formalism's characteristics are particularly relevant to our proof technique. *Firstly*, the CIRCAL composition operator fulfills the partial synchronisation requirement necessary for the composition-based property verification technique.

Secondly, the CIRCAL composition operator is a multi-way operator in which an action shared by two processes remains visible in the composite process, enabling additional processes to participate in the event. This allows processes that implement behavioural constraints, diagnostic "probes" (see for example [18]), and correctness properties to be composed into a system model without having to modify the original processes.

Thirdly, the fact that transitions are labelled with *sets* of events allows arbitrary finite relations and functions to be constructed and incorporated into a model. These can be used to connect and adapt process components, or as model components in their own right.

3 Modelling and Verification Methodology

In this section we outline our modelling and verification methodology, then illustrate the methodology by application to a timing-dependent concurrent mutual-exclusion protocol. The methodology proceeds in three phases.

1. The first phase consists of identifying critical actions in the system being modelled and constructing processes that capture the essential details of the system's behaviour. This involves constructing explicit transition systems for parts of the system that can be modelled as simple finite state behaviours, and using concurrent composition and abstraction operations to construct larger, more complex systems in a hierarchical fashion. This phase is illustrated in section 3.2. At this stage the detailed time-critical aspects of the model may be ignored.
2. In the second phase, the model events that delimit critical timing intervals are identified. Timing constraint processes that specify the necessary relationships between these intervals are then constructed and composed together to obtain a timed system. This phase is illustrated in this paper in section 3.3.
3. The third phase consists of the definition and verification of required system properties, which is accomplished by the construction of property processes and application of the constraint-based verification technique. This phase is illustrated in section 3.4.

3.1 Modelling the Fischer Protocol

The Fischer Protocol [15] is a distributed algorithm for ensuring critical section mutual exclusion between a number of concurrent processes. The protocol is simple yet relies on timing constraints among its processes for correct operation. It has become a standard for demonstrating verification techniques for timed systems, see for example [3, 14, 24].

We demonstrate our property verification methodology by treating part of the specification for correct operation of a Fischer protocol system as a safety property. We model both the system and the protocol's essential correctness property (mutual exclusion) as processes, and verify that the modelled system satisfies the property.

System Description. A Fischer protocol system consists of N *workers*. Each worker goes about some independent activity (not modelled here) and occasionally attempts to perform some activity which needs to be protected by a *critical section*. It is assumed that in order to operate correctly, the system must have the property that at most one worker is performing its critical section activity at any instant.

To enact the Fischer protocol, the workers interact by reading from and writing to a shared register. The register can take on one of $N+1$ values, one for each process plus an "empty" state Z. Figure 2 shows the basic operational cycle of a Fischer protocol worker. Workers wait (or perform their non-critical activity) in the *start* state (A) until the register becomes empty. They may then indicate their intention to enter their critical section moving to the *request* state (B), in which case they must set the register to indicate the fact, and then make the transition to the *wait* state (C) within a certain time period. In the wait state the worker will either notice that another worker has made a later request, in which case this worker aborts its attempt to enter its critical section and returns to the start state; or the waiting period will elapse and the worker enters the *critical section* state (D). Eventually the worker exits its critical section and returns to the start state, setting the shared register to the empty state.

3.2 Process Models of System Components

In the construction of our model of a Fischer protocol system, we utilise processes to model two quite different classes of object. In the following section we use processes to model abstract *temporal constraints* needed for the correct operation of Fischer's protocol. This leaves us free to model, in this section, the physical elements of the protocol system without regard to timed behaviour.

Worker processes are modelled in CIRCAL as behavioural processes in a straightforward way: a diagram of the worker process model is shown in Figure 3. The process has four states A, B, C and D. The transitions are labelled with two varieties of actions. There are actions of the form xy, where x and y are states; the purpose of these actions is to signal the activity of the process at every transition. As we shall see later, these actions will be shared with constraint and property processes in order to refine and analyse the system model.

Each transition is also labelled with an additional actions that indicate the worker's interaction with the shared register (which is also modelled as a process). These actions take the form $k := a$, where the worker writes a process name a to the register; or $k == a$ (or $k! = a$), where the worker reads and tests the value of the register. These actions are shared with the process model of the register, and coordinate the activity of the worker process with the register process.

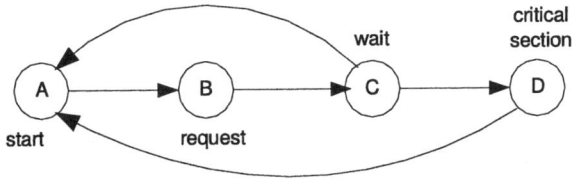

Fig. 2. The Fischer protocol worker process states

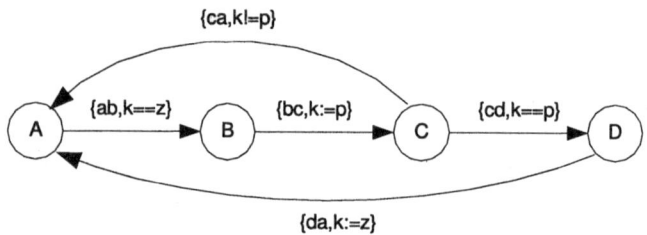

Fig. 3. The Fischer worker process model

```
Process Fischer(Event ab,bc,ca,cd,da,ksetz,keqz,ksetp,
                      keqp,kneqp) {
  Process A, B, C, D;
  A <- (ab keqz) B
  B <- (bc ksetp) C
  C <- (ca kneqp) A + (cd keqp) D
  D <- (da ksetz)
  return A
}
```

Fig. 4. The XCircal code for the worker process

The XCircal code for constructing a worker process is given in Figure 4.[1] This prototypical worker process is instantiated with events named to indicate the worker process in which they occur. For reasons that will become clear later, actions involving the empty register state also tagged with the worker's name. For example, the action $pk == z$ indicates that process P is testing to see if the register's value has value Z.

```
FischerP <- Fischer(pab,pbc,pca,pcd,pda,pksetz,pkeqz,ksetp,
                    keqp,kneqp)
FischerQ <- Fischer(qab,qbc,qca,qcd,qda,pksetz,qkeqz,ksetq,
                    keqq,kneqq)
```

The Shared Register Model. Figure 5 shows a process which models the shared register for a system of two worker processes. The process has one state for each worker process, plus one state representing the "empty" state of the register (labelled z). *Write* actions of the form $k := a$ lead from every state to the state a. For each state a, *read* actions of the form $k == a$ lead from a to itself. For clarity, Figure 5 omits the read transitions of the form $k!=a$: for each A these are present as looping transitions for all states other than A. Worker processes performing write actions cause the register to change state, and worker processes will only be able to perform read actions if the register is in a compatible state. For brevity, we have omitted XCircal code for the remainder of the transition systems.

---
[1] Since XCircal does not allow them in event names, the non-alphabetic characters are transcribed to mnemonic characters in an obvious way.

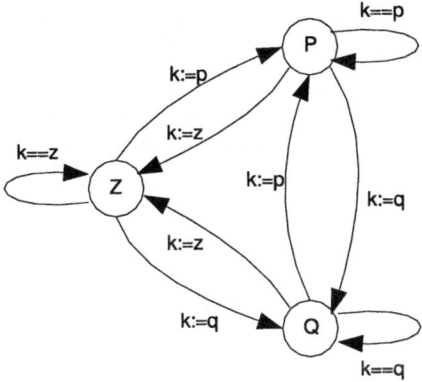

Fig. 5. The shared register process for a system with two worker processes P and Q

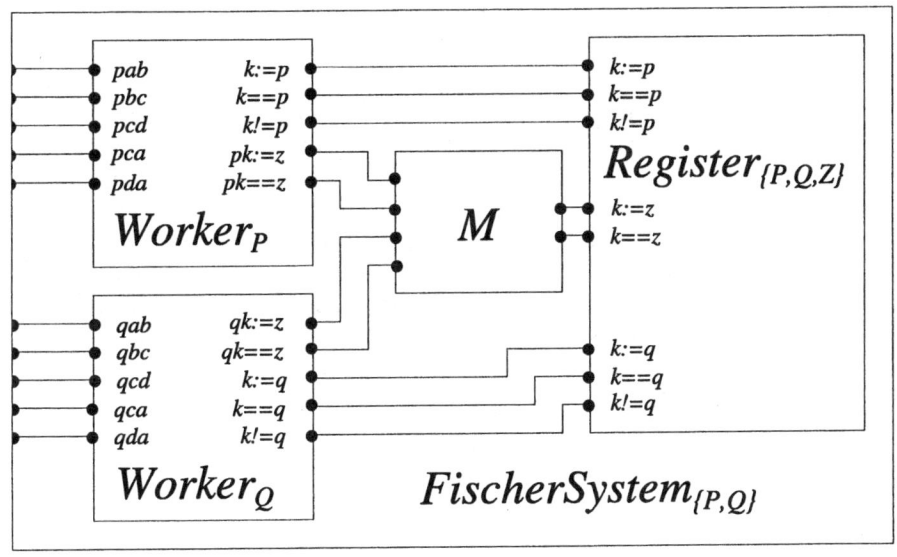

Fig. 6. Diagram of untimed Fischer protocol system

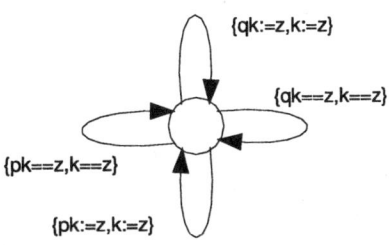

Fig. 7. Register multiplexer process M

The Untimed System. Figure 6 shows the Fischer protocol system of two worker processes, using a simple but powerful (and fully formal) diagramming notation introduced in [6]. In this notation, each rectangle represents an abstraction boundary containing one or more processes: all actions other than those appearing as "ports" on the rectangle's perimeter are abstracted and hidden from the exterior. In a simplified version of the notation, employed here, lines simply connect ports with identical names (thus denoting a single shared action). At the innermost level, processes are ultimately represented by transition diagrams. For reasons of space, we only show a single level of nesting in a diagram: the internal structure of internal processes are represented instead by process names.

There are several things to note about the composite system.

- The complete Fischer protocol system consists of the *concurrent composition* of the worker processes, the shared register process, and a register-access mediation process (see below).
- For actions which involve the empty state Z, communication between the register and worker processes are mediated by an additional process M (pictured in
  Figure 7). If these each of these events were modelled by a single system-wide action, this would force each action to be synchronised across all worker processes. This is clearly incorrect, since it would require all workers to rendezvous for reads or writes involving the Z register value. Considering the intended behaviour more carefully, we can see that outside of the register itself, the action of each worker setting (or checking) a particular register value are distinct events which can occur independently. Process M acts as a junction that allows asynchronous access to shared register actions.
- All the register actions are abstracted from the *FischerSystem* process. What remains visible to the outside are the transition-marking actions for each worker process.

The XCircal code that defines an (untimed) Fischer system with two workers is:

```
FischerSystem <- (FischerP * FischerQ * Register * Multiport) -
(pksetz pkeqz qksetz qkeqz kneqp kneqq kneqz
  ksetp ksetq ksetz keqp keqq keqz)
```

3.3 Process Models of Timing Constraints

Since the Fischer protocol relies on timing constraints among its worker processes for correct operation, the untimed model of the Fischer protocol presented above is inadequate. Specifically, after indicating its intention to enter its critical section, a worker process P needs to wait "long enough" to ensure that all other workers are either (a) back at the start state, or (b) have already followed P, usurped Ps place, and have sent P back to the start state.

One approach to modelling the timed behaviour of a Fischer protocol system is to equip each worker with its own local clock, and predicate certain transitions

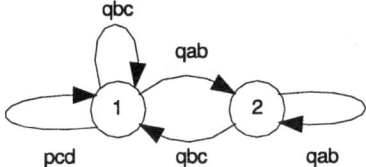

Fig. 8. Fischer protocol timing constraint between processes P and Q

on clock values. This is the Timed Automata approach, described for example in [14].

Applying our methodology, we express the "workers wait long enough in state C" condition purely in terms of the sequences of events allowed (or disallowed) by timing interval restrictions. The condition that worker P waits long enough for worker Q can be enforced by the requirement that the interval between the qab and qbc event be longer than the interval from qab to any pcd event. In other words, once a qab event has occurred, a pcd event may not occur (i.e. P must wait) until qbc has occurred. A process that enforces this constraint is shown in Figure 8.

The process shown in Figure 8 is an instance of a family of processes which have the effect of disallowing a specific sequence of actions. In this case the process disallows the subsequence $qab \to pcd$ in the set of all sequences of events drawn from $\{qab, qbc, pcd\}$. Constraints based on disallowing longer sequences of events can easily be generated, using an algorithm based on the Knuth-Morris-Pratt string searching algorithm [13]. This process expresses the constraint that requires P to wait for worker Q. To fully express the timing constraints for the whole system a constraint process is needed for every ordered pair of distinct workers, so $n(n-1)$ constraint processes are required for an n worker system.[2] For our two-worker example, the two instantiated constraint processes are:

```
TimingPQ <- TimingConstraint(pcd,qab,qbc)
TimingQP <- TimingConstraint(qcd,pab,pbc)
```

Applying these timing constraints to our untimed system yields the process:

```
TimedFischer <- FischerSystem * TimingPQ * Timing QP
```

The relative timing interval constraint technique employed here is more generic and less concrete than the use of clock variables in timed automata. Unlike clock variables, relative timing interval constraints do not directly suggest an implementation in terms of local clocks used by concurrent processes. It is interesting to note that the nature of the CIRCAL composition operator allows the timing interval constraint processes given in this subsection to be replaced

---

[2] By using slightly more complex processes, this can be reduced to n constraint processes for an n worker system. There are a number of different constraint processes that correctly enforce the Fischer protocol's timing requirements; the constraint process used here is one of the simplest.

by an alternative set of processes which express the necessary timing constraints in another idiom – as discrete local clocks for each process for example – without requiring modification to either the worker processes or the correctness property process (described in the next section).

3.4 Process Models of Behavioural Properties

The mutual exclusion property says that only one process may be in its critical section at a time. In our model, this property can be expressed in terms of the events that mark each worker process entering (cd events) and leaving (da events) its critical section. For a system of n worker processes, a simple $n+1$ state property process indicates what sequences of events are compatible with the mutual exclusion property. The two-worker version of this property process is show in Figure 9.

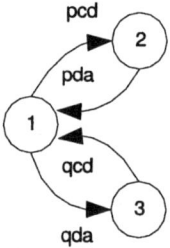

Fig. 9. Mutual-exclusion property for two processes P and Q

3.5 Verification

The behaviour of a protocol system (including the shared register and timing constraint processes) for two or three workers is simple enough that the mutual exclusion property can be verified by printing out the critical section behaviour and inspecting it. Figure 10 shows the complete behaviour of a two-worker protocol system, with all actions except critical section actions hidden by the abstraction operator. It clearly conforms to the two-worker mutual exclusion property (the two being in fact identical). Larger systems can be verified by using the technique described in section 2. Treating the mutual exclusion property as a safety condition (it expresses the *allowable* behaviours for a correct system), our correctness condition is

$$\texttt{TimedFischer} * \texttt{MutexProperty} \cong \texttt{TimedFischer}$$

where *TimedFischer* is the system model process (including timing constraint processes) and *MutexProperty* is the mutual exclusion property for the appropriate number of workers. Using the current generation of CircalSystem tools we have successfully performed this verification for systems of at most 5 workers.

```
Start State      Transition Label       End State
-----------      ----------------       ---------
     1              ["Pcd"]      ->        2
     1              ["Qcd"]      ->        3
     2              ["Pda"]      ->        1
     3              ["Qda"]      ->        1
```

Fig. 10. Critical section behaviour of worker, register and timing constraint processes

4 Discussion

The ability of a modelling formalism to accurately represent timing information is becoming increasingly significant when designing a range of complex, concurrent systems such as asynchronous digital logic circuits [8, 23, 5] and network communication protocols [4].

In this paper we present a practical modelling and verification methodology which exploits the characteristics of a specific process algebraic composition operator. This approach differs from existing methodologies.

Rather than augment an automata model with clocks and timed transitions, temporal constraints are expressed as relative timing interval constraint processes. The primary requirements for use of the interval timing constraints technique are that (a) the critical states and time intervals in the system are cleanly delimited by actions, and that (b) timing constraints can be expressed as relationships between these intervals. For the example in this paper the constraint relationship takes the form a relative differences in interval duration for two intervals that start at the same moment. Other timing properties known to be amenable to expression as interval constraints include intervals required to be overlapping (or non-overlapping); and intervals required to be entirely contained within other intervals. Cowie [7] describes a methodology for translating a class of constraints normally expressed in an interval algebra to constraint processes.

Our methodology contrasts with previously described methodologies for modelling and verifying timing-dependent systems. Timed Automata [2] are formal automata models which include a real-valued local clock value for each process, and allow transitions to be predicated on clock values. The Uppaal and TVS systems are toolsets that include model-checkers for Timed Automata (Fischer protocol verification examples for each are reported in [14] and [3]).

Timed process algebra [20] extend untimed process algebra (such as CCS, CSP or ACP) with operators for expressing the possibility that transitions may be delayed a certain period after they become active. [24] describes the Fischer protocol in terms of a discrete-time and a real-time process algebra.

A third approach to modelling and analysing timed systems is to introduce timing components (e.g. clock processes and "clock tick" actions) into an untimed framework such as an untimed process algebra – an example of this approach is given in this is given in [4].

The methodology described in this paper contributes to the state of the art of formal methods by providing (1) an alternative technique for defining constraints in timing-critical systems: separate constraint processes which define relationships between critical timing intervals; and (2) an alternative technique for verifying properties in such systems: the composition-based verification technique, which does not require the introduction of temporal logic, model-checking or refinement relation checking.

This elegant approach does not introduce any additional mathematical concepts, and capitalises on a concept already very familiar to engineers: processes described by state transition diagrams. The use of state-machine based property and constraint definition does not, of course, guarantee superior expressiveness and comprehensibility in all cases: it depends very much on the system and properties in question. The methodology presented in this paper does however present a lower barrier of entry to a population design engineers that would otherwise be unlikely to adopt formal methods techniques, and provides an additional set of tools for the experienced formal methods practitioner.

The example presented here is simple, due to space constraints. We can report a number of observations about the application of the methodology to larger systems (for example, see [12]).

Firstly, increasing structural and behavioural complexity of systems does not appear to present a major problem in system modelling. We find that the encapsulation of system processes as components with well defined interfaces (the process signature) and encapsulated state provides an "object oriented" environment that allows the construction of clean, hierarchical models.

Secondly, whilst some entities such as finite variables and logical relations can be naturally modelled as component processes, this does not appear to be the case for arithmetic or dynamically sized data structures (even when restricted to finitely bounded versions).

We see this methodology being used, as in the Fischer protocol example, to analyse complex systems in terms of sequences of critical events. Experimentation and modelling at this level can be used to develop correct algorithms and protocols.

We would like to acknowledge that this research has been funded in part by the Australian Research Council.

References

1. Martín Abadi and Leslie Lamport. Conjoining specifications. *ACM Transactions on Programming Languages*, 17(3), 1995.
2. Rajeev Alur and David L. Dill. A theory of timed automata. *Theoretical Computer Science*, 126(2):183–235, 1994.
3. Marcel Ammerlaan, Ronald Lutje Spelberg, and Hans Toetenel. XTG - an engineering approach to modelling and analysis of real-time systems. In *10th Euromicro Workshop on Real Time Systems*, pages 88–97. IEEE Computer Society Press, jun 1998.
4. A. Cerone, A. J. Cowie, G. J. Milne, and P. A. Moseley. Modelling a time-dependant protocol using the CIRCAL process algebra. *Lecture Notes in Computer Science*, 2102:124–138, 1997.

5. A. Cerone, D. A. Kearney, and G. J. Milne. Integrating the verification of timing, performance and correctness properties of concurrent systems. In *The International Conference on Application of Concurrency to System Design*, pages 109–119. IEEE Computer Society Press, 1998.
6. A. Cerone and G. J. Milne. A methodology for the formal analysis of asynchronous micropipelines. In *International Conference on Formal Methods in Computer-Aided Design (FMCAD'00)*, number 1954 in Lecture Notes in Computer Science, pages 246–262. Springer-Verlag, 2000.
7. Alex Cowie. *The Modelling of Temporal Properties in a Process Algebra Framework*. PhD thesis, University of South Australia, 1999.
8. S. B. Furber and P. Day. Four-phase micropipeline latch control circuit. *IEEE Transactions on VLSI Systems*, 4(2):247–253, June 1996.
9. C. A. R. Hoare. *Communicating Sequential Processes*. International Series in Computer Science. Prentice Hall, 1985.
10. Joel Kelso. Proof of the soundness of the concurrent composition property checking technique. Technical Report Report-05-003, School of Computer Science and Software Engineering, Univeristy of Western Australia, 2005.
11. Joel Kelso and George Milne. The prototype Haskell CIRCAL system. http://www.csse.uwa.edu.au/FormalSpecification/HaskellCircal/, 2003.
12. Joel Kelso and George Milne. An interacting automata model of a fault-tolerant scada system. Technical Report Report-05-004, School of Computer Science and Software Engineering, Univeristy of Western Australia, 2005.
13. D.E. Knuth, J.H. Morris, and V.R. Pratt. Fast pattern matching in strings. *SIAM Journal on Computing*, 6(1):323–350, 1997.
14. K. J. Kristoffersen, F. Laroussinie, K. G. Larsen, P. Pettersson, and Wang Yi. A composition proof of a real-time mutual exclusion protocol. Technical Report RS-96-55, Aalborg University, Denmark, 1996.
15. Leslie Lamport. A fast mutual exclusion algorithm. *ACM Transactions on Computer Systems*, 5(1):1–11, 1987.
16. Leslie Lamport. The temporal logic of actions. *ACM Transactions on Programming Languages and Systems*, 16(3):872–923, 1994.
17. George J. Milne. CIRCAL and the representation of communication, concurrency and time. *ACM Transactions on Programming Languages and Systems*, 7(2):270–298, 1985.
18. George J. Milne. *Formal Specification and Verification of Digital Systems*. McGraw-Hill, 1994.
19. Robin Milner. *Communication and Concurrency*. International Series in Computer Science. Prentice Hall, 1989.
20. Xavier Nicollin and Joseph Sifakis. An overview and synthesis on timed process algebras. In Kim Guldstrand Larsen and Arne Skou, editors, *Computer Aided Verification, 3rd International Workshop, CAV '91*, volume 575 of *Lecture Notes in Computer Science*, pages 376–398. Springer, 1992.
21. G. Plotkin. Structural operational semantics. Technical Report DAIMI FN-19, Aahus University, 1981 (reprinted in 1991).
22. A. W. Roscoe. *The Theory and Practice of Concurrency*. Prentice Hall, 1997.
23. Ivan E. Sutherland. Micropipelines. *Communications of the ACM*, 32(6):720–738, 1989.
24. J. Vereijken. Fischer's protocol in timed process algebra. Technical Report CSR 94/32, Eindhoven University of Technology, Computing Science Department, 1994.

Epoch Distance of the Random Waypoint Model in Mobile Ad Hoc Networks

Yueh-Ting Wu, Wanjiun Liao, and Cheng-Lin Tsao

Department of Electrical Engineering,
National Taiwan University,
Taipei, Taiwan
wjliao@ntu.edu.tw

Abstract. In this paper, we model the epoch distance of the random waypoint model in mobile ad hoc networks. In the random waypoint model, each node selects a target location (i.e., waypoint) to move at a speed selected from an interval. Once the target is reached, the node pauses for a random time and then selects another target with another speed to move again. The movement between two waypoints is referred to as an epoch. In this paper, we derive the probability distribution of the epoch distance for the random waypoint model. Such a study is important as the epoch length distribution may be required for the derivation of the link duration distribution or node spatial distribution for mobile ad hoc networks. The analytical result is then verified via simulation.

Keywords: Random waypoint model, epoch distance, ad hoc networks.

1 Introduction

Mobile ad hoc networks have received much attention in recent years. In such a network, no infrastructures such as base stations exist, and data are relayed by intermediate mobile hosts if the receiver is beyond the transmission range of the sender.

There have been many mobility models available for evaluating the performance of mobile ad hoc networks, including the random waypoint model [1], random walk [2], and group model [3]. In this paper, we focus on the random waypoint model. With this mobility model, each node selects a target location (i.e., waypoint) to move at a speed selected from a uniformly distributed interval [V_{min}, V_{max}]. Once the target is reached, the node pauses for a random time and then selects another target with another speed to move again.

In this paper, we model the epoch distance (length) of the random waypoint model, and derive the probability distribution of the distance between two waypoints in mobile ad hoc networks. Such a study is important as the epoch length distribution may be required for the derivation of the link duration distribution [4] or node spatial distribution [5] for mobile ad hoc networks. The analytical result is then verified by simulations.

The rest of the paper is organized as follows. Sec. II gives the analytical model of epoch distance in the random waypoint model. Sec. III provides the simulation results to verify the analytical model. Finally, the paper is concluded in Sec. IV.

2 Epoch Distance in Random Waypoint Model

In our analysis, the movement area Q is a two-dimensional unit square area $[0, 1]^2$, and each node moves based on the random waypoint model with the same parameters. Nodes are assumed uniformly distributed in the area. Given two waypoints (x_1, y_1) and (x_2, y_2), there are four cases to consider, each with an equal probability: (i) $x_1 \leq x_2$ and $y_1 \leq y_2$, (ii) $x_1 \leq x_2$ and $y_1 > y_2$, (iii) $x_1 > x_2$ and $y_1 \leq y_2$, and (iv) $x_1 > x_2$ and $y_1 > y_2$. To save space, we will derive the epoch length distribution based on the conditions $x_1 \leq x_2$ and $y_1 \leq y_2$. The other cases can be obtained similarly.

Let D_E denote the random variable of an epoch distance for the random waypoint model. The probability of $D_E \leq d$ is equal to the probability that the distance of two random points in a unit square less than or equal to d (i.e., $\leq d$). The probability of $D_E \leq d$ given the first point placed at (x_1, y_1) is equal to the probability that the second point falls inside the circle centered at (x_1, y_1) with radius d. We only consider the probability under the condition that (x_2, y_2) is at the upper right direction of (x_1, y_1), which is equivalent to the condition $x_1 \leq x_2$ and $y_1 \leq y_2$. Since the second point is uniformly placed on the movement area Q at random, the probability that the condition $D_E \leq d$ is satisfied is equivalent to the area for the second point to locate on Q that satisfies the condition. To derive the probability of $D_E \leq d$, we need to further consider two cases: (i) $d \leq 1$ and (ii) $1 \leq d \leq \sqrt{2}$.

i) $d \leq 1$

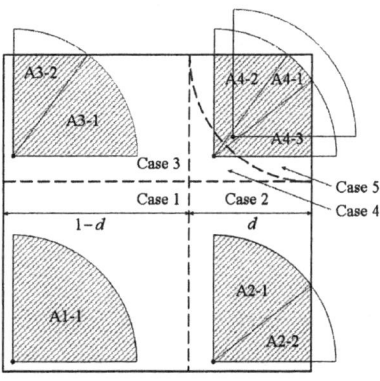

Fig. 1. The conditional probability of $D_E \leq d$ given $d \leq 1$

The probability of $D_E \leq d$ given $d \leq 1$ is illustrated in the shaded areas shown in Fig 1. The lowest-leftmost point of each shaded area is a possible location of (x_1, y_1), and the shaded area is the corresponding area for (x_2, y_2) to locate in Q, which satisfies $D_E \leq d$ given $d \leq 1$. There are five different sub-cases to derive the conditional probability of $D_E \leq d$ given $d \leq 1$, as shown in Fig. 1.

Case 1: $x_1 \leq 1-d$ and $y_1 \leq 1-d$

Case 1 states that as long as the first point (x_1, y_1) stays in the area with $x_1 \leq 1-d$, and $y_1 \leq 1-d$, where $d \leq 1$, the possible area at which the second point (x_2, y_2) is located (see the shaded area in A1-1 in Fig. 1) will entirely fall in the movement area Q. Therefore, we have

$$\Pr\{D_E \leq d \mid d \leq 1, x_1 \leq 1-d, y_1 \leq 1-d\} = \frac{1}{4}\pi d^2 \quad (1)$$

Case 2: $x_1 \geq 1-d$ and $y_1 \leq 1-d$

Case 2 states that once x_1 exceeds 1-d, x_2 must be limited to 1 to avoid the second point move out of the movement area Q. Consequently, the possible area in which the second point may be located is composed of a fan shape and a triangle as given by the shaded areas A2-1 and A2-2, respectively, in Fig. 1. Therefore, we have

$$\Pr\{D_E \leq d \mid d \leq 1, x_1 \geq 1-d, y_1 \leq 1-d\} = \frac{d^2 \sin^{-1}(\frac{1-x}{d})}{2} + \frac{(1-x)\sqrt{d^2-(1-x)^2}}{2} \quad (2)$$

Case 3: $x_1 \leq 1-d$ and $y_1 \geq 1-d$

Case 3 states that once y_1 exceeds 1-d, y_2 must be limited to 1 to avoid the second point move out of the movement area Q. Consequently, the possible area in which the second point may be located is also composed of a fan shape and a triangle as given by the shaded areas A3-1 and A3-2, respectively, in Fig. 1. Therefore, we have.

$$\Pr\{D_E \leq d \mid d \leq 1, x_1 \leq 1-d, y_1 \geq 1-d\} = \frac{d^2 \sin^{-1}(\frac{1-y}{d})}{2} + \frac{(1-y)\sqrt{d^2-(1-y)^2}}{2} \quad (3)$$

Case 4: $x_1 \geq 1-d$ and $y_1 \geq 1-d$.

Case 4 states that since both x_1 and y_1 exceeds 1-d, both x_2 and y_2 must be limited to 1 to avoid the second point move out of the movement area Q. In Case 4, $\sqrt{(1-x_1)^2+(1-y_1)^2} \geq d$, so that the arc of the quarter circle still intersects the upper and right boundaries of the movement area Q. The possible location of the second point is composed of a fan shape and two triangles, as given by the shaded areas A4-1, A4-2, and A4-3, respectively, in Fig. 1. Hence, we have

$$\Pr\{D_E \leq d \mid d \leq 1, x_1 \geq 1-d, y_1 \geq 1-d, \sqrt{(1-x_1)^2+(1-y_1)^2} \geq d\}$$
$$= \frac{d^2\left(\frac{\pi}{2}-\cos^{-1}(\frac{1-x}{d})-\cos^{-1}(\frac{1-y}{d})\right)}{2} + \frac{(1-y)\sqrt{d^2-(1-y)^2}}{2} + \frac{(1-x)\sqrt{d^2-(1-x)^2}}{2} \quad (4)$$

Case 5: $x_1 \geq 1-d$ and $y_1 \geq 1-d$

Similar to Case 4, but with $\sqrt{(1-x_1)^2+(1-y_1)^2} \leq d$, the arc of the quarter circle will not intersect any boundary of area Q. Thus, the possible location of the second point to stay is just a rectangular (i.e., the intersection the quarter circle and the unit square Q) as shown in Fig. 1. It yields

$$\Pr\{D_E \leq d \mid d \leq 1, \sqrt{(1-x_1)^2+(1-y_1)^2} \leq d\} = (1-x_1)(1-y_1) \qquad (5)$$

From (1) to (5), we obtain

$$\Pr\{D_E \leq d \mid d \leq 1, x_1 \leq x_2, y_1 \leq y_2\} = \frac{\pi}{4}d^2 - \frac{2}{3}d^3 + \frac{1}{8}d^4 \qquad (6)$$

Therefore,

$$\Pr\{D_E \leq d \mid d \leq 1\} = 4\Pr\{D_E \leq d \mid d \leq 1, x_1 \leq x_2, y_1 \leq y_2\} = \pi d^2 - \frac{8}{3}d^3 + \frac{1}{2}d^4 \qquad (7)$$

ii) $1 \leq d \leq \sqrt{2}$

Given (x_1, y_1), the conditional probability of $D_E \leq d$ given $1 \leq d \leq \sqrt{2}$ is the shaded areas shown in Fig 2. Like in the case $d \leq 1$, the lowest-leftmost point of each shaded area is a possible location of (x_1, y_1), the shaded areas are the corresponding area for (x_2, y_2) to locate in Q, which satisfies $D_E \leq d$ given that $1 \leq d \leq \sqrt{2}$.

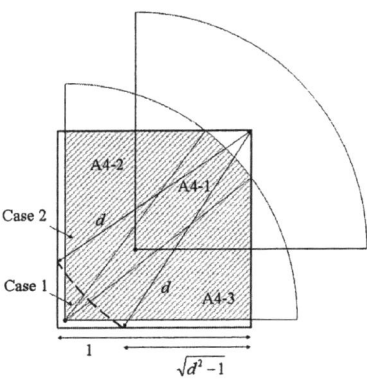

Fig. 2. The conditional probability of $D_E \leq d$ given $1 \leq d \leq \sqrt{2}$

There are two different sub-cases to derive the probability of $D_E \leq d$ given $1 \leq d \leq \sqrt{2}$, as shown in Fig. 2, which are similar to Cases 4 and 5 when $d \leq 1$.

Case 1: Since $\sqrt{(1-x_1)^2 + (1-y_1)^2} \geq d$, the arc of the quarter circle will intersect the boundaries of the movement area Q. The possible location of the second point is composed of a fan shape and two triangles, as given by the shaded areas A4-1, A4-2, and A4-3, respectively, in Fig. 2. Thus,

$$\Pr\{D_E \leq d \mid 1 \leq d \leq \sqrt{2}, \sqrt{(1-x_1)^2 + (1-y_1)^2} \geq d\} \quad (8)$$

$$= \frac{d^2\left(\frac{\pi}{2} - \cos^{-1}(\frac{1-x}{d}) - \cos^{-1}(\frac{1-y}{d})\right)}{2} + \frac{(1-y)\sqrt{d^2-(1-y)^2}}{2} + \frac{(1-x)\sqrt{d^2-(1-x)^2}}{2}$$

Case 2: Since $\sqrt{(1-x_1)^2 + (1-y_1)^2} \leq d$, the arc of the quarter circle will not intersect any boundary of area Q. The possible location of the second point is just a rectangular (i.e., the intersection the quarter circle and the unit square Q) as in Fig. 2. Hence, we have

$$\Pr\{D_E \leq d \mid 1 \leq d \leq \sqrt{2}, \sqrt{(1-x_1)^2 + (1-y_1)^2} \leq d\} = (1-x)(1-y) \quad (9)$$

From (8) and (9), we obtain

$$\Pr\{D_E \leq d \mid 1 \leq d \leq \sqrt{2}, x_1 \leq x_2, y_1 \leq y_2\} = \frac{1}{12} + (\frac{\pi}{4} - \frac{1}{2} - \cos^{-1}(\frac{1}{d}))d^2 - \frac{1}{8}d^4 + \sqrt{d^2-1}(\frac{1}{3} + \frac{2}{3}d^2) \quad (10)$$

Therefore,

$$\Pr\{D_E \leq d \mid 1 \leq d \leq \sqrt{2}\} \quad (11)$$

$$= 4\Pr\{D_E \leq d \mid 1 \leq d \leq \sqrt{2}, x_1 \leq x_2, y_1 \leq y_2\} = \frac{1}{3} + (\pi - 2 - 4\cos^{-1}(\frac{1}{d}))d^2 - \frac{1}{2}d^4 + \sqrt{d^2-1}(\frac{4}{3} + \frac{8}{3}d^2)$$

Based on (7) and (11), we can obtain the probability distribution of D_E, i.e. the distance between two destinations as follows.

$$F_{D_E}(d) = \Pr\{D_E \leq d\} \quad (12)$$

$$= \begin{cases} \pi d^2 - \frac{8}{3}d^3 + \frac{1}{2}d^4 & \text{if } d \leq 1 \\ \frac{1}{3} + (\pi - 2 - 4\cos^{-1}(\frac{1}{d}))d^2 - \frac{1}{2}d^4 + \sqrt{d^2-1}(\frac{4}{3} + \frac{8}{3}d^2) & \text{otherwis} \end{cases}$$

$$f_{D_E}(d) = \frac{dF_{D_E}(d)}{dd} \quad (13)$$

$$= \begin{cases} 2\pi d - 8d^2 + 2d^3 & \text{if } d \leq 1 \\ (2\pi - 4 - 8\cos^{-1}(\frac{1}{d}))d - 2d^3 + 8d\sqrt{d^2-1} & \text{otherwis} \end{cases}$$

3 Performance Evaluation

In this section, we verify our analytical model via simulation. In our simulation, there are 300 nodes initially distributed in a unit square as in [6,7]. The parameter settings are listed in Table I.

Table 1. Simulation parameters

Parameter	Value
number of nodes	300
transmission range r	0.15
nodal speed V_{fix}	0.01 (1/sec)
movement area Q	$[0, 1]^2$
simulation duration	600,000 (sec)

Fig. 3 plots the analytical probability density functions (pdf) of DE in comparison to the simulation. The figure shows that the analytical curves match the simulation results very well.

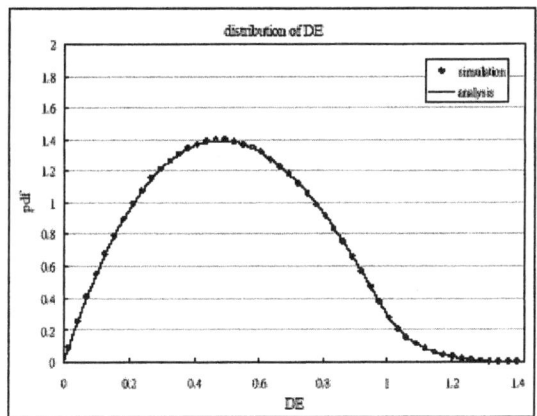

Fig. 3. The distribution of DE

4 Conclusion

In this paper, we model the epoch distance of the random waypoint model for mobile ad hoc networks. In particular, the probability distribution of the distance between two waypoints is derived. The analytical results are also verified via simulations. The results show that the analytical and simulation curves match well.

Acknowledgement

This work was supported partly by National Science Council under a Center Excellence Grant NSC93-2752-E-002-006-PAE, and in part by the National Science Council, Taiwan, under grant number NSC93-2213-E-002-132.

References

[1] D. B. Johnson and D. A. Maltz, "Dynamic Source Routing in Ad Hoc Wireless Networks," Mobile Computing, T. Imelinsky and H. Korth, eds., Kluwer Academic Publishers, 1996, pp. 153-181
[2] A. B. McDonald and T. Znati, "A Path Availability Model for Wireless Ad-Hoc Networks," Wireless Communications and Networking Conference (WCNC 1999), Sep. 1999, pp.35-40
[3] X. Hong, M. Gerla, G. Pei, and C.-C. Chiang, "A group mobility model for ad hoc wireless networks," Proceedings of the 2nd ACM international Workshop on Modeling, Analysis and Simulation of Wireless and Mobile Systems (MSWiM), Aug. 1999
[4] Yu Yueh-Ting Wu, Wanjiun Liao, Cheng-Lin Tsao, and Jia-Chun Kuo, "Link Duration of the Random Way Point Model in Mobile Ad Hoc Networks," submitted to IEEE PIMRC 2005.
[5] Jia-Chun Kuo and Wanjiun Liao, "Modeling Forwarding Progress for One Hop in Wireless Ad Hoc Networks," submitted to IEEE Wirelesscom 2005.
[6] F. Bai, Narayanan Sadagopan, and A. Helmy, "IMPORTANT: a framework to systematically analyze the Impact of Mobility on Performance of RouTing protocols for Adhoc NeTworks," Twenty-Second Annual Joint Conference of the IEEE Computer and Communications Societies (INFOCOM 2003), Mar.-Apr. 2003, pp. 825-835
[7] W. Navidi and T. Camp, "Stationary Distributions for the Random Waypoint Mobility Model," IEEE Transactions on Mobile Computing, Jan.-Mar. 2004, pp. 99-108

Automatic Partitioner for Behavior Level Distributed Logic Simulation

Kai-Hui Chang[1], Jeh-Yen Kang[1], Han-Wei Wang[2], Wei-Ting Tu[2], Yi-Jong Yeh[1], and Sy-Yen Kuo[2]

[1] Avery Design Systems, Inc., Andover, MA 01810, USA
[2] Graduate Institute of Electronics Engineering, National Taiwan University, 1, Sec. 4, Roosevelt Rd., Taipei, Taiwan 106, ROC
sykuo@cc.ee.ntu.edu.tw

Abstract. As the complexity of circuit design increases, verification through simulation has become a bottleneck of the IC design process. Distributed parallel simulation is one way to solving the problem. In order to distribute the simulation workload to multiple processors, the design must be carefully partitioned first. While most previous work focus on gate level partitioning, our work extends a previously implemented Verilog gate-level partitioner to support RTL and behavior level partitioning. Techniques to partition special constructs specific to these levels, such as global access, function calls and memory access, are described in this paper. The experimental results show that our techniques are capable of finding partitions which can accelerate simulation.

Keywords: distributed simulation, parallel simulation, RTL level partitioner, behavior level partitioner.

1 Introduction

As the complexity of circuit design increases, verification through simulation has become a bottleneck of chip design process. Large designs, such as System on Chip (SOP), may take several days to simulate. Sitting for simulation to finish is a waste of time and increases the chip's time to market. Therefore the Field Programmable Gate Array(FPGA) prototyping, such as an emulator, has been proposed to solve this problem. However, emulators are expensive and hard to use.

Memory usage is another problem that arises when a design gets larger. The physical memory of a computer is limited, so it may not be possible to simulate large designs that exceed the computer's capacity of memory.

Several Electronic Design Automation (EDA) tool vendors now provide distributed simulation solutions to solve the problem, e.g. the Simcluster [1]. Through distributed simulation, the workload can be distributed among several processors and improve the turnaround time of simulation. By dividing a design into several smaller pieces, each piece needs less memory for simulation and can easily fit into a modern computer. However, for better performance, partitioning must be done carefully.

Partitioning has been studied for several decades and many algorithms have been proposed and solved the partitioning problems successfully. However, most of them focus on flattened gate-level partitioning. As chips get larger, RTL and behavior level simulation have also become bottlenecks in the IC design process, and the demand for parallel simulation is increasing. Furthermore, in a large project, it is often necessary to simulate a design containing several levels of abstraction. For example, part of a chip may be in gate-level while another part in RTL-level; or part of the design may be hierarchical while the other part is flattened. This emerging demand for mixed abstraction level of parallel logic simulation is beyond the capability of existing gate-level partitioning algorithms.

In this paper, a partitioner that can perform the partitioning at all abstraction levels is proposed. It can find partitions for a design from behavior level to gate level, no matter it is hierarchical or flattened.

2 Previous Work

The goal of the distributed simulation partitioner is to make the workload shared among processors as balanced as possible and make the communication overhead as small as possible. A good survey on this topic is given by Bailey, Briner and Chamberlain [2]. While most previous work focuses on gate-level, Guettaf et al. [3] proposed a behavior level partitioner for VHDL. However, they did not address how to handle special constructs like function call, global access and memory access, and these issues are addressed in our work.

The multi-level partitioner proposed in this paper is relied on our previous work on gate-level partitioning. It supports two partitioner modes, *normal mode* and *regroup mode*, and utilizes techniques to flatten the design for finer-grained partitioning. Please refer to [4] for more details on this work.

3 Behavior and RTL Level Partitioning

Our proposed workload estimation technique and RTL/behavior level partitioning algorithm are discussed in this section.

3.1 Workload Estimation

Workload in a simulation consists of processing signal changes, scheduling the affected behaviors, and executing the affected behaviors. In general, it is difficult to estimate workload accurately, and approximations are needed. In gate level designs, the number of gates are often used to estimate workload in each partition. In this paper, we use the number of variables and nets in a partition to estimate the workload, which is similar to the use of gate count in gate-level designs.

3.2 Partition Algorithm

The gate-level partitioner we based on is only capable of partitioning gates (or instances in Verilog). In order to handle RTL/behavior level code, we need to convert them to instances first, and the algorithm is given below.

For each *initial block, always block,* and *continuous assignments*, an instance is created. The variables used at the LHS(left hand side) of the assignments will become output ports, and the variables used at the RHS of the assignments will become input ports. Then it can be partitioned with any gate-level partitioning algorithm.

Task and *function* definitions are duplicated to all the partitions where they are called. Since Verilog *task* and *function* calls are not reentrant, this approach will not cause any problem.

Global accesses which cross partitions will be replaced by *channel commands* provided by Simcluster. In Simcluster, *channel commands* are provided to set, view, force and release variables in a remote partition. For example, "a= b.c.d;" will be converted to "$channel_variable("b.c.d", a)".

Memory accesses are handled differently from variables because a memory cannot become a port. Task and function are used to handle memory accesses that cross partitions, and the template is given in Figure 1. In the template,

---

When memory access to "a.b.mem" appears on the LHS and is in another partition:
a.b.mem[i]= RHS;
will become:
set_mem(i, RHS);

```
task set_mem;
input index;
input RHS;
$channel_memory_set("a.b.mem", index, RHS);
endtask
```

When memory access to "a.b.mem" appears on the RHS and is in another partition:
LHS= a.b.mem[i];
will become:
LHS= fetch_mem(i);

```
function fetch_mem;
input index;
reg result;
begin
$channel_memory("a.b.mem", index, result);
fetch_mem= result;
end
endfunction
```

Fig. 1. Remote Memory Access Template

$channel\_memory$ is used to get data from the memory in a remote partition, and $channel\_memory\_set$ is used to send data to the remote memory.

4 Experimental Results

The design is part of the CF FFT project from Opencores [5]. It is a fast Fourier transform converter. The FFT architecture is pipelined on a rank basis; each rank has its own butterfly and ranks are isolated from each other using memory interleavers. The design is in RTL level. The "large testbench" provided in the project is used as the testbench and is also in RTL level. The cf_fft_4096_16 configuration (4K point FFT, 16 bit precision) is used as the design under test. The top-level module instantiates the testbench and the design under test. Our partitioner is used to partition the design into two partitions at top module.

The simulator used is VCK, and the platform is Redhat Linux 8.0 running on a workstation with dual AMD MP 1.8GHz CPU. The partitioner run time is 0.6 seconds. The single process run time is 118 seconds. After partitioning, the distributed run time becomes 71 seconds with 1.66X speed up.

Aside from this benchmark, our partitioner has also been used by Avery Design Systems to partition several commercial designs successfully.

5 Conclusion

In this paper, we extended a gate-level partitioner to support RTL and behavior level partitioning. We proposed techniques to convert RTL/behavior level code to gates and described how to handle constructs specific to these levels. Unlike other partitioners, which usually focus on gate-level circuits only, our partitioner can partition any design in any level of abstraction, as long as it is written in Verilog. From the results of the experiment, it can be concluded that the partitioner proposed in our work can indeed find good partitions that accelerate circuit simulation by distributed simulation. With this partitioner, distributed simulation tools will become easier to use and greatly save circuit designers' and verifiers' time.

References

1. Avery Design Systems, "VCK/Simlib User's Guide", Rev. 1.1.0, May 2002
2. M. L. Bailey, J. V. Briner, Jr., and R. D. Chamberlain, "Parallel logic simulation of VLSI systems", *ACM Computing Surveys*(1994)
3. A. Guettaf and P. Bazargan-Sabet, "Efficient Partitioning Method For Distributed Logic Simulation of VLSI Circuits", *Annual Simulation Symposium*, 1998, pp. 196-201.
4. K. H. Chang, H. W. Wang, Y. J. Yeh, and S. Y. Kuo, "Automatic Partitioner for Distributed Parallel Logic Simulation", *IASTED International Conference on Modeling, Simulation and Optimization(MSO'03)*, Kauai, Hawaii, USA, 2004.
5. CF FFT Project, http://www.opencores.org/

Expressive Completeness of an Event-Pattern Reactive Programming Language*

César Sánchez, Matteo Slanina, Henny B. Sipma, and Zohar Manna

Computer Science Department,
Stanford University, Stanford,CA 94305, USA
{cesar, matteo, sipma,zm}@CS.Stanford.EDU

Abstract. Event-pattern reactive programs serve reactive components by pre-processing the input event stream and generating notifications according to temporal patterns. The declarative language PAR allows the expression of complex event-pattern reactions. Despite its simplicity and deterministic nature, PAR is expressively complete in the following sense: *every event-pattern reactive system that can be described and implemented using finite memory can also be expressed in PAR*.

1 Introduction

Event-pattern reactive (EPR) programs are software components that recognize temporal patterns of events and respond by generating output notifications. Such components are increasingly used in middleware for publish-subscribe architectures to provide services such as event correlation (see, for example [6, 2]). EPR programs process an input stream of events, possibly generating an output after each event is read. The process of generating an output stream from input is called a **behavior**. Similar to regular languages, behaviors can be specified operationally by means of state machines or declaratively. Although state machines are usually the model of choice for implementation, a declarative representation is preferred for specification, because

(1) it is often more concise and readable. For example, the expression *"notify all occurrences of* alarm *after* fire *with no interleaving* false-alarm*"* is clearer than an equivalent state machine;
(2) it permits algebraic treatment for common operations and for proving equivalences and entailments;
(3) it avoids the "implementation bias," thus enabling to delay space/time tradeoffs until the system construction phase.

In [3] we presented a machine-oriented approach to describe EPR programs. In [4] we proposed PAR, a declarative language to specify EPR programs, and built the formal framework to define its semantics in terms of output and completion status (a pattern is recognized or it is realized that the pattern will never occur, and no more output is produced).

---

* This research was supported in part by NSF grants CCR-01-21403, CCR-02-20134, CCR-02-09237, CNS-0411363, and CCF-0430102, by ARO grant DAAD19-01-1-0723, and by NAVY/ONR contract N00014-03-1-0939.

In this paper we prove that PAR has full expressive power: any behavior that can be implemented by a finite-state machine, also called a **finite behavior**, can be specified by a PAR expression. This result mirrors the well-known result in automata theory that regular expressions are equally expressive as finite-state automata, and our proof borrows ideas from that proof [1], but is technically more challenging. First, the semantic domain is more complex since output, completion and synchronization with the input have to be considered. Second, PAR is deterministic while regular expressions contain + for non-deterministic choice, and ∗ for arbitrary repetition. This simplifies the proof of expressive completeness of regular expressions since different paths can be easily merged.

Below we briefly summarize the semantic domain for EPR programs and the PAR syntax and semantics. More details can be found in [4] and the full version of this paper [5].

The Semantic Domain. The input stream is formed from input symbols taken from a finite set Σ. Output notifications $\mathcal{O}$ consist of subsets of a finite set of output symbols. The empty notification $\varnothing$ is allowed, and notifications can be combined by set union if two patterns are recognized simultaneously. The combination of two or more of the same output A, is A itself.

An event-pattern behavior is defined by the immediate response to all input stream prefixes, characterized by two aspects: the output and the *completion status*. There are three completion statuses: (1) **success** ($\top$): the pattern has *just* been observed; (2) **failure** ($\bot$): the pattern cannot be observed in any stream that extends the current prefix; and (3) **incomplete** (ι): more input is needed or the input symbol is not relevant. We call $\mathcal{C} = \{\top, \iota, \bot\}$ the *completion domain*. The presence of completion statuses allows a compositional definition of behaviors: expressions can use the completion statuses of their subexpressions to preempt or restart them.

In [4] we defined *Event Pattern Machines* (EPM) to describe behaviors. An EPM $\mathcal{M} : \langle S, o, \alpha, \partial \rangle$ consists of a set of states S and three maps—o, α and ∂—such that, for any state and input symbol: (1) o returns an output value, (2) α returns a completion status, and (3) ∂ gives a "next" state. We require that if a state s is reached from q with input a, and $\alpha_a q \neq \iota$ then s is silent in the sense that all states reachable from s generate no output and declare ι status. Under these conditions, each state in S is associated with a unique behavior.

If S is a finite set of states (basically a Mealy-style machine with input Σ and output $\mathcal{O} \times \mathcal{C}$) we call such a machine a finite EPM, and the behaviors defined by them are called finite behaviors. The framework, however, is not restricted to finite machines. Any set, for example, the (infinite) set of all PAR programs, if equipped with o, α and ∂ function, receives unique semantics: each PAR program is assigned a unique behavior.

PAR Syntax. A *simple* PAR expression is an equality test for an input symbol: for each input symbol a there is an expression **a**. If A is an output notification and x and y are PAR expressions, then so are:

$x \mid y$ $x \,; y$ $\overline{x}$ $x[A]$ **repeat** x **try** x **unless** y **silent**

PAR Semantics. The semantics of PAR is defined in terms of the maps o, α and ∂. First, for every PAR expression x and input a, if $\alpha_a x \neq \iota$ then $\partial_a x = $ **silent**. Let x and y be PAR expressions. The semantics of the constructs are:

- *simple*: the expression **a** waits for an a event to succeed.
- *selection*: the expression $(x \mid y)$ evaluates x and y in parallel, succeeding as soon as one succeeds and failing when both have failed. Unlike $+$ for regular expressions, selection does not nondeterministically choose between the two branches.
- *sequential*: $(x\,;y)$ evaluates x and, upon successful completion, evaluates y.
- *complementation*: $\overline{x}$ reverses completion statuses upon termination.
- *output*: $x[A]$ generates the output A when x successfully completes.
- *repetition*: the expression (**repeat** x) evaluates x. If x fails, then the repetition fails; if x succeeds then repeat restarts the body.
- *preemption*: the expression (**try** x **unless** y) evaluates both x and y in parallel, trying to check whether x succeeds before y. Hence, if the try part x succeeds then the whole expression succeeds. It fails if x fails, or if y succeeds and x does not succeed.
- *silent*: **silent** always outputs ∅ and declares incomplete.

2 Expressive Completeness

Every PAR expression x describes a finite behavior since the set $\{\partial_w x\}$ is finite. The converse also holds:

Theorem. *Every finite behavior can be described with a PAR expression.*

Proof. (Sketch; the full formal proof can be found in the full version of this paper [5]). Let $\mathcal{M}$ be an EPM with state set $S : \{v_1, \ldots, v_n, v_{n+1}\}$, where, without loss of generality, we assume that v_{n+1} is the only silent state (all silent states are bisimilar). The goal is to construct PAR expressions $\Phi_1, \ldots, \Phi_n$ such that each Φ_i exactly describes the behavior associated with state v_i. Following the approach of the proof of the equivalence of regular expressions and finite automata [1], we do so by incrementally constructing a set of intermediate expressions that more and more accurately capture the behavior of the states. We show that after n rounds we can define the desired expressions $\Phi_1, \ldots, \Phi_n$.

Incremental Construction. At round k we build a set of expressions φ_{ij}^k that simulate the behavior of node v_i for input strings that, visiting only nodes labeled less than v_k along the way, either never reach v_j or reach it for the first time. During the construction all expressions φ_{ij}^k satisfy the following invariant: if v_l is the state reached from v_i after reading a, and A is the output generated:
(1) if $v_l = v_j$ then φ_{ij}^k succeeds on a and outputs A;
(2) if $v_l \neq v_j$ and $l > k$ then φ_{ij}^k fails and outputs nothing; and
(3) if $v_l \neq v_j$ and $l \leq k$ then φ_{ij}^k is incomplete on a, outputs A and $\partial_a(\varphi_{ij}^k) = \varphi_{lj}^k$.

Base case: The expression φ_{ij}^0 succeeds on a and outputs A, if there is a direct edge from v_i to v_j labeled with input a and output A; otherwise φ_{ij}^0 fails without generating output. This can simply be achieved with the expression a[A] enclosed in a **try-unless** whose unless case succeeds immediately.

Inductive step: The expression φ_{ij}^k is defined using previously defined expressions. For $j = k$, $\varphi_{ij}^k = \varphi_{ij}^{k-1}$. For $j \neq k$ we need to consider two sets of paths (see figure): those that do not visit v_k (captured by φ_{ij}^{k-1}), and and those that do. In the latter case, v_k can be visited multiple times. Therefore, we need to define a PAR expression $\varphi_{kk}^{k-1} * \varphi_{kj}^{k-1}$ that (based on φ_{kk}^{k-1} and φ_{kj}^{k-1}) behaves: (1) as v_k for paths that lead to v_j using nodes at most v_{k-1}, (2) fails as soon as the the machine visits a node larger than v_k, and (3) restarts if a visit to v_k is produced. Note that this is trivial to achieve with regular expressions, but not that easy in PAR. In the full version [5] we show that this construct can be defined by the expression $x * y \stackrel{\text{def}}{=} \textbf{try repeat } \overline{(y \mathcal{W} x)} \textbf{ unless repeat } \overline{x}$.

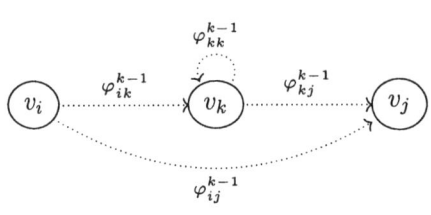

Final Expressions. Using the expressions φ_{ij}^n we can now define expressions Φ_i, for states v_i, $i = 1, \ldots, n$. The behavior of the silent state v_{n+1}, if present, is modeled by the expression **silent**. We introduce the auxiliary expressions $Kleene_i^\top$ (and $Kleene_i^\bot$) that upon an input a, succeed if v_i succeeds (resp. fails), and become $Kleene_j^\top$ (resp. become $Kleene_j^\bot$) if v_i leads to v_j. This is achieved with the use of $*$ defined above. Finally, Φ_i is defined by composing all possible paths from v_i:

$$\Phi_i \stackrel{\text{def}}{=} \begin{pmatrix} \textbf{try} & Kleene_i^\top \mid \mid_j \varphi_{ij}^n\,;\,Kleene_j^\top \\ \textbf{unless} \, Kleene_i^\bot \mid \mid_j \varphi_{ij}^n\,;\,Kleene_j^\bot \end{pmatrix}.$$

References

1. J. E. Hopcroft and J. D. Ullman. *Introduction to automata theory, languages and computation.* Addison-Wesley, 1979.
2. P. R. Pietzuch, B. Shand, and J. Bacon. Composite event detection as a generic middleware extension. *IEEE Network*, 18(1), 2004.
3. C. Sánchez, S. Sankaranarayanan, H. B. Sipma, T. Zhang, D. Dill, and Z. Manna. Event correlation: Language and semantics. In *EMSOFT'03*, pages 323–339, 2003.
4. C. Sánchez, H. B. Sipma, M. Slanina, and Z. Manna. Final semantics for event-pattern reactive programs. In *CALCO'05*, pages 364–378, 2005.
5. C. Sánchez, M. Slanina, H. B. Sipma, and Z. Manna. Expressive completeness of an event-pattern reactive programming language. http://Theory.Stanford.EDU/~cesar/papers/completeness.html, Stanford CS REACT Technical Report 2005.
6. B. Segall and S. Arnold. Elvin has left the building: A publish/subscribe notification service with quenching. In *Queensland AUUG Summer Tech. Conf.*, 1997.

Formalizing Interoperability Testing: Quiescence Management and Test Generation

Alexandra Desmoulin and César Viho

IRISA/Université de Rennes 1, Campus de Beaulieu,
35042 Rennes Cedex, France
{adesmoul, viho}@irisa.fr
http://www.irisa.fr/armor

Abstract. This paper gives formal definitions of the different existing interoperability notions called *interoperability criteria*. The equivalence between two of them leads to a method for interoperability test generation that avoids the state explosion problem of classical approaches.

1 Introduction

Despite a large literature on the interest of providing a formal approach for interoperability testing [1, 2], only few tentative have been proposed. Therefore, the aims of this study presented in this paper are double. First, we give formal definitions of interoperability testing called *interoperability criteria* (*iop criteria* for short in the following). The second contribution of this work is a new method to generate automatically interoperability test cases. It uses a theorem proving the equivalence between two iop criteria. It avoids the well-known state-explosion problem due to the classical construction of the specification composition. Thus, the proposed method is a real solution that provides an easy and efficient way to derive effectively interoperability test cases.

2 Interoperability Definitions

One-to-One Interoperability Testing Architecture. In this study, we consider the one-to-one interoperability context : the System Under Test (SUT) is composed of two Implementation Under Test (IUT). There are two kind of interfaces. The lower interfaces used for the interaction of the IUTs and the upper interfaces used for the communication with their environment. Depending on the access to the different interfaces, different architectures can be distinguished.

Formal Background. The well-known IOLTS (Input-Output Labeled Transition System) model will be used to model specifications and to define interoperability criteria. We note $p?m$ ($p!a$) for an input (output) of message m on the interface p. Figure 1 gives an example of two specifications using this model.

Quiescence and ioco. Three main situations lead to quiescence of a system : *deadlock* (a state after which no event is possible), *outputlock* (a state after which

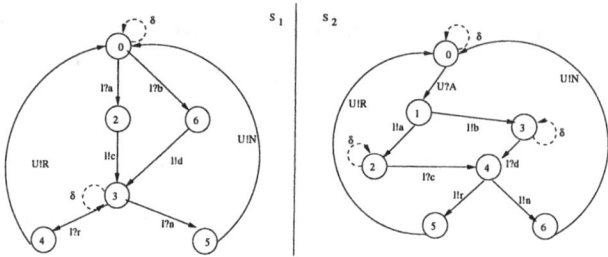

Fig. 1. Specifications S_1 and S_2

only transitions labeled with input exist) and *livelock* (a loop of internal events). Quiescence is modeled by δ and is treated as an observable output event. The obtained IOLTS is called suspensive IOLTS [3] and noted $\Delta(M)$. The **ioco** conformance relation [3] is used for the formal interoperability definitions. It says that an IUT I is **ioco**-conformant to its specification S if I can never produce an output that could not be produced by S after the same suspension trace.

Interaction. We need a model of the asynchronous interaction of the implementations. This is noted $M_1 \|_A M_2$ and obtained as usual by a synchronous composition of $\Delta(M_1)$, $\Delta(M_2)$ and FIFO queues modeling the asynchronous environment. Quiescence is preserved and $\delta(i)$ corresponds to quiescence of M_i and δ of the two IOLTS.

Projection. In interoperability testing, we usually need to observe some specific events of an IUT. M/X represents the projection of the behavior of the implementation M reduced to a set X of expected messages.

Model of an Implementation: iop-Input Completion. In the context of interoperability testing, tester can only observe the events on the lower interfaces. But these testers can not differenciate events received by an IUT from events effectively treated. A completion is needed for inputs corresponding to the output alphabet of the other IUT specification. It is called the iop-input completion leading the IOLTS into an error deadlock state.

Formal Definition of Interoperability Criteria. According to the chosen testing architecture, different notions of interoperability can be used [4]. We will focus here on two *interoperability (iop) criteria*. The **global iop criterion** iop_G says that two implementations are considered interoperable if, after a suspensive trace of the asynchronous interaction of the specifications, all outputs and quiescence observed during the asynchronous interaction of the implementations are foreseen in the specifications. The **bilateral iop criterion** iop_B says that after a suspensive trace of S_1 observed during the asynchronous interaction of the implementations, all outputs and quiescence observed in I_1 are foreseen in S_1, and the same in the point of view of I_2 implementing the specification S_2.

The most important result is the following theorem 1 stating that iop_G is equivalent to the bilateral total iop criterion iop_B.

Theorem 1. $I_1 \, iop_G \, I_2 \Leftrightarrow I_1 \, iop_B \, I_2$

3 Interoperability Test Generation

The goal of an interoperability test generation algorithm is to generate interoperability Test Cases (TC) that can be executable on the SUT composed of the two IUT to be tested. The inputs of such algorithms are the specifications S_1 and S_2 on which the two IUT (I_1 and I_2) are based, and a Test Purpose (TP) which is a particular property (in the shape of incomplete sequences of actions that have to be observed or sent to the SUT) to be tested.

Interoperability Verdicts. The execution of an iop test case TC on $SUT(I_1\|_A I_2)$ gives a verdict : $verdict(TC, SUT) \in \{PASS, FAIL, INC\}$. The interoperability verdict PASS means that no interoperability error was detected, FAIL means that the iop criterion is not verified, and INC (for Inconclusive) means that the behavior of the SUT seems valid but it is not the purpose of the test case.

The Classical Approach and the State-Space Explosion Problem. In the classical approach based on a criteria like iop_G, the test generation algorithm begins with the construction of the asynchronous interaction $S_1 \|_A S_2$. Then $S_1 \|_A S_2$ is composed with the TP. The consistency of TP is checked in parallel and TC is generated. Yet, the construction of $S_1 \|_A S_2$ can cause the well-known state-space explosion, as building $S_1 \|_A S_2$ is exponential in the number of states of S_1 and S_2 and the FIFO queues size. Thus, interoperability test generation based on the global iop criterion may be impossible even for small specifications.

A New Method Based on the Bilateral iop Criterion iop_B. The equivalence of iop_B and iop_G (cf. therorem 1) suggests to study a method for iop test cases generation based on the bilateral iop criterion iop_B. The idea is to derive TP_{S_i} from an iop test purpose TP. Each TP_{S_i} represents TP in the point of view of S_i. This step is described in the following algorithm (see figure 2). The second step is to use a conformance test generation tool $\mathcal{F}$ such that $\mathcal{F} : (S_1, TP_{S_1}) \to TC_1$ and $\mathcal{F} : (S_2, TP_{S_2}) \to TC_2$. We obtain two unilateral iop test cases TC_1 and TC_2. The obtained test cases obtained are modified in order to take into account the differences between upper and lower interfaces in interoperability testing. For example, an event $l!m$ (resp. $l?m$) in the obtained test case will be replaced by $?(l?m)$ (resp. $?(l!m)$) in the interoperability test case. This means that the unilateral interoperability tester observes that a message m is received from (resp. sent to) the other IUT on the lower interface l. No changes are made on the test cases for events on the upper interfaces. According to the theorem 1, $verdict(TC, I_1 \|_A I_2) = verdict(TC_1, I_1 \|_A I_2) \wedge verdict(TC_2, I_1 \|_A I_2)$. The rules for the combination of these two verdicts to obtain the final iop_B verdict are given by : $PASS \wedge PASS = PASS$, $PASS \wedge INC = INC$, $INC \wedge INC = INC$, and $FAIL \wedge (FAIL \vee INC \vee PASS) = FAIL$.

Applying the Method to an Example. Let us consider the two specifications S_1 and S_2 of figure 1 and the interoperability testing purpose $TP = l1?a.U2!N$. This test purpose is interesting because it contains events on both interfaces

Input: TP: test purpose; **Output:** $\{TP_{S_i}\}_{i=1,2}$;
Invariant: $S_k = S_{3-i}$ (* S_k is the other specification *); $TP = \mu_1...\mu_n$
Initialization: $\mu_0 = \epsilon$; $TP_{S_i} = \epsilon$;
for (i=0;$i \leq n$;i++) do
  if ($\mu_i \in \Sigma^{S_i}$) then $TP_{S_i} = TP_{S_i}.\mu_i$ (* just add *)
  if ($\mu_i \in \Sigma_L^{S_k}$) then $TP_{S_i} = TP_{S_i}.\bar{\mu}_i$ (* just add the mirror *)
  if ($\mu_i \in \Sigma_U^{S_k} \cup \{\tau\}$)
    $\sigma_1 := TP_{S_i}$; a_j =last_event(σ_1)
    while $a_j \in \Sigma_U^{S_k} \cup \{\tau\}$ do σ_1=remove_last_event(σ_1)
      a_{j-1} =last_event(σ_1) (* a_{j-1} is the last event added to TP_{S_i} and
    end   a mirror event $\bar{a}_{j-1}$ may exist in S_k *)
    $M_{S_k} = \{q \in Q^{S_k}$ such that $q \overset{\bar{a}_{j-1}}{\to}$ and $\sigma = \bar{a}_{j-1}.\omega.\mu_i \in Traces(q)\}$
    if ($\forall q \in M_{S_k}$, $q \overset{\sigma}{\not\to}$) then error(TP not valid : no path to μ_i)
    while (e=last_event(ω) $\notin \Sigma_L^{S_k} \cup \{\epsilon\}$) do ω=remove_last_event(ω) end
    if (e $\in \Sigma_L^{S_k}$) then $TP_{S_i} = TP_{S_i}.\bar{e}$
  else error(TP not valid : $\mu_i \notin \Sigma^{S_1} \cup \Sigma^{S_2}$)

Fig. 2. Algorithm to derive TP_{S_i} from TP

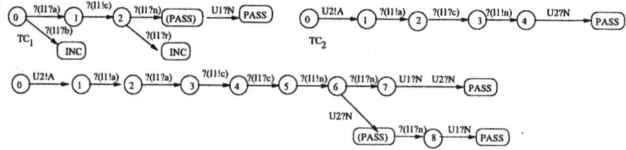

Fig. 3. Interoperability test cases obtained for $TP = l1?a.U2!N$

and both IUTs. Applying the algorithm of figure 2, we obtain : $TP_{S_1} = l1!a.l1?n$ and $TP_{S_2} = \bar{\mu}_1.\mu_2 = l2!a.U2!N$. The obtained test cases TC_1 and TC_2 are given in upper side of figure 3. For interoperability test case generation based on the global relation, the obtained TC (cf. the third test case in figure 3) comes from the composition of $S_1\|_A S_2$ with TP. According to the theorem 1, final interoperability verdicts obtained with TC_1 and TC_2 should be the same as the verdict obtained with TC. The proof is not given here but a look at glance to TC_1 and TC_2 shows the same paths and verdicts in TC.

4 Conclusion

In this paper, *interoperability criteria* taking quiescence into account are defined, describing the conditions under which two IUT can be considered interoperable. A theorem proving that two of them are equivalent allows a new method for interoperability test generation that avoids the classical state-explosion problem. Further studies will consider a distributed approach for interoperability testing of architectures composed of more than two implementations.

References

[1] O. Rafiq and R. Castanet. From conformance testing to interoperability testing. In *Protocol Test Systems*, volume III, pages 371–385, North-Holland, 1991. IFIP, Elsevier sciences publishers B. V.

[2] S. Seol, M. Kim, S. Kang, and J. Ryu. Fully automated interoperability test suite derivation for communication protocols. *Comp. Networks*, 43(6):735–759, 2003.

[3] J. Tretmans. Testing concurrent systems: A formal approach. In J.C.M Baeten and S. Mauw, editors, *CONCUR'99 - 10th Int. Conference on Concurrency Theory*, volume 1664 of *LNCS*, pages 46–65. Springer-Verlag, 1999.

[4] S. Barbin, L. Tanguy, and C. Viho. Towards a formal framework for interoperability testing. In M. Kim, B. Chin, S. Kang, and D. Lee, editors, *FORTE' 2001*, pages 53–68, Cheju Island, Korea, 2001.

Formal Description of Mobile IPv6 Protocol

Yujun Zhang and Zhongcheng Li

Institute of Computing Technology, Chinese Academy of Sciences, 100080,
Beijing, P.R. China
zhmj@ict.ac.cn

Abstract. Formal technique is the basis of automatic test generation. Mobile IPv6 is a complicated and distributed protocol with many discrete behaviors. It is difficult to describe the entire protocol by some formal model. The idea of hierarchical protocol description is proposed. Finite state machine (FSM) and multi-node finite state machine (MN-FSM) are defined. Mobile IPv6 protocol is divided into four layers. FSM and MN-FSM are used to describe network system, mobile IPv6 nodes, inner data structure management and discrete behaviors. Test sequences can be generated automatically based on these formal models.

1 Introduction

Mobile IPv6 is the mobility solution in network layer [1]. Conformance testing is very necessary to guarantee an implementation consistent to its standard specification [2]. Mobile IPv6 is in its growing stage, so it is necessary to study mobile IPv6 conformance testing.

Test generation is the key issue in conformance testing. Formal technique is the basis of automatic test generation. How to describe mobile IPv6 by formal technique must be solved before test generation. Considering state explosion and plentiful discrete behaviors, it is not practical to describe the entire mobile IPv6 protocol by some formal model. We propose the idea of hierarchical protocol description. Finite state machine (FSM) and multi-node finite state machine (MN-FSM) are defined to describe mobile IPv6.

2 Hierarchical Protocol Description

Mobile IPv6 protocol can be described in four sections, which are network system, nodes, inner data structure (IDS) management and discrete behaviors. Four types of nodes, including mobile node (MN), correspondent node (CN), home agent (HA) and common router (CR), are defined. Each type of node is also a self-governed system. Also, three types of IDSs, including binding cache (BC), binding update list (BUL) and home agent list (HAL), are defined.

For distributed system, compared to trying to describe entire protocol by single formal model, hierarchical description can reduce complexity [3]. Mobile IPv6 protocol can be described in four layers (Fig 1).

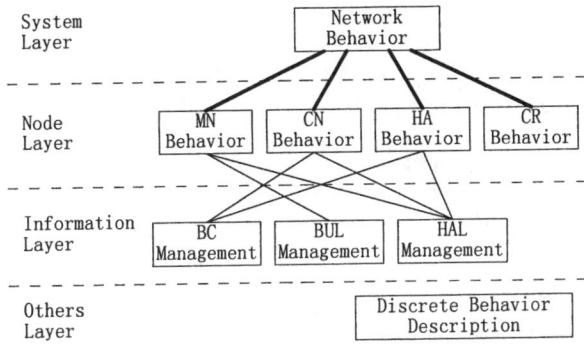

Fig. 1. The composition of mobile IPv6 protocol. Four types of nodes (MN, CN, HA and CR) are the core section. Mobile IPv6 network is composed of these types of nodes. IDS management is the most important mission that these nodes must perform. Discrete behavior description is the necessary section.

Finite state machine (FSM) is the most popular model for describing network protocols [4]. We add a behavior function to the traditional FSM definition, which is used to describe behaviors that don't change state nor generate output event.

2.1 Description for Network System (NS)

The state of mobile IPv6 network system can be described by the following properties.
1. M_p: location of mobile node. $M_p = \{home, foreign\}$.
2. HR_{flag}: flag of home registration (HR). $HR_{flag} = \{0, 1\}$.
3. CR_{flag}: flag of common registration (CR). $CR_{flag} = \{0, 1\}$.

Let S be the set of states for network system. $S = M_p \times HR_{flag} \times CR_{flag}$. Removing the invalid or unstable states from S, only three valid states remain is S. For mobile IPv6 network, all input events are manual behaviors. Under any circumstance, no output event happens, but related behaviors will happen. State transition graph for network system is shown in Fig 2.

2.2 Description for Mobile IPv6 Nodes

We take MN description as an example to present how to describe mobile IPv6 nodes. The MN's main task is to maintain its current location on home agent and correspondent nodes. In one lifecycle of movement, MN's behaviors can be presented as follows (Fig 3).

1. At first, MN attaches at home link and is in stable state.
2. MN detects movement from home link, and then generates care-of address.
3. Mobile node performs HR, and then is in stable state.
4. MN receives a tunnel packet, performs CR, and then is in stable state.
5. MN receives another tunnel packet, repeat last step.
6. MN detects itself returning to home link, and then de-registers HR and all CRs.
7. Then MN completes one lifecycle of movement.

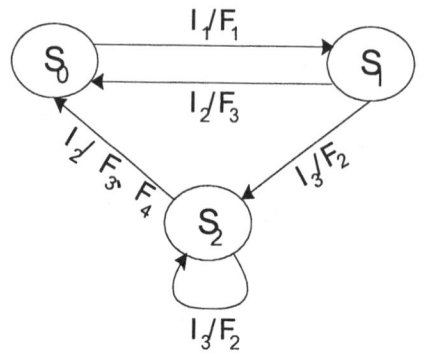

Fig. 2. State transition graph for NS   **Fig. 3.** State transition graph for MN

2.3 Description for Inner Data Structure Management

We take BC management as an example to present how to describe IDS management. BC is composed of many BC entries (BCE). BCE's state is determined by its remaining lifetime. In CN, each BCE stands for a mobile node. Let FSM $M = (S_e, I_e, O_e, of, tf, bf)$ be the formal model for single BCE management (Fig 4).

Based on description for single BCE management, we propose multi-nodes finite state machine (MN-FSM) to describe BC management in a particular mobile IPv6 network (Def 1).

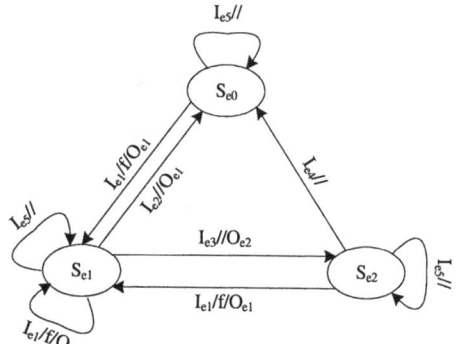

Fig. 4. State transition graph for BCE management

Definition 1. Multi-Nodes Finite State Machine

MN-FSM is used to describe BC management by CN in a particular mobile IPv6 network. Let MN-FSM $M = (S, I, O, N, of, tf, V, bf, sf, SB_{0B})$, in which:
- N: the set of mobile nodes. If there are n mobile nodes, $N = \{1, 2, ..., n\}$.
- S: the set of states. Each state is the combination of all BCEs' current states.
- S_0: the initial state. $S_0 = \{<1, S_{e0}>, ..., <n, S_{e0}>\}$.
- I: the set of input events. $I \subseteq N \times I_e$.
- O: the set of output events. $O \subseteq N \times O_e$.
- of: the output function. $of: S \times I \to O$.
- tf: the state transition function. $tf: S \times I \to S$.
- V: a n-column vector. Each element stores the related BCE's lifetime that has been updated latest.
- bf: the behavior function. bf resets the vector V based on the valid binding updates latest.
- Sf: the signal generation function.

BC management with two BCEs is described (Fig 5), in which tf and of are defined as follows.

If in Fig 4
$$S_{ei} \rightarrow I_{ea}/f/O_{eb} \rightarrow S_{ej}$$
Then in Fig 5
$$\{<1,S_{ei}>,<2,*>\} \rightarrow <1,I_{ea}>/bf/<1,O_{eb}> \rightarrow \{<1,S_{ej}>,<2,*>\}$$
And
$$\{<1,*>,<2,S_{ei}>\} \rightarrow <2,I_{ea}>/bf/<2,O_{eb}> \rightarrow \{<1,*>,<2,S_{ej}>\}$$

3 Conclusion

Formal description is the base of conformance testing. This paper proposes the method of hierarchical description. The entire mobile IPv6 protocol is divided into four layers and each layer is described separately. Based on formal description for mobile IPv6 protocol, we can use test generation method for FSM model to generate mobile IPv6 test sequences, such as T-method, U-method etc. We also have developed test system, and tested many kinds of mobile IPv6 devices and obtained some valuable results [5].

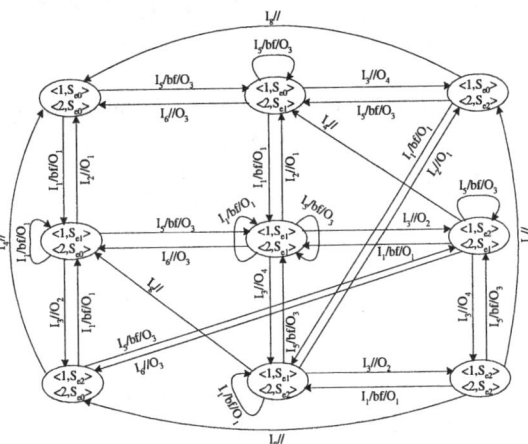

Fig. 5. State transition graph for BC management with two BCEs

References

1. D.Johnson, C.Perkins, J.Arkko: Mobility Support in IPv6. IETF RFC 3775 (2004)
2. ISO/IEC 9646: IT-OSI-Conformance Testing Methodology and Framework. (1996)
3. J.Wu: Formal Methods for Protocol Engineering and Distributed Systems. Kluwer Academic Publishers (2001)
4. D.Lee, M.Yannakakis: Principles and Methods of Testing Finite State Machines - a survey. Proceedings of the IEEE, Vol. 8 (1996) 1090-1123
5. Y.Zhang, Z.Li: IPv6 Conformance Testing: Theory and Practice. IEEE ITC (2004) 719-727

Incremental Modeling Under Large-Scale Distributed Interaction

Horst F. Wedde, Arnim Wedig, Anca Lazarescu,
Ralf Paaschen, and Elisei Rotaru

University of Dortmund, Informatik III, 44221 Dortmund, Germany
isystems@ls3.cs.uni-dortmund.de

Abstract. We present I–Systems as a formal constraint-based approach for modeling and analyzing both autonomous and reactive behavior in a distributed system. Essentially it is a formalism of *interacting finite automata*. We demonstrate its incremental potential by stepwise modeling a solution for a synchronous communication problem.

1 I–Systems

In practice, interaction in a distributed system is based on local (or regional) cooperation between a small number of components. Global effects arise from a propagation of influences originating from constraints on local or regional cooperation. The component behavior exhibits two different types of events: *enforced* events *will* occur, either due to local control decisions or through external influences that trigger these events, *free* events *may* (or may never) occur based on autonomous local decisions, or because of incomplete information about yet unknown external influences.

Based on the observation that components in distributed systems may be reactive or active, we distinguish between *reactive (inert)* and *autonomous* components called *parts*. Parts have a constituting set of local states (that are relevant for the interaction) which are called *phases*. Also, parts are in exactly one *phase at any time*. In this way *parts are finite automata*. In contrast to communicating automata the cooperation, influences, decisions and their propagation, even the internal behavioral details within a component are defined based only on two types of binary relations (denoted as *coupling and excitement relation*, see section 2) between parts. It turns out that the I-System model has a higher specificational power than communicating finite automata.

We Will Present I-Systems as Interacting Finite Automata. The interaction is specified though local *action rules* which describe the frame of actions in parts (i.e. occurrences of phase transitions), as well as the ensuing influence on, or from, other parts. A technical comprehensive presentation of the static structure, the dynamics, and the semantics of I-Systems can be found in [3,4].

2 Modeling of Sequential Processes

As mentioned above each part of an I–System can be interpreted as a finite automaton. In order to specify its transition structure we focus on installing *interaction primitives* (instead of communication primitives for communicating automata). As a result, free and enforced phase transitions, as well as their enforcing influences, can be modeled explicitly.

As an example let us assume an autonomous part b_1 with four phases $p_1, \ldots, p_4$. Our goal is to impose a cyclic behavior structure in b1 such that only free phase transitions from p_1 to p_2 and from p_3 to p_4, and enforced phase transitions from p_2 to p_3 and from p_4 to p_1 may/will occur. We realize this by simply adding an additional inert part $\underline{b}_2$ with phases $e_1, \ldots, e_4$, and by stepwise adapting the coupling and excitement relation as depicted in Fig. 1.

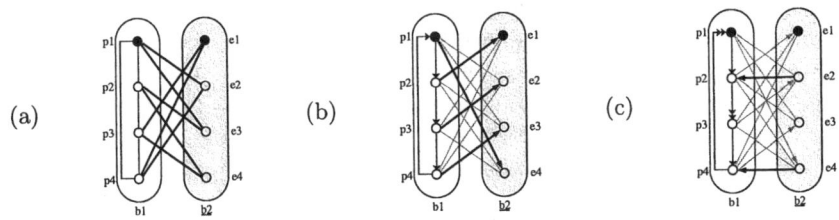

Fig. 1. Incremental Design of Sequential Processes

Step 1 (Fig. 1.a): Adding coupling relations between b_1 and $\underline{b}_2$
The symmetrical coupling relation specifies pairs of *mutually exclusive phases*.
Result: We restrict the local behavior to phase transitions between p_i and $p_{(i+1) \bmod 4}$ and back, induced by the reactive part $\underline{b}_2$.

Step 2 (Fig. 1.b): Adding excitement relations directed from b_1 to b_2
In general, an element $(p, q) \in E$ where E is the *excitement relation* expresses a *potential excitation from phase p in part b to phase q in part b'*. The main idea is that if b is in p and b' is in q then b exerts an influence on b' to leave p, and b' will leave p unless prevented through other external influences. B, in turn, has to stay in p as long as b' is in q.
Result: We install directions in b_1, i.e. phase transitions only occur from p_i to $p_{(i+1) \bmod 4}$.

Step 3 (Fig. 1.c): Adding excitement relations directed from b_2 to b_1
Result: We enforce outgoing phase transitions from p_2 as well as from p_4.

Major Result: *In general each organizational form of behavior in a part as specified through autonomous decision effects or dutiful steps according to an organizational role can be modeled through the incremental standard construction explained in the example above [3,4].*

3 Application: Synchronous Communication

We model, for a correct implementation, the synchronous communication concept of CSP, cf. [1,2]. In order to establish such a communication between a process (part) P_1 and a process (part) P_2, P_1 executes a *tie* command (when arriving in phase ti_1). As a result a virtual channel is opened which would be connected to a corresponding virtual channel on the side of P_2 (in phase ti_2). In this way the real communication between P_1 and P_2 could start (phases co_1, co_2). After completion the virtual channels will be abandoned by executing an *untie* command (in phases un_1, un_2).

The **synchronization conditions for P_1** are formulated in the following way. They must hold **symmetrically for P_2**.

SC1: If P_1 has arrived in ti_1 while P_2 has not entered ti_2 or co_2, P_1 has to wait.
SC2: If P_1 has arrived in co_1 while P_2 is still in ti_2 then P_1 cannot proceed, and P_1 exerts an influence on P_2 as to leaving ti_2.
SC3: If P_1 has arrived in un_1 while P_2 is still in co_2 then P_1 cannot proceed, and P_1 exerts an influence on P_2 as to leaving co_2.
SC4: If P_1 is in ti_1 and P_2 is outside of its communication section (i.e. P_2 is in a remainder phase re_2) then there is no influence on P_2 from P_1 as to enter its communication section.

The local behavior in the parts P_1 and P_2 can be realized as in section 2, detailing free and enforced phase transitions. We stepwise realize SC1 - SC4 through the symmetric construction shown in the screenshot of Fig. 1.

Step 1: SC2 is realized through connecting P_1 and P_2 through the inert part $\boldsymbol{VE_1}$.

Step 2: SC3 is realized through connecting P_1 and P_2 through the inert part $\boldsymbol{VE_2}$.

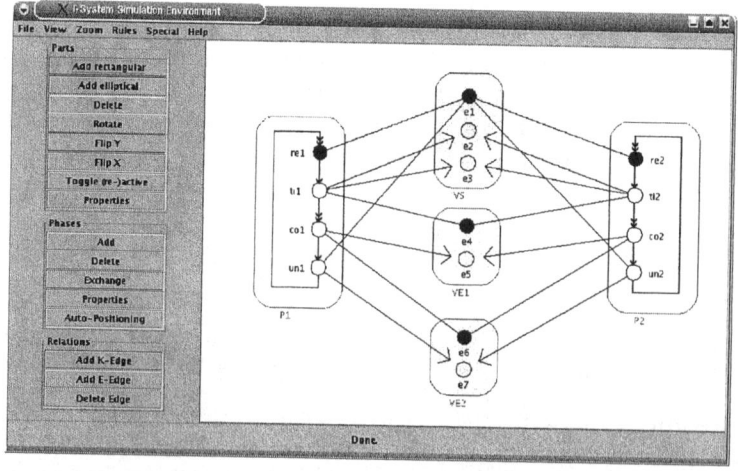

Fig. 2. Incremental Realization of Synchronous Communication

Step 3: SC1 and SC4 are both realized through connecting P_1 and P_2 through the inert part $\underline{VS}$.

Major Property: *The interaction is minimal in the sense that through this connection no further restriction is imposed on P_1 or P_2.*

As we readily verify this property is easy to achieve through the explicit specification utilized above while in other models, including communicating automata, this has always been the weakest part of the proposed solutions (see e.g. [1]).

4 Conclusion

We have presented the advantages of I–Systems in modeling distributed interaction, a formalism corresponding to an extended model of interacting finite automata (as opposed to communicating finite automata).

We have demonstrated the stepwise realization of a local behavior structure through primitive interaction constructions, connecting the involved parts through a reactive component. An I–System model for a distributed system reflecting all kinds of cooperative requirements or constraints can be incrementally constructed in this way such that the absence of undesirable influences in subsystems can be guaranteed.

We have developed a fundamental formal framework for I–Systems, e.g.:

- We have developed a novel abstract axiom system for specifying and deriving the behavior of an I–System. Behavioral steps (phase transitions) are derived by local checks of the local constraint structure. The axiom system is motivated through a *distributed implementation* and an *efficient animator*.
- We have defined a trace-semantics that documents the effects of influences and allows to distinguish between *free* and *enforced actions* (phase transitions).
- We have defined a finite behavior graph that is equivalent to the (infinite) trace semantics in that they describe the same behavior.
- We currently investigate efficient analysis and model-checking techniques for I–Systems, i.e. finding cycles in the behavior graph in order to identify infinite traces in the trace-semantics.

The presentation of formal details is out of the scope of this short paper. They can be found in [3,4]. *An on-line animation including the examples as well as the example constructions described will be demonstrated at the conference.*

References

1. Castelli, G., De Cindio, F., De Michelis, G., Simone, C.: The GCP Language and its Implementation. In Proc. of the IFIP workshop *Languages for Automation*, New Orleans, October 1984.
2. Hoare, C. A. R.: Communicating Sequential Processes. CACM, vol. 21, no. 8, 1978.

3. Wedde, H. F., Wedig, A.: Explicit Modeling of Influences, and of Their Absence, in Distributed Systems. In *Tools and Algorithms for the Construction and Analysis of Systems (ETAPS/TACAS'02)*, volume 2280 of LNCS, pages 127–141. Springer, 2002. Ext. Version: http://ls3-www.cs.uni-dortmund.de/I-Systems/P/techrep742.pdf
4. Wedde, H. F., Wedig, A., Lazarescu, A., Paaschen, R., Rotaru, E.: Model Building and Model Checking under Large-Scale Distributed Interaction. Technical report, University of Dortmund, April 2005. http://ls3-www.cs.uni-dortmund.de/I-Systems/P/techrep795.pdf

The Inductive Approach to Strand Space*

Yongjian Li[1,2]

[1] Key Laboratory of Computer Science
[2] The State Key Laboratory of Information Security, Institute of Software,
Chinese Academy of Sciences, P.O.Box 8718, Beijing, China
lyj238@ios.ac.cn

Abstract. Strand space is a promising technique developed by Guttman et al. from MITRE company, and it provides us an intuitive and clear framework to analyze security protocols, but its mechanics of the proof tend to be quite intricate and not necessarily easy to be formalized. In this paper, we combine the inductive approach with strand space. We introduce an inductive definition for bundles, and it not only provides us a constructive illustration for a bundle, but also introduces an effective and rigorous technique of rule induction to prove properties of bundles. Using this induction principle, we not only prove that a bundle is a casually well-founded graph, but also give a rigorous proof for results of authentication tests. Our result of authentication test extends Guttman's result to a more general case, and its proof is also much easier and clearer. As a trivial case study, we prove authentication properties of Needham-Schroeder-Lowe protocol. Our approach has been mechanized using Isabelle/HOL.

1 Introduction

Strand space is a promising technique developed by Guttman et al. from MITRE company [1]. The most important of all for analysis is carried out on the notion of bundles. A bundle is a casually well-founded set of nodes and arrows of both kinds, which sufficiently formalizes a session of a protocol. In a bundle, it must be insured that a node is included only if all nodes that proceed it are already included. For the strand corresponding to the principal in a given protocol run, we construct all possible bundles containing nodes of the strand. In fact, this set of bundles encodes all possible interactions of the environment with that principal in the run. Reasoning about the protocol takes place on this set of bundles. Typically, for the protocol to be correct, each such bundle must contain one strand of each legitimate principals apparently participating this session, all agreeing on principals, nonces, and session keys. Penetrator strands may also be entangled in a bundle, even in a correct protocol, but they should not prevent legitimate parties from agreeing on the data values, or from maintaining the secrecy of the value chosen. The key to this approach is the fact that a bundle

---

* This work is supported by NSF project of China under Grant No.60173020, 60421001, 60223005.

form a finite, well-founded sets under the relation, and each non-empty subset of the bundle has a $\preceq$-minimal element. A powerful idea, authentication test, is also introduced by Guttman et al [2]. This is basically a formalization of the basic challenge-response style primitive that is a building block for many protocols. An agent transmits a so-called test component, and later receives back another term that is in some transformed form of the component, then only a regular principal, not penetrator can have transformed it. In favorable circumstances, it can only be one regular participant, the intended one, who has thereby been authenticated.

Although strand space provides us an intuitive and clear framework to analyze why security protocols are correct, it seemed that the mechanics of the proof tend to be quite intricate and not necessarily easy to be formalized. To our knowledge, no one has ever formalized strand space theory in a theorem prover since the theory was introduced in 1998. Note that almost 7 years has passed, which is not a short time. Special attention should be paid to consider why it is so difficult to formalize strand space. In our opinion, two problems are due to this difficulty. Firstly, as the cornerstone in strand space theory, bundle's definition is not suitable for formal reasoning. It is just a sketchy property description of a graph about a protocol session, that is, a bundle is a casually well-founded graph. However, it does not tell us how this graph is constructed. Secondly, many concepts and proofs are very informal and complicated, and it is far away from being mechanized. One evidence is results about authentication tests. Authentication tests provide a general and powerful idea to prove authentication properties in a wide range of security protocols, and they are easy to apply themselves, but the proofs justifying them are quite complicated and difficult to be formalized. In order to prove these results, Guttman has introduced normal bundles and efficient bundles, which place more restriction on the operations of penetrator, and he has proved two important lemmas: a normal form lemma and an efficient form lemma. Many definitions are involved in his proof, such as graph operations, rising and falling paths, bridges, and it is too tedious to formally define them in a theorem prover, and proofs of the two lemmas are so complicated that it is hard to follow even in paper proof, let alone to formalize them and present formal proofs in theorem provers.

The main contributions of this paper are as following: (1) We introduce an inductive definition for bundles, and it not only provides us a constructive illustration for a bundle, but also introduces an effective and rigorous technique of rule induction to prove properties of bundles. (2) We formalize the semantics to fresh assumption, that is certain data items, such as nonces and session keys, are fresh and never arise in more than one protocol run. We also introduce a notion of complete transforming path. Roughly speaking, a complete transforming path p for a data item a is a path such that record necessary transforming information about a. Suppose a uniquely originates in n, and n' is a node containing a in a bundle b, then there is a complete transforming path from n to n' through b about a. (3) We extend Guttman's authentication results to a more general case, and use results of well-foundedness of bundle and complete path to give an easier and clearer proof. (4) We formalized our theory in Isabelle/HOL, and prove authentication results of Needham-Schroeder-Lowe protocol as a trivial case study. The remainder of this paper is organized as follows: Section 2 formalizes preliminary definitions such as messages, agents, and strands, strand spaces. Section 3 introduces the inductive definition of bundle and the corresponding induction principle. Section 4 introduces the notion of complete path and authentication results. Section 5 is related work and conclusion.

2 Strands and Strand Space

The notions in this subsection are mainly from Guttman's original definition, and we just formalize them straightforward in Isabelle.
  datatype sign=positive ("+" 100) |negative (" − " 100)
  types signed_msg= "sign × msg"
  typedecl sigma
  types node= " sigma × nat"
  types strand_space="sigma ⇒ signed_msg list "
  consts Sigma_set :: "sigma set" (" $\sum$ ")"
    SP :: "strand_space"
    attr::"sigma ⇒ agent"
  constdefs Domain::"node set"
    "Domain=={(s,i). s ∈ $\sum$ ∧ i < length (SP s)}"
  constdefs casual1::"(node × node) set"
  "casual1 == $\left\{ \begin{array}{l} \text{(n1,n2) . n1} \in \text{Domain} \land \text{n2} \in \text{Domain} \land \\ \text{node\_sign n1} = + \land \text{node\_sign n2} = - \land \\ \land \text{ node\_term n1} = \text{node\_term n2} \land \text{fst n1} \neq \text{fst n2} \end{array} \right\}$
  syntax "_casual1":: "node ⇒node⇒bool" (infix "→" 100)
  translations "n1→n2 "=="(n1, n2)∈casual1"
  constdefs casual2::"(node × node) set"
  "casual2 == $\left\{ \begin{array}{l} \text{(n1, n2) . n1} \in \text{Domain} \land \text{n2} \in \text{Domain} \land \\ \land \text{ (fst n1)} = \text{(fst n2)} \land \text{Suc(snd n1)} = \text{snd n2} \end{array} \right\}$
  syntax "_casual2"::" node ⇒node⇒bool" (infix "⇒" 50)
  translations "n1⇒n2 "=="(n1, n2)∈casual2"
  edge="node × node"
  graph="node set × edge set"

A signed message such as $(+, m)$ is a pair of a sign and a message. We define an abstract type sigma to define the type of signatures of strands. A node (s, i) is just a pair of a strand signature and an integer index. A strand space is just a trace mapping function which maps a strand signature to a list of signed messages. In our discussion, we usually fix a given strand signature set and strand space, so we define them as arbitrary but fixed consts $\sum$ and SP respectively. Given $\sum$ and SP, we are only interested in those nodes which is in the image of $\sum$ under the trace mapping function SP, and these nodes are defined by the const $Domain$. Two kinds of casual relation, denoted by → and ⇒, are introduced on the nodes in $Domain$. In the definition of →, $node\_term$ n, $node\_sign$ n are defined to return n's message term and sign respectively.

3 Bundles

Rather than following the way Guttman defined, we introduce a brand-new definition for bundles. It is totally an inductive definition, as shown as follows.

    consts bundles ::" graph set"
    inductive "bundles" intros
    Nil: "$(\emptyset, \emptyset) \in$ bundles"
    Add_Positive1:"[| b$\in$ bundles; node_sign n2 = +; n2$\in$Domain; n2$\notin$ fst b;
    0 < snd n2; n1$\in$ fst b; n1$\Rightarrow$n2 |] $\Longrightarrow$ ({n2} $\cup$ fst b, (n1, n2) $\cup$ snd b)$\in$bundles"
    Add_Positive2:"[| b$\in$ bundles; node_sign n2=+; n2$\notin$fst b; n2$\in$Domain;
    snd n2=0 |] $\Longrightarrow$({n2} $\cup$ fst b, snd b)$\in$bundles"
    Add_negtive1: "[| b$\in$ bundles; node_sign n2=−; n2 $\notin$ fst b;
              n1 $\rightarrow$ n2 $\wedge$ n1 $\in$ fst b $\wedge$ ($\forall$ n3. n3 $\in$ fst b$\longrightarrow$(n1,n3)$\notin$ snd b);
              0 < snd n2 ; n1' $\in$ (fst b); n1' $\Rightarrow$n2 |]
              $\Longrightarrow$ ({n2} $\cup$ fst b, {(n1, n2), (n1' , n2)} $\cup$ snd b) $\in$ bundles"
    Add_negtive2: "[| b$\in$ bundles; node_sign n2=−; n2 $\notin$ (fst b);
              n1 $\rightarrow$ n2 $\wedge$ n1 $\in$ fst b $\wedge$ ($\forall$ n3. n3 $\in$fst b$\longrightarrow$(n1,n3)$\notin$ snd b);
              snd n2=0 |] $\Longrightarrow$({n2} $\cup$ fst b, {(n1, n2)} $\cup$ snd b)$\in$bundles"

Our motivation here is two-folded. The more apparent is to introduce a more constructive definition to formalize a graph of a protocol session, rather that just saying that it is a casually well-defined graph. The other is to take advantage of the strong ability of induction principle supported by Isabelle to reason about inductively defined set. For the set of bundles, the induction principle says that $P(b)$ holds for each bundle b provided that P is preserved under all the rules for creating bundles.

4 Path and Authentication Tests

Definition 1. *A path p through bundle b is a list of nodes such that $p = []$, or $p_0 \in b$ and $(p_i, p_{i+1}) \in (\rightarrow \cap \text{ snd } b)$ or $(p_i, p_{i+1}) \in (\Rightarrow \cap \text{ snd } b)^+$ for any i such that $0 \leq i < \text{length } p - 1$.*

If a is uniquely originating from n, and n' is a node which contains a, and n' is in bundle b, then there exists a path p through b from n to n', moreover, and if p is across a positive node m such that $a \sqsubset node\_term\ m$ and m is in a non_originating strand for term a, then p also crosses all nodes in $fst\ m$ such that $m' \Rightarrow^+ m$ and $a \sqsubset node\_term\ m'$; in particular, p must cross a node m'', which is the first node containing a in non-originating strand $fst\ m$;.

Lemma 1
$[|b \in bundles|] \Longrightarrow uniquely\_originate\ a\ n \longrightarrow$
$\forall n'.n' \in fst\ b \wedge a \sqsubset node\_term\ n' \longrightarrow$
$$\left(\begin{array}{l} \exists p.\ path\ (n\#p)\ b \wedge (n\#p)!(length\ p) = n' \\ \wedge \left(\begin{array}{l} \forall m.\ \left(\begin{array}{l} m \in set\ (n\#p) \wedge node\_sign\ m = + \\ \wedge fst\ m \neq fst\ n \wedge a \sqsubset node\_term\ m \end{array} \right) \longrightarrow \\ \left(\begin{array}{l} (\exists m'.\ m' \in set\ (n\#p) \wedge is\_first\_node\ a\ m'\ (fst\ m)) \\ \wedge (\forall m'.m' \Rightarrow^+ m \wedge a \sqsubset node\_term\ m' \longrightarrow m' \in set\ (n\#p)) \end{array} \right) \end{array} \right) \end{array} \right)$$

, where *set xs* returns the set of all elements in list xs.

Proofs given by Guttman are extraordinarily complicated, we could not just follow his way to formalize results of authentication tests. Instead, we present authentication tests in a different style. Suppose that atom a uniquely originates on n, and given a term set T such that for all terms t in T, if $a \sqsubset M$, then $t = Crypt\ K\ M$, and $invKey\ K$ can not be obtained by the penetrator for some K, M; $synth\ T$ are terms that the penetrator can build up from T; if n' is another node containing a, and n' contains a new a-component which can not be built by $synth\ T$, furthermore, if we also assume that each component t' of each positive node on the originating strand is built by $synth\ T$, i.e., the originating strand does not help this transformation, then some regular strand except the originating one performs some transformation about a.

Lemma 2 (outgoing-authentication-test).
$[\![b \in bundles;\ uniquely\_originate\ a\ n; T \neq \varnothing; a \in Atoms;$
$\forall t \in T.\exists K\ M.a \sqsubset t \longrightarrow t = Crypt\ K\ M;$
$\forall t.a \not\sqsubset t \longrightarrow t \in T;\ \forall k.a \neq Key\ k;$
$\forall t \in T.a \sqsubset t \longrightarrow \forall K\ M.\begin{pmatrix} t = Crypt\ K\ M \longrightarrow \\ \forall n.(node\_term\ n = invKey\ K \rightarrow attr\ n \notin bad) \end{pmatrix};$
$\forall m.\begin{pmatrix} fst\ m = fst\ n \wedge node\_sign\ m = + \wedge a \sqsubset node\_term\ m \longrightarrow \\ node\_term\ m \in synth\ T \end{pmatrix};$
$a \sqsubset (node\_term\ m') \wedge node\_term\ m' \notin synth\ T]\!] \Longrightarrow$
$\exists p\ m\ m'.\begin{pmatrix} path\ n\#p\ b \wedge\ (n\#p)!\ (length\ p) = n' \wedge \\ m \Rightarrow^+ m' \wedge m \in set\ (n\#p) \wedge m' \in set\ (n\#p) \wedge \\ node\_sign\ m = - \wedge\ node\_sign\ m' = + \wedge \\ attr\ (fst\ m') \notin bad \wedge fst\ m \neq fst\ n \\ \wedge node\_term\ m \in synth\ T \\ \wedge node\_term\ m' \notin synth\ T \\ \wedge a \sqsubset node\_term\ m \wedge a \sqsubset node\_term\ m' \end{pmatrix}$

5 Related Work and Conclusions

Our work in this paper fruitfully borrows techniques from two popular approaches: strand space and the inductive method. Firstly, strand space model provides us a natural and efficient representation for the problem domain, and it has the advantage that it contains the exact casual relation information, and precise formulation about freshness assumption, and much more intuitive formulation of protocol's properties, and much simpler proofs. Our initial aim is just using Isabelle to formalise original strand space theory. But during this process, we find many concepts are too informal and many proofs needs a lot of human insight, and they are far away from being mechanized. In particular, when we try to formalise results of authentication tests, we find we could not overcome this difficulty if we do not extend their model. The definitions involved in results about normal form lemma and efficient form lemma are too tedious to formulate, and it is very hard to follow proofs even in paper proof, let alone to formalize them. Because all these problems are about bundles, they have given us the intuition that the crux lies in the definition of bundles, which is just a sketchy property specification, and not enough to support formal reasoning. But how to give a more tractable definition for bundles? Fortunately, Paulson's work in the inductive approach has inspired us to go ahead [3]. Paulson's intuition behind his work has taught us that the principles of mathematical induction is not only simple, but also very powerful, especially to handle problems with infinite states. Besides, Isabelle's built-in support for inductive set and rule induction make it very convenient to apply induction principle. All these acted as stimuli for us to introduce the inductive approach to formalising strand space. The key to our approach is introducing an inductive definition for bundles, and it not only provides us a constructive illustration for a bundle, but also introduces an effective and rigorous technique of rule induction to prove properties of bundles. Using this induction principle, we can prove that a bundle is a casually well-founded graph. We also clearly formalize the semantics to fresh assumption, and introduce the notion of complete transforming path and prove the existence of a a-complete transforming path through a bundle from its originating node to any nodes containing a. Combining the above results we give a rigorous proof for results of authentication tests. Our result of authentication test not only extends Guttman's result to a more general case, but also its proof is much easier and clearer, because we need not introduce normal bundles and efficient bundles. Our formulation and proof techniques are applicable generally. Analyzing a protocol case only requires definition about traces of regular strands, and our results of authentication tests make it very easy to prove authentication properties. As a trivial case study, we show how to use our results by proving authentication properties of Needham-Schroeder-Lowe protocol.

References

1. F. Javier Thayer Fabrega, Jonathan C. Herzog, Joshua D. Guttman. Strand Spaces: Proving Security Protocols Correct. Journal of Computer Security, 7 (1999), pages 191-230.
2. Guttman, J. D., Thayer Fabrega, F. J., 2000a. Authentication tests. In: Proceedings, 2000 IEEE Symposium on Security and Privacy. May, IEEE Computer Society Press.
3. L. C. Paulson. The Inductive Approach to Verifying Cryptographic Protocols. Journal of Computer Security, 6:85–128, 1998.

Appendix. Due to space limitation, we have to omit many details and references. Interesting readers can see http://lcs.ios.ac.cn/~lyj238/strand.html for them.

Compositional Modelling and Verification of IPv6 Mobility[*]

Peng Wu[1] and Dongmei Zhang[2]

[1] Lab of Computer Science, Institute of Software, Chinese Academy of Sciences,
Graduate School of the Chinese Academy of Sciences, Beijing 100080, China
wp@ios.ac.cn
[2] School of Computer Science & Technology,
Beijing University of Posts and Telecommunications, Beijing 100876, China
zhangdm@bupt.edu.cn

Abstract. An enhanced compositional framework is presented for modelling network protocols with symbolic transition graphs. In the context of the modelling framework, a sufficient condition for deadlock freedom of network protocols, namely interoperability, is reconstructed in a more concise way with an advantage that it allows for symbolic verification without referring to protocol states. Furthermore, a case study with Mobile IPv6 illustrates the effectiveness of the improved modelling framework and also discloses some infrangibilities of Mobile IPv6 in the sense that it can not maintain the binding coherency all the time, which may result in unreachable or unstable routes.

1 Introduction

Internet Protocol version 6 (IPv6), as a backbone of the Next Generation Internet, supports mobility as one of its fundamental features, which aims to make the global mobile Internet possible [1,2]. Research efforts have been devoted to analyze Mobile IPv6 quantitatively with respect to its performance. However, qualitative analysis of Mobile IPv6, with respect to its functionality, is of little concern.

This paper presents an enhanced version of modelling framework for network protocols using symbolic transition graphs with assignment (STGA), and extends our case study on Mobile IPv4 [3] to analyze the inherent mobility of IPv6 from a viewpoint of a complete network topology. The case study discloses some infrangibilities in the routing capability of Mobile IPv6, that is, it can not maintain the binding coherency all the time, which may result in unreachable or unstable routes. Such defects have not been reported before, even in Mobile IPv6 testing [4].

---

[*] The work is supported by grants 60223005 and 60242002 from the National Natural Science Foundation of China, a grant from the Chinese Academy of Sciences and a grant from the EYTT of MOE.

2 Model Checking Mobile IPv6

Formally, Mobile IPv6 can be described as a tuple $MIP6^{n_{ha}, n_{mh}} = (\mathbb{E}_6, \mathbb{C}_6^e, \mathbb{C}_6^p)$ with $\mathbb{E}_6 = \{HA6[0..n_{ha}-1], MH6[0..n_{mh}-1]\}$. $HA6$ and $MH6$ are STGA models of home agents and mobile hosts in Mobile IPv6, respectively; n_{ha} and n_{mh} are the number of home agents and mobile hosts, respectively. $\mathbb{C}_6^e$ is a finite set of channel connecting protocol entities with the external environment of $MIP6$. $\mathbb{C}_6^p$ is a finite set of channel connecting protocol entities with each other.

From the viewpoint of functionality, Mobile IPv6 should always be able to route IP datagrams to mobile nodes roaming outside of their home networks, which can be described as the conjunction of μ-calculus formulae: DF, AR_h, AR_f and ToD. DF means the protocol can always evolve. $AR_h(AR_f)$ means whenever a mobile host becomes stable at its home network(a foreign network), all datagrams destined for the mobile host should be forwarded without a tunnel(via a tunnel). ToD means a tunnel should be used only when the mobile host is roaming.

For details of the definitions of $MIP6$ and formulae mentioned above, one can refer to [5]. Especially, $MIP6$ can be easily proved to be interoperable. With Theorem 2.3 and 2.4 in [5], the deadlock freedom of $MIP6^{1,1}$ can be concluded without explicitly enumerating its state space exhaustively.

As far as AR and ToD are concerned, the model checking experiments end unexpectedly with negative results, which disclose the infrangibility of Mobile IPv6 in its routing capability.

2.1 Adaptive Routing

Fig. 1(a) illustrates a counterexample for the property AR_f, where a mobile host is to register its binding information. Although having acknowledged the mobile host with OK, the home agent updates its local binding list after it has forwarded a datagram received previously to the mobile host according to its current binding list, where the mobile host is supposed to be still home. Therefore the datagram will never reach the mobile host. Similarly one can find a corresponding counterexample for the property AR_h.

One way to avoid the case of datagram loss illustrated above is to switch the order between actions reg_rep_hm and $set\_hbinding$. A model checking experiment shows the resulted model does still not satisfy AR_h, with a counterexample illustrated in Fig. 1(b), where a mobile host has moved out of its home network. Before the mobile host becomes stable at the foreign network, that is, receives a Binding Acknowledgement from its home agent, a datagram has been forwarded to its new care-of address coa that is not yet enabled. In such case, the behavior of the mobile host is undefined in the specification of Mobile IPv6. Similarly one can find a corresponding counterexample for the property AR_f with respect to the modified model.

2.2 Tunnel on Demand

The binding incoherency also ruins the property ToD. Fig. 2(a) illustrates a counterexample for ToD, where a mobile host is to deregister its binding in-

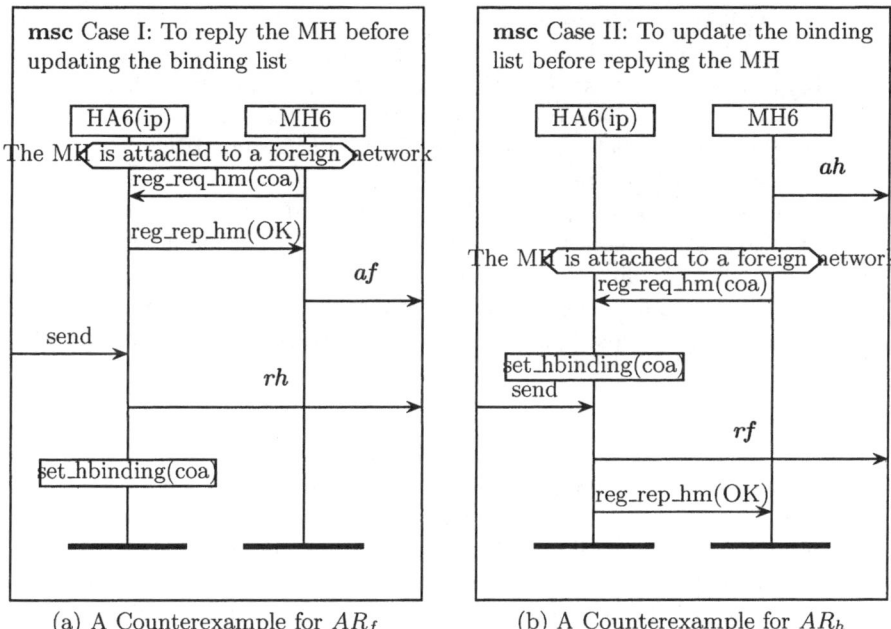

Fig. 1. Counterexamples for Adaptive Routing

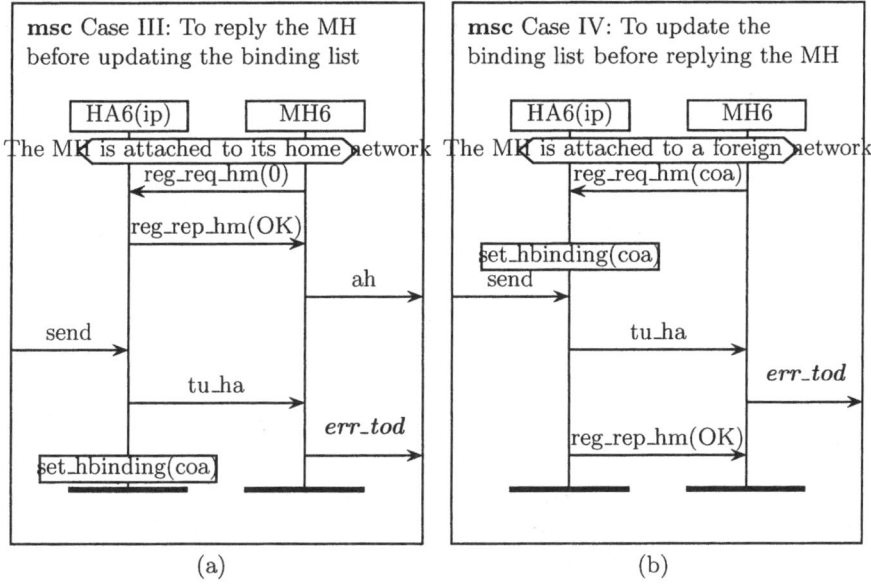

Fig. 2. Counterexamples for Tunnel-On-Demand

formation. Although having acknowledged the mobile host with OK, the home agent updates its local binding list after it has forwarded a datagram received previously to the mobile host according to its current binding list, where the mobile host is supposed to be out of its home network. In such case, the behavior of the mobile host is undefined in the specification of Mobile IPv6.

The modified model resulted by switching the order between actions reg_rep_hm and $set\_hbinding$ does still not satisfy ToD. A counterexample is illustrated in Fig. 2(b), where a mobile host is to register its binding information. Before receiving a Binding Acknowledgement from its home agent, it receives a datagram via a tunnel, which has not yet been enabled. In such case, the behavior of the mobile host is undefined in the specification of Mobile IPv6.

3 Conclusion

An enhanced compositional framework was presented in this paper for modelling network protocols using STGA. It inherits the reactive nature of network protocols and render interoperability checking static on symbolic transition graphs. A case study on Mobile IPv6 has been conducted, respecting the deadlock-free design paradigm of the modelling framework. The case study not only shows the effectiveness of the modelling framework, but also detects some infrangibilities of Mobile IPv6 in its binding incoherency, which may make a datagram unreachable to its destination or being forwarded to an unstable mobile host.

As future work, the framework can be extended for parameterized verification. The inherent parameterized nature of the modelling framework can help verify concrete network protocols or other reactive systems in a more cost-effective way.

References

1. Johnson, D., Perkins, C.: Mobility support in IPv6. In: Second ACM International Conference On Mobile Computing And Networking (MobiCom'96), ACM (1996) 27–37
2. Johnson, D., Perkins, C., Arkko, J.: Mobility support in IPv6. Internet-Draft, IETF Mobile IP Working Group (2003)
3. Wu, P., Zhang, D.: Compositional analysis of mobile IP with symbolic transition graphs. In: 16th International Conference on Computer Communication. (2004) 1481–1488
4. ZHANG, Y.J., TIAN, J., LI, Z.C.: Mobile IPv6 and its conformance testing (2002)
5. Wu, P., Zhang, D.: Compositional analysis of mobile network protocols. Technical Report ISCAS-LCS-05-02, Lab of Computer Science, Institute of Software, Chinese Academy of Sciences (2005)

Author Index

Arun-Kumar, S.   320

Balaban, Ittai   1
Billington, Jonathan   143
Bochmann, Gregor V.   396
Bollig, Benedikt   53

Chang, Chi-Lan   233
Chang, Kai-Hui   525
Chatain, Thomas   489
Chen, J.   219
Chiu, Yun-Peng   233
Ciaffaglione, Alberto   335
Cleaveland, Rance   83
Couvreur, Jean-Michel   443

Daou, Bassel   396
Desmoulin, Alexandra   533
Dorofeeva, Rita   204
Dssouli, Rachida   366

El-Fakih, Khaled   204

Gill, Christopher   159

Haddad, Serge   189
Hammal, Youcef   38
Hassine, Jameleddine   366
Heitmeyer, Constance   13
Helke, Steffen   305
Hélouët, Loïc   489
Hennessy, Matthew   335
Hermanns, Holger   98
Hierons, R.M.   219
Higashino, Teruo   20
Hsiung, Pao-Ann   290

Ilié, Jean-Michel   189
Imine, Abdessamado   411

Jansen, David N.   98
Jard, Claude   489
Jhumka, Arshad   428

Kammüller, Florian   305
Kang, Jeh-Yen   525

Kelso, Joel   503
Kiehn, Astrid   320
Klai, Kais   189
Kongprakaiwoot, Tul   143
Krumm, Heiko   247
Kuo, Sy-Yen   525

Lakos, Charles A.   174
Langerak, Rom   24
Lazarescu, Anca   542
Lei, Chin-Laung   233
Leucker, Martin   53
Liao, Wanjiun   518
Lin, Yen-Hung   290
Li, Yongjian   547
Li, Zhongcheng   538

Majster-Cederbaum, Mila   351
Mandrioli, Dino   381
Manna, Zohar   159, 529
Milne, George   503
Molli, Pascal   411

Nymeyer, Albert   275

Oster, Gérald   411

Paaschen, Ralf   542
Parrow, Joachim   128
Pears, Arnold   128
Pnueli, Amir   1
Pradella, Matteo   381

Qian, Junyan   261
Qian, Kairong   275

Rathke, Julian   335
Rilling, Juergen   366
Rossi, Matteo   381
Rotaru, Elisei   542
Rothmaier, Gerrit   247
Rusinowitch, Michaël   411

Sánchez, César   159, 529
Sipma, Henny B.   159, 529
Sistla, A. Prasad   68
Slanina, Matteo   529

Strubbe, Stefan 24
Subramonian, Venkita 159
Suri, Neeraj 428
Susanto, Steven 275

Thierry-Mieg, Yann 443
Tsao, Cheng-Lin 518
Turner, Kenneth J. 473
Tu, Wei-Ting 525

Ural, H. 219

Vanit-Anunchai, Somsak 143
Viho, César 533

Wang, Bow-Yaw 113
Wang, Han-Wei 525
Wedde, Horst F. 542
Wedig, Arnim 542

Wibling, Oskar 128
Wu, Peng 553
Wu, Yueh-Ting 518

Xu, Baowen 261

Yamaguchi, Hirozumi 20
Yeh, Yi-Jong 525
Yen, Li-Hsing 458
Yevtushenko, Nina 204
Yu, Chang Wu 458

Zhan, Naijun 351
Zhang, Dezhuang 83
Zhang, Dongmei 553
Zhang, Lijun 98
Zhang, Yujun 538
Zhou, Min 68
Zuck, Lenore D. 1

Lecture Notes in Computer Science

For information about Vols. 1–3636

please contact your bookseller or Springer

Vol. 3739: W. Fan, Z. Wu, J. Yang (Eds.), Advances in Web-Age Information Management. XXII, 930 pages. 2005.

Vol. 3738: V.R. Syrotiuk, E. Chávez (Eds.), Ad-Hoc, Mobile, and Wireless Networks. XI, 360 pages. 2005.

Vol. 3731: F. Wang (Ed.), Formal Techniques for Networked and Distributed Systems - FORTE 2005. XII, 558 pages. 2005.

Vol. 3728: V. Paliouras, J. Vounckx, D. Verkest (Eds.), Integrated Circuit and System Design. XV, 753 pages. 2005.

Vol. 3726: L.T. Yang, O.F. Rana, B. Di Martino, J. Dongarra (Eds.), High Performance Computing and Communcations. XXVI, 1116 pages. 2005.

Vol. 3725: D. Borrione, W. Paul (Eds.), Correct Hardware Design and Verification Methods. XII, 412 pages. 2005.

Vol. 3724: P. Fraigniaud (Ed.), Distributed Computing. XIV, 520 pages. 2005.

Vol. 3718: V.G. Ganzha, E.W. Mayr, E.V. Vorozhtsov (Eds.), Computer Algebra in Scientific Computing. XII, 502 pages. 2005.

Vol. 3717: B. Gramlich (Ed.), Frontiers of Combining Systems. X, 321 pages. 2005. (Subseries LNAI).

Vol. 3715: E. Dawson, S. Vaudenay (Eds.), Progress in Cryptology – Mycrypt 2005. XI, 329 pages. 2005.

Vol. 3714: H. Obbink, K. Pohl (Eds.), Software Product Lines. XIII, 235 pages. 2005.

Vol. 3713: L. Briand, C. Williams (Eds.), Model Driven Engineering Languages and Systems. XV, 722 pages. 2005.

Vol. 3712: R. Reussner, J. Mayer, J.A. Stafford, S. Overhage, S. Becker, P.J. Schroeder (Eds.), Quality of Software Architectures and Software Quality. XIII, 289 pages. 2005.

Vol. 3711: F. Kishino, Y. Kitamura, H. Kato, N. Nagata (Eds.), Entertainment Computing - ICEC 2005. XXIV, 540 pages. 2005.

Vol. 3710: M. Barni, I. Cox, T. Kalker, H.J. Kim (Eds.), Digital Watermarking. XII, 485 pages. 2005.

Vol. 3708: J. Blanc-Talon, W. Philips, D. Popescu, P. Scheunders (Eds.), Advanced Concepts for Intelligent Vision Systems. XXII, 725 pages. 2005.

Vol. 3707: D.A. Peled, Y.-K. Tsay (Eds.), Automated Technology for Verification and Analysis. XII, 506 pages. 2005.

Vol. 3706: H. Fuks, S. Lukosch, A.C. Salgado (Eds.), Groupware: Design, Implementation, and Use. XII, 378 pages. 2005.

Vol. 3703: F. Fages, S. Soliman (Eds.), Principles and Practice of Semantic Web Reasoning. VIII, 163 pages. 2005.

Vol. 3702: B. Beckert (Ed.), Automated Reasoning with Analytic Tableaux and Related Methods. XIII, 343 pages. 2005. (Subseries LNAI).

Vol. 3701: M. Coppo, E. Lodi, G. M. Pinna (Eds.), Theoretical Computer Science. XI, 411 pages. 2005.

Vol. 3699: C.S. Calude, M.J. Dinneen, G. Păun, M. J. Pérez-Jiménez, G. Rozenberg (Eds.), Unconventional Computation. XI, 267 pages. 2005.

Vol. 3698: U. Furbach (Ed.), KI 2005: Advances in Artificial Intelligence. XIII, 409 pages. 2005. (Subseries LNAI).

Vol. 3697: W. Duch, J. Kacprzyk, E. Oja, S. Zadrożny (Eds.), Artificial Neural Networks: Formal Models and Their Applications – ICANN 2005, Part II. XXXII, 1045 pages. 2005.

Vol. 3696: W. Duch, J. Kacprzyk, E. Oja, S. Zadrożny (Eds.), Artificial Neural Networks: Biological Inspirations – ICANN 2005, Part I. XXXI, 703 pages. 2005.

Vol. 3695: M.R. Berthold, R. Glen, K. Diederichs, O. Kohlbacher, I. Fischer (Eds.), Computational Life Sciences. XI, 277 pages. 2005. (Subseries LNBI).

Vol. 3694: M. Malek, E. Nett, N. Suri (Eds.), Service Availability. VIII, 213 pages. 2005.

Vol. 3693: A.G. Cohn, D.M. Mark (Eds.), Spatial Information Theory. XII, 493 pages. 2005.

Vol. 3692: R. Casadio, G. Myers (Eds.), Algorithms in Bioinformatics. X, 436 pages. 2005. (Subseries LNBI).

Vol. 3691: A. Gagalowicz, W. Philips (Eds.), Computer Analysis of Images and Patterns. XIX, 865 pages. 2005.

Vol. 3690: M. Pěchouček, P. Petta, L.Z. Varga (Eds.), Multi-Agent Systems and Applications IV. XVII, 667 pages. 2005. (Subseries LNAI).

Vol. 3688: R. Winther, B.A. Gan, G. Dahll (Eds.), Computer Safety, Reliability, and Security. XI, 405 pages. 2005.

Vol. 3687: S. Singh, M. Singh, C. Apte, P. Perner (Eds.), Pattern Recognition and Image Analysis, Part II. XXV, 809 pages. 2005.

Vol. 3686: S. Singh, M. Singh, C. Apte, P. Perner (Eds.), Pattern Recognition and Data Mining, Part I. XXVI, 689 pages. 2005.

Vol. 3685: V. Gorodetsky, I. Kotenko, V. Skormin (Eds.), Computer Network Security. XIV, 480 pages. 2005.

Vol. 3684: R. Khosla, R.J. Howlett, L.C. Jain (Eds.), Knowledge-Based Intelligent Information and Engineering Systems, Part IV. LXXIX, 933 pages. 2005. (Subseries LNAI).

Vol. 3683: R. Khosla, R.J. Howlett, L.C. Jain (Eds.), Knowledge-Based Intelligent Information and Engineering Systems, Part III. LXXX, 1397 pages. 2005. (Subseries LNAI).

Vol. 3682: R. Khosla, R.J. Howlett, L.C. Jain (Eds.), Knowledge-Based Intelligent Information and Engineering Systems, Part II. LXXIX, 1371 pages. 2005. (Subseries LNAI).

Vol. 3681: R. Khosla, R.J. Howlett, L.C. Jain (Eds.), Knowledge-Based Intelligent Information and Engineering Systems, Part I. LXXX, 1319 pages. 2005. (Subseries LNAI).

Vol. 3679: S.d.C. di Vimercati, P. Syverson, D. Gollmann (Eds.), Computer Security – ESORICS 2005. XI, 509 pages. 2005.

Vol. 3678: A. McLysaght, D.H. Huson (Eds.), Comparative Genomics. VIII, 167 pages. 2005. (Subseries LNBI).

Vol. 3677: J. Dittmann, S. Katzenbeisser, A. Uhl (Eds.), Communications and Multimedia Security. XIII, 360 pages. 2005.

Vol. 3676: R. Glück, M. Lowry (Eds.), Generative Programming and Component Engineering. XI, 448 pages. 2005.

Vol. 3675: Y. Luo (Ed.), Cooperative Design, Visualization, and Engineering. XI, 264 pages. 2005.

Vol. 3674: W. Jonker, M. Petković (Eds.), Secure Data Management. X, 241 pages. 2005.

Vol. 3673: S. Bandini, S. Manzoni (Eds.), AI*IA 2005: Advances in Artificial Intelligence. XIV, 614 pages. 2005. (Subseries LNAI).

Vol. 3672: C. Hankin, I. Siveroni (Eds.), Static Analysis. X, 369 pages. 2005.

Vol. 3671: S. Bressan, S. Ceri, E. Hunt, Z.G. Ives, Z. Bellahsène, M. Rys, R. Unland (Eds.), Database and XML Technologies. X, 239 pages. 2005.

Vol. 3670: M. Bravetti, L. Kloul, G. Zavattaro (Eds.), Formal Techniques for Computer Systems and Business Processes. XIII, 349 pages. 2005.

Vol. 3669: G.S. Brodal, S. Leonardi (Eds.), Algorithms – ESA 2005. XVIII, 901 pages. 2005.

Vol. 3668: M. Gabbrielli, G. Gupta (Eds.), Logic Programming. XIV, 454 pages. 2005.

Vol. 3666: B.D. Martino, D. Kranzlmüller, J. Dongarra (Eds.), Recent Advances in Parallel Virtual Machine and Message Passing Interface. XVII, 546 pages. 2005.

Vol. 3665: K. S. Candan, A. Celentano (Eds.), Advances in Multimedia Information Systems. X, 221 pages. 2005.

Vol. 3664: C. Türker, M. Agosti, H.-J. Schek (Eds.), Peer-to-Peer, Grid, and Service-Orientation in Digital Library Architectures. X, 261 pages. 2005.

Vol. 3663: W.G. Kropatsch, R. Sablatnig, A. Hanbury (Eds.), Pattern Recognition. XIV, 512 pages. 2005.

Vol. 3662: C. Baral, G. Greco, N. Leone, G. Terracina (Eds.), Logic Programming and Nonmonotonic Reasoning. XIII, 454 pages. 2005. (Subseries LNAI).

Vol. 3661: T. Panayiotopoulos, J. Gratch, R. Aylett, D. Ballin, P. Olivier, T. Rist (Eds.), Intelligent Virtual Agents. XIII, 506 pages. 2005. (Subseries LNAI).

Vol. 3660: M. Beigl, S. Intille, J. Rekimoto, H. Tokuda (Eds.), UbiComp 2005: Ubiquitous Computing. XVII, 394 pages. 2005.

Vol. 3659: J.R. Rao, B. Sunar (Eds.), Cryptographic Hardware and Embedded Systems – CHES 2005. XIV, 458 pages. 2005.

Vol. 3658: V. Matoušek, P. Mautner, T. Pavelka (Eds.), Text, Speech and Dialogue. XV, 460 pages. 2005. (Subseries LNAI).

Vol. 3657: F.S. de Boer, M.M. Bonsangue, S. Graf, W.-P. de Roever (Eds.), Formal Methods for Components and Objects. VIII, 325 pages. 2005.

Vol. 3656: M. Kamel, A. Campilho (Eds.), Image Analysis and Recognition. XXIV, 1279 pages. 2005.

Vol. 3655: A. Aldini, R. Gorrieri, F. Martinelli (Eds.), Foundations of Security Analysis and Design III. VII, 273 pages. 2005.

Vol. 3654: S. Jajodia, D. Wijesekera (Eds.), Data and Applications Security XIX. X, 353 pages. 2005.

Vol. 3653: M. Abadi, L. de Alfaro (Eds.), CONCUR 2005 – Concurrency Theory. XIV, 578 pages. 2005.

Vol. 3652: A. Rauber, S. Christodoulakis, A M. Tjoa (Eds.), Research and Advanced Technology for Digital Libraries. XVIII, 545 pages. 2005.

Vol. 3651: R. Dale, K.-F. Wong, J. Su, O.Y. Kwong (Eds.), Natural Language Processing – IJCNLP 2005. XXI, 1031 pages. 2005. (Subseries LNAI).

Vol. 3650: J. Zhou, J. Lopez, R.H. Deng, F. Bao (Eds.), Information Security. XII, 516 pages. 2005.

Vol. 3649: W.M. P. van der Aalst, B. Benatallah, F. Casati, F. Curbera (Eds.), Business Process Management. XII, 472 pages. 2005.

Vol. 3648: J.C. Cunha, P.D. Medeiros (Eds.), Euro-Par 2005 Parallel Processing. XXXVI, 1299 pages. 2005.

Vol. 3646: A. F. Famili, J.N. Kok, J.M. Peña, A. Siebes, A. Feelders (Eds.), Advances in Intelligent Data Analysis VI. XIV, 522 pages. 2005.

Vol. 3645: D.-S. Huang, X.-P. Zhang, G.-B. Huang (Eds.), Advances in Intelligent Computing, Part II. XIII, 1010 pages. 2005.

Vol. 3644: D.-S. Huang, X.-P. Zhang, G.-B. Huang (Eds.), Advances in Intelligent Computing, Part I. XXVII, 1101 pages. 2005.

Vol. 3643: R. Moreno Díaz, F. Pichler, A. Quesada Arencibia (Eds.), Computer Aided Systems Theory – EUROCAST 2005. XIV, 629 pages. 2005.

Vol. 3642: D. Ślezak, J. Yao, J.F. Peters, W. Ziarko, X. Hu (Eds.), Rough Sets, Fuzzy Sets, Data Mining, and Granular Computing, Part II. XXIII, 738 pages. 2005. (Subseries LNAI).

Vol. 3641: D. Ślezak, G. Wang, M. Szczuka, I. Düntsch, Y. Yao (Eds.), Rough Sets, Fuzzy Sets, Data Mining, and Granular Computing, Part I. XXIV, 742 pages. 2005. (Subseries LNAI).

Vol. 3639: P. Godefroid (Ed.), Model Checking Software. XI, 289 pages. 2005.

Vol. 3638: A. Butz, B. Fisher, A. Krüger, P. Olivier (Eds.), Smart Graphics. XI, 269 pages. 2005.

Vol. 3637: J. M. Moreno, J. Madrenas, J. Cosp (Eds.), Evolvable Systems: From Biology to Hardware. XI, 227 pages. 2005.